What They Said

The Ultimate Authoritative Book of Quotations

What They Said

The Ultimate Authoritative Book of Quotations

Edited by
Nicholas Augustus Phillips

SWEETWATER
PRESS

SWEETWATER
PRESS

What They Said

Produced by arrangement with Sweetwater Press

ISBN–13: 978–1-58173-679-3
ISBN–10: 1-58173-679-7

Design by Miles Parsons and Nick Phillips

Printed in China

Table of Contents

Preface 7

Quotations 9

Index by Author or Source 899

Index by Subject 1131

PREFACE

Quotations offer insight into different times, distant places, and strange cultures, as well as provide springboards for new ideas. They can yield points for meditation or inspiration, soothe a broken heart, and help give congratulations at a wedding or graduation ceremony.

This collection of quotations acts like a time capsule, capturing for the ages the knowledge, wit, and insight of society's most prominent and even lesser known members. Spanning thirty centuries of human history, *What They Said* not only includes the words of more than 4,000 scholars, wise men, scientists, philosophers, and leaders, but among its pages readers will also find brilliant passages from the world's most heralded literary works, along with quotes from actors, artists, musicians, and playwrights. All 15,000 quotations are classified into more than 1,000 subject categories and organized into two indexes—one by author or source, the second by subject—to facilitate easy reference.

The quotations in this volume were selected for their profundity, humor, irony, or historical significance. Classic sources such as Shakespeare, the Bible, and Homer's *The Odyssey* are cited along with more up-to-date references, including popular movies, songs, and television shows.

With a compilation that is as historical as it is contemporary, *What They Said* is the most comprehensive and extensive collection of its kind. The advice of sages, the foresight of philosophers, the spiritual words of clergymen, the pandering of politicians, the observations of scientists, and the musings of poets all come into focus within its pages.

From the ancient wisdom of Plato and Aristotle to the modern comic wit of Robin Williams and Bill Cosby, *What They Said* represents an extensive body of knowledge, which, in times of celebration, hardship, joy, or grief, will help readers find just the right words to console a loved one, liven up a speech, give authority to term papers, or simply deepen a conversation.

NICHOLAS AUGUSTUS PHILLIPS

Ability

The difference between one man and another is not mere ability… it is energy.
THOMAS ARNOLD (1795–1842)

Just do what you do best.
RED AUERBACH (1917–2006)

Natural abilities are like natural plants; they need pruning by study.
SIR FRANCIS BACON (1561–1626)

I thought [Sir Winston Churchill] was a young man of promise, but it appears he is a young man of promises.
ARTHUR JAMES BALFOUR (1848–1930)

Knowing what you cannot do is more important than knowing what you can do. In fact, that's good taste.
LUCILLE BALL (1911–1989)

To become an able and successful man in any profession, three things are necessary, nature, study, and practice.
HENRY WARD BEECHER (1813–1887)

The king is the man who can.
THOMAS CARLYLE (1795–1881)

No amount of ability is of the slightest avail without honor.
ANDREW CARNEGIE (1835–1919)

You have to have confidence in your ability, and then be tough enough to follow through.
ROSALYNN CARTER (1927–)

When it is a question of God's almighty Spirit, never say, "I can't."
OSWALD CHAMBERS (1874–1917)

I have learnt that I am me, that I can do the things that, as one might put it, me can do, but I cannot do the things that me would like to do.
AGATHA CHRISTIE (1890–1976)

Ability without honor is useless.
CICERO (106–43 BC)

Natural ability without education has more often attained to glory and virtue than education without natural ability.
CICERO (106–43 BC)

Aptitude found in the understanding is often inherited. Genius coming from reason and imagination, rarely.
SAMUEL TAYLOR COLERIDGE (1772–1834)

To sentence a man of true genius, to the drudgery of a school is to put a racehorse on a treadmill.
CHARLES CALEB COLTON (1780–1832)

The first requisite for success is the ability to apply your physical and mental energies to one problem incessantly without growing weary.
THOMAS A. EDISON (1847–1931)

When I examine myself and my methods of thought, I come to the conclusion that the gift of fantasy has meant more to me than my talent for absorbing positive knowledge.
ALBERT EINSTEIN (1879–1955)

People with great gifts are easy to find, but symmetrical and balanced ones never.
RALPH WALDO EMERSON (1803–1882)

Big jobs usually go to the men who prove their ability to outgrow small ones.
RALPH WALDO EMERSON (1803–1882)

Each man has his own vocation; his talent is his call. There is one direction in which all space is open to him.
RALPH WALDO EMERSON (1803–1882)

The fox has many tricks. The hedgehog has but one. But that is the best of all.
DESIDERIUS ERASMUS (C. 1466–1536)

Others have done it before me. I can, too.
CORPORAL JOHN FAUNCE (1897–1962)

Genius is the ability to put into effect what is on your mind.
F. Scott Fitzgerald (1896–1940)

The test of a first-rate intelligence is the ability to hold two opposed ideas in the mind at the same time, and still retain the ability to function. One should, for example, be able to see that things are hopeless and yet be determined to make them otherwise.
F. Scott Fitzgerald (1896–1940)

Vitality shows not only in the ability to persist, but in the ability to start over.
F. Scott Fitzgerald (1896–1940)

Ability will never catch up with the demand for it.
Malcolm S. Forbes (1919–1990)

The question "Who ought to be boss?" is likely as "Who ought to be the tenor in the quartet?" Obviously, the man who can sing tenor.
Henry Ford (1863–1947)

Whether you think that you can, or that you can't, you are usually right.
Henry Ford (1863–1947)

As we advance in life we learn the limits of our abilities.
James A. Froude (1818–1894)

The real contest is always between what you've done and what you're capable of doing. You measure yourself against yourself and nobody else.
Geoffrey Gaberino (1962–)

I know I have the ability to do so much more than just stand in front of the camera the rest of my life.
Jennie Garth (1972–)

The winds and waves are always on the side of the ablest navigators.
Edward Gibbon (1737–1794)

Our work is the presentation of our capabilities.
Johann Wolfgang von Goethe (1749–1832)

People are so constituted that everybody would rather undertake what they see others do, whether they have an aptitude for it or not.
Johann Wolfgang von Goethe (1749–1832)

The really unhappy person is the one who leaves undone what they can do, and starts doing what they don't understand; no wonder they come to grief.
Johann Wolfgang von Goethe (1749–1832)

Life has been compared to a race, but the illusion improves by observing that the most swift are usually the least manageable and the most likely to stray from the course. Great abilities have always been less serviceable to the possessors than moderate ones.
Oliver Goldsmith (1728–1774)

I think luck is the sense to recognize an opportunity and the ability to take advantage of it.... The man who can smile at his breaks and grab his chances gets on.
Samuel Goldwyn (1882–1974)

Great ability develops and reveals itself increasingly with every new assignment.
Baltasar Gracian (1601–1658)

The less their ability, the more their conceit.
Ahad Ha'am (1856–1927)

There is something that is much more scarce, something rarer than ability. It is the ability to recognize ability.
Robert Half (1918–)

Every person is responsible for all the good within the scope of his abilities, and for no more, and none can tell whose sphere is the largest.
Gail Hamilton (1833–1896)

You are searching for the magic key that will unlock the door to the source of power; and yet you have the key in your own hands, and you may use it the moment you learn to control your thoughts.
Napoleon Hill (1883–1970)

As life is action and passion, it is required of a man that he should share the passion and action of his time, at the peril of being judged not to have lived.
OLIVER WENDELL HOLMES SR. (1809–1894)

Ability is what you're capable of doing. Motivation determines what you do. Attitude determines how well you do it.
LOU HOLTZ (1937–)

It is a fine thing to have ability, but the ability to discover ability in others is the true test.
ELBERT HUBBARD (1856–1915)

Perhaps the most valuable result of all education is the ability to make yourself do the thing you have to do, when it ought to be done, whether you like it or not; it is the first lesson that ought to be learned; and however early a man's training begins, it is probably the last lesson that he learns thoroughly.
THOMAS H. HUXLEY (1825–1895)

Alone we can do so little; together we can do so much.
HELEN KELLER (1880–1968)

As the eagle was killed by the arrow winged with his own feather, so the hand of the world is wounded by its own skill.
HELEN KELLER (1880–1968)

It is a great ability to be able to conceal one's ability.
FRANÇOIS DE LA ROCHEFOUCAULD (1613–1680), *Maxims*

The height of ability consists in a thorough knowledge of the real value of things, and of the genius of the age in which we live.
FRANÇOIS DE LA ROCHEFOUCAULD (1613–1680)

The Army has carried the American … ideal to its logical conclusion. Not only do they prohibit discrimination on the grounds of race, creed, and color, but also on ability.
TOM LEHRER (1928–)

Certainly we're not satisfied with just winning games. We've been playing some pretty good hockey, but we think we can play much better.
MARIO LEMIEUX (1965–)

The Creator has not given you a longing to do that which you have no ability to do.
ORISON SWETT MARDEN (1850–1924)

We are not in a position in which we have nothing to work with. We already have capacities, talents, direction, missions, callings.
ABRAHAM MASLOW (1908–1970)

Analyzing what you haven't got as well as what you have is a necessary ingredient of a career.
GRACE MOORE (1898–1947)

Ability is of little account without opportunity.
NAPOLÉON I (1769–1821)

Men take only their needs into consideration, never their abilities.
NAPOLÉON I (1769–1821)

Ability hits the mark where presumption overshoots and diffidence falls short.
JOHN HENRY NEWMAN (1801–1890)

Ability is sexless.
CHRISTABEL PANKHURST (1880–1958)

Man cannot live by incompetence alone.
DR. LAURENCE J. PETER (1919–1990)

Executive ability is deciding quickly and getting somebody else to do the work.
JOHN G. POLLARD (1871–1937)

As simple as it sounds, we all must try to be the best person we can: by making the best choices, by making the most of the talents we've been given.
MARY LOU RETTON (1968–)

Put yourself in a state of mind where you say to yourself, "Here is an opportunity for me to celebrate like never before, my own power, my own ability to get myself to do whatever is necessary."
ANTHONY ROBBINS (1960–)

Do what you can, with what you have, where you are.
THEODORE ROOSEVELT (1858–1919)

No great intellectual thing was ever done by great effort.
JOHN RUSKIN (1819–1900)

The principle of all successful effort is to try to do not what is absolutely the best, but what is easily within our power, and suited for our temperament and condition.
JOHN RUSKIN (1819–1900)

When love and skill work together, expect a masterpiece.
JOHN RUSKIN (1819–1900)

Anything you're good at contributes to happiness.
BERTRAND RUSSELL (1872–1970)

Natural abilities can almost compensate for the want of every kind of cultivation, but no cultivation of the mind can make up for the want of natural abilities.
ARTHUR SCHOPENHAUER (1788–1860)

Martyrdom … is the only way in which a man can become famous without ability.
GEORGE BERNARD SHAW (1856–1950), *The Devil's Disciple*

The abilities of man must fall short on one side or the other, like too scanty a blanket when you are abed. If you pull it upon your shoulders, your feet are left bare; if you thrust it down to your feet, your shoulders are uncovered.
SIR WILLIAM TEMPLE (1628–1699)

Be faithful in small things because it is in them that your strength lies.
MOTHER TERESA (1910–1997)

He is the best sailor who can steer within fewest points of the wind, and exact a motive power out of the greatest obstacles.
HENRY DAVID THOREAU (1817–1862)

I know of no more encouraging fact than the unquestioned ability of a man to elevate his life by conscious endeavor.
HENRY DAVID THOREAU (1817–1862)

Not many men have both good fortune and good sense.
TITUS LIVIUS (59 BC–AD 17)

It's not the size of the dog in the fight, it's the size of the fight in the dog.
MARK TWAIN (1835–1910)

Wicked people are always surprised to find ability in those that are good.
MARQUIS DE VAUVENARGUES (1715–1747)

They are able because they think they are able.
VIRGIL (C. 70–19 BC)

The ability to delude yourself may be an important survival tool.
JANE WAGNER (1935–)

The world cares very little about what a man or woman knows; it is what a man or woman is able to do that counts.
BOOKER T. WASHINGTON (1856–1915)

Intelligence is quickness to apprehend as distinct from ability, which is capacity to act wisely on the thing apprehended.
ALFRED NORTH WHITEHEAD (1861–1947)

Whatever women do they must do twice as well as men to be thought half as good. Luckily, this is not difficult.
CHARLOTTE WHITTON (1896–1975)

I think that God in creating Man somewhat overestimated his ability.
OSCAR WILDE (1854–1900)

Charm is the ability to make someone else think that both of you are pretty wonderful.
KATHLEEN WINSOR (1919–2003)

We all have ability. The difference is how we use it.
STEVIE WONDER (1950–)

Ability may get you to the top, but it takes character to keep you there.
JOHN WOODEN (1910–)

Don't measure yourself by what you have accomplished, but by what you should have accomplished with your ability.
JOHN WOODEN (1910–)

It is possible to fly without motors, but not without knowledge and skill.
WILBUR WRIGHT (1867–1912)

You are the only one who can use your ability. It is an awesome responsibility.
ZIG ZIGLAR (1926–)

Success is the maximum utilization of the ability that you have.
ZIG ZIGLAR (1926–)

God does not ask about our ability, but our availability.
ANONYMOUS

Behind every able man, there are always other able men.
CHINESE PROVERB

Abortion

Abolition of a woman's right to abortion, when and if she wants it, amounts to compulsory maternity: a form of rape by the State.
EDWARD ABBEY (1927–1989)

They credited us [rock band Cream] with the birth of that sort of heavy metal thing. Well, if that's the case, there should be an immediate abortion.
GINGER BAKER (1939–)

But I've been the leader in the Senate, as you may know, to protect the right to choose. Not because I thought abortion was nice and kind, but I think nobody should put themselves in the position of the woman and her husband and her doctor and her minister when decisions like that are made.
BIRCH BAYH (1928–)

The states are not free, under the guise of protecting maternal health or potential life, to intimidate women into continuing pregnancies.
JUSTICE HARRY A. BLACKMUN (1908–1999), *Roe v. Wade*

However much I dislike the idea of abortion, you should not criminalize a woman who, in very difficult circumstances, makes that choice.
TONY BLAIR (1953–)

The freedom that women were supposed to have found in the Sixties largely boiled down to easy contraception and abortion; things to make life easier for men, in fact.
JULIE BURCHILL (1959–)

The biggest obstacle was mixing abortion with overpopulation. These are two things that have nothing to do with each other.
JACQUES COUSTEAU (1910–1997)

The issue is not abortion. The issue is whether women can make up their own [minds] instead of some right-wing pastor, some right-wing politician telling them what to do.
HOWARD DEAN (1948–)

Expanding eligibility of family planning services to low-income women will maximize cost-savings to both federal and state governments, reduce the disparities in access to family planning services for low-income women, and decrease the incidence of abortion in the U.S.
ROSA DELAURO (1943–)

I want to know how these very people who are against war because of loss of life can possibly be the same people who are for abortion? They are the same people who are for animal rights, but they are not for the rights of the unborn.
JIM GIBBONS (1944–)

The emphasis must be not on the right to abortion but on the right to privacy and reproductive control.
RUTH BADER GINSBERG (1933–)

In the case of abortion, one pits the life of the fetus against the interests of the pregnant woman.
LEON KASS (1939–)

The abortion controversy is important for what it says about our stance toward procreation and children altogether.
LEON KASS (1939–)

If men could get pregnant, abortion would be a sacrament.
FLORYNCE R. KENNEDY (1916–2000)

Too many people in America believe that if you are pro-choice that means pro-abortion. It doesn't. I don't want abortion. Abortion should be the rarest thing in the world. I am actually personally opposed to abortion. But I don't believe that I have a right to take what is an article of faith to me and legislate it to other people. That's not how it works in America.
JOHN KERRY (1943–)

Abortion … was probably regarded by the average Roman of the later days of Paganism much as Englishmen in the last century regarded convivial excesses, as certainly wrong, but so venial as scarcely to deserve censure.
W. E. H. LECKY (1838–1903)

I really didn't know there was two sides to the abortion issue.
NORMA MCCORVEY (1947–)

If your neighbor has a completely different view on abortion, gay marriage, stem cell research, all of those things, you still are both Americans. Neither one of you is necessarily more patriotic than the other. Neither loves their country any more than the other one does.
PHIL MCGRAW (1950–)

I've noticed that everybody that is for abortion has already been born.
RONALD REAGAN (1911–2004)

The most merciful thing that a family does to one of its infant members is to kill it.
MARGARET SANGER (1879–1966)

[I]t's hopeless expecting that neutrality will occur at an abortion clinic.
JENNY SHIPLEY (1952–)

Abortion is inherently different from other medical procedures because no other procedure involves the purposeful termination of a potential life.
POTTER STEWART (1915–1985)

If we accept that a mother can kill even her own child, how can we tell other people to not kill each other? Any country that accepts abortion is not teaching its people to love, but to use any violence to get what they want.
MOTHER TERESA (1910–1997)

These concerns (for orphan children in India and elsewhere in the world) are very good, but often these same people are not concerned with the millions that are killed by the deliberate decision of their own mothers. And this is what is the greatest destroyer of peace today, Abortion.… For the pregnant women who don't want their children, give them to me.
MOTHER TERESA (1910–1997)

If the anti-abortion movement took a tenth of the energy they put into noisy theatrics and devoted it to improving the lives of children who have been born into lives of poverty, violence, and neglect, they could make a world shine.
MICHAEL J. TUCKER (1957–)

Abstinence

Abstinence from sins is better than seeking help afterwards.
ALI IBN ABI TALIB (C. 599–661)

Total abstinence is easier than perfect moderation.
SAINT AUGUSTINE (354–430), *On the Good of Marriage*

Abstinence sows sand all over
The ruddy limbs & flaming hair,
But Desire Gratified
Plants fruits of life & beauty there.
WILLIAM BLAKE (1757–1827)

Courtly love-poetry may first have been written during long periods of abstinence on the Crusades, but it would not have flourished in the cold of northern Europe without some help from the chimney.
JAMES BURKE (1936–)

Half the vices which the world condemns most loudly have seeds of good in them and require moderate use rather than total abstinence.
SAMUEL BUTLER (1835–1902)

There is a great deal of political pressure to only talk about abstinence, and to deny support for condoms and education on using them. This policy will lead to the unnecessary deaths of many people.
HILLARY CLINTON (1947–)

Great sorrow or great joy should bring intense hunger—not abstinence from food, as our novelists will have it.
ARTHUR CONAN DOYLE SR. (1859–1930)

The old notion that any strict attempt to adhere to sexual abstinence is beset by terrible risks, insanity and so forth, has no foundation, at all events where we are concerned with reasonably sound and healthy people.
HENRY HAVELOCK ELLIS (1859–1939)

Against Diseases here, the strongest Fence,
Is the defensive Virtue, Abstinence.
BENJAMIN FRANKLIN (1706–1790)

I'm tired of hearing about temperance instead of abstinence, in order to please the cocktail crowd in church congregations.
VANCE HAVNER (1901–1986)

A rich man cannot enjoy a sound mind nor a sound body without exercise and abstinence; and yet these are truly the worst ingredients of poverty.
HENRY HOME (1696–1782)

You never see animals going through the absurd and often horrible fooleries of magic and religion. Dogs do not ritually urinate in the hope of persuading heaven to do the same and send down rain. Asses do not bray a liturgy to cloudless skies. Nor do cats attempt, by abstinence from cat's meat, to wheedle the feline spirits into benevolence. Only man behaves with such gratuitous folly. It is the price he has to pay for being intelligent but not, as yet, quite intelligent enough.
ALDOUS HUXLEY (1894–1963)

Peace and abstinence from European interferences are our objects, and so will continue while the present order of things in America [remains] uninterrupted.
THOMAS JEFFERSON (1743–1826)

Abstinence is as easy to me, as temperance would be difficult.
SAMUEL JOHNSON (1709–1784)

Tea's proper use is to amuse the idle, and relax the studious, and dilute the full meals of those who cannot use exercise, and will not use abstinence.
SAMUEL JOHNSON (1709–1784)

My experience through life has convinced me that, while moderation and temperance in all things are commendable and beneficial, abstinence from spirituous liquors is the best safeguard of morals and health.
ROBERT E. LEE (1807–1870)

Abstinence is a perversion.
BILL MAHER (1956–)

Abstinence is the surety of temperance.
PLATO (C. 428–348 BC)

The importance of great strictness of life and abstinence from various pleasures and indulgences was a familiar thought.
ROBERT RAINY (1826–1906)

The few bad poems which occasionally are created during abstinence are of no great interest.
WILHELM REICH (1897–1957)

Abstinence is easier than temperance.
SENECA (5 BC–AD 65)

Abstinence engenders maladies.
WILLIAM SHAKESPEARE (1564–1616), *Love's Labour's Lost*

Abstinence is the great strengthener and clearer of reason.
ROBERT SOUTH (1634–1716)

She belongs to a Temperance Society and wears one of those badges in the shape of a bow of ribbon to show that she would never take a drink, not even brandy if she were dying. Of course by temperance they all mean the opposite—total abstinence.
ELIZABETH TAYLOR (1932–)

If a man earnestly seeks a righteous life, his first act of abstinence is from animal food.
LEO TOLSTOY (1828–1910)

Use, do not abuse; neither abstinence nor excess ever renders man happy.
VOLTAIRE (1694–1778)

And must I wholly banish hence these red and golden juices, and pay my vows to Abstinence, that pallidest of Muses?
WILLIAM WATSON (1858–1935)

Temperance is moderation in the things that are good and total abstinence from the things that are foul.
FRANCES E. WILLARD (1839–1898)

I didn't practice abstinence, I perfected it.
DENNIS WOLFBERG (1946–1994)

Abstinence makes the heart grow fonder for someone else.
ANONYMOUS

Absurdity

Absurdity, n.: A statement or belief manifestly inconsistent with one's own opinion.
AMBROSE BIERCE (1842–1914), *The Devil's Dictionary*

My turn of mind is so given to taking things in the absurd point of view, that it breaks out in spite of me every now and then.
LORD BYRON (1788–1824)

At any street corner the feeling of absurdity can strike any man in the face.
ALBERT CAMUS (1913–1960)

It is not funny that anything else should fall down; only that a man should fall down. Why do we laugh? Because it is a gravely religious matter: it is the Fall of Man. Only man can be absurd: for only man can be dignified.
G. K. CHESTERTON (1874–1936)

The privilege of absurdity; to which no living creature is subject, but man only.
THOMAS HOBBES (1588–1679)

The irrationality of a thing is no argument against its existence, rather a condition of it.
FRIEDRICH NIETZSCHE (1844–1900)

In the consciousness of the truth he has perceived, man now sees everywhere only the awfulness or the absurdity of existence and loathing seizes him.
FRIEDRICH NIETZSCHE (1844–1900)

In the sphere of thought, absurdity and perversity remain the masters of the world, and their dominion is suspended only for brief periods.
ARTHUR SCHOPENHAUER (1788–1860)

Abundance

Abundance is not something we acquire. It is something we tune into.
WAYNE D. DYER (1940–)

Everything you need you already have. You are complete right now, you are a whole, total person, not an apprentice person on the way to someplace else. Your completeness must be understood by you and experienced in your thoughts as your own personal reality.
WAYNE D. DYER (1940–)

You can never get enough of what you don't want.
WAYNE D. DYER (1940–)

He who is plenteously provided for from within, needs but little from without.
JOHANN WOLFGANG VON GOETHE (1749–1832)

Acceptance

The antiquity and general acceptance of an opinion is not assurance of its truth.
PIERRE BAYLE (1647–1706)

You have to know how to accept rejection and reject acceptance.
RAY BRADBURY (1920–)

The first step toward change is awareness. The second step is acceptance.
NATHANIEL BRANDEN (1930–)

If the conditions were right there could be great acceptance. Often it is only when they pose an economic or political threat that it turns really ugly.
IRIS CHANG (1968–2004)

After an argument, silence may mean acceptance or the continuation of resistance by other means.
MASON COOLEY (1927–2002)

What we need is not more distrust and division. What we need now is acceptance.
TOM DASCHLE (1947–)

Acceptance by government of a dissident press is a measure of the maturity of a nation.
WILLIAM ORVILLE DOUGLAS (1898–1980)

Give love and unconditional acceptance to those you encounter, and notice what happens.
WAYNE D. DYER (1940–)

If I could define enlightenment briefly I would say it is "the quiet acceptance of what is."
WAYNE D. DYER (1940–)

Only by acceptance of the past, can you alter it.
T. S. ELIOT (1888–1965)

Acceptance is not love. You love a person because he or she has lovable traits, but you accept everybody just because they're alive and human.
ALBERT ELLIS (1913–2007)

Sometimes the solutions will require acknowledgement of past mistakes, and acceptance of insights for which none of our learning has prepared us.
MALCOLM FRASER (1930–)

Familiarity with evil breeds not contempt but acceptance.
ROY HATTERSLEY (1932–)

Acceptance of what has happened is the first step to overcoming the consequences of any misfortune.
WILLIAM JAMES (1842–1910)

Lukewarm acceptance is more bewildering than outright rejection.
MARTIN LUTHER KING JR. (1929–1968)

The art of acceptance is the art of making someone who has just done you a small favor wish that he might have done you a greater one.
MARTIN LUTHER KING JR. (1929–1968)

The primary joy of life is acceptance, approval, the sense of appreciation and companionship of our human comrades. Many men do not understand that the need for fellowship is really as deep as the need for food, and so they go through life accepting many substitutes for genuine, warm, simple.
JOSHUA LOTH LIEBMAN (1907–1948)

Reasonable acceptance, our way of living, is imperfect. But God, if God exists, must be perfect and beyond reason.
BARRY LONG (1926–2003)

The first thing a kindness deserves is acceptance, the second, transmission.
GEORGE MACDONALD (1824–1905)

Living apart and at peace with myself, I came to realize more vividly the meaning of the doctrine of acceptance. To refrain from giving advice, to refrain from meddling in the affairs of others, to refrain, even though the motives be the highest, from tampering with another's way of life—so simple, yet so difficult for an active spirit. Hands off!
HENRY MILLER (1891–1980)

Bad humor is an evasion of reality; good humor is an acceptance of it.
MALCOLM MUGGERIDGE (1902–1990)

Generally speaking, the Way of the warrior is resolute acceptance of death.
MIYAMOTO MUSASHI(1584–1645)

Happiness can exist only in acceptance.
GEORGE ORWELL (1903–1950)

Human beings, like plants, grow in the soil of acceptance, not in the atmosphere of rejection.
JOHN POWELL (1963–)

Understanding is the first step to acceptance, and only with acceptance can there be recovery.
J. K. ROWLING (1965–)

The greatest gift that you can give to others is the gift of unconditional love and acceptance.
BRIAN TRACY (1944–)

Acceptance of others, their looks, their behaviors, their beliefs, [brings] you an inner peace and tranquility—instead of anger and resentment.
ANONYMOUS

Accidents

The ideal man bears the accidents of life with dignity and grace, making the best of circumstances.
ARISTOTLE (384–322 BC)

Beware of undertaking too much at the start. Be content with quite a little. Allow for accidents. Allow for human nature, especially your own.
ARNOLD BENNETT (1867–1931)

The most likely way for the world to be destroyed, most experts agree, is by accident. That's where we come in; we're computer professionals. We cause accidents.
NATHANIEL BORENSTEIN (1957–)

Accidents will occur in the best regulated families.
CHARLES DICKENS (1812–1870)

Accidents ruled every corner of the universe except the chambers of the human heart.
DAVID GUTERSON (1956–), *Snow Falling on Cedars*

The good neighbor looks beyond the external accidents and discerns those inner qualities that make all men human and, therefore, brothers.
MARTIN LUTHER KING JR. (1929–1968), *Strength to Love*

It happens fast for some people and slow for some, accidents or gravity, but we all end up mutilated.
CHUCK PALAHNIUK (1962–), *Invisible Monsters*

Beautiful young people are accidents of nature, but beautiful old people are works of art.
ELEANOR ROOSEVELT (1884–1962)

Of course there is no formula for success except perhaps an unconditional acceptance of life and what it brings.
ARTHUR RUBINSTEIN (1886–1982)

Passive acceptance of the teacher's wisdom is easy to most boys and girls. It involves no effort of independent thought, and seems rational because the teacher knows more than his pupils; it is moreover the way to win the favour of the teacher unless he is a very exceptional man. Yet the habit of passive acceptance is a disastrous one in later life. It causes man to seek and to accept a leader, and to accept as a leader whoever is established in that position.
BERTRAND RUSSELL (1872–1970)

When anyone asks me how I can best describe my experience in nearly forty years at sea, I merely say, uneventful. Of course there have been winter gales, and storms and fog and the like. But in all my experience, I have never been in any accident … or

any sort worth speaking about. I have seen but one vessel in distress in all my years at sea. I never saw a wreck and never have been wrecked nor was I ever in any predicament that threatened to end in disaster of any sort.
Captain E. J. SMITH (1850–1912), RMS *Titanic*

Achievement

You can have anything you want—if you want it badly enough. You can be anything you want to be, do anything you set out to accomplish if you hold to that desire with singleness of purpose.
WILLIAM ADAMS (1706–1789)

Optimism is essential to achievement and it is also the foundation of courage and true progress.
LLOYD ALEXANDER (1924–)

Nothing splendid has ever been achieved except by those who dared to believe that something inside of them was superior to circumstance.
BRUCE BARTON (1886–1967)

Great things are accomplished by talented people who believe they will accomplish them.
WARREN G. BENNIS (1925–)

Life is all one piece. Men err when they think they can be inhuman exploiters in their business life, and loving husbands and fathers at home. For achievement without love is a cold and tight-lipped murderer of human happiness everywhere.
SMILEY BLANTON (1882–1966)

What looks like a loss may be the very event which is subsequently responsible for helping to produce the major achievement of your life.
SRULLY D. BLOTNICK (1941–)

I don't confuse greatness with perfection. To be great anyhow is … the higher achievement.
LOIS MCMASTER BUJOLD (1949–), *Mirror Dance*

"I can't do it" never yet accomplished anything; "I will try" has performed wonders.
GEORGE P. BURNHAM (1868–1939)

Nothing stops the man who desires to achieve. Every obstacle is simply a course to develop his achievement muscle. It's a strengthening of his powers of accomplishment.
ERIC BUTTERWORTH (1916–2003)

Most of the important things in the world have been accomplished by people who have kept on trying when there seemed to be no hope at all.
DALE CARNEGIE (1888–1955)

If you fear making anyone mad, then you ultimately probe for the lowest common denominator of human achievement.
JIMMY CARTER (1924–)

I don't measure America by its achievement but by its potential.
SHIRLEY CHISHOLM (1924–2005)

The best current evidence is that media are mere vehicles that deliver instruction, but do not influence student achievement any more than the truck that delivers groceries causes change in our nutrition.
RICHARD CLARK (1951–)

Nothing great will ever be achieved without great men, and men are great only if they are determined to be so.
CHARLES DE GAULLE (1890–1970)

None of us will ever accomplish anything excellent or commanding except when he listens to this whisper which is heard by him alone.
RALPH WALDO EMERSON (1803–1882)

Death comes to all
But great achievements raise a monument
Which shall endure until the sun grows old.
GEORG FABRICIUS (1516–1571), "In Praise of Georgius Agricola"

There is joy in work. There is no happiness except in the realization that we have accomplished something.
HENRY FORD (1863–1947)

To accomplish great things, we must not only act but also dream. Not only plan but also believe.
Anatole France (1844–1926)

My mother drew a distinction between achievement and success. She said that "achievement is the knowledge that you have studied and worked hard and done the best that is in you. Success is being praised by others, and that's nice, too, but not as important or satisfying. Always aim for achievement and forget about success."
Helen Hayes (1900–1993)

Our achievements speak for themselves. What we have to keep track of are our failures, discouragements, and doubts. We tend to forget the past difficulties, the many false starts, and the painful groping. We see our past achievements as the end results of a clean forward thrust, and our present difficulties as signs of decline and decay.
Eric Hoffer (1902–1983)

They who lack talent expect things to happen without effort. They ascribe failure to a lack of inspiration or ability, or to misfortune, rather than to insufficient application. At the core of every true talent there is an awareness of the difficulties inherent in any achievement, and the confidence that by persistence and patience something worthwhile will be realized. Thus talent is a species of vigor.
Eric Hoffer (1902–1983)

In studying the history of the human mind one is impressed again and again by the fact that the growth of the mind is the widening of the range of consciousness, and that each step forward has been a most painful and laborious achievement. One could almost say that nothing is more hateful to man than to give up even a particle of his unconsciousness. Ask those who have tried to introduce a new idea!
Carl Jung (1875–1961)

I long to accomplish a great and noble task, but it is my chief duty to accomplish small tasks as if they were great and noble.
Helen Keller (1880–1968)

Only those who dare to fail greatly can ever achieve greatly.
Robert F. Kennedy (1925–1968)

The controversial overachiever is someone whose grasp exceeds his reach. This is possible but not attractive.
Fran Lebowitz (1950–)

Ideas are the beginning of all achievement.
Bruce Lee (1940–1973)

A successful individual typically sets his next goal somewhat but not too much above his last achievement. In this way he steadily raises his level of aspiration.
Kurt Lewin (1890–1947)

Failures are finger posts on the road to achievement.
C. S. Lewis (1898–1963)

If you'll not settle for anything less than your best, you will be amazed at what you can accomplish in your lives.
Vince Lombardi (1913–1970)

The achievements of an organization are the results of the combined effort of each individual.
Vince Lombardi (1913–1970)

I never did anything alone. Whatever was accomplished in this country was accomplished collectively.
Golda Meir (1898–1978)

Lord grant that I might always desire more than I can accomplish.
Michelangelo (1475–1564)

The greater danger for most of us lies not in setting our aim too high and falling short, but in setting our aim too low, and achieving our mark.
Michelangelo (1475–1564)

Achievement is largely the product of steadily raising one's levels of aspiration and expectation.
Jack Nicklaus (1940–), *My Story*

Don't let the fear of the time it will take to accomplish something stand in the way of your doing it. The time will pass anyway; we might just as well put that passing time to the best possible use.
EARL NIGHTINGALE (1921–1989)

Nor is it always in the most distinguished achievements that men's virtues or vices may be best discovered: but very often an action of small note, a short saying, or a jest, shall distinguish a person's real character more than the greatest sieges, or the most important battle.
PLUTARCH (AD 46–120)

Happiness is that state of consciousness which proceeds from the achievement of one's values.
AYN RAND (1905–1982)

Happiness lies in the joy of achievement and the thrill of creative effort.
FRANKLIN D. ROOSEVELT (1882–1945)

It is not the critic who counts; not the man who points out how the strong man stumbles, or where the doer of deeds could have done them better. The credit belongs to the man who is actually in the arena, whose face is marred by dust and sweat and blood, who strives valiantly; who errs and comes short again and again; because there is no effort without error and shortcomings; but who does actually strive to do the deed; who knows the great enthusiasm, the great devotion, who spends himself in a worthy cause, who at the best knows in the end the triumph of high achievement and who at the worst, if he fails, at least he fails while daring greatly. So that his place shall never be with those cold and timid souls who know neither victory nor defeat.
THEODORE ROOSEVELT (1858–1919)

Whereas in art nothing worth doing can be done without genius, in science even a very moderate capacity can contribute to a supreme achievement.
BERTRAND RUSSELL (1872–1970)

How my achievements mock me!
WILLIAM SHAKESPEARE (1564–1616), *Troilus and Cressida*

The roots of true achievement lie in the will to become the best that you can become.
HAROLD TAYLOR (1914–1993)

The awareness of the ambiguity of one's highest achievements (as well as one's deepest failures) is a definite symptom of maturity.
PAUL TILLICH (1886–1965)

The greatest achievement of the human spirit is to live up to one's opportunities and make the most of one's resources.
MARQUIS DE VAUVENARGUES (1715–1747)

You are not here merely to make a living. You are here to enable the world to live more amply, with greater vision, and with a finer spirit of hope and achievement. You are here to enrich the world. You impoverish yourself if you forget this errand.
WOODROW WILSON (1856–1924)

Accomplish something for yourself, not others.
ANONYMOUS

Instead of solid accomplishments, the man pursues pleasures and self-gratification. He will never achieve anything so long as he is surrounded by dissipating temptations.
THE I CHING

When clouds form in the skies we know that rain will follow but we must not wait for it. Nothing will be achieved by attempting to interfere with the future before the time is ripe. Patience is needed.
THE I CHING

Acting

Look up the definition of rejection in the dictionary, get really comfortable with it, and then maybe you can go into acting.
LONI ANDERSON (1946–)

Acting is all about honesty. If you can fake that, you've got it made.
GEORGE BURNS (1896–1996)

The most difficult character in comedy is that of a fool, and he must be no simpleton who plays the part.
MIGUEL DE CERVANTES (1547–1616), *Don Quixote*

Acting is the most minor of gifts and not a very high-class way to earn a living. After all, Shirley Temple could do it at the age of four.
KATHARINE HEPBURN (1907–2003)

I enjoy being a highly overpaid actor.
ROGER MOORE (1927–)

Acting is not being emotional, but being able to express emotion.
KATE REID (1930–1993)

Acting is merely the art of keeping a large group of people from coughing.
SIR RALPH RICHARDSON (1902–1983)

Talk low, talk slow, and don't talk too much.
JOHN WAYNE (1907–1979)

I love acting. It is so much more real than life.
OSCAR WILDE (1854–1900), *The Picture of Dorian Gray*

Actions

All human actions have one or more of these seven causes: chance, nature, compulsion, habit, reason, passion, and desire.
ARISTOTLE (384–322 BC)

Men acquire a particular quality by constantly acting a particular way … you become just by performing just actions, temperate by performing temperate actions, brave by performing brave actions.
ARISTOTLE (384–322 BC)

Action is the antidote to despair.
JOAN BAEZ (1941–)

The superior man is modest in his speech, but exceeds in his actions.
CONFUCIUS (551–479 BC), *The Confucian Analects*

I have long since come to believe that people never mean half of what they say, and that it is best to disregard their talk and judge only their actions.
DOROTHY DAY (1897–1980), *The Long Loneliness*

You cannot have a proud and chivalrous spirit if your conduct is mean and paltry; for whatever a man's actions are, such must be his spirit.
DEMOSTHENES (384–322 BC), *Third Olynthiac*

Don't be too timid and squeamish about your actions. All life is an experiment. The more experiments you make the better.
RALPH WALDO EMERSON (1803–1882)

Words without actions are the assassins of idealism.
HERBERT HOOVER (1874–1964)

The actions of men are the best interpreters of their thoughts.
JOHN LOCKE (1632–1704)

You ask me why I do not write something.… I think one's feelings waste themselves in words, they ought all to be distilled into actions and into actions which bring results.
FLORENCE NIGHTINGALE (1820–1910)

What is the use in not actively engaging life? It passes anyhow.
MARGE PIERCY (1936–)

Only actions give life strength; only moderation gives it a charm.
JEAN PAUL RICHTER (1763–1825)

Great thoughts speak only to the thoughtful mind, but great actions speak to all mankind.
THEODORE ROOSEVELT (1858–1919)

Action is eloquence.
WILLIAM SHAKESPEARE (1564–1616), *Coriolanus*

Strong reasons make strong actions.
WILLIAM SHAKESPEARE (1564–1616), *King John*

I must lose myself in action, lest I wither in despair.
ALFRED, LORD TENNYSON (1809–1892)

Actions lie louder than words.
CAROLYN WELLS (1862–1942)

Many men feel that they should act according to the time or the moment they are facing, and thus are in confusion when something goes beyond this and some difficulty arises.
SHIBA YOSHIMASA (1350–1410)

Activity

During [these] periods of relaxation after concentrated intellectual activity, the intuitive mind seems to take over and can produce the sudden clarifying insights which give so much joy and delight.
FRITJOF CAPRA (1939–)

I'm struck by the insidious, computer-driven tendency to take things out of the domain of muscular activity and put them into the domain of mental activity. The transfer is not paying off. Sure, muscles are unreliable, but they represent several million years of accumulated finesse.
BRIAN ENO (1948–)

We must learn to be still in the midst of activity and to be vibrantly alive in repose.
INDIRA GANDHI (1917–1984)

Happiness consists in activity. It is a running steam, not a stagnant pool.
JOHN MASON GOOD (1764–1827)

Enjoyment is not a goal, it is a feeling that accompanies important ongoing activity.
PAUL GOODMAN (1911–1972)

Love is that splendid triggering of human vitality … the supreme activity which nature affords anyone for going out of himself toward someone else.
JOSÉ ORTEGA Y GASSET (1883–1955)

Any activity becomes creative when the doer cares about doing it right, or better.
JOHN UPDIKE (1932–)

Actors

If there's anything unsettling to the stomach, it's watching actors on television talk about their personal lives.
MARLON BRANDO (1924–2004)

Actors search for rejection. If they don't get it they reject themselves.
CHARLIE CHAPLIN (1889–1977)

I do not regret one professional enemy I have made. Any actor who doesn't dare to make an enemy should get out of the business.
BETTE DAVIS (1908–1989), *The Lonely Life*

Modesty in an actor is as fake as passion in a call girl.
JACKIE GLEASON (1916–1987)

You've got to be original, because if you're like someone else, what do they need you for?
BERNADETTE PETERS (1948–)

Acting is a form of deception, and actors can mesmerize themselves almost as easily as an audience.
LEO ROSTEN (1908–1997)

Our revels now are ended. These our actors,
As I foretold you, were all spirits, and
Are melted into air, into thin air:
And, like the baseless fabric of this vision,
The cloud-capp'd towers, the gorgeous palaces,
The solemn temples, the great globe itself,
Yea, all which it inherit, shall dissolve,
And, like this insubstantial pageant faded,
Leave not a rack behind. We are such stuff
As dreams are made on; and our little life
Is rounded with a sleep….
WILLIAM SHAKESPEARE (1564–1616), *The Tempest*

We're actors—we're the opposite of people.
TOM STOPPARD (1937–), *Rosencrantz and Guildenstern Are Dead*

All programmers are playwrights and all computers are lousy actors.
ANONYMOUS

Addiction

All sins tend to be addictive, and the terminal point of addiction is damnation.
W. H. AUDEN (1907–1973)

I stopped smoking cigarettes over 15 years ago. That's an addiction, a sick addiction.
MIKHAIL BARYSHNIKOV (1948–)

Nothing is more singular about this generation than its addiction to music.
ALLAN BLOOM (1930–1992)

We need to reduce or at least limit U.S. demand for oil as quickly as possible, and we need to develop new technologies that can further help address our addiction to oil in the future.
SHERWOOD BOEHLERT (1936–)

Most kids turn to drug addiction, alcoholism, and even suicide. It's very tragic. Child actors have a lot of tragedy.
MORGAN BRITTANY (1951–)

I had not taken a bath in a year nor changed my clothes or removed them except to stick a needle every hour in the fibrous grey wooden flesh of heroin addiction. I did absolutely nothing.
WILLIAM S. BURROUGHS (1914–1997)

She goes from one addiction to another. All are ways for her to not feel her feelings.
ELLEN BURSTYN (1932–)

Feeding our addiction to fossil fuels is how we got in this mess in the first place.
LOIS CAPPS (1938–)

Just cause you got the monkey off your back doesn't mean the circus has left town.
GEORGE CARLIN (1937–)

I got invited to Japan by a Dr. Wu, who wanted me to talk about nicotine addiction.
ALLAN CARR (1937–1999)

If you're happy, you eat. If you're sad, you eat. You lose a job, you eat. You get a job, you eat. It's, you know, it's addiction.
BARBARA COOK (1927–)

A moderate addiction to money may not always be hurtful; but when taken in excess it is nearly always bad for the health.
CLARENCE DAY (1874–1935)

You can change a person's life in an instant; put him in a movie, and you start thinking differently, you want to be in another movie. It's like an addiction almost.
DENNIS FARINA (1944–)

I hope they find the DNA, the one that will fix alcoholism and drug addiction.
MELANIE GRIFFITH (1957–)

It is hard to understand addiction unless you have experienced it.
KEN HENSLEY (1945–)

Every form of addiction is bad, no matter whether the narcotic be alcohol, morphine or idealism.
CARL JUNG (1875–1961)

No one is immune from addiction; it afflicts people of all ages, races, classes, and professions.
PATRICK J. KENNEDY (1967–)

I admire addicts. In a world where everybody is waiting for some blind, random disaster, or some sudden disease, the addict has the comfort of knowing what will most likely wait for him down the road. He's taken some control over his ultimate fate, and his addiction keeps the cause of death from being a total surprise.
CHUCK PALAHNIUK (1962–)

I love making people laugh. It's an addiction and it's probably dysfunctional, but I am addicted to it and there's no greater pleasure for me than sitting in a theater and feeling a lot of people losing control of themselves.
JAY ROACH (1957–)

Avant-gardism is an addiction that can be appeased only by a revolution in permanence.
HAROLD ROSENBERG (1906–1978)

I remain convinced that obstinate addiction to ordinary language in our private thoughts is one of the main obstacles to progress in philosophy.
BERTRAND RUSSELL (1872–1970)

We may think there is willpower involved, but more likely … change is due to want power. Wanting the new addiction more than the old one. Wanting the new me in preference to the person I am now.
GEORGE SHEEHAN (1918–1993)

Secrecy, once accepted, becomes an addiction.
EDWARD TELLER (1908–2003)

Everyone knows the health consequences at this point. What people fail to acknowledge is their addiction—people think they can stop at any time, that it's easy—it's not.
CHRISTY TURLINGTON (1969–)

The addiction to sports, therefore, in a peculiar degree marks an arrested development in man's moral nature.
THORSTEIN VEBLEN (1857–1929)

This dark diction has become America's addiction.
KANYE WEST (1977–)

Adjustment

A man is not rightly conditioned until he is a happy, healthy, and prosperous being; and happiness, health, and prosperity are the result of a harmonious adjustment of the inner with the outer of the man with his surroundings.
JAMES ALLEN (1864–1912)

To harmonize the One with the Many, this is indeed a difficult adjustment, perhaps the most difficult of all, and so important, withal, that nations have perished from their failure to achieve it.
IRVING BABBITT (1865–1933)

The adjustment of reality to the masses and of the masses to reality is a process of unlimited scope, as much for thinking as for perception.
WALTER BENJAMIN (1892–1940)

In the adjustment of the new order of things, we women demand an equal voice; we shall accept nothing less.
CARRIE CHAPMAN CATT (1859–1947)

Freedom is an internal achievement rather than an external adjustment.
POWELL CLAYTON (1833–1914)

All biologic phenomena act to adjust: there are no biologic actions other than adjustments. Adjustment is another name for Equilibrium. Equilibrium is the Universal, or that which has nothing external to derange it.
CHARLES FORT (1874–1932)

There may be some difficulties during a period of adjustment. Specifically, picking up their life again and making their own truly independent decisions.
RICK ROSS (1952–)

In other words the inhibitory process was found capable of no less delicate quantitative adjustment than is the excitatory process.
CHARLES SCOTT SHERRINGTON (1857–1952)

I think I'm constantly in a state of adjustment.
PATTI SMITH (1946–)

Life is the continuous adjustment of internal relations to external relations.
HERBERT SPENCER (1820–1903)

Happiness comes from … some curious adjustment to life.
HUGH WALPOLE (1884–1941)

Admiration

Admiration is a very short-lived passion that immediately decays upon growing familiar with its object, unless it be still fed with fresh discoveries,

and kept alive by a perpetual succession of miracles rising into view.
JOSEPH ADDISON (1672–1719)

Familiarity breeds contempt, while rarity wins admiration.
APULEIUS (124–170)

Men go abroad to admire the heights of mountains, the mighty billows of the sea, the broad tides of rivers, the compass of the ocean, and the circuits of the stars, and pass themselves by.
SAINT AUGUSTINE (354–430)

If we want our children to possess the traits of character we most admire, we need to teach them what those traits are and why they deserve both admiration and allegiance. Children must learn to identify the forms and content of those traits.
WILLIAM BENNETT (1943–)

Admiration, n.: Our polite recognition of another's resemblance to ourselves.
AMBROSE BIERCE (1842–1914), *The Devil's Dictionary*

Enthusiastic Admiration is the first Principle of Knowledge and its last.
WILLIAM BLAKE (1757–1827)

Ignorance is the mother of admiration.
GEORGE CHAPMAN (1559–1634)

Great is our admiration of the orator who speaks with fluency and discretion.
CICERO (106-43 BC)

The poet never asks for admiration; he wants to be believed.
JEAN COCTEAU (1889–1963)

In wonder all philosophy began, in wonder it ends, and admiration fill up the interspace; but the first wonder is the offspring of ignorance, the last is the parent of adoration.
SAMUEL TAYLOR COLERIDGE (1772–1834)

Distance is a great promoter of admiration!
DENIS DIDEROT (1713–1784)

My religion consists of a humble admiration of the illimitable superior spirit who reveals himself in the slight details we are able to perceive with our frail and feeble mind.
ALBERT EINSTEIN (1879–1955)

The youth, intoxicated with his admiration of a hero, fails to see, that it is only a projection of his own soul, which he admires.
RALPH WALDO EMERSON (1803–1882)

Admiration is the daughter of ignorance.
BENJAMIN FRANKLIN (1706–1790)

To love is to admire with the heart; to admire is to love with the mind.
THÉOPHILE GAUTIER (1811–1872)

Though familiarity may not breed contempt, it takes the edge off admiration.
WILLIAM HAZLITT (1778–1830)

It is better in some respects to be admired by those with whom you live, than to be loved by them. And this is not on account of any gratification of vanity, but because admiration is so much more tolerant than love.
SIR ARTHUR HELPS (1813–1875)

If you want to sacrifice the admiration of many men for the criticism of one, go ahead, get married.
KATHARINE HEPBURN (1907–2003)

Our admiration is so given to dead martyrs that we have little time for living heroes.
ELBERT HUBBARD (1856–1915)

Admiration begins where acquaintance ceases.
SAMUEL JOHNSON (1709–1784)

When a nation gives birth to a man who is able to produce a great thought, another is born who is able to understand and admire it.
JOSEPH JOUBERT (1754–1824)

Don't accept your dog's admiration as conclusive evidence that you are wonderful.
ANN LANDERS (1918–2002)

I have always been an admirer. I regard the gift of admiration as indispensable if one is to amount to something; I don't know where I would be without it.
FRANÇOIS DE LA ROCHEFOUCAULD (1613–1680)

You always admire what you really don't understand.
BLAISE PASCAL (1623–1662)

What I have known with respect to myself, has tended much to lessen both my admiration, and my contempt, of others.
JOSEPH PRIESTLEY (1733–1804)

The only things one can admire at length are those one admires without knowing why.
JEAN ROSTAND (1894–1977)

Tell me who admires you and loves you, and I will tell you who you are.
CHARLES AUGUSTIN SAINTE-BEUVE (1804–1869)

Admiration and familiarity are strangers.
GEORGE SAND (1804–1876)

The secret of happiness is to admire without desiring.
CARL SANDBURG (1878–1967)

Whenever you commend, add your reasons for doing so; it is this which distinguishes the approbation of a man of sense from the flattery of sycophants and admiration of fools.
SIR RICHARD STEELE (1672–1729)

To be rich in admiration and free from envy, to rejoice greatly in the good of others, to love with such generosity of heart that your love is still a dear possession in absence or unkindness—these are the gifts which money cannot buy.
ROBERT LOUIS STEVENSON (1850–1894)

We live by admiration, hope and love.
WILLIAM WORDSWORTH (1770–1850)

Besides mutual admiration, the first requisite for Platonic friendship is a subtle trace of disdain.
ANONYMOUS

Adolescence

What laughter is to childhood, sex is to adolescence.
MARTHA BECK (1962–)

There is a weirdness about having a famous pre-pubescent in the house when you are going through the trials and tribulations of adolescence.
DANNY BONADUCE (1959–)

I am in an adolescence in reverse, as mysterious as the first, except that this time I feel it as a decay of the odds that I might live for a while, that I can sleep it off.
HAROLD BRODKEY (1930–1996)

Adolescence is just one big walking pimple.
CAROL BURNETT (1933–)

Adolescence is a drastic time for anyone. I grew four inches, for heaven's sake.
TIA CARRERE (1966–)

Elegance is not the prerogative of those who have just escaped from adolescence, but of those who have already taken possession of their future.
COCO CHANEL (1883–1971)

You don't have to suffer to be a poet; adolescence is enough suffering for anyone.
JOHN CIARDI (1916–1986)

I have always had a sense that we are all pretty much alone in life, particularly in adolescence.
ROBERT CORMIER (1925–2000)

Premature burial works just fine as a cure for adolescence.
GEORGE ALEC EFFINGER (1947–2002)

With any child entering adolescence, one hunts for signs of health, is desperate for the smallest indication that the child's problems will never be important enough for a television movie.
NORA EPHRON (1941–)

Maturity is only a short break in adolescence.
JULES FEIFFER (1929–)

Adolescence is a new birth, for the higher and more completely human traits are now born.
G. STANLEY HALL (1844–1924)

Adolescence is the time when an individual "recapitulates" the savage stage of the race's past.
G. STANLEY HALL (1844–1924)

The four stages of man are infancy, childhood, adolescence, and obsolescence.
ART LINKLETTER (1912–), *A Child's Garden of Misinformation*

Adolescence isn't just about prom or wearing sparkly dresses.
JENA MALONE (1984–)

Poetry is adolescence fermented, and thus preserved.
JOSÉ ORTEGA Y GASSET (1883–1955)

Hemingway never grew out of adolescence. His scope and depth stayed shallow because he had no idea what women are for.
REX STOUT (1886–1975)

I never killed anybody or anything, but I certainly had my nightmarish adolescence.
ETHAN SUPLEE (1976–)

Snow and adolescence are the only problems that disappear if you ignore them long enough.
EARL WILSON (1934–2005)

Adolescence is the stage between infancy and adultery.
ANONYMOUS

Adultery

Affairs are easier of entrance than of exit; and it is but common prudence to see our way out before we venture in.
AESOP (620–560 BC)

Passion is the evil in adultery. If a man has no opportunity of living with another man's wife, but if it is obvious for some reason that he would like to do so, and would do so if he could, he is no less guilty than if he was caught in the act.
SAINT AUGUSTINE (354–430)

As a musician I tell you that if you were to suppress adultery, fanaticism, crime, evil, the supernatural, there would no longer be the means for writing one note.
GEORGES BIZET (1838–1875)

Christ and The Church: If he were to apply for a divorce on the grounds of cruelty, adultery and desertion, he would probably get one.
SAMUEL BUTLER (1835–1902)

What men call gallantry and gods adultery
Is much more common where the climate's sultry.
LORD BYRON (1788–1824)

I've looked on many women with lust. I've committed adultery in my heart many times. God knows I will do this and forgives me.
JIMMY CARTER (1924–)

The task of an American writer is not to describe the misgivings of a woman taken in adultery as she looks out of a window at the rain but to describe four hundred people under the lights reaching for a foul ball. This is ceremony.
JOHN CHEEVER (1912–1982)

I do not believe we can blame genetics for adultery, homosexuality, dishonesty and other character flaws.
JERRY FALWELL (1933–2005)

French novels generally treat of the relations of women to the world and to lovers, after marriage; consequently there is a great deal in French novels about adultery, about improper relations between the sexes, about many things which the English public would not allow.
LAFCADIO HEARN (1850–1904)

Adultery is the application of democracy to love.
H. L. MENCKEN (1880–1956)

But, you know, there's still an argument, there's still ten states that outlaw premarital sex, and many more states where adultery is still outlawed and a crime.
LIAM NEESON (1952–)

Adultery—which is the only grounds for divorce in New York—is not grounds for divorce in California. As a matter of fact, adultery in Southern California is grounds for marriage.
ALLAN SHERMAN (1924–1973)

The first breath of adultery is the freest; after it, constraints aping marriage develop.
JOHN UPDIKE (1932–)

Adults

The twenties are tryout years and what motivates young people are two contradictory impulses. The urge to create a structure that will serve their needs into the (barely) foreseeable future and the fear of being locked into a life pattern that will ultimately prove unsatisfying or limited.
JANE ADDAMS (1860–1935)

Another belief of mine: that everyone else my age is an adult, whereas I am merely in disguise.
MARGARET ATWOOD (1939–)

I was a young person once, shortly after the polar ice caps retreated, and I distinctly recall believing that virtually all adults were clueless goobers.
DAVE BARRY (1947–)

If you treat a sick child like an adult and a sick adult like a child, everything usually works out pretty well.
RUTH CARLISLE (1908–)

Too many people grow up. That's the real trouble with the world, too many people grow up. They forget. They don't remember what it's like to be 12 years old. They patronize, they treat children as inferiors. Well I won't do that.
WALT DISNEY (1901–1966)

What a distressing contrast there is between the radiant intelligence of the child and the feeble mentality of the average adult.
SIGMUND FREUD (1856–1939)

Adults are obsolete children.
THEODOR SEUSS GEISEL (1904–1991)

We have not passed that subtle line between childhood and adulthood until … we have stopped saying, "It got lost," and say, "I lost it."
SYDNEY J. HARRIS (1917–1986)

A boy becomes an adult three years before his parents think he does, and about two years after he thinks he does.
LEWIS HERSHEY (1893–1977)

I have always thought it would be a blessing if each person could be blind and deaf for a few days during his early adult life. Darkness would make him appreciate sight; silence would teach him the joys of sound.
HELEN KELLER (1880–1968)

The average, healthy, well-adjusted adult gets up at seven-thirty in the morning feeling just plain terrible.
JEAN KERR (1922–2003)

I must take issue with the term "a mere child," for it has been my invariable experience that the company of a mere child is infinitely preferable to that of a mere adult.
FRAN LEBOWITZ (1950–)

The creative adult is the child who has survived.
URSULA K. LE GUIN (1929–)

Thirty was so strange for me. I've really had to come to terms with the fact that I am now a walking and talking adult.
C. S. LEWIS (1898–1963)

The day the child realizes that all adults are imperfect, he becomes an adolescent; the day he forgives them, he becomes an adult; the day he forgives himself, he becomes wise.
ALDEN NOWLAN (1933–1983)

If you are young and you drink a great deal it will spoil your health, slow your mind, make you fat—in other words, turn you into an adult.
P. J. O'ROURKE (1947–)

Adults are always asking little kids what they want to be when they grow up because they're looking for ideas.
PAULA POUNDSTONE (1959–)

To be a healthy person, you have to be sympathetic to the child you once were and maintain the continuity between you as a child and you as an adult.
MAURICE SENDAK (1928–)

The great challenge of adulthood is holding on to your idealism after you lose your innocence.
BRUCE SPRINGSTEEN (1949–)

A child becomes an adult when he realizes that he has a right not only to be right but also to be wrong.
THOMAS S. SZASZ (1920–)

Every time I see an adult on a bicycle, I no longer despair for the future of the human race.
H. G. WELLS (1866–1946)

Adventure

An adventure is only an inconvenience rightly considered. An inconvenience is only an adventure wrongly considered.
G. K. CHESTERTON (1874–1936)

Adventure is worthwhile.
AMELIA EARHART (1897–1937)

One way to get the most out of life is to look upon it as an adventure.
WILLIAM FEATHER (1908–1976)

It is only in adventure that some people succeed in knowing themselves—in finding themselves.
ANDRÉ GIDE (1869–1951)

Adversity

Certainly virtue is like precious odors, most fragrant when they are incensed, or crushed: for prosperity doth best discover vice, but adversity doth best discover virtue.
SIR FRANCIS BACON (1561–1626)

Prosperity is the blessing of the Old Testament; adversity is the blessing of the New.
SIR FRANCIS BACON (1561–1626)

If we had no winter, the spring would not be so pleasant: if we did not sometimes taste of adversity, prosperity would not be so welcome.
ANNE BRADSTREET (1612–1672), *Meditations Divine and Moral*

Adversity does teach who your real friends are.
LOIS MCMASTER BUJOLD (1949–), *A Civil Campaign*

In prosperity prepare for a change; in adversity hope for one.
JAMES BURGH (1714–1775)

Adversity is the diamond dust Heaven polishes its jewels with.
THOMAS CARLYLE (1795–1881)

What you see, but can't see over is as good as infinite.
THOMAS CARLYLE (1795–1881)

Be more prompt to go to a friend in adversity than in prosperity.
CHILO (C. 620–550 BC)

Friendship makes prosperity more shining and lessens adversity by dividing and sharing it.
CICERO (106–43 BC), *On Friendship*

It is the character of a brave and resolute man not to be ruffled by adversity and not to desert his post.
CICERO (106–43 BC)

In prosperity our friends know us; in adversity we know our friends.
JOHN CHURTON COLLINS (1848–1908)

The reason why great men meet with so little pity or attachment in adversity, would seem to be this: the friends of a great man were made by his fortune, his enemies by himself, and revenge is a much more punctual paymaster than gratitude.
CHARLES CALEB COLTON (1780–1832)

Adversity is the trial of principle. Without it a man hardly knows whether he is honest or not.
HENRY FIELDING (1707–1754)

He that can heroically endure adversity will bear prosperity with equal greatness of the soul; for the mind that cannot be dejected by the former is not likely to be transported without the latter.
HENRY FIELDING (1707–1754)

Memory tempers prosperity, mitigates adversity, controls youth, and delights old age.
FIRMIANUS LACTANTIUS (C. 240–320)

Adversity is like a strong wind. It tears away from us all but the things that cannot be torn, so that we see ourselves as we really are.
ARTHUR GOLDEN (1956–), *Memoirs of a Geisha*

Prosperity is a great teacher; adversity a greater.
WILLIAM HAZLITT (1778–1830)

It is not the mountain we conquer but ourselves.
EDMUND HILLARY (1919–)

In adversity remember to keep an even mind.
HORACE (65–8 BC), *Odes*

Adversity reveals genius, prosperity conceals it.
HORACE (65–8 BC)

Adversity makes men, and prosperity makes monsters.
VICTOR HUGO (1802–1885)

Adversity has ever been considered the state in which a man most easily becomes acquainted with himself.
SAMUEL JOHNSON (1709–1784)

He knows not his own strength that hath not met adversity.
BEN JONSON (1572–1637)

Nearly all men can stand adversity, but if you want to test a man's character, give him power.
ABRAHAM LINCOLN (1809–1865)

Always seek out the seed of triumph in every adversity.
OG MANDINO (1923–1996)

Sometimes I get the feeling the whole world is against me, but deep down I know that's not true. Some smaller countries are neutral.
ROBERT ORBEN (1927–)

Nothing is harder to direct than a man in prosperity; nothing more easily managed than one in adversity.
PLUTARCH (AD 46–120)

Prosperity is no just scale; adversity is the only balance to weigh friends.
PLUTARCH (AD 46–120)

Adversity is sometimes hard upon a man; but for one man who can stand prosperity, there are a hundred that will stand adversity.
ELVIS PRESLEY (1935–1977)

Prosperity makes friends, adversity tries them.
PUBLILIUS SYRUS (C. 100 BC), *Maxims*

Fire is the test of gold, adversity, of strong men.
SENECA (5 BC–AD 65), *Epistles*

The good things which belong to prosperity are to be wished, but the good things that belong to adversity are to be admired.
SENECA (5 BC–AD 65)

Sweet are the uses of adversity,
Which, like a toad, though ugly and venomous,
Wears yet a precious jewel in its head.
WILLIAM SHAKESPEARE (1564–1616), *As You Like It*

A wretched soul, bruised with adversity,
We bid be quiet when we hear it cry;
But were we burdened with like weight of pain,
As much or more we should ourselves complain.
WILLIAM SHAKESPEARE (1564–1616) *The Comedy of Errors*

Remember that there is nothing stable in human affairs; therefore avoid undue elation in prosperity, or undue depression in adversity.
SOCRATES (469–399 BC)

The sufferings that fate inflicts on us should be borne with patience, what enemies inflict with manly courage.
THUCYDIDES (C. 460–395 BC)

By trying we can easily learn to endure adversity. Another man's, I mean.
MARK TWAIN (1835–1910), *Following the Equator*

Be courteous to all, but intimate with few, and let those few be well tried before you give them your confidence. True friendship is a plant of slow growth, and must undergo and withstand the shocks of adversity before it is entitled to the appellation.
GEORGE WASHINGTON (1732–1799)

A smooth sea never made a skillful mariner, neither do uninterrupted prosperity and success qualify for usefulness and happiness. The storms of adversity, like those of the ocean, rouse the faculties, and excite the invention, prudence, skill and fortitude of the voyager. The martyrs of ancient times, in bracing their minds to outward calamities, acquired a loftiness of purpose and a moral heroism worth a lifetime of softness and security.
ANONYMOUS

By courage I repel adversity.
ANONYMOUS

Adversity is the touchstone of friendship.
FRENCH PROVERB

Advertising

Advertising is fundamentally persuasion, and persuasion happens to be not a science, but an art.
WILLIAM BERNBACH (1911–1982)

There is no such thing as a good or bad ad in isolation. What is good at one moment is bad at another. Research can trap you into the past.
WILLIAM BERNBACH (1911–1982)

Chess is as elaborate a waste of human intelligence as you can find outside an advertising agency.
RAYMOND CHANDLER (1888–1959)

The very first law in advertising is to avoid the concrete promise and cultivate the delightfully vague.
BILL COSBY (1937–)

Magazines and advertising are flogging the idea that you have to keep changing things and get something new. I think that's evil. But obviously that's your livelihood.
ROBIN DAY (1923–2000)

You can tell the ideals of a nation by its advertisements.
NORMAN DOUGLAS (1868–1952), *South Wind*

The advertising industry is one of our most basic forms of communication and, allegedly, of information. Yet, obviously, much of this ostensible information is not purveyed to inform but to manipulate and to achieve a result—to make somebody think he needs something that very possibly he doesn't need, or to make him think one version of something is better than another version when the ground for such a belief really doesn't exist.
MARVIN E. FRANKEL (1921–2002)

I read no newspaper now but Ritchie's, and in that chiefly the advertisements, for they contain the only truths to be relied on in a newspaper.
THOMAS JEFFERSON (1743–1826)

Advertising may be described as the science of arresting the human intelligence long enough to get money from it.
STEPHEN LEACOCK (1869–1944)

Advertising is a valuable economic factor because it is the cheapest way of selling goods, particularly if the goods are worthless.
SINCLAIR LEWIS (1885–1951)

Advertising people who ignore research are as dangerous as generals who ignore decodes of enemy signals.
DAVID OGILVY (1911–1999)

Advertising is the modern substitute for argument; its function is to make the worse appear the better.
GEORGE SANTAYANA (1863–1952)

What is the difference between unethical and ethical advertising? Unethical advertising uses falsehoods to deceive the public; ethical advertising uses truth to deceive the public.
VILHJALMUR STEFANSSON (1879–1962), *Discovery*

Many a small thing has been made large by the right kind of advertising.
MARK TWAIN (1835–1910), *A Connecticult Yankee in King Arthur's Court*

Half the money I spend on advertising is wasted; the trouble is I don't know which half.
JOHN WANAMAKER (1838–1922)

Advice

Never trust the advice of a man in difficulties.
AESOP (620–560 BC)

People who ask our advice almost never take it. Yet we should never refuse to give it, upon request, for it often helps us to see our own way more clearly.
BRENDAN FRANCIS BEHAN (1923–1964)

The advice of friends must be received with a judicious reserve; we must not give ourselves up to it and follow it blindly, whether right or wrong.
PIERRE CHARRON (1541–1603)

I owe my success to having listened respectfully to the very best advice, and then going away and doing the exact opposite.
G. K. CHESTERTON (1874–1936)

Advice is like snow—the softer it falls, the longer it dwells upon, and the deeper it sinks into the mind.
SAMUEL TAYLOR COLERIDGE (1772–1834)

Some people like my advice so much that they frame it upon the wall instead of using it.
GORDON R. DICKSON (1923–2001)

Advice is what we ask for when we already know the answer but wish we didn't.
ERICA JONG (1942–)

Good advice is something a man gives when he is too old to set a bad example.
FRANÇOIS DE LA ROCHEFOUCAULD (1613–1680)

Please give me some good advice in your next letter. I promise not to follow it.
EDNA ST. VINCENT MILLAY (1892–1950)

Many receive advice, few profit by it.
PUBLILIUS SYRUS (C. 100 BC), *Maxims*

The true secret of giving advice is, after you have honestly given it, to be perfectly indifferent whether it is taken or not, and never persist in trying to set people right.
HANNAH WHITALL SMITH (1832–1911)

In giving advice, seek to help, not please, your friend.
SOLON (638–559 BC)

I have found the best way to give advice to your children is to find out what they want and then advise them to do it.
HARRY S TRUMAN (1884–1972)

It is very difficult to live among people you love and hold back from offering them advice.
ANNE TYLER (1941–), *Celestial Navigation*

There is no human problem which could not be solved if people would simply do as I advise.
GORE VIDAL (1925–)

The only thing to do with good advice is pass it on. It is never any use to oneself.
OSCAR WILDE (1854–1900)

Ask advice only of your equals.
DANISH PROVERB

Write down the advice of him who loves you, though you like it not at present.
ENGLISH PROVERB

Never give advice unless asked.
GERMAN PROVERB

Never advise anyone to go to war or to marry.
SPANISH PROVERB

Affection

Does it really matter what these affectionate people do, so long as they don't do it in the streets and frighten the horses?
MRS. PATRICK CAMPBELL (1865–1940)

With affection beaming out of one eye, and calculation shining out of the other.
CHARLES DICKENS (1812–1870)

Let grace and goodness be the principal loadstone of thy affections. For love which hath ends, will have an end; whereas that which is founded on true virtue, will always continue.
JOHN DRYDEN (1631–1700)

A woman's whole life is a history of the affections.
WASHINGTON IRVING (1783–1859)

I am certain of nothing but the holiness of the heart's affections and the truth of imagination. What the imagination seizes as beauty must be truth, whether it existed before or not.
JOHN KEATS (1795–1821)

The affections are like lightning; you cannot tell where they will strike till they have fallen.
JEAN-BAPTISTE LACORAIRE (1802–1861)

Affection is responsible for nine-tenths of whatever solid and durable happiness there is in our lives.
C. S. LEWIS (1898–1963)

Nonsense and noise will oft prevail,
When honour and affection fail.
ROBERT LLOYD (1733–1764)

Talk not of wasted affection, affection never was wasted,
If it enrich not the heart of another, its waters returning
Back to their springs, like the rain shall fill them full of refreshment;
That which the fountain sends forth returns again to the fountain.
HENRY WADSWORTH LONGFELLOW (1807–1882)

Good men must be affectionate men.
SAMUEL RICHARDSON (1689–1761)

We are a spectacular, splendid manifestation of life. We have language. We have affection. We have genes for usefulness, and usefulness is about as close to a "common goal" of nature as I can guess at. And finally, and perhaps best of all, we have music.
LEWIS THOMAS (1913–1993), *The Medusa and the Snail*

African-Americans

What the Nazis did to the Jews in Europe, plantation owners and law enforcement were doing to the African-Americans.
MORRIS DEES (1936–)

Make sure to try to bring something interesting that will keep everyone's attention. Not just African-Americans, but everyone.
KENNETH EDMONDS (1958–)

I am always inspired by the community spirit and leadership I witness from African-Americans in New York and around the country.
ELIOT ENGEL (1947–)

It is my hope that as we commemorate Black History Month in the future, we will continue to celebrate the many achievements and rich culture of African-Americans.
ELIOT ENGEL (1947–)

From politics and business to music and food to culture, African-Americans have helped to shape our state's [Lousiana's] colorful past and its future.
MARY LANDRIEU (1955–)

Eight generations of African-Americans are still waiting to achieve their rights, compensation and restitution for the hundreds of years during which they were bought and sold on the market.
CYNTHIA MCKINNEY (1955–)

Out of 30 years of Second City I was probably the third African-American with the main stage cast. I was surprised when I first heard that. I think part of the reason that improvisation has never been popular with African-Americans is that it isn't popular in the inner cities.
TIM MEADOWS (1961–)

When you are the only two African-Americans among 14 clearly Caucasians, you could say that's a handicap.
JEFF PROBST (1962–)

Clearly, African-Americans and other African and Afro-descendant populations would see the uplifting of a black cartoon character, with monkey-like lips and head and a childish demeanor, as an attempt to malign them.
CHARLES RANGEL (1930–)

The challenges African-Americans are facing today are rooted in the system of slavery.
CHARLES RANGEL (1930–)

The Klan had used fear, intimidation and murder to brutally oppress over African-Americans who sought justice and equality and it sought to respond to the young workers of the civil rights movement in Mississippi in the same way.
CHARLES RANGEL (1930–)

Take the time to discover how African-Americans have had a great impact on this country. In science, education, literature, art, and politics.
LYNN SWANN (1952–)

We talk about freedoms for African-Americans but unless you have more than one option politically, how free are you?
LYNN SWANN (1952–)

Ray Charles' revolutionary approach to music was also reflected in his politics and his deep and abiding commitment to Martin Luther King and the plight of African-Americans. Ray Charles may not have been on the front lines, but he put his money where his mouth was.
DIANE WATSON (1933–)

What comes forth from you as an artist cannot be controlled. But you have responsibilities as a global citizen. Your history dictates your duty. And by writing about black people, you are not limiting yourself. The experiences of African-Americans are as wide open as God's closet.
AUGUST WILSON (1945–2005)

Afternoon

The majority of people perform well in a crisis and when the spotlight is on them; it's on the Sunday afternoons of this life, when nobody is looking, that the spirit falters.
ALAN BENNETT (1934–)

We should live our lives as though Christ were coming this afternoon.
JIMMY CARTER (1924–)

There's a certain Slant of light,
Winter Afternoons—
That oppresses, like the Heft
Of Cathedral Tunes—
EMILY DICKINSON (1830–1886), "No. 258"

Millions long for immortality who don't know what to do with themselves on a rainy Sunday afternoon.
SUSAN ERTZ (1894–1985), *Anger in the Sky*

Summer afternoon ... the two most beautiful words in the English language.
HENRY JAMES (1843–1916)

If you can spend a perfectly useless afternoon in a perfectly useless manner, you have learned how to live.
LIN YUTANG (1895–1976)

Age

You can only perceive real beauty in a person as they get older.
ANOUK AIMEE (1932–)

To keep the heart unwrinkled, to be hopeful, kindly, cheerful, reverent, that is to triumph over old age.
THOMAS BAILEY ALDRICH (1836–1907)

In case you're worried about what's going to become of the younger generation, it's going to grow up and start worrying about the younger generation.
ROGER ALLEN (1857–)

Young people are in a condition like permanent intoxication, because youth is sweet and they are growing.
ARISTOTLE (384–322 BC), *Nicomachean Ethics*

People who say you're just as old as you feel are all wrong, fortunately.
RUSSELL BAKER (1925–)

The secret of staying young is to live honestly, eat slowly, and lie about your age.
LUCILLE BALL (1911–1989)

To me, old age is always 15 years older than I am.
BERNARD M. BARUCH (1870–1965)

As for me, except for an occasional heart attack, I feel as young as I ever did.
ROBERT BENCHLEY (1889–1945)

Childhood, n.: The period of human life intermediate between the idiocy of infancy and the folly of youth—two removes from the sin of manhood and three from the remorse of age.
AMBROSE BIERCE (1842–1914), *The Devil's Dictionary*

To resist the frigidity of old age one must combine the body, the mind and the heart, and to keep them in parallel vigor one must exercise, study and love.
KARL VON BONSTETTEN (1745–1832)

Age to me means nothing. I can't get old; I'm working. I was old when I was twenty-one and out of work. As long as you're working, you stay young. When I'm in front of an audience, all that love and vitality sweeps over me and I forget my age.
GEORGE BURNS (1896–1996)

I was always taught to respect my elders and I've now reached the age when I don't have anybody to respect.
GEORGE BURNS (1896–1996)

Sure I'm for helping the elderly. I'm going to be old myself some day.
LILLIAN CARTER (1898–1983)

I am an old man, but in many senses a very young man. And this is what I want you to be, young, young all your life.
PABLO CASALS (1876–1973)

Old age is not so bad when you consider the alternatives.
MAURICE CHEVALIER (1888–1972)

I have enjoyed greatly the second blooming … suddenly you find, at the age of 50, say, that a whole new life has opened before you.
AGATHA CHRISTIE (1890–1976)

Always be nice to those younger than you, because they are the ones who will be writing about you.
CYRIL CONNOLLY (1903–1974)

As we grow old … the beauty steals inward.
RALPH WALDO EMERSON (1803–1882)

Of all the self-fulfilling prophecies in our culture, the assumption that aging means decline and poor health is probably the deadliest.
MARILYN FERGUSON (1938–), *The Aquarian Conspiracy*

Beware of the young doctor and the old barber.
BENJAMIN FRANKLIN (1706–1790)

Aging is not "lost youth" but a new stage of opportunity and strength.
BETTY FRIEDAN (1921–2006)

Though it sounds absurd, it is true to say I felt younger at sixty than I felt at twenty.
ELLEN GLASGOW (1873–1945), *The Woman Within*

A person is always startled when he hears himself seriously called an old man for the first time.
OLIVER WENDELL HOLMES SR. (1809–1894)

To be 70 years young is sometimes far more cheerful and hopeful than to be 40 years old.
OLIVER WENDELL HOLMES SR. (1809–1894)

Young men's minds are always changeable, but when an old man is concerned in a matter, he looks both before and after.
HOMER (800–700 BC), *The Iliad*

A young man is embarrassed to question an older one.
HOMER (800–700 BC), *The Odyssey*

The surprising thing about young fools is how many survive to become old fools.
DOUG LARSON (1902–1981)

The great secret that all old people share is that you really haven't changed in 70 or 80 years. Your body changes, but you don't change at all.
DORIS LESSING (1919–)

Age is not a particularly interesting subject. Anyone can get old. All you have to do is live long enough.
GROUCHO MARX (1890–1977)

There is no old age. There is, as there always was, just you.
CAROL MATTHAU (1924–2003)

When you have loved as she has loved, you grow old beautifully.
W. SOMERSET MAUGHAM (1874–1965)

The older I grow the more I distrust the familiar doctrine that age brings wisdom.
H. L. MENCKEN (1880–1956)

The young have aspirations that never come to pass, the old have reminiscences of what never happened.
H. H. MUNRO (1870–1916)

Middle age is when you've met so many people that every new person you meet reminds you of someone else.
OGDEN NASH (1902–1971)

I never feel age. If you have creative work, you don't have age or time.
LOUISE NEVELSON (1900–1988)

He who is of calm and happy nature will hardly feel the pressure of age, but to him who is of an opposite disposition youth and age are equally a burden.
PLATO (C. 428–348 BC), *The Republic*

An old doting fool, with one foot already in the grave.
PLUTARCH (AD 46–120), *Morals*

It is a mistake to regard age as a downhill grade toward dissolution. The reverse is true. As one grows older, one climbs with surprising strides.
GEORGE SAND (1804–1876)

Before you contradict an old man, my fair friend, you should endeavor to understand him.
GEORGE SANTAYANA (1863–1952)

The denunciation of the young is a necessary part of the hygiene of older people, and greatly assists in the circulation of their blood.
LOGAN PEARSALL SMITH (1865–1946), *Afterthoughts*

With age comes the inner, the higher life. Who would be forever young, to dwell always in externals?
ELIZABETH CADY STANTON (1815–1902)

I think age is a very high price to pay for maturity.
TOM STOPPARD (1937–)

Wisdom doesn't automatically come with old age. Nothing does, except wrinkles. It's true, some wines improve with age. But only if the grapes were good in the first place.
ABIGAIL VAN BUREN (1918–2002)

I'm very pleased with each advancing year. It stems back to when I was forty. I was a bit upset about

reaching that milestone, but an older friend consoled me. "Don't complain about growing old, many, many people do not have that privilege."
EARL WARREN (1891–1974)

You're never too old to become younger.
MAE WEST (1892–1980)

In spite of illness, in spite even of the archenemy sorrow, one can remain alive long past the usual date of disintegration if one is unafraid of change, insatiable in intellectual curiosity, interested in big things, and happy in small ways.
EDITH WHARTON (1862–1937)

Old age, calm, expanded, broad with the haughty breadth of the universe, old age flowing free with the delicious near-by freedom of death.
EDITH WHARTON (1862–1937)

The deepest definition of youth is life as yet untouched by tragedy.
ALFRED NORTH WHITEHEAD (1861–1947)

To get back my youth I would do anything in the world, except take exercise, get up early, or be respectable.
OSCAR WILDE (1854–1900), *The Picture of Dorian Gray*

I am not young enough to know everything.
OSCAR WILDE (1854–1900)

The longer I live the more beautiful life becomes.
FRANK LLOYD WRIGHT (1869–1959)

Aging

We should so provide for old age that it may have no urgent wants of this world to absorb it from meditation on the next. It is awful to see the lean hands of dotage making a coffer of the grave.
SIR EDWARD G. BULWER–LYTTON (1803–1873)

The excess of our youth are checks written against our age and they are payable with interest thirty years later.
CHARLES CALEB COLTON (1780–1832)

The worst old age is that of the mind.
WILLIAM HAZLITT (1778–1830)

To be happy, we must be true to nature, and carry our age along with us.
WILLIAM HAZLITT (1778–1830)

As you get older it is harder to have heroes, but it is sort of necessary.
ERNEST HEMINGWAY (1898–1961)

He that is not handsome at 20, nor strong at 30, nor rich at 40, nor wise at 50, will never be handsome, strong, rich or wise.
GEORGE HERBERT (1593–1632)

I am not afraid of aging, but more afraid of people's reactions to my aging.
BARBARA HERSHEY (1948–)

Old age equalizes—we are aware that what is happening to us has happened to untold numbers from the beginning of time. When we are young we act as if we were the first young people in the world.
ERIC HOFFER (1902–1983)

The end comes when we no longer talk with ourselves. It is the end of genuine thinking and the beginning of the final loneliness.
ERIC HOFFER (1902–1983)

A person is always startled when he hears himself called old for the first time.
OLIVER WENDELL HOLMES SR. (1809–1894)

Age, like distance lends a double charm.
OLIVER WENDELL HOLMES SR. (1809–1894)

To be seventy years young is sometimes far more cheerful and hopeful than to be forty years old.
OLIVER WENDELL HOLMES SR. (1809–1894)

Forty is the old age of youth, fifty is the youth of old age.
VICTOR HUGO (1802–1885)

When grace is joined with wrinkles, it is adorable. There is an unspeakable dawn in happy old age.
VICTOR HUGO (1802–1885)

How can the moribund old man reason back to himself the romance, the mystery, the imminence of great things with which our old earth tingled for him in the days when he was young and well?
WILLIAM JAMES (1842–1910)

My only fear is that I may live too long. This would be a subject of dread to me.
THOMAS JEFFERSON (1743–1826)

At seventy-seven it is time to be in earnest.
SAMUEL JOHNSON (1709–1784)

When I was as you are now, towering in the confidence of twenty-one, little did I suspect that I should be at forty-nine, what I now am.
SAMUEL JOHNSON (1709–1784)

Talking is the disease of age.
BEN JONSON (1572–1637)

From the middle of life onward, only he remains vitally alive who is ready to die with life.
CARL JUNG (1875–1961)

Old age realizes the dreams of youth: look at Dean Swift; in his youth he built an asylum for the insane, in his old age he was himself an inmate.
SØREN KIERKEGAARD (1813–1855)

The quality, not the longevity, of one's life is what is important.
MARTIN LUTHER KING JR. (1929–1968)

As one grows older, one becomes wiser and more foolish.
FRANÇOIS DE LA ROCHEFOUCAULD (1613–1680)

Few people know how to be old.
FRANÇOIS DE LA ROCHEFOUCAULD (1613–1680)

Old age is a tyrant, who forbids, under pain of death, the pleasures of youth.
FRANÇOIS DE LA ROCHEFOUCAULD (1613–1680)

Old people love to give good advice to console themselves for no longer being able to set a bad example.
FRANÇOIS DE LA ROCHEFOUCAULD (1613–1680)

The great secret that all old people share is that you really haven't changed in seventy or eighty years. Your body changes, but you don't change at all. And that, of course, causes great confusion.
DORIS LESSING (1919–)

One is rarely an impulsive innovator after the age of sixty, but one can still be a very fine orderly and inventive thinker. One rarely procreates children at that age, but one is all the more skilled at educating those who have already been procreated, and education is procreation of another kind.
GEORG C. LICHTENBERG (1742–1799)

Old age. It's the only disease … you don't look forward to being cured of.
HERMAN J. MANKIEWICZ (1897–1953) and ORSON WELLS (1915–1985), *Citizen Kane*

Agnosticism

I do not consider it an insult, but rather a compliment to be called an agnostic. I do not pretend to know where many ignorant men are sure—that is all that agnosticism means.
CLARENCE DARROW (1857–1938)

The mystery of the beginning of all things is insoluble by us; and I for one must be content to remain an agnostic.
CHARLES DARWIN (1809–1882)

What the world needs today is a definite, spiritual mobilization of the nations who believe in God against this tide of Red agnosticism.... And in rejecting an atheistic other world, I am confident that the Almighty God will be with us.
HERBERT HOOVER (1874–1964)

Agnosticism simply means that a man shall not say he knows or believes that for which he has no grounds for professing to believe.
THOMAS H. HUXLEY (1825–1895)

The Old Testament is responsible for more atheism, agnosticism, disbelief—call it what you will—than any book ever written; it has emptied more churches than all the counterattractions of cinema, motor bicycle and golf course.
A. A. MILNE (1882–1956)

I have a great love and respect for religion, great love and respect for atheism. What I hate is agnosticism, people who do not choose.
ORSON WELLES (1915–1985)

Agriculture

The diligent farmer plants trees, of which he himself will never see the fruit.
CICERO (106–43 BC)

The first farmer was the first man, and all historic nobility rests on possession and use of land.
RALPH WALDO EMERSON (1803–1882)

Ye rigid Ploughman! bear in mind
Your labor is for future hours.
Advance! spare not! nor look behind!
Plough deep and straight with all your powers!
RICHARD HENGIST HORNE (1802–1884)

Agriculture not only gives riches to a nation, but the only riches she can call her own.
SAMUEL JOHNSON (1709–1784)

He allows very readily, that the eyes and footsteps of the master are things most salutary to the land.
LUCIUS JUNIUS MODERATUS COLUMELLA (C. 100)

Adam, well may we labour, still to dress
This garden, still to tend plant, herb, and flower.
JOHN MILTON (1608–1674)

A field becomes exhausted by constant tillage.
OVID (43 BC–AD 17)

Our fathers used to say that the master's eye was the best fertilizer.
PLINY THE ELDER (AD 23–79)

Where grows—where grows it not? If vain our toil,
We ought to blame the culture, not the soil.
ALEXANDER POPE (1688–1744), *Epistle IV*

Airplanes

Airplanes are interesting toys but of no military value.
MARSHAL FERDINAND FOCH (1851–1929)

When everything seems to be going against you, remember that the airplane takes off against the wind, not with it.
HENRY FORD (1863–1947)

I feel about airplanes the way I feel about diets. It seems to me they are wonderful things for other people to go on.
JEAN KERR (1922–2003)

I realized that if I had to choose, I would rather have birds than airplanes.
CHARLES LINDBERGH (1902–1974)

Airplanes may kill you, but they ain't likely to hurt you.
LEROY "SATCHEL" PAIGE (1906–1982)

Alcohol

One reason I don't drink is that I want to know when I am having a good time.
NANCY ASTOR (1879–1964)

Electricity is actually made up of extremely tiny particles called electrons, that you cannot see with the naked eye unless you have been drinking.
DAVE BARRY (1947–), *The Taming of the Screw*

The good news is that parents are the leading influence on kids' [decisions] not to drink alcohol.
XAVIER BECERRA (1958–)

If we burn ourselves out with drugs or alcohol, we won't have long to go in this business.
JOHN BELUSHI (1949–1982)

Drinking makes such fools of people, and people are such fools to begin with, that it's compounding a felony.
ROBERT BENCHLEY (1889–1945)

For the same reason we don't allow kids to buy pornography, for the same reason we don't allow kids to buy cigarettes, for the same reason we don't allow kids to buy alcohol, we shouldn't allow them to go to stores and buy video games.
ROD BLAGOJEVICH (1956–)

When I lived in Seattle and Oregon, we partied, which is a large reason I don't know drugs or alcohol now because I saw the destruction of so many great musicians and artists.
MEREDITH BROOKS (1958–)

I think people tend to see the bigger point, which is maybe not fitting in and feeling like you didn't have the childhood that you expected you would have, or that you felt lonely or struggled with drugs and alcohol or just that you were able to achieve your dreams.
AUGUSTEN BURROUGHS (1909–)

Our national drug is alcohol. We tend to regard the use any other drug with special horror.
WILLIAM S. BURROUGHS (1914–1997)

If the headache would only precede the intoxication, alcoholism would be a virtue.
SAMUEL BUTLER (1835–1902)

I'm very serious about no alcohol, no drugs. Life is too beautiful.
JIM CARREY (1962–)

Alcohol is like love. The first kiss is magic, the second is intimate, the third is routine. After that you take the girl's clothes off.
RAYMOND CHANDLER (1888–1959)

I have taken more out of alcohol than alcohol has taken out of me.
SIR WINSTON CHURCHILL (1874–1965)

My rule of life prescribed as an absolutely sacred rite smoking cigars and also the drinking of alcohol before, after and if need be during all meals and in the intervals between them.
SIR WINSTON CHURCHILL (1874–1965)

Man seeks to escape himself in myth, and does so by any means at his disposal. Drugs, alcohol, or lies. Unable to withdraw into himself, he disguises himself. Lies and inaccuracy give him a few moments of comfort.
JEAN COCTEAU (1889–1963)

I have never even had a sip of alcohol, never have done drugs. The hardest thing I have ever done would be Pepsi.
DANE COOK (1972–)

An American Monkey after getting drunk on Brandy would never touch it again, and thus is much wiser than most men.
CHARLES DARWIN (1809–1882)

Drugs, alcohol and ego. They are a bad mix.
DON DOKKEN (1953–)

Drugs and alcohol can be so destructive.
KYAN DOUGLAS (1970–)

You got to realise that when I was 20 years old, I had a house, a Mercedes, a Corvette and a million dollars in the bank before I could buy alcohol legally.
DR. DRE (1965–)

Alcohol is necessary for a man so that he can have a good opinion of himself, undisturbed by the facts.
FINLEY PETER DUNNE (1867–1936)

Alcohol doesn't console, it doesn't fill up anyone's psychological gaps, all it replaces is the lack of God. It doesn't comfort man. On the contrary, it encourages him in his folly, it transports him to the supreme regions where he is master of his own destiny.
MARGUERITE DURAS (1914–1996)

Alcohol is barren. The words a man speaks in the night of drunkenness fade like the darkness itself at the coming of day.
MARGUERITE DURAS (1914–1996)

I'm glad now, at age 66, that I never used alcohol or tobacco…. I've buried a lot of friends who used tobacco or alcohol.
JERRY FALWELL (1933–2005)

Reminds me of my safari in Africa. Somebody forgot the corkscrew and for several days we had to live on nothing but food and water.
W. C. FIELDS (1880–1946)

Let me be the first to tell you, drinking alcohol is the worst thing to do in cold weather. Hot soup is the best because the process of digesting food helps to warm you up.
MORGAN FREEMAN (1937–)

Bacchus hath drowned more men than Neptune.
THOMAS FULLER (1608–1661), *Gnomologia*

But when alcohol comes in, start running. Because there's a demon there, and it goes back to her childhood.
DAVID GEST (1953–)

If they took all the drugs, nicotine, alcohol and caffeine off the market for six days, they'd have to bring out the tanks to control you.
DICK GREGORY (1932–)

If you are a sensitive person like me, you turn to something that makes you feel good. For me it was alcohol and cocaine.
MELANIE GRIFFITH (1957–)

Here's to alcohol: the cause of, and answer to, all of life's problems.
MATT GROENING (1954–)

Always do sober what you said you'd do drunk. That will teach you to keep your mouth shut.
ERNEST HEMINGWAY (1899–1961)

It is better to hide ignorance, but it is hard to do this when we relax over wine.
HERACLITUS (C. 535–475 BC)

The wine urges me on, the bewitching wine, which sets even a wise man to singing and to laughing gently and rouses him up to dance and brings forth words which were better unspoken.
HOMER (800–700 BC), *The Odyssey*

And malt does more than Milton can
To justify God's ways to man.
A. E. HOUSMAN (1859–1936)

Every form of addiction is bad, no matter whether the narcotic be alcohol, morphine, or idealism.
CARL JUNG (1875–1961)

My peers, lately, have found companionship through means of intoxication—it makes them sociable. I, however, cannot force myself to use drugs to cheat on my loneliness—it is all that I have—and when the drugs and alcohol dissipate, will be all that my peers have as well.
FRANZ KAFKA (1883–1924)

Ice cubes likely sell more alcohol for the distilling industry than attractive models in cheesecake poses. The inconspicuous ice cubes often hide the invisible sell—invisible, that is, to the conscious mind.
WILSON BRYAN KEY (1925–)

Great people talk about ideas, average people talk about things, and small people talk about wine.
FRAN LEBOWITZ (1950–)

I envy people who drink. At least they have something to blame everything on.
OSCAR LEVANT (1906–1972)

If you drink, don't drive. Don't even putt.
DEAN MARTIN (1917–1995)

Alcohol is a very patient drug. It will wait for the alcoholic to pick it up one more time.
MERCEDES MCCAMBRIDGE (1916–2004)

The trouble with jogging is that the ice falls out of your glass.
MARTIN MULL (1943–)

Two great European narcotics: alcohol and Christianity.
FRIEDRICH NIETZSCHE (1844–1900)

Scientists announced that they have located the gene for alcoholism. Scientists say they found it at a party, talking way too loudly.
CONAN O'BRIEN (1963–)

There is more refreshment and stimulation in a nap, even of the briefest, than in all the alcohol ever distilled.
OVID (43 BC–AD 17)

All excess is ill, but drunkenness is of the worst sort. It spoils health, dismounts the mind, and unmans men. It reveals secrets, is quarrelsome, lascivious, impudent, dangerous and bad.
WILLIAM PENN (1644–1718)

With such compelling information, the question is why haven't we been able to do more to prevent the crisis of underage drinking? The answer is: the alcohol industry.
LUCILLE ROYBAL-ALLARD (1941–)

Drunkenness is temporary suicide.
BERTRAND RUSSELL (1872–1970)

Alcohol is the anesthesia by which we endure the operation of life.
GEORGE BERNARD SHAW (1856–1950)

Alcohol may be man's worst enemy, but the Bible says love your enemy.
FRANK SINATRA (1915–1988)

That's all drugs and alcohol do, they cut off your emotions in the end.
RINGO STARR (1940–)

An alcoholic is someone you don't like who drinks as much as you do.
DYLAN THOMAS (1914–1953)

I hate to advocate drugs, alcohol, violence, or insanity to anyone, but they've always worked for me.
HUNTER S. THOMPSON (1937–2005)

[Water is] the only drink for a wise man.
HENRY DAVID THOREAU (1817–1862)

Work is the curse of the drinking classes.
OSCAR WILDE (1854–1900)

My Grandmother is over eighty and still doesn't need glasses. Drinks right out of the bottle.
HENNY YOUNGMAN (1906–1998)

When I read about the evils of drinking, I gave up reading.
HENNY YOUNGMAN (1906–1998)

Alcoholism

Drunkenness is nothing but voluntary madness.
SENECA (5 BC–AD 65)

O God, that men should put an enemy in their mouths to steal away their brains! That we should with joy, pleasance, revel, and applause transform ourselves into beasts!
WILLIAM SHAKESPEARE (1564–1616), *Othello*

Better belly burst than good liquor be lost.
JONATHAN SWIFT (1667–1745)

Sometimes too much drink is barely enough.
MARK TWAIN (1835–1910)

Alienation

Passion cuts everything else, it blocks all, it's what psychologists call unhealthy. It's what one calls total alienation.
ISABELLE ADJANI (1955–)

When you stop to think about it, so many films today where we don't have that kind of contact are films about alienation. About alienated feelings. We are much more alienated from our colleagues nowadays.
ELMER BERNSTEIN (1922–2004)

There is no religion in which everyday life is not considered a prison; there is no philosophy or ideology that does not think that we live in alienation.
EUGÈNE IONESCO (1909–1994)

The historical experience of socialist countries has sadly demonstrated that collectivism does not do away with alienation but rather increases it, adding to it a lack of basic necessities and economic inefficiency.
POPE JOHN PAUL II (1920–2005)

Without alienation, there can be no politics.
ARTHUR MILLER (1915–2005)

Young alienation, disappointment, and heartache is all a part of the first real growing up that we do.
JUDD NELSON (1959–)

Those English songs tend to sound like they have a connection. A lot of these songs are written in the past, and I proceeded to write more about alienation.
PAUL SIMON (1941–)

I think the degree of alienation and despair is more universal.
TERRY SOUTHERN (1924–1995)

Another cause for the increase in alienation and cynicism is a feeling that too many policy decisions that affect individuals have been taken out of any system that has accountability or that they can influence.
ROBERT TEETER (1939–2004)

Alliances

It is probably not love that makes the world go around, but rather those mutually supportive alliances through which partners recognize their dependence on each other for the achievement of shared and private goals.
FRED ALLEN (1894–1956)

Beware of sentimental alliances where the consciousness of good deeds is the only compensation for noble sacrifices.
OTTO VON BISMARCK (1815–1898)

To avoid entangling alliances has been a maxim of our policy ever since the days of Washington, and it's wisdom no one will attempt to dispute.
JAMES BUCHANAN (1791–1868)

An understanding is perhaps better than an alliance, which may stereotype arrangements which cannot be regarded as permanent in view of the changing circumstances from day to day.
EDWARD GREY (1862–1933)

Our alliances should be understood as a means to expand our influence, not as a constraint on our power. The expansion of democracy and freedom in the world should be a shared interest and value with all nations.
CHUCK HAGEL (1946–)

The 21st century will require a re-affirmation and re-definition of our alliances and international organizations.
CHUCK HAGEL (1946–)

Peace, commerce, and honest friendship with all nations; entangling alliances with none.
THOMAS JEFFERSON (1743–1826)

I know that military alliances and armament have been the reliance for peace for centuries, but they do not produce peace; and when war comes, as it inevitably does under such conditions, these armaments and alliances but intensify and broaden the conflict.
FRANK B. KELLOGG (1856–1937)

Community means engaging constructively with like-minded nations to build strong, sustaining institutions and alliances, and bringing emerging powers into this community so future conflict becomes less likely.
JOE LIEBERMAN (1942–)

[We] are a nation with some conscience. It means alliances are extremely important when they're

based on a national interest. We have to have the ability to sustain our presence within those alliances.
MALCOLM WALLOP (1933–)

It is our true policy to steer clear of entangling alliances with any portion of the foreign world.
GEORGE WASHINGTON (1732–1799)

Ambassadors

An ambassador is not simply an agent; he is also a spectacle.
WALTER BAGEHOT (1826–1877)

The function of a briefing paper is to prevent the ambassador from saying something dreadfully indiscreet. I sometimes think its true object is to prevent the ambassador from saying anything at all.
KINGMAN BREWSTER JR. (1919–1988)

The popular song is America's greatest ambassador.
SAMMY CAHN (1913–1993)

He who plays advisor is no longer ambassador.
PIERRE CORNEILLE (1606–1684)

If I could give some advice to the White House, it would be that President Bush should be his own ambassador more.
PETER MANDELSON (1953–)

An ambassador is an honest man sent abroad to lie and intrigue for the benefit of his country.
HENRY WOTTON (1568–1639)

Ambition

A man without ambition is dead. A man with ambition but no love is dead. A man with ambition and love for his blessings here on earth is ever so alive. Having been alive, it won't be so hard in the end to lie down and rest.
PEARL BAILEY (1918–1990)

Ambition—it is the last infirmity of noble minds.
JAMES M. BARRIE (1860–1937)

A noble man compares and estimates himself by an idea which is higher than himself; and a mean man, by one lower than himself. The one produces aspiration; the other ambition, which is the way in which a vulgar man aspires.
HENRY WARD BEECHER (1813–1887)

Ambition is a poor excuse for not having sense enough to be lazy.
EDGAR BERGEN (1903–1978)

Like dogs in a wheel, birds in a cage, or squirrels on a chain, ambitious men still climb and climb, with great labor, and incessant anxiety, but never reach the top.
ROBERT BURTON (1577–1640)

All ambitions are lawful except those which climb upward on the miseries or credulities of mankind.
WILLIAM CONGREVE (1670–1729)

I feel that you [Americans] are justified in looking into the future with true assurance, because you have a mode of living in which we find the joy of life and the joy of work harmoniously combined. Added to this is the spirit of ambition, which pervades your very being, and seems to make the day's work like a happy child at play.
ALBERT EINSTEIN (1879–1955)

Without ambition one starts nothing. Without work one finishes nothing. The prize will not be sent to you. You have to win it. The man who knows how will always have a job. The man who also knows why will always be his boss. As to methods there may be a million and then some, but principles are few. The man who grasps principles can successfully select his own methods. The man who tries methods, ignoring principles, is sure to have trouble.
RALPH WALDO EMERSON (1803–1882)

When I was young, my ambition was to be one of the people who made a difference in this world. My hope still is to leave the world a little bit better for my having been here. It's a wonderful life and I love it.
JIM HENSON (1936–1990)

Where ambition can cover its enterprises, even to the person himself, under the appearance of principle, it is the most incurable and inflexible of passions.
DAVID HUME (1711–1776)

Men are more often bribed by their loyalties and ambitions than by money.
ROBERT JACKSON (1892–1954)

A wise man is cured of ambition by ambition itself; his aim is so exalted that riches, office, fortune and favor cannot satisfy him.
SAMUEL JOHNSON (1709–1784)

An ounce of hypocrisy is worth a pound of ambition.
MICHAEL KORDA (1933–)

What seems to be generosity is often no more than disguised ambition, which overlooks a small interest in order to secure a great one.
FRANÇOIS DE LA ROCHEFOUCAULD (1613–1680)

Women who seek to be equal with men lack ambition.
TIMOTHY LEARY (1920–1996)

Most people would succeed in small things if they were not troubled with great ambitions.
HENRY WADSWORTH LONGFELLOW (1807–1882), *Driftwood; Table Talk*

He who, blinded by ambition, raises himself to a position whence he cannot mount higher, must thereafter fall with the greatest loss.
NICCOLÒ MACHIAVELLI (1469–1527)

Ambition is not a vice of little people.
MICHEL DE MONTAIGNE (1533–1592)

Live neither in the past nor in the future, but let each day's work absorb your entire energies, and satisfy your widest ambition.
SIR WILLIAM OSLER (1849–1919)

Though ambition itself be a vice, yet it is often times the cause of virtues.
QUINTILIAN (C. AD 35–100)

I had no ambition to make a fortune. Mere money making has never been my goal: I had an ambition to build.
JOHN D. ROCKEFELLER (1839–1937)

The universe is not required to be in perfect harmony with human ambition.
CARL SAGAN (1934–1996)

Ambition drove many men to become false; to have one thought locked in the breast, another ready on the tongue.
SALLUST (86–34 BC), *The War with Catiline*

It is the nature of ambition to make men liars and cheats, to hide the truth in their breasts, and show, like jugglers, another thing in their mouths, to cut all friendships and enmities to the measure of their own interest, and to make a good countenance without the help of good will.
SALLUST (86–34 BC)

It is a good idea to be ambitious, to have goals, to want to be good at what you do, but it is a terrible mistake to let drive and ambition get in the way of treating people with kindness and decency. The point is not that they will then be nice to you. It is that you will feel better about yourself.
ROBERT SOLOW (1924–)

Ambition often puts men upon doing the meanest offices; so climbing is performed in the same posture with creeping.
JONATHAN SWIFT (1667–1745), *Miscellanies*

Keep away from people who try to belittle your ambitions. Small people always do that, but the really great make you feel that you, too, can become great.
MARK TWAIN (1835–1910)

Ambition is putting a ladder against the sky.
AMERICAN PROVERB

Where ambition ends happiness begins.
ANONYMOUS

America

I always consider the settlement of America with reverence and wonder, as the opening of a grand scene and design in providence, for the illumination of the ignorant and the emancipation of the slavish part of mankind all over the earth.
JOHN ADAMS (1735–1826)

What a pity, when Christopher Colombus discovered America, that he ever mentioned it.
MARGOT ASQUITH (1864–1945)

I just want to say this. I want to say it gently but I want to say it firmly: There is a tendency for the world to say to America, "the big problems of the world are yours, you go, and sort them out," and then to worry when America wants to sort them out.
TONY BLAIR (1953–)

There's the country of America, which you have to defend, but there's also the idea of America. America is more than just a country, it's an idea. An idea that's supposed to be contagious.
BONO (1960–)

America has believed that in differentiation, not in uniformity, lies the path of progress. It acted on this belief; it has advanced human happiness, and it has prospered.
LOUIS D. BRANDEIS (1856–1941)

America has never been an empire. We may be the only great power in history that had the chance, and refused, preferring greatness to power and justice to glory.
GEORGE W. BUSH (1946–)

America has never been united by blood or birth or soil. We are bound by ideals that move us beyond our backgrounds, lift us above our interests, and teach us what it means to be citizens.
GEORGE W. BUSH (1946 –)

Our American values are not luxuries but necessities, not the salt in our bread, but the bread itself. Our common vision of a free and just society is our greatest source of cohesion at home and strength abroad, greater than the bounty of our material blessings.
JIMMY CARTER (1924–)

I don't measure America by its achievement but by its potential.
SHIRLEY CHISHOLM (1924–2005)

There is nothing wrong with America that cannot be cured by what is right with America.
BILL CLINTON (1946–)

You see, we're America the Beautiful, not America "Well, at Least She Has a Great Personality."
STEPHEN COLBERT (1964–)

The discovery of America was the occasion of the greatest outburst of cruelty and reckless greed known in history.
JOSEPH CONRAD (1857–1924)

America is the greatest, freest, and most decent society in existence. It is an oasis of goodness in a desert of cynicism and barbarism. This country, once an experiment unique in the world, is now the last best hope for the world.
DINESH D'SOUZA (1961–)

The thing that impresses me the most about America is the way parents obey their children.
KING EDWARD VIII (1894–1972)

There is nothing wrong with America that the faith, love of freedom, intelligence, and energy of her citizens cannot cure.
DWIGHT D. EISENHOWER (1890–1969)

What's right about America is that although we have a mess of problems, we have great capacity, intellect and resources, to do something about them.
HENRY FORD II (1917–1987)

America is a mistake, a giant mistake.
SIGMUND FREUD (1856–1939)

From slavery to segregation, we remember that America did not always live up to its ideals. In fact,

we often fell far short of them. But we also learned that fundamental to our national character is the drive to live out the true meaning of our creed.
BILL FRIST (1952–)

America's one of the finest countries anyone ever stole.
BOBCAT GOLDTHWAITE (1962–)

America is therefore the land of the future, where, in the ages that lie before us, the burden of the World's History shall reveal itself.
GEORG W. HEGEL (1770–1831)

It is now the moment when by common consent we pause to become conscious of our national life and to rejoice in it, to recall what our country has done for each of us, and to ask ourselves what we can do for our country in return.
OLIVER WENDELL HOLMES JR. (1841–1935)

America, a great social and economic experiment, noble in motive, and far-reaching in purpose.
HERBERT HOOVER (1874–1964)

America is not merely a nation but a nation of nations.
LYNDON B. JOHNSON (1908–1973)

This is the story of America. Everybody's doing what they think they're supposed to do.
JACK KEROUAC (1922–1969), *On the Road*

I believe America's best days are ahead of us because I believe that the future belongs to freedom, not to fear.
JOHN KERRY (1943–)

In this remarkable time for the world, I refuse to believe it's time to stop believing in the possibilities of our remarkable country. I refuse to accept the downsizing of the American Dream. I refuse to bet against American entrepreneurial spirit and American ingenuity.
JOHN KERRY (1943–)

Intellectually, I know that America is no better than any other country; emotionally I know she is better than every other country.
SINCLAIR LEWIS (1885–1951)

The trouble with America is that there are far too many wide-open spaces surrounded by teeth.
CHARLES LUCKMAN (1909–1999)

There are three social classes in America: upper middle class, middle class, and lower middle class.
JUDITH MARTIN (1938–)

The strength of the United States is not the gold at Fort Knox or the weapons of mass destruction that we have, but the sum total of the education and the character of our people.
CLAIBORNE PELL (1918–)

America is a country that doesn't know where it is going but is determined to set a speed record getting there.
DR. LAURENCE J. PETER (1919–1990)

All great change in America begins at the dinner table.
RONALD REAGAN (1911–2004)

I see America, not in the setting sun of a black night of despair ahead of us, I see America in the crimson light of a rising sun fresh from the burning, creative hand of God. I see great days ahead, great days possible to men and women of will and vision.
CARL SANDBURG (1878–1967)

America is a young country with an old mentality.
GEORGE SANTAYANA (1863–1952)

England and America are two countries separated by a common language.
GEORGE BERNARD SHAW (1856–1950)

In the United States there is more space where nobody is than where anybody is. That is what makes America what it is.
GERTRUDE STEIN (1874–1946), *The Geographical History of America*

In America, any boy may become President; and I suppose it's just one of the risks he takes.
ADLAI E. STEVENSON II (1900–1965)

There is a New America every morning when we wake up. It is upon us whether we will it or not.
ADLAI E. STEVENSON II (1900–1965)

Europe was created by history. America was created by philosophy.
MARGARET THATCHER (1925–)

America is a large, friendly dog in a very small room. Every time it wags its tail, it knocks over a chair.
ARNOLD J. TOYNBEE (1889–1975)

It was wonderful to find America, but it would have been more wonderful to miss it.
MARK TWAIN (1835–1910)

America is a vast conspiracy to make you happy.
JOHN UPDIKE (1932–)

America's greatest strength, and its greatest weakness, is our belief in second chances, our belief that we can always start over, that things can be made better.
ANTHONY WALTON (1962–)

The preservation of the sacred fire of liberty and the destiny of the republican model of government are justly considered … deeply, … finally, staked on the experiment entrusted to the hands of the American people.
GEORGE WASHINGTON (1732–1799)

How much longer are we going to think it necessary to be "American" before (or in contradistinction to) being cultivated, being enlightened, being humane, and having the same intellectual discipline as other civilized countries?
EDITH WHARTON (1862–1937)

Other lands have their vitality in a few, a class, but we have it in the bulk of our people.
WALT WHITMAN (1819–1892)

The genius of the United States is not best or most in its executives or legislatures, nor in its ambassadors or authors, or colleges, or churches, or parlors, nor even in its newspapers or inventors, but always most in the common people.
WALT WHITMAN (1819–1892)

Perhaps, after all, America never has been discovered. I myself would say that it had merely been detected.
OSCAR WILDE (1854–1900), *The Picture of Dorian Gray*

America had often been discovered before Columbus, but it had always been hushed up.
OSCAR WILDE (1854–1900)

America is the only country that went from barbarism to decadence without civilization in between.
OSCAR WILDE (1854–1900)

America lives in the heart of every man everywhere who wishes to find a region where he will be free to work out his destiny as he chooses.
WOODROW WILSON (1856–1924)

Just what is it that America stands for? If she stands for one thing more than another it is for the sovereignty of self-governing people.
WOODROW WILSON (1856–1924)

The United States is a nation of laws: badly written and randomly enforced.
FRANK ZAPPA (1940–1993)

Amnesty

Amnesty, n.: The state's magnanimity to those offenders whom it would be too expensive to punish.
AMBROSE BIERCE (1842–1914), *The Devil's Dictionary*

[G]ranting amnesty by legalizing illegal immigrants is detrimental to our national and economic security.
ELTON GALLEGLY (1944–)

Amnesty is the magnet. Other magnets that you mentioned are anchor babies who get benefits in this country and employer deductions for employees, even if they are here illegally.
VIRGIL GOODE (1946–)

The American people likewise want to see enforcement first, no tricks, no triggers, no amnesty, enforcing existing laws and closing loopholes to reaffirm that our great Republic is, in fact, a nation of laws.
J. D. HAYWORTH (1952–)

Amnesty is not the answer as it will only encourage more illegal immigrants to enter.
TIMOTHY MURPHY (1952–)

That is why I proposed, in my first speech as head of state, an amnesty for those who have been led astray by terrorism.
JALAL TALABANI (1933–)

Amnesty is a terrible policy, and it's terrible politics. It's a terrible policy because you are rewarding people for breaking the law.
TOM TANCREDO (1945–)

Anarchy

Anarchism is founded on the observation that since few men are wise enough to rule themselves, even fewer are wise enough to rule others.
EDWARD ABBEY (1927–1989)

Neither a life of anarchy nor one beneath a despot should you praise; to all that lies in the middle a god has given excellence.
AESCHYLUS (C. 525–456 BC)

The worst thing in this world, next to anarchy, is government.
HENRY WARD BEECHER (1813–1887)

Tyranny and anarchy are never far apart.
JEREMY BENTHAM (1748–1832)

The events of September 11 and what has happened since have made people understand that even a small, distant and far away country like Afghanistan cannot be left to break up into anarchy and chaos without consequences for the whole world.
LAKHDAR BRAHIMI (1934–)

Our government … teaches the whole people by its example. If the government becomes the lawbreaker, it breeds contempt for law; it invites every man to become a law unto himself; it invites anarchy.
LOUIS D. BRANDEIS (1856–1941)

There is a certain combination of anarchy and discipline in the way I work.
ROBERT DE NIRO (1943–)

As soon as liberty is complete it dies in anarchy.
WILL DURANT (1885–1981)

Anarchy may await America, due to the daily injustices suffered by the people.
LOUIS FARRAKHAN (1933–)

Without an advocate for the poor, without a new state of mind in America, the country lies on the brink of anarchy.
LOUIS FARRAKHAN (1933–)

Justice is the end of government. It is the end of civil society. It ever has been and ever will be pursued until it be obtained, or until liberty be lost in the pursuit. In a society under the forms of which the stronger faction can readily unite and oppress the weaker, anarchy may as truly be said to reign as in a state of nature, where the weaker individual is not secured against the violence of the stronger; and as, in the latter state, even the individuals are prompted, by the uncertainty of their condition, to submit to a government which may protect the weak as well as themselves; so, in the former state, will the more powerful factions or parties be gradually induced, by a like motive to wish for a government which will protect all parties, the weaker as well as the more powerful.
ALEXANDER HAMILTON (1755–1804)

Four years of world war, at a cost in human suffering which our minds are mercifully too limited to imagine, led to the very clear realization that international anarchy must be abandoned if civilization was to survive.
ARTHUR HENDERSON (1863–1945)

I do not believe that the values which the Western democracies consider essential to civilization can survive in a world rent by the international anarchy of nationalism and the economic anarchy of competitive enterprise.
ARTHUR HENDERSON (1863–1945)

Anarchy is the only slight glimmer of hope.
MICK JAGGER (1943–)

In liberal democracy and anxious anarchy, the traditional classic dance, compact of aristocratic authority and absolute freedom in a necessity of order, has never been so promising as an independent expression as it is today.
LINCOLN KIRSTEIN (1907–1996)

A culture without property, or in which creators can't get paid, is anarchy, not freedom.
LAWRENCE LESSIG (1961–)

Anarchy is not what I advance here.
LAWRENCE LESSIG (1961–)

The entire world, the much-praised European civilization, is falling into ruins through the anarchy which has been let loose by the world war.
KARL LIEBKNECHT (1871–1919)

We have two American flags always: one for the rich and one for the poor. When the rich fly it means that things are under control; when the poor fly it means danger, revolution, anarchy.
HENRY MILLER (1891–1980)

Are not laws dangerous which inhibit the passions? Compare the centuries of anarchy with those of the strongest legalism in any country you like and you will see that it is only when the laws are silent that the greatest actions appear.
MARQUIS DE SADE (1740–1814)

I uphold the defense invoking the Fourteenth Amendment to guarantee the federal right of free speech against a state criminal anarchy statute.
EDWARD T. SANFORD (1865–1930)

I was the only guy with any bit of anarchy left.
SID VICIOUS (1957–1979)

Undermine their pompous authority, reject their moral standards, make anarchy and disorder your trademarks. Cause as much chaos and disruption as possible but don't let them take you alive.
SID VICIOUS (1957–1979)

Mere anarchy is loosed upon the world,
The blood-dimmed tide is loosed, and everywhere
The ceremony of innocence is drowned....
WILLIAM BUTLER YEATS (1869–1935), "The Second Coming"

Anarchy, it's not the law, it's just a good idea.
ANONYMOUS

Ancestors

Humans are not proud of their ancestors, and rarely invite them round to dinner.
DOUGLAS ADAMS (1952–2001)

Tradition means giving votes to the most obscure of all classes, our ancestors. It is the democracy of the dead. Tradition refuses to submit to the small and arrogant oligarchy of those who merely happen to be walking about.
G. K. CHESTERTON (1874–1936), *Orthodoxy*

Gentility is what is left over from rich ancestors after the money is gone.
JOHN CIARDI (1916–1986)

Some people are your relatives but others are your ancestors, and you choose the ones you want to have as ancestors. You create yourself out of those values.
RALPH ELLISON (1914–1994)

There is no escape, we pay for the violence of our ancestors.
FRANK HERBERT (1920–1986)

To us, the moment 8:17 a.m. means something, something very important, if it happens to be the starting time of our daily train. To our ancestors, such an odd eccentric instant was without significance, did not even exist. In inventing the locomotive, Watt and Stevenson were part inventors of time.
ALDOUS HUXLEY (1894–1963)

There is no king who has not had a slave among his ancestors, and no slave who has not had a king among his.
HELEN KELLER (1880–1968)

Men can know more than their ancestors did if they start with a knowledge of what their ancestors had already learned.... That is why a society can be progressive only if it conserves its traditions.
WALTER LIPPMANN (1889–1974)

It is certainly desirable to be well descended, but the glory belongs to our ancestors.
PLUTARCH (AD 46–120), *Morals*

He who boasts of his ancestry is praising the deeds of another.
SENECA (5 BC–AD 65), *Hercules Furens*

Some families can trace their ancestors back three hundred years, but can't tell you where their children were last night.
ANONYMOUS

Ancestry

Genealogy, n.: An account of one's descent from an ancestor who did not particularly care to trace his own.
AMBROSE BIERCE (1842–1914), *The Devil's Dictionary*

Good breeding is the result of good sense, some good nature, and a little self-denial for the sake of others.
LORD CHESTERFIELD (1694–1773)

The scholar without good breeding is a nitpicker; the philosopher a cynic; the soldier a brute and everyone else disagreeable.
LORD CHESTERFIELD (1694–1773)

Breed is stronger than pasture.
GEORGE ELIOT (1819–1880)

Good breeding, a union of kindness and independence.
RALPH WALDO EMERSON (1803–1882)

Every man is an omnibus in which his ancestors ride.
OLIVER WENDELL HOLMES SR. (1809–1894)

Stillness and steadiness of features are signal marks of good breeding. Vulgar persons can't sit still, or at least must always work their limbs and features.
OLIVER WENDELL HOLMES SR. (1809–1894)

I don't know who my grandfather was; I am much more concerned to know what his grandson will be.
ABRAHAM LINCOLN (1809–1865)

They talk about their Pilgrim blood, their birthright high and holy! a mountain—stream that ends in mud methinks is melancholy.
JAMES RUSSELL LOWELL (1819–1891)

The sharp thorn often produces delicate roses.
OVID (43 BC–AD 17)

Angels

As I was walking among the fires of Hell,
Delighted with the enjoyments of Genius;
Which to Angels look like torment and insanity.
I collected some of their Proverbs.
WILLIAM BLAKE (1757–1827), "The Marriage of Heaven and Hell"

Music is well said to be the speech of angels.
THOMAS CARLYLE (1795–1881)

We shall find peace. We shall hear the angels, we shall see the sky sparkling with diamonds.
ANTON CHEKHOV (1860–1904)

We are, each of us angels with only one wing; and we can only fly by embracing one another.
LUCIANO DE CRESCENZO (1928–)

The golden moments in the stream of life rush past us and we see nothing but sand; the angels come to visit us, and we only know them when they are gone.
GEORGE ELIOT (1819–1880)

If men were angels, no government would be necessary.
JAMES MADISON (1751–1836)

Character is what God and the angels know of us; reputation is what men and women think of us.
HORACE MANN (1796–1859)

[To] emphasize the afterlife is to deny life. To concentrate on Heaven is to create hell. In their desperate longing to transcend the disorderliness, friction, and unpredictability that pesters life; in their desire for a fresh start in a tidy habitat, germ-free and secured by angels, religious multitudes are gambling the only life they may ever have on a dark horse in a race that has no finish line.
TOM ROBBINS (1936–), *Skinny Legs and All*

Now cracks a noble heart. Good night sweet
prince:
And flights of angels sing thee to thy rest!
WILLIAM SHAKESPEARE (1564–1616), *Hamlet*

It would be absurd if we did not understand both angels and devils, since we invented them.
JOHN STEINBECK (1902–1968), *East of Eden*

It would take battalions of angels to protect us from our dreaded dangers, though in a long lifetime few of the dangers come to anything.
ANONYMOUS

Do not forget to show hospitality to strangers, for by so doing some people have shown hospitality to angels without knowing it.
THE BIBLE, Hebrews 13:2

Anger

Anyone can become angry—that is easy, but to be angry with the right person at the right time, and for the right purpose and in the right way—that is not within everyone's power and that is not easy.
ARISTOTLE (384–322 BC)

Never forget what a man says to you when he is angry.
HENRY WARD BEECHER (1813–1887)

Anger repressed can poison a relationship as surely as the cruelest words.
DR. JOYCE BROTHERS (1928–)

Anger will never disappear so long as thoughts of resentment are cherished in the mind. Anger will disappear just as soon as thoughts of resentment are forgotten.
THE BUDDHA (563–483 BC)

Holding on to anger is like grasping a hot coal with the intent of throwing it at someone else; you are the one who gets burned.
THE BUDDHA (563–483 BC)

Anger is not bad. Anger can be a very positive thing, the thing that moves us beyond the acceptance of evil.
JOAN CHITTISTER (1936–)

A man is about as big as the things that make him angry.
SIR WINSTON CHURCHILL (1874–1965)

I know of no more disagreeable sensation than to be left feeling generally angry without anybody in particular to be angry at.
FRANK MOORE COLBY (1865–1925)

Speak the truth, do not yield to anger; give, if thou art asked for little; by these three steps thou wilt go near the gods.
CONFUCIUS (551–479 BC)

When anger rises, think of the consequences.
CONFUCIUS (551–479 BC)

Anger as soon as fed is dead—
'Tis starving makes it fat.
EMILY DICKINSON (1830–1886), *Poems, Second Series*

Anger dwells only in the bosom of fools.
ALBERT EINSTEIN (1879–1955)

Anger makes dull men witty, but it keeps them poor.
ELIZABETH I (1533–1603)

For every minute you are angry you lose sixty seconds of happiness.
RALPH WALDO EMERSON (1803–1882)

If you do not wish to be prone to anger, do not feed the habit; give it nothing which may tend to its increase.
EPICTETUS (AD 55–135)

If you would cure anger, do not feed it. Say to yourself: 'I used to be angry every day; then every other day; now only every third or fourth day.' When you reach thirty days offer a sacrifice of thanksgiving to the gods.
EPICTETUS (AD 55–135)

When you are offended at any man's fault, turn to yourself and study your own failings. Then you will forget your anger.
EPICTETUS (AD 55–135)

Anger at lies lasts forever. Anger at truth can't last.
GREG EVANS (1947–)

Anger is never without a reason, but seldom with a good one.
BENJAMIN FRANKLIN (1706–1790)

Whatever is begun in anger ends in shame.
BENJAMIN FRANKLIN (1706–1790)

In a controversy, the instant we feel anger, we have already ceased striving for truth and have begun striving for ourselves.
ABRAHAM J. HESCHEL (1907–1972)

Anger blows out the lamp of the mind.
ROBERT GREEN INGERSOLL (1833–1899)

Holding on to anger, resentment, and hurt only gives you tense muscles, a headache, and a sore jaw from clenching your teeth. Forgiveness gives you back the laughter and the lightness in your life.
JOAN LUNDEN (1950–)

Usually when people are sad, they don't do anything. They just cry over their condition. But when they get angry, they bring about a change.
MALCOLM X (1925–1965), *Malcolm X Speaks*

How much more grievous are the consequences of anger than the causes of it.
MARCUS AURELIUS ANTONINUS (121–180)

Speak when you are angry, and you will make the best speech you'll ever regret.
DR. LAURENCE J. PETER (1919–1990)

There are two things a person should never be angry at, what they can help, and what they cannot.
PLATO (C. 428–348 BC)

You should make a woman angry if you wish her to love.
PUBLILIUS SYRUS (C. 100 BC)

Never get angry. Never make a threat. Reason with people.
MARIO PUZO (1920–1999), *The Godfather*

Try as much as possible to be wholly alive, with all your might, and when you laugh, laugh like hell and when you get angry, get good and angry. Try to be alive. You will be dead soon enough.
WILLIAM SAROYAN (1908–1981)

Anger, if not restrained, is frequently more hurtful to us than the injury that provokes it.
SENECA (5 BC–AD 65)

The greatest remedy for anger is delay.
SENECA (5 BC–AD 65)

Anger is a great force. If you control it, it can be transmuted into a power which can move the whole world.
WILLIAM SHENSTONE (1714–1763)

Let us not look back in anger, nor forward in fear, but around in awareness.
JAMES THURBER (1894–1961)

When angry, count to four. When very angry, swear.
MARK TWAIN (1835–1910)

It is wise to direct your anger towards problems—not people; to focus your energies on answer—not excuses.
WILLIAM ARTHUR WARD (1921–1994)

I have a right to my anger, and I don't want anybody telling me I shouldn't be, that it's not nice to be, and that something's wrong with me because I get angry.
MAXINE WATERS (1938–)

Anger is only one letter short of danger.
ANONYMOUS

If you are patient in one moment of anger, you will escape a hundred days of sorrow.
CHINESE PROVERB

So long as a man is angry he cannot be in the right.
CHINESE PROVERB

Eat a third and drink a third and leave the remaining third of your stomach empty. Then, when you get angry, there will be sufficient room for your rage.
THE TALMUD

Animals

Man perfected by society is the best of all animals; he is the most terrible of all when he lives without law, and without justice.
ARISTOTLE (384–322 BC)

Man is an animal, which alone among the animals, refuses to be satisfied by the fulfillment of animal desires.
ALEXANDER GRAHAM BELL (1847–1922)

I'm not a vegetarian because I love animals. I'm a vegetarian because I hate plants.
A. WHITNEY BROWN (1952–)

Animals are such agreeable friends, they ask no questions, they pass no criticisms.
GEORGE ELIOT (1819–1880)

Wild animals never kill for sport. Man is the only one to whom the torture and death of his fellow creatures is amusing in itself.
JAMES A. FROUDE (1818–1894)

Often and often afterwards, the beloved Aunt would ask me why I had never told anyone how I was being treated. Children tell little more than animals, for what comes to them they accept as eternally established.
RUDYARD KIPLING (1865–1936)

Men are the only animals that devote themselves, day in and day out, to making one another unhappy. It is an art like any other. Its virtuosi are called altruists.
H. L. MENCKEN (1880–1956)

Humans are the only animals that have children on purpose with the exception of guppies, who like to eat theirs.
P. J. O'ROURKE (1947–)

All animals are equal, but some animals are more equal than others.
GEORGE ORWELL (1903–1950), *Animal Farm*

The desire to take medicine is perhaps the greatest feature which distinguishes man from animals.
SIR WILLIAM OSLER (1849–1919)

Man … is a tame or civilized animal; never-the-less, he requires proper instruction and a fortunate nature, and then of all animals he becomes the most divine and most civilized; but if he be insufficiently or ill-educated he is the most savage of earthly creatures.
PLATO (C. 428–348 BC)

We call them dumb animals, and so they are, for they cannot tell us how they feel, but they do not suffer less because they have no words.
ANNA SEWELL (1820–1878), *Black Beauty*

My music is best understood by children and animals.
IGOR STRAVINSKY (1882–1971)

We have been God-like in our planned breeding of our domesticated plants and animals, but we have been rabbit-like in our unplanned breeding of ourselves.
ARNOLD J. TOYNBEE (1889–1975)

The animals of the planet are in desperate peril.... Without free animal life I believe we will lose the spiritual equivalent of oxygen.
ALICE WALKER (1944–), *Living by the Word*

Anti-Semitism

Anti-Semitism is the rumor about the Jews.
THEODOR W. ADORNO (1903–1969)

In addition I could feel the growing anti-Semitism in school as well as among my friends and comrades.
LEON ASKIN (1907–2005)

Anti-Semitism has no historical, political, and certainly no philosophical origins. Anti-Semitism is a disease.
DANIEL BARENBOIM (1942–)

I feel that the Christian experience and the Jewish one have much to give each other. If this open society continues and there is no return to political anti-Semitism, then this encounter, deeper than any theology, may happen.
LIONEL BLUE (1930–)

[N]early six decades after the Holocaust concluded, anti-Semitism still exists as the scourge of the world.
ELIOT ENGEL (1947–)

I myself think anti-Semitism is about envy.
JOSEPH EPSTEIN (1911–1944)

Even in the Western world, one cannot argue that the ideal has been achieved given the existence of issues like the integration, participation, and representation of Muslim citizens, and occasional but lingering anti-Semitism.
RECEP TAYYIP ERDOGAN (1959–)

State-run television stations contribute to the resurgent anti-Semitism, crying only over Palestinian deaths while playing down Israeli deaths, glossing over them in unwilling tones.
ORIANA FALLACI (1929–2006)

I think anti-Semitism is the meal ticket of the organizations that fight it.
ARTHUR HERTZBERG (1921–2006)

In Paris, as I have said, I achieved a freer attitude toward anti-Semitism, which I now began to understand historically and to pardon.
THEODOR HERZL (1860–1904)

When two drivers curse each other on the road, and one of them happens to be a Jew, you can't define that as anti-Semitism.
JEAN-MARIE LE PEN (1928–)

The worst mistake I made was that stupid, suburban prejudice of anti-Semitism.
EZRA POUND (1885–1972)

Anxiety

Learn the art of patience. Apply discipline to your thoughts when they become anxious over the outcome of a goal. Impatience breeds anxiety, fear, discouragement and failure.
BRIAN ADAMS (1964–)

A crust eaten in peace is better than a banquet partaken in anxiety.
AESOP (620–560 BC), *The Town Mouse and the Country Mouse*

Like dogs in a wheel, birds in a cage, or squirrels on a chain, ambitious men still climb and climb, with great labor, and incessant anxiety, but never reach the top.
ROBERT BURTON (1577–1640)

Beware lest in your anxiety to avoid war you obtain a master.
DEMOSTHENES (384–322 BC)

Man is tormented by no greater anxiety than to find someone quickly to whom he can hand over that great gift of freedom with which the ill-fated creature is born.
FYODOR DOSTOEVSKY (1821–1881), *The Brothers Karamazov*

Anxiety is the rust of life, destroying its brightness and weakening its power. A childlike and abiding trust in Providence is its best preventive and remedy.
TYRON EDWARDS (1808–1894)

Innately, children seem to have little true realistic anxiety. They will run along the brink of water, climb on the windowsill, play with sharp objects and with fire, in short, do everything that is bound to damage them and to worry those in charge of them, that is wholly the result of education; for they cannot be allowed to make the instructive experiences themselves.
SIGMUND FREUD (1856–1939)

Americans are the only people in the world known to me whose status anxiety prompts them to advertise their college and university affiliations in the rear window of their automobiles.
PAUL FUSSELL (1924–)

Anxiety is the dizziness of freedom.
SØREN KIERKEGAARD (1813–1855)

Anxiety is love's greatest killer. It makes others feel as you might when a drowning man holds on to you. You want to save him, but you know he will strangle you with his panic.
ANAÏS NIN (1903–1977), *The Diary of Anaïs Nin*

There is no such thing as pure pleasure; some anxiety always goes with it.
OVID (43 BC–AD 17)

Every tomorrow has two handles. We can take hold of it by the handle of anxiety, or by the handle of faith.
ANONYMOUS

Apathy

Indifference may not wreck a man's life at any one turn, but it will destroy him with a kind of dry–rot in the long run.
BLISS CARMAN (1861 1929)

My generation's apathy. I'm disgusted with it. I'm disgusted with my own apathy too, for being spineless and not always standing up against racism, sexism and all those other -isms the counterculture has been whining about for years.
KURT COBAIN (1967–1994)

I was faced more with apathy than opposition.
ADRIAN CRONAUER (1938–)

It is not opposition but indifference which separates men.
MARY PARKER FOLLETT(1942–)

The apathy of the people is enough to make every statue leap from its pedestal and hasten the resurrection of the dead.
WILLIAM LLOYD GARRISON (1805–1879)

Some people confuse acceptance with apathy, but there's all the difference in the world. Apathy fails to distinguish between what can and what cannot be helped; acceptance makes that distinction. Apathy paralyzes the will-to-action; acceptance frees it by relieving it of impossible burdens.
ARTHUR GORDON (1909–1974)

Apathy is a sort of living oblivion.
HORACE GREELEY (1811–1872)

The death of democracy is not likely to be an assassination from ambush. It will be a slow extinction from apathy, indifference, and undernourishment.
ROBERT M. HUTCHINS (1899–1977)

There can be no transforming of darkness into light and of apathy into movement without emotion.
CARL JUNG (1875–1961)

Science may have found a cure for most evils; but it has found no remedy for the worst of them all, the apathy of human beings.
HELEN KELLER (1880–1968), *My Religion*

Hate is not the opposite of love, apathy is.
ROLLO MAY (1909–1994)

There is nothing harder than the softness of indifference.
JUAN ECUADOREAN MONTALVO (1832–1889)

By far the most dangerous foe we have to fight is apathy—indifference from whatever cause, not from a lack of knowledge, but from carelessness, from absorption in other pursuits, from a contempt bred of self satisfaction.
SIR WILLIAM OSLER (1849–1919)

So much attention is paid to the aggressive sins, such as violence and cruelty and greed with all their tragic effects, that too little attention is paid to the passive sins, such as apathy and laziness, which in the long run can have a more devastating effect.
ELEANOR ROOSEVELT (1884–1962)

Is sloppiness in speech caused by ignorance or apathy? I don't know and I don't care.
WILLIAM SAFIRE (1929–)

No one cares. Apathy is a disease and some days I long for it.
ZOE TROPE (1986–)

People can be so apathetic. They continue to ignore the real people trapped in poverty and homelessness. It's almost maddening.
DAPHNE ZUNIGA (1962–)

Appearances

Appearances often are deceiving.
AESOP (620–560 BC), *The Wolf in Sheep's Clothing*

Do not judge men by mere appearances; for the light laughter that bubbles on the lip often mantles over the depths of sadness, and the serious look may be the sober veil that covers a divine peace and joy.
EDWARD CHAPIN (1831–1863)

Beware so long as you live, of judging people by appearances.
JEAN DE LA FONTAINE (1621–1665)

Fashion is the science of appearances, and it inspires one with the desire to seem rather than to be.
MICHEL DE MONTAIGNE (1533–1592)

Do not hover always on the surface of things, nor take up suddenly, with mere appearances; but penetrate into the depth of matters, as far as your time and circumstances allow, especially in those things which relate to your profession.
ISAAC WATTS (1674–1748)

The world is governed more by appearances than realities, so that it is fully as necessary to seem to know something as to know it.
DANIEL WEBSTER (1782–1852)

It is only shallow people who do not judge by appearances.
OSCAR WILDE (1854–1900)

By listening to his language of his locality the poet begins to learn his craft. It is his function to lift, by use of imagination and the language he hears, the material conditions and appearances of his environment to the sphere of the intelligence where they will have new currency.
WILLIAM CARLOS WILLIAMS (1883–1963)

Appeasement

The idea of reasoning with terrorists without force or with appeasement is naive, and I think it's dangerous.
GEORGE ALLEN (1952–)

You may gain temporary appeasement by a policy of concession to violence, but you do not gain lasting peace that way.
ANTHONY EDEN (1897–1977)

I seem to smell the stench of appeasement in the air.
MARGARET THATCHER (1925–)

Appreciation

Everyone wants to be appreciated, so if you appreciate someone, don't keep it a secret.
MARY KAY ASH (1918–2001)

I would rather be able to appreciate things I cannot have than to have things I am not able to appreciate.
ELBERT HUBBARD (1856–1915)

Appreciation is a wonderful thing. It makes what is excellent in others belong to us as well.
VOLTAIRE (1694–1778)

Architects

I hope that America as a whole, and especially its architects, will become more seriously involved in producing a new architectural culture that would bring the nation to the apex, where it has stood before, and lead the world.
TADAO ANDO (1941–)

Where do architects and designers get their ideas? The answer, of course, is mainly from other architects and designers, so is it mere casuistry to distinguish between tradition and plagiarism?
STEPHEN BAYLEY (1951–)

Architects themselves tend to shy away from the word, preferring instead to talk about the manipulation of space.
ALAIN DE BOTTON (1969–)

Designed by architects with honorable intentions but hands of palsy.
JIMMY BRESLIN (1930–)

Women are the real architects of society.
CHER (1946–)

Let architects sing of aesthetics that bring
Rich clients in hordes to their knees;
Just give me a home, in a great circle dome
Where stresses and strains are at ease.
R. BUCKMINSTER FULLER (1895–1983)

We are called to be architects of the future, not its victims.
R. BUCKMINSTER FULLER (1895–1983)

Architects of grandeur are often the master builders of disillusionment.
BRYANT H. MCGILL (1969–)

Architects in the past have tended to concentrate their attention on the building as a static object. I believe dynamics are more important: the dynamics of people, their interaction with spaces, and environmental condition.
JOHN PORTMAN (1924–)

American architects in the 19th century followed the English and French prevalent stylisms until the Industrial Revolution when dramatic advances were made technically and aesthetically.
HARRY SEIDLER (1923–2006)

Architects today tend to depreciate themselves, to regard themselves as no more than just ordinary citizens without the power to reform the future.
KENZO TANGE (1913–2005)

Architecture

Nothing is as dangerous in architecture as dealing with separated problems. If we split life into

separated problems we split the possibilities to make good building art.
ALVAR AALTO (1898–1976)

Architecture is inhabited sculpture.
CONSTANTIN BRANCUSI (1876–1957)

All architecture is great architecture after sunset; perhaps architecture is really a nocturnal art, like the art of fireworks.
G. K. CHESTERTON (1874–1936)

The intellectual architecture means focusing on doing great work instead of focusing on agency politics.
JAY CHIAT (1931–2002)

Architecture should speak of its time and place, but yearn for timelessness.
FRANK GEHRY (1929–)

I call architecture frozen music.
JOHANN WOLFGANG VON GOETHE (1749–1832)

Architecture tends to consume everything else, it has become one's entire life.
ARNE JACOBSEN (1902–1971)

All architecture is shelter, all great architecture is the design of space that contains, cuddles, exalts, or stimulates the persons in that space.
PHILIP JOHNSON (1906–2005)

Architecture is the art of how to waste space.
PHILIP JOHNSON (1906–2005)

The architecture of our future is not only unfinished; the scaffolding has hardly gone up.
GEORGE LAMMING (1927–)

Architecture is the learned game, correct and magnificent, of forms assembled in the light.
LE CORBUSIER (1887–1965)

To create architecture is to put in order. Put what in order? Function and objects.
LE CORBUSIER (1887–1965)

To provide meaningful architecture is not to parody history but to articulate it.
DANIEL LIBESKIND (1946–)

Architecture starts when you carefully put two bricks together. There it begins.
LUDWIG MIES VAN DER ROHE (1886–1969)

Architecture is a visual art, and the buildings speak for themselves.
JULIA MORGAN (1872–1957)

Architecture is not a private affair; even a house must serve a whole family and its friends, and most buildings are used by everybody, people of all walks of life. If a building is to meet the needs of all the people, the architect must look for some common ground of understanding and experience.
JOHN PORTMAN (1924–)

Notre Dame depicts nothing less than the whole natural universe as it was known at the start of the thirteenth century.
ALLEN TEMKO (1924–2006)

The architect should strive continually to simplify; the ensemble of the rooms should then be carefully considered that comfort and utility may go hand in hand with beauty.
FRANK LLOYD WRIGHT (1869–1959)

Arguments

Arguments out of a pretty mouth are unanswerable.
JOSEPH ADDISON (1672–1719), *Women and Liberty*

I argue very well. Ask any of my remaining friends. I can win an argument on any topic, against any opponent. People know this, and steer clear of me at parties. Often, as a sign of their great respect, they don't even invite me.
DAVE BARRY (1947–)

Silence is one of the hardest arguments to refute.
JOSH BILLINGS (1818–1885)

Fear not those who argue but those who dodge.
DALE CARNEGIE (1888–1955)

With reasonable men I will reason; with humane men I will plea; but to tyrants I will give no quarter, nor waste arguments where they will certainly be lost.
WILLIAM LLOYD GARRISON (1805–1879)

If you can't answer a man's arguments, all is not lost; you can still call him vile names.
ELBERT HUBBARD (1856–1915)

An Argument needs no reason; Nor any friendship.
IBYCUS (C. 400 BC)

The most perfidious way of harming a cause consists of defending it deliberately with faulty arguments.
FRIEDRICH NIETZSCHE (1844–1900), *The Gay Science*

Truth often suffers more by the heat of its defenders than from the arguments of its opposers.
WILLIAM PENN (1644–1718)

Arguments derived from probabilities are idle.
PLATO (C. 428–348 BC)

Arguments, like men, are often pretenders.
PLATO (C. 428–348 BC)

Discussion is an exchange of knowledge; an argument an exchange of ignorance.
ROBERT QUILLEN (1887–1948)

Nothing sways the stupid more than arguments they can't understand.
CARDINAL DE RETZ (1614–1679)

For they are yet ear-kissing arguments.
WILLIAM SHAKESPEARE (1564–1616), *King Lear*

The moment we want to believe something, we suddenly see all the arguments for it, and become blind to the arguments against it.
GEORGE BERNARD SHAW (1856–1950)

There is a principle which is a bar against all information, which is proof against all arguments and which cannot fail to keep a man in everlasting ignorance—that principle is contempt prior to investigation.
HERBERT SPENCER (1820–1903)

I love argument, I love debate. I don't expect anyone just to sit there and agree with me, that's not their job.
MARGARET THATCHER (1925–)

How beggarly appear arguments before a defiant deed!
WALT WHITMAN (1819–1892)

Arguments are to be avoided; they are always vulgar and often convincing.
OSCAR WILDE (1854–1900)

Use soft words and hard arguments.
ENGLISH PROVERB

Aristocracy

Most people go through life dreading they'll have a traumatic experience. Freaks were born with their trauma. They've already passed their test in life. They're aristocrats.
DIANE ARBUS (1923–1971)

It is already possible to imagine a society in which the majority of the population, that is to say, its laborers, will have almost as much leisure as in earlier times was enjoyed by the aristocracy. When one recalls how aristocracies in the past actually behaved, the prospect is not cheerful.
W. H. AUDEN (1907–1973)

In literature as in ethics, there is danger, as well as glory, in being subtle. Aristocracy isolates us.
CHARLES BAUDELAIRE (1821–1867)

The present aristocracy of western culture, at the moment when it most clearly dominates the world, is being imitated rapidly and successfully in every eastern country.
JOHN DESMOND BERNAL (1901–1971)

Democracy means government by the uneducated, while aristocracy means government by the badly educated.
G. K. CHESTERTON (1874–1936)

The aristocrat is the democrat ripe and gone to seed.
RALPH WALDO EMERSON (1803–1882)

There is a natural aristocracy among men. The grounds of this are virtue and talents.
THOMAS JEFFERSON (1743–1826)

If the rabble were lopped off at one end and the aristocrats at the other, all would be well with the country.
ANDREW JOHNSON (1808–1875)

Actual aristocracy cannot be abolished by any law: all the law can do is decree how it is to be imparted and who is to acquire it.
GEORG C. LICHTENBERG (1742–1799)

An aristocracy in a republic is like a chicken whose head has been cut off; it may run about in a lively way, but in fact it is dead.
NANCY MITFORD (1904–1973)

Common sense, in so far as it exists, is all for the bourgeoisie. Nonsense is the privilege of the aristocracy. The worries of the world are for the common people.
GEORGE JEAN NATHAN (1882–1958)

Aristocracy is always cruel.
WENDELL PHILLIPS (1811–1884)

I am an aristocrat. I love liberty; I hate equality.
JOHN RANDOLPH (1773–1833)

We are the only real aristocracy in the world: the aristocracy of money.
GEORGE BERNARD SHAW (1856–1950)

We stand a better chance with aristocracy, whether hereditary or elective, than with monarchy.
EZRA STILES (1727–1797)

The old interests of aristocracy—the romance of action, the exalted passions of chivalry and war—faded into the background, and their place was taken by the refined and intimate pursuits of peace and civilization.
LYTTON STRACHEY (1880–1932)

Our aristocracy, unlike that of Europe, is open to all comers.
JOSIAH STRONG (1847–1916)

Wherever magistrates were appointed from among those who complied with the injunctions of the laws, Socrates considered the government to be an aristocracy.
XENOPHON (C. 431–335 BC)

Arrogance

No one is more arrogant toward women, more aggressive or scornful, than the man who is anxious about his virility.
SIMONE DE BEAUVOIR (1908–1986)

The insufferable arrogance of human beings to think that Nature was made solely for their benefit, as if it was conceivable that the sun had been set afire merely to ripen men's apples and head their cabbages.
CYRANO DE BERGERAC (1619–1655)

All too often arrogance accompanies strength, and we must never assume that justice is on the side of the strong. The use of power must always be accompanied by moral choice.
THEODORE BIKEL (1924–)

The arrogance of age must submit to be taught by youth.
EDMUND BURKE (1729–1797)

The truest characters of ignorance are vanity, and pride and arrogance.
SAMUEL BUTLER (1835–1902)

There's nothing more arrogant or conceited than youth, and there's nothing other than machinery that can replace youth.
ELLIOTT GOULD (1938–)

The most important scientific revolutions all include, as their only common feature, the dethronement of human arrogance from one pedestal after another of previous convictions about our centrality in the cosmos.
STEPHEN JAY GOULD (1941–2002)

Nobody can be so amusingly arrogant as a young man who has just discovered an old idea and thinks it is his own.
SYDNEY J. HARRIS (1917–1986)

When men are most sure and arrogant they are commonly most mistaken, giving views to passion without that proper deliberation which alone can secure them from the grossest absurdities.
DAVID HUME (1711–1776)

Stupidity combined with arrogance and a huge ego will get you a long way.
CHRIS LOWE (1959–)

Arrogance on the part of the meritorious is even more offensive to us than the arrogance of those without merit: for merit itself is offensive.
FRIEDRICH NIETZSCHE (1844–1900)

Arrogance is the worst kind of ignorance.
GARY ROLANDO (1982–)

Like, the kind of arrogance that some of the policy makers and world leaders are carrying with them right now is, I think, reflective of the very worst of the United States. It's that teenage arrogance, as a young country, the know-it-all kind of thing. That makes me crazy.
MICHAEL STIPE (1960–)

The offspring of riches: Pride, vanity, ostentation, arrogance, tyranny.
MARK TWAIN (1835–1910)

Arrogance is a kingdom without a crown.
AMERICAN PROVERB

Arrogance diminishes wisdom.
ARABIAN PROVERB

Art

Let each man exercise the art he knows.
ARISTOPHANES (C. 448–380 BC)

Simplicity is nature's first step, and the last of art.
PHILIP JAMES BAILEY (1816–1902)

Every artist dips his brush in his own soul, and paints his own nature into his pictures.
HENRY WARD BEECHER (1813–1887), *Proverbs from Plymouth Pulpit*

Art and Religion are, then, two roads by which men escape from circumstance to ecstasy. Between aesthetic and religious rapture there is a family alliance. Art and Religion are means to similar states of mind.
CLIVE BELL (1881–1964)

Painting, n.: The art of protecting flat surfaces from the weather and exposing them to the critic.
AMBROSE BIERCE (1842–1914), *The Devil's Dictionary*

Illusions are art, for the feeling person, and it is by art that you live, if you do.
ELIZABETH BOWEN (1899–1973)

Simplicity is not an objective in art, but one achieves simplicity despite one's self by entering into the real sense of things.
CONSTANTIN BRANCUSI (1876–1957)

Art is moral passion married to entertainment. Moral passion without entertainment is propaganda, and entertainment without moral passion is television.
RITA MAE BROWN (1944–)

[Abstract art is] a product of the untalented, sold by the unprincipled to the utterly bewildered.
AL CAPP (1909–1979)

At its best, entertainment is going to be a subjective thing that can't win for everyone, while at worst, a particular game just becomes a random symbol for petty tribal behavior.
JOHN CARMACK (1970–)

Art, like morality, consists of drawing the line somewhere.
G. K. CHESTERTON (1874–1936)

Art is born of the observation and investigation of nature.
CICERO (106–43 BC)

Art forms of the past were really considered elitist. Bach did not compose for the masses, neither did Beethoven. It was always for patrons, aristocrats, and royalty. Now we have a sort of democratic version of that, which is to say that the audience is so splintered in its interests.
DAVID CRONENBERG (1943–)

We are all hungry and thirsty for concrete images. Abstract art will have been good for one thing: to restore its exact virginity to figurative art.
SALVADOR DALÍ (1904–1989)

In art the hand can never execute anything higher than the heart can inspire.
RALPH WALDO EMERSON (1803–1882)

I don't believe in total freedom for the artist. Left on his own, free to do anything he likes, the artist ends up doing nothing at all. If there's one thing that's dangerous for an artist, it's precisely this question of total freedom, waiting for inspiration and all the rest of it.
FEDERICO FELLINI (1920–1993)

Works of art, in my opinion, are the only objects in the material universe to possess internal order, and that is why, though I don't believe that only art matters, I do believe in Art for Art's sake.
E. M. FORSTER (1879–1970)

Art arises when the secret vision of the artist and the manifestation of nature agree to find new shapes.
KAHLIL GIBRAN (1883–1931)

Art is a collaboration between God and the artist, and the less the artist does the better.
ANDRÉ GIDE (1869–1951)

A painting in a museum hears more ridiculous opinions than anything else in the world.
EDMOND DE GONCOURT (1822–1896)

Art may make a suit of clothes: but nature must produce a man.
DAVID HUME (1711–1776)

I paint my own reality. The only thing I know is that I paint because I need to, and I paint whatever passes through my head without any other consideration.
FRIDA KAHLO (1907–1954)

Art is never finished, only abandoned.
LEONARDO DA VINCI (1452–1519)

Even in literature and art, no man who bothers about originality will ever be original: whereas if you simply try to tell the truth (without caring twopence how often it has been told before) you will, nine times out of ten, become original without ever having noticed it.
C. S. LEWIS (1898–1963)

Art is the desire of a man to express himself, to record the reactions of his personality to the world he lives in.
AMY LOWELL (1874–1925)

I believe entertainment can aspire to be art, and can become art, but if you set out to make art you're an idiot.
STEVE MARTIN (1945–)

What I dream of is an art of balance.
HENRI MATISSE (1869–1954)

Art is merely the refuge which the ingenious have invented, when they were supplied with food and women, to escape the tediousness of life.
W. SOMERSET MAUGHAM (1874–1965), *Of Human Bondage*

Art enables us to find ourselves and lose ourselves at the same time.
THOMAS MERTON (1915–1968)

Art is essentially the affirmation, the blessing, and the deification of existence.
FRIEDRICH NIETZSCHE (1844–1900)

We have art to save ourselves from the truth.
FRIEDRICH NIETZSCHE (1844–1900)

Art has two constant, two unending concerns: It always meditates on death and thus always creates

life. All great, genuine art resembles and continues the Revelation of St. John.
BORIS PASTERNAK (1890–1960)

The painting has a life of its own. I try to let it come through.
JACKSON POLLOCK (1912–1956)

Art is contemplation. It is the pleasure of the mind which searches into nature and which there divines the spirit of which Nature herself is animated.
AUGUSTE RODIN (1840–1917)

All art is an imitation of nature.
SENECA (5 BC–AD 65)

Without art, the crudeness of reality would make the world unbearable.
GEORGE BERNARD SHAW (1856–1950)

Love the art in yourself, not yourself in the art.
KONSTANTIN STANISLAVSKY (1863–1938)

Painting is an attempt to come to terms with life. There are as many solutions as there are human beings.
GEORGE TOOKER (1920–)

Another unsettling element in modern art is that common symptom of immaturity, the dread of doing what has been done before.
EDITH WHARTON (1862–1937)

Art is on the side of the oppressed. Think before you shudder at the simplistic dictum and its heretical definition of the freedom of art. For if art is freedom of the spirit, how can it exist within the oppressors?
EDITH WHARTON (1862–1937)

Art is the imposing of a pattern on experience, and our aesthetic enjoyment is recognition of the pattern.
ALFRED NORTH WHITEHEAD (1861–1947), *Dialogues*

Art is the most intense mode of individualism that the world has known.
OSCAR WILDE (1854–1900)

It is the spectator, and not life, that art really mirrors.
OSCAR WILDE (1854–1900)

It is through Art, and through Art only, that we can realise our perfection.
OSCAR WILDE (1854–1900)

One should either be a work of art, or wear a work of art.
OSCAR WILDE (1854–1900)

The moment you think you understand a great work of art, it's dead for you.
OSCAR WILDE (1854–1900)

The secret of life is in art.
OSCAR WILDE (1854–1900)

But all art is sensual and poetry particularly so. It is directly, that is, of the senses, and since the senses do not exist without an object for their employment all art is necessarily objective. It doesn't declaim or explain, it presents.
WILLIAM CARLOS WILLIAMS (1883–1963)

Simplicity and repose are qualities that measure the true value of any work of art.
FRANK LLOYD WRIGHT (1867–1959)

Art is making something out of nothing and selling it.
FRANK ZAPPA (1940–1993)

Artists

I'm not a driven businessman, but a driven artist. I never think about money. Beautiful things make money.
LORD ACTON (1834–1902)

In Italy the artist is a god. Now if the artist is a god, the scientist is likewise a god.
JOSEF ALBERS (1888–1976)

It betrays hubris on the part of the artist to think his medium is limiting him, and I think we all recognize this.
STEVE ALBINI (1962–)

As an artist I'd choose the thing that's beautiful more than the one that's true.
LAURIE ANDERSON (1947–)

All works of art are commissioned in the sense that no artist can create one by a simple act of will but must wait until what he believes to be a good idea for a work comes to him.
W. H. AUDEN (1907–1973)

Of all possible subjects, travel is the most difficult for an artist, as it is the easiest for a journalist.
W. H. AUDEN (1907–1973)

An artist cannot do anything slovenly.
JANE AUSTEN (1775–1817)

I was being an artist, being sensitive and technical as artists are. I'm sure Leonardo Da Vinci did that. Artists don't always feel the same as others feel about their work.
ROY AYERS (1940–)

Being a cover artist is not like being a real artist. That's just copying what someone else did.
SEBASTIAN BACH (1968–)

The job of the artist is always to deepen the mystery.
SIR FRANCIS BACON (1561–1626)

Memory is the greatest of artists, and effaces from your mind what is unnecessary.
MAURICE BARING (1874–1945)

An artist has every right—one may even say a duty—to exhibit his productions as prominently as he can.
JACQUES BARZUN (1907–)

Every artist dips his brush in his own soul, and paints his own nature into his pictures.
HENRY WARD BEECHER (1813–1887)

Every man is an artist.
JOSEPH BEUYS (1921–1986)

The great artist is a slave to his ideals.
CHRISTIAN NESTELL BOVÉE (1820–1904)

To say that an artist sells out means that an artist is making a conscious choice to compromise his music, to weaken his music for the sake of commercial gain.
KEN BURNS (1953–)

You are born an artist or you are not. And you stay an artist, dear, even if your voice is less of a fireworks. The artist is always there.
MARIA CALLAS (1923–1977)

Doubtless there are things in nature which have not yet been seen. If an artist discovers them, he opens the way for his successors.
PAUL CÉZANNE (1839–1906)

The artist makes things concrete and gives them individuality.
PAUL CÉZANNE (1839–1906)

The most seductive thing about art is the personality of the artist himself.
PAUL CÉZANNE (1839–1906)

The man who throws a bomb is an artist, because he prefers a great moment to everything.
G. K. CHESTERTON (1874–1936)

An artist carries on throughout his life a mysterious, uninterrupted conversation with his public.
MAURICE CHEVALIER (1888–1972)

I set my sights upon becoming the kind of artist who would make a contribution to art history.
JUDY CHICAGO (1939–)

And moreover, to succeed, the artist must possess the courageous soul ... the brave soul. The soul that dares and defies.
KATE CHOPIN (1850–1904)

Before everything they are about freedom. Nobody needs this work but the artist.
CHRISTO (1935–)

I think most paintings are a record of the decisions that the artist made. I just perhaps make them a little clearer than some people have.
CHUCK CLOSE (1940–)

An artist cannot speak about his art any more than a plant can discuss horticulture.
JEAN COCTEAU (1889–1963)

An original artist is unable to copy. So he has only to copy in order to be original.
JEAN COCTEAU (1889–1963)

The expression of beauty is in direct ratio to the power of conception the artist has acquired.
GUSTAVE COURBET (1819–1877)

To give a body and a perfect form to one's thought, this—and only this—is to be an artist.
JACQUES-LOUIS DAVID (1748–1825)

Artists who seek perfection in everything are those who cannot attain it in anything.
EUGÈNE DELACROIX (1798–1863)

A great artist is never poor.
ISAK DINESEN (1885–1962)

I am enough of an artist to draw freely upon my imagination. Imagination is more important than knowledge. Knowledge is limited. Imagination encircles the world.
ALBERT EINSTEIN (1879–1955)

True art is characterized by an irresistible urge in the creative artist.
ALBERT EINSTEIN (1879 1955)

The progress of an artist is a continual self-sacrifice, a continual extinction of personality.
T. S. ELIOT (1888–1965)

To be a true artist you have to play the way you feel—not the way others think you should feel.
DON ELLIS (1934–1978)

Every artist was first an amateur.
RALPH WALDO EMERSON (1803–1882)

By keenly confronting the enigmas that surround us, and by considering and analyzing the observations that I have made, I ended up in the domain of mathematics, Although I am absolutely without training in the exact sciences, I often seem to have more in common with mathematicians than with my fellow artists.
M. C. ESCHER (1898–1972)

The aim of every artist is to arrest motion, which is life, by artificial means and hold it fixed so that a hundred years later, when a stranger looks at it, it moves again since it is life.
WILLIAM FAULKNER (1897–1962)

Artists can color the sky red because they know it's blue. Those of us who aren't artists must color things the way they really are or people might think we're stupid.
JULES FEIFFER (1929–)

The artist must be in his work as God is in creation, invisible and all-powerful; one must sense him everywhere but never see him.
GUSTAVE FLAUBERT (1821–1880)

I think any artistic child of a businessman is prone to a sense of the slightness of what he or she is doing. Of the uselessness of art.
JONATHAN FRANZEN (1959–)

The artist alone sees spirits. But after he has told of their appearing to him, everybody sees them.
JOHANN WOLFGANG VON GOETHE (1749–1832)

That terrible mood of depression of whether it's any good or not is what is known as The Artist's Reward.
ERNEST HEMINGWAY (1899–1961)

The individual, the great artist when he comes, uses everything that has been discovered or known about his art up to that point, being able to accept or reject in a time so short it seems that the knowledge was born with him.
ERNEST HEMINGWAY (1899–1961)

Great art is the outward expression of an inner life in the artist, and this inner life will result in his personal vision of the world.
EDWARD HOPPER (1882–1967)

A culture is only as great as its dreams, and its dreams are dreamed by artists.
L. Ron Hubbard (1911–1986)

The artist, like the God of the creation, remains within or behind or beyond or above his handiwork, invisible, refined out of existence, indifferent, paring his fingernails.
James Joyce (1882–1941)

The artist must train not only his eye but also his soul.
Wassily Kandinsky (1866–1944)

Nature is garrulous to the point of confusion, let the artist be truly taciturn.
Paul Klee (1879–1940)

The highest art is always the most religious, and the greatest artist is always a devout person.
Abraham Lincoln (1809–1865)

Sorrowful and great is the artist's destiny.
Franz Liszt (1811–1886)

An artist must never be a prisoner. Prisoner? An artist should never be a prisoner of himself, prisoner of style, prisoner of reputation, prisoner of success, etc.
Henri Matisse (1869–1954)

The artist must summon all his energy, his sincerity, and the greatest modesty in order to shatter the old clichés that come so easily to hand while working, which can suffocate the little flower that does not come, ever, the way one expects.
Henri Matisse (1869–1954)

Those who work in a preconceived style, deliberately turning their backs on nature, miss the truth. An artist must recognize, when he is reasoning, that his picture is an artifice; but when he is painting, he should feel that he has copied nature.
Henri Matisse (1869–1954)

Lavish promotional campaigns are meant to blind audiences to the uselessness of an artist. If an artist is no good, why is it necessary to have that artist repeatedly rammed in our face?
Steven Morrissey (1959–)

An artist has no home in Europe except in Paris.
Friedrich Nietzsche (1844–1900)

The artist need not know very much; best of all let him work instinctively and paint as naturally as he breathes or walks.
Emil Nolde (1867–1956)

Being an artist means ceasing to take seriously that very serious person we are when we are not an artist.
José Ortega y Gasset (1883–1955)

Every child is an artist. The problem is how to remain an artist once he grows up.
Pablo Picasso (1881–1973)

The artist is a receptacle for emotions that come from all over the place: from the sky, from the earth, from a scrap of paper, from a passing shape....
Pablo Picasso (1881–1973)

The modern artist is working with space and time, and expressing his feelings rather than illustrating.
Jackson Pollock (1912–1956)

The artist's job is to be a witness to his time in history.
Robert Rauschenberg (1925–)

I paint what cannot be photographed, that which comes from the imagination or from dreams, or from an unconscious drive.
Man Ray (1890–1976)

Only a bad artist thinks he has a good idea. A good artist does not need anything.
Ad Reinhardt (1913–1967)

An artist, under pain of oblivion, must have confidence in himself, and listen only to his real master: Nature.
Auguste Renoir (1841–1919)

The artist is the confidant of nature … flowers carry on dialogues with him through the graceful bending of their stems and the harmoniously tinted nuances of their blossoms…. Every flower has a cordial word which nature directs towards him.
AUGUSTE RODIN (1840–1917)

The aim of every authentic artist is not to conform to the history of art, but to release himself from it in order to replace it with his own history.
HAROLD ROSENBERG (1906–1978)

An artist's only concern is to shoot for some kind of perfection, and on his own terms, not anyone else's.
J. D. SALINGER (1919–)

I believe that if it were left to artists to choose their own labels, most would choose none.
BEN SHAHN (1898–1969)

No art is any good unless you can feel how it's put together. By and large it's the eye, the hand and if it's any good, you feel the body. Most of the best stuff seems to be a complete gesture, the totality of the artist's body; you can really lean on it.
FRANK STELLA (1936–)

The real essence of art turned out to be not something high up and far off—it was right inside my ordinary daily self. If a musician wants to become a finer artist, he must first become a finer person.
SHINICHI SUZUKI (1898–1998)

The test of the artist does not lie in the will with which he goes to work, but in the excellence of the work he produces.
SAINT THOMAS AQUINAS (1225–1274)

The Artist is he who detects and applies the law from observation of the works of Genius, whether of man or Nature. The Artisan is he who merely applies the rules which others have detected.
HENRY DAVID THOREAU (1817–1862)

Art is not a handicraft, it is the transmission of feeling the artist has experienced.
LEO TOLSTOY (1828–1910)

An artist needn't be a clergyman or a churchwarden, but he certainly must have a warm heart for his fellow men.
VINCENT VAN GOGH (1853–1890)

It is only too true that a lot of artists are mentally ill. It's a life which, to put it mildly, makes one an outsider. I'm all right when I completely immerse myself in work, but I'll always remain half crazy.
VINCENT VAN GOGH (1853–1890)

I say in speeches that a plausible mission of artists is to make people appreciate being alive at least a little bit. I am then asked if I know of any artists who pulled that off. I reply, "The Beatles did."
KURT VONNEGUT JR. (1922–2007), *Timequake*

An artist is someone who produces things that people don't need to have but that he—for some reason—thinks it would be a good idea to give them.
ANDY WARHOL (1927–1987)

A good artist should be isolated. If he isn't isolated, something is wrong.
ORSON WELLES (1915–1985)

It is Nature who makes our artists for us, though it may be Art who taught them their right mode of expression.
OSCAR WILDE (1854–1900)

The artist is nothing without the gift, but the gift is nothing without work.
ÉMILE ZOLA (1840–1902)

Assassination

Assassination has never changed the history of the world.
BENJAMIN DISRAELI (1804–1881)

Demoralize the enemy from within by surprise, terror, sabotage, assassination. This is the war of the future.
ADOLF HITLER (1889–1945)

Assassination is the extreme form of censorship.
GEORGE BERNARD SHAW (1856–1950)

Those who want the Government to regulate matters of the mind and spirit are like men who are so afraid of being murdered that they commit suicide to avoid assassination.
HARRY S TRUMAN (1884–1972)

The best government is a benevolent tyranny tempered by an occasional assassination.
VOLTAIRE (1694–1778)

Every culture has its distinctive and normal system of government. Yours is democracy, moderated by corruption. Ours is totalitarianism, moderated by assassination.
ANONYMOUS (Russian)

Astrology

Astrology, or when the stars enlighten illuminated who dazzle a bunch of lunatics.
PAUL CARVEL (1964–)

I don't believe in astrology; I'm a Sagittarius and we're skeptical.
ARTHUR C. CLARKE (1917–)

The only function of economic forecasting is to make astrology look respectable.
JOHN KENNETH GALBRAITH (1908–2006)

I know nothing of the science of astrology and I consider it to be a science, if it is a science, of doubtful value, to be severely left alone by those who have any faith in Providence.
MAHATMA GANDHI (1869–1948)

If one were to bring ten of the wisest men in the world together and ask them what was the most stupid thing in existence, they would not be able to discover anything so stupid as astrology.
DAVID HILBERT (1862–1943)

A physician without a knowledge of Astrology has no right to call himself a physician.
HIPPOCRATES (460–370 BC)

If the people were a little more ignorant, astrology would flourish—if a little more enlightened, religion would perish.
ROBERT GREEN INGERSOLL (1833–1899)

[M]y evenings are taken up very largely with astrology, I make horoscopic calculations in order to find a clue to the core of psychological truth.
CARL JUNG (1875–1961)

We are born at a given moment, in a given place and, like vintage years of wine, we have the qualities of the year and of the season of which we are born. Astrology does not lay claim to anything more.
CARL JUNG (1875–1961)

Superstition is to religion what astrology is to astronomy: the mad daughter of a wise mother.
VOLTAIRE (1694–1778)

About astrology and palmistry: they are good because they make people vivid and full of possibilities. They are communism at its best. Everybody has a birthday and almost everybody has a palm.
KURT VONNEGUT JR. (1922–2007)

Atheism

Ask a deeply religious Christian if he'd rather live next to a bearded Muslim that may or may not be plotting a terror attack, or an atheist that may or may not show him how to set up a wireless network in his house. On the scale of prejudice, atheists don't seem so bad lately.
SCOTT ADAMS (1957–)

How can I believe in God when just last week I got my tongue caught in the roller of an electric typewriter?
WOODY ALLEN (1935–)

If it turns out that there is a God, I don't think that he's evil. But the worst that you can say about him is that basically he's an underachiever.
WOODY ALLEN (1935–)

To you I'm an atheist; to God, I'm the Loyal Opposition.
WOODY ALLEN (1935–)

No philosophy, no religion, has ever brought so glad a message to the world as this good news of Atheism.
ANNIE BESANT (1847–1933)

Nobody talks so constantly about God as those who insist that there is no God.
HEYWOOD BROUN (1888–1939)

An atheist is a man who has no invisible means of support.
JOHN BUCHAN (1875–1940)

I'm still an atheist, thank God.
LUIS BUÑUEL (1900–1983)

If there were no God, there would be no Atheists.
G. K. CHESTERTON (1874–1936)

Atheism: the religion devoted to the worship of one's own smug sense of superiority.
STEPHEN COLBERT (1964–)

We are all atheists about most of the gods that societies have ever believed in. Some of us just go one god further.
RICHARD DAWKINS (1941–)

It is the final proof of God's omnipotence that he need not exist in order to save us.
PETER DE VRIES (1910–1993)

I have too much respect for the idea of God to make it responsible for such an absurd world.
GEORGES DUHAMEL (1884–1966)

The opposite of the religious fanatic is not the fanatical atheist but the gentle cynic who cares not whether there is a god or not.
ERIC HOFFER (1902–1983)

Shake off all the fears of servile prejudices, under which weak minds are servilely crouched. Fix reason firmly in her seat, and call on her tribunal for every fact, every opinion. Question with boldness even the existence of a God; because, if there be one, he must more approve of the homage of reason than that of blindfolded fear.
THOMAS JEFFERSON (1743–1826)

I don't know if God exists, but it would be better for His reputation if He didn't.
JULES RENARD (1864–1910)

The worst moment for the atheist is when he is really thankful and has nobody to thank.
DANTE GABRIEL ROSSETTI (1828–1882)

I'm a born-again atheist.
GORE VIDAL (1925–)

If God did not exist, it would be necessary to invent him.
VOLTAIRE (1694–1778)

I believe in God, only I spell it Nature.
FRANK LLOYD WRIGHT (1869–1959)

I once wanted to become an atheist, but I gave up, they have no holidays.
HENNY YOUNGMAN (1906–1998)

Attitude

There are no menial jobs, only menial attitudes.
WILLIAM BENNETT (1943–)

Weakness of attitude becomes weakness of character.
ALBERT EINSTEIN (1879–1955)

Whether you think you can or whether you think you can't, you're right!
HENRY FORD (1863–1947)

The greatest discovery of my generation is that a man can alter his life simply by altering his attitude of mind.
WILLIAM JAMES (1842–1910)

Nothing can stop the man with the right mental attitude from achieving his goal; nothing on earth can help the man with the wrong mental attitude.
THOMAS JEFFERSON (1743–1826)

Excellence is not a skill. It is an attitude.
RALPH MARSTON (1900–1965)

Our attitude toward life determines life's attitude toward us.
EARL NIGHTINGALE (1921–1989)

Any fact facing us is not as important as our attitude toward it, for that determines our success or failure.
NORMAN VINCENT PEALE (1898–1993)

Human beings can alter their lives by altering their attitudes.
NORMAN VINCENT PEALE (1898–1993)

There is little difference in people, but that little difference makes a big difference. That little difference is attitude. The big difference is whether it is positive or negative.
W. CLEMENT STONE (1902–2002)

A healthy attitude is contagious, but don't wait to catch it from others. Be a carrier.
ANONYMOUS

Authority

The man who prefers his country before any other duty shows the same spirit as the man who surrenders every right to the state. They both deny that right is superior to authority.
LORD ACTON(1834–1902)

Truth is the secret of eloquence and of virtue, the basis of moral authority; it is the highest summit of art and life.
HENRI-FRÉDÉRIC AMIEL (1821–1881)

No moral system can rest solely on authority.
A. J. AYER (1910–1989), *Humanist Outlook*

The best government rests on the people, and not on the few, on persons and not on property, on the free development of public opinion and not on authority.
GEORGE BANCROFT (1800–1891)

A quotation in a speech, article, or book is like a rifle in the hands of an infantryman. It speaks with authority.
BRENDAN FRANCIS BEHAN (1923–1964)

The peaceful transfer of authority is rare in history, yet common in our country. With a simple oath, we affirm old traditions and make new beginnings.
GEORGE W. BUSH (1946–)

Men decide far more problems by hate, love, lust, rage, sorrow, joy, hope, fear, illusion, or some other inward emotion than by reality, authority, any legal standard, judicial precedent, or statute.
CICERO (106–43 BC)

You can delegate authority, but not responsibility.
STEPHEN W. COMISKEY (1947–)

The essence of independence has been to think and act according to standards from within, not without. Inevitably anyone with an independent mind must become "one who resists or opposes authority or established conventions": a rebel. If enough people come to agree with, and follow, the Rebel, we now have a Devil. Until, of course, still more people agree. And then, finally, we have Greatness.
ALEISTER CROWLEY (1875–1947)

I love quotations because it is a joy to find thoughts one might have, beautifully expressed with much authority by someone recognized wiser than oneself.
MARLENE DIETRICH (1901–1992)

To punish me for my contempt for authority, fate made me an authority myself.
ALBERT EINSTEIN (1879–1955)

The faith that stands on authority is not faith.
RALPH WALDO EMERSON (1803–1882)

The reliance on authority measures the decline of religion, the withdrawal of the soul.
RALPH WALDO EMERSON (1803–1882)

Wherever there is authority, there is a natural inclination to disobedience.
THOMAS C. HALIBURTON (1796–1865)

Every great advance in natural knowledge has involved the absolute rejection of authority.
THOMAS H. HUXLEY (1825–1895)

Ours is an age of criticism, to which everything must be subjected. The sacredness of religion, and the authority of legislation, are by many regarded as grounds for exemption from the examination by this tribunal. But, if they are exempted, and cannot lay claim to sincere respect, which reason accords only to that which has stood the test of a free and public examination.
IMMANUEL KANT (1724–1804)

Whoever in discussion adduces authority uses not intellect but memory.
LEONARDO DA VINCI (1452–1519)

Believe nothing against another but on good authority; and never report what may hurt another, unless it be a greater hurt to some other to conceal it.
WILLIAM PENN (1644–1718)

Justice requires that to lawfully constituted Authority there be given that respect and obedience which is its due; that the laws which are made shall be in wise conformity with the common good; and that, as a matter of conscience, all men shall render obedience to these laws.
POPE PIUS XI (1857–1939)

The young know how truly difficult and dreadful youth can be. Their youth is wasted on everyone else, that's the horror. The young have no authority, no respect.
ANNE RICE (1941–), *Tale of the Body Thief*

If you're going to kick authority in the teeth, you might as well use two feet.
KEITH RICHARDS (1943–)

Liberty is the possibility of doubting, the possibility of making a mistake, the possibility of searching and experimenting, the possibility of saying No to any authority, literary, artistic, philosophic, religious, social, and even political.
IGNAZIO SILONE (1900–1978), *The God That Failed*

Show me the man who keeps his house in hand,
He's fit for public authority.
SOPHOCLES (496–406 BC), *Antigone*

Would you who judge of the lawfulness or unlawfulness of pleasure, take this rule; whatever weakens your reason, impairs the tenderness of your conscience, obscures your sense of God, or takes off the relish of spiritual things; in short, whatever increases the strength and authority of your body over your mind, that is sin to you; however innocent it may be in itself.
ROBERT SOUTHEY (1774–1843)

Always acknowledge a fault. This will throw those in authority off their guard and give you an opportunity to commit more.
MARK TWAIN (1835–1910)

Liberty is the proper end and object of authority, and cannot subsist without it; and it is liberty to that which is good, just, and honest.
JOHN WINTHROP (1587–1649)

If you wish to know what a man is, place him in authority.
YUGOSLAV PROVERB

Automobiles

I'd ban all automobiles from the central part of the city. You see, the automobile was just a passing fad. It's got to go. It's got to go a long way from here.
LAWRENCE FERLINGHETTI (1919–)

I know a lot about cars. I can look at a car's headlights and tell you exactly which way it's coming.
MITCH HEDBERG (1968–2005)

I thought that automobiles were going to have mufflers and go fast and airplanes were going to fly fast.
JACK VANCE (1916–)

I would never kill a living thing, although I probably have inadvertently while driving automobiles.
DON VAN VLIET (1941–)

If we were driving pure hydrogen automobiles, that automobile would actually help clean up the air because the air coming out of the exhaust would be cleaner than the air going into the engine intake.
DENNIS WEAVER (1924–2006)

Autumn

The leaves fall, the wind blows, and the farm country slowly changes from the summer cottons into its winter wools.
HENRY BESTON (1888–1968), *Northern Farm*

Autumn is a second spring when every leaf is a flower.
ALBERT CAMUS (1913–1960)

I cannot endure to waste anything as precious as autumn sunshine by staying in the house. So I spend almost all the daylight hours in the open air.
NATHANIEL HAWTHORNE (1804–1864)

It was one of those perfect English autumnal days which occur more frequently in memory than in life.
P. D. JAMES (1920–)

There is a harmony
In autumn, and a lustre in its sky,
Which through the summer is not heard or seen,
As if it could not be, as if it had not been!
PERCY BYSSHE SHELLEY (1792–1822)

For man, autumn is a time of harvest, of gathering together.
For nature, it is a time of sowing, of scattering abroad.
EDWIN WAY TEALE (1899–1980)

Avarice

We have no government armed with power capable of contending with human passions unbridled by morality and religion. Avarice, ambition, revenge, or gallantry would break the strongest cords of our Constitution as a whale goes through a net. Our Constitution is designed only for a moral and religious people. It is wholly inadequate for any other.
JOHN ADAMS (1735–1826)

The avarice of mankind is insatiable.
ARISTOTLE (384–322 BC)

If you would abolish avarice, you must abolish its mother, luxury.
CICERO (106–43 BC)

The avarice of the old: it's absurd to increase one's luggage as one nears the journey's end.
CICERO (106–43 BC)

Avarice has ruined more souls than extravagance.
CHARLES CALEB COLTON (1780–1832)

Avarice, envy, pride,
Three fatal sparks, have set the hearts of all
On Fire.
DANTE ALIGHIERI (1265–1321), *The Divine Comedy*

We are a puny and fickle folk. Avarice, hesitation, and following are our diseases.
RALPH WALDO EMERSON (1803–1882)

The avarice person is ever in want; let your desired aim have a fixed limit.
HORACE (65–8 BC)

Avarice, the spur of industry.
DAVID HUME (1711–1776)

Avarice is always poor.
SAMUEL JOHNSON (1709–1784)

Avarice is generally the last passion of those lives of which the first part has been squandered in pleasure, and the second devoted to ambition.
SAMUEL JOHNSON (1709–1784)

Avarice increases with the increasing pile of gold.
JUVENAL (AD 55–127)

Ambition is but avarice on stilts, and masked.
WALTER SAVAGE LANDOR (1775–1864)

Passions often produce their contraries: avarice sometimes leads to prodigality, and prodigality to avarice; we are often obstinate through weakness and daring though timidity.
FRANÇOIS DE LA ROCHEFOUCAULD (1613–1680)

All social rules and all relations between individuals are eroded by a cash economy, avarice drags Pluto himself out of the bowels of the earth.
KARL MARX (1818–1883)

Poverty wants much; but avarice, everything.
PUBLILIUS SYRUS (C. 100 BC)

There is no evil that does not promise inducements. Avarice promises money; luxury, a varied assortment of pleasures; ambition, a purple robe and applause. Vices tempt you by the rewards they offer.
SENECA (5 BC–AD 65)

Pride, avarice, and envy are in every home.
THORNTON WILDER (1897–1975)

Gambling is the son of avarice and the father of despair.
FRENCH PROVERB

Awe

Scientific views end in awe and mystery, lost at the edge in uncertainty, but they appear to be so deep and so impressive that the theory that it is all arranged as a stage for God to watch man's struggle for good and evil seems inadequate.
RICHARD FEYNMAN (1918–1988)

Awe is an intuition for the dignity of all things, a realization that things not only are what they are but also stand, however remotely, for something supreme.
ABRAHAM J. HESCHEL (1907–1972)

Two things fill the mind with ever new and increasing wonder and awe—the starry heavens above me and the moral law within me.
IMMANUEL KANT (1724–1804)

Awe and respect are two different things.
OLIVER REED (1938–1999)

I stand in awe of my body.
HENRY DAVID THOREAU (1817–1862)

If you can't be in awe of Mother Nature, there's something wrong with you.
ALEX TREBEK (1940–)

Babies

Father asked us what was God's noblest work. Anna said men, but I said babies. Men are often bad, but babies never are.
LOUISA MAY ALCOTT (1832–1888)

When the first baby laughed for the first time, the laugh broke into a thousand pieces and they all went skipping about.
JAMES M. BARRIE (1860–1937)

If a woman has to choose between catching a fly ball and saving an infant's life, she will choose to save the infant's life without even considering if there are men on base.
DAVE BARRY (1947–)

If you were to open up a baby's head—and I am not for a moment suggesting that you should—you would find nothing but an enormous drool gland.
DAVE BARRY (1947–)

The old system of having a baby was much better than the new system, the old system being characterized by the fact that the man didn't have to watch.
DAVE BARRY (1947–)

Having a baby changes the way you view your in-laws. I love it when they come to visit now. They can hold the baby and I can go out.
MATTHEW BRODERICK (1962–)

People who say they sleep like a baby usually don't have one.
LEO J. BURKE (1911–1980)

It is the nature of babies to be in bliss.
DEEPAK CHOPRA (1947–)

There is no finer investment for any community than putting milk into babies.
SIR WINSTON CHURCHILL (1874–1965)

A baby is born with a need to be loved and never outgrows it.
FRANK A. CLARK (1915–2003)

One of the most obvious results of having a baby around the house is to turn two good people into complete idiots who probably wouldn't have been much worse than mere imbeciles without it.
GEORGES COURTELINE (1858–1929)

Every baby born into the world is a finer one than the last.
CHARLES DICKENS (1812–1870)

In the evening, after she has gone to sleep, I kneel beside the crib and touch her face, where it is pressed against the slats, with mine.
JOAN DIDION (1934–)

My illness is due to my doctor's insistence that I drink milk, a whitish fluid they force down helpless babies.
W. C. FIELDS (1880–1946)

Babies are such a nice way to start people.
DON HEROLD (1889–1966)

The worst feature of a new baby is its mother's singing.
KIN HUBBARD (1868–1930)

Now the thing about having a baby—and I can't be the first person to have noticed this—is that thereafter you have it.
JEAN KERR (1923–2003)

I was much distressed by next door people who had twin babies and played the violin; but one of the twins died, and the other has eaten the fiddle—so all is peace.
EDWARD LEAR (1812–1888)

In the sheltered simplicity of the first days after a baby is born, one sees again the magical closed circle, the miraculous sense of two people existing only for each other.
ANNE MORROW LINDBERGH (1906–2001)

I didn't know how babies were made until I was pregnant with my fourth child.
LORETTA LYNN (1934–)

War will never cease until babies begin to come into the world with larger cerebums and smaller adrenal glands.
H. L. MENCKEN (1880–1956)

Babies are always more trouble than you thought—and more wonderful.
CHARLES OSGOOD (1933–)

Having a baby is definitely a labor of love.
JOAN RIVERS (1933–)

A baby is God's opinion that life should go on.
CARL SANDBURG (1878–1967)

Women have babies and men provide the support. If you don't like the way we're made you've got to take it up with God.
PHYLLIS SCHLAFLY (1924–)

The more people have studied different methods of bringing up children the more they have come to the conclusion that what good mothers and fathers instinctively feel like doing for their babies is the best after all.
BENJAMIN SPOCK (1903–)

I don't think Christians should use birth control. You consummate your marriage as often as you like and if you have babies, you have babies.
RANDALL TERRY (1959–)

Some things I never learned to like. I didn't like to kiss babies, though I didn't mind kissing their mothers.
PIERRE TRUDEAU (1919–2000)

A babe in a house is a well-spring of pleasure, a messenger of peace and love.
MARTIN FARQUHAR TUPPER (1810–1889)

A baby is an inestimable blessing and bother.
MARK TWAIN (1835–1910)

Adam and Eve had many advantages, but the principal one was that they escaped teething.
MARK TWAIN (1835–1910)

I stood in the hospital corridor the night after she was born. Through a window I could see all the small, crying newborn infants, and somewhere among them slept the one who was mine. I stood there for hours filled with happiness until the night nurse sent me to bed.
LIV ULLMAN (1938–)

If one feels the need of something grand, something infinite, something that makes one feel aware of God, one need not go far to find it. I think that I see something deeper, more infinite, more eternal than the ocean in the expression of the eyes of a little baby when it wakes in the morning and coos or laughs because it sees the sun shining on its cradle.
VINCENT VAN GOGH (1853–1890)

An ugly baby is a very nasty object—and the prettiest is frightful.
QUEEN VICTORIA (1819–1901)

Babies don't need a vacation but I still see them at the beach. I'll go over to them and say, "What are you doing here? You've never worked a day in your life!"
STEVEN WRIGHT (1955–)

My friend has a baby. I'm recording all the noises he makes so later I can ask him what he meant.
STEVEN WRIGHT (1955–)

A baby is an angel whose wings decrease as his legs increase.
ANONYMOUS

A baby will make love stronger, days shorter, nights longer, bankroll smaller, home happier, clothes shabbier, the past forgotten, and the future worth living for.
ANONYMOUS

Take a sprinkling of fairy dust, an angel's single feather. Also a dash of love and care, then mix them both together. Add a sentiment or two, a thoughtful wish or line. A touch of stardust, a sunshine ray. It's a recipe, for a Baby Girl truly fine.
ANONYMOUS

Ten fingers, ten toes. She's laughter and teardrops so small and brand new and amazingly angelic. She's sent to bless you; she's one special baby. The best of life's treasure and will grant and bless you many hours of great pleasure.
ANONYMOUS

This baby is your blessing. I wish happiness in every way. Good luck, God bless, I say. And many blessings and wishes to welcome baby into your life today.
ANONYMOUS

Bachelors

The only good husbands stay bachelors. They're too considerate to get married.
FINLEY PETER DUNNE (1867–1936)

Summer bachelors, like summer breezes, are never as cool as they pretend to be.
NORA EPHRON (1941–)

Though bachelors be the strongest stakes, married men are the best binders, in the hedge of the commonwealth.
THOMAS FULLER (1608–1661)

Bachelors have consciences; married men have wives.
SAMUEL JOHNSON (1709–1784)

Cary Grant and Randolph Scott famously lived together as bachelors; to prove it, they double-dated.
ARTHUR LAURENTS (1918–)

Bachelors know more about women than married men; if they didn't they'd be married too.
H. L. MENCKEN (1880–1956)

Look at your bachelors, and see if they do not strive as much for wealth, and attend as steadily to business as married men.
ERNESTINE ROSE (1810–1892)

Nowadays, all the married men live like bachelors, and all the bachelors like married men.
HELEN ROWLAND (1876–1950)

Rich bachelors should be heavily taxed. It is not fair that some men should be happier than others.
OSCAR WILDE (1854–1900)

Bankers

Because bankers measure their self-worth in money, and pay themselves a lot of it, they think they're fine fellows and don't need to explain themselves.
JAMES BUCHAN (1954–)

Bankers cannot afford to be concerned with only the economic aspects of projects. There may be serious implications on the natural environment, the urban environment, on human culture.
ARTHUR ERICKSON (1954–)

Always be nice to bankers. Always be nice to pension fund managers. Always be nice to the media. In that order.
JOHN GOTTI (1940–2002)

Another paradox of banking practice arose from the fact that bankers, who loved deflation, often acted in an inflationary fashion from their eagerness to lend money at interest.
CARROLL QUIGLEY (1910–1977)

The bankers made loans to business so that the volume of money increased faster than the increase in goods. The result was inflation.
CARROLL QUIGLEY (1910–1977)

A banker is a fellow who lends you his umbrella when the sun is shining, but wants it back the minute it begins to rain.
MARK TWAIN (1835–1910)

I went to the bank and proposed that they lend money to the poor people. The bankers almost fell over.
MUHAMMAD YUNUS (1940–)

Banks

Central banks don't have divine wisdom. They try to do the best analysis they can and must be prepared to stand or fall by the quality of that analysis.
MARY KAY ASH (1918–2001)

When I saw my friends were earning just seven or eight dollars a week in banks I thought I'd better try acting.
RICHARD BARTHELMESS (1895–1963)

If you go back to the time of J. P. Morgan, the world of high finance was completely wholesale. The prestigious investment banks on Wall Street appealed exclusively to large corporations, governments, and to extremely wealthy individuals.
RON CHERNOW (1949–)

I rob banks for a living, what do you do?
JOHN DILLINGER (1903–1934)

The process by which banks create money is so simple that the mind is repelled.
JOHN KENNETH GALBRAITH (1908–2006)

A bank is a place that will lend you money if you can prove that you don't need it.
BOB HOPE (1903–2003)

Before the arrival of the Credit Union, people who were from the poor background or a working class background couldn't borrow from banks.
JOHN HUME (1937–)

I have always been afraid of banks.
ANDREW JACKSON (1767–1845)

I believe that banking institutions are more dangerous to our liberties than standing armies. Already they have raised up a monied aristocracy that has set the government at defiance. The issuing power should be taken from the banks and restored to the people to whom it properly belongs.
THOMAS JEFFERSON (1743–1826)

Banks have a new image. Now you have "a friend," your friendly banker. If the banks are so friendly, how come they chain down the pens?
ALAN KING (1927–2004)

Banks introduced the installment plan. The disappearance of cash and the coming of the credit card changed the shape of life in the United States.
JERZY KOSINSKI (1933–1991)

I don't want to glorify robbing banks, but I come from a world that shares Willis's [Willis Newton, Texas Bank Robber] view, that banks and so on are the biggest crooks of them all.
RICHARD LINKLATER (1960–)

I am afraid that the ordinary citizen will not like to be told that the banks can and do create and destroy money. And they who control the credit of a nation direct the policy of governments, and hold in the hollow of their hands the destiny of the people.
RICHARD MCKENNA (1913–1964)

The trade of banks is the buying and selling of interest and exchange.
WILLIAM PETTY (1623–1687)

I don't have a bank account, because I don't know my mother's maiden name.
PAULA POUNDSTONE (1959–)

But if you want to continue to be slaves of the banks and pay the cost of your own slavery, then let bankers continue to create money and control credit.
JOSIAH STAMP (1880–1941)

Banks properly established and conducted are highly useful to the business of the country, and will doubtless continue to exist in the States so long as they conform to their laws and are found to be safe and beneficial.
MARTIN VAN BUREN (1782–1862)

The connection which formerly existed between the Government and banks was in reality injurious to both, as well as to the general interests of the community at large.
MARTIN VAN BUREN (1782–1862)

Baseball

Baseball is 90% mental, the other half is physical.
YOGI BERRA (1925–)

Any pitcher who throws at a batter and deliberately tries to hit him is a communist.
ALVIN DARK (1922–)

If it weren't for baseball, many kids wouldn't know what a millionaire looked like.
PHYLLIS DILLER (1917–)

Baseball is like church. Many attend, few understand.
LEO DUROCHER (1905–1991)

Every day is a new opportunity. You can build on yesterday's success or put its failures behind and start over again. That's the way life is, with a new game every day, and that's the way baseball is.
BOB FELLER (1918–)

A young ballplayer looks on his first spring training trip as a stage struck young woman regards the theater.
CHRISTY MATHEWSON (1880–1925)

Opera in English is, in the main, just about as sensible as baseball in Italian.
H. L. MENCKEN (1880–1956)

Baseball is a skilled game. It's America's game, it, and high taxes.
WILL ROGERS (1879–1935)

Baseball has the great advantage over cricket of being sooner ended.
GEORGE BERNARD SHAW (1856–1950)

Canada is a country whose main exports are hockey players and cold fronts. Our main imports are baseball players and acid rain.
PIERRE TRUDEAU (1919–2000)

We're supposed to be perfect our first day on the job and then show constant improvement.
ED VARGO (1930–)

Basketball

Basketball is like war in that offensive weapons are developed first, and it always takes a while for the defense to catch up.
RED AUERBACH (1917–2006)

If I weren't earning $3 million a year to dunk a basketball, most people on the street would run in the other direction if they saw me coming.
CHARLES BARKLEY (1963–)

Not only do I admire Jordan's accomplishments and his phenomenal basketball ability, but also the way he has conducted himself on and off the court. I don't think there will ever be another player to have the same impact on the game of basketball as Michael Jordan.
ELGIN BAYLOR (1934–)

Trying to take money out of politics is like trying to take jumping out of basketball.
BILL BRADLEY (1943–)

Scoring 100 points is a lot, but … I maybe could have scored 140 if they had played straight-up basketball.
WILT CHAMBERLAIN (1936–)

I think I started learning lessons about being a good person long before I ever knew what basketball was. And that starts in the home, it starts with the parental influence.
JULIUS ERVING (1950–)

I started out as a football player. I liked to inflict pain. In basketball, it was the same thing.
SHAQUILLE O'NEAL (1972–)

I feel like I'm a basketball player in a football uniform.
TERRELL OWENS (1973–)

Hockey is a sport for white men. Basketball is a sport for black men. Golf is a sport for white men dressed like black pimps.
TIGER WOODS (1975–)

Bathrooms

I don't think people need to come into the bathroom with me. I don't understand why they should be interested.
JULIE ANDREWS (1935–)

I never sing in the shower, but sometimes I sing in the bathroom, since bathrooms usually have great acoustics.
JOSE CARRERAS (1946–)

I grew up with six brothers. That's how I learned to dance, waiting for the bathroom.
BOB HOPE (1903–2003)

Having two bathrooms ruined the capacity to co-operate.
MARGARET MEAD (1901–1978)

I couldn't even go to the bathroom alone. My mother or a social worker always went with me.
NATALIE WOOD (1938–1981)

Beauty

You can only perceive real beauty in a person as they get older.
ANOUK AIMEE (1932–)

Beauty: the adjustment of all parts proportionately so that one cannot add or subtract or change without impairing the harmony of the whole.
LEON BATTISTA ALBERTI (1404–1472)

It sometimes happens that a woman is handsomer at twenty-nine than she was ten years before.
JANE AUSTEN (1775–1817)

There is no excellent beauty that hath not some strangeness in the proportion.
SIR FRANCIS BACON (1561–1626), "Of Beauty"

[I]t's hard to stay mad when there's so much beauty in the world. Sometimes I feel like I'm seeing it all at once, and it's too much. My heart fills up like a balloon that's about to burst.
ALAN BALL (1957–), *American Beauty*

Order is the shape upon which beauty depends.
PEARL S. BUCK (1892–1973)

The first question I ask myself when something doesn't seem to be beautiful is why do I think it's not beautiful. And very shortly you discover that there is no reason.
JOHN CAGE (1912–1992)

Beauty is unbearable, drives us to despair, offering us for a minute the glimpse of an eternity that we should like to stretch out over the whole of time.
ALBERT CAMUS (1913–1960)

I've always been a big fan of beauty. Sure, you can't judge a book by its cover but who wants to have sex with a book?
STEPHEN COLBERT (1964–)

Everything has its beauty, but not everyone sees it.
CONFUCIUS (551–479 BC)

I never saw an ugly thing in my life: for let the form of an object be what it may—light, shade, and perspective will always make it beautiful.
JOHN CONSTABLE (1776–1837)

Beauty is not caused. It is.
EMILY DICKINSON (1830–1886)

The absence of flaw in beauty is itself a flaw.
HENRY HAVELOCK ELLIS (1859–1939), *Impressions and Comments*

Love of beauty is Taste. The creation of beauty is Art.
RALPH WALDO EMERSON (1803–1882)

Think of all the beauty still left around you and be happy.
ANNE FRANK (1929–1945), *Diary of a Young Girl*

Beauty is in the eye of the beer holder
KINKY FRIEDMAN (1944–)

When I'm working on a problem, I never think about beauty. I think only how to solve the problem. But when I have finished, if the solution is not beautiful, I know it is wrong.
R. BUCKMINSTER FULLER (1895–1983)

Ugliness is in a way superior to beauty because it lasts.
SERGE GAINSBOURG (1928–1991)

Beauty is not in the face; beauty is a light in the heart.
KAHLIL GIBRAN (1883–1931)

We live only to discover beauty. All else is a form of waiting.
KAHLIL GIBRAN (1883–1931)

When you reach the heart of life you shall find beauty in all things, even in the eyes that are blind to beauty.
KAHLIL GIBRAN (1883–1931)

I love it when ugliness is beautiful. I love character flaws.
MARCIA GAY HARDEN (1959–)

People often say that "beauty is in the eye of the beholder," and I say that the most liberating thing about beauty is realizing that you are the beholder. This empowers us to find beauty in places where others have not dared to look, including inside ourselves.
SALMA HAYEK (1966–)

Youth is happy because it has the ability to see beauty. Anyone who keeps the ability to see beauty never grows old.
FRANZ KAFKA (1883–1924)

Beauty is truth, truth beauty.
JOHN KEATS (1795–1821), "Ode on a Grecian Urn"

The most beautiful things in the world cannot be seen or even touched, they must be felt with the heart.
HELEN KELLER (1880–1968)

I'm tired of all this nonsense about beauty being only skin-deep. That's deep enough. What do you want, an adorable pancreas?
JEAN KERR (1922–2003)

The words that enlighten the soul are more precious than jewels.
HAZRAT INAYAT KHAN (1882–1927)

When the people of the world all know beauty as
beauty,
There arises the recognition of ugliness.
When they all know the good as good,
There arises the recognition of evil.
LAO-TZU (C. 600 BC), *The Way of Lao-tzu*

Beauty is how you feel inside, and it reflects in your eyes. It is not something physical.
SOPHIA LOREN (1934–)

Whatever is in any way beautiful hath its source of beauty in itself, and is complete in itself; praise forms no part of it. So it is none the worse nor the better for being praised.
MARCUS AURELIUS ANTONINUS (121–180), *Meditations*

The essence of the beautiful is unity in variety.
W. SOMERSET MAUGHAM (1874–1965)

Beauty is the radiance of truth and the fragrance of goodness.
VINCENT MCNABB (1868–1943)

Develop interest in life as you see it; in people, things, literature, music—the world is so rich, simply throbbing with rich treasures, beautiful souls and interesting people. Forget yourself.
HENRY MILLER (1891–1980)

For every beauty there is an eye somewhere to see it. For every truth there is an ear somewhere to hear it. For every love there is a heart somewhere to receive it.
IVAN PANIN (1855–1942)

Beauty is only skin deep, but ugly goes clean to the bone.
DOROTHY PARKER (1893–1967)

Rarely do great beauty and great virtue dwell together.
PETRARCH (1304–1374), *De Remedies*

Beautiful young people are accidents of nature, but beautiful old people are works of art.
ELEANOR ROOSEVELT (1884–1962)

She's beautiful, and therefore to be woo'd;
She is a woman, therefore to be won;
WILLIAM SHAKESPEARE (1564–1616), *King Henry VI*

Time takes the ugliness and horror out of death and turns it into beauty.
DODIE SMITH (1896–1990)

A beauty is a woman you notice; a charmer is one who notices you.
ADLAI E. STEVENSON II (1900–1965)

Beauty is truth's smile when she beholds her own face in a perfect mirror.
RABINDRANATH TAGORE (1861–1941)

By plucking her petals, you do not gather the beauty of the flower.
RABINDRANATH TAGORE (1861–1941)

Like anyone else, there are days I feel beautiful and days I don't, and when I don't, I do something about it.
CHERYL TIEGS (1947–)

It is amazing how complete is the delusion that beauty is goodness.
LEO TOLSTOY (1828–1910)

It is better to be beautiful than to be good, but it is better to be good than to be ugly.
OSCAR WILDE (1854–1900)

No object is so beautiful that, under certain conditions, it will not look ugly.
OSCAR WILDE (1854–1900)

The true beauty of a woman is her inherent ability to make better a man in every way.
DON WILLIAMS JR. (1968–)

Your beauty should not come from outward adornment, such as braided hair and the wearing of gold jewelry and fine clothes. Instead, it should be that of your inner self, the unfading beauty of a gentle and quiet spirit, which is of great worth in God's sight.
THE BIBLE, 1 Peter 3:3

Beauty is the wisdom of women. Wisdom is the beauty of men.
CHINESE PROVERB

Bedrooms

It is not I who have been consigned to the bedroom of history.
CORAZON AQUINO (1933–)

There are quite a few honest songwriters out there writing about relationships and their own personality traits. But for some reason, once they step out of the bedroom, their honesty doesn't seem to come with them.
BILLY BRAGG (1957–)

The perception is that I'm going to be something in the bedroom that they can't compete with, but that's their loss. Only the brave need apply.
KIM CATTRALL (1956–)

I'm recording our history now on the bedroom wall, and when we leave the landlord will come and paint over it all.
ANI DIFRANCO (1970–)

Radical conservatives want to police bedrooms.
ROBERT REICH (1946–)

You remember some bedrooms you have slept in. There are bedrooms you like to remember and others you would like to forget.
CARL SANDBURG (1878–1967)

The state has no business in the bedrooms of the nation.
PIERRE TRUDEAU (1919–2000)

Beds

In bed we laugh, in bed we cry; and born in bed, in bed we die; the near approach a bed may show, of human bliss to human woe.
ISAAC DE BENSERADE (1613–1691)

No one ever died from sleeping in an unmade bed. I have known mothers who remake the bed after their children do it because there is a wrinkle in the spread or the blanket is on crooked. This is sick.
ERMA BOMBECK (1927–1996)

The bed comprehends our whole life, for we were born in it, we live in it, and we shall die in it.
GUY DE MAUPASSANT (1850–1893)

The bed has become a place of luxury to me! I would not exchange it for all the thrones in the world.
NAPOLÉON I (1769–1821)

The bed is a bundle of paradoxes: we go to it with reluctance, yet we quit it with regret; we make up our minds every night to leave it early, but we make up our bodies every morning to keep it late.
OGDEN NASH (1902–1971)

Bed is the poor man's opera.
ITALIAN PROVERB

Beer

Religions change; beer and wine remain.
HERVEY ALLEN (1889–1949)

Not all chemicals are bad. Without chemicals such as hydrogen and oxygen, for example, there would be no way to make water, a vital ingredient in beer.
DAVE BARRY (1947–)

I look like the kind of guy who has a bottle of beer in my hand.
CHARLES BRONSON (1921–2003)

Paintings are like a beer, only beer tastes good and it's hard to stop drinking beer.
BILLY CARTER (1937–1988)

Beer. Now there's a temporary solution.
DAN CASTELLANETA (1957–)

I do like beer, but lately I've started drinking non-alcoholic beer and I like the taste of it and I don't get the alcohol, so that's a good alternative also.
MIKE DITKA (1939–)

All right, brain, you don't like me, and I don't like you, but let's just get me through this, and I can get back to killing you with beer.
MATT GROENING (1954–)

Whiskey's too tough, Champagne costs too much, Vodka puts my mouth in gear. I hope this refrain, Will help me explain, As a matter of fact, I like beer.
TOM T. HALL (1936–)

Beer makes you feel the way you ought to feel without beer.
HENRY LAWSON (1867–1922)

Marriage is based on the theory that when man discovers a brand of beer exactly to his taste he should at once throw up his job and go work in the brewery.
GEORGE JEAN NATHAN (1882–1958)

Beer, it's the best damn drink in the world.
JACK NICHOLSON (1937–)

Beer is the Danish national drink, and the Danish national weakness is another beer.
CLEMENTINE PADDLEFORD (1898–1967)

Cover a war in a place where you can't drink beer or talk to a woman? Hell no!
HUNTER S. THOMPSON (1939–2005)

Give me a woman who loves beer and I will conquer the world.
KAISER WILHELM II (1859–1941)

Beggars

God ordains that beggars should beg for greatness, as for all else, when greatness shines out of them, and they don't know it.
GEORGES BERNANOS (1888–1948)

Beggar, n.: One who has relied on the assistance of his friends.
AMBROSE BIERCE (1842–1914), *The Devil's Dictionary*

And love is love in beggars and in kings.
SIR EDWARD DYER (1543–1607)

I would rather be a beggar and single than a queen and married.
ELIZABETH I (1533–1603)

Without the rich heart, wealth is an ugly beggar.
RALPH WALDO EMERSON (1803–1882)

Pride is as loud a beggar as want, and a great deal more saucy.
BENJAMIN FRANKLIN (1706–1790)

The poor have little, beggars none, the rich too much, enough not one.
BENJAMIN FRANKLIN (1706–1790)

I know that a man who shows me his wealth is like the beggar who shows me his poverty; they are both looking for alms from me, the rich man for the alms of my envy, the poor man for the alms of my guilt.
BEN HECHT (1893–1964)

All strangers and beggars are from Zeus, and a gift, though small, is precious.
HOMER (800–700 BC), *The Odyssey*

Beggars should be abolished entirely! Verily, it is annoying to give to them and it is annoying not to give to them.
FRIEDRICH NIETZSCHE (1844–1900)

Conceit, more rich in matter than in words, brags of his substance: they are but beggars who can count their worth.
WILLIAM SHAKESPEARE (1564–1616), *Romeo and Juliet*

A court is an assembly of noble and distinguished beggars.
CHARLES MAURICE DE TALLEYRAND (1754–1838)

Neither beg of him who has been a beggar, nor serve him who has been a servant.
ANONYMOUS

Beginnings

But all endings are also beginnings. We just don't know it at the time.
MITCH ALBOM (1959–), *The Five People You Meet in Heaven*

The ultimate wisdom which deals with beginnings, remains locked in a seed. There it lies, the simplest fact of the universe and at the same time the one which calls faith rather than reason.
HAL BORLAND (1900–1978)

Genuine beginnings begin within us, even when they are brought to our attention by external opportunities.
WILLIAM BRIDGES (1797–1872)

All great deeds and all great thoughts have a ridiculous beginning. Great works are often born on a street corner or in a restaurant's revolving door.
ALBERT CAMUS (1913–1960)

Small opportunities are often the beginning of great enterprises.
DEMOSTHENES (384–322 BC)

Youth, what man's age is like to be, doth show;
We may our ends by our beginnings know.
JOHN DENHAM (1953–)

The beginnings and endings of all human undertakings are untidy.
JOHN GALSWORTHY (1867–1933)

Men often become what they believe themselves to be. If I believe I cannot do something, it makes me incapable of doing it. But when I believe I can, then I acquire the ability to do it even if I didn't have it in the beginning.
MAHATMA GANDHI (1869–1948)

Perplexity is the beginning of knowledge.
KAHLIL GIBRAN (1883–1931)

At the beginning and at the end of love, the two lovers are embarrassed to find themselves alone.
JEAN DE LA BRUYÈRE (1645–1696)

There will come a time when you believe everything is finished. That will be the beginning.
LOUIS L'AMOUR (1908–1988)

People in their handling of affairs often fail when they are about to succeed. If one remains as careful at the end as he was at the beginning, there will be no failure.
LAO-TZU (C. 600 BC)

There are always beginnings for me that are wonderful—the Albert Hall, the first time on stage, the Carnegie Hall.
NANA MOUSKOURI (1934–)

From the end spring new beginnings.
PLINY THE ELDER (AD 23–79)

The world is round and the place which may seem like the end may also be only the beginning.
IVY BAKER PRIEST (1905–1975)

It is a tremendous act of violence to begin anything. I am not able to begin. I simply skip what should be the beginning.
RAINER MARIA RILKE (1875–1926)

Nourish beginnings, let us nourish beginnings. Not all things are blest, but the seeds of all things are blest. The blessing is in the seed.
MURIEL RUKEYSER (1913–1980)

The time to stop a revolution is at the beginning, not the end.
ADLAI E. STEVENSON II (1900–1965)

Let us always meet each other with smile, for the smile is the beginning of love.
MOTHER TERESA (1910–1997)

Laughter is not at all a bad beginning for a friendship, and it is far the best ending for one.
OSCAR WILDE (1854–1900)

Belief

Unless you believe, you will not understand.
SAINT AUGUSTINE (354–430), *De Libero Arbitrio*

The worst derangement of the spirit is to believe things because we want them to be so, not because we have seen them for what they are.
JACQUES BOSSUET (1627–1704)

Do not believe in anything simply because you have heard it. Do not believe in anything simply because it is spoken and rumored by many. Do not believe in anything simply because it is found written in your religious books. Do not believe in anything merely on the authority of your teachers and elders. Do not believe in traditions because they have been handed down for many generations. But after observation and analysis, when you find that anything agrees with reason and is conducive to the good and benefit of one and all, then accept it and live up to it.
THE BUDDHA (563–483 BC)

Men willingly believe what they wish.
JULIUS CAESAR (100–44 BC), *De Bello Gallico*

Sometimes I've believed as many as six impossible things before breakfast.
LEWIS CARROLL (1832–1898), *Alice in Wonderland*

Man is what he believes.
ANTON CHEKHOV (1860–1904)

A new way of thinking has become the necessary condition for responsible living and acting. If we maintain obsolete values and beliefs, a fragmented consciousness and self-centered spirit, we will continue to hold onto outdated goals and behaviors.
THE DALAI LAMA (1935–)

They were so strong in their beliefs that there came a time when it hardly mattered what exactly those beliefs were; they all fused into a single stubbornness.
LOUISE ERDRICH (1954–)

If I have the belief that I can do it, I shall surely acquire the capacity to do it even if I may not have it at the beginning.
MAHATMA GANDHI (1869–1948)

You have to admit beliefs are odd.
BILL HICKS (1961–1994)

Some things have to be believed to be seen.
RALPH HODGSON (1871–1962)

Isms in my opinion are not good. A person should not believe in an ism—he should believe in himself.
JOHN HUGHES (1950–), *Ferris Bueller's Day Off*

Beliefs are dangerous. Beliefs allow the mind to stop functioning. A non-functioning mind is clinically dead. Believe in nothing.
MAYNARD JAMES KEENAN (1964–)

Tolerance implies no lack of commitment to one's own beliefs. Rather it condemns the oppression or persecution of others.
JOHN F. KENNEDY (1917–1963)

There are two ways to slide easily through life; to believe everything or to doubt everything. Both ways save us from thinking.
ALFRED KORZYBSKI (1879–1950)

First there is a time when we believe everything, then for a little while we believe with discrimination, then we believe nothing whatever, and then we believe everything again—and, moreover, give reasons why we believe.
GEORG C. LICHTENBERG (1742–1799)

With most men, unbelief in one thing springs from blind belief in another.
GEORG C. LICHTENBERG (1742–1799)

In the province of the mind, what one believes to be true either is true or becomes true.
JOHN LILLY (1915–2001)

Faith may be defined briefly as an illogical belief in the occurrence of the improbable.
H. L. MENCKEN (1880–1956)

Oh, what a tangled web we weave when first we practice to believe.
DR. LAURENCE J. PETER (1919–1990)

Remember that what you believe will depend very much on what you are.
NOAH PORTER (1811–1892)

I came to the realization that there were certain public issues that were most usefully dealt with within some sort of framework of at least my private beliefs, if not my private life.
ANNA QUINDLEN (1953–)

I never cease being dumbfounded by the unbelievable things people believe.
LEO ROSTEN (1908–1997)

I would never die for my beliefs because I might be wrong.
BERTRAND RUSSELL (1872–1970)

The fact that a believer is happier than a skeptic is no more to the point than the fact that a drunken man is happier than a sober one.
GEORGE BERNARD SHAW (1856–1950)

The public will believe anything, so long as it is not founded on truth.
EDITH SITWELL (1887–1964)

I would rather have a mind opened by wonder than one closed by belief.
GERRY SPENCE (1929–)

What do I believe? As an American I believe in generosity, in liberty, in the rights of man. These are social and political faiths that are part of me, as they are, I suppose, part of all of us. Such beliefs are easy to express.
ADLAI E. STEVENSON II (1900–1965)

Live your beliefs and you can turn the world around.
HENRY DAVID THOREAU (1817–1862)

If I have any beliefs about immortality, it is that certain dogs I have known will go to heaven, and very, very few persons.
JAMES THURBER (1894–1961)

Religious superstition consists in the belief that the sacrifices, often of human lives, made to the imaginary being are essential, and that men may and should be brought to that state of mind by all methods, not excluding violence.
LEO TOLSTOY (1828–1910)

Beliefs are what divide people. Doubt unites them.
PETER USTINOV (1921–2004)

Believe one who has proved it. Believe an expert.
VIRGIL (C. 70–19 BC), *Aeneid*

They can conquer who believe they can.
VIRGIL (C. 70–19 BC)

Those who can make you believe absurdities can make you commit atrocities.
VOLTAIRE (1694–1778)

I can believe anything, provided that it is quite incredible.
OSCAR WILDE (1854–1900), *The Picture of Dorian Gray*

The thing always happens that you really believe in; and the belief in a thing makes it happen.
FRANK LLOYD WRIGHT (1869–1959)

Benevolence

The lessons of prudence have charms,
And slighted, may lead to distress;
But the man whom benevolence warms
Is an angel who lives but to bless.
ROBERT BLOOMFIELD (1766–1823)

Thus it appears that there is no peculiar contrariety between self-love and benevolence; no greater competition between these than between any other particular affections and self-love.
JOSEPH BUTLER (1692–1752)

Benevolence alone will not make a teacher, nor will learning alone do it. The gift of teaching is a peculiar talent, and implies a need and a craving in the teacher himself.
JOHN JAY CHAPMAN (1862–1933)

Let the professors of Christianity recommend their religion by deeds of benevolence, by Christian meekness, by lives of temperance and holiness.
RICHARD MENTOR JOHNSON (1780–1850)

When virtue is lost, benevolence appears; when benevolence is lost, right conduct appears; when right conduct is lost, expedience appears. Expediency is the mere shadow of right and truth; it is the beginning of disorder.
LAO-TZU (C. 600 BC)

Generosity during life is a very different thing from generosity in the hour of death; one proceeds from genuine liberality and benevolence, the other from pride or fear.
HORACE MANN (1796–1859)

It is not from the benevolence of the butcher, the brewer, or the baker that we expect our dinner, but from their regard to their own interest.
ADAM SMITH (1723–1790)

Peace is not an absence of war, it is a virtue, a state of mind, a disposition for benevolence, confidence, justice.
BENEDICT DE SPINOZA (1632–1677)

The Bible

No one ever became, or can become truly eloquent without being a reader of the Bible, and an admirer of the purity and sublimity of its language.
FISHER AMES (1758–1808)

Prosperity is the blessing of the Old Testament; adversity is the blessing of the New.
SIR FRANCIS BACON (1561–1626)

Dude, read your bible. This is what it says is going to happen. The Bible, you know, B-asic I-nstruction B-efore L-eaving E-earth.
STEPHEN BALDWIN (1966–)

The Bible, as a revelation from God, was not designed to give us all the information we might desire, nor to solve all the questions about which the human soul is perplexed, but to impart enough to be a safe guide to the haven of eternal rest.
ALBERT BARNES (1798–1870)

Both read the Bible day and night, but thou read black where I read white.
WILLIAM BLAKE (1757–1827)

We follow the rules laid out in the Bible for running our church.
WILLIAM BREWSTER (1566–1644)

If the Bible had said that Jonah swallowed the whale, I would believe it.
WILLIAM JENNINGS BRYAN (1860–1925)

The Bible may be the truth, but it is not the whole truth and nothing but the truth.
SAMUEL BUTLER (1835–1902)

The Bible says, as a man thinketh in his heart, so is he.
DYAN CANNON (1937–)

The Bible tells us to love our neighbors, and also to love our enemies; probably because they are generally the same people.
G. K. CHESTERTON (1874–1936)

I know the Bible is inspired because it finds me at greater depths of my being than any other book.
SAMUEL TAYLOR COLERIDGE (1772–1834)

I don't care if the Bible says it. It's wrong. It's wrong to divide people on the basis of sexual preference, of sexual orientation. It's wrong to say that women are unequal, if the Bible says so. It's wrong to say that Blacks are unequal even if the Hammite myth supports it or suggests it. The Bible is often wrong. It is often right. Of course, it is often brilliantly right.
ALAN M. DERSHOWITZ (1938–)

Those who talk of the Bible as a "monument of English prose" are merely admiring it as a monument over the grave of Christianity.
T. S. ELIOT (1888–1965)

I take the Bible as the standard.
JERRY FALWELL (1933–)

It is very pious to say and prudent to affirm that the holy Bible can never speak untruth—whenever its true meaning is understood. But I believe nobody will deny that it is often very abstruse.
GALILEO GALILEI (1564–1642)

The Bible shows the way to go to heaven, not the way the heavens go.
GALILEO GALILEI (1564–1642)

I've read the last page of the Bible. It's all going to turn out all right.
BILLY GRAHAM (1918–)

The Bible warns us clearly that we must not attack men of God no matter how sinful they may have become or wicked in our eyes.
BENNY HINN (1952–)

The Bible account of the creation of Eve is a preposterous fable.
THOMAS H. HUXLEY (1825–1895)

The Bible was written by barbarians in a barbarous, coarse and vulgar age.
ROBERT GREEN INGERSOLL (1833–1899)

I've often thought the Bible should have a disclaimer in the front saying this is fiction.
IAN MCKELLEN (1939–)

The Bible is a book that has been read more and examined less than any book that ever existed.
THOMAS PAINE (1737–1809)

When I see throughout this book, called the Bible, a history of the grossest vices and a collection of the most paltry and contemptible tales and stories, I could not so dishonor my Creator by calling it by His name.
THOMAS PAINE (1737–1809)

Whenever we read the obscene stories, the voluptuous debaucheries, the cruel and torturous executions, the unrelenting vindictiveness, with which more than half the Bible is filled, it would seem more consistent that we called it the word of a demon than the Word of God. It is a history of wickedness that has served to corrupt and brutalize mankind.
THOMAS PAINE (1737–1809)

No man ever believes that the Bible means what it says: He is always convinced that it says what he means.
GEORGE BERNARD SHAW (1856–1950)

The Bible is a mass of fables and traditions, mere mythology.
MARK TWAIN (1835–1910)

Bigotry

Perhaps travel cannot prevent bigotry, but by demonstrating that all peoples cry, laugh, eat, worry, and die, it can introduce the idea that if we try and understand each other, we may even become friends.
MAYA ANGELOU (1928–)

Bigotry dwarfs the soul by shutting out the truth.
EDWIN CHAPIN (1814–1880)

It is not bigotry to be certain we are right; but it is bigotry to be unable to imagine how we might possibly have gone wrong.
G. K. CHESTERTON (1874–1936)

The world knows of Rosa Parks because of a single, simple act of dignity and courage that struck a lethal blow to the foundations of legal bigotry.
BILL CLINTON (1946–)

Bigotry murders religion to frighten fools with her ghost.
CHARLES CALEB COLTON (1780–1832)

Too small is our world to allow discrimination, bigotry, and intolerance to thrive in any corner of it, let alone in the United States of America.
ELIOT ENGEL (1947–)

There is no bigotry like that of "free thought" run to seed.
HORACE GREELEY (1811–1872)

Bigotry and judgment are the height of insecurity.
JASMINE GUY (1964–)

Bigotry is the sacred disease.
HERACLITUS (C. 535–475 BC)

I believe all Americans who believe in freedom, tolerance and human rights have a responsibility to oppose bigotry and prejudice based on sexual orientation.
CORETTA SCOTT KING (1927–2006)

Bigotry or prejudice in any form is more than a problem; it is a deep-seated evil within our society.
JUDITH LIGHT (1949–)

The rising sun can dispel the darkness of night, but it cannot banish the blackness of malice, hatred, bigotry, and selfishness from the hearts of humanity.
DAVID O. MCKAY (1873–1970)

Bigotry's birthplace is the sinister back room of the mind where plots and schemes are hatched for the persecution and oppression of other human beings.
BAYARD RUSTIN (1912–1987)

Bigotry and intolerance, silenced by argument, endeavor to silence by persecution, in old days by fire and sword, in modern days by the tongue.
CHARLES SIMMONS (1951–)

It is an infectious disease, and we must all be on our guard against intolerance, bigotry and the pretension of invidious distinction.
HENRY A. WALLACE (1888–1965)

Billiards

I learned to approach racing like a game of billiards. If you bash the ball too hard, you get nowhere. As you handle the cue properly, you drive with more finesse.
JUAN MANUEL FANGIO (1911–1995)

It is impossible to imagine Goethe or Beethoven being good at billiards or golf.
H. L. MENCKEN (1880–1956)

To play billiards well was a sign of an ill-spent youth.
HERBERT SPENCER (1820–1903)

Biological Clock

I needed to nurture someone in my life. I had never done that. My life had been about me. It was like the biological clock exploded. I needed to be a mother.
SHEENA EASTON (1959–)

I don't know if the biological clock thing was thrown in too, [but] I knew I wanted to have a family so I think there was a sort of natural instinct in all of us to take a break.
SUSANNA HOFFS (1959–)

Biology

Very few people in the history of biology could have seen as much of the actual things that I have, and the sad thing is that I do so little with it. I'm so

busy gobbling it up that I don't sort of digest it.
DAVID ATTENBOROUGH (1926–)

If the relationship of father to son could really be reduced to biology, the whole earth would blaze with the glory of fathers and sons.
JAMES ARTHUR BALDWIN (1924–1987)

Biology has progressed tremendously due to the model that Darwin put forth. But the black boxes Darwin accepted are now being opened, and our view of the world is again being shaken.
MICHAEL BEHE (1952–)

Novel technologies and ideas that impinge on human biology and their perceived impact on human values have renewed strains in the relationship between science and society.
PAUL BERG (1926–)

Biology is the science. Evolution is the concept that makes biology unique.
JARED DIAMOND (1937–)

Nothing in biology makes sense except in the light of evolution.
THEODOSIUS DOBZHANSKY (1900–1975)

Biology will relate every human gene to the genes of other animals and bacteria, to this great chain of being.
WALTER GILBERT (1912–)

Politics is applied biology.
ERNST HAECKEL (1834–1919)

Biology has at least 50 more interesting years.
JAMES D. WATSON (1928–)

The human mind evolved to believe in the gods. It did not evolve to believe in biology.
EDWARD O. WILSON (1929–)

Biology is the least of what makes someone a mother.
OPRAH WINFREY (1954–)

Birds

I value my garden more for being full of blackbirds than of cherries, and very frankly give them fruit for their songs.
JOSEPH ADDISON (1672–1719), *The Spectator*

It is not only fine feathers that make fine birds.
AESOP (620–560 BC), *The Jay and the Peacock*

One swallow does not make a summer.
ARISTOTLE (384–322 BC), *Nichomachean Ethics*

The moment a little boy is concerned with which is a jay and which is a sparrow, he can no longer see thc birds or hcar thcm sing.
ERIC BERNE (1910–1970)

No bird soars too high if he soars with his own wings.
WILLIAM BLAKE (1757–1827)

When thou seest an eagle, thou seest a portion of genius; lift up thy head!
WILLIAM BLAKE (1757–1827)

The very idea of a bird is a symbol and a suggestion to the poet. A bird seems to be at the top of the scale, so vehement and intense his life.... The beautiful vagabonds, endowed with every grace, masters of all climes, and knowing no bounds, how many human aspirations are realized in their free, holiday-lives, and how many suggestions to the poet in their flight and song!
JOHN BURROUGHS (1837–1921), *Birds and Poets*

God loved the birds and invented trees. Man loved the birds and invented cages.
JACQUES DEVAL (1745–1794)

I hope you love birds too. It is economical. It saves going to heaven.
EMILY DICKINSON (1830–1886)

You cannot fly like an eagle with the wings of a wren.
WILLIAM H. HUDSON (1841–1922), *Afoot in England*

Birds sing after a storm; why shouldn't people feel as free to delight in whatever sunlight remains to them?
ROSE F. KENNEDY (1890–1995)

Fall is my favorite season in Los Angeles, watching the birds change color and fall from the trees.
DAVID LETTERMAN (1947–)

I realized that if I had to choose, I would rather have birds than airplanes.
CHARLES LINDBERGH (1902–1974)

There is nothing in which the birds differ more from man than the way in which they can build and yet leave a landscape as it was before.
ROBERT LYND (1879–1949), *The Blue Lion and Other Essays*

How helpless we are, like netted birds, when we are caught by desire!
BELVA PLAIN (1919–)

I once had a sparrow alight upon my shoulder for a moment, while I was hoeing in a village garden, and I felt that I was more distinguished by that circumstance than I should have been by any epaulet I could have worn.
HENRY DAVID THOREAU (1817–1862)

Use what talents you possess: the woods would be very silent if no birds sang there except those that sang best.
HENRY VAN DYKE (1852–1933)

Those little nimble musicians of the air, that warble forth their curious ditties, with which nature hath furnished them to the shame of art.
IZAAK WALTON (1593–1683)

I know of only one bird, the parrot, that talks; and it can't fly very high.
WILBUR WRIGHT (1867–1912)

A bird does not sing because it has an answer. It sings because it has a song.
CHINESE PROVERB

Birth

When I was born I was so surprised I didn't talk for a year and a half.
GRACIE ALLEN (1906–1964)

He not busy being born is busy dying.
BOB DYLAN (1941–)

Somewhere on this globe, every ten seconds, there is a woman giving birth to a child. She must be found and stopped.
SAM LEVENSON (1911–1980)

We are born charming, fresh and spontaneous and must be civilized before we are fit to participate in society.
JUDITH MARTIN (1938–)

To my embarrassment I was born in bed with a lady.
WILSON MIZNER (1876–1933)

There is no cure for birth and death save to enjoy the interval.
GEORGE SANTAYANA (1863–1952)

Some people are born on third base and go through life thinking they hit a triple.
BARRY SWITZER (1937–)

It is true that I was born in Iowa, but I can't speak for my twin sister.
ABIGAIL VAN BUREN (1918–)

Birth Control

One year they asked me to be poster boy … for birth control.
RODNEY DANGERFIELD (1921–2004)

Contraception is important. Making contraception available doesn't lead to promiscuity. But much more is needed than just contraception.
JANE FONDA (1937–)

What's more important? Life after death or birth control? What is more important? God's forgiving love or premarital sex?
ANDREW GREELEY (1928–)

My best birth control now is just to leave the lights on.
JOAN RIVERS (1933–)

Too many people use abortion as a form of birth control. And that's very wrong. I could never, ever have an abortion.
BROOKE SHIELDS (1965–)

Blame

The man who backbites an absent friend, nay, who does not stand up for him when another blames him, the man who angles for bursts of laughter and for the repute of a wit, who can invent what he never saw, who cannot keep a secret—that man is black at heart: mark and avoid him.
CICERO (106–43 BC)

If you reveal your secrets to the wind you should not blame the wind for revealing them to the trees.
KAHLIL GIBRAN (1883–1931)

It is no use to blame the looking glass if your face is awry.
NIKOLAI GOGOL (1809–1852)

I envy people who drink. At least they have something to blame everything on.
OSCAR LEVANT (1906–1972)

To err is human, and to blame it on a computer is even more so.
ROBERT ORBEN (1927–)

Democracy is a process by which the people are free to choose the man who will get the blame.
DR. LAURENCE J. PETER (1919–1990)

If your daily life seems poor, do not blame it; blame yourself, tell yourself that you are not poet enough to call forth its riches.
RAINER MARIA RILKE (1875–1926)

Blame someone else and get on with your life.
ALAN WOODS (1944–)

When you point your finger at someone, three fingers are pointing back at you.
ANONYMOUS

Blessings

The unthankful heart discovers no mercies; but the thankful heart will find, in every hour, some heavenly blessings.
HENRY WARD BEECHER (1813–1887)

Ye fearful saints fresh courage take, The clouds you so much dread Are big with mercy and shall break, With blessings on your head.
WILLIAM COWPER (1731–1800)

Reflect on your present blessings, of which every man has many; not on your past misfortunes, of which all men have some.
CHARLES DICKENS (1812–1870)

A bad neighbor is a misfortune, as much as a good one is a great blessing.
HESIOD (C. 800 BC), *Works and Days*

A wise man should consider that health is the greatest of human blessings, and learn how by his own thought to derive benefit from his illnesses.
HIPPOCRATES (460–377 BC), *Regimen in Health*

The hardest arithmetic to master is that which enables us to count our blessings.
ERIC HOFFER (1902–1983)

Thus have the gods spun the thread for wretched mortals: that they live in grief while they themselves are without cares; for two jars stand on the floor of Zeus of the gifts which he gives, one of evils, and another of blessings.
HOMER (800–700 BC), *The Iliad*

It is not the rich man you should properly call happy, but him who knows how to use with wisdom the blessings of the gods, to endure hard poverty,

and who fears dishonor worse than death, and is not afraid to die for cherished friends or fatherland.
HORACE (65–8 BC), *Odes*

A single good government is a blessing to the whole earth.
THOMAS JEFFERSON (1762–1826)

A true friend is the greatest of all blessings, and that which we take the least care of all to acquire.
FRANÇOIS DE LA ROCHEFOUCAULD (1613–1680)

When we lose one blessing, another is often most unexpectedly given in its place.
C. S. LEWIS (1898–1963)

We should certainly count our blessings, but we should also make our blessings count.
NEIL A. MAXWELL (1926–2004)

In reality, serendipity accounts for one percent of the blessings we receive in life, work, and love. The other 99 percent is due to our efforts.
PETER MCWILLIAMS (1949–2000)

Living in the moment brings you a sense of reverence for all of life's blessings.
OPRAH WINFREY (1954–)

Bliss

Let me go to hell, that's all I ask, and go on cursing them there, and them look down and hear me, that might take some of the shine off their bliss.
SAMUEL BECKETT (1906–1989)

If not bliss, ignorance can at least be fun.
CARTER BURWELL (1955–)

Follow your bliss and doors will open where there were no doors before.
JOSEPH CAMPBELL (1904 –1987)

I always feel the greatest bliss when I recollect those I have caught in my snares, for they generally are insolent, and so self-conceited that they challenge wit.
GIACOMO CASANOVA (1725–1798)

It is the nature of babies to be in bliss.
DEEPAK CHOPRA (1946–)

Ignorance is not bliss, it is oblivion.
PHILIP WYLIE (1902–1971)

Blood

Boxing is just show business with blood.
FRANK BRUNO (1961–)

Aristotle was famous for knowing everything. He taught that the brain exists merely to cool the blood and is not involved in the process of thinking. This is true only of certain persons.
WILL CUPPY (1884–1949)

To knock a thing down, especially if it is cocked at an arrogant angle, is a deep delight of the blood.
GEORGE SANTAYANA (1863–1952)

In peace there's nothing so becomes a man
As modest stillness and humility;
But when the blast of war blows in our ears,
Then imitate the action of the tiger:
Stiffen the sinews, summon up the blood.
WILLIAM SHAKESPEARE (1564–1616), *King Henry V*

The denunciation of the young is a necessary part of the hygiene of older people, and greatly assists in the circulation of their blood.
LOGAN PEARSALL SMITH (1865–1946), *Afterthoughts*

See, the problem is that God gives men a brain and a penis, and only enough blood to run one at a time.
ROBIN WILLIAMS (1951–)

Blunders

Nature never makes any blunders, when she makes a fool she means it.
ARCHIBALD ALEXANDER (1772–1871)

During the Second World War, the Germans took four years to build the Atlantic Wall. On four

beaches it held up the Allies for about an hour; at Omaha it held up the U.S. for less than one day. The Atlantic Wall must therefore be regarded as one of the greatest blunders in military history.
STEPHEN AMBROSE (1936–2002), *D-Day*

The best advisers, helpers, and friends, always are not those who tell us how to act in special cases, but who give us, out of themselves, the ardent spirit and desire to act right, and leave us then, even through many blunders, to find out what our own form of right action is.
PHILLIPS BROOKS (1835–1893)

Finish each day and be done with it. You have done what you could. Some blunders and absurdities no doubt crept in; forget them as soon as you can. Tomorrow is a new day; begin it well and serenely and with too high a spirit to be encumbered with your old nonsense.
RALPH WALDO EMERSON (1803–1882)

Blessed are the forgetful, for they get the better even of their blunders.
FRIEDRICH NIETZSCHE (1844–1900)

Which is it, is man one of God's blunders or is God one of man's?
FRIEDRICH NIETZSCHE (1844–1900)

Body

Each body has its art…
GWENDOLYN BROOKS (1917–)

It's also helpful to realize that this very body that we have, that's sitting right here right now … with its aches and it pleasures … is exactly what we need to be fully human, fully awake, fully alive.
PEMA CHODRON (1936–)

Be sure that it is not you that is mortal, but only your body. For that man whom your outward form reveals is not yourself; the spirit is the true self, not that physical figure which can be pointed out by your finger.
CICERO (106–43 BC)

Safeguard the health both of body and soul.
CLEOBULUS (C. 500 BC)

I live in company with a body, a silent companion, exacting and eternal.
EUGÈNE DELACROIX (1798–1863)

Over the years your bodies become walking autobiographies, telling friends and strangers alike of the minor and major stresses of your lives.
MARILYN FERGUSON (1938–)

But the body is deeper than the soul and its secrets inscrutable.
E. M. FORSTER (1879–1970)

I am convinced that life in a physical body is meant to be an ecstatic experience.
SHAKTI GAWAIN (1948–)

Our bodies communicate to us clearly and specifically, if we are willing to listen to them.
SHAKTI GAWAIN (1948–)

The body is a sacred garment.
MARTHA GRAHAM (1894–1991)

The body is shaped, disciplined, honored, and in time, trusted.
MARTHA GRAHAM (1894–1991)

The body says what words cannot.
MARTHA GRAHAM (1894–1991)

[The body is] a marvelous machine … a chemical laboratory, a power-house. Every movement, voluntary or involuntary, full of secrets and marvels!
THEODOR HERZL (1860–1904)

You should pray for a sound mind in a sound body.
JUVENAL (AD 55–127), *Satires*

All we actually have is our body and its muscles that allow us to be under our own power.
ALLEGRA KENT (1937–), *Once a Dancer…*

He who loves the world as his body may be entrusted with the empire.
LAO-TZU (C. 600 BC), *The Way of Lao-tzu*

A sound mind in a sound body is a short but full description of a happy state in this world.
JOHN LOCKE (1632–1704)

Our own physical body possesses a wisdom which we who inhabit the body lack.
HENRY MILLER (1891–1980)

There is but one temple in the universe and that is the body of man.
NOVALIS (1772–1801)

Bodily exercise, when compulsory, does no harm to the body; but knowledge which is acquired under compulsion obtains no hold on the mind.
PLATO (C. 428–348 BC), *The Republic*

Choose rather to be strong of soul than strong of body.
PYTHAGORAS (C. 582–500 BC)

The body is an instrument, the mind its function, the witness and reward of its operation.
GEORGE SANTAYANA (1863–1952)

Oh, darling, let your body in, let it tie you in, in comfort.
ANNE SEXTON (1928–1974)

Our bodies are our gardens to which our wills are gardeners.
WILLIAM SHAKESPEARE (1564–1616), *Othello*

The mind's first step to self-awareness must be through the body.
GEORGE SHEEHAN (1918–1993)

Reading is to the mind what exercise is to the body.
SIR RICHARD STEELE (1672–1729)

Each individual woman's body demands to be accepted on its own terms.
GLORIA STEINEM (1934–)

Every man is the builder of a temple called his body.
HENRY DAVID THOREAU (1817–1862)

I stand in awe of my body.
HENRY DAVID THOREAU (1817–1862)

If any thing is sacred the human body is sacred.
WALT WHITMAN (1819–1892)

I finally realized that being grateful to my body was key to giving more love to myself.
OPRAH WINFREY (1954–)

Boldness

Boldness in business is the first, second, and third thing.
H. G. BOHN (1796–1884)

It requires a great deal of boldness and a great deal of caution to make a great fortune, and when you have it, it requires ten times as much skill to keep it.
RALPH WALDO EMERSON (1803–1882)

A man must have a good deal of vanity who believes, and a good deal of boldness who affirms, that all the doctrines he holds are true, and all he rejects are false.
BENJAMIN FRANKLIN (1706–1790)

If the mass of people hesitate to act, strike swiftly and with boldness, the brave heart that understands and seizes opportunity can accomplish everything.
JOHANN WOLFGANG VON GOETHE (1749–1832)

Whatever you can do or dream you can, begin it. Boldness has genius, power, and magic in it.
JOHANN WOLFGANG VON GOETHE (1749–1832)

The first symptom of love in a young man is shyness; the first symptom in a woman, is boldness.
VICTOR HUGO (1802–1885)

Shake off all the fears of servile prejudices, under which weak minds are servilely crouched. Fix reason firmly in her seat, and call on her tribunal for every fact, every opinion. Question with boldness even the existence of a God; because, if there be

one, he must more approve of the homage of reason than that of blindfolded fear.
THOMAS JEFFERSON (1743–1826)

Maps encourage boldness. They're like cryptic love letters. They make anything seem possible.
MARK JENKINS (1943–), *To Timbuktu*

Be bold. If you are going to make an error, make a doozy, and don't be afraid to hit the ball.
BILLIE JEAN KING (1943–)

It is strange that modesty is the rule for women when what they most value in men is boldness.
NINON DE LENCLOS (1620–1705)

Fortune and love befriend the bold.
OVID (43 BC–AD 17)

The mind, ever the willing servant, will respond to boldness, for boldness, in effect, is a command to deliver mental resources.
NORMAN VINCENT PEALE (1898–1993)

Be bold, be bold, and everywhere be bold.
HERBERT SPENCER (1820–1903)

How I like the boldness of the English, how I like the people who say what they think!
VOLTAIRE (1694–1778)

Books

Learn as much by writing as by reading.
LORD ACTON (1834–1902)

Books are the legacies that a great genius leaves to mankind, which are delivered down from generation to generation as presents to the posterity of those who are yet unborn.
JOSEPH ADDISON (1672–1719)

Some books are undeservedly forgotten; none are undeservedly remembered.
W. H. AUDEN (1907–1973)

Read not to contradict and confute, nor to find talk and discourse, but to weigh and consider.
SIR FRANCIS BACON (1561–1626)

Some books are to be tasted, others to be swallowed, and some few to be chewed and digested: that is, some books are to be read only in parts, others to be read, but not curiously, and some few to be read wholly, and with diligence and attention.
SIR FRANCIS BACON (1561–1626)

Where is human nature so weak as in the bookstore?
HENRY WARD BEECHER (1813–1887)

The covers of this book are too far apart.
AMBROSE BIERCE (1842–1914), *The Devil's Dictionary*

Given pounds and five years, an ordinary man can in the ordinary course, without any undue haste or putting any pressure upon his taste, surround himself with books, all in his own language, and thence forward have at least one place in the world.
AUGUSTINE BIRRELL (1850–1933)

Reading well is one of the great pleasures that solitude can afford you.
HAROLD BLOOM (1930–)

I still find each day too short for all the thoughts I want to think, all the walks I want to take, all the books I want to read, and all the friends I want to see.
JOHN BURROUGHS (1837–1921)

Many books require no thought from those who read them, and for a very simple reason; they made no such demand upon those who wrote them.
CHARLES CALEB COLTON (1780–1832)

A good novel tells us the truth about its hero; but a bad novel tells us the truth about its author.
G. K. CHESTERTON (1874–1936)

There is a great deal of difference between an eager man who wants to read a book and the tired man who wants a book to read.
G. K. CHESTERTON (1874–1936)

A room without books is like a body without a soul.
CICERO (106–43 BC)

To be a book-collector is to combine the worst characteristics of a dope fiend with those of a miser.
ROBERTSON DAVIES (1913–1995), *The Table Talk of Samuel Marchbanks*

A truly great book should be read in youth, again in maturity, and once more in old age, as a fine building should be seen by morning light, at noon, and by moonlight.
ROBERTSON DAVIES (1913–1995)

Reading, after a certain age, diverts the mind too much from its creative pursuits. Any man who reads too much and uses his own brain too little falls into lazy habits of thinking.
ALBERT EINSTEIN (1879–1955)

Don't join the book burners. Don't think you're going to conceal faults by concealing evidence that they ever existed. Don't be afraid to go in your library and read every book...
DWIGHT D. EISENHOWER (1890–1969)

Books are the quietest and most constant of friends; they are the most accessible and wisest of counsellors, and the most patient of teachers.
CHARLES W. ELIOT (1834–1926), *The Happy Life*

In the highest civilization, the book is still the highest delight. He who has once known its satisfactions is provided with a resource against calamity.
RALPH WALDO EMERSON (1803–1882), *Letters and Social Aims: Quotation and Originality*

Nature and Books belong to the eyes that see them.
RALPH WALDO EMERSON (1803–1882)

Most new books are forgotten within a year, especially by those who borrow them.
EVAN ESAR (1899–1995)

I read part of it all the way through.
SAMUEL GOLDWYN (1882–1974)

Reading is sometimes an ingenious device for avoiding thought.
SIR ARTHUR HELPS (1813–1875)

Woe be to him that reads but one book.
GEORGE HERBERT (1593–1633)

This paperback is very interesting, but I find it will never replace a hardcover book—it makes a very poor doorstop.
ALFRED HITCHCOCK (1899–1980)

Life-transforming ideas have always come to me through books.
BELL HOOKS (1952–)

The only obligation to which in advance we may hold a novel, without incurring the accusation of being arbitrary, is that it be interesting.
HENRY JAMES (1843–1916)

You can cover a great deal of country in books.
ANDREW LANG (1844–1912)

Books to the ceiling,
Books to the sky,
My pile of books is a mile high.
How I love them! How I need them!
I'll have a long beard by the time I read them.
ARNOLD LOBEL (1933–1987)

The love of learning, the sequestered nooks,
And all the sweet serenity of books.
HENRY WADSWORTH LONGFELLOW (1807–1882), "Morituri Salutamus"

It was a book to kill time for those who like it better dead.
DAME ROSE MACAULAY (1881–1958)

Resolve to edge in a little reading every day, if it is but a single sentence. If you gain fifteen minutes a day, it will make itself felt at the end of the year.
HORACE MANN (1796–1859)

The pleasure of all reading is doubled when one lives with another who shares the same books.
KATHERINE MANSFIELD (1888–1923)

From the moment I picked up your book until I laid it down, I was convulsed with laughter. Some day I intend reading it.
GROUCHO MARX (1890–1977)

I find television very educating. Every time somebody turns on the set, I go into the other room and read a book.
GROUCHO MARX (1890–1977)

Outside of a dog, a book is man's best friend. Inside of a dog it's too dark to read.
GROUCHO MARX (1890–1977)

When I read a book I seem to read it with my eyes only, but now and then I come across a passage, perhaps only a phrase, which has a meaning for me, and it becomes part of me.
W. SOMERSET MAUGHAM (1874–1965), *Of Human Bondage*

When I am attacked by gloomy thoughts, nothing helps me so much as running to my books. They quickly absorb me and banish the clouds from my mind.
MICHEL DE MONTAIGNE (1533–1592)

There is no mistaking a real book when one meets it. It is like falling in love.
CHRISTOPHER MORLEY (1890–1957)

Just the knowledge that a good book is awaiting one at the end of a long day makes that day happier.
KATHLEEN NORRIS (1880–1966), *Hands Full of Living*

Always read stuff that will make you look good if you die in the middle of it.
P. J. O'ROURKE (1947–)

This is not a novel to be tossed aside lightly. It should be thrown with great force.
DOROTHY PARKER (1893–1967)

The books that help you most are those which make you think the most. The hardest way of learning is that of easy reading; but a great book that comes from a great thinker is a ship of thought, deep freighted with truth and beauty.
THEODORE PARKER (1810–1860)

Wear the old coat and buy the new book.
AUSTIN PHELPS (1820–1890)

Properly, we should read for power. Man reading should be man intensely alive. The book should be a ball of light in one's hand.
EZRA POUND (1885–1972)

There's a certain kind of conversation you have from time to time at parties in New York about a new book. The word "banal" sometimes rears its by-now banal head; you say "underedited," I say "derivative." The conversation goes around and around various literary criticisms, and by the time it moves on one thing is clear: No one read the book; wc just read the reviews.
ANNA QUINDLEN (1953–)

A book is a version of the world. If you do not like it, ignore it; or offer your own version in return.
SALMAN RUSHDIE (1947–)

Books … are like lobster shells, we surround ourselves with 'em, then we grow out of 'em and leave 'em behind, as evidence of our earlier stages of development.
DOROTHY L. SAYERS (1893–1957)

I've never known any trouble that an hour's reading didn't assuage.
CHARLES DE SECONDAT (1689–1755)

Knowing I lov'd my books, he furnish'd me
From mine own library with volumes that
I prize above my dukedom….
WILLIAM SHAKESPEARE (1564–1616), *The Tempest*

I aimed at the public's heart, and by accident I hit it in the stomach.
UPTON SINCLAIR (1878–1968)

My personal hobbies are reading, listening to music, and silence.
EDITH SITWELL (1887–1964)

People say that life is the thing, but I prefer reading.
LOGAN PEARSALL SMITH (1865–1946), *Afterthoughts*

Live always in the best company when you read.
SYDNEY SMITH (1771–1845)

Reading is to the mind what exercise is to the body.
SIR RICHARD STEELE (1672–1729)

Books are the carriers of civilization. Without books, history is silent, literature dumb, science crippled, thought and speculation at a standstill. I think that there is nothing, not even crime, more opposed to poetry, to philosophy, ay, to life itself than this incessant business.
HENRY DAVID THOREAU (1817–1862)

How many a man has dated a new era in his life from the reading of a book.
HENRY DAVID THOREAU (1817–1862)

Neither books nor people have Velcro sides; there must be a bonding agent, someone who attaches child to book.
JIM TRELEASE (1941–)

Be careful about reading health books. You may die of a misprint.
MARK TWAIN (1835–1910)

Just the omission of Jane Austen's books alone would make a fairly good library out of a library that hadn't a book in it.
MARK TWAIN (1835–1910)

The man who doesn't read good books has no advantage over the man who can't read them.
MARK TWAIN (1835–1910)

The multitude of books is making us ignorant.
VOLTAIRE (1694–1778)

You despise books; you whose lives are absorbed in the vanities of ambition, the pursuit of pleasure or indolence; but remember that all the known world, excepting only savage nations, is governed by books.
VOLTAIRE (1694–1778)

There is no such thing as a moral or an immoral book. Books are well written or badly written.
OSCAR WILDE (1854–1900), *The Picture of Dorian Gray*

Oh for a book and a shady nook…
JOHN WILSON (1785–1854)

Never read a book through merely because you have begun it.
JOHN WITHERSPOON (1723–1794)

I think it is good that books still exist, but they do make me sleepy.
FRANK ZAPPA (1940–1993)

Boredom

I don't believe in an afterlife, so I don't have to spend my whole life fearing hell, or fearing heaven even more. For whatever the tortures of hell, I think the boredom of heaven would be even worse.
ISAAC ASIMOV (1920–1992)

The penalty for success is to be bored by the people who used to snub you.
NANCY ASTOR (1879–1964)

Bore, n.: A person who talks when you wish him to listen.
AMBROSE BIERCE (1842–1914), *The Devil's Dictionary*

Every improvement in communication makes the bore more terrible.
FRANK MOORE COLBY (1865–1925)

Virtuous people often revenge themselves for the constraints to which they submit by the boredom which they inspire.
CONFUCIUS (551–479 BC)

Every hero becomes a bore at last.
RALPH WALDO EMERSON (1803–1882)

[S]he refused to be bored chiefly because she wasn't boring.
ZELDA FITZGERALD (1900–1948)

A bore is a man who deprives you of solitude without providing you with company.
GIAN VINCENZO GRAVINA (1664–1718)

I fell asleep reading a dull book and dreamed I kept on reading, so I awoke from sheer boredom.
SIR HEINRICH HEINE (1797–1856)

Is boredom anything less than the sense of one's faculties slowly dying?
SIR ARTHUR HELPS (1813–1875)

Your true traveller finds boredom rather agreeable than painful. It is the symbol of his liberty—his excessive freedom. He accepts his boredom, when it comes, not merely philosophically, but almost with pleasure.
ALDOUS HUXLEY (1894–1963)

The nice thing about being a celebrity is that when you bore people, they think it's their fault.
HENRY KISSINGER (1923–)

The essence of life is the smile of round female bottoms, under the shadow of cosmic boredom.
GUY DE MAUPASSANT (1850–1893)

The capacity of human beings to bore one another seems to be vastly greater than that of any other animal.
H. L. MENCKEN (1880–1956)

A subject for a great poet would be God's boredom after the seventh day of creation.
FRIEDRICH NIETZSCHE (1844–1900)

The cure for boredom is curiosity. There is no cure for curiosity.
DOROTHY PARKER (1893–1967)

The chief product of an automated society is a widespread and deepening sense of boredom.
C. NORTHCOTE PARKINSON (1909–1993)

Good-bye. I am leaving because I am bored.
GEORGE SAUNDERS (1958–), last words

Life is as tedious as a twice-told tale
Vexing the dull ear of a drowsy man.
WILLIAM SHAKESPEARE (1564–1616), *King John*

Boredom is just the reverse side of fascination: both depend on being outside rather than inside a situation, and one leads to the other.
ARTHUR SCHOPENHAUER (1788–1860)

The two foes of human happiness are pain and boredom.
ARTHUR SCHOPENHAUER (1788–1860)

The life of the creative man is led, directed and controlled by boredom. Avoiding boredom is one of our most important purposes.
SUSAN SONTAG (1933–2004)

He who seeks rest finds boredom. He who seeks work finds rest.
DYLAN THOMAS (1914–1953)

Someone's boring me. I think it's me.
DYLAN THOMAS (1914–1953)

Boredom: the desire for desires.
LEO TOLSTOY (1828–1910)

A healthy male adult bore consumes each year one and a half times his own weight in other people's patience.
JOHN UPDIKE (1932–), *Assorted Prose*

Who wants a world in which the guarantee that we shall not die of starvation entails the risk of dying of boredom?
RAOUL VANEIGEM (1934–)

The secret of being a bore is to tell everything.
VOLTAIRE (1694–1778), *Discours en vers sur l'homme*

Work spares us from three evils: boredom, vice, and need.
VOLTAIRE (1694–1778)

Bosses

Without ambition one starts nothing. Without work one finishes nothing. The prize will not be sent to you. You have to win it. The man who knows how will always have a job. The man who also knows why will always be his boss. As to methods there may be a million and then some, but principles are few. The man who grasps principles can successfully select his own methods. The man who tries methods, ignoring principles, is sure to have trouble.
RALPH WALDO EMERSON (1803–1882)

By working faithfully eight hours a day, you may eventually get to be a boss and work twelve hours a day.
ROBERT FROST (1874–1963)

I want to share something with you: The three little sentences that will get you through life. Number 1: Cover for me. Number 2: Oh, good idea, Boss! Number 3: It was like that when I got here.
MATT GROENING (1954–)

The speed of the boss is the speed of the team.
LEE IACOCCA (1924–)

Accomplishing the impossible means only that the boss will add it to your regular duties.
DOUG LARSON (1902–1981)

Grasp your opportunities, no matter how poor your health; nothing is worse for your health than boredom.
MIGNON MCLAUGHLIN (1913–1983)

The person who knows how will always have a job. The person who knows why will always be his boss.
DIANE RAVITCH (1938–)

Botany

I decided that my means were sufficient to enable me to devote myself to botany, a determination which I never, during the long period of my subsequent career, had on any occasion any reason to repent of.
GEORGE BENTHAM (1800–1884)

Botany, n.: The science of vegetables—those that are not good to eat, as well as those that are. It deals largely with their flowers, which are commonly badly designed, inartistic in color, and ill-smelling.
AMBROSE BIERCE (1842–1914), *The Devil's Dictionary*

Love not the flower they pluck and know it not,
And all their botany is Latin names.
RALPH WALDO EMERSON (1803–1882)

The grounding in natural sciences which I obtained in the course of my medical studies, including preliminary examinations in botany, zoology, physics, and chemistry, was to become decisive in determining the trend of my literary work.
JOHANNES VILHELM JENSEN (1873–1950)

Just as the science and art of agriculture depend upon chemistry and botany, so the art of education depends upon physiology and psychology.
EDWARD THORNDIKE (1874–1949)

It is, I find, in zoology as it is in botany: all nature is so full, that that district produces the greatest variety which is the most examined.
GILBERT WHITE (1720–1793)

Boxing

Boxing is a lot of white men watching two black men beat each other up.
MUHAMMAD ALI (1942–)

I am the astronaut of boxing. Joe Louis and Dempsey were just jet pilots. I'm in a world of my own.
MUHAMMAD ALI (1942–)

Boxing gave me the opportunities to grow into the person that I am today.
ALEXIS ARGUELLO (1952–)

I'd say the most memorable thing for me was my dedication and motivation in how I got so involved in boxing.
ALEXIS ARGUELLO (1952–)

See, I respect boxing because it has given me so much and that's why I will never allow anyone to mistreat the sport of boxing if I can help it.
ALEXIS ARGUELLO (1952–)

In those days, boxing was very glamorous and romantic. You listened to fights on the radio, and a good announcer made it seem like a contest between gladiators.
JOSEPH BARBERA (1911–)

Boxing is the toughest and loneliest sport in the world.
FRANK BRUNO (1961–)

When I came into boxing, I brought it to the next level with adverts and doing pantomime and people just got jealous of me doing that.
FRANK BRUNO (1961–)

Attack is only one half of the art of boxing.
GEORGES CARPENTIER (1894–1975)

All of the sports have a safety net, but boxing is the only sport that has none. So when the fighter is through, he is through. While he was fighting his management was very excited for him, but now that he is done, that management team is moving on.
GERRY COONEY (1956–)

Boxing was not the sport that I thought it was due to all the politics.
GERRY COONEY (1956–)

Boxing, for me, it's the beginning of all sports. I'm willing to bet that the first sport was a man against another man in a fight, so I think that's something innate in all of us.
OMAR EPPS (1973–)

Boxing is like jazz. The better it is, the less people appreciate it.
GEORGE FOREMAN (1949–)

I've seen George Foreman shadow boxing and the shadow won.
GEORGE FOREMAN (1949–)

Boxing is the only sport you can get your brain shook, your money took and your name in the undertaker book.
JOE FRAZIER (1944–)

To me, boxing is like a ballet, except there's no music, no choreography, and the dancers hit each other.
JACK HANDY (1949–)

In boxing, everybody has their favorites.
THOMAS HEARNS (1958–)

Well, of course a boxing match is hard because boxing isn't set for you to do good. You have to force your will upon someone, but dancing you don't have to force your will. It should be a lot easier because if I make a mistake I don't get hit.
EVANDER HOLYFIELD (1962–)

Boxing brings out my aggressive instinct, not necessarily a killer instinct.
SUGAR RAY LEONARD (1956–)

Boxing is the ultimate challenge. There's nothing that can compare to testing yourself the way you do every time you step in the ring.
SUGAR RAY LEONARD (1956–)

Boxing was not something I truly enjoyed. Like a lot of things in life, when you put the gloves on, it's better to give than to receive.
SUGAR RAY LEONARD (1956–)

A boxing match is like a cowboy movie. There's got to be good guys and there's got to be bad guys. And that's what people pay for—to see the bad guys get beat.
SONNY LISTON (1932–1970)

Boxing has become America's tragic theater.
JOYCE CAROL OATES (1938–)

Boxing is about being hit rather more than it is about hitting, just as it is about feeling pain, if not devastating psychological paralysis, more than it is about winning.
JOYCE CAROL OATES (1938–)

Boxing is a celebration of the lost religion of masculinity all the more trenchant for its being lost.
JOYCE CAROL OATES (1938–)

The third man in the ring makes boxing possible.
JOYCE CAROL OATES (1938–)

The boxing world is full of all kinds of corruption.
AL SHARPTON (1954–)

[I] started my ring career as a terrific hitter; then my hands cracked up and I had to resort to boxing and tricks to win.
GENE TUNNEY (1897–1978)

Brains

Ideas must work through the brains and arms of men, or they are no better than dreams.
RALPH WALDO EMERSON (1803–1882)

I'm not sure I've even got the brains to be President.
BARRY GOLDWATER (1909–1998)

Do not think of knocking out another person's brains because he differs in opinion from you. It would be as rational to knock yourself on the head because you differ from yourself ten years ago.
HORACE MANN (1796–1859)

Brains, like hearts, go where they are appreciated.
ROBERT S. MCNAMARA (1916–)

A man paints with his brains and not with his hands.
MICHELANGELO (1475–1564)

Not Hercules could have knock'd out his brains, for he had none.
WILLIAM SHAKESPEARE (1564–1616), *Cymbeline*

Oh God, that men should put an enemy in their mouths to steal away their brains!
WILLIAM SHAKESPEARE (1564–1616), *Othello*

I believe in an open mind, but not so open that your brains fall out.
ARTHUR HAYS SULZBERGER (1891–1968)

I not only use all the brains that I have, but all that I can borrow.
WOODROW WILSON (1856–1924)

Nature abhors a vacuum. When a head lacks brains, nature fills it with conceit.
ANONYMOUS

A handful of patience is worth more than a bushel of brains.
DUTCH PROVERB

Bravery

Moral excellence comes about as a result of habit. We become just by doing just acts, temperate by doing temperate acts, brave by doing brave acts.
ARISTOTLE (384–322 BC)

When their adventures do not succeed, however, they run away; but it was the mark of a brave man to face things that are, and seem, terrible for a man, because it is noble to do so and disgraceful not to do so.
ARISTOTLE (384–322 BC)

Bravery is the capacity to perform properly even when scared half to death.
OMAR BRADLEY (1893–1981)

Brave men are all vertebrates; they have their softness on the surface and their toughness in the middle.
G. K. CHESTERTON (1874–1936)

Bravery has no place where it can avail nothing.
SAMUEL JOHNSON (1709–1784)

Bravery is being the only one who knows you're afraid.
FRANKLIN P. JONES (1887–1929)

Few men are willing to brave the disapproval of their fellows, the censure of their colleagues, the wrath of their society. Moral courage is a rarer commodity than bravery in battle or great intelligence. Yet it is the one essential, vital quality

for those who seek to change a world which yields most painfully to change.
ROBERT F. KENNEDY (1925–1968)

True bravery is shown by performing without witness what one might be capable of doing before all the world.
FRANÇOIS DE LA ROCHEFOUCAULD (1613–1680)

Let bravery be thy choice, but not bravado.
MENANDER (342–292 BC)

You can't be brave if you've only had wonderful things happen to you.
MARY TYLER MOORE (1936–)

No matter whether a person belongs to the upper or lower ranks, if he has not put his life on the line at least once he has cause for shame.
NABESHIMA NAOSHIGE (1538–1618)

Bravery is believing in yourself, and that thing nobody can teach you.
MANUEL BENÍTEZ PÉREZ (1936–)

Like timidity, bravery is also contagious.
MUNSHI PREMCHAND (1880–1936)

Alexander received more bravery of mind by the pattern of Achilles, than by hearing the definition of fortitude.
SIR PHILIP SIDNEY (1554–1586)

Curiosity will conquer fear even more than bravery will.
JAMES STEPHENS (1882–1950)

Bravery never goes out of fashion.
WILLIAM MAKEPEACE THACKERAY (1811–1863)

The bravest are surely those who have the clearest vision of what is before them, glory and danger alike and, yet notwithstanding, go out to meet it.
THUCYDIDES (C. 460–395 BC)

Breakfast

Life … is like a grapefruit. It's orange and squishy, and has a few pips in it, and some folks have half a one for breakfast.
DOUGLAS ADAMS (1952–2001)

Sometimes I've believed as many as six impossible things before breakfast.
LEWIS CARROLL (1832–1898), *Alice in Wonderland*

Eat breakfast like a king, lunch like a prince, and dinner like a pauper.
ADELLE DAVIS (1904–1974)

A simple enough pleasure, surely, to have breakfast alone with one's husband, but how seldom married people in the midst of life achieve it.
ANNE MORROW LINDBERGH (1906–2001)

Only dull people are brilliant at breakfast.
OSCAR WILDE (1854–1900), *An Ideal Husband*

Brides

Brides aren't happy, they are just triumphant.
JOHN BARRYMORE (1882–1942)

In Hollywood, brides keep the bouquets and throw away the groom.
GROUCHO MARX (1890–1977)

A bride at her second marriage does not wear a veil. She wants to see what she is getting.
HELEN ROWLAND (1876–1950)

A happy bridesmaid makes a happy bride.
ALFRED, LORD TENNYSON (1809–1892)

Brotherhood

The world is now too small for anything but brotherhood.
ARTHUR POWELL DAVIES (1902–1957)

Whoever in prayer can say, "Our Father," acknowledges and should feel the brotherhood of the whole race of mankind.
TYRON EDWARDS (1809–1894)

The good neighbor looks beyond the external accidents and discerns those inner qualities that make all men human and, therefore, brothers.
MARTIN LUTHER KING JR. (1929–1968), *Strength to Love*

The hope of a secure and livable world lies with disciplined nonconformists who are dedicated to justice, peace, and brotherhood.
MARTIN LUTHER KING JR. (1929–1968), *Strength to Love*

We must learn to live together as brothers or perish together as fools.
MARTIN LUTHER KING JR. (1929–1968)

I believe that if we really want human brotherhood to spread and increase until it makes life safe and sane, we must also be certain that there is no one true faith or path by which it may spread.
ADLAI E. STEVENSON II (1900–1965)

The universal brotherhood of man is our most precious possession, what there is of it.
MARK TWAIN (1835–1910), *Following the Equator*

The brotherhood of man is not a mere poet's dream: it is a most depressing and humiliating reality.
OSCAR WILDE (1854–1900)

The opportunity for brotherhood presents itself every time you meet a human being.
JANE WYMAN (1914–)

The mystical bond of brotherhood makes all men brothers.
THOMAS CARLYLE (1795–1881)

Let us at all times remember that all American citizens are brothers of a common country, and should dwell together in bonds of fraternal feeling.
ABRAHAM LINCOLN (1809–1865)

To see the earth as it truly is, small and blue and beautiful in that eternal silence where it floats, is to see ourselves as riders on the earth together, brothers on that bright loveliness in the eternal cold.
ARCHIBALD MACLEISH (1892–1982)

If you wish to be brothers, let the arms fall from your hands. One cannot love while holding offensive arms.
POPE PAUL VI (1897–1978)

Unless man is committed to the belief that all mankind are his brothers, then he labors in vain and hypocritically in the vineyards of equality.
ADAM CLAYTON POWELL JR. (1908–1972)

We are all brothers under the skin—and I, for one, would be willing to skin humanity to prove it.
AYN RAND (1905–1982)

Brothers

You can only help one of your luckless brothers by trampling down a dozen others.
BERTOLT BRECHT (1898–1956)

We few, we happy few, we band of brothers. For he today that sheds his blood with me shall be my brother; be never so vile. This day shall gentle his condition. And gentlemen in England now abed shall think themselves accursed they were not here, and hold their manhoods cheap whiles any speaks that fought with us upon Saint Crispin's day.
WILLIAM SHAKESPEARE (1564–1616), *Henry V*

You should never do anything wicked and lay it on your brother, when it is just as convenient to lay it on some other boy.
MARK TWAIN (1835–1910)

It takes two men to make one brother.
ISRAEL ZANGWILL (1864–1926)

Live together like brothers and do business like strangers.
ARABIAN PROVERB

Buddhism

A text of Tibetan Buddhism describes the time of death as a unique opportunity for spiritual liberation from the cycles of death and rebirth and a period that determines our next incarnation.
STANISLAV GROF (1931–)

I feel a lot more secure about the directions I take, than I might have, had I not practiced Buddhism.
HERBIE HANCOCK (1940–)

[O]ne of [Buddhism's] main practices is understanding and experiencing compassion, and how that ultimately is a road to happiness.
GOLDIE HAWN (1945–)

One thing that Buddhism teaches you is that every moment is an opportunity to change.
RON REAGAN (1958–)

Buddhism teaches you to embrace change.
KOO STARK (1956–)

Zen Buddhism is a discipline where belief isn't necessary.
DAVID SYLVIAN (1958–)

Buddhism has in it no idea of there being a moral law laid down by some kind of cosmic lawgiver.
ALAN W. WATTS (1914–1973)

Buddhism is not essentially moralistic.
ALAN W. WATTS (1914–1973)

Burdens

Great heroes need great sorrows and burdens, or half their greatness goes unnoticed.
PETER S. BEAGLE (1939–)

Thinking is hard work. One can't bear burdens and ideas at the same time.
RÉMY DE GOURMONT (1858–1915)

We are not living in a paradise where no one has any problems or anything to do any longer, where there are no hurdles, weariness or burdens.
ROBERT LEY (1890–1945)

People become attached to their burdens sometimes more than the burdens are attached to them.
GEORGE BERNARD SHAW (1856–1950)

The marvel of all history is the patience with which men and women submit to burdens unnecessarily laid upon them by their governments.
GEORGE WASHINGTON (1732–1799)

Bureaucracy

A memorandum is written not to inform the reader but to protect the writer.
DEAN ACHESON (1893–1971)

Temporary teams of trusted people are generally sent to all Departments and to major agencies of government to assist in planning and to acquaint the incoming administration with the civil servants and bureaucracy that will remain in place in the new Administration.
RICHARD V. ALLEN (1936–)

I've never been married and I've no more desire to be married now than I ever have. I hate bureaucracy and I am not religious.
FRANCESCA ANNIS (1945–)

The perfect bureaucrat everywhere is the man who manages to make no decisions and escape all responsibility.
BROOKS ATKINSON (1894–1984), *Once Around the Sun*

Not only does a bureaucracy tend to under-government in point of quality; it tends to over-government in point of quantity.
WALTER BAGEHOT (1826–1877)

What the world really needs is more love and less paperwork.
PEARL BAILEY (1918–1990)

And thus Bureaucracy, the giant power wielded by pygmies, came into the world.
HONORÉ DE BALZAC (1799–1850)

I'm against big bureaucracy in Washington making health care decisions. I just have an aversion to bureaucrats. But it's not just government bureaucrats. I don't like HMO bureaucrats and insurance company bureaucrats either.
GARY BAUER (1946–)

Pedantry and bureaucracy—of an unintelligent respect for the past—are at present real dangers, but, once their genesis is understood, they can be made to vanish.
JOHN DESMOND BERNAL (1901–1971)

The challenge is to manage the Web in an open way—not too much bureaucracy, not subject to political or commercial pressures. The U.S. should demonstrate that it is prepared to share control with the world.
TIM BERNERS-LEE (1955–)

Modern democracy was no doubt the most wholesome and needed reaction against the abuses of absolutism and of a selfish, often corrupt, bureaucracy.
FRANZ BOAS (1858–1942)

Misdirected focus on paperwork, on procedures, and on bureaucracy frustrates teachers and fails to give children the education they need.
CHRISTOPHER BOND (1939–)

We can lick gravity, but sometimes the paperwork is overwhelming.
WERNHER VON BRAUN (1912–1977)

Too often I find that the volume of paper expands to fill the available briefcases.
JERRY BROWN (1938–)

The best way to deal with bureaucrats is with stealth and sudden violence.
BUTROS BUTROS-GHALI (1922–)

Any plan of administration which contemplates a concentrating of responsibility is open to the dangers which follow the creation of a bureaucracy.
ARTHUR CAPPER (1865–1951)

Every year the Federal Government wastes billions of dollars as a result of overpayments of government agencies, misuse of government credit cards, abuse of the Federal entitlement programs, and the mismanagement of the Federal bureaucracy.
CHRIS CHOCOLA (1962–)

A bureaucrat is the most despicable of men, though he is needed as vultures are needed, but one hardly admires vultures whom bureaucrats so strangely resemble. I have yet to meet a bureaucrat who was not petty, dull, almost witless, crafty or stupid, an oppressor or a thief, a holder of little authority in which he delights, as a boy delights in possessing a vicious dog. Who can trust such creatures?
CICERO (106–43 BC)

"Corpocracy" is large-scale corporate America's tendency to be like the government bureaucracy.
RICHARD DARMAN (1943–)

The search of the young today is more specific than the ancient search for the Holy Grail. The search of the youth today is for ways and means to make the machine—and the vast bureaucracy of the corporation state and of government that runs that machine—the servant of man.... That is the revolution that is coming.... It could be a revolution in the nature of an explosive political regeneration. It depends on how wise the Establishment is. If, with its stockpile of arms, it resolves to suppress the dissenters, America will face, I fear, an awful ordeal.
WILLIAM ORVILLE DOUGLAS (1898–1980)

I wanted to have some kind of evening at the White House to honor the art of the story, but the bureaucracy was so tough, it just never happened.
RITA DOVE (1952–)

Bureaucracy is the death of all sound work.
ALBERT EINSTEIN (1879–1955)

German businessmen are overwhelmed by the high cost of doing business. Inflexible rules, enforced by a burgeoning bureaucracy, discourage entrepreneurship.
SUZANNE FIELDS (1950–)

The bureaucracy is not great. I don't think Rick Santorum who is not one for being a big proponent of large bureaucracies would be as enthusiastic a supporter of it.
HAROLD FORD (1970–)

Hell hath no fury like a bureaucrat scorned.
MILTON FRIEDMAN (1912–2006)

Such schemes take money from people who can least afford to spend it to support an unneeded bureaucracy that eats money people thought they were providing for education.
JESSE HELMS (1921–)

An official man is always an official man, and he has a wild belief in the value of reports.
SIR ARTHUR HELPS (1813–1875)

A mayor is a symbol and a public face of what a city bureaucracy provides its citizens.
JOHN HICKENLOOPER (1952–)

Well, that's true… to me, communism is a… it's a graveyard of skulls, of very unhappy people, below the level of the top bureaucracy.
E. HOWARD HUNT (1918–2007)

A democracy which makes or even effectively prepares for modern, scientific war must necessarily cease to be democratic. No country can be really well prepared for modern war unless it is governed by a tyrant, at the head of a highly trained and perfectly obedient bureaucracy.
ALDOUS HUXLEY (1894–1963)

A civil servant doesn't make jokes.
EUGÈNE IONESCO (1909–1994)

Every revolution evaporates and leaves behind only the slime of a new bureaucracy
FRANZ KAFKA (1883–1924)

Too many vital education dollars that should be spent in the classroom are bouncing around in the federal bureaucracy.
MARK KENNEDY (1957–)

Bureaucracies are inherently antidemocratic. Bureaucrats derive their power from their position in the structure, not from their relations with the people they are supposed to serve. The people are not masters of the bureaucracy, but its clients.
ALAN KEYES (1950–)

Government machinery has been described as a marvelous labor saving device which enables ten men to do the work of one.
JOHN MAYNARD KEYNES (1883–1946)

Without general elections, without unrestricted freedom of press and assembly, without a free struggle of opinion, life dies out in every public institution, becomes a mere semblance of life, in which only the bureaucracy remains as the active element. Public life gradually falls asleep, a few dozen party leaders of inexhaustible energy and boundless experience direct and rule. Such conditions must inevitably cause a brutalization of public life: attempted assassinations, shootings of hostages, etc.
ROSA LUXEMBURG (C. 1870–1919)

The bureaucracy is a circle from which one cannot escape. Its hierarchy is a hierarchy of knowledge. The top entrusts the understanding of detail to the lower levels, whilst the lower levels credit the top with understanding of the general, and so all are mutually deceived.
KARL MARX (1818–1883)

The only thing that saves us from the bureaucracy is its inefficiency. An efficient bureaucracy is the greatest threat to liberty.
EUGENE J. MCCARTHY (1916–2005)

Bureaucracy, the rule of no one, has become the modern form of despotism.
MARY MCCARTHY (1912–1989)

The disease which inflicts bureaucracy and what they usually die from is routine.
JOHN STUART MILL (1806–1873)

When I appointed the Minister of the Environment to major cabinet status, the Planning and Priorities committee, the signals that that sent through Ottawa were major, because that's what the bureaucracy understands.
BRIAN MULRONEY (1939–)

What we have now is democracy without citizens. No one is on the public's side. All the buyers are on the corporation's side. And the bureaucrats in the administration don't think the government belongs to the people.
RALPH NADER (1934–)

Any change is resisted because bureaucrats have a vested interest in the chaos in which they exist.
RICHARD M. NIXON (1913–1994)

Government proposes, bureaucracy disposes. And the bureaucracy must dispose of government proposals by dumping them on us.
P. J. O'ROURKE (1947–)

Bureaucracy defends the status quo long past the time when the quo has lost its status.
DR. LAURENCE J. PETER (1919–1990)

Bureaucracy defends the status quo long past the time when the quo has lost its status.
DR. LAURENCE J. PETER (1919–1990)

Bureaucrats write memoranda both because they appear to be busy when they are writing and because the memos, once written, immediately become proof that they were busy.
CHARLES PETERS (1952–)

More harm was done in the 20th century by faceless bureaucrats than tyrant dictators.
DENNIS PRAGER (1948–)

The larger the state, the more callous it becomes… the colder its heart. It is also true that the bigger the corporation, the more callous its heart. But unlike the state, corporations have competition and have no police powers.
DENNIS PRAGER (1948–)

We need to remind our core supporters that we have not forgotten their concern with the way our democracy is being replaced by European bureaucracy in so many areas.
JOHN REDWOOD (1951–)

Powers once assumed are never relinquished, just as bureaucracies, once created, never die.
CHARLEY REESE (1937–)

There is an increasingly pervasive sense not only of failure, but of futility. The legislative process has become a cruel shell game and the service system has become a bureaucratic maze, inefficient, incomprehensible, and inaccessible.
ELLIOT RICHARDSON (1920–1999)

If you are going to sin, sin against God, not the bureaucracy. God will forgive you but the bureaucracy won't.
HYMAN RICKOVER (1900–1986)

Congress, the press, and the bureaucracy too often focus on how much money or effort is spent, rather than whether the money or effort actually achieves the announced goal.
DONALD H. RUMSFELD (1932–)

Strive to make proposed solutions as self-executing as possible. As the degree of discretion increases, so too does bureaucracy, delay, and expense.
DONALD H. RUMSFELD (1932–)

Gay activist groups are already starting to instruct same-sex couples to file joint income tax returns, so the Bush Administration should establish procedures right now in order that the bureaucracy will know how to handle the paperwork.
PHYLLIS SCHLAFLY (1924–)

Bureaucracy is not an obstacle to democracy but an inevitable complement to it.
JOSEPH A. SCHUMPETER (1883–1950)

It is amazing that people who think we cannot afford to pay for doctors, hospitals, and medication somehow think that we can afford to pay for doctors, hospitals, medication and a government bureaucracy to administer it.
THOMAS SOWELL (1930–)

Mystical references to society and its programs to help may warm the hearts of the gullible but what it really means is putting more power in the hands of bureaucrats.
THOMAS SOWELL (1930–)

You will never understand bureaucracies until you understand that for bureaucrats procedure is everything and outcomes are nothing.
THOMAS SOWELL (1930–)

Major policy decisions that affect them are now made by the courts, the bureaucracy and "The Headquarters" of various organizations.
ROBERT TEETER (1939–2004)

Most managers were trained to be the thing they most despise—bureaucrats.
ALVIN TOFFLER (1928–)

It's a poor bureaucrat who can't stall a good idea until even its sponsor is relieved to see it dead and officially buried.
ROBERT TOWNSEND (1957–)

[The Bill of Rights is] designed to protect individuals and minorities against the tyranny of the majority, but it's also designed to protect the people against bureaucracy, against the government.
JUDGE LAWRENCE TRIBE (1941–)

Bureaucracy strangles; informality liberates. Creating an informal atmosphere is a competitive advantage.
JACK WELCH (1935–)

Any sufficiently advanced bureaucracy is indistinguishable from molasses.
ANONYMOUS

If an idea can survive a bureaucratic review and be implemented it wasn't worth doing.
ANONYMOUS

If there is a way to delay an important decision, the good bureaucracy, public or private, will find it.
ANONYMOUS

If you are going to sin, sin against God, not the bureaucracy. God will forgive you but the bureaucracy won't.
ANONYMOUS

In any bureaucracy, paper work increases as you spend more and more time reporting on the less and less you are doing.
ANONYMOUS

Join in the new game that's sweeping the country. It's called "Bureaucracy." Everybody stands in a circle. The first person to do anything loses.
ANONYMOUS

Business

I ran the wrong kind of business, but I did it with integrity.
SYDNEY BIDDLE BARROWS (1952–)

The gambling known as business looks with austere disfavor upon the business known as gambling.
AMBROSE BIERCE (1842–1914), *The Devil's Dictionary*

In the business world, the rearview mirror is always clearer than the windshield.
WARREN BUFFETT (1930–)

I find it rather easy to portray a businessman. Being bland, rather cruel, and incompetent comes naturally to me.
JOHN CLEESE (1939–)

The chief business of the American people is business.
CALVIN COOLIDGE (1872–1933)

Here's my theory about meetings and life; the three things you can't fake are erections, competence and creativity. That's why meetings become toxic: they put uncreative people in a situation in which they have to be something they can never be. And the more effort they put into concealing their inabilities, the more toxic the meeting becomes. One of the most common creativity-faking tactics is when someone puts their hands in prayer position and conceals their mouth while they nod at you and say, "Mmmmmm. Interesting." If pressed, they'll add, "I'll have to get back to you on that." Then they don't say anything else.
DOUGLAS COUPLAND (1961–)

So much of what we call management consists in making it difficult for people to work.
PETER F. DRUCKER (1909–2005)

Drive thy business or it will drive thee.
BENJAMIN FRANKLIN (1706–1790)

It is an immutable law in business that words are words, explanations are explanations, promises are promises but only performance is reality.
HAROLD S. GENEEN (1910–1997)

Letting your customers set your standards is a dangerous game, because the race to the bottom is pretty easy to win. Setting your own standards, and living up to them is a better way to profit. Not to mention a better way to make your day worth all the effort you put into it.
SETH GODIN (1960–)

Dressing up is inevitably a substitute for good ideas. It is no coincidence that technically inept business types are known as "suits."
PAUL GRAHAM (1964–)

Management is nothing more than motivating other people.
LEE IACOCCA (1924–)

More business is lost every year through neglect than through any other cause.
ROSE F. KENNEDY (1890–1995)

There's no business like show business, but there are several businesses like accounting.
DAVID LETTERMAN (1947–)

Talk of nothing but business, and dispatch that business quickly.
ALDUS MANUTIUS (1449–1515)

In the modern world of business, it is useless to be a creative original thinker unless you can also sell what you create. Management cannot be expected to recognize a good idea unless it is presented to them by a good salesman.
DAVID M. OGILVY (1911–1999)

Success in business requires training and discipline and hard work. But if you're not frightened by these things, the opportunities are just as great today as they ever were.
DAVID ROCKEFELLER (1915–)

You never really hear the truth from your subordinates until after 10 in the evening.
JURGEN SCHREMPP (1944–)

The key to being a good manager is keeping the people who hate me away from those who are still undecided.
CASEY STENGEL (1890–1975)

No one travelling on a business trip would be missed if he failed to arrive.
THORSTEIN VEBLEN (1857–1929)

My own business always bores me to death; I prefer other people's.
OSCAR WILDE (1854–1900), *Lady Windermere's Fan*

Caffeine

Widespread caffeine use explains a lot about the twentieth century.
GREG EGA (1961–)

Caffeine. The gateway drug.
EDDIE VEDDER (1964–)

If it weren't for caffeine I'd have no personality whatsoever!
ANONYMOUS

California

California is a fine place to live—if you happen to be an orange.
FRED ALLEN (1894–1956)

California is like an artificial limb the rest of the country doesn't really need.
SAUL BELLOW (1915–2005)

In California everyone goes to a therapist, is a therapist, or is a therapist going to a therapist.
TRUMAN CAPOTE (1924–1984)

It's a scientific fact that if you stay in California you lose one point of your IQ every year.
TRUMAN CAPOTE (1924–1984)

California, the department store state.
RAYMOND CHANDLER (1888–1959)

Californians invented the concept of life-style. This alone warrants their doom.
DON DELILLO (1936–)

California: The west coast of Iowa.
JOAN DIDION (1934–)

California is the only state in the union where you can fall asleep under a rose bush in full bloom and freeze to death.
W. C. FIELDS (1880–1946)

Nothing is wrong with California that a rise in the ocean level wouldn't cure.
ROSS MACDONALD (1915 –1983)

Living in California adds ten years to a man's life. And those extra ten years I'd like to spend in New York.
HARRY RUBY (1895–1984)

Campaigns

[T]o some extent the election campaigns never stop except for about three months after an election. There is a heightened level of interest in opinion polls and politics around the world.
JIM BOLGER (1935–)

The Court made an exception, however, in the case of candidates contributing to their own campaigns because of the rather reasonable presumption that a candidate is incapable of corrupting himself.
JAMES L. BUCKLEY (1923–)

What we have [are] two important values in conflict: freedom of speech and our desire for healthy campaigns in a healthy democracy. You can't have both.
DICK GEPHARDT (1941–)

There's enormous progressive activism and, more often than not, success at the grassroots level—everything from living wage campaigns to efforts to finance our elections are having terrific success.
JIM HIGHTOWER (1943–)

Some campaigns are not worth waging if you can't win; others have to be fought on grounds of principle regardless of the chances for success.
PATRICIA IRELAND (1945–)

Almost all political campaigns involve falsity and playacting.
RICH LOWRY (1968–)

In constant pursuit of money to finance campaigns, the political system is simply unable to function. Its deliberative powers are paralyzed.
JOHN RAWLS (1921–2002)

Political campaigns are designedly made into emotional orgies which endeavor to distract attention from the real issues involved, and they actually paralyze what slight powers of cerebration man can normally muster.
JAMES HARVEY ROBINSON (1863–1936)

Camping

Camping is nature's way of promoting the motel business.
DAVE BARRY (1947–)

The ultimate camping trip was the Lewis and Clark expedition.
DAVE BARRY (1947–)

Some national parks have long waiting lists for camping reservations. When you have to wait a year to sleep next to a tree, something is wrong.
GEORGE CARLIN (1937–)

I went camping for 33 days, and now everybody seems to care.
COLLEEN HASKELL (1976–)

Is that weird, taking my Louis Vuitton bag camping?
JESSICA SIMPSON (1980–)

Cancer

Growth for the sake of growth is the ideology of the cancer cell.
EDWARD ABBEY (1927–1989)

Bitterness is like cancer. It eats upon the host. But anger is like fire. It burns it all clean.
MAYA ANGELOU (1928–)

Cancer, like any other illness, is a bore.
ALAN BENNETT (1934–)

Anyone with cancer and their families and their friends, free of charge, [should] get emotional support—emotional and psychological support.
GENE WILDER (1933–)

Cannibalism

I believe that if ever I had to practice cannibalism, I might manage if there were enough tarragon around.
JAMES BEARD (1903–1985)

Monty Python was well-known for pushing and breaking comedy taboos and raising a stir… we were also the first show to do cannibalism as a schtick.
GRAHAM CHAPMAN (1941–1989)

If you were to destroy in mankind the belief in immortality, not only love but every living force maintaining the life of the world would at once be dried up. Moreover, nothing then would be immoral, everything would be permissible, even cannibalism.
FYODOR DOSTOEVSKY (1821–1881), *Brothers Karamazov*

I believe in compulsory cannibalism. If people were forced to eat what they killed, there would be no more wars.
ABBIE HOFFMAN (1936–1989)

One day it's going to dawn on the human race that war is as barbaric a means of resolving conflict as cannibalism is as a means of coping with diet deficiencies.
BRUCE KENT (1929–)

Nothing more strongly arouses our disgust than cannibalism, yet we make the same impression on Buddhists and vegetarians, for we feed on babies, though not our own.
ROBERT LOUIS STEVENSON (1850–1894)

The people of the future will say "meat-eaters" in disgust and regard us in the same way that we regard cannibals and cannibalism.
DENNIS WEAVER (1924–2006)

Capitalism

Liberal capitalism is not at all the good of humanity. Quite the contrary; it is the vehicle of savage, destructive nihilism.
ALAIN BADIOU (1937–)

Socialism failed because it couldn't tell the economic truth; capitalism may fail because it couldn't tell the ecological truth.
LESTER R. BROWN (1934–)

The inherent vice of capitalism is the unequal sharing of blessings; the inherent virtue of socialism is the equal sharing of miseries.
SIR WINSTON CHURCHILL (1874–1965)

Under capitalism, man exploits man. Under communism, it's just the opposite.
JOHN KENNETH GALBRAITH (1908–2006)

The market is not an invention of capitalism. It has existed for centuries. It is an invention of civilization.
MIKHAIL GORBACHEV (1931–)

Capitalism is the astounding belief that the most wickedest of men will do the most wickedest of things for the greatest good of everyone
JOHN MAYNARD KEYNES (1883–1946)

The forces in a capitalist society, if left unchecked, tend to make the rich richer and the poor poorer.
JAWAHARLAL NEHRU (1889–1964)

The spread of evil is the symptom of a vacuum. Whenever evil wins, it is only by default: by the moral failure of those who evade the fact that there can be no compromise on basic principles.
AYN RAND (1905–1982), *Capitalism: The Unknown Ideal*

Socialism is nothing but the capitalism of the lower classes.
OSWALD SPENGLER (1880–1936), *The Hour of Decision*

Catholicism

Protestantism has the method of Jesus with His secret too much left out of mind; Catholicism has His secret with His method too much left out of mind; neither has His unerring balance, His intuition, His sweet reasonableness. But both have hold of a great truth, and get from it a great power.
MATTHEW ARNOLD (1822–1888)

If I were going to convert to any religion I would probably choose Catholicism because it at least has female saints and the Virgin Mary.
MARGARET ATWOOD (1939–)

The Catholic imagination is metaphorical or sacramental. It sees God as present in the world. The Protestant imagination, the dialectical imagination, wants to preserve God from the possibility of idolatry by identifying with His creatures. Catholicism has no problem with that.
ANDREW GREELEY (1928–)

You know, Catholicism, we believed in the teachings of Cathol, and everything it stood for.
EDDIE IZZARD (1962–)

Well, I think that Catholicism's basic foundation of faith is personal conscience. I think it's between you and God, not you and the Church.
MARTIN SHEEN (1940–)

Cats

One of the problems of taking things apart and seeing how they work—supposing you're trying to find out how a cat works—you take that cat apart to see how it works, what you've got in your hands is a non-working cat. The cat wasn't a sort of clunky mechanism that was susceptible to our available tools of analysis.
DOUGLAS ADAMS (1952–2001)

Never play cat and mouse games if you're a mouse.
DON ADDIS (1964–)

But buds will be roses, and kittens, cats—more's the pity!
LOUISA MAY ALCOTT (1832–1888)

Two cats can live as cheaply as one, and their owner has twice as much fun. Most cats do not approach humans recklessly. The possibility of concealed weapons, clods or sticks, tends to make them reserved. Homeless cats in particular—with some justification, unfortunately—consider humans their natural enemies. Much ceremony must be observed, and a number of diplomatic feelers put out before establishing a state of truce.
LLOYD ALEXANDER (1924–2007)

As anyone who has ever been around a cat for any length of time well knows, cats have enormous patience with the limitations of the human kind.
CLEVELAND AMORY (1917–1998)

Cats talk with their tails.
CLEVELAND AMORY (1917–1998)

To anyone who has ever been owned by a cat, it will come as no surprise that there are all sorts of things about your cat you will never, as long as you live, forget. Not the least of these is the first sight of him or her.
CLEVELAND AMORY (1917–1998)

To bathe a cat takes brute force, perseverance, courage of conviction—and a cat. The last ingredient is usually hardest to come by.
STEPHEN BAKER (1964–)

Both ardent lovers and austere scholars, when once they come to the years of discretion, love cats, so strong and gentle, the pride of the household, who like them are sensitive to the cold, and sedentary.
CHARLES BAUDELAIRE (1821–1867)

Drowsing, [cats] take the noble attitude of a great sphinx, who, in a desert land, sleeps always, dreaming dreams that have no end.
CHARLES BAUDELAIRE (1821–1867)

There is something about the presence of a cat … that seems to take the bite out of being alone.
DR. LOUIS J. CAMUTI (1894–1981)

Work—other people's work—is an intolerable idea to a cat. Can you picture cats herding sheep or agreeing to pull a cart? They will not inconvenience themselves to the slightest degree.
DR. LOUIS J. CAMUTI (1894–1981)

Quite obviously a cat trusts human beings; but she doesn't trust a cat because she knows her better than we do.
KAREL CAPEK (1890–1938)

Cats can be cooperative when something feels good, which, to a cat, is the way everything is supposed to feel as much of the time as possible.
ROGER A. CARAS (1928–)

Cats don't like change without their consent.
ROGER A. CARAS (1928–)

There is no more intrepid explorer than a kitten. He makes perilous voyages into cellar and attic, he scales the roofs of neighboring houses, he thrusts his little inquiring nose into half-shut doors…he gets himself into every kind of trouble, and he's always sorry when it is too late.
JULES CHAMPFLEURY (1820–1889)

Two things are aesthetically perfect in the world—the clock and the cat.
ÉMILE-AUGUSTE CHARTIER (1868–1951)

The cat lives alone. He has no need of society. He obeys only when he wishes, he pretends to sleep the better to see, and scratches everything he can scratch.
FRANÇOIS-RENÉ DE CHATEAUBRIAND (1768–1848)

I like pigs. Dogs look up to us. Cats look down on us. Pigs treat us as equals.
SIR WINSTON CHURCHILL (1874–1965)

The thing about cats, as you may find, is that no one knows what they have in mind.
JOHN CIARDI (1916–1986)

The cat is the animal to whom the Creator gave the biggest eye, the softest fur, the most supremely delicate nostrils, a mobile ear, an unrivaled paw and a curved claw borrowed from the rose-tree.
SIDONIE GABRIELLE COLETTE (1873–1954)

There stands before you, gray like all the other grays but one whom you won't confuse, having seen her once, with any other gray cat, she who rejects the names of queens, the childish diminutives, and is called—as if she were the only one in the world—Cat.
SIDONIE GABRIELLE COLETTE (1873–1954)

A poet's cat, sedate and grave as a poet well could wish to have…. Time, that spoils all things, will, I suppose, make her also a cat…. For no wisdom that she may gain by experience and reflection hereafter will compensate for the loss of her present hilarity.
WILLIAM COWPER (1731–1800)

To respect the cat is the beginning of the aesthetic sense.
ERASMUS DARWIN (1731–1802)

The great charm of cats is their rampant egotism, their devil-may-care attitude toward responsibility, their disinclination to earn an honest dollar … cats are disdainful of everything but their own immediate interests.
ROBERTSON DAVIES (1913–1995)

I don't care what color the cat is, as long as it catches the rat.
DENG XIAOPING (1904–1997)

Cats are independent, but completely loyal friends for life.
ANTHONY EDWARDS (1962–)

When a cat adopts you there is nothing to be done about it except to put up with it until the wind changes.
T. S. ELIOT (1888–1965)

A creature that never cries over spilt milk: a cat.
EVAN ESAR (1899–1995)

The cat: an animal that's so unpredictable, you can never tell in advance how it will ignore you the next time.
EVAN ESAR (1899–1995)

Cats are peaceful and tranquil—they bring calmness with their serene personalities.
CHRIS EVERT (1954–)

Nothing's more playful than a young cat, nor more grave than an old one.
THOMAS FULLER (1608–1661)

The cat is the only non-gregarious domestic animal.
FRANCIS GALTON (1822–1911)

It is a matter to gain the affection of a cat. He is a philosophical animal, tenacious of his own habits, fond of order and neatness, and disinclined to extravagant sentiment. He will be your friend, if he finds you worthy of friendship, but not your slave. He keeps his free will though he loves, and will not do for you what he thinks unreasonable; but if he once gives himself to you, it is with absolute confidence and fidelity of affection. God has created the cat to give man the pleasure of caressing the tiger.
THÉOPHILE GAUTIER (1811–1872)

The cat is a dilettante in fur.
THÉOPHILE GAUTIER (1811–1872)

For a dyed-in-the-wool author nothing is as dead as a book once it is written.… She is rather like a cat whose kittens have grown up. While they were a-growing she was passionately interested in them but now they seem hardly to belong to her—and probably she is involved with another batch of kittens as I am involved with other writing.
RUMER GODDEN (1907–1998)

How we behave towards cats here below determines our status in heaven. Women and cats will do as they please, and men and dogs should relax and get used to the idea.
ROBERT A. HEINLEIN (1907–1988)

A cat has absolute emotional honesty: human beings, for one reason or another, may hide their feelings, but a cat does not.
ROBERT HERRICK (1591–1674)

Cats are connoisseurs of comfort.
JAMES HERRIOT (1916–1995)

I have noticed that what cats most appreciate in a human being is not the ability to produce food which they take for granted—but his or her entertainment value.
GEOFFREY HOUSEHOLD (1900–1988)

No man has ever dared to manifest his boredom so insolently as does a Siamese tomcat.
ALDOUS HUXLEY (1894–1963)

Cats and monkeys; monkeys and cats; all human life is there.
HENRY JAMES (1843–1916)

Cats keep their cool, no matter what. Even when they do things like fall or lose their balance, they'll walk away with an attitude that seems to say, "I meant to do that."
MICHAEL JORDAN (1963–)

All cats are possessed of a proud spirit, and the surest way to forfeit the esteem of a cat is to treat him as an inferior being.
MICHAEL JOSEPH (1872–1940)

Cats seem to go on the principle that it never does any harm to ask for what you want.
JOSEPH WOOD KRUTCH (1893–1970)

A dog is like a liberal. He wants to please everybody. A cat doesn't need to know that everybody loves him.
WILLIAM KUNSTLER (1919–1995)

Of all animals, the cat alone attains to the contemplative life. He regards the wheel of existence from without, like the Buddha.
ANDREW LANG (1844–1912)

I've never understood why women love cats. Cats are independent, they don't listen, they don't come in when you call, they like to stay out all night, and when they're home they like to be left alone and sleep. In other words, every quality that women hate in a man, they love in a cat.
JAY LENO (1950–)

If a fish is the movement of water embodied, given shape, then a cat is a diagram and pattern of subtle air.
DORIS LESSING (1919–)

No matter how much the cats fight, there always seem to be plenty of kittens.
ABRAHAM LINCOLN (1809–1865)

Cats are possessed of a shy, retiring nature, cajoling, haughty, and capricious, difficult to fathom. They reveal themselves only to certain favored individuals, and are repelled by the faintest suggestion of insult or even by the most trifling deception.
PIERRE LOTI (1850–1923)

I will admit to feeling exceedingly proud when any cat has singled me out for notice; for, of course, every cat is really the most beautiful woman in the room. That is part of their deadly fascination.
E. V. LUCAS (1868–1938)

If a cat can detect no self-advantage in what it is being told to do, it says the hell with it, and, if pressure is brought to bear, it will grow increasingly surly and irritable to the point where it is hopeless to continue.
JOHN D. MACDONALD (1916–1986)

The only mystery about the cat is why it ever decided to become a domesticated animal.
SIR COMPTON MACKENZIE (1883–1972)

A black cat crossing your path signifies that the animal is going somewhere.
GROUCHO MARX (1890–1977)

Cats do not have to be shown how to have a good time, for they are unfailingly ingenious in that respect.
JAMES MASON (1909–1984)

Looking at a cat, like looking at clouds or stars or the ocean, makes it difficult to believe there is nothing miraculous in this world.
LEONARD MICHAELS (1933–2003)

Cats always seem so very wise, when staring with their half-closed eyes. Can they be thinking, "I'll be nice, and maybe she will feed me twice"?
BETTE MIDLER (1945–)

Cats regard people as warm-blooded furniture.
JACQUELYN MITCHARD (1955–), *The Deep End of the Ocean*

The cat is domestic only as far as suits its own ends; it will not be kennelled or harnessed nor suffer any dictation as to its goings out or comings in. Long contact with the human race has developed in it the art of diplomacy, and no Roman Catholic in medieval days knew better how to ingratiate himself with his surroundings than a cat with a saucer of cream on its mental horizon.
H. H. MUNRO (1870–1916)

A cat is never a presentation, but an innocent happening.
ALWIN NIKOLAIS (1910–1993)

Cats are autocrats of naked self-interest. They are both amoral and immoral, consciously breaking rules. Their "evil" look at such times is no human projection: the cat may be the only animal who savors the perverse or reflects upon it.
CAMILLE PAGLIA (1947–)

I wish I could write as mysterious as a cat.
EDGAR ALLAN POE (1809–1849)

Cats have a curious effect on people. They seem to excite more extreme sentiments than any other animals. There are people who cannot remain in the room with a cat—who feel instinctively the presence of a cat even though they do not actually see it. On the other hand, there are people who, whatever they may be doing, will at once get up and fondle a cat immediately [when] they see it.
ARTHUR PONSONBY (1871–1946)

It's funny how dogs and cats know the inside of folks better than other folks do, isn't it?
ELEANOR H. PORTER (1868–1920), *Pollyanna*

In ancient times cats were worshipped as gods; they have not forgotten this.
TERRY PRATCHETT (1948–)

Watch a cat when it enters a room for the first time. It searches and smells about, it is not quiet for a moment, it trusts nothing until it has examined and made acquaintance with everything.
JEAN-JACQUES ROUSSEAU (1712–1778)

Dogs eat. Cats dine.
ANN TAYLOR (1782–1866)

If animals could speak the dog would be a blundering outspoken fellow, but the cat would have the rare grace of never saying a word too much.
MARK TWAIN (1835–1910)

Ignorant people think it is the noise which fighting cats make that is so aggravating, but it ain't so; it is the sickening grammar that they use.
MARK TWAIN (1835–1910)

A computer and a cat are somewhat alike—they both purr, and like to be stroked, and spend a lot of the day motionless. They also have secrets they don't necessarily share.
JOHN UPDIKE (1932–)

The cat is the only animal without visible means of support who still manages to find a living in the city.
CARL VAN VECHTEN (1880–1964)

If a dog jumps in your lap, it is because he is fond of you; but if a cat does the same thing, it is because your lap is warmer.
ALFRED NORTH WHITEHEAD (1861–1947)

Cats love one so much—more than they will allow. But they have so much wisdom they keep it to themselves.
MARY WILKINS (1852–1930)

Like a graceful vase, a cat, even when motionless, seems to flow.
GEORGE F. WILL (1941–)

The trouble with cats is that they've got no tact.
P. G. WODEHOUSE (1881–1975)

If toast always lands butter-side down, and cats always land on their feet, what happens if you strap toast on the back of a cat and drop it?
STEVEN WRIGHT (1955–)

A cat knows exactly what you are, and treats you accordingly.
ANONYMOUS

Cats are so unpredictable. You just never know how they'll ignore you next.
ANONYMOUS

Cats are intended to teach us that not everything in nature has a function.
ANONYMOUS
Curiosity was framed. Ignorance killed the cat.
ANONYMOUS

Dogs have owners, cats have staff.
ANONYMOUS

I got rid of my husband. The cat was allergic.
ANONYMOUS

Cause and Effect

It is common error to infer that things which are consecutive in order of time have necessarily the relation of cause and effect.
JACOB BIGELOW (1787–1879)

To all facts there are laws,
The effect has its cause, and I mount to the cause.
ROBERT BULWER-LYTTON (1831–1891), *Lucile*

It becomes extremely hard to disentangle our idea of the cause from the effect by which we know it.
EDMUND BURKE (1729–1797)

The cause ceasing, the effect ceases also.
EDWARD COKE (1552–1634)

To legislate each duty, were to count
Drops of a stream that issue from one fount.
God gives, since all effects are in their cause,
For narrow prescripts universal laws.
ABRAHAM COLES (1813–1891), "The Marriage in Cana"

We know the effects of many things, but the cause of few; experience, therefore, is a surer guide than imagination, and inquiry than conjecture.
CHARLES CALEB COLTON (1780–1832)

Nothing happens until something moves.
ALBERT EINSTEIN (1879–1955)

Cause and effect, means and ends, seed and fruit cannot be severed; for the effect already blooms in the cause, the end preexists in the means, the fruit in the seed.
RALPH WALDO EMERSON (1803–1882)

Life is a perpetual instruction in cause and effect.
RALPH WALDO EMERSON (1803–1882)

Shallow men believe in luck. Strong men believe in cause and effect.
RALPH WALDO EMERSON (1803–1882)

No game in the world is as tidy and dramatically neat as baseball, with cause and effect, crime and punishment, motive and result, so cleanly defined.
PAUL GALLICO (1897–1976)

The thinker makes a great mistake when he asks after cause and effect. They both together make up the indivisible phenomenon.
JOHANN WOLFGANG VON GOETHE (1749–1832)

Every effect doth, after a sort, contain, or at least resemble, the cause from which it proceedeth.
RICHARD HOOKER (1554–1600)

The general idea of cause is that without which another thing, called the effect, cannot be. The final cause is that for the sake of which anything is done.
GEORGE WILLIAM HOWARD (1892–1964)

Study carefully the law of cause and effect.
VERNON HOWARD (1918–1992)

We cannot live only for ourselves. A thousand fibers connect us with our fellow men; and among those fibers, as sympathetic threads, our actions run as causes, and they come back to us as effects.
HERMAN MELVILLE (1819–1891)

Before the effect one believes in different causes than one does after the effect.
FRIEDRICH NIETZSCHE (1844–1900)

Cause and effect: such a duality will probably never exist. In truth we are faced by a continuum out of which we isolate a couple of pieces, just as we perceive a motion only as isolated points without really seeing it but then infer [a motion]. The

suddenness with which many effects are standing out, misleading us; but it is only a suddenness for us. There are an infinite number of processes in this second of suddenness which elude us. An intellect that could see cause and effect as a continuum. and not see it in our way as arbitrary division and dismemberment, would reject the concept of cause and effect and deny all conditionality.
FRIEDRICH NIETZSCHE (1844–1900)

The so called unconscious inferences can be traced back to the all-preserving memory, which presents us with parallel experiences and hence already knows the consequences of an action. It is not anticipation of the effects; rather, it is the feeling: identical causes, identical effects.
FRIEDRICH NIETZSCHE (1844–1900)

The cause is hidden, but the result is known.
OVID (43 BC–AD 17), *Metamorphoses*

Everything has something to do with it.
TOM ROBBINS (1936–)

Mad let us grant him them, and now remains
That we find out the cause of this effect—
Or rather say, the cause of this defect,
For this effect defective comes by cause.
Thus it remains, and the remainder thus.
WILLIAM SHAKESPEARE (1564–1616), *Hamlet*

Every cause produces more than one effect.
HERBERT SPENCER (1820–1903)

It is an enduring truth, which can never be altered, that every infraction of the Law of nature must carry its punitive consequences with it. We can never get beyond that range of cause and effect.
THOMAS TROWARD (1847–1916)

The will is not free—it is a phenomenon bound by cause and effect—but there is something behind the will which is free.
SWAMI VIVEKANANDA (1863–1902)

Writing a story or a novel is one way of discovering sequence in experience, of stumbling upon cause and effect in the happenings of a writer's own life.
EUDORA WELTY (1909–2001)

God created the law of free will, and God created the law of cause and effect. And he himself will not violate the law. We need to be thinking less in terms of what God did and more in terms of whether or not we are following those laws.
MARIANNE WILLIAMSON (1952–)

A life without cause is a life without effect.
ANONYMOUS

If you want to understand the causes that existed in the past, look at the results as they are manifested in the present. And if you want to understand what results will be manifested in the future, look at the causes that exist in the present.
BUDDHIST PROVERB

Caution

Be slow of tongue and quick of eye.
MIGUEL DE CERVANTES (1547–1616)

The cautious seldom err.
CONFUCIUS (551–479 BC)

The timid man calls himself cautious, the sordid man thrifty.
PUBLILIUS SYRUS (C. 100 BC)

Of all forms of caution, caution in love is perhaps the most fatal to true happiness.
BERTRAND RUSSELL (1872–1970)

He that is over-cautious will accomplish little.
FRIEDRICH VON SCHILLER (1759–1805)

Caution is the confidential agent of selfishness.
WOODROW WILSON (1856–1924)

Caution is not cowardly. Carelessness is not courage
ANONYMOUS

Caution is the parent of safety.
ANONYMOUS

Celebrities

Living in L.A., everyone likes to mold you and change you. I don't care about fame, I don't care about being a celebrity. I know that's part of the job, but I don't feed into anyone's idea of who I should be.
JESSICA ALBA (1981–)

A celebrity is a person who works hard all his life to become well known, then wears dark glasses to avoid being recognized.
FRED ALLEN (1894–1956)

A sign of celebrity is that his name is often worth more than his services.
DANIEL J. BOORSTIN (1914–)

When once a man has made celebrity necessary to his happiness, he has put it in the power of the weakest and most timorous malignity, if not to take away his satisfaction, at least to withhold it. His enemies may indulge their pride by airy negligence and gratify their malice by quiet neutrality.
SAMUEL JOHNSON (1709–1784)

The nice thing about being a celebrity is that when you bore people, they think it's their fault.
HENRY KISSINGER (1923–)

A celebrity is one who is known to many persons he is glad he doesn't know.
H. L. MENCKEN (1880–1956)

I had an epiphany a few years ago where I was out at a celebrity party and it suddenly dawned on me that I had yet to meet a celebrity who is as smart and interesting as any of my friends.
MOBY (1965–)

Celibacy

Celibacy is not a matter of compulsion. Someone is accepted as a priest only when he does it of his own accord.
POPE BENEDICT XVI (1927–)

Celibacy is the worst form of self-abuse.
PETER DE VRIES (1910–1993)

Celibacy? Nine months. But once you start doing it again, it's all over.
RACHEL HUNTER (1969–)

The vow of celibacy is a matter of keeping one's word to Christ and the Church. A duty and a proof of the priest's inner maturity; it is the expression of his personal dignity.
POPE JOHN PAUL II (1920–2005)

Marriage may often be a stormy lake, but celibacy is almost always a muddy horse pond.
THOMAS LOVE PEACOCK (1785–1866)

As to marriage or celibacy, let a man take which course he will, he will be sure to repent.
SOCRATES (469–399 BC)

In the domain of religious celibacy, an interdiction serves to mythologize repression and energize lust.
WILLIAM I. THOMPSON (1938–)

Cell Phones

People are very protective of their cell phones, how it's used, where it's used and how much it costs. It has become a very personal issue for a whole lot of people in this country.
STEVE LARGENT (1954–)

E-mail, instant messaging, and cell phones give us fabulous communication ability, but because we live and work in our own little worlds, that communication is totally disorganized.
MARILYN VOS SAVANT (1946–)

Censorship

To choose a good book, look in an inquisitor's prohibited list.
JOHN AIKIN (1747–1822)

The paper burns, but the words fly away.
AKIBA BEN JOSEPH (C. AD 50–135)

If you can't annoy somebody with what you write, I think there's little point in writing.
KINGSLEY AMIS (1922–1995)

You need only reflect that one of the best ways to get yourself a reputation as a dangerous citizen these days is to go about repeating the very phrases which our founding fathers used in the great struggle for independence.
CHARLES AUSTIN BEARD (1874–1948)

As long as I don't write about the government, religion, politics, and other institutions, I am free to print anything.
PIERRE-AUGUSTIN BEAUMARCHAIS (1732–1799)

If censorship reigns there cannot be sincere flattery, and only small men are afraid of small writings.
PIERRE-AUGUSTIN BEAUMARCHAIS (1732–1799)

You can cage the singer but not the song.
HARRY BELAFONTE (1927–)

The test of democracy is freedom of criticism.
DAVID BEN-GURION (1886–1973)

As to the evil which results from a censorship, it is impossible to measure it, for it is impossible to tell where it ends.
JEREMY BENTHAM (1748–1832)

I am still against any kind of censorship. It's a subject in my life that has been very important.
BERNARDO BERTOLUCCI (1940–)

Revolution, n.: A bursting of the boilers which usually takes place when the safety valve of public discussion is closed.
AMBROSE BIERCE (1842–1914), *The Devil's Dictionary*

Freedom of speech means that you shall not do something to people either for the views they have, or the views they express, or the words they speak or write.
HUGO L. BLACK (1886–1971)

The de facto censorship which leaves so many Americans functionally illiterate about the history of U.S. foreign affairs may be all the more effective because it is not official, heavy-handed or conspiratorial, but woven artlessly into the fabric of education and media. No conspiracy is needed.
WILLIAM BLUM (1933–)

Let children read whatever they want and then talk about it with them. If parents and kids can talk together, we won't have as much censorship because we won't have as much fear.
JUDY BLUME (1938–)

I look upon those who would deny others the right to urge and argue their position, however irksome and pernicious they may seem, as intellectual and moral cowards.
WILLIAM E. BORAH (1865–1940)

There is more than one way to burn a book. And the world is full of people running about with lit matches. Every minority … feels it has the will, the right, the duty to douse the kerosene, light the fuse. Every dimwit editor who sees himself as the source of all dreary blanc-mange plain porridge unleavened literature, licks his guillotine and eyes the neck of any author who dares to speak above a whisper or write above a nursery rhyme….
RAY BRADBURY (1920–)

Without free speech no search for truth is possible … no discovery of truth is useful…. Better a thousandfold abuse of free speech than denial of free speech. The abuse dies in a day, but the denial slays the life of the people, and entombs the hope of the race.
CHARLES BRADLAUGH (1833–1891)

Fear of serious injury cannot alone justify suppression of free speech and assembly. Men feared witches and burned women. It is the function of speech to free men from the bondage of irrational fears.
LOUIS D. BRANDEIS (1856–1941)

When the conspiracy of lies surrounding me demands of me to silence the one word of truth given to me, *that word becomes the one word I wish to utter above all others.*
ANDRE P. BRINK (1935–)

A free press can be good or bad, but, most certainly, without freedom a press will never be anything but bad.
ALBERT CAMUS (1913–1960)

Every human being has a right to hear what other wise human beings have spoken to him. It is one of the Rights of Men; a very cruel injustice if you deny it to a man!
THOMAS CARLYLE (1795–1881)

Censorship feeds the dirty mind more than the four-letter word itself.
DICK CAVETT (1936–)

If we don't believe in freedom of expression for people we despise, we don't believe in it at all.
NOAM CHOMSKY (1928–)

The press is easier to strangle than to look in the eyes.
SIR WINSTON CHURCHILL (1874–1965)

The fact is that censorship always defeats its own purpose, for it creates, in the end, the kind of society that is incapable of exercising real discretion.
HENRY STEELE COMMAGER (1902–1998)

Freedom of the press is not just important to democracy, it *is* democracy.
WALTER CRONKITE (1916–)

We are willing enough to praise freedom when she is safely tucked away in the past and cannot be a nuisance. In the present, amidst dangers whose outcome we cannot foresee, we get nervous about her, and admit censorship.
E. E. CUMMINGS (1894–1962)

Restriction on free thought and free speech is the most dangerous of all subversions. It is the one un-American act that could most easily defeat us.
WILLIAM ORVILLE DOUGLAS (1898–1980)

Every burned book enlightens the world.
RALPH WALDO EMERSON (1803–1882)

Censorship is advertising paid by the government.
FEDERICO FELLINI (1920–1993)

What progress we are making. In the Middle Ages they would have burned me. Now they are content with burning my books.
SIGMUND FREUD (1856–1939)

Exile as a mode of genius no longer exists; in place of Joyce we have the fragments of work appearing in Index on Censorship.
NADINE GORDIMER (1923–)

Books won't stay banned. They won't burn. Ideas won't go to jail. In the long run of history, the censor and the inquisitor have always lost. The only weapon against bad ideas is better ideas.
ALFRED WHITNEY GRISWOLD (1906–1963)

Wherever they burn books they will also, in the end, burn human beings.
HEINRICH HEINE (1797–1856), *Almansor*

Limiting the freedom of news "just a little bit" is in the same category with the classic example "a little bit pregnant."
ROBERT A. HEINLEIN (1907–1988), *A Rabble in Arms*

To limit the press is to insult a nation; to prohibit reading of certain books is to declare the inhabitants to be either fools or slaves.
CLAUDE-ADRIEN HELVÉTIUS (1715–1771)

A censor is a man who knows more than he thinks you ought to.
GRANVILLE HICKS (1901–1982)

Fear of corrupting the mind of the younger generation is the loftiest of cowardice.
HOLBROOK JACKSON (1874–1948)

Did you ever hear anyone say, "That work had better be banned because I might read it and it might be very damaging to me?"
JOSEPH HENRY JACKSON (1894–1955)

I am opposed to any form of tyranny over the mind of man.
THOMAS JEFFERSON (1743–1826)

Our liberty depends on the freedom of the press, and that cannot be limited without being lost.
THOMAS JEFFERSON (1743–1826)

We are not afraid to entrust the American people with unpleasant facts, foreign ideas, alien philosophies, and competitive values. For a nation that is afraid to let its people judge the truth and falsehood in an open market is a nation that is afraid of its people.
JOHN F. KENNEDY (1917–1963)

To reject the word is to reject the human search.
MAX LERNER (1902–1992)

Freedom of the press is guaranteed only to those who own one.
A. J. LIEBLING (1904–1963)

Censorship, like charity, should begin at home; but unlike charity, it should end there.
CLARE BOOTH LUCE (1903–1987)

Our whole constitutional heritage rebels at the thought of giving government the power to control men's minds.
THURGOOD MARSHALL (1908–1993)

If you don't have this freedom of the press, then all these little fellows are weaseling around and doing their monkey business and they never get caught.
HAROLD R. MEDINA (1888–1990)

If all mankind minus one were of one opinion, mankind would be no more justified in silencing that one person than he, if he had the power, would be justified in silencing mankind.
JOHN STUART MILL (1806–1873), *On Liberty*

The peculiar evil of silencing the expression of an opinion is that it is robbing the human race; posterity as well as the existing generation; those who dissent from the opinion, still more than those who hold it. If the opinion is right, they are deprived of the opportunity of exchanging error for truth: if wrong, they lose, what is almost as great a benefit, the clearer perception and livelier impression of truth, produced by its collision with error.
JOHN STUART MILL (1806–1873), *On Liberty*

We can never be sure that the opinion we are endeavoring to stifle is a false opinion; and if we were sure, stifling it would be an evil still.
JOHN STUART MILL (1806–1873), *On Liberty*

You have not converted a man because you have silenced him.
JOHN MORLEY (1838–1923)

Censorship of anything, at any time, in any place, on whatever pretense, has always been and always be the last resort of the boob and the bigot.
EUGENE O'NEILL (1888–1953)

Freedom of the Press, if it means anything at all, means the freedom to criticize and oppose.
GEORGE ORWELL (1903–1950)

Free speech is life itself.
SALMAN RUSHDIE (1947–)

Obscenity is not a quality inherent in a book or picture, but is solely and exclusively a contribution of the reading mind, and hence cannot be defined in terms of the qualities of a book or picture.
THEODORE SCHROEDER (1864–1953)

All censorships exist to prevent anyone from challenging current conceptions and existing institutions. All progress is initiated by challenging current conceptions, and executed by supplanting existing institutions. Consequently the first condition of progress is the removal of censorships.
GEORGE BERNARD SHAW (1856–1950)

Censorship ends in logical completeness when nobody is allowed to read any books except the books that nobody reads.
GEORGE BERNARD SHAW (1856–1950)

The ultimate form of censorship is assassination.
GEORGE BERNARD SHAW (1856–1950)

The only valid censorship of ideas is the right of people not to listen.
TOMMY SMOTHERS (1937–)

There is a fine line between censorship and good taste and moral responsibility.
STEVEN SPIELBERG (1946–)

Censorship reflects society's lack of confidence in itself. It is a hallmark of an authoritarian regime.
POTTER STEWART (1915–1985)

Nature knows no indecencies; man invents them.
MARK TWAIN (1835–1910), *Notebook*

It is called the First Amendment.... Simple words marching in seried ranks. Compact, concise. To the point. Clear and pure. It's freedom's music.
JACK VALENTI (1921–2007)

We have a natural right to make use of our pens as of our tongue, at our peril, risk and hazard.
VOLTAIRE (1694–1778), *Dictionnaire Philosophique*

I disapprove of what you say, but I will defend to the death your right to say it.
VOLTAIRE (1694–1778)

Think for yourselves and let others enjoy the privilege to do so, too.
VOLTAIRE (1694–1778)

I believe in censorship. I made a fortune out of it.
MAE WEST (1893–1980)

God forbid that any book should be banned. The practice is as indefensible as infanticide.
REBECCA WEST (1892–1983)

Vietnam was the first war ever fought without any censorship. Without censorship, things can get terribly confused in the public mind.
WILLIAM C. WESTMORELAND (1914–2005)

The dirtiest book of all is the expurgated book.
WALT WHITMAN (1819–1892)

Intelligence is the capacity to receive, decode and transmit information efficiently. Stupidity is blockage of this process at any point. Bigotry, ideologies etc. block the ability to receive; robotic reality-tunnels block the ability to decode or integrate new signals; censorship blocks transmission.
ROBERT ANTON WILSON (1932–)

Free speech not only lives, it rocks!
OPRAH WINFREY (1954–)

Censure

It is folly for an eminent man to think of escaping censure, and a weakness to be affected with it. All the illustrious persons of antiquity, and indeed of every age in the world, have passed through this fiery persecution.
JOSEPH ADDISON (1672–1719)

I listen to them freely and with all the respect merited by their intelligence, their character, their knowledge, reserving always my incontestable right of criticism and censure.
MIKHAIL BAKUNIN (1814–1876)

The readiest and surest way to get rid of censure, is to correct ourselves.
DEMOSTHENES (384–322 BC)

Censure acquits the raven, but pursues the dove.
JUVENAL (AD 55–127)

You do ill if you praise, but worse if you censure, what you do not understand.
LEONARDO DA VINCI (1452–1519)

It is salutary to train oneself to be no more affected by censure than by praise.
W. SOMERSET MAUGHAM (1874–1965)

They have a right to censure that have a heart to help.
WILLIAM PENN (1644–1718)

He who would acquire fame must not show himself afraid of censure. The dread of censure is the death of genius.
WILLIAM GILMORE SIMMS (1806–1870)

Censure is the tax a man pays to the public for being eminent.
JONATHAN SWIFT (1667–1745)

Certainty

Certainty is the mother of quiet and repose, and uncertainty the cause of variance and contentions.
EDWARD COKE (1552–1634)

I am certain there is too much certainty in the world.
MICHAEL CRICHTON (1942–), *State of Fear*

Only one absolute certainty is possible to man, namely that at any given moment the feeling which he has exists.
THOMAS H. HUXLEY (1825–1895)

To believe with certainty we must begin with doubting.
STANISLAW LESZCZYNSKI (1677–1766)

Science has proof without any certainty. Creationists have certainty without any proof.
ASHLEY MONTAGU (1905–1999)

In these matters the only certainty is that nothing is certain.
PLINY THE ELDER (AD 23–79)

When one admits that nothing is certain one must, I think, also admit that some things are much more nearly certain than others.
BERTRAND RUSSELL (1872–1970), *Am I an Atheist or an Agnostic?*

The minute one utters a certainty, the opposite comes to mind.
MAY SARTON (1912–1995), *Mrs. Stevens Hears the Mermaids Singing*

Doubt is not a pleasant condition, but certainty is absurd.
VOLTAIRE (1694–1778)

Do not expect to arrive at certainty in every subject which you pursue. There are a hundred things wherein we mortals … must be content with probability, where our best light and reasoning will reach no farther.
ISAAC WATTS (1674–1748)

No great deed, private or public, had ever been undertaken in a bliss of certainty.
LEON WIESELTIER (1952–)

Challenges

It's lack of faith that makes people afraid of meeting challenges, and I believe in myself.
MUHAMMAD ALI (1942–)

When you've got something to prove, there's nothing greater than a challenge.
TERRY BRADSHAW (1948–)

There are no great people in this world, only great challenges that ordinary people rise to meet.
WILLIAM FREDERICK HALSEY JR. (1882–1959)

Champions

Champions aren´t made in the gyms. Champions are made from something they have deep inside them—a desire, a dream, a vision.
MUHAMMAD ALI (1942–)

I hated every minute of training, but I said, "Don't quit. Suffer now and live the rest of your life as a champion."
MUHAMMAD ALI (1942–)

A champion is someone who gets up when he can't.
JACK DEMPSEY (1895–1983)

I am a member of a team, and I rely on the team, I defer to it and sacrifice for it, because the team, not the individual, is the ultimate champion.
MIA HAMM (1972–)

A champion is afraid of losing. Everyone else is afraid of winning.
BILLIE JEAN KING (1943–)

Champions keep playing until they get it right.
BILLIE JEAN KING (1943–)

I have been wounded but not yet slain. I shall lie here and bleed awhile. Then I shall rise and fight again. The title of champion may from time to time fall to others more than ourselves. But the heart, the spirit, and the soul of champions remains in Green Bay.
VINCE LOMBARDI (1913–1970)

Inches make a champion.
VINCE LOMBARDI (1913–1970)

Winning is great, sure, but if you are really going to do something in life, the secret is learning how to lose. Nobody goes undefeated all the time. If you can pick up after a crushing defeat, and go on to win again, you are going to be a champion someday.
WILMA RUDOLPH (1940–1994)

Chance

It is my job to make sure that these kids who are talented get every chance they can and not to be passed over; this is life or death for them.
PAULA ABDUL (1962–)

Learning is not attained by chance, it must be sought for with ardor and diligence.
ABIGAIL ADAMS (1744–1818)

All human actions have one or more of these seven causes: chance, nature, compulsions, habit, reason, passion, desire.
ARISTOTLE (384–322 BC)

The first time Adam had a chance, he laid the blame on women.
NANCY ASTOR (1879–1964)

Happiness in marriage is entirely a matter of chance.
JANE AUSTEN (1774–1817)

Work and acquire, and thou hast chained the wheel of Chance.
RALPH WALDO EMERSON (1803–1882)

Chance fights ever on the side of the prudent.
EURIPIDES (C. 480–406 BC)

Fortune can, for her pleasure, fools advance,
And toss them on the wheels of Chance.
JUVENAL (AD 55–127)

Chance is always powerful. Let your hook be always cast; in the pool where you least expect it, there will be a fish.
OVID (43 BC–AD 17)

In the field of observation, chance favors only the prepared mind.
LOUIS PASTEUR (1822–1895)

There is no such thing as chance; and what [seems] to us merest accident springs from the deepest source of destiny.
FRIEDRICH VON SCHILLER (1759–1805)

No man ever became wise by chance.
SENECA (5 BC–AD 65)

Change

Even God cannot change the past.
AGATHON (448–400 BC)

Our generation has an incredible amount of realism, yet at the same time it loves to complain and not really change. Because, if it does change, then it won't have anything to complain about.
TORI AMOS (1963–)

People can cry much easier than they can change.
JAMES ARTHUR BALDWIN (1924–1987)

Change your life today. Don't gamble on the future, act now, without delay.
SIMONE DE BEAUVOIR (1908–1986)

Any transition serious enough to alter your definition of self will require not just small adjustments in your way of living and thinking but a full-on metamorphosis.
MARTHA BECK (1962–)

To exist is to change, to change is to mature, to mature is to go on creating oneself endlessly
HENRI BERGSON (1859–1941)

Everything changes, nothing remains without change.
THE BUDDHA (563–483 BC)

In prosperity prepare for a change; in adversity hope for one.
JAMES BURGH (1714–1775)

We must all obey the great law of change. It is the most powerful law of nature.
EDMUND BURKE (1729–1797)

Only I can change my life. No one can do it for me.
CAROL BURNETT (1933–)

By nature man hates change; seldom will he quit his old home till it has actually fallen around his ears.
THOMAS CARLYLE (1795–1881)

All major changes are like death. You can't see to the other side until you're there.
MICHAEL CRICHTON (1942–), *Jurassic Park*

To improve is to change; to be perfect is to change often.
SIR WINSTON CHURCHILL (1874–1965)

Turbulence is life force. It is opportunity. Let's love turbulence and use it for change.
RAMSAY CLARK (1927–)

It is not the strongest of the species that survive, nor the most intelligent, but the one most responsive to change.
CHARLES DARWIN (1809–1882)

We all have big changes in our lives that are more or less a second chance.
HARRISON FORD (1942–)

You must be the change you wish to see in the world.
MAHATMA GANDHI (1869–1948)

Nothing endures but change.
HERACLITUS (C. 535–475 BC)

The charm of history and its enigmatic lesson consist in the fact that, from age to age, nothing changes and yet everything is completely different.
ALDOUS HUXLEY (1894–1963)

I guess it's hard for people who are so used to things the way they are—even if they're bad—to change. 'Cause they kind of give up. And when they do, everybody kind of loses.
CATHERINE RYAN HYDE (1955–), *Pay it Forward*

Change is the law of life. And those who look only to the past or present are certain to miss the future.
JOHN F. KENNEDY (1917–1963)

Every moment of one's existence one is growing into more or retreating into less. One is always living a little more or dying a little bit.
NORMAN MAILER (1923–2007)

There is nothing like returning to a place that remains unchanged to find the ways in which you yourself have altered.
NELSON MANDELA (1918–), *A Long Walk to Freedom*

The universe is change; our life is what our thoughts make it.
MARCUS AURELIUS ANTONINUS (121–180), *Meditations*

If you don't get what you want, you suffer; if you get what you don't want, you suffer; even when you get exactly what you want, you still suffer because you can't hold on to it forever. Your mind is your predicament. It wants to be free of change. Free of pain, free of the obligations of life and death. But change is a law, and no amount of pretending will alter that reality.
DAN MILLMAN (1946–), *The Way of the Peaceful Warrior*

A mind not to be changed by place or time, the mind is its own place, and in itself can make a Heaven of Hell, a Hell of Heaven.
JOHN MILTON (1608–1674)

All things change, nothing is extinguished. There is nothing in the whole world which is permanent. Everything flows onward; all things are brought into being with a changing nature; the ages themselves glide by in constant movement.
OVID (43 BC–AD 17)

Change your thoughts and you change your world.
NORMAN VINCENT PEALE (1898–1993)

Be not the first by which a new thing is tried, or the last to lay the old aside.
ALEXANDER POPE (1688–1744)

Things do not change; we change.
HENRY DAVID THOREAU (1817–1862), *Walden*

Change, like sunshine, can be a friend or a foe, a blessing or a curse, a dawn or a dusk.
WILLIAM ARTHUR WARD (1921–1994)

They always say time changes things, but you actually have to change them yourself.
ANDY WARHOL (1928–1987), *The Philosophy of Andy Warhol*

To change and to change for the better are two different things.
GERMAN PROVERB

Chaos

In the midst of movement and chaos, keep stillness inside of you.
DEEPAK CHOPRA (1947–)

A schedule defends from chaos and whim.
ANNIE DILLARD (1945–)

Civilization begins with order, grows with liberty, and dies with chaos.
WILL DURANT (1885–1981)

Here is the world, sound as a nut, perfect, not the smallest piece of chaos left, never a stitch nor an end, not a mark of haste, or botching, or second thought; but the theory of the world is a thing of shreds and patches.
RALPH WALDO EMERSON (1803–1882)

We adore chaos because we love to produce order.
M. C. ESCHER (1898–1972)

Freedom is just Chaos, with better lighting.
ALAN DEAN FOSTER (1946–), "To the Vanishing Point"

It's pretty clear now that what looked like it might have been some kind of counterculture is, in reality, just the plain old chaos of undifferentiated weirdness.
JERRY GARCIA (1942–1995)

When the mind withdraws into itself and dispenses with facts it makes only chaos.
EDITH HAMILTON (1868–1963)

He who every morning plans the transaction of the day and follows out that plan, carries a thread that will guide him through the maze of the most busy life. But where no plan is laid, where the disposal of time is surrendered merely to the chance of incidence, chaos will soon reign.
VICTOR HUGO (1802–1885)

A life lived in chaos is an impossibility…
MADELEINE L'ENGLE (1918–)

Chaos in the midst of chaos isn't funny, but chaos in the midst of order is.
STEVE MARTIN (1945–)

Chaos is the score upon which reality is written.
HENRY MILLER (1891–1980)

One must still have chaos in oneself to be able to give birth to a dancing star.
FRIEDRICH NIETZSCHE (1844–1900)

The overman … has organized the chaos of his passions, given style to his character, and become creative. Aware of life's terrors, he affirms life without resentment.
FRIEDRICH NIETZSCHE (1844–1900)

You need chaos in your soul to give birth to a dancing star.
FRIEDRICH NIETZSCHE (1844–1900)

Too little liberty brings stagnation and too much brings chaos.
BERTRAND RUSSELL (1872–1970)

Excellent wretch! Perdition catch my soul,
But I do love thee! and when I love thee not,
Chaos is come again…
WILLIAM SHAKESPEARE (1564–1616), *Othello*

Sport is imposing order on what was chaos.
ANTHONY STARR (1975–)

The Internet has no such organization—files are made available at random locations. To search through this chaos, we need smart tools, programs that find resources for us.
CLIFFORD STOLL (1950–), *Silicon Snake Oil*

What we imagine is order is merely the prevailing form of chaos.
KERRY THORNLEY (1938–1998)

Before the beginning of great brilliance, there must be chaos. Before a brilliant person begins something great, they must look foolish in the crowd.
THE I CHING

Character

Poverty is the schoolmaster of character.
ANTIPHANES (408–334 BC)

Character may almost be called the most effective means of persuasion.
ARISTOTLE (384–322 BC)

To enjoy the things we ought and to hate the things we ought has the greatest bearing on excellence of character.
ARISTOTLE (384–322 BC)

One can acquire everything in solitude—except character.
MARIE HENRI BEYLE (1783–1842)

Our character is what we do when we think no one is looking.
H. JACKSON BROWN JR. (1948–)

Show class, have pride, and display character. If you do, winning takes care of itself.
PAUL "BEAR" BRYANT (1913–1983)

Forming characters! Whose? Our own or others? Both. And in that momentous fact lies the peril and responsibility of our existence.
ELIHU BURRITT (1810–1879)

Temperament lies behind mood; behind will lies the fate of character. Then behind both, the influence of family; the tyranny of culture; and finally the power of climate and environment; and we are free, only to the extent we rise above these.
JOHN BURROUGHS (1837–1921)

Strong feelings do not necessarily make a strong character. The strength of a man is to be measured by the power of the feelings he subdues, not by the power of those [who] subdue him.
WILLIAM CARLETON (1794–1869)

Any fool can criticize, condemn, and complain, but it takes character and self-control to be understanding and forgiving.
DALE CARNEGIE (1888–1955)

Everyone has the obligation to ponder well his own specific traits of character. He must also regulate them adequately and not wonder whether someone else's traits might suit him better. The more definitely his own a man's character is, the better it fits him.
CICERO (106–43 BC)

Without an acquaintance with the rules of propriety, it is impossible for the character to be established.
CONFUCIUS (551–479 BC), *The Confucian Analects*

Our character is basically a composite of our habits. Because they are consistent, often unconscious patterns, they constantly, daily, express our character.
STEPHEN R. COVEY (1932–)

Influence follows close upon the heels of character, and whatever we are, that we shall in the end be acknowledged to be.
CAROLINE DALL (1822–1912)

Character—the willingness to accept responsibility for one's own life—is the source from which self respect springs.
JOAN DIDION (1934–), *Slouching Towards Bethlehem*

Weakness of attitude becomes weakness of character.
ALBERT EINSTEIN (1879–1955)

Nature magically suits a man to his fortunes, by making them the fruit of his character.
RALPH WALDO EMERSON (1803–1882)

People seem not to see that their opinion of the world is also a confession of their character.
RALPH WALDO EMERSON (1803–1882)

Hard work spotlights the character of people: some turn up their sleeves, some turn up their noses, and some don't turn up at all.
SAM EWING (1921–)

You cannot dream yourself into a character; you must hammer and forge yourself one.
JAMES A. FROUDE (1818–1894)

Character develops itself in the stream of life.
JOHANN WOLFGANG VON GOETHE (1749–1832)

Character, in great and little things, means carrying through what you feel able to do.
JOHANN WOLFGANG VON GOETHE (1749–1832)

Men show their characters in nothing more clearly than in what they think laughable.
JOHANN WOLFGANG VON GOETHE (1749–1832)

A man is what he is, not what men say he is. His character no man can touch. His character is what he is before his God and his Judge; and only he himself can damage that. His reputation's what men say he is. That can be damaged; but reputation is for time, character is for eternity
JOHN BALLANTINE GOUGH (1817–1886)

A man's character is his fate.
HERACLITUS (C. 535–475 BC), *On the Universe*

People with courage and character always seem sinister to the rest.
HERMANN HESSE (1877–1962)

The character of every act depends upon the circumstances in which it is done.
OLIVER WENDELL HOLMES JR. (1841–1935)

Character is the result of two things: mental attitude and the way we spend our time.
ELBERT HUBBARD (1856–1915)

Many a man's reputation would not know his character if they met on the street.
ELBERT HUBBARD (1856–1915)

The true measure of a man is how he treats someone who can do him absolutely no good.
SAMUEL JOHNSON (1709–1784)

Character cannot be developed in ease and quiet. Only through experience of trial and suffering can the soul be strengthened, ambition inspired, and success achieved.
HELEN KELLER (1880–1968)

By constant self-discipline and self-control you can develop greatness of character.
GRENVILLE KLEISER (1868–1953)

Personality can open doors, but only character can keep them open.
ELMER G. LETTERMAN (1897–1982)

Underneath this flabby exterior is an enormous lack of character.
OSCAR LEVANT (1906–1972)

A person reveals his character by nothing so clearly as the joke he resents.
GEORG C. LICHTENBERG (1742–1799)

Character is like a tree and reputation like its shadow. The shadow is what we think of it; the tree is the real thing.
ABRAHAM LINCOLN (1809–1865), *Lincoln's Own Stories*

Nearly all men can stand adversity, but if you want to test a man's character, give him power.
ABRAHAM LINCOLN (1809–1865)

Sometimes people carry to such perfection the mask they have assumed that in due course they actually become the person they seem.
W. SOMERSET MAUGHAM (1874–1965), *The Moon and Sixpence*

The character of a man is known from his conversations.
MENANDER (342–292 BC)

Reputation is what men and women think of us; character is what God and angels know of us.
THOMAS PAINE (1737–1809)

You can tell a lot about a fellow's character by his way of eating jellybeans.
RONALD REAGAN (1911–2004)

We learn our virtues from our friends who love us; our faults from the enemy who hates us. We cannot easily discover our real character from a friend. He is a mirror, on which the warmth of our breath impedes the clearness of the reflection.
JEAN PAUL RICHTER (1763–1825)

The four cornerstones of character on which the structure of this nation was built are initiative, imagination, individuality, and independence.
EDWARD VERNON RICKENBACKER (1890–1973)

People grow through experience if they meet life honestly and courageously. This is how character is built.
ELEANOR ROOSEVELT (1884–1962), *My Day*

Character, in the long run, is the decisive factor in the life of an individual and of nations alike.
THEODORE ROOSEVELT (1858–1919)

Our character … is an omen of our destiny, and the more integrity we have and keep, the simpler and nobler that destiny is likely to be.
GEORGE SANTAYANA (1863–1952), *The German Mind: A Philosophical Diagnosis*

You can tell the character of every man when you see how he receives praise.
SENECA (5 BC–AD 65), *Epistles*

Moral cowardice that keeps us from speaking our minds is as dangerous to this country as irresponsible talk. The right way is not always the popular and easy way. Standing for right when it is unpopular is a true test of moral character.
MARGARET CHASE SMITH (1897–1995)

Put more trust in nobility of character than in an oath.
SOLON (638–559 BC)

In attempts to improve your character, know what is in your power and what is beyond it.
FRANCIS THOMPSON (1859–1907)

Character is a by-product; it is produced in the great manufacture of daily duty.
WOODROW WILSON (1856–1924)

Character is always lost when a high ideal is sacrificed on the altar of conformity and popularity.
ANONYMOUS

The test of any man's character is how he takes praise.
ANONYMOUS

When the character of a man is not clear to you, look at his friends.
JAPANESE PROVERB

Charisma

Let the others have the charisma. I've got the class.
GEORGE H. W. BUSH (1924–)

Personality is essential. It is in every work of art. When someone walks on stage for a performance and has charisma, everyone is convinced that he has personality. I find that charisma is merely a form of showmanship. Movie stars usually have it. A politician has to have it.
LUKAS FOSS (1922–)

That whole process of somebody who has all that charisma and talent, to be able to break through and make it in America is fabulous.
TAYLOR HACKFORD (1944–)

Lack of charisma can be fatal.
JENNY HOLZER (1950–)

The reason we're successful, darling? My overall charisma, of course.
FREDDIE MERCURY (1946–1991)

[A] man who might not have enormous charisma, who could be president 40 years ago, and who was a deserving president, I don't know that George Washington would be a president today, I don't know that Abe Lincoln would, I don't know that Roosevelt would.
SYDNEY POLLACK (1934–)

If you are a person of great charisma, as [Ingmar] Bergman is, people demand from him a lot of things which he probably doesn't have. That is a terribly frustrating situation.
MAX VON SYDOW (1929–)

We need less posturing and more genuine charisma. Charisma was originally a religious term, meaning "of the spirit" or "inspired." It's about letting God's light shine through us. It's about a sparkle in people that money can't buy. It's an invisible energy with visible effects. To let go, to just love, is not to fade into the wallpaper. Quite the contrary, it's when we truly become bright. We're letting our own light shine.
MARIANNE WILLIAMSON (1952–)

Charity

In charity there is no excess.
SIR FRANCIS BACON (1561–1626), *Of Goodness*

He that defers his charity until he is dead is, if a man weighs it rightly, rather liberal of another man's goods than his own.
SIR FRANCIS BACON (1561–1626)

The best thing to give to your enemy is forgiveness; to an opponent, tolerance; to a friend, your heart; to your child, a good example; to a father, deference; to your mother, conduct that will make her proud of you; to yourself, respect; to all men, charity.
FRANCIS MAITLAND BALFOUR (1851–1882)

Every charitable act is a stepping stone towards heaven.
HENRY WARD BEECHER (1813–1887)

Be charitable before wealth makes thee covetous.
SIR THOMAS BROWNE (1605–1682)

The highest exercise of charity is charity towards the uncharitable.
J. S. BUCKMINSTER (1797–1812)

Too many have dispensed with generosity in order to practice charity.
ALBERT CAMUS (1913–1960)

One of the serious obstacles to the improvement of our race is indiscriminate charity.
ANDREW CARNEGIE (1835–1919)

Charity begins at home, and justice begins next door.
CHARLES DICKENS (1812–1870)

Not he who has much is rich, but he who gives much.
ERICH FROMM (1900–1980)

What we frankly give, forever is our own.
GEORGE GRANVILLE (1815–1891)

If you haven't got any charity in your heart, you have the worst kind of heart trouble.
BOB HOPE (1903–2003)

As the purse is emptied, the heart is filled.
VICTOR HUGO (1802–1885)

The charity that hastens to proclaim its good deeds, ceases to be charity, and is only pride and ostentation.
WILLIAM HUTTON (1723–1815)

A bone to the dog is not charity. Charity is the bone shared with the dog, when you are just as hungry as the dog.
JACK LONDON (1876–1916)

Christian life consists of faith and charity.
MARTIN LUTHER (1483–1546)

Boards of public charity were invented by the devil to prevent real individual charity.
AUSTIN O'MALLEY (1858–1932)

Charity begins at home.
TERENCE (185–159 BC), *Andria*

In all the ages, three-fourths of the support of the great charities has been conscience money.
MARK TWAIN (1835–1910)

Charity and pride have different aims, yet both feed the poor.
ANONYMOUS

Charity begins at home, but should not end there.
ANONYMOUS

May your charity increase as much as your wealth.
ANONYMOUS

Charity sees the need not the cause.
GERMAN PROVERB

Charm

Charm is the quality in others that makes us more satisfied with ourselves.
HENRI-FRÉDÉRIC AMIEL (1821–1881)

There is something in a woman beyond all human delight; a magnetic virtue, a charming quality, an occult and powerful motive.
ROBERT BURTON (1577–1640)

Charm is a way of getting the answer yes without asking a clear question.
ALBERT CAMUS (1913–1960)

Brevity is a great charm of eloquence.
CICERO (106–43 BC)

All charming people have something to conceal, usually their total dependence on the appreciation of others.
CYRIL CONNOLLY (1903–1974), *Enemies of Promise*

Modesty: the gentle art of enhancing your charm by pretending not to be aware of it.
OLIVER HERFORD (1863–1935)

We are born charming, fresh and spontaneous and must be civilized before we are fit to participate in society.
JUDITH MARTIN (1938–)

Only actions give life its strength, as only moderation gives it its charm.
JEAN PAUL RICHTER (1763–1825)

No siren did ever so charm the ear of the listener as the listening ear has charmed the soul of the siren.
HENRY TAYLOR (1800–1866)

It is absurd to divide people into good and bad. People are either charming or tedious.
OSCAR WILDE (1854–1900), *Lady Windermere's Fan*

Chastity

We may eventually come to realize that chastity is no more a virtue than malnutrition.
ALEX COMFORT (1920–2000)

Chastity: the most unnatural of the sexual perversions.
ALDOUS HUXLEY (1894–1963)

For the preservation of chastity, an empty and rumbling stomach and fevered lungs are indispensable.
SAINT JEROME (C. 342–420)

Chastity always takes its toll. In some it produces pimples; in others, sex laws.
KARL KRAUS (1874–1936)

Skepticism, like chastity, should not be relinquished too readily.
GEORGE SANTAYANA (1863–1952)

Chastity is a monkish and evangelical superstition, a greater foe to natural temperance even than unintellectual sensuality; it strikes at the root of all domestic happiness, and consigns more than half of the human race to misery.
PERCY BYSSHE SHELLEY (1792–1822)

Chauvinism

The fact remains; chauvinism is prevailing.
EMMA BONINO (1948–)

Everywhere I go I'm being reminded that I need to be voiceless and certainly powerless. It sounds like jealousy or male chauvinism. That's why I have to fight back.
ANNETTE LU (1944–)

It was male chauvinism, as you must realize, in the 1960s, particularly in the entertainment business, which was pretty repulsive.
PATRICK MACNEE (1922–)

Independence did not mean chauvinism and narrow nationalism.
SAID MUSA (1944–)

Cheating

I was thrown out of college for cheating on the metaphysics exam; I looked into the soul of the boy sitting next to me.
WOODY ALLEN (1935–)

Love is a game in which one always cheats.
HONORÉ DE BALZAC (1799–1850)

In order to preserve your self-respect, it is sometimes necessary to lie and cheat.
ROBERT BYRNE (1928–)

'Tis my opinion every man cheats in his own way, and he is only honest who is not discovered.
SUSANNAH CENTLIVRE (1669–1723)

A thing worth having is a thing worth cheating for.
W. C. FIELDS (1880–1946)

Forget your personal tragedy. We are all bitched from the start and you especially have to be hurt like hell before you can write seriously. But when you get the damned hurt, use it—don't cheat with it.
ERNEST HEMINGWAY (1899–1961)

Someone who thinks the world is always cheating him is right. He is missing that wonderful feeling of trust in someone or something.
ERIC HOFFER (1902–1983)

It is better to suffer wrong than to do it, and happier to be sometimes cheated than not to trust.
SAMUEL JOHNSON (1709–1784)

If you marry a man who cheats on his wife, you'll be married to a man who cheats on his wife.
ANN LANDERS (1918–2002)

He who purposely cheats his friend, would cheat his God.
JOHANN KASPAR LAVATER (1741–1801)

I would prefer even to fail with honor than to win by cheating.
SOPHOCLES (495–406 BC)

If you know how to cheat, start now.
EARL WEAVER (1930–)

He that will cheat at play, will cheat you any way.
ANONYMOUS

Childhood

When childhood dies, its corpses are called adults and they enter society, one of the politer names of hell. That is why we dread children, even if we love them, they show us the state of our decay.
BRIAN W. ALDISS (1925–)

Blessed be childhood, which brings down something of heaven into the midst of our rough earthliness.
HENRI-FRÉDÉRIC AMIEL (1821–1881)

When we were children we were grateful to those who filled our stockings at Christmas time. Why are we not grateful to God for filling our stockings with legs?
G. K. CHESTERTON (1874–1936)

A happy childhood is one of the best gifts that parents have it in their power to bestow.
MARY CHOLMONDELEY (1859–1925)

There is always one moment in childhood when the door opens and lets the future in.
DEEPAK CHOPRA (1947–)

The essence of childhood, of course, is play, which my friends and I did endlessly on streets that we reluctantly shared with traffic.
BILL COSBY (1937–)

I was coming home from kindergarten—well they told me it was kindergarten. I found out later I had been working in a factory for ten years. It's good for a kid to know how to make gloves.
ELLEN DEGENERES (1958–)

When you finally go back to your old hometown, you find it wasn't the old home you missed but your childhood.
SAM EWING (1921–)

Our whole life is but a greater and longer childhood.
BENJAMIN FRANKLIN (1706–1790)

I cannot think of any need in childhood as strong as the need for a father's protection.
SIGMUND FREUD (1856–1939)

The things which the child loves remain in the domain of the heart until old age. The most beautiful thing in life is that our souls remain over the places where we once enjoyed ourselves.
KAHLIL GIBRAN (1883–1931)

We have not passed that subtle line between childhood and adulthood until … we have stopped saying "It got lost," and say "I lost it."
SYDNEY J. HARRIS (1917–1986)

Childhood is a short season.
HELEN HAYES (1900–1993)

Man is most nearly himself when he achieves the seriousness of a child at play.
HERACLITUS (C. 535–475 BC)

The highlight of my childhood was making my brother laugh so hard that food came out of his nose.
GARRISON KEILLOR (1942–)

There is a garden in every childhood, an enchanted place where colors are brighter, the air softer, and the morning more fragrant than ever again.
ELIZABETH LAWRENCE (1904–1985)

Childhood is the kingdom where nobody dies. Nobody that matters, that is.
EDNA ST. VINCENT MILLAY (1892–1950)

The childhood shows the man, as morning shows the day.
JOHN MILTON (1608–1674) (1608–1674)

We plan our lives according to a dream that came to us in our childhood, and we find that life alters our plans. And yet, at the end, from a rare height, we also see that our dream was our fate. It's just that providence had other ideas as to how we would get there. Destiny plans a different route, or turns the dream around, as if it were a riddle, and fulfills the dream in ways we couldn't have expected.
BEN OKRI (1959–)

All those writers who write about their childhood! Gentle God, if I wrote about mine you wouldn't sit in the same room with me.
DOROTHY PARKER (1893–1967)

Childhood is not only the childhood we really had but also the impressions we formed of it in our adolescence and maturity. That is why childhood seems so long. Probably every period of life is multiplied by our reflections upon the next.
CESARE PAVESE (1908–1950)

There are perhaps no days of our childhood we lived so fully as those we spent with a favorite book.
MARCEL PROUST (1871–1922)

It is never too late to have a happy childhood.
TOM ROBBINS (1936–)

Arguably, no artist grows up: If he sheds the perceptions of childhood, he ceases being an artist.
NED ROREM (1923–)

Childhood is the sleep of reason.
JEAN-JACQUES ROUSSEAU (1712–1778)

There is no absurdity so obvious that it cannot be firmly planted in the human head if you only begin to impose it before the age of five, by constantly repeating it with an air of great solemnity.
ARTHUR SCHOPENHAUER (1788–1860)

If you carry your childhood with you, you never become older.
TOM STOPPARD (1937–)

My childhood was a period of waiting for the moment when I could send everyone and everything connected with it to hell.
IGOR STRAVINSKY (1882–1971)

For most of us, dreams come true only after they do not matter. Only in childhood do we ever have the chance of making dreams come true when they mean everything.
ANONYMOUS

Children

If you can give your son or daughter only one gift, let it be enthusiasm.
BRUCE BARTON (1886–1967)

Mothers—especially single mothers—are heroic in their efforts to raise our nation's children, but men must also take responsibility for their children and recognize the impact they have on their families' well-being.
EVAN BAYH (1955–)

Children are the hands by which we take hold of heaven.
HENRY WARD BEECHER (1813–1887)

Who in their infinite wisdom decreed that Little League uniforms be white? Certainly not a mother.
ERMA BOMBECK (1927–1996)

[M]y opinion is that the future good or bad conduct of a child depends on its mother.
MARIA LETIZIA BONAPARTE (1750–1836)

The test of the morality of a society is what it does for its children.
DIETRICH BONHOEFFER (1906–1945)

Loving a child doesn't mean giving in to all his whims; to love him is to bring out the best in him, to teach him to love what is difficult.
NADIA BOULANGER (1887–1979)

A woman with a child rediscovers the world. All is changed: politics, loyalties, needs. For now all is judged by the life of the child … and of all children.
PAM BROWN (1948–)

There was a time when we expected nothing of our children but obedience, as opposed to the present, when we expect everything of them but obedience.
ANATOLE BROYARD (1920–1990)

Children might or might not be a blessing, but to create them and then fail them was surely damnation.
LOIS MCMASTER BUJOLD (1949–), *Barrayar*

Our children change us … whether they live or not.
LOIS MCMASTER BUJOLD (1949–), *Barrayar*

Some men just aren't cut out for paternity. Better they should realize it before and not after they become responsible for a son.
LOIS MCMASTER BUJOLD (1949–), *Ethan of Athos*

People who say they sleep like a baby usually don't have one.
LEO J. BURKE (1911–1980)

Children who are read to learn two things: First, that reading is worthwhile, and second, that they are worthwhile.
LAURA BUSH (1946–)

Learning to dislike children at an early age saves a lot of expense and aggravation later in life.
ROBERT BYRNE (1928–)

If I had influence with the good fairy who is supposed to preside over the christening of all children, I should ask that her gift to each child in the world be a sense of wonder so indestructible that it would last throughout life.
RACHEL CARSON (1907–1964)

There are two lasting bequests we can hope to give our children. One of these is roots, the other, wings.
HODDING CARTER JR. (1907–1972)

The child must know that he is a miracle, that since the beginning of the world there hasn't been, and until the end of the world there will not be, another child like him.
PABLO CASALS (1876–1973)

If your parents never had children, chances are you won't, either.
DICK CAVETT (1936–)

There is nothing more thrilling in this world, I think, than having a child that is yours, and yet is mysteriously a stranger.
AGATHA CHRISTIE (1890–1976)

Always end the name of your child with a vowel, so that when you yell the name it will carry.
BILL COSBY (1937–)

Human beings are the only creatures that allow their children to come back home.
BILL COSBY (1937–)

The childless experts on child-raising also bring tears of laughter to my eyes when they say, "I love children because they're so honest." There is not an agent in the CIA or the KGB who knows how to conceal the theft of food, how to fake being asleep, or how to forge a parent's signature like a child.
BILL COSBY (1937–)

The first half of our lives is ruined by our parents, and the second half by our children.
CLARENCE DARROW (1857–1938)

Discipline is a symbol of caring to a child. He needs guidance. If there is love, there is no such thing as being too tough with a child.
BETTE DAVIS (1908–1989)

A child is the root of the heart.
CAROLINA MARIA DE JESUS (1914–1977)

Always be nice to your children because they are the ones who will choose your rest home.
PHYLLIS DILLER (1917–)

It would seem that something which means poverty, disorder, and violence every single day should be avoided entirely, but the desire to beget children is a natural urge.
PHYLLIS DILLER (1917–)

Children are not casual guests in our home. They have been loaned to us temporarily for the purpose of loving them and instilling a foundation of values on which their future lives will be built.
JAMES DOBSON (1936–)

Children represent God's most generous gift to us.
JAMES DOBSON (1936–)

The soul is healed by being with children.
FYODOR DOSTOEVSKY (1821–1881)

The trouble with children is that they are not returnable.
FYODOR DOSTOEVSKY (1821–1881)

If you want to see what children can do, you must stop giving them things.
NORMAN DOUGLAS (1868–1952)

The finest inheritance you can give to a child is to allow it to make its own way, completely on its own feet.
ISADORA DUNCAN (1877–1927)

If we don't stand up for children, then we don't stand up for much.
MARIAN WRIGHT EDELMAN (1939–)

The thing that impresses me the most about America is the way parents obey their children.
KING EDWARD VIII (1894–1972)

Little children are still the symbol of the eternal marriage between love and duty.
GEORGE ELIOT (1819–1880)

Children are all foreigners.
RALPH WALDO EMERSON (1803–1882)

There never was a child so lovely but his mother was glad to get him asleep.
RALPH WALDO EMERSON (1803–1882)

To speak truly, few adult persons can see nature. Most persons do not see the sun. At least they have a very superficial seeing. The sun illuminates only the eye of the man, but shines into the eye and heart of the child.
RALPH WALDO EMERSON (1803–1882)

We find delight in the beauty and happiness of children that make the heart too big for the body.
RALPH WALDO EMERSON (1803–1882)

It will be gone before you know it. The fingerprints on the wall appear higher and higher. Then suddenly they disappear.
DOROTHY EVSLIN (1923–)

Upon our children—how they are taught—rests the fate, or fortune, of tomorrow's world.
B. C. FORBES (1880–1954)

To nourish children and raise them against odds is in any time, any place, more valuable than to fix bolts in cars or design nuclear weapons.
MARILYN FRENCH (1929–)

Strange new problems are being reported in the growing generations of children whose mothers were always there, driving them around, helping them with their homework—an inability to endure pain or discipline or pursue any self-sustained goal of any sort, a devastating boredom with life.
BETTY FRIEDAN (1921–2006)

Don't worry that children never listen to you; worry that they are always watching you.
ROBERT FULGHUM (1937–)

It is not giving children more that spoils them; it is giving them more to avoid confrontation.
JOHN GRAY (1951–), *Children Are from Heaven*

The best thing you can give children, next to good habits, are good memories.
SYDNEY J. HARRIS (1917–1986)

Children are the keys of paradise.
ERIC HOFFER (1898–1983)

The Paleolithic hunters who painted the unsurpassed animal murals on the ceiling of the cave at Altamira had only rudimentary tools. Art is older than production for use, and play older than work. Man was shaped less by what he had to do than by what he did in playful moments. It is the child in man that is the source of his uniqueness and creativeness, and the playground is the optimal milieu for the unfolding of his capacities.
ERIC HOFFER (1902–1983)

All the honest truth telling in the world is done by children.
OLIVER WENDELL HOLMES JR. (1841–1935)

Children, aye forsooth, they bring their own love with them when they come.
JEAN INGELOW (1820–1897)

Children are likely to live up to what you believe in them.
LADY BIRD JOHNSON (1912–2007)

You can learn many things from children. How much patience you have, for instance.
FRANKLIN P. JONES (1887–1929)

Be gentle with the young.
JUVENAL (AD 55–127)

Children are the true connoisseurs. What's precious to them has no price, only value.
BEL KAUFMAN (1911–)

Nothing you do for children is ever wasted.
GARRISON KEILLOR (1942–)

Often and often afterwards, the beloved Aunt would ask me why I had never told anyone how I was being treated. Children tell little more than animals, for what comes to them they accept as eternally established.
RUDYARD KIPLING (1865–1936)

A sweet child is the sweetest thing in nature.
CHARLES LAMB (1775–1834)

Loving a child is a circular business … the more you give, the more you get, the more you get, the more you give.
PENELOPE LEACH (1937–)

Ask your child what he wants for dinner only if he's buying.
FRAN LEBOWITZ (1950–)

Even when freshly-washed and relieved of all obvious confections, children tend to be sticky.
FRAN LEBOWITZ (1950–)

I must take issue with the term "a mere child," for it has been my invariable experience that the company of a mere child is infinitely preferable to that of a mere adult.
FRAN LEBOWITZ (1950–)

The creative adult is the child who has survived.
URSULA K. LE GUIN (1929–)

The reason grandparents and grandchildren get along so well is that they have a common enemy.
SAM LEVENSON (1911–1980)

Curiosity in children, is but an appetite for knowledge. One great reason why children abandon themselves wholly to silly pursuits and trifle away their time insipidly is, because they find their curiosity balked, and their inquiries neglected.
JOHN LOCKE (1632–1704)

My mother loved children—she would have given anything if I had been one.
GROUCHO MARX (1890–1977)

This would be a better world for children if parents had to eat the spinach.
GROUCHO MARX (1890–1977)

D'you call life a bad job? Never! We've had our ups and downs, we've had our struggles, we've always been poor, but it's been worth it, ay, worth it a hundred times I say when I look round at my children.
W. SOMERSET MAUGHAM (1874–1965), *Of Human Bondage*

Your children tell you casually years later what it would have killed you with worry to know at the time.
MIGNON MCLAUGHLIN (1913–1983)

Children aren't happy with nothing to ignore, and that's what parents were created for.
OGDEN NASH (1902–1971)

Kids are life's only guaranteed, bona fide upside surprise.
JACK NICHOLSON (1937–)

Humans are the only animals that have children on purpose with the exception of guppies, who like to eat theirs.
P. J. O'ROURKE (1947–)

I take my children everywhere, but they always find their way back home.
ROBERT ORBEN (1927–)

Never raise your hand to your children; it leaves your midsection unprotected.
ROBERT ORBEN (1927–)

The best way to keep children home is to make the home atmosphere pleasant—and let the air out of the tires.
DOROTHY PARKER (1893–1967)

When I approach a child, he inspires in me two sentiments; tenderness for what he is, and respect for what he may become.
LOUIS PASTEUR (1822–1895)

Every child is an artist. The problem is how to remain an artist once we grow up.
PABLO PICASSO (1881–1973)

To show a child what once delighted you, to find the child's delight added to your own, this is happiness.
J. B. PRIESTLEY (1894–1994)

I would be the most content if my children grew up to be the kind of people who think decorating consists mostly of building enough bookshelves.
ANNA QUINDLEN (1953–)

Children possess a remarkable amount of passion. They throw themselves completely, heart and soul, into everything.
MARY LOU RETTON (1968–)

The smallest children are nearest to God, as the smallest planets are nearest the sun.
JEAN PAUL RICHTER (1763–1825)

I always wanted children, but not until they were actually part of my life did I realize that I could love that fiercely, or get that angry.
COKIE ROBERTS (1943–)

The world is not always a kind place. That's something all children learn for themselves, whether we want them to or not, but it's something they really need our help to understand.
FRED ROGERS (1928–2003)

I think, at a child's birth, if a mother could ask a fairy godmother to endow it with the most useful gift, that gift should be curiosity.
ELEANOR ROOSEVELT (1884–1962)

All grown-ups were once children, though few of them remember it.
ANTOINE DE SAINT-EXUPÉRY (1900–1944)

How sharper than a serpent's tooth it is
To have a thankless child!
WILLIAM SHAKESPEARE (1564–1616), *King Lear*

It is a wise father that knows his own child.
WILLIAM SHAKESPEARE (1564–1616), *The Merchant of Venice*

In early childhood you may lay the foundation of poverty or riches, industry or idleness, good or evil, by the habits to which you train your children. Teach them right habits then, and their future life is safe.
LYDIA SIGOURNEY (1791–1865)

Children today are tyrants. They contradict their parents, gobble their food, and tyrannize their teachers.
SOCRATES (469–399 BC)

Children require guidance and sympathy far more than instruction.
ANNIE SULLIVAN (1866–1936)

Children learn to smile from their parents.
SHINICHI SUZUKI (1898–1998)

A child becomes an adult when he realizes that he has a right not only to be right but also to be wrong.
THOMAS S. SZASZ (1920–)

Every child comes with the message that God is not yet discouraged of man.
RABINDRANATH TAGORE (1861–1941)

I have found the best way to give advice to your children is to find out what they want and then advise them to do it.
HARRY S TRUMAN (1884–1972)

Children are the only form of immortality that we can be sure of.
PETER USTINOV (1921–2004)

Never have children, only grandchildren.
GORE VIDAL (1925–)

Young people are more hopeful at a certain age than adults, but I suspect that's glandular. As for children, I keep as far from them as possible. I don't like the sight of them. The scale is all wrong. The heads tend to be too big for the bodies, and the hands and feet are a disaster. They keep falling into things. The nakedness of their bad character! We adults have learned how to disguise our terrible character, but children, well, they are like grotesque

drawings of us. They should be neither seen nor heard, and no one must make another one.
GORE VIDAL (1925–)

People who get nostalgic about childhood were obviously never children.
BILL WATTERSON (1958–)

Children are the living messages we send to a time we will not see.
JOHN W. WHITEHEAD (1946–)

Every child born into the world is a new thought of God, an ever fresh and radiant possibility.
KATE DOUGLAS WIGGIN (1856–1923)

Children begin by loving their parents; as they grow older they judge them; sometimes they forgive them.
OSCAR WILDE (1854–1900), *The Picture of Dorian Gray*

The best way to make children good is to make them happy.
OSCAR WILDE (1854–1900)

What is a home without children? Quiet.
HENNY YOUNGMAN (1906–1998)

A child can ask questions that a wise man cannot answer.
ANONYMOUS

Anyone who uses the phrase "easy as taking candy from a baby" has never tried taking candy from a baby.
ANONYMOUS

A child's life is like a piece of paper on which every person leaves a mark.
CHINESE PROVERB

Every child born has innate goodness.
CHINESE PROVERB

There is only one pretty child in the world, and every mother has it.
CHINESE PROVERB

Children are poor men's riches.
ENGLISH PROVERB

Who takes the child by the hand takes the mother by the heart.
GERMAN PROVERB

Don't limit a child to your own learning, for he was born in another time.
JEWISH PROVERB

Children are the bridge to heaven.
PERSIAN PROVERB

Chocolate

I owe it all to little chocolate donuts.
JOHN BELUSHI (1949–1982)

I adore chocolate. But then just lately I started to become allergic to it, so I've had to be careful. Apart from all that, life is wonderful. So it's really a small sacrifice.
JULIETTE BINOCHE (1964–)

Research tells us fourteen out of any ten individuals likes chocolate.
SANDRA BOYNTON (1953–)

Anything is good if it's made of chocolate.
JO BRAND (1957 –)

Venice is like eating an entire box of chocolate liqueurs in one go.
TRUMAN CAPOTE (1924–1984)

I began to realise that the large chocolate companies actually did possess inventing rooms, and they took their inventing very seriously.
ROALD DAHL (1916–1990)

My momma always said life was like a box of chocolates. You never know what you're gonna get.
WINSTON GROOM (1944–), *Forrest Gump*

Researchers have discovered that chocolate produces some of the same reactions in the brain as

marijuana. The researchers also discovered other similarities between the two but can't remember what they are.
MATT LAUER (1957–)

Choice

To live is to choose. But to choose well, you must know who you are and what you stand for, where you want to go and why you want to get there.
KOFI ANNAN (1938–)

Allow the world to live as it chooses, and allow yourself to live as you choose.
RICHARD BACH (1936–)

Some choices we live not only once but a thousand times over, remembering them for the rest of our lives.
RICHARD BACH (1936–)

Your life is the sum result of all the choices you make, both consciously and unconsciously. If you can control the process of choosing, you can take control of all aspects of your life. You can find the freedom that comes from being in charge of yourself.
ROBERT F. BENNETT (1927–2000)

Life is a sum of all your choices.
ALBERT CAMUS (1913–1960)

While we are free to choose our actions, we are not free to choose the consequences of our actions.
STEPHEN R. COVEY (1932–)

When you have to make a choice and don't make it, that is in itself a choice.
WILLIAM JAMES (1842–1910)

I believe that we are solely responsible for our choices, and we have to accept the consequences of every deed, word, and thought throughout our lifetime.
ELISABETH KÜBLER-ROSS (1926–2004)

We must make the choices that enable us to fulfill the deepest capacities of our real selves.
THOMAS MERTON (1915–1968)

It's choice, not chance, that determines your destiny.
JEAN NIDETCH (1923–)

You have a choice. Live or die. Every breath is a choice. Every minute is a choice. To be or not to be.
CHUCK PALAHNIUK (1962–)

Man is a being with free will; therefore, each man is potentially good or evil, and it's up to him and only him (through his reasoning mind) to decide which he wants to be.
AYN RAND (1905–1982)

One's philosophy is not best expressed in words; it is expressed in the choices one makes … and the choices we make are ultimately our responsibility.
ELEANOR ROOSEVELT (1884–1962)

It is our choices … that show what we truly are, far more than our abilities.
J. K. ROWLING (1965–), *Harry Potter and the Chamber of Secrets*

Character is the sum and total of a person's choices.
ANONYMOUS

I discovered I always have choices and sometimes it's only a choice of attitude.
ANONYMOUS

Christianity

Christianity is completed Judaism, or it is nothing.
BENJAMIN DISRAELI (1804–1881)

He who shall introduce into public affairs the principles of Christianity, will revolutionize the world.
BENJAMIN FRANKLIN (1706–1790)

It is unnatural for Christianity to be popular.
BILLY GRAHAM (1918–)

The greatness of Christianity did not lie in attempted negotiations for compromise with any similar philosophical opinions in the ancient world, but in its inexorable fanaticism in preaching and fighting for its own doctrine.
ADOLF HITLER (1889–1945)

Christianity neither is, nor ever was a part of the common law.
THOMAS JEFFERSON (1762–1826)

To the frivolous, Christianity is certainly not glad tidings, for it wishes first of all to make them serious.
SØREN KIERKEGAARD (1813–1855)

Yes, I see the Church as the body of Christ. But, oh! How we have blemished and scarred that body through social neglect and through fear of being nonconformists.
MARTIN LUTHER KING JR. (1929–1968)

I know the greatness of Christianity; it is a past greatness.... I live in 1924, and the Christian venture is done.
D. H. LAWRENCE (1885–1930)

[T]hat people often say about Him: "I'm ready to accept Jesus as a great moral teacher, but I don't accept His claim to be God." That is the one thing we must not say. A man who was merely a man and said the sort of things Jesus said would not be a great moral teacher. He would either be a lunatic—on a level with the man who says he is a poached egg—or else he would be the Devil of Hell. You must make your choice. Either this man was, and is, the Son of God: or else a madman or something worse. You can shut Him up for a fool, you can spit at Him and kill Him as a demon; or you can fall at His feet and call Him Lord and God. But let us not come with any patronizing nonsense about His being a great human teacher. He has not left that open to us. He did not intend to.
C. S. LEWIS (1898–1963), *Mere Christianity*

Christianity is called the religion of pity.
FRIEDRICH NIETZSCHE (1844–1900), *The Antichrist*

In Christianity neither morality nor religion come into contact with reality at any point.
FRIEDRICH NIETZSCHE (1844–1900), *The Antichrist*

Of all the systems of religion that ever were invented, there is none more derogatory to the Almighty, more unedifying to man, more repugnant to reason, and more contradictory to itself than this thing called Christianity.
THOMAS PAINE (1737–1809)

Christianity is the greatest intellectual system the mind of man has ever touched.
FRANCIS SCHAEFFER (1912–1984)

Christianity does not remove you from the world and its problems; it makes you fit to live in it, triumphantly and usefully.
CHARLES TEMPLETON (1915–2001)

Christianity, with its doctrine of humility, of forgiveness, of love, is incompatible with the state, with its haughtiness, its violence, its punishment, its wars.
LEO TOLSTOY (1828–1910)

Christianity is the most ridiculous, the most absurd, and bloody religion that has ever infected the world.
VOLTAIRE (1694–1778)

Of all religions, Christianity is without a doubt the one that should inspire tolerance most, although, up to now, the Christians have been the most intolerant of all men.
VOLTAIRE (1694–1778)

Church

No religion can long continue to maintain its purity when the church becomes the subservient vassal of the state.
FELIX ADLER (1851–1933)

Therefore, the church is not absolutely necessary as an object of faith, not even for us today, for then Abraham and the other prophets would not have given assent to those things which were revealed to them from God without any intervening help of the church.
WILLIAM AMES (1576–1633)

The church is challenging such negative cultural elements as superstition, rugged individualism, materialism, hedonism, permissiveness, and utilitarianism.
FRANCIS ARINZE (1932–)

We have taken a giant step forward in correcting some of the misconceptions people have about the church. I think that we've made a lot of friends.
M. RUSSELL BALLARD (1928–)

In the Church of Jesus Christ there can and should be no non-theologians.
KARL BARTH (1886–1968)

The Church is not a gallery for the exhibition of eminent Christians, but a school for the education of imperfect ones.
HENRY WARD BEECHER (1813–1887)

You go to church and they tell you to do good and help others, and then you go home and they tell you to do good and help others—but then you have to decide what to do.
DONNA BRAZILE (1959–)

The church is so subnormal that if it ever got back to the New Testament normal it would seem to people to be abnormal.
VANCE HAVNER (1901–1986)

All Church power arises from the indwelling of the Spirit; therefore those in whom the Spirit dwells are the seat of Church power. But the Spirit dwells in the whole Church, and therefore the whole Church is the seat of Church power.
CHARLES HODGE (1797–1878)

The Church is everywhere represented as one. It is one body, one family, one fold, one kingdom. It is one because pervaded by one Spirit. We are all baptized into one Spirit so as to become, says the apostle, one body.
CHARLES HODGE (1797–1878)

The Church is supposed to be fellowship and healing.
JENNIFER O'NEILL (1948–)

The Church has ever proved indestructible. Her persecutors have failed to destroy her; in fact, it was during times of persecution that the Church grew more and more; while the persecutors themselves, and those whom the Church would destroy, are the very ones who came to nothing.
SAINT THOMAS AQUINAS (1225–1274)

There is but one Church in which men find salvation, just as outside the ark of Noah it was not possible for anyone to be saved.
SAINT THOMAS AQUINAS (1225–1274)

Running is my church.
JOAN VAN ARK (1943–)

People don't come to church for preachments, of course, but to daydream about God.
KURT VONNEGUT JR. (1922–2007)

Cinema

If my film makes one more person miserable, I've done my job.
WOODY ALLEN (1935–)

I also wanted to express the strength of cinema to hide reality, while being entertaining. Cinema can fill in the empty spaces of your life and your loneliness.
PEDRO ALMODOVAR (1951–)

Today's cinema is a global art form, it is impossible to make movies for a market the size of France, representing no more than 4 percent of the world's total.
JEAN-JACQUES ANNAUD (1943–)

In American cinema, people will take a chance on you, though they'll often remind you that really, they always liked you.
KIM BASINGER (1953–)

The "Western" is the only genre whose origins are almost identical with those of the cinema itself.
ANDRE BAZIN (1918–1958)

Movies are open doors, and at every door, I change character and life.... I live for the present always. I accept this risk. I don't deny the past, but it's a page to turn.
JULIETTE BINOCHE (1964–)

This film business, perhaps more so in America than in Europe, has always been about young sexuality. It's not true of theatre, but in America, film audiences are young. It's not an intellectual cinema in America.
JACQUELINE BISSET (1956–)

It's so easy to manipulate an audience, but it's nearly always clear that you are being manipulated. I think even people that are not critically attuned are aware of cynical manipulation in film.
JOHN BOORMAN (1933–)

You can lose in cinema too if you don't put on a good performance.
ERIC CANTONA (1966–)

Cinema will always have an important role to play in society.
LESLIE CARON (1931–)

Strangers used to gather together at the cinema and sit together in the dark, like Ancient Greeks participating in the mysteries, dreaming the same dream in unison.
ANGELA CARTER (1940–1992)

I think cinema, movies, and magic have always been closely associated. The very earliest people who made film were magicians.
FRANCIS FORD COPPOLA (1939–)

Cinema explains American society. It's like a Western, with good guys and bad guys, where the weak don't have a place.
JACQUES DELORS (1925–)

Movies can and do have tremendous influence in shaping young lives in the realm of entertainment towards the ideals and objectives of normal adulthood.
WALT DISNEY (1901–1966)

[I]n painting the form arises from abstract elements of line and color, while in cinema the material concreteness of the image within the frame presents—as an element—the greatest difficulty in manipulation.
SERGEI EISENSTEIN (1898–1948)

Now why should the cinema follow the forms of theater and painting rather than the methodology of language, which allows wholly new concepts of ideas to arise from the combination of two concrete denotations of two concrete objects?
SERGEI EISENSTEIN (1898–1948)

Cinema is an old whore, like circus and variety, who knows how to give many kinds of pleasure. Besides, you can't teach old fleas new dogs.
FEDERICO FELLINI (1920–1993)

I discovered that what's really important for a creator isn't what we vaguely define as inspiration or even what it is we want to say, recall, regret, or rebel against. No, what's important is the way we say it. Art is all about craftsmanship. Others can interpret craftsmanship as style if they wish. Style is what unites memory or recollection, ideology, sentiment, nostalgia, presentiment, to the way we express all that. It's not what we say but how we say it that matters.
FEDERICO FELLINI (1920–1993)

Realism is always subjective in film. There's no such thing as cinema verité.
CRISPIN GLOVER (1964–)

Cinema is the most beautiful fraud in the world.
JEAN-LUC GODARD (1930–)

In films murders are always very clean. I show how difficult it is and what a messy thing it is to kill a man.
ALFRED HITCHCOCK (1899–1980)

The length of a film should be directly related to the endurance of the human bladder.
ALFRED HITCHCOCK (1899–1980)

In cinema, the leading player is the director.
BEN KINGSLEY (1943–)

A film is—or should be—more like music than like fiction. It should be a progression of moods and feelings. The theme, what's behind the emotion, the meaning, all that comes later.
STANLEY KUBRICK (1928–1999)

The screen is a magic medium. It has such power that it can retain interest as it conveys emotions and moods that no other art form can hope to tackle.
STANLEY KUBRICK (1928–1999)

Mainstream movies cost so much money to make and so much more to market.
LEONARD MALTIN (1950–)

Directing, I realize, on film is far more personal, you know. Cinema really is a director's medium.
SAM MENDES (1965–)

Cinema should make you forget you are sitting in a theater.
ROMAN POLANSKI (1933–)

The movies are the only business where you can go out front and applaud yourself.
WILL ROGERS (1879–1935)

There is only one thing that can kill the movies, and that is education.
WILL ROGERS (1879–1935)

Movies have to handle time very efficiently. They're about stringing scenes together in the present. Novels aren't necessarily about that.
RICHARD RUSSO (1949–)

If cinema has burgeoned, it's also thanks to the fact that democracy—not economic democracy, but at least political democracy—has returned to a great part of the continent.
WALTER SALLES (1956–)

I do believe that movies are subject to a million interpretations.
OLIVER STONE (1946–)

Movies give me an opportunity to go places. I'm not only a Swede but an American, not just a man of my time, but I've been living 2,000 years ago—and not just in a new country, America, but in the Holy Land, too.
MAX VON SYDOW (1929–)

I like it when somebody tells me a story, and I actually really feel that that's becoming like a lost art in American cinema.
QUENTIN TARANTINO (1963–)

Movies are not about the weekend that they're released, and in the grand scheme of things, that's probably the most unimportant time of a film's life.
QUENTIN TARANTINO (1963–)

To me, all movies are very personal.
QUENTIN TARANTINO (1963–)

Juxtaposing a person with an environment that is boundless, collating him with a countless number of people passing by close to him and far away, relating a person to the whole world, that is the meaning of cinema.
ANDREI TARKOVSKY (1932–1986)

Cinema is a worldwide phenomenon.
WIM WENDERS (1945–)

Entertainment today constantly emphasises the message that things are wonderful the way they are. But there is another kind of cinema, which says that change is possible and necessary and it's up to you.
WIM WENDERS (1945–)

Everything is entertainment; criticism is now entertainment and it seems that the French directors have woken up one day and suddenly realised that they were not backed up any more.
WIM WENDERS (1945–)

China's cinema has been rising for some time; it has more exposure, so my chances of becoming internationally known are better. But the first thing I have to do is learn English. If I can grasp the language, then perhaps I can think about the U.S.
ZIYI ZHANG (1979–)

Circumstances

Men are the sport of circumstances when it seems circumstances are the sport of men.
LORD BYRON (1788–1824)

Circumstances are beyond human control, but our conduct is in our own power.
BENJAMIN DISRAELI (1804–1881)

Man is more powerful than matter.
BENJAMIN DISRAELI (1804–1881)

Man is not the creature of circumstances, circumstances are the creatures of men. We are free agents, and man is more powerful than matter.
BENJAMIN DISRAELI (1804–1881)

A man with a surplus can control circumstances, but a man without a surplus is controlled by them, and often has no opportunity to exercise judgment.
HARVEY S. FIRESTONE (1868–1938)

That which resembles most living one's life over again, seems to be to recall all the circumstances of it; and, to render this remembrance more durable, to record them in writing.
BENJAMIN FRANKLIN (1706–1790)

He is happy whom circumstances suit his temper; but he is more excellent who suits his temper to any circumstance.
DAVID HUME (1711–1776)

To hell with circumstances; I create opportunities.
BRUCE LEE (1940–1973)

Consider that thou dost not even understand whether men are doing wrong or not, for many things are done with a certain reference to circumstance. And, in short, a man must learn a great deal to enable him to pass a correct judgment on another man's acts.
MARCUS AURELIUS ANTONINUS (121–180)

Living is like working out a long addition sum, and if you make a mistake in the first two totals you will never find the right answer. It means involving oneself in a complicated chain of circumstances.
CESARE PAVESE (1908–1950)

People are always blaming their circumstances for what they are. I don't believe in circumstances. The people who get on in this world are the people who get up and look for the circumstances they want, and if they can't find them, make them.
GEORGE BERNARD SHAW (1856–1950)

Character, not circumstances, make the man.
BOOKER T. WASHINGTON (1856–1915)

No person is either as happy or as unhappy as they imagine. Things are never as good or as bad as they seem.
ANONYMOUS

The one who complains about the way the ball bounces is likely the one who dropped it
ANONYMOUS

Cities

The cities of the world are concentric, isomorphic, synchronic. Only one exists and you are always in the same one. It's the effect of their permanent revolution, their intense circulation, their instantaneous magnetism.
JEAN BAUDRILLARD (1929–2007)

What I like about cities is that everything is king size, the beauty and the ugliness.
JOSEPH BRODSKY (1940–1996)

Cities, like cats, will reveal themselves at night.
RUPERT BROOKE (1887–1915)

In cities no one is quiet but many are lonely; in the country, people are quiet but few are lonely.
Geoffrey Fisher (1887–1972)

Big cities are chaotic. And chaos for humans—who have experience from their ancestors—is the last step before conflict. So, in the park, every kind of visual contradiction has been eliminated.
John Hench (1908–2004)

The people should fight for the law as for their city wall.
Heraclitus (c. 535–475 BC)

The mobs of the great cities add just so much to the support of pure government, as sores do to the strength of the human body.
Thomas Jefferson (1762–1826)

Cities are the greatest creations of humanity.
Daniel Libeskind (1946–)

In a real estate man's eye, the most expensive part of the city is where he has a house to sell.
Will Rogers (1879–1935)

Cities are the abyss of the human species.
Jean-Jacques Rousseau (1712–1778)

Cities are, first of all, seats of the highest economic division of labor.
Georg Simmel (1858–1918)

A great city is that which has the greatest men and women.
Walt Whitman (1819–1892)

Civil War

All wars are civil wars, because all men are brothers.
François de Fénelon (1651–1715)

I declare that civil war is inevitable and is near at hand. When it comes the descendants of the heroes of Lexington and Bunker Hill will be found equal in patriotism, courage, and heroic endurance with the descendants of the heroes of Cowpens and York.
Sam Houston (1793–1863)

Civil war? What does that mean? Is there any foreign war? Isn't every war fought between men, between brothers?
Victor Hugo (1802–1885)

Now we are engaged in a great civil war, testing whether that nation, or any nation so conceived and so dedicated, can long endure. We are met on a great battlefield of that war. We have come to dedicate a portion of that field, as a final resting place for those who here gave their lives that that nation might live. It is altogether fitting and proper that we should do this.
Abraham Lincoln (1809–1865), *The Gettysburg Address*

Civilization

Civilization is a method of living, an attitude of equal respect for all men.
Jane Addams (1860–1935)

Civilization degrades the many to exalt the few.
Amos Bronson Alcott (1799–1888), *Table Talk*

The three great elements of modern civilization: Gun powder, Printing, and the Protestant religion.
Thomas Carlyle (1795–1881)

Underlying the whole scheme of civilization is the confidence men have in each other, confidence in their integrity, confidence in their honesty, confidence in their future.
Bourke Cockran (1854–1923)

Civilization and profit go hand in hand.
Calvin Coolidge (1872–1933)

Increased means and increased leisure are the two civilizers of man.
Benjamin Disraeli (1804–1881)

Civilization begins with order, grows with liberty, and dies with chaos.
Will Durant (1885–1981)

The more rapidly a civilization progresses, the sooner it dies for another to rise in its place.
HENRY HAVELOCK ELLIS (1859–1939), *The Dance of Life*

As long as our civilization is essentially one of property, of fences, of exclusiveness, it will be mocked by delusions. Our riches will leave us sick; there will be bitterness in our laughter; and our wine will burn our mouth. Only that good profits, which we can taste with all doors open, and which serves all men.
RALPH WALDO EMERSON (1803–1882)

Civilization depends on morality.
RALPH WALDO EMERSON (1803–1882)

Sunday is the core of our civilization, dedicated to thought and reverence.
RALPH WALDO EMERSON (1803–1882)

The end of the human race will be that it will eventually die of civilization.
RALPH WALDO EMERSON (1803–1882)

One of the indictments of civilizations is that happiness and intelligence are so rarely found in the same person.
WILLIAM FEATHER (1908–1976)

Civilization is a process in the service of Eros, whose purpose is to combine single human individuals, and after that families, then races, peoples and nations, into one great unity, the unity of mankind. Why this has to happen, we do not know; the work of Eros is precisely this.
SIGMUND FREUD (1856–1939)

The path of civilization is paved with tin cans.
ELBERT HUBBARD (1856–1915)

The quantity of civilization is measured by the quality of imagination.
VICTOR HUGO (1802–1885), *Les Miserables*

The true civilization is where every man gives to every other every right that he claims for himself.
ROBERT GREEN INGERSOLL (1833–1899)

One might enumerate the items of high civilization, as it exists in other countries, which are absent from the texture of American life, until it should become a wonder to know what was left.
HENRY JAMES (1843–1916)

Civilization is the art of living in towns of such size that everyone does not know everyone else.
JULIAN JAYNES (1920–1997), *The Origin of Consciousness*

Illusions mistaken for truth are the pavement under our feet. They are what we call civilization.
BARBARA KINGSOLVER (1955–), *The Poisonwood Bible*

Every civilization when it loses its inner vision and its cleaner energy, falls into a new sort of sordidness, more vast and more stupendous than the old savage sort. An Augean stable of metallic filth.
D. H. LAWRENCE (1885–1930)

Every new stroke of civilization has cost the lives of countless brave men, who have fallen defeated by the "dragon," in their efforts to win the apples of the Hesperides, or the fleece of gold. Fallen in their efforts to overcome the old, half sordid savagery of the lower stages of creation, and win the next stage.
D. H. LAWRENCE (1885–1930)

Civilization is built on a number of ultimate principles … respect for human life, the punishment of crimes against property and persons, the equality of all good citizens before the law … or, in a word, justice.
MAX NORDAU (1849–1923)

Civilization is the progress toward a society of privacy. The savage's whole existence is public, ruled by the laws of his tribe. Civilization is the process of setting man free from men.
AYN RAND (1905–1982)

You can't say that civilization don't advance, however, for in every war they kill you in a new way.
WILL ROGERS (1879–1935)

Civilizations die from suicide, not by murder.
ARNOLD J. TOYNBEE (1889–1975)

America is the only country that went from barbarism to decadence without civilization in between.
OSCAR WILDE (1854–1900)

Class

The class distinctions proper to a democratic society are not those of rank or money, still less, as is apt to happen when these are abandoned, of race, but of age.
W. H. AUDEN (1907–1973)

The fears of one class of men are not the measure of the rights of another.
GEORGE BANCROFT (1800–1891)

Race and class are the easiest divisions. It's very stupid.
LYNDA BARRY (1956–)

Broadly speaking, human beings may be divided into three classes: those who are billed to death, those who are worried to death, and those who are bored to death.
SIR WINSTON CHURCHILL (1874–1965)

All history has been a history of class struggles between dominated classes at various stages of social development.
FRIEDRICH ENGELS (1820–1895)

The Constitution is colorblind, and neither knows nor tolerates classes among citizens.
JOHN MARSHALL (1755–1835)

There are three social classes in America: upper middle class, middle class, and lower middle class.
JUDITH MARTIN (1938–)

The class struggle necessarily leads to the dictatorship of the proletariat.
KARL MARX (1818–1883)

Class in society is determined by voice.
MARSHALL MCLUHAN (1911–1980)

Aerial flight is one of that class of problems with which men will never have to cope.
SIMON NEWCOMB (1835–1909)

Patriotism is usually stronger than class hatred, and always stronger than internationalism.
GEORGE ORWELL (1903–1950)

I divide all readers into two classes: Those who read to remember and those who read to forget.
WILLIAM LYON PHELPS (1865–1943)

There are only two classes in good society in England: the equestrian classes and the neurotic classes.
GEORGE BERNARD SHAW (1856–1950)

All mankind is divided into three classes: those that are immovable, those that are movable, and those that move.
ARABIAN PROVERB

Clergy

It will, I believe, be everywhere found, that as the clergy are, or are not what they ought to be, so are the rest of the nation.
JANE AUSTEN (1775–1817), *Mansfield Park*

Clergyman, n.: A man who undertakes the management of our spiritual affairs as a method of bettering his temporal ones.
AMBROSE BIERCE (1842–1914), *The Devil's Dictionary*

If lawyers are disbarred and clergymen defrocked, doesn't it follow that electricians can be delighted, musicians denoted?
GEORGE CARLIN (1937–)

You must believe in God in spite of what the clergy say.
BENJAMIN JOWETT (1817–1893)

A celibate clergy is an especially good idea, because it tends to suppress any hereditary propensity toward fanaticism.
CARL SAGAN (1934–1996), *Contact*

A clergyman is one who feels himself called upon to live without working at the expense of the rascals who work to live.
VOLTAIRE (1694–1778)

Cleverness

An ounce of loyalty is worth a pound of cleverness.
ELBERT HUBBARD (1856–1915)

The height of cleverness is to be able to conceal it.
FRANÇOIS DE LA ROCHEFOUCAULD (1613–1680)

Ignorance of all things is an evil neither terrible nor excessive, nor yet the greatest of all; but great cleverness and much learning, if they be accompanied by a bad training, are a much greater misfortune.
PLATO (C. 428–348 BC)

All religions are founded on the fear of the many and the cleverness of the few.
STENDHAL (1783–1842)

A man likes his wife to be just clever enough to comprehend his cleverness, and just stupid enough to admire it.
ISRAEL ZANGWILL (1864–1926)

Clothes

To say something nice about yourself, this is the hardest thing in the world for people to do. They'd rather take their clothes off.
NANCY FRIDAY (1933–)

It has always been the prerogative of children and half-wits to point out that the emperor has no clothes. But the half-wit remains a half-wit, and the emperor remains an emperor.
NEIL GAIMAN (1960–), *Sandman*

Normal is getting dressed in clothes that you buy for work and driving through traffic in a car that you are still paying for—in order to get to the job you need to pay for the clothes and the car, and the house you leave vacant all day so you can afford to live in it.
ELLEN GOODMAN (1941–)

Dressing up is inevitably a substitute for good ideas. It is no coincidence that technically inept business types are known as "suits."
PAUL GRAHAM (1964–)

Nerds don't just happen to dress informally. They do it too consistently. Consciously or not, they dress informally as a prophylactic measure against stupidity.
PAUL GRAHAM (1964–)

Art may make a suit of clothes: but nature must produce a man.
DAVID HUME (1711–1776)

Patience serves as a protection against wrongs as clothes do against cold. For if you put on more clothes as the cold increases, it will have no power to hurt you. So in like manner you must grow in patience when you meet with great wrongs, and they will then be powerless to vex your mind.
LEONARDO DA VINCI (1452–1519)

Beware of all enterprises that require new clothes.
HENRY DAVID THOREAU (1817–1862), *Walden*

It is an interesting question how far men would retain their relative rank if they were divested of their clothes.
HENRY DAVID THOREAU (1817–1862), *Walden*

However mean your life is, meet it and live it: do not shun it and call it hard names. Cultivate poverty like a garden herb, like sage. Do not trouble yourself much to get new things, whether clothes or friends. Things do not change, we change. Sell your clothes and keep your thoughts.
HENRY DAVID THOREAU (1817–1862)

Clothes make the man. Naked people have little or no influence on society.
MARK TWAIN (1835–1910)

We buy our way out of jail but we can't buy freedom,
We buy a lot of clothes when we don't really need them,
Things we buy to cover up what's inside.
KANYE WEST (1977–)

Clouds

The fear that was on me so long was gone, and when thunder clouds appeared I was always glad to see them, for they came as relatives now to visit me.
BLACK ELK (1863–1950)

Scatter the clouds that hide
The face of heaven, and show,
Where sweet peace doth abide,
Where Truth and Beauty grow.
ROBERT BRIDGES (1844–1930)

Heavy hearts, like heavy clouds in the sky, are best relieved by the letting of a little water.
CHRISTOPHER MORLEY (1890–1957)

Clouds come floating into my life, no longer to carry rain or usher storm, but to add color to my sunset sky.
RABINDRANATH TAGORE (1861–1941)

Coffee

This coffee plunges into the stomach … the mind is aroused, and ideas pour forth like the battalions of the Grand Army on the field of battle…. Memories charge at full gallop … the light cavalry of comparisons deploys itself magnificently; the artillery of logic [hurries] in with their train of ammunition; flashes of wit pop up like sharp-shooters.
HONORÉ DE BALZAC (1799–1850)

If this is coffee, please bring me some tea; but if this is tea, please bring me some coffee.
ABRAHAM LINCOLN (1809–1865)

Good communication is as stimulating as black coffee and just as hard to sleep after.
ANNE MORROW LINDBERGH (1906–2001), *Gift from the Sea*

There are three intolerable things in life—cold coffee, lukewarm champagne, and overexcited women.
ORSON WELLES (1915–1985)

The Cold War

The Cold War was over. The global standoff between superpowers was at an end. The world saw America and the West triumphant, freedom preserved, and the promises of Marx and Lenin and Stalin discredited.
SPENCER ABRAHAM (1952–)

It is true the Cold War has ended and that our big bosses think that relieves them of the obligation to cover the world.
CHRISTIANE AMANPOUR (1958–)

America won the Cold War by protecting our strategic resources from the threat of foreign control. We must bring the same attitude to our trade relationship with China.
JO ANN EMERSON (1950–)

During the Cold War, we gathered information by listening to the Soviets, taking pictures of the Soviets, and we allowed our human intelligence to decline.
BOB GRAHAM (1936–)

The Cold War was waged in a particularly brutal and cynical way in Africa, and Africa seemed powerless to do anything to stop it.
RYSZARD KAPUSCINSKI (1932–2007)

During the Cold War, we lived in coded times when it wasn't easy and there were shades of grey and ambiguity.
JOHN LE CARRÉ (1931–)

The Cold War was over long before it was officially declared dead.
JOHN LE CARRÉ (1931–)

Since the end of the Cold War, Soviet aggression had been replaced by a number of particularly venomous threats, from Timothy McVeigh to Osama bin Laden.
BARBARA OLSON (1955–2001)

College

I was thrown out of college for cheating on the metaphysics exam; I looked into the soul of the boy sitting next to me.
WOODY ALLEN (1935–)

It takes most men five years to recover from a college education, and to learn that poetry is as vital to thinking as knowledge.
BROOKS ATKINSON (1894–1984)

I believe that we parents must encourage our children to become educated, so they can get into a good college that we cannot afford.
DAVE BARRY (1947–)

A university is what a college becomes when the faculty loses interest in students.
JOHN CIARDI (1916–1986)

Colleges hate geniuses, just as convents hate saints.
RALPH WALDO EMERSON (1803–1882)

Never get married in college; it's hard to get a start if a prospective employer finds you've already made one mistake.
ELBERT HUBBARD (1856–1915)

An old tutor of a college said to one of his pupils: "Read over your compositions, and wherever you meet with a passage which you think is particularly fine, strike it out."
SAMUEL JOHNSON (1709–1784)

College isn't the place to go for ideas.
HELEN KELLER (1880–1968)

Everybody can be great because anybody can serve. You don't have to have a college degree to serve. You don't have to make your subject and verb agree to serve. You only need a heart full of grace. A soul generated by love.
MARTIN LUTHER KING JR. (1929–1968)

Some people get an education without going to college; the rest get it after they get out.
MARK TWAIN (1835–1910)

Commanders

Any commander who fails to exceed his authority is not of much use to his subordinates.
ARLEIGH BURKE (1901–1996)

In war, when a commander becomes so bereft of reason and perspective that he fails to understand the dependence of arms on Divine guidance, he no longer deserves victory.
GENERAL DOUGLAS MACARTHUR (1880–1964)

The commander in the field is always right and the rear echelon is wrong, unless proved otherwise.
COLIN POWELL (1937–)

Comedy

The difference between tragedy and comedy: Tragedy is something awful happening to somebody else, while comedy is something awful happening to somebody else.
AARON ALLSTON (1960–)

Friends applaud, the comedy is over.
LUDWIG VAN BEETHOVEN (1770–1827), last words

Good taste is the enemy of comedy.
MEL BROOKS (1926–)

Tragedy is when I cut my finger. Comedy is when you walk into an open sewer and die.
MEL BROOKS (1926–)

Comedy is tragedy plus time.
CAROL BURNETT (1933–)

When someone who is known for being comedic does something straight, it's always "a big breakthrough" or a "radical departure." Why is it no one ever says that if a straight actor does comedy? Are they presuming comedy is easier?
CAROL BURNETT (1933–)

I think it's the duty of the comedian to find out where the line is drawn and cross it deliberately.
GEORGE CARLIN (1937–)

There's so much comedy on television. Does that cause comedy in the streets?
DICK CAVETT (1936–)

The most difficult character in comedy is that of a fool, and he must be no simpleton who plays the part.
MIGUEL DE CERVANTES (1547–1616), *Don Quixote*

All I need to make a comedy is a park, a policeman and a pretty girl.
CHARLIE CHAPLIN (1889–1977), *My Autobiography*

Life is a tragedy when seen in close-up, but a comedy in long-shot
CHARLIE CHAPLIN (1889–1977)

The essence of all jokes, of all comedy, seems to be an honest or well intended halfness; a non performance of that which is pretended to be performed, at the same time that one is giving loud pledges of performance. The balking of the intellect is comedy, and it announces itself in the pleasant spasms we call laughter.
RALPH WALDO EMERSON (1803–1882)

In tragedy, every moment is eternity; in comedy, eternity is a moment.
CHRISTOPHER FRY (1907–2005)

Dying is easy. Comedy is difficult.
EDMUND GWENN (1877–1959)

Once you can laugh at your own weaknesses, you can move forward. Comedy breakes down walls. It opens up people. If you're good, you can fill up those openings with something positive. Maybe … combat some of the ugliness in the world.
GOLDIE HAWN (1945–)

Comedy is nothing more than tragedy deferred.
PICO IYER (1957–)

There are so many different ways lives work out, so many stories, and every one of them is precious: full of joy and heartbreak, and a fair amount of situation comedy.
SEAN STEWART (1965–), *Perfect Circle*

The only rules comedy can tolerate are those of taste, and the only limitations those of libel.
JAMES THURBER (1894–1961)

Comedy is simply a funny way of being serious.
PETER USTINOV (1921–2004)

The world is a tragedy to those who feel, but a comedy to those who think.
HORACE WALPOLE (1717–1797)

Honest vulgarity is in the central tradition of English humour—the humour of the music-hall. Uninhibitedness is the essence of comedy.
KENNETH WILLIAMS (1926–1988)

Comedy is acting out optimism.
ROBIN WILLIAMS (1951–)

Commerce

By virtue of exchange, one man's prosperity is beneficial to all others.
FRÉDÉRIC BASTIAT (1801–1850)

Let peace, descending from her native heaven, bid her olives spring amidst the joyful nations; and plenty, in league with commerce, scatter blessings from her copious hand!
DANIEL BOONE (1734–1820)

The lessons taught in great books are misleading. The commerce in life is rarely so simple and never so just.
ANITA BROOKNER (1938–)

In day-to-day commerce, television is not so much interested in the business of communications as in the business of delivering audiences to advertisers. People are the merchandise, not the shows. The shows are merely the bait.
LES BROWN (1945–)

But I am committed to keeping this city a strong and viable center for commerce and industry, for continuing to make it a place of opportunity for its citizens.
JANE BYRNE (1934–)

In matters of commerce the fault of the Dutch
Is offering too little and asking too much.
The French are with equal advantage content,
So we clap on Dutch bottoms just twenty per cent.
GEORGE CANNING (1770–1827)

A magazine or a newspaper is a shop. Each is an experiment and represents a new focus, a new ratio between commerce and intellect.
JOHN JAY CHAPMAN (1862–1933)

Wars have ever been but another aristocratic mode of plundering and oppressing commerce.
RICHARD COBDEN (1804–1865)

Commerce flourishes by circumstances, precarious, transitory, contingent, almost as the winds and waves that bring it to our shores.
CHARLES CALEB COLTON (1780–1832)

Commerce is against morality. Morality is going to lose every time.
ROBIN DAY (1923–2000)

Commerce is of trivial import; love, faith, truth of character, the aspiration of man, these are sacred.
RALPH WALDO EMERSON (1803–1882)

Whoever controls the volume of money in any country is absolute master of all industry and commerce.
JAMES A. GARFIELD (1831–1881)

Honour sinks where commerce long prevails.
OLIVER GOLDSMITH (1730–1774)

Commerce changes the fate and genius of nations.
THOMAS GRAY (1716–1771)

Commerce has become very extensive since the invention of steam, and the countries of the West have in consequence become rich.
TOWNSEND HARRIS (1804–1878)

Perfect freedom is as necessary to the health and vigor of commerce as it is to the health and vigor of citizenship.
PATRICK HENRY (1736–1799)

Commerce with all nations, alliance with none, should be our motto.
THOMAS JEFFERSON (1743–1826)

Money, not morality, is the principle commerce of civilized nations.
THOMAS JEFFERSON (1743–1826)

The whole commerce between master and slave is a perpetual exercise of the most boisterous passions, the most unremitting despotism on the one part, and degrading submissions on the other. Our children see this, and learn to imitate it.
THOMAS JEFFERSON (1743–1826)

To the extent that these advanced weapons or their components are treated as articles of commerce, perhaps for peaceful uses as in the Plowshare program, their cost would be well within the resources available to many large private organizations.
HERMAN KAHN (1922–1983)

Not just in commerce but in the world of ideas too our age is putting on a veritable clearance sale. Everything can be had so dirt cheap that one begins to wonder whether in the end anyone will want to make a bid.
SØREN KIERKEGAARD (1813–1855)

What prudent merchant will hazard his fortunes in any new branch of commerce when he knows not that his plans may be rendered unlawful before they can be executed?
JAMES MADISON (1751–1836)

If the other fellow sells cheaper than you, it is called dumping. 'Course, if you sell cheaper than him, that's mass production.
WILL ROGERS (1879–1935)

Common Sense

The last time anybody made a list of the top hundred character attributes of New Yorkers, common sense snuck in at number 79.
DOUGLAS ADAMS (1952–2001), *Mostly Harmless*

Common sense is the measure of the possible; it is composed of experience and prevision; it is calculation applied to life.
HENRI-FRÉDÉRIC AMIEL (1821–1881)

The freethinking of one age is the common sense of the next.
MATTHEW ARNOLD (1822–1888), *God and the Bible*

The philosophy of one century is the common sense of the next.
HENRY WARD BEECHER (1813–1887)

Common sense is the knack of seeing things as they are, and doing things as they ought to be done.
JOSH BILLINGS (1818–1885)

Common sense is only a modification of talent. Genius is an exaltation of it. The difference is, therefore, in degree, not nature.
SIR EDWARD G. BULWER-LYTTON (1803–1873)

[Common sense] is the best sense I know of.
LORD CHESTERFIELD (1694–1773)

Common sense is the collection of prejudices acquired by age eighteen.
ALBERT EINSTEIN (1879–1955)

Nothing astonishes men so much as common sense and plain dealing.
RALPH WALDO EMERSON (1803–1882), *Art*

I do not feel obliged to believe that the same God who has endowed us with sense, reason, and intellect has intended us to forgo their use.
GALILEO GALILEI (1564–1642)

Science is nothing but trained and organized common sense, differing from the latter only as a veteran may differ from a raw recruit: and its methods differ from those of common sense only as far as the guardsman's cut and thrust differ from the manner in which a savage wields his club.
THOMAS H. HUXLEY (1825–1895)

Everybody gets so much information all day long that they lose their common sense.
GERTRUDE STEIN (1874–1946)

Nowadays most people die of a sort of creeping common sense, and discover when it is too late that the only things one never regrets are one's mistakes.
OSCAR WILDE (1854–1900), *The Picture of Dorian Gray*

Communication

Every improvement in communication makes the bore more terrible.
FRANK MOORE COLBY (1865–1925)

I wish people who have trouble communicating would just shut up.
TOM LEHRER (1928–)

Good communication is as stimulating as black coffee and just as hard to sleep after.
ANNE MORROW LINDBERGH (1906–2001), *Gift from the Sea*

Let us make a special effort to stop communicating with each other, so we can have some conversation.
JUDITH MARTIN (1938–)

Think like a wise man but communicate in the language of the people.
WILLIAM BUTLER YEATS (1865–1939)

Communism

I am for socialism, disarmament, and, ultimately, for abolishing the state itself.... I seek the social ownership of property, the abolition of the propertied class, and the sole control of those who produce wealth. Communism is the goal.
ROGER BALDWIN (1884–1981)

Communism is like one big phone company.
LENNY BRUCE (1923–1966)

It is popular to call it a crisis of the Western world. It is in fact a crisis of the whole world. Communism, which claims to be a solution of the crisis, is itself a symptom and an irritant of the crisis.
WHITTAKER CHAMBERS (1901–1961)

A communist is like a crocodile: when it opens its mouth you cannot tell whether it is trying to smile or preparing to eat you up.
SIR WINSTON CHURCHILL (1874–1965)

The terrible thing is that one cannot be a Communist and not let oneself in for the shameful act of recantation. One cannot be a Communist and preserve an iota of one's personal integrity.
MILOVAN DJILAS (1911–1995)

One strength of the communist system of the East is that it has some of the character of a religion and inspires the emotions of a religion.
ALBERT EINSTEIN (1879–1955)

What is a Communist? One who hath yearnings for equal division of unequal earnings. Idler or bungler, or both, he is willing to fork out his copper and pocket a shilling.
EBENEZER ELLIOTT (1781–1849)

Under capitalism, man exploits man. Under communism, it's just the opposite.
JOHN KENNETH GALBRAITH (1908–2006)

Communism possesses a language which every people can understand—its elements are hunger, envy, and death.
HEINRICH HEINE (1797–1856)

There may be community of material possessions, but there can never be community of love or esteem.
SAMUEL JOHNSON (1709–1784), *The Great Charm of Literature*

Communism has never come to power in a country that was not disrupted by war or corruption, or both.
JOHN F. KENNEDY (1917–1963)

To those people in the huts and villages of half the globe struggling to break the bonds of mass misery, we pledge our best efforts to help them help themselves, for whatever period is required, not because the Communists may be doing it, not because we seek their votes, but because it is right. If a free society cannot help the many who are poor, it cannot save the few who are rich.
JOHN F. KENNEDY (1917–1963)

What we want is some sort of communism not based on wages, nor profits, nor any sort of buying and selling but on a religion of life.
D. H. LAWRENCE (1885–1930)

Among the masses of the people, we [the communists] are but drops in the ocean, and we will be able to govern only when we properly express that which the people appreciate. Without this the communist party will not lead the proletariat, the proletariat will not take the lead of the masses, and the whole machine will fall to pieces.
VLADIMIR I. LENIN (1870–1924)

Communism is Soviet power plus the electrification of the whole country
VLADIMIR I. LENIN (1870–1924)

Communism means barbarism.
JAMES RUSSELL LOWELL (1819–1891)

Communism is the opiate of the intellectuals with no cure except as a guillotine might be called a cure for dandruff.
CLARE BOOTHE LUCE (1903–1987)

Communism destroys democracy. Democracy can also destroy Communism.
ANDRÉ MALRAUX (1901–1976)

Communism is not love. Communism is a hammer which we use to crush the enemy.
MAO TSE-TUNG (1893–1976)

Every Communist must grasp the truth, "Political power grows out of the barrel of a gun." Our principle is that the Communist Party commands the gun and the gun will never be allowed to command the Party.
MAO TSE-TUNG (1893–1976)

All I know is I'm not a Marxist.
KARL MARX (1818–1883)

In a higher phase of communist society ... only then can the narrow horizon of bourgeois right be fully left behind and society inscribe on its banners: from each according to his ability, to each according to his needs.
KARL MARX (1818–1883)

In communist society, where nobody has one exclusive sphere of activity but each can become accomplished in any branch he wishes, society regulates the general production and thus makes it possible for me to do one thing today and another tomorrow, to hunt in the morning, fish in the afternoon, rear cattle in the evening, criticize after dinner, just as I have a mind, without ever becoming hunter, fisherman, shepherd or critic.
KARL MARX (1818–1883)

Let the ruling classes tremble at a Communist revolution. The proletarians have nothing to lose, but their chains.... Workers of the world unite!
KARL MARX (1818–1883)

The theory of Communism may be summed up in one sentence: Abolish all private property.
KARL MARX (1818–1883)

Communists have always played an active role in the fight by colonial countries for their freedom, because the short-term objects of Communism would always correspond with the long-term objects of freedom movements.
NELSON MANDELA (1918–)

Communism, like any other revealed religion, is largely made up of prophecies.
H. L. MENCKEN (1880–1956)

I never agree with Communists or any other kind of kept men.
H. L. MENCKEN (1880–1956)

The Catholic and the Communist are alike in assuming that an opponent cannot be both honest and intelligent.
GEORGE ORWELL (1903–1950)

Communism teaches and seeks two objectives: unrelenting class warfare and the complete eradication of private ownership.
POPE PIUS XI (1857–1939)

You cannot place mediocrity on a par with culture and intelligence; consequently communism is impossible.
BENJAMIN PERLEY POORE (1820–1887)

Communism is a society where each one works according to his abilities and gets according to his needs.
PIERRE-JOSEPH PROUDHON (1809–1865)

Communism is inequality, but not as property is. Property is exploitation of the weak by the strong. Communism is exploitation of the strong by the weak.
PIERRE-JOSEPH PROUDHON (1809–1865)

How do you tell a communist? Well, it's someone who reads Marx and Lenin. And how do you tell an anti-Communist? It's someone who understands Marx and Lenin.
RONALD REAGAN (1911–2004)

Communism is in conflict with human nature.
ERNEST RENAN (1823–1892)

Communism is like prohibition, it's a good idea but it won't work.
WILL ROGERS (1879–1935)

The economy of Communism is an economy which grows in an atmosphere of misery and want.
ELEANOR ROOSEVELT (1884–1962)

I do not believe in Communism any more than you do but there is nothing wrong with the Communists in this country; several of the best friends I have got are Communists.
FRANKLIN D. ROOSEVELT (1882–1945)

Socialism is the same as Communism, only better English.
GEORGE BERNARD SHAW (1856–1950)

Most people who read "The Communist Manifesto" probably have no idea that it was written by a couple of young men who had never worked a day in their lives, and who nevertheless spoke boldly in the name of "the workers."
THOMAS SOWELL (1930–)

Communists are people who fancied that they had an unhappy childhood.
GERTRUDE STEIN (1874–1946)

Communism is the corruption of a dream of justice.
ADLAI E. STEVENSON II (1900–1965)

Communism is the death of the soul. It is the organization of total conformity—in short, of tyranny—and it is committed to making tyranny universal.
ADLAI E. STEVENSON II (1900–1965)

Marxism is the opium of the intellectuals.
EDMUND WILSON (1895–1972)

Let's not talk about Communism. Communism was just an idea, just pie in the sky.
BORIS YELTSIN (1931–)

Communism doesn't work because people like to own stuff.
FRANK ZAPPA (1940–1993)

Communists should be the first to be concerned about other people and country and the last to enjoy themselves.
ZHAO ZIYANG (1919–2005)

Community

The most perfect political community is one in which the middle class is in control, and outnumbers both of the other classes.
ARISTOTLE (384–322 BC), *Politics*

It is vain to talk of the interest of the community, without understanding what is the interest of the individual.
JEREMY BENTHAM (1748–1832)

There is no finer investment for any community than putting milk into babies.
SIR WINSTON CHURCHILL (1874–1965)

The benefits of education and of useful knowledge, generally diffused through a community, are essential to the preservation of a free government.
SAM HOUSTON (1793–1863)

A community is like a ship; everyone ought to be prepared to take the helm.
HENRIK IBSEN (1828–1906)

Community means engaging constructively with like-minded nations to build strong, sustaining institutions and alliances, and bringing emerging powers into this community so future conflict becomes less likely.
JOE LIEBERMAN (1942–)

God creates men, but they choose each other.
NICCOLÒ MACHIAVELLI (1469–1527)

Never doubt that a small group of thoughtful, committed citizens can change the world. Indeed, it is the only thing that ever has.
MARGARET MEAD (1901–1978)

There can be no vulnerability without risk; there can be no community without vulnerability; there can be no peace, and ultimately no life, without community.
M. SCOTT PECK (1936–2005)

A healthy social life is found only, when in the mirror of each soul the whole community finds its

reflection, and when in the whole community the virtue of each one is living.
RUDOLF STEINER (1861–1925)

Law; an ordinance of reason for the common good, made by him who has care of the community.
SAINT THOMAS AQUINAS (1225–1274)

Community cannot for long feed on itself; it can only flourish with the coming of others from beyond, their unknown and undiscovered brothers.
HOWARD THURMAN (1900–1981)

The universal brotherhood of man is our most precious possession.
MARK TWAIN (1835–1910)

What should young people do with their lives today? Many things, obviously. But the most daring thing is to create stable communities in which the terrible disease of loneliness can be cured.
KURT VONNEGUT JR. (1922–2007)

Compassion

How far you go in life depends on your being tender with the young, compassionate with the aged, sympathetic with the striving, and tolerant of the weak and the strong—because someday you will have been all of these.
GEORGE WASHINGTON CARVER (1864–1943)

If you want others to be happy, practice compassion. If you want to be happy, practice compassion.
THE DALAI LAMA (1935–)

A human being is part of a whole, called by us the Universe, a part limited in time and space. He experiences himself, his thoughts and feelings, as something separated from the rest—a kind of optical delusion of his consciousness. This delusion is a kind of prison for us, restricting us to our personal desires and to affection for a few persons nearest us. Our task must be to free ourselves from this prison by widening our circles of compassion to embrace all living creatures and the whole of nature in its beauty.
ALBERT EINSTEIN (1879–1955)

The measure of a country's greatness is its ability to retain compassion in times of crisis.
THURGOOD MARSHALL (1908–1993)

Compassion is the basis of all morality.
ARTHUR SCHOPENHAUER (1788–1860)

Until he extends his circle of compassion to include all living things, man will not himself find peace.
DR. ALBERT SCHWEITZER (1875–1965)

Competition

Competition is a painful thing, but it produces great results.
JERRY FLINT (1931–)

Competition is the keen cutting edge of business, always shaving away at costs.
HENRY FORD (1863–1947)

My grandfather once told me that there were two kinds of people: those who do the work and those who take the credit. He told me to try to be in the first group; there was much less competition.
INDIRA GANDHI (1917–1984)

The ultimate good desired is better reached by free trade in ideas [and] the best test of truth is the power of the thought to get itself accepted in the competition of the market.
OLIVER WENDELL HOLMES JR. (1841–1935)

Competition is not only the basis of protection to the consumer, but is the incentive to progress.
HERBERT HOOVER (1874–1964)

Science would be ruined if (like sports) it were to put competition above everything else, and if it were to clarify the rules of competition by withdrawing entirely into narrowly defined specialties. The rare scholars who are nomads-by-choice are essential to the intellectual welfare of the settled disciplines.
BENOIT MANDELBROT (1924–)

The more the division of labor and the application of machinery extend, the more does competition extend among the workers, the more do their wages shrink together.
KARL MARX (1818–1883)

Friendships born on the field of athletic strife are the real gold of competition. Awards become corroded, friends gather no dust.
JESSE OWENS (1913–1980)

Competition is a sin.
JOHN D. ROCKEFELLER (1839–1937)

Life is nothing but a competition to be the criminal rather than the victim.
BERTRAND RUSSELL (1872–1970)

Competition is easier to accept if you realize it is not an act of oppression or abrasion—I've worked with my best friends in direct competition.
DIANE SAWYER (1945–)

The biggest things are always the easiest to do because there is no competition.
WILLIAM VAN HORNE (1843–1915)

Complaints

There are times in life when, instead of complaining, you do something about your complaints.
RITA DOVE (1952–)

We took risks. We knew we took them. Things have come out against us. We have no cause for complaint.
ROBERT FROST (1874–1963)

Complaints about content about a program that doesn't even exist is like complaining about a referee's call in a game that has not yet been played.
MARK E. HYMAN (1958–)

To hear complaints is tiresome to the miserable and the happy.
SAMUEL JOHNSON (1709–1784)

Take away your opinion, and then there is taken away the complaint, "I have been harmed." Take away the complaint, "I have been harmed," and the harm is taken away.
MARCUS AURELIUS ANTONINUS (121–180)

Our present time is indeed a criticizing and critical time, hovering between the wish, and the inability to believe. Our complaints are like arrows shot up into the air at no target: and with no purpose they only fall back upon our own heads and destroy ourselves.
SIR WILLIAM TEMPLE (1628–1699)

Computers

The computer offers another kind of creativity. You cannot ignore the creativity that computer technology can bring. But you need to be able to move between those two different worlds.
TADAO ANDO (1941–)

I do not fear computers. I fear the lack of them.
ISAAC ASIMOV (1920–1992)

Part of the inhumanity of the computer is that, once it is competently programmed and working smoothly, it is completely honest.
ISAAC ASIMOV (1920–1992)

The most likely way for the world to be destroyed, most experts agree, is by accident. That's where we come in; we're computer professionals. We cause accidents.
NATHANIEL BORENSTEIN (1957–)

Programming today is a race between software engineers striving to build bigger and better idiot-proof programs, and the Universe trying to produce bigger and better idiots. So far, the Universe is winning.
RICK COOK (1944–), *The Wizardry Compiled*

Computer Science is no more about computers than astronomy is about telescopes.
EDSGER W. DIJKSTRA (1930–2002)

The computer is a moron.
PETER F. DRUCKER (1909–2005)

The great thing about a computer notebook is that no matter how much you stuff into it, it doesn't get bigger or heavier.
BILL GATES (1955–), *Business @ The Speed of Thought*

I think computer viruses should count as life. I think it says something about human nature that the only form of life we have created so far is purely destructive. We've created life in our own image.
STEPHEN HAWKING (1942–)

Home computers are being called upon to perform many new functions, including the consumption of homework formerly eaten by the dog.
DOUG LARSON (1902–1981)

Not even computers will replace committees, because committees buy computers.
EDWARD SHEPHERD MEAD (1914–1994)

There is no reason for any individual to have a computer in his home.
KEN OLSEN (1926–)

To err is human—and to blame it on a computer is even more so.
ROBERT ORBEN (1927–)

The computing field is always in need of new clichés.
ALAN PERLIS (1922–1990)

Computers are useless. They can only give you answers.
PABLO PICASSO (1881–1973)

Imagine if every Thursday your shoes exploded if you tied them the usual way. This happens to us all the time with computers, and nobody thinks of complaining.
JEF RASKIN (1943–2005)

Computers make it easier to do a lot of things, but most of the things they make it easier to do don't need to be done.
ANDY ROONEY (1919–)

All programmers are playwrights and all computers are lousy actors.
ANONYMOUS

In a few minutes a computer can make a mistake so great that it would have taken many men many months to equal it.
ANONYMOUS

Conceit

Self-conceit may lead to self destruction.
AESOP (620–560 BC)

The smaller the mind the greater the conceit.
AESOP (620–560 BC)

Conceit spoils the finest genius. There is not much danger that real talent or goodness will be overlooked long; even if it is, the consciousness of possessing and using it well should satisfy one, and the great charm of all power is modesty.
LOUISA MAY ALCOTT (1832–1888)

Conceit is God's gift to little men.
BRUCE BARTON (1886–1967)

The first sin in our universe was Lucifer's self conceit.
THOMAS CARLYLE (1795–1881)

We can bear to be deprived of everything but our self-conceit.
WILLIAM HAZLITT (1778–1830)

Conceit causes more conversation than wit.
FRANÇOIS DE LA ROCHEFOUCAULD (1613–1680)

Pride and conceit were the original sins of man.
ALAIN-RENÉ LESAGE (1668–1747)

Whenever nature leaves a hole in a person's mind, she generally plasters it over with a thick coat of self-conceit.
HENRY WADSWORTH LONGFELLOW (1807–1882)

Let your actions always speak for you, but be forever on guard against the terrible traps of false pride and conceit that can halt your progress. The next time you are tempted to boast, just place your fist in a full pail of water, and when you remove it, the hole remaining will give you a correct measure of your importance.
OG MANDINO (1923–1996)

Conceit may puff a man up, but never prop him up.
JOHN RUSKIN (1819–1900)

Conceit in weakest bodies works the strongest.
WILLIAM SHAKESPEARE (1564–1616), *Hamlet*

Conceit, more rich in matter than in words, brags of his substance: they are but beggars who can count their worth.
WILLIAM SHAKESPEARE (1564–1616), *Romeo and Juliet*

Conceit is incompatible with understanding.
LEO TOLSTOY (1828–1910)

There is a difference between conceit and confidence. Conceit is bragging about yourself. Confidence means you believe you can get the job done.
JOHNNY UNITAS (1933–2002)

Talent is God given. Be humble. Fame is man-given. Be grateful. Conceit is self-given. Be careful.
JOHN WOODEN (1910–)

Confessions

Because interrogations are intended to coerce confessions, interrogators feel themselves justified in using their coercive means. Consistency regarding the technique is not important; inducing anxiety and fear is the point.
ALDRICH AMES (1941–)

Where all are guilty, no one is; confessions of collective guilt are the best possible safeguard against the discovery of culprits, and the very magnitude of the crime the best excuse for doing nothing.
HANNAH ARENDT (1906–1975)

Confess your sins to the Lord and you will be forgiven; confess them to man and you will be laughed at.
JOSH BILLINGS (1818–1885)

Confession is good for the soul only in the sense that a tweed coat is good for dandruff—it is a palliative rather than a remedy.
PETER DE VRIES (1910–1993)

All confessions are Odysseys.
RAYMOND QUENEAU (1903–1976)

Every conceivable cruel method of blackmail was used against me to obtain by force and at all costs confessions and statements both about comrades who had been arrested, and about political activities.
ERNST THALMANN (1886–1944)

There is no refuge from confession but suicide; and suicide is confession.
DANIEL WEBSTER (1782–1852)

It is the confession, not the priest, that gives us absolution
OSCAR WILDE (1854–1900)

Confession is the first step to repentance.
ENGLISH PROVERB

Confidence

It seems to me that people have vast potential. Most people can do extraordinary things if they have the confidence or take the risks. Yet most people don't. They sit in front of the telly and treat life as if it goes on forever.
PHILIP ADAMS (1939–)

Having once decided to achieve a certain task, achieve it at all costs of tedium and distaste. The gain in self-confidence of having accomplished a tiresome labor is immense.
ARNOLD BENNETT (1867–1931)

One who has lost confidence can lose nothing more.
PIERRE-CLAUDE-VICTOR BOISTE (1765–1824)

You have to have confidence in your ability, and then be tough enough to follow through.
ROSALYNN CARTER (1927–)

If I have lost confidence in myself, I have the universe against me.
RALPH WALDO EMERSON (1803–1882)

I was always looking outside myself for strength and confidence, but it comes from within. It is there all the time.
ANNA FREUD (1895–1982)

If you have no confidence in self, you are twice defeated in the race of life. With confidence, you have won even before you have started.
MARCUS GARVEY (1887–1940)

Every time you don't follow your inner guidance, you feel a loss of energy, loss of power, a sense of spiritual deadness.
SHAKTI GAWAIN (1948–)

There are admirable potentialities in every human being. Believe in your strength and your youth. Learn to repeat endlessly to yourself, "It all depends on me."
ANDRÉ GIDE (1869–1951)

Attempt easy tasks as if they were difficult, and difficult as if they were easy; in the one case that confidence may not fall asleep, in the other that it may not be dismayed.
BALTASAR GRACIAN (1601–1658)

As is our confidence, so is our capacity.
WILLIAM HAZLITT (1778–1830)

Skill and confidence are an unconquered army.
GEORGE HERBERT (1593–1633)

Self-confidence is the first requisite to great undertakings.
SAMUEL JOHNSON (1709–1784)

The confidence which we have in ourselves gives birth to much of that which we have in others.
FRANÇOIS DE LA ROCHEFOUCAULD (1613–1680)

Confidence is contagious. So is lack of confidence.
VINCE LOMBARDI (1913–1970)

Getting ahead in a difficult profession requires avid faith in yourself. That is why some people with mediocre talent, but with great inner drive, go much further than people with vastly superior talent.
SOPHIA LOREN (1934–)

Confidence is courage at ease.
DANIEL MAHER (1881–1916)

Confidence imparts a wonderful inspiration to its possessor.
JOHN MILTON (1608–1674)

Concentration comes out of a combination of confidence and hunger.
ARNOLD PALMER (1929–)

Believe in yourself! Have faith in your abilities! Without a humble but reasonable confidence in your own powers you cannot be successful or happy
NORMAN VINCENT PEALE (1898–1993)

Confidence … thrives only on honesty, on honor, on the sacredness of obligation, on faithful performance. Without them, it cannot live.
FRANKLIN D. ROOSEVELT (1882–1945)

Confidence awakens confidence.
FRIEDRICH VON SACHSEN (1463–1525)

Experience tells you what to do; confidence allows you to do it.
STAN SMITH (1946–)

All you need in this life is ignorance and confidence; then success is sure.
MARK TWAIN (1835–1910)

Confidence cannot find a place wherein to rest in safety.
VIRGIL (C. 70–19 BC)

The man who has confidence in himself gains the confidence of others.
HASIDIC PROVERB

Conflict

If we were to wake up some morning and find that everyone was the same race, creed and color, we would find some other cause for prejudice by noon.
GEORGE D. AIKEN (1892–1984)

What begins with the failure to uphold the dignity of one life all too often ends with a calamity for entire nations.
KOFI ANNAN (1938–)

I count him braver who overcomes his desires than him who conquers his enemies; for the hardest victory is the victory over self.
ARISTOTLE (384–322 BC)

An eye for an eye only leads to more blindness.
MARGARET ATWOOD (1939–)

My wife, Mary, and I have been married for forty-seven years and not once have we had an argument serious enough to consider divorce. Murder, yes, but divorce, never.
JACK BENNY (1894–1974)

Nothing is given to man on earth—struggle is built into the nature of life, and conflict is possible—the hero is the man who lets no obstacle prevent him from pursuing the values he has chosen.
ANDREW BERNSTEIN (1949–)

The greatest conflicts are not between two people but between one person and himself.
GARTH BROOKS (1956–)

Arguments are like firearms which a man may keep at home but should not carry about with him.
SAMUEL BUTLER (1835–1902)

Difficulties are meant to rouse, not discourage. The human spirit is to grow strong by conflict.
WILLIAM ELLERY CHANNING (1780–1842)

An appeaser is one who feeds a crocodile, hoping it will eat him last.
SIR WINSTON CHURCHILL (1874–1965)

I have benefited greatly from criticism, and at no time have I suffered a lack thereof.
SIR WINSTON CHURCHILL (1874–1965)

The hottest places in Hell are reserved for those who in time of great moral crises maintain their neutrality.
DANTE ALIGHIERI (1265–1321)

Conflict is the gadfly of thought. It stirs us to observation and memory. It instigates to invention. It shocks us out of sheeplike passivity, and sets us at noting and contriving.
JOHN DEWEY (1859–1952)

We are not going to deal with the violence in our communities, our homes, and our nation, until we learn to deal with the basic ethic of how we resolve our disputes and to place an emphasis on peace in the way we relate to one another.
MARIAN WRIGHT EDELMAN (1939–)

Great ideas often receive violent opposition from mediocre minds.
ALBERT EINSTEIN (1879–1955)

Whenever two good people argue over principles, they are both right.
MARIE VON EBNER-ESCHENBACH (1830–1916)

There are three ways of dealing with difference: domination, compromise, and integration. By domination only one side gets what it wants; by compromise neither side gets what it wants; by integration we find a way by which both sides may get what they wish.
MARY PARKER FOLLETT (1868–1933)

You can't shake hands with a clenched fist.
INDIRA GANDHI (1917–1984)

Every fight is on some level a fight between differing "angles of vision" illuminating the same truth.
MAHATMA GANDHI (1869–1948)

Non-cooperation is a measure of discipline and sacrifice, and it demands respect for the opposite views.
MAHATMA GANDHI (1869–1948)

Truth springs from argument amongst friends.
DAVID HUME (1711–1776)

Whenever you're in conflict with someone, there is one factor that can make the difference between damaging your relationship and deepening it. That factor is attitude.
WILLIAM JAMES (1842–1910)

True peace is not merely the absence of tension: it is the presence of justice.
MARTIN LUTHER KING JR. (1929–1968)

Pick battles big enough to matter, small enough to win.
JONATHAN KOZOL (1936–), *On Being a Teacher*

All married couples should learn the art of battle as they should learn the art of making love. Good battle is objective and honest—never vicious or cruel. Good battle is healthy and constructive, and brings to a marriage the principle of equal partnership.
ANN LANDERS (1918–2002)

Conflict is inevitable, but combat is optional.
MAX LUCADO (1955–)

Conflict itself is, of course, a sign of health as you would know if you ever met really apathetic people, really hopeless people, people who have given up hoping, striving, coping.
ABRAHAM MASLOW (1908–1970)

There is no squabbling so violent as that between people who accepted an idea yesterday and those who will accept the same idea tomorrow.
CHRISTOPHER MORLEY (1890–1957)

'Tis the business of little minds to shrink; but he whose heart is firm, and whose conscience approves his conduct, will pursue his principles unto death.
THOMAS PAINE (1737–1809)

The truth is that our finest moments are most likely to occur when we are feeling deeply uncomfortable, unhappy, or unfulfilled. For it is only in such moments, propelled by our discomfort, that we are likely to step out of our ruts and start searching for different ways or truer answers.
M. SCOTT PECK (1936–2005)

I found one day in school a boy of medium size ill-treating a smaller boy. I expostulated, but he replied: "The bigs hit me, so I hit the babies; that's fair." In these words he epitomized the history of the human race.
BERTRAND RUSSELL (1872–1970)

Peace is not the absence of conflict but the presence of creative alternatives for responding to conflict—alternatives to passive or aggressive responses, alternatives to violence.
DOROTHY THOMPSON (1893–1961)

A good manager doesn't try to eliminate conflict; he tries to keep it from wasting the energies of his people. If you're the boss and your people fight you openly when they think that you are wrong—that's healthy.
ROBERT TOWNSEND (1957–)

Have you learned lessons only of those who admired you, and were tender with you, and stood aside for you? Have you not learned great lessons from those who braced themselves against you, and disputed the passage with you?
WALT WHITMAN (1819–1892)

Conformity

The real end of prayer is not so much to get this or that single desire granted, as to put human life into full and joyful conformity with the will of God.
CHARLES BENT (1799–1847)

Has there ever been a society which has died of dissent? Several have died of conformity in our lifetime.
JACOB BRONOWSKI (1908–1974)

The reward for conformity was that everyone liked you except yourself.
RITA MAE BROWN (1944–), *Venus Envy*

To seek understanding before taking action, yet to trust my instincts when action is called for. Never to avoid danger from fear, never to seek out danger for its own sake. Never to conform to fashion from fear of eccentricity, never to be eccentric from fear of conformity.
STEVEN BRUST (1955–)

How I hate those who are dedicated to producing conformity.
WILLIAM S. BURROUGHS (1914–1997)

Case by case, we find that conformity is the easy way, and the path to privilege and prestige; dissidence carries personal costs.
NOAM CHOMSKY (1928–)

A self that is only differentiated—not integrated—may attain great individual accomplishments, but risks being mired in self-centered egotism. By the same token, a person whose self is based exclusively on integration will be well connected and secure, but lack autonomous individuality. Only when a person invests equal amounts of psychic energy in these two processes and avoids both selfishness and conformity is the self likely to reflect complexity.
MIHALY CSIKSZENTMIHALYI (1934–), *Flow: The Psychology of Optimal Experience*

Follow the path of the unsafe, independent thinker. Expose your ideas to the dangers of controversy. Speak your mind and fear less the label of "crackpot" than the stigma of conformity. And on issues that seem important to you, stand up and be counted at any cost.
CHAUNCEY DEPEW (1834–1928)

We do not quite say that the new is more valuable because it fits in; but its fitting in is a test of its value—a test, it is true, which can only be slowly and cautiously applied, for we are none of us infallible judges of conformity.
T. S. ELIOT (1888–1965)

A man must consider what a rich realm he abdicates when he becomes a conformist.
RALPH WALDO EMERSON (1803–1882)

Society everywhere is in conspiracy against the manhood of every one of its members. The virtue in most request is conformity. Self-reliance is its aversion. It loves not realities and creators, but names and customs.
RALPH WALDO EMERSON (1803–1882)

I, for one, hope that youth will again revolt and again demoralize the dead weight of conformity that now lies upon us.
HOWARD MUMFORD JONES (1892–1980)

Conformity is the jailer of freedom and the enemy of growth.
JOHN F. KENNEDY (1917–1963)

I find the earth to be a place of misery in which I am surrounded by the conformity that kills society.
MATT LEBLANC (1967–)

If religion were true, its followers would not try to bludgeon their young into an artificial conformity; but would merely insist on their unbending quest for truth, irrespective of artificial backgrounds or practical consequences.
H. P. LOVECRAFT (1890–1937)

I have a high state of resentment for the conformity in this country. If you're not married and having children, it's like your life is empty or you're a communist meanie.
BILL MAHER (1956–)

The opposite of courage in our society is not cowardice, it is conformity.
ROLLO MAY (1909–1994)

Group conformity scares the pants off me because it's so often a prelude to cruelty towards anyone who doesn't want to—or can't—join the Big Parade.
BETTE MIDLER (1945–)

It may be that we are puppets-puppets controlled by the strings of society. But at least we are puppets with perception, with awareness. And perhaps our awareness is the first step to our liberation.
STANLEY MILGRAM (1933–1984)

The surest way to corrupt a youth is to instruct him to hold in higher esteem those who think alike than those who think differently.
FRIEDRICH NIETZSCHE (1844–1900)

There is a level of cowardice lower than that of the conformist: the fashionable non-conformist.
AYN RAND (1905–1982)

A big element of what they regard as conformity is simply a desire to have an audience.
KAREL REISZ (1926–2002)

Morality is a test of our conformity rather than our integrity.
JANE RULE (1931–)

It's both rebellion and conformity that attack you with success.
AMY TAN (1952–)

Endeavor to be always patient of the faults and imperfections of others for thou has many faults and imperfections of thine own that require forbearance. If thou are not able to make thyself that which thou wishest, how canst thou expect to mold another in conformity to thy will?
THOMAS À KEMPIS (1380–1471)

Any fool can make a rule, and every fool will mind it.
HENRY DAVID THOREAU (1817–1862)

Whenever you find yourself on the side of the majority, it is time to pause and reflect.
MARK TWAIN (1835–1910)

In America, through pressure of conformity, there is freedom of choice, but nothing to choose from.
PETER USTINOV (1921–2004)

The race of man, while sheep in credulity, are wolves for conformity.
CARL VAN DOREN (1885–1950)

If there is anything the nonconformist hates worse than a conformist, it's another nonconformist who doesn't conform to the prevailing standard of nonconformity.
BILL VAUGHN (1915–1977)

Our wretched species is so made that those who walk on the well-trodden path always throw stones at those who are showing a new road.
VOLTAIRE (1694–1778)

To be one's self, and unafraid whether right or wrong, is more admirable than the easy cowardice of surrender to conformity.
IRVING WALLACE (1916–1990)

We are half ruined by conformity, but we should be wholly ruined without it.
CHARLES DUDLEY WARNER (1829–1900)

If you stand up and be counted, from time to time you may get yourself knocked down. But remember this: A man flattened by an opponent can get up again. A man flattened by conformity stays down for good.
THOMAS J. WATSON (1874–1956)

A red rose is not selfish because it wants to be a red rose. It would be horribly selfish if it wanted all the other flowers in the garden to be both red and roses.
OSCAR WILDE (1954–1900)

The so-called modern education, with all its defects, however, does others so much more good than it does the Negro, because it has been worked out in conformity to the needs of those who have enslaved and oppressed weaker peoples.
CARTER G. WOODSON (1875–1950)

Conscience

Conscience and reputation are two things. Conscience is due to yourself, reputation to your neighbour.
SAINT AUGUSTINE (354–430)

Conscience is the perfect interpreter of life.
KARL BARTH (1886–1968)

If all the world hated you and believed you wicked, while your own conscience approved of you and absolved you from guilt, you would not be without friends.
CHARLOTTE BRONTË (1816–1855), *Jane Eyre*

Destiny is but a phrase of the weak human heart—the dark apology for every error. The strong and virtuous admit no destiny. On earth conscience guides; in heaven God watches. And destiny is but the phantom we invoke to silence the one and dethrone the other.
SIR EDWARD G. BULWER-LYTTON (1803–1873)

All a man can betray is his conscience.
JOSEPH CONRAD (1857–1924)

The conscience of a people is their power.
JOHN DRYDEN (1631–1700)

Conscience is what makes a boy tell his mother before his sister does.
EVAN ESAR (1899–1995)

There is one thing alone that stands the brunt of life throughout its course: a quiet conscience.
EURIPIDES (C. 480–406 BC), *Hippolytus*

Conscience is a coward, and those faults it has not strength enough to prevent it seldom has justice enough to accuse.
OLIVER GOLDSMITH (1730–1774)

I cannot and will not cut my conscience to fit this year's fashions.
LILLIAN HELLMAN (1905–1984)

Courage without conscience is a wild beast.
ROBERT GREEN INGERSOLL (1833–1899)

The real satisfaction which praise can afford, is when what is repeated aloud agrees with the whispers of conscience, by showing us that we have not endeavored to deserve well in vain.
SAMUEL JOHNSON (1709–1784)

I submit that an individual who breaks a law that conscience tells him is unjust, and who willingly accepts the penalty of imprisonment in order to arouse the conscience of the community over its injustice, is in reality expressing the highest respect for the law.
MARTIN LUTHER KING JR. (1929–1968)

A lot of people mistake a short memory for a clear conscience.
DOUG LARSON (1902–1981)

Before I can live with other folks, I've got to live with myself. The one thing that doesn't abide by majority rule is a person's conscience.
HARPER LEE (1926–), *To Kill a Mockingbird*

Conscience is the inner voice that warns us somebody may be looking.
H. L. MENCKEN (1880–1956), *A Mencken Chrestomathy*

Give me the liberty to know, to utter, and to argue freely according to conscience, above all liberties.
JOHN MILTON (1608–1674)

Justice requires that to lawfully constituted Authority there be given that respect and obedience which is its due; that the laws which are made shall be in wise conformity with the common good; and that, as a matter of conscience all men shall render obedience to these laws.
POPE PIUS XI (1857–1939)

There is no witness so dreadful, no accuser so terrible as the conscience that dwells in the heart of every man.
POLYBIUS (205–118 BC), *History*

Cowardice asks: Is it safe? Expediency asks: Is it politic? But Conscience asks: Is it right?
WILLIAM PUNSHON (1824–1881)

Fear is the tax that conscience pays to guilt.
GEORGE SEWELL (1924–2007)

The play's the thing
Wherein I'll catch the conscience of the king.
WILLIAM SHAKESPEARE (1564–1616), *Hamlet*

I feel within me a peace above all earthly dignities, a still and quiet conscience.
WILLIAM SHAKESPEARE (1564–1616), *Henry VIII*

All Reformers, however strict their social conscience, live in houses just as big as they can pay for.
LOGAN PEARSALL SMITH (1865–1946), *Afterthoughts*

Most people sell their souls, and live with a good conscience on the proceeds.
LOGAN PEARSALL SMITH (1865–1946), *Afterthoughts*

Senescent judges show how patriotic they are by passing out hard sentences for tearing up a draft card or following one's conscience according to the principles established by our country at the Nuremburg trials.
ALBERT SZENT-GYORGYI (1893–1986), *The Crazy Ape*

It is by the goodness of God that in our country we have those three unspeakably precious things: freedom of speech, freedom of conscience, and the prudence never to practice either of them.
MARK TWAIN (1835–1910), *Following the Equator*

[T]he safest course is to do nothing against one's conscience. With this secret, we can enjoy life and have no fear from death.
VOLTAIRE (1694–1778)

Labor to keep alive in your breast that little spark of celestial fire called conscience.
GEORGE WASHINGTON (1732–1799)

Conscience and cowardice are really the same things. Conscience is the trade-name of the firm. That is all.
OSCAR WILDE (1854–1900)

Consciousness

Dignity consists not in possessing honors, but in the consciousness that we deserve them.
ARISTOTLE (384–322 BC)

The real questions are the ones that obtrude upon your consciousness whether you like it or not, the ones that make your mind start vibrating like a jackhammer, the ones that you "come to terms with" only to discover that they are still there. The real questions refuse to be placated. They barge into your life at the times when it seems most important for them to stay away. They are the questions asked most frequently and answered most inadequately, the ones that reveal their true natures slowly, reluctantly, most often against your will.
INGRID BENGIS (1944–)

Beware of sentimental alliances where the consciousness of good deeds is the only compensation for noble sacrifices.
OTTO VON BISMARCK (1815–1898)

Our unconscious is not more animal than our conscious, it is often even more human.
EDWARD BOND (1934–)

An unconscious consciousness is no more a contradiction in terms than an unseen case of seeing.
FRANZ CLEMENS BRENTANO (1838–1917)

When we quit thinking primarily about ourselves and our own self-preservation, we undergo a truly heroic transformation of consciousness.
JOSEPH CAMPBELL (1904–1987)

Inspiration may be a form of superconsciousness, or perhaps of subconsciousness—I wouldn't know. But I am sure it is the antithesis of self-consciousness.
AARON COPLAND (1900–1990)

Entropy is the normal state of consciousness—a condition that is neither useful nor enjoyable.
MIHALY CSIKSZENTMIHALYI (1934–), *Flow: The Psychology of Optimal Experience*

Pleasure is an important component of the quality of life, but by itself it does not bring happiness. Pleasure helps to maintain order, but by itself cannot create a new order in consciousness.
MIHALY CSIKSZENTMIHALYI (1934–), *Flow: The Psychology of Optimal Experience*

The defining function of the artist is to cherish consciousness.
MAX EASTMAN (1883–1969)

A human being is part of a whole, called by us the Universe, a part limited in time and space. He experiences himself, his thoughts and feelings, as something separated from the rest—a kind of optical delusion of his consciousness. This delusion is a kind of prison for us, restricting us to our personal desires and to affection for a few persons nearest us. Our task must be to free ourselves from this prison by widening our circles of compassion to embrace all living creatures and the whole of nature in its beauty.
ALBERT EINSTEIN (1879–1955)

Knowledge is not a series of self-consistent theories that converges toward an ideal view; it is rather an ever increasing ocean of mutually incompatible (and perhaps even incommensurable) alternatives, each single theory, each fairy tale, each myth that is part of the collection forcing the others into greater articulation and all of them contributing, via this process of competition, to the development of our consciousness.
PAUL FEYERABEND (1924–1994)

Life is consciousness.
EMMET FOX (1886–1951)

God must become an activity in our consciousness.
JOEL S. GOLDSMITH (1892–1964)

Human consciousness arose but a minute before midnight on the geological clock. Yet we mayflies try to bend an ancient world to our purposes, ignorant perhaps of the messages buried in its long history. Let us hope that we are still in the early morning of our April day.
STEPHEN JAY GOULD (1941–2002)

Consciousness is a phase of mental life which arises in connection with the formation of new habits. When habit is formed, consciousness only interferes to spoil our performance.
WILLIAM RALPH INGE (1860–1954)

In studying the history of the human mind one is impressed again and again by the fact that the growth of the mind is the widening of the range of consciousness, and that each step forward has been a most painful and laborious achievement. One could almost say that nothing is more hateful to man than to give up even a particle of his unconsciousness. Ask those who have tried to introduce a new idea!
CARL JUNG (1875–1961)

A loving person lives in a loving world. A hostile person lives in a hostile world. Everyone you meet is your mirror.
KEN KEYES JR. (1921–1995), *Handbook of Higher Consciousness*

I never took hallucinogenic drugs because I never wanted my consciousness expanded one unnecessary iota.
FRAN LEBOWITZ (1950–)

That consciousness is everything and that all things begin with a thought. That we are responsible for our own fate, we reap what we sow, we get what we give, we pull in what we put out. I know these things for sure.
MADONNA (1958–)

Every extension of knowledge arises from making the conscious the unconscious.
FRIEDRICH NIETZSCHE (1844–1900)

That which you call your soul or spirit is your consciousness, and that which you call "free will" is your mind's freedom to think or not, the only will you have, your only freedom, the choice that controls all the choices you make and determines your life and your character.
AYN RAND (1905–1982), *Atlas Shrugged*

Happiness is that state of consciousness which proceeds from the achievement of one's values.
AYN RAND (1905–1982)

I used to wake up at 4 a.m. and start sneezing, sometimes for five hours. I tried to find out what sort of allergy I had but finally came to the conclusion that it must be an allergy to consciousness.
JAMES THURBER (1894–1961)

The only thing that sustains one through life is the consciousness of the immense inferiority of everybody else, and this is a feeling that I have always cultivated.
OSCAR WILDE (1854–1900), *The Remarkable Rocket*

Conservation

True conservation provides for wise use by the general public. The American people do not want our resources preserved for the exclusive use of the wealthy. These land and water resources belong to the people, and people of all income levels should have easy access to them.
GEORGE D. AIKEN (1892–1984)

Energy conservation is the foundation of energy independence.
TOM ALLEN (1945–)

Conservation is a state of harmony between men and land.
ALDO LEOPOLD (1887–1948)

By encouraging conservation, increasing investments in clean, renewable sources of energy, and promoting increased domestic production of oil and gas, we can build a more secure future for our country.
RON LEWIS (1946–)

Conservation is humanity caring for the future.
NANCY NEWHALL (1908–1974)

Conservation means the wise use of the earth and its resources for the lasting good of men.
GIFFORD PINCHOT (1865–1946)

The outgrowth of conservation, the inevitable result, is national efficiency.
GIFFORD PINCHOT (1865–1946)

Conservatives

The most radical revolutionary will become a conservative the day after the revolution.
HANNAH ARENDT (1906–1975)

A conservative government is an organized hypocrisy.
BENJAMIN DISRAELI (1804–1881)

I am a Conservative to preserve all that is good in our constitution, a Radical to remove all that is bad. I seek to preserve property and to respect order, and I equally decry the appeal to the passions of the many or the prejudices of the few.
BENJAMIN DISRAELI (1804–1881)

Men are conservatives when they are least vigorous, or when they are most luxurious. They are conservatives after dinner.
RALPH WALDO EMERSON (1803–1882), *New England Reformers*

I never dared to be radical when young
For fear it would make me conservative when old.
ROBERT FROST (1874–1963), "Ten Mills"

When you are right you cannot be too radical; when you are wrong, you cannot be too conservative.
MARTIN LUTHER KING JR. (1929–1968)

Radical conservatives want to police bedrooms.
ROBERT REICH (1946–)

A conservative is a man with two perfectly good legs who, however, has never learned to walk forward.
FRANKLIN D. ROOSEVELT (1882–1945)

The true conservative is the man who has a real concern for injustices and takes thought against the day of reckoning.
FRANKLIN D. ROOSEVELT (1882–1945)

Conservatism is the blind and fear-filled worship of dead radicals.
MARK TWAIN (1835–1910)

The radical of one century is the conservative of the next. The radical invents the views. When he has worn them out the conservative adopts them.
MARK TWAIN (1835–1910)

It only takes 20 years for a liberal to become a conservative without changing a single idea.
ROBERT ANTON WILSON (1932–2007)

A conservative is a man who sits and thinks, mostly sits.
WOODROW WILSON (1856–1924)

Consistency

One isn't necessarily born with courage, but one is born with potential. Without courage, we cannot practice any other virtue with consistency. We can't be kind, true, merciful, generous, or honest.
MAYA ANGELOU (1928–)

Consistency requires you to be as ignorant today as you were a year ago.
BERNARD BERENSON (1865–1959)

The man who sees consistency in things is a wit; the man who sees the inconsistency in things is a humorist.
G. K. CHESTERTON (1874–1936)

There must be consistency in direction.
W. EDWARDS DEMING (1900–1993)

A foolish consistency is the hobgoblin of little minds, adored by little statesmen and philosophers and divines.
RALPH WALDO EMERSON (1803–1882), *Self-Reliance*

Consistency is the quality of a stagnant mind.
JOHN SLOAN (1871–1951)

What, then, is the true Gospel of consistency? Change. Who is the really consistent man? The man who changes. Since change is the law of his being, he cannot be consistent if stuck in a rut.
MARK TWAIN (1835–1910)

Consistency is the last refuge of the unimaginative.
OSCAR WILDE (1854–1900)

Consumerism

Violence is hidden within democratic structures because they are not radically democratic—Western democracy is merely a domestic convenience of consumerism.
EDWARD BOND (1934–)

My first rule of consumerism is never to buy anything you can't make your children carry.
BILL BRYSON (1951–)

It is the logic of consumerism that undermines the values of loyalty and permanence and promotes a different set of values that is destructive of family life.
CHRISTOPHER LASCH (1932–1994)

The corruption of the American soul is consumerism.
BEN NICHOLSON (1894–1982)

By continually pushing the message that we have the right to gratification now, consumerism at its most expansive encouraged a demand for fulfillment that could not so easily be contained by products.
ELLEN WILLIS (1941–2006)

Contemplation

I live not in dreams but in contemplation of a reality that is perhaps the future.
RAINER MARIA RILKE (1875–1926), *Selected Letters of Rainer Maria Rilke*

Art is contemplation. It is the pleasure of the mind which searches into nature and which there divines the spirit of which Nature herself is animated.
AUGUSTE RODIN (1840–1917)

I pray you bear me henceforth from the noise and
 rumour of the field,
Where I may think the remnant of my thoughts in
 peace,
And part of this body and my soul with
Contemplation and devout desires.
WILLIAM SHAKESPEARE (1564–1616), *King John*

Contempt

Of all afflictions, the worst is self-contempt.
BERTHOLD AUERBACH (1812–1882)

An appeal is when you ask one court to show its contempt for another court.
FINLEY PETER DUNNE (1867–1936)

He had heard people speak contemptuously of money: he wondered if they had ever tried to do without it.
W. SOMERSET MAUGHAM (1874–1965), *Of Human Bondage*

If there be no great love in the beginning, yet heaven may decrease it upon better acquaintance, when we are married and have more occasion to know one another: I hope, upon familiarity will grow more contempt.
WILLIAM SHAKESPEARE (1564–1616), *The Merry Wives of Windsor*

I have nothing but contempt for the kind of governor who is afraid, for whatever reason, to follow the course that he knows is best for the State; and as for the man who sets private friendship above the public welfare—I have no use for him either.
SOPHOCLES (496–406 BC), *Antigone*

Familiarity breeds contempt—and children.
MARK TWAIN (1835–1910)

Conversation

Good nature is more agreeable in conversation than wit, and gives a certain air to the countenance which is more amiable than beauty.
JOSEPH ADDISON (1672–1719)

Method is not less requisite in conversation than in writing, provided a man would talk to make himself understood.
JOSEPH ADDISON (1672–1719)

Too often travel, instead of broadening the mind, merely lengthens the conversation.
ELIZABETH DREW (1935–)

The great secret of succeeding in conversation is to admire little, to hear much; always to distrust our own reason, and sometimes that of our friends; never to pretend to wit, but to make that of others appear as much as possibly we can; to hearken.
BENJAMIN FRANKLIN (1706–1790)

Education begins a gentleman, conversation completes him.
THOMAS FULLER (1608–1661), *Gnomologia*

Wit is the salt of conversation, not the food.
WILLIAM HAZLITT (1778–1830)

Don't knock the weather. If it didn't change once in a while, nine out of ten people couldn't start a conversation.
KIN HUBBARD (1868–1930)

Questioning is not the mode of conversation among gentlemen.
SAMUEL JOHNSON (1709–1784)

No animal should ever jump up on the dining-room furniture unless absolutely certain that he can hold his own in the conversation.
FRAN LEBOWITZ (1950–)

Let us make a special effort to stop communicating with each other, so we can have some conversation.
JUDITH MARTIN (1938–)

Most conversations are simply monologues delivered in the presence of witnesses.
MARGARET MILLAR (1915–1994)

There is no conversation more boring than the one where everybody agrees.
MICHEL DE MONTAIGNE (1533–1592)

The real art of conversation is not only to say the right thing at the right place but to leave unsaid the wrong thing at the tempting moment.
DOROTHY NEVILL (1826–1913)

I often quote myself. It adds spice to my conversation.
GEORGE BERNARD SHAW (1856–1950)

Argument, as usually managed, is the worst sort of conversation, as in books it is generally the worst sort of reading.
JONATHAN SWIFT (1667–1745)

Talking with you is sort of the conversational equivalent of an out of body experience.
BILL WATTERSON (1958–)

Ultimately the bond of all companionship, whether in marriage or in friendship, is conversation.
OSCAR WILDE (1854–1900)

A single conversation across the table with a wise person is worth a month's study of books.
CHINESE PROVERB

To listen well, is as powerful a means of influence as to talk well, and is as essential to all true conversation.
CHINESE PROVERB

Conviction

The one serious conviction that a man should have is that nothing is to be taken too seriously.
NICHOLAS BUTLER (1862–1947)

At 18 our convictions are hills from which we look. At 45 they are caves in which we hide.
F. SCOTT FITZGERALD (1896–1940)

One needs to be slow to form convictions, but once formed they must be defended against the heaviest odds.
MAHATMA GANDHI (1869–1948)

The most important scientific revolutions all include, as their only common feature, the dethronement of human arrogance from one pedestal after another of previous convictions about our centrality in the cosmos.
STEPHEN JAY GOULD (1941–2002)

Don't sacrifice your political convictions for the convenience of the hour.
EDWARD M. KENNEDY (1932–)

Men never do evil so completely and cheerfully as when they do it from a religious conviction.
BLAISE PASCAL (1623–1662)

Every man, wherever he goes, is encompassed by a cloud of comforting convictions, which move with him like flies on a summer day.
BERTRAND RUSSELL (1872–1970), *Sceptical Essays*

Patriotism is your conviction that this country is superior to all other countries because you were born in it.
GEORGE BERNARD SHAW (1856–1950)

In religion and politics, people's beliefs and convictions are in almost every case gotten at second hand, and without examination.
MARK TWAIN (1835–1910)

A strong conviction that something must be done is the parent of many bad measures.
DANIEL WEBSTER (1782–1852)

Cooking

When compelled to cook, I produce a meal that would make a sword swallower gag.
RUSSELL BAKER (1925–)

I feel a recipe is only a theme, which an intelligent cook can play each time with a variation.
JEHANE BENOIT (1904–1987)

Cooking is one of the oldest arts and one which has rendered us the most important service in civic life.
JEAN-ANTHELME BRILLAT-SAVARIN (1755–1826)

When we no longer have good cooking in the world, we will have no literature, nor high and sharp intelligence, nor friendly gatherings, no social harmony.
MARIE-ANTOINE CARÊME (1784–1833)

I was 32 when I started cooking; up until then, I just ate.
JULIA CHILD (1912–2004)

Noncooks think it's silly to invest two hours' work in two minutes' enjoyment; but if cooking is evanescent, so is the ballet.
JULIA CHILD (1912–2004)

Some people like to paint pictures, or do gardening, or build a boat in the basement. Other people get a tremendous pleasure out of the kitchen, because cooking is just as creative and imaginative an activity as drawing, or woodcarving, or music.
JULIA CHILD (1912–2004)

Cooking is at once child's play and adult joy. And cooking done with care is an act of love.
CRAIG CLAIBORNE (1920–2000)

No one who cooks, cooks alone. Even at her most solitary, a cook in the kitchen is surrounded by generations of cooks past, the advice and menus of cooks present, the wisdom of cookbook writers.
LAURIE COLWIN (1944–1992)

My mother was a good recreational cook, but what she basically believed about cooking was that if you worked hard and prospered, someone else would do it for you.
NORA EPHRON (1941–)

Cooking is an art and patience a virtue.... Careful shopping, fresh ingredients and an unhurried approach are nearly all you need. There is one more thing—love. Love for food and love for those you invite to your table. With a combination of these things you can be an artist—not perhaps in the representational style of a Dutch master, but rather more like Gauguin, the naïve, or Van Gogh, the impressionist. Plates or pictures of sunshine taste of happiness and love.
KEITH FLOYD (1943–), *A Feast of Floyd*

There is one thing more exasperating than a wife who can cook and won't and that's a wife who can't cook and will.
ROBERT FROST (1847–1963)

Cooking is an art, but you eat it too.
MARCELLA HAZAN (1924–)

Cooking is like love, it should be entered into with abandon or not at all.
HARRIET VAN HORNE (1920–1998)

She did not so much cook as assassinate food.
MARGARET STORM JAMESON (1891–1986)

A good cook is the peculiar gift of the gods. He must be a perfect creature from the brain to the palate, from the palate to the finger's end.
WALTER SAVAGE LANDOR (1775–1864)

What is literature compared with cooking? The one is shadow, the other is substance.
E. V. LUCAS (1868–1938), *365 Days and One More*

You will never get out of pot or pan anything fundamentally better than what went into it. Cooking is not alchemy; there is no magic in the pot.
MARTHA MCCULLOCH-WILLIAMS (1848–1934), *Dishes & Beverages of the Old South*

Kissing don't last: cookery do.
GEORGE MEREDITH (1963–)

Strange to see how a good dinner and feasting reconciles everybody.
SAMUEL PEPYS (1633–1703)

Light, refined, learned and noble, harmonious and orderly, clear and logical, the cooking of France is, in some strange manner, intimately linked to the genius of her greatest men.
MARCEL ROUFF (1877–1936)

'Tis an ill cook that cannot lick his own fingers.
WILLIAM SHAKESPEARE (1564–1616), *Romeo and Juliet*

When men reach their sixties and retire, they go to pieces. Women go right on cooking.
GAIL SHEEHY (1937–)

A good meal makes a man feel more charitable toward the world than any sermon.
WILLIAM MAKEPEACE THACKERY (1811–1863)

Cooking should be a carefully balanced reflection of all the good things of the earth.
JEAN TROISGROS (1926–) and PIERRE TROISGROS (1928–)

Savory seasonings stimulate the appetite.
LATIN PROVERB

Fish, to taste right, must swim three times—in water, in butter, and in wine.
POLISH PROVERB

Cooperation

Great discoveries and improvements invariably involve the cooperation of many minds. I may be given credit for having blazed the trail, but when I look at the subsequent developments I feel the credit is due to others rather than to myself.
ALEXANDER GRAHAM BELL (1847–1922)

"Management" means, in the last analysis, the substitution of thought for brawn and muscle, of knowledge for folklore and superstition, and of cooperation for force....
PETER F. DRUCKER (1909–2005), *People and Performance*

Every kind of peaceful cooperation among men is primarily based on mutual trust and only secondarily on institutions such as courts of justice and police.
ALBERT EINSTEIN (1879–1955)

We must be willing to learn the lesson that cooperation may imply compromise, but if it brings a world advance it is a gain for each individual nation.
ELEANOR ROOSEVELT (1884–1962)

The only thing that will redeem mankind is cooperation.
BERTRAND RUSSELL (1872–1970)

One man may hit the mark, another blunder; but heed not these distinctions. Only from the alliance of the one, working with and through the other, are great things born.
ANTOINE DE SAINT-EXUPÉRY (1900–1944)

Willingness to compromise with others' ways of living and cooperation in common tasks, these make living happy and fruitful.
SRI SATHYA SAI BABA (1926–)

You must cultivate unity, cooperation and mutual trust.
SRI SATHYA SAI BABA (1926–)

Leadership is based on inspiration, not domination; on cooperation, not intimidation.
WILLIAM ARTHUR WARD (1921–1994)

Power consists in one's capacity to link his will with the purpose of others, to lead by reason and a gift of cooperation.
WOODROW WILSON (1856–1924)

Corporations

American corporations hate to give away money.
STEPHEN AMBROSE (1936–2002)

The Republicans would like to take us back to a darker time, when corporations ruled and the underserved had no rights.
JOE BACA (1947–)

Corporations are social organizations, the theater in which men and women realize or fail to realize purposeful and productive lives.
LESTER BANGS (1948–1982)

Rather than point fingers at corporations, we came to the conclusion that we should strengthen our own ceremonies, strengthen what we do.
DENNIS BANKS (1932–)

Scientific corporations might well become almost independent states and be enabled to undertake their largest experiments without consulting the outside world—a world which would be less and less able to judge what the experiments were about.
JOHN DESMOND BERNAL (1901–1971)

Punk is not dead. Punk will only die when corporations can exploit and mass produce it.
JELLO BIAFRA (1958–)

If both parents must work, I think it is more important that the mother has proximity to the child to therefore establish a childcare situation at the big corporations not once a day, but many times a day.
ERIC BRAEDEN (1941–)

Multinational corporations do control. They control the politicians. They control the media. They control the pattern of consumption, entertainment, thinking. They're destroying the planet and laying the foundation for violent outbursts and racial division.
JERRY BROWN (1938–)

Who gets the risks? The risks are given to the consumer, the unsuspecting consumer and the poor work force. And who gets the benefits? The benefits are only for the corporations, for the money makers.
CESAR CHAVEZ (1927–1993)

If you go back to the time of J. P. Morgan, the world of high finance was completely wholesale. The prestigious investment banks on Wall Street appealed exclusively to large corporations, governments, and to extremely wealthy individuals.
RON CHERNOW (1949–)

The fall of the dollar may be good news for American corporations, but it is very bad news for American tourists.
NICK CLOONEY (1934–)

Of the five House Calendars, the Private Calendar is the one to which all Private Bills are referred. Private Bills deal with specific individuals, corporations, institutions, and so forth, as distinguished from public bills which deal with classes only.
HOWARD COBLE (1931–)

Corporations cannot commit treason, nor be outlawed, nor excommunicated, for they have no souls.
EDWARD COKE (1552–1634)

It is unfair to spend millions of dollars in tax breaks that benefit corporations importing Chinese ceiling fans as well as Starbucks.
SUSAN COLLINS (1952–)

In every case, the environmental hazards were made known only by independent scientists, who were often bitterly opposed by the corporations responsible for the hazards.
BARRY COMMONER (1917–)

The way that a handful of corporations in Los Angeles dictate how our stories are told creates a real poverty of imagination and it's a big problem.
ALEX COX (1954–)

The most important is to loosen the grasp of corporations and special interests from buying politicians and their votes.
DAVID CROSS (1964–)

Chicago is not separate or independent from the state of Illinois. We have major corporations here. Look at our business community.
RICHARD M. DALEY (1942–)

Our supporters can send the message that it's wrong for politically connected corporations to make millions while people doing an honest day's work are being cheated out of an honest day's pay.
MORRIS DEES (1936–)

And we've become very doubtful of our information sources, because they're all controlled by these huge multilateral corporations.
BRIAN DE PALMA (1940–)

I have lately with some others been discussing cults, and their consequences when they arrive in organizations brought together for other purposes. For instance, in large corporations they can distract workers from their normal work.
MARY DOUGLAS (1921–)

There were some entrepreneurial Du Ponts that are a little different from the heads of the corporations today.
PETE DU PONT (1935–)

In all large corporations, there is a pervasive fear that someone, somewhere is having fun with a computer on company time. Networks help alleviate that fear.
JOHN C. DVORAK (1952–)

Well, I don't think that the role of the pharmaceutical industry is any different from that of other transnational corporations.
PAUL FARMER (1909–)

What is not fair now is that corporations pay less and less tax, which means that you and I pay more because we're rooted somewhere, they've got our address, right?
SUSAN GEORGE (1950–)

Whatever we want to say about the growing power of global agencies like the IMF and World Bank or global corporations with respect to decisive questions, everywhere there is one nation-state that doesn't mean to go gently into erosion, and that is of course the United States of America.
TODD GITLIN (1943–)

Pension-fund wealth is thus being mobilized as financial leverage to break up the narrow-minded thinking of finance capital and to confront the antisocial behavior of corporations.
WILLIAM GREIDER (1936–)

Obviously we're a consumer nation and you have the power to influence these big corporations who are running the world right now through what you chose to, or not to, purchase.
DARYL HANNAH (1960–)

And also, more and more businesses really want to do the right thing. They feel better about themselves, their workers feel better, and so do their customers. I think this is equally true in the transnational corporations, but it is harder to express in those situations.
PAUL HAWKEN (1946–)

The financial capital is being concentrated by corporations, institutional investors, and even our pension funds, and being reinvested in companies that repeat this process because it provides the highest return on that financial capital.
PAUL HAWKEN (1946–)

April is tax month. If you are having trouble filing your taxes, then you should hire an accountant. They'll give you the same advice that they've given hundreds of corporations—taxes are for douche bags.
ED HELMS (1974–)

The corporations don't have to lobby the government anymore. They are the government.
JIM HIGHTOWER (1943–)

Groups are corporations now. They have pension plans. Musicians have saw the daylight.
JOHN LEE HOOKER (1917–2001)

Corporate corruption, as exhibited by the Enron scandal, is a serious problem and investing in the stock market is risky.
STEVE ISRAEL (1958–)

I hope we shall crush in its birth the aristocracy of our monied corporations which dare already to challenge our government to a trial by strength, and bid defiance to the laws of our country.
THOMAS JEFFERSON (1743–1826)

We're all corporations and contractors and production companies now.
BILLY JOEL (1949–)

In a time of serious budget deficits, immense war costs and a sluggish economy, we cannot afford to grant such outlandish subsidies to some of our Nation's largest corporations.
RON KIND (1963–)

TV that people will never see, that giant international corporations will never touch, will never pay your salary.
NORMAN LEAR (1922–)

In the steel industry the corporations generally have accepted collective bargaining and negotiated wage agreements with the Committee for Industrial Organization.
JOHN L. LEWIS (1880–1969)

Five of the corporations in the steel industry elected to resist collective bargaining and undertook to destroy the steel workers' union.
JOHN L. LEWIS (1880–1969)

I see in the near future a crisis approaching that unnerves me and causes me to tremble for the safety of my country.... Corporations have been enthroned, an era of corruption in high places will follow, and the money-power of the country will endeavor to prolong its reign by working upon the prejudices of the people until the wealth is aggregated in a few hands and the Republic is destroyed.
ABRAHAM LINCOLN (1809–1865)

People like me have to have the discipline only to work for clients, corporations, political people, products, services, networks that we believe in and we want to see succeed.
FRANK LUNTZ (1962–)

Thirty years after drafting the US Declaration of Independence, Thomas Jefferson warned of the dangers posed by the corporation, writing of the need to "crush in its birth the aristocracy of our moneyed corporations, which dare already to challenge our government to a trial of strength and bid defiance to the laws of our country." Today, instead, the aristocracy of the corporation has grown to full maturity, wielding power over the state and its laws in the service of corporate aims.
BEN MANSKI (1974–)

Were the radical democratic impulses of the American Revolution still driving U.S. politics, it would be difficult to imagine corporatization of the kind witnessed today. But that impulse has weakened, and the relationship between the people and the corporation has reversed.
BEN MANSKI (1974–)

So Indian policy has become institutionalized and the result has been that American people have become more dependent on government and that the American people have become more dependent on corporations.
RUSSELL MEANS (1939–)

Give tax breaks to large corporations, so that money can trickle down to the general public, in the form of extra jobs.
ANDREW MELLON (1855–1937)

The motivation for war is simple. The U.S. government started the war with Iraq in order to make it easy for U.S. corporations to do business in other countries. They intend to use cheap labor in those countries, which will make Americans rich.
MICHAEL MOORE (1954–)

The great corporations of this country were not founded by ordinary people. They were founded by people with extraordinary intelligence, ambition, and aggressiveness.
DANIEL P. MOYNIHAN (1927–2003)

[George W. Bush's] administration is not sympathetic to corporations, it is indentured to corporations.
RALPH NADER (1934–)

I don't think meals have any business being deductible. I'm for separation of calories and corporations.
RALPH NADER (1934–)

The only difference between the Republican and Democratic parties is the velocities with which their knees hit the floor when corporations knock on their door. That's the only difference.
RALPH NADER (1934–)

A lot of the time, now, it would seem that the power doesn't reside with politicians. So much power has been given over to corporations.
ED O'BRIEN (1968–)

I was endorsed by many corporations to work with their people. Since I had several hundred successful case histories, I realized that it was really valuable and everybody should have access to the information, so I started teaching seminars to groups of people.
LEONARD ORR (1938–)

We are going through tough economic times but things are looking up, and the indicators are

improving not only for large corporations but also for small business.
GEORGE PATAKI (1945–)

To survive, men and business and corporations must serve.
JOHN H. PATTERSON (1844–1922)

Basically, what Economic Hit Men are trained to do is to build up the American empire. To create situations where as many resources as possible flow into this country, to our corporations, and our government, and in fact we've been very successful.
JOHN PERKINS (1945–)

[O]ur country really needs to understand, if people in this nation understood what our foreign policy is really about, what foreign aid is about, how our corporations work, where our tax money goes, I know we will demand change.
JOHN PERKINS (1909–)

Media corporations have a civic responsibility not only to prevent fraud and financial abuse, but also to not corrupt or degrade our culture.
CHARLES W. PICKERING (1937–)

Why do otherwise sane, competent, strong men, men who can wrestle bears or raid corporations, shrink away in horror at the thought of washing a dish or changing a diaper?
FRANK PITTMAN (1935–)

The larger the state, the more callous it becomes… the colder its heart. It is also true that the bigger the corporation, the more callous its heart. But unlike the state, corporations have competition and have no police powers.
DENNIS PRAGER (1948–)

I can't justify taking money away from hungry kids and needy schools to pay for the Games when corporations are willing to write the checks.
MARY LOU RETTON (1968–)

These corporations have to sell something new and they find these bands. Just because people in offices haven't heard this music, doesn't mean that other people haven't. It's a little insulting to the bands and to the kids.
CHRIS ROBINSON (1966–)

I suspect that many corporations have begun to understand that they have an important role to play in the lives of their communities, and that allocating funds to support local groups helps them discharge that function and also burnish their image.
DAVID ROCKEFELLER (1915–)

Vigilante consumers are working with human rights groups, environmental groups—the grassroots movement—and are definitely challenging corporations.
ANITA RODDICK (1942–)

And when the customers demand technology we move and adopt it. And right now since we're focused mostly on corporations they are not demanding it.
KEVIN ROLLINS (1953–)

Most of the services staff is for the larger corporations, not so much for small and medium businesses because they cannot afford an extensive services army.
KEVIN ROLLINS (1953–)

My work gives me the opportunity to travel around the world and try to convince corporations and countries to take a serious look at how this new world disorder can affect them.
PIERRE SALINGER (1925–2004)

In the United States, corporations are very concerned about securing natural resources for them to profit from.
JUSTIN SANE (1973–)

Turning corporations loose and letting the profit motive run amok is not a prescription for a more livable world.
TOM SCHOLZ (1947–)

A criminal is a person with predatory instincts who has not sufficient capital to form a corporation.
HOWARD SCOTT (1890–1970)

Like the government, corporations must be bound with the chains of the Constitution, and especially of the Bill of Rights.
L. NEIL SMITH (1946–)

We must start with the reality that corporations cannot guarantee anyone a lifetime job any more than corporations have a guarantee of immortality.
JOHN W. SNOW (1939–)

It's an incredible con job when you think about it, to believe something now in exchange for something after death. Even corporations with their reward systems don't try to make it posthumous.
GLORIA STEINEM (1934–)

I am on the board of corporations who contribute both to environmental problems and their solutions. And I am on the NGO side: the Earth Council and other organizations.
MAURICE STRONG (1929–)

Not to say that corporations are perfect today, but even grand corporations like Dupont have made immense progress in translating some of their past environmentally damaging practices into new profit opportunities.
MAURICE STRONG (1929–)

Even President Bush has cited the need to outlaw the practice of corporations making loans to their officers. Strangely enough, when the President was a corporate officer, he took out several loans from the company.
BENNIE THOMPSON (1948–)

Yet, individuals and corporations in Puerto Rico pay no federal income tax.
DICK THORNBURGH (1932–)

Now you have people in Washington who have no interest in the country at all. They're interested in their companies, their corporations grabbing Caspian oil.
GORE VIDAL (1925–)

Large corporations and unions know the power of being big enough to bargain for better rates.
GREG WALDEN (1957–)

We must remember that for many, many women, work does not represent liberation, modernization, or market success. Most women are not upper income professionals and certainly not executives of large corporations and banks; most women work in the expanding low-wage service sector of our economy.
PAUL WELLSTONE (1944–2002)

Now, having dealt with both Universal and EMI, I can say that I directly know that two major corporations are run by idiots who have no knowledge of music and little understanding even of basic bourgeois economics.
MALCOLM WILSON (1914–2000)

The corporations and the media don't need power; they already have it.
JOSE LUIS RODRIGUEZ ZAPATERO (1960–)

Corruption

A government, for protecting business only, is but a carcass, and soon falls by its own corruption and decay.
AMOS BRONSON ALCOTT (1799–1888)

The first sign of corruption in a society that is still alive is that the end justifies the means.
GEORGES BERNANOS (1888–1948), *Why Freedom?*

It is said that power corrupts, but actually it's more true that power attracts the corruptible. The sane are usually attracted by other things than power.
DAVID BRIN (1950–)

Corruption is like a ball of snow, once it's set a rolling it must increase.
CHARLES CALEB COLTON (1780–1832)

Corruption never has been compulsory.
ANTHONY EDEN (1897–1977)

The only way to escape the personal corruption of praise is to go on working.
ALBERT EINSTEIN (1879–1955)

Corruption and hypocrisy ought not to be inevitable products of democracy, as they undoubtedly are today.
MAHATMA GANDHI (1869–1948)

Corporate corruption, as exhibited by the Enron scandal, is a serious problem and investing in the stock market is risky.
STEVE ISRAEL (1958–)

Communism has never come to power in a country that was not disrupted by war or corruption, or both.
JOHN F. KENNEDY (1917–1963)

I see in the near future a crisis approaching that unnerves me and causes me to tremble for the safety of my country. Corporations have been enthroned, an era of corruption in high places will follow, and the money-power of the country will endeavor to prolong its reign by working upon the prejudices of the people until the wealth is aggregated in a few hands and the Republic is destroyed.
ABRAHAM LINCOLN (1809–1865)

The surest way to corrupt a youth is to instruct him to hold in higher esteem those who think alike than those who think differently.
FRIEDRICH NIETZSCHE (1844–1900)

In a state where corruption abounds, laws must be very numerous.
PUBLILIUS SYRUS (C. 100 BC)

I hate ingratitude more in a man
Than lying, vainness, babbling, drunkenness,
Or any taint of vice whose strong corruption
Inhabits our frail blood.
WILLIAM SHAKESPEARE (1564–1616)

Communism is the corruption of a dream of justice.
ADLAI E. STEVENSON II (1900–1965)

Politics, as the word is commonly understood, are nothing but corruption.
JONATHAN SWIFT (1667–1745)

Corruption is nature's way of restoring our faith in democracy.
PETER USTINOV (1921)

Every culture has its distinctive and normal system of government. Yours is democracy, moderated by corruption. Ours is totalitarianism, moderated by assassination.
ANONYMOUS (RUSSIAN)

Countries

When I am abroad, I always make it a rule never to criticize or attack the government of my own country. I make up for lost time when I come home.
SIR WINSTON CHURCHILL (1874–1965)

A great country worthy of the name does not have any friends.
CHARLES DE GAULLE (1890–1970)

How can you govern a country which has 246 varieties of cheese?
CHARLES DE GAULLE (1890–1970)

I have never belonged wholeheartedly to a country, a state, nor to a circle of friends, nor even to my own family.
ALBERT EINSTEIN (1879–1955)

America's one of the finest countries anyone ever stole.
BOBCAT GOLDTHWAITE (1962–)

America is a country that doesn't know where it is going but is determined to set a speed record getting there.
DR. LAURENCE J. PETER (1919–1990)

England and America are two countries separated by a common language.
GEORGE BERNARD SHAW (1856–1950)

Ask not what you can do for your country. Ask what's for lunch.
ORSON WELLES (1915–1985)

America is the only country that went from barbarism to decadence without civilization in between.
OSCAR WILDE (1854–1900)

A country can be judged by the quality of its proverbs.
GERMAN PROVERB

Courage

Courage and perseverance have a magical talisman, before which difficulties disappear and obstacles vanish into air.
JOHN QUINCY ADAMS (1767–1848)

Courage is of no value unless accompanied by justice; yet if all men became just, there would be no need for courage.
AGESILAUS II (C. 444–360 BC)

Courage is just fear, plus prayers, plus understanding.
EDWARD ALBERT (1951–)

One isn't necessarily born with courage, but one is born with potential. Without courage, we cannot practice any other virtue with consistency. We can't be kind, true, merciful, generous, or honest.
MAYA ANGELOU (1928–)

Courage is fear that has said its prayers.
DOROTHY BERNARD (1890–1955)

Live as brave men; and if fortune is adverse, front its blows with brave hearts.
CICERO (106–43 BC)

Courage and grace are a formidable mixture. The only place to see it is in the bullring.
MARLENE DIETRICH (1901–1992)

Courage is the price that Life exacts for granting peace.
AMELIA EARHART (1897–1937), *Courage*

The qualities of a great man are vision, integrity, courage, understanding, the power of articulation, and profundity of character.
DWIGHT D. EISENHOWER (1890–1969)

A hero is no braver than an ordinary man, but he is braver five minutes longer.
RALPH WALDO EMERSON (1803–1882)

Courage consists in the power of self-recovery.
RALPH WALDO EMERSON (1803–1882)

A coward turns away, but a brave man's choice is danger.
EURIPIDES (C. 480–406 BC), *Iphigenia in Tauris*

I would rather be a coward than brave because people hurt you when you are brave.
E. M. FORSTER (1879–1970)

Despair gives courage to a coward.
THOMAS FULLER (1608–1661)

Many would be cowards if they had courage enough.
THOMAS FULLER (1608–1661)

Some have been thought brave because they were afraid to run away.
THOMAS FULLER (1608–1661)

The bravest thing you can do when you are not brave is to profess courage and act accordingly.
CORRA HARRIS (1869–1935)

It is from numberless diverse acts of courage and belief that human history is shaped. Each time a man stands up for an ideal, or acts to improve the lot of others, or strikes out against injustice, he sends forth a tiny ripple of hope, and crossing each other from a million different centers of energy and daring, those ripples build a current that can sweep down the mightiest walls of oppression and resistance.
ROBERT F. KENNEDY (1925–1968), *South Africa*

I wanted you to see what real courage is, instead of getting the idea that courage is a man with a gun in his hand. It's when you know you're licked before

you begin but you begin anyway and you see it through no matter what.
HARPER LEE (1926–), *To Kill a Mockingbird*

Courage is the ladder on which all the other virtues mount.
CLARE BOOTH LUCE (1903–1987)

The only courage that matters is the kind that gets you from one moment to the next.
MIGNON MCLAUGHLIN (1913–1983), *The Second Neurotic's Notebook*

Let bravery be thy choice, but not bravado.
MENANDER (342–292 BC)

Take chances. Make mistakes. That's how you grow. Pain nourishes your courage. You have to fail in order to practice being brave.
MARY TYLER MOORE (1936–)

Life shrinks or expands in proportion to one's courage.
ANAÏS NIN (1903–1977), *The Diary of Anaïs Nin*

And the day came when the risk to remain tight in a bud was more painful than the risk it took to blossom.
ANAÏS NIN (1903–1977)

Why do they always teach us that it's easy and evil to do what we want and that we need discipline to restrain ourselves? It's the hardest thing in the world—to do what we want. And it takes the greatest kind of courage. I mean, what we really want.
AYN RAND (1905–1982)

A timid person is frightened before a danger, a coward during the time, and a courageous person afterward.
JEAN PAUL RICHTER (1763–1825)

Courage is doing what you're afraid to do. There can be no courage unless you're scared.
EDWARD VERNON RICKENBACKER (1890–1973)

When you meet your antagonist, do everything in a mild and agreeable manner. Let your courage be as keen, but at the same time as polished, as your sword.
RICHARD BRINSLEY SHERIDAN (1751–1816)

Keep your fears to yourself, but share your courage with others.
ROBERT LOUIS STEVENSON (1850–1894)

Fortune helps the brave.
TERENCE (185–159 BC), *Phormio*

The bravest are surely those who have the clearest vision of what is before them, glory and danger alike, and yet notwithstanding, go out to meet it.
THUCYDIDES (C. 460–395 BC)

The secret of happiness is freedom. The secret of freedom is courage.
THUCYDIDES (C. 460–395 BC)

Courage is resistance to fear, mastery of fear—not absence of fear.
MARK TWAIN (1835–1910)

It is curious that physical courage should be so common in the world and moral courage so rare.
MARK TWAIN (1835–1910)

Fortune favors the brave.
VIRGIL (C. 70 BC–19 BC), *Aeneid*

Courage is being scared to death—but saddling up anyway.
JOHN WAYNE (1907–1979)

True courage is not the brutal force of vulgar heroes, but the firm resolve of virtue and reason.
ALFRED NORTH WHITEHEAD (1861–1947)

Courage is the art of being the only one who knows you're scared to death.
HAROLD WILSON (1916–1995)

Courtesy

The grace of God is courtesy.
HILAIRE BELLOC (1870–1953)

All doors open to courtesy.
THOMAS FULLER (1608–1661)

There is a courtesy of the heart; it is allied to love. From it springs the purest courtesy in the outward behavior.
JOHANN WOLFGANG VON GOETHE (1749–1832)

Courtesy is a silver lining around the dark clouds of civilization; it is the best part of refinement and in many ways, an art of heroic beauty in the vast gallery of man's cruelty and baseness.
BRYANT H. MCGILL (1969–)

Courtesy is as much a mark of a gentleman as courage.
THEODORE ROOSEVELT (1858–1919)

Courtesy is the one coin you can never have too much of or be stingy with.
JOHN WANAMAKER (1838–1922)

Cowardice

As the ostrich when pursued hideth his head, but forgetteth his body; so the fears of a coward expose him to danger.
AKHENATON (C. 1400 BC)

A high heart ought to bear calamities and not flee them, since in bearing them appears the grandeur of the mind and in fleeing them the cowardice of the heart.
PIETRO ARETINO (1492–1556)

To run away from trouble is a form of cowardice and, while it is true that the suicide braves death, he does it not for some noble object but to escape some ill.
ARISTOTLE (384–322 BC)

Cowardice and courage are never without a measure of affectation. Nor is love. Feelings are never true. They play with their mirrors.
JEAN BAUDRILLARD (1929–2007)

Coward, n.: One who, in a perilous emergency, thinks with his legs.
AMBROSE BIERCE (1842–1914), *The Devil's Dictionary*

Courage enlarges, cowardice diminishes resources. In desperate straits the fears of the timid aggravate the dangers that imperil the brave.
CHRISTIAN NESTELL BOVÉE (1820–1904)

No coward soul is mine,
No trembler in the world's storm-troubled sphere;
I see Heaven's glories shine,
And, Faith shines equal, arming me from Fear.
EMILY BRONTË (1818–1848)

He who despairs of the human condition is a coward, but he who has hope for it is a fool.
ALBERT CAMUS (1913–1960), *The Rebel*

At the bottom of not a little of the bravery that appears in the world, there lurks a miserable cowardice. Men will face powder and steel because they have not the courage to face public opinion.
EDWIN HUBBEL CHAPIN (1814–1880)

The real hero is always a hero by mistake; he dreams of being an honest coward like everybody else.
UMBERTO ECO (1932–), *Travels in Hyperreality*

Any coward can fight a battle when he's sure of winning, but give me the man who has pluck to fight when he's sure of losing. That's my way, sir; and there are many victories worse than a defeat.
GEORGE ELIOT (1819–1880)

Despair gives courage to a coward.
THOMAS FULLER (1608–1661)

A coward is incapable of exhibiting love; it is the prerogative of the brave.
MAHATMA GANDHI (1869–1948)

The coward threatens when he is safe.
JOHANN WOLFGANG VON GOETHE (1749–1832)

Conscience is a coward, and those faults it has not strength enough to prevent it seldom has justice enough to accuse.
OLIVER GOLDSMITH (1730–1774)

Cowardice, as distinguished from panic, is almost always simply a lack of ability to suspend the functioning of the imagination.
ERNEST HEMINGWAY (1899–1961)

It is better to be the widow of a hero than the wife of a coward.
DOLORES IBARRURI (1895–1989)

The brave man inattentive to his duty, is worth little more to his country than the coward who deserts in the hour of danger.
ANDREW JACKSON (1767–1845)

A coward is much more exposed to quarrels than a man of spirit.
THOMAS JEFFERSON (1762–1826)

God is the brave man's hope, and not the coward's excuse.
PLUTARCH (AD 46–120)

That man is not truly brave who is afraid either to seem or to be, when it suits him, a coward.
EDGAR ALLAN POE (1809–1849)

There is a level of cowardice lower than that of the conformist: the fashionable non-conformist.
AYN RAND (1905–1982)

A timid person is frightened before a danger, a coward during the time, and a courageous person afterwards.
JEAN PAUL RICHTER (1763–1825)

They tell us that suicide is the greatest piece of cowardice … that suicide is wrong; when it is quite obvious that there is nothing in the world to which every man has a more unassailable title than to his own life and person.
ARTHUR SCHOPENHAUER (1788–1860)

Hatred is the coward's revenge for being intimidated.
GEORGE BERNARD SHAW (1856–1950)

Moral cowardice that keeps us from speaking our minds is as dangerous to this country as irresponsible talk. The right way is not always the popular and easy way. Standing for right when it is unpopular is a true test of moral character.
MARGARET CHASE SMITH (1897–1995)

You are a coward when you even seem to have backed down from a thing you openly set out to do.
MARK TWAIN (1835–1910)

It is vain for the coward to flee; death follows close behind; it is only by defying it that the brave escape.
VOLTAIRE (1694–1778)

Conscience and cowardice are really the same things. Conscience is the trade-name of the firm. That is all.
OSCAR WILDE (1854–1900)

Yet each man kills the thing he loves,
By each let this be heard,
Some do it with a bitter look,
Some with a flattering word.
The coward does it with a kiss,
The brave man with a sword!
OSCAR WILDE (1854–1900)

It is better to be a coward for a minute than dead for the rest of your life.
IRISH PROVERB

Creativity

I think creativity is spiritual. I absolutely believe that.
F. MURRAY ABRAHAM (1939–)

No man has the right to dictate what other men should perceive, create or produce, but all should be encouraged to reveal themselves, their perceptions and emotions, and to build confidence in the creative spirit.
ANSEL ADAMS (1902–1984)

Creativity is allowing yourself to make mistakes. Art is knowing which ones to keep.
SCOTT ADAMS (1957–)

Whatever creativity is, it is in part a solution to a problem.
BRIAN W. ALDISS (1925–)

Your brain has an in-built mechanism for finding patterns you've programmed because of where you've put your attention. Solutions, innovations, and success come not from greater intelligence or creativity but from what we notice because of where we point those attributes.
DAVID ALLEN (1945–)

The computer offers another kind of creativity. You cannot ignore the creativity that computer technology can bring. But you need to be able to move between those two different worlds.
TADAO ANDO (1941–)

Creativity is a great motivator because it makes people interested in what they are doing. Creativity gives hope that there can be a worthwhile idea. Creativity gives the possibility of some sort of achievement to everyone. Creativity makes life more fun and more interesting.
EDWARD DE BONO (1933–)

Creativity comes from trust. Trust your instincts.
RITA MAE BROWN (1944–)

Curiosity about life in all of its aspects, I think, is still the secret of great creative people.
LEO BURNETT (1891–1971)

Creativity—like human life itself—begins in darkness.
JULIA CAMERON (1948–)

A hunch is creativity trying to tell you something.
FRANK CAPRA (1897–1991)

Creativity is essentially a lonely art. An even lonelier struggle. To some a blessing. To others a curse. It is in reality the ability to reach inside yourself and drag forth from your very soul an idea.
LOU DORFSMAN (1918–)

I lived in solitude in the country and noticed how the monotony of a quiet life stimulates the creative mind.
ALBERT EINSTEIN (1879–1955)

Creativity requires the courage to let go of certainties.
ERICH FROMM (1900–1980)

The creative individual has the capacity to free himself from the web of social pressures in which the rest of us are caught. He is capable of questioning the assumptions that the rest of us accept.
JOHN W. GARDNER (1912–2002)

Creativity and artistic endeavors have a mission that goes far beyond just making music for the sake of music.
HERBIE HANCOCK (1940–)

Creativity is discontent translated into arts.
ERIC HOFFER (1902–1983)

The Paleolithic hunters who painted the unsurpassed animal murals on the ceiling of the cave at Altamira had only rudimentary tools. Art is older than production for use, and play older than work. Man was shaped less by what he had to do than by what he did in playful moments. It is the child in man that is the source of his uniqueness and creativeness, and the playground is the optimal milieu for the unfolding of his capacities.
ERIC HOFFER (1902–1983)

Creative powers can just as easily turn out to be destructive. It rests solely with the moral personality whether they apply themselves to good things or to bad. And if this is lacking, no teacher can supply it or take its place.
CARL JUNG (1875–1961)

The creation of something new is not accomplished by the intellect but by the play instinct acting from inner necessity. The creative mind plays with the objects it loves.
CARL JUNG (1875–1961)

Above all, we are coming to understand that the arts incarnate the creativity of a free people. When the creative impulse cannot flourish, when it cannot

freely select its methods and objects, when it is deprived of spontaneity, then society severs.
JOHN F. KENNEDY (1917–1963)

Creativity can solve almost any problem. The creative act, the defeat of habit by originality, overcomes everything.
GEORGE LOIS (1937–)

Creativity is not the finding of a thing, but the making something out of it after it is found.
JAMES RUSSELL LOWELL (1819–1891)

Creativity is more than just being different. Anybody can plan weird; that's easy. What's hard is to be as simple as Bach. Making the simple, awesomely simple, that's creativity.
CHARLES MINGUS (1922–1979)

I never feel age. If you have creative work, you don't have age or time.
LOUISE NEVELSON (1900–1988)

Creativity is a natural extension of our enthusiasm.
EARL NIGHTINGALE (1921–1989)

Thoughts give birth to a creative force that is neither elemental nor sidereal. Thoughts create a new heaven, a new firmament, a new source of energy, from which new arts flow. When a man undertakes to create something, he establishes a new heaven, as it were and from it the work that he desires to create flows into him. For such is the immensity of man that he is greater than heaven and earth.
PARACELSUS (1493–1541)

Creativity is the power to connect the seemingly unconnected.
WILLIAM PLOMER (1903–1973)

The way of the Creative works through change and transformation, so that each thing receives its true nature and destiny and comes into permanent accord with the Great Harmony: this is what furthers and what perseveres.
ALEXANDER POPE (1688–1744)

Creativity is to think more efficiently.
PIERRE REVERDY (1889–1960)

Happiness lies in the joy of achievement and the thrill of creative effort.
FRANKLIN D. ROOSEVELT (1882–1945)

Whoever undertakes to create soon finds himself engaged in creating himself. Self-transformation and the transformation of others have constituted the radical interest of our century, whether in painting, psychiatry, or political action.
HAROLD ROSENBERG (1906—1978)

Imagination is the beginning of creation. You imagine what you desire, you will what you imagine and at last you create what you will.
GEORGE BERNARD SHAW (1856–1950)

Creativity is much better when it's free. Someone can take it and sell it if that's what it needs, and from that standpoint, you have to have a label. If you could make your music and just give it away and somehow make a living—that would be the best scenario.
MATTHEW SWEET (1964–)

Confidence in nonsense is a requirement for the creative process.
ANONYMOUS

Crime

Organized crime in America takes in over forty billion dollars a year and spends very little on office supplies.
WOODY ALLEN (1935–)

Poverty is the parent of revolution and crime.
ARISTOTLE (384–322 BC)

Murder is unique in that it abolishes the party it injures, so that society has to take the place of the victim and on his behalf demand atonement or grant forgiveness; it is the one crime in which society has a direct interest.
W. H. AUDEN (1907–1973)

Behind every great fortune there is a crime.
HONORÉ DE BALZAC (1799–1850)

There is no den in the wide world to hide a rogue. Commit a crime and the earth is made of glass. Commit a crime, and it seems as if a coat of snow fell on the ground, such as reveals in the woods the track of every partridge, and fox, and squirrel.
RALPH WALDO EMERSON (1803–1882)

History is indeed little more than the register of the crimes, follies, and misfortunes of mankind.
EDWARD GIBBON (1737–1794)

Crime is naught but misdirected energy.
EMMA GOLDMAN (1869–1940), *Anarchism*

Obviously crime pays, or there'd be no crime.
G. GORDON LIDDY (1930–)

A crime which is the crime of many none avenge.
LUCAN (AD 39–65)

My loathings are simple: stupidity, oppression, crime, cruelty, soft music.
VLADIMIR NABOKOV (1899–1977)

Crooks are early adopters.
CRAIG NEWMARK (1952–)

The judge is condemned when the criminal is absolved.
PUBLILIUS SYRUS (C. 100 BC), *Maxims*

Crime butchers innocence to secure a throne, and innocence struggles with all its might against the attempts of crime.
MAXIMILIEN ROBESPIERRE (1758–1794)

Life is nothing but a competition to be the criminal rather than the victim.
BERTRAND RUSSELL (1872–1970)

A criminal is a person with predatory instincts who has not sufficient capital to form a corporation.
HOWARD SCOTT (1890–1970)

When you think of the long and gloomy history of man, you will find more hideous crimes have been committed in the name of obedience than have ever been committed in the name of rebellion.
C. P. SNOW (1905–1980)

Going to trial with a lawyer who considers your whole life-style a Crime in Progress is not a happy prospect.
HUNTER S. THOMPSON (1939–2005)

Indeed, history is nothing more than a tableau of crimes and misfortunes.
VOLTAIRE (1694–1778)

Starvation, not sin, is the parent of modern crime.
OSCAR WILDE (1854–1900)

Crisis

There is a human capital crisis in the federal government. Not only are we losing the decades of talent as civil servants retire, we are not doing enough to develop and nurture the next generation of public servants.
DANIEL AKAKA (1923–)

Yet, today, we see what is becoming a constitutional crisis which is completely unprecedented, and that is the use of the filibuster to basically stop the confirmation process both for circuit court and Supreme Court nominations.
TODD AKIN (1947–)

In times of life crisis, whether wild fires or smoldering stress, the first thing I do is go back to basics … am I eating right, am I getting enough sleep, am I getting some physical and mental exercise everyday.
EDWARD ALBERT (1951–)

The wise man does not expose himself needlessly to danger, since there are few things for which he cares sufficiently; but he is willing, in great crises, to give even his life—knowing that under certain conditions it is not worth-while to live.
ARISTOTLE (384–322 BC)

It doesn't mean we shouldn't mention a Lebanese cabinet crisis, for example, but we don't have to spend two minutes with it from the Middle East.
ROONE ARLEDGE (1931–)

Real style is not having a program—it's how one behaves in a crisis.
FRANK AUERBACH (1931–)

I really do think that any deep crisis is an opportunity to make your life extraordinary in some way.
MARTHA BECK (1962–)

Why is it that men who can go through severe accidents, air raids, and any other major crisis always seems to think that they are at death's door when they have a simple head cold?
SHIRLEY BOOTH (1907–1992)

Try to relax and enjoy the crisis.
ASHLEIGH BRILLIANT (1933–)

If you have a crisis, whether on a ship or wherever, there are heroes who rise above it.
JERRY BRUCKHEIMER (1945–)

In a crisis, don't hide behind anything or anybody. They're going to find you anyway.
PAUL "BEAR" BRYANT (1913–1983)

Well, I have also believed in empowering the individual and believe there is a degree of inertia in big government that hampers the ability to respond to a rapidly evolving crisis.
MICHAEL BURGESS (1950–)

Sexual abuse of children now presents society with the ultimate crisis of patriarchy, when children refuse to protect their fathers by keeping secrets.
BEATRIX CAMPBELL (1947–)

An act of terrorism totally outside the bounds of international law and diplomatic tradition. a crisis that calls for firmness and restraint.
JIMMY CARTER (1924–)

In short, our response as a party should be to work to solve the crises that produce crisis pregnancies, and work to make life worth living for mother and child, rather than victimize the child as a way of dealing with the crisis.
ROBERT CASEY (1932–2000)

Crises refine life. In them you discover what you are.
ALLAN K. CHALMERS (1915–1990)

It is popular to call it a crisis of the Western world. It is in fact a crisis of the whole world. Communism, which claims to be a solution of the crisis, is itself a symptom and an irritant of the crisis.
WHITTAKER CHAMBERS (1901–1961)

Racism is always there underneath, but usually it is exploited in these times of economic crisis, and it's hard to find out when one slides into another.
IRIS CHANG (1968–2004)

Any idiot can face a crisis—it's day to day living that wears you out.
ANTON CHEKHOV (1860–1904)

We've got to be judged by how we do in times of crisis.
JOHNNIE COCHRAN (1937–2005)

Successful people recognize crisis as a time for change—from lesser to greater, smaller to bigger.
EDWIN LOUIS COLE (1922–2002)

Man is not imprisoned by habit. Great changes in him can be wrought by crisis—once that crisis can be recognized and understood.
NORMAN COUSINS (1915–1990)

Perhaps two million years ago the creatures of a planet in some remote galaxy faced a musical crisis similar to that which we earthly composers face today.
GEORGE CRUMB (1929–)

Every great crisis of human history is a pass of Thermopylae, and there is always a Leonidas and his three hundred to die in it, if they can not conquer.
GEORGE WILLIAM CURTIS (1824–1892)

Being on a movie set is like one long financial crisis.
JOHN CUSACK (1966–)

You can't relate to a superhero, to a superman, but you can identify with a real man who in times of crisis draws forth some extraordinary quality from within himself and triumphs but only after a struggle.
TIMOTHY DALTON (1946–)

The darkest places in hell are reserved for those who maintain their neutrality in times of moral crisis.
DANTE ALIGHIERI (1265–1321)

Faced with crisis, the man of character falls back on himself. He imposes his own stamp of action, takes responsibility for it, makes it his own.
CHARLES DE GAULLE (1890–1970)

There's nothing like a family crisis, especially a divorce, to force a person to re-evaluate his life.
MICHAEL DOUGLAS (1944–)

It takes a lot of experience of life to see why some relationships last and others do not. But we do not have to wait for a crisis to get an idea of the future of a particular relationship. Our behavior in little everyday incidents tells us a great deal.
EKNATH EASWARAN (1910–1999)

I totally relate to Tom Cruise. He's not crazy, it's just the litany of the mid-life crisis.
BRET EASTON ELLIS (1964–)

In a kind of middle-aged crisis, it dawned upon me that there was a possibility that music might not even be an art form.
MORTON FELDMAN (1926–1987)

A crisis is a close encounter of the third kind.
GUY FINLEY (1949–)

Many viewed New York City as highly intense, fast-paced, and cynical. But on September 11, we saw a city that pulled together in a time of crisis.
RANDY FORBES (1952–)

Nobody but radicals have ever accomplished anything in a great crisis.
JAMES A. GARFIELD (1831–1881)

Unless, therefore, there should come a crisis far more terrible than the present one in Germany, a crisis, indeed, far exceeding the horrors of any other crises that ever were before, the poor peasants in Western Europe will side with Capitalism, as long as it has any life left.
HERMAN GORTER (1864–1927)

I believe it is essential for our planetary future to develop tools that can change the consciousness which has created the crisis that we are in.
STANISLAV GROF (1931–)

The greatest possible pressure against the enemy's whole front must be maintained, especially when the crisis of the battle approaches.
DOUGLAS HAIG (1861–1928)

Every new adjustment is a crisis in self-esteem.
ERIC HOFFER (1902–1983)

When is a crisis reached? When questions arise that can't be answered.
RYSZARD KAPUSCINSKI (1932–)

When written in Chinese, the word "crisis" is composed of two characters. One represents danger and the other represents opportunity.
JOHN F. KENNEDY (1917–1963)

Actually, this seems to be the basic need of the human heart in nearly every great crisis—a good hot cup of coffee.
ALEXANDER KING (1899–1965)

In crises the most daring course is often safest.
HENRY KISSINGER (1923–)

There cannot be a crisis today; my schedule is already full.
HENRY KISSINGER (1923–)

Crisis alone is not enough. There must also be a basis, though it need be neither rational nor ultimately correct, for faith in the particular candidate chosen.
THOMAS KUHN (1922–1996)

In every war zone that I've been in, there has been a reality and then there has been the public perception of why the war was being fought. In every crisis, the issues have been far more complex than the public has been allowed to know.
JOHN LE CARRÉ (1931–)

I'm trying to use the language of today to express a general existential crisis that I think the world and I are going through.
SEAN LENNON (1975–)

I find it inconceivable that we're meeting for five and a half days, and there isn't one moment on the agenda to deal with the greatest crisis we've ever had in the church since 1789.
ROGER MAHONY (1936–)

Close scrutiny will show that most "crisis situations" are opportunities to either advance, or stay where you are.
MAXWELL MALTZ (1899–1975)

Fashion is never in crisis because clothes are always necessary.
ACHILLE MARAMOTTI (1927–2005)

A leader or a man of action in a crisis almost always acts subconsciously and then thinks of the reasons for his action.
JAWAHARLAL NEHRU (1889–1964)

Crises and deadlocks when they occur have at least this advantage, that they force us to think.
JAWAHARLAL NEHRU (1889–1964)

Every crisis offers you extra desired power.
WILLIAM MOULTON MARSTON (1893–1947)

Every little thing counts in a crisis.
JAWAHARLAL NEHRU (1889–1964)

Life isn't meant to be easy. It's hard to take being on the top—or on the bottom. I guess I'm something of a fatalist. You have to have a sense of history, I think, to survive some of these things.... Life is one crisis after another.
RICHARD M. NIXON (1913–1994)

In prehistoric times, mankind often had only two choices in crisis situations: fight or flee. In modern times, humor offers us a third alternative; fight, flee—or laugh.
ROBERT ORBEN (1927–)

These are the times that try men's souls.
THOMAS PAINE (1737–1809)

What one decides to do in crisis depends on one's philosophy of life, and that philosophy cannot be changed by an incident. If one hasn't any philosophy in crises, others make the decision.
JEANETTE RANKIN (1880–1973)

In the present crisis, government is not the solution to our problem; government is the problem.
RONALD REAGAN (1911–2004)

There is a crisis of public morality. Instead of policing bedrooms, we ought to be doing a better job policing boardrooms.
ROBERT REICH (1946–)

A man has no more character than he can command in a time of crisis.
RALPH W. SOCKMAN (1889–1970)

We are in such a slump that even the ones that are drinking aren't hitting.
CASEY STENGEL (1890–1975)

When you have a crisis, the crisis itself becomes one of your biggest assets if that crisis is bad enough. Everyone gets very modest and humble and listens. If you need to do rough things, you do rough things.
CARL-HENRIC SVANBERG (1952–)

Seeds of faith are always within us; sometimes it takes a crisis to nourish and encourage their growth.
SUSAN TAYLOR (1946–)

The whole life of an American is passed like a game of chance, a revolutionary crisis, or a battle.
ALEXIS DE TOCQUEVILLE (1805–1859)

We stand today poised on a pinnacle of wealth and power, yet we live in a land of vanishing beauty, of increasing ugliness, of shrinking open space and of an overall environment that is diminished daily by pollution and noise and blight. This, in brief, is the quiet conservation crisis.
STEWART UDALL (1920–)

The crisis of today is the joke of tomorrow.
H. G. WELLS (1866–1946)

Great occasions do not make heroes or cowards; they simply unveil them to the eyes of men. Silently and imperceptibly, as we wake or sleep, we grow strong or weak; and at last some crisis shows what we have become.
BROOKE FOSS WESTCOTT (1825–1901)

The human crisis is always a crisis of understanding: what we genuinely understand we can do.
RAYMOND WILLIAMS (1921–1988)

At every crisis in one's life, it is absolute salvation to have some sympathetic friend to whom you can think aloud without restraint or misgiving.
WOODROW WILSON (1856–1924)

But for every part of the world, instability, migration, crime, health becomes our issue, and it is just too late to wait for the crisis.
JAMES WOLFENSOHN (1933–)

Criticism

Sympathy is the first condition of criticism.
HENRI-FRÉDÉRIC AMIEL (1821–1881)

One cannot review a bad book without showing off.
W. H. AUDEN (1907–1973)

Critics are like eunuchs in a harem; they know how its done, they've seen it done every day, but they're unable to do it themselves.
BRENDAN FRANCIS BEHAN (1923–1964)

Silence is sometimes the severest criticism.
CHARLES BUXTON (1823–1871)

Any fool can criticize, condemn, and complain—and most fools do.
DALE CARNEGIE (1888–1955)

By a curious confusion, many modern critics have passed from the proposition that a masterpiece may be unpopular to the other proposition that unless it is unpopular it cannot be a masterpiece.
G. K. CHESTERTON (1874–1936)

It is better to correct your own faults than those of another.
DEMOCRITUS (460–370 BC)

How much easier it is to be critical than to be correct.
BENJAMIN DISRAELI (1804–1881)

The artist doesn't have time to listen to the critics. The ones who want to be writers read the reviews, the ones who want to write don't have the time to read reviews.
WILLIAM FAULKNER (1897–1962)

Now, in reality, the world has paid too great a compliment to critics, and has imagined them to be men of much greater profundity than they really are.
HENRY FIELDING (1707–1754)

Against criticism a man can neither protest nor defend himself; he must act in spite of it, and then it will gradually yield to him.
JOHANN WOLFGANG VON GOETHE (1749–1832)

He who wishes to exert a useful influence must be careful to insult nothing. Let him not be troubled by what seems absurd, but concentrate his energies to the creation of what is good. He must not demolish, but build. He must raise temples where mankind may come and partake of the purest pleasure.
JOHANN WOLFGANG VON GOETHE (1749–1832)

Asking a working writer what he thinks about critics is like asking a lamppost how it feels about dogs.
CHRISTOPHER HAMPTON (1946–)

He only profits from praise who values criticism.
HEINRICH HEINE (1797–1856)

The most destructive criticism is indifference.
EDGAR WATSON HOWE (1853–1937)

To avoid criticism do nothing, say nothing, be nothing.
ELBERT HUBBARD (1856–1915)

Honest criticism is hard to take, particularly from a relative, a friend, an acquaintance, or a stranger.
FRANKLIN P. JONES (1887–1929)

He has the right to criticize who has the heart to help.
ABRAHAM LINCOLN (1809–1865)

Music critics get their records for free so their opinions usually don't matter.
MARILYN MANSON (1969–)

People ask for criticism, but they only want praise.
W. SOMERSET MAUGHAM (1874–1965)

Criticism is prejudice made plausible.
H. L. MENCKEN (1880–1956)

I never met anybody who said when they were a kid, "I wanna grow up and be a critic."
RICHARD PRYOR (1940–2005)

Do what you feel in your heart to be right—for you'll be criticized anyway. You'll be damned if you do, and damned if you don't.
ELEANOR ROOSEVELT (1884–1962)

No degree of dullness can safeguard a work against the determination of critics to find it fascinating.
HAROLD ROSENBERG (1906–1978)

If you are not criticized, you may not be doing much.
DONALD H. RUMSFELD (1932–)

Pay no attention to what the critics say.... Remember, a statue has never been set up in honor of a critic!
JEAN SIBELIUS (1865–1957)

There's nothing more exhilarating than pointing out the shortcomings of others, is there?
KEVIN SMITH (1970–), *Clerks*

The trade of critic, in literature, music, and the drama, is the most degraded of all trades.
MARK TWAIN (1835–1910)

Critics are like pigs at the pastry cart.
JOHN UPDIKE (1932–)

Critics search for ages for the wrong word, which, to give them credit, they eventually find.
PETER USTINOV (1921–2004)

Any reviewer who expresses rage and loathing for a novel is preposterous. He or she is like a person who has put on full armor and attacked a hot fudge sundae.
KURT VONNEGUT JR. (1922–2007)

Having the critics praise you is like having the hangman say you've got a pretty neck.
ELI WALLACH (1915–)

Everything is entertainment; criticism is now entertainment and it seems that the French directors have woken up one day and suddenly realised that they were not backed up any more.
WIM WENDERS (1945–)

After all, one knows one's weak points so well, that it's rather bewildering to have the critics overlook them and invent others.
EDITH WHARTON (1862–1937)

Criticism comes easier than craftsmanship.
ZEUXIS (C. 400 BC)

It is usually best to be generous with praise, but cautious with criticism.
ANONYMOUS

Never criticize a man until you've walked a mile in his moccasins.
NATIVE AMERICAN PROVERB

Crowds

Spare me the whispering, crowded room, the friends who come and gape and go, the ceremonious air of gloom—all, which makes death a hideous show.
MATTHEW ARNOLD (1822–1888)

A crowd is not company, and faces are but a gallery of pictures.
SIR FRANCIS BACON (1561–1626)

The desert has its holiness of silence, the crowd its holiness of conversation.
WALTER ELLIOT (1842–1928)

It is easy in the world to live after the world's opinions; it is easy in solitude to live after your own; but the great man is he who in the midst of the crowd keeps with perfect sweetness the independence of solitude.
RALPH WALDO EMERSON (1803–1882)

He who reforms himself has done more toward reforming the public than a crowd of noisy, impotent patriots.
JOHANN KASPAR LAVATER (1741–1801)

The mass, whether it be a crowd or an army, is vile.
BENITO MUSSOLINI (1883–1945)

In a crowd, on a journey, at a banquet even, a line of thought can itself provide its own seclusion.
QUINTILIAN (C. AD 35–100)

Two's company, three's a crowd.
AMERICAN PROVERB

A born leader sees which way the crowd is going and steps in ahead.
ANONYMOUS

Cruelty

What beauty in childhood, what purity, what openness before one lets oneself be killed and cruelty recloses all.
ISABELLE ADJANI (1955–)

To insult someone we call him "bestial." For deliberate cruelty and nature, "human" might be the greater insult.
ISAAC ASIMOV (1920–1992)

Cruelty is, perhaps, the worst kind of sin. Intellectual cruelty is certainly the worst kind of cruelty.
G. K. CHESTERTON (1874–1936)

Men feel that cruelty to the poor is a kind of cruelty to animals. They never feel that it is an injustice to equals; nay it is treachery to comrades.
G. K. CHESTERTON (1874–1936)

The discovery of America was the occasion of the greatest outburst of cruelty and reckless greed known in history.
JOSEPH CONRAD (1857–1924)

I believe in preventing cruelty to all living beings in any form.
MORARJI DESAI (1896–1995)

Cruelty, like every other vice, requires no motive outside of itself; it only requires opportunity.
GEORGE ELIOT (1819–1880)

Cruelty is a tyrant that's always attended with fear.
THOMAS FULLER (1608–1661)

Cruelty is the law pervading all nature and society; and we can't get out of it if we would.
THOMAS HARDY (1840–1928)

My loathings are simple: stupidity, oppression, crime, cruelty, soft music.
VLADIMIR NABOKOV (1899–1977)

The infliction of cruelty with a good conscience is a delight to moralists—that is why they invented hell.
BERTRAND RUSSELL (1872–1970)

War is cruelty. There's no use trying to reform it, the crueler it is the sooner it will be over.
WILLIAM TECUMSEH SHERMAN (1820–1891)

Cruelty towards others is always also cruelty towards ourselves.
PAUL TILLICH (1886–1965)

Cults

When theology erodes and organization crumbles, when the institutional framework of religion begins to break up, the search for a direct experience which people can feel to be religious facilitates the rise of cults.
DANIEL BELL (1919–)

The history of the Church of Rome is a constant leakage of members into such breakaway cults, which go on splitting.
MARY DOUGLAS (1921–)

Cult recruiting methods based on dosing victims with the brain chemicals released during capture bonding would make cults even more of a problem than they are now.
KEITH HENSON (1942–)

Cults, or related social movements such as the Taliban in Afghanistan, result in massive military expenses.
KEITH HENSON (1942–)

Culture

Television is the first truly democratic culture—the first culture available to everybody and entirely governed by what the people want. The most terrifying thing is what people do want.
CLIVE BARNES (1927–)

All over the place, from the popular culture to the propaganda system, there is constant pressure to make people feel that they are helpless, that the only role they can have is to ratify decisions and to consume.
NOAM CHOMSKY (1928–)

I will go further, and assert that nature without culture can often do more to deserve praise than culture without nature.
CICERO (106–43 BC)

The highest possible stage in moral culture is when we recognize that we ought to control our thoughts.
CHARLES DARWIN (1809–1882)

Of all the self-fulfilling prophecies in our culture, the assumption that aging means decline and poor health is probably the deadliest.
MARILYN FERGUSON (1938–), *The Aquarian Conspiracy*

I do not want my house to be walled in on all sides and my windows to be stuffed. I want the cultures of all the lands to be blown about my house as freely as possible. But I refuse to be blown off my feet by any
MAHATMA GANDHI (1869–1948)

It's pretty clear now that what looked like it might have been some kind of counterculture is, in reality, just the plain old chaos of undifferentiated weirdness.
JERRY GARCIA (1942–1995)

A culture is only as great as its dreams, and its dreams are dreamed by artists.
L. RON HUBBARD (1911–1986), *Science of Survival*

I think that one possible definition of our modern culture is that it is one in which nine-tenths of our intellectuals can't read any poetry.
RANDALL JARRELL (1914–1965)

Culture makes all men gentle.
MENANDER (342–292 BC)

To give an accurate description of what has never occurred is not merely the proper occupation of the historian, but the inalienable privilege of any man of parts and culture.
OSCAR WILDE (1854–1900), *The Critic as Artist*

Noble life demands a noble architecture for noble uses of noble men. Lack of culture means what it has always meant: ignoble civilization and therefore imminent downfall.
FRANK LLOYD WRIGHT (1869–1959)

Cunning

Nothing doth more hurt in a state than that cunning men pass for wise.
SIR FRANCIS BACON (1561–1626)

Man's unhappiness, as I construe, comes of his greatness; it is because there is an Infinite in him, which with all his cunning he cannot quite bury under the Finite.
THOMAS CARLYLE (1795–1881)

I recognize in thieves, traitors and murderers, in the ruthless and the cunning, a deep beauty—a sunken beauty.
JEAN GENET (1910–1986)

Nature is beneficent. I praise her and all her works. She is silent and wise. She is cunning, but for good ends. She has brought me here and will also lead me away. She may scold me, but she will not hate her work. I trust her.
JOHANN WOLFGANG VON GOETHE (1749–1832)

Cunning is the art of concealing our own defects, and discovering other people's weaknesses.
WILLIAM HAZLITT (1778–1830)

Art is the final cunning of the human soul which would rather do anything than face the gods.
IRIS MURDOCH (1919–1999)

Cunning leads to knavery. It is but a step from one to the other, and that very slippery. Only lying makes the difference; add that to cunning, and it is knavery.
OVID (43 BC–AD 17)

Cunning … is but the low mimic of wisdom.
PLATO (C. 428–348 BC)

Many men have been capable of doing a wise thing, more a cunning thing, but very few a generous thing.
ALEXANDER POPE (1688–1744)

Cunning is a short blanket—if you pull it over your face, you expose your feet.
ANONYMOUS

Curiosity

Curiosity begins as an act of tearing to pieces or analysis.
SAMUEL ALEXANDER (1859–1938)

The first and simplest emotion which we discover in the human mind, is curiosity
EDMUND BURKE (1729–1797)

Curiosity about life in all of its aspects, I think, is still the secret of great creative people.
LEO BURNETT (1891–1971)

Curiosity does, no less than devotion, pilgrims make.
ABRAHAM COWLEY (1618–1667)

Be less curious about people and more curious about ideas.
MARIE CURIE (1867–1934)

Creatures whose mainspring is curiosity enjoy the accumulating of facts far more than the pausing at times to reflect on those facts.
CLARENCE DAY (1874–1935)

We keep moving forward, opening new doors, and doing new things, because we're curious and curiosity keeps leading us down new paths.
WALT DISNEY (1901–1966)

When you're curious, you find lots of interesting things to do.
WALT DISNEY (1901–1966)

It is a miracle that curiosity survives formal education.
ALBERT EINSTEIN (1879–1955)

The important thing is not to stop questioning. Curiosity has its own reason for existing. One cannot help but be in awe when he contemplates the mysteries of eternity, of life, of the marvelous structure of reality. It is enough if one tries merely to comprehend a little of this mystery every day. Never lose a holy curiosity.
ALBERT EINSTEIN (1879–1955)

Curiosity is lying in wait for every secret.
RALPH WALDO EMERSON (1803–1882)

Curiosity is one of the lowest of the human faculties. You will have noticed in daily life that when people are inquisitive they nearly always have bad memories and are usually stupid at bottom.
E. M. FORSTER (1879–1970)

The greatest virtue of man is perhaps curiosity.
ANATOLE FRANCE (1844–1924)

Many a secret that cannot be pried out by curiosity can be drawn out by indifference.
SYDNEY J. HARRIS (1917–1986)

Curiosity is, in great and generous minds, the first passion and the last.
SAMUEL JOHNSON (1709–1784)

Curiosity is one of the permanent and certain characteristics of a vigorous mind.
SAMUEL JOHNSON (1709–1784)

Human curiosity the urge to know, is a powerful force and is perhaps the best secret weapon of all in the struggle to unravel the workings of the natural world.
AARON KLUG (1926–)

Curiosity in children, is but an appetite for knowledge. One great reason why children abandon themselves wholly to silly pursuits and trifle away their time insipidly is, because they find their curiosity balked, and their inquiries neglected.
JOHN LOCKE (1632–1704)

Let's just say I was testing the bounds of reality. I was curious to see what would happen. That's all it was: curiosity.
JIM MORRISON (1943–1971)

Curiosity killed the cat, but satisfaction brought it back.
EUGENE O'NEILL (1888–1953)

The cure for boredom is curiosity. There is no cure for curiosity.
DOROTHY PARKER (1893–1967)

What we have to do is to be forever curiously testing new opinions and courting new impressions.
WALTER PATER (1839–1894)

Satisfaction of one's curiosity is one of the greatest sources of happiness in life.
LINUS PAULING (1901–1994)

To be curious about that which is not one's concern while still in ignorance of oneself is ridiculous.
PLATO (C. 428–348 BC)

A person who is too nice an observer of the business of the crowd, like one who is too curious in observing the labor of bees, will often be stung for his curiosity.
ALEXANDER POPE (1688–1744)

A good scientist is a person in whom the childhood quality of perennial curiosity lingers on. Once he gets an answer, he has other questions.
FREDERICK SEITZ (1911–)

Curiosity will conquer fear even more than bravery will.
JAMES STEPHENS (1882–1950)

Curiosity is the wick in the candle of learning.
WILLIAM ARTHUR WARD (1921–1994)

The public have an insatiable curiosity to know everything, except what is worth knowing.
OSCAR WILDE (1854–1900)

Only the curious will learn and only the resolute overcome the obstacles to learning. The quest quotient has always excited me more than the intelligence quotient.
EUGENE S. WILSON (1900–1981)

Seize the moment of excited curiosity on any subject to solve your doubts; for if you let it pass, the desire may never return, and you may remain in ignorance.
WILLIAM WIRT (1772–1834)

Curiosity killed the cat, but for a while I was a suspect.
STEVEN WRIGHT (1955–)

Custom

Custom is second nature.
SAINT AUGUSTINE (354–430)

Custom reconciles us to everything.
EDMUND BURKE (1729–1797)

Without the aid of prejudice and custom I should not be able to find my way across the room.
WILLIAM HAZLITT (1778–1830)

Have a place for everything and keep the thing somewhere else; this is not advice, it is merely custom.
MARK TWAIN (1835–1910)

Be not so bigoted to any custom as to worship it at the expense of truth.
JOHANN GEORG VON ZIMMERMANN (1728–1795)

Cynicism

A cynic is not merely one who reads bitter lessons from the past, he is one who is prematurely disappointed in the future.
SYDNEY J. HARRIS (1917–1986)

Cynicism is an unpleasant way of saying the truth.
LILLIAN HELLMAN (1905–1984), *The Little Foxes*

Never be a cynic, even a gentle one. Never help out a sneer, even at the devil.
VACHEL LINDSAY (1879–1931)

A cynic is a man who, when he smells flowers, looks around for a coffin.
H. L. MENCKEN (1880–1956)

Cynicism is not realistic and tough. It's unrealistic and kind of cowardly because it means you don't have to try.
PEGGY NOONAN (1950–)

My pessimism extends to the point of even suspecting the sincerity of the pessimists.
JEAN ROSTAND (1894–1977), *Journal of a Character*

The power of accurate observation is commonly called cynicism by those who have not got it.
GEORGE BERNARD SHAW (1856–1950)

Another cause for the increase in alienation and cynicism is a feeling that too many policy decisions that affect individuals have been taken out of any system that has accountability or that they can influence.
ROBERT TEETER (1939–2004)

No matter how cynical you get, it is impossible to keep up.
LILY TOMLIN (1939–)

What is a cynic? A man who knows the price of everything and the value of nothing.
OSCAR WILDE (1854–1900), *Lady Windermere's Fan*

Cynics regarded everybody as equally corrupt.... Idealists regarded everybody as equally corrupt, except themselves.
ROBERT ANTON WILSON (1932–2007)

Idealism is what precedes experience; cynicism is what follows.
DAVID T. WOLF (1943–)

Dance

I don't want people who want to dance; I want people who have to dance.
GEORGE BALANCHINE (1904–1983)

Nobody cares if you can't dance well. Just get up and dance.
DAVE BARRY (1947–)

A sympathetic Scot summed it all up very neatly in the remark, "You should make a point of trying every experience once, excepting incest and folk dancing."
SIR ARNOLD BAX (1883–1953), *Farewell My Youth*

There comes a pause, for human strength will not endure to dance without cessation; and everyone must reach the point at length of absolute prostration.
LEWIS CARROLL (1832–1898)

Custom has made dancing sometimes necessary for a young man; therefore mind it while you learn it, that you may learn to do it well, and not be ridiculous, though in a ridiculous act.
LORD CHESTERFIELD (1694–1773)

Never give a sword to a man who can't dance.
CONFUCIUS (551–479 BC)

Human beings, vegetables, or comic dust, we all dance to a mysterious tune, intoned in the distance by an invisible player.
ALBERT EINSTEIN (1879–1955)

Dance is the hidden language of the soul.
MARTHA GRAHAM (1894–1991)

Almost nobody dances sober, unless they happen to be insane.
H. P. LOVECRAFT (1890–1937)

Wives are people who feel they don't dance enough.
GROUCHO MARX (1890–1977)

The dance is a poem of which each movement is a word.
MATA HARI (1876–1917)

I would not know what the spirit of a philosopher might wish more to be than a good dancer.
FRIEDRICH NIETZSCHE (1844–1900), *The Gay Science*

And let that day be lost to us on which we did not dance once! And let that wisdom be false to us that brought no laughter with it!
FRIEDRICH NIETZSCHE (1844–1900)

Dancing in all its forms cannot be excluded from the curriculum of all noble education; dancing with the feet, with ideas, with words, and, need I add that one must also be able to dance with the pen?
FRIEDRICH NIETZSCHE (1844–1900)

I do not know what the spirit of a philosopher could more wish to be than a good dancer. For the dance is his ideal, also his fine art, finally also the only kind of piety he knows, his "divine service."
FRIEDRICH NIETZSCHE (1844–1900)

Without music, life would be a mistake.... I would only believe in a God who knew how to dance.
FRIEDRICH NIETZSCHE (1844–1900)

If you can't make your heart dance because you are too depressed, do something that makes someone else's heart dance. If you keep doing that ... it changes your life. One day perhaps we will get together and all dance.
YOKO ONO (1933–)

Poetry is an echo, asking a shadow to dance.
CARL SANDBURG (1878–1967)

A perpendicular expression of a horizontal desire.
GEORGE BERNARD SHAW (1856–1950)

If you cannot get rid of the family skeleton, you may as well make it dance.
GEORGE BERNARD SHAW (1856–1950)

We sing in a church, why can we not dance there?
GEORGE BERNARD SHAW (1856–1950)

Dancing is silent poetry.
SIMONIDES (556–468 BC)

Kids: they dance before they learn there is anything that isn't music.
WILLIAM STAFFORD (1914–1993)

On with dance, let joy be unconfined, is my motto; whether there's any dance to dance or any joy to be unconfined.
MARK TWAIN (1835–1910)

Let us read and let us dance—two amusements that will never do any harm to the world.
VOLTAIRE (1694–1778)

Every day brings a chance for you to draw in a breath, kick off your shoes, and dance.
OPRAH WINFREY (1954–)

He who cannot dance will say: "The drum is bad."
AFRICAN PROVERB

When the music changes, so does the dance.
AFRICAN PROVERB

Don't dance on a volcano.
French Proverb

We're fools whether we dance or not, so we might as well dance.
Japanese Proverb

Danger

I may be compelled to face danger, but never fear it, and while our soldiers can stand and fight, I can stand and feed and nurse them.
Clara Barton (1821–1912)

To seek understanding before taking action, yet to trust my instincts when action is called for. Never to avoid danger from fear, never to seek out danger for its own sake. Never to conform to fashion from fear of eccentricity, never to be eccentric from fear of conformity.
Steven Brust (1955–)

All generalizations are dangerous, even this one.
Alexandre Dumas (1802–1870)

As soon as there is life, there is danger.
Ralph Waldo Emerson (1803–1882)

I believe that banking institutions are more dangerous to our liberties than standing armies.
Thomas Jefferson (1743–1826)

The Chinese use two brush strokes to write the word "crisis." One brush stroke stands for danger; the other for opportunity. In a crisis, be aware of the danger—but recognize the opportunity.
John F. Kennedy (1917–1963)

Nothing in the world is more dangerous than a sincere ignorance and conscientious stupidity.
Martin Luther King Jr. (1929–1968)

Through danger safety comes—through trouble rest.
John Marston (1576–1634)

The greater danger for most of us lies not in setting our aim too high and falling short; but in setting our aim too low, and achieving our mark.
Michelangelo (1475–1564)

Between the great things we cannot do and the small things we will not do, the danger is that we shall do nothing.
Adolph Monod (1802–1856)

Believe me! The secret of reaping the greatest fruitfulness and the greatest enjoyment from life is to live dangerously!
Friedrich Nietzsche (1844–1900)

Wherever there is danger, there lurks opportunity; whenever there is opportunity, there lurks danger. The two are inseparable. They go together.
Earl Nightingale (1921–1989)

A rite of passage that doesn't involve some danger is too much a gift to create confidence.
Marge Piercy (1936–)

A timid person is frightened before a danger, a coward during the time, and a courageous person afterward.
Jean Paul Richter (1763–1825)

When we are afraid we ought not to occupy ourselves with endeavoring to prove that there is no danger, but in strengthening ourselves to go on in spite of the danger.
Mark Rutherford (1831–1913)

It is dangerous to be sincere unless you are also stupid.
George Bernard Shaw (1856–1950), *Man and Superman*

I'm all in favor of keeping dangerous weapons out of the hands of fools. Let's start with typewriters.
Solomon Short (1789–1867)

If you are out of trouble, watch for danger.
Sophocles (496–406 BC)

Considering how dangerous everything is, nothing is really very frightening.
GERTRUDE STEIN (1874–1946)

I am opposed to millionaires, but it would be dangerous to offer me the position.
MARK TWAIN (1835–1910)

It is dangerous to be right when the government is wrong.
VOLTAIRE (1694–1778)

A little sincerity is a dangerous thing, and a great deal of it is absolutely fatal.
OSCAR WILDE (1854–1900), *The Critic as Artist*

Anger is only one letter short of danger.
AMERICAN PROVERB

A danger foreseen is half avoided.
ANONYMOUS

The greater the fear the nearer the danger.
DANISH PROVERB

Danger can only be overcome by more danger.
GREEK PROVERB

The thief is no danger to the beggar.
IRISH PROVERB

Darkness

When it is dark enough, you can see the stars.
CHARLES AUSTIN BEARD (1874–1948)

When you close your doors, and make darkness within, remember never to say that you are alone, for you are not alone; nay, God is within, and your genius is within. And what need have they of light to see what you are doing?
EPICTETUS (AD 55–135), *Discourses*

The guilty one is not he who commits the sin, but the one who causes the darkness.
VICTOR HUGO (1802–1885)

Everything has its wonders, even darkness and silence, and I learn whatever state I am in, therein to be content.
HELEN KELLER (1880–1968)

Darkness is only driven out with light, not more darkness.
MARTIN LUTHER KING JR. (1929–1968)

Returning violence for violence multiplies violence, adding deeper darkness to a night already devoid of stars.... Hate cannot drive out hate: only love can do that.
MARTIN LUTHER KING JR. (1929–1968)

I will love the light for it shows me the way, yet I will endure the darkness for it shows me the stars.
OG MANDINO (1923–1996)

Light thinks it travels faster than anything but it is wrong. No matter how fast light travels, it finds the darkness has always got there first, and is waiting for it.
TERRY PRATCHETT (1948–)

It is the unknown we fear when we look upon death and darkness, nothing more.
J. K. ROWLING (1965–), *Harry Potter and the Half-Blood Prince*

In darkness one may be ashamed of what one does, without the shame of disgrace.
SOPHOCLES (496–406 BC)

Our deepest fear is not that we are inadequate. Our deepest fear is that we are powerful beyond measure. It is our Light, not our Darkness, that most frightens us.
MARIANNE WILLIAMSON (1952–), *Return to Love*

It's always darkest before the dawn.
ANONYMOUS

Dating

Nothing defines humans better than their willingness to do irrational things in the pursuit of

phenomenally unlikely payoffs. This is the principle behind lotteries, dating, and religion.
SCOTT ADAMS (1957–)

Bisexuality immediately doubles your chances for a date on Saturday night.
WOODY ALLEN (1935–)

Watching your daughter being collected by her date feels like handing over a million dollar Stradivarius to a gorilla.
JIM BISHOP (1907–1987)

Computer dating is fine, if you're a computer.
RITA MAE BROWN (1944–)

I've been dating since I was fifteen. I'm exhausted. Where is he?
KRISTIN DAVIS (1965–)

I think more dating stuff is scheduling. It's needing people who understand your work schedule.
JENNIFER LOVE HEWITT (1979–)

I'm dating a woman now who, evidently, is unaware of it.
GARY SHANDLING (1949–)

Employees make the best dates. You don't have to pick them up and they're always tax-deductible.
ANDY WARHOL (1928–1987)

Daughters

Well, knowledge is a fine thing, and mother Eve thought so; but she smarted so severely for hers, that most of her daughters have been afraid of it since.
ABIGAIL ADAMS (1744–1818)

Certain is it that there is no kind of affection so purely angelic as of a father to a daughter. In love to our wives there is desire; to our sons, ambition; but to our daughters there is something which there are no words to express.
JOSEPH ADDISON (1672–1719)

Mothers don't let your daughters grow up to be models unless you're present.
JANICE DICKINSON (1953–)

The mother is only really the mistress of her daughter upon the condition of continually representing herself to her as a model of wisdom and type of perfection.
ALEXANDRE DUMAS (1802–1870)

You teach your daughters the diameters of the planets and wonder when you are done that they do not delight in your company.
SAMUEL JOHNSON (1709–1784)

A fluent tongue is the only thing a mother doesn't like her daughter to resemble her in.
RICHARD BRINSLEY SHERIDAN (1751–1816)

We've begun to raise daughters more like sons ... but few have the courage to raise our sons more like our daughters.
GLORIA STEINEM (1934–)

I have three daughters and I find as a result I played King Lear almost without rehearsal.
PETER USTINOV (1921–)

If I had a choice of educating my daughters or my sons because of opportunity constraints, I would choose to educate my daughters.
BRIGHAM YOUNG (1801–1877)

A son is a son till he takes him a wife; a daughter is a daughter all of her life.
IRISH PROVERB

Days

Why are our days numbered and not, say, lettered?
WOODY ALLEN (1935–)

These are not dark days: these are great days—the greatest days our country has ever lived.
SIR WINSTON CHURCHILL (1874–1965)

The Dead

By a series of violent shocks, the nations in succession have struggled to shake off the Past, to reverse the action of Time and the verdict of success, and to rescue the world from the reign of the dead.
Lord Acton (1834–1902)

I'm spending a year dead for tax reasons.
Douglas Adams (1952–2001)

Woman absent is woman dead.
Walter Bagehot (1826- 1877)

A man without ambition is dead. A man with ambition but no love is dead. A man with ambition and love for his blessings here on earth is ever so alive.
Pearl Bailey (1918–1990)

War would end if the dead could return.
Stanley Baldwin (1867–1947)

You are either alive and proud or you are dead, and when you are dead, you can't care anyway.
Steven Biko (1946–1977)

The dead cannot cry out for justice. It is a duty of the living to do so for them.
Lois McMaster Bujold (1949–)

Rather be dead than cool.
Kurt Cobain (1967–1994), "Stay Away"

The dead governs the living.
Auguste Comte (1798–1857)

The past is the only dead thing that smells sweet.
Cyril Connolly (1903–1974)

In Spain, the dead are more alive than the dead of any other country in the world.
Federico Garcia Lorca (1898–1936)

I never go to funerals. To me a person is dead when he breathes for the last time. After that, your memories should be personal.
Hedy Lamarr (1913–2000)

Being dead is being weak and walled off.
Richard McKenna (1913–1964)

Excess of grief for the dead is madness; for it is an injury to the living, and the dead know it not.
Xenophon (c. 431–335 BC)

Death

Death is better, a milder fate than tyranny.
Aeschylus (c. 525–456 BC), *Agamemnon*

I don't want to achieve immortality through my work. I want to achieve it through not dying.
Woody Allen (1935–)

It is impossible to experience one's death objectively and still carry a tune.
Woody Allen (1935–)

On the plus side, death is one of the few things that can be done just as easily lying down.
Woody Allen (1935–)

There are worse things in life than death. Have you ever spent an evening with an insurance salesman?
Woody Allen (1935–)

We do not die because we have to die; we die because one day, and not so long ago, our consciousness was forced to deem it necessary.
Antonin Artaud (1896–1948)

Life is pleasant. Death is peaceful. It's the transition that's troublesome.
Isaac Asimov (1920–1992)

Death by starvation is slow.
Mary Austin (1868–1934)

Do not fear death so much, but rather the inadequate life.
Bertolt Brecht (1898–1956), *The Mother*

The dead cannot cry out for justice. It is a duty of the living to do so for them.
Lois McMaster Bujold (1949–)

If you live to be one hundred, you've got it made. Very few people die past that age.
GEORGE BURNS (1896–1996)

For three days after death hair and fingernails continue to grow but phone calls taper off.
JOHNNY CARSON (1925–2005)

There was something awesome in the thought of the solitary mortal standing by the open window and summoning in from the gloom outside the spirits of the nether world.
SIR ARTHUR CONAN DOYLE (1859–1930)

He not busy being born is busy dying.
BOB DYLAN (1941–)

Death is nothing to us, since when we are, death has not come, and when death has come, we are not.
EPICURUS (341–270 BC)

Death comes to all
But great achievements raise a monument
Which shall endure until the sun grows old.
GEORG FABRICIUS (1516–1571), "In Praise of Georgius Agricola"

Death most resembles a prophet who is without honor in his own land or a poet who is a stranger among his people.
KAHLIL GIBRAN (1883–1931)

Life isn't fair. It's just fairer than death, that's all.
WILLIAM GOLDMAN (1931–), *The Princess Bride*

If I could drop dead right now, I'd be the happiest man alive.
SAMUEL GOLDWYN (1882–1974)

I think about death a lot, like I think we all do. I don't think of suicide as an option, but as fun. It's an interesting idea that you can control how you go. It's this thing that's looming, and you can control it.
RYAN GOSLING (1980–)

What makes life worth living? Better surely, to yield to the stain of suicide blood in me and seek forgetfulness in the embrace of cold dark death.
ZANE GREY (1872–1939)

For any culture which is primarily concerned with meaning, the study of death—the only certainty that life holds for us—must be central, for an understanding of death is the key to liberation in life.
STANISLAV GROF (1931–)

Madame, all stories, if continued far enough, end in death, and he is no true story-teller who would keep that from you.
ERNEST HEMINGWAY (1899–1961)

It is a sign of a creeping inner death when we no longer can praise the living.
ERIC HOFFER (1902–1983)

Pale Death with impartial tread beats at the poor man's cottage door and at the palaces of kings.
HORACE (65–8 BC), *Odes*

Almost everything—all external expectations, all pride, all fear of embarrassment or failure—these things just fall away in the face of death, leaving only what is truly important. Remembering that you are going to die is the best way I know to avoid the trap of thinking you have something to lose. You are already naked. There is no reason not to follow your heart.
STEVE JOBS (1955–)

I hope the leaving is joyful; and I hope never to return.
FRIDA KAHLO (1907–1954)

As a well-spent day brings happy sleep, so life well used brings happy death.
LEONARDO DA VINCI (1452–1519)

Think not disdainfully of death, but look on it with favor; for even death is one of the things that Nature wills.
MARCUS AURELIUS ANTONINUS (121–180), *Meditations*

Dying is a very dull, dreary affair. And my advice to you is to have nothing whatever to do with it.
W. SOMERSET MAUGHAM (1874–1965)

Those who welcome death have only tried it from the ears up.
WILSON MIZNER (1876–1933)

Generally speaking, the Way of the warrior is resolute acceptance of death.
MIYAMOTO MUSASHI (1584–1645)

Must not all things at the last be swallowed up in death?
PLATO (C. 428–348 BC), *Dialogues*

The fear of death is more to be dreaded than death itself.
PUBLILIUS SYRUS (C. 100 BC), *Maxims*

As men, we are all equal in the presence of death.
PUBLILIUS SYRUS (C. 100 BC), *Moral Sayings*

It's sad when our daddies die. Makes us one less person inside.
PAMELA RIBON (1975–), *Why Girls Are Weird*

To the well-organized mind, death is but the next great adventure.
J. K. ROWLING (1965–), *Harry Potter and the Sorcerer's Stone*

There is no cure for birth and death save to enjoy the interval.
GEORGE SANTAYANA (1863–1952), *Soliloquies in England*

To be, or not to be: that is the question:
Whether 'tis nobler in the mind to suffer
The slings and arrows of outrageous fortune,
Or to take arms against a sea of troubles,
And by opposing end them? To die: to sleep:
No more; and by a sleep to say we end
The heartache and the thousand natural shocks
That flesh is heir to,—'t is a consummation
Devoutly to be wish'd. To die, to sleep;
To sleep: perchance to dream: ay, there's the rub:
For in that sleep of death what dreams may come,
When we have shuffled off this mortal coil,
Must give us pause: there's the respect
That makes calamity of so long life;
For who would bear the whips and scorns of time,
The oppressor's wrong, the proud man's contumely,
The pangs of despised love, the law's delay,
The insolence of office and the spurns
That patient merit of the unworthy takes,
When he himself might his quietus make
With a bare bodkin? who would fardels bear,
To grunt and sweat under a weary life,
But that the dread of something after death,
The undiscover'd country from whose bourn
No traveller returns, puzzles the will
And makes us rather bear those ills we have
Than fly to others that we know not of?
Thus conscience does make cowards of us all;
And thus the native hue of resolution
Is sicklied o'er with the pale cast of thought,
And enterprises of great pith and moment
With this regard their currents turn awry,
And lose the name of action.
WILLIAM SHAKESPEARE (1564–1616), *Hamlet*

Life does not cease to be funny when people die any more than it ceases to be serious when people laugh.
GEORGE BERNARD SHAW (1856–1950)

Death is not the worst; rather, in vain
To wish for death, and not to compass it.
SOPHOCLES (496–406 BC), *Electra*

A single death is a tragedy; a million deaths is a statistic.
JOSEPH STALIN (1879–1953)

It is impossible that anything so natural, so necessary, and so universal as death, should ever have been designed by Providence as an evil to mankind.
JONATHAN SWIFT (1667–1745)

Many that live deserve death. And some die that deserve life. Can you give it to them? Then be not too eager to deal out death in the name of justice, fearing for your own safety. Even the wise cannot see all ends.
J. R. R. TOLKIEN (1892–1973), *The Lord of the Rings*

The report of my death was an exaggeration.
MARK TWAIN (1835–1910)

We all end up dead, the question is how and why.
RANDALL WALLACE (1949–), *Braveheart*

I suppose that I shall have to die beyond my means.
OSCAR WILDE (1854–1900), upon being told the cost of an operation

As we look deeply within, we understand our perfect balance. There is no fear of the cycle of birth, life and death. For when you stand in the present moment, you are timeless.
RODNEY YEE (1957–)

For certain is death for the born
And certain is birth for the dead;
Therefore over the inevitable
Thou shouldst not grieve.
THE BHAGAVAD GITA

Debate

Debate is masculine, conversation is feminine.
AMOS BRONSON ALCOTT (1799–1888)

Debate and divergence of views can only enrich our history and culture.
IBRAHIM BABANGIDA (1941–)

Healthy disagreement, debate, leading to compromise has always been the American way.
DONALD L. CARCIERI (1942–)

Historically, the claim of consensus has been the first refuge of scoundrels; it is a way to avoid debate by claiming that the matter is already settled.
MICHAEL CRICHTON (1942–)

Debate is almost non-existent and no one is apparently accountable to anybody apart from their political party bosses. It is bad news for democracy in this country.
HELEN SUZMAN (1917–)

I love argument, I love debate. I don't expect anyone just to sit there and agree with me, that's not their job.
MARGARET THATCHER (1925–)

Debt

Interest works night and day in fair weather and in foul. It gnaws at a man's substance with invisible teeth.
HENRY WARD BEECHER (1813–1887)

Debt, n.: An ingenious substitute for the chain and whip of the slavedriver.
AMBROSE BIERCE (1842–1914), *The Devil's Dictionary*

Forgetfulness, n.: A gift of God bestowed upon debtors in compensation for their destitution of conscience.
AMBROSE BIERCE (1842–1914), *The Devil's Dictionary*

Always live within your income, even if you have to borrow money to do so.
JOSH BILLINGS (1818–1885)

You don't pay back your parents. You can't. The debt you owe them gets collected by your children, who hand it down in turn. It's a sort of entailment. Or if you don't have children of the body, it's left as a debt to your common humanity. Or to your God, if you possess or are possessed by one.
LOIS MCMASTER BUJOLD (1949–), *A Civil Campaign*

It is very iniquitous to make me pay my debts — you have no idea of the pain it gives one.
LORD BYRON (1788–1824)

There are but two ways of paying debt: Increase of industry in raising income, increase of thrift in laying out.
THOMAS CARLYLE (1795–1881)

Credit is a system whereby a person who can not pay gets another person who can not pay to guarantee that he can pay.
CHARLES DICKENS (1812–1870)

It is said that the world is in a state of bankruptcy, that the world owes the world more than the world can pay.
RALPH WALDO EMERSON (1803–1882)

Creditors have better memories than debtors.
BENJAMIN FRANKLIN (1706–1790), *Poor Richard's Almanac*

Rather go to bed without dinner than to rise in debt.
BENJAMIN FRANKLIN (1706–1790)

To the generous mind the heaviest debt is that of gratitude, when it is not in our power to repay it.
BENJAMIN FRANKLIN (1706–1790)

Debt is the worst poverty.
THOMAS FULLER (1608–1661)

A national debt, if it is not excessive, will be to us a national blessing.
ALEXANDER HAMILTON (1755–1804)

A creditor is worse than a slave owner; for the master owns only your person, but a creditor owns your dignity, and can command it.
VICTOR HUGO (1802–1885)

The world is indebted for all triumphs which have been gained by reason and humanity over error and oppression.
THOMAS JEFFERSON (1743–1826)

Small debts are like small gun shot; they are rattling around us on all sides and one can scarcely escape being wounded. Large debts are like cannons, they produce a loud noise, but are of little danger.
SAMUEL JOHNSON (1709–1784)

Money is a poor man's credit card.
MARSHALL MCLUHAN (1911–1980)

The spirit in which a thing is given determines that in which the debt is acknowledged; it's the intention, not the face-value of the gift, that's weighed.
SENECA (5 BC–AD 65), *Letters to Lucilius*

I can get no remedy against this consumption of the purse: borrowing only lingers and lingers it out, but the disease is incurable.
WILLIAM SHAKESPEARE (1564–1616), *Henry IV*

He that dies pays all his debts.
WILLIAM SHAKESPEARE (1564–1616), *The Tempest*

Words pay no debts.
WILLIAM SHAKESPEARE (1564–1616), *Troilus and Cressida*

Decency

God's most lordly gift to man is decency of mind.
AESCHYLUS (C. 525–456 BC)

I've had to hold back certain things for legal reasons, or just out of common decency, but I think autobiography has got to be selected confessions, hasn't it? I could have said jolly things about some of the dreadful people I've spent my life with, but it would have been a cheat.
TOM BAKER (1934–)

I had a marketing idea that everybody hated, decency is sexy.
JAMES L. BROOKS (1940–)

Morals are private. Decency is public.
RITA MAE BROWN (1944–)

Each person has inside a basic decency and goodness. If he listens to it and acts on it, he is giving a great deal of what it is the world needs most. It is not complicated but it takes courage. It takes courage for a person to listen to his own goodness and act on it.
PABLO CASALS (1876–1973)

As for plenty, we had not only for necessity, conveniency and decency, but for delight and pleasure to superfluity.
MARGARET CAVENDISH (1623–1673)

Justice consists in doing no injury to men; decency in giving them no offense.
CICERO (106–43 BC)

Decency must be an even more exhausting state to maintain than its opposite. Those who succeed seem to need a stupefying amount of sleep.
QUENTIN CRISP (1908–1999)

With all their faults, trade unions have done more for humanity than any other organization of men that ever existed. They have done more for decency, for honesty, for education, for the betterment of the race, for the developing of character in man, than any other association of men.
CLARENCE DARROW (1857–1938)

Is there decency left in American politics?
BYRON DORGAN (1942–)

Everything goes by the board—honor, pride, decency—to get the book written.
WILLIAM FAULKNER (1897–1962)

A woman drove me to drink and I didn't even have the decency to thank her.
W. C. FIELDS (1880–1946)

On matters of race, on matters of decency, baseball should lead the way.
A. BARTLETT GIAMATTI (1938–1989)

I believe that we should die with decency so that at least decency will survive.
DAG HAMMARSKJÖLD (1905–1961)

People who don't know how to keep themselves healthy ought to have the decency to get themselves buried, and not waste time about it.
HENRIK IBSEN (1828–1906)

Western civilization, Christianity, decency are struggling for their very lives. In this worldwide civil war, race prejudice is our most dangerous enemy, for it is a disease at the very root of our democratic life.
MORDECAI WYATT JOHNSON (1890–1976)

Above all, it is not decency or goodness or gentleness that impresses the Middle East, but strength.
MEIR KAHANE (1932–1990)

As much as we need a prosperous economy, we also need a prosperity of kindness and decency.
CAROLINE KENNEDY (1957–)

I respect anyone who has to fight and howl for his decency.
DEBORAH KERR (1921–2007)

Decency is the least of all laws, but yet it is the law which is most strictly observed.
FRANÇOIS DE LA ROCHEFOUCAULD (1613–1680)

If you don't believe in God, all you have to believe in is decency. Decency is very good. Better decent than indecent. But I don't think it's enough.
HAROLD MACMILLAN (1894–1986)

Today's Constitution is a realistic document of freedom only because of several corrective amendments. Those amendments speak to a sense of decency and fairness that I and other Blacks cherish.
THURGOOD MARSHALL (1908–1993)

That past is still within our living memory, a time when neighbour helped neighbour, sharing what little they had out of necessity, as well as decency.
MARY MCALEESE (1951–)

The extent to which all people in our society are made to count, and believe that they count, is not just a measure of decency; it makes sound economic sense.
MARY MCALEESE (1951–)

Don't overestimate the decency of the human race.
H. L. MENCKEN (1880–1956)

It is inaccurate to say that I hate everything. I am strongly in favor of common sense, common honesty, and common decency. This makes me forever ineligible for public office.
H. L. MENCKEN (1880–1956)

There can be no compromise with war; it cannot be reformed or controlled; cannot be disciplined into decency or codified into common sense.
JEANETTE RANKIN (1880–1973)

The most practical kind of politics is the politics of decency.
THEODORE ROOSEVELT (1858–1919)

You can't reason with people blinded by hate. They hate the power of the individual. They hate the progress of women. They hate the religious freedom of others. They hate the liberating breeze of democracy. But ladies and gentlemen, their hate is no match for America's decency.
ARNOLD SCHWARZENEGGER (1947–)

The practice of executing such offenders is a relic of the past and is inconsistent with evolving standards of decency in a civilized society.
JOHN PAUL STEVENS (1920–)

I've always felt, in all my books, that there's a deep decency in the American people and a native intelligence—providing they have the facts, providing they have the information.
LOUIS "STUDS" TERKEL (1912–)

Deception

Deceivers are the most dangerous members of society. They trifle with the best affections of our nature, and violate the most sacred obligations.
GEORGE CRABBE (1754–1832)

Deception is a cruel act. It often has many players on different stages that corrode the soul.
DONNA A. FAVORS (1955–)

We are never deceived; we deceive ourselves.
JOHANN WOLFGANG VON GOETHE (1749–1832)

Acting is a form of deception, and actors can mesmerize themselves almost as easily as an audience.
LEO ROSTEN (1908–1997)

And thus I clothe my naked villainy
With old odd ends, stol'n forth of holy writ;
And seem a saint, when most I play the devil.
WILLIAM SHAKESPEARE (1564–1616), *Richard III*

All deception in the course of life is indeed nothing else but a lie reduced to practice, and falsehood passing from words into things.
ROBERT SOUTHEY (1774–1843)

A military operation involves deception. Even though you are competent, appear to be incompetent. Though effective, appear to be ineffective.
SUN-TZU (C. 544–496 BC), *The Art of War*

All warfare is based on deception. There is no place where espionage is not used. Offer the enemy bait to lure him.
SUN-TZU (C. 544–496 BC), *The Art of War*

The only charm of marriage is that it makes a life of deception necessary for both parties.
OSCAR WILDE (1854–1900)

Decisions

Informed decision-making comes from a long tradition of guessing and then blaming others for inadequate results.
SCOTT ADAMS (1957–)

Men decide far more problems by hate, love, lust, rage, sorrow, joy, hope, fear, illusion, or some other inward emotion than by reality, authority, any legal standard, judicial precedent, or statute.
CICERO (106–43 BC)

The self is not something ready-made, but something in continuous formation through choice of action.
JOHN DEWEY (1859–1952)

The strongest principle of growth lies in human choice.
GEORGE ELIOT (1819–1880)

When it is not necessary to make a decision, it is necessary not to make a decision.
LORD FALKLAND (1610–1643)

Truly successful decision making relies on a balance between deliberate and instinctive thinking.
MALCOLM GLADWELL (1963–), *Blink: The Power of Thinking Without Thinking*

If I had to sum up in one word what makes a good manager, I'd say decisiveness. You can use the fanciest computers to gather the numbers, but in the end you have to set a timetable and act.
LEE IACOCCA (1924–)

Failures of perspective in decision-making can be due to aspects of the social utility paradox, but more often result from simple mistakes caused by inadequate thought.
HERMAN KAHN (1922–1983)

A weak man has doubts before a decision, a strong man has them afterwards.
KARL KRAUS (1874–1936)

He who lets the world, or his own portion of it, choose his plan of life for him, has no need of any other faculty than the ape-like one of imitation. He who chooses his plan for himself, employs all his faculties. He must use observation to see, reasoning and judgment to foresee, activity to gather materials for decision, discrimination to decide, and when he has decided, firmness and self-control to hold to his deliberate decision.
JOHN STUART MILL (1806–1873), *On Liberty*

An executive is a person who always decides; sometimes he decides correctly, but he always decides.
JOHN H. PATTERSON (1844–1922)

Give no decision till both sides thou'st heard.
PHOCYLIDES (C. 550 BC)

We must give lengthy deliberation to what has to be decided once and for all.
PUBLILIUS SYRUS (C. 100 BC)

Democracies are based on the principle that their citizens participate actively in the decision-making processes of the government.
CHARLES RANGEL (1930–)

I think that somehow, we learn who we really are and then live with that decision.
ELEANOR ROOSEVELT (1884–1962)

It is our choices … that show what we truly are, far more than our abilities.
J. K. ROWLING (1965–), *Harry Potter and the Chamber of Secrets*

The first step to getting the things you want out of life is this: Decide what you want.
BEN STEIN (1944–)

When you see how the President makes political or policy decisions, you see who he is. The essence of the Presidency is decision-making.
BOB WOODWARD (1943–)

Deeds

The ideal life is in our blood and never will be still. Sad will be the day for any man when he becomes contented with the thoughts he is thinking and the deeds he is doing—where there is not forever beating at the doors of his soul some great desire to do something larger, which he knows that he was meant and made to do.
PHILLIPS BROOKS (1835–1893)

All great deeds and all great thoughts have a ridiculous beginning.
ALBERT CAMUS (1913–1960), *The Myth of Sisyphus*

For blessings ever wait on virtuous deeds,
And though a late, a sure reward succeeds.
WILLIAM CONGREVE (1670–1729), *The Mourning Bride*

Our deeds follow us, and what we have been makes us what we are.
JOHN DYKES (1823–1876)

Our deeds determine us, as much as we determine our deeds.
GEORGE ELIOT (1819–1880)

Deeds, not words shall speak me.
JOHN FLETCHER (1579–1625)

Pleasure and love are the pinions of great deeds.
CHARLES FOX (1749–1806)

Great deeds are usually wrought at great risks.
HERODOTUS (484–430 BC), *The Histories of Herodotus*

You will certainly not be able to take the lead in all things yourself, for to one man a god has given deeds of war, and to another the dance, to another lyre and song, and in another wide-sounding Zeus puts a good mind.
HOMER (800–700 BC), *The Iliad*

Evil deeds do not prosper; the slow man catches up with the swift.
HOMER (800–700 BC), *The Odyssey*

There is nothing more dread and more shameless than a woman who plans such deeds in her heart as the foul deed which she plotted when she contrived her husband's murder.
HOMER (800–700 BC), *The Odyssey*

The charity that hastens to proclaim its good deeds, ceases to be charity, and is only pride and ostentation.
WILLIAM HUTTON (1723–1815)

Do not let your deeds belie your words, lest when you speak in church someone may say to himself, "Why do you not practice what you preach?"
SAINT JEROME (C. 342–420)

We would frequently be ashamed of our good deeds if people saw all of the motives that produced them.
FRANÇOIS DE LA ROCHEFOUCAULD (1613–1680)

Such evil deeds could religion prompt.
LUCRETIUS (C. 99–55 BC), *De Rerum Natura*

Deeds, not stones, are the true monuments of the great.
JOHN L. MOTLEY (1814–1877)

Memories of our lives, of our works and our deeds will continue in others.
ROSA PARKS (1913–2005)

Words have a longer life than deeds.
PINDAR (522–443 BC), *Nemean Odes*

It is not the critic who counts; not the man who points out how the strong man stumbles, or where the doer of deeds could have done them better. The credit belongs to the man who is actually in the arena, whose face is marred by dust and sweat and blood, who strives valiantly; who errs and comes short again and again; because there is not effort without error and shortcomings; but who does actually strive to do the deed; who knows the great enthusiasm, the great devotion, who spends himself in a worthy cause, who at the best knows in the end the triumph of high achievement and who at the worst, if he fails, at least he fails while daring greatly. So that his place shall never be with those cold and timid souls who know neither victory nor defeat.
THEODORE ROOSEVELT (1858–1919)

He who boasts of his ancestry is praising the deeds of another.
SENECA (5 BC–AD 65), *Hercules Furens*

'Tis a kind of good deed to say well; and yet words are not deeds.
WILLIAM SHAKESPEARE (1564–1616), *Henry VIII*

The bitterest tears shed over graves are for words left unsaid and deeds left undone.
HARRIET BEECHER STOWE (1811–1896)

Every minute you are thinking of evil, you might have been thinking of good instead. Refuse to pander to a morbid interest in your own misdeeds. Pick yourself up, be sorry, shake yourself, and go on again.
EVELYN UNDERHILL (1875–1941)

Vile deeds like poison weeds bloom well in prison air, It is only what is good in man, that wastes and withers there.
OSCAR WILDE (1854–1900), "The Ballad of Reading Gaol"

Do not be wise in words—be wise in deeds.
JEWISH PROVERB

If you disclose your alms, even then it is well done, but if you keep them secret, and give them to the poor, then that is better still for you; and this wipes off from you some of your evil deeds.
THE KORAN

He who carries out one good deed acquires one advocate in his own behalf, and he who commits one transgression acquires one accuser against himself. Repentance and good works are like a shield against calamity.
THE TALMUD

Man has three friends on whose company he relies. First, wealth which goes with him only while good fortune lasts. Second, his relatives; they go only as far as the grave, leave him there. The third friend, his good deeds, go with him beyond the grave.
THE TALMUD

Defeat

Exile, for no other motive than ease, would be the last defeat, with no seed of future victory in it.
LOIS MCMASTER BUJOLD (1949–), *Shards of Honor*

Any coward can fight a battle when he's sure of winning, but give me the man who has pluck to fight when he's sure of losing. That's my way, sir, and there are many victories worse than a defeat.
GEORGE ELIOT (1819–1880)

Victory attained by violence is tantamount to a defeat, for it is momentary.
MAHATMA GANDHI (1869–1948)

Before success in any man's life he is sure to meet with much temporary defeat and, perhaps, some failure. When defeat overtakes a man, the easiest and most logical thing to do is to quit. That is exactly what the majority of men do.
NAPOLEON HILL (1883–1970)

There are some defeats more triumphant than victories.
MICHEL DE MONTAIGNE (1533–1592)

What is defeat? Nothing but education; nothing but the first step to something better.
WENDELL PHILLIPS (1811–1884)

When defeat is inevitable, it is wisest to yield.
QUINTILIAN (C. AD 35–100)

Far better it is to dare mighty things, to win glorious triumphs even though checkered by failure, than to rank with those poor spirits who neither enjoy nor suffer much because they live in the gray twilight that knows neither victory nor defeat.
THEODORE ROOSEVELT (1858–1919)

A good man would prefer to be defeated than to defeat injustice by evil means.
SALLUST (86–34 BC), *Jugurthine War*

Be careful that victories do not carry the seed of future defeats.
RALPH W. SOCKMAN (1889–1970)

Victorious warriors win first and then go to war, while defeated warriors go to war first and then seek to win.
SUN-TZU (C. 544–496 BC), *The Art of War*

Defiance

These bickerings of opposite parties, and their mutual reproaches, their declamations, their sing-song, their triumphs and defiance, their dismal and prophecies, are all delusion.
JOHN ADAMS (1735–1826)

The defiance of established authority, religious and secular, social and political, as a worldwide phenomenon may well one day be accounted the outstanding event of the last decade.
HANNAH ARENDT (1906–1975)

There comes a time when deceit and defiance must be seen for what they are. At that point, a gathering danger must be directly confronted. At that point,

we must show that beyond our resolutions is actual resolve.
DICK CHENEY (1941–)

In war, resolution; in defeat, defiance; in victory, magnanimity
SIR WINSTON CHURCHILL (1874–1965)

Comedy is defiance. It's a snort of contempt in the face of fear and anxiety. And it's the laughter that allows hope to creep back on the inhale.
WILL DURST (1952–)

There is no person in this room whose basic rights are not involved in any successful defiance to the carrying out of court orders.
DWIGHT D. EISENHOWER (1890–1969)

Pride in their port, defiance in their eye
I see the Lords of human kind pass by.
OLIVER GOLDSMITH (1730–1774)

A religious man is a person who holds God and man in one thought at one time, at all times, who suffers harm done to others, whose greatest passion is compassion, whose greatest strength is love and defiance of despair.
ABRAHAM J. HESCHEL (1907–1972)

I believe that banking institutions are more dangerous to our liberties than standing armies. Already they have raised up a monied aristocracy that has set the government at defiance. The issuing power should be taken from the banks and restored to the people to whom it properly belongs.
THOMAS JEFFERSON (1743–1826)

I soon found that wit, like every other power, has its boundaries; that its success depends upon the aptitude of others to receive impressions; and that as some bodies, indissoluble by heat, can set the furnace and crucible at defiance, there are minds upon which the rays of fancy may be pointed without effect, and which no fire of sentiment can agitate or exalt.
SAMUEL JOHNSON (1709–1784)

We know that if gold, if fraud, if force can defeat us, they will all be used. And we have resolved that they shall not defeat us. We shall arm. We shall meet fraud and falsehood with defiance, and force with force, if need be.
DENIS KEARNEY (1847–1907)

With the pride of the artist, you must blow against the walls of every power that exists the small trumpet of your defiance.
NORMAN MAILER (1923–2007)

Today the majority of South Africans, black and white, recognize that apartheid has no future. It has to be ended by our own decisive mass action in order to build peace and security. The mass campaign of defiance and other actions of our organizations and people can only culminate in the establishment of democracy.
NELSON MANDELA (1918–)

Serious art has been the work of individual artists whose art has had nothing to do with style because they were not in the least connected with the style or the needs of the masses. Their work arose rather in defiance of their times.
FRANZ MARC (1880–1916)

Mrs. Parks' act of brave defiance rocked the foundation of American society and inspired generations of civil rights leaders and created a sense of hope for every American facing legal discrimination in this country.
KENDRICK MEEK (1966–)

I am certain that I speak on behalf of my entire nation when I say: On September 11th we are all Americans—in grief, as in defiance.
BENJAMIN NETANYAHU (1949–)

I am making this statement as an act of wilful defiance of military authority, because I believe that the War is being deliberately prolonged by those who have the power to end it.
SIEGFRIED SASSOON (1886–1967)

Shall I tell you what the real evil is? To cringe to the things that are called evils, to surrender to them our freedom, in defiance of which we ought to face any suffering.
SENECA (5 BC–AD 65)

The bold defiance of a woman is the certain sign of her shame—when she has once ceased to blush, it is because she has too much to blush for.
CHARLES MAURICE DE TALLEYRAND (1754–1838)

Nothing short of self-respect and that justice which is essential to a national character ought to involve us in war; for sure I am, if this country is preserved in tranquillity twenty years longer, it may bid defiance, in a just cause, to any power.
GEORGE WASHINGTON (1732–1799)

There is no week nor day nor hour when tyranny may not enter upon this country, if the people lose their roughness and spirit of defiance.
WALT WHITMAN (1819–1892)

For men tied fast to the absolute, bled of their differences, drained of their dreams by authoritarian leeches until nothing but pulp is left, become a massive, sick Thing whose sheer weight is used ruthlessly by ambitious men. Here is the real enemy of the people: our own selves dehumanized into "the masses." And where is the David who can slay this giant?
LILLIAN SMITH (1897–1966)

I am human because you are human. My humanity is caught up in yours and if you are dehumanized, I am dehumanized, and anger and resentment and retribution are corrosive of this great good, the harmony that has got to exist between people.
DESMOND TUTU (1931–)

Dehumanization

The film has succeeded in transforming subjects so indistinguishably into social functions, that those wholly encompassed, no longer aware of any conflict, enjoy their own dehumanization as something human, as the joy of warmth. The total interconnectedness of the culture industry, omitting nothing, is one with total social delusion.
THEODOR W. ADORNO (1903–1969)

I believe that the horrifying deterioration in the ethical conduct of people today stems from the mechanization and dehumanization of our lives—the disastrous by-product of the scientific and technical mentality. Nostra culpa. Man grows cold faster than the planet he inhabits.
ALBERT EINSTEIN (1879–1955)

Too much organization transforms men and women into automatia, suffocates the creative spirit and abolishes the very possibility of freedom.... The dehumanizing effects of over-organization are reinforced by the dehumanizing effects of over-population. Industry, as it expands, draws an ever greater proportion of humanity's increasing numbers into large cities.
ALDOUS HUXLEY (1894–1963)

Delay

Never think that God's delays are God's denials. Hold on; hold fast; hold out. Patience is genius.
GEORGE-LOUIS DE BUFFON (1707–1788)

Never do today what you can put off till tomorrow. Delay may give clearer light as to what is best to be done.
AARON BURR (1756–1836)

Grant us a brief delay; impulse in everything is but a worthless servant.
CAECILIUS STATIUS (220–168 BC)

Foolish men imagine that because judgment for an evil thing is delayed, there is no justice; but only accident here below. Judgment for an evil thing is many times delayed some day or two, some century or two, but it is sure as life, it is sure as death.
THOMAS CARLYLE (1795–1881)

Delay always breeds danger; and to protract a great design is often to ruin it.
MIGUEL DE CERVANTES (1547–1616)

Where duty is plain, delay is both foolish and hazardous; where it is not, delay may provide both wisdom and safety.
TYRON EDWARDS (1809–1894)

You may delay, but time will not.
BENJAMIN FRANKLIN (1706–1790)

Justice delayed, is justice denied.
WILLIAM GLADSTONE (1809–1898)

You must dare to disassociate yourself from those who would delay your journey.... Leave, depart, if not physically, then mentally. Go your own way, quietly, undramatically, and venture toward trueness at last.
VERNON HOWARD (1848–1921)

Delay is preferable to error.
THOMAS JEFFERSON (1743–1826)

Delay not; swift the flight of fortune's greatest favours.
SENECA (5 BC–AD 65)

The greatest loss of time is delay and expectation, which depend upon the future. We let go the present, which we have in our power, and look forward to that which depends upon chance, and so relinquish a certainty for an uncertainty.
SENECA (5 BC–AD 65)

The greatest remedy for anger is delay.
SENECA (5 BC–AD 65)

An incompetent attorney can delay a trial for months or years. A competent attorney can delay one even longer.
EVELLE J. YOUNGER (1918–1989)

There are no thanks for a kindness which has been delayed.
ANONYMOUS

Delusion

All are lunatics, but he who can analyze his delusion is called a philosopher.
AMBROSE BIERCE (1842–1914)

The ignorant mind, with its infinite afflictions, passions, and evils, is rooted in the three poisons. Greed, anger, and delusion.
BODHIDHARMA (470–543)

Getting rid of a delusion makes us wiser than getting hold of a truth.
LUDWIG BORNE (1786–1837)

No man is happy without a delusion of some kind. Delusions are as necessary to our happiness as realities.
CHRISTIAN NESTELL BOVÉE (1820–1904)

The people never give up their liberties but under some delusion.
EDMUND BURKE (1729–1797)

From the viewpoint of absolute truth, what we feel and experience in our ordinary daily life is all delusion. Of all the various delusions, the sense of discrimination between oneself and others is the worst form, as it creates nothing but unpleasant.
THE DALAI LAMA (1935–)

A human being is part of a whole, called by us the Universe, a part limited in time and space. He experiences himself, his thoughts and feelings, as something separated from the rest—a kind of optical delusion of his consciousness. This delusion is a kind of prison for us, restricting us to our personal desires and to affection for a few persons nearest us. Our task must be to free ourselves from this prison by widening our circles of compassion to embrace all living creatures and the whole of nature in its beauty.
ALBERT EINSTEIN (1879–1955)

There are men who would quickly love each other if once they were to speak to each other; for when they spoke they would discover that their souls had only separated by phantoms and delusions.
ERNEST HELLO (1828–1885)

It is a common delusion that you make things better by talking about them.
DAME ROSE MACAULAY (1881–1958)

Fishing is a delusion entirely surrounded by liars in old clothes.
DON MARQUIS (1878–1937)

Love is the delusion that one woman differs from another
H. L. MENCKEN (1880–1956)

Let no man in the world live in delusion. Without a Guru none can cross over to the other shore.
GURU NANAK (1469–1539)

When all else fails there's always delusion.
CONAN O'BRIEN (1963–)

If we ever pass out as a great nation we ought to put on our tombstone "America died from a delusion that she had moral leadership."
WILL ROGERS (1879–1935)

It is far better to grasp the Universe as it really is than to persist in delusion, however satisfying and reassuring.
CARL SAGAN (1934–1996)

It is amazing how complete is the delusion that beauty is goodness.
LEO TOLSTOY (1828–1910)

Delusions of grandeur make me feel a lot better about myself.
JANE WAGNER (1935–)

Delusion arises from anger. The mind is bewildered by delusion. Reasoning is destroyed when the mind is bewildered. One falls down when reasoning is destroyed.
THE BHAGAVAD GITA

Democracy

Democracy … while it lasts is more bloody than either [aristocracy or monarchy]. Remember, democracy never lasts long. It soon wastes, exhausts, and murders itself. There is never a democracy that did not commit suicide.
JOHN ADAMS (1735–1826)

Remember one thing about democracy. We can have anything we want and at the same time, we always end up with exactly what we deserve.
EDWARD ALBEE (1928–)

A democracy is a government in the hands of men of low birth, no property, and vulgar employment.
ARISTOTLE (384–322 BC)

Democracy arose from men's thinking that if they are equal in any respect, they are equal absolutely.
ARISTOTLE (384–322 BC)

Democracy is when the indigent, and not the men of property, are the rulers.
ARISTOTLE (384–322 BC)

If liberty and equality, as is thought by some, are chiefly to be found in democracy, they will be best attained when all persons alike share in the government to the utmost.
ARISTOTLE (384–322 BC), *Politics*

In a democracy the poor will have more power than the rich, because there are more of them, and the will of the majority is supreme.
ARISTOTLE (384–322 BC)

Democracy means government by discussion, but it is only effective if you can stop people talking.
CLEMENT ATLEE (1883–1967)

Democracy is being allowed to vote for the candidate you dislike least.
ROBERT BYRNE (1928–)

Democracy means government by the uneducated, while aristocracy means government by the badly educated.
G. K. CHESTERTON (1874–1936)

Propaganda is to a democracy what the bludgeon is to a totalitarian state.
NOAM CHOMSKY (1928–)

Nothing can be more abhorrent to democracy than to imprison a person or keep him in prison because he is unpopular. This is really the test of civilization.
SIR WINSTON CHURCHILL (1874–1965)

The best argument against democracy is a five minute conversation with the average voter.
SIR WINSTON CHURCHILL (1874–1965)

Many forms of Government have been tried, and will be tried in this world of sin and woe. No one pretends that democracy is perfect or all-wise. Indeed, it has been said that democracy is the worst form of government except all those other forms that have been tried from time to time
SIR WINSTON CHURCHILL (1874–1965)

Nor is the people's judgment always true: the most may err as grossly as the few.
JOHN DRYDEN (1631–1700)

The whole dream of democracy is to raise the proletarian to the level of stupidity attained by the bourgeois.
GUSTAVE FLAUBERT (1821–1880)

An honest election, under democracy, is an act of innocence which does not take place more than once in the history of a given nation.
JOSÉ MARÍA GIL ROBLES Y QUIÑONES (1898–1980)

Democracy is the only system that persists in asking the powers that be whether they are the powers that ought to be.
SYDNEY J. HARRIS (1917–1986)

The freeman, casting with unpurchased hand the vote that shakes the turrets of the land.
OLIVER WENDELL HOLMES SR. (1809–1894)

All democracies are based on the proposition that power is very dangerous and that it is extremely important not to let any one person or small group have too much power for too long a time.
ALDOUS HUXLEY (1894–1963)

A democracy is nothing more than mob rule, where fifty-one percent of the people may take away the rights of the other forty-nine.
THOMAS JEFFERSON (1762–1826)

The democracy will cease to exist when you take away from those who are willing to work and give to those who would not.
THOMAS JEFFERSON (1762–1826)

People often say that, in a democracy, decisions are made by a majority of the people. Of course, that is not true. Decisions are made by a majority of those who make themselves heard and who vote—a very different thing.
WALTER H. JUDD (1898–1994)

The ignorance of one voter in a democracy impairs the security of all.
JOHN F. KENNEDY (1917–1963)

Now is the time to make real the promise of democracy.
MARTIN LUTHER KING JR. (1929–1968)

Democracy means the opportunity to be everyone's slave.
KARL KRAUS (1874–1936)

To make democracy work, we must be a nation of participants, not simply observers. One who does not vote has no right to complain.
LOUIS L'AMOUR (1908–1988)

You must drop all your democracy. You must not believe in "the people." One class is no better than another. It must be a case of Wisdom, or Truth. Let the working classes be working classes. That is the truth. There must be an aristocracy of people who have wisdom, and there must be a Ruler: a Kaiser: no Presidents and democracies.
D. H. LAWRENCE (1885–1930)

As I would not be a slave, so I would not be a master. This expresses my idea of democracy.
ABRAHAM LINCOLN (1809–1865)

Democracy is the government of the people, by the people, for the people.
ABRAHAM LINCOLN (1809–1865)

No man is good enough to govern another man without the other's consent.
ABRAHAM LINCOLN (1809–1865)

Democracy is the road to socialism.
KARL MARX (1818–1883)

Democracy is also a form of worship. It is the worship of Jackals by Jackasses.
H. L. MENCKEN (1880–1956)

Democracy is the theory that the common people know what they want and deserve to get it good and hard.
H. L. MENCKEN (1880–1956)

Giving every man a vote has no more made men wise and free than Christianity has made them good.
H. L. MENCKEN (1880–1956)

Under democracy one party always devotes its chief energies to trying to prove that the other party is unfit to rule—and both commonly succeed, and are right.
H. L. MENCKEN (1880–1956)

The love of democracy is that of equality.
CHARLES DE MONTESQUIEU (1689–1755)

Democracy is a process by which the people are free to choose the man who will get the blame.
DR. LAURENCE J. PETER (1919–1990)

Democracies are based on the principle that their citizens participate actively in the decision-making processes of the government.
CHARLES RANGEL (1930–)

On account of being a democracy and run by the people, we are the only nation in the world that has to keep a government four years, no matter what it does.
WILL ROGERS (1879–1935)

The liberty of a democracy is not safe if the people tolerate the growth of private power to a point where it comes stronger than their democratic state itself. That, in its essence, is fascism—ownership of government by an individual, by a group.
FRANKLIN D. ROOSEVELT (1882–1945)

A great democracy must be progressive or it will soon cease to be a great democracy.
THEODORE ROOSEVELT (1858–1919)

You can't reason with people blinded by hate. They hate the power of the individual. They hate the progress of women. They hate the religious freedom of others. They hate the liberating breeze of democracy. But ladies and gentlemen, their hate is no match for America's decency.
ARNOLD SCHWARZENEGGER (1947–)

The three main sources of skepticism are, first, that not every people desires freedom; second, that democracy in certain parts of the world would be dangerous; and third, that there is little the world's democracies can do to advance freedom outside their countries.
NATAN SHARANSKY (1948–)

Democracy is a device that ensures we shall be governed no better than we deserve.
GEORGE BERNARD SHAW (1856–1950)

Democracy substitutes election by the incompetent many for appointment by the corrupt few.
GEORGE BERNARD SHAW (1856–1950), *Man and Superman*

Democracy's a very fragile thing. You have to take care of democracy. As soon as you stop being responsible to it and allow it to turn into scare tactics, it's no longer democracy, is it? It's something else. It may be an inch away from totalitarianism.
SAM SHEPARD (1943–)

Democracy encourages the majority to decide things about which the majority is blissfully ignorant.
JOHN SIMON (1873–1954)

It's not the voting that's democracy, it's the counting.
TOM STOPPARD (1937–), *Jumpers*

Democracy is the recurrent suspicion that more than half of the people are right more than half the time.
E. B. WHITE (1899–1985)

Democracy means simply the bludgeoning of the people by the people for the people.
OSCAR WILDE (1854–1900)

Democrats

The Democrats seem to be basically nicer people, but they have demonstrated time and again that they have the management skills of celery.
DAVE BARRY (1947–)

What is a democrat? One who believes that the republicans have ruined the country. What is a republican? One who believes that the democrats would ruin the country.
AMBROSE BIERCE (1842–1914)

Republicans have nothing but bad ideas, and Democrats have no ideas.
LEWIS BLACK (1948–)

Republicans believe largely in the market working, Democrats believe stereotypically that you've got to give people something. So why not give people a chance to let the market work for them.
HAROLD FORD (1970–)

If you want to live like a Republican, you have to vote for Democrats.
RICHARD GEPHARDT (1941–)

I never said all Democrats were saloonkeepers; what I said was all saloonkeepers are Democrats.
HORACE GREELEY (1811–1872)

Simply put, Republican economic policies let Americans keep more of their own money to spend, save and invest, while Democrats want to take it away.
J. D. HAYWORTH (1958–)

You get fifteen democrats in a room, and you get twenty opinions.
PATRICK LEAHY (1940–)

The only difference between the Democrats and the Republicans is that the Democrats allow the poor to be corrupt, too.
OSCAR LEVANT (1906–1972)

All people are born alike—except Republicans and Democrats.
GROUCHO MARX (1890–1977)

The Democrats are the party that says government will make you smarter, taller, richer, and remove the crabgrass on your lawn. The Republicans are the party that says government doesn't work and then they get elected and prove it.
P. J. O'ROURKE (1947–)

Republicans believe every day is the Fourth of July, but the Democrats believe every day is April 15.
RONALD REAGAN (1911–2004)

You can never underestimate the ability of the Democrats to wet their finger and hold it to the wind.
RONALD REAGAN (1911–2004)

Democrats never agree on anything, that's why they're Democrats. If they agreed with each other, they would be Republicans.
WILL ROGERS (1879–1935)

The Democrats and Republicans are equally corrupt—it's only in the amount where the Republicans excel.
WILL ROGERS (1879–1935)

The difference between a Republican and a Democrat is the Democrat is a cannibal—they have to live off each other—while the Republicans, why, they live off the Democrats.
WILL ROGERS (1879–1935)

I have been thinking that I would make a proposition to my Republican friends … that if they will stop telling lies about the Democrats, we will stop telling the truth about them.
ADLAI E. STEVENSON II (1900–1965)

Depression

The best cure for worry, depression, melancholy, brooding, is to go deliberately forth and try to lift

with one's sympathy the gloom of somebody else.
ARNOLD BENNETT (1867 –1931)

Just like other illnesses, depression can be treated so that people can live happy, active lives.
TOM BOSLEY (1927–)

The term clinical depression finds its way into too many conversations these days. One has a sense that a catastrophe has occurred in the psychic landscape.
LEONARD COHEN (1934–)

You largely constructed your depression. It wasn't given to you. Therefore, you can deconstruct it.
ALBERT ELLIS (1913–2007)

If you suffer from depression, anything that makes you feel has to be the most important thing in your life, because it's the only thing that can save you.
SIOBHAN FAHEY (1957–)

Depression is close to me, but suicide hasn't been.
CLAIRE FORLANI (1972–)

That terrible mood of depression of whether it's any good or not is what is known as The Artist's Reward.
ERNEST HEMINGWAY (1899–1961)

Instead of seeing depression as a dysfunction, it is a functioning phenomenon. It stops you cold, sets you down, makes you damn miserable.
JAMES HILLMAN (1926–)

In addition to my other numerous acquaintances, I have one more intimate confidant. My depression is the most faithful mistress I have known—no wonder, then, that I return the love.
SØREN KIERKEGAARD (1813–1855)

Depression is rage spread thin.
GEORGE SANTAYANA (1863–1952)

Remember that there is nothing stable in human affairs; therefore avoid undue elation in prosperity, or undue depression in adversity.
SOCRATES (469–399 BC)

Depression is melancholy minus its charms—the animation, the fits.
SUSAN SONTAG (1933–2004)

That's the thing about depression: A human being can survive almost anything, as long as she sees the end in sight. But depression is so insidious, and it compounds daily, that it's impossible to ever see the end. The fog is like a cage without a key.
ELIZABETH WURTZEL (1967–)

Concern should drive us into action and not into depression.
ANONYMOUS

Desire

The wise man will love; all others will desire.
AFRANIUS (C. 90 BC)

It is the nature of desire not to be satisfied, and most men live only for the gratification of it.
ARISTOTLE (384–322 BC), *Politics*

[M]en in general desire the good, and not merely what their fathers had.
ARISTOTLE (384–322 BC), *Politics*

I count him braver who overcomes his desires than him who overcomes his enemies.
ARISTOTLE (384–322 BC)

If you greatly desire something, have the guts to stake everything on obtaining it.
BRENDAN FRANCIS BEHEN (1923–1964)

Man is an animal, which, alone among the animals, refuses to be satisfied by the fulfilment of animal desires.
ALEXANDER GRAHAM BELL (1847–1922)

Those who restrain desire, do so because theirs is weak enough to be restrained.
WILLIAM BLAKE (1757–1827), *The Marriage of Heaven and Hell*

Some prices are just too high, no matter how much you may want the prize. The one thing you can't trade for your heart's desire is your heart.
LOIS MCMASTER BUJOLD (1949–), *Memory*

In men of the highest character and noblest genius there is to be found an insatiable desire for honour, command, power, and glory.
CICERO (106–43 BC)

Let your desires be ruled by reason.
CICERO (106–43 BC)

He who desires is always poor.
CLAUDIANUS (C. 350)

One must desire something to be alive.
MARGARET DELAND (1857–1945)

Desire awakens only those things that are thought possible.
RENÉ DESCARTES (1596–1650)

Freedom is not procured by a full enjoyment of what is desired, but by controlling the desire.
EPICTETUS (AD 55–135)

Man is the only animal whose desires increase as they are fed; the only animal that is never satisfied.
HENRY GEORGE (1839–1897)

Desire is half of life; indifference is half of death.
KAHLIL GIBRAN (1883–1931)

What makes the engine go? Desire, desire, desire.
STANLEY KUNITZ (1905–2006)

Manifest plainness,
Embrace simplicity,
Reduce selfishness,
Have few desires.
LAO-TZU (C. 600 BC), *The Way of Lao-tzu*

There is no calamity greater than lavish desires.
There is no greater guilt than discontentment.
And there is no greater disaster than greed.
LAO-TZU (C. 600 BC), *The Way of Lao-tzu*

Lord, grant that I may always desire more than I accomplish.
MICHELANGELO (1475–1564)

How helpless we are, like netted birds, when we are caught by desire!
BELVA PLAIN (1919–)

We desire nothing so much as what we ought not to have.
PUBLILIUS SYRUS (C. 100 BC), *Maxims*

Every man has business and desire,
Such as it is…
WILLIAM SHAKESPEARE (1564–1616), *Hamlet*

There are two tragedies in life. One is not to get your heart's desire. The other is to get it.
GEORGE BERNARD SHAW (1856–1950), *Man and Superman*

The stoical scheme of supplying our wants by lopping off our desires is like cutting off our feet when we want shoes.
JONATHAN SWIFT (1667–1745)

A human being has a natural desire to have more of a good thing than he needs.
MARK TWAIN (1835–1910), *Following the Equator*

Life ought to be a struggle of desire toward adventures whose nobility will fertilize the soul.
REBECCA WEST (1892–1983)

Dwell not upon thy weariness, thy strength shall be according to the measure of thy desire.
ARAB PROVERB

Despair

He who learns must suffer, and, even in our sleep, pain that cannot forget falls drop by drop upon the

heart, and in our own despair, against our will,
comes wisdom to us by the awful grace of God.
AESCHYLUS (C. 525–456 BC)

More than any other time in history, mankind faces a crossroads. One path leads to despair and utter hopelessness. The other, to total extinction. Let us pray we have the wisdom to choose correctly.
WOODY ALLEN (1935–)

Action is the antidote to despair.
JOAN BAEZ (1941–)

It is necessary to work, if not from inclination, at least from despair. Everything considered, work is less boring than amusing oneself.
CHARLES BAUDELAIRE (1821–1867)

Every composer knows the anguish and despair occasioned by forgetting ideas which one had no time to write down.
LOUIS-HECTOR BERLIOZ (1803–1869)

Love seeketh not itself to please,
Nor for itself hath any care,
But for another gives its ease,
And builds a Heaven in Hell's despair.
WILLIAM BLAKE (1757–1827)

Never despair; but if you do, work on in despair.
EDMUND BURKE (1729–1797)

He who despairs over an event is a coward, but he who holds hope for the human condition is a fool.
ALBERT CAMUS (1913–1960)

If there is a sin against life, it consists perhaps not so much in despairing of life as in hoping for another life and in eluding the implacable grandeur of this life.
ALBERT CAMUS (1913–1960)

In idleness there is a perpetual despair.
THOMAS CARLYLE (1795–1881)

I like living. I have sometimes been wildly, despairingly, acutely miserable, racked with sorrow, but through it all I still know quite certainly that just to be alive is a grand thing.
AGATHA CHRISTIE (1890–1976)

I can't tell if a straw ever saved a drowning man, but I know that a mere glance is enough to make despair pause. For in truth we who are creatures of impulse are creatures of despair.
JOSEPH CONRAD (1857–1924)

What we call our despair is often only the painful eagerness of unfed hope.
GEORGE ELIOT (1819–1880), *Middlemarch*

Discouragement is simply the despair of wounded self-love.
FRANÇOIS DE FÉNELON (1651–1715)

Lord, make me an instrument of Your peace!
Where there is hatred let me sow love;
Where there is injury, pardon;
Where there is doubt, faith;
Where there is despair, hope;
Where there is darkness, light;
Where there is sadness, joy.
SAINT FRANCIS OF ASSISI (1181–1226)

Whoever feels pain in hearing a good character of his neighbor, will feel a pleasure in the reverse. And those who despair to rise in distinction by their virtues, are happy if others can be depressed to a level of themselves.
BENJAMIN FRANKLIN (1706–1790)

Despair gives courage to a coward.
THOMAS FULLER (1608–1661)

When I despair, I remember that all through history the ways of truth and love have always won. There have been tyrants, and murderers, and for a time they can seem invincible, but in the end they always fall. Think of it—always.
MAHATMA GANDHI (1869–1948)

Tenderness and kindness are not signs of weakness and despair, but manifestations of strength and resolutions.
KAHLIL GIBRAN (1883–1931)

Appetite, with an opinion of attaining, is called hope; the same, without such opinion, despair.
THOMAS HOBBES (1588–1679)

My views and feelings [are] in favor of the abolition of war—and I hope it is practicable, by improving the mind and morals of society, to lessen the disposition to war; but of its abolition I despair.
THOMAS JEFFERSON (1743–1826)

Melancholy and sadness are the start of doubt … doubt is the beginning of despair; despair is the cruel beginning of the differing degrees of wickedness.
ISIDORE DUCASSE LAUTREAMONT (1846–1870)

Mortal lovers must not try to remain at the first step; for lasting passion is the dream of a harlot and from it we wake in despair.
C. S. LEWIS (1898–1963), *The Pilgrim's Regress*

If you look for truth, you may find comfort in the end; if you look for comfort you will not get either comfort or truth, only soft soap and wishful thinking to begin, and in the end, despair.
C. S. LEWIS (1898–1963)

He who labors diligently need never despair; for all things are accomplished by diligence and labor.
MENANDER (342–292 BC)

Despair is vinegar from the wine of hope.
AUSTIN O'MALLEY (1858–1932)

To be thoroughly conversant with a man's heart, is to take our final lesson in the iron-clasped volume of despair.
EDGAR ALLAN POE (1809–1849)

Oft expectation fails, and most oft there
Where most it promises; and oft it hits
Where hope is coldest; and despair most fits.
WILLIAM SHAKESPEARE (1564–1616), *All's Well That Ends Well*

He who has never hoped can never despair.
GEORGE BERNARD SHAW (1856–1950), *Caesar and Cleopatra*

Sometimes you feel other people's pain worse than your own. We're armored against our own troubles. We can't afford to give in to despair. Then you see someone else struggling, and it breaks your … heart.
SEAN STEWART (1965–), *Perfect Circle*

I must lose myself in action, lest I wither in despair.
ALFRED, LORD TENNYSON (1809–1892)

I can endure my own despair,
but not another's hope.
WILLIAM WALSH (1663–1708)

Desperation

Desperation is the raw material of drastic change. Only those who can leave behind everything they have ever believed in can hope to escape.
WILLIAM S. BURROUGHS (1914–1997)

My interest in desperation lies only in that sometimes I find myself having become desperate. Very seldom do I start out that way. I can see of course that, in the abstract, thinking and all activity is rather desperate.
WILLEM DE KOONING (1904–1997)

Desperation is sometimes as powerful an inspirer as genius.
BENJAMIN DISRAELI (1804–1881)

In life you need either inspiration or desperation.
ANTHONY ROBBINS (1960–)

Men of my age live in a state of continual desperation.
VITA SACKVILLE-WEST (1892–1962)

Who knows where inspiration comes from. Perhaps it arises from desperation. Perhaps it comes from the flukes of the universe, the kindness of the muses.
AMY TAN (1952–)

Nowadays men lead lives of noisy desperation.
JAMES THURBER (1894–1961)

The mass of men lead lives of quiet desperation.
HENRY DAVID THOREAU (1817–1862), *Walden*

What is called resignation is confirmed desperation.
HENRY DAVID THOREAU (1817–1862), *Walden*

A dog in desperation will leap over a wall.
CHINESE PROVERB

Dessert

Comedy just pokes at problems, rarely confronts them squarely. Drama is like a plate of meat and potatoes, comedy is rather the dessert, a bit like meringue.
WOODY ALLEN (1935–)

Just think of all those women on the *Titanic* who said, "No, thank you," to dessert that night. And for what!
ERMA BOMBECK (1927–1996)

It's so difficult. Sometimes if I have dessert, I think, "Well, I blew it." That's something I need to work on and control. But still there's nothing like a buffet.
DONNA DIXON (1957–)

It's nice to eat a good hunk of beef but you want a light dessert, too.
ARTHUR FIEDLER (1894–1979)

Work is the meat of life, pleasure the dessert.
B. C. FORBES (1880–1954)

Thus the public use of reason and freedom is nothing but a dessert, a sumptuous dessert.
JOHANN G. HAMANN (1730–1788)

I remember one dinner for which I had relied upon a form of ice as the principal feature of the dessert.
JULIA WARD HOWE (1819–1910)

I try to eat low-fat, but once a week I'll have a major dessert or an oily pasta. Mostly I eat fresh fruits and vegetables, chicken and fish.
CHRISTINE LAHTI (1950–)

I don't always prepare such rich meals. Sometimes I'll just serve a simple quiche, salad and dessert for dinner. During the week I try to eat lightly.
PAUL LYNDE (1926–1982)

Chocolate's okay, but I prefer a really intense fruit taste. You know when a peach is absolutely perfect … it's sublime. I'd like to capture that and then use it in a dessert.
KATHY MATTEA (1959–)

For me the ideal date would be to drink wine in the backyard under the stars, listen to music and just talk. Then we'd eat steak and, later, dessert. If all went as planned, we'd save some of the dessert and play with it while making out.
KAREN MCDOUGAL (1971–)

Dessert is probably the most important stage of the meal, since it will be the last thing your guests remember before they pass out all over the table.
WILLIAM POWELL (1892–1984)

Life is uncertain. Eat dessert first.
ERNESTINE ULMER (1925–)

Destiny

Destiny waits alike for the free man as well as for him enslaved by another's might.
AESCHYLUS (C. 525–456 BC), *The Libation Bearers*

Woman is the salvation or the destruction of the family. She carries its destiny in the folds of her mantle.
HENRI-FRÉDÉRIC AMIEL (1821–1881)

Destiny is no matter of chance. It is a matter of choice. It is not a thing to be waited for, it is a thing to be achieved.
WILLIAM JENNINGS BRYAN (1860–1925)

Destiny is but a phrase of the weak human heart—the dark apology for every error. The strong and virtuous admit no destiny. On earth conscience guides; in heaven God watches. And destiny is but the phantom we invoke to silence the one and dethrone the other.
SIR EDWARD G. BULWER-LYTTON (1803–1873)

To accomplish our destiny it is not enough to merely guard prudently against road accidents. We

must also cover before nightfall the distance assigned to each of us.
ALEXIS CARREL (1873–1944)

Great people and great athletes realize early in their lives their destiny, and accept it. Even if they do not consciously realize the how, the where, the what.
PERCY CERUTTY (1895–1975)

It is a mistake to try to look too far ahead. The chain of destiny can only be grasped one link at a time.
SIR WINSTON CHURCHILL (1874–1965)

The man of virtue makes the difficulty to be overcome his first business, and success only a subsequent consideration.
CONFUCIUS (551–479 BC), *The Confucian Analects*

No trumpets sound when the important decisions of our life are made. Destiny is made known silently.
AGNES DE MILLE (1909–1993)

Thoughts lead on to purposes; purposes go forth in action; actions form habits; habits decide character; and character fixes our destiny.
TYRON EDWARDS (1809–1894)

The best years of your life are the ones in which you decide your problems are your own. You don't blame them on your mother, the ecology, or the President. You realize that you control your own destiny.
ALBERT ELLIS (1913–2007)

The bitterest tragic element in life to be derived from an intellectual source is the belief in a brute Fate or Destiny.
RALPH WALDO EMERSON (1803–1882), *Natural History of Intellect*

There is no difficulty that enough love will not conquer; no disease that enough love will not heal; no door that enough love will not open.
EMMET FOX (1886–1951)

Anatomy is destiny.
SIGMUND FREUD (1856–1939), *Collected Writings*

Men heap together the mistakes of their lives and create a monster they call destiny.
JOHN OLIVER HOBBES (1867–1906)

Our problems are man-made, therefore they may be solved by man. No problem of human destiny is beyond human beings.
JOHN F. KENNEDY (1917–1963)

[P]eace does not rest in the charters and covenants alone. It lies in the hearts and minds of all people. So let us not rest all our hopes on parchment and on paper, let us strive to build peace, a desire for peace, a willingness to work for peace in the hearts and minds of all of our people. I believe that we can. I believe the problems of human destiny are not beyond the reach of human beings.
JOHN F. KENNEDY (1917–1963)

Fame comes only when deserved, and then is as inevitable as destiny, for it is destiny.
HENRY WADSWORTH LONGFELLOW (1807–1852)

It's choice, not chance, that determines your destiny.
JEAN NIDETCH (1923–)

I almost think it is the ultimate destiny of science to exterminate the human race.
THOMAS LOVE PEACOCK (1785–1866)

Real, constructive mental power lies in the creative thought that shapes your destiny, and your hour-by-hour mental conduct produces power for change in your life. Develop a train of thought on which to ride. The nobility of your life as well as your happiness depends upon the direction in which that train of thought is going.
DR. LAURENCE J. PETER (1919–1990)

You and I have a rendezvous with destiny. We will preserve for our children this, the last best hope of man on earth, or we will sentence them to take the first step into a thousand years of darkness. If we fail, at least let our children and our children's children say of us we justified our brief moment here. We did all that could be done.
RONALD REAGAN (1911–2004)

Our character … is an omen of our destiny, and the more integrity we have and keep, the simpler and nobler that destiny is likely to be.
GEORGE SANTAYANA (1863–1952), *The German Mind: A Philosophical Diagnosis*

There is no such thing as chance; and what seem to us merest accident springs from the deepest source of destiny.
FRIEDRICH VON SCHILLER (1759–1805)

Ideals are like stars: you will not succeed in touching them with your hands, but like the seafaring man on the ocean desert of waters, you choose them as your guides, and following them, you reach your destiny.
CARL SCHURZ (1829–1906)

I don't know what your destiny will be, but one thing I do know: the only ones among you who will be really happy are those who have sought and found how to serve.
DR. ALBERT SCHWEITZER (1875–1965)

It is not in the stars to hold our destiny but in ourselves.
WILLIAM SHAKESPEARE (1564–1616), *Macbeth*

What is life but a series of inspired follies? The difficulty is to find them to do. Never lose a chance: it doesn't come every day.
GEORGE BERNARD SHAW (1856–1950), *Pygmalion*

It is perhaps a more fortunate destiny to have a taste for collecting shells than to be born a millionaire.
ROBERT LOUIS STEVENSON (1850–1894)

Man is asked to make of himself what he is supposed to become to fulfill his destiny.
PAUL TILLICH (1886–1965)

The preservation of the sacred fire of liberty and the destiny of the republican model of government are justly considered … deeply, … finally, staked on the experiment entrusted to the hands of the American people.
GEORGE WASHINGTON (1732–1799)

America lives in the heart of every man everywhere who wishes to find a region where he will be free to work out his destiny as he chooses.
WOODROW WILSON (1856–1924)

If you begin the day with love in your heart, peace in your nerves, and truth in your mind, you not only benefit by their presence but also bring them to others, to your family and friends, and to all those whose destiny draws across your path that day.
ANONYMOUS

Determination

People of mediocre ability sometimes achieve outstanding success because they don't know when to quit. Most men succeed because they are determined to.
GEORGE ALLEN (1952–)

Desire is the key to motivation, but it's determination and commitment to an unrelenting pursuit of your goal—a commitment to excellence—that will enable you to attain the success you seek.
MARIO ANDRETTI (1940–)

It's easier to go down a hill than up it but the view is much better at the top.
HENRY WARD BEECHER (1813–1887)

Never mind what others do; do better than yourself, beat your own record from day to day, and you are a success.
WILLIAM J. H. BOETCKER (1873–1962)

It's the constant and determined effort that breaks down all resistance and sweeps away all obstacles.
CLAUDE M. BRISTOL (1891–1951)

In the confrontation between the stream and the rock, the stream, always, wins—not through strength but by perseverance.
H. JACKSON BROWN JR. (1948–)

Destiny is not a matter of chance, it is a matter of choice; it is not a thing to be waited for, it is a thing to be achieved.
WILLIAM JENNINGS BRYAN (1860–1925)

Most of the important things in the world have been accomplished by people who have kept on trying when there seemed to be no help at all.
DALE CARNEGIE (1888–1955)

It is a mistake to look too far ahead. Only one link of the chain of destiny can be handled at a time.
SIR WINSTON CHURCHILL (1874–1965)

Never give in! Never give in! Never, never, never, never—in nothing great or small, large or petty. Never give in except to convictions of honor and good sense.
SIR WINSTON CHURCHILL (1874–1965)

Determination and perseverance move the world; thinking that others will do it for you is a sure way to fail.
MARVA COLLINS (1936–)

Nothing in this world can take the place of persistence. Talent will not; nothing is more common than unsuccessful people with talent. Genius will not; unrewarded genius is almost a proverb. Education will not; the world is full of educated derelicts. Persistence and determination alone are omnipotent. The slogan "press on" has solved and always will solve the problems of the human race.
CALVIN COOLIDGE (1872–1933)

Begin with the end in mind.
STEPHEN R. COVEY (1932–)

The person who makes a success of living is the one who sees his goal steadily and aims for it unswervingly. That is dedication.
CECIL B. DEMILLE (1881–1959)

What counts is not necessarily the size of the dog in the fight—it's the size of the fight in the dog.
DWIGHT D. EISENHOWER (1890–1969)

Hard work spotlights the character of people: some turn up their sleeves, some turn up their noses, and some don't turn up at all.
SAM EWING (1921–)

Thinking is the hardest work there is, which is the probable reason so few engage in it.
HENRY FORD (1863–1947)

In three words I can sum up everything I've learned about life. It goes on.
ROBERT FROST (1874–1963)

The best way out is always through.
ROBERT FROST (1874–1963)

An invincible determination can accomplish almost anything, and in this lies the great distinction between great men and little men.
THOMAS FULLER (1608–1661)

Whatever you can do, or dream you can, begin it. Boldness has genius, power, and magic in it.
JOHANN WOLFGANG VON GOETHE (1749–1832)

I am only one, but I am one. I cannot do everything, but I can do something. And because I cannot do everything, I will not refuse to do the something that I can do. What I can do, I should do. And what I should do, by the grace of God, I will do.
EDWARD EVERETT HALE (1822–1909)

A man may fulfill the object of his existence by asking a question he cannot answer and attempting a task he cannot achieve.
OLIVER WENDELL HOLMES SR. (1809–1894)

You must pay the price if you wish to secure the blessing.
ANDREW JACKSON (1767–1845)

I'm a great believer in luck, and I find that the harder I work, the more I have of it.
THOMAS JEFFERSON (1743–1826)

Although the world is full of suffering, it is also full of overcoming of it.
HELEN KELLER (1880–1968)

The difference between the impossible and the possible lies in a person's determination.
TOMMY LASORDA (1927–)

Obstacles cannot crush me. Every obstacle yields to stern resolve. He who is fixed to a star does not change his mind.
LEONARDO DA VINCI (1452–1519)

Once a man has made a commitment to a way of life, he puts the greatest strength in the world behind him. It's something we call heart power. Once a man has made this commitment, nothing will stop him short of success.
VINCE LOMBARDI (1913–1970)

The harder you work, the harder it is to surrender.
VINCE LOMBARDI (1913–1970)

A will finds a way.
ORISON SWETT MARDEN (1850–1924)

Most of our obstacles would melt away if, instead of cowering before them, we should make up our minds to walk boldly through them.
ORISON SWETT MARDEN (1850–1924)

He who labors diligently need never despair; for all things are accomplished by diligence and labor.
MENANDER (342–292 BC)

On the mountains of truth you can never climb in vain: either you will reach a point higher up today, or you will be training your powers so that you will be able to climb higher tomorrow.
FREDERICK NIETZSCHE (1844–1900)

Never let your head hang down. Never give up and sit down and grieve. Find another way. And don't pray when it rains if you don't pray when the sun shines.
LEROY "SATCHEL" PAIGE (1906–1982)

If you want to get somewhere you have to know where you want to go and how to get there. Then never, never, never give up.
NORMAN VINCENT PEALE (1898–1993)

The more you venture to live greatly, the more you will find within you what it takes to get on top of the things and stay there.
NORMAN VINCENT PEALE (1898–1993)

It is common sense to take a method and try it. If it fails, admit it frankly and try another. But above all, try something.
FRANKLIN D. ROOSEVELT (1882–1945)

Tough times never last, but tough people do.
ROBERT H. SCHULLER(1926–)

People are always blaming their circumstances for what they are. I don't believe in circumstances. The people who get on in the world are the people who get up and look for the circumstances they want, and if they can't find them, make them.
GEORGE BERNARD SHAW (1856–1950)

The miracle, or the power, that elevates the few is to be found in their industry, application, and perseverance under the prompting of a brave, determined spirit.
MARK TWAIN (1835–1910)

Determination gives you the resolve to keep going in spite of the roadblocks that lay before you.
DENIS WAITLEY (1933–)

I was the kind nobody thought could make it. I had a funny Boston accent. I couldn't pronounce my R's. I wasn't a beauty.
BARBARA WALTERS (1929–)

Winning is not everything, but the effort to win is.
ZIG ZIGLAR (1926–)

Success is a ladder you cannot climb with your hands in your pockets.
AMERICAN PROVERB

A diamond is a chunk of coal that made good under pressure.
ANONYMOUS

If you think you are too small to be effective, you have never been in the dark with a mosquito.
ANONYMOUS

Nobody trips over mountains. It is the small pebble that causes you to stumble. Pass all the pebbles in your path and you will find that you have crossed the mountain.
ANONYMOUS

There are no shortcuts to any place worth going.
ANONYMOUS

Fall seven times; stand up eight.
JAPANESE PROVERB

Devotion

Devotion, when it does not lie under the check of reason, is apt to degenerate into enthusiasm.
JOSEPH ADDISON (1672–1719)

To feel, to love, to suffer, to devote herself, will always be the text of the life of woman.
HONORÉ DE BALZAC (1799–1850)

Devotion is like the candle which Michaelangelo used to take in his pasteboard cap, so as not to throw his shadow upon the work in which he was engaged.
PHILLIPS BROOKS (1835–1893)

Destruction is a true sign of devotion. As I always tell my girlfriend when she threatens to kill me, "You should kill me and it would tell me that you love me."
BILLY CORGAN (1967–)

Nothing truly valuable arises from ambition or from a mere sense of duty; it stems rather from love and devotion towards men and towards objective things.
ALBERT EINSTEIN (1879–1955)

Man may content himself with the applause of the world and the homage paid to his intellect, but woman's heart has holier idols.
GEORGE ELIOT (1819–1880)

The best part of a woman's love is worship; but it is hard to her to be sent away with her precious spikenard rejected, and her long tresses, too, that were let fall, ready to soothe the wearied feet.
GEORGE ELIOT (1819–1880)

The days of chivalry are not gone, notwithstanding Burke's grand dirge over them; they live still in that far-off worship paid by many a youth and man to the woman of whom he never dreams that he shall touch so much as her little finger, or the hem of her robe.
GEORGE ELIOT (1819–1880)

All is holy where devotion kneels.
OLIVER WENDELL HOLMES JR. (1841–1935)

Real inward devotion knows no prayer but that arising from the depths of its own feelings.
WILHELM VON HUMBOLDT (1767–1835)

All who wait upon the Lord shall rise higher and higher upon the mighty pinions of strong devotion, and with the unblinking eye of faith, into the regions of heavenly-mindedness, and shall approach nearer and nearer to God, the Sun of our spiritual day.
JOHN ANGELL JAMES (1785–1859)

To succeed in your mission, you must have single-minded devotion to your goal.
ABDUL KALAM (1931–)

The energy, the faith, the devotion which we bring this endeavor will light our bounty and all who serve it, and the glow from that fire can truly light the world.
JOHN F. KENNEDY (1917–1963)

Oh, only those whose souls have felt this one idolatry can tell how precious is the slightest thing affection gives and hallows.
LETITIA ELIZABETH LANDON (1802–1838)

Complete self-devotion is woman's part.
LORD THOMAS BABINGTON MACAULAY (1800–1859)

True strength lies in submission which permits one to dedicate his life, through devotion, to something beyond himself.
HENRY MILLER (1891–1980)

I find no quality so easy for a man to counterfeit as devotion, though his life and manner are not conformable to it; the essence of it is abstruse and occult, but the appearances easy and showy.
MICHEL DE MONTAIGNE (1533–1592)

The secret heart is fair devotion's temple; there the saint, even on that living altar, lights the flame of purest sacrifice, which burns unseen, not unaccepted.
HANNAH MORE (1745–1833)

The need for devotion to something outside ourselves is even more profound than the need for companionship. If we are not to go to pieces or wither away, we must have some purpose in life; for no man can live for himself alone.
ROSS PARMENTER (1912–1999)

People think I am disciplined. It is not discipline. It is devotion. There is a great difference.
LUCIANO PAVAROTTI (1935–2007)

Devotion's self shall steal a thought from heaven.
ALEXANDER POPE (1688–1744)

That fabric rises high as heaven whose basis on devotion stands.
MATTHEW PRIOR (1664–1721)

If devotion to the truth is the hallmark of morality, then there is no greater, nobler, more heroic form of devotion than the act of a man who assumes the responsibility of thinking.
AYN RAND (1905–1982)

The woman who too easily and ardently yielded her devotion will find that its vitality, like a bright fire, soon consumes itself.
ANTOINE DE RIVAROL (1753–1801)

It is not the critic who counts; not the man who points out how the strong man stumbles, or where the doer of deeds could have done them better. The credit belongs to the man who is actually in the arena, whose face is marred by dust and sweat and blood, who strives valiantly; who errs and comes short again and again; because there is not effort without error and shortcomings; but who does actually strive to do the deed; who knows the great enthusiasm, the great devotion, who spends himself in a worthy cause, who at the best knows in the end the triumph of high achievement and who at the worst, if he fails, at least he fails while daring greatly. So that his place shall never be with those cold and timid souls who know neither victory nor defeat.
THEODORE ROOSEVELT (1858–1919), *Man in the Arena*

Love without reverence and enthusiasm is only friendship.
GEORGE SAND (1804–1876)

Love is not love Which alters when it alteration finds; … Love alters not with his brief hours and weeks, But bears it out even to the edge of doom.
WILLIAM SHAKESPEARE (1564–1616), "Sonnet 116"

Perpetual devotion to what a man calls his business, is only to be sustained by perpetual neglect of many other things.
ROBERT LOUIS STEVENSON (1850–1895)

There is always the danger that we may just do the work for the sake of the work. This is where the respect and the love and the devotion come in—that we do it to God, to Christ, and that's why we try to do it as beautifully as possible.
MOTHER TERESA (1910–1997)

I delight in men over seventy. They always offer one the devotion of a lifetime.
OSCAR WILDE (1854–1900)

There's nothing in the world like the devotion of a married woman. It's a thing no married man knows anything about.
OSCAR WILDE (1854–1900)

I know the price of success: dedication, hard work, and an unremitting devotion to the things you want to see happen
FRANK LLOYD WRIGHT (1867–1959)

Whatever I am offered in devotion with a pure heart—a leaf, a flower, fruit, or water—I accept with joy.
THE BHAGAVAD GITA

Diet

'Tis a superstition to insist on a special diet. All is made at last of the same chemical atoms.
RALPH WALDO EMERSON (1803–1882)

To safeguard one's health at the cost of too strict a diet is a tiresome illness indeed.
FRANÇOIS DE LA ROCHEFOUCAULD (1613–1680)

I'm one stomach flu away from reaching my goal weight.
ALINE BROSH MCKENNA (1967–) and
LAREN WEISBERGER (1977–), *The Devil Wears Prada*

Dieters—People that are thick and tired of it.
ANONYMOUS

Nothing arouses more hope than the first four hours of a diet.
ANONYMOUS

Difficulty

Conquering any difficulty always gives one a secret joy, for it means pushing back a boundary-line and adding to one's liberty.
HENRI-FRÉDÉRIC AMIEL (1821–1881)

Deep down, no one really believes they have a right to live. But this death sentence generally stays tucked away, hidden beneath the difficulty of living. If that difficulty is removed from time to time, death is suddenly there, unintelligibly.
JEAN BAUDRILLARD (1929–2007)

Troubles are often the tools by which God fashions us for better things.
HENRY WARD BEECHER (1813–1887)

If we wait until our lives are free from sorrow or difficulty, then we wait forever. And miss the entire point.
DIRK BENEDICT (1945–)

Give yourself an even greater challenge than the one you are trying to master and you will develop the powers necessary to overcome the original difficulty.
WILLIAM BENNETT (1943–)

Every great and deep difficulty bears in itself its own solution. It forces us to change our thinking in order to find it.
NIELS BOHR (1885–1962)

Difficulty, my brethren, is the nurse of greatness—a harsh nurse—who roughly rocks her fosterchildren into strength and athletic proportion.
WILLIAM C. BRYANT (1794–1878)

Difficulties are meant to rouse, not discourage. The human spirit is to grow strong by conflict.
WILLIAM ELLERY CHANNING (1780–1842)

A pessimist sees the difficulty in every opportunity; an optimist sees the opportunity in every difficulty.
SIR WINSTON CHURCHILL (1874–1965)

Difficulties mastered are opportunities won.
SIR WINSTON CHURCHILL (1874–1965)

The greater the difficulty, the greater the glory.
CICERO (106–43 BC)

The best way to avoid a bad action is by doing a good one, for there is no difficulty in the world like that of trying to do nothing.
JOHN CLARE (1793–1864)

Perpetual pushing and assurance put a difficulty out of countenance and make a seeming difficulty gives way.
JEREMY COLLIER (1650–1726)

Times of great calamity and confusion have been productive for the greatest minds. The purest ore is produced from the hottest furnace. The brightest thunder-bolt is elicited from the darkest storm.
CHARLES CALEB COLTON (1780–1832)

The superior man makes the difficulty to be overcome his first interest; success only comes later.
CONFUCIUS (551–479 BC)

It seems that the greatest difficulty is to find the end. Don't try to find it, it's there already.
TOM CORA (1909–1998)

A man of character finds a special attractiveness in difficulty, since it is only by coming to grips with difficulty that he can realize his potentialities.
CHARLES DE GAULLE (1890–1970)

Divide each difficulty into as many parts as is feasible and necessary to resolve it.
RENÉ DESCARTES (1596–1650)

In the middle of difficulty lies opportunity.
ALBERT EINSTEIN (1879–1955)

Bad times have a scientific value. These are occasions a good learner would not miss.
RALPH WALDO EMERSON (1803–1882)

There are always difficulties arising that tempt you to believe your critics are right.
RALPH WALDO EMERSON (1803–1882)

Difficulties show men what they are. In case of any difficulty remember that God has pitted you against a rough antagonist that you may be a conqueror, and this cannot be without toil.
EPICTETUS (C. AD 55–135)

I am trying to do two things: dare to be a radical and not a fool, which is a matter of no small difficulty.
JAMES A. GARFIELD (1831–1881)

It is not always by plugging away at a difficulty and sticking to it that one overcomes it; often it is by working on the one next to it. Some things and some people have to be approached obliquely, at an angle.
ANDRÉ GIDE (1869–1951)

Man needs difficulties; they are necessary for health.
CARL JUNG (1875–1961)

The difficulty lies, not in the new ideas, but in escaping the old ones, which ramify, for those brought up as most of us have been, into every corner of our minds.
JOHN MAYNARD KEYNES (1883–1946)

Where there is no choice, we do well to make no difficulty.
GEORGE MACDONALD (1824–1905)

The difficulty in life is the choice.
GEORGE A. MOORE (1852–1933)

Difficulty is the excuse history never accepts.
EDWARD R. MURROW (1908–1965)

Almost any difficulty will move in the face of honesty. When I am honest I never feel stupid. And when I am honest I am automatically humble.
HUGH PRATHER (1906–1975)

The best way out of a difficulty is through it.
WILL ROGERS (1879–1935)

It is not because things are difficult that we do not dare; it is because we do not dare that they are difficult.
SENECA (5 BC–AD 65)

The apprenticeship of difficulty is one which the greatest of men have had to serve.
SAMUEL SMILES (1812–1904)

Men govern nothing with more difficulty than their tongues, and can moderate their desires more than their words.
BENEDICT DE SPINOZA (1632–1677)

Have the courage to face a difficulty lest it kick you harder than you bargain for.
STANISLAUS I (1677–1766)

Dignity

Dignity consists not in possessing honors, but in the consciousness that we deserve them.
ARISTOTLE (384–322 BC)

Be mild with the mild, shrewd with the crafty, confiding to the honest, rough to the ruffian, and a

thunderbolt to the liar. But in all this, never be unmindful of your own dignity.
JOHN BROWN (1800–1859)

Dignity is like a perfume; those who use it are scarcely conscious of it.
CHRISTINA OF SWEDEN (1626–1689)

Where is there dignity unless there is honesty?
CICERO (106–43 BC)

Let not a man guard his dignity, but let his dignity guard him.
RALPH WALDO EMERSON (1803–1882)

One's dignity may be assaulted, vandalized, and cruelly mocked, but it cannot be taken away unless it is surrendered.
MICHAEL J. FOX (1961–)

The only kind of dignity which is genuine is that which is not diminished by the indifference of others.
DAG HAMMARSKJÖLD (1905–1961)

There is only one terminal dignity—love.
HELEN HAYES (1900–1993)

Self-respect is the fruit of discipline; the sense of dignity grows with the ability to say no to oneself.
ABRAHAM J. HESCHEL (1907–1972)

When decorum is repression, the only dignity free men have is to speak out.
ABBIE HOFFMAN (1936–1989)

Dignity is a mask we wear to hide our ignorance.
ELBERT HUBBARD (1856–1915)

There is a healthful hardiness about real dignity that never dreads contact and communion with others, however humble.
WASHINGTON IRVING (1783–1859)

Remember this—that there is a proper dignity and proportion to be observed in the performance of every act of life.
MARCUS AURELIUS ANTONINUS (121–180)

It is not wealth one asks for, but just enough to preserve one's dignity, to work unhampered, to be generous, frank and independent.
W. SOMERSET MAUGHAM (1874–1965), *Of Human Bondage*

Dignity and love do not blend well, nor do they continue long together.
OVID (43 BC–AD 17)

Our vanity is the constant enemy of our dignity.
ANNE SOPHIE SWETCHINE (1782–1857)

Human Dignity has gleamed only now and then and here and there, in lonely splendor, throughout the ages, a hope of the better men, never an achievement of the majority.
JAMES THURBER (1894–1961)

No race can prosper till it learns that there is as much dignity in tilling a field as in writing a poem.
BOOKER T. WASHINGTON (1856–1915)

Diplomacy

Diplomacy, n.: The patriotic art of lying for one's country.
AMBROSE BIERCE (1842–1914), *The Devil's Dictionary*

In the defense of our nation, a president must be a clear-eyed realist. There are limits to the smiles and scowls of diplomacy. Armies and missiles are not stopped by stiff notes of condemnation. They are held in check by strength and purpose and the promise of swift punishment.
GEORGE W. BUSH (1946–)

Diplomacy without arms is like music without instruments.
FREDERICK THE GREAT (1712–1786)

Diplomacy is to do and say, the nastiest thing in the nicest way.
ISAAC GOLDBERG (1887–1938)

The art of life is to show your hand. There is no diplomacy like candor. You may lose by it now and then, but it will be a loss well gained if you do.

In archaeology you uncover the unknown. In diplomacy you cover the known.
THOMAS PICKERING (1931–)

I think that anyone who comes upon a Nautilus machine suddenly will agree with me that its prototype was clearly invented at some time in history when torture was considered a reasonable alternative to diplomacy.
ANNA QUINDLEN (1953–)

Diplomacy is the art of saying "Nice doggie" until you can find a rock.
WILL ROGERS (1879–1935)

Take the diplomacy out of war and the thing would fall flat in a week.
WILL ROGERS (1879–1935)

Diplomacy is a continuation of war by other means.
ZHOU ENLAI (1898–1976)

Diplomacy is the art of letting someone else have your way.
AMERICAN PROVERB

Disability

One always overcompensates for disabilities. I'm thinking of having my entire body surgically removed.
DOUGLAS ADAMS (1952–2001)

It is a waste of time to be angry about my disability. One has to get on with life and I haven't done badly. People won't have time for you if you are always angry or complaining.
STEPHEN HAWKING (1942–)

Disability is a matter of perception. If you can do just one thing well, you're needed by someone.
MARTINA NAVRATILOVA (1956–)

Even this disability from which I suffer I have assumed by the very fact that I live; I surpass it toward my own projects, I make of it the necessary obstacle for my being and I cannot be crippled without choosing myself as crippled. This means that I choose the way I constitute my disability (as "unbearable," "humiliating," "to be hidden," "to be revealed to all").
JEAN-PAUL SARTRE (1905–1980)

Disaster

Treat all disasters as if they were trivialities but never treat a triviality as if it were a disaster.
QUENTIN CRISP (1908–1999)

Do not seek evil gains; evil gains are the equivalent of disaster.
HESIOD (C. 800 BC), *Works and Days*

There is no calamity greater than lavish desires. There is no greater guilt than discontentment. And there is no greater disaster than greed.
LAO-TZU (C. 600 BC), *The Way of Lao-tzu*

Any effort that has self-glorification as its final endpoint is bound to end in disaster.
ROBERT M. PIRSIG (1928–)

LA needs the cleansing of a great disaster or founding of a barricaded commune.
PETER PLAGENS (1941–)

I always tried to turn every disaster into an opportunity.
JOHN D. ROCKEFELLER (1839–1937)

A clash of doctrines is not a disaster—it is an opportunity.
ALFRED NORTH WHITEHEAD (1861–1947)

Do not let your heart envy sinners, but always be zealous for the fear of the LORD.
THE BIBLE, Proverbs 23:17

Discipline

Some people regard discipline as a chore. For me, it is a kind of order that sets me free to fly.
JULIE ANDREWS (1935–)

Discipline is remembering what you want.
DAVID CAMPBELL (1948–)

Error is discipline through which we advance.
WILLIAM ELLERY CHANNING (1780–1842)

Repression is not the way to virtue. When people restrain themselves out of fear, their lives are by necessity diminished. Only through freely chosen discipline can life be enjoyed and still kept within the bounds of reason.
MIHALY CSIKSZENTMIHALYI (1934–), *Flow: The Psychology of Optimal Experience*

Discipline is a symbol of caring to a child. He needs guidance. If there is love, there is no such thing as being too tough with a child.
BETTE DAVIS (1908–1989)

He that cannot obey, cannot command.
BENJAMIN FRANKLIN (1706–1790)

Discipline is simply the art of making the soldiers fear their officers more than the enemy.
CLAUDE-ADRIEN HELVÈTIUS (1715–1771)

Without discipline, there's no life at all.
KATHARINE HEPBURN (1907–2003)

Seek freedom and become captive of your desires. Seek discipline and find your liberty.
FRANK HERBERT (1920–1986)

Self-respect is the fruit of discipline; the sense of dignity grows with the ability to say no to oneself.
ABRAHAM J. HESCHEL (1907–1972)

Man must be disciplined, for he is by nature raw and wild.
IMMANUEL KANT (1724–1804)

Discipline must come through liberty.... We do not consider an individual disciplined only when he has been rendered as artificially silent as a mute and as immovable as a paralytic. He is an individual annihilated, not disciplined.
MARIA MONTESSORI (1870–1952)

Discipline in art is a fundamental struggle to understand oneself, as much as to understand what one is drawing.
HENRY MOORE (1898–1986)

People think I am disciplined. It is not discipline. It is devotion. There is a great difference.
LUCIANO PAVAROTTI (1935–2007)

Discipline is wisdom and vice versa.
M. SCOTT PECK (1936–2005)

With self-discipline most anything is possible.
THEODORE ROOSEVELT (1858–1919)

Right discipline consists, not in external compulsion, but in the habits of mind which lead spontaneously to desirable rather than undesirable activities.
BERTRAND RUSSELL (1872–1970)

Dreams are what get you started. Discipline is what keeps you going.
JIM RYUN (1947–)

No evil propensity of the human heart is so powerful that it may not be subdued by discipline.
SENECA (5 BC–AD 65)

The main source of good discipline is growing up in a loving family, being loved, and learning to love in return.
BENJAMIN SPOCK (1903–1998)

If I want to be great I have to win the victory over myself ... self-discipline.
HARRY S TRUMAN (1884–1972)

Nothing can be more hurtful to the service, than the neglect of discipline; for that discipline, more than numbers, gives one army the superiority over another.
GEORGE WASHINGTON (1732–1799)

Discovery

There is a theory which states that if ever anybody discovers exactly what the Universe is for and why

it is here, it will instantly disappear and be replaced by something even more bizarre and inexplicable. There is another theory which states that this has already happened.
DOUGLAS ADAMS (1952–2001)

The most exciting phrase to hear in science, the one that heralds new discoveries, is not "Eureka!" (I found it!) but "That's funny...."
ISAAC ASIMOV (1920–1992)

The greatest obstacle to discovery is not ignorance—it is the illusion of knowledge.
DANIEL J. BOORSTIN (1914–)

There is no harm in doubt and skepticism, for it is through these that new discoveries are made.
RICHARD FEYNMAN (1918–1988)

All truths are easy to understand once they are discovered; the point is to discover them.
GALILEO GALILEI (1564–1642)

Man cannot discover new oceans unless he has the courage to lose sight of the shore.
ANDRÉ GIDE (1869–1951)

The beginning of knowledge is the discovery of something we do not understand.
FRANK HERBERT (1920–1986)

Mistakes are the portals of discovery.
JAMES JOYCE (1882–1941)

No pessimist ever discovered the secret of the stars or sailed an uncharted land, or opened a new doorway for the human spirit.
HELEN KELLER (1880–1968)

The more original a discovery, the more obvious it seems afterwards.
ARTHUR KOESTLER (1905–1983)

One of the advantages of being disorderly is that one is constantly making exciting discoveries.
A. A. MILNE (1882–1956)

I do not know what I may appear to the world; but to myself I seem to have been only like a boy playing on the seashore, and diverting myself in now and then finding a smoother pebble or a prettier shell than ordinary, whilst the great ocean of truth lay all undiscovered before me.
SIR ISAAC NEWTON (1642–1727)

If I have ever made any valuable discoveries, it has been owing more to patient attention, than to any other talent.
SIR ISAAC NEWTON (1642–1727)

The real voyage of discovery consists not in seeking new landscapes but in having new eyes.
MARCEL PROUST (1871–1922)

He who never made a mistake never made a discovery.
SAMUEL SMILES (1812–1904)

A discovery is said to be an accident meeting a prepared mind.
ALBERT SZENT-GYORGYI (1893–1986)

Discovery consists of seeing what everybody has seen and thinking what nobody has thought.
ALBERT SZENT-GYORGYI (1893–1986)

The art of teaching is the art of assisting discovery.
MARK VAN DOREN (1894–1972)

Disease

For somehow this is tyranny's disease, to trust no friends.
AESCHYLUS (C. 525–456 BC), *Prometheus Bound*

Words are the physicians of the mind diseased.
AESCHYLUS (C. 525–456 BC), *Prometheus Bound*

Health consists of having the same diseases as one's neighbors.
QUENTIN CRISP (1908–1999)

As I see it, every day you do one of two things: build health or produce disease in yourself.
ADELLE DAVIS (1904–1974)

The doctor of the future will give no medicine, but will interest her or his patients in the care of the human frame, in a proper diet, and in the cause and prevention of disease.
THOMAS A. EDISON (1847–1931)

There is no difficulty that enough love will not conquer; no disease that enough love will not heal; no door that enough love will not open.
EMMET FOX (1886–1951)

A bodily disease which we look upon as whole and entire within itself, may, after all, be but a symptom of some ailment in the spiritual part.
NATHANIEL HAWTHORNE (1804–1864)

As to diseases make a habit of two things—to help, or at least, to do no harm.
HIPPOCRATES (460–377 BC), *Epidemics*

Life is a sexually transmitted disease.
R. D. LAING (1927–1989)

To know that you do not know is the best.
To pretend to know when you do not know is a disease.
LAO-TZU (C. 600 BC), *The Way of Lao-tzu*

Do not listen to those who weep and complain, for their disease is contagious.
OG MANDINO (1923–1996)

To study the phenomenon of disease without books is to sail an uncharted sea, while to study books without patients is not to go to sea at all.
SIR WILLIAM OSLER (1849–1919)

They certainly give very strange names to diseases.
PLATO (C. 428–348 BC)

What some call health, if purchased by perpetual anxiety about diet, isn't much better than tedious disease.
GEORGE DENNISON PRENTICE (1802–1870)

There are some remedies worse than the disease.
PUBLILIUS SYRUS (C. 100 BC), *Maxims*

The art of medicine consists in amusing the patient while nature cures the disease.
VOLTAIRE (1694–1778)

Dishonesty

Dishonesty is so grasping it would deceive God himself, were it possible.
GEORGE BANCROFT (1800–1891)

Honesty may be the best policy, but it's important to remember that apparently, by elimination, dishonesty is the second-best policy.
GEORGE CARLIN (1937–)

There is no kind of dishonesty into which otherwise good people more easily and frequently fall than that of defrauding the government.
BENJAMIN FRANKLIN (1706–1790)

Men are able to trust one another, knowing the exact degree of dishonesty they are entitled to expect.
STEPHEN LEACOCK (1869–1944)

Honesty is for the most part less profitable than dishonesty.
PLATO (C. 428–348 BC)

The discipline of the written word punishes both stupidity and dishonesty.
JOHN STEINBECK (1902–1968)

Dissatisfaction

The problem lay buried, unspoken for many years in the minds of American women. It was a strange stirring, a sense of dissatisfaction, a yearning that women suffered in the middle of the twentieth century in the United States. Each suburban housewife struggled with it alone. As she made the beds, shopped for groceries, matched slipcover material, ate peanut butter sandwiches with her children, chauffeured Cub Scouts and Brownies, lay beside her husband at night, she was afraid to ask even of herself the silent question: "Is this all?"
BETTY FRIEDAN (1921–2006)

The weight of the world is love. Under the burden of solitude, under the burden of dissatisfaction.
ALLEN GINSBERG (1926–1997)

Society expects man to be a passive social animal who believes like the People of the Field in "Jurgen" that "to do what you always have done" and "what is expected of you" are the twin rules of life. This, is course, is not true. The wanton crucifixion of impulses, the unnecessary blocking and frustration of the drives and urges, are an evil that reflects itself in sophistication, ennui and boredom, dissatisfaction, melancholy, fatigue, anxiety and neurosis.
ABRAHAM MYERSON (1881–1948)

Dissent

If our democracy is to flourish, it must have criticism; if our government is to function it must have dissent.
HENRY COMMAGER (1902–1998)

In a democracy dissent is an act of faith. Like medicine, the test of its value is not in its taste, but in its effects.
J. WILLIAM FULBRIGHT (1905–1995)

We must dare to think "unthinkable" thoughts. We must learn to explore all the options and possibilities that confront us in a complex and rapidly changing world. We must learn to welcome and not to fear the voices of dissent. We must dare to think about "unthinkable things" because when things become unthinkable, thinking stops and action becomes mindless.
J. WILLIAM FULBRIGHT (1905–1995)

Distrust

The man who trusts men will make fewer mistakes that he who distrusts them.
CAMILLO BENSO, CONTE DI CAVOUR (1810–1861)

The people I distrust most are those who want to improve our lives but have only one course of action.
FRANK HERBERT (1920–1986)

The older I grow the more I distrust the familiar doctrine that age brings wisdom.
H. L. MENCKEN (1880–1956)

If nations could overcome the mutual fear and distrust whose somber shadow is now thrown over the world, and could meet with confidence and good will to settle their possible differences, they would easily be able to establish a lasting peace.
FRIDJOF NANSEN (1861–1930)

But thus do I counsel you, my friends: distrust all in whom the impulse to punish is powerful!
FRIEDRICH NIETZSCHE (1844–1900), *Thus Spoke Zarathustra*

How frequently are the honesty and integrity of a man disposed of by a smile or a shrug. How many good and generous actions have been sunk into oblivion by a distrustful look, or stamped with the imputation of bad motives, by a mysterious and seasonable whisper!
LAWRENCE STERNE (1713–1768)

The chief lesson I have learned in a long life is that the only way to make a man trustworthy is to trust him; and the surest way to make him untrustworthy is to distrust him and show your distrust.
HENRY L. STIMSON (1867–1950)

You can use all the quantitative data you can get, but you still have to distrust it and use your own intelligence and judgment.
ALVIN TOFFLER (1928–)

The best rules to form a young man, are, to talk little, to hear much, to reflect alone upon what has passed in company, to distrust one's own opinions, and value others that deserve it.
SIR WILLIAM TEMPLE (1628–1699)

Seek simplicity, and distrust it.
ALFRED NORTH WHITEHEAD (1861–1947)

We have to distrust each other. It's our only defense against betrayal.
TENNESSEE WILLIAMS (1911–1983)

Courage is always greatest when blended with meekness; intellectual ability is most admired when it sparkles in the setting of modest self-distrust; and never does the human soul appear so strong as when it foregoes revenge and dares to forgive any injury.
ANONYMOUS

Divorce

For a while we pondered whether to take a vacation or get a divorce. We decided that a trip to Bermuda is over in two weeks, but a divorce is something you always have.
WOODY ALLEN (1935–)

If divorce has increased by one thousand percent, don't blame the women's movement. Blame the obsolete sex roles on which our marriages were based.
BETTY FRIEDAN (1921–2006)

Getting divorced just because you don't love a man is almost as silly as getting married just because you do.
ZSA ZSA GABOR (1919–)

The happiest time of anyone's life is just after the first divorce.
JOHN KENNETH GALBRAITH (1908–2006)

American husbands are the best in the world; no other husbands are so generous to their wives, or can be so easily divorced.
ELINOR GLYN (1864–1943)

In our family we don't divorce our men—we bury them.
RUTH GORDON (1896–1985)

Remarriage is an excellent test of just how amicable your divorce was.
MARGO KAUFMAN (1954–2000)

A bachelor is a selfish, undeserving guy who has cheated some woman out of a divorce.
DON QUINN (1900–1967)

Divorces are made in heaven.
OSCAR WILDE (1854–1900)

Ah yes, divorce, from the Latin word meaning to rip out a man's genitals through his wallet.
ROBIN WILLIAMS (1951–)

Doctors

Doctors are the same as lawyers; the only difference is that lawyers merely rob you, whereas doctors rob you and kill you too.
ANTON CHEKHOV (1860–1904)

A careful physician, before he attempts to administer a remedy to his patient, must investigate not only the malady of the man he wishes to cure, but also his habits when in health, and his physical constitution.
CICERO (106–43 BC)

Nature can do more than physicians.
OLIVER CROMWELL (1599–1658)

Surgeons must be very careful. When they take the knife!, underneath their fine incisions, stirs the Culprit—Life!
EMILY DICKINSON (1830–1886)

The best doctor is the one you run to and can't find.
DENIS DIDEROT (1713–1784)

The more ignorant, reckless and thoughtless a doctor is, the higher his reputation soars even amongst powerful princes.
DESIDERIUS ERASMUS (1469–1536)

God heals and the doctor takes the fee.
BENJAMIN FRANKLIN (1706–1790)

The doctor should be opaque to his patients and, like a mirror, should show them nothing but what is shown to him.
SIGMUND FREUD (1856–1939)

I have noticed that doctors who fail in the practice of medicine have a tendency to seek one another's company and aid in consultation. A doctor who cannot take out your appendix properly will recommend you to a doctor who will be unable to remove your tonsils with success.
ERNEST HEMINGWAY (1898–1961)

Deceive not thy physician, confessor, nor lawyer.
GEORGE HERBERT (1593–1632)

He felt about books as doctors feel about medicines, or managers about plays—cynical, but hopeful.
DAME ROSE MACAULAY (1881–1958), *Crewe Train*

Doctors will have more lives to answer for in the next world than even we generals.
NAPOLÉON I (1769–1821)

The physician who killed me,
Neither bled, purged or pilled me,
Nor counted my pulse but it comes to the same,
In the height of my fever I thought of his name.
NICARCHUS (C. 100)

Some people imagine that nuclear war will mean instant and painless death. But for millions this will not be the case. The accounts of the injured at Hiroshima and Nagasaki, and of the doctors who tried to tend them, witness to the horrors and torments which would be magnified thousands of times over in the kinds of attack we analyze here....
STAN OPENSHAW (1946–), *Doomsday*

It is as expedient that a wicked man be punished as that a sick man be cured by a physician; for all chastisement is a kind of medicine.
PLATO (C. 428–348 BC)

If you believe the doctors, nothing is wholesome; if you believe the theologians, nothing is innocent; if you believe the military, nothing is safe.
LORD SALISBURY (1563–1612)

Doctors don't know everything really. They understand matter, not spirit. And you and I live in spirit.
WILLIAM SAROYAN (1908–1981), *The Human Comedy*

I had rather follow you to your grave than see you owe your life to any but a regular-bred physician.
RICHARD BRINSLEY SHERIDAN (1751–1816)

Doctors are men who prescribe medicines of which they know little, to cure diseases of which they know less, in human beings of whom they know nothing.
VOLTAIRE (1694–1778)

A recent survey was said to prove that the people we Americans most admire are our politicians and doctors. I don't believe it. They are simply the people we are most afraid of. And with the most reason.
ANONYMOUS

Nature, time, and patience are the three great physicians.
ANONYMOUS

Don't live in a town where there are no doctors.
JEWISH PROVERB

Though physician to others, yet himself full of sores.
LATIN PROVERB

Dogma

The best teacher is the one who suggests rather than dogmatizes, and inspires his listener with the wish to teach himself.
SIR EDWARD G. BULWER-LYTTON (1803–1873)

Then he saw also that it matters little what profession, whether of religion or irreligion, a man may make, provided only he follows it out with charitable inconsistency, and without insisting on it to the bitter end. It is in the uncompromisingness with which dogma is held and not in the dogma or want of dogma that the danger lies.
SAMUEL BUTLER (1835–1902), *The Way of All Flesh*

All formal dogmatic religions are fallacious and must never be accepted by self-respecting persons as final.
HYPATIA OF ALEXANDRIA (C. 360–415)

Your time is limited, so don't waste it living someone else's life. Don't be trapped by dogma—which is living with the results of other people's thinking. Don't let the noise of other's opinions drown out your own inner voice. And most important, have the courage to follow your heart and intuition. They somehow already know what you truly want to become. Everything else is secondary.
STEVE JOBS (1955–)

The greater the ignorance the greater the dogmatism.
SIR WILLIAM OSLER (1849–1919)

All dogmas perish the thinking mind, especially ones you agree with.
ADAM RICHARDSON (1967–)

I think we ought always to entertain our opinions with some measure of doubt. I shouldn't wish people dogmatically to believe any philosophy, not even mine.
BERTRAND RUSSELL (1872–1970)

What the world needs is not dogma but an attitude of scientific inquiry combined with a belief that the torture of millions is not desirable, whether inflicted by Stalin or by a Deity imagined in the likeness of the believer.
BERTRAND RUSSELL (1872–1970)

My karma ran over your dogma.
ANONYMOUS

Dogs

The more I know about men the more I like dogs.
GLORIA ALLRED (1941–)

I have no dog, but it must be somewhere there's one belongs to me—a little chap with wagging tail, and dark brown eyes that never quail, but look you through, and through, and through, with love unspeakable and true.
JOHN KENDRICK BANGS (1862–1922)

The dog was created especially for children. He is the god of frolic.
HENRY WARD BEECHER (1813–1887)

A boy can learn a lot from a dog: obedience, loyalty, and the importance of turning around three times before lying down.
ROBERT BENCHLEY (1889–1945)

Dachshunds are ideal dogs for small children, as they are already stretched and pulled to such a length that the child cannot do much harm one way or the other.
ROBERT BENCHLEY (1889–1945)

The factory of the future will have only two employees, a man and a dog. The man will be there to feed the dog. The dog will be there to keep the man from touching the equipment.
WARREN G. BENNIS (1925–)

Dog, n.: A subsidiary Deity designed to catch the overflow and surplus of the world's worship.... [H]is master works for the means wherewith to purchase the idle wag of the Solomonic tail, seasoned with a look of tolerant recognition.
AMBROSE BIERCE (1842–1914), *The Devil's Dictionary*

A dog is the only thing on earth that loves you more than he loves himself.
JOSH BILLINGS (1818–1885)

Newfoundland dogs are good to save children from drowning, but you must have a pond of water handy and a child, or else there will be no profit in boarding a Newfoundland.
JOSH BILLINGS (1818–1885)

Dogs come when they are called. Cats take a message and get back to you.
MARY BLY (1962–)

When a dog bites a man, that is not news, because it happens so often. But if a man bites a dog, that is news.
JOHN B. BOGART (1848–1921)

When you leave them in the morning, they stick their noses in the door crack and stand there like a portrait until you turn the key eight hours later.
ERMA BOMBECK (1927–1996)

An animal's eyes have the power to speak a great language.
MARTIN BUBER (1878–1965)

Dogs are indeed the most affectionate, and amiable animals of the whole brute creation.
EDMUND BURKE (1729–1797)

The great pleasure of a dog is that you may make a fool of yourself with him and not only will he not scold you, but he will make a fool of himself too.
SAMUEL BUTLER (1835–1902)

Dogs are not our whole life, but they make our lives whole.
ROGER A. CARAS (1929–2001)

Generally, or at least very often, people with a deep interest in animals are the best people around.
ROGER A. CARAS (1929–2001)

If you don't own a dog, at least one, there is not necessarily anything wrong with you, but there may be something wrong with your life.
ROGER A. CARAS (1929–2001)

I like pigs. Dogs look up to us. Cats look down on us. Pigs treat us as equals.
SIR WINSTON CHURCHILL (1874–1965)

Our perfect companions never have fewer than four feet.
SIDONIE GABRIELLE COLETTE (1873–1954)

When a dog bites a man that is not news, but when a man bites a dog that is news.
CHARLES ANDERSON DANA (1819–1897)

You ask of my companions. Hills, sir, and the sundown, and a dog as large as myself that my father bought me. They are better than human beings, because they know but do not tell.
EMILY DICKINSON (1830–1886)

Dogs laugh, but they laugh with their tails. What puts man in a higher state of evolution is that he has got his laugh on the right end.
MAX EASTMAN (1883–1969)

We long for an affection altogether ignorant of our faults. Heaven has accorded this to us in the uncritical canine attachment.
GEORGE ELIOT (1819–1880)

Old age means realizing you will never own all the dogs you wanted to.
JOE GORES (1931–)

Women and cats will do as they please, and men and dogs should relax and get used to the idea.
ROBERT A. HEINLEIN (1907–1988)

To his dog, every man is Napoleon; hence the constant popularity of dogs.
ALDOUS HUXLEY (1894–1963)

They [dogs] never talk about themselves but listen to you while you talk about yourself, and keep up an appearance of being interested in the conversation.
JEROME K. JEROME (1859–1927)

Dogs have not the power of comparing. A dog will take a small piece of meat as readily as a large, when both are before him.
SAMUEL JOHNSON (1709–1784)

Scratch a dog and you'll find a permanent job.
FRANKLIN P. JONES (1887–1929)

When a dog barks at the moon, then it is religion; but when he barks at strangers, it is patriotism!
DAVID STARR JORDAN (1851–1931)

Know yourself. Don't accept your dog's admiration as conclusive evidence that you are wonderful.
ANN LANDERS (1918–2002)

If you are a dog and your owner suggests that you wear a sweater … suggest that he wear a tail.
FRAN LEBOWITZ (1950–)

No animal should ever jump up on the dining-room furniture unless absolutely certain that he can hold his own in the conversation.
FRAN LEBOWITZ (1950–)

What kind of life a dog … acquires. I have sometimes tried to imagine by kneeling or lying full length on the ground and looking up. The world then becomes strangely incomplete; one sees little but legs.
E. V. LUCAS (1868–1938)

We are alone, absolutely alone on this chance planet: and, amid all the forms of life that surround us, not one, excepting the dog, has made an alliance with us
MAURICE MAETERLINCK (1862–1949)

Dogs are very different from cats in that they can be images of human virtue. They are like us.
IRIS MURDOCH (1919–1999)

A door is what a dog is perpetually on the wrong side of.
OGDEN NASH (1902–1971)

The world was conquered through the understanding of dogs; the world exists through the understanding of dogs.
FRIEDRICH NIETZCHE (1844–1900)

It's funny how dogs and cats know the inside of folks better than other folks do, isn't it?
ELEANOR H. PORTER (1868–1920), *Pollyanna*

Our dogs will love and admire the meanest of us, and feed our colossal vanity with their uncritical homage.
AGNES REPPLIER (1855–1950)

Dogs are getting bigger, according to a leading dog manufacturer.
LEO ROSTEN (1908–1997)

I wonder if other dogs think poodles are members of a weird religious cult.
RITA RUDNER (1956–)

My husband and I are either going to buy a dog or have a child. We can't decide whether to ruin our carpet or ruin our lives.
RITA RUDNER (1956–)

If you eliminate smoking and gambling, you will be amazed to find that almost all an Englishman's pleasures can be, and mostly are, shared by his dog.
GEORGE BERNARD SHAW (1856–1950)

I loathe people who keep dogs. They are cowards who haven't got the guts to bite people themselves.
AUGUST STRINDBERG (1849–1912), *A Madman's Diary*

Every dog must have his day.
JONATHAN SWIFT (1667–1745)

Some of my best leading men have been dogs and horses.
ELIZABETH TAYLOR (1932–)

When a dog runs at you, whistle for him.
HENRY DAVID THOREAU (1817–1862)

I am not a cat man, but a dog man, and all felines can tell this at a glance—a sharp, vindictive glance.
JAMES THURBER (1894–1961)

The dog has seldom been successful in pulling man up to its level of sagacity, but man has frequently dragged the dog down to his.
JAMES THURBER (1894–1961)

A hungry dog hunts best.
LEE TREVINO (1939–)

Children and dogs are as necessary to the welfare of the country as Wall Street and the railroads.
HARRY S TRUMAN (1884–1972)

If you pick up a starving dog and make him prosperous, he will not bite you. This is the principal difference between a dog and a man.
MARK TWAIN (1835–1910)

Ever consider what they must think of us? I mean, here we come back from a grocery store with the most amazing haul—chicken, pork, half cow. They must think we're the greatest hunters on earth!
ANNE TYLER (1941–)

If a dog jumps in your lap, it is because he is fond of you; but if a cat does the same thing, it is because your lap is warmer.
ALFRED NORTH WHITEHEAD (1861–1947)

There is no psychiatrist in the world like a puppy licking your face.
BEN WILLIAMS (1982–)

I can train any dog in five minutes. It's training the owner that takes longer.
BARBARA WOODHOUSE (1910–1988)

It is no coincidence that man's best friend cannot talk.
ANONYMOUS

Never judge a dog's pedigree by the kind of books he does not chew.
ANONYMOUS

To err is human, to forgive, canine.
ANONYMOUS

A dog owns nothing, yet is seldom dissatisfied.
IRISH PROVERB

Doubt

I show you doubt, to prove that faith exists.
ROBERT BROWNING (1812–1889)

Doubt is the vestibule through which all must pass before they can enter the temple of wisdom. When we are in doubt and puzzle out the truth by our own exertions, we have gained something that will stay by us and will serve us again. But if to avoid the trouble of the search we avail ourselves of the superior information of a friend, such knowledge will not remain with us; we have not bought, but borrowed it.
CHARLES CALEB COLTON (1780–1832)

Just think of the tragedy of teaching children not to doubt.
CLARENCE DARROW (1857–1938)

If you would be a real seeker after truth, it is necessary that at least once in your life you doubt, as far as possible, all things.
RENÉ DESCARTES (1596–1650)

Freedom of speech and freedom of action are meaningless without freedom to think. And there is no freedom of thought without doubt.
BERGEN EVANS (1904–1978)

Doubt is a pain too lonely to know that faith is his twin brother.
KAHLIL GIBRAN (1883–1931)

A mind troubled by doubt cannot focus on the course to victory.
ARTHUR GOLDEN (1956–), *Memoirs of a Geisha*

Doubt 'til thou canst doubt no more … doubt is thought and thought is life. Systems which end doubt are devices for drugging thought.
ALBERT GUERARD (1914–2000)

To have doubted one's own first principles is the mark of a civilized man.
OLIVER WENDELL HOLMES JR. (1841–1935)

Doubt yourself and you doubt everything you see. Judge yourself and you see judges everywhere. But if you listen to the sound of your own voice, you can rise above doubt and judgment. And you can see forever.
NANCY KERRIGAN (1969–)

There are two ways to slide easily through life; to believe everything or to doubt everything. Both ways save us from thinking.
ALFRED KORZYBSKI (1879–1950)

A weak man has doubts before a decision, a strong man has them afterwards.
KARL KRAUS (1874–1936)

Melancholy and sadness are the start of doubt … doubt is the beginning of despair; despair is the

cruel beginning of the differing degrees of wickedness.
ISIDORE DUCASSE LAUTREAMONT (1846–1870)

To believe with certainty we must begin with doubting.
STANISLAW LESZCZYNSKI (1677–1766)

I respect faith, but doubt is what gets you an education.
WILSON MIZNER (1876–1933)

Knowledge and personality make doubt possible, but knowledge is also the cure of doubt; and when we get a full and adequate sense of personality we are lifted into a region where doubt is almost impossible, for no man can know himself as he is, and all fullness of his nature, without also knowing God.
T. T. MUNGER (1883–1975)

The only limit to our realization of tomorrow will be our doubts of today.
FRANKLIN D. ROOSEVELT (1882–1945)

I think we ought always to entertain our opinions with some measure of doubt. I shouldn't wish people dogmatically to believe any philosophy, not even mine.
BERTRAND RUSSELL (1872–1970)

The whole problem with the world is that fools and fanatics are always so certain of themselves, but wiser people so full of doubts.
BERTRAND RUSSELL (1872–1970)

Our doubts are traitors,
And make us lose the good we oft might win
By fearing to attempt.
WILLIAM SHAKESPEARE (1564–1616), *Measure for Measure*

Suspicion and doubt lead to animosity and hatred.
RALPH STEADMAN (1936–)

Beliefs are what divide people. Doubt unites them.
PETER USTINOV (1921–2004)

Doubt is not a pleasant condition, but certainty is absurd.
VOLTAIRE (1694–1778)

Dreams

He felt that his whole life was some kind of dream and he sometimes wondered whose it was and whether they were enjoying it.
DOUGLAS ADAMS (1952–2001), *The Hitchhiker's Guide to the Galaxy*

I know how men in exile feed on dreams of hope.
AESCHYLUS (C. 525–456 BC), *Agamemnon*

Our dreams drench us in senses, and senses steps us again in dreams.
AMOS BRONSON ALCOTT (1799–1888)

Dream lofty dreams, and as you dream, so shall you become.
JAMES ALLEN (1864–1912)

What if nothing exists and we're all in somebody's dream? Or what's worse, what if only that fat guy in the third row exists?
WOODY ALLEN (1935–), *Without Feathers*

When you stop having dreams and ideals—well, you might as well stop altogether.
MARIAN ANDERSON (1897–1993)

Hope is a waking dream.
ARISTOTLE (384–322 BC)

Dream manfully and nobly, and thy dreams shall be prophets.
SIR EDWARD G. BULWER-LYTTON (1803–1873)

Dreams that do come true can be as unsettling as those that don't.
BRETT BUTLER (1958–), *Knee Deep in Paradise*

One of the characteristics of the dream is that nothing surprises us in it. With no regret, we agree to live in it with strangers, completely cut off from our habits and friends.
JEAN COCTEAU (1889–1963)

Last night I dreamed I ate a ten-pound marshmallow, and when I woke up the pillow was gone.
TOMMY COOPER (1921–1984)

Dream as if you'll live forever. Live as if you'll die today.
JAMES DEAN (1931–1955)

Dreaming permits each and every one of us to be quietly and safely insane every night of our lives.
WILLIAM DEMENT (1928–)

When I consider this carefully, I find not a single property which with certainty separates the waking state from the dream. How can you be certain that your whole life is not a dream?
RENÉ DESCARTES (1596–1650)

Dreams are unbridled thought.
AUGUSTUS DURANT (1982–)

A dream is a scripture, and many scriptures are nothing but dreams.
UMBERTO ECO (1932–)

It is never too late to be what you might have been.
GEORGE ELIOT (1819–1880)

There are some people who live in a dream world, and there are some who face reality; and then there are those who turn one into the other.
DOUGLAS EVERETT (1927–)

Always dream and shoot higher than you know you can do. Don't bother just to be better than your contemporaries or predecessors. Try to be better than yourself.
WILLIAM FAULKNER (1897–1962)

The end of wisdom is to dream high enough to lose the dream in the seeking of it.
WILLIAM FAULKNER (1897–1962)

To accomplish great things, we must dream as well as act.
ANATOLE FRANCE (1844–1924)

Trust the dreams, for hidden in them is the gate to eternity.
KAHLIL GIBRAN (1883–1931)

It is difficult to say what is impossible, for the dream of yesterday is the hope of today and the reality of tomorrow.
ROBERT H. GODDARD (1882–1945)

Dream no small dreams for they have no power to move the hearts of men.
JOHANN WOLFGANG VON GOETHE (1749–1832)

Man, alone, has the power to transform his thoughts into physical reality; man, alone, can dream and make his dreams come true.
NAPOLEON HILL (1883–1970)

We do not really feel grateful toward those who make our dreams come true; they ruin our dreams.
ERIC HOFFER (1902–1983)

Dreams surely are difficult, confusing, and not everything in them is brought to pass for mankind. For fleeting dreams have two gates: one is fashioned of horn and one of ivory. Those which pass through the one of sawn ivory are deceptive, bringing tidings which come to nought, but those which issue from the one of polished horn bring true results when a mortal sees them.
HOMER (800–700 BC), *The Odyssey*

Hold fast to dreams, for if dreams die, life is a broken winged bird that cannot fly.
LANGSTON HUGHES (1902–1967)

There is nothing like dream to create the future. Utopia to-day, flesh and blood tomorrow.
VICTOR HUGO (1802–1885), *Les Miserables*

Ideologies separate us. Dreams and anguish bring us together.
EUGÈNE IONESCO (1909–1994)

I like the dreams of the future better than the history of the past.
THOMAS JEFFERSON (1743–1826)

It is on the whole probably that we continually dream, but that consciousness makes such a noise that we do not hear it.
CARL JUNG (1875–1961)

We need men who can dream of things that never were.
JOHN F. KENNEDY (1917–1963)

Now, I say to you today, my friends, even though we face the difficulties of today and tomorrow, I still have a dream. It is a dream deeply rooted in the American dream. I have a dream that one day this nation will rise up and live out the true meaning of its creed: we hold these truths to be self-evident, that all men are created equal.
MARTIN LUTHER KING JR. (1929–1968)

Those who dream by night in the dusty recesses of their minds wake in the day to find that it was vanity, but the dreamers of the day are dangerous men, for they may act on their dreams with open eyes to make it possible.
T. E. LAWRENCE (1888–1935)

A dream will always triumph over reality, once it is given the chance.
STANISLAW LEM (1921–2006)

Those who dream by day are cognizant of many things which escape those who dream only by night.
EDGAR ALLAN POE (1809–1849), "Eleonora"

Only in our dreams are we free. The rest of the time we need wages.
TERRY PRATCHETT (1948–)

If a little dreaming is dangerous, the cure for it is not to dream less but to dream more, to dream all the time.
MARCEL PROUST (1871–1922)

It has never been my object to record my dreams, just to realize them.
MAN RAY (1890–1976)

So many of our dreams at first seem impossible, then they seem improbable, and then when we summon the will, they soon become inevitable.
CHRISTOPHER REEVE (1952–2004)

It does not do to dwell on dreams and forget to live.
J. K. ROWLING (1965–), *Harry Potter and the Sorcerer's Stone*

Dreams are what get you started. Discipline is what keeps you going.
JIM RYUN (1947–)

I have had dreams, and I have had nightmares. I overcame the nightmares because of my dreams.
JONAS SALK (1914–1995)

Nothing happens unless first a dream.
CARL SANDBURG (1878–1967)

Keep true to the dreams of thy youth.
FRIEDRICH VON SCHILLER (1759–1805)

I will! I am! I can! I will actualize my dream. I will press ahead. I will settle down and see it through. I will solve the problems. I will pay the price. I will never walk away from my dream until I see my dream walk away: Alert! Alive! Achieved!
ROBERT H. SCHULLER(1926–)

You can often measure a person by the size of his dream.
ROBERT H. SCHULLER(1926–)

There are more things in heaven and earth,
  Horatio,
Than are dreamt of in your philosophy.
WILLIAM SHAKESPEARE (1564–1616), *Hamlet*

You see things; and you say, "Why?" But I dream things that never were; and I say, "Why not?"
GEORGE BERNARD SHAW (1856–1950), *Back to Methuselah*

Dreams are the touchstones of our characters.
HENRY DAVID THOREAU (1817–1862)

Our truest life is when we are in our dreams awake.
HENRY DAVID THOREAU (1817–1862)

Dreams come true. Without that possibility, nature would not incite us to have them.
JOHN UPDIKE (1932–)

Have you ever had a dream … that you were so sure was real? What if you were unable to wake from that dream? How would you know the difference between the dream world and the real world?
ANDY WACHOWSKI (1967–) and LARRY WACHOWSKI (1965–), *The Matrix*

You have all the reason in the world to achieve your grandest dreams. Imagination plus innovation equals realization.
DENIS WAITLEY (1933–)

A dreamer is one who can only find his way by moonlight, and his punishment is that he sees the dawn before the rest of the world.
OSCAR WILDE (1854–1900)

Dreamers … see things in the soft haze of a spring day or in the red fire of a long winter's evening. Some of us let these great dreams die, but others … bring them to the sunshine … which comes always to those who sincerely hope that their dreams will come true.
WOODROW WILSON (1856–1924)

I have spread my dreams beneath your feet. Tread softly because you tread on my dreams.
WILLIAM BUTLER YEATS (1865–1939)

Keep dreaming, for as long as you dream that dream might come true.
ANONYMOUS

The poorest man is not without a cent but without a dream.
ANONYMOUS

To those who can dream, there is no such place as faraway.
ANONYMOUS

The longer the night lasts, the more our dreams will be.
CHINESE PROVERBS

Yesterday is but a dream, tomorrow but a vision. But today well lived makes every yesterday a dream of happiness, and every tomorrow a vision of hope. Look well, therefore, to this day. Such is the salutation to the dawn.
SANSKRIT PROVERB

Drugs

If we burn ourselves out with drugs or alcohol, we won't have long to go in this business.
JOHN BELUSHI (1949–1982)

The last time somebody said, "I find I can write much better with a word processor," I replied, "They used to say the same thing about drugs."
ROY BLOUNT JR. (1941–)

I always keep a supply of stimulant handy in case I see a snake—which I also keep handy.
W. C. FIELDS (1880–1946)

[I] don't do drugs anymore…. But I'll tell you something honestly about drugs, and I know it's not a very popular idea, you don't hear it very often anymore, but it is the truth: I had a great time doing drugs. Never murdered anyone, never robbed anyone, never raped anyone, never beat anyone, never lost a job, a car, a house, a wife or kids … laughed my ass off, and went about my day.
BILL HICKS (1961–1994)

I never took hallucinogenic drugs because I never wanted my consciousness expanded one unnecessary iota.
FRAN LEBOWITZ (1950–)

I hate to advocate drugs, alcohol, violence, or insanity to anyone, but they've always worked for me.
HUNTER S. THOMPSON (1939–2005)

Reality is a crutch for people who can't cope with drugs.
LILY TOMLIN (1939–)

Duty

I take it as a man's duty to restrain himself.
LOIS MCMASTER BUJOLD (1949–), *Ethan of Athos*

I think it's the duty of the comedian to find out where the line is drawn and cross it deliberately.
GEORGE CARLIN (1937–)

Where duty is plain, delay is both foolish and hazardous; where it is not, delay may provide both wisdom and safety.
TYRON EDWARDS (1809–1894)

It is the duty of every citizen according to his best capacities to give validity to his convictions in political affairs.
ALBERT EINSTEIN (1879–1955), *Treasury for the Free World*

The reward of one duty is the power to fulfill another.
GEORGE ELIOT (1819–1880)

How can you come to know yourself? Never by thinking, always by doing. Try to do your duty, and you'll know right away what you amount to.
JOHANN WOLFGANG VON GOETHE (1749–1832)

The first duty of a revolutionary is to get away with it.
ABBIE HOFFMAN (1936–1989)

The first duty of a leader is to make himself be loved without courting love. To be loved without "playing up" to anyone—even to himself.
ANDRÉ MALRAUX (1901–1976)

I believe that every right implies a responsibility; every opportunity an obligation; every possession a duty.
JOHN D. ROCKEFELLER JR. (1874–1960)

The strongest is never strong enough to be always the master, unless he transforms strength into right, and obedience into duty.
JEAN-JACQUES ROUSSEAU (1712–1778), *The Social Contract*

A sense of duty is useful in work, but offensive in personal relations. People wish to be liked, not be endured with patient resignation.
BERTRAND RUSSELL (1872–1970), *Conquest of Happiness*

If you have no friends to share or rejoice in your success in life—if you cannot look back to those whom you owe gratitude, or forward to those to whom you ought to afford protection, still it is no less incumbent on you to move steadily in the path of duty; for your active excretions are due not only to society; but in humble gratitude to the Being who made you a member of it, with powers to save yourself and others.
SIR WALTER SCOTT (1771–1832)

I want to be thoroughly used up when I die, for the harder I work the more I love. I rejoice in life for its own sake. Life is no brief candle to me; it is a sort of splendid torch which I've got a hold of for the moment and I want to make it burn as brightly as possible before handing it on to future generations.
GEORGE BERNARD SHAW (1856–1950)

When a stupid man is doing something he is ashamed of, he always declares that it is his duty.
GEORGE BERNARD SHAW (1856–1950), *Caesar and Cleopatra*

Self-development is a higher duty than self-sacrifice.
ELIZABETH CADY STANTON (1815–1902)

I came to realize that life lived to help others is the only one that matters and that it is my duty.... This is my highest and best use as a human.
BEN STEIN (1944–)

The paths of glory at least lead to the grave, but the paths of duty may not get you anywhere.
JAMES THURBER (1894–1961)

The first duty of love is to listen.
PAUL TILLICH (1886–1965)

Do something every day that you don't want to do; this is the golden rule for acquiring the habit of doing your duty without pain.
MARK TWAIN (1835–1910)

Evil when we are in its power is not felt as evil but as a necessity, or even a duty.
SIMONE WEIL (1909–1943), *Gravity and Grace*

It's the soul's duty to be loyal to its own desires. It must abandon itself to its master passion.
REBECCA WEST (1892–1983)

[I]t is as hard to do your duty when men are sneering at you as when they are shooting at you.
WOODROW WILSON (1856–1924)

Earth

We are here on Earth to do good to others. What the others are here for, I don't know.
W. H. AUDEN (1907–1973)

What's the earth
With all its art, verse, music, worth—
Compared with love, found, gained, and kept?
ROBERT BROWNING (1812–1889)

Genius hath electric power which earth can never tame.
LYDIA M. CHILD (1802–1880)

The meek shall inherit the Earth, but not its mineral rights.
J. PAUL GETTY (1892–1976)

And forget not that the earth delights to feel your bare feet and the winds long to play with your hair.
KAHLIL GIBRAN (1883–1931)

The Earth needs rebels!
DAVID ICKE (1952–)

There is no security on this earth, there is only opportunity.
GENERAL DOUGLAS MACARTHUR (1880–1964)

Pity the meek, for they shall inherit the earth.
DON MARQUIS (1878–1937)

Thank God men cannot as yet fly and lay waste the sky as well as the earth!
HENRY DAVID THOREAU (1817–1862)

The earth is the general and equal possession of all humanity and therefore cannot be the property of individuals.
LEO TOLSTOY (1828–1910)

I really wonder what gives us the right to wreck this poor planet of ours.
KURT VONNEGUT JR. (1922–2007)

I tell you, we are here on Earth to fart around, and don't let anybody tell you different.
KURT VONNEGUT JR. (1922–2007)

Now I see the secret of the making of the best persons. It is to grow in the open air and to eat and sleep with the earth.
WALT WHITMAN (1819–1892), "Song of the Open Road"

Earthquakes

Mr. Speaker, from hurricanes and floods in Latin America to earthquakes in Asia, natural disasters are increasingly becoming a regular feature of life for large numbers of people around the globe.
EARL BLUMENAUER (1948–)

There are two big forces at work, external and internal. We have very little control over external forces such as tornadoes, earthquakes, floods, disasters, illness and pain. What really matters is the internal force. How do I respond to those disasters? Over that I have complete control.
LEO F. BUSCAGLIA (1924–1998)

When it comes to two of the big social earthquakes in the last fifty years—which are the gay movement and the women's movement—I think there is a direct line from Kinsey to those.
BILL CONDON (1955–)

We learn geology the morning after the earthquake
RALPH WALDO EMERSON (1803–1882)

I was married once—in San Francisco. I haven't seen her for many years. The great earthquake and fire in 1906 destroyed the marriage certificate.

There's no legal proof. Which proves that earthquakes aren't all bad.
W. C. FIELDS (1880–1946)

If they'd lower the taxes and get rid of the smog and clean up the traffic mess, I really believe I'd settle here until the next earthquake.
GROUCHO MARX (1890–1977)

The pleasure of going to a laboratory and seeing what they're doing, listening to the scientists talking, listening to the scientists gossip, and visiting like volcanoes, earthquakes, geysers, all that.
FREDERIK POHL (1919–)

What emerged, of course, was that the magnitude scale presupposed that all earthquakes were alike except for a constant scaling factor. And this proved to be closer to the truth than we expected.
CHARLES FRANCIS RICHTER (1900–1985)

There is a lot that happens around the world we cannot control. We cannot stop earthquakes, we cannot prevent droughts, and we cannot prevent all conflict, but when we know where the hungry, the homeless and the sick exist, then we can help.
JAN SCHAKOWSKY (1944–)

Japan's humid and warm summer climate, as well as frequent earthquakes resulted in lightweight timber buildings raised off the ground that are resistant to earth tremors.
HARRY SEIDLER (1923–)

An earthquake achieves what the law promises but does not in practice maintain—the equality of all men.
IGNAZIO SILONE (1900–1978)

When distant cities are hit by earthquakes, it is the United States that hurries into help.... Managua Nicaragua is one of the most recent examples.
GORDON SINCLAIR (1900–1984)

Opinion has caused more trouble on this little earth than plagues or earthquakes.
VOLTAIRE (1694–1778)

Eccentricity

Eccentricity, n.: A method of distinction so cheap that fools employ it to accentuate their incapacity.
AMBROSE BIERCE (1842–1914), *The Devil's Dictionary*

The surest defense against Evil is extreme individualism, originality of thinking, whimsicality, even ... eccentricity. That is, something that can't be feigned, faked, imitated; something even a seasoned imposter couldn't be happy with.
JOSEPH BRODSKY (1940–1996)

To seek understanding before taking action, yet to trust my instincts when action is called for. Never to avoid danger from fear, never to seek out danger for its own sake. Never to conform to fashion from fear of eccentricity, never to be eccentric from fear of conformity.
STEVEN BRUST (1955–)

The world thinks eccentricity in great things is genius, but in small things, only crazy.
SIR EDWARD G. BULWER-LYTTON (1803–1873)

The English like eccentrics. They just don't like them living next door.
JULIAN CLARY (1959–)

A civilized society is one which tolerates eccentricity to the point of doubtful sanity.
ROBERT FROST (1874–1963)

No one can be profoundly original who does not avoid eccentricity.
ANDRÉ MAUROIS (1885–1967)

Eccentricity has always abounded when and where strength of character had abounded; and the amount of eccentricity in a society has generally been proportional to the amount of genius, mental vigor, and courage which it contained.
JOHN STUART MILL (1806–1873)

That so few now dare to be eccentric marks the chief danger of the time.
JOHN STUART MILL (1806–1873)

Graphic design is the paradise of individuality, eccentricity, heresy, abnormality, hobbies and humors.
George Santayana (1863–1952)

My mother was the concert master of the symphony. Absurdity and eccentricity were not criticized.
Martin Short (1950–)

Eccentricity is not, as dull people would have us believe, a form of madness. It is often a kind of innocent pride, and the man of genius and the aristocrat are frequently regarded as eccentrics because genius and aristocrat are entirely unafraid of and uninfluenced by the opinions and vagaries of the crowd.
Edith Sitwell (1887–1964)

There's not much room for eccentricity in Hollywood, and eccentricity is what's sexy in people.
Rachel Weisz (1971–)

Economics

A study of economics usually reveals that the best time to buy anything is last year.
Marty Allen (1922–)

You always want to try to make something new, and, of course, America is the world leader in economics today.
Tadao Ando (1941–)

The whole industry is so screwed up by economics. It's disgusting to me.
Armand Assante (1949–)

A strong economy causes an increase in the demand for housing; the increased demand for housing drives real-estate prices and rentals through the roof. And then affordable housing becomes completely inaccessible.
William Baldwin (1963–)

Marriages are under strain today in terms of economics. There are social cross-currents. We see failed marriages. But it is not under attack by our gay and lesbian citizens.
Earl Blumenauer (1948–)

There can be no real individual freedom in the presence of economic insecurity.
Chester Bowles (1901–1986)

Socialism failed because it couldn't tell the economic truth; capitalism may fail because it couldn't tell the ecological truth.
Lester Brown (1934–)

It's the economy, stupid.
James Carville (1944–)

An economist is a surgeon with an excellent scalpel and a rough-edged lancet, who operates beautifully on the dead and tortures the living.
Nicolas Chamfort (1741–1794)

I had become interested in economics, an interest that was transformed into a lifetime dedication when I met with the mathematical theory of general economic equilibrium.
Gerard Debreu (1921–2004)

In all recorded history there has not been one economist who has had to worry about where the next meal would come from.
Peter F. Drucker (1909–2005)

Too many people think that economics is this subject that should wait until the university level. But it can't wait that long.
Robert Duvall (1931–)

Listen, there is no courage or any extra courage that I know of to find out the right thing to do. Now, it is not only necessary to do the right thing, but to do it in the right way and the only problem you have is what is the right thing to do and what is the right way to do it. That is the problem. But this economy of ours is not so simple that it obeys to the opinion of bias or the pronouncements of any particular individual, even to the President. This is an economy that is made up of 173 million people and it reflects their desires, they're ready to buy, they're ready to spend, it is a thing that is too

complex and too big to be affected adversely or advantageously just by a few words or any particular—say a little this and that, or even a panacea so alleged.
DWIGHT D. EISENHOWER (1890–1969)

I'd call it a new version of voodoo economics, but I'm afraid that would give witch doctors a bad name.
GERALDINE FERRARO (1935–)

There are 10^{11} stars in the galaxy. That used to be a huge number. But it's only a hundred billion. It's less than the national deficit! We used to call them astronomical numbers. Now we should call them economical numbers.
RICHARD FEYNMAN (1918–1988)

The most powerful argument of all for saving open space is economics; in most states, tourism is the number two industry.
JIM FOWLER (1932–)

Economics is extremely useful as a form of employment for economists.
JOHN KENNETH GALBRAITH (1908–2006)

I think it is just stupid economics for a government to approach economic management from a strand of thinking regarding unions as enemies.
BOB HAWKE (1929–)

Religion and art spring from the same root and are close kin. Economics and art are strangers.
NATHANIEL HAWTHORNE (1804–1864)

The art of economics consists in looking not merely at the immediate but at the longer effects of any act or policy; it consists in tracing the consequences of that policy not merely for one group but for all groups.
HENRY HAZLITT (1894–1983)

And one of the worst effects was that by suppressing critical thought, it also suppressed critical thought in the field of economics and hampered the development of economics—and the country would fall back further and further in the economic competition with the West.
STEFAN HEYM (1913–2001)

If ignorance paid dividends, most Americans could make a fortune out of what they don't know about economics.
LUTHER H. HODGES (1898–1974)

People want economy and they will pay any price to get it.
LEE IACOCCA (1924–)

Did you ever think that making a speech on economics is a lot like pissing down your leg? It seems hot to you, but it never does to anyone else.
LYNDON B. JOHNSON (1908–1973)

The long run is a misleading guide to current affairs. In the long run we are all dead. Economists set themselves too easy, too useless a task if in tempestuous seasons they can only tell us that when the storm is past the ocean is flat again.
JOHN MAYNARD KEYNES (1883–1946), *A Tract on Monetary Reform*

Economics is a subject that does not greatly respect one's wishes.
NIKITA KHRUSHCHEV (1894–1971)

We believe that economics does not necessarily have to be a zero-sum game; it can be a win-win proposition for everyone involved so long as they have the tools in which to succeed.
RON KIND (1963–)

An economist is a man who states the obvious in terms of the incomprehensible.
ALFRED A. KNOPF (1892–1984)

Economics has as its purpose firstly to acquire knowledge for its own sake, and secondly to throw light on practical issues. But though we are bound, before entering on any study, to consider carefully what are its uses, we should not plan out our work with direct reference to them.
ALFRED MARSHALL (1842–1924)

Classic economic theory, based as it is on an inadequate theory of human motivation, could be revolutionized by accepting the reality of higher human needs, including the impulse to self-actualization and the love for the highest values.
ABRAHAM MASLOW (1908–1970)

Manufacturing and commercial monopolies owe their origin not to a tendency imminent in a capitalist economy but to governmental interventionist policy directed against free trade and laissez-faire.
LUDWIG VON MISES (1881–1973)

An economist is an expert who will know tomorrow why the things he predicted yesterday didn't happen today.
DR. LAURENCE J. PETER (1919–1990)

The government's view of the economy could be summed up in a few short phrases: If it moves, tax it. If it keeps moving, regulate it. And if it stops moving, subsidize it.
RONALD REAGAN (1911–2004)

Whoever claims that economic competition represents "survival of the fittest" in the sense of the law of the jungle, provides the clearest possible evidence of his lack of knowledge of economics.
GEORGE REISMAN (1937–)

Economics has never been a science—and it is even less now than a few years ago.
PAUL A. SAMUELSON (1915–)

Profit is the ignition system of our economic engine.
CHARLES SAWYER (1868–1954)

If all economists were laid end to end, they would not reach a conclusion.
GEORGE BERNARD SHAW (1856–1950)

The first lesson of economics is scarcity: there is never enough of anything to fully satisfy all those who want it. The first lesson of politics is to disregard the first lesson of economics.
THOMAS SOWELL (1930–)

Start with the idea that you can't repeal the laws of economics. Even if they are inconvenient.
LARRY SUMMERS (1954–)

Editors

Editors, for the most part, don't care "what" you've done, or how astounding the physical event may have been. You need to write well. Many others are capable of doing what you have done (probably), so you must write better than they….
TIM CAHILL (1943–)

Some editors are failed writers, but so are most writers.
T. S. ELIOT (1888–1965)

Democracy becomes a government of bullies tempered by editors.
RALPH WALDO EMERSON (1803–1882)

The real literary editors have mostly been fired. Those that remain are all "bottom line" editors; everything depends on the money.
LAWRENCE FERLINGHETTI (1919–)

Editors may think of themselves as dignified headwaiters in a well-run restaurant but more often they operate a snack bar and expect you to be grateful that at least they got the food to the table warm.
THOMAS GRIFFITH (1915–)

I have never had an editor ask me to explain anything more than was already down on the paper. I've done work for five major publishers, and countless editors, and it's never come up.
LAURELL K. HAMILTON (1963–)

I think editors have to come out of a certain kind of community.
BILL JOY (1954–)

Newspaper editors are men who separate the wheat from the chaff, and then print the chaff.
ADLAI E. STEVENSON II (1835–1914)

[E]ditors and publishers will never be obsolete: a reader wants someone with taste and authority to point them in the direction of the good stuff, and to keep the awful stuff away from their door.
WALTER J. WILLIAMS (1953–)

Education

There are two educations. One should teach us how to make a living and the other how to live.
JOHN ADAMS (1735–1826)

What sculpture is to a block of marble, education is to the soul.
JOSEPH ADDISON (1672–1719)

Education is the best provision for old age.
ARISTOTLE (384–322 BC)

It is the mark of an educated mind to be able to entertain a thought without accepting it.
ARISTOTLE (384–322 BC)

Education is the movement from darkness to light.
ALLAN BLOOM (1930–1992)

She knows what is the best purpose of education: not to be frightened by the best but to treat it as part of daily life.
JOHN MASON BROWN (1900–1969)

Education is simply the soul of a society as it passes from one generation to another.
G. K. CHESTERTON (1874–1936)

Natural ability without education has more often attained to glory and virtue than education without natural ability.
CICERO (106–43 BC)

The present structure of rewards in high schools produces a response on the part of an adolescent social system which effectively impedes the process of education.
JAMES S. COLEMAN (1926–)

The number of books will grow continually, and one can predict that a time will come when it will be almost as difficult to learn anything from books as from the direct study of the whole universe. It will be almost as convenient to search for some bit of truth concealed in nature as it will be to find it hidden away in an immense multitude of bound volumes.
DENIS DIDEROT (1713–1784)

The foundation of every state is the education of its youth.
DIOGENES LAERTIUS (C. 200)

Education is a state-controlled manufactory of echoes.
NORMAN DOUGLAS (1868–1952)

Education is a progressive discovery of our own ignorance.
WILL DURANT (1885–1981)

Bear in mind that the wonderful things you learn in your schools are the work of many generations. All this is put in your hands as your inheritance in order that you may receive it, honor it, add to it, and one day faithfully hand it on to your children.
ALBERT EINSTEIN (1879–1955)

Only the educated are free.
EPICTETUS (AD 55–135), *Discourses*

America believes in education: the average professor earns more money in a year than a professional athlete earns in a whole week.
EVAN ESAR (1899–1995)

Education's purpose is to replace an empty mind with an open one.
MALCOLM S. FORBES (1919–1990)

An education isn't how much you have committed to memory, or even how much you know. It's being able to differentiate between what you do know and what you don't.
ANATOLE FRANCE (1844–1924)

Genius without education is like silver in the mine.
BENJAMIN FRANKLIN (1706–1790)

Education is helping the child realize his potentialities.
ERICH FROMM (1900–1980)

Education is the ability to listen to almost anything without losing your temper or your self-confidence.
ROBERT FROST (1874–1963)

Education begins a gentleman, conversation completes him.
THOMAS FULLER (1608–1661), *Gnomologia*

Next in importance to freedom and justice is popular education, without which neither freedom nor justice can be permanently maintained.
JAMES A. GARFIELD (1831–1881)

Good teaching is one-fourth preparation and three-fourths theater.
GAIL GODWIN (1937–)

To be able to be caught up into the world of thought—that is being educated.
EDITH HAMILTON (1867–1963)

The whole purpose of education is to turn mirrors into windows.
SYDNEY J. HARRIS (1917–1986)

He who opens a school door closes a prison.
VICTOR HUGO (1802–1885)

Education is a kind of continuing dialogue, and a dialogue assumes, in the nature of the case, different points of view.
ROBERT M. HUTCHINS (1899–1977)

Education is not to reform students or amuse them or to make them expert technicians. It is to unsettle their minds, widen their horizons, inflame their intellects, teach them to think straight, if possible.
ROBERT M. HUTCHINS (1899–1977)

My idea of education is to unsettle the minds of the young and inflame their intellects.
ROBERT M. HUTCHINS (1899–1977)

Perhaps the most valuable result of all education is the ability to make yourself do the thing you have to do, when it ought to be done, whether you like it or not; it is the first lesson that ought to be learned; and however early a man's training begins, it is probably the last lesson that he learns thoroughly.
THOMAS H. HUXLEY (1825–1895)

Everyone has a right to a university degree in America, even if it's in Hamburger Technology.
CLIVE JAMES (1939–)

Above all things I hope the education of the common people will be attended to, convinced that on their good sense we may rely with the most security for the preservation of a due degree of liberty.
THOMAS JEFFERSON (1743–1826)

College isn't the place to go for ideas.
HELEN KELLER (1880–1968)

The highest result of education is tolerance.
HELEN KELLER (1880–1968)

Education can give you a skill, but a liberal education can give you dignity.
ELLEN KEY (1849–1926)

A college degree is not a sign that one is a finished product but an indication a person is prepared for life.
REVEREND EDWARD A. MALLOY (1941–), *Monk's Reflections*

Anyone who tries to make a distinction between education and entertainment doesn't know the first thing about either.
MARSHALL MCLUHAN (1911–1980)

The plain fact is that education is itself a form of propaganda—a deliberate scheme to outfit the pupil, not with the capacity to weigh ideas, but with a simple appetite for gulping ideas ready-made. The aim is to make "good" citizens, which is to say, docile and uninquisitive citizens.
H. L. MENCKEN (1880–1956)

I respect faith, but doubt is what gets you an education.
WILSON MIZNER (1876–1933)

I prefer the company of peasants because they have not been educated sufficiently to reason incorrectly.
MICHEL DE MONTAIGNE (1533–1592)

In large states, public education will always be mediocre, for the same reason that in large kitchens the cooking is usually bad.
FRIEDRICH NIETZSCHE (1844–1900)

The strength of the United States is not the gold at Fort Knox or the weapons of mass destruction that we have, but the sum total of the education and the character of our people.
CLAIBORNE PELL (1918–)

Education is a method whereby one acquires a higher grade of prejudices.
DR. LAURENCE J. PETER (1919–1990)

The direction in which education starts a man will determine his future life.
PLATO (C. 428–348 BC), *The Republic*

The very spring and root of honesty and virtue lie in good education.
PLUTARCH (AD 46–120), *Morals*

Real education must ultimately be limited to men who insist on knowing; the rest is mere sheep-herding.
EZRA POUND (1885–1972)

It is only the ignorant who despise education.
PUBLILIUS SYRUS (C. 100 BC), *Maxims*

To educate a man in mind, and not in morals, is to educate a menace to society.
THEODORE ROOSEVELT (1858–1919)

Education is when you read the fine print. Experience is what you get if you don't.
PETE SEEGER (1919–)

A fool's brain digests philosophy into folly, science into superstition, and art into pedantry. Hence University education.
GEORGE BERNARD SHAW (1856–1950)

Education is what survives when what has been learned has been forgotten.
B. F. SKINNER (1904–1990)

Education has for its object the formation of character.
HERBERT SPENCER (1820–1903)

The great aim of education is not knowledge but action.
HERBERT SPENCER (1820–1903)

Education … has produced a vast population able to read but unable to distinguish what is worth reading.
G. M. TREVELYAN (1876–1962)

Training is everything. The peach was once a bitter almond; cauliflower is nothing but cabbage with a college education.
MARK TWAIN (1835–1910), *Pudd'nhead Wilson*

I have never let my schooling interfere with my education.
MARK TWAIN (1835–1910)

Human history becomes more and more a race between education and catastrophe.
H. G. WELLS (1866–1946), *Outline of History*

Education is like a double-edged sword. It may be turned to dangerous uses if it is not properly handled.
WU TING-FANG (1842–1922)

It'll be a great day when education gets all the money it wants, and the Air Force has to hold a bake sale to buy bombers.
ANONYMOUS

Efficiency

Efficiency is doing things right; effectiveness is doing the right things.
PETER F. DRUCKER (1909–2005)

It's pretty hard to be efficient without being obnoxious.
KIN HUBBARD (1868–1930)

Washington is a city of Southern efficiency and Northern charm.
JOHN F. KENNEDY (1917–1963)

The only thing that saves us from the bureaucracy is inefficiency. An efficient bureaucracy is the greatest threat to liberty.
EUGENE J. MCCARTHY (1916–2005)

We have a criminal jury system which is superior to any in the world; and its efficiency is only marred by the difficulty of finding twelve men every day who don't know anything and can't read.
MARK TWAIN (1835–1910)

Efficiency is intelligent laziness.
ANONYMOUS

Effort

A positive attitude may not solve all your problems, but it will annoy enough people to make it worth the effort.
HERM ALBRIGHT (1876–1944)

Don't stay in bed, unless you can make money in bed.
GEORGE BURNS (1896–1996)

For the great mass of mankind, the only saving grace needed is a steady fidelity to what is nearest to hand and heart for the short moment of each human effort.
JOSEPH CONRAD (1857–1924)

All growth depends upon activity. There is no development physically or intellectually without effort, and effort means work.
CALVIN COOLIDGE (1872–1933)

He was a genius—that is to say, a man who does superlatively and without obvious effort something that most people cannot do by the uttermost exertion of their abilities.
ROBERTSON DAVIES (1913–1995), *Fifth Business*

Well done is better than well said.
BENJAMIN FRANKLIN (1706–1790)

Never mistake motion for action.
ERNEST HEMINGWAY (1899–1961)

Great effort is required to arrest decay and restore vigor. One must exercise proper deliberation, plan carefully before making a move, and be alert in guarding against relapse following a renaissance.
HORACE (65–8 BC)

How many a man has thrown up his hands at a time when a little more effort, a little more patience would have achieved success?
ELBERT HUBBARD (1856–1915)

I find that the harder I work, the more luck I seem to have.
THOMAS JEFFERSON (1743–1826)

What is written without effort is in general read without pleasure.
SAMUEL JOHNSON (1709–1784)

Let us make a special effort to stop communicating with each other, so we can have some conversation.
JUDITH MARTIN (1938–)

Nothing of me is original. I am the combined effort of everybody I've ever known.
CHUCK PALAHNIUK (1962–), *Invisible Monsters*

If a man does his best, what else is there?
GEORGE S. PATTON (1885–1945)

Any effort that has self-glorification as its final endpoint is bound to end in disaster.
ROBERT M. PIRSIG (1928–)

Happiness lies in the joy of achievement and the thrill of creative effort.
FRANKLIN D. ROOSEVELT (1882–1945)

It is hard to fail, but it is worse never to have tried to succeed. In this life we get nothing save by effort.
THEODORE ROOSEVELT (1858–1919)

Fanaticism consists in redoubling your effort when you have forgotten your aim.
GEORGE SANTAYANA (1863–1952), *Life of Reason*

The effort to understand the universe is one of the very few things that lifts human life a little above the level of farce, and gives it some of the grace of tragedy.
STEVEN WEINBERG (1933–)

This I do know beyond any reasonable doubt. Regardless of what you are doing, if you pump long enough, hard enough and enthusiastically enough, sooner or later the effort will bring forth the reward.
ZIG ZIGLAR (1926–)

You know you're getting old when it takes too much effort to procrastinate.
ANONYMOUS

Ego

The great corrupter of public man is the ego.... Looking at the mirror distracts one's attention from the problem.
DEAN ACHESON (1893–1791)

If there's anything more important than my ego around, I want it caught and shot now.
DOUGLAS ADAMS (1952–2001), *Hitchhiker's Guide to the Galaxy*

When science discovers the center of the universe, a lot of people will be disappointed to find they are not it.
BERNARD BAILY (1916–1996)

If you develop an ear for sounds that are musical it is like developing an ego. You begin to refuse sounds that are not musical and that way cut yourself off from a good deal of experience.
JOHN CAGE (1912–1992)

In any influence, will, a self, the ego, the I AM is the greater force to be dealt with, but as numbers do influence, a knowledge of same certainly gives an individual a foresight into relationships.
EDGAR CAYCE (1877–1945)

We are all worms, but I do believe I am a glowworm.
SIR WINSTON CHURCHILL (1874–1965)

A self that is only differentiated—not integrated—may attain great individual accomplishments, but risks being mired in self-centered egotism. By the same token, a person whose self is based exclusively on integration will be well connected and secure, but lack autonomous individuality. Only when a person invests equal amounts of psychic energy in these two processes and avoids both selfishness and conformity is the self likely to relfect complexity.
MIHALY CSIKSZENTMIHALYI (1934–), *Flow: The Psychology of Optimal Experience*

The perfection preached in the Gospels never yet built up an empire. Every man of action has a strong dose of egotism, pride, hardness, and cunning. But all those things will be forgiven him, indeed, they will be regarded as high qualities, if he can make of them the means to achieve great ends.
CHARLES DE GAULLE (1890–1970)

Blushing is the color of virtue.
DIOGENES LAERTIUS (C. 200)

He was like a cock who thought the sun had risen to hear him crow.
GEORGE ELIOT (1819–1880), *Adam Bede*

Take egotism out and you would castrate the benefactors.
RALPH WALDO EMERSON (1803–1882)

Too many people overvalue what they are not and undervalue what they are.
MALCOLM S. FORBES (1919–1990)

A man wrapped up in himself makes a very small bundle.
BENJAMIN FRANKLIN (1706–1790)

Many could forgo heavy meals, a full wardrobe, a fine house, et cetera; it is the ego they cannot forgo.
JOHN KENNETH GALBRAITH (1908–2006)

True merit, like a river, the deeper it is, the less noise it makes.
EDWARD FREDERICK HALIFAX (1881–1959)

Modesty is the lowest of the virtues, and is a confession of the deficiency it indicates. He who undervalues himself is justly overvalued by others.
WILLIAM HAZLITT (1778–1830)

Modesty is the gentle art of enhancing your charm by pretending not to be aware of it.
OLIVER HERFORD (1863–1935)

Egotism is the art of seeing in yourself what others cannot see.
GEORGE V. HIGGINS (1939–1999)

Glory is largely a theatrical concept. There is no striving for glory without a vivid awareness of an audience.
ERIC HOFFER (1902–1983), *The True Believer*

Most of us retain enough of the theological attitude to think that we are little gods.
OLIVER WENDELL HOLMES JR. (1841–1935)

Religion is a monumental chapter in the history of human egotism.
WILLIAM JAMES (1842–1910)

An inflated consciousness is always egocentric and conscious of nothing but its own existence. It is incapable of learning from the past, incapable of understanding contemporary events, and incapable of drawing right conclusions about the future. It is hypnotized by itself and therefore cannot be argued with. It inevitably dooms itself to calamities that must strike it dead.
CARL JUNG (1875–1961)

Egotism is the anesthetic that dulls the pain of stupidity.
FRANK LEAHY (1907–1973)

What kills a skunk is the publicity it gives itself.
ABRAHAM LINCOLN (1809–1865)

My father always wanted to be the corpse at every funeral, the bride at every wedding, and the baby at every christening.
ALICE ROOSEVELT LONGWORTH (1884–1980)

Lying increases the creative faculties, expands the ego, and lessens the frictions of social contacts.
CLARE BOOTH LUCE (1903–1987)

It is not titles that honor men, but men that honor titles.
NICCOLÒ MACHIAVELLI (1469–1527)

Lord, where we are wrong, make us willing to change; where we are right, make us easy to live with.
PETER MARSHALL (1902–1949)

It wasn't until quite late in life that I discovered how easy it is to say "I don't know!"
W. SOMERSET MAUGHAM (1874–1965)

Don't talk about yourself; it will be done when you leave.
WILSON MIZNER (1876–1933)

Any party which takes credit for the rain must not be surprised if its opponents blame it for the drought.
DWIGHT MORROW (1873–1931)

To have a thing is little, if you're not allowed to show it, to know a thing is nothing, unless others know you know it.
CHARLES NEAVES (1800–1876)

You shouldn't gloat about anything you've done; you ought to keep going and find something better to do.
DAVID PACKARD (1912–1996)

There are two kinds of egotists: Those who admit it, and the rest of us.
DR. LAURENCE J. PETER (1919–1990)

Avoid having your ego so close to your position that when your position falls, your ego goes with it.
COLIN POWELL (1937–)

With people of only moderate ability modesty is mere honesty; but with those who possess great talent it is hypocrisy.
ARTHUR SCHOPENHAUER (1788–1860)

Humility is to make a right estimate of one's self.
CHARLES H. SPURGEON (1834–1892)

Flattery is all right so long as you don't inhale.
ADLAI E. STEVENSON II (1900–1965)

Some people are born on third base and go through life thinking they hit a triple.
BARRY SWITZER (1937–)

Humility does not mean thinking less of yourself than of other people, nor does it mean having a low opinion of your own gifts. It means freedom from thinking about yourself at all.
SIR WILLIAM TEMPLE (1628–1699)

Don't let that chip on your shoulder be your only reason for walking erect.
JAMES THURBER (1894–1961)

If I only had a little humility, I would be perfect.
TED TURNER (1938–)

I'm the stuff men are made of.
JOHN WAYNE (1907–1979)

None are so empty as those who are full of themselves.
BENJAMIN WHICHCOTE (1609–1683)

The man who thinks he can live without others is mistaken; the one who thinks others can't live without him is even more deluded.
HASIDIC PROVERB

If every fool wore a crown, we should all be kings.
WELSH PROVERB

Elections

The one pervading evil of democracy is the tyranny of the party that succeeds, by force or fraud, in carrying elections.
LORD ACTON (1834–1902)

Elections are won by men and women chiefly because most people vote against somebody rather than for somebody.
FRANKLIN P. ADAMS (1881–1960), *Nods and Becks*

Where annual elections end, slavery begins.
JOHN QUINCY ADAMS (1767–1848)

These endless legal challenges that define elections in New York are a joke in this country, and they are the reason why it is so expensive, or one of the reasons, it's so expensive to run here and why so many people decide not to run.
MICHAEL BLOOMBERG (1942–)

Elections are … about the future—the pledges that we are making for [Britain]. For those who care about equality and fairness in the UK, and beyond, Labour really is the only choice.
ANNE CAMPBELL (1940–)

No wonder Americans hate politics when, year in and year out, they hear politicians make promises that won't come true because they don't even mean them—campaign fantasies that win elections but don't get nations moving again.
BILL CLINTON (1946–)

Federal elections happen every two years in this country. Presidential elections every four years. And four years just isn't long enough to dismantle all the environmental laws we've got in this country.
JARED DIAMOND (1937–)

An honest election, under democracy, is an act of innocence which does not take place more than once in the history of a given nation.
José María Gil Robles y Quiñones (1898–1980)

The recent successful elections in Iraq and Afghanistan have shown us that freedom is the best antidote to terror.
Lindsey Graham (1955–)

Elections are about choosing sides, but inaugurations are about closing ranks.
Ted Kulongoski (1940–)

Every election is a sort of advance auction sale of stolen goods.
H. L. Mencken (1880–1956)

Elections should be held on April 16th—the day after we pay our income taxes. That is one of the few things that might discourage politicians from being big spenders.
Thomas Sowell (1930–)

Our elections are free, it's in the results where eventually we pay.
Bill Stern (1907–1971)

Electricity

Electricity is actually made up of extremely tiny particles called electrons, that you cannot see with the naked eye unless you have been drinking.
Dave Barry (1947–), *The Taming of the Screw*

Reason and Justice tell me that there is more love of man in electricity and steam, than in chastity and refusal to eat meat.
Anton Chekov (1860–1904)

Her own mother lived the latter years of her life in the horrible suspicion that electricity was dripping invisibly all over the house.
James Thurber (1894–1961), *My Life and Hard Times*

All power corrupts, but we need the electricity.
Anonymous

Eloquence

Discretion in speech is more than eloquence.
Sir Francis Bacon (1561–1626)

The finest eloquence is that which gets things done; the worst is that which delays them.
David Lloyd George (1863–1945)

So it is that the gods do not give all men gifts of grace—neither good looks nor intelligence nor eloquence.
Homer (800–700 BC), *The Odyssey*

Talking and eloquence are not the same thing: to speak, and to speak well, are two things. A fool may talk, but a wise man speaks.
Ben Jonson (1572–1637), *Timber; or, Discoveries Made Upon Men and Matter*

Oh, how one wishes sometimes to escape from the meaningless dullness of human eloquence, from all those sublime phrases, to take refuge in nature, apparently so inarticulate, or in the wordlessness of long grinding labor, of sound sleep, of true music, or of a human understanding, rendered speechless by emotion!
Boris Pasternak (1890 –1960), *Dr. Zhivago*

His intelligence seized on a subject, his genius embraced it, his eloquence illuminated it.
Paterculus (19 BC–AD 31)

Eloquence is in the assembly, not merely in the speaker.
William Pitt (1759–1806)

Action is eloquence.
William Shakespeare (1564–1616), *Coriolanus*

Well-timed silence hath more eloquence than speech.
Martin Fraquhar Tupper (1810–1889)

I am from a state that raises corn and cotton and cocklebures and Democrats, and frothy eloquence neither convinces nor satisfies me. I am from

Missouri. You have got to show me.
WILLIAM DUNCAN VANDIVER (1854–1932)

Emotions

No man has the right to dictate what other men should perceive, create or produce, but all should be encouraged to reveal themselves, their perceptions and emotions, and to build confidence in the creative spirit.
ANSEL ADAMS (1902–1984)

The true meaning of religion is thus not simply morality, but morality touched by emotion.
MATTHEW ARNOLD (1822–1888)

When dealing with people, let us remember we are not dealing with creatures of logic. We are dealing with creatures of emotion, creatures bustling with prejudices and motivated by pride and vanity.
DALE CARNEGIE (1888–1955)

I have enjoyed greatly the second blooming that comes when you finish the life of the emotions and of personal relations; and suddenly find—at the age of fifty, say—that a whole new life has opened before you, filled with things you can think about, study, or read about.... It is as if a fresh sap of ideas and thoughts was rising in you.
AGATHA CHRISTIE (1890–1976), *An Autobiography*

Men decide far more problems by hate, love, lust, rage, sorrow, joy, hope, fear, illusion, or some other inward emotion, than by reality, authority, any legal standard, judicial precedent, or statute.
CICERO (106–43 BC)

Poetry is not a turning loose of emotion, but an escape from emotion; it is not the expression of personality, but an escape from personality. But, of course, only those who have personality and emotions know what it means to want to escape from these things.
T. S. ELIOT (1888–1965), *Tradition and the Individual Talent*

Never feel self-pity, the most destructive emotion there is. How awful to be caught up in the terrible squirrel cage of self.
MILLICENT FENWICK (1910–1992)

It is the mind which creates the world about us, and even though we stand side by side in the same meadow, my eyes will never see what is beheld by yours, my heart will never stir to the emotions with which yours is touched.
GEORGE GISSING (1857–1903)

The face is not a secondary billboard for our internal feelings. It is an equal partner in the emotional process.
MALCOLM GLADWELL (1963–), *Blink: The Power of Thinking Without Thinking*

Cherish your own emotions and never undervalue them.
ROBERT HENRI (1865–1929)

There can be no transforming of darkness into light and of apathy into movement without emotion.
CARL JUNG (1875–1961)

Intellectually, I know that America is no better than any other country; emotionally, I know she is better than every other country.
SINCLAIR LEWIS (1885–1951)

The sign of an intelligent people is their ability to control emotions by the application of reason.
MARYA MANNES (1904–1990)

When you are not physically starving, you have the luxury to realize psychic and emotional starvation.
CHERRIE MORAGA (1952–)

Hatred is a very underestimated emotion.
JIM MORRISON (1943–1971)

The artist is a receptacle for emotions that come from all over the place: from the sky, from the earth, from a scrap of paper, from a passing shape.
PABLO PICASSO (1881–1973)

Acting is not being emotional, but being able to express emotion.
KATE REID (1930–)

Where we have strong emotions, we're liable to fool ourselves.
CARL SAGAN (1934–1996), *Cosmos (Blues for a Red Planet)*

The advantage of the emotions is that they lead us astray, and the advantage of science is that it is not emotional.
OSCAR WILDE (1854–1900), *The Picture of Dorian Gray*

Employment

The celebrated Galen said that employment was nature's physician. It is indeed so important to happiness that indolence is justly considered the parent of misery.
CHARLES CALEB COLTON (1780–1832)

More people out of work leads to higher unemployment.
CALVIN COOLIDGE (1872–1933)

Never fear the want of business. A man who qualifies himself well for his calling, never fails of employment.
THOMAS JEFFERSON (1743–1826)

Think enthusiastically about everything; but especially about your job. If you do, you'll put a touch of glory in your life. If you love your job with enthusiasm, you'll shake it to pieces. You'll love it into greatness.
NORMAN VINCENT PEALE (1898–1993)

Most are engaged in business the greater part of their lives, because the soul abhors a vacuum and they have not discovered any continuous employment for man's nobler faculties.
HENRY DAVID THOREAU (1817–1862)

There is no trade or employment but the young man following it may become a hero.
WALT WHITMAN (1819–1892)

Encouragement

God brings men into deep waters, not to drown them, but to cleanse them.
JOHN AUGHEY (1828–1911)

The art of living lies less in eliminating our troubles than in growing with them.
BERNARD M. BARUCH (1870–1965)

God uses suffering as a whetstone, to make men sharp with.
HENRY WARD BEECHER (1813–1887)

The world is more malleable than you think and it's waiting for you to hammer it into shape.
BONO (1960–)

Be grateful for what you have now. As you begin to think about all the things in your life you are grateful for, you will be amazed at the never ending thoughts that come back to you of more things to be grateful for. You have to make a start, and then the law of attraction will receive those grateful thoughts and give you more just like them.
RHONDA BYRNE (1955–)

The soul would have no rainbow had the eyes no tears.
JOHN VANCE CHENEY (1848–1922)

I have sometimes been wildly, despairingly, acutely miserable, but through it all I still know quite certainly that just to be alive is a grand thing.
AGATHA CHRISTIE (1890–1976)

Never give in … never, never, never, never, in nothing great or small, large or petty, never give in except to convictions of honour and good sense. Never yield to force … never yield to the apparently overwhelming might of the enemy.
SIR WINSTON CHURCHILL (1874–1965)

What lies behind us and what lies before us are tiny matters compared to what lies within us.
RALPH WALDO EMERSON (1803–1882)

Man performs and engenders so much more than he can or should have to bear. That's how he finds that he can bear anything.
WILLIAM FAULKNER (1897–1962)

Most of us, swimming against the tides of trouble the world knows nothing about, need only a bit of praise or encouragement—and we will make the goal.
JEROME FLEISHMAN (1922–)

Instruction does much, but encouragement does everything.
JOHANN WOLFGANG VON GOETHE (1749–1832)

Some luck lies in not getting what you thought you wanted but getting what you have, which once you have got it you may be smart enough to see is what you would have wanted had you known.
GARRISON KEILLOR (1942–)

When you come to the end of your rope, tie a knot and hang on.
FRANKLIN D. ROOSEVELT (1882–1945)

A word of encouragement during a failure is worth more than an hour of praise after success.
ANONYMOUS

Endings

[A]ll endings are also beginnings. We just don't know it at the time.
MITCH ALBOM (1959–), *The Five People You Meet in Heaven*

I don't believe in happy endings, but I do believe in happy travels, because ultimately, you die at a very young age, or you live long enough to watch your friends die. It's a mean thing, life.
GEORGE CLOONEY (1961–)

The beginnings and endings of all human undertakings are untidy.
JOHN GALSWORTHY (1867–1933)

What the caterpillar calls the end, the rest of the world calls a butterfly.
LAO-TZU (C. 600 BC)

That's something I think is growing on me as I get older: happy endings.
ALICE MUNRO (1931–)

Endurance

I learned from the example of my father that the manner in which one endures what must be endured is more important than the thing that must be endured.
DEAN ACHESON (1893–1971)

Endurance is not just the ability to bear a hard thing, but to turn it into glory.
WILLIAM BARCLAY (1907–1978)

Endurance is one of the most difficult disciplines, but it is to the one who endures that the final victory comes.
THE BUDDHA (563–483 BC)

Endurance is patience concentrated.
THOMAS CARLYLE (1795–1881)

A fight is not won by one punch or kick. Either learn to endure or hire a bodyguard.
BRUCE LEE (1940–1973)

Endurance is the crowning quality, And patience all the passion of great hearts.
JAMES RUSSELL LOWELL (1819–1891)

Endurance is nobler than strength and patience than beauty.
JOHN RUSKIN (1819–1900)

Patient endurance attaineth to all things; who God possesseth in nothing is wanting; alone God sufficeth.
SAINT TERESA OF AVILA (1515–1582)

Enemies

The moment at which two people, approaching from opposite ends of a long passageway, recognize each other and immediately pretend they haven't. This is to avoid the ghastly embarrassment of having to continue recognizing each other the whole length of the corridor.
DOUGLAS ADAMS (1952–2001)

The shaft of the arrow had been feathered with one of the eagle's own plumes. We often give our enemies the means of our own destruction.
AESOP (620–560 BC), *The Eagle and the Arrow*

He who has a thousand friends has not a friend to spare,
And he who has one enemy will meet him everywhere.
ALI IBN ABI TALIB (C. 599–661), *A Hundred Sayings*

Observe your enemies, for they first find out your faults.
ANTISTHENES (445–365 BC)

It is easier to forgive an enemy than to forgive a friend.
WILLIAM BLAKE (1757–1827)

When a sinister person means to be your enemy, they always start by trying to become your friend.
WILLIAM BLAKE (1757–1827)

It is difficult to say who do you the most harm: enemies with the worst intentions or friends with the best.
SIR EDWARD G. BULWER-LYTTON (1803–1873)

He hasn't an enemy in the world—but all his friends hate him.
EDDIE CANTOR (1892–1964)

If there be no enemy there's no fight. If no fight, no victory and if no victory there is no crown.
THOMAS CARLYLE (1795–1881)

Our greatest foes, and whom we must chiefly combat, are within.
MIGUEL DE CERVANTES (1547–1616)

Let your enemies be disarmed by the gentleness of your manner, but at the same time let them feel, the steadiness of your resentment.
LORD CHESTERFIELD (1694–1773)

You shall judge a man by his foes as well as by his friends.
JOSEPH CONRAD (1857–1924)

I do not regret one professional enemy I have made. Any actor who doesn't dare to make an enemy should get out of the business.
BETTE DAVIS (1908–1989), *The Lonely Life*

If you want to make peace, you don't talk to your friends. You talk to your enemies.
MOSHE DAYAN (1915–1981)

As a matter of self-preservation, a man needs good friends or ardent enemies, for the former instruct him and the latter take him to task.
DIOGENES LAERTIUS (C. 200)

There is nothing like the sight of an old enemy down on his luck.
EURIPIDES (C. 480–406 BC)

No prudent antagonist thinks light of his adversaries.
JOHANN WOLFGANG VON GOETHE (1749–1832)

A wise man gets more use from his enemies than a fool from his friends.
BALTASAR GRACIAN (1601–1658)

The enemy is anybody who's going to get you killed, no matter which side he's on.
JOSEPH HELLER (1923–1999), *Catch-22*

You can discover what your enemy fears most by observing the means he uses to frighten you.
ERIC HOFFER (1902–1983)

Never explain—your friends do not need it and your enemies will not believe you anyway.
ELBERT HUBBARD (1856–1915)

Friends may come and go, but enemies accumulate.
THOMAS JONES (1892–1969)

It is hard to fight an enemy who has outposts in your head.
SALLY KEMPTON (1943–)

Forgive your enemies, but never forget their names.
JOHN F. KENNEDY (1917–1963)

In the End, we will remember not the words of our enemies, but the silence of our friends.
MARTIN LUTHER KING JR. (1929–1968)

The best way to destroy your enemy is to make him your friend.
ABRAHAM LINCOLN (1809–1865)

Above all things, never be afraid. The enemy who forces you to retreat is himself afraid of you at that very moment.
ANDRÉ MAUROIS (1885–1967)

Money can't buy friends, but it can get you a better class of enemy.
SPIKE MILLIGAN (1918–2002)

Never interrupt your enemy when he is making a mistake.
NAPOLÉON I (1769–1821)

At times one remains faithful to a cause only because its opponents do not cease to be insipid.
FRIEDRICH NIETZSCHE (1844–1900)

He who lives by fighting with an enemy has an interest in the preservation of the enemy's life.
FRIEDRICH NIETZSCHE (1844–1900)

We can learn even from our enemies.
OVID (43 BC–AD 17), *Metamorphoses*

Treat your friend as if he might become an enemy.
PUBLILIUS SYRUS (C. 100 BC), *Maxims*

Never hate your enemies, it affects your judgment.
MARIO PUZO (1999–), *The Godfather*

Know thy self, know thy enemy. A thousand battles, a thousand victories.
SUN-TZU (C. 544–496 BC)

The rule is perfect: in all matters of opinion our adversaries are insane.
MARK TWAIN (1835–1910)

I have never made but one prayer to God, a very short one: "O Lord, make my enemies ridiculous." And God granted it.
VOLTAIRE (1694–1778)

A man cannot be too careful in the choice of his enemies.
OSCAR WILDE (1854–1900), *The Picture of Dorian Gray*

Always forgive your enemies; nothing annoys them so much.
OSCAR WILDE (1854–1900)

Rejoice not at thine enemy's fall—but don't rush to pick him up either.
JEWISH PROVERB

Use your enemy's hand to catch a snake.
PERSIAN PROVERB

Energy

[H]appiness gives us the energy which is the basis of health.
HENRI-FRÉDÉRIC AMIEL (1821–1881)

Life engenders life. Energy creates energy. It is by spending oneself that one becomes rich.
SARAH BERNHARDT (1844–1923)

Energy is eternal delight.
WILLIAM BLAKE (1757–1827)

Energy and persistence conquer all things.
BENJAMIN FRANKLIN (1706–1790)

Crime is naught but misdirected energy.
EMMA GOLDMAN (1869–1940), *Anarchism*

Love the moment, and the energy of that moment will spread beyond all boundaries.
CORITA KENT (1918–1986)

Engineering

Engineering is not merely knowing and being knowledgeable, like a walking encyclopedia; engineering is not merely analysis; engineering is not merely the possession of the capacity to get elegant solutions to non-existent engineering problems; engineering is practicing the art of the organized forcing of technological change … Engineers operate at the interface between science and society….
GORDON S. BROWN (1908–1996)

Architecture begins where engineering ends.
WALTER GROPIUS (1883–1969)

Engineering is a great profession. There is the satisfaction of watching a figment of the imagination emerge through the aid of science to a plan on paper. Then it moves to realization in stone or metal or energy. Then it brings homes to men or women. Then it elevates the standard of living and adds to the comforts of life. This is the engineer's high privilege.
HERBERT HOOVER (1874–1964)

For decades engineers have stood accused that their buildings do not have any cultural value. We have attempted to liberate engineering of this accusation.
FRITZ TODT (1891–1942)

England

He was born an Englishman and remained one for years.
BRENDAN FRANCIS BEHAN (1923–1964), *Hostage*

This royal throne of kings, this sceptred isle,
This earth of majesty, this seat of Mars,
This other Eden, demi-paradise,
This fortress built by Nature for herself
Against infection and the hand of war,
This happy breed of men, this little world,
This precious stone set in the silver sea,
Which serves it in the office of a wall
Or as a moat defensive to a house,
Against the envy of less happier lands,—
This blessed plot, this earth, this realm, this England.
WILLIAM SHAKESPEARE (1564–1616), *King Richard II*

This England never did, nor never shall,
Lie at the proud foot of a conqueror.
WILLIAM SHAKESPEARE (1564–1616), *King John*

England and America are two countries separated by a common language.
GEORGE BERNARD SHAW (1856–1950)

We don't bother much about dress and manners in England, because as a nation we don't dress well and we've no manners.
GEORGE BERNARD SHAW (1856–1950), *You Never Can Tell*

We have really everything in common with America nowadays except, of course, language.
OSCAR WILDE (1854–1900), *The Canterville Ghost*

English

Even if you do learn to speak correct English, whom are you going to speak it to?
CLARENCE DARROW (1857–1938)

Every English poet should master the rules of grammar before he attempts to bend or break them.
ROBERT GRAVES (1895–1985)

Summer afternoon—the two most beautiful words in the English language.
HENRY JAMES (1843–1916)

If the English language made any sense, a catastrophe would be an apostrophe with fur.
DOUG LARSON (1926–)

Here will be an old abusing of God's patience and the king's English.
WILLIAM SHAKESPEARE (1564–1616), *The Merry Wives of Windsor*

England and America are two countries separated by a common language.
GEORGE BERNARD SHAW (1856–1950)

The English have no respect for their language, and will not teach their children to speak it.
GEORGE BERNARD SHAW (1856–1950), *Pygmalion*

Enjoyment

If a man who enjoys a lesser happiness beholds a greater one, let him leave aside the lesser to gain the greater.
THE BUDDHA (563–483 BC)

He has spent his life best who has enjoyed it most. God will take care that we do not enjoy it any more than is good for us.
SAMUEL BUTLER (1612–1680)

You never achieve real success unless you like what you are doing.
DALE CARNEGIE (1888–1955)

Enjoy what thou has inherited from thy sires if thou wouldn't really possess it. What we employ and use is never an oppressive burden; what the moment brings forth, that only can it profit by.
JOHANN WOLFGANG VON GOETHE (1749–1832)

He who enjoys doing and enjoys what he has done is happy.
JOHANN WOLFGANG VON GOETHE (1749–1832)

Enjoyment is not a goal, it is a feeling that accompanies important ongoing activity.
PAUL GOODMAN (1911–1972)

Everyone enjoys doing the kind of work for which he is best suited.
NAPOLEON HILL (1883–1970)

No man can succeed in a line of endeavor which he does not like.
NAPOLEON HILL (1883–1970)

Listen to the cry of a woman in labor at the hour of giving birth—look at the dying man's struggle at his last extremity, and then tell me whether something that begins and ends thus could be intended for enjoyment.
SØREN KIERKEGAARD (1813–1855)

People who like this sort of thing will find this the sort of thing they like.
ABRAHAM LINCOLN (1809–1865)

It is what we do easily and what we like to do that we do well.
ORISON SWETT MARDEN (1850–1924)

No man can be ideally successful until he has found his place. Like a locomotive he is strong on the track, but weak anywhere else.
ORISON SWETT MARDEN (1850–1924)

The man who has no money is poor, but one who has nothing but money is poorer. He only is rich who can enjoy without owning; he is poor who though he has millions is is covetous.
ORISON SWETT MARDEN (1850–1924)

You have not found your place until all your faculties are roused, and your whole nature consents and approves of the work you are doing.
ORISON SWETT MARDEN (1850–1924)

Believe me! The secret of reaping the greatest fruitfulness and the greatest enjoyment from life is to live dangerously!
FRIEDRICH NIETZSCHE (1844–1900)

I have always said and felt that true enjoyment can not be described.
JEAN-JACQUES ROUSSEAU (1712–1778)

Doing is the great thing, for if people resolutely do what is right, they come in time to like doing it.
JOHN RUSKIN (1819–1900)

Enjoy yourself—it's later than you think.
SOCRATES (469–399 BC)

The first half of life consists of the capacity to enjoy without the chance; the last half consists of the chance without the capacity.
MARK TWAIN (1835–1910)

Enlightenment

Not creating delusions is enlightenment.
BODHIDHARMA (470–543)

To enjoy good health, to bring true happiness to one's family, to bring peace to all, one must first discipline and control one's own mind. If a man can control his mind he can find the way to Enlightenment, and all wisdom and virtue will naturally come to him.
THE BUDDHA (563–483 BC)

There is probably no more terrible instant of enlightenment than the one in which you discover your father is a man—with human flesh.
FRANK HERBERT (1920–1986), *Dune*

The real meaning of enlightenment is to gaze with undimmed eyes on all darkness.
NIKOS KAZANTZAKIS (1883–1957)

Nirvana or lasting enlightenment or true spiritual growth can be achieved only through persistent exercise of real love.
M. SCOTT PECK (1936–2005)

Peace has never come from dropping bombs. Real peace comes from enlightenment and educating people to behave more in a divine manner.
CARLOS SANTANA (1947–)

Enlightenment must come little by little—otherwise it would overwhelm.
IDRIES SHAH (1924–1996)

Entertainment

Art is moral passion married to entertainment. Moral passion without entertainment is propaganda, and entertainment without moral passion is television.
RITA MAE BROWN (1944–)

At its best, entertainment is going to be a subjective thing that can't win for everyone, while at worst, a particular game just becomes a random symbol for petty tribal behavior.
JOHN CARMACK (1970–)

The delusion of entertainment is devoid of meaning. It may amuse us for a bit, but after the initial hit we are left with the dark feeling of desolation.
ARTHUR ERICKSON (1924–)

Maybe entertainment is not supposed to be reality.
VICTORIA JACKSON (1959–)

I believe entertainment can aspire to be art, and can become art, but if you set out to make art you're an idiot.
STEVE MARTIN (1945–)

Anyone who tries to make a distinction between education and entertainment doesn't know the first thing about either.
MARSHALL MCLUHAN (1911–1980)

The entertainment is in the presentation.
JOHN MCTIERNAN (1951–)

No entertainment is so cheap as reading, nor any pleasure so lasting. She will not want new fashions nor regret the loss of expensive diversions or variety of company if she can be amused with an author in her closet.
LADY MARY WORTLEY MONTAGU (1689–1762)

It seems that entertainment is what most excites us and what we value above everything else.
CARROLL O'CONNOR (1922–2001)

Entertainment today constantly emphasises the message that things are wonderful the way they are. But there is another kind of cinema, which says that change is possible and necessary and it's up to you.
WIM WENDERS (1945–)

Everything is entertainment; criticism is now entertainment and it seems that the French directors have woken up one day and suddenly realised that they were not backed up any more.
WIM WENDERS (1945–)

Enthusiasm

A mediocre idea that generates enthusiasm will go further than a great idea that inspires no one.
MARY KAY ASH (1918–2001)

The enthusiasm of a woman's love is even beyond the biographer's.
JANE AUSTEN (1775–1817), *Mansfield Park*

Fires can't be made with dead embers, nor can enthusiasm be stirred by spiritless men. Enthusiasm in our daily work lightens effort and turns even labor into pleasant tasks.
JAMES ARTHUR BALDWIN (1924–1987)

If you can give your son or daughter only one gift, let it be enthusiasm.
BRUCE BARTON (1886–1967)

In things pertaining to enthusiasm, no man is sane who does not know how to be insane on proper occasions.
HENRY WARD BEECHER (1813–1887)

Enthusiasm, n.: A distemper of youth, curable by small doses of repentance in connection with outward applications of experience.
AMBROSE BIERCE (1842–1914), *The Devil's Dictionary*

Enthusiasm is the genius of sincerity and truth accomplishes no victories without it.
SIR EDWARD G. BULWER-LYTTON (1803–1873)

The prudent person may direct a state, but it is the enthusiast who regenerates or ruins it.
SIR EDWARD G. BULWER-LYTTON (1803–1873)

One man has enthusiasm for 30 minutes, another for 30 days, but it is the man who has it for 30 years who makes a success of his life.
EDWARD B. BUTLER (1853–1928)

To find your own way is to follow your bliss. This involves analysis, watching yourself and seeing where real deep bliss is—not the quick little excitement, but the real deep, life-filling bliss.
JOSEPH CAMPBELL (1904–1987)

The condition of the most passionate enthusiast is to be preferred over the individual who, because of the fear of making a mistake, won't in the end affirm or deny anything.
THOMAS CARLYLE (1795–1881)

Flaming enthusiasm, backed up by horse sense and persistence, is the quality that most frequently makes for success.
DALE CARNEGIE (1888–1955)

If you want to be enthusiastic, act enthusiastic.
DALE CARNEGIE (1888–1955)

I feel sorry for the person who can't get genuinely excited about his work. Not only will he never be satisfied, but he will never achieve anything worthwhile.
WALTER CHRYSLER (1875–1940)

Success is the ability to go from one failure to another with no loss of enthusiasm.
SIR WINSTON CHURCHILL (1874–1965)

You will do foolish things, but do them with enthusiasm.
SIDONIE GABRIELLE COLETTE (1873–1954)

The people of England are the most enthusiastic in the world.
BENJAMIN DISRAELI (1804–1881)

Every production of genius must be the production of enthusiasm.
BENJAMIN DISRAELI (1804–1881)

Love what you do. Do what you love.
WAYNE D. DYER (1940–)

Every great and commanding moment in the annals of the world is the triumph of some enthusiasm.
RALPH WALDO EMERSON (1803–1882)

Nothing great was ever achieved without enthusiasm.
RALPH WALDO EMERSON (1803–1882)

I prefer the folly of enthusiasm to the indifference of wisdom.
ANATOLE FRANCE (1844–1926)

Do not be afraid of enthusiasm. You need it. You can do nothing effectively without it.
FRANÇOIS-PIERRE-GUILLAUME GUIZOT (1787–1874)

Like what you do. If you don't like it, do something else.
PAUL HARVEY (1918–)

Life is to be lived. If you have to support yourself, you had bloody well better find some way that is going to be interesting.
KATHARINE HEPBURN (1907–2003)

Enthusiasm, if fueled by inspiration and perseverance, travels with passion, and its destination is excellence.
NAPOLEON HILL (1883–1970)

Enthusiasm is the great hill-climber.
ELBERT HUBBARD (1856–1915)

We act as though comfort and luxury were the chief requirements of life, when all that we need to make us happy is something to be enthusiastic about.
CHARLES KINGSLEY (1819–1875)

Happiness is excitement that has found a settling down place. But there is always a little corner that keeps flapping around.
E. L. KONIGSBURG (1930–)

If you aren't fired with enthusiasm, you will be fired with enthusiasm.
VINCE LOMBARDI (1913–1970)

If you are not getting as much from life as you want to, then examine the state of your enthusiasm.
NORMAN VINCENT PEALE (1898–1993)

If you have zest and enthusiasm you attract zest and enthusiasm. Life does give back in kind.
NORMAN VINCENT PEALE (1898–1993)

Life's blows cannot break a person whose spirit is warmed at the fire of enthusiasm.
NORMAN VINCENT PEALE (1898–1993)

There is real magic in enthusiasm. It spells the difference between mediocrity and accomplishment.
NORMAN VINCENT PEALE (1898–1993)

Think enthusiastically about everything; but especially about your job. If you do, you'll put a touch of glory in your life. If you love your job with enthusiasm, you'll shake it to pieces. You'll love it into greatness.
NORMAN VINCENT PEALE (1898–1993)

Do not stop thinking of life as an adventure. You have no security unless you can live bravely, excitingly, imaginatively, unless you can choose a challenge instead of a competence.
ELEANOR ROOSEVELT (1884–1962)

It is not the critic who counts; not the man who points out how the strong man stumbles, or where the doer of deeds could have done them better. The credit belongs to the man who is actually in the arena, whose face is marred by dust and sweat and blood, who strives valiantly; who errs and comes short again and again; because there is not effort without error and shortcomings; but who does actually strive to do the deed; who knows the great enthusiasm, the great devotion, who spends himself in a worthy cause, who at the best knows in the end the triumph of high achievement and who at the worst, if he fails, at least he fails while daring greatly. So that his place shall never be with those cold and timid souls who know neither victory nor defeat.
THEODORE ROOSEVELT (1858–1919)

It is always with excitement that I wake up in the morning wondering what my intuition will toss up to me, like gifts from the sea. I work with it and rely on it. It's my partner.
JONAS SALK (1914–1995)

Faith is an excitement and an enthusiasm: it is a condition of intellectual magnificence to which we must cling as to a treasure, and not squander on our way through life in the small coin of empty words, or in exact and priggish argument.
GEORGE SAND (1804–1876)

A man can succeed at almost anything for which he has unlimited enthusiasm.
CHARLES M. SCHWAB (1862–1939)

The ability to understand a question from all sides meant one was totally unfit for action. Fanatical enthusiasm was the mark of the real man.
THUCYDIDES (C. 460–395 BC)

I found that the men and women who got to the top were those who did the jobs they had in hand, with everything they had of energy and enthusiasm and hard work.
HARRY S TRUMAN (1884–1972)

Let us endeavor to live so that when we come to die even the undertaker will be sorry.
MARK TWAIN (1835–1910)

The best way to cheer yourself up is to try to cheer somebody else up.
MARK TWAIN (1835–1910)

Nobody grows old merely by living a number of years. We grow old by deserting our ideals. Years may wrinkle the skin, but to give up enthusiasm wrinkles the soul.
SAMUEL ULLMAN (1840–1924)

How do you go from where you are to where you want to be? I think you have to have an enthusiasm for life. You have to have a dream, a goal and you have to be willing to work for it.
JIM VALVANO (1946–1993)

Do not quench your inspiration and your imagination; do not become the slave of your model.
VINCENT VAN GOGH (1853–1890)

Get excited and enthusiastic about your own dream. This excitement is like a forest fire— you can smell it, taste it, and see it from a mile away.
DENIS WAITLEY (1933–)

Catch on fire with enthusiasm and people will come from miles to watch you burn.
JOHN WESLEY (1703–1791)

Enthusiasm is that kindling spark which marks the difference between the leaders in every activity and the laggards who put in just enough to "get by."
ANONYMOUS

Enthusiasm is very good lubrication for the mind.
ANONYMOUS

Genius is nothing more than inflamed enthusiasm.
ANONYMOUS

Jumping for joy is good exercise.
ANONYMOUS

Environment

We shall never understand the natural environment until we see it as a living organism. Land can be healthy or sick, fertile or barren, rich or poor, lovingly nurtured or bled white. Our present attitudes and laws governing the ownership and use of land represent an abuse of the concept of private property.... Today you can murder land for private profit. You can leave the corpse for all to see and nobody calls the cops.
PAUL BROOKS (1959–), *The Pursuit of Wilderness*

I can find God in nature, in animals, in birds and the environment.
PAT BUCKLEY (1952–)

Environmental protection doesn't happen in a vacuum. You can't separate the impact on the environment from the impact on our families and communities.
JIM CLYBURN (1940–)

The sharp rise in environmental pollution in the 20 years following World War II could be traced to such new technologies of production: new ways of producing electric power, transportation and food that, while they generated these valuable goods, now violently assaulted the environment as well.
BARRY COMMONER (1917–)

The environment is everything that isn't me.
ALBERT EINSTEIN (1879–1955)

We do not know, in most cases, how far social failure and success are due to heredity, and how far to environment. But environment is the easier of the two to improve.
J. B. S. HALDANE (1892–1964)

The destruction of our environment and resources cannot be stemmed unless the growth of the world's population is stemmed and ultimately reduced.
HENRY W. KENDALL (1926–1999)

We must conserve our environment and pass it on to our children in as good or better condition than it was passed to us.
MARK KENNEDY (1957–)

Nature favors those organisms which leave the environment in better shape for their progeny to survive.
JAMES LOVELOCK (1919–)

Envy

It is in the character of very few men to honor without envy a friend who has prospered.
AESCHYLUS (C. 525–456 BC), *Agamemnon*

As iron is eaten by rust, so are the envious consumed by envy.
ANTISTHENES (444–371 BC)

Love looks through a telescope; envy, through a microscope.
JOSH BILLINGS (1818–1885)

Envy is like a fly that passes all the body's sounder parts, and dwells upon the sores.
ARTHUR CHAPMAN (1873–1935)

There is a diabolical trio existing in the natural man, implacable, inextinguishable, co-operative and consentaneous: pride, envy, and hate. Pride that makes us fancy we deserve all the goods that others possess; envy that some should be admired while we are overlooked; and hate, because all that is bestowed on others, diminishes the sum we think due to ourselves.
CHARLES CALEB COLTON (1780–1832)

There are three things which the superior man guards against. In youth, lust. When he is strong, quarrelsomeness. When he is old, covetousness.
CONFUCIUS (551–479 BC), *The Confucian Analects*

There is no credulity so eager and blind as the credulity of covetness, which, in its universal extent, measures the moral misery and the intellectual destitution of mankind.
JOSEPH CONRAD (1857–1924), *Nostromo*

Avarice, envy, pride,
Three fatal sparks, have set the hearts of all
On Fire.
DANTE ALIGHIERI (1265–1321), *The Divine Comedy*

Whoever cultivates the golden mean avoids both the poverty of a hovel and the envy of a palace.
HORACE (65–8 BC), *Odes*

The truest mark of being born with great qualities, is being born without envy.
FRANÇOIS DE LA ROCHEFOUCAULD (1613–1680)

I envy people who drink. At least they have something to blame everything on.
OSCAR LEVANT (1906–1972)

They envy the distinction I have won; let them therefore, envy my toils, my honesty, and the methods by which I gained it.
SALLUST (86–34 BC)

Envy is the ulcer of the soul.
SOCRATES (469–399 BC)

Our envy of others devours us most of all.
ALEXANDER SOLZHENITSYN (1918–)

If we did but know how little some enjoy of the great things that they possess, there would not be much envy in the world.
ANONYMOUS

The only person worth envying is the person who doesn't envy.
ANONYMOUS

There are many roads to hate, but envy is the shortest of them all.
ANONYMOUS

Do not let your heart envy sinners, but always be zealous for the fear of the LORD.
THE BIBLE, Proverbs 23:17

Epitaphs

I have somewhere met with the epitaph on a charitable man which has pleased me very much. I cannot recollect the words, but here is the sense of it: "What I spent I lost; what I possessed is left to others; what I gave away remains with me."
JOSEPH ADDISON (1672–1719)

Epitaph, n.: An inscription on a tomb, showing that virtues acquired by death have a retroactive effect. Following is a touching example: "Here lie the bones of Parson Platt, Wise, pious, humble and all that, Who showed us life as all should live it; Let that be said —and God forgive it!"
AMBROSE BIERCE (1842–1914), *The Devil's Dictionary*

I want no epitaphs of profound history and all that type of thing. I contributed. I would hope they would say that, and I would hope somebody liked me.
BRIAN CLOUGH (1935–2004)

An epitaph is a belated advertisement for a line of goods that has been discontinued.
IRVIN S. COBB (1876–1944)

Reading the epitaphs, our only salvation lies in resurrecting the dead and burying the living.
PAUL ELDRIDGE (1888–1982)

It is my aim, and every effort bent, that the sum and history of my life, which in the same sentence is my obit and epitaph too, shall be them both: He made the books and he died.
WILLIAM FAULKNER (1897–1962)

This is the epitaph I want on my tomb: "Here lies one of the most intelligent animals who ever appeared on the face of the earth."
BENITO MUSSOLINI (1883–1945)

Wit is the epitaph of an emotion.
FRIEDRICH NIETZSCHE (1844–1900)

I always remember an epitaph which is in the cemetery at Tombstone, Arizona. It says: "Here lies Jack Williams. He done his damnedest." I think that is the greatest epitaph a man can have.
HARRY S TRUMAN (1884–1972)

If the whole human race lay in one grave, the epitaph on its headstone might well be: "It seemed a good idea at the time."
REBECCA WEST (1892–1983)

Equality

Equality ... is the result of human organization. We are not born equal.
HANNAH ARENDT (1906–1975)

If liberty and equality, as is thought by some are chiefly to be found in democracy, they will be best attained when all persons alike share in the government to the utmost.
ARISTOTLE (384–322 BC), *Politics*

The only stable state is the one in which all men are equal before the law.
ARISTOTLE (384–322 BC)

Before God we are all equally wise—and equally foolish.
ALBERT EINSTEIN (1879–1955)

That all men are equal is a proposition which, at ordinary times, no sane individual has ever given his assent.
ALDOUS HUXLEY (1894–1963)

In the state of nature…all men are born equal, but they cannot continue in this equality. Society makes

them lose it, and they recover it only by the protection of the law.
CHARLES DE MONTESQUIEU (1689–1755)

The love of democracy is that of equality.
CHARLES DE MONTESQUIEU (1689–1755)

All animals are equal but some animals are more equal than others.
GEORGE ORWELL (1903–1950), *Animal Farm*

Unless man is committed to the belief that all mankind are his brothers, then he labors in vain and hypocritically in the vineyards of equality.
ADAM CLAYTON POWELL JR. (1908–1972), *Black Power: A Form of Godly Power*

As men, we are all equal in the presence of death.
PUBLILIUS SYRUS (C. 100 BC), *Moral Sayings*

It was not their irritating assumption of equality that annoyed Nicholai so much as their cultural confusions. The Americans seemed to confuse standard of living with quality of life, equal opportunity with institutionalized mediocrity, bravery with courage, machismo with manhood, liberty with freedom, wordiness with articulation, fun with pleasure, in short, all of the misconceptions common to those who assume that justice implies equality for all, rather than equality for equals.
TREVANIAN (1931–2005) *Shibumi*

It is not true that equality is a law of nature. Nature has no equality. Its sovereign law is subordination and dependence.
MARQUIS DE VAUVENARGUES (1715–1747)

Men are equal; it is not birth but virtue that makes the difference.
VOLTAIRE (1694–1778)

We hold these truths to be self-evident that all men are created equal; that they are endowed by their Creator with certain inalienable rights; that among these are life, liberty, and the pursuit of happiness.
U.S. DECLARATION OF INDEPENDENCE

Error

An error is the more dangerous the more truth it contains.
HENRI-FRÉDÉRIC AMIEL (1821–1881)

Destiny is but a phrase of the weak human heart—the dark apology for every error. The strong and virtuous admit no destiny. On earth conscience guides; in heaven God watches. And destiny is but the phantom we invoke to silence the one and dethrone the other.
SIR EDWARD G. BULWER-LYTTON (1803–1873)

The only man, woman, or child who ever wrote a simple declarative sentence with seven grammatical errors is dead.
E. E. CUMMINGS (1894–1962), on the death of Warren G. Harding

There are sadistic scientists who hurry to hunt down errors instead of establishing the truth.
MARIE CURIE (1867–1934)

Great services are not canceled by one act or by one single error.
BENJAMIN DISRAELI (1804–1881)

Perhaps the history of the errors of mankind, all things considered, is more valuable and interesting than that of their discoveries. Truth is uniform and narrow; it constantly exists, and does not seem to require so much an active energy, as a passive aptitude of the soul in order to encounter it. But error is endlessly diversified; it has no reality, but is the pure and simple creation of the mind that invents it. In this field the soul has room enough to expand herself, to display all her boundless faculties, and all her beautiful and interesting extravagancies and absurdities.
BENJAMIN FRANKLIN (1706–1790)

If all else fails, immortality can always be assured by spectacular error.
JOHN KENNETH GALBRAITH (1908–2006)

Irrationally held truths may be more harmful than reasoned errors.
THOMAS H. HUXLEY (1825–1895)

Delay is preferable to error.
THOMAS JEFFERSON (1743–1826)

There are, in every age, new errors to be rectified and new prejudices to be opposed.
SAMUEL JOHNSON (1709–1784)

Don't be discouraged by a failure. It can be a positive experience. Failure is, in a sense, the highway to success, inasmuch as every discovery of what is false leads us to seek earnestly after what is true, and every fresh experience points out some form of error which we shall afterwards carefully avoid.
JOHN KEATS (1795–1821)

There are grammatical errors even in his silence.
STANISLAW LEC (1909–1966), *Unkempt Thoughts*

Any man whose errors take ten years to correct is quite a man.
J. ROBERT OPPENHEIMER (1904–1967), speaking of Albert Einstein

The first step towards amendment is the recognition of error.
SENECA (5 BC–AD 65)

Errors to be dangerous must have a great deal of truth mingled with them. It is only from this alliance that they can ever obtain an extensive circulation.
SYDNEY SMITH (1771–1845)

Anyone nit-picking enough to write a letter of correction to an editor doubtless deserves the error that provoked it.
ALVIN TOFFLER (1928–)

Love truth, and pardon error.
VOLTAIRE (1694–1778)

Eternity

A teacher affects eternity; he can never tell where his influence stops.
HENRY ADAMS (1838–1918), *The Education of Henry Adams*

To see a world in a Grain of Sand,
And a Heaven in a Wild Flower,
Hold Infinity in the palm of your hand,
And eternity in an hour.
WILLIAM BLAKE (1757–1827), "Auguries of Innocence"

Eternity has nothing to do with the hereafter.... This is it.... If you don't get it here, you won't get it anywhere. The experience of eternity right here and now is the function of life. Heaven is not the place to have the experience; here's the place to have the experience.
JOSEPH CAMPBELL (1904–1987)

Under all speech that is good for anything there lies a silence that is better. Silence is deep as Eternity; speech is shallow as Time.
THOMAS CARLYLE (1795–1881)

Every action of our lives touches on some chord that will vibrate in eternity.
EDWIN CHAPIN (1814–1880)

Equations are more important to me, because politics is for the present, but an equation is something for eternity.
ALBERT EINSTEIN (1879–1955)

History is a voice forever sounding across the centuries the laws of right and wrong. Opinions alter, manners change, creeds rise and fall, but the moral law is written on the tablets of eternity.
JAMES A. FROUDE (1818–1894)

In tragedy, every moment is eternity; in comedy, eternity is a moment.
CHRISTOPHER FRY (1907–2005)

Eternity is not something that begins after you are dead. It is going on all the time. We are in it now.
CHARLOTTE P. GILMAN (1860–1935)

A man is what he is, not what men say he is. His character no man can touch. His character is what he is before his God and his Judge; and only he himself can damage that. His reputation's what men

say he is. That can be damaged; but reputation is for time, character is for eternity
JOHN BALLANTINE GOUGH (1817–1886)

Eternity is a mere moment, just long enough for a joke.
HERMANN HESSE (1877–1962)

The few little years we spend on earth are only the first scene in a Divine Drama that extends into Eternity.
EDWIN MARKHAM (1852–1940)

Every action of our lives touches on some chord that will vibrate in eternity.
SEAN O'CASEY (1880–1964)

What nature delivers to us is never stale. Because what nature creates has eternity in it.
ISAAC BASHEVIS SINGER (1904–1991)

Eternity's a terrible thought. I mean, where's it all going to end?
TOM STOPPARD (1937–), *Rosencrantz and Guildenstern Are Dead*

We don't have an eternity to realize our dreams, only the time we are here.
SUSAN TAYLOR (1946–)

As if you could kill time without injuring eternity.
HENRY DAVID THOREAU (1817–1862)

Time is but the stream I go a-fishing in. I drink at it; but while I drink, I see the sandy bottom and detect how shallow it is. Its thin current slides away, but eternity remains. I would drink deeper; fish fill the sky, whose bottom is pebbly with stars. I cannot count one. I know not the first letter of the alphabet. I have always been regretting that I was not as wise as the day I was born.
HENRY DAVID THOREAU (1817–1862)

A dreamer lives for eternity.
ANONYMOUS

Ethics

The needs of society determine its ethics.
MAYA ANGELOU (1928–)

Never let your sense of morals get in the way of doing what's right.
ISAAC ASIMOV (1920–1992)

There is a concept which corrupts and upsets all others. I refer not to Evil, whose limited realm is that of ethics; I refer to the infinite.
JORGE LUIS BORGES (1899–1986)

Grub first, then ethics.
BERTOLT BRECHT (1898–1956)

A man without ethics is a wild beast loosed upon this world.
ALBERT CAMUS (1913–1960)

Non-violence leads to the highest ethics, which is the goal of all evolution. Until we stop harming all other living beings, we are still savages.
THOMAS A. EDISON (1847–1931)

A man's ethical behavior should be based effectually on sympathy, education, and social ties; no religious basis is necessary. Man would indeed be in a poor way if he had to be restrained by fear of punishment and hope of reward after death.
ALBERT EINSTEIN (1879–1955)

Relativity applies to physics, not ethics.
ALBERT EINSTEIN (1879–1955)

The ideals which have always shone before me and filled me with the joy of living are goodness, beauty, and truth. To make a goal of comfort or happiness has never appealed to me; a system of ethics built on this basis would be sufficient only for a herd of cattle.
ALBERT EINSTEIN (1879–1955)

I consider ethics, as well as religion, as supplements to law in the government of man.
THOMAS JEFFERSON (1762–1826)

In law a man is guilty when he violates the rights of others. In ethics he is guilty if he only thinks of doing so.
IMMANUEL KANT (1724–1804)

Ethics is nothing else than reverence for life.
DR. ALBERT SCHWEITZER (1875–1965)

Ethics is the activity of man directed to secure the inner perfection of his own personality.
DR. ALBERT SCHWEITZER (1875–1965)

I can do no other than be reverent before everything that is called life. I can do no other than to have compassion for all that is called life. That is the beginning and the foundation of all ethics.
DR. ALBERT SCHWEITZER (1875–1965)

The first step in the evolution of ethics is a sense of solidarity with other human beings.
DR. ALBERT SCHWEITZER (1875–1965)

Ethics is not definable, is not implementable, because it is not conscious; it involves not only our thinking, but also our feeling.
VALDEMAR W. SETZER (1940–)

Even the most rational approach to ethics is defenseless if there isn't the will to do what is right.
ALEXANDER SOLZHENITSYN (1918–)

Etiquette

Politeness, n.: The most acceptable hypocrisy.
AMBROSE BIERCE (1842–1914), *The Devil's Dictionary*

One of the greatest victories you can gain over someone is to beat him at politeness.
JOSH BILLINGS (1818–1885)

It is wise to apply the oil of refined politeness to the mechanisms of friendship.
SIDONIE GABRIELLE COLETTE (1873–1954)

Cleanliness and order are not matters of instinct; they are matters of education, and like most great things, you must cultivate a taste for them.
BENJAMIN DISRAELI (1804–1881)

Rudeness is the weak man's imitation of strength.
ERIC HOFFER (1902–1983)

We don't bother much about dress and manners in England, because as a nation we don't dress well and we've no manners.
GEORGE BERNARD SHAW (1856–1950), *You Never Can Tell*

Politeness and consideration for others is like investing pennies and getting dollars back.
THOMAS SOWELL (1930–), *Creators Syndicate*

To have respect for ourselves guides our morals; and to have a deference for others governs our manners.
LAWRENCE STERNE (1713–1768)

Good manners will open doors that the best education cannot.
CLARENCE THOMAS (1948–)

Associate with well-mannered persons and your manners will improve. Run around with decent folk and your own decent instincts will be strengthened.
STANLEY WALKER (1898–1962)

Manners maketh man.
WILLIAM OF WYKEHAM (1324–1404)

Evening

My evening visitors, if they cannot see the clock, should find the time in my face.
RALPH WALDO EMERSON (1803–1882)

I've had a perfectly wonderful evening. But this wasn't it.
GROUCHO MARX (1890–1977)

Our evenings are farewells. Our parties are testaments. So that the secret stream of suffering may warm the cold of life.
BORIS PASTERNAK (1890–1960)

Evil

We must as second best … take the least of the evils.
ARISTOTLE (384–322 BC), *Nichomachean Ethics*

Evil draws men together.
ARISTOTLE (384–322 BC), *Rhetoric*

The evils of the body are murder, theft, and adultery; of the tongue, lying, slander, abuse, and idle talk; of the mind, covetousness, hatred, and error.
THE BUDDHA (563–483 BC)

All that is necessary for the triumph of evil is that good men do nothing.
EDMUND BURKE (1729–1797)

The evil that is in the world almost always comes of ignorance, and good intentions may do as much harm as malevolence if they lack understanding.
ALBERT CAMUS (1913–1960)

The belief in a supernatural source of evil is not necessary; men alone are quite capable of every wickedness.
JOSEPH CONRAD (1857–1924), *Under Western Eyes*

Nothing is easier than to denounce the evildoer; nothing is more difficult than to understand him.
FYODOR DOSTOEVSKY (1821–1881)

Evil to him who evil thinks.
KING EDWARD III (1312–1377)

Every sweet has its sour; every evil its good.
RALPH WALDO EMERSON (1803–1882)

I know indeed what evil I intend to do,
but stronger than all my afterthoughts is my fury,
fury that brings upon mortals the greatest evils.
EURIPIDES (C. 480–406 BC), *Medea*

The disease of an evil conscience is beyond the practice of all the physicians of all the countries in the world.
WILLIAM E. GLADSTONE (1809–1898)
Don't let us make imaginary evils, when you know we have so many real ones to encounter.
OLIVER GOLDSMITH (1730–1774)

Do not seek evil gains; evil gains are the equivalent of disaster.
HESIOD (C. 800 BC), *Works and Days*

He harms himself who does harm to another, and the evil plan is most harmful to the planner.
HESIOD (C. 800 BC), *Works and Days*

Often an entire city has suffered because of an evil man.
HESIOD (C. 800 BC), *Works and Days*

Evil deeds do not prosper; the slow man catches up with the swift.
HOMER (800–700 BC), *The Odyssey*

Whenever evil befalls us, we ought to ask ourselves, after the first suffering, how we can turn it into good. So shall we take occasion, from one bitter root, to raise perhaps many flowers.
LEIGH HUNT (1784–1859)

Melancholy and sadness are the start of doubt … doubt is the beginning of despair; despair is the cruel beginning of the differing degrees of wickedness.
ISIDORE DUCASSE LAUTREAMONT (1846–1870)

All things may corrupt when minds are prone to evil.
OVID (43 BC–AD 17)

I have discovered that all human evil comes from this, man's being unable to sit still in a room.
BLAISE PASCAL (1623–1662)

Men never do evil so completely and cheerfully as when they do it from a religious conviction.
BLAISE PASCAL (1623–1662)

No evil can happen to a good man, either in life or after death.
PLATO (C. 428–348 BC), *Dialogues*

Of two evils we must always choose the least.
THOMAS À KEMPIS (1380–1471)

The evil of the world is made possible by nothing but the sanction you give it.
AYN RAND (1905–1982), *Atlas Shrugged*

The spread of evil is the symptom of a vacuum. Whenever evil wins, it is only by default: by the moral failure of those who evade the fact that there can be no compromise on basic principles.
AYN RAND (1905–1982), *Capitalism: The Unknown Ideal*

It is bitter to lose a friend to evil, before one loses him to death.
MARY RENAULT (1905–1983), *The Praise Singer*

No man is justified in doing evil on the ground of expediency.
THEODORE ROOSEVELT (1858–1919), *The Strenuous Life*

The end excuses any evil.
SOPHOCLES (496–406 BC), *Electra*

Evil is obvious only in retrospect.
GLORIA STEINEM (1934–), *Outrageous Acts and Everyday Rebellions*

The evil that we know is best.
TITUS MACCIUS PLAUTUS (254–184 BC)

Every minute you are thinking of evil, you might have been thinking of good instead. Refuse to pander to a morbid interest in your own misdeeds. Pick yourself up, be sorry, shake yourself, and go on again.
EVELYN UNDERHILL (1875–1941)

Evil when we are in its power is not felt as evil but as a necessity, or even a duty.
SIMONE WEIL (1909–1943), *Gravity and Grace*

Indifference, to me, is the epitome of evil.
ELIE WIESEL (1928–)

Evolution

God may be a matter of indifference to the evolutionists, and a life beyond may have no charm for them, but the mass of mankind will continue to worship their creator and continue to find comfort in the promise of their Savior that he has gone to prepare a place for them.
WILLIAM JENNINGS BRYAN (1860–1925)

In the survival of favoured individuals and races, during the constantly-recurring struggle for existence, we see a powerful and ever-acting form of selection.
CHARLES DARWIN (1809–1882)

It is not the strongest of the species that survives, nor the most intelligent that survives. It is the one that is the most adaptable to change.
CHARLES DARWIN (1809–1882)

The theory of evolution by cumulative natural selection is the only theory we know of that is in principle capable of explaining the existence of organized complexity.
RICHARD DAWKINS (1941–)

Non-violence leads to the highest ethics, which is the goal of all evolution. Until we stop harming all other living beings, we are still savages.
THOMAS A. EDISON (1847–1931)

Nothing will benefit human health and increase the chances for survival of life on Earth as much as the evolution to a vegetarian diet.
ALBERT EINSTEIN (1879–1955)

It is curious how there seems to be an instinctive disgust in Man for his nearest ancestors and relations. If only Darwin could conscientiously have traced man back to the Elephant or the Lion or the Antelope, how much ridicule and prejudice would have been spared to the doctrine of Evolution.
HENRY HAVELOCK ELLIS (1859–1939)

Creationist critics often charge that evolution cannot be tested, and therefore cannot be viewed as a properly scientific subject at all. This claim is rhetorical nonsense.
STEPHEN JAY GOULD (1941–2002)

If we are going to teach creation science as an alternative to evolution, then we should also teach the stork theory as an alternative to biological reproduction.
JUDITH HAYES (1945–)

It is an error to imagine that evolution signifies a constant tendency to increased perfection. That process undoubtedly involves a constant remodelling of the organism in adaptation to new conditions; but it depends on the nature of those conditions whether the directions of the modifications effected shall be upward or downward.
THOMAS H. HUXLEY (1825–1895)

There is no law of progress. Our future is in our own hands, to make or to mar. It will be an uphill fight to the end, and would we have it otherwise? Let no one suppose that evolution will ever exempt us from struggles. "You forget," said the Devil, with a chuckle, "that I have been evolving too."
WILLIAM RALPH INGE (1860–1954)

Scripture suggests that the elements in space were created for the benefit of earth, while evolution suggests that earth is an insignificant speck in vast space.
WALTER LANG (1896–1972)

Today, the theory of evolution is an accepted fact for everyone but a fundamentalist minority, whose objections are based not on reasoning but on doctrinaire adherence to religious principles.
JAMES D. WATSON (1928–)

My theory of evolution is that Darwin was adopted.
STEVEN WRIGHT (1955–)

Excellence

The sad truth is that excellence makes people nervous.
SHANA ALEXANDER (1925–2005)

To enjoy the things we ought and to hate the things we ought has the greatest bearing on excellence of character.
ARISTOTLE (384–322 BC), *Nichomachean Ethics*

With regard to excellence, it is not enough to know, but we must try to have and use it.
ARISTOTLE (384–322 BC), *Nichomachean Ethics*

We are what we repeatedly do. Excellence, then, is not an act, but a habit.
ARISTOTLE (384–322 BC)

In every power, of which taste is the foundation, excellence is pretty fairly divided between the sexes.
JANE AUSTEN (1775–1817), *Northanger Abbey*

Excellence is a better teacher than mediocrity. The lessons of the ordinary are everywhere. Truly profound and original insights are to be found only in studying the exemplary.
WARREN G. BENNIS (1925–)

Strive for excellence, not perfection.
H. JACKSON BROWN JR. (1948–)

The secret of joy in work is contained in one word—excellence. To know how to do something well is to enjoy it.
PEARL S. BUCK (1892–1973), *The Joy of Children*

It's not enough that we do our best; sometimes we have to do what's required.
SIR WINSTON CHURCHILL (1874–1965)

Excellence is not an act but a habit. The things you do the most are the things you will do best.
MARVA COLLINS (1936–)

Find something that you're really interested in doing in your life. Pursue it, set goals, and commit

yourself to excellence. Do the best you can.
CHRIS EVERT (1954–)

I am careful not to confuse excellence with perfection. Excellence, I can reach for; perfection is God's business.
MICHAEL J. FOX (1961–)

Excellence is doing ordinary things extraordinarily well.
JOHN W. GARDNER (1912–2002)

No man ever reached to excellence in any one art or profession without having passed through the slow and painful process of study and preparation.
HORACE (65–8 BC)

Excellence in any department can be attained only by the labor of a lifetime; it is not to be purchased at a lesser price.
SAMUEL JOHNSON (1709–1784)

The ancient Greek definition of happiness was the full use of your powers along lines of excellence.
JOHN F. KENNEDY (1917–1963)

Excellence always sells.
EARL NIGHTINGALE (1921–1989)

Excellence means when a man or woman asks of himself more than others do.
JOSÉ ORTEGA Y GASSET (1883–1955)

Losing a game is heartbreaking. Losing your sense of excellence or worth is a tragedy.
JOE PATERNO (1924–)

Excellence is the unlimited ability to improve the quality of what you have to offer.
RICK PITINO (1952–)

Excellent things are rare.
PLATO (C. 428–348 BC)

If you are going to achieve excellence in big things, you develop the habit in little matters. Excellence is not an exception, it is a prevailing attitude.
COLIN POWELL (1937–)

It takes a long time to bring excellence to maturity.
PUBLILIUS SYRUS (C. 100 BC), *Maxims*

Excellence is the gradual result of always striving to do better.
PAT RILEY (1945–)

The renown which riches or beauty confer is fleeting and frail; mental excellence is a splendid and lasting possession.
SALLUST (86–34 BC), *The War with Catiline*

Life's like a play; it's not the length but the excellence of the acting that matters.
SENECA (5 BC–AD 65)

Next to excellence is the appreciation of it.
WILLIAM MAKEPEACE THACKERAY (1811–1863)

By appreciation, we make excellence in others our own property.
VOLTAIRE (1694–1778)

Sports serve society by providing vivid examples of excellence.
GEORGE F. WILL (1941–)

Excess

In charity there is no excess.
SIR FRANCIS BACON (1561–1626), *Of Goodness, and Goodness of Nature*

As scarce as truth is, the supply has always been in excess of the demand.
JOSH BILLINGS (1818–1885)

The best things carried to excess are wrong.
CHARLES CHURCHILL (1731–1764)

Never go to excess, but let moderation be your guide.
CICERO (106–43 BC)

There can never be a complete confidence in a power which is excessive.
CORNELIUS TACITUS (AD 55–117)

Minds, like bodies, will often fall into a pimpled, ill-conditioned state from mere excess of comfort.
CHARLES DICKENS (1812–1870)

When love is in excess it brings a man no honor nor worthiness.
EURIPIDES (C. 480–406 BC), *Medea*

In battling evil, excess is good; for he who is moderate in announcing the truth is presenting half-truth. He conceals the other half out of fear of the people's wrath.
KAHLIL GIBRAN (1883–1931)

Everything in excess! To enjoy the flavor of life, take big bites. Moderation is for monks.
ROBERT A. HEINLEIN (1907–1988)

I was simply furnishing a home. I love music ... and I don't think a $130,000 indoor-outdoor stereo system is extravagant.
LEONA HELMSLEY (1920–)

Excess on occasion is exhilarating. It prevents moderation from acquiring the deadening effect of a habit.
W. SOMERSET MAUGHAM (1874–1965)

All excess is ill, but drunkenness is of the worst sort. It spoils health, dismounts the mind, and unmans men. It reveals secrets, is quarrelsome, lascivious, impudent, dangerous and bad.
WILLIAM PENN (1644–1718)

Use, do not abuse; neither abstinence nor excess ever renders man happy.
VOLTAIRE (1694–1778)

Moderation is a fatal thing. Nothing succeeds like excess.
OSCAR WILDE (1854–1900)

Americans are overreachers; overreaching is the most admirable of the many American excesses.
GEORGE F. WILL (1941–), *Statecraft as Soulcraft*

Excitement

Enthusiasm is excitement with inspiration, motivation, and a pinch of creativity.
BO BENNETT (1972–)

The language of excitement is at best picturesque merely. You must be calm before you can utter oracles.
HENRY DAVID THOREAU (1817–1862)

Get excited and enthusiastic about your own dream. This excitement is like a forest fire—you can smell it, taste it, and see it from a mile away.
DENIS WAITLEY (1933–)

Excuses

Ninety-nine percent of all failures come from people who have the habit of making excuses.
GEORGE WASHINGTON CARVER (1864–1943)

He that is good for making excuses is seldom good for anything else.
BENJAMIN FRANKLIN (1706–1790)

The trick is not how much pain you feel—but how much joy you feel. Any idiot can feel pain. Life is full of excuses to feel pain, excuses not to live, excuses, excuses, excuses.
ERICA JONG (1942–)

The end excuses any evil.
SOPHOCLES (496–406 BC), *Electra*

It is wise to direct your anger towards problems—not people; to focus your energies on answers—not excuses.
WILLIAM ARTHUR WARD (1921–1994)

Executives

There are many highly successful businesses in the United States. There are also many highly paid executives. The policy is not to intermingle the two.
NORMAN R. AUGUSTINE (1935–)

Executives owe it to the organization and to their fellow workers not to tolerate nonperforming individuals in important jobs.
PETER F. DRUCKER (1909–2005)

Executives who get there and stay suggest solutions when they present the problems.
MALCOLM S. FORBES (1917–1990)

The worst disease which can afflict executives in their work is not, as popularly supposed, alcoholism; it's egotism.
ROBERT FROST (1874–1963)

Good executives never put off until tomorrow what they can get someone else to do today.
JOHN C. MAXWELL (1947–)

The best executive is one who has sense enough to pick good people to do what he wants done, and self-restraint enough to keep from meddling with them while they do it.
THEODORE ROOSEVELT (1858–1919)

Dealing with network executives is like being nibbled to death by ducks.
ERIC SEVAREID (1912–1992)

Exercise

Exercise ferments the humors, casts them into their proper channels, throws off redundancies, and helps nature in those secret distributions, without which the body cannot subsist in its vigor, nor the soul act with cheerfulness.
JOSEPH ADDISON (1672–1719)

I believe that every human has a finite number of heartbeats. I don't intend to waste any of mine running around doing exercises.
BUZZ ALDRIN (1930–)

Exercise is bunk. If you are healthy, you don't need it: if you are sick you should not take it.
HENRY FORD (1863–1947)

Walking is the best possible exercise. Habituate yourself to walk very far.
THOMAS JEFFERSON (1743–1826)

Why do strong arms fatigue themselves with frivolous dumbbells? To dig a vineyard is worthier exercise for men.
MARCUS VALERIUS MARTIALIS (AD 40–103)

In general, any form of exercise, if pursued continuously, will help train us in perseverance. Long-distance running is particularly good training in perseverance.
MAO TSE-TUNG (1893–1976)

I think that anyone who comes upon a Nautilus machine suddenly will agree with me that its prototype was clearly invented at some time in history when torture was considered a reasonable alternative to diplomacy.
ANNA QUINDLEN (1953–)

I don't excercise. If God had wanted me to bend over, he would have put diamonds on the floor.
JOAN RIVERS (1935–)

Exercise is done against one's wishes and maintained only because the alternative is worse.
GEORGE SHEEHAN (1918–1993)

Reading is to the mind what exercise is to the body.
SIR RICHARD STEELE (1672–1729)

I have never taken any exercise except sleeping and resting.
MARK TWAIN (1835–1910)

Existentialism

For an individual animal, plant, or man, existence (to be or not to be) is of quite decisive importance; an individual man has not after all a conceptual existence.
SØREN KIERKEGAARD (1813–1855), *Journals*

We run heedlessly into the abyss after putting something in front of us to stop us seeing it.
BLAISE PASCAL (1623–1662), *Pensées*

Man is nothing else but what he makes of himself. Such is the first principle of existentialism.
JEAN-PAUL SARTRE (1905–1980), *Existentialism*

Every existing thing is born without reason, prolongs itself out of weakness, and dies by chance.
JEAN-PAUL SARTRE (1905–1980), *Nausea*

Existence precedes essence.
JEAN-PAUL SARTRE (1905–1980)

The existentialist says at once that man is anguish.
JEAN-PAUL SARTRE (1905–1980)

Expectations

That is a good book which is opened with expectation and closed with profit.
AMOS BRONSON ALCOTT (1799–1888), *Table Talk*

Carry out a random act of kindness, with no expectation of reward, safe in the knowledge that one day someone might do the same for you.
PRINCESS DIANA (1961–1997)

A great obstacle to happiness is the expectation of too great a happiness.
FONTENELLE (1657–1757)

For [a product] to surprise me, it must be satisfying expectations I didn't know I had. No focus group is going to discover those. Only a great designer can.
PAUL GRAHAM (1964–), *Made in USA*

Life is largely a matter of expectation.
HORACE (65–8 BC)

Almost everything—all external expectations, all pride, all fear of embarrassment or failure—these things just fall away in the face of death, leaving only what is truly important. Remembering that you are going to die is the best way I know to avoid the trap of thinking you have something to lose. You are already naked. There is no reason not to follow your heart.
STEVE JOBS (1955–)

A master can tell you what he thinks of you. A teacher, though awakens your own expectations.
PARTRICIA NEAL (1926–)

Achievement is largely the product of steadily raising one's levels of aspiration and expectation.
JACK NICKLAUS (1940–), *My Story*

We tend to live up to our expectations.
EARL NIGHTINGALE (1921–1989)

If you paint in your mind a picture of bright and happy expectations, you put yourself into a condition conducive to your goal.
NORMAN VINCENT PEALE (1898–1993)

I am not in this world to live up to other people's expectations, nor do I feel that the world must live up to mine.
FRITZ PERLS (1893–1970)

Simplicity is not the goal. It is the by-product of a good idea and modest expectations.
PAUL RAND (1914–1996)

The greatest loss of time is delay and expectation, which depend upon the future. We let go the present, which we have in our power, and look forward to that which depends upon chance, and so relinquish a certainty for an uncertainty.
SENECA (5 BC–AD 65)

Oft expectation fails, and most oft
Where most it promises; and oft it hits
Where hope is coldest; and despair most sits.
WILLIAM SHAKESPEARE (1564–1616), *Twelfth Night*

We never live; we are always in the expectation of living.
VOLTAIRE (1694–1778)

High expectations are the key to everything.
SAM WALTON (1918–1992)

Experience

Human beings, who are almost unique in having the ability to learn from the experience of others, are also remarkable for their apparent disinclination to do so.
DOUGLAS ADAMS (1952–2001), *Last Chance to See*

By far the best proof is experience.
SIR FRANCIS BACON (1561–1626)

An expert is a person who has made all the mistakes that can be made in a very narrow field.
NIELS BOHR (1885–1962)

Judgment comes from experience, and experience comes from bad judgment.
SIMON BOLÍVAR (1783–1830)

Men are wise in proportion, not to their experience, but to their capacity for experience.
JAMES BOSWELL (1740–1795), *Life of Samuel Johnson*

Don't learn to do, but learn in doing. Let your falls not be on a prepared ground, but let them be bona fide falls in the rough and tumble of the world.
SAMUEL BUTLER (1612–1680)

You cannot acquire experience by making experiments. You cannot create experience. You must undergo it.
ALBERT CAMUS (1913–1960)

Experience which was once claimed by the aged is now claimed exclusively by the young.
G. K. CHESTERTON (1874–1936)

When you have really exhausted an experience you always reverence and love it. The two things that nearly all of us have thoroughly and really been through are childhood and youth. And though we would not have them back again on any account, we feel that they are both beautiful, because we have drunk them dry.
G. K. CHESTERTON (1874–1936)

The wise are instructed by reason; ordinary minds by experience; the stupid, by necessity; and brutes by instinct.
CICERO (106–43 BC)

The only source of knowledge is experience.
ALBERT EINSTEIN (1879–1955)

But human experience is usually paradoxical, that means incongruous with the phrases of current talk or even current philosophy.
GEORGE ELIOT (1819–1880)

Is it not rather what we expect in men, that they should have numerous strands of experience lying side by side and never compare them with each other?
GEORGE ELIOT (1819–1880)

Our knowledge is the amassed thought and experience of innumerable minds.
RALPH WALDO EMERSON (1803–1882)

The more experiments you make the better.
RALPH WALDO EMERSON (1803–1882)

If you take all the experience and judgment of men over fifty out of the world, there wouldn't be enough left to run it.
HENRY FORD (1863–1947)

Experience keeps a school, yet fools will learn in no other.
BENJAMIN FRANKLIN (1706–1790)

Experience teaches slowly and at the cost of mistakes.
JAMES A. FROUDE (1818–1894)

Seek you counsel of the aged for their eyes have looked on the faces of the years and their ears have hardened to the voices of Life. Even if their counsel is displeasing to you, pay heed to them.
KAHLIL GIBRAN (1883–1931)

It takes half your life before you discover life is a do-it-yourself project.
NAPOLEON HILL (1883–1970)

Experience is not what happens to a man; it is what a man does with what happens to him.
ALDOUS HUXLEY (1894–1963), *Texts and Pretexts*

Experience teaches only the teachable.
ALDOUS HUXLEY (1894–1963)

From their experience or from the recorded experience of others (history), men learn only what their passions and their metaphysical prejudices allow them to learn.
ALDOUS HUXLEY (1894–1963)

Words form the thread on which we string our experiences.
ALDOUS HUXLEY (1894–1963)

Experience is never limited, and it is never complete; it is an immense sensibility, a kind of huge spider-web of the finest silken threads suspended in the chamber of consciousness, and catching every air-borne particle in its tissue.
HENRY JAMES (1843–1916)

The power to guess the unseen from the seen, to trace the implications of things, to judge the whole piece by the pattern, the condition of feeling life in general so completely that you are well on your way to knowing any particular corner of it—this cluster of gifts may almost be said to constitute experience.
HENRY JAMES (1843–1916)

Experience is that marvelous thing that enables you to recognize a mistake when you make it again.
FRANKLIN P. JONES (1906–)

Nothing ever becomes real till it is experienced—even a proverb is no proverb to you till your life has illustrated it.
JOHN KEATS (1795–1821)

Experience is a hard teacher because she gives the test first, the lesson afterwards.
VERNON SANDERS LAW (1930–)

Experience does not err. Only your judgments err by expecting from her what is not in her power.
LEONARDO DA VINCI (1452–1519)

You gain strength, courage, and confidence by every experience in which you really stop to look fear in the face. You are able to say to yourself, "I have lived through this horror. I can take the next thing that comes along." You must do the thing you think you cannot do.
ELEANOR ROOSEVELT (1884–1962)

An expert is a person who avoids small error as he sweeps on to the grand fallacy.
BENJAMIN STOLBERG (1891–1951)

In the beginner's mind there are many possibilities. In the expert's mind there are few.
SHUNRYU SUZUKI (1904–1971)

If the world should blow itself up, the last audible voice would be that of an expert saying it can't be done.
PETER USTINOV (1921–2004)

Believe one who has proved it. Believe an expert.
VIRGIL (C. 70–19 BC), *Aeneid*

Experience is the name everyone gives to their mistakes.
OSCAR WILDE (1854–1900), *Lady Windermere's Fan*

Experts

An expert is a person who has made all the mistakes that can be made in a very narrow field.
NIELS BOHR (1885–1962)

An expert is someone called in at the last minute to share the blame.
SAM EWING (1921–)

Always listen to experts. They'll tell you what can't be done and why. Then do it.
ROBERT A. HEINLEIN (1907–1988)

I have learned the novice can often see things that the expert overlooks. All that is necessary is not to be afraid of making mistakes, or of appearing naive.
ABRAHAM MASLOW (1908–1970)

Don't be buffaloed by experts and elites. Experts often possess more data than judgment. Elites can become so inbred that they produce haemophiliacs who bleed to death as soon as they are nicked by the real world.
COLIN POWELL (1937–)

An expert is a person who avoids small error as he sweeps on to the grand fallacy.
BENJAMIN STOLBERG (1914–1951)

In the beginner's mind there are many possibilities. In the expert's mind there are few.
SHUNRYU SUZUKI (1904–1971)

Whenever there is a simple error that most laymen fall for, there is always a slightly more sophisticated version of the same problem that experts fall for.
AMOS TVERSKY (1937–1996)

If the world should blow itself up, the last audible voice would be that of an expert saying it can't be done.
PETER USTINOV (1921–2004)

Believe one who has proved it. Believe an expert.
VIRGIL (C. 70–19 BC)

Eyes

You know, I can see two tiny pictures of myself.
And there's one in each of your eyes.
And they're doin' everything I do.
Every time I light a cigarette, they light up theirs.
I take a drink and I look in and they're drinkin' too.
It's drivin' me crazy. It's drivin' me nuts.
LAURIE ANDERSON (1947–), "Sharkey's Night"

The mind has a thousand eyes.
And the heart but one;
Yet the life of a whole life dies
When love is done.
FRANCIS WILLIAM BOURDILLON (1852–1921)

We sometimes laugh from ear to ear, but it would be impossible for a smile to be wider than the distance between our eyes.
CHAZAL (1956–)

All action is of the mind, and the mirror of the mind is the face, its index the eyes.
CICERO (106–43 BC)

Men are born with two eyes, but only one tongue, in order that they should see twice as much as they say.
CHARLES CALEB COLTON (1780–1832)

It's extraordinary how we go through life with eyes half shut, with dull ears, with dormant thoughts. Perhaps it's just as well; and it may be that it is this very dullness that makes life to the incalculable majority so supportable and so welcome.
JOSEPH CONRAD (1857–1924), *Lord Jim*

(i do not know what it is about you that closes
and opens; only something in me understands
the voice of your eyes is deeper than all roses)
nobody, not even the rain, has such small hands
E. E. CUMMINGS (1894–1962)

Nature and Books belong to the eyes that see them.
RALPH WALDO EMERSON (1803–1882)

One of the most wonderful things in nature is a glance of the eye; it transcends speech; it is the bodily symbol of identity.
RALPH WALDO EMERSON (1803–1882)

I shut my eyes in order to see.
PAUL GAUGUIN (1848–1903)

Who can believe that there is no soul behind those luminous eyes!
THÉOPHILE GAUTIER (1811–1872)

Young cat, if you keep your eyes open enough, oh, the stuff you would learn! The most wonderful stuff!
THEODOR SEUSS GEISEL (1904–1991), *Seuss-isms*

Men trust their ears less than their eyes.
HERODOTUS (484–430 BC), *The Histories of Herodotus*

Originality is simply a pair of fresh eyes.
THOMAS WENTWORTH HIGGINSON (1823–1911)

For visions come not to polluted eyes.
MARY HOWITT (1799–1888)

The face is the mirror of the mind, and eyes without speaking confess the secrets of the heart.
SAINT JEROME (C. 342–420)

Drink to me only with thine eyes,
And I will pledge with mine;
Or leave a kiss but in the cup,
And I'll not look for wine.
BENJAMIN JOHNSON (1665–1742)

Living is easy with eyes closed, misunderstanding all you see.
JOHN LENNON (1940–1980), "Strawberry Fields"

What a blessing it would be if we could open and shut our ears as easily as we open and shut our eyes!
GEORG C. LICHTENBERG (1742–1799)

But O the truth, the truth. The
many eyes
That look on it! The diverse things
they see.
GEORGE MEREDITH (1828–1909)

There is no end to the adventures that we can have if only we seek them with our eyes open.
JAWAHARLAL NEHRU (1889–1964)

To find everything profound—that is an inconvenient trait. It makes one strain one's eyes all the time, and in the end one finds more than one might have wished.
FRIEDRICH NIETZSCHE (1844–1900), *The Gay Science*

Any one who has common sense will remember that the bewilderments of the eyes are of two kinds, and arise from two causes, either from coming out of the light or from going into the light, which is true of the mind's eye, quite as much as of the bodily eye; and he who remembers this when he sees any one whose vision is perplexed and weak, will not be too ready to laugh; he will first ask whether that soul of man has come out of the brighter light, and is unable to see because unaccustomed to the dark, or having turned from darkness to the day is dazzled by excess of light.
PLATO (C. 428–348 BC), *The Republic*

It is said that your life flashes before your eyes just before you die. That is true, it's called Life.
TERRY PRATCHETT (1948–)

The real voyage of discovery consists not in seeking new landscapes but in having new eyes.
MARCEL PROUST (1871–1922)

The eyes are not responsible when the mind does the seeing.
PUBLILIUS SYRUS (C. 100 BC)

Keep your eyes on the stars, and your feet on the ground.
THEODORE ROOSEVELT (1858–1919)

A man's feet should be planted in his country, but his eyes should survey the world.
GEORGE SANTAYANA (1863–1952)

Love looks not with the eyes, but with the mind.
WILLIAM SHAKESPEARE (1564–1616), *A Midsummer Night's Dream*

You cannot depend on your eyes when your imagination is out of focus.
MARK TWAIN (1835–1910), *A Connecticut Yankee in King Arthur's Court*

TV is chewing gum for the eyes.
FRANK LLOYD WRIGHT (1869–1959)

Few cases of eyestrain have been developed by looking on the bright side of things.
ANONYMOUS

True friendship is seen through the heart not through the eyes.
ANONYMOUS

When you go to buy, use your eyes, not your ears.
CZECH PROVERB

One may have good eyes and yet see nothing.
ITALIAN PROVERB

What you don't see with your eyes, don't invent with your mouth.
JEWISH PROVERB

Eyes that see do not grow old.
NICARAGUAN PROVERB

Faces

My face looks like a wedding cake left out in the rain.
W. H. AUDEN (1907–1973)

People remain what they are even if their faces fall apart.
BERTOLT BRECHT (1898–1956)

Alas after a certain age, every man is responsible for his own face.
ALBERT CAMUS (1913–1960)

He had a face like a blessing.
MIGUEL DE CERVANTES (1547–1616)

A man finds room in the few square inches of the face for the traits of all his ancestors; for the expression of all his history, and his wants.
RALPH WALDO EMERSON (1803–1882)

A good face they say, is a letter of recommendation. O Nature, Nature, why art thou so dishonest, as ever to send men with these false recommendations into the World!
HENRY FIELDING (1707–1754)

I am the family face; flesh perishes, I live on, projecting trait and trace through time to times anon, and leaping from place to place over oblivion.
THOMAS HARDY (1840–1928)

We can see nothing whatever of the soul unless it is visible in the expression of the countenance; one might call the faces at a large assembly of people a history of the human soul written in a kind of Chinese ideograms.
GEORG C. LICHTENBERG (1742–1799)

Facts

Facts are stubborn things; and whatever may be our wishes, our inclinations, or the dictates of our passion, they cannot alter the state of facts and evidence.
JOHN ADAMS (1735–1826)

I'm not a fan of facts. You see, the facts can change, but my opinion will never change, no matter what are the facts.
STEPHEN COLBERT (1964–)

The trouble with facts is that there are so many of them.
SAMUEL MCCHORD CROTHERS (1857–1927), *The Gentle Reader*

We can have facts without thinking but we cannot have thinking without facts.
JOHN DEWEY (1859–1952)

If the facts don't fit the theory, change the facts.
ALBERT EINSTEIN (1879–1955)

Get the facts, or the facts will get you. And when you get them, get them right, or they will get you wrong.
THOMAS FULLER (1608–1661), *Gnomologia*

Count Hermann Keyserling once said truly that the greatest American superstition was belief in facts.
JOHN GUNTHER (1901–1970)

Facts do not cease to exist because they are ignored.
ALDOUS HUXLEY (1894–1963), *Proper Studies*

Facts are facts and will not disappear on account of your likes.
JAWAHARLAL NEHRU (1889–1964)

Let us take things as we find them: let us not attempt to distort them into what they are not. We cannot make facts. All our wishing cannot change them. We must use them.
JOHN HENRY NEWMAN (1801–1890)

There are no facts, only interpretations.
FRIEDRICH NIETZSCHE (1844–1900)

Facts are the air of scientists. Without them you can never fly.
LINUS PAULING (1901–1994)

Science is facts; just as houses are made of stones, so is science made of facts; but a pile of stones is not a house and a collection of facts is not necessarily science.
HENRI POINCARÉ (1854–1912)

Facts are stupid things.
RONALD REAGAN (1911–2004)

If a man is offered a fact which goes against his instincts, he will scrutinize it closely, and unless the evidence is overwhelming, he will refuse to believe it. If, on the other hand, he is offered something which affords a reason for acting in accordance to his instincts, he will accept it even on the slightest evidence. The origin of myths is explained in this way.
BERTRAND RUSSELL (1872–1970)

He is indebted to his memory for his jests and to his imagination for his facts.
RICHARD BRINSLEY SHERIDAN (1751–1816)

Get your facts first, and then you can distort them as much as you please.
MARK TWAIN (1835–1910)

I am not one of those who in expressing opinions confine themselves to facts.
MARK TWAIN (1835–1910)

If it is a Miracle, any sort of evidence will answer, but if it is a Fact, proof is necessary.
MARK TWAIN (1835–1910)

There is something fascinating about science. One gets such wholesale returns of conjecture out of such a trifling investment of fact.
MARK TWAIN (1835–1910)

Failure

It is possible to fail in many ways. While to succeed is possible only in one way.
ARISTOTLE (384–322 BC), *Nichomachean Ethics*

Act as if it were impossible to fail.
DOROTHEA BRANDE (1893–1948)

A minute's success pays the failure of years.
ROBERT BROWNING (1812–1889)

The important thing to recognize is that it takes a team, and the team ought to get credit for the wins and the losses. Successes have many fathers, failures have none.
PHILIP CALDWELL (1920–)

Success is the ability to go from one failure to another with no loss of enthusiasm.
SIR WINSTON CHURCHILL (1874–1965)

If at first you don't succeed, failure may be your style.
QUENTIN CRISP (1908–1999)

Try as hard as we may for perfection, the net result of our labors is an amazing variety of imperfectness. We are surprised at our own versatility in being able to fail in so many different ways.
SAMUEL MCCHORD CROTHERS (1857–1927)

Success isn't permanent, and failure isn't fatal.
MIKE DITKA (1939–)

I have not failed. I've just found 10,000 ways that won't work.
THOMAS A. EDISON (1847–1931)

Many of life's failures are people who did not realize how close they were to success when they gave up.
THOMAS A. EDISON (1847–1931)

I'm proof against that word failure. I've seen behind it. The only failure a man ought to fear is failure of cleaving to the purpose he sees to be best.
T. S. ELIOT (1888–1965)

It's how you deal with failure that determines how you achieve success.
DAVID FEHERTY (1958–)

Of course, our failures are a consequence of many factors, but possibly one of the most important is the fact that society operates on the theory that specialization is the key to success, not realizing that specialization precludes comprehensive thinking.
R. BUCKMINSTER FULLER (1895–1983), *Operating Manual for Spaceship Earth*

Before success in any man's life he is sure to meet with much temporary defeat and, perhaps, some failure. When defeat overtakes a man, the easiest and most logical thing to do is to quit. That is exactly what the majority of men do.
NAPOLEON HILL (1883–1970)

Edison failed 10,000 times before he made the electric light. Do not be discouraged if you fail a few times.
NAPOLEON HILL (1883–1970)

Failure is nature's plan to prepare you for great responsibilities.
NAPOLEON HILL (1883–1970)

No man is ever whipped until he quits in his own mind.
NAPOLEON HILL (1883–1970)

When defeat comes, accept it as a signal that your plans are not sound, rebuild those plans, and set sail once more toward your coveted goal.
NAPOLEON HILL (1883–1970)

There is no loneliness greater than the loneliness of a failure. The failure is a stranger in his own house.
ERIC HOFFER (1902–1983)

A failure is a man who has blundered, but is not able to cash in on the experience.
ELBERT HUBBARD (1856–1915)

There is but one cause of human failure. And that is man's lack of faith in his true Self.
WILLIAM JAMES (1842–1910)

Nothing has a stronger influence psychologically on their environment and especially on their children than the unlived life of the parent.
CARL JUNG (1875–1961)

Don't be discouraged by a failure. It can be a positive experience. Failure is, in a sense, the highway to success, inasmuch as every discovery of what is false leads us to seek earnestly after what is true, and every fresh experience points out some form of error which we shall afterwards carefully avoid.
JOHN KEATS (1795–1821)

I would sooner fail than not be among the greatest.
JOHN KEATS (1795–1821)

There is not a fiercer hell than the failure in a great object.
JOHN KEATS (1795–1821)

Only those who dare to fail greatly can ever achieve greatly.
ROBERT F. KENNEDY (1925–1968)

Believe and act as if it were impossible to fail.
CHARLES KETTERING (1876–1958)

No persons are more frequently wrong, than those who will not admit they are wrong.
FRANÇOIS DE LA ROCHEFOUCAULD (1613–1680)

My great concern is not whether you have failed, but whether you are content with your failure.
ABRAHAM LINCOLN (1809–1865)

The probability that we may fail in the struggle ought not to deter us from the support of a cause we believe to be just.
ABRAHAM LINCOLN (1809–1865)

However things may seem, no evil thing is success and no good thing is failure.
HENRY WADSWORTH LONGFELLOW (1807–1882)

Not in the clamor of the crowded street, not in the shouts and plaudits of the throng, but in ourselves, are triumph and defeat.
HENRY WADSWORTH LONGFELLOW (1807–1882)

If at first you don't succeed, find out if the loser gets anything.
BILL LYON (1865–1943)

When we can begin to take our failures seriously, it means we are ceasing to be afraid of them. It is of immense importance to learn to laugh at ourselves.
KATHERINE MANSFIELD (1888–1923)

Many a man has finally succeeded only because he has failed after repeated efforts. If he had never met defeat he would never have known any great victory.
ORISON SWETT MARDEN (1850–1924)

There is no failure for the man who realizes his power, who never knows when he is beaten; there is no failure for the determined endeavor; the unconquerable will. There is no failure for the man who gets up every time he falls, who rebounds like a rubber ball, who persists when everyone else gives up, who pushes on when everyone else turns back.
ORISON SWETT MARDEN (1850–1924)

You cannot measure a man by his failures. You must know what use he makes of them. What did they mean to him. What did he get out of them.
ORISON SWETT MARDEN (1850–1924)

He's not the finest character that ever lived. But he's a human being, and a terrible thing is happening to him. So attention must be paid.
ARTHUR MILLER (1915–2005)

The world itself is pregnant with failure, is the perfect manifestation of imperfection, of the consciousness of failure.
HENRY MILLER (1891–1980)

If you have made mistakes, even serious ones, there is always another chance for you. What we call failure is not the falling down but the staying down.
MARY PICKFORD (1893–1979)

You always pass failure on the way to success.
MICKEY ROONEY (1920–)

If it fails, admit it frankly and try another. But above all, try something.
FRANKLIN D. ROOSEVELT (1882–1945)

It is hard to fail, but it is worse never to have tried to succeed. In this life we get nothing save by effort.
THEODORE ROOSEVELT (1858–1919)

The boy who is going to make a great man must not make up his mind merely to overcome a thousand obstacles, but to win in spite of a thousand repulses and defeats.
THEODORE ROOSEVELT (1858–1919)

Good people are good because they've come to wisdom through failure.
WILLIAM SAROYAN (1908–1981)

If thou art a man, admire those who attempt great things, even though they fail.
SENECA (5 BC–AD 65)

You may be disappointed if you fail, but you are doomed if you don't try.
BEVERLY SILLS (1929–2007)

Our business in this world is not to succeed, but to continue to fail, in good spirits.
ROBERT LOUIS STEVENSON (1850–1894)

I can't give you a sure-fire formula for success, but I can give you a formula for failure: try to please everybody all the time.
HERBERT BAYARD SWOPE (1882–1958)

Men are born to succeed, not fail.
HENRY DAVID THOREAU (1817–1862)

It is not enough to succeed. Others must fail.
GORE VIDAL (1925–)

Have you heard that it was good to gain the day? I also say it is good to fall—battles are lost in the same spirit in which they are won.
WALT WHITMAN (1819–1892)

Think like a queen. A queen is not afraid to fail. Failure is another steppingstone to greatness.
OPRAH WINFREY (1954–)

Act as though it is impossible to fail.
ANONYMOUS

Faith

It's lack of faith that makes people afraid of meeting challenges, and I believe in myself.
MUHAMMAD ALI (1942–)

Any dogma, primarily based on faith and emotionalism, is a dangerous weapon to use on others, since it is almost impossible to guarantee that the weapon will never be turned on the user.
ISAAC ASIMOV (1920–1992), *Foundation*

Faith is a cop-out. If the only way you can accept an assertion is by faith, then you are conceding that it can't be taken on its own merits.
DAN BARKER (1949–), *Losing Faith in Faith*

On life's journey faith is nourishment, virtuous deeds are a shelter, wisdom is the light by day and right mindfulness is the protection by night. If a man lives a pure life, nothing can destroy him.
THE BUDDHA (563–483 BC)

To believe in God or in a guiding force because someone tells you to is the height of stupidity. We are given senses to receive our information within. With our own eyes we see, and with our own skin we feel. With our intelligence, it is intended that we understand. But each person must puzzle it out for himself or herself.
SOPHY BURNHAM (1936–)

Hold faithfulness and sincerity as first principles.
CONFUCIUS (551–479 BC), *The Confucian Analects*

Faith, as well intentioned as it may be, must be built on facts, not fiction—faith in fiction is a damnable false hope.
THOMAS A. EDISON (1847–1931)

The faith that stands on authority is not faith.
RALPH WALDO EMERSON (1803–1882)

Doubt is a pain too lonely to know that faith is his twin brother.
KAHLIL GIBRAN (1883–1931)

If you think you can win, you can win. Faith is necessary to victory.
WILLIAM HAZLITT (1778–1830)

Faith must have adequate evidence, else it is mere superstition.
ALEXANDER HODGE (1823–1886)

Faith is the strength by which a shattered world shall emerge into the light.
HELEN KELLER (1880–1968)

Take the first step in faith. You don't have to see the whole staircase, just take the first step.
MARTIN LUTHER KING JR. (1929–1968)

Faith is, at one and the same time, absolutely necessary and altogether impossible.
STANISLAW LEM (1921–2006)

Life is only a long and bitter suicide, and faith alone can transform this suicide into a sacrifice.
FRANZ LISZT (1811–1886)

I respect faith, but doubt is what gets you an education.
WILSON MIZNER (1876–1933)

He wears his faith but as the fashion of his hat.
WILLIAM SHAKESPEARE (1564–1616), *Much Ado About Nothing*

Faith is the bird that sings when the dawn is still dark.
RABINDRANATH TAGORE (1861–1941)

Faithless is he that says farewell when the road darkens.
J. R. R. TOLKIEN (1892–1973)

If you can't have faith in what is held up to you for faith, you must find things to believe in yourself, for a life without faith in something is too narrow a space to live.
GEORGE E. WOODBERRY (1855–1930)

When you have come to the edge of all the light that you know and are about to step off into the darkness of the unknown, faith is knowing one of

two things will happen: there will be something to stand on, or you will be taught to fly.
ANONYMOUS

Fallibility

Fear of error which everything recalls to me at every moment of the flight of my ideas, this mania for control, makes men prefer reason's imagination to the imagination of the senses. And yet it is always the imagination alone which is at work.
LOUIS ARAGON (1897–1982)

We all carry within us our places of exile, our crimes, and our ravages. But our task is not to unleash them on the world; it is to fight them in ourselves and in others.
ALBERT CAMUS (1913–1960)

Once we know our weaknesses they cease to do us any harm.
GEORG C. LICHTENBERG (1742–1799)

If I have any justification for having lived it's simply, I'm nothing but faults, failures and so on, but I have tried to make a good pair of shoes. There's some value in that.
ARTHUR MILLER (1915–2005)

It says nothing against the ripeness of a spirit that it has a few worms.
FRIEDRICH NIETZSCHE (1844–1900)

The first faults are theirs that commit them, the second theirs that permit them.
ENGLISH PROVERB

Falsity

Contradiction is not a sign of falsity, nor the lack of contradiction a sign of truth.
BLAISE PASCAL (1623–1662)

I know that most men, including those at ease with problems of the greatest complexity, can seldom accept even the simplest and most obvious truth if it be such as would oblige them to admit the falsity of conclusions which they have delighted in explaining to colleagues, which they have proudly taught to others, and which they have woven, thread by thread, into the fabric of their lives.
LEO TOLSTOY (1828–1910)

Fame

It is folly for an eminent person to think of escaping censure, and a weakness to be affected by it. All the illustrious persons of antiquity, and indeed of every age, have passed through this fiery persecution. There is no defense against reproach but obscurity; it is a kind of concomitant to greatness, as satires and invectives were an essential part of a Roman triumph.
JOSEPH ADDISON (1672–1719)

Living in L.A., everyone likes to mold you and change you. I don't care about fame, I don't care about being a celebrity. I know that's part of the job, but I don't feed into anyone's idea of who I should be.
JESSICA ALBA (1981–)

He who pursues fame at the risk of losing his self is not a scholar.
CHUANG-TZU (369–286 BC), *The Great Supreme*

The love of fame is the last weakness which even the wise resign.
CORNELIUS TACITUS (AD 55–117)

Fame is proof that the people are gullible.
RALPH WALDO EMERSON (1803–1882)

Never suffer youth to be an excuse for inadequacy, nor age and fame to be an excuse for indolence.
BENJAMIN HAYDON (1786- 1846)

I'm a bit of an abstract figure that people can project their fantasies on; it's pretty much what we all are, otherwise we wouldn't be stars, and people wouldn't be interested. But people project things on you that have nothing to do with what you really are, or they see a little something and then

exaggerate it. And you can't really control that.
SALMA HAYEK (1966–)

Popularity? It is glory's small change.
VICTOR HUGO (1802–1885)

When once a man has made celebrity necessary to his happiness, he has put it in the power of the weakest and most timorous malignity, if not to take away his satisfaction, at least to withhold it. His enemies may indulge their pride by airy negligence and gratify their malice by quiet neutrality.
SAMUEL JOHNSON (1709–1784)

The glory of great men should always be measured by the means they have used to acquire it.
FRANÇOIS DE LA ROCHEFOUCAULD (1613–1680)

Fame comes only when deserved, and then is as inevitable as destiny, for it is destiny.
HENRY WADSWORTH LONGFELLOW (1807–1852)

Fame is an illusive thing—here today, gone tomorrow. The fickle, shallow mob raises its heroes to the pinnacle of approval today and hurls them into oblivion tomorrow at the slightest whim; cheers today, hisses tomorrow; utter forgetfulness in a few months.
HENRY MILLER (1891–1980)

All the fame you should look for in life is to have lived it quietly.
MICHEL DE MONTAIGNE (1533–1592)

Glory is fleeting, but obscurity is forever.
NAPOLÉON I (1769–1821)

The love of glory gives an immense stimulus.
OVID (BC 43–AD 18)

Even those who write against fame wish for the fame of having written well, and those who read their works desire the fame of having read them.
BLAISE PASCAL (1623–1662)

The charm of fame is so great that we like every object to which it is attached, even death.
BLAISE PASCAL (1623–1662)

Now there is fame! Of all—hunger, misery, the incomprehension by the public—fame is by far the worst. It is the castigation of God by the artist. It is sad. It is true.
PABLO PICASSO (1881–1973)

What's fame? a fancy'd life in other's breath.
A thing beyond us, even before our death.
ALEXANDER POPE (1688–1744)

Fame is a constant effort.
JULES RENARD (1864–1910)

Oblivion is the rule and fame the exception, of humanity.
ANTOINE RIVAROL (1753–1801)

Fame is but the breath of people, and that often unwholesome.
JEAN-JACQUES ROUSSEAU (1712–1778)

The highest form of vanity is love of fame.
GEORGE SANTAYANA (1863–1952)

Of all the possessions of this life fame is the noblest; when the body has sunk into the dust the great name still lives.
FRIEDRICH VON SCHILLER (1759–1805)

Fame is something that must be won. Honor is something that must not be lost.
ARTHUR SCHOPENHAUER (1788–1860)

The longer a man's fame is likely to last, the longer it will be in coming.
ARTHUR SCHOPENHAUER (1788–1860)

Glory is like a circle in the water,
Which never ceaseth to enlarge itself,
Till by broad spreading it disperses to naught.
WILLIAM SHAKESPEARE (1564–1616), *Henry VI*

Fame is the perfume of heroic deeds.
SOCRATES (469–399 BC)

Fame has also this great drawback, that if we pursue it, we must direct our lives so as to please the fancy of men.
BENEDICT DE SPINOZA (1632–1677)

Even the best things are not equal to their fame.
HENRY DAVID THOREAU (1817–1862)

Rather than love, than money, than fame, give me truth.
HENRY DAVID THOREAU (1817–1862)

What a heavy burden is a name that has become famous too soon.
VOLTAIRE (1694–1778)

The day will come when everyone will be famous for fifteen minutes.
ANDY WARHOL (1930–1987)

Riches: A dream in the night. Fame: A gull floating on water.
CHINESE PROVERB

Familiarity

All objects lose by too familiar a view.
JOHN DRYDEN (1631–1700)

The hues of the opal, the light of the diamond, are not to be seen if the eye is too near.
RALPH WALDO EMERSON (1803–1882)

Though familiarity may not breed contempt, it takes off the edge of admiration.
WILLIAM HAZLITT (1778–1830)

Familiarity breeds contempt.
PUBLILIUS SYRUS (C. 100 BC)

Sweets grown common lose their dear delight.
WILLIAM SHAKESPEARE (1564–1616), "Sonnet 102"

Family

The family is the school of duties—founded on love.
FELIX ADLER (1851–1933)

Woman is the salvation or the destruction of the family. She carries its destiny in the folds of her mantle.
HENRI-FRÉDÉRIC AMIEL (1821–1881)

The bond that links your true family is not one of blood, but of respect and joy in each other's life. Rarely do members of one family grow up under the same roof.
RICHARD BACH (1936–)

Mothers are the pivot on which the family spins.
PAM BROWN (1948–)

Happiness is having a large, loving, caring, close-knit family in another city.
GEORGE BURNS (1896–1996)

The strength of a nation derives from the integrity of the home.
CONFUCIUS (551–479 BC)

Fate chooses your relations, you choose your friends.
JACQUES DELILLE (1738–1813)

The family is the nucleus of civilization.
ARIEL DURANT (1898–1981) and WILL DURANT (1885–1981)

If you ever start feeling like you have the goofiest, craziest, most dysfunctional family in the world, all you have to do is go to a state fair. Because five minutes at the fair, you'll be going, "You know, we're alright. We are dang near royalty."
JEFF FOXWORTHY (1958–)

In every conceivable manner, the family is a link to our past, a bridge to our future.
ALEX HALEY (1921–1992)

Family has always been the most important thing in my life. The only real goal that I ever had was to be a good mother.
GOLDIE HAWN (1945–)

Call it a clan, call it a network, call it a tribe, call it a family. Whatever you call it, whoever you are, you need one.
JANE HOWARD (1935–1996), *Families*

No matter what you've done for yourself or for humanity, if you can't look back on having given love and attention to your own family, what have you really accomplished?
ELBERT HUBBARD (1856–1915)

Blood relatives often have nothing to do with family, and similarly, family is about who you choose to make your life with.
OLIVER HUDSON (1976–)

No matter what you've done for yourself or for humanity, if you can't look back on having given love and attention to your own family, what have you really accomplished?
LEE IACOCCA (1924–)

So much of what is best in us is bound up in our love of family, that it remains the measure of our stability because it measures our sense of loyalty. All other pacts of love or fear derive from it and are modeled upon it.
HANIEL LONG (1888–1956)

Woman knows what man has long forgotten, that the ultimate economic and spiritual unit of any civilization is still the family.
CLARE BOOTHE LUCE (1903–1987)

The Family is the Country of the heart. There is an angel in the Family who, by the mysterious influence of grace, of sweetness, and of love, renders the fulfilment of duties less wearisome, sorrows less bitter. The only pure joys unmixed with sadness.
GIUSEPPE MAZZINI (1805–1872)

God gives us relatives; thank God we can choose our friends.
ETHEL MUMFORD (1878–1940)

A family is a unit composed not only of children but of men, women, an occasional animal, and the common cold.
OGDEN NASH (1902–1971)

Family love is messy, clinging, and of an annoying and repetitive pattern, like bad wallpaper.
FRIEDRICH NIETZSCHE (1844–1900)

Family isn't about whose blood you have. It's about who you care about.
TREY PARKER (1969–) and MATT STONE (1971–)

I can't think of anything to write about except families. They are a metaphor for every other part of society.
ANNA QUINDLEN (1953–)

The family is one of nature's masterpieces.
GEORGE SANTAYANA (1863–1952)

If you cannot get rid of the family skeleton, you may as well make it dance.
GEORGE BERNARD SHAW (1856–1950)

Perhaps the greatest social service that can be rendered by anybody to the country and to mankind is to bring up a family.
GEORGE BERNARD SHAW (1856–1950)

Happy families are all alike; every unhappy family is unhappy in its own way.
LEO TOLSTOY (1828–1910), *Anna Karenina*

You don't choose your family. They are God's gift to you, as you are to them.
DESMOND TUTU (1931–)

Govern a family as you would cook a small fish, very gently.
CHINESE PROVERB

Famine

Whosoever shall not fall by the sword or by famine, shall fall by pestilence, so why bother shaving?
WOODY ALLEN (1935–), *Without Feathers*

In Ethiopia during the famine, I saw stuff there that reorganized how I saw the world. I didn't quite know what to do about it. At a certain point, I felt God is not looking for alms. God is looking for action.
BONO (1960–)

To prevent famine, one plow is worth a million sermons, and even patent medicines will cure more diseases than all the prayers uttered since the beginning of the world.
ROBERT GREEN INGERSOLL (1833–1899)

Abundance does not spread; famine does.
ZULU PROVERB

Fantasy

Men live in a fantasy world. I know this because I am one, and I actually receive my mail there.
SCOTT ADAMS (1957–)

I consider it useless and tedious to represent what exists, because nothing that exists satisfies me. Nature is ugly, and I prefer the monsters of my fancy to what is positively trivial.
CHARLES BAUDELAIRE (1821–1867)

The mind can make substance, and people planets of its own with beings brighter than have been, and give a breath to forms which can outlive all flesh.
LORD BYRON (1788–1824)

When I examine myself and my methods of thought, I come to the conclusion that the gift of fantasy has meant more to me than any talent for abstract, positive thinking.
ALBERT EINSTEIN (1879–1955)

I like nonsense, it wakes up the brain cells. Fantasy is a necessary ingredient in living, It's a way of looking at life through the wrong end of a telescope. Which is what I do. And that enables you to laugh at life's realities.
THEODOR SEUSS GEISEL (1904–1991)

To be matter of fact about the world is to blunder into fantasy—and dull fantasy at that, as the real world is strange and wonderful.
ROBERT A. HEINLEIN (1907–1988)

On a lazy Saturday morning when you're lying in bed, drifting in and out of sleep, there is a space where fantasy and reality become one. Are you awake, or are you dreaming? You see people and things; some are familiar; some are strange. You talk, you feel, but you move without walking; you fly without wings. Your mind and your body exist, but on separate planes. Time stands still. For me, this is the feeling I have when ideas come.
LYNN JOHNSTON (1947–)

All the works of man have their origin in creative fantasy. What right have we then to depreciate imagination?
CARL JUNG (1875–1961)

The pleasures of the imagination are as it were only drawings and models which are played with by poor people who cannot afford the real thing.
GEORG C. LICHTENBERG (1742–1799)

But fantasy kills imagination, pornography is death to art.
IRIS MURDOCH (1919–1999)

The poet is in command of his fantasy, while it is exactly the mark of the neurotic that he is possessed by his fantasy.
LIONEL TRILLING (1905–1975), *The Liberal Imagination*

One's real life is so often the life that one does not lead.
OSCAR WILDE (1854–1900)

Farming

There are three easy ways of losing money—racing is the quickest, women the most pleasant, and

farming the most certain.
JEFFREY, BARON AMHERST (1717–1797)

It is thus with farming: if you do one thing late, you will be late in all your work.
CATO THE ELDER (234–149 BC)

Farming as we do it is hunting, and in the sea we act like barbarians.
JACQUES COUSTEAU (1910–1997)

Farming looks mighty easy when your plow is a pencil, and you're a thousand miles from the cornfield.
DWIGHT D. EISENHOWER (1890–1969)

Farming in our rural communities is not just an economic industry, but a way of life.
SUE KELLY (1936–)

Farming with live animals is a 7 day a week, legal form of slavery.
GEORGE SEGAL (1934–)

Fascism

Fascism is itself less ideological, in so far as it openly proclaims the principle of domination that is elsewhere concealed.
THEODOR W. ADORNO (1903–1969)

Fascism is fascism. Terrorism is terrorism. Oppression is oppression.
HARRY BELAFONTE (1927–)

Fascism is not in itself a new order of society. It is the future refusing to be born.
ANEURIN BEVAN (1897–1960)

Fascism will come at the hands of perfectly authentic Americans.
JOHN T. FLYNN (1882–1964)

Fascism is capitalism in decay.
VLADIMIR I. LENIN (1870–1924)

Fascism is a religion. The twentieth century will be known in history as the century of Fascism.
BENITO MUSSOLINI (1883–1945)

Fascism should more appropriately be called Corporatism because it is a merger of state and corporate power.
BENITO MUSSOLINI (1883–1945)

The liberty of a democracy is not safe if the people tolerate the growth of private power to a point where it comes stronger than their democratic state itself. That, in its essence, is fascism—ownership of government by an individual, by a group.
FRANKLIN D. ROOSEVELT (1882–1945)

Fascism was a counter-revolution against a revolution that never took place.
IGNAZIO SILONE (1900–1978)

Fascism is capitalism plus murder.
UPTON SINCLAIR (1878–1968)

Fashion

All fashions are charming, or rather relatively charming, each one being a new striving, more or less well conceived, after beauty, an approximate statement of an ideal, the desire for which constantly teases the unsatisfied human mind.
CHARLES BAUDELAIRE (1821–1867)

You don't have to signal a social conscience by looking like a frump. Lace knickers won't hasten the holocaust, you can ban the bomb in a feather boa just as well as without, and a mild interest in the length of hemlines doesn't necessarily disqualify you from reading *Das Kapital* and agreeing with every word.
ELIZABETH BIBESCO (1897–1945)

Fashion, n.: A despot whom the wise ridicule and obey.
AMBROSE BIERCE (1842–1914), *The Devil's Dictionary*

If the cut of the costume indicates intellect and talent, then the color indicates temper and heart.
THOMAS CARLYLE (1795–1881)

Society is founded upon cloth.
THOMAS CARLYLE (1795–1881)

Fashion fades, only style remains the same.
COCO CHANEL (1883–1971)

There's never a new fashion but it's old.
GEOFFREY CHAUCER (1342–1400)

When a person is in fashion, all they do is right.
LORD CHESTERFIELD (1694–1773)

Fashion is the science of appearance, and it inspires one with the desire to seem rather than to be.
HENRY FIELDING (1707–1754)

Only men who are not interested in women are interested in women's clothes. Men who like women never notice what they wear.
ANATOLE FRANCE (1844–1924)

Eat to please thyself, but dress to please others.
BENJAMIN FRANKLIN (1706–1790)

I cannot and will not cut my conscience to fit this year's fashions.
LILLIAN HELLMAN (1905–1984)

Even truth needs to be clad in new garments if it is to appeal to a new age.
GEORG C. LICHTENBERG (1742–1799)

Fashion is the science of appearances, and it inspires one with the desire to seem rather than to be.
MICHEL DE MONTAIGNE (1533–1592)

I who have been involved with all styles of painting can assure you that the only things that fluctuate are the waves of fashion which carry the snobs and speculators; the number of true connoisseurs remains more or less the same.
PABLO PICASSO (1881–1973)

I base my fashion taste on what doesn't itch.
GILDA RADNER (1946–1989)

Fashions fade, style is eternal.
YVES SAINT-LAURENT (1940–)

Fashion is something barbarous, for it produces innovation without reason and imitation without benefit.
GEORGE SANTAYANA (1863–1952)

What a deformed thief this fashion is.
WILLIAM SHAKESPEARE (1564–1616), *Much Ado About Nothing*

A fashion is nothing but an induced epidemic.
GEORGE BERNARD SHAW (1856–1950)

Every generation laughs at the old fashions, but follows religiously the new.
HENRY DAVID THOREAU (1817–1862), *Walden*

I once had a sparrow alight upon my shoulder for a moment, while I was hoeing in a village garden, and I felt that I was more distinguished by that circumstance that I should have been by any epaulet I could have worn.
HENRY DAVID THOREAU (1817–1862)

Fashion is a form of ugliness so intolerable that we have to alter it every six months.
OSCAR WILDE (1854–1900)

Fashion is something that goes in one year and out the other.
ANONYMOUS

Fate

Destiny has two ways of crushing us—by refusing our wishes and by fulfilling them.
HENRI-FRÉDÉRIC AMIEL (1821–1881)

Ill fortune never crushed that man whom good fortune deceived not.
SIR FRANCIS BACON (1561–1626)

Fortune is like the market, where, many times, if you can stay a little, the price will fall.
SIR FRANCIS BACON (1561–1626)

Chance happens to all, but to turn chance to account is the gift of few.
SIR EDWARD G. BULWER-LYTTON (1803–1873)

There is but one philosophy and its name is fortitude! To bear is to conquer our fate.
SIR EDWARD G. BULWER-LYTTON (1803–1873)

Tempted fate will leave the loftiest star.
LORD BYRON (1788–1824)

There is no fate that cannot be surmounted by scorn.
ALBERT CAMUS (1913–1960)

Death and life have their determined appointments; riches and honors depend upon heaven.
CONFUCIUS (551–479 BC)

The wheel of fortune turns round incessantly, and who can say to himself, "I shall today be uppermost."
CONFUCIUS (551–479 BC)

When you go into court you are putting your fate into the hands of twelve people who weren't smart enough to get out of jury duty.
NORM CROSBY (1927–)

Fate chooses your relations, you choose your friends.
JACQUES DELILLE (1738–1813)

We make our fortunes and we call them fate.
BENJAMIN DISRAELI (1804–1881)

All things are subject to decay and when fate summons, monarchs must obey.
JOHN DRYDEN (1631–1700)

Seek not to know what must not be revealed,
For joy only flows where fate is most concealed.
A busy person would find their sorrows much more;
If future fortunes were known before!
JOHN DRYDEN (1631–1700)

Concern for man himself and his fate must always form the chief interest of all technical endeavor. Never forget this in the midst of your diagrams and equations.
ALBERT EINSTEIN (1879–1955)

The individual must not merely wait and criticize, he must defend the cause the best he can. The fate of the world will be such as the world deserves.
ALBERT EINSTEIN (1879–1955)

To punish me for my contempt for authority, fate made me an authority myself.
ALBERT EINSTEIN (1879–1955)

The bitterest tragic element in life to be derived from an intellectual source is the belief in a brute Fate or Destiny.
RALPH WALDO EMERSON (1803–1882), *Natural History of Intellect*

Fate is nothing but the deeds committed in a prior state of existence.
RALPH WALDO EMERSON (1803–1882)

If you believe in fate, believe in it, at least, for your good.
RALPH WALDO EMERSON (1803–1882)

Whatever limits us we call fate.
RALPH WALDO EMERSON (1803–1882)

A strict belief, fate is the worst kind of slavery; on the other hand there is comfort in the thought that God will be moved by our prayers.
EPICURUS (341–270 BC)

You were a stranger to sorrow: therefore Fate has cursed you.
EURIPIDES (C. 480–406 BC), *Alcestis*

I have found power in the mysteries of thought,
exaltation in the changing of the Muses;
I have been versed in the reasonings of men;
but Fate is stronger than anything I have known.
EURIPIDES (C. 480–406 BC), *Alcestis*

Man is his own star and the soul that can render an honest and perfect man commands all light, all influence, all fate.
JOHN FLETCHER (1579–1625)

Yet ah! why should they know their fate,
Since sorrow never comes too late,
And happiness too swiftly flies?

Thought would destroy their paradise.
No more; where ignorance is bliss,
'Tis folly to be wise.
THOMAS GRAY (1716–1771), "On a Distant Prospect of Eton College"

Riches and power are but gifts of blind fate, whereas goodness is the result of one's own merits.
HÉLOÏSE (1098–1164)

A man's character is his fate.
HERACLITUS (C. 535–475 BC), *On the Universe*

The fates have given mankind a patient soul.
HOMER (800–700 BC), *The Iliad*

The lofty pine is oftenest shaken by the winds;
High towers fall with a heavier crash;
And the lightning strikes the highest mountain.
HORACE (65–8 BC)

How a person masters his fate is more important than what his fate is.
WILHELM VON HUMBOLDT (1767–1835)

Chance generally favors the prudent.
JOSEPH JOUBERT (1754–1824)

When an inner situation is not made conscious, it appears outside as fate.
CARL JUNG (1875–1961)

Let us, then be up and doing,
With a heart for any fate;
Still achieving, still pursuing,
Learn to labour and to wait.
HENRY WADSWORTH LONGFELLOW (1807–1882)

If fate means you to lose, give him a good fight anyhow.
WILLIAM MCFEE (1881–1966)

Man is never honestly the fatalist, nor even the stoic. He fights his fate, often desperately. He is forever entering bold exceptions to the rulings of the bench of gods. This fighting, no doubt, makes for human progress, for it favors the strong and the brave. It also makes for beauty, for lesser men try to escape from a hopeless and intolerable world by creating a more lovely one of their own.
H. L. MENCKEN (1880–1956)

Question: Why are we Masters of our Fate, the captains of our souls? Because we have the power to control our thoughts, our attitudes. That is why many people live in the withering negative world. That is why many people live in the Positive Faith world. And you don't have to be a poet or a philosopher to know which is best.
ALFRED A. MONTAPERT (1906–)

At the bottom no one in life can help anyone else in life; this one experiences over and over in every conflict and every perplexity: that one is alone. That isn't as bad as it may first appear; and again it is the best thing in life that each should have everything in himself; his fate, his future, his whole expanse and world.
RAINER MARIA RILKE (1875–1926)

Men are not prisoners of fate, but only prisoners of their own minds.
FRANKLIN D. ROOSEVELT (1882–1945)

Full of wisdom are the ordinations of fate.
FRIEDRICH VON SCHILLER (1759–1805)

Fate gives us the hand, and we play the cards.
ARTHUR SCHOPENHAUER (1788–1860)

Fate leads the willing, and drags along the reluctant.
SENECA (5 BC–AD 65)

Fate rules the affairs of men, with no recognizable order.
SENECA (5 BC–AD 65)

While the fates permit, live happily; life speeds on with hurried step, and with winged days the wheel of the headlong year is turned.
SENECA (5 BC–AD 65)

Be extremely subtle, even to the point of formlessness. Be extremely mysterious, even to the point of soundlessness. Thereby you can be the director of the opponent's fate.
SUN-TZU (C. 544–496 BC), *The Art of War*

If you can't change your fate, change your attitude.
AMY TAN (1952–)

Public opinion is a weak tyrant compared with our own private opinion. What a man thinks of himself, that is which determines, or rather indicates, his fate.
HENRY DAVID THOREAU (1817–1862)

The sufferings that fate inflicts on us should be borne with patience, what enemies inflict with manly courage.
THUCYDIDES (C. 460–395 BC)

I am not an adventurer by choice but by fate.
VINCENT VAN GOGH (1853–1890)

The ritual of marriage is not simply a social event; it is a crossing of threads in the fabric of fate. Many strands bring the couple and their families together and spin their lives into a fabric that is woven on their children.
JEWISH WEDDING CEREMONY (PORTUGAL)

Fathers

Again, men in general desire the good, and not merely what their fathers had.
ARISTOTLE (384–322 BC), *Politics*

Mothers are fonder than fathers of their children because they are more certain they are their own.
ARISTOTLE (384–322 BC)

Mothers—especially single mothers—are heroic in their efforts to raise our nation's children, but men must also take responsibility for their children and recognize the impact they have on their families' well-being.
EVAN BAYH (1955–)

Life is all one piece. Men err when they think they can be inhuman exploiters in their business life, and loving husbands and fathers at home. For achievement without love is a cold and tight-lipped murderer of human happiness everywhere.
SMILEY BLANTON (1882–1966)

The important thing to recognize is that it takes a team, and the team ought to get credit for the wins and the losses. Successes have many fathers, failures have none.
PHILIP CALDWELL (1920–)

Blessed indeed is the man who hears many gentle voices call him father!
LYDIA M. CHILD (1802–1880)

No one would be foolish enough to choose war over peace.
CROESUS OF LYDIA (595–546 BC)

The gods visit the sins of the fathers upon the children.
EURIPIDES (C. 480–406 BC), *Phrixus*

Not a tenth of us who are in business are doing as well as we could if we merely followed the principles that were known to our grandfathers.
WILLIAM FEATHER (1908–1976)

I grew up to have my father's looks, my father's speech patterns, my father's posture, my father's walk, my father's opinions, and my mother's contempt for my father.
JULES FEIFER (1929–)

In peace the sons bury their fathers, but in war the fathers bury their sons.
HERODOTUS (484–430 BC)

The most important thing a father can do for his children is to love their mother.
THEODORE HESBURGH (1917–)

For rarely are sons similar to their fathers: most are worse, and a few are better than their fathers.
HOMER (800–700 BC), *The Odyssey*

All we have of freedom—all we use or know—
This our fathers bought for us, long and long ago.
RUDYARD KIPLING (1865–1936)

It is a wise father who knows his own child.
WILLIAM SHAKESPEARE (1564–1616), *The Merchant of Venice*

The more people have studied different methods of bringing up children the more they have come to the conclusion that what good mothers and fathers instinctively feel like doing for their babies is the best after all.
BENJAMIN SPOCK (1903–)

A father is someone who carries pictures where his money used to be.
ANONYMOUS

Fatigue

When one is happy there is no time to be fatigued; being happy engrosses the whole attention.
E. F. BENSON (1867–1940)

Our fatigue is often caused not by work, but by worry, frustration and resentment.
DALE CARNEGIE (1888–1955)

Men weary as much of not doing the things they want to do as of doing the things they do not want to do.
ERIC HOFFER (1902–1983)

Our greatest weariness comes from work not done.
ERIC HOFFER (1902–1983)

Nothing is so fatiguing as the eternal hanging on of an uncompleted task.
WILLIAM JAMES (1842–1910)

One of the amusements of idleness is reading without the fatigue of attention, and the world, therefore, swarms with writers whose wish is not to be studied but to be read.
SAMUEL JOHNSON (1709–1784)

Why do strong arms fatigue themselves with frivolous dumbbells? To dig a vineyard is worthier exercise for men.
MARCUS VALERIUS MARTIALIS (AD 40–103)

Faults

Our friends don't see our faults, or conceal them, or soften them.
JOSEPH ADDISON (1672–1719)

The greatest of all faults, I should say, is to be conscious of none.
THOMAS CARLYLE (1795–1881)

Not to alter one's faults is to be faulty indeed.
CONFUCIUS (551–479 BC)

The faults of a superior person are like the sun and moon. They have their faults, and everyone sees them; they change and everyone looks up to them.
CONFUCIUS (551–479 BC)

The real fault is to have faults and not amend them.
CONFUCIUS (551–479 BC)

When you have faults, do not fear to abandon them.
CONFUCIUS (551–479 BC)

He has not a single redeeming defect.
BENJAMIN DISRAELI (1804–1881)

A man's personal defects will commonly have with the rest of the world precisely that importance which they have to himself. If he makes light of them, so will other men.
RALPH WALDO EMERSON (1803–1882)

Don't find fault, find a remedy.
HENRY FORD (1863–1947)

A benevolent man should allow a few faults in himself, to keep his friends in countenance.
BENJAMIN FRANKLIN (1706–1790)

A good garden may have some weeds.
THOMAS FULLER (1608–1661)

Certain defects are necessary for the existence of individuality.
JOHANN WOLFGANG VON GOETHE (1749–1832)

It is well that there is no one without a fault; for he would not have a friend in the world.
WILLIAM HAZLITT (1778–1830)

While fools shun one set of faults they run into the opposite one.
HORACE (BC 65–8)

Everyone has his faults which he continually repeats: neither fear nor shame can cure them.
JEAN DE LA FONTAINE (1621–1695)

If we had no faults of our own, we should not take so much pleasure in noticing those in others.
FRANÇOIS DE LA ROCHEFOUCAULD (1613–1680)

Only the great can afford to have great defects.
FRANÇOIS DE LA ROCHEFOUCAULD (1613–1680)

We forget our faults easily when they are known to ourselves alone.
FRANÇOIS DE LA ROCHEFOUCAULD (1613–1680)

Trust no friend without faults, and love a woman, but no angel.
DORIS LESSING (1919–)

Humankind's chief fault is that they have so many small ones.
JEAN PAUL RICHTER (1763–1825)

We are all full of weakness and errors; let us mutually pardon each other our follies; it is the first law of nature.
VOLTAIRE (1691 1778)

None of us can stand other people having the same faults as ourselves.
OSCAR WILDE (1854–1900)

Favors

Our friends are generally ready to do everything for us, except the very thing we wish them to do.
WILLIAM HAZLITT (1778–1830)

The person whose doors I enter with most pleasure, and quit with most regret, never did me the smallest favor.
WILLIAM HAZLITT (1778–1830)

The pleasure we derive from doing favors is partly in the feeling it gives us that we are not altogether worthless. It is a pleasant surprise to ourselves.
ERIC HOFFER (1902–1983)

Benefits should be conferred gradually; and in that way they will taste better.
NICCOLÒ MACHIAVELLI (1469–1527)

The person who receives the most favors is the one who knows how to return them.
PUBLILIUS SYRUS (C. 100 BC)

To refuse graciously is to confer a favor.
PUBLILIUS SYRUS (C. 100 BC)

When you confer a benefit on those worthy of it, you confer a favor on all.
PUBLILIUS SYRUS (C. 100 BC)

O how wretched is that poor man that hangs on princes' favors! There is betwixt that smile we would aspire to, that sweet aspect of princes, and their ruin, more pangs and fears than wars or women have, and when he falls, he falls like Lucifer, never to hope again.
WILLIAM SHAKESPEARE (1564–1616), *King Henry VIII*

Fear

Courage is just fear, plus prayers, plus understanding.
EDWARD ALBERT (1951–)

It is a miserable state of mind to have few things to desire and many things to fear.
SIR FRANCIS BACON (1561–1626)

Men fear death as children fear to go in the dark; and as that natural fear in children is increased with tales, so is the other.
SIR FRANCIS BACON (1561–1626)

Fear secretes acids; but love and trust are sweet juices.
HENRY WARD BEECHER (1813–1887)

Courage is fear that has said its prayers.
DOROTHY BERNARD (1890–1955)

The whole secret of existence is to have no fear. Never fear what will become of you, depend on no one. Only the moment you reject all help are you freed.
THE BUDDHA (563–483 BC)

When one has the feeling of dislike for evil, when one feels tranquil, one finds pleasure in listening to good teachings; when one has these feelings and appreciates them, one is free of fear.
THE BUDDHA (563–483 BC)

No passion so effectually robs the mind of all its powers of acting and reasoning as fear.
EDMUND BURKE (1729–1797), *A Philosophical Inquiry into the Origin of Our Ideas of the Sublime and Beautiful*

The first duty of man is to conquer fear; he must get rid of it, he cannot act till then.
THOMAS CARLYLE (1795–1881)

Do the thing you fear to do and keep on doing it … that is the quickest and surest way ever yet discovered to conquer fear.
DALE CARNEGIE (1888–1955)

Inaction breeds doubt and fear. Action breeds confidence and courage. If you want to conquer fear, do not sit home and think about it. Go out and get busy.
DALE CARNEGIE (1888–1955)

You can conquer almost any fear if you will only make up your mind to do so. For remember, fear doesn't exist anywhere except in the mind.
DALE CARNEGIE (1888–1955)

Fear has many eyes and can see things underground.
MIGUEL DE CERVANTES (1547–1616)

The timidity of the child or the savage is entirely reasonable; they are alarmed at this world, because this world is a very alarming place. They dislike being alone because it is verily and indeed an awful idea to be alone. Barbarians fear the unknown for the same reason that Agnostics worship it—because it is a fact.
G. K. CHESTERTON (1874–1936)

It is better to be frightened now than killed hereafter.
SIR WINSTON CHURCHILL (1874–1965)

One need not be a Chamber—to be haunted—
One need not be a House—
The Brain has Corridors—surpassing
Material place—
EMILY DICKINSON (1830–1886), "No. 670"

Fear not those who argue but those who dodge.
MARIE VON EBNER-ESCHENBACH (1830–1916), *Aphorisms*

Our tragedy today is a general and universal physical fear so long sustained by now that we can even bear it. There are no longer problems of the spirit. There is only the question: When will I be blown up? Because of this, the young man or woman writing today has forgotten the problems of the human heart in conflict with itself which alone can make good writing because only that is worth writing about, worth the agony and the sweat.
WILLIAM FAULKNER (1897–1962)

Fear is a question: What are you afraid of, and why? Just as the seed of health is in illness, because illness contains information, your fears are a treasure house of self-knowledge if you explore them.
MARILYN FERGUSON (1938–)

None but a coward dares to boast that he has never known fear.
MARSHALL FERDINAND FOCH (1851–1929)

Become so wrapped up in something that you forget to be afraid.
LADY BIRD JOHNSON (1912–2007)

Normal fear protects us; abnormal fear paralyses us. Normal fear motivates us to improve our individual and collective welfare; abnormal fear constantly poisons and distorts our inner lives. Our problem is not to be rid of fear but, rather, to harness and master it.
MARTIN LUTHER KING JR. (1929–1968)

I must not fear. Fear is the mind-killer. Fear is the little-death that brings total obliteration. I will face my fear. I will permit it to pass over me and through me. And when it has gone past I will turn the inner eye to see its path. Where the fear has gone there will be nothing. Only I will remain.
FRANK HERBERT (1920–1986), *Dune*

It's just a ride and we can change it any time we want. It's only a choice. No effort, no work, no job, no savings and money, a choice, right now, between fear and love. The eyes of fear want you to put bigger locks on your door, buy guns, close yourself off. The eyes of love instead see all of us as one.
BILL HICKS (1961–1994)

It is when power is wedded to chronic fear that it becomes formidable.
ERIC HOFFER (1902–1983), *The Passionate State of Mind*

You can discover what your enemy fears most by observing the means he uses to frighten you.
ERIC HOFFER (1902–1983)

Fear is the path to the dark side. Fear leads to anger. Anger leads to hate. Hate leads to suffering.
GEORGE LUCAS (1944–), *The Phantom Menace*

The more I traveled the more I realized that fear makes strangers of people who would be friends.
SHIRLEY MACLAINE (1934–)

He who fears being conquered is sure of defeat.
NAPOLÉON I (1769–1821)

Men are moved by two levers only: fear and self interest.
NAPOLÉON I (1769–1821)

The fear of death is more to be dreaded than death itself.
PUBLILIUS SYRUS (C. 100 BC), *Maxims*

Valor grows by daring, fear by holding back.
PUBLILIUS SYRUS (C. 100 BC)

Let the fear of danger be a spur to prevent it; he that fears not, gives advantage to the danger.
FRANCIS QUARLES (1592–1644)

A timid person is frightened before a danger, a coward during the time, and a courageous person afterward.
JEAN PAUL RICHTER (1763–1825)

You gain strength, courage, and confidence by every experience in which you really stop to look fear in the face. You are able to say to yourself, "I have lived through this horror. I can take the next thing that comes along." You must do the thing you think you cannot do.
ELEANOR ROOSEVELT (1884–1962)

First of all, let me assert my firm belief that the only thing we have to fear is fear itself, nameless, unreasoning, unjustified terror which paralyzes needed efforts to convert retreat into advance.
FRANKLIN D. ROOSEVELT (1882–1945)

Fear of a name increases fear of the thing itself.
J. K. ROWLING (1965–), *Harry Potter and the Sorcerer's Stone*

Fear is the main source of superstition, and one of the main sources of cruelty. To conquer fear is the beginning of wisdom.
BERTRAND RUSSELL (1872–1970), *Unpopular Essays*

Never let the fear of striking out get in your way.
GEORGE HERMAN "BABE" RUTH JR. (1895–1948)

Fear is the tax that conscience pays to guilt.
GEORGE SEWELL (1924–2007)

Curiosity will conquer fear even more than bravery will.
JAMES STEPHENS (1882–1950)

Keep your fears to yourself, but share your courage with others.
ROBERT LOUIS STEVENSON (1850–1894)

Courage is resistance to fear, mastery of fear—not absence of fear.
MARK TWAIN (1835–1910)

Fear follows crime, and is its punishment.
VOLTAIRE (1694–1778)

Our deepest fear is not that we are inadequate. Our deepest fear is that we are powerful beyond measure. It is our Light, not our Darkness, that most frightens us.
MARIANNE WILLIAMSON (1952–), *Return to Love*

The greater the fear the nearer the danger.
DANISH PROVERB

Feelings

See that each hour's feelings, and thoughts and actions are pure and true; then your life will be also.
HENRY WARD BEECHER (1813–1887)

To have in general but little feeling, seems to be the only security against feeling too much on any particular occasion.
GEORGE ELIOT (1819–1880)

Do not give in too much to feelings. An overly sensitive heart is an unhappy possession on this shaky earth.
JOHANN WOLFGANG VON GOETHE (1749–1832)

Individuality is founded in feeling; and the recesses of feeling, the darker, blinder strata of character, are the only places in the world in which we catch real fact in the making, and directly perceive how events happen, and how work is actually done.
WILLIAM JAMES (1842–1910)

When I do good, I feel good. When I do bad, I feel bad. And that's my religion.
ABRAHAM LINCOLN (1809–1865)

Not to expose your true feelings to an adult seems to be instinctive from the age of seven or eight onwards.
GEORGE ORWELL (1903–1950)

Feet

And forget not that the earth delights to feel your bare feet and the winds long to play with your hair.
KAHLIL GIBRAN (1883–1931)

First it is necessary to stand on your own two feet. But the minute a man finds himself in that position, the next thing he should do is reach out his arms.
KRISTIN HUNTER (1931–)

Feet, why do I need them if I have wings to fly?
FRIDA KAHLO (1907–1954)

The journey of a thousand leagues begins from beneath your feet.
LAO-TZU (C. 600 BC)

When you jump for joy, beware that no one moves the ground from beneath your feet.
STANISLAW LEC (1909–1966), *Unkempt Thoughts*

If you're going to kick authority in the teeth, you might as well use two feet.
KEITH RICHARDS (1943–)

Keep your eyes on the stars, and your feet on the ground.
THEODORE ROOSEVELT (1858–1919)

A man's feet should be planted in his country, but his eyes should survey the world.
GEORGE SANTAYANA (1863–1952)

The stoical scheme of supplying our wants by lopping off our desires is like cutting off our feet when we want shoes.
JONATHAN SWIFT (1667–1745)

Cultivate the habit of early rising. It is unwise to keep the head long on a level with the feet.
HENRY DAVID THOREAU (1817–1862)

Why isn't there a special name for the tops of your feet?
LILY TOMLIN (1939–)

Though I am grateful for the blessings of wealth, it hasn't changed who I am. My feet are still on the ground. I'm just wearing better shoes.
OPRAH WINFREY (1954–)

It is better to die on your feet than live on your knees.
EMILIANO ZAPATA (1877–1919)

No one tests the depth of a river with both feet.
AFRICAN PROVERB

A closed mouth gathers no feet.
ANONYMOUS

I have but one lamp by which my feet are guided, and that is the lamp of experience. I know no way of judging the future but by the past.
ANONYMOUS

Imagination is the pontoon bridge making way for the timid feet of reason.
ANONYMOUS

Feminism

If particular care and attention is not paid to the ladies, we are determined to foment a rebellion, and will not hold ourselves bound by any laws in which we have no voice or representation.
ABIGAIL ADAMS (1744–1818)

When we abolish the slavery of half of humanity, together with the whole system of hypocrisy it implies, then the "division" of humanity will reveal its genuine significance and the human couple will find its true form.
SIMONE DE BEAUVOIR (1908–1986), *The Second Sex*

We've got a generation now who were born with semiequality. They don't know how it was before, so they think, this isn't too bad. We're working. We have our attaché cases and our three piece suits. I get very disgusted with the younger generation of women. We had a torch to pass, and they are just sitting there. They don't realize it can be taken away. Things are going to have to get worse before they join in fighting the battle.
ERMA BOMBECK (1927–1996)

Feminism is hated because women are hated. Anti-feminism is a direct expression of misogyny; it is the political defense of women hating.
ANDREA DWORKIN (1946–2005)

If divorce has increased by one thousand percent, don't blame the women's movement. Blame the obsolete sex roles on which our marriages were based.
BETTY FRIEDAN (1921–2006)

It's important to remember that feminism is no longer a group of organizations or leaders. It's the expectations that parents have for their daughters, and their sons, too. It's the way we talk about and treat one another. It's who makes the money and who makes the compromises and who makes the dinner. It's a state of mind. It's the way we live now.
ANNA QUINDLEN (1953–)

[N]ever fear, gentlemen; castration was really not the point of feminism, and we women are too busy eviscerating one another to take you on.
ANNA QUINDLEN (1953–)

[Feminism is] a socialist, anti-family, political movement that encourages women to leave their husbands, kill their children, practice witchcraft, destroy capitalism and become lesbians.
PAT ROBERTSON (1930–)

This is no simple reform. It really is a revolution. Sex and race because they are easy and visible differences have been the primary ways of organizing human beings into superior and inferior groups and into the cheap labour on which this system still depends. We are talking about a society in which there will be no roles other than those chosen or those earned. We are really talking about humanism.
GLORIA STEINEM (1934–)

I myself have never been able to find out precisely what feminism is: I only know that people call me a feminist whenever I express sentiments that differentiate me from a doormat.
REBECCA WEST (1892–1983)

Remember, Ginger Rogers did everything Fred Astaire did, but she did it backwards and in high heels.
FAITH WHITTLESEY (1939–)

Fiction

The best part of the fiction in many novels is the notice that the characters are purely imaginary.
FRANKLIN P. ADAMS (1881–1960)

Fiction is a piece of truth that turns lies to meaning.
DOROTHY ALLISON (1949–)

Truth is so hard to tell, it sometimes needs fiction to make it plausible.
SIR FRANCIS BACON (1561–1626)

Our interest's on the dangerous edge of things. The honest thief, the tender murderer, the superstitious atheist.
ROBERT BROWNING (1812 –1889)

But I hate things all fiction… there should always be some foundation of fact for the most airy fabric—and pure invention is but the talent of a liar.
LORD BYRON (1788–1824)

For truth is always strange; stranger than fiction.
LORD BYRON (1788–1824)

Romances never read like those I have seen.
LORD BYRON (1788–1824)

Literature is a luxury; fiction is a necessity.
G. K. CHESTERTON (1874–1936), *Defendant*

Truth must necessarily be stranger than fiction, for fiction is the creation of the human mind and therefore congenial to it.
G. K. CHESTERTON (1874–1936)

Politicians should read science fiction, not westerns and detective stories.
ARTHUR C. CLARKE (1917–)

What is a novel if not a conviction of our fellow-men's existence strong enough to take upon itself a form of imagined life clearer than reality and whose accumulated verisimilitude of selected episodes puts to shame the pride of documentary history?
JOSEPH CONRAD (1857–1924)

I at least have so much to do in unraveling certain human lots, and seeing how they were woven and interwoven, that all the light I can command must be concentrated on this particular web, and not dispersed over that tempting range of relevancies called the universe.
GEORGE ELIOT (1819–1880)

The life of man is the true romance, which when it is valiantly conduced, will yield the imagination a higher joy than any fiction.
RALPH WALDO EMERSON (1803–1882)

Writing a novel is not merely going on a shopping expedition across the border to an unreal land: it is hours and years spent in the factories, the streets, the cathedrals of the imagination.
JANET FRAME (1924–2004)

When writing a novel a writer should create living people; people not characters. A character is a caricature.
ERNEST HEMINGWAY (1898–1961)

The function of science fiction is not always to predict the future but sometimes to prevent it.
FRANK HERBERT (1920–1986)

It's with bad sentiments that one makes good novels.
ALDOUS HUXLEY (1894–1963)

The only reason for the existence of a novel is that it does attempt to represent life.
HENRY JAMES (1843–1916)

Would you not like to try all sorts of lives—one is so very small—but that is the satisfaction of

writing—one can impersonate so many people.
KATHERINE MANSFIELD (1888–1923)

The really great novel tends to be the exact negative of its author's life.
ANDRÉ MAUROIS (1885–1967)

For if the proper study of mankind is man, it is evidently more sensible to occupy yourself with the coherent, substantial and significant creatures of fiction than with the irrational and shadowy figures of real life.
W. SOMERSET MAUGHAM (1874–1965)

Thus, in a real sense, I am constantly writing autobiography, but I have to turn it into fiction in order to give it credibility.
KATHERINE PATERSON (1932–), *The Spying Heart*

There are certain themes of which the interest is all-absorbing, but which are too entirely horrible for the purposes of legitimate fiction.
EDGAR ALLAN POE (1809–1849), *The Premature Burial*

The acceptance that all that is solid has melted into the air, that reality and morality are not givens but imperfect human constructs, is the point from which fiction begins.
SALMAN RUSHDIE (1947–)

The novel does not seek to establish a privileged language but it insists upon the freedom to portray and analyze the struggle between the different contestants for such privileges.
SALMAN RUSHDIE (1947–)

If this were played upon a stage now, I could condemn it as an improbable fiction.
WILLIAM SHAKESPEARE (1564–1616), *Twelfth Night*

Fiction is obliged to stick to possibilities. Truth isn't.
MARK TWAIN (1835–1910)

Persons attempting to find a motive in this narrative will be prosecuted; persons attempting to find a moral in it will be banished; persons attempting to find a plot in it will be shot.
MARK TWAIN (1835–1910)

Why shouldn't truth be stranger than fiction? Fiction, after all, has to make sense.
MARK TWAIN (1835–1910)

There is something else which has the power to awaken us to the truth. It is the works of writers of genius. They give us, in the guise of fiction, something equivalent to the actual density of the real, that density which life offers us every day but which we are unable to grasp because we are amusing ourselves with lies.
SIMONE WEIL (1910–1943)

Henry James writes fiction as if it were a painful duty.
OSCAR WILDE (1854–1900)

One should not be too severe on English novels; they are the only relaxation of the intellectually unemployed.
OSCAR WILDE (1854–1900)

The good ended happily, and the bad unhappily. That is what Fiction means.
OSCAR WILDE (1854–1900)

Income tax returns are the most imaginative fiction being written today.
HERMAN WOUK (1915–)

Victory is a political fiction.
ANONYMOUS

Fidelity

Fidelity, n.: A virtue peculiar to those who are about to be betrayed.
AMBROSE BIERCE (1842–1914), *The Devil's Dictionary*

Constancy … that small change of love, which people exact so rigidly, receive in such counterfeit coin, and repay in baser metal.
LORD BYRON (1788–1824)

Nothing is more noble, nothing more venerable than fidelity. Faithfulness and truth are the most sacred excellences and endowments of the human mind.
CICERO (106–43 BC)

For the great mass of mankind, the only saving grace needed is a steady fidelity to what is nearest to hand and heart for the short moment of each human effort.
JOSEPH CONRAD (1857–1924)

Many persons have a wrong idea of what constitutes true happiness. It is not attained through self-gratification but through fidelity to a worthy purpose.
HELEN KELLER (1880–1968)

What a fuss people make about fidelity! Why, even in love it is purely a question for physiology. It has nothing to do with our own will. Young men want to be faithful, and are not; old men want to be faithless, and cannot: that is all one can say.
OSCAR WILDE (1854–1900)

Fighting

The full value of this life can only be got by fighting; the violent take it by storm. And if we have accepted everything we have missed something—war. This life of ours is a very enjoyable fight, but a very miserable truce.
G. K. CHESTERTON (1874–1936)

You cannot love a thing without wanting to fight for it.
G. K. CHESTERTON (1874–1936)

Let him that is without stone among you cast the first thing he can lay his hands on.
ROBERT FROST (1875–1963)

I'm not going to get into the ring with Tolstoy.
ERNEST HEMINGWAY (1898–1961)

No matter how much the cats fight, there always seem to be plenty of kittens.
ABRAHAM LINCOLN (1809–1865)

He who fights with monsters might take care lest he thereby become a monster. And if you gaze for long into an abyss, the abyss gazes also into you.
FRIEDRICH NIETZSCHE (1844–1900)

That is the whole secret of successful fighting. Get your enemy at a disadvantage; and never, on any account, fight him on equal terms.
GEORGE BERNARD SHAW (1856–1950)

There is such a thing as a man being too proud to fight.
WOODROW WILSON (1856–1924)

Acts of kindness may soon be forgotten, but the memory of an offense remains.
ANONYMOUS

Finance

The objects of a financier are, then, to secure an ample revenue; to impose it with judgment and equality; to employ it economically; and, when necessity obliges him to make use of credit, to secure its foundations in that instance, and for ever, by the clearness and candor of his proceedings, the exactness of his calculations, and the solidity of his funds.
EDMUND BURKE (1729–1797)

We estimate the wisdom of nations by seeing what they did with their surplus capital.
RALPH WALDO EMERSON (1803–1882)

When it comes to finances, remember that there are no withholding taxes on the wages of sin.
MAE WEST (1892–1980)

Fish

Fish and visitors smell in three days.
BENJAMIN FRANKLIN (1706–1790), *Poor Richard's Almanack*

A countryman between two lawyers is like a fish between two cats.
BENJAMIN FRANKLIN (1706–1790)

No one can feel as helpless as the owner of a sick goldfish.
KIN HUBBARD (1868–1930)

Give a man a fish and he will eat for a day. Teach a man to fish and he will eat for a lifetime. Teach a man to create an artificial shortage of fish and he will eat steak.
JAY LENO (1950–)

Fish is the only food that is considered spoiled once it smells like what it is.
P. J. O'ROURKE (1947–)

A woman without a man is like a fish without a bicycle.
GLORIA STEINEM (1934–)

Two people kissing always look like fish.
ANDY WARHOL (1928–1987)

At high tide fish eat ants; at low tide ants eat fish.
THAI PROVERB

Fishing

Fishing is boring, unless you catch an actual fish, and then it is disgusting.
DAVE BARRY (1947–)

Work, n.: A dangerous disorder affecting high public functionaries who want to go fishing.
AMBROSE BIERCE (1842–1914), *The Devil's Dictionary*

If fishing is a religion, fly-fishing is high church.
TOM BROKAW (1940–)

The charm of fishing is that it is the pursuit of that which is elusive but attainable, a perpetual series of occasions for hope.
JOHN BUCHAN (1875–1940)

Fishing, with me, has always been an excuse to drink in the daytime.
JIMMY CANNON (1910–1973)

Hell, if I'd jumped on all the dames I'm supposed to have jumped on, I'd have had no time to go fishing.
CLARK GABLE (1901–1960)

You know when they have a fishing show on TV? They catch the fish and then let it go. They don't want to eat the fish, they just want to make it late for something.
MITCH HEDBERG (1968–2005)

Somebody just back of you while you are fishing is as bad as someone looking over your shoulder while you write a letter to your girl.
ERNEST HEMINGWAY (1899–1961)

The only thing bad about winning the pennant is that you have to manage the All-Star Game the next year. I'd rather go fishing for three years.
WHITEY HERZOG (1931–)

Fishing is much more than fish. It is the great occasion when we may return to the fine simplicity of our forefathers.
HERBERT HOOVER (1874–1964)

Fishing seems to be the favorite form of loafing.
EDGAR WATSON HOWE (1853–1937)

There is certainly something in fishing that tends to produce a gentleness of spirit, a pure serenity of mind.
WASHINGTON IRVING (1783–1859)

Fishing is a delusion entirely surrounded by liars in old clothes.
DON MARQUIS (1878–1937)

If fishing is interfering with your business, give up your business.
ALFRED W. MILLER (1892–1983)

In cross-examination, as in fishing, nothing is more ungainly than a fisherman pulled into the water by his catch.
LOUIS NIZER (1902–1994)

Many men go fishing all of their lives without knowing it is not fish they are after.
HENRY DAVID THOREAU (1817–1862)

Last year I went fishing with Salvador Dali. He was using a dotted line. He caught every other fish.
STEVEN WRIGHT (1955–)

There's a fine line between fishing and just standing on the shore like an idiot.
STEVEN WRIGHT (1955–)

A bad day's fishing is better than a good day at work.
ANONYMOUS

Caution is a most valuable asset in fishing, especially if you are the fish.
ANONYMOUS

Even if you've been fishing for 3 hours and haven't gotten anything except poison ivy and sunburn, you're still better off than the worm.
ANONYMOUS

Give a man a fish and you feed him for a day. Teach a man to fish and you feed him for a lifetime.
CHINESE PROVERB

Flattery

Flattery is like cologne water, to be smelt of, not swallowed.
JOSH BILLINGS (1818–1885)

Listening, not imitation, may be the sincerest form of flattery.
DR. JOYCE BROTHERS (1928–)

A fool flatters himself, a wise man flatters the fool.
SIR EDWARD G. BULWER-LYTTON (1803–1873)

Flattery corrupts both the receiver and the giver.
EDMUND BURKE (1729–1797)

The reason that adulation is not displeasing is that, though untrue, it shows one to be of consequence enough, in one way or other, to induce people to lie.
LORD BYRON (1788–1824)

Women who are either indisputably beautiful, or indisputably ugly, are best flattered upon the score of their understandings; but those who are in a state of mediocrity are best flattered upon their beauty, or at least their graces: for every woman who is not absolutely ugly, thinks herself handsome.
LORD CHESTERFIELD (1694–1773)

To ask for advice is in nine cases out of ten to ask for flattery.
JOHN CHURTON COLLINS (1848–1908)

Imitation is the sincerest of flattery.
CHARLES CALEB COLTON (1780–1832), *Lacon*

We swallow with one gulp the lie that flatters us, and drink drop by drop the truth which is bitter to us.
DENIS DIDEROT (1713–1784)

Commend a fool for his wit, or a rogue for his honesty and he will receive you into his favor.
HENRY FIELDING (1707–1754)

Look closely at those who patronize you. Half are unfeeling, half untaught.
JOHANN WOLFGANG VON GOETHE (1749–1832)

Just praise is only a debt, but flattery is a present.
SAMUEL JOHNSON (1709–1784)

Nothing flatters a man as much as the happiness of his wife; he is always proud of himself as the source of it.
SAMUEL JOHNSON (1709–1784)

Every flatterer lives at the expense of him who listens to him.
JEAN DE LA FONTAINE (1621–1695)

Self-love is the greatest of all flatterers.
FRANÇOIS DE LA ROCHEFOUCAULD (1613–1680)

He who says he hates every kind of flattery, and says it in earnest, certainly does not yet know every kind of flattery.
GEORG C. LICHTENBERG (1742–1799)

It is possible to be below flattery as well as above it.
LORD THOMAS BABINGTON MACAULAY (1800–1859)

There is no other way of guarding oneself against flattery than by letting men understand that they will not offend you by speaking the truth; but when everyone can tell you the truth, you lose their respect.
NICCOLÒ MACHIAVELLI (1469–1527), *The Prince*

I hate careless flattery, the kind that exhausts you in your effort to believe it.
WILSON MIZNER (1876–1933)

Immigration is the sincerest form of flattery.
JACK PAAR (1918–2004)

To make a man perfectly happy tell him he works too hard, that he spends too much money, that he is "misunderstood" or that he is "different"; none of this is necessarily complimentary, but it will flatter him infinitely more that merely telling him that he is brilliant, or noble, or wise, or good.
HELEN ROWLAND (1875–1950)

What really flatters a man is that you think him worth flattering.
GEORGE BERNARD SHAW (1856–1950)

Baloney is the lie laid on so thick you hate it. Blarney is flattery laid on so thin you love it.
BISHOP FULTON J. SHEEN (1895–1979)

The aim of flattery is to soothe and encourage us by assuring us of the truth of an opinion we have already formed about ourselves.
EDITH SITWELL (1887–1964)

None are more taken in by flattery than the proud, who wish to be the first and are not.
BENEDICT DE SPINOZA (1632–1677)

Whenever you commend, add your reasons for doing so; it is this which distinguishes the approbation of a man of sense from the flattery of sycophants and admiration of fools.
SIR RICHARD STEELE (1672–1729)

Flattery looks like friendship, just like a wolf looks like a dog.
ANONYMOUS

If we did not flatter ourselves the flattery from others would not harm us.
ANONYMOUS

He that flatters you more than you desire either has deceived you or wishes to deceive.
ITALIAN PROVERB

Flattery makes friends and truth makes enemies.
SPANISH PROVERB

Flirting

God created the flirt as soon as he made the fool.
VICTOR HUGO (1802–1885)

There are few things that we so unwillingly give up, even in advanced age, as the supposition that we still have the power of ingratiating ourselves with the fair sex.
SAMUEL JOHNSON (1709–1784)

All women are flirts, but some are restrained by shyness, and others by sense.
FRANÇOIS DE LA ROCHEFOUCAULD (1613–1680)

No matter how happily a woman may be married, it always pleases her to discover that there is a nice man who wishes that she were not.
H. L. MENCKEN (1880–1956)

Flirting is the gentle art of making a man feel pleased with himself.
HELEN ROWLAND (1875–1950)

The hardest task of a girl's life, nowadays, is to prove to a man that his intentions are serious.
HELEN ROWLAND (1875–1950)

Why does a man take it for granted that a girl who flirts with him wants him to kiss her—when, nine times out of ten, she only wants him to want to kiss her?
HELEN ROWLAND (1875–1950)

Whoever loves above all the approach of love will never know the joy of attaining it.
ANTOINE DE SAINT-EXUPÉRY (1900–1944)

The amount of women in London who flirt with their own husbands is perfectly scandalous. It looks so bad. It is simply washing one's clean linen in public.
OSCAR WILDE (1854–1900)

When a flirt fishes for a man, she fishes merely for the sport.
ANONYMOUS

Floods

The only thing that stops God from sending another flood is that the first one was useless.
NICOLAS CHAMFORT (1741–1794)

Eventually, all things merge into one, and a river runs through it. The river was cut by the world's great flood and runs over rocks from the basement of time. On some of the rocks are timeless raindrops. Under the rocks are the words, and some of the words are theirs. I am haunted by waters.
NORMAN MACLEAN (1902–1990), *A River Runs Through It*

There is a tide in the affairs of men,
Which, taken at the flood, leads on to fortune;
Omitted, all the voyage of their life
Is bound in shallows and in miseries.
WILLIAM SHAKESPEARE (1564–1616), *The Tragedy of Julius Caesar*

What need the bridge much broader than the flood?
WILLIAM SHAKESPEARE (1564–1616), *Much Ado About Nothing*

Flowers

What sunshine is to flowers, smiles are to humanity. These are but trifles, to be sure; but, scattered along life's pathway, the good they do is inconceivable.
JOSEPH ADDISON (1672–1719)

Gardens and flowers have a way of bringing people together, drawing them from their homes.
CLARE ANSBERRY (1957–), *The Women of Troy Hill*

Flowers are the sweetest things God ever made and forgot to put a soul into.
HENRY WARD BEECHER (1813–1887)

Stretching his hand out to catch the stars, he forgets the flowers at his feet.
JEREMY BENTHAM (1748–1832)

To create a little flower is the labor of ages.
WILLIAM BLAKE (1757–1827)

Flowers are words even a baby can understand.
QUENTIN CRISP (1908–1999)

Earth laughs in flowers.
RALPH WALDO EMERSON (1803–1882)

Flowers are a proud assertion that a ray of beauty out-values all the utilities of the world.
RALPH WALDO EMERSON (1803–1882)

Flowers are restful to look at. They have neither emotions nor conflicts.
SIGMUND FREUD (1856–1939)

The flower is the poetry of reproduction. It is the example of the eternal seductiveness of life.
JEAN GIRAUDOUX (1882–1944)

The most precious gift we can offer others is our presence. When mindfulness embraces those we love, they will bloom like flowers.
THICH NHAT HAHN (1926–)

Money is a powerful aphrodisiac. But flowers work almost as well.
ROBERT A. HEINLEIN (1907–1988)

The Amen of nature is always a flower.
OLIVER WENDELL HOLMES SR. (1809–1894)

Whenever evil befalls us, we ought to ask ourselves, after the first suffering, how we can turn it into good. So shall we take occasion, from one bitter

root, to raise perhaps many flowers.
LEIGH HUNT (1784–1859)

The fairest thing in nature, a flower, still has its roots in earth and manure.
D. H. LAWRENCE (1885–1930)

Arranging a bowl of flowers in the morning can give a sense of quiet in a crowded day— like writing a poem, or saying a prayer.
ANNE MORROW LINDBERGH (1906–2001)

I have seen flowers come in stony places
And kind things done by men with ugly faces
And the gold cup won by the worst horse at the
races,
So I trust too.
JOHN MASEFIELD (1878–1967)

A cynic is a man who, when he smells flowers, looks around for a coffin.
H. L. MENCKEN (1880–1956)

Flowers never emit so sweet and strong a fragrance as before a storm. When a storm approaches thee, be as fragrant as a sweet-smelling flower.
JEAN PAUL RICHTER (1763–1825)

The artist is the confidant of nature, flowers carry on dialogues with him through the graceful bending of their stems and the harmoniously tinted nuances of their blossoms, Every flower has a cordial word which nature directs towards him.
AUGUSTE RODIN (1840–1917)

One of the most attractive things about the flowers is their beautiful reserve.
HENRY DAVID THOREAU (1817–1862)

He does not care for flowers. Calls them rubbish, and cannot tell one from another, and thinks it is superior to feel like that.
MARK TWAIN (1835–1910)

A morning glory at my window satisfies me more than the metaphysics of books.
WALT WHITMAN (1819–1892)

You must not know too much or be too precise or scientific about birds and trees and flowers and watercraft; a certain free-margin, and even vagueness—ignorance, credulity—helps your enjoyment of these things.
WALT WHITMAN (1819–1892)

Flowers are as common in the country as people are in London.
OSCAR WILDE (1854–1900)

Let the minor genius go his light way and enjoy his life—the great nature cannot so live, he is never really in holiday mood, even though he often plucks flowers by the wayside and ties them into knots and garlands like little children and lays out on a sunny morning.
WILLIAM BUTLER YEATS (1865–1935)

Fair flowers are not left standing along the wayside long.
GERMAN PROVERB

Fog

[T]he fog is rising.
EMILY DICKINSON (1830–1886), last words

Derive happiness in oneself from a good day's work, from illuminating the fog that surrounds us.
HENRI MATISSE (1869–1954)

The fog comes
on little cat feet.
It sits looking
over harbor and city
on silent haunches
and then moves on.
CARL SANDBURG (1878–1967), "Fog"

When anyone asks me how I can best describe my experience in nearly forty years at sea, I merely say, uneventful. Of course there have been winter gales, and storms and fog and the like. But in all my experience, I have never been in any accident … or any sort worth speaking about. I have seen but one vessel in distress in all my years at sea. I never saw a

wreck and never have been wrecked nor was I ever in any predicament that threatened to end in disaster of any sort.
CAPTAIN E. J. SMITH (1850–1912), *RMS Titanic*

Food

Food is our common ground, a universal experience.
JAMES BEARD (1903–1989)

Tell me what you eat, and I will tell you what you are.
ANTHELME BRILLAT-SAVARIN (1755–1826), *The Physiology of Taste*

Tomatoes and oregano make it Italian; wine and tarragon make it French. Sour cream makes it Russian; lemon and cinnamon make it Greek. Soy sauce makes it Chinese; garlic makes it good.
ALICE MAY BROCK (1941–)

At my age the bones are water in the morning until food is given them.
PEARL S. BUCK (1892–1973)

Music with dinner is an insult both to the cook and the violinist.
G. K. CHESTERTON (1874–1936)

You don't have to cook fancy or complicated masterpieces—just good food from fresh ingredients.
JULIA CHILD (1912–2004)

Eat breakfast like a king, lunch like a prince, and dinner like a pauper.
ADELLE DAVIS (1904–1974)

We are indeed much more than what we eat, but what we eat can nevertheless help us to be much more than what we are.
ADELLE DAVIS (1904–1974)

Nothing will benefit human health and increase the chances for survival of life on Earth as much as the evolution to a vegetarian diet.
ALBERT EINSTEIN (1879–1955)

Bear in mind that you should conduct yourself in life as at a feast.
EPICTETUS (AD 55–135)

Preach not to others what they should eat, but eat as becomes you, and be silent.
EPICTETUS (AD 55–135)

When a man's stomach is full it makes no difference whether he is rich or poor.
EURIPIDES (C. 480–406 BC)

Man is what he eats.
LUDWIG FEUERBACH (1804–1872)

I've been on a diet for two weeks and all I've lost is two weeks.
TOTIE FIELDS (1930–1978)

Food is the most primitive form of comfort.
SHEILA GRAHAM (1908–1988)

Eating everything you want is not that much fun. When you live a life with no boundaries, there's less joy. If you can eat anything you want to, what's the fun in eating anything you want to?
TOM HANKS (1956–)

I like rice. Rice is great if you're hungry and want 2000 of something.
MITCH HEDBERG (1968–2005)

Never eat more than you can lift.
JIM HENSON (1936–1990), as Miss Piggy on *The Muppet Show*

We seldom report of having eaten too little.
THOMAS JEFFERSON (1743–1826)

A man seldom thinks with more earnestness of anything than he does of his dinner.
SAMUEL JOHNSON (1709–1784)

He who does not mind his belly, will hardly mind anything else.
SAMUEL JOHNSON (1709–1784)

Food is an important part of a balanced diet.
FRAN LEBOWITZ (1950–)

My favorite animal is steak.
FRAN LEBOWITZ (1950–)

Food probably has a very great influence on the condition of men. Wine exercises a more visible influence, food does it more slowly but perhaps just as surely. Who knows if a well-prepared soup was not responsible for the pneumatic pump or a poor one for a war?
GEORG C. LICHTENBERG (1742–1799)

If there were only turnips and potatoes in the world, someone would complain that plants grow the wrong way.
GEORG C. LICHTENBERG (1742–1799)

What is food to one, is to others bitter poison.
LUCRETIUS (C. 99–55 BC), *De Rerum Natura*

At a dinner party one should eat wisely but not too well, and talk well but not too wisely.
W. SOMERSET MAUGHAM (1874–1965)

I no longer prepare food or drink with more than one ingredient.
CYRA MCFADDEN (1939–)

You can travel fifty thousand miles in America without once tasting a piece of good bread.
HENRY MILLER (1891–1980)

The art of dining well is no slight art, the pleasure not a slight pleasure.
MICHEL DE MONTAIGNE (1533–1592)

Fish is the only food that is considered spoiled once it smells like what it is.
P. J. O'ROURKE (1947–)

We may find in the long run that tinned food is a deadlier weapon than the machine-gun.
GEORGE ORWELL (1903–1950)

What some call health, if purchased by perpetual anxiety about diet, isn't much better than tedious disease.
GEORGE DENNISON PRENTICE (1802–1870)

You can tell a lot about a fellow's character by his way of eating jellybeans.
RONALD REAGAN (1911–2004)

The only man who is really free is the one who can turn down an invitation to dinner without giving an excuse.
JULES RENARD (1864–1910)

He who comes first, eats first. [Familiar as: First come first served.]
EIKE VON REPKOW (C. 1220), *Sachsenspiegel*

It's amazing how pervasive food is. Every second commercial is for food. Every second TV episode takes place around a meal. In the city, you can't go ten feet without seeing or smelling a restaurant. There are 20 foot high hamburgers up on billboards. I am acutely aware of food, and its omnipresence is astounding.
ADAM SCOTT (1980–), *The Monkey Chow Diaries*

He hath eaten me out of house and home.
WILLIAM SHAKESPEARE (1564–1616), *King Henry IV*

There is no love sincerer than the love of food.
GEORGE BERNARD SHAW (1856–1950), *Man and Superman*

Bad men live that they may eat and drink, whereas good men eat and drink that they may live.
SOCRATES (469–399 BC)

Thou shouldst eat to live; not live to eat.
SOCRATES (469–399 BC)

There ain't no such thing as wrong food.
SEAN STEWART (1965–), *Perfect Circle*

A dinner lubricates business.
LORD WILLIAM STOWELL (1745–1836)

If more of us valued food and cheer and song above hoarded gold, it would be a merrier world.
J. R. R. TOLKIEN (1892–1973)

Health food makes me sick.
CALVIN TRILLIN (1935–)

The most remarkable thing about my mother is that for thirty years she served the family nothing but leftovers. The original meal has never been found.
CALVIN TRILLIN (1935–)

Make hunger thy sauce, as a medicine for health.
THOMAS TUSSER (1524–1580)

Part of the secret of success in life is to eat what you like and let the food fight it out inside.
MARK TWAIN (1835–1910)

There are people who strictly deprive themselves of each and every eatable, drinkable, and smokable which has in any way acquired a shady reputation. They pay this price for health. And health is all they get for it. How strange it is. It is like paying out your whole fortune for a cow that has gone dry.
MARK TWAIN (1835–1910)

Ask not what you can do for your country. Ask what's for lunch.
ORSON WELLES (1915–1985)

My doctor told me to stop having intimate dinners for four. Unless there are three other people.
ORSON WELLES (1915–1985)

Only dull people are brilliant at breakfast.
OSCAR WILDE (1854–1900)

One cannot think well, love well, sleep well, if one has not dined well.
VIRGINIA WOOLF (1882–1941)

Fools

A common mistake that people make when trying to design something completely foolproof is to underestimate the ingenuity of complete fools.
DOUGLAS ADAMS (1952–2001), *Mostly Harmless*

Silence is the virtue of fools.
SIR FRANCIS BACON (1561–1626)

Nature makes only dumb animals. We owe the fools to society.
HONORÉ DE BALZAC (1799–1850)

Drinking makes such fools of people, and people are such fools to begin with, that it's compounding a felony.
ROBERT BENCHLEY (1889–1945)

Take all the fools out of this world and there wouldn't bc any fun living in it, or profit.
JOSH BILLINGS (1818–1885)

The best way to convince a fool that he is wrong is to let him have his way.
JOSH BILLINGS (1818–1885)

There are two kinds of fools: those who can't change their opinions and those who won t.
JOSH BILLINGS (1818–1885)

A fool sees not the same tree that a wise man sees.
WILLIAM BLAKE (1757–1827)

The world is full of fools; and he who would not wish to see one, must not only shut himself up alone, but must also break his looking-glass.
NICOLAS BOILEAU-DESPRÉAUX (1636–1711)

There are more fools than knaves in the world, else the knaves would not have enough to live upon.
SAMUEL BUTLER (1612–1680)

I'll publish right or wrong.
Fools are my theme, let satire be my song.
LORD BYRON (1788–1824)

He who despairs of the human condition is a coward, but he who has hope for it is a fool.
ALBERT CAMUS (1913–1960), *The Rebel*

Any fool can criticize, condemn, and complain — and most fools do.
DALE CARNEGIE (1888–1955)

The fool inherits, but the wise must get.
WILLIAM CARTWRIGHT (1611–1643)

Wise men profit more from fools than fools from wise men; for the wise men shun the mistakes of fools, but fools do not imitate the successes of the wise.
CATO THE ELDER (234–149 BC)

The most difficult character in comedy is that of a fool, and he must be no simpleton who plays the part.
MIGUEL DE CERVANTES (1547–1616), *Don Quixote*

He is mad past recovery, but yet he has lucid intervals.
MIGUEL DE CERVANTES (1547–1616)

Great use they have, when in the hands
Of one like me, who understands,
Who understands the time and place,
The person, manner, and the grace,
Which fools neglect; so that we find,
If all the requisites are join'd,
From whence a perfect joke must spring,
A joke's a very serious thing.
CHARLES CHURCHILL (1731–1764), "The Ghost"

The greatest lesson in life is to know that even fools are right sometimes.
SIR WINSTON CHURCHILL (1874–1965)

It is the peculiar quality of a fool to perceive the faults of others and to forget his own.
CICERO (106–43 BC)

A fool despises good counsel, but a wise man takes it to heart.
CONFUCIUS (551–479 BC)

Get all the fools on your side and you can be elected to anything.
FRANK DANE (1981–)

In the vain laughter of folly wisdom hears half its applause.
GEORGE ELIOT (1819–1880)

Fools are without number.
DESIDERIUS ERASMUS (1469–1536)

The entire world is my temple, and a very fine one too, if I'm not mistaken, and I'll never lack priests to serve it as long as there are men.
DESIDERIUS ERASMUS (1469–1536)

There are two fools in this world. One is the millionaire who thinks that by hoarding money he can somehow accumulate real power, and the other is the penniless reformer who thinks that if only he can take the money from one class and give it to another, all the world's ills will be cured.
HENRY FORD (1863–1947)

Experience is a dear teacher, but fools will learn at no other.
BENJAMIN FRANKLIN (1706–1790)

Most fools think they are only ignorant.
BENJAMIN FRANKLIN (1706–1790)

The world is full of fools and faint hearts; and yet everyone has courage enough to bear the misfortunes, and wisdom enough to manage the affairs of his neighbor.
BENJAMIN FRANKLIN (1706–1790)

A mother takes twenty years to make a man of her boy, and another woman makes a fool of him in twenty minutes.
ROBERT FROST (1875–1963)

It seems to never occur to fools that merit and good fortune are closely united.
JOHANN WOLFGANG VON GOETHE (1749–1832)

There are more fools in the world than there are people.
HEINRICH HEINE (1797–1856)

By their own follies they perished, the fools.
HOMER (800–700 BC), *The Odyssey*

Mix a little foolishness with your serious plans. It is lovely to be silly at the right moment.
HORACE (65–8 BC)

Only fools are positive.
MOE HOWARD (1897–1975)

Fortune can, for her pleasure, fools advance,
And toss them on the wheels of Chance.
JUVENAL (AD 55–127)

Ten thousand fools proclaim themselves into obscurity, while one wise man forgets himself into immortality.
MARTIN LUTHER KING JR. (1929–1968)

We must learn to live together as brothers or perish together as fools.
MARTIN LUTHER KING JR. (1929–1968)

The surprising thing about young fools is how many survive to become old fools.
DOUG LARSON (1902–1981)

A clever child brought up with a foolish one can itself become foolish. Man is so perfectible and corruptible he can become a fool through good sense.
GEORG C. LICHTENBERG (1742–1799)

Better to remain silent and be thought a fool, than to speak and remove all doubt.
ABRAHAM LINCOLN (1809–1865)

Who loves not women, wine and song remains a fool his whole life long.
MARTIN LUTHER (1483–1546)

Last words are for fools who haven't said enough.
KARL MARX (1818–1883)

Fortune, seeing that she could not make fools wise, has made them lucky.
MICHEL DE MONTAIGNE (1533–1592)

Impossible is a word only to be found in the dictionary of fools.
NAPOLÉON I (1769–1821)

Wise men talk because they have something to say; fools, because they have to say something.
PLATO (C. 428–348 BC)

Fools admire, but men of sense approve.
ALEXANDER POPE (1688–1744)

Fools rush in where Angels fear to tread.
ALEXANDER POPE (1688–1744)

Those who wish to appear wise among fools, among the wise seem foolish.
QUINTILIAN (C. AD 35–100), *De Institutione Oratoria*

If fifty million people say a foolish thing, it is still a foolish thing.
BERTRAND RUSSELL (1872–1970)

Folly is perennial, yet the human race has survived.
BERTRAND RUSSELL (1872–1970)

The whole problem with the world is that fools and fanatics are always so certain of themselves, but wiser people so full of doubts.
BERTRAND RUSSELL (1872–1970)

The person who writes for fools is always sure of a large audience.
ARTHUR SCHOPENHAUER (1788–1860)

A foolishness is inflicted with a hatred of itself.
SENECA (5 BC–AD 65)

The fool thinks himself to be wise, but the wise man knows himself to be a fool.
WILLIAM SHAKESPEARE (1564–1616), *As You Like It*

When we are born, we cry, that we are come
To this great stage of fools…
WILLIAM SHAKESPEARE (1564–1616), *King Lear*

To-morrow, and to-morrow, and to-morrow,
Creeps in this petty pace from day to day
To the last syllable of recorded time,
And all our yesterdays have lighted fools
The way to dusty death. Out, out, brief candle!
Life's but a walking shadow, a poor player
That struts and frets his hour upon the stage
And then is heard no more: it is a tale
Told by an idiot, full of sound and fury,
Signifying nothing.
WILLIAM SHAKESPEARE (1564–1616), *Macbeth*

Lord, what fools these mortals be!
WILLIAM SHAKESPEARE (1564–1616), *A Midsummer Night's Dream*

Do you think that the things people make fools of themselves about are any less real and true than the

things they behave sensibly about? They are more true: they are the only things that are true.
GEORGE BERNARD SHAW (1856–1950), *Candida*

Build a system that even a fool can use, and only a fool will want to use it.
GEORGE BERNARD SHAW (1856–1950)

Ridicule is the first and last argument of fools.
CHARLES SIMMONS (1924–)

Wind buffs up empty bladders; opinion, fools.
SOCRATES (469–399 BC)

The ultimate result of shielding men from the effects of folly is to fill the world with fools.
HERBERT SPENCER (1820–1903)

Wisdom is the right use of knowledge. To know is not to be wise. Many men know a great deal, and are all the greater fools for it. There is no fool so great a fool as a knowing fool. But to know how to use knowledge is to have wisdom.
CHARLES H. SPURGEON (1834–1892)

Whenever you commend, add your reasons for doing so; it is this which distinguishes the approbation of a man of sense from the flattery of sycophants and admiration of fools.
SIR RICHARD STEELE (1672–1729)

I was young and foolish then; now I am old and foolisher.
MARK TWAIN (1835–1910)

It is better to keep your mouth closed and let people think you are a fool than to open it and remove all doubt.
MARK TWAIN (1835–1910)

Let us be thankful for the fools. But for them the rest of us could not succeed.
MARK TWAIN (1835–1910)

Statistics show that we lose more fools on this day than on all other days of the year put together. This proves, by the numbers left in stock, that one Fourth of July per year is now inadequate, the country has grown so.
MARK TWAIN (1835–1910)

Looking foolish does the spirit good. The need not to look foolish is one of youth's many burdens; as we get older we are exempted from more and more, and float upward in our heedlessness, singing Gratia Dei sum quod sum.
JOHN UPDIKE (1932–)

A fool and his money are soon parted.
ANONYMOUS

Fools rush in where fools have been before.
ANONYMOUS

Great minds think alike, and fools seldom differ.
ANONYMOUS

Prejudice is the reasoning of fools.
ANONYMOUS

The fool is always beginning to live.
ANONYMOUS

Fools mock at making amends for sin, but goodwill is found among the upright.
THE BIBLE, Proverbs 14:9

Do not answer a fool according to his folly, or you will be like him yourself.
THE BIBLE, Proverbs 26:4

He who asks is a fool for five minutes, but he who does not ask remains a fool forever.
CHINESE PROVERB

If a man fools me once, shame on him. If he fools me twice, shame on me.
CHINESE PROVERB

Fools build houses, and wise men buy them.
ENGLISH PROVERB

He is a fool that kisseth the maid when he may kiss the mistress.
ENGLISH PROVERB

Football

Anybody who watches three games of football in a row should be declared brain dead.
ERMA BOMBECK (1927–1996)

Gerry Ford is a nice guy, but he played too much football with his helmet off.
LYNDON B. JOHNSON (1908–1973)

Being in politics is like being a football coach. You have to be smart enough to understand the game, and dumb enough to think it's important.
EUGENE J. MCCARTHY (1916–2005)

College football would be more interesting if the faculty played instead of the students—there would be a great increase in broken arms, legs and necks.
H. L. MENCKEN (1880–1956)

For when the One Great Scorer comes
To write against your name,
He marks—not that you won or lost—
But how you played the game.
GRANTLAND RICE (1880–1954), "Alumunus Football"

Some people think football is a matter of life and death. I don't like that attitude. I can assure them it is much more serious than that.
BILL SHANKLY (1913–1981)

Nobody in the game of football should be called a genius. A genius is somebody like Norman Einstein.
JOE THEISMANN (1949–)

Football is a mistake. It combines the two worst elements of American life. Violence and committee meetings.
GEORGE F. WILL (1941–)

Force

The use of force alone is but temporary. It may subdue for a moment; but it does not remove the necessity of subduing again: and a nation is not governed, which is perpetually to be conquered.
EDMUND BURKE (1729–1797)

Force works on servile natures, not the free.
BEN JONSON (1572–1637)

Whatever needs to be maintained through force is doomed.
HENRY MILLER (1891–1980)

Force is as pitiless to the man who possesses it, or thinks he does, as it is to its victims; the second it crushes, the first it intoxicates. The truth is, nobody really possesses it.
SIMONE WEIL (1910–1943)

Who were the fools who spread the story that brute force cannot kill ideas? Nothing is easier. And once they are dead they are no more than corpses.
SIMONE WEIL (1910–1943)

Force without forecast is to little avail.
ANONYMOUS

Forests

A woodland in full color is awesome as a forest fire, in magnitude at least, but a single tree is like a dancing tongue of flame to warm the heart.
HAL BORLAND (1900–1978)

When the oak is felled the whole forest echoes with its fall, but a hundred acorns are sown in silence by an unnoticed breeze.
THOMAS CARLYLE (1795–1881)

The heart of another is a dark forest, always, no matter how close it has been to one's own.
WILLA CATHER (1873–1947)

As a single withered tree, if set aflame, causes a whole forest to burn, so does a rascal son destroy a whole family.
CHANAKYA (350–275 BC)

As you sit on the hillside, or lie prone under the trees of the forest, or sprawl wet-legged by a mountain stream, the great door, that does not look like a door, opens.
STEPHEN GRAHAM (1884–1975)

The mountains, the forest, and the sea, render men savage; they develop the fierce, but yet do not destroy the human.
VICTOR HUGO (1802–1885)

This is what I believe: That I am I. That my soul is a dark forest. That my known self will never be more than a little clearing in the forest. That gods, strange gods, come forth from the forest into the clearing of my known self, and then go back. That I must have the courage to let them come and go. That I will never let mankind put anything over me, but that I will try always to recognize and submit to the gods in me and the gods in other men and women. There is my creed.
D. H. LAWRENCE (1885–1930)

[E]ach day mankind and the claims of mankind slipped farther from him. Deep in the forest a call was sounding, and as often as he heard this call, mysteriously thrilling and luring, he felt compelled to turn his back upon the fire and the beaten earth around it, and to plunge into the forest, and on and on, he knew not where or why; nor did he wonder where or why, the call sounding imperiously, deep in the forest.
JACK LONDON (1876–1916), *The Call of the Wild*

It is not so much for its beauty that the forest makes a claim upon men's hearts, as for that subtle something, that quality of air that emanation from old trees, that so wonderfully changes and renews a weary spirit.
ROBERT LOUIS STEVENSON (1850–1894)

If you tell a joke in the forest, but nobody laughs, was it a joke?
STEVEN WRIGHT (1955–)

He can't see the forest for the trees.
ANONYMOUS

Some men go through a forest and see no firewood.
ENGLISH PROVERB

Forgetfulness

I've learned that people will forget what you said, people will forget what you did, but people will never forget how you made them feel.
MAYA ANGELOU (1928–)

Forgetfulness is the drug that heals our sorrow.
APPIANUS (C. 200)

Remember your humanity and forget the rest.
ALBERT EINSTEIN (1879–1955)

There is an ecstasy that marks the summit of life, and beyond which life cannot rise. And such is the paradox of living, this ecstasy comes when one is most alive, and it comes as a complete forgetfulness that one is alive.
JACK LONDON (1876–1916), *The Call of the Wild*

Blessed are the forgetful: for they get the better even of their blunders.
FRIEDRICH NIETZSCHE (1844–1900)

To forget one's purpose is the commonest form of stupidity.
FRIEDRICH NIETZSCHE (1844–1900)

That you may please others you must be forgetful of yourself.
OVID (43 BC–AD 17)

Age is foolish and forgetful when it underestimates youth.
J. K. ROWLING (1965–), *Harry Potter and the Half-Blood Prince*

Do not forget to show hospitality to strangers, for by so doing some people have shown hospitality to angels without knowing it.
THE BIBLE, Herbrews 13:2

Forgiveness

To err is human; to forgive, infrequent.
FRANKLIN P. ADAMS (1881–1960)

Forgiveness is the remission of sins. For it is by this that what has been lost, and was found, is saved from being lost again.
SAINT AUGUSTINE (354–430)

Forgive many things in others; nothing in yourself.
AUSONIUS (C. 310–395)

This is certain, that a man that studieth revenge keeps his wounds green, which otherwise would heal and do well.
SIR FRANCIS BACON (1561–1626)

The heart of a mother is a deep abyss at the bottom of which you will always find forgiveness.
HONORÉ DE BALZAC (1799–1850)

Every man should keep a fair-sized cemetery in which to bury the faults of his friends.
HENRY WARD BEECHER (1813–1887)

God pardons like a mother, who kisses the offense into everlasting forgiveness.
HENRY WARD BEECHER (1813–1887)

"I can forgive, but I cannot forget," is only another way of saying, "I will not forgive." Forgiveness ought to be like a canceled note—torn in two, and burned up, so that it never can be shown against one.
HENRY WARD BEECHER (1813–1887)

The best thing to give to your enemy is forgiveness.
HENRY WARD BEECHER (1813–1887)

To apologize is to lay the foundation for a future offense.
AMBROSE BIERCE (1842–1914)

There is no revenge so complete as forgiveness.
JOSH BILLINGS (1818–1885)

It is easier to forgive an enemy than to forgive a friend.
WILLIAM BLAKE (1757–1827)

We all like to forgive, and love best not those who offend us least, nor who have done most for us, but those who make it most easy for us to forgive them.
SAMUEL BUTLER (1612–1680)

Absolute virtue is impossible and the republic of forgiveness leads, with implacable logic, to the republic of the guillotine.
ALBERT CAMUS (1913–1960)

The more a man knows, the more he forgives.
CATHERINE THE GREAT (1729–1796)

Wrongs are often forgiven, but contempt never is. Our pride remembers it forever. It implies a discovery of weakness, which we are more careful to conceal than a crime. Many a man will confess his crimes to a friend; but I never knew a man that would tell his silly weaknesses to his most intimate one.
LORD CHESTERFIELD (1694–1773)

Love thy neighbor as thyself: Do not to others what thou would not wish be done to thyself: Forgive injuries. Forgive thy enemy, be reconciled to him, give him assistance, invoke God in his behalf.
CONFUCIUS (551–479 BC)

Life is an adventure in forgiveness.
NORMAN COUSINS (1915–1990)

Would not love see returning penitence afar off, and fall on its neck and kiss it?
GEORGE ELIOT (1819–1880)

Forgive, son; men are men; they needs must err.
EURIPIDES (C. 480–406 BC)

To be social is to be forgiving.
ROBERT FROST (1874–1963)

The weak can never forgive. Forgiveness is the attribute of the strong.
MAHATMA GANDHI (1869–1948)

If a good person does you wrong, act as though you had not noticed it. They will make note of this and not remain in your debt long.
JOHANN WOLFGANG VON GOETHE (1749–1832)

He that cannot forgive others, breaks the bridge over which he himself must pass if he would ever reach heaven; for everyone has need to be forgiven.
GEORGE HERBERT (1593–1632)

If you haven't forgiven yourself something, how can you forgive others?
DOLORES HUERTA (1930–)

The condition of being forgiven is self-abandonment. The proud man prefers self-reproach, however painful—because the reproached self isn't abandoned; it remains intact.
ALDOUS HUXLEY (1894–1963)

If I owe Smith ten dollars and God forgives me, that doesn't pay Smith.
ROBERT GREEN INGERSOLL (1833–1899)

Forgiveness is the needle that knows how to mend.
JEWEL (1974–)

He who is devoid of the power to forgive, is devoid of the power to love.
MARTIN LUTHER KING JR. (1929–1968)

We pardon to the extent that we love.
FRANÇOIS DE LA ROCHEFOUCAULD (1613–1680)

If we could read the secret history of our enemies, we would find in each person's life sorrow and suffering enough to disarm all hostility.
HENRY WADSWORTH LONGFELLOW (1807–1882)

Holding on to anger, resentment and hurt only gives you tense muscles, a headache, and a sore jaw from clenching your teeth. Forgiveness gives you back the laughter and the lightness in your life.
JOAN LUNDEN (1950–)

Forgiveness is God's command.
MARTIN LUTHER (1483–1546)

The best thing about giving of ourselves is that what we get is always better than what we give. The reaction is greater than the action.
ORISON SWETT MARDEN (1850–1924)

A woman can forgive a man for the harm he does her ... but she can never forgive him for the sacrifices he makes on her account.
W. SOMERSET MAUGHAM (1874–1965), *The Moon and Sixpence*

There is no love without forgiveness, and there is no forgiveness without love.
BRYANT H. MCGILL (1969–)

To forgive is the highest, most beautiful form of love. In return, you will receive untold peace and happiness.
ROBERT MULLER (1944–)

And if your friend does evil to you, say to him, "I forgive you for what you did to me, but how can I forgive you for what you did to yourself?"
FRIEDRICH NIETZSCHE (1844–1900)

When a deep injury is done us, we never recover until we forgive.
ALAN PATON (1903–1988)

How shall I lose the sin, yet keep the sense, and love the offender, yet detest the offence?
ALEXANDER POPE (1688–1744)

To err is human, to forgive is divine.
ALEXANDER POPE (1688–1744)

Humanity is never so beautiful as when praying for forgiveness, or else forgiving another.
JEAN PAUL RICHTER (1763–1825)

People find it far easier to forgive others for being wrong than for being right.
J. K. ROWLING (1965–)

To forgive all is as inhuman as to forgive none.
SENECA (5 BC–AD 65)

Pray you now, forget and forgive.
WILLIAM SHAKESPEARE (1564–1616), *King Lear*

Forgive him, for he believes that the customs of his tribe are the laws of nature!
GEORGE BERNARD SHAW (1856–1950)

The secret of forgiving everything is to understand nothing.
GEORGE BERNARD SHAW (1856–1950)

'Tis the most tender part of love, each other to forgive.
JOHN SHEFFIELD (1648–1721)

To forgive is to set a prisoner free and discover that the prisoner was you.
LEWIS B. SMEDES (1921–2002)

Only the brave know how to forgive; it is the most refined and generous pitch of virtue human nature can arrive at.
LAURENCE STERNE (1713–1768)

I believe in the forgiveness of sin and the redemption of ignorance.
ADLAI E. STEVENSON II (1900–1965)

The stupid neither forgive nor forget; the naive forgive and forget; the wise forgive but do not forget.
THOMAS S. SZASZ (1920–), *The Second Sin*

Let us forgive each other—only then will we live in peace.
LEO TOLSTOY (1828–1910)

Without forgiveness, there's no future.
DESMOND TUTU (1931–)

Forget and forgive. This is not difficult when properly understood. It means forget inconvenient duties, then forgive yourself for forgetting. By rigid practice and stern determination, it comes easy.
MARK TWAIN (1835–1910)

Forgiveness is the fragrance that the violet sheds on the heel that has crushed it.
MARK TWAIN (1835–1910)

Love is an act of endless forgiveness, a tender look which becomes a habit.
PETER USTINOV (1921–)

Forgiveness is a funny thing. It warms the heart and cools the sting.
WILLIAM ARTHUR WARD (1921–1994)

Always forgive your enemies; nothing annoys them so much.
OSCAR WILDE (1854–1900)

Fortune

The fortune which nobody sees makes a person happy and unenvied.
SIR FRANCIS BACON (1561–1626)

Therefore if a man look sharply and attentively, he shall see Fortune; for though she be blind, yet she is not invisible.
SIR FRANCIS BACON (1561–1626)

Behind every great fortune there is a crime.
HONORE DE BALZAC (1799–1850)

It is madness to make fortune the mistress of events, because by herself she is nothing and is ruled by prudence.
JOHN DRYDEN (1631–1700)

Nature magically suits a man to his fortunes, by making them the fruit of his character.
RALPH WALDO EMERSON (1803–1882)

Fortune truly helps those who are of good judgment.
EURIPIDES (C. 480–406 BC)

He that waits upon fortune, is never sure of a dinner.
BENJAMIN FRANKLIN (1706–1790)

Only learn to seize good fortune, for good fortune's always here.
JOHANN WOLFGANG VON GOETHE (1749–1832)

Fortune makes a fool of those she favors too much.
HORACE (65–8 BC)

If a man's fortune does not fit him, it is like the shoe in the story; if too large it trips him up, if too small it pinches him.
HORACE (65–8 BC)

There is a kind of elevation which does not depend on fortune; it is a certain air which distinguishes us, and seems to destine us for great things; it is a price which we imperceptibly set upon ourselves.
FRANÇOIS DE LA ROCHEFOUCAULD (1613–1680)

Fortune is the rod of the weak, and the staff of the brave.
JAMES RUSSELL LOWELL (1819–1891)

I am above being injured by fortune, though she steals away much, more will remain with me. The blessing I now enjoy transcend fear.
OVID (43 BC–AD 17)

Fortune is like glass—the brighter the glitter, the more easily broken.
PUBLILIUS SYRUS (C. 100 BC)

We do not know what is really good or bad fortune.
JEAN-JACQUES ROUSSEAU (1712–1778)

Large fortunes are all founded either on the occupation of land, or lending or the taxation of labor.
JOHN RUSKIN (1819–1900)

Fortune favors the brave.
TERENCE (185–159 BC)

Fortune knocks at every man's door once in a life, but in a good many cases the man is in a neighboring saloon and does not hear her.
MARK TWAIN (1835–1910)

Henceforth I ask not good fortune. I myself am good fortune.
WALT WHITMAN (1819–1892)

France

France, mother of arts, of warfare, and of laws.
JOACHIM DU BELLAY (1522–1560)

France cannot be France without greatness.
CHARLES DE GAULLE (1890–1970)

I was France.
CHARLES DE GAULLE (1890–1970)

We always have been, we are, and I hope that we always shall be detested in France.
ARTHUR WELLESLEY (1769–1852)

Frankness

Frank and explicit—that is the right line to take when you wish to conceal your own mind and confuse the minds of others.
BENJAMIN DISRAELI (1804–1881)

We are franker towards others than towards ourselves.
FRIEDRICH NIETZSCHE (1844–1900)

The great consolation in life is to say what one thinks.
VOLTAIRE (1694–1778)

All faults may be forgiven of him who has perfect candor.
WALT WHITMAN (1819–1892)

All cruel people describe themselves as paragons of frankness.
TENNESSEE WILLIAMS (1911–1983)

Fraud

The first and worst of all frauds is to cheat oneself.
PHILIP JAMES BAILEY (1816–1902)

Fraud is the ready minister of injustice.
EDMUND BURKE (1729–1797)

There are some frauds so well conducted that it would be stupidity not to be deceived by them.
CHARLES CALEB COLTON (1780–1832)

Fraud is the homage that force pays to reason.
CHARLES CURTIS (1860–1936)

Whoever is detected in a shameful fraud is ever after not believed even if they speak the truth.
PHAEDRUS (15 BC–AD 50)

It is a fraud to borrow what we are unable to pay.
PUBLILIUS SYRUS (C. 100 BC)

Freedom

But a Constitution of Government once changed from Freedom, can never be restored. Liberty, once lost, is lost forever.
JOHN ADAMS (1735–1826)

Any existence deprived of freedom is a kind of death.
MICHEL AOUN (1935–)

Freedom is not something that anybody can be given; Freedom is something that people take and people are as free as they want to be.
JAMES ARTHUR BALDWIN (1924–1987)

Freedom is nothing but a chance to be better.
ALBERT CAMUS (1913–1960)

The only way to deal with an unfree world is to become so absolutely free that your very existence is an act of rebellion.
ALBERT CAMUS (1913–1960)

The name of peace is sweet, and the thing itself is beneficial, but there is a great difference between peace and servitude. Peace is freedom in tranquillity, servitude is the worst of all evils, to be resisted not only by war, but even by death.
CICERO (106–43 BC)

Freedom is an internal achievement rather than an external adjustment.
POWELL CLAYTON (1833–1914)

While we are free to choose our actions, we are not free to choose the consequences of our actions.
STEPHEN R. COVEY (1932–)

There is no such thing as a little freedom. Either you are all free, or you are not free.
WALTER CRONKITE (1916–)

Man is tormented by no greater anxiety than to find someone quickly to whom he can hand over that great gift of freedom with which the ill-fated creature is born.
FYODOR DOSTOEVSKY (1821–1881), *The Brothers Karamazov*

I think of a hero as someone who understands the degree of responsibility that comes with his freedom.
BOB DYLAN (1941–)

Everything that is really great and inspiring is created by the individual who can labor in freedom.
ALBERT EINSTEIN (1879–1955), *Out of My Later Years*

Only the educated are free.
EPICTETUS (AD 55–135), *Discourses*

Freedom is not procured by a full enjoyment of what is desired, but by controlling the desire.
EPICTETUS (AD 55–135)

Freedom is just Chaos, with better lighting.
ALAN DEAN FOSTER (1946–), *To the Vanishing Point*

Freedom lies in being bold.
ROBERT FROST (1874–1963)

Freedom is not worth having if it does not include the freedom to make mistakes.
MAHATMA GANDHI (1869–1948)

The outward freedom that we shall attain will only be in exact proportion to the inward freedom to which we may have grown at a given moment. And if this is a correct view of freedom, our chief energy must be concentrated on achieving reform from within.
MAHATMA GANDHI (1869–1948)

Next in importance to freedom and justice is popular education, without which neither freedom nor justice can be permanently maintained.
JAMES A. GARFIELD (1831–1881)

They have exiled me now from their society and I am pleased, because humanity does not exile except the one whose noble spirit rebels against despotism and oppression. He who does not prefer exile to slavery is not free by any measure of freedom, truth, and duty.
KAHLIL GIBRAN (1883–1931), *Spirits Rebellious*

To know how to free oneself is nothing; the arduous thing is to know what to do with one's freedom.
ANDRÉ GIDE (1869–1951)

[Y]ou are in control of your life. Don't ever forget that. You are what you are because of the conscious and subconscious choices you have made.
BARBARA HALL (1946), *A Summons to New Orleans*

Indignation boils my blood at the thought of the heritage we are throwing away; at the thought that, with few exceptions, the fight for freedom is left to the poor, forlorn and defenseless, and to the few radicals and revolutionaries who would make use of liberty to destroy … American institutions.
ARTHUR GARFIELD HAYS (1881–1954)

Seek freedom and become captive of your desires, seek discipline and find your liberty.
FRANK HERBERT (1920–1986), *Dune*

The basic test of freedom is perhaps less in what we are free to do than in what we are free not to do.
ERIC HOFFER (1902–1983)

The First Amendment is often inconvenient. But that is besides the point. Inconvenience does not absolve the government of its obligation to tolerate speech.
ANTHONY KENNEDY (1936–)

The cost of freedom is always high, but Americans have always paid it. And one path we shall never choose, and that is the path of surrender, or submission.
JOHN F. KENNEDY (1917–1963)

People demand freedom of speech as a compensation for the freedom of thought which they seldom use.
SØREN KIERKEGAARD (1813–1855)

Freedom is never voluntarily given by the oppressor; it must be demanded by the oppressed.
MARTIN LUTHER KING JR. (1929–1968)

While the State exists, there can be no freedom. When there is freedom there will be no State.
VLADIMIR I. LENIN (1870–1924), *State and Revolution*

Freedom is not the right to do what we want, but what we ought. Let us have faith that right makes might and in that faith let us, to the end, dare to do our duty as we understand it.
ABRAHAM LINCOLN (1809–1865)

Those who deny freedom to others, deserve it not for themselves.
ABRAHAM LINCOLN (1809–1865)

Nobody can give you freedom. Nobody can give you equality or justice or anything. If you're a man, you take it.
MALCOLM X (1925–1965), *Malcolm X Speaks*

You can't separate peace from freedom because no one can be at peace unless he has his freedom.
MALCOLM X (1925–1965), *Malcolm X Speaks*

The only freedom which deserves the name is that of pursuing our own good in our own way, so long as we do not attempt to deprive others of theirs, or impede their efforts to obtain it. Each is the proper guardian of his own health, whether bodily, or mental or spiritual. Mankind are greater gainers by suffering each other to live as seems good to themselves, than by compelling each to live as seems good to the rest.
JOHN STUART MILL (1806–1873), *On Liberty*

Freedom is the will to be responsible to ourselves.
FRIEDRICH NIETZSCHE (1844–1900)

There are only two kinds of freedom in the world; the freedom of the rich and powerful, and the freedom of the artist and the monk who renounces possessions.
ANAÏS NIN (1903–1977)

Freedom is the right to tell people what they do not want to hear.
GEORGE ORWELL (1903–1950)

It's only after we've lost everything that we're free to do anything.
CHUCK PALAHNIUK (1962–), *Fight Club*

To give up the task of reforming society is to give up one's responsibility as a free man.
ALAN PATON (1903–1988)

In the truest sense, freedom cannot be bestowed; it must be achieved.
FRANKLIN D. ROOSEVELT (1882–1945)

True individual freedom cannot exist without economic security and independence. People who are hungry and out of a job are the stuff of which dictatorships are made.
FRANKLIN D. ROOSEVELT (1882–1945)

Freedom in general may be defined as the absence of obstacles to the realization of desires.
BERTRAND RUSSELL (1872–1970)

I know but one freedom and that is the freedom of the mind.
ANTOINE DE SAINT-EXUPÉRY (1900–1944)

The more freedom we enjoy, the greater the responsibility we bear, toward others as well as ourselves.
OSCAR ARIAS SANCHEZ (1941–)

If you want to be free, there is but one way; it is to guarantee an equally full measure of liberty to all your neighbors. There is no other.
CARL SCHURZ (1829–1906)

He who is brave is free.
SENECA (5 BC–AD 65)

My definition of a free society is a society where it is safe to be unpopular.
ADLAI E. STEVENSON II (1900–1965)

To know what you prefer instead of humbly saying Amen to what the world tells you you ought to prefer, is to have kept your soul alive.
ROBERT LOUIS STEVENSON (1850–1894)

Every renaissance comes to the world with a cry, the cry of the human spirit to be free.
ANNIE SULLIVAN (1866–1936)

All good things are wild, and free.
HENRY DAVID THOREAU (1817–1862)

The law will never make men free, it is men that have to make the law free.
HENRY DAVID THOREAU (1817–1862)

The secret of happiness is freedom. The secret of freedom is courage.
THUCYDIDES (C. 460–395 BC)

It is by the goodness of God that in our country we have those three unspeakably precious things: freedom of speech, freedom of conscience, and the prudence never to practice either of them.
MARK TWAIN (1835–1910), *Following the Equator*

It is hard to free fools from the chains they revere.
VOLTAIRE (1694–1778)

Man is free at the moment he wishes to be.
VOLTAIRE (1694–1778)

The true character of liberty is independence, maintained by force.
VOLTAIRE (1694–1778)

[F]ight and you may die. Run, and you'll live … at least a while. And dying in your beds, many years from now, would you be willing to trade all of that from this day to that, for one chance, just one chance, to come back here and tell our enemies that they may take away our lives, but they'll never take our freedom!
RANDALL WALLACE (1949–), *Braveheart*

The time is near at hand which must determine whether Americans are to be free men or slaves.
GEORGE WASHINGTON (1732–1799)

Freedom—to walk free and own no superior.
WALT WHITMAN (1819–1892)

A slave is a free man if he is content with his lot; a free man is a slave if he seeks more than that.
ANONYMOUS

Freedom also includes the right to mismanage your own affairs.
ANONYMOUS

It is my right to be uncommon. For I do not choose to be a common man. If I can, I seek opportunity. I do not wish to be a kept citizen, humbled and dulled by having the government look after me. I choose to take the calculated risk, to dream, to build, to fail or succeed. I choose not to barter incentive for a dole, I prefer the challenges of life to a guaranteed existence, the thrill of fulfillment to the state calm of Utopia. I will not trade my freedom for beneficence nor my dignity for a handout.
ANONYMOUS

It is quite impossible to guarantee world peace. But is should be possible to guarantee world freedom.
ANONYMOUS

Liberty is the right to choose. Freedom is the result of the right choice.
ANONYMOUS

Free Will

This doctrine, that of the ghost in the machine, strictly separates the mind or soul from the body. And by doing so it takes the soul outside the sphere of mechanical or scientific explanation. It splits the world of the mind from the world of science. It is often supposed to protect our cherished free will.
SIMON BLACKBURN (1944–)

Whereas the Greeks gave to will the boundaries of reason, we have come to put the will's impulse in the very center of reason, which has, as a result, become deadly.
ALBERT CAMUS (1913–1960)

Human freedom is not an illusion; it is an objective phenomenon, distinct from all other biological conditions and found in only one species, us.
DANIEL DENNETT (1942–)

A man may be a pessimistic determinist before lunch and an optimistic believer in the will's freedom after it.
ALDOUS HUXLEY (1894–1963)

Man is a masterpiece of creation if for no other reason than that, all the weight of evidence for determinism notwithstanding, he believes he has free will.
GEORG C. LICHTENBERG (1742–1799)

God is not willing to do everything, and thus take away our free will and that share of glory which belongs to us.
NICCOLÒ MACHIAVELLI (1469–1527)

Free will. It's like butterfly wings: once touched, they never get off the ground. No, I only set the stage. You pull your own strings.
JOHN MILTON (1608–1674)

Life is like a game of cards. The hand that is dealt you is determinism; the way you play it is free will.
JAWAHARLAL NEHRU (1889–1964)

The strongest knowledge (that of the total freedom of the human will) is nonetheless the poorest in successes: for it always has the strongest opponent, human vanity.
FRIEDRICH NIETZSCHE (1844–1900)

That which you call your soul or spirit is your consciousness, and that which you call "free will" is your mind's freedom to think or not, the only will you have, your only freedom, the choice that controls all the choices you make and determines your life and your character.
AYN RAND (1905–1982), *Atlas Shrugged*

Man is a being with free will; therefore, each man is potentially good or evil, and it's up to him and only him (through his reasoning mind) to decide which he wants to be.
AYN RAND (1905–1982)

We have to believe in free will. We've got no choice.
ISAAC BASHEVIS SINGER (1904–1991), *The Times*

Free will is not the liberty to do whatever one likes, but the power of doing whatever one sees ought to be done, even in the very face of otherwise overwhelming impulse. There lies freedom, indeed.
ANONYMOUS

Friendship

Friends are born, not made.
HENRY ADAMS (1838–1918)

Friendship improves happiness, and abates misery, by doubling our joys, and dividing our grief.
JOSEPH ADDISON (1672–1719)

The greatest sweetener of human life is friendship. To raise this to the highest pitch of enjoyment is a secret which but few discover.
JOSEPH ADDISON (1672–1719)

True happiness is of a retired nature, and an enemy to pomp and noise; it arises, in the first place, from the enjoyment of one's self, and in the next from the friendship and conversation of a few select companions.
JOSEPH ADDISON (1672–1719)

Friendship is a very taxing and arduous form of leisure activity.
MORTIMER ADLER (1902–2001)

Little friends may prove great friends.
AESOP (620–560 BC)

What brings joy to the heart is not so much the friend's gift as the friend's love.
SAINT AETHELRED OF RIEVAULX (C. 1110–1167)

He who has a thousand friends has not a friend to spare,
And he who has one enemy will meet him everywhere.
ALI IBN ABI TALIB (602–661), *A Hundred Sayings*

The most called-upon prerequisite of a friend is an accessible ear.
MAYA ANGELOU (1928–)

I keep my friends as misers do their treasure, because, of all the things granted us by wisdom, none is greater or better than friendship.
PIETRO ARETINO (1492–1556)

Misfortune shows those who are not really friends.
ARISTOTLE (384–322 BC), *Eudemian Ethics*

Without friends no one would choose to live, though he had all other goods.
ARISTOTLE (384–322 BC), *Nichomachean Ethics*

Friends keep the young out of mischief; to the old they are a comfort and aid in their weakness; and those in the prime of life, they incite to noble deeds.
ARISTOTLE (384–322 BC)

Friendship is essentially a partnership.
ARISTOTLE (384–322 BC)

In poverty and other misfortunes of life, true friends are a sure refuge.
ARISTOTLE (384–322 BC)

The antidote for fifty enemies is one friend.
ARISTOTLE (384–322 BC)

If two friends ask you to judge a dispute, don't accept, because you will lose one friend; on the other hand, if two strangers come with the same request, accept because you will gain one friend.
SAINT AUGUSTINE (354-430)

Friendship is certainly the finest balm for the pangs of disappointed love.
JANE AUSTEN (1775–1817), *Northanger Abbey*

Every gift from a friend is a wish for your happiness.
RICHARD BACH (1936–)

Without friends the world is but a wilderness.
SIR FRANCIS BACON (1561–1626)

The best time to make friends is before you need them.
ETHEL BARRYMORE (1879–1959)

It is easier to forgive an enemy than to forgive a friend.
WILLIAM BLAKE (1757–1827)

A companion loves some agreeable qualities which a man may possess, but a friend loves the man himself.
JAMES BOSWELL (1740–1795)

We cannot tell the precise moment when friendship is formed. As in filling a vessel drop by drop, there is at last a drop which makes it run over. So in a series of kindness there is, at last, one which makes the heart run over.
JAMES BOSWELL (1740–1795)

A good friend can tell you what is the matter with you in a minute. He may not seem such a good friend after telling.
ARTHUR BRISBANE (1864–1946), *The Book of Today*

How delightful to find a friend in everyone.
JOSEPH BRODSKY (1940–1996)

If we would build on a sure foundation in friendship, we must love friends for their sake rather than for our own.
CHARLOTTE BRONTË (1816–1855)

A friendship can weather most things and thrive in thin soil; but it needs a little mulch of letters and phone calls and small, silly presents every so often—just to save it from drying out completely.
PAM BROWN (1948–)

Friendship is not diminished by distance or time, by imprisonment or war, by suffering or silence. It is in these things that it roots most deeply. It is from these things that it flowers.
PAM BROWN (1948–)

In loneliness, in sickness, in confusion—the mere knowledge of friendship makes it possible to endure, even if the friend is powerless to help. It is enough that they exist.
PAM BROWN (1948–)

When friends stop being frank and useful to each other, the whole world loses some of its radiance.
ANATOLE BROYARD (1920–1990)

An insincere and evil friend is more to be feared than a wild beast; a wild beast may wound your body, but an evil friend will wound your mind.
THE BUDDHA (563–483 BC)

The rule of friendship means there should be mutual sympathy between them, each supplying what the other lacks and trying to benefit the other, always using friendly and sincere words.
THE BUDDHA (563–483 BC)

Friendship is a strong and habitual inclination in two persons to promote the good and happiness of one another.
EUSTACE BUDGELL (1686–1737)

Adversity does teach who your real friends are.
LOIS MCMASTER BUJOLD (1949–), *A Civil Campaign*

If you make it plain you like people, it's hard for them to resist liking you back.
LOIS MCMASTER BUJOLD (1949–), *Diplomatic Immunity*

A good friend of my son's is a son to me.
LOIS MCMASTER BUJOLD (1949–), *Ethan of Athos*

True friendship brings sunshine to the shade and shade to the sunshine.
THOMAS BURKE (1910–1973)

Friends are treasures.
HORACE BURNS (1915–2000)

I still find each day too short for all the thoughts I want to think, all the walks I want to take, all the books I want to read, and all the friends I want to see.
JOHN BURROUGHS (1837–1921)

False friendship, like the ivy, decays and ruins the walls it embraces, but true friendship gives new life and animation to the object it supports.
RICHARD BURTON (1925–1984)

A friend is known when needed.
LEO F. BUSCAGLIA (1924–1998)

A single rose can be my garden … a single friend, my world.
LEO F. BUSCAGLIA (1924–1998)

Friendship is like money—easier made than kept.
SAMUEL BUTLER (1835–1902)

Friendship is love, without his wings.
LORD BYRON (1788–1824)

You can make more friends in two months by becoming interested in other people than you can in two years by trying to get other people interested in you.
DALE CARNEGIE (1888–1955)

The advice of friends must be received with a judicious reserve; we must not give ourselves up to it and follow it blindly, whether right or wrong.
PIERRE CHARRON (1541–1603)

Treat your friends as you do your pictures, and place them in their best light.
JENNIE JEROME CHURCHILL (1854–1921)

Friendship makes prosperity more shining and lessens adversity by dividing and sharing it.
CICERO (106–43 BC), *On Friendship*

The shifts of Fortune test the reliability of friends.
CICERO (106–43 BC), *On Friendship*

Friendship was given by nature to be an assistant to virtue, not a companion to vice.
CICERO (106–43 BC)

He removes the greatest ornament of friendship, who takes away from it respect.
CICERO (106–43 BC)

The man who backbites an absent friend, nay, who does not stand up for him when another blames him, the man who angles for bursts of laughter and for the repute of a wit, who can invent what he never saw, who cannot keep a secret—that man is black at heart: mark and avoid him.
CICERO (106–43 BC)

The rule of friendship means there should be mutual sympathy between them, each supplying what the other lacks and trying to benefit the other, always using friendly and sincere words.
CICERO (106–43 BC)

Thus nature has no love for solitude and always leans, as it were, on some support; and the sweetest support is found in the most intimate friendship.
CICERO (106–43 BC)

What sweetness is left in life, if you take away friendship? Robbing life of friendship is like robbing the world of the sun. A true friend is more to be esteemed than kinsfolk.
CICERO (106–43 BC)

It is wise to apply the oil of refined politeness to the mechanisms of friendship.
SIDONIE GABRIELLE COLETTE (1873–1954), *The Pure and the Impure*

In prosperity our friends know us; in adversity we know our friends.
JOHN CHURTON COLLINS (1848–1908)

True friendship is like sound health; the value of it is seldom known until it is lost.
CHARLES CALEB COLTON (1780–1832)

Have no friends not equal to yourself.
CONFUCIUS (551–479 BC), *The Confucian Analects*

What is a friend? I will tell you. It is someone with whom you dare to be yourself.
FRANK CRANE (1861–1928)

Old friends pass away; new friends appear. It is just like the days. An old day passes; a new day arrives. The important thing is to make it meaningful: a meaningful friend, or a meaningful day.
THE DALAI LAMA (1935–)

A man's friendships are one of the best measures of his worth.
CHARLES DARWIN (1809–1882)

Fate chooses your relations, you choose your friends.
JACQUES DELILLE (1738–1813)

Friends are relatives you make for yourself.
EUSTACHE DESCHAMPS (1346–1406)

It is the friends you can call up at 4 a.m. that matter.
MARLENE DIETRICH (1901–1992)

As a matter of self-preservation, a man needs good friends or ardent enemies, for the former instruct him and the latter take him to task.
DIOGENES LAERTIUS (C. 200)

It is better to have one friend of great value than many friends who are good for nothing.
DIOGENES LAERTIUS (C. 200)

Wherever we are, it is our friends that make our world.
HENRY DRUMMOND (1851–1897)

Friendship consists in forgetting what one gives, and remembering what one receives.
ALEXANDRE DUMAS (1802–1870)

Friends are helpful not only because they will listen to us, but because they will laugh at us.
WILL DURANT (1885–1981)

Friendship is the inexpressible comfort of feeling safe with a person, having neither to weigh thoughts nor measure words.
GEORGE ELIOT (1819–1880)

A friend is a person with whom I may be sincere. Before him I may think aloud. I am arrived at last in the presence of a man so real and equal, that I may drop even those undermost garments of dissimulation, courtesy, and second thought.
RALPH WALDO EMERSON (1803–1882)

A man's growth is seen in the successive choirs of his friends.
RALPH WALDO EMERSON (1803–1882)

I awoke with devout thanksgiving for my friends.
RALPH WALDO EMERSON (1803–1882)

I do not wish to treat friendships daintily, but with the roughest courage. When they are real, they are not glass threads or frost-work, but the solidest thing we know.
RALPH WALDO EMERSON (1803–1882)

It is one of the blessings of old friends that you can afford to be stupid with them.
RALPH WALDO EMERSON (1803–1882)

The glory of friendship is not the outstretched hand, nor the kindly smile, nor the joy of companionship; it is the spiritual inspiration that comes to one when he discovers that someone else believes in him and is willing to trust him with friendship.
RALPH WALDO EMERSON (1803–1882)

The ornament of a house is the friends who frequent it.
RALPH WALDO EMERSON (1803–1882)

It is not so much our friends help that help us, as the confidence of their help.
EPICURUS (C. 341–270 BC)

Of all the things which wisdom provides to make life entirely happy, much the greatest is the possession of friendship.
EPICURUS (C. 341–270 BC)

Life has no blessing like a prudent friend.
EURIPIDES (C. 480–406 BC)

My mother used to say that there are no strangers, only friends you haven't met yet. She's now in a maximum security twilight home in Australia.
DAME EDNA EVERAGE (1934–)

I have learned that to have a good friend is the purest of all God's gifts, for it is a love that has no exchange of payment.
FRANCES FARMER (1913–1970)

Life has taught me that respect, caring and love must be shared, for it's only through sharing that friendships are born.
DONNA A. FAVORS (1955–)

Let us learn to show our friendship for a man when he is alive and not after he is dead.
F. SCOTT FITZGERALD (1896–1940)

The most beautiful discovery true friends make is that they can grow separately without growing apart.
ELISABETH FOLEY (1965–)

My best friend is the one who brings out the best in me.
HENRY FORD (1863–1947)

If I had to choose between betraying my country and betraying my friend, I hope I should have the guts to betray my country.
E. M. FORSTER (1879–1970)

Trouble is a sieve through which we sift our acquaintances. Those too big to pass through are our friends.
ARLENE FRANCIS (1907–2001)

'Tis a great confidence in a friend to tell him your faults; greater to tell him his.
BENJAMIN FRANKLIN (1706–1790)

The beauty of friendship is in security.
ROBERT FROST (1874–1963)

No man can be happy without a friend, nor be sure of his friend till he is unhappy.
THOMAS FULLER (1608–1661)

Purchase not friends by gifts; when thou ceasest to give, such will cease to love.
THOMAS FULLER (1608–1661)

There is a scarcity of friendship, but not of friends.
THOMAS FULLER (1608–1661)

And in the sweetness of friendship let there be laughter and the sharing of pleasures. For in the dew of little things the heart finds its morning and is refreshed.
KAHLIL GIBRAN (1883–1931), *The Prophet*

A friend who is far away is sometimes much nearer than one who is at hand. Is not the mountain far more awe-inspiring and more clearly visible to one passing through the valley than to those who inhabit the mountain?
KAHLIL GIBRAN (1883–1931)

[I]n the sweetness of friendship let there be laughter and the sharing of pleasures. For in the dew of little things, the heart finds its morning and is refreshed.
KAHLIL GIBRAN (1883–1931)

Since there is nothing so well worth having as friends, never lose a chance to make them.
FRANCESCO GUICCIARDINI (1483–1540)

The making of friends, who are real friends, is the best token we have of a man's success in life.
EDWARD EVERETT HALE (1822–1909)

A friend should be one in whose understanding and virtue we can equally confide, and whose opinion we can value at once for its justness and its sincerity.
ROBERT HALL (1764–1831)

Friendship needs no words; it is solitude delivered from the anguish of loneliness.
DAG HAMMARSKJÖLD (1905–1961)

There is nothing better than the encouragement of a good friend.
KATHARINE BUTLER HATHAWAY (1890–1942)

Don't flatter yourself that friendship authorizes you to say disagreeable things to your intimates. The nearer you come into relation with a person, the more necessary do tact and courtesy become. Except in cases of necessity, which are rare, leave your friend to learn unpleasant things from his enemies; they are ready enough to tell them.
OLIVER WENDELL HOLMES SR. (1809–1894), *The Autocrat of the Breakfast-Table*

There is no friend like an old friend who has shared
our morning days,
No greeting like his welcome,
No homage like his praise; Fame is the scentless
sunflower, with gaudy crown of gold;
But friendship is the breathing rose, with sweets in
every fold.
OLIVER WENDELL HOLMES SR. (1809–1894)

A sympathetic friend can be quite as dear as a brother.
HOMER (800–700 BC)

The difficulty is not so great to die for a friend , as to find a friend worth dying for.
HOMER (800–700 BC)

Two friends, two bodies with one soul inspired.
HOMER (800–700 BC)

If a friend is in trouble, don't annoy him by asking him if there's anything you can do. Think of something appropriate and do it.
EDGAR WATSON HOWE (1853–1937)

The little trouble in the world that is not due to love is due to friendship.
EDGAR WATSON HOWE (1853–1937)

Never explain—your friends do not need it and your enemies will not believe you anyway.
ELBERT HUBBARD (1856–1915)

The friend is the man who knows all about you and still likes you.
ELBERT HUBBARD (1856–1915)

Blessed are they who have the gift of making friends, for it is one of God's best gifts. It involves many things, but above all, the power of going out of one's self, and appreciating whatever is noble and loving in another.
THOMAS HUGHES (1822–1896)

Do you know what friendship is ... it is to be brother and sister; two souls which touch without mingling, two fingers on one hand.
VICTOR HUGO (1802–1885), *The Hunchback of Notre Dame*

At the shrine of friendship never say die;
Let the wine of friendship never run dry.
VICTOR HUGO (1802–1885)

The greatest gift of life is friendship, and I have received it.
HUBERT H. HUMPHREY (1911–1978)

For memory has painted this perfect day
With colors that never fade,
And we find at the end of a perfect day
The soul of a friend we've made.
CARRIE JACOBS-BOND (1862–1946)

I find friendship to be like wine, raw when new, ripened with age, the true old man's milk and restorative cordial.
THOMAS JEFFERSON (1762–1826)

Peace and friendship with all mankind is our wisest policy, and I wish we may be permitted to pursue it.
THOMAS JEFFERSON (1762–1826)

The friendship that can cease has never been real.
SAINT JEROME (C. 342–420)

If a man does not make new acquaintances, as he advances through life, he soon will find himself alone. A man should keep his friendship in constant repair.
SAMUEL JOHNSON (1709–1784)

Nothing changes your opinion of a friend so surely as success—yours or his.
FRANKLIN P. JONES (1887–1929)

Friends may come and go, but enemies accumulate.
THOMAS JONES (1892–1969)

There is no substitute for flesh-and-blood friends if we are to understand and learn to love ourselves.
TIMOTHY JONES (1962–)

The meeting of two personalities is like the contact of two chemical substances: if there is any reaction, both are transformed.
CARL JUNG (1875–1961)

Walking with a friend in the dark is better than walking alone in the light.
HELEN KELLER (1880–1968)

A blessed thing it is for any man or woman to have a friend, one human soul whom we can trust utterly, who knows the best and worst of us, and who loves us in spite of all our faults.
CHARLES KINGSLEY (1819–1875)

The friend who holds your hand and says the wrong thing is made of dearer stuff than the one who stays away.
BARBARA KINGSOLVER (1955–)

We cannot always assure the future of our friends; we have a better chance of assuring our future if we remember who our friends are.
HENRY KISSINGER (1923–)

'Tis the privilege of friendship to talk nonsense, and have her nonsense respected.
CHARLES LAMB (1775–1834)

A true friend is the greatest of all blessings, and that which we take the least care to acquire.
FRANÇOIS DE LA ROCHEFOUCAULD (1613–1680)

What men have called friendship is only a social arrangement, a mutual adjustment of interests, an interchange of services given and received; it is, in sum, simply a business from which those involved propose to derive a steady profit for their own self-love.
FRANCOIS DE LA ROCHEFOUCAULD (1613–1680)

A true friend is one who overlooks your failures and tolerates your success!
DOUG LARSON (1902–1981)

Go through your phone book, call people and ask them to drive you to the airport. The ones who will drive you are your true friends. The rest aren't bad people; they're just acquaintances.
JAY LENO (1950–)

Friendship is unnecessary, like philosophy, like art. It has no survival value; rather it is one of those things that give value to survival.
C. S. LEWIS (1898–1963)

Ah, how good it feels! The hand of an old friend.
HENRY WADSWORTH LONGFELLOW (1807–1882)

Many a person has held close, throughout their entire lives, two friends that always remained strange to one another, because one of them attracted by virtue of similarity, the other by difference.
EMIL LUDWIG (1881–1948)

If instead of a gem, or even a flower, we should cast the gift of a loving thought into the heart of a friend, that would be giving as the angels give.
GEORGE MACDONALD (1824–1905)

I always felt that the great high privilege, relief, and comfort of friendship was that one had to explain nothing.
KATHERINE MANSFIELD (1888–1923)

I am treating you as my friend, asking you to share my present minuses in the hope that I can ask you to share my future pluses.
KATHERINE MANSFIELD (1888–1923)

When you choose your friends, don't be short-changed by choosing personality over character.
W. SOMERSET MAUGHAM (1874–1965)

No friendship can cross the path of our destiny without leaving some mark on it forever.
FRANÇOIS MAURIAC (1885–1970)

We are keenly aware of the faults of our friends, but if they like us enough it doesn't matter.
MIGNON MCLAUGHLIN (1913–1983)

A true friend is one who thinks you are a good egg even if you are half-cracked.
BERNARD MELTZER (1917–1998)

The best way to keep your friends is not to give them away.
WILSON MIZNER (1876–1933)

God gives us our relatives. Thank God we can choose our friends.
MICHEL DE MONTAIGNE (1533–1592)

True friends are always together in spirit.
LUCY MAUD MONTGOMERY (1874–1942)

A friend is someone who lets you have total freedom to be yourself.
JIM MORRISON (1943–1971)

Strangers are just friends waiting to happen.
NAPOLÉON I (1769–1821)

Each friend represents a world in us, a world possibly not born until they arrive, and it is only by this meeting that a new world is born.
ANAÏS NIN (1903–1977)

When we honestly ask ourselves which person in our lives mean the most to us, we often find that it is those who, instead of giving advice, solutions, or cures, have chosen rather to share our pain and touch our wounds with a warm and tender hand. The friend who can be silent with us in a moment of despair or confusion, who can stay with us in an hour of grief and bereavement, who can tolerate not knowing, not curing, not healing and face with us the reality of our powerlessness, that is a friend who cares.
HENRI NOUWEN (1932–1996), *Out of Solitude*

Nobody sees a flower—really—it is so small it takes time—we haven't time—and to see takes time, like to have a friend takes time.
GEORGIA O'KEEFFE (1887–1986)

Constant use will not wear ragged the fabric of friendship.
DOROTHY PARKER (1893–1967)

A true friend unbosoms freely, advises justly, assists readily, adventures boldly, takes all patiently, defends courageously, and continues a friend unchangeably.
WILLIAM PENN (1644–1718)

You can always tell a real friend. When you've made a fool of yourself, he doesn't feel you've done a permanent job.
DR. LAURENCE J. PETER (1919–1990)

Suspicion is the cancer of friendship.
PETRARCH (1304–1374)

Friends have all things in common.
PLATO (C. 428–348 BC), *Dialogues*

Prosperity is no just scale; adversity is the only balance to weigh friends.
PLUTARCH (AD 46–120)

Let us be grateful to people who make us happy. They are the charming gardeners who make our souls blossom.
MARCEL PROUST (1871–1922)

Prosperity makes friends, adversity tries them.
PUBLILIUS SYRUS (C. 100 BC), *Maxims*

Treat your friend as if he might become an enemy.
PUBLILIUS SYRUS (C. 100 BC), *Maxims*

Friends are as companions on a journey, who ought to aid each other to persevere on the road to a happier life.
PYTHAGORAS (C. 582–500 BC)

We learn our virtues from our friends who love us; our faults from the enemy who hates us. We cannot easily discover our real character from a friend. He is a mirror, on which the warmth of our breath impedes the clearness of the reflection.
JEAN PAUL RICHTER (1763–1825)

I would rather have a million friends than a million dollars.
EDWARD VERNON RICKENBACKER (1890–1973)

Friendship with one's self is all important, because without it one cannot be friends with anyone else in the world.
ELEANOR ROOSEVELT (1884–1962)

Many people will walk in and out of your life, but only true friends will leave footprints in your heart.
ELEANOR ROOSEVELT (1884–1962)

Reveal not every secret you have to a friend, for how can you tell but that friend may hereafter become an enemy. And bring not all mischief you are able to upon an enemy, for he may one day become your friend.
SAADI (1184–1291)

The friend within the man is that part of him which belongs to you and opens to you a door which never, perhaps, is opened to another. Such a friend is true, and all he says is true; and he loves you even if he hates you in other mansions of his heart.
ANTOINE DE SAINT-EXUPÉRY (1900–1944)

The tender friendships one gives up, on parting, leave their bite on the heart, but also a curious feeling of a treasure somewhere buried.
ANTOINE DE SAINT-EXUPÉRY (1900–1944)

To like and dislike the same things, that is indeed true friendship.
SALLUST (86–34 BC), *The War with Catiline*

Friendship is almost always the union of a part of one mind with the part of another; people are friends in spots.
GEORGE SANTAYANA (1863–1952)

Friends need not agree in everything or go always together, or have no comparable other friendships of the same intimacy. On the contrary, in friendship union is more about ideal things: and in that sense it is more ideal and less subject to trouble than marriage is.
GEORGE SANTAYANA (1863–1952)

One's friends are that part of the human race with which one can be human.
GEORGE SANTAYANA (1863–1952)

Though friendship is not quick to burn, it is explosive stuff.
MAY SARTON (1912–1995)

One of the most beautiful qualities of true friendship is to understand and to be understood.
SENECA (5 BC–AD 65)

The comfort of having a friend may be taken away—but not that of having had one.
SENECA (5 BC–AD 65)

True friendship is never serene.
MARQUISE DE SÉVIGNÉ (1626–1696)

We are advertis'd by our loving friends.
WILLIAM SHAKESPEARE (1564–1616), *King Henry VI*

Get not your friends by bare compliments, but by giving them sensible tokens of your love.
SOCRATES (469–399 BC)

No distance of place or lapse of time can lessen the friendship of those who are throughout persuaded of each other's worth.
ROBERT SOUTHEY (1774–1843)

The loss of a friend is like that of a limb; time may heal the anguish of the wound, but the loss cannot be repaired.
ROBERT SOUTHEY (1774–1843)

Friendship is one of the sweetest joys of life. Many might have failed beneath the bitterness of their trial had they not found a friend.
CHARLES H. SPURGEON (1834–1892)

No man is useless while he has a friend.
ROBERT LOUIS STEVENSON (1850–1894)

Of what shall a man be proud, if he is not proud of his friends?
ROBERT LOUIS STEVENSON (1850–1894)

We are all travellers in the wilderness of this world, and the best we can find in our travels is an honest friend.
ROBERT LOUIS STEVENSON (1850–1894)

The essence of true friendship is to make allowances for another's little lapses.
DAVID STOREY (1933–)

The ideal friendship is to feel as one while remaining two.
ANNE-SOPHIE SWETCHINE (1782–1857)

Friends make life a lot more fun.
CHARLES R. SWINDOLL (1934–)

I cannot even imagine where I would be today were it not for that handful of friends who have given me a heart full of joy.
CHARLES R. SWINDOLL (1934–)

Depth of friendship does not depend on length of acquaintance.
RABINDRANATH TAGORE (1861–1941)

Never refuse any advance of friendship, for if nine out of ten bring you nothing, one alone may repay you.
MADAME DE TENCIN (1682–1749)

No birth certificate is issued when friendship is born. There is nothing tangible. There is just a feeling that your life is different and that your capacity to love and care has miraculously been enlarged without any effort on your part.
STEVE TESICH (1942–1996)

Friendship is the source of the greatest pleasures, and without friends, even the most agreeable pursuits become tedious.
SAINT THOMAS AQUINAS (1225–1274)

There is nothing on this earth more to be prized than true friendship.
SAINT THOMAS AQUINAS (1225–1274)

A friend is one who takes me for what I am.
HENRY DAVID THOREAU (1817–1862)

The language of friendship is not words but meanings.
HENRY DAVID THOREAU (1817–1862)

We secure our friends not by accepting favors but by doing them.
THUCYDIDES (C. 460–395 BC)

Nothing but heaven itself is better than a friend who is really a friend.
TITUS MACCIUS PLAUTUS (254–184 BC)

Where there are friends, there is wealth.
TITUS MACCIUS PLAUTUS (254–184 BC)

Indeed, we do not really live unless we have friends surrounding us like a firm wall against the winds of the world.
CHARLES HANSON TOWNE (1877–1949)

The holy passion of Friendship is of so sweet and steady and loyal and enduring a nature that it will last through a whole lifetime, if not asked to lend money.
MARK TWAIN (1835–1910)

The proper office of a friend is to side with you when you are wrong. Nearly anybody will side with you when you are right.
MARK TWAIN (1835–1910)

A friend is what the heart needs all the time.
HENRY VAN DYKE (1852–1933)

A true friend knows your weaknesses but shows you your strengths; feels your fears but fortifies your faith; sees your anxieties but frees your spirit; recognizes your disabilities but emphasizes your possibilities.
WILLIAM ARTHUR WARD (1921–1994)

One discovers a friend by chance, and cannot but feel regret that 20 or 30 years of life may have been spent without the least knowledge of him.
CHARLES DUDLEY WARNER (1829–1900)

Associate yourself with men of good quality if you esteem your own reputation for 'tis better to be alone than in bad company.
GEORGE WASHINGTON (1732–1799)

Be courteous to all, but intimate with few, and let those few be well tried before you give them your confidence. True friendship is a plant of slow growth, and must undergo and withstand the shocks of adversity before it is entitled to the appellation.
GEORGE WASHINGTON (1732–1799)

We cherish our friends not for their ability to amuse us, but for ours to amuse them.
EVELYN WAUGH (1903–1966)

There was a definite process by which one made people into friends, and it involved talking to them and listening to them for hours at a time.
REBECCA WEST (1892–1983)

There is one friend in the life of each of us who seems not a separate person, however dear and beloved, but an expansion, an interpretation, of one's self, the very meaning of one's soul.
EDITH WHARTON (1862–1937)

I no doubt deserved my enemies, but I don't believe I deserved my friends.
WALT WHITMAN (1819–1892)

Anyone can sympathize with the sufferings of a friend, but it requires a very fine nature to sympathize with a friend's success.
OSCAR WILDE (1854–1900)

I always like to know everything about my new friends, and nothing about my old ones.
OSCAR WILDE (1854–1900)

Friendship is the only cement that will ever hold the world together.
WOODROW WILSON (1856–1924)

You cannot be friends upon any other terms than upon the terms of equality.
WOODROW WILSON (1856–1924)

Our friends should be companions who inspire us, who help us rise to our best.
JOSEPH B. WIRTHLIN (1917–)

A good friend is a connection to life—a tie to the past, a road to the future, the key to sanity in a totally insane world.
LOIS WYSE (1926–2007)

Winning has always meant much to me, but winning friends has meant the most.
BABE DIDRIKSON ZAHARIAS (1911–1956)

Before borrowing money from a friend, decide which you need most.
AMERICAN PROVERB

A friend accepts us as we are yet helps us to be what we should.
ANONYMOUS

A friend comes to mind with a smile and memories of a sweet fragrance, like a rose pressed in the pages of a favorite book.
ANONYMOUS

A friend is a feeling of forever in the heart.
ANONYMOUS

A good friend is cheaper than therapy.
ANONYMOUS

A real friend is someone who would feel lost if you jumped on a train or in front of one.
ANONYMOUS

A true friend reaches for your hand and touches your heart.
ANONYMOUS

Don't walk behind me, I may not lead. Don't walk in front of me, I may not follow. Just walk beside me and be my friend.
ANONYMOUS

Friends are the ones who lift us from our feet when our wings forget how to fly.
ANONYMOUS

Friends are those rare people who ask how you are and then wait for the answer.
ANONYMOUS

Friendship is a living thing that lasts only as long as it is nourished with kindness, empathy, and understanding.
ANONYMOUS

Friendship isn't a big thing. It's a million little things.
ANONYMOUS

It is by chance we met; by choice we became friends.
ANONYMOUS

Make new friends, but keep the old; one is silver, and the other's gold.
ANONYMOUS

One who looks for a friend without faults will have none.
ANONYMOUS

The best rule of friendship is to keep your heart a little softer than your head.
ANONYMOUS

True friendship is seen through the heart not through the eyes.
ANONYMOUS

Greater love has no one than this, that he lay down his life for his friends.
THE BIBLE, John 15:13

With true friends … even water drunk together is sweet enough.
CHINESE PROVERB

Do not protect yourself by a fence, but rather by your friends.
CZECH PROVERB

The road to a friend's house is never long.
DANISH PROVERB

When the character of a man is not clear to you, look at his friends.
JAPANESE PROVERB

Who finds a faithful friend, finds a treasure.
JEWISH PROVERB

A friend in need is a friend indeed.
LATIN PROVERB

Hold a true friend with both your hands.
NIGERIAN PROVERB

Be slow in choosing a friend, but slower in changing him.
SCOTTISH PROVERB

Fruit

Life … is like a grapefruit. It's orange and squishy, and has a few pips in it, and some folks have half a one for breakfast.
DOUGLAS ADAMS (1952–2001)

I value my garden more for being full of blackbirds than of cherries, and very frankly give them fruit for their songs.
JOSEPH ADDISON (1672–1719), *The Spectator*

Patience is bitter, but its fruit is sweet.
ARISTOTLE (384–322 BC)

A mind without instruction can no more bear fruit than can a field, however fertile, without cultivation.
CICERO (106–43 BC)

Nature magically suits a man to his fortunes, by making them the fruit of his character.
RALPH WALDO EMERSON (1803–1882)

One that would have the fruit must climb the tree.
THOMAS FULLER (1608–1661)

I have always found that mercy bears richer fruits than strict justice.
ABRAHAM LINCOLN (1809–1865)

Time flies like an arrow. Fruit flies like a banana.
GROUCHO MARX (1890–1977)

The trees that are slow to grow bear the best fruit.
MOLIÈRE (1622–1673)

He that climbs the tall tree has won right to the fruit.
SIR WALTER SCOTT (1771–1832)

Live each season as it passes; breathe the air, drink the drink, taste the fruit, and resign yourself to the influences of each.
HENRY DAVID THOREAU (1817–1862), *Walden*

The finest qualities of our nature, like the bloom on fruits, can be preserved only by the most delicate handling. Yet we do not treat ourselves nor one another thus tenderly.
HENRY DAVID THOREAU (1817–1862), *Walden*

Your descendants shall gather your fruits.
VIRGIL (C. 70–19 BC)

Ignorance is like a delicate exotic fruit; touch it and the bloom is gone.
OSCAR WILDE (1854–1900)

The fruits of all our labors have left us as we started. To grow without is not to grow within.
DAVE WINER (1955–)

If you enjoy the fruit, pluck not the flower.
ANONYMOUS

On action alone be thy interest,
Never on its fruits.
Let not the fruits of action be thy motive,
Nor be thy attachment to inaction.
THE BHAGAVAD GITA

Each tree is recognized by its own fruit. People do not pick figs from thornbushes, or grapes from briers.
THE BIBLE, Luke 6:44

We must learn not to disassociate the airy flower from the earthy root, for the flower that is cut off from its root fades, and its seeds are barren, whereas the root, secure in mother earth, can produce flower after flower and bring their fruit to maturity.
THE KABBALAH

Fun

Fun I love, but too much fun is of all things the most loathsome. Mirth is better than fun, and happiness is better than mirth.
WILLIAM BLAKE (1757–1827)

Fun is about as good a habit as there is.
JIMMY BUFFETT (1946–)

All animals, except man, know that the principal business of life is to enjoy it.
SAMUEL BUTLER (1612–1680)

People rarely succeed unless they have fun in what they are doing.
DALE CARNEGIE (1888–1955)

Horse-play, romping, frequent and loud fits of laughter, jokes, and indiscriminate familiarity, will sink both merit and knowledge into a degree of contempt. They compose at most a merry fellow; and a merry fellow was never yet a respectable man.
LORD CHESTERFIELD (1694–1773)

If you do not feel yourself growing in your work and your life broadening and deepening, if your task is not a perpetual tonic to you, you have not found your place.
ORISON SWETT MARDEN (1850–1924)

Fun is a good thing but only when it spoils nothing better.
GEORGE SANTAYANA (1863–1952)

Funerals

A funeral is a pageant whereby we attest our respect for the dead by enriching the undertaker.
AMBROSE BIERCE (1842–1914)

Worldly faces never look so worldly as at a funeral. They have the same effect of grating incongruity as the sound of a coarse voice breaking the solemn silence of night.
GEORGE ELIOT (1819–1880)

The chief mourner does not always attend the funeral.
RALPH WALDO EMERSON (1803–1882)

They say such nice things about people at their funerals that it makes me sad to realize that I'm going to miss mine by just a few days.
GARRISON KEILLOR (1942–)

Funeral pomp is more for the vanity of the living than for the honor of the dead.
FRANÇOIS DE LA ROCHEFOUCAULD (1613–1680)

Not by lamentations and mournful chants ought we to celebrate the funeral of a good man, but by hymns, for in ceasing to be numbered with mortals he enters upon the heritage of a diviner life.
PLUTARCH (AD 46–120)

Let no one weep for me, or celebrate my funeral with mourning; for I still live, as I pass to and fro through the mouths of men.
QUINTUS ENNIUS (239–169 BC)

You can have money piled to the ceiling but the size of your funeral is still going to depend on the weather.
CHUCK TANNER (1929–)

Where a blood relation sobs, an intimate friend should choke up, a distant acquaintance should sigh, a stranger should merely fumble sympathetically with his handkerchief.
MARK TWAIN (1835–1910)

Why is it that we rejoice at a birth and grieve at a funeral? It is because we are not the person involved.
MARK TWAIN (1835–1910)

Animals have these advantages over man: they never hear the clock strike, they die without any idea of death, they have no theologians to instruct them, their last moments are not disturbed by unwelcome and unpleasant ceremonies, their funerals cost them nothing, and no one starts lawsuits over their wills.
VOLTAIRE (1694–1778)

The Future

The past is a source of knowledge, and the future is a source of hope. Love of the past implies faith in the future.
STEPHEN AMBROSE (1936–2002)

The future ain't what it used to be.
YOGI BERRA (1925–)

The future is an opaque mirror. Anyone who tries to look into it sees nothing but the dim outlines of an old and worried face.
JIM BISHOP (1907–1987)

Prediction is very difficult, especially about the future.
NIELS BOHR (1885–1962)

Every experience God gives us, every person he puts in our lives, is the perfect preparation for the future that only he can see.
CORRIE TEN BOOM (1892–1983)

The empires of the future are the empires of the mind.
SIR WINSTON CHURCHILL (1874–1965)

The world is full of people whose notion of a satisfactory future is, in fact, a return to the idealised past.
ROBERTSON DAVIES (1913–1995), *A Voice from the Attic*

I never think of the future—it comes soon enough.
ALBERT EINSTEIN (1879–1955)

I have seen the future and it doesn't work.
ROBERT FULFORD (1932–)

The future depends on what we do in the present.
MAHATMA GANDHI (1869–1948)

The future is here. It's just not widely distributed yet.
WILLIAM GIBSON (1948–)

You control your future, your destiny. What you think about comes about. By recording your dreams and goals on paper, you set in motion the process of becoming the person you most want to be. Put your future in good hands—your own.
MARK VICTOR HANSEN (1948–)

A preoccupation with the future not only prevents us from seeing the present as it is but often

prompts us to rearrange the past.
ERIC HOFFER (1902–1983), *The Passionate State of Mind*

There is nothing like dream to create the future. Utopia to-day, flesh and blood tomorrow.
VICTOR HUGO (1802–1885), *Les Misérables*

The best way to predict the future is to invent it.
ALAN KAY (1940–)

Never let the future disturb you. You will meet it, if you have to, with the same weapons of reason which today arm you against the present.
MARCUS AURELIUS ANTONINUS (121–180), *Meditations*

Life wouldn't be worth living if I worried over the future as well as the present.
W. SOMERSET MAUGHAM (1874–1965), *Of Human Bondage*

He who controls the present, controls the past. He who controls the past, controls the future.
GEORGE ORWELL (1903–1950)

The future you have tomorrow won't be the same future you had yesterday.
CHUCK PALAHNIUK (1962–)

The present is never our goal: the past and present are our means: the future alone is our goal. Thus, we never live but we hope to live; and always hoping to be happy, it is inevitable that we will never be so.
BLAISE PASCAL (1623–1662)

The future will be better tomorrow.
DAN QUAYLE (1947–)

The future is much like the present, only longer.
DAN QUISENBERRY (1953–1998)

The future belongs to those who believe in the beauty of their dreams.
ELEANOR ROOSEVELT (1884–1962)

The future, according to some scientists, will be exactly like the past, only far more expensive.
JOHN SLADEK (1937–2000)

Without forgiveness, there's no future.
DESMOND TUTU (1931–)

The trouble with our times is that the future is not what it used to be.
PAUL VALÉRY (1871–1945)

In the future everyone will be famous for fifteen minutes.
ANDY WARHOL (1928–1987)

Gambling

Gambling with cards or dice or stocks is all one thing. It's getting money without giving an equivalent for it.
HENRY WARD BEECHER (1813–1887)

The gambling known as business looks with austere disfavor upon the business known as gambling.
AMBROSE BIERCE (1842–1914), *The Devil's Dictionary*

I have a notion that gamblers are as happy as most people, being always excited; women, wine, fame, the table, even ambition, sate now and then, but every turn of the card and cast of the dice keeps the gambler alive—besides one can game ten times longer than one can do anything else.
LORD BYRON (1788–1824)

The world is the house of the strong. I shall not know until the end what I have lost or won in this place, in this vast gambling den where I have spent more than sixty years, dicebox in hand, shaking the dice.
DENIS DIDEROT (1713–1784)

I can't believe that God plays dice with the universe.
ALBERT EINSTEIN (1879–1955)

I like to play blackjack. I'm not addicted to gambling, I'm addicted to sitting in a semi-circle.
MITCH HEDBERG (1968–2005)

Gambling is a disease of barbarians superficially civilized.
WILLIAM RALPH INGE (1860–1954)

Sir, I do not call a gamester a dishonest man; but I call him an unsociable man, an unprofitable man. Gaming is a mode of transferring property without producing any intermediate good.
SAMUEL JOHNSON (1709–1784)

Gambling: The sure way of getting nothing for something.
WILSON MIZNER (1876–1933)

Millions of words are written annually purporting to tell how to beat the races, whereas the best possible advice on the subject is found in the three monosyllables: "Do not try."
DAN PARKER (1781–1844)

You cannot get anything out of nature or from God by gambling; only out of your neighbor.
JOHN RUSKIN (1819–1900)

Gambling promises the poor what property performs for the rich, something for nothing.
GEORGE BERNARD SHAW (1856–1950)

[Gambling] is the child of avarice, the brother of iniquity, and the father of mischief.
GEORGE WASHINGTON (1732–1799)

One should always play fair when one has the winning cards.
OSCAR WILDE (1854–1900)

Rule: Never perform card tricks for the people you play poker with.
ANONYMOUS

The best throw of the dice is to throw them away.
ENGLISH PROVERB

The Garden of Eden

Who loves a garden still his Eden keeps,
Perennial pleasures plants, and wholesome harvest reaps.
AMOS BRONSON ALCOTT (1799–1888)

It gets to seem as if way back in the Garden of Eden after the Fall, Adam and Eve had begged the Lord to forgive them and He, in his boundless exasperation, had said, "All right, then. Stay. Stay in the Garden. Get civilized. Procreate. Muck it up." And they did.
DIANE ARBUS (1923–1971)

There was never such a gigantic lie told as the fable of the Garden of Eden.
HENRY WARD BEECHER (1813–1887)

Relate it to what should happen; fuse it into the long morality play that began, really, in the Garden of Eden.
WILLIAM F. BUCKLEY JR. (1925–)

I've learned a lot about women. I think I've learned exactly how the fall of man occured in the Garden of Eden. Adam and Eve were in the Garden of Eden, and Adam said one day, "Wow, Eve, here we are, at one with nature, at one with God, we'll never age, we'll never die, and all our dreams come true the instant that we have them." And Eve said, "Yeah… it's just not enough is it?"
BILL HICKS (1961–)

She will promise you more
Than the Garden of Eden
Then she'll carelessly cut you
And laugh while you're bleeding.
BILLY JOEL (1949–)

For centuries people have attempted to find the location of the Garden of Eden, placing it in such divergent places as Florida and Babylonia.
WALTER LANG (1913–2004)

[The] unwillingness to admit guilt is traced back to the Garden of Eden. Adam blamed Eve and she blamed the serpent. It is an ingrained trait because of sin.
WALTER LANG (1913–2004)

The male has been persuaded to assume a certain onerous and disagreeable role with the promise of rewards—material and psychological. Women may in the first place even have put it into his head. BE A MAN! may have been, metaphorically, what Eve

uttered at the critical moment in the garden of Eden.
WYNDHAM LEWIS (1882–1957)

The flame from the angel's sword in the garden of Eden has been catalyzed into the atom bomb; God's thunderbolt became blunted, so man's thunderbolt has become the steel star of destruction.
SEAN O'CASEY (1880–1964)

Did perpetual happiness in the Garden of Eden maybe get so boring that eating the apple was justified?
CHUCK PALAHNIUK (1962–)

The LORD God took the man and put him in the Garden of Eden to work it and take care of it.
THE BIBLE, Genesis 2:15

Gardens

Gardening is not a rational act.
MARGARET ATWOOD (1939–)

The glory of gardening: hands in the dirt, head in the sun, heart with nature. To nurture a garden is to feed not just on the body, but the soul.
ALFRED AUSTIN (1835–1913)

Show me your garden and I shall tell you what you are.
ALFRED AUSTIN (1835–1913)

There is no gardening without humility. Nature is constantly sending even its oldest scholars to the bottom of the class for some egregious blunder.
ALFRED AUSTIN (1835–1913)

A garden is half-made when it is well planned. The best gardener is the one who does the most gardening by the winter fire.
LIBERTY HYDE BAILEY (1858–1954)

We learn from our gardens to deal with the most urgent question of the time: How much is enough?
WENDELL BERRY (1934–)

But well-a-day, the gardener careless grew,
The maids and fairies both were kept away,
And in a drought the caterpillars threw
Themselves upon the bud and every spray.
God shield the stock! if Heaven send no supplies,
The fairest blossom of the garden dies.
WILLIAM BROWNE OF TAVISTOCK (1591–1643)

A hundred objective measurements didn't sum the worth of a garden; only the delight of its users did that. Only the use made it mean something.
LOIS MCMASTER BUJOLD (1949–), *A Civil Campaign*

E'vn in the stifling bosom of the town,
A garden, in which nothing thrives, has charms
That soothes the rich possessor; much consol'd,
That here and there some sprigs of mournful mint,
Or nightshade, or valerian, grace the well He
cultivates.
WILLIAM COWPER (1731–1800)

Strength may wield the ponderous spade,
May turn the clod, and wheel the compost home;
But elegance, chief grace the garden shows,
And most attractive, is the fair result
Of thought, the creature of a polished mind.
WILLIAM COWPER (1731–1800)

The more help a man has in his garden, the less it belongs to him.
WILLIAM M. DAVIES (1850–1934)

I don't like formal gardens. I like wild nature. It's just the wilderness instinct in me, I guess.
WALT DISNEY (1901–1966)

How fair is a garden amid the toils and passions of existence.
BENJAMIN DISRAELI (1804–1881)

In green old gardens, hidden away
From sight of revel and sound of strife,
Here I have leisure to breathe and move,
And to do my work in a nobler way;
To sing my songs, and to say my say;
To Dream my dreams, and to love my love;
To hold my faith, and to live my life.
Making the most of its shadowy day.
VIOLET FANE (1843–1905), "Green Old Gardens"

All through the long winter, I dream of my garden. On the first day of spring, I dig my fingers deep into the soft earth. I can feel its energy, and my spirits soar.
HELEN HAYES (1900–1993)

A garden must be looked into, and dressed as the body.
GEORGE HERBERT (1593–1632)

No occupation is so delightful to me as the culture of the earth, and no culture comparable to that of the garden.
THOMAS JEFFERSON (1743–1826)

The love of gardening is a seed once sown that never dies.
GERTRUDE JEKYLL (1843–1932)

All gardening is landscape painting.
WILLIAM KENT (1685–1748)

Where you have a plot of land, however small, plant a garden. Staying close to the soil is good for the soul.
SPENCER W. KIMBALL (1895–1973)

In the garden, Autumn is, indeed the crowning glory of the year, bringing us the fruition of months of thought and care and toil. And at no season, safe perhaps in Daffodil time, do we get such superb colour effects as from August to November.
ROSE G. KINGSLEY (1845–1908), *The Autumn Garden*

Gardens are not made by singing "Oh, how beautiful," and sitting in the shade.
RUDYARD KIPLING (1865–1936)

Cultivate the garden within. What was Paradise? but a garden, an orchard of trees and herbs, full of pleasure and nothing there but delights.
WILLIAM LAWSON (1774–1850)

That God once loved a garden we learn in Holy writ. And seeing gardens in the Spring I well can credit it.
WINIFRED MARY LETTS (1882–1936)

He who makes a garden works hand-in-hand with God.
DOUGLAS MALLOCH (1877–1938)

Gardening is the art that uses flowers and plants as paint, and the soil and sky as canvas.
ELIZABETH MURRAY (1940–)

My garden will never make me famous,
I'm a horticultural ignoramus.
OGDEN NASH (1902–1971)

How often I admire the taste shown in the garden which, within the house, may be indifferent. Here is an art which is today probably more perfect than at any previous time, one which does not break with the past, while it brings a sense of comely order, and a radiant beauty, to cottage and manor alike.
WILLIAM ROTHENSTEIN (1872–1945)

When your heart becomes the grave of your secrets, that desire of yours will be gained more quickly. The prophet said that anyone who keeps secret his inmost thought will soon attain the object of his desire. When seeds are buried in the earth, their inward secrets become the flourishing garden.
MEVLANA RUMI (1207–1273)

Our gardens are symbols of home rather than seduction. Young people with fire in their blood are seldom found in them. The garden is the scene of middle age, of the slow passage from sexual excitement to domestic routine.
ROGER SCRUTON (1944–)

Now 'tis the spring, and weeds are shallow-rooted;
Suffer them now and they'll o'ergrow the garden.
WILLIAM SHAKESPEARE (1564–1616)

The best place to seek God is in a garden. You can dig for him there.
GEORGE BERNARD SHAW (1856–1950)

A vegetable garden in the beginning looks so promising and then after all little by little it grows nothing but vegetables, nothing, nothing but vegetables.
GERTRUDE STEIN (1874–1946)

It is a golden maxim to cultivate the garden for the nose, and the eyes will take care of themselves.
ROBERT LOUIS STEVENSON (1850–1895)

Give me odorous at sunrise a garden of beautiful flowers where I can walk undisturbed.
WALT WHITMAN (1819–1892), *Give Me That Splendid Silent Sun*

A garden is a friend you can visit anytime.
ANONYMOUS

A healthy garden is a reflection of a healthy soul.
ANONYMOUS

Wherever man exists, he finds the need to redesign, to recreate the world. A more beautiful world, purer, sweeter smelling and more colorful. A garden is probably the spot where the hopes for civilization are best captured. In fact, man defines himself by his garden.
ANONYMOUS

More grows in the garden than the gardener knows he has sown.
SPANISH PROVERB

Gender

We are all androgynous, not only because we are all born of a woman impregnated by the seed of a man but because each of us, helplessly and forever, contains the other—male in female, female in male, white in black and black in white. We are a part of each other. Many of my countrymen appear to find this fact exceedingly inconvenient and even unfair, and so, very often, do I. But none of us can do anything about it.
JAMES ARTHUR BALDWIN (1924–1987)

The loss of sex polarity is part and parcel of the larger disintegration, the reflex of the soul's death, and coincident with the disappearance of great men, great deeds, great causes, great wars, etc.
HENRY MILLER (1891–1980)

Different though the sexes are, they inter-mix. In every human being a vacillation from one sex to the other takes place, and often it is only the clothes that keep the male or female likeness, while underneath the sex is very opposite of what it is above.
VIRGINIA WOOLF (1882–1941)

Generalizations

To generalize is to be an idiot. To particularize is the alone distinction of merit. General knowledge is the knowledge that idiots possess.
WILLIAM BLAKE (1757–1827)

We are more prone to generalize the bad than the good. We assume that the bad is more potent and contagious.
ERIC HOFFER (1902–1983)

Generalization is necessary to the advancement of knowledge; but particularly is indispensable to the creations of the imagination. In proportion as men know more and think more they look less at individuals and more at classes. They therefore make better theories and worse poems.
LORD THOMAS BABBINGTON MACAULAY (1800–1859)

Generals

Generals think war should be waged like the tourneys of the Middle Ages. I have no use for knights; I need revolutionaries.
ADOLF HITLER (1889–1945)

I think with the Romans, that the general of today should be a soldier tomorrow if necessary.
THOMAS JEFFERSON (1743–1826)

The Creator has not thought proper to mark those in the forehead who are of stuff to make good generals. We are first, therefore, to seek them blindfold, and then let them learn the trade at the expense of great losses.
THOMAS JEFFERSON (1743–1826)

Tell me what brand of whiskey that Grant drinks. I would like to send a barrel of it to my other generals.
ABRAHAM LINCOLN (1809–1865)

I made all my generals out of mud.
NAPOLÉON I (1769–1821)

Soldiers generally win battles; generals get credit for them.
NAPOLÉON I (1769–1821)

To a surprising extent the war-lords in shining armor, the apostles of the martial virtues, tend not to die fighting when the time comes. History is full of ignominious getaways by the great and famous.
GEORGE ORWELL (1903–1950)

To conquer the enemy without resorting to war is the most desirable. The highest form of generalship is to conquer the enemy by strategy.
SUN-TZU (C. 544–496 BC)

Dead battles, like dead generals, hold the military mind in their dead grip and Germans, no less than other peoples, prepare for the last war.
BARBARA TUCHMAN (1912–1989)

As for being a General, well, at the age of four with paper hats and wooden swords, we're all Generals. Only some of us never grow out of it.
PETER USTINOV (1921–2004)

Generosity

That's what I consider true generosity. You give your all, and yet you always feel as if it costs you nothing.
SIMONE DE BEAUVOIR (1908–1986)

A really great man is known by three signs … generosity in the design, humanity in the execution, moderation in success.
OTTO VON BISMARCK (1815–1898)

Real generosity toward the future lies in giving all to the present.
ALBERT CAMUS (1913–1960)

Too many have dispensed with generosity in order to practice charity.
ALBERT CAMUS (1913–1960)

To be able under all circumstances to practice five things constitutes perfect virtue; these five things are gravity, generosity of soul, sincerity, earnestness and kindness.
CONFUCIUS (551–479 BC)

He had a certain frankness and generosity, qualities indeed which turn to a man's ruin, unless tempered with discretion.
CORNELIUS TACITUS (AD 55–117)

It is always so pleasant to be generous, though very vexatious to pay debts.
RALPH WALDO EMERSON (1803–1882)

To generous souls every task is noble.
EURIPIDES (C. 480–406 BC)

Lavishness is not generosity.
THOMAS FULLER (1608–1661)

Generosity is giving more than you can, and pride is taking less than you need.
KAHLIL GIBRAN (1883–1931)

Giving is the business of the rich.
JOHANN WOLFGANG VON GOETHE (1749–1832)

The act of nutrition is not a purely physiological event…. The family meal is a formality that cultivates in us … a capacity for sharing, generosity, thoughtfulness, a talent for civilized conversation.
FRANCINE DU PLESSIX GRAY (1930–)

There is sublime thieving in all giving. Someone gives us all he has and we are his.
ERIC HOFFER (1902–1983)

Sir, he throws away his money without thought and without merit. I do not call a tree generous that sheds its fruit at every breeze.
SAMUEL JOHNSON (1709–1784)

Generosity lies less in giving much than in giving at the right moment.
JEAN DE LA BRUYÈRE (1645–1696)

Liberality consists less in giving a great deal than in gifts well-timed.
JEAN DE LA BRUYÈRE (1645–1696)

What is called generosity is usually only the vanity of giving; we enjoy the vanity more than the thing given.
FRANÇOIS DE LA ROCHEFOUCAULD (1613–1680)

Generosity during life is a very different thing from generosity in the hour of death; one proceeds from genuine liberality and benevolence, the other from pride or fear.
HORACE MANN (1796–1859)

Generosity with strings is not generosity; it is a deal.
MARYA MANNES (1904–1990)

Many people are capable of doing a wise thing, more a cunning thing, but very few a generous thing.
ALEXANDER POPE (1688–1744)

Generosity is nothing else than a craze to possess. All which I abandon, all which I give, I enjoy in a higher manner through the fact that I give it away. To give is to enjoy possessively the object which one gives.
JEAN-PAUL SARTRE (1905–1980)

The poor don't know that their function in life is to exercise our generosity.
JEAN-PAUL SARTRE (1905–1980)

He who gives what he would as readily throw away, gives without generosity; for the essence of generosity is in self sacrifice.
HENRY TAYLOR (1800–1886)

Romans, never forget that government is your medium! Be this your art: to practice men in habit of peace, generosity to the conquered, and firmness against aggressors.
VIRGIL (C. 70–19 BC), *Aeneid*

Genius

We know that the nature of genius is to provide idiots with ideas twenty years later.
LOUIS ARAGON (1897–1982)

There is no great genius without a mixture of madness.
ARISTOTLE (384–322 BC)

Geniuses are the luckiest of mortals because what they must do is the same as what they most want to do.
W. H. AUDEN (1907–1973)

Genius is no more than childhood recaptured at will, childhood equipped now with man's physical means to express itself, and with the analytical mind that enables it to bring order into the sum of experience, involuntarily amassed.
CHARLES BAUDELAIRE (1821–1867)

One is not born a genius, one becomes a genius.
SIMONE DE BEAUVOIR (1908–1986)

Genius unexerted is no more genius than a bushel of acorns is a forest of oaks.
HENRY WARD BEECHER (1813–1887)

Talent does what it can; genius does what it must.
SIR EDWARD G. BULWER-LYTTON (1803–1873)

Genius might be described as a supreme capacity for getting its possessors into trouble of all kinds.
SAMUEL BUTLER (1835–1902)

Genius is an infinite capacity for taking pains.
THOMAS CARLYLE (1795–1881)

Genius hath electric power which earth can never tame.
LYDIA M. CHILD (1802–1880)

Genius is of no country.
CHARLES CHURCHILL (1731–1764)

True genius resides in the capacity for evaluation of uncertain, hazardous, and conflicting information.
SIR WINSTON CHURCHILL (1874–1965)

Intelligence recognizes what has happened. Genius recognizes what will happen.
JOHN CIARDI (1916–1986)

He was a genius—that is to say, a man who does superlatively and without obvious effort something that most people cannot do by the uttermost exertion of their abilities.
ROBERTSON DAVIES (1913–1995), *Fifth Business*

Genius is present in every age, but the men carrying it within them remain benumbed unless extraordinary events occur to heat up and melt the mass so that it flows forth.
DENIS DIDEROT (1713–1784)

Genius, when young, is divine.
BENJAMIN DISRAELI (1804–1881)

Patience is a necessary ingredient of genius.
BENJAMIN DISRAELI (1804–1881)

Mediocrity knows nothing higher than itself, but talent instantly recognizes genius.
SIR ARTHUR CONAN DOYLE (1859–1930), *The Valley of Fear*

Great wits are sure to madness near allied,
And thin partitions do their bounds divide.
JOHN DRYDEN (1631–1700)

Time, place, and action may with pains be wrought,
But genius must be born; and never can be taught.
JOHN DRYDEN (1631–1700)

His genius he was quite content in one brief sentence to define;
Of inspiration one percent, of perspiration, ninety nine.
THOMAS A. EDISON (1847–1931)

Genius is one percent inspiration and ninety-nine percent perspiration.
THOMAS A. EDISON (1847–1931)

Genius at first is little more than a great capacity for receiving discipline.
GEORGE ELIOT (1819–1880)

Accept your genius and say what you think.
RALPH WALDO EMERSON (1803–1882)

A man of genius is privileged only as far as he is genius. His dullness is as insupportable as any other dullness.
RALPH WALDO EMERSON (1803–1882)

Coffee is good for talent, but genius wants prayer.
RALPH WALDO EMERSON (1803–1882)

In every work of genius we recognize our own rejected thoughts; they come back to us with a certain alienated majesty.
RALPH WALDO EMERSON (1803–1882)

The greatest genius is the most indebted person.
RALPH WALDO EMERSON (1803–1882)

To believe your own thought, to believe that what is true for you in your private heart is true for all men—that is genius.
RALPH WALDO EMERSON (1803–1882)

When Nature has work to be done, she creates a genius to do it.
RALPH WALDO EMERSON (1803–1882)

Everybody hates a prodigy, detests an old head on young shoulders.
DESIDERIUS ERASMUS (1469–1536)

Genius without education is like silver in the mine.
BENJAMIN FRANKLIN (1706–1790)

Men of genius do not excel in any profession because they labor in it, but they labor in it because they excel.
WILLIAM HAZLITT (1778–1830)

Genius may have its limitations, but stupidity is not thus handicapped.
ELBERT HUBBARD (1856–1915)

Men of lofty genius when they are doing the least work are most active.
LEONARDO DA VINCI (1452–1519)

There's a fine line between genius and insanity. I have erased this line.
OSCAR LEVANT (1906–1972)

Everyone is a genius at least once a year; a real genius has his original ideas closer together.
GEORG LICHTENBERG (1742–1799)

Neither a lofty degree of intelligence nor imagination nor both together go to the making of genius. Love, love, love, that is the soul of genius.
WOLFGANG AMADEUS MOZART (1756–1791)

[T]he fact that some geniuses were laughed at does not imply that all who are laughed at are geniuses. They laughed at Columbus, they laughed at Fulton, they laughed at the Wright brothers. But they also laughed at Bozo the Clown.
CARL SAGAN (1934–1996)

There is no great genius without some touch of madness.
SENECA (5 BC–AD 65), *Epistles*

Genius always gives its best at first; prudence, at last.
SENECA (5 BC–AD 65)

Everyone is born with genius, but most people only keep it a few minutes.
EDGARD VARÈSE (1883–1965)

The public is wonderfully tolerant. It forgives everything except genius.
OSCAR WILDE (1854–1900), *The Critic as Artist*

I have nothing to declare except my genius.
OSCAR WILDE (1854–1900)

Ghosts

Ghosts, like ladies, never speak till spoke to.
RICHARD HARRIS BARHAM (1788–1845)

A ghost is someone who hasn't made it—in other words, who died, and they don't know they're dead. So they keep walking around and thinking that you're inhabiting their—let's say, their domain. So they're aggravated with you.
SYLVIA BROWNE (1943–)

No ghost was ever seen by two pair of eyes.
THOMAS CARLYLE (1795–1881)

But psychoanalysis has taught that the dead—a dead parent, for example—can be more alive for us, more powerful, more scary, than the living. It is the question of ghosts.
JACQUES DERRIDA (1930–2004)

At first cock-crow the ghosts must go
Back to their quiet graves below.
THEODOSIA GARRISON (1874–1944)

Chat to the ghosts! That's what I do!
LEE RYAN (1983–)

Gifts

"Know thyself," said the old philosopher, "improve thyself," saith the new. Our great object in time is not to waste our passions and gifts on the things external that we must leave behind, but that we cultivate within us all that we can carry into the eternal progress beyond.
SIR EDWARD G. BULWER-LYTTON (1803–1873)

The only gift is a portion of thyself.
RALPH WALDO EMERSON (1803–1882)

I care for riches, to make gifts
To friends, or lead a sick man back to health
With ease and plenty. Else small aid is wealth
For daily gladness; once a man be done
With hunger, rich and poor are all as one.
EURIPIDES (C. 480–406 BC), *Electra*

There is no benefit in the gifts of a bad man.
EURIPIDES (C. 480–406 BC)

Purchase not friends by gifts; when thou ceasest to give, such will cease to love.
THOMAS FULLER (1608–1661)

Riches and power are but gifts of blind fate, whereas goodness is the result of one's own merits.
HÉLOÏSE (1098–1164)

The glorious gifts of the gods are not to be cast aside.
HOMER (800–700 BC), *The Iliad*

So it is that the gods do not give all men gifts of grace—neither good looks nor intelligence nor eloquence.
HOMER (800–700 BC), *The Odyssey*

Blessed are they who have the gift of making friends, for it is one of God's best gifts. It involves many things, but above all, the power of going out of one's self, and appreciating whatever is noble and loving in another.
THOMAS HUGHES (1822–1896)

We are all born with wonderful gifts. We use these gifts to express ourselves, to amuse, to strengthen, and to communicate. We begin as children to explore and develop our talents, often unaware that we are unique, that not everyone can do what we're doing!
LYNN JOHNSTON (1947–), *Lynn on Ideas*

Gifts are like hooks.
MARCUS VALERIUS MARTIALIS (AD 40–103)

Gifts, believe me, captivate both men and Gods, Jupiter himself was won over and appeased by gifts.
OVID (43 BC–AD 17)

Anyone can revolt. It is more difficult silently to obey our own inner promptings, and to spend our lives finding sincere and fitting means of expression for our temperament and our gifts.
GEORGES ROUAULT (1871–1958)

There is only one real deprivation, I decided this morning, and that is not to be able to give one's gifts to those one loves most.
MAY SARTON (1912–1995)

A gift consists not in what is done or given, but in the intention of the giver or doer.
SENECA (5 BC–AD 65)

Rich gifts wax poor when givers prove unkind.
WILLIAM SHAKESPEARE (1564–1616), *Hamlet*

We are always too busy for our children; we never give them the time or interest they deserve. We lavish gifts upon them; but the most precious gift, our personal association, which means so much to them, we give grudgingly.
MARK TWAIN (1835–1910)

Whatever it is, I fear Greeks even when they bring gifts.
VIRGIL (C. 70–19 BC), *Aeneid*

Each day provides its own gifts.
AMERICAN PROVERB

Gifts dissolve rocks.
ANONYMOUS

Gifts make their way through stone walls.
ANONYMOUS

Giving

It is in giving that I connect with others, with the world, and with the divine.
ISABEL ALLENDE (1942–)

You try to give away what you want yourself.
LOIS MCMASTER BUJOLD (1949–), *Memory*

We make a living by what we get, we make a life by what we give.
SIR WINSTON CHURCHILL (1874–1965)

If you want to see what children can do, you must stop giving them things.
NORMAN DOUGLAS (1868–1952)

One must be poor to know the luxury of giving.
GEORGE ELIOT (1819–1880)

There is no benefit in the gifts of a bad man.
EURIPIDES (C. 480–406 BC), *Medea*

Purchase not friends by gifts; when thou ceasest to give, such will cease to love.
THOMAS FULLER (1608–1661)

Generosity is giving more than you can, and pride is taking less than you need.
KAHLIL GIBRAN (1883–1931)

The great art of giving consists in this: the gift should cost very little and yet be greatly coveted, so that it may be the more highly appreciated.
BALTASAR GRACIAN (1601–1658)

Do give books—religious or otherwise—for Christmas. They're never fattening, seldom sinful, and permanently personal.
LENORE HERSHEY (1919–1997)

You give before you get.
NAPOLEON HILL (1883–1970)

What a child doesn't receive he can seldom later give.
P. D. JAMES (1920–), *Time to Be in Earnest*

Give what you have. To someone, it may be better than you dare to think.
HENRY WADSWORTH LONGFELLOW (1807–1882)

He doubly benefits the needy who gives quickly.
PUBLILIUS SYRUS (C. 100 BC), *Maxims*

A gift in season is a double favor to the needy.
PUBLILIUS SYRUS (C. 100 BC), *Moral Sayings*

Giving is the secret of a healthy life. Not necessarily money, but whatever a person has of encouragement, sympathy, and understanding.
JOHN D. ROCKEFELLER (1839–1937)

You must give some time to your fellow men. Even if it's a little thing, do something for others—something for which you get no pay but the privilege of doing it.
DR. ALBERT SCHWEITZER (1875–1965)

The spirit in which a thing is given determines that in which the debt is acknowledged; it's the intention, not the face-value of the gift, that's weighed.
SENECA (5 BC–AD 65), *Letters to Lucilius*

We should give as we would receive, cheerfully, quickly, and without hesitation; for there is no grace in a benefit that sticks to the fingers.
SENECA (5 BC–AD 65)

Rich gifts wax poor when givers prove unkind.
WILLIAM SHAKESPEARE (1564–1616), *Hamlet*

The excellence of a gift lies in its appropriateness rather than in its value.
CHARLES DUDLEY WARNER (1829–1900)

Make all you can, save all you can, give all you can.
JOHN WESLEY (1703–1791)

Glory

The object of government in peace and in war is not the glory of rulers or of races, but the happiness of the common man.
LORD WILLIAM BEVERIDGE (1879–1963)

Suicidal glory is the luxury of the irresponsible. We're not giving up. We're waiting for a better opportunity to win.
LOIS MCMASTER BUJOLD (1949–), *Barrayar*

America has never been an empire. We may be the only great power in history that had the chance, and refused—preferring greatness to power and justice to glory.
GEORGE W. BUSH (1946–)

Who tracks the steps of glory to the grave?
LORD BYRON (1788–1824)

Every day you may make progress. Every step may be fruitful. Yet there will stretch out before you an ever-lengthening, ever-ascending, ever-improving path. You know you will never get to the end of the journey. But this, so far from discouraging, only adds to the joy and glory of the climb.
SIR WINSTON CHURCHILL (1874–1965)

In men of the highest character and noblest genius there is to be found an insatiable desire for honour, command, power, and glory.
CICERO (106–43 BC)

Natural ability without education has more often attained to glory and virtue than education without natural ability.
CICERO (106–43 BC)

Our greatest glory is not in never falling, but in getting up every time we do.
CONFUCIUS (551–479 BC)

To win without risk is to triumph without glory.
PIERRE CORNEILLE (1606–1684), *The Cid*

Glory built on selfish principles is shame and guilt.
WILLIAM COWPER (1731–1800)

For glory gives herself only to those who have always dreamed of her.
CHARLES DE GAULLE (1890–1970)

The greater difficulty, the more glory in surmounting it. Skillful pilots gain their reputation from storms and tempests.
EPICURUS (C. 341–270 BC)

I never set out to write a book to change women's lives, to change history. It's like, "Who, me?" Yes, me. I did it. And I'm not that different from other women. Maybe my power and glory was that I could speak my truth as a woman and it was the truth of every woman.
BETTY FRIEDAN (1921–2006)

Glory is largely a theatrical concept. There is no striving for glory without a vivid awareness of an audience.
ERIC HOFFER (1902–1983)

Of men who have a sense of honor, more come through alive than are slain, but from those who flee comes neither glory nor any help.
HOMER (800–700 BC), *The Iliad*

Popularity? It is glory's small change.
VICTOR HUGO (1802–1885)

The glory of great men should always be measured by the means they have used to acquire it.
FRANÇOIS DE LA ROCHEFOUCAULD (1613–1680)

Glory is fleeting, but obscurity is forever.
NAPOLÉON I (1769–1821)

True glory consists in doing what deserves to be written; in writing what deserves to be read; and in so living as to make the world happier for our living in it.
PLINY THE ELDER (AD 23–79)

It is certainly desirable to be well descended, but the glory belongs to our ancestors.
PLUTARCH (AD 46–120), *Morals*

Man: the glory, jest, and riddle of the world.
ALEXANDER POPE (1688–1744)

Glory is like a circle in the water,
Which never ceaseth to enlarge itself,
Till by broad spreading it disperses to naught.
WILLIAM SHAKESPEARE (1564–1616), *Henry VI*

O, how this spring of love resembleth
The uncertain glory of an April day!
WILLIAM SHAKESPEARE (1564–1616), *The Two Gentlemen of Verona*

My poems are hymns of praise to the glory of life.
EDITH SITWELL (1887–1964)

The nearest way to glory is to strive to be what you wish to be thought to be.
SOCRATES (469–399 BC)

Real glory springs from the silent conquest of ourselves.
JOSEPH P. THOMPSON (1937–)

The bravest are surely those who have the clearest vision of what is before them, glory and danger alike, and yet notwithstanding, go out to meet it.
THUCYDIDES (C. 460–395 BC)

The paths of glory at least lead to the grave, but the paths of duty may not get you anywhere.
JAMES THURBER (1894–1961)

And say my glory was I had such friends.
William Butler Yeats (1865–1939)

We rise in glory as we sink in pride.
Edward Young (1683–1765)

True glory lies in noble deeds.
Anonymous

Gray hair is a crown of splendor; it is attained by a righteous life.
The Bible, Proverbs 16:31

Gluttony

In love, as in gluttony, pleasure is a matter of the utmost precision.
Italo Calvino (1923–1985)

Not addicted to gluttony or drunkenness, this people who incur no expense in food or dress, and whose minds are always bent upon the defense of their country, and on the means of plunder, are wholly employed in the care of their horses and furniture.
Giraldus Cambrensis (c. 1146–1220)

Gluttony is an emotional escape, a sign something is eating us.
Peter De Vries (1910–1993)

The flesh endures the storms of the present alone; the mind, those of the past and future as well as the present. Gluttony is a lust of the mind.
Thomas Hobbes (1588–1679)

Gluttony is not a secret vice.
Orson Welles (1915–1985)

Goals

Man is a goal seeking animal. His life only has meaning if he is reaching out and striving for his goals.
Aristotle (384–322 BC)

A man without a goal is like a ship without a rudder.
Thomas Carlyle (1795–1881)

I am doomed to an eternity of compulsive work. No set goal achieved satisfies. Success only breeds a new goal. The golden apple devoured has seeds. It is endless.
Bette Davis (1908–1989), *The Lonely Life*

The person who makes a success of living is the one who sees his goal steadily and aims for it unswervingly. That is dedication.
Cecil B. DeMille (1881–1959)

It is a very high goal which, with our weak powers, we can reach only very inadequately, but which gives a sure foundation to our aspirations and valuations.
Albert Einstein (1879–1955)

A distracted existence leads us to no goal.
Johann Wolfgang von Goethe (1749–1832)

In the absence of clearly-defined goals, we become strangely loyal to performing daily trivia until ultimately we become enslaved by it.
Robert A. Heinlein (1907–1988)

A goal is a dream with a deadline.
Napoleon Hill (1883–1970)

A successful individual typically sets his next goal somewhat but not too much above his last achievement. In this way he steadily raises his level of aspiration.
Kurt Lewin (1890–1947)

We find no real satisfaction or happiness in life without obstacles to conquer and goals to achieve.
Maxwell Maltz (1899–1975)

People with goals succeed because they know where they are going. It's as simple as that.
Earl Nightingale (1921–1989)

Before you begin a thing, remind yourself that difficulties and delays quite impossible to foresee are ahead. If you could see them clearly, naturally you could do a great deal to get rid of them but

you can't. You can only see one thing clearly and that is your goal. Form a mental vision of that and cling to it through thick and thin.
KATHLEEN NORRIS (1880–1966)

Let me tell you the secret that has led me to my goal. My strength lies solely in my tenacity.
LOUIS PASTEUR (1822–1895)

Do not turn back when you are just at the goal.
PUBLILIUS SYRUS (C. 100 BC), *Maxims*

A goal without a plan is just a wish.
ANTOINE DE SAINT-EXUPÉRY (1900–1944)

It is a paradoxical but profoundly true and important principle of life that the most likely way to reach a goal is to be aiming not at that goal itself but at some more ambitious goal beyond it.
ARNOLD J. TOYNBEE (1889–1975)

The goal of life is living in agreement with nature.
ZENO (335–264 BC)

God

The question before the human race is whether the God of nature shall govern the world by His own laws, or whether priests and kings shall rule it by fictitious miracles.
JOHN ADAMS (1735–1826)

This only is denied to God: the power to undo the past.
AGATHON (448–400 BC)

The gods too are fond of a joke.
ARISTOTLE (384–322 BC)

God has been replaced, as he has all over the West, with respectability and air conditioning.
IMAMU AMIRI BARAKA (1934–)

It is the creative potential itself in human beings that is the image of God.
MARY DALY (1928–)

They say that God is everywhere, and yet we always think of Him as somewhat of a recluse.
EMILY DICKINSON (1830–1886)

At any rate, I am convinced that He [God] does not play dice.
ALBERT EINSTEIN (1879–1955)

Before God we are all equally wise—and equally foolish.
ALBERT EINSTEIN (1879–1955)

I cannot imagine a God who rewards and punishes the objects of his creation, whose purposes are modeled after our own—a God, in short, who is but a reflection of human frailty. Neither can I believe that the individual survives the death of his body, although feeble souls harbor such thoughts through fear or ridiculous egotisms.
ALBERT EINSTEIN (1879–1955)

Slow but sure moves the might of the gods.
EURIPIDES (C. 480–406 BC), *The Bacchae*

I could prove God statistically.
GEORGE GALLUP (1901–1984)

God must become an activity in our consciousness.
JOEL S. GOLDSMITH (1892–1964)

God gives every bird its food, but He does not throw it into its nest.
J. G. HOLLAND (1819–1881)

The glorious gifts of the gods are not to be cast aside.
HOMER (800–700 BC), *The Iliad*

Whoever obeys the gods, to him they particularly listen.
HOMER (800–700 BC), *The Iliad*

The gods, likening themselves to all kinds of strangers, go in various disguises from city to city, observing the wrongdoing and the righteousness of men.
HOMER (800–700 BC), *The Odyssey*

Everyone ought to worship God according to his own inclinations, and not to be constrained by force.
JOSEPHUS (AD 37–100), *Life*

What can you say about a society that says that God is dead and Elvis is alive?
IRV KUPCINET (1912–2003)

He who purposely cheats his friend, would cheat his God.
JOHANN KASPAR LAVATER (1741–1801)

Let none turn over books, or roam the stars in quest of God, who sees him not in man.
JOHANN KASPAR LAVATER (1741–1801)

God is only a great imaginative experience.
D. H. LAWRENCE (1885–1930)

God is a concept by which we measure our pain.
JOHN LENNON (1940–1980)

The God of this world is riches, pleasure and pride.
MARTIN LUTHER (1483–1546)

God is the immemorial refuge of the incompetent, the helpless, the miserable. They find not only sanctuary in His arms, but also a kind of superiority, soothing to their macerated egos: He will set them above their betters.
H. L. MENCKEN (1880–1956)

I cannot believe in a God who wants to be praised all the time.
FRIEDRICH NIETZSCHE (1844–1900)

Which is it, is man one of God's blunders or is God one of man's?
FRIEDRICH NIETZSCHE (1844–1900)

All God does is watch us and kill us when we get boring. We must never, ever be boring.
CHUCK PALAHNIUK (1962–), *Invisible Monsters*

We must accept that this creative pulse within us is God's creative pulse itself.
JOSEPH CHILTON PEARCE (1926–)

Men must be governed by God, or they will be ruled by tyrants.
WILLIAM PENN (1644–1718)

God is really only another artist. He invented the giraffe, the elephant, and the cat. He has no real style. He just keeps on trying other things.
PABLO PICASSO (1881–1973)

God is the brave man's hope, and not the coward's excuse.
PLUTARCH (AD 46–120)

God does not play dice with the universe; He plays an ineffable game of his own devising, which might be compared, from the perspective of any of the other players, to being involved in an obscure and complex version of poker in a pitch dark room, with blank cards, for infinite stakes, with a dealer who won't tell you the rules, and who smiles all the time.
TERRY PRATCHETT (1948–), *Good Omens*

Pray as if everything depended upon God and work as if everything depended upon man.
CARDINAL FRANCIS SPELLMAN (1889–1967)

I know God will not give me anything I can't handle. I just wish that He didn't trust me so much.
MOTHER TERESA (1910–1997)

There is one evident, indubitable manifestation of the Divinity, and that is the laws of right which are made known to the world through Revelation.
LEO TOLSTOY (1828–1910)

Think of yourself as an incandescent power, illuminated and perhaps forever talked to by God and his messengers.
BRENDA UELAND (1891–1985)

God is not on the side of the big battalions, but on the side of those who shoot best.
VOLTAIRE (1694–1778)

It is only the impossible that is possible for God. He has given over the possible to the mechanics of matter and the autonomy of his creatures.
SIMONE WEIL (1910–1943)

We can only know one thing about God—that he is what we are not. Our wretchedness alone is an image of this. The more we contemplate it, the more we contemplate him.
SIMONE WEIL (1910–1943)

In the faces of men and women I see God, and in my own face in the glass, I find letters from God dropped in the street, and every one is signed by God's name. And I leave them where they are, for I know that wherever I go, others will punctually come forever and ever.
WALT WHITMAN (1819–1892)

I think that God in creating Man somewhat overestimated his ability.
OSCAR WILDE (1854–1900)

All your Western theologies, the whole mythology of them, are based on the concept of God as a senile delinquent.
TENNESSEE WILLIAMS (1911–1983)

God is not dead but alive and well and working on a much less ambitious project.
ANONYMOUS

Call on God, but row away from the rocks.
INDIAN PROVERB

If God lived on earth, people would break his windows.
JEWISH PROVERB

Gold

Silence is golden when you can't think of a good answer.
MUHAMMAD ALI (1942–), *More Than a Hero*

Recommend to your children virtue; that alone can make them happy, not gold.
LUDWIG VAN BEETHOVEN (1770–1827)

A man that hoards up riches and enjoys them not, is like an ass that carries gold and eats thistles.
SIR RICHARD FRANCIS BURTON (1821–1890)

Do not hold as gold all that shines as gold.
ALAIN DE LILLE (C. 1202), *Parabolae*

Treasure the love you have received above all. It will survive long after your gold and good health have vanished.
OG MANDINO (1923–1996)

They wonder much to hear that gold, which in itself is so useless a thing, should be everywhere so much esteemed, that even men for whom it was made, and by whom it has its value, should yet be thought of less value than it is.
SIR THOMAS MORE (1478–1535), *Utopia*

'Tis better to be lowly born,
And range with humble livers in content,
Than to be perked up in a glistering grief,
And wear a golden sorrow.
WILLIAM SHAKESPEARE (1564–1616), *King Henry VIII*

Gold is worse poison to a man's soul, doing more murders in this loathsome world, than any mortal drug.
WILLIAM SHAKESPEARE (1564–1616) *Romeo and Juliet*

All that is gold does not glitter; not all those that wander are lost.
J. R. R. TOLKIEN (1892–1973), *The Lord of the Rings*

If more of us valued food and cheer and song above hoarded gold, it would be a merrier world.
J. R. R. TOLKIEN (1892–1973)

Truth, like gold, is to be obtained not by its growth, but by washing away from it all that is not gold.
LEO TOLSTOY (1828–1910)

An inch of time cannot be bought with an inch of gold.
CHINESE PROVERB

The Golden Rule

The golden rule is that there are no golden rules.
GEORGE BERNARD SHAW (1856–1950), *Man and Superman*

Practicing the Golden Rule is not a sacrifice; it is an investment.
ANONYMOUS

Golf

Although golf was originally restricted to wealthy, overweight Protestants, today it's open to anybody who owns hideous clothing.
DAVE BARRY (1947–)

Golf is a game whose aim is to hit a very small ball into an even smaller hole, with weapons singularly ill-designed for the purpose.
SIR WINSTON CHURCHILL (1874–1965)

Golf and sex are about the only things you can enjoy without being good at.
JIMMY DEMARET (1910–1983)

If you watch a game, it's fun. If you play at it, it's recreation. If you work at it, it's golf.
BOB HOPE (1903–2003)

It is impossible to imagine Goethe or Beethoven being good at billiards or golf.
H. L. MENCKEN (1880–1956)

The income tax has made more liars out of the American people than golf has.
WILL ROGERS (1879–1935)

The place of the father in the modern suburban family is a very small one, particularly if he plays golf.
BERTRAND RUSSELL (1872–1970)

Golf is a good walk spoiled.
MARK TWAIN (1835–1910)

Hockey is a sport for white men. Basketball is a sport for black men. Golf is a sport for white men dressed like black pimps.
TIGER WOODS (1975–)

Life is a game but golf is serious.
ANONYMOUS

Gossip

We cannot control the evil tongues of others; but a good life enables us to disregard them.
CATO THE ELDER (234–149 BC)

Gossip is what no one claims to like, but everybody enjoys.
JOSEPH CONRAD (1857–1924)

Gossip is a sort of smoke that comes from the dirty tobacco-pipes of those who diffuse it: it proves nothing but the bad taste of the smoker.
GEORGE ELIOT (1819–1880)

There is so much good in the worst of us,
And so much bad in the best of us,
That it hardly behooves any of us
To talk about the rest of us.
EDWARD WALLIS HOCH (1849–1925)

Gossip is always a personal confession of malice or imbecility; it is a low, frivolous, and too often a dirty business. There are neighborhoods where it rages like a pest; churches are split in pieces by it, and neighbors made enemies for life. Let the young avoid or cure it while they may.
JACK HOLLAND (1947–2004)

Avoid inquisitive persons, for they are sure to be gossips, their ears are open to hear, but they will not keep what is entrusted to them.
HORACE (65–8 BC)

Never tell evil of a man, if you do not know it for certainty, and if you know it for a certainty, then ask yourself, "Why should I tell it?"
JOHANN KASPAR LAVATER (1741–1801)

Have I inadvertently said some evil thing?
PHOCION (402–318 BC)

Live in such a way that you would not be ashamed to sell your parrot to the town gossip.
WILL ROGERS (1879–1935)

Rumor travels faster, but it don't stay put as long as truth.
WILL ROGERS (1879–1935)

The only time people dislike gossip is when you gossip about them.
WILL ROGERS (1879–1935)

No one gossips about other people's secret virtues.
BERTRAND RUSSELL (1872–1970)

Ill deeds are doubled with an evil word.
WILLIAM SHAKESPEARE (1564–1616), *The Comedy of Errors*

No sword bites so fiercely as an evil tongue.
SIR PHILIP SIDNEY (1554–1586)

Scandal is gossip made tedious by morality.
OSCAR WILDE (1854–1900), *Lady Windermere's Fan*

May no portent of evil be attached to the words I say.
ANONYMOUS

To harken to evil conversation is the road to wickedness.
ANONYMOUS

Whoever gossips to you will gossip about you.
SPANISH PROVERB

Government

[A] Constitution of Government once changed from Freedom, can never be restored. Liberty, once lost, is lost forever.
JOHN ADAMS (1735–1826)

The essence of a free government consists in an effectual control of rivalries.
JOHN ADAMS (1735–1826)

The only maxim of a free government ought to be to trust no man living with power to endanger the public liberty.
JOHN ADAMS (1735–1826)

We have no government armed with power capable of contending with human passions unbridled by morality and religion. Avarice, ambition, revenge, or gallantry would break the strongest cords of our Constitution as a whale goes through a net. Our Constitution is designed only for a moral and religious people. It is wholly inadequate for any other.
JOHN ADAMS (1735–1826)

The best government rests on the people, and not on the few, on persons and not on property, on the free development of public opinion and not on authority.
GEORGE BANCROFT (1800–1891)

The worst thing in the world next to anarchy, is government.
HENRY WARD BEECHER (1813–1887)

To have a popular government we must, first of all, and before all else, have good citizens.
CHARLES JOSEPH BONAPARTE (1851–1921)

The marvel of all history is the patience with which men and women submit to burdens unnecessarily laid upon them by their governments.
WILLIAM E. BORAH (1865–1940)

Government is too big and too important to be left to the politicians.
CHESTER BOWLES (1901–1986)

Nothing turns out to be so oppressive and unjust as a feeble government.
EDMUND BURKE (1729–1797)

Too bad the only people who know how to run the country are busy driving cabs and cutting hair.
GEORGE BURNS (1896–1996)

You know what's interesting about Washington? It's the kind of place where second-guessing has become second nature.
GEORGE W. BUSH (1946–)

By definition, a government has no conscience. Sometimes it has a policy, but nothing more.
ALBERT CAMUS (1913–1960)

In the long-run every Government is the exact symbol of its People, with their wisdom and unwisdom; we have to say, Like People like Government.
THOMAS CARLYLE (1795–1881)

Thou camest out of thy mother's belly without government, thou hast liv'd hitherto without government, and thou mayst be carried to thy long home without government, when it shall please the Lord. How many people in this world live without government, yet do well enough, and are well look'd upon?
MIGUEL DE CERVANTES (1547–1616)

Many forms of Government have been tried, and will be tried in this world of sin and woe. No one pretends that democracy is perfect or all-wise. Indeed, it has been said that democracy is the worst form of Government except all those others that have been tried from time to time.
SIR WINSTON CHURCHILL (1874–1965)

So they [the Government] go on in strange paradox, decided only to be undecided, resolved to be irresolute, adamant for drift, solid for fluidity, all-powerful to be impotent.
SIR WINSTON CHURCHILL (1874–1965)

Nations it may be have fashioned their Governments, but the Governments have paid them back in the same coin.
JOSEPH CONRAD (1857–1924)

The less government we have the better.
RALPH WALDO EMERSON (1803–1882)

In rivers and bad governments, the lightest things swim at the top.
BENJAMIN FRANKLIN (1706–1790)

You will find that the State is the kind of organization which, though it does big things badly, does small things badly, too.
JOHN KENNETH GALBRAITH (1908–2006)

The best government is that which teaches us to govern ourselves.
JOHANN WOLFGANG VON GOETHE (1749–1832)

Justice is the end of government. It is the end of civil society. It ever has been and ever will be pursued until it be obtained, or until liberty be lost in the pursuit. In a society under the forms of which the stronger faction can readily unite and oppress the weaker, anarchy may as truly be said to reign as in a state of nature, where the weaker individual is not secured against the violence of the stronger; and as, in the latter state, even the individuals are prompted, by the uncertainty of their condition, to submit to a government which may protect the weak as well as themselves; so, in the former state, will the more powerful factions or parties be gradually induced, by a like motive to wish for a government which will protect all parties, the weaker as well as the more powerful.
ALEXANDER HAMILTON (1755–1804)

Nothing is more surprising than the easiness with which the many are governed by the few.
DAVID HUME (1711–1776)

Some men look at constitutions with sanctimonious reverence, and deem them like the ark of the covenant, too sacred to be touched.
THOMAS JEFFERSON (1743–1826), *Resolutions*

My reading of history convinces me that most bad government results from too much government.
THOMAS JEFFERSON (1743–1826)

That government is the strongest of which every man feels himself a part.
THOMAS JEFFERSON (1743–1826)

The natural progress of things is for liberty to yield and government to gain ground.
THOMAS JEFFERSON (1762–1826)

Whenever the people are well informed, they can be trusted with their own government; that whenever things get so far wrong as to attract their notice, they may be relied on to set them to rights.
THOMAS JEFFERSON (1743–1826)

A Government of the people, by the people and for the people, shall not perish from the earth.
ABRAHAM LINCOLN (1809–1865)

Government has no other end, but the preservation of property.
JOHN LOCKE (1632–1704)

A strong government always wars on the superior man. Its regimenting of the inferior goes on too, but is harmless; they can't be made worse. But its enmity to the superior does real damage. Converting a million serfs into slaves merely changes their name, but wrecking one potential Goethe or Darwin may be a capital disaster to the race.
H. L. MENCKEN (1880–1956)

Every decent man is ashamed of the government he lives under.
H. L. MENCKEN (1880–1956)

Good government is that which delivers the citizen from the risk of being done out of his life and property too arbitrarily and violently—one that relieves him sufficiently from the barbaric business of guarding them…
H. L. MENCKEN (1880–1956)

Government is actually the worst failure of civilized man. There has never been a really good one, and even those that are most tolerable are arbitrary, cruel, grasping and unintelligent.
H. L. MENCKEN (1880–1956)

I believe that all government is evil, and that trying to improve it is largely a waste of time.
H. L. MENCKEN (1880–1956)

The government consists of a gang of men exactly like you and me. They have, taking one with another, no special talent for the business of government; they have only a talent for getting and holding office.
H. L. MENCKEN (1880–1956)

The art of government is not to let me grow stale.
NAPOLÉON I (1769–1821)

Sure there are dishonest men in local government. But there are dishonest men in national government too.
RICHARD M. NIXON (1913–1994)

The mystery of government is not how Washington works but how to make it stop.
P. J. O'ROURKE (1947–)

The punishment which the wise suffer, who refuse to take part in government, is to live under the government of worse men.
PLATO (C. 428–348 BC)

Disbelief in magic can force a poor soul into believing in government and business.
TOM ROBBINS (1936–)

I don't make jokes. I just watch the government and report the facts.
WILL ROGERS (1879–1935)

There's no trick to being a humorist when you have the whole government working for you.
WILL ROGERS (1879–1935)

This country has come to feel the same when Congress is in session as when the baby gets hold of a hammer.
WILL ROGERS (1879–1935)

The government is us; we are the government, you and I.
THEODORE ROOSEVELT (1858–1919)

There is something to be said for government by a great aristocracy which has furnished leaders to the nation in peace and war for generations; even a democrat like myself must admit this. But there is absolutely nothing to be said for government by a plutocracy, for government by men very powerful in certain lines and gifted with the "money touch," but with ideals which in their essence are merely those of so many glorified pawnbrokers.
THEODORE ROOSEVELT (1858–1919)

There is no nonsense so errant that it cannot be made the creed of the vast majority by adequate governmental action.
BERTRAND RUSSELL (1872–1970)

No man undertakes a trade he has not learned, even the meanest; yet every one thinks himself sufficiently qualified for the hardest of all trades—that of government.
SOCRATES (469–399 BC)

Every government is run by liars. Nothing they say should be believed.
I. F. STONE (1907–1989)

After two years in Washington, I often long for the realism and sincerity of Hollywood.
FRED THOMPSON (1942–)

[G]overnment in which the majority rule in all cases can not be based on justice, even as far as men understand it.
HENRY DAVID THOREAU (1817–1862), *Civil Disobedience*

That government is best which governs least.
HENRY DAVID THOREAU (1817–1862)

The state has no business in the bedrooms of the nation.
PIERRE TRUDEAU (1919–2000)

Those who want the Government to regulate matters of the mind and spirit are like men who are so afraid of being murdered that they commit suicide to avoid assassination.
HARRY S TRUMAN (1884–1972)

Whenever you have an efficient government you have a dictatorship.
HARRY S TRUMAN (1884–1972)

We have the best government that money can buy.
MARK TWAIN (1835–1910)

It is dangerous to be right when the government is wrong.
VOLTAIRE (1694–1778)

The best government is a benevolent tyranny tempered by an occasional assassination.
VOLTAIRE (1694–1778)

Government is not reason and it is not eloquence. It is force! Like fire it is a dangerous servant and a fearful master. Never for a moment should it be left to irresponsible action.
GEORGE WASHINGTON (1732–1799)

For every action there is an equal and opposite government program.
BOB WELLS (1966–)

Every culture has its distinctive and normal system of government. Yours is democracy, moderated by corruption. Ours is totalitarianism, moderated by assassination.
ANONYMOUS (Russian)

Grace

[G]race is a gift for the fallen.
SAM BEAM (1974–), "An Angry Blade"

Courage and grace are a formidable mixture. The only place to see it is in the bullring.
MARLENE DIETRICH (1901–1992)

No spring nor summer beauty hath such grace as I have seen in one autumnal face.
JOHN DONNE (1572–1631)

Let grace and goodness be the principal loadstone of thy affections. For love which hath ends, will have an end; whereas that which is founded on true virtue, will always continue.
JOHN DRYDEN (1631–1700)

Set all things in their own peculiar place, and know that order is the greatest grace.
JOHN DRYDEN (1631–1700)

Beauty without grace is the hook without the bait.
RALPH WALDO EMERSON (1803–1882)

Grace has been defined as the outward expression of the inward harmony of the soul.
WILLIAM HAZLITT (1778–1830)

Grace is the absence of everything that indicates pain or difficulty, hesitation or incongruity.
WILLIAM HAZLITT (1778–1830)

By "guts" I mean, grace under pressure.
ERNEST HEMINGWAY (1899–1961)

So it is that the gods do not give all men gifts of grace—neither good looks nor intelligence nor eloquence.
HOMER (800–700 BC), *The Odyssey*

Grace is in garments, in movements, in manners; beauty in the nude, and in forms. This is true of bodies; but when we speak of feelings, beauty is in their spirituality, and grace in their moderation.
JOSEPH JOUBERT (1754–1824)

I do not at all understand the mystery of grace—only that it meets us where we are but does not leave us where it found us.
ANNE LAMOTT (1954–)

Grace is to the body, what good manners are to the mind.
FRANÇOIS DE LA ROCHEFOUCAULD (1613–1680)

Gracefulness is to the body what understanding is to the mind.
FRANÇOIS DE LA ROCHEFOUCAULD (1613–1680)

Grace is given to heal the spiritually sick, not to decorate spiritual heroes.
MARTIN LUTHER (1483–1546)

I seek constantly to improve my manners and graces, for they are the sugar to which all are attracted.
OG MANDINO (1923–1996)

God, give us grace to accept with serenity the things that cannot be changed, courage to change the things which should be changed, and the wisdom to distinguish the one from the other.
REINHOLD NIEBUHR (1892–1971)

Grace tried is better than grace, and more than grace; it is glory in its infancy.
SAMUEL RUTHERFORD (1600–1661)

The winds of grace are always blowing, but it is you that must raise your sails.
RABINDRANATH TAGORE (1861–1941)

Rain is grace; rain is the sky condescending to the earth; without rain, there would be no life.
JOHN UPDIKE (1932–)

Grammar

From now on, ending a sentence with a preposition is something up with which I will not put.
SIR WINSTON CHURCHILL (1874–1965)

You can be a little ungrammatical if you come from the right part of the country.
ROBERT FROST (1875–1963)

My attitude toward punctuation is that it ought to be as conventional as possible. The game of golf would lose a good deal if croquet mallets and billiard cues were allowed on the putting green. You ought to be able to show that you can do it a good deal better than anyone else with the regular tools before you have a license to bring in your own improvements.
ERNEST HEMINGWAY (1898–1961)

I never made a mistake in grammar but once in my life and as soon as I done it I seen it.
CARL SANDBURG (1878–1967)

Cut out all these exclamation points. An exclamation point is like laughing at your own joke.
ANONYMOUS

Grandfathers

The Grandfathers had sprinkled fresh soil on the nation's hoop that they had made in there with the red and black roads across it, and all around this little circle of the nation's hoop we saw the prints

of tiny pony hoofs as though the spirit horses had been dancing while we danced.
BLACK ELK (1863–1950)

Our grandfathers had to run, run, run. My generation's out of breath. We ain't running no more.
STOKELY CARMICHAEL (1941–1998)

Not a tenth of us who are in business are doing as well as we could if we merely followed the principles that were known to our grandfathers.
WILLIAM FEATHER (1908–1976)

There are fathers who do not love their children; there is no grandfather who does not adore his grandson.
VICTOR HUGO (1802–1885)

Every generation revolts against its fathers and makes friends with its grandfathers.
LEWIS MUMFORD (1895–1990)

Grandmothers

My grandmother started walking five miles a day when she was sixty. She's ninety-seven now, and we don't know where the hell she is.
ELLEN DEGENERES (1958–)

To reform a man, you must begin with his grandmother.
VICTOR HUGO (1802–1885)

When the grandmothers of today hear the word "Chippendales," they don't necessarily think of chairs.
JEAN KERR (1922–2003)

My grandmother was a very tough woman. She buried three husbands and two of them were just napping.
RITA RUDNER (1955–)

My grandmothers are full of memories
Smelling of soap and onions and wet clay
With veins rolling roughly over quick hands
They have many clean words to say.
My grandmothers were strong.
MARGARET WALKER (1915–1998), "Lineage"

A mother becomes a true grandmother the day she stops noticing the terrible things her children do because she is so enchanted with the wonderful things her grandchildren do.
LOIS WYSE (1926–2007)

My grandmother is over eighty and still doesn't need glasses. Drinks right out of the bottle.
HENRY YOUNGMAN (1906–1998)

Gratitude

Thankfulness is the beginning of gratitude. Gratitude is the completion of thankfulness. Thankfulness may consist merely of words. Gratitude is shown in acts.
HENRI-FRÉDÉRIC AMIEL (1821–1881)

Gratitude is the fairest blossom which springs from the soul.
HENRY WARD BEECHER (1813–1887)

It's a sign of mediocrity when you demonstrate gratitude with moderation.
ROBERTO BENIGNI (1952–)

Gratitude is not only the greatest of virtues, but the parent of all others.
CICERO (106–43 BC), *Pro Plancio*

I awoke this morning with devout thanksgiving for my friends, the old and new.
RALPH WALDO EMERSON (1803–1882)

Maybe the only thing worse than having to give gratitude constantly is having to accept it.
WILLIAM FAULKNER (1897–1962)

Gratitude is born in hearts that take time to count up past mercies.
CHARLES E. JEFFERSON (1860–1937)

Gratitude is merely the secret hope of further favors.
FRANÇOIS DE LA ROCHEFOUCAULD (1613–1680)

Gratitude is the most exquisite form of courtesy.
JACQUES MARITAIN (1882–1973), *Reflections on America*

Gratitude—the meanest and most sniveling attribute in the world.
DOROTHY PARKER (1893–1967)

Gratitude is a duty which ought to be paid, but which none have a right to expect.
JEAN-JACQUES ROUSSEAU (1712–1778)

The more you recognize and express gratitude for the things you have, the more you will have to express gratitude for.
ZIG ZIGLAR (1926–)

Greatness

Great men are true men, the men in whom nature has succeeded. They are not extraordinary—they are in the true order. It is the other species of men who are not what they ought to be.
HENRI-FRÉDÉRIC AMIEL (1821–1881)

No one who has come to true greatness has not felt in some degree that his life belongs to the people, and what God has given them he gives it for mankind.
PHILLIPS BROOKS (1835–1893)

Great men are the guideposts and landmarks in the state.
EDMUND BURKE (1729–1797)

The great must submit to the dominion of prudence and of virtue, or none will long submit to the dominion of the great.
EDMUND BURKE (1729–1797)

Sighing that Nature formed but one such man, and broke the die.
LORD BYRON (1788–1824)

All great deeds and all great thoughts have a ridiculous beginning.
ALBERT CAMUS (1913–1960)

No great man lives in vain. The history of the world is but the biography of great men.
THOMAS CARLYLE (1795–1881)

The difference between Socrates and Jesus? The great conscious and the immeasurably great unconscious.
THOMAS CARLYLE (1795–1881)

Great merit, or great failings, will make you respected or despised; but trifles, little attentions, mere nothings, either done or neglected, will make you either liked or disliked in the general run of the world.
LORD CHESTERFIELD (1694–1773)

There is a great man who makes every man feel small. But the real great man is the man who makes every man feel great.
G. K. CHESTERTON (1874–1936)

Great and good are seldom the same man.
SIR WINSTON CHURCHILL (1874–1965)

It is a melancholy truth that even great men have their poor relations.
CHARLES DICKENS (1812–1870)

A great person is one who affects the minds of their generation.
BENJAMIN DISRAELI (1804–1881)

Man is only truly great when he acts from his passions.
BENJAMIN DISRAELI (1804–1881)

No great thing is created suddenly.
EPICTETUS (AD 50–120)

Great people are they who see that spiritual is stronger than any material force, that thoughts rule the world.
RALPH WALDO EMERSON (1803–1882)

He is great who is what he is from nature, and who never reminds us of others.
RALPH WALDO EMERSON (1803–1882)

No great man ever complains of want of opportunity.
RALPH WALDO EMERSON (1803–1882)

Not he is great who can alter matter, but he who can alter my state of mind.
RALPH WALDO EMERSON (1803–1882)

The essence of greatness is the perception that virtue is enough.
RALPH WALDO EMERSON (1803–1882)

The search after the great men is the dream of youth, and the most serious occupation of manhood.
RALPH WALDO EMERSON (1803–1882)

To be great is to be misunderstood.
RALPH WALDO EMERSON (1803–1882)

There never was a truly great man that was not at the same time truly virtuous.
BENJAMIN FRANKLIN (1706–1790)

No man is truly great who is great only in his lifetime. The test of greatness is the page of history.
WILLIAM HAZLITT (1778–1830)

There would be no great men if there were no little ones.
GEORGE HERBERT (1593–1632)

A great man's greatest good luck is to die at the right time.
ERIC HOFFER (1902–1983)

To have a great man for a friend seems pleasant to those who have never tried it; those who have, fear it.
HORACE (65–8 BC)

There is a sacred horror about everything grand. It is easy to admire mediocrity and hills; but whatever is too lofty, a genius as well as a mountain, an assembly as well as a masterpiece, seen too near, is appalling.
VICTOR HUGO (1802–1885)

He was dull in a new way, and that made many think him great.
SAMUEL JOHNSON (1709–1784)

The superiority of some men is merely local. They are great because their associates are little.
SAMUEL JOHNSON (1709–1784)

Everybody can be great … because anybody can serve. You don't have to have a college degree to serve. You don't have to make your subject and verb agree to serve. You only need a heart full of grace. A soul generated by love.
MARTIN LUTHER KING JR. (1929–1968)

A position of eminence makes a great person greater and a small person less.
JEAN DE LA BRUYÈRE (1645–1696)

False greatness is unsociable and remote: conscious of its own frailty, it hides, or at least averts its face, and reveals itself only enough to create an illusion and not be recognized as the meanness that it really is. True greatness is free, kind, familiar and popular; it lets itself be touched and handled, it loses nothing by being seen at close quarters; the better one knows it, the more one admires it.
JEAN DE LA BRUYÈRE (1645–1696)

Neither wealth or greatness render us happy.
JEAN DE LA FONTAINE (1621–1695)

To achieve greatness one should live as if they will never die.
FRANÇOIS DE LA ROCHEFOUCAULD (1613–1680)

There are people who possess not so much genius as a certain talent for perceiving the desires of the century, or even of the decade, before it has done so itself.
GEORG C. LICHTENBERG (1742–1799)

Whatever you are, be a good one.
ABRAHAM LINCOLN (1809–1865)

The world isn't kept running because it's a paying proposition. (God doesn't make a cent on the deal.) The world goes on because a few men in every generation believe in it utterly, accept it

unquestioningly; they underwrite it with their lives.
HENRY MILLER (1891–1980)

Great people are meteors designed to burn so that the earth may be lighted.
NAPOLÉON I (1769–1821)

Greatness be nothing unless it be lasting.
NAPOLÉON I (1769–1821)

The herd seek out the great, not for their sake but for their influence; and the great welcome them out of vanity or need.
NAPOLÉON I (1769–1821)

Those who intend on becoming great should love neither themselves or their own things, but only what is just, whether it happens to be done by themselves or others.
PLATO (C. 428–348 BC)

Great men never make bad use of their superiority. They see it and feel it and are not less modest. The more they have, the more they know their own deficiencies.
JEAN-JACQUES ROUSSEAU (1712–1778)

A great thing can only be done by a great person; and they do it without effort.
JOHN RUSKIN (1819–1900)

Great men are like eagles, and build their nest on some lofty solitude.
ARTHUR SCHOPENHAUER (1788–1860)

It is the nature of man to rise to greatness if greatness is expected of him.
JOHN STEINBECK (1902–1968)

The Great Depression

No one can possibly have lived through the Great Depression without being scarred by it. No amount of experience since the depression can convince someone who has lived through it that the world is safe economically.
ISAAC ASIMOV (1920–1992)

The Great Depression, like most other periods of severe unemployment, was produced by government mismanagement rather than by any inherent instability of the private economy.
MILTON FRIEDMAN (1912–2006)

During the Depression, people were getting evicted, ten a day. We used to come along and break the lock and put the furniture back in again.
AL LEWIS (1910–2006)

We're the middle children of history, man. No purpose or place. We have no Great War. No Great Depression. Our Great War's a spiritual war … our Great Depression is our lives.
CHUCK PALAHNIUK (1962–), *Fight Club*

I'm really glad that our young people missed the Depression, and missed the great big war. But I do regret that they missed the leaders that I knew. Leaders who told us when things were tough, and that we would have to sacrifice, and these difficulties might last awhile. They didn't tell us things were hard for us because we were different, or isolated, or special interests. They brought us together and they gave us a sense of national purpose.
ANN RICHARDS (1933–2006)

Greed

Do not follow vain desires; for verily he who prospers is preserved from lust, greed, and anger.
ABU BAKR (C. 573–634)

The ignorant mind, with its infinite afflictions, passions, and evils, is rooted in the three poisons. Greed, anger, and delusion.
BODHIDHARMA (470–543)

Greed, like the love of comfort, is a kind of fear.
CYRIL CONNOLLY (1903–1974)

The discovery of America was the occasion of the greatest outburst of cruelty and reckless greed known in history.
JOSEPH CONRAD (1857–1924)

It is partly to avoid consciousness of greed that we prefer to associate with those who are at least as greedy as we ourselves. Those who consume much less are a reproach.
CHARLES HORTON COOLEY (1864–1929)

Greed is a bottomless pit which exhausts the person in an endless effort to satisfy the need without ever reaching satisfaction.
ERICH FROMM (1900–1980)

Greed and globalization aren't just America's fault.
ARLO GUTHRIE (1947–)

Seek not happiness too greedily, and be not fearful of happiness.
LAO-TZU (C. 600 BC)

Greed has taken the whole universe, and nobody is worried about their soul.
LITTLE RICHARD (1932–)

The main source of our wealth is goodness. The affections and the generous qualities that God admires in a world full of greed.
ALFRED A. MONTAPERT (1906–)

The chief weapon of sea pirates … was their capacity to astonish. Nobody else could believe, until it was too late, how heartless and greedy they were.
KURT VONNEGUT JR. (1922–2007), *Breakfast of Champions*

One of the weaknesses of our age is our apparent inability to distinguish our need from our greed.
ANONYMOUS

We are born brave, trusting and greedy, and most of us remain greedy.
ANONYMOUS

Greedy eaters dig their graves with their teeth.
FRENCH PROVERB

Grief

Grief is the agony of an instant, the indulgence of grief the blunder of a life.
BENJAMIN DISRAELI (1804–1881)

He is a wise man who does not grieve for the things which he has not, but rejoices for those which he has.
EPICURUS (341–270 BC)

Waste not fresh tears over old griefs.
EURIPIDES (C. 480–406 BC)

Even his griefs are a joy long after to one that remembers all that he wrought and endured.
HOMER (800–700 BC), *The Odyssey*

While grief is fresh, every attempt to divert only irritates. You must wait till it be digested, and then amusement will dissipate the remains of it.
SAMUEL JOHNSON (1709–1784)

The only cure for grief is action.
GEORGE HENRY LEWES (1817–1878)

[W]hat's gone and what's past help
Should be past grief…
WILLIAM SHAKESPEARE, *The Winter's Tale*

Grief teaches the steadiest minds to waver.
SOPHOCLES (496–406 BC), *Antigone*

The greatest griefs are those we cause ourselves.
SOPHOCLES (496–406 BC), *Oedipus Rex*

It is light grief that can take counsel.
ANONYMOUS

Growth

If we don't change, we don't grow. If we don't grow, we aren't really living.
ANATOLE FRANCE (1844–1924)

Strength and growth come only through continuous effort and struggle…
NAPOLEON HILL (1883–1970)

The minute a man ceases to grow, no matter what his years, that minute he begins to be old.
WILLIAM JAMES (1842–1910)

You will either step forward into growth or you will step back into safety.
ABRAHAM MASLOW (1908–1970)

All growth is a leap in the dark, a spontaneous, unpremeditated act without benefit of experience.
HENRY MILLER (1891–1980)

Be not afraid of growing slowly. Be afraid only of standing still.
CHINESE PROVERB

Guilt

If all the world hated you and believed you wicked, while your own conscience approved of you and absolved you from guilt, you would not be without friends.
CHARLOTTE BRONTË (1816–1855), *Jane Eyre*

Glory built on selfish principles is shame and guilt.
WILLIAM COWPER (1731–1800)

Short is the joy that guilty pleasure brings.
EURIPIDES (C. 480–406 BC)

Peace visits not the guilty mind.
JUVENAL (AD 55–127)

There is no calamity greater than lavish desires. There is no greater guilt than discontentment. And there is no greater disaster than greed.
LAO-TZU (C. 600 BC), *The Way of Lao-tzu*

Guilt is a rope that wears thin.
AYN RAND (1905–1982)

Fear is the tax that conscience pays to guilt.
GEORGE SEWELL (1924–2007)

So full of artless jealousy is guilt,
It spills itself in fearing to be spilt.
WILLIAM SHAKESPEARE (1564–1616), *Hamlet*

Suspicion always haunts the guilty mind.
WILLIAM SHAKESPEARE (1564–1616), *King Henry IV*

Nothing is more wretched than the mind of a man conscious of guilt.
TITUS MACCIUS PLAUTUS (254–184 BC)

Every man is guilty of all the good he didn't do.
VOLTAIRE (1694–1778)

Whoever destroys a single life is as guilty as though he had destroyed the entire world; and whoever rescues a single life earns as much merit as though he had rescued the entire world.
THE TALMUD

Guns

Guns are evil! And very little good comes from the availability of a bullet designed to kill human beings!
MACKENZIE ASTIN (1973–)

Gun control means being able to hit your target. If I have a "hot button" issue, this is definitely it. Don't even think about taking my guns. My rights are not negotiable, and I am totally unwilling to compromise when it comes to the Second Amendment.
MICHAEL BADNARIK (1954–)

I don't shoot guns. I don't know how to do that. I grew up in Upstate New York, so I fought with my fists.
JIMMY FALLON (1974–)

Banning guns addresses a fundamental right of all Americans to feel safe.
DIANNE FEINSTEIN (1933–)

Guns will make us powerful; butter will only make us fat.
HERMANN GOERING (1893–1946)

Guns are neat little things, aren't they? They can kill extraordinary people with very little effort.
JOHN W. HINCKLEY JR. (1955–)

Guns don't kill people, people kill people, and monkeys do too (if they have a gun).
EDDIE IZZARD (1962–)

Giving kids a gun and feeling confident they're not going to go near it, this is a way for the NRA to make sure they have people purchasing guns.
NITA LOWEY (1937–)

[T]he guns were there to help capture the imagination of the people. But more important, since we knew that you couldn't observe the police without guns, we took our guns with us to let the police know that we have an equalizer.
BOBBY SEALE (1936–)

Habits

We are what we repeatedly do. Excellence, then, is not an act, but a habit.
ARISTOTLE (384–322 BC)

Curious things, habits. People themselves never knew they had them.
AGATHA CHRISTIE (1890–1976)

Great is the power of habit. It teaches us to bear fatigue and to despise wounds and pain.
CICERO (106–43 BC)

Our character is basically a composite of our habits. Because they are consistent, often unconscious patterns, they constantly, daily, express our character.
STEPHEN R. COVEY (1932–)

My problem lies in reconciling my gross habits with my net income.
ERROL FLYNN (1909–1959)

Each year one vicious habit rooted out, in time might make the worst man good throughout.
BENJAMIN FRANKLIN (1706–1790)

Cultivate only the habits that you are willing should master you.
ELBERT HUBBARD (1856–1915)

Habit converts luxurious enjoyments into dull and daily necessities.
ALDOUS HUXLEY (1894–1963)

The chains of habit are too weak to be felt until they are too strong to be broken.
SAMUEL JOHNSON (1709–1784)

Habit and routine have an unbelievable power to waste and destroy.
HENRI DE LUBAC (1896–1991)

Habit is a cable; we weave a thread of it every day, and at last we cannot break it.
HORACE MANN (1796–1859)

Nothing is stronger than habit.
OVID (43 BC–AD 17), *Ars Amatoria*

Character is long-standing habit.
PLUTARCH (AD 46–120)

Habit is stronger than reason
GEORGE SANTAYANA (1863–1952)

How use doth breed a habit in a man!
WILLIAM SHAKESPEARE (1564–1616), *The Two Gentlemen of Verona*

Habit is habit and not to be flung out of the window by any man, but coaxed downstairs a step at a time.
MARK TWAIN (1835–1910)

Bad habits are like a comfortable bed, easy to get into, but hard to get out of.
ANONYMOUS

Good habits result from resisting temptation.
ANONYMOUS

Habits are cobwebs at first; cables at last.
CHINESE PROVERBS

A nail is driven out by another nail; habit is overcome by habit.
LATIN PROVERB

Hair

Too bad the only people who know how to run the country are busy driving cabs and cutting hair.
GEORGE BURNS (1896–1996)

For three days after death hair and fingernails continue to grow but phone calls taper off.
JOHNNY CARSON (1925–2005)

Nancy Reagan fell down and broke her hair.
JOHNNY CARSON (1925–2005)

Gray hair is God's graffiti.
BILL COSBY (1937–)

And forget not that the earth delights to feel your bare feet and the winds long to play with your hair.
KAHLIL GIBRAN (1883–1931)

It is not white hair that engenders wisdom.
MENANDER (342–292 BC)

Some of the worst mistakes of my life have been haircuts.
JIM MORRISON (1943–1971), *No One Here Gets Out Alive*

[Long hair] is considered bohemian, which may be why I grew it, but I keep it long because I love the way it feels, part cloak, part fan, part mane, part security blanket.
MARGE PIERCY (1936–)

I get a lot of cracks about my hair, mostly from men who don't have any.
ANN RICHARDS (1933–2006)

You do not lament the loss of hair of one who has been beheaded.
JOSEPH STALIN (1879–1953)

But Jacob said, "My son will not go down there with you; his brother is dead and he is the only one left. If harm comes to him on the journey you are taking, you will bring my gray head down to the grave in sorrow."
THE BIBLE, Genesis 42:38

And even the very hairs of your head are all numbered.
THE BIBLE, Matthew 10:30

A hair on the head is worth two on the brush.
IRISH PROVERB

Happiness

Friendship improves happiness, and abates misery, by doubling our joys, and dividing our grief.
JOSEPH ADDISON (1672–1719)

True happiness is of a retired nature, and an enemy to pomp and noise; it arises, in the first place, from the enjoyment of one's self, and in the next from the friendship and conversation of a few select companions.
JOSEPH ADDISON (1672–1719)

Now and then it's good to pause in our pursuit of happiness and just be happy.
GUILLAUME APOLLINAIRE (1880–1918)

Happiness depends upon ourselves.
ARISTOTLE (384–322 BC)

Happiness is an expression of the soul in considered actions.
ARISTOTLE (384–322 BC)

Happiness, n.: An agreeable sensation arising from contemplating the misery of another.
AMBROSE BIERCE (1842–1914), *The Devil's Dictionary*

Laughing is the sensation of feeling good all over and showing it principally in one spot.
JOSH BILLINGS (1818–1885)

The world's literature and folklore are full of stories that point out how futile it can be to seek happiness. Rather, happiness is a blessing that comes to you as you go along; a treasure that you incidentally find.
LOUIS BINSTOCK (1896–1974)

I cannot believe that the inscrutable universe turns on an axis of suffering; surely the strange beauty of the world must somewhere rest on pure joy!
LOUISE BOGAN (1897–1970)

Always remember to forget the things that made you sad, but never forget to remember the things that made you glad.
VICTOR BORGE (1909–2000)

The discovery of a new dish does more for human happiness than the discovery of a new star.
ANTHELME BRILLAT-SAVARIN (1755–1826), *Physiologie du Gout*

One of the keys to happiness is a bad memory.
RITA MAE BROWN (1944–)

Happiness is having a large, loving, caring, close-knit family in another city.
GEORGE BURNS (1896–1996)

In order for people to be happy, sometimes they have to take risks. It's true these risks can put them in danger of being hurt.
MEG CABOT (1967–), *The Boy Next Door*

Slow down and enjoy life. It's not only the scenery you miss by going too fast—you also miss the sense of where you are going and why.
EDDIE CANTOR (1892–1964)

The only true happiness comes from squandering ourselves for a purpose.
WILLIAM COWPER (1731–1800)

Happiness is always a by-product. It is probably a matter of temperament, and for anything I know it may be glandular. But it is not something that can be demanded from life, and if you are not happy you had better stop worrying about it and see what treasures you can pluck from your own brand of unhappiness.
ROBERTSON DAVIES (1913–1995)

Happiness resides not in possessions, and not in gold, happiness dwells in the soul.
DEMOCRITUS (460–370 BC)

It is only a poor sort of happiness that could ever come by caring very much about our own pleasures. We can only have the highest happiness such as goes along with being a great man, by having wide thoughts and much feeling for the rest of the world as well as ourselves.
GEORGE ELIOT (1819–1880)

Happiness is a perfume which you cannot pour on someone without getting some on yourself.
RALPH WALDO EMERSON (1803–1882)

If we cannot live so as to be happy, let us at least live so as to deserve it.
IMMANUEL HERMANN FICHTE (1797–1879)

To be stupid, selfish, and have good health are three requirements for happiness, though if stupidity is lacking, all is lost.
GUSTAVE FLAUBERT (1821–1880)

A great obstacle to happiness is the expectation of too great a happiness.
FONTENELLE (1657–1757)

A person is never happy except at the price of some ignorance.
ANATOLE FRANCE (1844–1924)

We all live with the objective of being happy, our lives are all different and yet the same.
ANNE FRANK (1929–1945)

Happiness makes up in height for what it lacks in length.
ROBERT FROST (1874–1963)

Happiness is when what you think, what you say, and what you do are in harmony.
MAHATMA GANDHI (1869–1948)

Remember that happiness is a way of travel—not a destination.
ROY M. GOODMAN (1930–)

Happiness is as a butterfly which, when pursued, is always beyond our grasp, but which if you will sit down quietly, may alight upon you.
NATHANIEL HAWTHORNE (1804–1864)

At the height of laughter, the universe is flung into a kaleidoscope of new possibilities.
JEAN HOUSTON (1937–)

It is pretty hard to tell what does bring happiness; poverty and wealth have both failed.
KIN HUBBARD (1868–1930)

Life's greatest happiness is to be convinced we are loved.
VICTOR HUGO (1802–1885), *Les Miserables*

I am more and more convinced that our happiness or unhappiness depends more on the way we meet the events of life than on the nature of those events themselves.
ALEXANDER VON HUMBOLDT (1769–1859)

Happiness is an endowment and not an acquisition. It depends more upon temperament and disposition than environment.
JOHN J. INGALLS (1833–1900)

Happiness comes of the capacity to feel deeply, to enjoy simply, to think freely, to risk life, to be needed.
MARGARET STORM JAMESON (1891–1986)

It is neither wealth nor splendor, but tranquility and occupation which give happiness.
THOMAS JEFFERSON (1743–1826)

The order of nature is that individual happiness shall be inseparable from the practice of virtue.
THOMAS JEFFERSON (1762–1826)

True happiness ... is not attained through self-gratification, but through fidelity to a worthy purpose.
HELEN KELLER (1880–1968)

Seek not happiness too greedily, and be not fearful of happiness.
LAO-TZU (C. 600 BC)

All sanity depends on this: that it should be a delight to feel heat strike the skin, a delight to stand upright, knowing the bones are moving easily under the flesh.
DORIS LESSING (1919–)

Happiness isn't something you experience; it's something you remember.
OSCAR LEVANT (1906–1972)

Most folks are about as happy as they make up their minds to be.
ABRAHAM LINCOLN (1809–1865)

Very little is needed to make a happy life.
MARCUS AURELIUS ANTONINUS (121–180), *Meditations*

Happiness is the interval between periods of unhappiness.
DON MARQUIS (1878–1937)

Happiness is not a matter of events; it depends upon the tides of the mind.
ALICE MEYNELL (1847–1922)

Cherish all your happy moments: they make a fine cushion for old age.
CHRISTOPHER MORLEY (1890–1957)

All I can say about life is, Oh God, enjoy it!
BOB NEWHART (1929–)

The foolish man seeks happiness in the distance, the wise grows it under his feet.
JAMES OPPENHEIM (1882–1932)

Men can only be happy when they do not assume that the object of life is happiness.
GEORGE ORWELL (1903–1950)

Our happiness depends on the habit of mind we cultivate. So practice happy thinking every day. Cultivate the merry heart, develop the happiness habit, and life will become a continual feast.
NORMAN VINCENT PEALE (1898–1993)

Happiness will come from materialism, not from meaning.
ANDREI PLATONOV (1899–1951)

Philosophers should consider the fact that the greatest happiness principle can easily be made an excuse for a benevolent dictatorship. We should replace it by a more modest and more realistic

principle—the principle that the fight against avoidable misery should be a recognized aim of public policy, while the increase of happiness should be left, in the main, to private initiative.
KARL POPPER (1902–1994)

No man is happy who does not think himself so.
PUBLILIUS SYRUS (C. 100 BC), *Maxims*

Happiness is that state of consciousness which proceeds from the achievement of one's values.
AYN RAND (1905–1982)

It is not easy to find happiness in ourselves and impossible to find it elsewhere.
AGNES REPPLIER (1855–1950)

Happiness: a good bank account, a good cook and a good digestion.
JEAN-JACQUES ROUSSEAU (1712–1778)

If there were in the world today any large number of people who desired their own happiness more than they desired the unhappiness of others, we could have paradise in a few years.
BERTRAND RUSSELL (1872–1970)

I am a kind of paranoiac in reverse. I suspect people of plotting to make me happy.
J. D. SALINGER (1919–)

Happiness is nothing more than good health and a bad memory.
DR. ALBERT SCHWEITZER (1875–1965)

All the joy the world contains is through wishing happiness for others.
SHANTIDEVA (C. 800)

A lifetime of happiness! No man alive could bear it: it would be hell on earth.
GEORGE BERNARD SHAW (1856–1950), *Man and Superman*

Happiness is different from pleasure. Happiness has something to do with struggling and enduring and accomplishing.
GEORGE SHEEHAN (1918–1993)

Happiness is essentially a state of going somewhere, wholeheartedly, one-directionally, without regret or reservation.
WILLIAM H. SHELDON (1898–1977)

The pursuit of happiness is a most ridiculous phrase; if you pursue happiness you'll never find it.
C. P. SNOW (1905–1980)

The happiness of a man in this life does not consist in the absence but in the mastery of his passions.
ALFRED, LORD TENNYSON (1809–1892)

Man is the artificer of his own happiness.
HENRY DAVID THOREAU (1817–1862)

The secret of happiness is freedom. The secret of freedom is courage.
THUCYDIDES (C. 460–395 BC)

Happiness does not depend on outward things, but on the way we see them.
LEO TOLSTOY (1828–1910)

I am still determined to be cheerful and happy, in whatever situation I may be; for I have also learned from experience that the greater part of our happiness or misery depends upon our dispositions, and not upon our circumstances.
MARTHA WASHINGTON (1732–1802)

Some cause happiness wherever they go; others whenever they go.
OSCAR WILDE (1854–1900)

I was happy but happy is an adult world. You don't have to ask a child about happy, you see it. They are or they are not. Adults talk about being happy because largely they are not. Talking about it is the same as trying to catch the wind. Much easier to let it blow all over you. This is where I disagree with the philosophers. They talk about passionate things but there is no passion in them.
JEANETTE WINTERSON (1959–), *The Passion*

Happiness is neither virtue nor pleasure nor this thing nor that but simply growth. We are happy when we are growing.
WILLIAM BUTLER YEATS (1865–1939)

Contentment is not the fulfillment of what you want, but the realization of how much you already have.
ANONYMOUS

Some pursue happiness—others create it.
ANONYMOUS

If one speaks or acts with a cruel mind, misery follows, as the cart follows the horse…. If one speaks or acts with a pure mind, happiness follows, as a shadow follows its source.
THE DHAMMAPADA

Hate

Hate no one; hate their vices, not themselves.
J. G. C. BRAINARD (1796–1828)

Hatred is the madness of the heart.
LORD BYRON (1788–1824)

We hate some persons because we do not know them; and we will not know them because we hate them.
CHARLES CALEB COLTON (1780–1832)

It is easy to hate and it is difficult to love. This is how the whole scheme of things works. All good things are difficult to achieve; and bad things are very easy to get.
RENÉ DESCARTES (1596–1650)

When love is suppressed hate takes its place.
HENRY HAVELOCK ELLIS (1859–1939)

It is better to be hated for what you are than to be loved for what you are not.
ANDRÉ GIDE (1869–1951)

If you hate a person, you hate something in him that is part of yourself. What isn't part of ourselves doesn't disturb us.
HERMANN HESSE (1877–1962)

Hate is too great a burden to bear. It injures the hater more than it injures the hated.
CORETTA SCOTT KING (1927–2006)

Hatred paralyses life; love releases it. Hatred confuses life; love harmonizes it. Hatred darkens life; love illuminates it.
MARTIN LUTHER KING JR. (1929–1968)

Like an unchecked cancer, hate corrodes the personality and eats away its vital unity. Hate destroys a man's sense of values and his objectivity. It causes him to describe the beautiful as ugly and the ugly as beautiful, and to confuse the true with the false and the false with the true.
MARTIN LUTHER KING JR. (1929–1968)

A true man hates no one.
NAPOLÉON I (1769–1821)

Always remember others may hate you but those who hate you don't win unless you hate them. And then you destroy yourself.
RICHARD M. NIXON (1913–1994)

When we don't know who to hate, we hate ourselves.
CHUCK PALAHNIUK (1962–)

Hatred comes from the heart; contempt from the head; and neither feeling is quite within our control.
ARTHUR SCHOPENHAUER (1788–1860)

You can't reason with people blinded by hate. They hate the power of the individual. They hate the progress of women. They hate the religious freedom of others. They hate the liberating breeze of democracy. But ladies and gentlemen, their hate is no match for America's decency.
ARNOLD SCHWARZENEGGER (1947–)

Hatred is the coward's revenge for being intimidated.
GEORGE BERNARD SHAW (1856–1950)

We have just enough religion to make us hate, but not enough to make us love one another.
JONATHAN SWIFT (1667–1745)

Those who hate most fervently must have once loved deeply; those who want to deny the world must have once embraced what they now set on fire.
KURT TUCHOLSKY (1890–1935)

Hatred can be nurtured anywhere, idealism can be perverted into sadism anywhere. If hatred and sadism combine with modern technology the inferno could erupt anew anywhere.
SIMON WIESENTHAL (1908–2005)

You cannot hate other people without hating yourself.
OPRAH WINFREY (1954–)

Healing

Sickness and healing are in every heart; death and deliverance in every hand.
ORSON SCOTT CARD (1951–), *Speaker for the Dead*

America's present need is not heroics, but healing; not nostrums but normalcy; not revolution, but restoration.
WARREN G. HARDING (1865–1923)

Healing is a matter of time, but it is sometimes also a matter of opportunity.
HIPPOCRATES (460–377 BC), *Precepts*

Everyone has a doctor in him or her; we just have to help it in its work. The natural healing force within each one of us is the greatest force in getting well. Our food should be our medicine. Our medicine should be our food. But to eat when you are sick, is to feed your sickness.
HIPPOCRATES (460–377 BC)

With the gift of listening comes the gift of healing.
CATHERINE DE HUECK (1896–1985)

To the soul, there is hardly anything more healing than friendship.
THOMAS MOORE (1779–1852)

When we honestly ask ourselves which person in our lives means the most to us, we often find that it is those who, instead of giving advice, solutions, or cures, have chosen rather to share our pain and touch our wounds with a warm and tender hand. The friend who can be silent with us in a moment of despair or confusion, who can stay with us in an hour of grief and bereavement, who can tolerate not knowing, not curing, not healing and face with us the reality of our powerlessness, that is a friend who cares.
HENRI NOUWEN (1932–1996), *Out of Solitude*

But for you who revere my name, the sun of righteousness will rise with healing in its rays. And you will go out and frolic like well-fed calves.
THE BIBLE, Malachi 4:2

Health

Exuberant health is always, as such, sickness also.
THEODOR W. ADORNO (1903–1969)

Safeguard the health both of body and soul.
CLEOBULUS (C. 500 BC)

All bodies are slow in growth but rapid in decay.
CORNELIUS TACITUS (55–117)

Health consists of having the same diseases as one's neighbors.
QUENTIN CRISP (1908–1999)

As I see it, every day you do one of two things: build health or produce disease in yourself.
ADELLE DAVIS (1904–1974)

Health nuts are going to feel stupid someday, lying in hospitals dying of nothing.
REDD FOXX (1922–1991)

Health is not valued till sickness comes.
THOMAS FULLER (1608–1661), *Gnomologia*

A hospital is no place to be sick.
SAMUEL GOLDWYN (1882–1974)

Health is not simply the absence of sickness.
HANNAH GREEN (1932–)

Keeping your body healthy is an expression of gratitude to the whole cosmos—the trees, the clouds, everything.
THICH NHAT HAHN (1926–)

Eating everything you want is not that much fun. When you live a life with no boundaries, there's less joy. If you can eat anything you want to, what's the fun in eating anything you want to?
TOM HANKS (1956–)

A wise man should consider that health is the greatest of human blessings, and learn how by his own thought to derive benefit from his illnesses.
HIPPOCRATES (460–377 BC), *Regimen in Health*

Health is worth more than learning.
THOMAS JEFFERSON (1743–1826)

One of the most sublime experiences we can ever have is to wake up feeling healthy after we have been sick.
RABBI HAROLD KUSHNER (1935–)

Preserving health by too severe a rule is a worrisome malady.
FRANÇOIS DE LA ROCHEFOUCAULD (1613–1680)

We should manage our fortunes as we do our health—enjoy it when good, be patient when it is bad, and never apply violent remedies except in an extreme necessity.
FRANÇOIS DE LA ROCHEFOUCAULD (1613–1680)

Now there are more overweight people in America than average-weight people. So overweight people are now average. Which means you've met your New Year's resolution.
JAY LENO (1950–)

It's no longer a question of staying healthy. It's a question of finding a sickness you like.
JACKIE MASON (1934–)

Quit worrying about your health. It'll go away.
ROBERT ORBEN (1927–)

The great majority of us are required to live a life of constant, systematic duplicity. Your health is bound to be affected if, day after day, you say the opposite of what you feel, if you grovel before what you dislike and rejoice at what brings you nothing but misfortune. Our nervous system isn't just a fiction, it's part of our physical body, and our soul exists in space and is inside us, like teeth in our mouth. It can't be forever violated with impunity.
BORIS PASTERNAK (1890–1960), *Doctor Zhivago*

Attention to health is life's greatest hindrance.
PLATO (C. 428–348 BC)

What some call health, if purchased by perpetual anxiety about diet, isn't much better than tedious disease.
GEORGE DENNISON PRENTICE (1802–1870)

Every patient carries her or his own doctor inside.
DR. ALBERT SCHWEITZER (1875–1965)

Happiness is nothing more than good health and a bad memory.
DR. ALBERT SCHWEITZER (1875–1965)

The preservation of health is a duty. Few seem conscious that there is such a thing as physical morality.
HERBERT SPENCER (1820–1903)

People who overly take care of their health are like misers. They hoard up a treasure which they never enjoy.
LAURENCE STERNE (1713–1768)

Must be out-of-doors enough to get experience of wholesome reality, as a ballast to thought and sentiment. Health requires this relaxation, this aimless life.
HENRY DAVID THOREAU (1817–1862)

Be careful about reading health books. You may die of a misprint.
MARK TWAIN (1835–1910)

Look to your health; and if you have it, praise God and value it next to conscience; for health is the second blessing that we mortals are capable of, a blessing money can't buy.
IZAAK WALTON (1593–1683)

Heart

I believe that every human has a finite number of heart-beats. I don't intend to waste any of mine running around doing exercises.
BUZZ ALDRIN (1930–)

Let us have a care not to disclose our hearts to those who shut up theirs against us.
FRANCIS BEAUMONT (1584–1616)

It is the heart that makes a man rich. He is rich according to what he is, not according to what he has.
HENRY WARD BEECHER (1813–1887)

Of all the music that reached farthest into heaven, it is the beating of a loving heart.
HENRY WARD BEECHER (1813–1887)

I have the heart of a child. I keep it in a jar on my shelf.
ROBERT BLOCH (1917–1994)

The way is not in the sky; the way is in the heart.
THE BUDDHA (563–483 BC)

It was never what I wanted to buy that held my heart's hope. It was what I wanted to be.
LOIS MCMASTER BUJOLD (1949–), *Memory*

Some prices are just too high, no matter how much you may want the prize. The one thing you can't trade for your heart's desire is your heart.
LOIS MCMASTER BUJOLD (1949–), *Memory*

Win hearts, and you have all men's hands and purses.
WILLIAM CECIL BURLEIGH (1520–1598)

The royal road to a man's heart is to talk to him about the things he treasures most.
DALE CARNEGIE (1888–1955)

The heart of another is a dark forest, always, no matter how close it has been to one's own.
WILLA CATHER (1873–1947)

[I]t's a fool that looks for logic in the chambers of the human heart.
ETHAN COEN (1957–) and JOEL COEN (1954–), *Oh Brother, Where Art Thou?*

What comes from the heart, goes to the heart.
SAMUEL TAYLOR COLERIDGE (1772–1834)

Wheresoever you go, go with all your heart.
CONFUCIUS (551–479 BC)

A loving heart is the truest wisdom.
CHARLES DICKENS (1812–1870)

Give all to love; obey thy heart.
RALPH WALDO EMERSON (1803–1882)

Great hearts steadily send forth the secret forces that incessantly draw great events.
RALPH WALDO EMERSON (1803–1882)

I have witnessed the softening of the hardest of hearts by a simple smile.
GOLDIE HAWN (1945–)

What other dungeon is so dark as one's own heart! What jailer so inexorable as one's self!
NATHANIEL HAWTHORNE (1804–1864)

Winter is on my head, but eternal spring is in my heart.
VICTOR HUGO (1802–1885)

A kind heart is a fountain of gladness, making everything in its vicinity freshen into smiles.
WASHINGTON IRVING (1783–1859)

The face is the mirror of the mind, and eyes without speaking confess the secrets of the heart.
SAINT JEROME (C. 342–420)

The best and most beautiful things in the world cannot be seen or even touched. They must be felt with the heart.
HELEN KELLER (1880–1968)

When the heart speaks, the mind finds it indecent to object.
MILAN KUNDERA (1929–), *The Unbearable Lightness of Being*

Before we set our hearts too much upon anything, let us examine how happy those are who already possess it.
FRANÇOIS DE LA ROCHEFOUCAULD (1613–1680)

My heart, which is so full to overflowing, has often been solaced and refreshed by music when sick and weary.
MARTIN LUTHER (1483–1546)

The human heart is like a ship on a stormy sea driven about by winds blowing from all four corners of heaven.
MARTIN LUTHER (1483–1546)

The family is the country of the heart.
GIUSEPPE MAZZINI (1805–1872)

Brains, like hearts, go where they are appreciated.
ROBERT S. MCNAMARA (1916–)

Those who don't know how to weep with their whole heart, don't know how to laugh either.
GOLDA MEIR (1898–1978)

The heart has its reasons which reason knows nothing of.
BLAISE PASCAL (1623–1662)

We know truth, not only by reason, but also by the heart.
BLAISE PASCAL (1623–1662)

Throw your heart over the fence and the rest will follow.
NORMAN VINCENT PEALE (1898–1993)

If your success is not on your own terms, if it looks good to the world but does not feel good in your heart, it is not success at all.
ANNA QUINDLEN (1953–)

Do what you feel in your heart to be right—for you'll be criticized anyway. You'll be damned if you do, and damned if you don't.
ELEANOR ROOSEVELT (1884–1962)

It is only with the heart that one can see rightly; what is essential is invisible to the eye.
ANTOINE DE SAINT-EXUPÉRY (1900–1944)

A light heart lives long.
WILLIAM SHAKESPEARE(1564–1616), *Love's Labour's Lost*

[G]o to your bosom;
Knock there, and ask your heart what it doth know.
WILLIAM SHAKESPEARE (1564–1616), *Measure for Measure*

There are two tragedies in life. One is not to get your heart's desire. The other is to get it.
GEORGE BERNARD SHAW (1856–1950), *Man and Superman*

A wise man should have money in his head, but not in his heart.
JONATHAN SWIFT (1667–1745)

To wear your heart on your sleeve isn't a very good plan; you should wear it inside, where it functions best.
MARGARET THATCHER (1925–)

There shall be eternal summer in the grateful heart.
CELIA THAXTER (1835–1894)

One learns people through the heart, not the eyes or the intellect.
MARK TWAIN (1835–1910)

Tears may be dried up, but the heart—never.
MARGUERITE DE VALOIS (1553–1615)

I have learned not to worry about love; but to honor its coming with all my heart.
ALICE WALKER (1944–)

A taste for irony has kept more hearts from breaking than a sense of humor, for it takes irony to appreciate the joke which is on oneself.
JESSAMYN WEST (1902–1984)

Everyone should carefully observe which way his heart draws him, and then choose that way with all his strength.
HASIDIC PROVERB

Heartbreak

Every instance of heartbreak can teach us powerful lessons about creating the kind of love we really want.
MARTHA BECK (1962–)

Blessed are the hearts that can bend; they shall never be broken.
ALBERT CAMUS (1913–1960)

Though you break your heart, men will go on as before.
MARCUS AURELIUS ANTONINUS (121–180)

Life will not break your heart. It'll crush it.
HENRY ROLLINS (1961–)

O! many a shaft, at random sent,
Finds mark the archer little meant!
And many a word, at random spoken,
May soothe or wound a heart that's broken!
SIR WALTER SCOTT (1771–1832)

There are so many different ways lives work out, so many stories, and every one of them is precious: full of joy and heartbreak, and a fair amount of situation comedy.
SEAN STEWART (1965–)

A taste for irony has kept more hearts from breaking than a sense of humor for it takes irony to appreciate the joke which is on oneself.
JESSAMYN WEST (1902–1984)

Love is like a puzzle. When you're in love, all the pieces fit but when your heart gets broken, it takes a while to get everything back together.
ANONYMOUS

When love is lost, do not bow your head in sadness; instead keep your head up high and gaze into heaven for that is where your broken heart has been sent to heal.
ANONYMOUS

God is closest to those with broken hearts.
JEWISH PROVERB

Heaven

Jean-Paul Sartre says in "No Exit" that hell is other people. Well, our task in life is to make it heaven. Or at least earth.
ALAN ALDA (1936–)

Children are the hands by which we take hold of heaven.
HENRY WARD BEECHER (1813–1887)

Those who enter heaven may find the outer walls plastered with creeds, but they won't find any on the inside.
JOSH BILLINGS (1818–1885)

Love seeketh not itself to please,
Nor for itself hath any care,
But for another gives its ease,
And builds a Heaven in Hell's despair.
WILLIAM BLAKE (1757–1827)

To see a world in a Grain of Sand,
And a Heaven in a Wild Flower,
Hold Infinity in the palm of your hand,
And eternity in an hour.
WILLIAM BLAKE (1757–1827)

Ah, but a man's reach should exceed his grasp—or what's a heaven for?
ROBERT BROWNING (1812–1889)

The poet only asks to get his head into the heavens. It is the logician who seeks to get the heavens into his head. And it is his head that splits.
G. K. CHESTERTON (1874–1936), *Orthodoxy*

Heaven has no rage like love to hatred turned,
Nor hell a fury like a woman scorned.
WILLIAM CONGREVE (1670–1729), *The Mourning Bride*

My life closed twice before its close—
It yet remains to see
If Immortality unveil
A third event to me.
So huge, so hopeless to concieve
As these that twice befell.

Parting is all we know of heaven,
And all we need of hell.
EMILY DICKINSON (1830–1886), "No. 1732"

I hope you love birds too. It is economical. It saves going to heaven.
EMILY DICKINSON (1830–1886)

What power would Hell have if those imprisoned there were not able to dream of Heaven?
NEIL GAIMAN (1960–)

By means of shrewd lies, unremittingly repeated, it is possible to make people believe that heaven is hell—and hell heaven. The greater the lie, the more readily it will be believed.
ADOLPH HITLER (1889–1945), *Mein Kampf*

Do not ask God the way to heaven; he will show you the hardest one.
STANISLAW LEC (1909–1966)

One single grateful thought raised to heaven is the most perfect prayer.
G. E. LESSING (1729–1781)

Aim at heaven and you will get earth thrown in.
Aim at earth and you get neither.
C. S. LEWIS (1898–1963)

Now hast thou but one bare hour to live,
And then thou must be damned perpetually.
Stand still, you ever-moving spheres of heaven,
That time may cease, and midnight never come.
CHRISTOPHER MARLOWE (1564–1593), *Doctor Faustus*

Sincerity is the way of Heaven.
MENCIUS (371–289 BC), *Works*

Sunday: A day given over by Americans to wishing they were dead and in heaven, and that their neighbors were dead and in hell.
H. L. MENCKEN (1880–1956)

The mind is its own place, and in itself can make a Heaven of Hell, a Hell of Heaven.
JOHN MILTON (1608–1674)

In heaven all the interesting people are missing.
FRIEDRICH NIETZSCHE (1844–1900)

Thoughts give birth to a creative force that is neither elemental nor sidereal. Thoughts create a new heaven, a new firmament, a new source of energy, from which new arts flow. When a man undertakes to create something, he establishes a new heaven, as it were and from it the work that he desires to create flows into him. For such is the immensity of man that he is greater than heaven and earth.
PARACELSUS (1493–1541)

[T]o emphasize the afterlife is to deny life. To concentrate on Heaven is to create hell. In their desperate longing to transcend the disorderliness, friction, and unpredictability that pesters life; in their desire for a fresh start in a tidy habitat, germ-free and secured by angels, religious multitudes are gambling the only life they may ever have on a dark horse in a race that has no finish line.
TOM ROBBINS (1936–), *Skinny Legs and All*

My words fly up, my thoughts remain below.
Words without thoughts never to heaven go.
WILLIAM SHAKESPEARE (1564–1616), *Hamlet*

O, my offence is rank, it smells to heaven;
It hath the primal eldest curse upon 't,
A brother's murder.
WILLIAM SHAKESPEARE (1564–1616), *Hamlet*

The peace of heaven is theirs that lift their swords, in such a just and charitable war.
WILLIAM SHAKESPEARE (1564–1616), *King John*

To love is to receive a glimpse of heaven.
KAREN SUNDE (1942–)

If I have any beliefs about immortality, it is that certain dogs I have known will go to heaven, and very, very few persons.
JAMES THURBER (1894–1961)

Go to Heaven for the climate, Hell for the company.
MARK TWAIN (1835–1910)

Heaven goes by favour. If it went by merit, you would stay out and your dog would go in.
MARK TWAIN (1835–1910)

Of the delights of this world man cares most for sexual intercourse, yet he has left it out of his heaven.
MARK TWAIN (1835–1910)

God has two dwellings: one in heaven, and the other in a meek and thankful heart.
IZAAK WALTON (1593–1683)

If heaven made him, earth can find some use for him.
CHINESE PROVERB

A child's tear rends the heavens.
YIDDISH PROVERB

Hell

Hell is a place, a time, a consciousness, in which there is no love.
RICHARD BACH (1936–)

Everybody's hell is different. It's not all fire and pain. The real hell is your life gone wrong.
RONALD BASS (1942–) and RICHARD MATHESON (1926–), *What Dreams May Come*

I cannot help thinking that the menace of Hell makes as many devils as the severe penal codes of inhuman humanity make villains.
LORD BYRON (1788–1824)

I'm not concerned about all hell breaking loose, but that a PART of hell will break loose… it'll be much harder to detect.
GEORGE CARLIN (1937–)

If you are going through hell, keep going.
SIR WINSTON CHURCHILL (1874–1965)

Man disavows, and Deity disowns me: hell might afford my miseries a shelter; therefore hell keeps her ever-hungry mouths all bolted against me.
WILLIAM COWPER (1731–1800)

The hottest places in hell are reserved for those who in times of great moral crises maintain their neutrality.
DANTE ALIGHIERI (1265–1321)

My life closed twice before its close—
It yet remains to see
If Immortality unveil
A third event to me.
So huge, so hopeless to concieve
As these that twice befell.
Parting is all we know of heaven,
And all we need of hell.
EMILY DICKINSON (1830–1886), "No. 1732"

Hell is oneself, Hell is alone, the other figures in it merely projections.
T. S. ELIOT (1888–1965)

Hell hath no fury like a bureaucrat scorned.
MILTON FRIEDMAN (1912–2006)

Hell is a half-filled auditorium.
ROBERT FROST (1874–1963)

What power would Hell have if those imprisoned there were not able to dream of Heaven?
NEIL GAIMAN (1960–)

In hell there is no other punishment than to begin over and over again the tasks left unfinished in your lifetime.
ANDRÉ GIDE (1869–1951)

By means of shrewd lies, unremittingly repeated, it is possible to make people believe that heaven is hell—and hell heaven. The greater the lie, the more readily it will be believed.
ADOLPH HITLER (1889–1945), *Mein Kampf*

Hell is an outrage on humanity. When you tell me that your deity made you in his image, I reply that he must have been very ugly.
VICTOR HUGO (1802–1885)

Hell isn't merely paved with good intentions, it is walled and roofed with them.
ALDOUS HUXLEY (1894–1963)

Maybe this world is another planet's hell.
ALDOUS HUXLEY (1894–1963)

The hottest place in Hell is reserved for those who remain neutral in times of great moral conflict.
MARTIN LUTHER KING JR. (1929–1968)

The road to hell is paved with adverbs.
STEPHEN KING (1947–)

The safest road to hell is the gradual one, the gentle slope, soft underfoot, without sudden turnings, without milestones, without signposts.
C. S. LEWIS (1898–1963)

Hell hath no limits, nor is circumscribed
In one self place, for where we are is hell,
And where hell is there must we ever be.
CHRISTOPHER MARLOWE (1564–1593)

Which way I fly is Hell; myself am Hell;
And in the lowest deep a lower deep
Still threat'ning to devour me opens wide,
To which the Hell I suffer seems a Heav'n.
JOHN MILTON (1608–1674), *Paradise Lost*

The mind is its own place, and in itself can make a Heaven of Hell, a Hell of Heaven.
JOHN MILTON (1608–1674)

I believe that I am in hell, therefore I am there.
ARTHUR RIMBAUD (1854–1891)

Hell is other people.
JEAN-PAUL SARTRE (1905–1980)

Hell is empty and all the devils are here.
WILLIAM SHAKESPEARE (1564–1616), *The Tempest*

A lifetime of happiness! No man alive could bear it: it would be hell on earth.
GEORGE BERNARD SHAW (1856–1950), *Man and Superman*

A perpetual holiday is a good working definition of hell.
GEORGE BERNARD SHAW (1856–1950), *Parents and Children*

Hell is full of musical amateurs.
GEORGE BERNARD SHAW (1856–1950)

Here there is no hope, and consequently no duty, no work, nothing to be gained by praying, nothing to be lost by doing what you like. Hell, in short, is a place where you have nothing to do but amuse yourself.
GEORGE BERNARD SHAW (1856–1950)

War is hell.
WILLIAM TECUMSEH SHERMAN (1820–1891)

If there is, in fact, a Heaven and a Hell, all we know for sure is that Hell will be a viciously overcrowded version of Phoenix….
HUNTER S. THOMPSON (1939–2005), *Generation of Swine*

I never did give them hell. I just told the truth, and they thought it was hell.
HARRY S TRUMAN (1884–1972)

Go to Heaven for the climate, Hell for the company.
MARK TWAIN (1835–1910)

Each of us bears his own Hell.
VIRGIL (C. 70–19 BC)

We are each our own devil, and we make this world our hell.
OSCAR WILDE (1854–1900)

Hell is yourself and the only redemption is when a person puts himself aside to feel deeply for another person.
TENNESSEE WILLIAMS (1911–1983)

It does not require a decision to go to hell.
ANONYMOUS

One of the horrors of hell is the undying memory of a misspent life.
ANONYMOUS

Heresy

From heresy, frenzy and jealousy, good Lord deliver me.
LUDOVICO ARIOSTO (1474–1533)

Progress, this great heresy of decay.
CHARLES BAUDELAIRE (1821–1867)

It is surely harmful to souls to make it a heresy to believe what is proved.
GALILEO GALILEI (1564–1642)

Heresy is another word for freedom of thought.
GRAHAM GREENE (1904–1991)

In the end it is worse to suppress dissent than to run the risk of heresy.
LEARNED HAND (1872–1961)

They that approve a private opinion, call it opinion; but they that dislike it, heresy; and yet heresy signifies no more than private opinion.
THOMAS HOBBES (1588–1679)

A heresy can spring only from a system that is in full vigor.
ERIC HOFFER (1902–1983)

The difference between heresy and prophecy is often one of sequence. Heresy often turns out to have been prophecy when properly aged.
HUBERT H. HUMPHREY (1911–1978)

There is no heresy or no philosophy which is so abhorrent to the church as a human being.
JAMES JOYCE (1882–1941)

The heresy of one age becomes the orthodoxy of the next.
HELEN KELLER (1880–1968)

According to Islamic principles, when a man is accused of heresy, he is given the choice between repentance and punishment.
NAGUIB MAHFOUZ (1911–2006)

If it squares with the Scripture, then let's go. If it's in conflict with the Scripture, then it's heresy.
RANDALL TERRY (1959–)

If forgers and malefactors are put to death by the secular power, there is much more reason for excommunicating and even putting to death one convicted of heresy.
SAINT THOMAS AQUINAS (1225–1274)

All this worldly wisdom was once the unamiable heresy of some wise man.
HENRY DAVID THOREAU (1817–1862)

Very few editors worry about heresy—their goals are much too commercial, thank goodness.
CHELSEA QUINN YARBRO (1942–)

Heroes

Everyone is necessarily the hero of his own life story.
JOHN BARTH (1930–)

The world's battlefields have been in the heart chiefly; more heroism has been displayed in the household and the closet, than on the most memorable battlefields in history.
HENRY WARD BEECHER (1813–1887)

Heroism is the divine relation which, in all times, unites a great man to other men.
THOMAS CARLYLE (1795–1881)

There are new words now that excuse everybody. Give me the good old days of heroes and villains. The people you can bravo or hiss. There was a truth to them that all the slick credulity of today cannot touch.
BETTE DAVIS (1908–1989), *The Lonely Life*

Nurture your mind with great thoughts; to believe in the heroic makes heroes.
BENJAMIN DISRAELI (1804–1881)

The legacy of heroes is the memory of a great name and the inheritance of a great example.
BENJAMIN DISRAELI (1804–1881)

I think of a hero as someone who understands the degree of responsibility that comes with his freedom.
BOB DYLAN (1941–)

The real hero is always a hero by mistake; he dreams of being an honest coward like everybody else.
UMBERTO ECO (1932–), *Travels in Hyperreality*

He who joyfully marches to music rank and file, has already earned my contempt. He has been given a large brain by mistake, since for him the spinal cord would surely suffice. This disgrace to civilization should be done away with at once. Heroism at command, how violently I hate all this, how despicable and ignoble war is; I would rather be torn to shreds than be a part of so base an action. It is my conviction that killing under the cloak of war is nothing but an act of murder.
ALBERT EINSTEIN (1879–1955)

A hero is no braver than an ordinary man, but he is braver five minutes longer.
RALPH WALDO EMERSON (1803–1882)

Every hero becomes a bore at last.
RALPH WALDO EMERSON (1803–1882)

Self-trust is the essence of heroism.
RALPH WALDO EMERSON (1803–1882)

The characteristic of genuine heroism is its persistency. All men have wandering impulses, fits and starts of generosity. But when you have resolved to be great, abide by yourself, and do not weakly try to reconcile yourself with the world. The heroic cannot be the common, nor the common the heroic.
RALPH WALDO EMERSON (1803–1882)

It is better to be the widow of a hero than the wife of a coward.
DOLORES IBARRURI (1895–1989)

The prudent see only the difficulties, the bold only the advantages, of a great enterprise; the hero sees both; diminishes the former and makes the latter preponderate, and so conquers.
JOHANN KASPAR LAVATER (1741–1801)

What is a hero without love for mankind.
DORIS LESSING (1919–)

Ultimately a hero is a man who would argue with the gods, and so awakens devils to contest his vision. The more a man can achieve, the more he may be certain that the devil will inhabit a part of his creation.
NORMAN MAILER (1923–2007)

In war the heroes always outnumber the soldiers ten to one.
H. L. MENCKEN (1880–1956)

The ordinary man is involved in action, the hero acts. An immense difference.
HENRY MILLER (1891–1980)

True heroism consists in being superior to the ills of life, in whatever shape they may challenge us to combat.
NAPOLÉON I (1769–1821)

I think a hero is an ordinary individual who finds strength to persevere and endure in spite of overwhelming obstacles.
CHRISTOPHER REEVE (1952–2004)

No heroine can create a hero through love of one, but she can give birth to one.
JEAN PAUL RICHTER (1763–1825)

Heroing is one of the shortest-lived professions there is.
WILL ROGERS (1879–1935)

We can't all be heroes because somebody has to sit on the curb and clap as they go by.
WILL ROGERS (1879–1935)

Heroes are not known by the loftiness of their carriage; the greatest braggarts are generally the merest cowards.
JEAN-JACQUES ROUSSEAU (1712–1778)

How many famous and high-spirited heroes have lived a day too long?
JEAN-JACQUES ROUSSEAU (1712–1778)

If we are marked to die, we are enough to do our country loss; and if to live, the fewer men, the greater share of honor.
WILLIAM SHAKESPEARE (1564–1616), *Henry V*

You cannot be a hero without being a coward.
GEORGE BERNARD SHAW (1856–1950)

A big man has no time really to do anything but just sit and be big.
ANONYMOUS

A smooth sea never made a skillful mariner, neither do uninterrupted prosperity and success qualify for usefulness and happiness. The storms of adversity, like those of the ocean, rouse the faculties, and excite the invention, prudence, skill and fortitude of the voyager. The martyrs of ancient times, in bracing their minds to outward calamities, acquired a loftiness of purpose and a moral heroism worth a lifetime of softness and security.
ANONYMOUS

Show me a hero and I will write you a tragedy.
ANONYMOUS

The great destroyers of nations and men are comfort, plenty and security. A coward gets scared and quits. A hero gets scared, but still goes on.
ANONYMOUS

A hero is a man who is afraid to run away.
ENGLISH PROVERB

Hesitation

Hesitation increases in relation to risk in equal proportion to age.
ERNEST HEMINGWAY (1899–1961)

Make up your mind to act decidedly and take the consequences. No good is ever done in this world by hesitation.
THOMAS H. HUXLEY (1825–1895)

To teach how to live without certainty, and yet without, being paralyzed by hesitation, is perhaps the chief thing that philosophy in our age can do for those who study it.
BERTRAND RUSSELL (1872–1970)

On the plains of hesitation lie the blackened bones of countless millions who at the dawn of victory lay down to rest, and in resting died.
ADLAI E. STEVENSON II (1900–1965)

History

History must be our deliverer not only from the undue influence of other times, but from the undue influence of our own, from the tyranny of environment and the pressures of the air we breathe.
LORD ACTON (1834–1902)

History, despite its wrenching pain, cannot be unlived, however, if faced with courage, need not be lived again.
MAYA ANGELOU (1928–)

Poetry is finer and more philosophical than history; for poetry expresses the universal, and history only the particular.
ARISTOTLE (384–322 BC)

History makes people wise.
SIR FRANCIS BACON (1561–1626)

History, n.: An account mostly false, of events unimportant, which are brought about by rulers mostly knaves, and soldiers mostly fools.
AMBROSE BIERCE (1842–1914), *The Devil's Dictionary*

History is moving, and it will tend toward hope, or tend toward tragedy.
GEORGE W. BUSH (1946–)

History is written by the victors.
SIR WINSTON CHURCHILL (1874–1965)

History will be kind to me for I intend to write it.
SIR WINSTON CHURCHILL (1874–1965)

The whole history of the world is summed up in the fact that, when nations are strong, they are not always just, and when they wish to be just, they are no longer strong.
SIR WINSTON CHURCHILL (1874–1965)

History is the witness that testifies to the passing of time; it illumines reality, vitalizes memory, provides guidance in daily life, and brings us tidings of antiquity.
CICERO (106–43 BC), *Pro Publio Sestio*

The principle office of history I take to be this: to prevent virtuous actions from being forgotten, and that evil words and deeds should fear an infamous reputation with posterity.
CORNELIUS TACITUS (AD 55–117)

In the long history of humankind (and animal kind, too) those who learned to collaborate and improvise most effectively have prevailed.
CHARLES DARWIN (1809–1882)

Some people make headlines while others make history.
PHILIP ELMER-DEWITT (1949–)

History is more or less bunk. It's tradition. We don't want tradition. We want to live in the present and the only history that is worth a tinker's damn is the history we made today.
HENRY FORD (1863–1947)

History is a voice forever sounding across the centuries the laws of right and wrong. Opinions alter, manners change, creeds rise and fall, but the moral law is written on the tablets of eternity.
JAMES A. FROUDE (1818–1894)

History never looks like history when you are living through it.
JOHN W. GARDNER (1912–2002)

History is indeed little more than the register of the crimes, follies and misfortunes of mankind.
EDWARD GIBBON (1737–1794)

History is a relentless master. It has no present, only the past rushing into the future. To try to hold fast is to be swept aside.
JOHN F. KENNEDY (1917–1963)

Few will have the greatness to bend history itself; but each of us can work to change a small portion of events, and in the total of all those acts will be written the history of this generation.
ROBERT F. KENNEDY(1925–1968)

Ideas shape the course of history.
JOHN MAYNARD KEYNES (1883–1946)

History is the version of past events that people have decided to agree upon.
NAPOLÉON I (1769–1821)

The history of mankind is the history of ideas.
LUIGI PIRANDELLO (1867–1936)

Those who cannot remember the past are condemned to repeat it.
GEORGE SANTAYANA (1863–1952), *The Life of Reason*

There is a history in all men's lives.
WILLIAM SHAKESPEARE (1564–1616), *Henry IV*

Hegel was right when he said that we learn from history that man can never learn anything from history.
GEORGE BERNARD SHAW (1856–1950)

When you think of the long and gloomy history of man, you will find more hideous crimes have been committed in the name of obedience than have ever been committed in the name of rebellion.
C. P. SNOW (1905–1980)

History is fables agreed upon.
VOLTAIRE (1694–1778)

[H]istory is nothing more than a tableau of crimes and misfortunes.
VOLTAIRE (1694–1778)

Human history becomes more and more a race between education and catastrophe.
H. G. WELLS (1866–1946), *Outline of History*

Studying history warns against making it.
ANONYMOUS

Holidays

How many observe Christ's birthday! How few, his precepts! O! 'tis easier to keep Holidays than Commandments.
BENJAMIN FRANKLIN (1706–1790)

Holidays are an expensive trial of strength. The only satisfaction comes from survival.
JONATHAN MILLER (1934–)

If all the year were playing holidays;
To sport would be as tedious as to work.
WILLIAM SHAKESPEARE (1564–1616), *King Henry IV*

I once wanted to become an atheist, but I gave up—they have no holidays.
HENNY YOUNGMAN (1906–1998)

Hollywood

Hollywood is a place where people from Iowa mistake each other for stars.
FRED ALLEN (1894–1956)

You can take all the sincerity in Hollywood, place it in the navel of a firefly and still have room enough for three caraway seeds and a producer's heart.
FRED ALLEN (1894–1956)

You can't find any true closeness in Hollywood, because everybody does the fake closeness so well.
CARRIE FISHER (1956–)

Behind the phony tinsel of Hollywood lies the real tinsel.
OSCAR LEVANT (1906–1972)

Hollywood is a place where they'll pay you a thousand dollars for a kiss and fifty cents for your soul.
MARILYN MONROE (1926–1962)

In Hollywood a marriage is a success if it outlasts milk.
RITA RUDNER (1956–)

A lot of people say that this town [Hollywood] is too liberal, out of touch with mainstream America, an atheistic pleasure dome, a modern-day, beachfront Sodom and Gomorrah, a moral black hole where innocence is obliterated in an endless orgy of sexual gratification and greed. I don't really have a joke here. I just thought you should know a lot of people are saying that.
JON STEWART (1962–)

After two years in Washington, I often long for the realism and sincerity of Hollywood.
FRED THOMPSON (1942–)

Hollywood is a place where they place you under contract instead of under observation.
WALTER WINCHELL (1897–1972)

Home

A man's homeland is wherever he prospers.
ARISTOPHANES (C. 448–380 BC), *Plutus*

My home is not a place, it is people.
LOIS MCMASTER BUJOLD (1949–), *Barrayar*

Home is where one starts from.
T. S. ELIOT (1888–1965)

Home is the place where, when you have to go there, they have to take you in.
ROBERT FROST (1874–1963)

The most important work you and I will ever do will be within the walls of our own homes.
HAROLD B. LEE (1899–1973)

A good home must be made, not bought.
JOYCE MAYNARD (1953–), *Domestic Affairs*

Life's a voyage that's homeward bound.
HERMAN MELVILLE (1819–1891)

A man travels the world over in search of what he needs and returns home to find it.
GEORGE EDWARD MOORE (1873–1958)

Mid pleasures and palaces though we may roam,
Be it ever so humble, there's no place like home.
JOHN HOWARD PAYNE (1791–1852)

Home is the girl's prison and the woman's workhouse.
GEORGE BERNARD SHAW (1856–1950)

Homelessness

As Secretary of Housing, I do have to express alarm, signal the alarm if you will, that the potential for homelessness to grow is there.
HENRY CISNEROS (1947–)

Homelessness is a part of our American system. There should be nothing wrong with this condition as long as the individual is not sentenced to unnecessary suffering and punishment.
JERZY KOSINSKI (1933–1991)

And homeless near a thousand homes I stood,
And near a thousand tables pined and wanted food.
WILLIAM WORDSWORTH (1770–1850)

Homosexuality

In itself, homosexuality is as limiting as heterosexuality: the ideal should be to be capable of loving a woman or a man; either, a human being, without feeling fear, restraint, or obligation.
SIMONE DE BEAUVOIR (1908–1986)

The topic of homosexuality is something I've grown up with and been aware of. I've always had a hard time expressing to my peers what it was like, that it was just something they needed to understand.
JENA MALONE (1984–)

Homosexuality is like the weather. It just is.
ANDREW SULLIVAN (1963–)

I don't think homosexuality is a choice. Society forces you to think it's a choice, but in fact, it's in one's nature. The choice is whether one expresses one's nature truthfully or spends the rest of one's life lying about it.
MARLO THOMAS (1937–)

Honesty

If the truth doesn't save us, what does that say about us?
LOIS MCMASTER BUJOLD (1949–), *Diplomatic Immunity*

Any fool can tell the truth, but it requires a man of some sense to know how to lie well.
SAMUEL BUTLER (1835–1902)

Concentration is my motto—first honesty, then industry, then concentration.
ANDREW CARNEGIE (1835–1919)

'Tis my opinion every man cheats in his own way, and he is only honest who is not discovered.
SUSANNAH CENTLIVRE (1669–1723)

Where is there dignity unless there is honesty?
CICERO (106–43 BC)

The best measure of a man's honesty isn't his income tax return. It's the zero adjust on his bathroom scale.
ARTHUR C. CLARKE (1917–)

The day is for honest men, the night for thieves.
EURIPIDES (C. 480–406 BC), *Iphigenia in Tauris*

Someone who thinks the world is always cheating him is right. He is missing that wonderful feeling of trust in someone or something.
ERIC HOFFER (1902–1983)

Honesty pays, but it doesn't seem to pay enough to suit some people.
KIN HUBBARD (1868–1930)

An honest man can feel no pleasure in the exercise of power over his fellow citizens.
THOMAS JEFFERSON (1743–1826)

Honesty is a good thing, but it is not profitable to its possessor unless it is kept under control.
DON MARQUIS (1878–1937)

Honesty is for the most part less profitable than dishonesty.
PLATO (C. 428–348 BC)

Son, always tell the truth. Then you'll never have to remember what you said the last time.
SAM RAYBURN (1882–1961)

When something that honest is said it usually needs a few minutes of silence to dissipate.
PAMELA RIBON (1975–), *Why Girls Are Weird*

No legacy is so rich as honesty.
WILLIAM SHAKESPEARE (1564–1616), *All's Well That Ends Well*

Though I am not naturally honest, I am so sometimes by chance.
WILLIAM SHAKESPEARE (1564–1616), *All's Well That Ends Well*

I thank God I am as honest as any man living that is an old man and no honester than I.
WILLIAM SHAKESPEARE (1564–1616), *Much Ado About Nothing*

Every man has his fault, and honesty is his.
WILLIAM SHAKESPEARE (1564–1616), *Timon of Athens*

It is possible that the scrupulously honest man may not grow rich so fast as the unscrupulous and dishonest one; but success will be of a truer kind, earned without fraud or injustice. And even though a man should for a time be unsuccessful, still he must be honest; better to lose all and save character. For character is itself a fortune.
SAMUEL SMILES (1812–1904)

There are only two ways of telling the complete truth—anonymously and posthumously.
THOMAS SOWELL (1930–)

Honesty is the best policy—when there is money in it.
MARK TWAIN (1835–1910)

If you tell the truth you don't have to remember anything.
MARK TWAIN (1835–1910)

When in doubt, tell the truth.
MARK TWAIN (1835–1910)

Honesty is the best image.
TOM WILSON (1931–1978)

Honor

Guard your honor. Let your reputation fall where it will. And outlive the bastards.
LOIS MCMASTER BUJOLD (1949–), *A Civil Campaign*

Reputation is what other people know about you. Honor is what you know about yourself.
LOIS MCMASTER BUJOLD (1949–), *A Civil Campaign*

An honor is not diminished for being shared.
LOIS MCMASTER BUJOLD (1949–), *Shards of Honor*

No person was ever honored for what they received. Honor was given for what they gave.
CALVIN COOLIDGE (1872–1933)

The louder he talked of his honor, the faster we counted our spoons.
RALPH WALDO EMERSON (1803–1882)

Be not ashamed of thy virtues; honor's a good brooch to wear in a man's hat at all times.
BEN JONSON (1572–1637)

So long as the great majority of men are not deprived of either property or honor, they are satisfied.
NICCOLÒ MACHIAVELLI (1469–1527)

The difference between a moral man and a man of honor is that the latter regrets a discreditable act, even when it has worked and he has not been caught.
H. L. MENCKEN (1880–1956), *Prejudices: Fourth Series*

If thou desire to purchase honor with thy wealth, consider first how that wealth became thine; if thy labor got it, let thy wisdom keep it; if oppression found it, let repentance restore it; if thy parent left it, let thy virtues deserve it; so shall thy honor be safer, better and cheaper.
FRANCIS QUARLES (1592–1644)

What is left when honor is lost?
PUBLILIUS SYRUS (C. 100 BC), *Maxims*

Honor does not have to be defended.
ROBERT J. SAWYER (1960–), *Calculating God*

Real integrity is doing the right thing, knowing that nobody's going to know whether you did it or not.
OPRAH WINFREY (1954–)

Where there is no shame, there is no honor.
AFRICAN PROVERB

Don't look for more honor than your learning merits.
JEWISH PROVERB

Be honorable yourself if you wish to associate with honorable people.
WELSH PROVERB

Hope

I know how men in exile feed on dreams of hope.
AESCHYLUS (C. 525–456 BC), *Agamemnon*

The past is a source of knowledge, and the future is a source of hope. Love of the past implies faith in the future.
STEPHEN AMBROSE (1936–2002)

Hope is only the love of life.
HENRI-FRÉDÉRIC AMIEL (1821–1881)

Hope is a waking dream.
ARISTOTLE (384–322 BC)

History is moving, and it will tend toward hope, or tend toward tragedy.
GEORGE W. BUSH (1946–)

Cease, every joy, to glimmer on my mind,
But leave—oh! leave the light of Hope behind.
THOMAS CAMPBELL (1777–1844)

He who despairs over an event is a coward, but he who holds hope for the human condition is a fool.
ALBERT CAMUS (1913–1960), *The Rebel*

Most of the important things in the world have been accomplished by people who have kept on trying when there seemed to be no hope at all.
DALE CARNEGIE (1888–1955)

While there's life, there's hope.
CICERO (106-43 BC), *Ad Atticum*

If you do not hope, you will not find what is beyond your hopes.
CLEMENT OF ALEXANDRIA (C. 150–211)

Hope is a dangerous thing. Hope can drive a man insane.
FRANK DARABONT (1959–) and STEPHEN KING (1947–), *The Shawshank Redemption*

"Hope" is the thing with feathers --
That perches in the soul --
And sings the tune without the words --
And never stops -- at all --
EMILY DICKINSON (1830–1886), "No. 254"

What we call our despair is often only the painful eagerness of unfed hope.
GEORGE ELIOT (1819–1880), *Middlemarch*

Do not spoil what you have by desiring what you have not; but remember that what you now have was once among the things you only hoped for.
EPICURUS (341–270 BC)

He that lives upon hope will die fasting.
BENJAMIN FRANKLIN (1706–1790)

It is difficult to say what is impossible, for the dream of yesterday is the hope of today and the reality of tomorrow.
ROBERT H. GODDARD (1882–1945)

The free expression of the hopes and aspirations of a people is the greatest and only safety in a sane society.
EMMA GOLDMAN (1869–1940), *Living My Life*

Hope, like the gleaming taper's light,
Adorns and cheers our way;
And still, as darker grows the night,
Emits a brighter ray.
OLIVER GOLDSMITH (1730–1774)

Appetite, with an opinion of attaining, is called hope; the same, without such opinion, despair.
THOMAS HOBBES (1588–1679)

Hope is necessary in every condition.
SAMUEL JOHNSON (1709–1784)

Hope begins in the dark, the stubborn hope that if you just show up and try to do the right thing, the dawn will come. You wait and watch and work: You don't give up.
ANNE LAMOTT (1954–)

Hope is a necessity for normal life and the major weapon against the suicide impulse.
DR. KARL A. MENNINGER (1893–1990)

Hope is nature's veil for hiding truth's nakedness.
ALFRED BERNHARD NOBEL (1833–1896)

Despair is vinegar from the wine of hope.
AUSTIN O'MALLEY (1858–1932)

Realize that there are not hopeless situations; there are only people who take hopeless attitudes.
NORMAN VINCENT PEALE (1898–1993)

For hope is but the dream of those who wake.
MATTHEW PRIOR (1664–1721)

Hope is beautiful, and so are those who have it.
CATHY ROWLAND (1950–)

Oft expectation fails, and most oft there
Where most it promises; and oft it hits
Where hope is coldest; and despair most fits.
WILLIAM SHAKESPEARE (1564–1616), *All's Well That Ends Well*

True hope is swift, and flies with swallow's wings;
Kings it makes gods, and meaner creatures kings.
WILLIAM SHAKESPEARE (1564–1616), *King Richard III*

He who has never hoped can never despair.
GEORGE BERNARD SHAW (1856–1950), *Caesar and Cleopatra*

I can endure my own despair,
but not another's hope.
WILLIAM WALSH (1663–1708)

Never lose hope.
POLISH PROVERB

Horses

Old minds are like old horses; you must exercise them if you wish to keep them in working order.
JOHN ADAMS (1735–1826)

You never know how a horse will pull until you hook him up to a heavy load.
PAUL "BEAR" BRYANT (1913–1983), *I Ain't Never Been Nothing but a Winner*

Did you ever see an unhappy horse? Did you ever see a bird that had the blues? One reason why birds and horses are not unhappy is because they are not trying to impress other birds and horses.
DALE CARNEGIE (1888–1955)

A wise man looks upon men as he does on horses; all their comparisons of title, wealth, and place, he consider but as harness.
ROBERT CECIL (1563–1612)

Horse sense is the thing a horse has which keeps it from betting on people.
W. C. FIELDS (1880–1946)

For the want of a nail, the shoe was lost; for the want of a shoe the horse was lost; and for the want of a horse the rider was lost, being overtaken and slain by the enemy, all for the want of care about a horseshoe nail.
BENJAMIN FRANKLIN (1706–1790)

A man may well bring a horse to the water but he cannot make him drink.
JOHN HEYWOOD (1497–1580)

I don't mind what Congress does, as long as they don't do it in the streets and frighten the horses.
VICTOR HUGO (1802–1885)

Never look a gift horse in the mouth.
SAINT JEROME (C. 342–420), *On the Epistle to the Ephesians*

Men are generally more careful of the breed of their horses and dogs than of their children.
WILLIAM PENN (1644–1718)

A horse! a horse! my kingdom for a horse!
WILLIAM SHAKESPEARE (1564–1616), *King Richard III*

Keep five yards from a carriage, ten yards from a horse, and a hundred yards from an elephant; but the distance one should keep from a wicked man cannot be measured.
INDIAN PROVERB

A good resolution is like an old horse, which is often saddled but rarely ridden.
MEXICAN PROVERB

It is not the horse that draws the cart, but the oats.
RUSSIAN PROVERB

Housework

Housework is what a woman does that nobody notices unless she hasn't done it.
EVAN ESAR (1899–1995)

Human Nature

There will be little rubs and disappointments everywhere, and we are all apt to expect too much; but then, if one scheme of happiness fails, human nature turns to another; if the first calculation is wrong, we make a second better: we find comfort somewhere.
JANE AUSTEN (1775–1817), *Mansfield Park*

One of the greatest pains to human nature is the pain of a new idea.
WALTER BAGEHOT (1826–1877)

Where is human nature so weak as in the bookstore?
HENRY WARD BEECHER (1813–1887)

Beware of undertaking too much at the start. Be content with quite a little. Allow for accidents. Allow for human nature, especially your own.
ARNOLD BENNETT (1867–1931)

It is human nature to hate him whom you have injured.
CORNELIUS TACITUS (C. AD 56–117)

Subdue your appetites, my dears, and you've conquered human nature.
CHARLES DICKENS (1812–1870)

It is human nature to think wisely and act foolishly.
ANATOLE FRANCE (1844–1924)

The most beautiful as well as the most ugly inclinations of man are not part of a fixed biologically given human nature, but result from the social process which creates man.
ERICH FROMM (1900–1980)

I think computer viruses should count as life. I think it says something about human nature that the only form of life we have created so far is purely destructive. We've created life in our own image.
STEPHEN HAWKING (1942–)

No doubt Jack the Ripper excused himself on the grounds that it was human nature.
A. A. MILNE (1882–1956)

Human nature is not of itself vicious.
THOMAS PAINE (1737–1809)

Human nature constitutes a part of the evidence in every case.
ELISHA POTTER (1811–1882)

You cannot slander human nature; it is worse than words can paint it.
CHARLES H. SPURGEON (1834–1892)

Humanism

For humanism also appeals to man as man. It seeks to liberate the universal qualities of human nature from the narrow limitations of blood and soil and class and to create a common language and a common culture in which men can realize their common humanity.
CHRISTOPHER DAWSON (1889–1970)

Humanism was a real historical movement, but it was never a philosophy or a religion.
CHRISTOPHER DAWSON (1889–1970)

That which is called humanism, but what would be more correctly called irreligious anthropocentrism, cannot yield answers to the most essential questions of our life.
ALEXANDER SOLZHENITSYN (1918–)

Humanism was not wrong in thinking that truth, beauty, liberty, and equality are of infinite value, but in thinking that man can get them for himself without grace.
SIMONE WEIL (1909–1943)

Humanity

What sunshine is to flowers, smiles are to humanity. These are but trifles, to be sure; but, scattered along life's pathway, the good they do is inconceivable.
JOSEPH ADDISON (1672–1719)

In every child who is born under no matter what circumstances and of no matter what parents, the potentiality of the human race is born again, and in him, too, once more, and each of us, our terrific responsibility toward human life: toward the utmost idea of goodness, of the horror of terrorism, and of God.
JAMES AGEE (1909–1955), *Let Us Now Praise Famous Men*

Liberty, equality—bad principles! The only true principle for humanity is justice; and justice to the feeble is protection and kindness.
HENRI-FRÉDÉRIC AMIEL (1821–1881)

It is better to be a beggar than ignorant; for a beggar only wants money, but an ignorant person wants humanity.
ARISTIPPUS (C. 435–366 BC)

Part of the inhumanity of the computer is that, once it is competently programmed and working smoothly, it is completely honest.
ISAAC ASIMOV (1920–1992)

Real education should educate us out of self into something far finer; into a selflessness which links us with all humanity.
NANCY ASTOR (1879–1964)

Humanity is not a gift of nature, it is a spiritual achievement to be earned.
RICHARD BACH (1936–)

All humanity is passion; without passion, religion, history, novels, art would be ineffectual.
HONORÉ DE BALZAC (1799–1850)

It's important that someone celebrate our existence.... People are the only mirror we have to see ourselves in. The domain of all meaning. All virtue, all evil, are contained only in people. There is none in the universe at large. Solitary confinement is a punishment in every human culture.
LOIS MCMASTER BUJOLD (1949–), *Mirror Dance*

Humanity can be quite cold to those whose eyes see the world differently.
ERIC A. BURNS (1968–)

A human being is part of a whole, called by us the Universe, a part limited in time and space. He experiences himself, his thoughts and feelings, as something separated from the rest, a kind of optical delusion of his consciousness. This delusion is a kind of prison for us, restricting us to our personal desires and to affection for a few persons nearest us. Our task must be to free ourselves from this prison

by widening our circles of compassion to embrace all living creatures and the whole of nature in its beauty.
ALBERT EINSTEIN (1879–1955)

Remember your humanity and forget the rest.
ALBERT EINSTEIN (1879–1955)

Every gun that is made, every warship launched, every rocket fired signifies, in the final sense, a theft from those who hunger and are not fed, those who are cold and not clothed. This world in arms is not spending money alone. It is spending the sweat of its laborers, the genius of its scientists, the hopes of its children. This is not a way of life at all in any true sense. Under the cloud of threatening war, it is humanity hanging from a cross of iron.
DWIGHT D. EISENHOWER (1890–1969)

The end of the human race will be that it will eventually die of civilization.
RALPH WALDO EMERSON (1803–1882)

We are at the very beginning of time for the human race. It is not unreasonable that we grapple with problems. But there are tens of thousands of years in the future. Our responsibility is to do what we can, learn what we can, improve the solutions, and pass them on.
RICHARD FEYNMAN (1918–1988)

Humanity is acquiring all the right technology for all the wrong reasons.
R. BUCKMINSTER FULLER (1895–1983)

As human beings, our greatness lies not so much in being able to remake the world … as in being able to remake ourselves.
MAHATMA GANDHI (1869–1948)

You must not lose faith in humanity. Humanity is an ocean; if a few drops of the ocean are dirty, the ocean does not become dirty.
MAHATMA GANDHI (1869–1948)

They have exiled me now from their society and I am pleased, because humanity does not exile except the one whose noble spirit rebels against despotism and oppression. He who does not prefer exile to slavery is not free by any measure of freedom, truth, and duty.
KAHLIL GIBRAN (1883–1931), *Spirits Rebellious*

So long as we live among men, let us cherish humanity.
ANDRÉ GIDE (1869–1951)

The most important scientific revolutions all include, as their only common feature, the dethronement of human arrogance from one pedestal after another of previous convictions about our centrality in the cosmos.
STEPHEN JAY GOULD (1941–2002)

Without words, without writing and without books there would be no history, there could be no concept of humanity.
HERMANN HESSE (1877–1962)

It is easier to love humanity as a whole than to love one's neighbor.
ERIC HOFFER (1902–1983)

There is always more misery among the lower classes than there is humanity in the higher.
VICTOR HUGO (1802–1885), *Les Miserables*

As far as we can discern, the sole purpose of human existence is to kindle a light in the darkness of mere being.
CARL JUNG (1875–1961)

The history of the human race, viewed as a whole may be regarded as the realization of a hidden plan of nature to bring about a political constitution, internally, and for this purpose, also externally perfect, as the only state in which all the capacities implanted by her in mankind can be fully developed.
IMMANUEL KANT (1724–1804)

Be ashamed to die until you have won some victory for humanity.
HORACE MANN (1796–1859)

Every day sees humanity more victorious in the struggle with space and time.
GUGLIELMO MARCONI (1874–1937)

The chief obstacle to the progress of the human race is the human race.
DON MARQUIS (1878–1937)

We owe to the Middle Ages the two worst inventions of humanity—gunpowder and romantic love.
ANDRÉ MAUROIS (1885–1967)

Of all the preposterous assumptions of humanity over humanity, nothing exceeds most of the criticisms made on the habits of the poor by the well-housed, well-warmed, and well-fed.
HERMAN MELVILLE (1819–1891)

Any man who afflicts the human race with ideas must be prepared to see them misunderstood.
H. L. MENCKEN (1880–1956)

I love humanity, but I hate people.
EDNA ST. VINCENT MILLAY (1892–1950)

Conservation is humanity caring for the future.
NANCY NEWHALL (1908–1974)

I have no faith in human perfectability. I think that human exertion will have no appreciable effect upon humanity. Man is now only more active—not more happy—nor more wise, than he was 6,000 years ago.
EDGAR ALLAN POE (1809–1849)

Humanity has advanced, when it has advanced, not because it has been sober, responsible, and cautious, but because it has been playful, rebellious, and immature.
TOM ROBBINS (1936–)

Someday I want to be rich. Some people get so rich they lose all respect for humanity. That's how rich I want to be.
RITA RUDNER (1956–)

A man is morally free when, in full possession of his living humanity, he judges the world, and judges other men, with uncompromising sincerity.
GEORGE SANTAYANA (1863–1952)

[S]earch and see if there is not some place where you may invest your humanity.
DR. ALBERT SCHWEITZER (1875–1965)

It is a denial of justice not to stretch out a helping hand to the fallen; that is the common right of humanity.
SENECA (5 BC–AD 65)

The worst sin toward our fellow creatures is not to hate them, but to be indifferent to them: that's the essence of inhumanity.
GEORGE BERNARD SHAW (1856–1950), *The Devil's Disciple*

Humanity is composed but of two categories, the invalids and the nurses.
RICHARD BRINSLEY SHERIDAN (1751–1816)

I am a man, and whatever concerns humanity is of interest to me.
TERENCE (185–159 BC)

We are a spectacular, splendid manifestation of life. We have language. We have affection. We have genes for usefulness, and usefulness is about as close to a "common goal" of nature as I can guess at. And finally, and perhaps best of all, we have music.
LEWIS THOMAS (1913–1993), *The Medusa and the Snail*

It was enough to make a body ashamed of the human race.
MARK TWAIN (1835–1910), *The Adventures of Huckleberry Finn*

[Humanity] has unquestionably one really effective weapon—laughter. Power, money, persuasion, supplication, persecution—these can lift at a colossal humbug—push it a little—weaken it a little, century by century; but only laughter can blow it to rags and atoms at a blast. Against the assault of laughter nothing can stand.
MARK TWAIN (1835–1910), *The Mysterious Stranger*

Every mammal on this planet instinctively develops a natural equilibrium with the surrounding environment, but you humans do not. You move to an area, and you multiply, and multiply, until every

natural resource is consumed. The only way you can survive is to spread to another area. There is another organism on this planet that follows the same pattern. A virus. Human beings are a disease, a cancer of this planet. You are a plague, and we are the cure.
ANDY WACHOWSKI (1967–) and LARRY WACHOWSKI (1965–), *The Matrix*

To the real artist in humanity, what are called bad manners are often the most picturesque and significant of all.
WALT WHITMAN (1819–1892)

Wherever you come near the human race there's layers and layers of nonsense.
THORNTON WILDER (1897–1975), *Our Town*

Man was designed for accomplishment, engineered for success, and endowed with the seeds of greatness.
ZIG ZIGLAR (1926–)

Nobody knows the age of the human race, but everybody agrees that it is old enough to know better.
ANONYMOUS

The human race is faced with a cruel choice: work or daytime television.
ANONYMOUS

Humility

Life is a long lesson in humility.
JAMES M. BARRIE (1860–1937)

It is no great thing to be humble when you are brought low; but to be humble when you are praised is a great and rare attainment.
SAINT BERNARD OF CLAIRVAUX (1090–1153)

You couldn't be that good and not know it, somewhere in your secret heart, however much you'd been abused into affecting public humility.
LOIS MCMASTER BUJOLD (1949–), *A Civil Campaign*

He who speaks without modesty will find it difficult to make his words good.
CONFUCIUS (551–479 BC), *The Confucian Analects*

The firm, the enduring, the simple, and the modest are near to virtue.
CONFUCIUS (551–479 BC), *The Confucian Analects*

The superior man is modest in his speech, but exceeds in his actions.
CONFUCIUS (551–479 BC), *The Confucian Analects*

Modesty is the citadel of beauty.
DEMADES (C. 380–318 BC)

Humility is no substitute for a good personality.
FRAN LEBOWITZ (1950–), *Metropolitan Life*

Pride makes us artificial and humility makes us real.
THOMAS MERTON (1915–1968)

Be modest! It is the kind of pride least likely to offend.
JULES RENARD (1864–1910)

In peace there's nothing so becomes a man
As modest stillness and humility.
WILLIAM SHAKESPEARE (1564–1616), *King Henry VI*

The longer I live the more I see that I am never wrong about anything, and that all the pains I have so humbly taken to verify my notions have only wasted my time.
GEORGE BERNARD SHAW (1856–1950)

I have often wished I had time to cultivate modesty.... But I am too busy thinking about myself.
EDITH SITWELL (1887–1964)

If I only had a little humility, I'd be perfect.
TED TURNER (1938–)

Always acknowledge a fault. This will throw those in authority off their guard and give you an opportunity to commit more.
MARK TWAIN (1835–1910)

When pride comes, then comes disgrace, but with humility comes wisdom.
THE BIBLE, Proverbs 11:2

Humor

Humor is the only test of gravity, and gravity of humor; for a subject which will not bear raillery is suspicious, and a jest which will not bear serious examination is false wit.
ARISTOTLE (384–322 BC)

Defining and analyzing humor is a pastime of humorless people.
ROBERT BENCHLEY (1889–1945)

Humor is by far the most significant activity of the human brain.
EDWARD DE BONO (1933–)

Humor is just another defense against the universe.
MEL BROOKS (1926–)

That is the saving grace of humor, if you fail no one is laughing at you.
A. WHITNEY BROWN (1952–)

All I need to make a comedy is a park, a policeman, and a pretty girl.
CHARLIE CHAPLIN (1889–1977), *My Autobiography*

Humor is always based on a modicum of truth. Have you ever heard a joke about a father-in-law?
DICK CLARK (1929–)

Total absence of humor renders life impossible.
SIDONIE GABRIELLE COLETTE (1873–1954), *Chance Acquaintances*

A sense of humor is part of the art of leadership, of getting along with people, of getting things done.
DWIGHT D. EISENHOWER (1890–1969)

Humor is also a way of saying something serious.
T. S. ELIOT (1888–1965)

Wit makes its own welcome, and levels all distinctions. No dignity, no learning, no force of character, can make any stand against good wit.
RALPH WALDO EMERSON (1803–1882), *Letters and Social Aims: The Comic*

Where humor is concerned there are no standards—no one can say what is good or bad, although you can be sure that everyone will.
JOHN KENNETH GALBRAITH (1908–2006)

If I had no sense of humor, I would long ago have committed suicide.
MAHATMA GANDHI (1869–1948)

One doesn't have a sense of humor. It has you.
LARRY GELBART (1928–)

Life is tough, and if you have the ability to laugh at it you have the ability to enjoy it.
SALMA HAYEK (1966–)

Comedy is nothing more than tragedy deferred.
PICO IYER (1957–)

Humor is our way of defending ourselves from life's absurdities by thinking absurdly about them.
LEWIS MUMFORD (1895–1990)

Humor is everywhere, in that there's irony in just about anything a human does.
BILL NYE (1955–)

There's no trick to being a humorist when you have the whole government working for you.
WILL ROGERS (1879–1935)

The only rules comedy can tolerate are those of taste, and the only limitations those of libel.
JAMES THURBER (1894–1961)

The wit makes fun of other persons; the satirist makes fun of the world; the humorist makes fun of himself.
JAMES THURBER (1894–1961)

Humor is the great thing, the saving thing. The minute it crops up, all our irritations and resentments slip away and a sunny spirit takes their place.
MARK TWAIN (1835–1910)

Comedy is simply a funny way of being serious.
PETER USTINOV (1921–2004)

The world is a tragedy to those who feel, but a comedy to those who think.
HORACE WALPOLE (1717–1797)

Humor can be dissected as a frog can, but the thing dies in the process and the innards are discouraging to any but the pure scientific mind.
E. B. WHITE (1899–1985), *Some Remarks on Humor*

Hunger

The most violent appetites in all creatures are lust and hunger; the first is a perpetual call upon them to propagate their kind, the latter to preserve themselves.
JOSEPH ADDISON (1672–1719)

Hunger is the best sauce in the world.
MIGUEL DE CERVANTES (1547–1616)

If only it was as easy to banish hunger by rubbing the belly as it is to masturbate.
DIOGENES LAERTIUS (C. 200)

There are people in the world so hungry, that God cannot appear to them except in the form of bread.
MAHATMA GANDHI (1869–1948)

As God is my witness, as God is my witness they're not going to lick me. I'm going to live through this and when it's all over, I'll never be hungry again. No, nor any of my folk. If I have to lie, steal, cheat, or kill. As God is my witness, I'll never be hungry again.
SIDNEY HOWARD (1891–1939) and MARGARET MITCHELL (1900–1949), *Gone with the Wind*

Emergencies have always been necessary to progress. It was darkness which produced the lamp. It was fog that produced the compass. It was hunger that drove us to exploration. And it took a depression to teach us the real value of a job.
VICTOR HUGO (1802–1885)

When you are not physically starving, you have the luxury to realize psychic and emotional starvation.
CHERRIE MORAGA (1952–)

Concentration comes out of a combination of confidence and hunger.
ARNOLD PALMER (1929–)

There is hunger for ordinary bread, and there is hunger for love, for kindness, for thoughtfulness; and this is the great poverty that makes people suffer so much.
MOTHER TERESA (1910–1997)

He who is dying of hunger must be fed rather than taught.
SAINT THOMAS AQUINAS (1225–1274)

Make hunger thy sauce, as a medicine for health.
THOMAS TUSSER, (1524–1580)

If your enemy is hungry, feed him; if he is thirsty, give him something to drink. In doing this, you will heap burning coals on his head.
THE BIBLE, Romans 12:20

Hunger is the best sauce.
ITALIAN PROVERB

Hunting

Certainly there is no hunting like the hunting of man and those who have hunted armed men long enough and liked it, never really care for anything else thereafter.
ERNEST HEMINGWAY (1899–1961)

Hunting is not a sport. In a sport, both sides should know they're in the game.
PAUL RODRIGUEZ (1955–)

You see I'm against hunting, in fact I'm a hunt saboteur. I go out the night before and shoot the fox.
TIM VINE (1966–)

Husbands

Pride is the chief cause in the decline in the number of husbands and wives.
NEIL DIAMOND (1941–), *Husbands and Wives*

Husbands are like fires—they go out when unattended.
ZSA ZSA GABOR (1919–)

American husbands are the best in the world; no other husbands are so generous to their wives, or can be so easily divorced.
ELINOR GLYN (1864–1943)

There are women whose infidelities are the only link they still have with their husbands.
SACHA GUITRY (1885–1957)

When you consider what a chance women have to poison their husbands, it's a wonder there isn't more of it done.
KIN HUBBARD (1868–1930)

American women expect to find in their husbands a perfection that English women only hope to find in their butlers.
W. SOMERSET MAUGHAM (1874–1965)

Husbands never become good; they merely become proficient.
H. L. MENCKEN (1880–1956)

If there were no husbands, who would look after our mistresses?
GEORGE EDWARD MOORE (1873–1958)

My mother buried three husbands, and two of them were just napping.
RITA RUDNER (1956–)

There is so little difference between husbands you might as well keep the first.
ADELA ROGERS ST. JOHNS (1894–1988)

Hypocrisy

As witnesses not of our intentions but of our conduct, we can be true or false, and the hypocrite's crime is that he bears false witness against himself. What makes it so plausible to assume that hypocrisy is the vice of vices is that integrity can indeed exist under the cover of all other vices except this one. Only crime and the criminal, it is true, confront us with the perplexity of radical evil; but only the hypocrite is really rotten to the core.
HANNAH ARENDT (1906–1975), *On Revolution*

When we abolish the slavery of half of humanity, together with the whole system of hypocrisy it implies, then the "division" of humanity will reveal its genuine significance and the human couple will find its true form.
SIMONE DE BEAUVOIR (1908–1986), *The Second Sex*

Politeness, n.: The most acceptable hypocrisy.
AMBROSE BIERCE (1842–1914), *The Devil's Dictionary*

Hypocrisy can afford to be magnificent in its promises; for never intending to go beyond promises, it costs nothing.
EDMUND BURKE (1729–1797)

Hypocrisy is the vaseline of political intercourse.
BILLY CONNOLLY (1942–)

A conservative government is an organized hypocrisy.
BENJAMIN DISRAELI (1804–1881)

An ounce of hypocrisy is worth a pound of ambition.
MICHAEL KORDA (1933–)

Hypocrisy is the homage which vice pays to virtue.
FRANÇOIS DE LA ROCHEFOUCAULD (1613–1680)

Idealism

An idealist is a person who helps other people to be prosperous.
HENRY FORD (1863–1947)

It's really a wonder that I haven't dropped all my ideals, because they seem so absurd and impossible to carry out. Yet I keep them, because in spite of everything, I still believe that people are really good at heart.
ANNE FRANK (1929–1945)

An idealist is one who, on noticing that a rose smells better than a cabbage, concludes that it will also make better soup.
H. L. MENCKEN (1880–1956)

We are like sculptors, constantly carving out of others the image we long for, need, love or desire, often against reality, against their benefit, and always, in the end, a disappointment, because it does not fit them.
ANAÏS NIN (1903–1977)

I'm an idealist. I don't know where I'm going, but I'm on my way.
CARL SANDBURG (1878–1967), *Incidentals*

Ideals are like stars: you will not succeed in touching them with your hands, but like the seafaring man on the ocean desert of waters, you choose them as your guides, and following them, you reach your destiny.
CARL SCHURZ (1829–1906)

When they come downstairs from their Ivory Towers, Idealists are very apt to walk straight into the gutter.
LOGAN PEARSALL SMITH (1865–1946), *Afterthoughts*

Cynics regarded everybody as equally corrupt.... Idealists regarded everybody as equally corrupt, except themselves.
ROBERT ANTON WILSON (1932–2007)

Idealism is what precedes experience; cynicism is what follows.
DAVID T. WOLF (1943–)

Ideas

The thinker dies, but his thoughts are beyond the reach of destruction. Men are mortal; but ideas are immortal.
RICHARD ADAMS (1626–1698)

Don't worry about people stealing an idea. If it's original, you will have to ram it down their throats.
HOWARD AIKEN (1900–1973)

There are pauses amidst study, and even pauses of seeming idleness, in which a process goes on which may be likened to the digestion of food. In those seasons of repose, the powers are gathering their strength for new efforts; as land which lies fallow recovers itself for tillage.
J. W. ALEXANDER (1888–1971)

In every great time there is some one idea at work which is more powerful than any other, and which shapes the events of the time and determines their ultimate issues.
SIR FRANCIS BACON (1561–1626)

One of the greatest pains to human nature is the pain of a new idea.
WALTER BAGEHOT (1826–1877)

No one has ever had an idea in a dress suit.
SIR FREDERICK G. BANTING (1891–1941)

Every composer knows the anguish and despair occasioned by forgetting ideas which one had no time to write down.
LOUIS-HECTOR BERLIOZ (1803–1869)

I can't understand why people are frightened of new ideas. I'm frightened of the old ones.
JOHN CAGE (1912–1992)

This is my answer to the gap between ideas and action—I will write it out.
HORTENSE CALISHER (1911–)

There are only two kinds of scholars; those who love ideas and those who hate them.
ÉMILE-AUGUSTE CHARTIER (1868–1951)

A committee is a cul-de-sac down which ideas are lured and then quietly strangled.
SIR BARNETT COCKS (1907–1989)

Be less curious about people and more curious about ideas.
MARIE CURIE (1867–1934)

The way to combat noxious ideas is with other ideas. The way to combat falsehoods is with truth.
WILLIAM ORVILLE DOUGLAS (1898–1980)

Ideas must work through the brains and arms of men, or they are no better than dreams.
RALPH WALDO EMERSON (1803–1882)

We are the prisoners of ideas.
RALPH WALDO EMERSON (1803–1882)

An idea is a feat of association, and the height of it is a good metaphor.
ROBERT FROST (1874–1963)

Daring ideas are like chessmen moved forward. They may be beaten, but they may start a winning game.
JOHANN WOLFGANG VON GOETHE (1749–1832)

Whenever I hear people talking about liberal ideas, I am always astounded that men should love to fool themselves with empty sounds. An idea should never be liberal; it must be vigorous, positive, and without loose ends so that it may fulfill its divine mission and be productive. The proper place for liberality is in the realm of the emotions.
JOHANN WOLFGANG VON GOETHE (1749–1832)

When ideas fail, words come in very handy.
JOHANN WOLFGANG VON GOETHE (1749–1832)

I had a monumental idea this morning, but I didn't like it.
SAMUEL GOLDWYN (1882–1974)

Ideas are not thoughts; the thought respects the boundaries that the idea ignores, thereby failing to realize itself.
FRANZ GRILLPARZER (1791–1872)

Lack of money is no obstacle. Lack of an idea is an obstacle.
KEN HAKUTA (1950–)

So many new ideas are at first strange and horrible, though ultimately valuable that a very heavy responsibility rests upon those who would prevent their dissemination.
J. B. S. HALDANE (1892–1964)

Do something. If it doesn't work, do something else. No idea is too crazy.
JIM HIGHTOWER (1943–)

Man's mind, once stretched by a new idea, never regains its original dimensions.
OLIVER WENDELL HOLMES SR. (1809–1894)

Many ideas grow better when transplanted into another mind than in the one where they sprung up.
OLIVER WENDELL HOLMES SR. (1809–1894)

An invasion of armies can be resisted, but not an idea whose time has come.
VICTOR HUGO (1802–1885)

Sometimes the simplest idea can make the biggest difference.
CATHERINE RYAN HYDE (1955–), *Pay It Forward*

A new idea is first condemned as ridiculous and then dismissed as trivial, until finally, it becomes what everybody knows.
WILLIAM JAMES (1842–1910)

On a lazy Saturday morning when you're lying in bed, drifting in and out of sleep, there is a space where fantasy and reality become one. Are you awake, or are you dreaming? You see people and things; some are familiar; some are strange. You talk, you feel, but you move without walking; you fly without wings. Your mind and your body exist, but on separate planes. Time stands still. For me, this is the feeling I have when ideas come.
LYNN JOHNSTON (1947–), *Lynn on Ideas*

College isn't the place to go for ideas.
HELEN KELLER (1880–1968)

Ideas shape the course of history.
JOHN MAYNARD KEYNES (1883–1946)

Ideas are the beginning of all achievement.
BRUCE LEE (1940–1973)

Ideas, like large rivers, never have just one source.
WILLY LEY (1906–1969)

Everyone is a genius at least once a year. The real geniuses simply have their bright ideas closer together.
GEORG C. LICHTENBERG (1742–1799)

Ideas too are a life and a world.
GEORG C. LICHTENBERG (1742–1799)

He can compress the most words into the smallest ideas of any man I ever met.
ABRAHAM LINCOLN (1809–1865)

The human mind treats a new idea the same way the body treats a strange protein; it rejects it.
P. B. MEDAWAR (1915–)

To die for an idea; it is unquestionably noble. But how much nobler it would be if men died for ideas that were true!
H. L. MENCKEN (1880–1956)

I said to myself, I have things in my head that are not like what anyone has taught me—shapes and ideas so near to me—so natural to my way of being and thinking that it hasn't occurred to me to put them down. I decided to start anew, to strip away what I had been taught.
GEORGIA O'KEEFFE (1887–1986)

The history of mankind is the history of ideas.
LUIGI PIRANDELLO (1867–1936)

Ideas aren't real estate, they grow collectively and that knocks out the egotistical loneliness that generally infects art.
ROBERT REDFORD (1937–)

Good ideas are not adopted automatically. They must be driven into practice with courageous patience.
HYMAN RICKOVER (1900–1986)

A good idea will keep you awake during the morning, but a great idea will keep you awake during the night.
MARILYN VOS SAVANT (1946–)

No matter what anybody tells you, words and ideas can change the world.
TOM SCHULMAN (1951–), *Dead Poets Society*

The best ideas are common property.
SENECA (5 BC–AD 65), *Epistles*

Ideas are like rabbits. You get a couple and learn how to handle them, and pretty soon you have a dozen.
JOHN STEINBECK (1902–1968)

If an idea's worth having once, it's worth having twice.
TOM STOPPARD (1937–)

The vitality of thought is in adventure. Ideas won't keep. Something must be done about them.
ALFRED NORTH WHITEHEAD (1861–1947)

An idea is salvation by imagination.
FRANK LLOYD WRIGHT (1869–1959)

Identity

Identity would seem to be the garment with which one covers the nakedness of the self, in which case, it is best that the garment be loose, a little like the robes of the desert, through which one's nakedness can always be felt, and, sometimes, discerned.
JAMES ARTHUR BALDWIN (1924–1987)

One of the most wonderful things in nature is a glance of the eye; it transcends speech; it is the bodily symbol of identity.
RALPH WALDO EMERSON (1803–1882)

Integrity simply means not violating one's own identity.
ERICH FROMM (1900–1980)

If you wake up at a different time, in a different place, could you wake up as a different person?
CHUCK PALAHNIUK (1962–)

Identity is such a crucial affair that one shouldn't rush into it.
DAVID QUAMMEN (1948–)

To be idle requires a strong sense of personal identity.
ROBERT LOUIS STEVENSON (1850–1894)

Be careful what you pretend to be because you are what you pretend to be.
KURT VONNEGUT JR. (1922–2007)

Ideology

Growth for the sake of growth is the ideology of the cancer cell.
EDWARD ABBEY (1927–1989)

He who stands aloof runs the risk of believing himself better than others and misusing his critique of society as an ideology for his private interest.
THEODOR W. ADORNO (1903–1969)

If across the Atlantic the ideology was pride, here it is delivering the goods.
THEODOR W. ADORNO (1903–1969)

Life has become the ideology of its own absence.
THEODOR W. ADORNO (1903–1969)

Ideology … is indispensable in any society if men are to be formed, transformed and equipped to respond to the demands of their conditions of existence.
LOUIS ALTHUSSER (1918–1990)

Ideology has very little to do with "consciousness"—it is profoundly unconscious.
LOUIS ALTHUSSER (1918–1990)

It did not occur to us that the Marxists' solution was fraudulent or that their vision was distorted, that whatever the wrongs in our society it was not the ideology of theirs that will cure them.
BARBARA AMIEL (1940–)

The Third World is not a reality but an ideology.
HANNAH ARENDT (1906–1979)

Faith in God's revelation has nothing to do with an ideology which glorifies the status quo.
KARL BARTH (1886–1968)

There has been a substitution of ideology for fact and scientific and engineering data in this administration.
VINTON CERF (1943–)

Killing the private property—that was the center of the Marxist economy and Marxist ideology. That was the center of the Lenin ideology.
ANATOLY CHUBAIS (1955–)

Ideology has shaped the very sofa on which I sit.
MASON COOLEY (1927–2002)

Ideology in the Soviet Union is both dead, and very much alive! Dead at the level of faith; alive as an indispensable rationale of policy.
MILOVAN DJILAS (1911–1995)

The ideology of this America wants to establish reassurance through Imitation. But profit defeats ideology, because the consumers want to be thrilled not only by the guarantee of the Good but also by the shudder of the Bad.
UMBERTO ECO (1932–)

Although, this is often used with negative connotations, I see ideology as an inherent part of culture.
DARIO FO (1926–)

You have your ideology and I have mine.
KAHLIL GIBRAN (1883–1931)

When I was in my teens, I had formulated the idea that the greatest advances in science arise where there has been resistance to progress. This is not so

much due to the intrinsic intellectual difficulty, but rather the fact that it might threaten the current ideology, whatever it might be.
Celia Green (1935–)

Pakistan not only means freedom and independence but the Muslim Ideology which has to be preserved, which has come to us as a precious gift and treasure and which, we hope others will share with us.
Muhammad Ali Jinnah (1876–1948)

Great ideology creates great times.
Kim Jong Il (1942–)

The truly powerful feed ideology to the masses like fast food while they dine on the most rarified delicacy of all: impunity.
Naomi Klein (1909–)

Those looking for ideology in the White House should consider this: For the men who rule our world, rules are for other people.
Naomi Klein (1909–)

Ideology and communication more often than not run into each other rather than complement each other. Principle and communication work together. Ideology and communication often work apart.
Frank Luntz (1962–)

To defeat the aggressors is not enough to make peace durable. The main thing is to discard the ideology that generates war.
Ludwig von Mises (1881–1973)

For the first time in our history, ideology and theology hold a monopoly of power in Washington.
Bill Moyers (1934–)

It's essential not to have an ideology, not to be a member of a political party. While the writer can have certain political views, he has to be careful not to have his hands tied.
Manuel Puig (1932–1990)

It has been demonstrated that no system, not even the most inhuman, can continue to exist without an ideology.
Joe Slovo (1926–1995)

Sometimes, if you wear suits for too long, it changes your ideology.
Joe Slovo (1926–1995)

How can you tell when a political ideology has become the equivalent of a religion?
Andrew Sullivan (1963–)

If any ideology is so serious that you can't have fun while you're doing it, it's probably too serious.
Larry Wall (1949–)

Political ideology can corrupt the mind, and science.
Edward O. Wilson (1929–)

Idleness

Idleness is a constant sin, and labor is a duty. Idleness is the devil's home for temptation and for unprofitable, distracting musings; while labor profiteth others and ourselves.
Anne Baxter (1923–1985)

In idleness there is a perpetual despair.
Thomas Carlyle (1795–1881)

Know the true value of time; snatch, seize, and enjoy every moment of it. No idleness; no laziness; no procrastination; never put off till tomorrow what you can do today.
Lord Chesterfield (1694–1773)

I don't think necessity is the mother of invention—invention, in my opinion, arises directly from idleness, possibly also from laziness. To save oneself trouble.
Agatha Christie (1890–1976), *An Autobiography*

Idleness is an inlet to disorder, and makes way for licentiousness. People who have nothing to do are quickly tired of their own company.
Jeremy Collier (1650–1726)

Idleness is not doing nothing. Idleness is being free to do anything.
Floyd Dell (1887–1969)

Idleness and lack of occupation tend—nay are dragged—towards evil.
HIPPOCRATES (460–377 BC), *Decorum*

Idleness, like kisses, to be sweet must be stolen.
JEROME K. JEROME (1859–1927)

Grief is a species of idleness.
SAMUEL JOHNSON (1709–1784)

Far from idleness being the root of all evil, it is rather the only true good.
SØREN KIERKEGAARD (1813–1855)

Certainly work is not always required of a man. There is such a thing as a sacred idleness —the cultivation of which is now fearfully neglected.
GEORGE MACDONALD (1824–1905)

Rather do what is nothing in the purpose than to be idle, that the devil may find thee doing. The bird that sits is easily shot when the fliers escape the fowler. Idleness is the Dead Sea that swallows all the virtues, and is the self-made sepulcher of a living man.
FRANCIS QUARLES (1592–1644)

To be idle requires a strong sense of personal identity.
ROBERT LOUIS STEVENSON (1850–1894)

Never be entirely idle; but either be reading, or writing, or praying or meditating or endeavoring something for the public good.
THOMAS À KEMPIS (1380–1471)

Idols

Idolatry is really not good for anyone. Not even the idols.
JOHN BACH (1946–)

God is not present in idols. Your feelings are your god. The soul is your temple.
CHANAKYA (350–275 BC)

I have no idols. I admire work, dedication and competence.
AYRTON SENNA (1960–1994)

Ignorance

We allow our ignorance to prevail upon us and make us think we can survive alone, alone in patches, alone in groups, alone in races, even alone in genders.
MAYA ANGELOU (1928–)

It is better to be a beggar than ignorant; for a beggar only wants money, but an ignorant person wants humanity.
ARISTIPPUS (C. 435–366 BC)

If knowledge can create problems, it is not through ignorance that we can solve them.
ISAAC ASIMOV (1920–1992)

A great deal of intelligence can be invested in ignorance when the need for illusion is deep.
SAUL BELLOW (1915–2005)(1915–)

Consistency requires you to be as ignorant today as you were a year ago.
BERNARD BERENSON (1865–1959)

The small part of ignorance that we arrange and classify we give the name of knowledge.
AMBROSE BIERCE (1842–1914)

Innocence dwells with Wisdom, but never with Ignorance.
WILLIAM BLAKE (1757–1827)

Ignorance is not innocence but sin.
ROBERT BROWNING (1812–1889)

If not bliss, ignorance can at least be fun.
CARTER BURWELL (1955–)

The truest characters of ignorance are vanity, and pride and arrogance.
SAMUEL BUTLER (1835–1902)

The evil that is in the world almost always comes of ignorance, and good intentions may do as much harm as malevolence if they lack understanding.
ALBERT CAMUS (1913–1960)

I do not believe in the collective wisdom of individual ignorance.
THOMAS CARLYLE (1795–1881)

That there should be one man die ignorant who had capacity for knowledge, this I call a tragedy.
THOMAS CARLYLE (1795–1881)

Ignorance is the mother of admiration.
GEORGE CHAPMAN (1559–1634)

I am not ashamed to confess I am ignorant of what I do not know.
CICERO (106–43 BC)

Ignorance is bliss. Oedipus ruined a great sex life by asking too many questions.
STEPHEN COLBERT (1964–)

Ignorance is the night of the mind, but a night without moon and star.
CONFUCIUS (551–479 BC)

I am an agnostic; I do not pretend to know what many ignorant men are sure of.
CLARENCE S. DARROW (1857–1938)

Ignorance more frequently begets confidence than does knowledge: it is those who know little, and not those who know much, who so positively assert that this or that problem will never be solved by science.
CHARLES DARWIN (1809–1882)

[I]t is always advisable to perceive clearly our ignorance.
CHARLES DARWIN (1809–1882)

To be conscious that you are ignorant is a great step to knowledge.
BENJAMIN DISRAELI (1804–1881), *Sybil*

Ignorance never settles a question.
BENJAMIN DISRAELI (1804–1881)

Where justice is denied, where poverty is enforced, where ignorance prevails, and where any one class is made to feel that society is in an organized conspiracy to oppress, rob, and degrade them, neither persons nor property will be safe.
FREDERICK DOUGLASS (1817–1895)

Education is a progressive discovery of our own ignorance.
WILL DURANT (1885–1981)

The highest form of ignorance is when you reject something you don't know anything about.
WAYNE D. DYER (1940–)

His ignorance is encyclopedic.
ABBA EBAN (1915–2002)

A little learning is a dangerous thing but a lot of ignorance is just as bad.
BOB EDWARDS (1947–)

Ignorance gives one a large range of probabilities.
GEORGE ELIOT (1819–1880)

There are many things of which a wise man might wish to be ignorant.
RALPH WALDO EMERSON (1803–1882)

Ignorance of one's misfortunes is clear gain.
EURIPIDES (C. 480–406 BC)

It is no good to try to stop knowledge from going forward. Ignorance is never better than knowledge.
ENRICO FERMI (1901–1954)

My whole career can be summed up with "Ignorance is bliss." When you do not know better, you do not really worry about failing.
JEFF FOXWORTHY (1958–)

A person is never happy except at the price of some ignorance.
ANATOLE FRANCE (1844–1924)

A learned blockhead is a greater blockhead than an ignorant one.
BENJAMIN FRANKLIN (1706–1790)

He was so learned that he could name a horse in nine languages; so ignorant that he bought a cow to ride on.
BENJAMIN FRANKLIN (1706–1790)

I do not feel obliged to believe that the same God who has endowed us with sense, reason, and intellect has intended us to forgo their use.
GALILEO GALILEI (1564–1642)

I have never met a man so ignorant that I couldn't learn something from him.
GALILEO GALILEI (1564–1642)

Nothing is worse than active ignorance.
JOHANN WOLFGANG VON GOETHE (1749–1832)

Ignorance of certain subjects is a great part of wisdom.
HUIGH DE GROOT (1583–1645)

It is better to confess ignorance than provide it.
HOMER HICKAM (1943–), *The Coalwood Way*

The recipe for perpetual ignorance is: be satisfied with your opinions and content with your knowledge.
ELBERT HUBBARD (1856–1915)

It is worse still to be ignorant of your ignorance.
SAINT JEROME (C. 342–420)

Nothing in all the world is more dangerous than sincere ignorance and conscientious stupidity.
MARTIN LUTHER KING JR. (1929–1968), *Strength to Love*

Ignorance breeds monsters to fill up the vacancies of the soul that are unoccupied by the verities of knowledge.
HORACE MANN (1796–1859)

It is impossible to defeat an ignorant man in argument.
WILLIAM G. MCADOO (1863–1941)

It's innocence when it charms us, ignorance when it doesn't.
MIGNON MCLAUGHLIN (1913–1983), *The Neurotic's Notebook*

The greater the ignorance the greater the dogmatism.
SIR WILLIAM OSLER (1849–1919)

Against logic there is no armor like ignorance.
DR. LAURENCE J. PETER (1919–1990)

Ignorance of all things is an evil neither terrible nor excessive, nor yet the greatest of all; but great cleverness and much learning, if they be accompanied by a bad training, are a much greater misfortune.
PLATO (C. 428–348 BC)

Ignorance, the root and the stem of every evil.
PLATO (C. 428–348 BC)

Better be ignorant of a matter than half know it.
PUBLILIUS SYRUS (C. 100 BC), *Maxims*

An ignorant person is one who doesn't know what you have just found out.
WILL ROGERS (1879–1935)

You know everybody is ignorant, only on different subjects.
WILL ROGERS (1879–1935)

Arrogance is the worst kind of ignorance.
GARY ROLANDO (1982–)

Most people would sooner die than think; in fact, they do so.
BERTRAND RUSSELL (1872–1970)

Nothing is so good for an ignorant man as silence; and if he was sensible of this he would not be ignorant.
SAADI (1184–1291)

Ignorance is degrading only when found in company with great riches.
ARTHUR SCHOPENHAUER (1788–1860)

Have the courage to be ignorant of a great number of things, in order to avoid the calamity of being ignorant of everything.
SYDNEY SMITH (1771–1845)

The only good is knowledge and the only evil is ignorance.
SOCRATES (469–399 BC)

Ignorant men don't know what good they hold in their hands until they've flung it away.
SOPHOCLES (496–406 BC)

I believe in the forgiveness of sin and the redemption of ignorance.
ADLAI E. STEVENSON II (1900–1965)

It is impossible to make people understand their ignorance; for it requires knowledge to perceive it and therefore he that can perceive it hath it not.
JEREMY TAYLOR (1613–1667)

Ignorance and inconsideration are the two great causes of the ruin of mankind.
JOHN TILLOTSON (1630–1694)

All you need in this life is ignorance and confidence; then success is sure.
MARK TWAIN (1835–1910)

The multitude of books is making us ignorant.
VOLTAIRE (1694–1778)

Ignorance is like a delicate exotic fruit; touch it and the bloom is gone.
OSCAR WILDE (1854–1900)

Ignorance is not bliss, it is oblivion.
PHILIP WYLIE (1902–1971)

Never forget public ignorance is the government's best friend.
ANONYMOUS

If ignorance is bliss, why aren't more people jumping up and down for joy.
ANONYMOUS

In the battle for survival the ignorant man has a considerable advantage.
ANONYMOUS

The mark of your ignorance is the depth of your belief in injustice and tragedy. What the caterpillar calls the end of the world, the master calls a butterfly.
ANONYMOUS

Illness

Refuse to be ill. Never tell people you are ill; never own it to yourself. Illness is one of those things which a man should resist on principle.
SIR EDWARD G. BULWER-LYTTON (1803–1873)

My illness is due to my doctor's insistence that I drink milk, a whitish fluid they force down helpless babies.
W. C. FIELDS (1880–1946)

A wise man should consider that health is the greatest of human blessings, and learn how by his own thought to derive benefit from his illnesses.
HIPPOCRATES (460–377 BC), *Regimen in Health*

To safeguard one's health at the cost of too strict a diet is a tiresome illness indeed.
FRANÇOIS DE LA ROCHEFOUCAULD (1613–1680)

Think of life as a terminal illness, because, if you do, you will live it with joy and passion, as it ought to be lived.
ANNA QUINDLEN (1953–), *A Short Guide to a Happy Life*

In spite of illness, in spite even of the archenemy sorrow, one can remain alive long past the usual date of disintegration if one is unafraid of change, insatiable in intellectual curiosity, interested in big things, and happy in small ways.
EDITH WHARTON (1862–1937)

Illusion

Time is an illusion. Lunchtime doubly so.
DOUGLAS ADAMS (1952–2001)

What if everything is an illusion and nothing exists? In that case, I definitely overpaid for my carpet.
WOODY ALLEN (1935–)

A great deal of intelligence can be invested in ignorance when the need for illusion is deep.
SAUL BELLOW (1915–2005)

The greatest obstacle to discovery is not ignorance—it is the illusion of knowledge.
DANIEL J. BOORSTIN (1914–)

Illusions are art, for the feeling person, and it is by art that you live, if you do.
ELIZABETH BOWEN (1899–1973)

If power was an illusion, wasn't weakness necessarily one also?
LOIS MCMASTER BUJOLD (1949–), *A Civil Campaign*

What is life? An illusion, a shadow, a story,
And the greatest good is little enough: for all life is a dream, and dreams themselves are only dreams.
PEDRO CALDERÓN DE LA BARCA (1600–1681), *Life Is a Dream*

I see many people die because they judge that life is not worth living. I see others paradoxically getting killed for the ideas or illusions that give them a reason for living (what is called a reason for living is also an excellent reason for dying). I therefore conclude that the meaning of life is the most urgent of questions.
ALBERT CAMUS (1913–1960), *The Myth of Sisyphus*

Reality is merely an illusion, albeit a very persistent one.
ALBERT EINSTEIN (1879–1955)

If we take in our hand any volume; of divinity or school metaphysics, for instance; let us ask, "Does it contain any abstract reasoning concerning quantity or number?" No. "Does it contain any experimental reasoning concerning matter of fact and existence?" No. Commit it then to the flames: for it can contain nothing but sophistry and illusion.
DAVID HUME (1711–1776)

Illusions mistaken for truth are the pavement under our feet. They are what we call civilization.
BARBARA KINGSOLVER (1955–), *The Poisonwood Bible*

It is an illusion that youth is happy, an illusion of those who have lost it; but the young know they are wretched for they are full of the truthless idealswhich have been instilled into them, and each time they come in contact with the real, they are bruised and wounded.
W. SOMERSET MAUGHAM (1874–1965), *Of Human Bondage*

[F]ree time is an illusion. It's what you get when you die and the gods reward you for a life spent working from dawn until midnight.
TAMORA PIERCE (1954–), *Alanna: The First Adventure*

Writing gives you the illusion of control, and then you realize it's just an illusion, that people are going to bring their own stuff into it.
DAVID SEDARIS (1956–)

What a strange illusion it is to suppose that beauty is goodness.
LEO TOLSTOY (1828–1910)

Don't part with your illusions. When they are gone you may still exist, but you have ceased to live.
MARK TWAIN (1835–1910)

I have realized that the past and future are real illusions, that they exist in the present, which is what there is and all there is.
ALAN W. WATTS (1915–1973)

Illusion is the first of all pleasures.
OSCAR WILDE (1854–1900)

Imagination

Man is an imagining being.
GASTON BACHELARD (1884–1962)

The soul without imagination is what an observatory would be without a telescope.
HENRY WARD BEECHER (1813–1887)

The imagination is not a State: it is the Human existence itself.
WILLIAM BLAKE (1757–1827)

Imagination is a poor matter when it has to part company with understanding.
THOMAS CARLYLE (1795–1881)

Not our logical faculty, but our imaginative one is king over us. I might say, priest and prophet to lead us to heaven-ward, or magician and wizard to lead us hellward.
THOMAS CARLYLE (1795–1881)

To me this world is all one continued vision of fancy or imagination, and I feel flattered when I am told so. What is it sets Homer, Virgil and Milton in so high a rank of art? Why is the Bible more entertaining and instructive than any other book? Is it not because they are addressed to the imagination, which is spiritual sensation, and but immediately to the understanding or reason?
WILLIAM BLAKE (1757–1827)

What is now proved was only once imagined.
WILLIAM BLAKE (1757–1827)

Only in men's imagination does every truth find an effective and undeniable existence. Imagination, not invention, is the supreme master of art as of life.
JOSEPH CONRAD (1857–1924)

To know is nothing at all; to imagine is everything.
ALBERT EINSTEIN (1879–1955)

Imagination is everything. It is the preview of life's coming attractions.
ALBERT EINSTEIN (1879–1955)

The most evident difference springs from the important part which is played in man by a relatively strong power of imagination and by the capacity to think, aided as it is by language and other symbolic devices.
ALBERT EINSTEIN (1879–1955)

I am enough of an artist to draw freely upon my imagination. Imagination is more important than knowledge. Knowledge is limited. Imagination encircles the world.
ALBERT EINSTEIN (1879–1955)

In that way imagination and intelligence enter into our existence in the part of servants of the primary instincts.
ALBERT EINSTEIN (1879–1955)

Imagination is more important than knowledge. For knowledge is limited to all we now know and understand, while imagination embraces the entire world, and all there ever will be to know and understand.
ALBERT EINSTEIN (1879–1955)

Imagination is not a talent of some people but is the health of everyone.
RALPH WALDO EMERSON (1803–1882)

Science does not know its debt to imagination.
RALPH WALDO EMERSON (1803–1882)

The quality of the imagination is to flow and not to freeze.
RALPH WALDO EMERSON (1803–1882)

We live by our imagination, our admiration, and our sentiments.
RALPH WALDO EMERSON (1803–1882)

What is the imagination? Only an arm or weapon of the interior energy; only the precursor of the reason.
RALPH WALDO EMERSON (1803–1882)

Imagination is the one weapon in the war against reality.
JULES DE GAULTIER (1858–1942)

There is nothing more dreadful than imagination without taste.
JOHANN WOLFGANG VON GOETHE (1749–1832)

First comes thought; then organization of that thought, into ideas and plans; then transformation of those plans into reality. The beginning, as you will observe, is in your imagination.
NAPOLEON HILL (1883–1970)

The quantity of civilization is measured by the quality of imagination.
VICTOR HUGO (1802–1885), *Les Miserables*

One who has imagination without learning has wings without feet.
JOSEPH JOUBERT (1754–1824)

All the works of man have their origin in creative fantasy. What right have we then to depreciate imagination.
CARL JUNG (1875–1961)

Without this playing with fantasy no creative work has ever yet come to birth. The debt we owe to the play of the imagination is incalculable.
CARL JUNG (1875–1961)

I am certain of nothing but the holiness of the heart's affections and the truth of imagination. What the imagination seizes as beauty must be truth, whether it existed before or not.
JOHN KEATS (1795–1821)

My imagination is a monastery and I am its monk.
JOHN KEATS (1795–1821)

Our imagination is the only limit to what we can hope to have in the future.
CHARLES F. KETTERING (1876–1958)

Our thoughts and imagination are the only real limits to our possibilities.
ORISON SWETT MARDEN (1850–1924)

It is impossible to imagine the universe run by a wise, just and omnipotent God, but it is quite easy to imagine it run by a board of gods. If such a board actually exists it operates precisely like the board of a corporation that is losing money.
H. L. MENCKEN (1880–1956)

Imagination is the voice of daring. If there is anything Godlike about God it is that. He dared to imagine everything.
HENRY MILLER (1891–1980)

The power of imagination makes us infinite.
JOHN MUIR (1838–1914)

Imagination rules the world.
NAPOLÉON I (1769–1821)

The human race is governed by its imagination.
NAPOLÉON I (1769–1821)

There is only one admirable form of the imagination: the imagination that is so intense that it creates a new reality, that it makes things happen.
SEAN O'FAOLAIN (1900–1991)

Reason clears and plants the wilderness of the imagination to harvest the wheat of art.
AUSTIN O'MALLEY (1858–1932)

Imagination decides everything.
BLAISE PASCAL (1623–1662)

Imagination disposes of everything; it creates beauty, justice, and happiness, which is everything in this world.
BLAISE PASCAL (1623–1662)

It is not that the child lives in a world of imagination, but that the child within us survives and starts into life only at rare moments of recollection, which makes us believe, and is it not true, that, as children, we were imaginative?
CESARE PAVESE (1908–1950)

Everything you can imagine is real.
PABLO PICASSO (1881–1973)

Imagination is the beginning of creation. You imagine what you desire, you will what you imagine and at last you create what you will.
GEORGE BERNARD SHAW (1856–1950)

Skill without imagination is craftsmanship and gives us many useful objects such as wickerwork picnic baskets. Imagination without skill gives us modern art.
TOM STOPPARD (1937–), *Artist Descending a Staircase*

Memory feeds imagination.
AMY TAN (1952–)

It is usually the imagination that is wounded first, rather than the heart; it being much more sensitive.
HENRY DAVID THOREAU (1817–1862)

You cannot depend on your eyes when your imagination is out of focus.
MARK TWAIN (1835–1910), *A Connecticut Yankee in King Arthur's Court*

Anyone who lives within their means suffers from a lack of imagination.
OSCAR WILDE (1854–1900)

An idea is salvation by imagination.
FRANK LLOYD WRIGHT (1869–1959)

Imagination is the pontoon bridge making way for the timid feet of reason.
ANONYMOUS

There is nothing that cannot be achieved by firm imagination.
JAPANESE PROVERB

Imitation

Imitation is the sincerest form of television.
FRED ALLEN (1894–1956)

It is by imitation, far more than by precept, that we learn everything; and what we learn thus, we acquire not only more efficiently, but more pleasantly. This forms our manners, our opinions, our lives.
EDMUND BURKE (1729–1797)

Trust yourself. Think for yourself. Act for yourself. Speak for yourself. Be yourself. Imitation is suicide.
MARVA COLLINS (1936–)

Imitation is the sincerest form of flattery.
CHARLES CALEB COLTON (1780–1832), *Lacon*

By three methods we may learn wisdom: first, by reflection, which is noblest; second, by imitation, which is easiest; and third by experience, which is the bitterest.
CONFUCIUS (551–479 BC)

Adaptability is not imitation. It means power of resistance and assimilation.
MAHATMA GANDHI (1869–1948)

I hardly know so true a mark of a little mind as the servile imitation of others.
FULKE GREVILLE (1554–1628)

Rudeness is the weak man's imitation of strength.
ERIC HOFFER (1902–1983)

Almost all absurdity of conduct arises from the imitation of those whom we cannot resemble.
SAMUEL JOHNSON (1709–1784)

To do just the opposite is also a form of imitation.
GEORG C. LICHTENBERG (1742–1799)

It is better to fail in originality than to succeed in imitation.
HERMAN MELVILLE (1819–1891)

He who lets the world, or his own portion of it, choose his plan of life for him, has no need of any other faculty than the ape-like one of imitation. He who chooses his plan for himself, employs all his faculties. He must use observation to see, reasoning and judgment to foresee, activity to gather materials for decision, discrimination to decide, and when he has decided, firmness and self-control to hold to his deliberate decision.
JOHN STUART MILL (1806–1873), *On Liberty*

Glamour, that trans-human aura or power to attract imitation, is a kind of vessel into which dreams are poured, and some vessels are simply worthier than others.... A beautiful woman can turn heads but real glamour has a deeper pull.... Glamour [is] the power to rearrange people's emotions, which, in effect, is the power to control one's environment.
ARTHUR MILLER (1915–2005)

All art is an imitation of nature.
SENECA (5 BC–AD 65)

Imitation causes us to leave natural ways to enter into artificial ones; it therefore makes slaves.
ALEXANDRE RODOLPHE VINET (1797–1847)

The Past: Our cradle, not our prison; there is danger as well as appeal in its glamour. The past is for inspiration, not imitation, for continuation, not repetition.
ISRAEL ZANGWILL (1864–1926)

Immortality

The influence of each human being on others in this life is a kind of immortality.
JOHN QUINCY ADAMS (1767–1848)

I don't want to achieve immortality through my work.... I want to achieve it through not dying.
WOODY ALLEN (1935–)

The only thing wrong with immortality is that it tends to go on forever.
HERB CAEN (1916–1997)

If you were to destroy in mankind the belief in immortality, not only love but every living force maintaining the life of the world would at once be dried up. Moreover, nothing then would be immoral, everything would be permissible, even cannibalism.
FYODOR DOSTOEVSKY, (1821–1881), *The Brothers Karamazov*

Immortality. I notice that as soon as writers broach this question they begin to quote. I hate quotation. Tell me what you know.
RALPH WALDO EMERSON (1803–1882)

Millions long for immortality who don't know what to do with themselves on a rainy Sunday afternoon.
SUSAN ERTZ (1894–1985), *Anger in the Sky*

The average man, who does not know what to do with his life, wants another one which will last forever.
ANATOLE FRANCE (1844–1924)

If all else fails, immortality can always be assured by spectacular error.
JOHN KENNETH GALBRAITH (1908–2006)

Ten thousand fools proclaim themselves into obscurity, while one wise man forgets himself into immortality.
MARTIN LUTHER KING JR. (1929–1968)

The first condition of immortality is death.
STANISLAW LEC (1909–1966), *Unkempt Thoughts*

Seek not, my soul, the life of the immortals; but enjoy to the full the resources that are within thy reach.
PINDAR (522–443 BC)

The soul of man is immortal and imperishable.
PLATO (C. 428–348 BC), *The Republic*

I have Immortal longings in me...
WILLIAM SHAKESPEARE (1564–1616), *Antony and Cleopatra*

Impatience

Intuition is a suspension of logic due to impatience.
RITA MAE BROWN (1944–)

Patience is the support of weakness; impatience the ruin of strength.
CHARLES CALEB COLTON (1780–1832)

In all evils which admit a remedy, impatience should be avoided, because it wastes that time and attention in complaints which, if properly applied, might remove the cause.
SAMUEL JOHNSON (1709–1784)

There are two main human sins from which all the others derive: impatience and indolence. It was because of impatience that they were expelled from Paradise, it is because of indolence that they do not return. Yet perhaps there is only one major sin: impatience. Because of impatience they were expelled, because of impatience they do not return.
FRANZ KAFKA (1883–1924)

Experience has taught me this, that we undo ourselves by impatience. Misfortunes have their life

and their limits, their sickness and their health.
MICHEL DE MONTAIGNE (1533–1592)

Impatience is the mark of independence, not of bondage.
MARIANNE MOORE (1887–1972)

Imperfection

This is the very perfection of a man, to find out his own imperfection.
SAINT AUGUSTINE (354–430)

It is only imperfection that complains of what is imperfect. The more perfect we are, the more gentle and quiet we become toward the defects of others.
FRANÇOIS DE FÉNELON (1651–1715)

Have patience with all things, but chiefly have patience with yourself. Do not lose courage in considering your own imperfections but instantly set about remedying them—every day begin the task anew.
SAINT FRANCIS DE SALES (1567–1622)

Endeavor to be always patient of the faults and imperfections of others for thou has many faults and imperfections of thine own that require forbearance. If thou are not able to make thyself that which thou wishest, how canst thou expect to mold another in conformity to thy will?
THOMAS À KEMPIS (1380–1471)

A diamond with a flaw is worth more than a pebble without imperfections.
CHINESE PROVERB

Imperialism

For behind all imperialism is ultimately the imperialistic individual, just as behind all peace is ultimately the peaceful individual.
IRVING BABBITT (1865–1933)

If there ever was in the history of humanity an enemy who was truly universal, an enemy whose acts and moves trouble the entire world, threaten the entire world, attack the entire world in any way or another, that real and really universal enemy is precisely Yankee imperialism.
FIDEL CASTRO (1926–)

Imperialism is not the creation of any one or any one group of states.
KARL LIEBKNECHT (1871–1919)

Imperialism was genuinely popular among Athenians who would expect to share in its profits, even if only indirectly and collectively, and not to have to bear its burdens.
J. M. ROBERTS (1928–2003)

It was the individual imperialism of the frontiersman-type that actually opened up and conquered the North American continent.
FRANCIS P. YOCKEY (1917–1960)

Impotence

It is only when the rich are sick that they fully feel the impotence of wealth.
CHARLES CALEB COLTON (1782–1830)

The impotence of God is infinite.
ANATOLE FRANCE (1844–1924)

It is better to be violent, if there is violence in our hearts, than to put on the cloak of nonviolence to cover impotence.
MAHATMA GANDHI (1869–1948)

The Argument from Intimidation is a confession of intellectual impotence.
AYN RAND (1905–1982), *The Virtue of Selfishness*

Indecision

Indecision may or may not be my problem.
JIMMY BUFFETT (1946–)

Indecision is like a stepchild: if he does not wash his hands, he is called dirty, if he does, he is wasting water.
AFRICAN PROVERB

Independence

America does not go abroad in search of monsters to destroy. She is the well-wisher to freedom and independence of all. She is the champion and vindicator only of her own.
JOHN QUINCY ADAMS (1767–1848)

You need only reflect that one of the best ways to get yourself a reputation as a dangerous citizen these days is to go about repeating the very phrases which our founding fathers used in the struggle for independence.
CHARLES AUSTIN BEARD (1874–1948)

Mad, adj.: Affected with a high degree of intellectual independence.
AMBROSE BIERCE (1842–1914), *The Devil's Dictionary*

The essence of independence has been to think and act according to standards from within, not without. Inevitably anyone with an independent mind must become "one who resists or opposes authority or established conventions": a rebel. If enough people come to agree with, and follow, the Rebel, we now have a Devil. Until, of course, still more people agree. And then, finally, we have—Greatness.
ALEISTER CROWLEY (1875–1947)

It is easy in the world to live after the world's opinion; it is easy in solitude to live after our own; but the great man is he who in the midst of the crowd keeps with perfect sweetness the independence of solitude.
RALPH WALDO EMERSON (1803–1882), *Self-Reliance*

If money is your hope for independence you will never have it. The only real security that a man will have in this world is a reserve of knowledge, experience, and ability.
HENRY FORD (1863–1947)

All in all, I am not surprised that the people who want to unravel the social contract start with young adults. Those who are urged to feel afraid, very afraid, have both the greatest sense of independence and the most finely honed skepticism about government.
ELLEN GOODMAN (1941–)

Dependence begets subservience and venality, suffocates the germ of virtue, and prepares fit tools for the designs of ambition.
THOMAS JEFFERSON (1762–1826)

Independence did not mean chauvinism and narrow nationalism.
SAID MUSA (1944–)

True individual freedom cannot exist without economic security and independence. People who are hungry and out of a job are the stuff of which dictatorships are made.
FRANKLIN D. ROOSEVELT (1882–1945)

Indifference

Nothing is so fatal to religion as indifference.
EDMUND BURKE (1729–1797)

The universe we observe has precisely the properties we should expect if there is, at bottom, no design, no purpose, no evil, no good, nothing but blind, pitiless indifference.
CHARLES DARWIN (1809–1882)

Desire is half of life; indifference is half of death.
KAHLIL GIBRAN (1883–1931)

Many a secret that cannot be pried out by curiosity can be drawn out by indifference.
SYDNEY J. HARRIS (1917–1986)

The most destructive criticism is indifference.
EDGAR WATSON HOWE (1853–1937)

At the bottom of enmity between strangers lies indifference.
SØREN KIERKEGAARD (1813–1855)

Tolerance is another word for indifference.
W. SOMERSET MAUGHAM (1874–1965)

Perhaps misguided moral passion is better than confused indifference.
IRIS MURDOCH (1919–1999)

The penalty good men pay for indifference to public affairs is to be ruled by evil men.
PLATO (C. 428–348 BC)

Indifference and neglect often do much more damage than outright dislike.
J. K. ROWLING (1965–), *Harry Potter and the Order of the Phoenix*

Disobedience, the rarest and most courageous of the virtues, is seldom distinguished from neglect, the laziest and commonest of the vices.
GEORGE BERNARD SHAW (1856–1950)

Indifference is the essence of inhumanity.
GEORGE BERNARD SHAW (1856–1950)

Politeness is organized indifference.
PAUL VALÉRY (1871–1945)

Indifference, to me, is the epitome of evil.
ELIE WIESEL (1928–)

The opposite of love is not hate, it's indifference. The opposite of art is not ugliness, it's indifference. The opposite of faith is not heresy, it's indifference. And the opposite of life is not death, it's indifference.
ELIE WIESEL (1928–)

Individualism

The age of individualism, laissez-faire industrialism and self-seeking capitalism is dead and gone.
DOROTHY DAY (1897–1980)

Individualism produces leaders, relies on them and gives them a lot of responsibility, but because they have little to say or do except to follow, that doesn't make them inhabit a hierarchy.
MARY DOUGLAS (1921–2007)

It is the individual's task to differentiate himself from all the others and stand on his own feet. All collective identities …vinterfere with the fulfillment of this task. Such collective identities are crutches for the lame, shields for the timid, beds for the lazy, nurseries for the irresponsible….
CARL JUNG (1875–1961), *Memories, Dreams, Reflections*

Risk! Risk anything! Care no more for the opinions of others, for those voices. Do the hardest thing on earth for you. Act for yourself. Face the truth.
KATHERINE MANSFIELD (1888–1923)

Art is the most intense mode of individualism that the world has known.
OSCAR WILDE (1854–1900)

Individuality

Learn to limit yourself, to content yourself with some definite thing, and some definite work; dare to be what you are, and learn to resign with a good grace all that you are not and to believe in your own individuality.
HENRI-FRÉDÉRIC AMIEL (1821–1881)

Trust yourself. Think for yourself. Act for yourself. Speak for yourself. Be yourself. Imitation is suicide.
MARVA COLLINS (1936–)

A self that is only differentiated—not integrated—may attain great individual accomplishments, but risks being mired in self-centered egotism. By the same token, a person whose self is based exclusively on integration will be well connected and secure, but lack autonomous individuality. Only when a person invests equal amounts of psychic energy in these two processes and avoids both selfishness and conformity is the self likely to reflect complexity.
MIHALY CSIKSZENTMIHALYI (1934–), *Flow: The Psychology of Optimal Experience*

To be yourself in a world that is constantly trying to make you something else is the greatest accomplishment.
RALPH WALDO EMERSON (1803–1882)

All Fords are exactly alike, but no two men are just alike. Every new life is a new thing under the sun; there has never been anything just like it before, never will be again. A young man ought to get that idea about himself; he should look for the single spark of individuality that makes him different from other folks, and develop that for all he is worth. Society and schools may try to iron it out of him; their tendency is to put it all in the same mold, but I say don't let that spark be lost; it is your only real claim to importance.
HENRY FORD (1863–1947)

Be who you are, and say what you feel because those who mind don't matter, and those who matter don't mind.
THEODORE SEUSS GEISEL (1904–1991)

It is those who concentrate on but one thing at a time who advance in this world. The great man or woman is the one who never steps outside his or her specialty or foolishly dissipates his or her individuality.
OG MANDINO (1923–1996)

The self is something which has a development; it is not initially there, at birth, but arises in the process of social experience and activity, that is, develops in the given individual as a result of his relations to that process as a whole and to other individuals within that process.
GEORGE H. MEAD (1863–1931)

To be one's self, and unafraid whether right or wrong, is more admirable than the easy cowardice of surrender to conformity.
IRVING WALLACE (1916–1990)

Individuals

A good marriage is one which allows for change and growth in the individuals and in the way they express their love.
PEARL S. BUCK (1892–1973)

You cannot hope to build a better world without improving the individuals. To that end each of us must work for his own improvement, and at the same time share a general responsibility for all humanity, our particular duty being to aid those to whom we think we can be most useful.
MARIE CURIE (1867–1934)

Individuals may form communities, but it is institutions alone that can create a nation.
BENJAMIN DISRAELI (1804–1881)

No amount of artificial reinforcement can offset the natural inequalities of human individuals.
HENRY P. FAIRCHILD (1880–1956)

Politics [is] the art of achieving the maximum amount of freedom for individuals that is consistent with the maintenance of social order.
BARRY GOLDWATER (1909–1998)

Insanity in individuals is something rare—but in groups, parties, nations and epochs, it is the rule.
FRIEDRICH NIETZSCHE (1844–1900)

There's a whiff of the lynch mob or the lemming migration about any overlarge concentration of like-thinking individuals, no matter how virtuous their cause.
P. J. O'ROURKE (1947–), *Parliament of Whores*

Industry

Concentration is my motto—first honesty, then industry, then concentration.
ANDREW CARNEGIE (1835–1919)

Almost everybody today believes that nothing in economic history has ever moved as fast as, or had a greater impact than, the Information Revolution. But the Industrial Revolution moved at least as fast in the same time span, and had probably an equal impact if not a greater one.
PETER F. DRUCKER (1909–2005)

Sloth makes all things difficult, but industry, all things easy. He that rises late must trot all day, and

shall scarce overtake his business at night, while laziness travels so slowly that poverty soon overtakes him.
BENJAMIN FRANKLIN (1706–1790)

Like the bee, we should make our industry our amusement.
JAMES GOLDSMITH (1933–1997)

Men are generally idle, and ready to satisfy themselves, and intimidate the industry of others, by calling that impossible which is only difficult.
SAMUEL JOHNSON (1709–1784), *Life of Boerhaave*

There are only two ways by which to rise in this world, either by one's own industry or by the stupidity of others.
JEAN DE LA BRUYÈRE (1645–1696)

That some should be rich, shows that others may become rich, and, hence, is just encouragement to industry and enterprise.
ABRAHAM LINCOLN (1809–1865)

If you have great talents, industry will improve them; if you have but moderate abilities, industry will supply their deficiency.
SIR JOSHUA REYNOLDS (1723–1792)

The miracle, or the power, that elevates the few is to be found in their industry, application, and perseverance under the prompting of a brave, determined spirit.
MARK TWAIN (1835–1910)

God has so made the mind of man that a peculiar deliciousness resides in the fruits of personal industry.
WILLIAM WILBERFORCE (1759–1833)

Inferiority

Exaggerated sensitiveness is an expression of the feeling of inferiority.
ALFRED ADLER (1870–1937)

Most people enjoy the inferiority of their friends.
LORD CHESTERFIELD(1694–1773)

The fact that man knows right from wrong proves his intellectual superiority to other creatures; but the fact that he can do wrong proves his moral inferiority to any creature that cannot.
MARK TWAIN (1835–1910), *What Is Man?*

The only thing that sustains one through life is the consciousness of the immense inferiority of everybody else, and this is a feeling that I have always cultivated.
OSCAR WILDE (1854–1900), *The Remarkable Rocket*

Infidelity

If you say, I love you, then you have already fallen in love with language, which is already a form of break up and infidelity.
JEAN BAUDRILLARD (1929–2007)

It is necessary to the happiness of man that he be mentally faithful to himself. Infidelity does not consist in believing, or in disbelieving, it consists in professing to believe what he does not believe.
THOMAS PAINE (1737–1809)

The honest man must be a perpetual renegade, the life of an honest man a perpetual infidelity. For the man who wishes to remain faithful must take himself perpetually unfaithful to all the continual, successive, indefatigable, renascent errors.
CHARLES PEGUY (1873–1914)

Physical infidelity is the signal, the notice given, that all fidelities are undermined.
KATHERINE ANNE PORTER (1890–1890)

One man's folly is another man's wife.
HELEN ROWLAND (1876–1950)

Inflation

The Great Inflation of the 1970s destroyed faith in paper assets, because if you held a bond, suddenly

the bond was worth much less money than it was before.
RON CHERNOW (1949–)

Inflation is when you pay fifteen dollars for the ten-dollar haircut you used to get for five dollars when you had hair.
SAM EWING (1921–)

Domestic inflation reflects domestic monetary policy.
MARTIN FELDSTEIN (1939–)

I believe that banking institutions are more dangerous to our liberties than standing armies. If the American people ever allow private banks to control the issue of their currency, first by inflation, then by deflation, the banks and corporations that will grow up around [the banks] will deprive the people of all property until their children wake up homeless on the continent their fathers conquered. The issuing power should be taken from the banks and restored to the people, to whom it properly belongs.
THOMAS JEFFERSON (1743–1826)

For all the gold and silver stolen and shipped to Spain did not make the Spanish people richer. It gave their kings an edge in the balance of power for a time, a chance to hire more mercenary soldiers for their wars. They ended up losing those wars anyway, and all that was left was a deadly inflation, a starving population, the rich richer, the poor poorer, and a ruined peasant class.
HANS KONIG (1586–1642)

Information

I find that a great part of the information I have was acquired by looking up something and finding something else on the way.
FRANKLIN P. ADAMS (1881–1960)

Almost everybody today believes that nothing in economic history has ever moved as fast as, or had a greater impact than, the Information Revolution. But the Industrial Revolution moved at least as fast in the same time span, and had probably an equal impact if not a greater one.
PETER F. DRUCKER (1909–2005)

The mind revels in conjecture. Where information is lacking, it will gladly fill in the gaps.
JAMES GEARY (1914–1989), *The World in a Phrase: A Brief History of the Aphorism*

Knowledge is of two kinds. We know a subject ourselves, or we know where we can find information on it.
SAMUEL JOHNSON (1709–1784)

I was brought up to believe that the only thing worth doing was to add to the sum of accurate information in the world.
MARGARET MEAD (1901–1978)

All of the books in the world contain no more information than is broadcast as video in a single large American city in a single year. Not all bits have equal value.
CARL SAGAN (1934–1996)

What information consumes is rather obvious: it consumes the attention of its recipients. Hence, a wealth of information creates a poverty of attention and a need to allocate that attention efficiently among the overabundance of information sources that might consume it.
HERBERT SIMON (1916–2001)

Everybody gets so much information all day long that they lose their common sense.
GERTRUDE STEIN (1874–1946)

We are drowning in information and starved for knowledge.
ANONYMOUS

Injustice

Where you find the laws most numerous, there you will find also the greatest injustice.
ARCESILAUS (316–241 BC)

Fraud is the ready minister of injustice.
EDMUND BURKE (1729–1797)

If it were not for injustice, men would not know justice.
HERACLITUS (C. 535–475 BC)

The world makes up for all its follies and injustices by being damnably sentimental.
THOMAS H. HUXLEY (1825–1895)

An injustice anywhere is an injustice everywhere.
SAMUEL JOHNSON (1709–1784)

It is from numberless diverse acts of courage and belief that human history is shaped. Each time a man stands up for an ideal, or acts to improve the lot of others, or strikes out against injustice, he sends forth a tiny ripple of hope, and crossing each other from a million different centers of energy and daring, those ripples build a current that can sweep down the mightiest walls of oppression and resistance.
ROBERT F. KENNEDY (1925–1968), *South Africa*

I submit that an individual who breaks a law that conscience tells him is unjust, and who willingly accepts the penalty of imprisonment in order to arouse the conscience of the community over its injustice, is in reality expressing the highest respect for the law.
MARTIN LUTHER KING JR. (1929–1968)

Segregation is the adultery of an illicit intercourse between injustice and immorality.
MARTIN LUTHER KING JR. (1929–1968)

Injustice is relatively easy to bear; what stings is justice.
H. L. MENCKEN (1880–1956)

Mankind censure injustice fearing that they may be the victims of it, and not because they shrink from committing it.
PLATO (C. 428–348 BC), *The Republic*

The true conservative is the man who has a real concern for injustices and takes thought against the day of reckoning.
FRANKLIN D. ROOSEVELT (1882–1945)

We must remember that any oppression, any injustice, any hatred, is a wedge designed to attack our civilization.
FRANKLIN D. ROOSEVELT (1882–1945)

In the part of this universe that we know, there is great injustice, and often the good suffer, and often the wicked prosper, and one hardly knows which of those is the more annoying.
BERTRAND RUSSELL (1872–1970)

A good man would prefer to be defeated than to defeat injustice by evil means.
SALLUST (86–34 BC), *Jugurthine War*

It is possible that the scrupulously honest man may not grow rich so fast as the unscrupulous and dishonest one; but success will be of a truer kind, earned without fraud or injustice. And even though a man should for a time be unsuccessful, still he must be honest; better to lose all and save character. For character is itself a fortune.
SAMUEL SMILES (1812–1904)

Innocence

Innocence dwells with Wisdom, but never with Ignorance.
WILLIAM BLAKE (1757–1827)

Ignorance is not innocence but sin.
ROBERT BROWNING (1812–1889)

Innocence most often is a good fortune and not a virtue.
ANATOLE FRANCE (1844–1924)

An honest election, under democracy, is an act of innocence which does not take place more than once in the history of a given nation.
JOSÉ MARÍA GIL ROBLES Y QUIÑONES (1898–1980)

In every American there is an air of incorrigible innocence, which seems to conceal a diabolical cunning.
A. E. HOUSMAN (1859–1936)

It's innocence when it charms us, ignorance when it doesn't.
MIGNON MCLAUGHLIN (1913–1983), *The Neurotic's Notebook*

No one is safe from slander. The best way is to pay no attention to it, but live in innocence and let the world talk.
MOLIÈRE (1622–1673)

Crime butchers innocence to secure a throne, and innocence struggles with all its might against the attempts of crime.
MAXIMILIEN ROBESPIERRE (1758–1794)

The trust I have is in mine innocence,
and therefore am I bold and resolute.
WILLIAM SHAKESPEARE (1564–1616), *King Henry VI*

Insanity

Love, n.: A temporary insanity curable by marriage.
AMBROSE BIERCE (1842–1914), *The Devil's Dictionary*

As I was walking among the fires of Hell,
Delighted with the enjoyments of Genius;
Which to Angels look like torment and insanity.
I collected some of their Proverbs.
WILLIAM BLAKE (1757–1827), "The Marriage of Heaven and Hell"

Insanity: doing the same thing over and over again and expecting different results.
ALBERT EINSTEIN (1879–1955)

When dealing with the insane, the best method is to pretend to be sane.
HERMANN HESSE (1877–1962)

Insanity is often the logic of an accurate mind overtaxed.
OLIVER WENDELL HOLMES SR. (1809–1894)

Insanity—a perfectly rational adjustment to an insane world.
R. D. LAING (1927–1989)

There's a fine line between genius and insanity. I have erased this line.
OSCAR LEVANT (1906–1972)

Insanity is hereditary; you get it from your children.
SAM LEVENSON (1911–1980)

Where does the violet tint end and the orange tint begin? Distinctly we see the difference of the colors, but where exactly does the one first blending enter into the other. So with sanity and insanity.
HERMAN MELVILLE (1819–1891)

Insanity in individuals is something rare—but in groups, parties, nations and epochs, it is the rule.
FRIEDRICH NIETZSCHE (1844–1900)

I hate to advocate drugs, alcohol, violence, or insanity to anyone, but they've always worked for me.
HUNTER S. THOMPSON (1939–2005)

Insects

A human being should be able to change a diaper, plan an invasion, butcher a hog, conn a ship, design a building, write a sonnet, balance accounts, build a wall, set a bone, comfort the dying, take orders, give orders, cooperate, act alone, solve equations, analyze a new problem, pitch manure, program a computer, cook a tasty meal, fight efficiently, die gallantly. Specialization is for insects.
ROBERT A. HEINLEIN (1907–1998)

Insects are my secret fear. That's what terrifies me more than anything—insects.
MICHAEL O'DONOGHUE (1940–1994)

There are scores of thousands of human insects who are ready at a moment's notice to reveal the will of God on every possible subject.
GEORGE BERNARD SHAW (1856–1950)

Speaking of insects, entomologists have found that life is pretty good for those insects that live as self-sufficient individuals; they have plenty of food, lots

of leisure and are good at protecting themselves from predators.
ROBERT SHEA (1933–1994)

I never kill insects. If I see ants or spiders in the room, I pick them up and take them outside. Karma is everything.
HOLLY VALANCE (1983–)

Inspiration

Inspiration is wonderful when it happens, but the writer must develop an approach for the rest of the time.... The wait is simply too long.
LEONARD BERNSTEIN (1918–1990)

Inspiration may be a form of superconsciousness, or perhaps of subconsciousness—I wouldn't know. But I am sure it is the antithesis of self-consciousness.
AARON COPLAND (1900–1990)

Desperation is sometimes as powerful an inspirer as genius.
BENJAMIN DISRAELI (1804–1881)

Genius is one per cent inspiration, ninety-nine per cent perspiration.
THOMAS A. EDISON (1847–1931)

You can't wait for inspiration. You have to go after it with a club.
JACK LONDON (1876–1916)

In life you need either inspiration or desperation.
ANTHONY ROBBINS (1960–)

I decided that it was not wisdom that enabled [poets] to write their poetry, but a kind of instinct or inspiration, such as you find in seers and prophets who deliver all their sublime messages without knowing in the least what they mean.
SOCRATES (469–399 BC), *Apology*

Insomnia is my greatest inspiration.
JON STEWART (1962–)

Who knows where inspiration comes from. Perhaps it arises from desperation. Perhaps it comes from the flukes of the universe, the kindness of the muses.
AMY TAN (1952–)

Instinct

Creativity comes from trust. Trust your instincts.
RITA MAE BROWN (1944–)

The wise are instructed by reason; ordinary minds by experience; the stupid, by necessity; and brutes by instinct.
CICERO (106–43 BC)

The very essence of instinct is that it's followed independently of reason.
CHARLES DARWIN (1809–1882)

Truly successful decision making relies on a balance between deliberate and instinctive thinking.
MALCOLM GLADWELL (1963–), *Blink: The Power of Thinking Without Thinking*

It is only by following your deepest instinct that you can lead a rich life, and if you let your fear of consequence prevent you from following your deepest instinct, then your life will be safe, expedient and thin.
KATHARINE BUTLER HATHAWAY (1890–1942)

If a man is offered a fact which goes against his instincts, he will scrutinize it closely, and unless the evidence is overwhelming, he will refuse to believe it. If, on the other hand, he is offered something which affords a reason for acting in accordance to his instincts, he will accept it even on the slightest evidence. The origin of myths is explained in this way.
BERTRAND RUSSELL (1872–1970)

I decided that it was not wisdom that enabled [poets] to write their poetry, but a kind of instinct or inspiration, such as you find in seers and prophets who deliver all their sublime messages without knowing in the least what they mean.
SOCRATES (469–399 BC), *Apology*

Insults

We are prepared for insults, but compliments leave us baffled.
MASON COOLEY (1927–2002)

The way to procure insults is to submit to them: a man meets with no more respect than he exacts.
WILLIAM HAZLITT (1778–1830)

There are two insults no human will endure. The assertion that he has no sense of humor and the doubly impertinent assertion that he has never known trouble.
SINCLAIR LEWIS (1885–1951)

Insults are pouring down on me as thick as hail.
EDOUARD MANET (1832–1883)

A wise man is superior to any insults which can be put upon him, and the best reply to unseemly behavior is patience and moderation.
MOLIÈRE (1622–1673)

Integrity

I ran the wrong kind of business, but I did it with integrity.
SYDNEY BIDDLE BARROWS (1952–)

Subtlety may deceive you; integrity never will.
OLIVER CROMWELL (1599–1658)

In silence man can most readily preserve his integrity.
MEISTER ECKHART (C. 1260–1328)

The qualities of a great man are vision, integrity, courage, understanding, the power of articulation, and profundity of character.
DWIGHT D. EISENHOWER (1890–1969)

Integrity simply means not violating one's own identity.
ERICH FROMM (1900–1980)

Integrity without knowledge is weak and useless, and knowledge without integrity is dangerous and dreadful.
SAMUEL JOHNSON (1709–1784)

If everyone were clothed with integrity, if every heart were just, frank, kindly, the other virtues would be well-nigh useless, since their chief purpose is to make us bear with patience the injustice of our fellows.
MOLIÉRE (1622–1673)

Our character … is an omen of our destiny, and the more integrity we have and keep, the simpler and nobler that destiny is likely to be.
GEORGE SANTAYANA (1863–1952), *The German Mind: A Philosophical Diagnosis*

Real integrity is doing the right thing, knowing that nobody's going to know whether you did it or not.
OPRAH WINFREY (1954–)

The most important persuasion tool you have in your entire arsenal is integrity.
ZIG ZIGLAR (1926–)

Intellectualism

We should take care not to make the intellect our god; it has, of course, powerful muscles, but no personality.
ALBERT EINSTEIN (1879–1955)

There is a real difference between intellectualism and intelligence. Intellectualism leaves out something that intelligence often had and what it really is is a kind of a part of the human spirit. You know many men will be highly intellectual and yet they will have absolutely terrible judgment.
THOMAS FORAN (1924–2000)

Only here, because of the illusion of intellectualism, our society separates the validity of human expression.
JOSEPH JARMAN (1937–)

Give me rampant intellectualism as a coping mechanism.
CHUCK PALAHNIUK (1962–)

Intellectualism came very late to America. That's why Americans are so proud of it. I found very few real intellectuals in America. But there are so many pseudo-intellectuals.
DOUGLAS SIRK (1897–1987)

Intellectuals

In the U.S. you have to be a deviant or exist in extreme boredom.... Make no mistake, all intellectuals are deviants in the U.S.
WILLIAM S. BURROUGHS (1914–1997), *Yage Letters*

I have no nationality—the best possible status for an intellectual.
E. M. CIORAN (1911–1995)

I think that one possible definition of our modern culture is that it is one in which nine-tenths of our intellectuals can't read any poetry.
RANDALL JARRELL (1914–1965)

If you explore beneath shyness or party chit-chat, you can sometimes turn a dull exchange into an intriguing one. I've found this to be particularly true in the case of professors or intellectuals, who are full of fascinating information, but need encouragement before they'll divulge it.
JOYCE CAROL OATES (1938–)

Intelligence

There is no such thing as an underestimate of average intelligence.
HENRY ADAMS (1838–1918)

I happen to feel that the degree of a person's intelligence is directly reflected by the number of conflicting attitudes she can bring to bear on the same topic.
LISA ALTHER (1944–), *Kinflicks*

It has yet to be proven that intelligence has any survival value.
ARTHUR C. CLARKE (1917–)

Beware when the great God lets loose a thinker on this planet.
RALPH WALDO EMERSON (1803–1882)

The test of a first-rate intelligence is the ability to hold two opposed ideas in the mind at the same time, and still retain the ability to function.
F. SCOTT FITZGERALD (1896–1940), *The Crack-Up*

I do not feel obliged to believe that the same God who has endowed us with sense, reason, and intellect has intended us to forgo their use.
GALILEO GALILEI (1564–1642)

It is not worth an intelligent man's time to be in the majority. By definition, there are already enough people to do that.
G. H. HARDY (1877–1947)

There is nobody so irritating as somebody with less intelligence and more sense than we have.
DON HEROLD (1889–1966)

Some people think only intellect counts: knowing how to solve problems, knowing how to get by, knowing how to identify an advantage and seize it. But the functions of intellect are insufficient without courage, love, friendship, compassion, and empathy.
DEAN KOONTZ (1945–)

The sign of an intelligent people is their ability to control emotions by the application of reason.
MARYA MANNES (1904–1990)

Intelligence is the flower of discrimination. There are many examples of the flower blooming but not bearing fruit.
NABESHIMA NAOSHIGE (1538–1618)

An intelligence test sometimes shows a man how smart he would have been not to have taken it.
DR. LAURENCE J. PETER (1919–1990)

A mind too active is no mind at all.
THEODORE ROETHKE (1908–1963)

Men fear thought as they fear nothing else on earth—more than ruin—more even than death.... Thought is subversive and revolutionary, destructive and terrible, thought is merciless to privilege, established institutions, and comfortable habit. Thought looks into the pit of hell and is not afraid. Thought is great and swift and free, the light of the world, and the chief glory of man.
BERTRAND RUSSELL (1872–1970)

So far as I can remember, there is not one word in the Gospels in praise of intelligence.
BERTRAND RUSSELL (1872–1970)

One man that has a mind and knows it can always beat ten men who haven't and don't.
GEORGE BERNARD SHAW (1856–1950), *The Apple Cart*

The ability to focus attention on important things is a defining characteristic of intelligence.
ROBERT J. SHILLER (1946–), *Irrational Exuberance*

Truly great madness cannot be achieved without significant intelligence.
HENRIK TIKKANEN (1924–1984)

Sometimes I think the surest sign that intelligent life exists elsewhere in the universe is that none of it has tried to contact us.
BILL WATTERSON (1958–)

The intelligent man who is proud of his intelligence is like the condemned man who is proud of his large cell.
SIMONE WEIL (1909–1943)

I not only use all the brains that I have, but all that I can borrow.
WOODROW WILSON (1856–1924)

The Internet

When I took office, only high energy physicists had ever heard of what is called the Worldwide Web.... Now even my cat has its own page.
BILL CLINTON (1946–)

The Internet is like alcohol in some sense. It accentuates what you would do anyway. If you want to be a loner, you can be more alone. If you want to connect, it makes it easier to connect.
ESTHER DYSON (1951–)

The Net is a waste of time, and that's exactly what's right about it.
WILLIAM GIBSON (1948–)

My favorite thing about the Internet is that you get to go into the private world of real creeps without having to smell them.
PENN JILLETTE (1955–)

Intolerance

Intolerance of ambiguity is the mark of an authoritarian personality.
THEODOR W. ADORNO (1903–1969)

It seems to me probable that anyone who has a series of intolerable positions to put up with must have been responsible for them in some extent; not that it was simply "their fault"—I don't mean that—but that they have contributed to it by impatience, or intolerance, or brusqueness—or some provocation.
ROBERT HUGH BENSON (1871–1914)

I have seen gross intolerance shown in support of tolerance.
SAMUEL TAYLOR COLERIDGE (1772–1834)

Intolerance itself is a form of egoism, and to condemn egoism intolerantly is to share it.
GEORGE SANTAYANA (1863–1952), *Winds of Doctrine*

Intoxication

Young people are in a condition like permanent intoxication, because youth is sweet and they are growing.
ARISTOTLE (384–322 BC), *Nicomachean Ethics*

If the headache would only precede the intoxication, alcoholism would be a virtue.
SAMUEL BUTLER (1835–1902)

Man, being reasonable, must get drunk; the best of life is but intoxication.
LORD BYRON (1788–1824)

The intoxication of anger, like that of the grape, shows us to others, but hides us from ourselves.
JOHN DRYDEN (1631–1700)

My peers, lately, have found companionship through means of intoxication—it makes them sociable. I, however, cannot force myself to use drugs to cheat on my loneliness—it is all that I have—and when the drugs and alcohol dissipate, will be all that my peers have as well.
FRANZ KAFKA (1883–1924)

For art to exist, for any sort of aesthetic activity or perception to exist, a certain physiological precondition is indispensable: intoxication.
FRIEDRICH NIETZSCHE (1844–1900)

I am an excitable person who only understands life lyrically, musically, in whom feelings are much stronger than reason. I am so thirsty for the marvelous that only the marvelous has power over me. Anything I can not transform into something marvelous, I let go. Reality doesn't impress me. I only believe in intoxication, in ecstasy, and when ordinary life shackles me, I escape, one way or another. No more walls.
ANAÏS NIN (1903–1977)

I have made an important discovery…that alcohol, taken in sufficient quantities, produces all the effect of intoxication.
OSCAR WILDE (1854–1900)

Intuition

The creative is the place where no one else has ever been. You have to leave the city of your comfort and go into the wilderness of your intuition. What you'll discover will be wonderful. What you'll discover will be yourself.
ALAN ALDA (1936–)

All great men are gifted with intuition. They know, without reasoning or analysis, what they need to know.
ALEXIS CARREL (1873–1944)

Intuition comes very close to clairvoyance; it appears to be the extrasensory perception of reality.
ALEXIS CARREL (1873–1944)

The intuitive mind is a sacred gift and the rational mind is a faithful servant. We have created a society that honors the servant and has forgotten the gift.
ALBERT EINSTEIN (1879–1955)

Proverbs are the literature of reason, or the statements of absolute truth, without qualification. Like the sacred books of each nation, they are the sanctuary of its intuitions.
RALPH WALDO EMERSON (1803–1882)

[W]e need to be willing to let our intuition guide us, and then be willing to follow that guidance directly and fearlessly.
SHAKTI GAWAIN (1948–)

Your time is limited, so don't waste it living someone else's life. Don't be trapped by dogma—which is living with the results of other people's thinking. Don't let the noise of others' opinions drown out your own inner voice. And most important, have the courage to follow your heart and intuition. They somehow already know what you truly want to become. Everything else is secondary.
STEVE JOBS (1955–)

For whereas the mind works in possibilities, the intuitions work in actualities, and what you intuitively desire, that is possible to you. Whereas what you mentally or "consciously" desire is nine times out of ten impossible; hitch your wagon to a star, or you will just stay where you are.
D. H. LAWRENCE (1885–1930)

The mind can assert anything and pretend it has proved it. My beliefs I test on my body, on my

intuitional consciousness, and when I get a response there, then I accept.
D. H. Lawrence (1885–1930)

I don't believe in intuition. When you get sudden flashes of perception, it is just the brain working faster than usual. But you've been getting ready to know it for a long time, and when it comes, you feel you've known it always.
Katherine Anne Porter (1894–1980)

Invention

Getting caught is the mother of invention.
Robert Byrne (1928–)

I don't think necessity is the mother of invention—invention, in my opinion, arises directly from idleness, possibly also from laziness. To save oneself trouble.
Agatha Christie (1890–1976), *An Autobiography*

To invent, you need a good imagination and a pile of junk.
Thomas A. Edison (1847–1931)

We are more ready to try the untried when what we do is inconsequential. Hence the fact that many inventions had their birth as toys.
Eric Hoffer (1902–1983)

The best way to predict the future is to invent it.
Alan Kay (1940–)

An inventor is simply a fellow who doesn't take his education too seriously.
Charles F. Kettering (1876–1958)

Invention is the mother of necessity.
Thorstein Veblen (1857–1929)

Irony

Irony is the hygiene of the mind.
Elizabeth Bibesco (1897–1945)

Neither irony or sarcasm is argument.
Samuel Butler (1835–1902)

The supreme irony of life is that hardly anyone gets out of it alive.
Robert A. Heinlein (1907–1988), *Job*

How is one to live a moral and compassionate existence when one is fully aware of the blood, the horror inherent in life, when one finds darkness not only in one's culture but within oneself? If there is a stage at which an individual life becomes truly adult, it must be when one grasps the irony in its unfolding and accepts responsibility for a life lived in the midst of such paradox. One must live in the middle of contradiction, because if all contradiction were eliminated at once life would collapse. There are simply no answers to some of the great pressing questions. You continue to live them out, making your life a worthy expression of leaning into the light.
Barry Lopez (1945–), *Arctic Dreams*

Humor is everywhere, in that there's irony in just about anything a human does.
Bill Nye (1955–)

A taste for irony has kept more hearts from breaking than a sense of humor, for it takes irony to appreciate the joke which is on oneself.
Jessamyn West (1902–1984)

Irrelevance

Very often the law of extremity demands an attention to irrelevance.
Janet Frame (1924–2004)

Poetry often enters through the window of irrelevance.
M. C. Richards (1916–1999)

Jealousy

It is better to be envied than pitied.
Herodotus (484–430 BC), *The Histories of Herodotus*

Jealousy is all the fun you think they had.
ERICA JONG (1942–), *Fear of Flying*

Jealousy feeds upon suspicion, and it turns into fury or it ends as soon as we pass from suspicion to certainty.
FRANÇOIS DE LA ROCHEFOUCAULD (1613–1680)

They envy the distinction I have won; let them therefore, envy my toils, my honesty, and the methods by which I gained it.
SALLUST (86–34 BC)

Everybody pities the weak; jealousy you have to earn.
ARNOLD SCHWARZENEGGER (1947–)

O, beware, my lord, of jealousy!
It is the green-eyed monster which doth mock
The meat it feeds on.
WILLIAM SHAKESPEARE (1564–1616), *Othello*

Envy is the ulcer of the soul.
SOCRATES (469–399 BC)

Moral indignation is jealousy with a halo.
H. G. WELLS (1866–1946), *The Wife of Sir Isaac Harman*

Jesus

If Jesus Christ were to come today, people would not even crucify him. They would ask him to dinner, and hear what he had to say, and make fun of it.
THOMAS CARLYLE (1795–1881)

Christmas is a time when people of all religions come together to worship Jesus Christ.
MATT GROENING (1954–)

[T]hat people often say about Him: "I'm ready to accept Jesus as a great moral teacher, but I don't accept His claim to be God." That is the one thing we must not say. A man who was merely a man and said the sort of things Jesus said would not be a great moral teacher. He would either be a lunatic—on a level with the man who says he is a poached egg—or else he would be the Devil of Hell. You must make your choice. Either this man was, and is, the Son of God: or else a madman or something worse. You can shut Him up for a fool, you can spit at Him and kill Him as a demon; or you can fall at His feet and call Him Lord and God. But let us not come with any patronising nonsense about His being a great human teacher. He has not left that open to us. He did not intend to.
C. S. LEWIS (1898–1963), *Mere Christianity*

Jesus died too soon. If he had lived to my age he would have repudiated his doctrine.
FRIEDRICH NIETZSCHE (1844–1900)

Jesus was a Jew, yes, but only on his mother's side.
STANLEY RALPH ROSS (1937–2000)

Jokes

Shall I crack any of those old jokes, master,
At which the audience never fail to laugh?
ARISTOPHANES (C. 448–380 BC), *Frogs*

Great use they have, when in the hands
Of one like me, who understands,
Who understands the time and place,
The person, manner, and the grace,
Which fools neglect, so that we find,
If all the requisites are join'd,
From whence a perfect joke must spring,
A joke's a very serious thing.
CHARLES CHURCHILL (1731–1764), *The Ghost*

The essence of all jokes, of all comedy, seems to be an honest or well intended halfness; a non performance of that which is pretended to be performed, at the same time that one is giving loud pledges of performance. The balking of the intellect, is comedy and it announces itself in the pleasant spasms we call laughter.
RALPH WALDO EMERSON (1803–1882)

Forgive, O Lord, my little jokes on Thee
And I'll forgive Thy great big joke on me.
ROBERT FROST (1874–1963), "In the Clearing"

The best ideas come as jokes. Make your thinking as funny as possible.
David M. Ogilvy (1911–1999)

I don't make jokes. I just watch the government and report the facts.
Will Rogers (1879–1935)

Well, the telling of jokes is an art of its own, and it always rises from some emotional threat. The best jokes are dangerous, and dangerous because they are in some way truthful.
Kurt Vonnegut Jr. (1922–2007)

He that jokes confesses.
Italian Proverb

Journalism

Rage is the only quality which has kept me, or anybody I have ever studied, writing columns for newspapers.
Jimmy Breslin (1930–)

You must have a room, or a certain hour or so a day, where you don't know what was in the newspapers that morning … a place where you can simply experience and bring forth what you are and what you might be.
Joseph Campbell (1904–1987)

Journalism largely consists of saying "Lord Jones is Dead" to people who never knew that Lord Jones was alive.
G. K. Chesterton (1874–1936)

Literature is the art of writing something that will be read twice; journalism what will be read once.
Cyril Connolly (1903–1974), *Enemies of Promise*

To read a newspaper is to refrain from reading something worthwhile. The first discipline of education must therefore be to refuse resolutely to feed the mind with canned chatter.
Aleister Crowley (1875–1947)

A newspaper consists of just the same number of words, whether there be any news in it or not.
Henry Fielding (1707–1754)

Trying to determine what is going on in the world by reading newspapers is like trying to tell the time by watching the second hand of a clock.
Ben Hecht (1893–1964)

Editor: a person employed by a newspaper, whose business it is to separate the wheat from the chaff, and to see that the chaff is printed.
Elbert Hubbard (1856–1915)

I do not take a single newspaper, nor read one a month, and I feel myself infinitely the happier for it.
Thomas Jefferson (1743–1826)

I read no newspaper now but Ritchie's, and in that chiefly the advertisements, for they contain the only truths to be relied on in a newspaper.
Thomas Jefferson (1743–1826)

The man who reads nothing at all is better educated than the man who reads nothing but newspapers.
Thomas Jefferson (1743–1826)

Newspapermen learn to call a murderer "an alleged murderer" and the King of England "the alleged King of England" to avoid libel suits.
Stephen Leacock (1869–1944)

People everywhere confuse what they read in newspapers with news.
A. J. Liebling (1904–1963)

Once a newspaper touches a story, the facts are lost forever, even to the protagonists.
Norman Mailer (1923–2007)

All successful newspapers are ceaselessly querulous and bellicose. They never defend anyone or anything if they can help it; if the job is forced on them, they tackle it by denouncing someone or something else.
H. L. Mencken (1880–1956)

I think there ought to be a club in which preachers and journalists could come together and have the sentimentalism of the one matched with the

cynicism of the other. That ought to bring them pretty close to the truth.
REINHOLD NIEBUHR (1892–1971)

It's amazing that the amount of news that happens in the world every day always just exactly fits the newspaper.
JERRY SEINFELD (1954–)

Half of the American people have never read a newspaper. Half never voted for President. One hopes it is the same half.
GORE VIDAL (1925–)

But what is the difference between literature and journalism? Journalism is unreadable and literature is not read. That is all.
OSCAR WILDE (1854–1900), *The Critic as Artist*

Rock journalism is people who can't write interviewing people who can't talk for people who can't read.
FRANK ZAPPA (1940–1993)

Journalists

Respect for journalists is like respect for doctors. It involves making your neutrality clear and being seen to be neutral.
KATE ADIE (1945–)

Here in the United States, our profession is much maligned, people simply don't trust or like journalists anymore and that's sad.
CHRISTIANE AMANPOUR (1958–)

Some of our best journalists take themselves even more seriously than the politicians they write about.
R. W. APPLE JR. (1934–)

I am satisfied that all politicians were meant to be journalists and all journalists meant to be politicians.
OWEN ARTHUR (1949–)

Doctors bury their mistakes. Lawyers hang them. But journalists put theirs on the front page.
MARGOT ASQUITH (1864–1945)

Journalists prize independence, not teamwork. Journalists understand waste is inherent to good journalism … that good reporting and writing is hard to quantify.
KEN AULETTA (1942–)

Reporters thrive on the world's misfortune. For this reason they often take an indecent pleasure in events that dismay the rest of humanity.
RUSSELL BAKER (1925–)

We journalists make it a point to know very little about an extremely wide variety of topics; this is how we stay objective.
DAVE BARRY (1947–)

Journalists say a thing that they know isn't true, in the hope that if they keep on saying it long enough it will be true.
ARNOLD BENNETT (1867–1931)

No news is good news. No journalists is even better….
NICOLAS BENTLEY (1907–1978)

The reporter is the daily prisoner of clocked facts. On all working days, he is expected to do his best in one swift swipe at each story.
JIM BISHOP (1907–1987)

A journalist is a person who has mistaken their calling.
OTTO VON BISMARCK (1815–1898)

My experience with journalists authorizes me to record that a very large number of them are ignorant, lazy, opinionated, intellectually dishonest and inadequately supervised.
CONRAD BLACK (1944–)

The smarter the journalists are, the better off society is. For to a degree, people read the press to inform themselves—and the better the teacher, the better the student body.
WARREN BUFFETT (1930–)

Journalists are supposed to be skeptical, that's what keeps them digging rather than simply accepting

the official line, whether it comes from government or corporate bureaucrats.
LINDA CHAVEZ (1947–)

I see journalists as the manual workers, the laborers of the word. Journalism can only be literature when it is passionate.
MARGUERITE DURAS (1914–1996)

U.S. journalists I don't think are very courageous. They tend to go along with the government's policy domestically and internationally. To question is seen as being unpatriotic, or potentially subversive.
ROBERT FISK (1909–)

I believe in equality for everyone, except reporters and photographers.
MAHATMA GANDHI (1869–1948)

It was when "reporters" became "journalists" and when "objectivity" gave way to "searching for truth," that an aura of distrust and fear arose around the New Journalist.
GEORGIE ANNE GEYER (1935–)

A petty reason perhaps why novelists more and more try to keep a distance from journalists is that novelists are trying to write the truth and journalists are trying to write fiction.
GRAHAM GREENE (1904–1991)

It is inexcusable for scientists to torture animals; let them make their experiments on journalists and politicians.
HENRIK IBSEN (1828–1906)

Journalists are accused of being lapdogs when they don't ask the hard questions, but then accused of being rude when they do. Good thing we have tough hides.
GWEN IFILL (1955–)

All of us learn to write by the second grade, then most of us go on to other things.
BOBBY KNIGHT (1940–)

A journalist is stimulated by a deadline: he writes worse when he has time.
KARL KRAUS (1874–1936)

How is the world ruled and how do wars start? Diplomats tell lies to journalists and then believe what they read.
KARL KRAUS (1874–1936)

Journalists write because they have nothing to say, and have something to say because they write.
KARL KRAUS (1874–1936)

Every journalist owes tribute to the evil one.
JEAN DE LA FONTAINE (1621–1695)

The serious, real journalists of this country are more needed now than they ever have been because the blogs and the mp3s and the iPods, they're all talking about the news, but where does the news originate? It originates with a reporter. It originates with a news organization.
JIM LEHRER (1934–)

The journalists have constructed for themselves a little wooden chapel, which they also call the Temple of Fame, in which they put up and take down portraits all day long and make such a hammering you can't hear yourself speak.
GEORGE C. LICHTENBERG (1742–1799)

You know journalists, they love a good story, there's nothing like a Grimm's fairytale book.
JAMES LOVELOCK (1919–)

Of necessity, we made the discovery that it is easier to turn poets into business journalists than to turn bookkeepers into writers.
HENRY R. LUCE (1898–1967)

Every journalist has a novel in him, which is an excellent place for it.
RUSSELL LYNES (1910–1991)

If a person is not talented enough to be a novelist, not smart enough to be a lawyer, and his hands are too shaky to perform operations, he becomes a journalist.
NORMAN MAILER (1923–2007)

Fidelity to the subject's thought and to his characteristic way of expressing himself is the sine

qua non of journalistic quotation.
JANET MALCOLM (1934–)

There aren't enough good journalists. There are too many who really weren't groomed to be reporters and, as a result, some of the reporting is shallow.
WILL MCDONOUGH (1935–2003)

There are honest journalists like there are honest politicians—they stay bought.
BILL MOYERS (1934–)

Journalists, who are skeptical to begin with, simply do not like to be lied to or made fools of.
ROGER MUDD (1928–)

Most journalists now believe that a person's privacy zone gets smaller and smaller as the person becomes more and more powerful.
ROGER MUDD (1928–)

I think there ought to be a club in which preachers and journalists could come together and have the sentimentalism of the one matched with the cynicism of the other. That ought to bring them pretty close to the truth.
REINHOLD NIEBUHR (1892–1971)

Journalists aren't supposed to praise things. It's a violation of work rules almost as serious as buying drinks with our own money or absolving the CIA of something.
P. J. O'ROURKE (1947–)

One of the problems that we have as American journalists is that we bring the American cultural baggage with us and we plop it down and it follows us around and that's just a fact of life.
JOHN POMFRET (1667–1702)

Journalists belong in the gutter because that is where the ruling classes throw their guilty secrets.
GERALD PRIESTLAND (1927–1991)

The power to mould the future of the Republic will be in the hands of the journalists of future generations.
JOSEPH PULITZER (1847–1911)

Being a reporter is as much a diagnosis as a job description.
ANNA QUINDLEN (1952–)

If you believe in journalism, you don't insult good journalists.
SYDNEY SCHANBERG (1934–)

Journalists are like dogs, whenever anything moves they begin to bark.
ARTHUR SCHOPENHAUER (1788–1860)

If I had my choice I would kill every reporter in the world, but I am sure we would be getting reports from Hell before breakfast.
WILLIAM TECUMSEH SHERMAN (1820–1891)

Journalists cover words and delude themselves into thinking they have committed journalism.
HEDRICK SMITH (1933–)

Journalists do not live by words alone, although sometimes they have to eat them.
ADLAI E. STEVENSON II (1900–1965)

We journalists tell the public which way the cat is jumping. The public will take care of the cat.
ARTHUR HAYS SULZBERGER (1891–1968)

In the real world, nothing happens at the right place at the right time. It is the job of journalists and historians to correct that.
MARK TWAIN (1835–1910)

General Sherman looked upon journalists as a nuisance and a danger at headquarters and in the field, and acted toward them accordingly, then as throughout his great war career.
HENRY VILLARD (1835–1900)

Bad manners make a journalist.
OSCAR WILDE (1856–1900)

You cannot hope to bribe or twist (thank God!) the British journalist. But, seeing what the man will do unbribed, there's no occasion to.
HUMBERT WOLFE (1885–1940)

I hate journalists. There is nothing in them but tittering jeering emptiness. They have all made what Dante calls the Great Refusal. The shallowest people on the ridge of the earth.
WILLIAM BUTLER YEATS (1865–1939)

Journals

A page of my journal is like a cake of portable soup. A little may be diffused into a considerable portion.
JAMES BOSWELL (1740–1795)

A word of advice: a person's journal is the raw material. A story is made from these events. Use the journal to craft the story.
TIM CAHILL (1979–)

After the writer's death, reading his journal is like receiving a long letter.
JEAN COCTEAU (1889–1963)

I write journals and would recommend journal writing to anyone who wishes to pursue a writing career. You learn a lot. You also remember a lot … and memory is important.
JUDY COLLINS (1939–)

I am enamoured of my journal.
SIR WALTER SCOTT (1771–1832)

When my journal appears, many statues must come down.
ARTHUR WELLESLEY (1769–1852)

Joy

I cannot believe that the inscrutable universe turns on an axis of suffering; surely the strange beauty of the world must somewhere rest on pure joy!
LOUISE BOGAN (1897–1970)

There is an alchemy in sorrow. It can be transmuted into wisdom, which, if it does not bring joy, can yet bring happiness.
PEARL S. BUCK (1892–1973)

Let there be more joy and laughter in your living.
EILEEN CADDY (1917–2006)

Cease, every joy, to glimmer on my mind,
But leave—oh! leave the light of Hope behind.
THOMAS CAMPBELL (1777–1844)

During [these] periods of relaxation after concentrated intellectual activity, the intuitive mind seems to take over and can produce the sudden clarifying insights which give so much joy and delight.
FRITJOF CAPRA (1939–)

My mind to me a kingdom is,
Such present joys therein I find,
That it excels all other bliss.
SIR EDWARD DYER (1543–1607)

Short is the joy that guilty pleasure brings.
EURIPIDES (C. 480–406 BC)

Where there is injury, pardon;
Where there is doubt, faith;
Where there is despair, hope;
Where there is darkness, light;
Where there is sadness, joy.
SAINT FRANCIS OF ASSISI (1181–1226)

We choose our joys and sorrows long before we experience them.
KAHLIL GIBRAN (1883–1931)

Real joy comes not from ease or riches or from the praise of men, but from doing something worthwhile.
SIR WILFRED GRENFELL (1865–1940)

Sometimes your joy is the source of your smile, but sometimes your smile can be the source of your joy.
THICH NHAT HAHN (1926–)

Winning is important to me, but what brings me real joy is the experience of being fully engaged in whatever I'm doing.
PHIL JACKSON (1945–)

We could never learn to be brave and patient, if there were only joy in the world.
HELEN KELLER (1880–1968)

When you jump for joy, beware that no one moves the ground from beneath your feet.
STANISLAW LEC (1909–1966), *Unkempt Thoughts*

The joy of a spirit is the measure of its power.
NINON DE LENCLOS (1620–1705)

Life is a tragedy full of joy.
BERNARD MALAMUD (1914–1986)

Joyfulness keeps the heart and face young. A good laugh makes us better friends with ourselves and everybody around us.
ORISON SWETT MARDEN (1850–1924)

There is no greater joy nor greater reward than to make a fundamental difference in someone's life.
SISTER MARY ROSE MCGEADY (1928–)

The most profound joy has more of gravity than of gaiety in it.
MICHEL DE MONTAIGNE (1533–1592)

The only joy in the world is to begin.
CESARE PAVESE (1908–1950)

Since you get more joy out of giving joy to others, you should put a good deal of thought into the happiness that you are able to give.
ELEANOR ROOSEVELT (1884–1962)

Things won are done; joy's soul lies in the doing.
WILLIAM SHAKESPEARE (1564–1616), *Troilus and Cressida*

This is the true joy in life, the being used for a purpose recognized by yourself as a mighty one; the being thoroughly worn out before you are thrown on the scrap heap; the being a force of Nature instead of a feverish selfish little clod of ailments and grievances complaining that the world will not devote itself to making you happy.
GEORGE BERNARD SHAW (1856–1950), *Man and Superman*

Joy is prayer. Joy is strength. Joy is love. Joy is a net of love by which you can catch souls.
MOTHER TERESA (1910–1997)

Grief can take care of itself, but to get the full value of a joy you must have somebody to divide it with.
MARK TWAIN (1835–1910)

Joy is not in things; it is in us.
RICHARD WAGNER (1813–1883)

One joy scatters a hundred griefs.
CHINESE PROVERB

Judaism

Judaism lives not in an abstract creed, but in its institutions.
BERTHOLD AUERBACH (1812–1882)

We realize that Judaism as a faith can survive only in an atmosphere of general faith.
LOUIS FINKELSTEIN (1895–1991)

Judaism is an intellectually based religion, and the single most important theme is that of study.
NORMAN LAMM (1927–)

Judaism boasts of no exclusive revelation of eternal truths that are indispensable to salvation, of no revealed religion in the sense in which that term is usually understood.
MOSES MENDELSSOHN (1729–1786)

Judges

Judges must beware of hard constructions and strained inferences, for there is no worse torture than that of laws.
SIR FRANCIS BACON (1561–1626)

Judges ought to be more learned than witty, more reverent than plausible, and more advised than confident. Above all things, integrity is their portion and proper virtue.
SIR FRANCIS BACON (1561–1626)

Judges don't age; time decorates them.
ENID BAGNOLD (1889–1981)

Take all the robes of all the good judges that have ever lived on the face of the earth, and they would not be large enough to cover the iniquity of one corrupt judge.
HENRY WARD BEECHER (1813–1887)

Our Constitution was not written in the sands to be washed away by each wave of new judges blown in by each successive political wind.
HUGO BLACK (1886–1971)

Those who made and endorsed our Constitution knew man's nature, and it is to their ideas, rather than to the temptations of utopia, that we must ask that our judges adhere.
ROBERT BORK (1927–)

Judges are appointed often through the political process.
STEPHEN BREYER (1938–)

Unfortunately, what many people forget is that judges are just lawyers in robes.
TAMMY BRUCE (1962–)

Judges rule on the basis of law, not public opinion, and they should be totally indifferent to pressures of the times.
WARREN E. BURGER (1907–1995)

We may have lured judges into roaming at large in the constitutional field.
WARREN E. BURGER (1907–1995)

The cold neutrality of an impartial judge.
EDMUND BURKE (1729–1797)

It is the function of a judge not to make but to declare the law, according to the golden mete-wand of the law and not by the crooked cord of discretion.
EDMUND BURKE (1729–1797)

It is better that a judge should lean on the side of compassion than severity.
MIGUEL DE CERVANTES (1547–1616)

The magistrates are the ministers for the laws, the judges their interpreters, the rest of us are servants of the law, that we all may be free.
CICERO (C. 106–43 BC)

Human judges can show mercy. But against the laws of nature, there is no appeal.
ARTHUR C. CLARKE (1917–)

Let judges secretly despair of justice: their verdicts will be more acute. Let generals secretly despair of triumph; killing will be defamed. Let priests secretly despair of faith: their compassion will be true.
LEONARD COHEN (1934–)

Judges must be free from political intervention or intimidation.
STOCKWELL DAY (1950–)

Judges are the weakest link in our system of justice, and they are also the most protected.
ALAN DERSHOWITZ (1938–)

The judges of England have rarely been original thinkers or great jurists. Many have been craftsmen rather than creators.
LORD PATRICK DEVLIN (1905–1992)

I never speak ill of dead people or live judges.
EDWIN EDWARDS (1927–)

The judge weighs the arguments and puts a brave face on the matter, and since there must be a decision, decides as he can, and hopes he has done justice and given satisfaction to the community.
RALPH WALDO EMERSON (1803–1882)

Judges are but men, and are swayed like other men by vehement prejudices. This is corruption in reality, give it whatever other name you please.
DAVID DUDLEY FIELD (1805–1894)

When the judges shall be obliged to go armed, it will be time for the courts to be closed.
STEPHEN J. FIELD (1816–1899)

Judging is a lonely job in which a man is, as near as may be, an island entire.
ABE FORTAS (1910–1982)

Judges who take the law into their own hands, who make up constitutional "rights" in order to strike down laws they oppose, undermine the people's right to have their values shape public policy and define the culture.
ORRIN HATCH (1934–)

I believe the two biggest mistakes made by the Founders were giving Federal judges life-time appointments and permitting them to be confirmed without the agreement of two-thirds of the members of the United States Senate.
JOHN JAY HOOKER (1930–)

A corrupt judge does not carefully search for the truth.
HORACE (65–8 BC)

We are under a Constitution, but the Constitution is what the judges say it is, and the judiciary is the safeguard of our liberty and our property under the Constitution.
CHARLES EVANS HUGHES (1862 1948)

To consider the judges as the ultimate arbiters of all constitutional questions is a very dangerous doctrine indeed, and one which would place us under the despotism of an oligarchy.
THOMAS JEFFERSON (1743–1826)

A judge's duty is to grant justice, but his practice is to delay it: even those judges who know their duty adhere to the general practice.
JEAN DE LA BRUYÈRE (1645–1696), *Les Caracteres*

Common Sense is that which judges the things given to it by other senses.
LEONARDO DA VINCI (1452–1519)

If judges would make their decisions just, they should behold neither plaintiff, defendant, nor pleader, but only the cause itself.
BROCKHOLST LIVINGSTON (1757–1823)

The acme of judicial distinction means the ability to look a lawyer straight in the eyes for two hours and not to hear a damned word he says.
NICCOLÒ MACHIAVELLI (1469–1527)

There should be many judges, for few will always do the will of few.
NICCOLÒ MACHIAVELLI (1469–1527)

A judge is a law student who marks his own examination papers.
H. L. MENCKEN (1880–1956)

The judge's duty is to inquire about the time, as well as the facts.
OVID (43 BC–AD 17)

The hungry judges soon the sentence sign,
And wretches hang that jurymen may dine.
ALEXANDER POPE (1688–1744)

Since twelve honest men have decided the cause,
And were judges of fact, tho' not judges of laws.
WILLIAM PULTENEY (1684–1764)

Many people have been fed up with judges for many years and for many different reasons, such as prayer in school, abortion, and capital punishment.
PHYLLIS SCHLAFLY (1924–)

Now that judges embrace forcibly starving someone to death, Congress should use its appropriation power to starve the judicial budget.
PHYLLIS SCHLAFLY (1924–)

Ideological warriors whether from the Left or the Right are bad news for the bench. They tend to make law, not interpret law. And that's not what any of us should want from our judges.
CHARLES SCHUMER (1950–)

Fairness in the justice system begins with the confirmation of capable judges.
LAMAR S. SMITH (1947–)

Judges have redefined marriage, deemed the Pledge of Allegiance unconstitutional, outlawed religious practices, and imposed their personal views on Americans.
LAMAR S. SMITH (1947–)

Judges hold a public trust, and like any other public official, they must be held accountable when they

abuse that trust.
LAMAR S. SMITH (1947–)

Judges should interpret the law, not make it.
LAMAR S. SMITH (1947–)

Judicial abuse occurs when judges substitute their own political views for the law.
LAMAR S. SMITH (1947–)

But one way or another, judges perform a very vital function in our society. They have a risky job and they are entitled to security.
ARLEN SPECTOR (1930–)

I love judges, and I love courts. They are my ideals, that typify on earth what we shall meet hereafter in heaven under a just God.
WILLIAM HOWARD TAFT (1857–1930)

Absent scandal, a federal judge can serve for decades on the bench, underscoring the importance of appointing judges who have a proper understanding of their constitutional role.
PAUL WEYRICH (1942–)

Judgment

Judgment comes from experience, and experience comes from bad judgment.
SIMON BOLÍVAR (1783–1830)

Judgment, not passion should prevail.
EPICHARMUS (C. 540–450 BC)

Doubt yourself and you doubt everything you see. Judge yourself and you see judges everywhere. But if you listen to the sound of your own voice, you can rise above doubt and judgment. And you can see forever.
NANCY KERRIGAN (1969–)

It is a great misfortune not to possess sufficient wit to speak well, nor sufficient judgment to keep silent.
JEAN DE LA BRUYÈRE (1645–1696)

When the judgement weak,
The prejudice is strong.
KANE O'HARA (1711–1782)

A man is morally free when, in full possession of his living humanity, he judges the world, and judges other men, with uncompromising sincerity.
GEORGE SANTAYANA (1863–1952)

How dreadful it is when the right judge judges wrong!
SOPHOCLES (496–406 BC), *Antigone*

Senescent judges show how patriotic they are by passing out hard sentences for tearing up a draft card or following one's conscience according to the principles established by our country at the Nuremburg trials.
ALBERT SZENT-GYORGYI (1893–1986), *The Crazy Ape*

If you judge people, you have no time to love them.
MOTHER TERESA (1910–1997)

Every judgment of conscience, be it right or wrong, be it about things evil in themselves or morally indifferent, is obligatory, in such wise that he who acts against his conscience always sins.
SAINT THOMAS AQUINAS (1225–1274)

Prejudice is opinion without judgment.
VOLTAIRE (1694–1778)

The poet judges not as a judge judges but as the sun falling around a helpless thing.
WALT WHITMAN (1819–1892)

One cool judgment is worth a thousand hasty counsels. The thing to do is to supply light and not heat.
WOODROW WILSON (1856–1924)

A fool judges people by the presents they give him.
CHINESE PROVERB

Juries

It is not only [the juror's] right, but his duty…to find the verdict according to his own best understanding, judgment, and conscience, though in direct opposition to the direction of the court.
JOHN ADAMS (1735–1826)

The jury has the right to determine both the law and the facts.
SAMUEL CHASE (1741–1811)

When you go into court you are putting your fate into the hands of twelve people who weren't smart enough to get out of jury duty.
NORM CROSBY (1927–)

A jury consists of twelve persons chosen to decide who has the better lawyer.
ROBERT FROST (1874–1963)

Jurors should acquit, even against the judge's instruction … if exercising their judgement with discretion and honesty they have a clear conviction that the charge of the court is wrong.
ALEXANDER HAMILTON (1755–1804)

It is presumed, that juries are the best judges of facts; it is, on the other hand, presumed that courts are the best judges of law. But still both objects are within your power of decision.… you have a right to take it upon yourselves to judge of both, and to determine the law as well as the fact in controversy.
JOHN JAY (1745–1829)

The jury has a right to judge both the law as well as the fact in controversy.
JOHN JAY (1745–1829)

I consider trial by jury as the only anchor ever yet imagined by man, by which a government can be held to the principles of its constitution.
THOMAS JEFFERSON (1743–1826)

[I]t is usual for the jurors to decide the fact, and to refer the law arising on it to the decision of the judges. But this division of the subject lies with their discretion only. And if the question relate to any point of public liberty, or if it be one of those in which the judges may be suspected of bias, the jury undertakes to decide both law and fact.
THOMAS JEFFERSON (1743–1826)

The juries are our judges of all fact, and of law when they choose it.
THOMAS JEFFERSON (1743–1826)

Jury: A group of 12 people, who, having lied to the judge about their health, hearing, and business engagements, have failed to fool him.
H. L. MENCKEN (1880–1956)

The jury, passing on the prisoner's life, may in the sworn twelve have a thief or two guiltier than him they try.
William Shakespeare (1564–1616), *Measure for Measure*

A jury is a group of twelve people of average ignorance.
HERBERT SPENCER (1820–1903)

Justice

Courage is of no value unless accompanied by justice; yet if all men became just, there would be no need for courage.
AGESILAUS II (C. 444–360 BC)

Liberty, equality—bad principles! The only true principle for humanity is justice; and justice to the feeble is protection and kindness.
HENRI-FRÉDÉRIC AMIEL (1821–1881)

It is in justice that the ordering of society is centered.
ARISTOTLE (384–322 BC)

The dead cannot cry out for justice; it is a duty of the living to do so for them.
LOIS MCMASTER BUJOLD (1949–), *Diplomatic Immunity*

Foolish men imagine that because judgment for an evil thing is delayed, there is no justice; but only accident here below. Judgment for an evil thing is many times delayed some day or two, some century or two, but it is sure as life, it is sure as death.
THOMAS CARLYLE (1795–1881)

Too much mercy … often resulted in further crimes which were fatal to innocent victims who need not have been victims if justice had been put first and mercy second.
AGATHA CHRISTIE (1890–1976)

Where justice is denied, where poverty is enforced, where ignorance prevails, and where any one class is made to feel that society is in an organized conspiracy to oppress, rob, and degrade them, neither persons nor property will be safe.
FREDERICK DOUGLASS (1817–1895)

Justice is a contract of expediency, entered upon to prevent men harming or being harmed.
EPICURUS (341–270 BC)

Next in importance to freedom and justice is popular education, without which neither freedom nor justice can be permanently maintained.
JAMES A. GARFIELD (1831–1881)

Justice delayed is justice denied.
WILLIAM GLADSTONE (1809–1898)

Justice does not come from the outside. It comes from inner peace.
BARBARA HALL (1946–)

Justice is the end of government. It is the end of civil society. It ever has been and ever will be pursued until it be obtained, or until liberty be lost in the pursuit. In a society under the forms of which the stronger faction can readily unite and oppress the weaker, anarchy may as truly be said to reign as in a state of nature, where the weaker individual is not secured against the violence of the stronger; and as, in the latter state, even the individuals are prompted, by the uncertainty of their condition, to submit to a government which may protect the weak as well as themselves; so, in the former state, will the more powerful factions or parties be gradually induced, by a like motive to wish for a government which will protect all parties, the weaker as well as the more powerful.
ALEXANDER HAMILTON (1755–1804)

If it were not for injustice, men would not know justice.
HERACLITUS (C. 535–475 BC)

Revenge is an act of passion; vengeance of justice. Injuries are revenged; crimes are avenged.
SAMUEL JOHNSON (1709–1784)

Injustice anywhere is a threat to justice everywhere.
MARTIN LUTHER KING JR. (1929–1968)

I have always found that mercy bears richer fruits than strict justice.
ABRAHAM LINCOLN (1809–1865)

The severest justice may not always be the best policy.
ABRAHAM LINCOLN (1809–1865)

Nobody can give you freedom. Nobody can give you equality or justice or anything. If you're a man, you take it.
MALCOLM X (1925–1965), *Malcolm X Speaks*

Military justice is to justice what military music is to music.
GROUCHO MARX (1890–1977)

Injustice is relatively easy to bear; what stings is justice.
H. L. MENCKEN (1880–1956)

Justice requires that to lawfully constituted Authority there be given that respect and obedience which is its due; that the laws which are made shall be in wise conformity with the common good; and that, as a matter of conscience all men shall render obedience to these laws.
POPE PIUS XI (1857–1939)

Justice consists not in being neutral between right and wrong, but in finding out the right and upholding it, wherever found, against the wrong.
THEODORE ROOSEVELT (1858–1919)

Many that live deserve death. And some die that deserve life. Can you give it to them? Then be not too eager to deal out death in the name of justice, fearing for your own safety. Even the wise cannot see all ends.
J. R. R. TOLKIEN (1892–1973), *The Lord of the Rings*

Justice is the constant and perpetual will to allot to every man his due.
ULPIAN (C. 228)

It is the spirit and not the form of law that keeps justice alive.
EARL WARREN (1891–1974)

Killing

War may sometimes be a necessary evil. But no matter how necessary, it is always an evil, never a good. We will not learn how to live together in peace by killing each other's children.
JIMMY CARTER (1924–)

One does not learn how to die by killing others.
VICOMTE DE CHATEAUBRIAND (1768–1848)

He who joyfully marches to music rank and file, has already earned my contempt. He has been given a large brain by mistake, since for him the spinal cord would surely suffice. This disgrace to civilization should be done away with at once. Heroism at command, how violently I hate all this, how despicable and ignoble war is; I would rather be torn to shreds than be a part of so base an action. It is my conviction that killing under the cloak of war is nothing but an act of murder.
ALBERT EINSTEIN (1879–1955)

So long as governments set the example of killing their enemies, private citizens will occasionally kill theirs.
ELBERT HUBBARD (1856–1915)

Arms are instruments of ill omen.... When one is compelled to use them, it is best to do so without relish. There is no glory in victory, and to glorify it despite this is to exult in the killing of men.... When great numbers of people are killed, one should weep over them with sorrow. When victorious in war, one should observe mourning rites.
LAO-TZU (C. 600 BC)

We can forgive you for killing our sons. But we will never forgive you for making us kill yours.
GOLDA MEIR (1898–1978)

To live without killing is a thought which could electrify the world, if men were only capable of staying awake long enough to let the idea soak in.
HENRY MILLER (1891–1980)

[The pamphlet] was very patriotic. That is, it talked about killing foreigners.
TERRY PRATCHETT (1948–), *Monstrous Regiment*

Patriots always talk of dying for their country but never of killing for their country.
BERTRAND RUSSELL (1872–1970)

I thoroughly disapprove of duels. If a man should challenge me, I would take him kindly and forgivingly by the hand and lead him to a quiet place and kill him.
MARK TWAIN (1835–1910)

Kindness

No act of kindness, no matter how small, is ever wasted.
AESOP (620–560 BC), *The Lion and the Mouse*

There is no duty more obligatory than the repayment of kindness.
CICERO (106–43 BC)

Recompense injury with justice, and recompense kindness with kindness.
CONFUCIUS (551–479 BC), *The Confucian Analects*

Forget injuries, never forget kindnesses.
CONFUCIUS (551–479 BC)

Carry out a random act of kindness, with no expectation of reward, safe in the knowledge that one day someone might do the same for you.
PRINCESS DIANA (1961–1997)

The ideals which have lighted my way, and time after time have given me new courage to face life cheerfully, have been Kindness, Beauty, and Truth. The trite subjects of human efforts, possessions, outward success, luxury have always seemed to me contemptible.
ALBERT EINSTEIN (1879–1955)

How beautiful a day can be when kindness touches it.
GEORGE SAMPSON ELLISTON (1875–1954)

You cannot do a kindness too soon, for you never know how soon it will be too late.
RALPH WALDO EMERSON (1803–1882)

I have learnt silence from the talkative, toleration from the intolerant, and kindness from the unkind; yet strange, I am ungrateful to these teachers.
KAHLIL GIBRAN (1883–1931)

Tenderness and kindness are not signs of weakness and despair, but manifestations of strength and resolutions.
KAHLIL GIBRAN (1883–1931)

I expect to pass through this world but once; any good thing therefore that I can do, or any kindness that I can show to any fellow creature, let me do it now; let me not defer or neglect it, for I shall not pass this way again.
ÉTIENNE DE GRELLET (1773–1855)

Three things in human life are important. The first is to be kind. The second is to be kind. And the third is to be kind.
HENRY JAMES (1843–1916)

Kindness in words creates confidence. Kindness in thinking creates profoundness. Kindness in giving creates love.
LAO-TZU (C. 600 BC)

What wisdom can you find that is greater than kindness?
JEAN-JACQUES ROUSSEAU (1712–1778)

Guard well within yourself that treasure, kindness. Know how to give without hesitation, how to lose without regret, how to acquire without meanness.
GEORGE SAND (1804–1876)

Compassion is the basis of all morality.
ARTHUR SCHOPENHAUER (1788–1860)

Constant kindness can accomplish much. As the sun makes ice melt, kindness causes misunderstanding, mistrust and hostility to evaporate.
DR. ALBERT SCHWEITZER (1875–1965)

[Y]et do I fear thy nature;
It is too full o' the milk of human kindness.
WILLIAM SHAKESPEARE (1564–1616), *Macbeth*

One who knows how to show and to accept kindness will be a friend better than any possession.
SOPHOCLES (496–406 BC)

I have always depended on the kindness of strangers.
TENNESSEE WILLIAMS (1911–1983), *A Streetcar Named Desire*

There are no thanks for a kindness which has been delayed.
ANONYMOUS

A word of kindness can warm three winter months.
JAPANESE PROVERB

Kingdoms

A little kingdom I possess, where thoughts and feelings dwell;
And very hard the task I find of governing it well.
LOUISA MAY ALCOTT (1832–1888)

For some years I deserted religion in favour of Marxism. The republic of goodness seemed more attainable than the Kingdom of God.
LIONEL BLUE (1930–)

The Kingdom of Heaven is not a place, but a state of mind.
JOHN BURROUGHS (1837–1921)

Almost in every kingdom the most ancient families have been at first princes' bastards.
ROBERT BURTON (1577–1640)

Not what I have, but what I do is my kingdom.
THOMAS CARLYLE (1795–1881)

Everything can be killed except nostalgia for the kingdom, we carry it in the color of our eyes, in every love affair, in everything that deeply torments and unties and tricks.
JULIO CORTAZAR (1914–1984)

The wooden walls are the best walls of this kingdom.
THOMAS COVENTRY (1578–1640)

My mind to me a kingdom is, such present joys therein I find, that it excels all other bliss.
SIR EDWARD DYER (1543–1607)

In the kingdom of the blind, the one-eyed man is king.
DESIDERIUS ERASMUS (1469–1536)

It is the childlike mind that finds the kingdom.
CHARLES FILLMORE (1854–1948)

The house represented the boundaries of the man's kingdom.
STEPHEN GARDINER (1497–1555)

You forget that the kingdom of heaven suffers violence: and the kingdom of heaven is like a woman.
JAMES JOYCE (1882–1941)

Rule a kingdom as though you were cooking a small fish—don't overdo it.
LAO-TZU (C. 600 BC)

As every divided kingdom falls, so every mind divided between many studies confounds and saps itself.
LEONARDO DA VINCI (1452–1519)

And all around is the desert; a corner of the mournful kingdom of sand.
PIERRE LOTI (1850–1923)

An earthly kingdom cannot exist without inequality of persons. Some must be free, some serfs, some rulers, some subjects.
MARTIN LUTHER (1483–1546)

Childhood is the kingdom where nobody dies. Nobody that matters, that is.
EDNA ST. VINCENT MILLAY (1892–1950)

If God is in a life, it doesn't have to be big to be happy and to be important in His kingdom.
KEITH MILLER (1919–2004)

There is little less trouble in governing a private family than a whole kingdom.
MICHEL DE MONTAIGNE (1533–1592)

No kingdom has shed more blood than the kingdom of Christ.
CHARLES DE MONTESQUIEU (1689–1755)

The trouble with kingdoms of heaven on earth is that they're liable to come to pass, and then their fraudulence is apparent for all to see. We need a kingdom of heaven in Heaven, if only because it can't be realized.
MALCOLM MUGGERIDGE (1903–1990)

Obsessed by a fairy tale, we spend our lives searching for a magic door and a lost kingdom of peace.
EUGENE O'NEILL (1888–1953)

My mind's my kingdom.
FRANCIS QUARLES (1592–1644)

A good mind possesses a kingdom.
SENECA (5 BC–AD 65)

A kingdom founded on injustice never lasts.
SENECA (5 BC–AD 65)

A kingdom that has once been destroyed can never come again into being; nor can the dead ever be brought back to life.
SUN-TZU (C. 544–496 BC)

It is the folly of too many to mistake the echo of a London coffee-house for the voice of the kingdom.
JONATHAN SWIFT (1667–1745)

In the animal kingdom, the rule is, eat or be eaten; in the human kingdom, define or be defined.
THOMAS SZASZ (1920–)

That is my major preoccupation, memory, the kingdom of memory. I want to protect and enrich that kingdom, glorify that kingdom and serve it.
ELIE WIESEL (1928–)

Our ambition should be to rule ourselves, the true kingdom for each one of us; and true progress is to know more, and be more, and to do more.
OSCAR WILDE (1854–1900)

That a peasant may become king does not render the kingdom democratic.
WOODROW WILSON (1856–1924)

Boredom is the legitimate kingdom of the philanthropic.
VIRGINIA WOOLF (1882–1941)

Kings

The question before the human race is whether the God of nature shall govern the world by His own laws, or whether priests and kings shall rule it by fictitious miracles.
JOHN ADAMS (1735–1826)

Kings will be tyrants from policy, when subjects are rebels from principle.
EDMUND BURKE (1729–1797)

The whole world is in revolt. Soon there will be only five Kings left—the King of England, the King of Spades, The King of Clubs, the King of Hearts, and the King of Diamonds.
KING FAROUK OF EGYPT (1920–1965)

If anybody thinks that kings, nobles, priests are good conservators of the public happiness, send him (to Europe).
THOMAS JEFFERSON (1762–1826)

In every country and in every age the priest has been hostile to liberty; he is always in allegiance to the despot, abetting his abuses in return for protection of his own.
THOMAS JEFFERSON (1762–1826)

Bishops move diagonally. That's why they often turn up where the kings don't expect them to be.
TERRY PRATCHETT (1948–), *Small Gods*

True hope is swift, and flies with swallow's wings;
Kings it makes gods, and meaner creatures kings.
WILLIAM SHAKESPEARE (1564–1616), *King Richard III*

The quality of mercy is not strain'd,
It droppeth as the gentle rain from heaven
Upon the place beneath. It is twice blest:
It blesseth him that gives and him that takes.
'Tis mightiest in the mightiest: it becomes
The throned monarch better than his crown;
His sceptre shows the force of temporal power,
The attribute to awe and majesty,
Wherein doth sit the dread and fear of kings;
But mercy is above this sceptred sway,
It is enthroned in the hearts of kings,
It is an attribute to God himself;
And earthly power doth then show likest God's,
When mercy seasons justice. Therefore, Jew,
Though justice be thy plea, consider this,
That in the course of justice none of us
Should see salvation: we do pray for mercy;
And that same prayer doth teach us all to render
The deeds of mercy.
WILLIAM SHAKESPEARE (1564–1616), *The Merchant of Venice*

Kisses

Kisses, even to the air, are beautiful.
DREW BARRYMORE (1975–)

God pardons like a mother, who kisses the offense into everlasting forgiveness.
HENRY WARD BEECHER (1813–1887)

A kiss is a lovely trick, designed by nature, to stop words when speech becomes unnecessary.
INGRID BERGMAN (1915–1982)

Some are kissing mothers and some are scolding mothers, but it is love just the same.
PEARL S. BUCK (1892–1973)

I married the first man I ever kissed. When I tell my children that, they just about throw up.
BARBARA BUSH (1925–)

Give me a thousand kisses, then a hundred, then a thousand more.
CATULLUS (84–54 BC)

He who kisses girl on hillside is not level.
CONFUCIUS (551–479 BC)

Kisses are a better fate than wisdom.
E. E. CUMMINGS (1894–1962)

To me, there is no greater act of courage than being the one who kisses first.
JANEANE GAROFALO (1964–)

God's wounds cure, sin's kisses kill.
WILLIAM GURNALL (1617–1679)

Oh, what lies there are in kisses.
HEINRICH HEINE (1797–1856)

What is a kiss? Why this, as some approve:
The sure, sweet cement, glue, and lime of love.
ROBERT HERRICK (1591–1674)

Stolen kisses are always sweetest.
LEIGH HUNT (1784–1859)

Idleness, like kisses, to be sweet must be stolen.
JEROME K. JEROME (1859–1927)

Drink to me only with thine eyes,
And I will pledge with mine;
Or leave a kiss but in the cup,
And I'll not look for wine.
BENJAMIN JOHNSON (1665–1742)

You are always new, The last of your kisses was ever the sweetest.
JOHN KEATS (1795–1821)

Every winter,
When the great sun has turned his face away,
The earth goes down into a vale of grief,
And fasts, and weeps, and shrouds herself in sables,
Leaving her wedding-garlands to decay—
Then leaps in spring to his returning kisses.
CHARLES KINGSLEY (1819–1875), *Saint's Tragedy*

A kiss may not be the truth, but it is what we wish were true.
STEVE MARTIN (1945–), *L.A. Story*

I wasn't kissing her, I was whispering in her mouth.
CHICO MARX (1891–1961)

A man loses his sense of direction after four drinks; a woman loses hers after four kisses.
H. L. MENCKEN (1880–1956)

The first kiss is stolen by the man; the last is begged by the woman.
H. L. MENCKEN (1880–1956)

When women kiss, it always reminds me of prizefighters shaking hands.
H. L. MENCKEN (1880–1956)

To a woman the first kiss is just the end of the beginning but to a man it is the beginning of the end.
HELEN ROWLAND (1876–1950)

A thousand kisses from your faithful bride.
CLARA SCHUMANN (1819–1896)

Come unto these yellow sands,
And then take hands:
Courtsied when you have, and kiss'd
The wild waves whist.
WILLIAM SHAKESPEARE (1564–1616), *The Tempest*

I wonder what fool it was that first invented kissing.
JONATHAN SWIFT (1667–1745)

I kissed my first girl and smoked my first cigarette on the same day. I haven't had time for tobacco since.
ARTURO TOSCANINI (1865–1957)

Some things I never learned to like. I didn't like to kiss babies, though I didn't mind kissing their mothers.
PIERRE TRUDEAU (1919–2000)

Everybody winds up kissing the wrong person good night.
ANDY WARHOL (1928–1987)

Two people kissing always look like fish.
ANDY WARHOL (1928–1987)

Women remember the first kiss, men remember the last.
ANONYMOUS

Love and faithfulness meet together; righteousness and peace kiss each other.
THE BIBLE, Pslam 85:10

Kisses that are easily obtained are easily forgotten.
ENGLISH PROVERB

In love, there is always one who kisses and one who offers the cheek.
FRENCH PROVERB

Kitchens

My kitchen is a mystical place, a kind of temple for me. It is a place where the surfaces seem to have significance, where the sounds and odors carry meaning that transfers from the past and bridges to the future.
PEARL BAILEY (1918–1990)

The kitchen is the great laboratory of the household, and much of the 'weal and woe' as far as regards bodily health, depends on the nature of the preparations concocted within its walls.
ISABELLA BEETON (1836–1865), *The Book of Household Management*

We owe much to the fruitful meditation of our sages, but a sane view of life is, after all, elaborated mainly in the kitchen.
JOSEPH CONRAD (1857–1924)

No chaos, no creation. Evidence: the kitchen at mealtime.
MASON COOLEY (1927–2002)

A fat kitchen makes a lean will.
BENJAMIN FRANKLIN (1706–1790)

Give me the provisions and whole apparatus of a kitchen, and I would starve.
MICHEL DE MONTAIGNE (1533–1592)

Bad cooks—and the utter lack of reason in the kitchen—have delayed human development longest and impaired it most.
FRIEDRICH NIETZSCHE (1844–1900)

The kitchen is a country in which there are always discoveries to be made.
GRIMOD DE LA REYNIÈRE (1758–1838)

Ladies and gentlemen are permitted to have friends in the kennel, but not in the kitchen.
GEORGE BERNARD SHAW (1856–1950)

If you can't stand the heat, get out of the kitchen.
HARRY S TRUMAN (1884–1972)

I saw him even now going the way of all flesh, that is to say towards the kitchen.
JOHN WEBSTER (1580–1632)

From morning till night, sounds drift from the kitchen, most of them familiar and comforting.... On days when warmth is the most important need of the human heart, the kitchen is the place you can find it; it dries the wet sock, it cools the hot little brain.
E. B. WHITE (1899–1985)

His passion has aroused the best and the beast in man. And the beast waited for him in the kitchen.
THEODORE H. WHITE (1915–1986)

Knights

In time of war the knight was, with his followers, in the camp of his sovereign, or commanding in the field, or holding some castle for him.
THOMAS BULFINCH (1796–1867)

Religion united its influence with those of loyalty and love, and the order of knighthood, endowed with all the sanctity and religious awe that attended the priesthood, became an object of ambition to the greatest sovereigns.
THOMAS BULFINCH (1796–1867)

The Knight's bones are dust,
And his good sword rust;
His soul is with the saints, I trust.
SAMUEL TAYLOR COLERIDGE (1772–1834)

As the knight of the quill never ventured into the fight, and only snuffed the battle afar, he knew nothing accurately of battles, but managed to pick up a few real or supposed incidents from the wounded and from stragglers.
DANIEL H. HILL (1821–1889)

And much more am I sorrier for my good knights' loss than for the loss of my fair queen; for queens I might have enough, but such a fellowship of good knights shall never be together in no company.
THOMAS MALORY (1405–1471)

The noir hero is a knight in blood-caked armor. He's dirty and he does his best to deny the fact that he's a hero the whole time.
FRANK MILLER (1957–)

Today the American knight holds the commercial supremacy of the world.
BETSY ROSS (1752–1836)

No lying knight or lying priest ever prospered in any age, but especially not in the dark ones. Men prospered then only in following an openly declared purpose, and preaching candidly beloved and trusted creeds.
JOHN RUSKIN (1819–1900)

A true knight is fuller of bravery in the midst, than in the beginning of danger.
SIR PHILIP SIDNEY (1554–1586)

And so I am become a knight of the Kingdom of Dreams and Shadows!
MARK TWAIN (1835–1910)

I started thinking about knighthood, and wondering why that period has an eternal fascination for us. Greek myth is laid in the Golden Age.
GENE WOLFE (1931–)

Knowledge

All men by nature desire knowledge.
ARISTOTLE (384–322 BC), *Metaphysics*

If knowledge can create problems, it is not through ignorance that we can solve them.
ISAAC ASIMOV (1920–1992)

God will not suffer man to have a knowledge of things to come; for if he had prescience of his prosperity, he would be careless; and if understanding of his adversity, he would be despairing and senseless.
SAINT AUGUSTINE (354–430)

To wisdom belongs the intellectual apprehension of things eternal; to knowledge, the rational apprehension of things temporal.
SAINT AUGUSTINE (354–430)

Knowledge is power.
SIR FRANCIS BACON (1561–1626), *Religious Meditations, Of Heresies*

The small part of ignorance that we arrange and classify we give the name of knowledge.
AMBROSE BIERCE (1842–1914)

The great obstacle to discovering the shape of the earth, the continents, and the ocean was not ignorance but the illusion of knowledge.
DANIEL J. BOORSTIN

That there should be one man die ignorant who had capacity for knowledge, this I call a tragedy.
THOMAS CARLYLE (1795–1881)

Knowledge is a comfortable and necessary retreat and shelter for us in advanced age, and if we do not plant it while young, it will give us no shade when we grow old.
LORD CHESTERFIELD (1694–1773)

When you know a thing, to hold that you know it; and when you do not know a thing, to allow that you do not know it—this is knowledge.
CONFUCIUS (551–479 BC), *The Confucian Analects*

There are three principal means of acquiring knowledge: observation of nature, reflection, and experimentation. Observation collects facts; reflection combines them; experimentation verifies the result of that combination.
DENIS DIDEROT (1713–1784)

To be conscious that you are ignorant is a great step to knowledge.
BENJAMIN DISRAELI (1804–1881), *Sybil*

I am enough of an artist to draw freely upon my imagination. Imagination is more important than knowledge. Knowledge is limited. Imagination encircles the world.
ALBERT EINSTEIN (1879–1955)

It is no good to try to stop knowledge from going forward. Ignorance is never better than knowledge.
ENRICO FERMI (1901–1954)

Knowledge is not a series of self-consistent theories that converges toward an ideal view; it is rather an ever increasing ocean of mutually incompatible (and perhaps even incommensurable) alternatives, each single theory, each fairy tale, each myth that is part of the collection forcing the others into greater articulation and all of them contributing, via this process of competition, to the development of our consciousness.
PAUL FEYERABEND (1924–1994)

I was born not knowing and have had only a little time to change that here and there.
RICHARD FEYNMAN (1918–1988)

You can know the name of a bird in all the languages of the world, but when you're finished, you'll know absolutely nothing whatever about the bird.... So let's look at the bird and see what it's doing—that's what counts. I learned very early the difference between knowing the name of something and knowing something.
RICHARD FEYNMAN (1918–1988)

The more the fruits of knowledge become accessible to men, the more widespread is the decline of religious belief.
SIGMUND FREUD (1856–1939), *The Future of an Illusion*

If you have knowledge, let others light their candles at it.
MARGARET FULLER (1810–1850)

Without self knowledge, without understanding the working and functions of his machine, man cannot be free, he cannot govern himself and he will always remain a slave.
G. I. GURDJIEFF (1872–1949)

Self-knowledge begins with the neighbor, the mirror, and just the same with true self-love; that goes from the mirror to the matter.
JOHANN G. HAMANN (1730–1788)

Thought is the wind, knowledge the sail, and mankind the vessel.
AUGUST HARE (1792–1834)

A complacent satisfaction with present knowledge is the chief bar to the pursuit of knowledge.
B. H. LIDDELL HART (1895–1970)

The beginning of knowledge is the discovery of something we do not understand.
FRANK HERBERT (1920–1986)

This is the bitterest pain among men, to have much knowledge but no power.
HERODOTUS (484–430 BC), *The Histories of Herodotus*

There are in fact two things, science and opinion; the former begets knowledge, the latter ignorance.
HIPPOCRATES (460–377 BC)

Knowledge and timber shouldn't be much used till they are seasoned.
OLIVER WENDELL HOLMES SR. (1809–1894), *The Autocrat of the Breakfast-Table*

Try to learn something about everything and everything about something.
THOMAS HENRY HUXLEY (1825–1895)

Integrity without knowledge is weak and useless, and knowledge without integrity is dangerous and dreadful.
SAMUEL JOHNSON (1709–1784)

Knowledge is of two kinds. We know a subject ourselves, or we know where we can find information on it.
SAMUEL JOHNSON (1709–1784)

Mankind have a great aversion to intellectual labor; but even supposing knowledge to be easily attainable, more people would be content to be ignorant than would take even a little trouble to acquire it.
SAMUEL JOHNSON (1709–1784)

People are difficult to govern because they have too much knowledge.
LAO-TZU (C. 600 BC), *The Way of Lao-tzu*

Curiosity in children, is but an appetite for knowledge. One great reason why children abandon themselves wholly to silly pursuits and trifle away their time insipidly is, because they find their curiosity balked, and their inquiries neglected.
JOHN LOCKE (1632–1704)

No man's knowledge here can go beyond his experience.
JOHN LOCKE (1632–1704)

Where there is much desire to learn, there of necessity will be much arguing, much writing, many opinions; for opinions in good men is but knowledge in the making.
JOHN MILTON (1608–1674)

Wisdom sets bounds even to knowledge.
FRIEDRICH NIETZSCHE (1844–1900)

Bodily exercise, when compulsory, does no harm to the body; but knowledge which is acquired under compulsion obtains no hold on the mind.
PLATO (C. 428–348 BC), *The Republic*

His priority did not seem to be to teach them what he knew, but rather to impress upon them that nothing, not even … knowledge, was foolproof.
J. K. ROWLING (1965–), *Harry Potter and the Order of the Phoenix*

Reports that say something hasn't happened are always interesting to me, because as we know, there are known knowns; there are things we know we know. We also know there are known unknowns; that is to say we know there are some things we do not know. But there are also unknown unknowns—the ones we don't know we don't know.
DONALD H. RUMSFELD (1932–)

Three passions, simple but overwhelmingly strong, have governed my life: the longing for love, the search for knowledge, and unbearable pity for the suffering of mankind.
BERTRAND RUSSELL (1872–1970), *Autobiography*

There is much pleasure to be gained from useless knowledge.
BERTRAND RUSSELL (1872–1970)

To acquire knowledge, one must study; but to acquire wisdom, one must observe.
MARILYN VOS SAVANT (1946–)

As we acquire more knowledge, things do not become more comprehensible but more mysterious.
DR. ALBERT SCHWEITZER (1875–1965)

What we want is to see the child in pursuit of knowledge, and not knowledge in pursuit of the child.
GEORGE BERNARD SHAW (1856–1950)

The larger the island of knowledge, the longer the shoreline of wonder.
RALPH W. SOCKMAN (1889–1970)

There is only one good, knowledge, and one evil, ignorance.
SOCRATES (469–399 BC)

True knowledge exists in knowing that you know nothing.
SOCRATES (469–399 BC)

Knowledge must come through action; you can have no test which is not fanciful, save by trial.
SOPHOCLES (496–406 BC), *Trachiniae*

Wisdom is the right use of knowledge. To know is not to be wise. Many men know a great deal, and are all the greater fools for it. There is no fool so great a fool as a knowing fool. But to know how to use knowledge is to have wisdom.
CHARLES H. SPURGEON (1834–1892)

The desire of knowledge, like the thirst for riches, increases ever with the acquisition of it.
LAURENCE STERNE (1713–1768)

If we value the pursuit of knowledge, we must be free to follow wherever that search may lead us. The free mind is not a barking dog, to be tethered on a ten-foot chain.
ADLAI E. STEVENSON II (1900–1965)

Language

High thoughts must have high language.
ARISTOPHANES (C. 448–380 BC), *Frogs*

Drawing on my fine command of the English language, I said nothing.
ROBERT BENCHLEY (1889–1945)

Language exerts hidden power, like a moon on the tides.
RITA MAE BROWN (1944–), *Starting from Scratch*

Works of imagination should be written in very plain language; the more purely imaginative they are the more necessary it is to be plain.
SAMUEL TAYLOR COLERIDGE (1772–1834)

Words ought to be a little wild, for they are the assaults of thought on the unthinking.
JOHN MAYNARD KEYNES (1883–1946)

The great enemy of clear language is insincerity. When there is a gap between one's real and one's declared aims, one turns as it were instinctively to long words and exhausted idioms, like a cuttlefish spurting out ink.
GEORGE ORWELL (1903–1950)

Speak properly, and in as few words as you can, but always plainly; for the end of speech is not ostentation, but to be understood.
WILLIAM PENN (1644–1718)

No one has a finer command of language than the person who keeps his mouth shut.
SAM RAYBURN (1882–1961)

Grammar and logic free language from being at the mercy of the tone of voice. Grammar protects us against misunderstanding the sound of an uttered name; logic protects us against what we say having double meaning.
EUGEN ROSENSTOCK-HUESSY (1888–1973)

Language is the source of misunderstandings.
ANTOINE DE SAINT-EXUPÉRY (1900–1944)

They have been at a great feast of languages, and stolen the scraps.
WILLIAM SHAKESPEARE (1564–1616), *Love's Labour's Lost*

Language is the tool of my trade—and I use them all, all the Englishes I grew up with.
AMY TAN (1952–)

We are a spectacular, splendid manifestation of life. We have language. We have affection. We have genes for usefulness, and usefulness is about as close to a "common goal" of nature as I can guess at. And finally, and perhaps best of all, we have music.
LEWIS THOMAS (1913–1993), *The Medusa and the Snail*

The great thing about human language is that it prevents us from sticking to the matter at hand.
LEWIS THOMAS (1913–1993)

Man invented language to satisfy his deep need to complain.
LILY TOMLIN (1939–)

We have really everything in common with America nowadays except, of course, language.
OSCAR WILDE (1854–1900), *The Canterville Ghost*

By listening to his language of his locality the poet begins to learn his craft. It is his function to lift, by use of imagination and the language he hears, the material conditions and appearances of his environment to the sphere of the intelligence where they will have new currency.
WILLIAM CARLOS WILLIAMS (1883–1963)

Think like a wise man but communicate in the language of the people.
WILLIAM BUTLER YEATS (1865–1939)

Let thy speech be short, comprehending much in a few words.
APOCRYPHA

Use soft words and hard arguments.
ENGLISH PROVERB

Laughter

If we may believe our logicians, man is distinguished from all other creatures by the faculty of laughter.
JOSEPH ADDISON (1672–1719)

Laughter, while it lasts, slackens and unbraces the mind, weakens the faculties and causes a kind of remissness and dissolution in all the powers of the soul; and thus it may be looked on as weakness in the composition of human nature. But if we consider the frequent reliefs we receive from it and how often it breaks the gloom which is apt to depress the mind and damp our spirits, with transient, unexpected gleams of joy, one would take care not to grow too wise for so great a pleasure of life.
JOSEPH ADDISON (1672–1719)

Among those whom I like or admire, I can find no common denominator, but among those whom I love, I can: all of them make me laugh.
W. H. AUDEN (1907–1973)

You grow up the day you have your first real laugh at yourself.
ETHEL BARRYMORE (1879–1959)

Mirth is God's medicine. Everybody ought to bathe in it.
HENRY WARD BEECHER (1813–1887)

The only cure for vanity is laughter, and the only fault that is laughable is vanity.
HENRI BERGSON (1859–1941)

Laughter is the shortest distance between two people.
VICTOR BORGE (1909–2000)

If we couldn't laugh, we would all go insane.
JIMMY BUFFETT (1946–), "Changes in Latitudes, Changes in Attitudes"

Always laugh when you can; it is cheap medicine. Merriment—it is the sunny side of existence.
LORD BYRON (1788–1824)

Let there be more joy and laughter in your living.
EILEEN CADDY (1917–2006)

The person who can bring the spirit of laughter into a room is indeed blessed.
BENNETT CERF (1898–1971)

A day without laughter is a day wasted.
CHARLIE CHAPLIN (1889–1977)

Total absence of humor renders life impossible.
SIDONIE GABRIELLE COLETTE (1873–1954), *Chance Acquaintances*

Through humor, you can soften some of the worst blows that life delivers. And once you find laughter, no matter how painful your situation might be, you can survive it.
BILL COSBY (1937–)

You can turn painful situations around through laughter. If you can find humor in anything, even poverty, you can survive it.
BILL COSBY (1937–)

Laughter is inner jogging.
NORMAN COUSINS (1915–1990)

The most wasted of all days is one without laughter.
E. E. CUMMINGS (1894–1962)

If you wish to glimpse inside a human soul and get to know a man, don't bother analyzing his ways of being silent, of talking, of weeping, of seeing how much he is moved by noble ideas; you will get better results if you just watch him laugh. If he laughs well, he's a good man.
FYODOR DOSTOEVSKY (1821–1881)

It is impossible for you to be angry and laugh at the same time. Anger and laughter are mutually exclusive and you have the power to choose either.
WAYNE D. DYER (1940–)

Earth laughs in flowers.
RALPH WALDO EMERSON (1803–1882)

I believe that imagination is stronger than knowledge—myth is more potent than history—dreams are more powerful than facts—hope always triumphs over experience—laughter is the cure for grief—love is stronger than death.
ROBERT FULGHUM (1937–)

One doesn't have a sense of humor. It has you.
LARRY GELBART (1928–)

In the sweetness of friendship let there be laughter, and sharing of pleasures. For in the dew of little things the heart finds its morning and is refreshed.
KAHLIL GIBRAN (1893–1931)

Nothing shows a man's character more than what he laughs at.
JOHANN WOLFGANG VON GOETHE (1749–1832)

At the height of laughter, the universe is flung into a kaleidoscope of new possibilities.
JEAN HOUSTON (1937–)

If you don't learn to laugh at trouble, you won't have anything to laugh at when you're old.
EDGAR WATSON HOWE (1853–1937)

Laughter is the sun that drives winter from the human face.
VICTOR HUGO (1802–1885)

One hearty laugh together will bring enemies into a closer communion of heart than hours spent on both sides in inward wrestling with the mental demon of uncharitable feeling.
WILLIAM JAMES (1842–1910)

You can't deny laughter; when it comes, it plops down in your favorite chair and stays as long as it wants.
STEPHEN KING (1947–)

Laughter is by definition healthy.
DORIS LESSING (1919–)

With the fearful strain that is on me night and day, if I did not laugh I should die.
ABRAHAM LINCOLN (1809–1865)

If I am not allowed to laugh in heaven, I don't want to go there.
MARTIN LUTHER (1483–1546)

The person who knows how to laugh at himself will never cease to be amused.
SHIRLEY MACLAINE (1934–)

Joyfulness keeps the heart and face young. A good laugh makes us better friends with ourselves and everybody around us.
ORISON SWETT MARDEN (1850–1924)

In this life he laughs longest who laughs last.
JOHN MASEFIELD (1878–1967), *Window in Bye Street*

Laugh at yourself first, before anyone else can.
ELSA MAXWELL (1883–1963)

Laughter gives us distance. It allows us to step back from an event, deal with it and then move on.
BOB NEWHART (1929–)

And let that day be lost to us on which we did not dance once! And let that wisdom be false to us that brought no laughter with it!
FRIEDRICH NIETZSCHE (1844–1900)

Perhaps I know best why it is man alone who laughs; he alone suffers so deeply that he had to invent laughter.
FRIEDRICH NIETZSCHE (1844–1900)

The more you find out about the world, the more opportunities there are to laugh at it.
BILL NYE (1955–)

If you can laugh at yourself loud and hard every time you fall, people will think you're drunk.
CONAN O'BRIEN (1963–)

Care to our coffin adds a nail, no doubt;
And every grin so merry, draws one out.
PETER PINDAR (1738–1819)

We cannot really love anybody with whom we never laugh.
AGNES REPPLIER (1855–1950), *Americans and Others*

I live by this credo: Have a little laugh at life and look around you for happiness instead of sadness. Laughter has always brought me out of unhappy situations. Even in your darkest moment, you usually can find something to laugh about if you try hard enough.
RICHARD BERNARD "RED" SKELTON (1913–1997)

I always knew looking back on my tears would bring me laughter, but I never knew looking back on my laughter would make me cry.
CAT STEVENS (1947–)

Men are happy to be laughed at for their humor, but not for their folly.
JONATHAN SWIFT (1667–1745)

A good laugh is sunshine in the house.
WILLIAM MAKEPEACE THACKERAY (1811–1863)

[Humanity] has unquestionably one really effective weapon—laughter. Power, money, persuasion, supplication, persecution—these can lift at a colossal humbug—push it a little—weaken it a little, century by century; but only laughter can blow it to rags and atoms at a blast. Against the assault of laughter nothing can stand.
MARK TWAIN (1835–1910), *The Mysterious Stranger*

I was irrevocably betrothed to laughter, the sound of which has always seemed to me to be the most civilized music in the world.
PETER USTINOV (1921–2004)

That is the best—to laugh with someone because you both think the same things are funny.
GLORIA VANDERBILT (1924–)

Laughter and tears are both responses to frustration and exhaustion. I myself prefer to laugh, since there is less cleaning up to do afterward.
KURT VONNEGUT JR. (1922–2007)

Laughter is the brush that sweeps away the cobwebs of your heart.
MORT WALKER (1923–)

Laughter is the hand of God on the shoulder of a troubled world.
ZIG ZIGLAR (1926–)

Laughter is the shock absorber that eases the blows of life.
ANONYMOUS

Laughter is the shortest distance between two people.
ANONYMOUS

Laughter is the spark of the soul.
ANONYMOUS

Time spent laughing is time spent with the gods.
JAPANESE PROVERB

He deserves Paradise who makes his companions laugh.
THE KORAN

Beware of too much laughter, for it deadens the mind and produces oblivion.
THE TALMUD

What soap is to the body, laughter is to the soul.
YIDDISH PROVERB

Laws

Good laws have their origins in bad morals.
AMBROSIUS MACROBIUS (C. 400 BC)

Where you find the laws most numerous, there you will find also the greatest injustice.
ARCESILAUS (C. 316–241 BC)

Even when laws have been written down, they ought not always to remain unaltered.
ARISTOTLE (384–322 BC), *Politics*

I have gained this by philosophy: that I do without being commanded what others do only from fear of the law.
ARISTOTLE (384–322 BC)

Law is mind without reason.
ARISTOTLE (384–322 BC)

Law is order, and good law is good order.
ARISTOTLE (384–322 BC), *Politics*

Laws and institutions must go hand in hand with the progress of the human mind.
SIR FRANCIS BACON (1561–1626)

Laws are like sausages. It's better not to see them being made.
OTTO VON BISMARCK (1815–1898)

It was the boast of Augustus that he found Rome of brick and left it of marble. But how much nobler will be the sovereign's boast when he shall have it to say that he found law … a sealed book and left it a living letter; found it the patrimony of the rich and left it the inheritance of the poor; found it the two-edged sword of craft and oppression and left it the staff of honesty and the shield of innocence.
HENRY BROUGHAM (1778–1868)

In law, nothing is certain but the expense.
SAMUEL BUTLER (1835–1902)

Sinners have to have the right to sin, up to the point, obviously, where it doesn't produce damage, at which point the law intervenes. The law doesn't touch upon the morality of our behaviour, but it touches upon the defense of the rights of the other. It's an old distinction that remains valid.
ROCCO BUTTIGLIONE (1948–)

Law stands mute in the midst of arms.
CICERO (106–43 BC), *Pro Milone*

The more laws, the less justice.
CICERO (106–43 BC)

The strictest law often causes the most serious wrong.
CICERO (106–43 BC)

The welfare of the people is the ultimate law.
CICERO (106–43 BC)

It is found by experience that admirable laws and right precedents among the good have their origin in the misdeeds of others.
CORNELIUS TACITUS (AD 55–117)

The law is a horrible business.
CLARENCE DARROW (1857–1938)

When men are pure, laws are useless; when men are corrupt, laws are broken.
BENJAMIN DISRAELI (1804–1881)

Common sense often makes good law.
WILLIAM ORVILLE DOUGLAS (1898–1980)

Laws alone can not secure freedom of expression; in order that every man present his views without penalty there must be spirit of tolerance in the entire population.
ALBERT EINSTEIN (1879–1955)

The law, in its majestic equality, forbids the rich as well as the poor to sleep under bridges, to beg in the streets, and to steal bread.
ANATOLE FRANCE (1844–1924), *The Red Lily*

Fragile as reason is and limited as law is as the institutionalized medium of reason, that's all we have between us and the tyranny of mere will and the cruelty of unbridled, undisciplined feelings.
FELIX FRANKFURTER (1882–1965)

What power has law where only money rules.
GAIUS PETRONIUS (C. AD 66)

To live as one likes is plebian; the noble man aspires to order and law.
JOHANN WOLFGANG VON GOETHE (1749–1832)

There exists, at the bottom of all abasement and misfortune, a last extreme which rebels and joins battle with the forces of law and respectability in a desperate struggle, waged partly by cunning and partly by violence, at once sick and ferocious, in which it attacks the prevailing social order with the pin-pricks of vice and the hammer-blows of crime.
VICTOR HUGO (1802–1885)

Law is order in liberty, and without order liberty is social chaos.
ARCHBISHOP JOHN IRELAND (1838–1918)

A strict observance of the written laws is doubtless one of the high virtues of a good citizen, but it is not the highest. The laws of necessity, of self-preservation, of saving our country when in danger, are of higher obligation.
THOMAS JEFFERSON (1743–1826)

In law a man is guilty when he violates the rights of others. In ethics he is guilty if he only thinks of doing so.
IMMANUEL KANT (1724–1804)

I submit that an individual who breaks a law that conscience tells him is unjust, and who willingly accepts the penalty of imprisonment in order to arouse the conscience of the community over its injustice, is in reality expressing the highest respect for the law.
MARTIN LUTHER KING JR. (1929–1968)

Never forget that everything Hitler did in Germany was legal.
MARTIN LUTHER KING JR. (1929–1968)

The more laws and order are made prominent,
The more thieves and robbers there will be.
LAO-TZU (C. 600 BC), *The Way of Lao-tzu*

Let me not be understood as saying that there are no bad laws, nor that grievances may not arise for the redress of which no legal provisions have been made. I mean to say no such thing. But I do mean to say that although bad laws, if they exist, should be repealed as soon as possible, still, while they continue in force, for the sake of example they should be religiously observed.
ABRAHAM LINCOLN (1809–1865)

A judge is a law student who marks his own examination papers.
H. L. MENCKEN (1880–1956)

The trouble with fighting for human freedom is that one spends most of one's time defending scoundrels. For it is against scoundrels that oppressive laws are first aimed, and oppression must be stopped at the beginning if it is to be stopped at all.
H. L. MENCKEN (1880–1956)

In the state of nature … all men are born equal, but they cannot continue in this equality. Society makes them lose it, and they recover it only by the protection of the law.
CHARLES DE MONTESQUIEU (1689–1755)

Good people do not need laws to tell them to act responsibly, while bad people will find a way around the laws.
PLATO (C. 428–348 BC)

The law must be stable, but it must not stand still.
ROSCOE POUND (1870–1964)

Where there is no law, but every man does what is right in his own eyes, there is the least of real liberty.
HENRY M. ROBERT (1837–1923)

Ignorance of the law excuses no man: Not that all men know the law, but because 'tis an excuse every man will plead, and no man can tell how to refute him.
JOHN SELDEN (1584–1654)

Nobody has a more sacred obligation to obey the law than those who make the law.
SOPHOCLES (496–406 BC)

It is not desirable to cultivate a respect for law, so much as a respect for right.
HENRY DAVID THOREAU (1817–1862)

Laws control the lesser man.... Right conduct controls the greater one.
MARK TWAIN (1835–1910)

It is the spirit and not the form of law that keeps justice alive.
EARL WARREN (1891–1974)

A law is something which must have a moral basis, so that there is an inner compelling force for every citizen to obey.
CHAIM WEIZMANN (1874–1952)

The United States is a nation of laws: badly written and randomly enforced.
FRANK ZAPPA (1940–1993)

Lawyers

Lawyers are the only persons in whom ignorance of the law is not punished.
JEREMY BENTHAM (1748–1832)

A lawyer's dream of heaven: every man reclaimed his property at the resurrection, and each tried to recover it from all his forefathers.
SAMUEL BUTLER (1835–1902)

If lawyers are disbarred and clergymen defrocked, doesn't it follow that electricians can be delighted, musicians denoted?
GEORGE CARLIN (1937–)

Upon the sacredness of property, civilization itself depends—the right of the laborer to his hundred dollars in the savings bank, and equally the legal right of the millionaire to his millions.
ANDREW CARNEGIE (1835–1919)

Doctors are the same as lawyers; the only difference is that lawyers merely rob you, whereas doctors rob you and kill you too.
ANTON CHEKHOV (1860–1904)

To some lawyers all facts are created equal.
FELIX FRANKFURTER (1882–1965)

A countryman between two lawyers is like a fish between two cats.
BENJAMIN FRANKLIN (1706–1790)

There is no better way to exercise the imagination than the study of the law. No artist ever interpreted nature as freely as a lawyer interprets the truth.
JEAN GIRADOUX (1882–1944)

Lawyers spend a great deal of their time shoveling smoke.
OLIVER WENDELL HOLMES JR. (1841–1935)

It is the trade of lawyers to question everything, yield nothing, and to talk by the hour.
THOMAS JEFFERSON (1762–1826)

A lawyer is never entirely comfortable with a friendly divorce, anymore than a good mortician wants to finish his job and then have the patient sit up on the table.
JEAN KERR (1922–2003)

He is no lawyer who cannot take two sides.
CHARLES LAMB (1775–1834)

Lawyers, I suppose, were children once.
CHARLES LAMB (1775–1834)

Lawyers are like rhinoceroses: thick skinned, short-sighted, and always ready to charge.
DAVID MELLOR (1949–)

Lawyers are like beavers. They get in the mainstream and damn it up.
JOHN NAISBITT (1929–)

A lawyer is a man who helps you get what is coming to him.
DR. LAURENCE J. PETER (1919–1990)

Marriage is really tough because you have to deal with feelings...and lawyers.
RICHARD PRYOR (1940–2005)

Lawyers are operators of the toll bridge across which anyone in search of justice has to pass.
JANE BRYANT QUINN (1939–)

Make crime pay. Become a Lawyer.
WILL ROGERS (1879–1935)

The first thing we do, let's kill all the lawyers.
WILLIAM SHAKESPEARE (1564–1616), *King Henry VI*

An incompetent attorney can delay a trial for months or years. A competent attorney can delay one even longer.
EVELLE J. YOUNGER (1918–1989)

When there are too many policemen, there is no liberty.
When there are too many soldiers, there is no peace.
When there are too many lawyers, there is no justice.
LIN YUTANG (1895–1976)

Be frank and explicit with your lawyer. It is his business to confuse the issue afterwards.
ANONYMOUS

If you laid all of the lawyers in the world, end to end, on the equator—It would be a good idea to just leave them there.
ANONYMOUS

Lawyers and painters can soon make what's black, white.
ANONYMOUS

Laziness

Ambition is a poor excuse for not having sense enough to be lazy.
EDGAR BERGEN (1903–1978)

I don't think necessity is the mother of invention—invention, in my opinion, arises directly from idleness, possibly also from laziness. To save oneself trouble.
AGATHA CHRISTIE (1890–1976), *An Autobiography*

Idleness is not doing nothing. Idleness is being free to do anything.
FLOYD DELL (1887–1969)

The laziest man I ever met put popcorn in his pancakes so they would turn over by themselves.
W. C. FIELDS (1880–1946)

Laziness travels so slowly that poverty soon overtakes him.
BENJAMIN FRANKLIN (1706–1790)

He that is busy is tempted by but one devil; he that is idle, by a legion.
THOMAS FULLER (1608–1661), *Gnomologia*

Indolence is a delightful but distressing state; we must be doing something to be happy.
MAHATMA GANDHI (1869–1948)

The path of least resistance makes all rivers, and some men, crooked.
NAPOLEON HILL (1883–1970)

Idleness and lack of occupation tend—nay, are dragged—towards evil.
HIPPOCRATES (460–377 BC), *Decorum*

People who throw kisses are mighty hopelessly lazy.
BOB HOPE (1903–2003)

Determine never to be idle.... It is wonderful how much may be done if we are always doing.
THOMAS JEFFERSON (1743–1826)

Far from idleness being the root of all evil, it is rather the only true good.
SØREN KIERKEGAARD (1813–1855)

Tomorrow is the only day in the year that appeals to a lazy man.
JIMMY LYONS (1931–1986)

That indolent but agreeable condition of doing nothing.
PLINY THE YOUNGER (AD 62–114), *Letters*

Failure is not the only punishment for laziness; there is also the success of others.
JULES RENARD (1864–1910)

Laziness is nothing more than the habit of resting before you get tired.
JULES RENARD (1864–1910)

Broad-minded is just another way of saying a fellow's too lazy to form an opinion.
WILL ROGERS (1879–1935)

There is no fatigue so wearisome as that which comes from lack of work.
CHARLES H. SPURGEON (1834–1892)

Never be entirely idle; but either be reading, or writing, or praying or meditating or endeavoring something for the public good.
THOMAS À KEMPIS (1380–1471)

The only thing wrong with doing nothing is that you never know when you're finished.
ANONYMOUS

The lazier a man is, the more he plans to do tomorrow.
NORWEGIAN PROVERB

Leadership

If your actions inspire others to dream more, learn more, do more, and become more, you are a leader.
JOHN QUINCY ADAMS (1767–1848)

He who has never learned to obey cannot be a good commander.
ARISTOTLE (384–322 BC)

Leadership is the capacity to translate vision into reality.
WARREN G. BENNIS (1925–)

Leaders keep their eyes on the horizon, not just on the bottom line.
WARREN G. BENNIS (1925–)

The most dangerous leadership myth is that leaders are born—that there is a genetic factor to leadership. This myth asserts that people simply either have certain charismatic qualities or not. That's nonsense; in fact, the opposite is true. Leaders are made rather than born.
WARREN G. BENNIS (1925–)

The art of leadership is saying no, not yes. It is very easy to say yes.
TONY BLAIR (1953–)

The key to successful leadership today is influence, not authority.
KENNETH BLANCHARD (1939–)

The task of leadership is not to put greatness into people, but to elicit it, for the greatness is there already.
JOHN BUCHAN (1875–1940)

A leader must have the courage to act against an expert's advice.
JAMES CALLAGHAN (1912–2005)

A leader takes people where they want to go. A great leader takes people where they don't necessarily want to go, but ought to be.
ROSALYNN CARTER (1927–)

Leaders are problem solvers by talent and temperament, and by choice.
HARLAN CLEVELAND (1918–)

Reason and judgment are the qualities of a leader.
CORNELIUS TACITUS (AD 55–117)

Effective leadership is putting first things first. Effective management is discipline, carrying it out.
STEPHEN R. COVEY (1932–)

Management is efficiency in climbing the leader of success; leadership determines whether the ladder is leaning against the right wall.
STEPHEN R. COVEY (1932–)

I never had much faith in leaders. I am willing to be charged with almost anything, rather than to be charged with being a leader. I am suspicious of leaders, and especially of the intellectual variety. Give me the rank and file every day in the week. If you go to the city of Washington, and you examine the pages of the Congressional Directory, you will

find that almost all of those corporation lawyers and cowardly politicians, members of Congress, and mis-representatives of the masses—you will find that almost all of them claim, in glowing terms, that they have risen from the ranks to places of eminence and distinction. I am very glad I cannot make that claim for myself. I would be ashamed to admit that I had risen from the ranks. When I rise it will be with the ranks, and not from the ranks.
EUGENE V. DEBS (1855–1926)

What you always do before you make a decision is consult. The best public policy is made when you are listening to people who are going to be impacted. Then, once policy is determined, you call on them to help you sell it.
ELIZABETH DOLE (1936–)

Leadership is not magnetic personality, that can just as well be a glib tongue. It is not "making friends and influencing people," that is flattery. Leadership is lifting a person's vision to higher sights, the raising of a person's performance to a higher standard, the building of a personality beyond its normal limitations.
PETER F. DRUCKER (1909–2005)

Management is doing things right; leadership is doing the right things.
PETER F. DRUCKER (1909–2005)

The leaders who work most effectively, it seems to me, never say "I." And that's not because they have trained themselves not to say "I." They don't think "I." They think "we"; they think "team." They understand their job to be to make the team function. They accept responsibility and don't sidestep it, but "we" gets the credit. This is what creates trust, what enables you to get the task done.
PETER F. DRUCKER (1909–2005)

What is the manager's job? It is to direct the resources and the efforts of the business toward opportunities for economically significant results. This sounds trite—and it is. But every analysis of actual allocation of resources and efforts in business that I have ever seen or made showed clearly that the bulk of time, work, attention, and money first goes to problems rather than to opportunities, and, secondly, to areas where even extraordinarily successful performance will have minimal impact on results.
PETER F. DRUCKER (1909–2005)

A sense of humor is part of the art of leadership, of getting along with people, of getting things done.
DWIGHT D. EISENHOWER (1890–1969)

Leadership is the art of getting someone else to do something you want done because he wants to do it.
DWIGHT D. EISENHOWER (1890–1969)

You do not lead by hitting people over the head—that's assault, not leadership.
DWIGHT D. EISENHOWER (1890–1969)

Our chief want is someone who will inspire us to be what we know we could be.
RALPH WALDO EMERSON (1803–1882)

Leadership can be thought of as a capacity to define oneself to others in a way that clarifies and expands a vision of the future.
EDWIN H. FRIEDMAN (1948–)

All of the great leaders have had one characteristic in common: it was the willingness to confront unequivocally the major anxiety of their people in their time. This, and not much else, is the essence of leadership.
JOHN KENNETH GALBRAITH (1908–2006)

[L]eaders can conceive and articulate goals that lift people out of their petty preoccupations and unite them in pursuit of objectives worthy of their best efforts.
JOHN GARDNER (1933–1982)

Pity the leader caught between unloving critics and uncritical lovers.
JOHN GARDNER (1933–1982)

Leadership is practiced not so much in words as in attitude and in actions.
HAROLD S. GENEEN (1910–1997)

Faith in the ability of a leader is of slight service unless it be united with faith in his justice.
GEORGE GOETHALS (1858–1928)

Good leaders must first become good servants.
ROBERT GREENLEAF (1904–1990)

The very essence of leadership is that you have to have a vision.
THEODORE HESBURGH (1917–)

What luck for rulers that men do not think.
ADOLF HITLER (1889–1945)

Management is nothing more than motivating other people.
LEE IACOCCA (1924–)

A community is like a ship; everyone ought to be prepared to take the helm.
HENRIK IBSEN (1828–1906)

Time is neutral and does not change things. With courage and initiative, leaders change things.
JESSE JACKSON (1941–)

Leadership and learning are indispensable to each other.
JOHN F. KENNEDY (1917–1963)

You don't lead by pointing and telling people some place to go. You lead by going to that place and making a case.
KEN KESEY (1935–2001)

The ultimate measure of a man is not where he stands in moments of comfort, but where he stands at times of challenge and controversy.
MARTIN LUTHER KING JR. (1929–1968)

Leaders must invoke an alchemy of great vision.
HENRY KISSINGER (1923–)

The task of the leader is to get his people from where they are to where they have not been.
HENRY KISSINGER (1923–)

The quality of a leader is reflected in the standards they set for themselves.
RAY KROC (1902–1984)

Leadership is getting someone to do what they don't want to do, to achieve what they want to achieve.
TOM LANDRY (1924–2000)

To lead people, walk beside them…As for the best leaders, the people do not notice their existence. The next best, the people honor and praise. The next, the people fear, and the next, the people hate.… When the best leader's work is done the people say, "We did it ourselves!"
LAO-TZU (C. 600 BC)

The final test of a leader is that he leaves behind him in other men the conviction and the will to carry on.
WALTER LIPPMAN (1889–1974)

Leaders aren't born, they are made. And they are made just like anything else, through hard work. And that's the price we'll have to pay to achieve that goal, or any goal.
VINCE LOMBARDI (1913–1970)

Leadership is based on a spiritual quality, the power to inspire the power to inspire others to follow.
VINCE LOMBARDI (1913–1970)

In this world a man must either be an anvil or hammer.
HENRY WADSWORTH LONGFELLOW (1807–1882)

Never give an order that can't be obeyed.
GENERAL DOUGLAS MACARTHUR (1880–1964)

The first duty of a leader is to make himself be loved without courting love. To be loved without "playing up" to anyone—even to himself.
ANDRÉ MALRAUX (1901–1976)

You can't lead anyone else farther than you have gone yourself.
GENE MAUCH (1925–2005)

A leader is one who knows the way, goes the way, and shows the way.
JOHN C. MAXWELL (1947–)

Leaders must be close enough to relate to others, but far enough ahead to motivate them.
JOHN C. MAXWELL (1947–)

Do not follow where the path may lead. Go instead where there is no path and leave a trail.
HAROLD R. MCALINDON (1940–)

A leader has the vision and conviction that a dream can be achieved. He inspires the power and energy to get it done.
RALPH NADER (1934–)

[T]he function of leadership is to produce more leaders, not more followers.
RALPH NADER (1934–)

A leader is a dealer in hope.
NAPOLÉON I (1769–1821)

If I have seen farther than others, it is because I was standing on the shoulders of giants.
SIR ISAAC NEWTON (1642–1727)

Don't tell people how to do things, tell them what to do and let them surprise you with their results.
GEORGE S. PATTON (1885–1945)

Inventories can be managed, but people must be led.
HENRY ROSS PEROT (1930–)

Great leaders are almost always great simplifiers, who can cut through argument, debate, and doubt to offer a solution everybody can understand.
COLIN POWELL (1937–)

You cannot be a leader, and ask other people to follow you, unless you know how to follow, too.
SAM RAYBURN (1882–1961)

Leadership is the ability of a single individual through his or her actions to motivate others to higher levels of achievement.
BUCK RODGERS (1938–)

The best executive is the one who has sense enough to pick good men to do what he wants done, and self-restraint to keep from meddling with them while they do it.
THEODORE ROOSEVELT (1858–1919)

Leadership is a combination of strategy and character. If you must be without one, be without the strategy.
NORMAN SCHWARZKOPF (1934–)

He who has great power should use it lightly.
SENECA (5 BC–AD 65)

It is impossible to imagine anything which better becomes a ruler than mercy.
SENECA (5 BC–AD 65)

The secret of a leader lies in the tests he has faced over the whole course of his life and the habit of action he develops in meeting those tests.
GAIL SHEEHY (1937–)

The key to being a good manager is keeping the people who hate me away from those who are still undecided.
CASEY STENGEL (1890–1975)

Men make history, and not the other way around. In periods where there is no leadership, society stands still. Progress occurs when courageous, skillful leaders seize the opportunity to change things for the better.
HARRY S TRUMAN (1884–1972)

The only safe ship in a storm is leadership.
FAYE WATTLETON (1943–)

Whoever is providing leadership needs to be as fresh and thoughtful and reflective as possible to make the very best fight.
FAYE WATTLETON (1943–)

Before you are a leader, success is all about growing yourself. When you become a leader, success is all about growing others.
JACK WELCH (1935–)

Whether a man is burdened by power or enjoys power; whether he is trapped by responsibility or made free by it; whether he is moved by other people and outer forces or moves them—this is of the essence of leadership.
THEODORE H. WHITE (1915–1986), *The Making of the President*

A leader leads by example, whether he intends to or not.
ANONYMOUS

An army of sheep led by a lion would defeat an army of lions led by a sheep.
ARAB PROVERB

Learning

Learning is not attained by chance; it must be sought for with ardor and attended to with diligence.
ABIGAIL ADAMS (1744–1818)

Human beings, who are almost unique in having the ability to learn from the experience of others, are also remarkable for their apparent disinclination to do so.
DOUGLAS ADAMS (1952–2001), *Last Chance to See*

We learn more by looking for the answer to a question and not finding it than we do from learning the answer itself.
LLOYD ALEXANDER (1924–)

Learning is an ornament in prosperity, a refuge in adversity, and a provision in old age.
ARISTOTLE (384–322 BC)

Learning is not child's play; we cannot learn without pain.
ARISTOTLE (384–322 BC)

Learning, n.: The kind of ignorance distinguishing the studious.
AMBROSE BIERCE (1842–1914), *The Devil's Dictionary*

The liberals can understand everything but people who don't understand them.
LENNY BRUCE (1925–1966)

Liberals claim to want to give a hearing to other views, but then are shocked and offended to discover that there are other views.
WILLIAM F. BUCKLEY JR. (1925–)

Liberals, it has been said, are generous with other people's money, except when it comes to questions of national survival when they prefer to be generous with other people's freedom and security.
WILLIAM F. BUCKLEY JR. (1925–)

Learn everything you can, anytime you can, from anyone you can—there will always come a time when you will be grateful you did.
SARAH CALDWELL (1924–2006)

Never seem more learned than the people you are with. Wear your learning like a pocket watch and keep it hidden. Do not pull it out to count the hours, but give the time when you are asked.
LORD CHESTERFIELD (1694–1773)

Learning without thought is labor lost; thought without learning is perilous.
CONFUCIUS (551–479 BC), *The Confucian Analects*

Learning is not compulsory … neither is survival.
W. EDWARDS DEMING (1900–1993)

The Liberals talk about a stable government but we don't know how bad the stable is going to smell.
T. C. DOUGLAS (1904–1986)

I never teach my pupils; I only attempt to provide the conditions in which they can learn.
ALBERT EINSTEIN (1879–1955)

Learn from yesterday, live for today, hope for tomorrow.
ALBERT EINSTEIN (1879–1955)

When a man is pushed, tormented, defeated, he has a chance to learn something.
RALPH WALDO EMERSON (1803–1882)

Whoso neglects learning in his youth,
Loses the past and is dead for the future.
EURIPIDES (C. 480–406 BC), *Phrixus*

Being ignorant is not so much a shame, as being unwilling to learn.
BENJAMIN FRANKLIN (1706–1790)

Live as if you were to die tomorrow. Learn as if you were to live forever.
MAHATMA GANDHI (1869–1948)

We learn by example and by direct experience because there are real limits to the adequacy of verbal instruction.
MALCOLM GLADWELL (1963–), *Blink: The Power of Thinking Without Thinking*

Much learning does not teach understanding.
HERACLITUS (C. 535–475 BC), *On the Universe*

Leadership and learning are indispensable to each other.
JOHN F. KENNEDY (1917–1963)

Liberty without learning is always in peril; learning without liberty is always in vain.
JOHN F. KENNEDY (1917–1963)

The beautiful thing about learning is that no one can take it away from you.
B. B. KING (1925–)

I am learning all the time. The tombstone will be my diploma.
EARTHA KITT (1927–)

That is what learning is. You suddenly understand something you've understood all your life, but in a new way.
DORIS LESSING (1919–)

Experience: that most brutal of teachers. But you learn, my God do you learn.
C. S. LEWIS (1898–1963)

The books that help you most are those which make you think the most. The hardest way of learning is that of easy reading; but a great book that comes from a great thinker is a ship of thought, deep freighted with truth and beauty.
THEODORE PARKER (1810–1860)

Ignorance of all things is an evil neither terrible nor excessive, nor yet the greatest of all; but great cleverness and much learning, if they be accompanied by a bad training, are a much greater misfortune.
PLATO (C. 428–348 BC)

It is no profit to have learned well, if you neglect to do well.
PUBLILIUS SYRUS (C. 100 BC)

Whenever you are asked if you can do a job, tell 'em, "Certainly I can!" Then get busy and find out how to do it.
THEODORE ROOSEVELT (1858–1919)

The wisest mind has something yet to learn.
GEORGE SANTAYANA (1863–1952)

While we teach, we learn.
SENECA (5 BC–AD 65)

If you hold a cat by the tail you learn things you cannot learn any other way.
MARK TWAIN (1835–1910)

One learns people through the heart, not the eyes or the intellect.
MARK TWAIN (1835–1910)

Beware of the man who works hard to learn something, learns it, and finds himself no wiser than before.
KURT VONNEGUT JR. (1922–2007)

Curiosity is the wick in the candle of learning.
WILLIAM ARTHUR WARD (1921–1994)

Only the curious will learn and only the resolute overcome the obstacles to learning. The quest quotient has always excited me more than the intelligence quotient.
EUGENE S. WILSON (1900–1981)

A wise man learns something new every day. The fool knows it already.
ANONYMOUS

Learning is a treasure that will follow its owner everywhere.
CHINESE PROVERB

Learning is like rowing upstream; not to advance is to drop back.
CHINESE PROVERB

Legends

Legends are material to be molded, and not facts to be recorded.
HERVEY ALLEN (1889–1949)

All the great legends are Templates for human behavior. I would define a myth as a story that has survived.
JOHN BOORMAN (1933–)

Legends die hard. They survive as truth rarely does.
HELEN HAYES (1900–1993)

Sometimes legends make reality, and become more useful than the facts.
SALMAN RUSHDIE (1947–)

When the legends die, the dreams end; there is no more greatness.
TECUMSEH (1768–1813)

Leisure

Friendship is a very taxing and arduous form of leisure activity.
MORTIMER ADLER (1902–2001)

The end of labor is to gain leisure.
ARISTOTLE (384–322 BC)

We give up leisure in order that we may have leisure, just as we go to war in order that we may have peace.
ARISTOTLE (384–322 BC)

Now hatred is by far the longest pleasure;
Men love in haste, but they detest at leisure.
LORD BYRON (1788–1824)

He does not seem to me to be a free man who does not sometimes do nothing.
CICERO (106–43 BC)

A poor life this if, full of care,
We have no time to stand and stare.
W. H. DAVIES (1871–1940)

We must beat the iron while it is hot, but we may polish it at leisure.
JOHN DRYDEN (1631–1700)

Employ thy time well, if thou meanest to get leisure.
BENJAMIN FRANKLIN (1706–1790)

The more we do, the more we can do; the more busy we are, the more leisure we have.
WILLIAM HAZLITT (1778–1830)

Leisure is the mother of philosophy.
THOMAS HOBBES (1588–1679)

Leisure only means a chance to do other jobs that demand attention.
OLIVER WENDELL HOLMES JR. (1841–1935)

They talk of the dignity of work. Bosh. The dignity is in leisure.
HERMAN MELVILLE (1819–1891)

The happiest people are those who think the most interesting thoughts. Those who decide to use leisure as a means of mental development, who love good music, good books, good pictures, good company, good conversation, are the happiest people in the world. And they are not only happy in themselves, they are the cause of happiness in others.
WILLIAM LYON PHELPS (1865–1943)

It is in his pleasure that a man really lives; it is from his leisure that he constructs the true fabric of self.
AGNES REPPLIER (1855–1950)

To be able to fill leisure intelligently is the last product of civilization, and at present very few people have reached this level.
BERTRAND RUSSELL (1872–1970), *Conquest of Happiness*

Nothing is as certain as that the vices of leisure are gotten rid of by being busy.
SENECA (5 BC–AD 65), *Moral Letters to Lucilius*

A day's work is a day's work, neither more nor less, and the man who does it needs a day's sustenance, a night's repose and due leisure, whether he be painter or ploughman.
GEORGE BERNARD SHAW (1856–1950)

If you are losing your leisure, look out; you may be losing your soul.
LOGAN PEARSALL SMITH (1865–1946)

Temptation rarely comes in working hours. It is in their leisure time that men are made or marred.
W. N. TAYLOR (1949–)

He enjoys true leisure who has time to improve his soul's estate.
HENRY DAVID THOREAU (1817–1862)

To be able to fill leisure intelligently is the last product of civilization.
ARNOLD J. TOYNBEE (1889–1975)

Conspicuous consumption of valuable goods is a means of reputability to the gentleman of leisure.
THORSTEIN VEBLEN (1857–1929), *Theory of the Leisure Class*

Leisure is a beautiful garment, but it will not do for constant wear.
ANONYMOUS

Say not, when I have leisure I will study; you may not have leisure.
THE MISHNAH

Liberals

The most radical revolutionary will become a conservative the day after the revolution.
HANNAH ARENDT (1906–1975)

Of all the varieties of virtues, liberalism is the most beloved.
ARISTOTLE (384–322 BC)

The liberals can understand everything but people who don't understand them.
LENNY BRUCE (1925–1966)

Any man who is under 30, and is not a liberal, has no heart; and any man who is over 30, and is not a conservative, has no brains.
SIR WINSTON CHURCHILL (1874–1965)

I am a Conservative to preserve all that is good in our constitution, a Radical to remove all that is bad. I seek to preserve property and to respect order, and I equally decry the appeal to the passions of the many or the prejudices of the few.
BENJAMIN DISRAELI (1804–1881)

My faith has been the driving thing of my life. I think it is important that people who are perceived as liberals not be afraid of talking about moral and community values.
MARIAN WRIGHT EDELMAN (1939–)

I never dared to be radical when young
For fear it would make me conservative when old.
ROBERT FROST (1874–1963), "Ten Mills"

A liberal is a man too broadminded to take his own side in a quarrel.
ROBERT FROST (1874–1963)

Liberalism is trust of the people, tempered by prudence; conservatism, distrust of people, tempered by fear.
WILLIAM GLADSTONE (1809–1898)

Whenever I hear people talking about "liberal ideas," I am always astounded that men should love to fool themselves with empty sounds. An idea

should never be liberal; it must be vigorous, positive, and without loose ends so that it may fulfill its divine mission and be productive. The proper place for liberality is in the realm of the emotions.
JOHANN WOLFGANG VON GOETHE (1749–1832)

A liberal is a conservative who's been arrested. A conservative is a liberal who's been mugged.
WENDY KAMINER (1950–)

When you are right, you cannot be too radical; when you are wrong, you cannot be too conservative.
MARTIN LUTHER KING JR. (1929–1968)

Liberalism is the supreme form of generosity; it is the right which the majority concedes to minorities and hence it is the noblest cry that has ever resounded on this planet.
JOSÉ ORTEGA Y GASSET (1883–1955)

A liberal is a person whose interests aren't at stake, at the moment.
WILLIS PLAYER (1915–)

Conservatives divide the world in terms of good and evil while liberals do it in terms of the rich and poor.
DENNIS PRAGER (1948–)

The essence of the Liberal outlook lies not in what opinions are held, but in how they are held: instead of being held dogmatically, they are held tentatively, and with a consciousness that new evidence may at any moment lead to their abandonment.
BERTRAND RUSSELL (1872–1970)

Liberals feel unworthy of their possessions. Conservatives feel they deserve everything they've stolen.
MORT SAHL (1927–)

Liberals seem to assume that, if you don't believe in their particular political solutions, then you don't really care about the people that they claim to want to help.
THOMAS SOWELL (1930–)

The radical of one century is the conservative of the next. The radical invents the views. When he has worn them out the conservative adopts them.
MARK TWAIN (1835–1910)

As Mankind becomes more liberal, they will be more apt to allow that all those who conduct themselves as worthy members of the community are equally entitled to the protections of civil government. I hope ever to see America among the foremost nations of justice and liberality.
GEORGE WASHINGTON (1732–1799)

It only takes 20 years for a liberal to become a conservative without changing a single idea.
ROBERT ANTON WILSON (1932–2007)

Liberals are very broadminded: they are always willing to give careful consideration to both sides of the same side.
ANONYMOUS

Liberation

Freeing oneself from words is liberation.
BODHIDHARMA (470–543)

Be a lamp unto yourself. Work out your liberation with diligence.
THE BUDDHA (563–483 BC)

Language is power, life and the instrument of culture, the instrument of domination and liberation.
ANGELA CARTER (1940–1992)

Nothing goes further toward a man's liberation than the act of surviving his need for character.
JOHN CIARDI (1916–1986)

Revenge only engenders violence, not clarity and true peace. I think liberation must come from within.
SANDRA CISNEROS (1954–)

I'm suspicious of any man or woman who approaches their own liberation with any kind of gender bias.
ANDREW COHEN (1955–)

We have to be willing to give up all the injustices of the past that did exist—and that do exist right now. When we become interested in liberation, we then become interested in that which transcends time.
ANDREW COHEN (1955–)

Gay Liberation? I ain't against it, it's just that there's nothing in it for me.
BETTE DAVIS (1908–1989)

Of all the nasty outcomes predicted for women's liberation… none was more alarming, from a feminist point of view, than the suggestion that women would eventually become just like men.
BARBARA EHRENREICH (1941–)

The true value of a human being can be found in the degree to which he has attained liberation from the self.
ALBERT EINSTEIN (1879–1955)

I work toward the liberation of women, but I'm not feminist. I'm just a woman.
BUCHI EMECHETA (1944–)

The liberation of those who commit murder and terrorism is unacceptable.
ALBERTO FUJIMORI (1938–)

The main object of a revolution is the liberation of man … interpretation and application of some transcendental ideology.
JEAN GENET (1910–1986)

This is what sexual liberation chiefly accomplishes—it liberates young women to pursue married men.
GEORGE GILDER (1939–)

It is the prayer of my innermost being to realize my supreme identity in the liberated play of consciousness, the Vast Expanse. Now is the moment, Here is the place of Liberation.
ALEX GREY (1953–)

Liberation is an ever shifting horizon, a total ideology that can never fulfill its promises. It has the therapeutic quality of providing emotionally charged rituals of solidarity in hatred—it is the amphetamine of its believers.
ARIANNA HUFFINGTON (1950–)

Liberation is not deliverance.
VICTOR HUGO (1802–1885)

Women's liberation is the liberation of the feminine in the man and the masculine in the woman.
CORITA KENT (1918–1986)

Despair and frustration will not shake our belief that the resistance is the only way of liberation.
EMILE LAHUD (1936–)

Long live the liberation of the workers of all countries from the infernal chasm of war, exploitation and slavery!
KARL LIEBKNECHT (1871–1919)

There are those who will say that the liberation of humanity, the freedom of man and mind is nothing but a dream. They are right. It is the American Dream.
ARCHIBALD MACLEISH (1892–1982)

Women's liberation is just a lot of foolishness. It's men who are discriminated against. They can't bear children. And no one is likely to do anything about that.
GOLDA MEIR (1898–1978)

I'm for human lib, the liberation of all people, not just black people or female people or gay people.
RICHARD PRYOR (1940–2005)

Only the liberation of the natural capacity for love in human beings can master their sadistic destructiveness.
WILHELM REICH (1897–1957)

My fellow revolutionaries, liberation is a noble cause. We must fight to obtain it.
GEORGE WEAH (1966–)

Liberty

By liberty I mean the assurance that every man shall be protected in doing what he believes is his duty against the influence of authority and majorities, custom and opinion.
LORD ACTON (1834–1902)

Liberty is not a means to a higher political end. It is itself the highest political end.
LORD ACTON (1834–1902)

The law of liberty tends to abolish the reign of race over race, of faith over faith, of class over class. It is not the realization of a political ideal; it is the discharge of a moral obligation.
LORD ACTON (1834–1902)

[A] Constitution of Government once changed from Freedom, can never be restored. Liberty, once lost, is lost forever.
JOHN ADAMS (1735–1826)

The only maxim of a free government ought to be to trust no man living with power to endanger the public liberty.
JOHN ADAMS (1735–1826)

If liberty and equality, as is thought by some, are chiefly to be found in democracy, they will be best attained when all persons alike share in the government to the utmost.
ARISTOTLE (384–322 BC), *Politics*

The basis of a democratic state is liberty.
ARISTOTLE (384–322 BC), *Politics*

In necessary things, unity; in doubtful things, liberty; in all things, charity.
RICHARD BAXTER (1615–1691)

Every law is an infraction of liberty.
JEREMY BENTHAM (1748–1832)

Experience should teach us to be most on our guard to protect liberty when the Government's purposes are beneficent. Men born to freedom are naturally alert to repel invasion of their liberty by evil-minded rulers. The greatest dangers to liberty lurk in insidious encroachment by men of zeal, well-meaning but without understanding.
LOUIS D. BRANDEIS (1856–1941)

But what is liberty without wisdom, and without virtue? It is the greatest of all possible evils; for it is folly, vice, and madness, without tuition or restraint.
EDMUND BURKE (1729–1797)

The people never give up their liberties but under some delusion.
EDMUND BURKE (1729–1797)

The advance of liberty is the path to both a safer and better world.
GEORGE W. BUSH (1946–)

Irresponsible power is inconsistent with liberty, and must corrupt those who exercise it.
JOHN CALHOUN (1782–1850)

Liberty is rendered even more precious by the recollection of servitude.
CICERO (106–43 BC)

Liberty will not descend to a people; a people must raise themselves to liberty; it is a blessing that must be earned before it can be enjoyed.
CHARLES CALEB COLTON (1780–1832)

Eternal vigilance is the price of liberty.
JOHN PHILPOT CURRAN (1750–1817)

The condition upon which God has given liberty to man is eternal vigilance.
JOHN PHILPOT CURRAN (1750–1817)

For what is liberty but the unhampered translation of will into act?
DANTE ALIGHIERI (1265–1321)

Civilization begins with order, grows with liberty, and dies with chaos.
WILL DURANT (1885–1981)

Education is a better safeguard of liberty than a standing army.
EDWARD EVERETT (1794–1865)

God grant that not only the love of liberty but a thorough knowledge of the rights of man may pervade all the nations of the earth, so that a philosopher may set his foot anywhere on its surface and say: "This is my country."
BENJAMIN FRANKLIN (1706–1790)

Sell not virtue to purchase wealth, nor liberty to purchase power.
BENJAMIN FRANKLIN (1706–1790)

Those who would give up essential liberty to purchase a little temporary safety deserve neither liberty nor safety.
BENJAMIN FRANKLIN (1706–1790)

What difference does it make to the dead, the orphans and the homeless, whether the mad destruction is wrought under the name of totalitarianism or the holy name of liberty or democracy?
MAHATMA GANDHI (1869–1948), *Non-Violence in Peace and War*

To deprive a man of his natural liberty and to deny to him the ordinary amenities of life is worse than starving the body; it is starvation of the soul…
MAHATMA GANDHI (1869–1948)

Liberty has restraints but no frontiers.
DAVID LLOYD GEORGE (1863–1945)

Life without liberty is like a body without spirit.
KAHLIL GIBRAN (1883–1931)

Justice is the end of government. It is the end of civil society. It ever has been and ever will be pursued until it be obtained, or until liberty be lost in the pursuit. In a society under the forms of which the stronger faction can readily unite and oppress the weaker, anarchy may as truly be said to reign as in a state of nature, where the weaker individual is not secured against the violence of the stronger; and as, in the latter state, even the individuals are prompted, by the uncertainty of their condition, to submit to a government which may protect the weak as well as themselves; so, in the former state, will the more powerful factions or parties be gradually induced, by a like motive to wish for a government which will protect all parties, the weaker as well as the more powerful.
ALEXANDER HAMILTON (1755–1804)

Indignation boils my blood at the thought of the heritage we are throwing away; at the thought that, with few exceptions, the fight for freedom is left to the poor, forlorn and defenseless, and to the few radicals and revolutionaries who would make use of liberty to destroy, rather than to maintain, American institutions.
ARTHUR GARFIELD HAYS (1881–1954)

The love of liberty is the love of others; the love of power is the love of ourselves.
WILLIAM HAZLITT (1778–1830)

Guard with jealous attention the public liberty. Suspect everyone who approaches that jewel. Unfortunately, nothing will preserve it but downright force. Whenever you give up that force, you are ruined.
PATRICK HENRY (1736–1799)

Is life so dear, or peace so sweet, as to be purchased at the price of chains or slavery? Forbid it, Almighty God! I know not what course others may take; but as for me, give me liberty or give me death!
PATRICK HENRY (1736–1799)

Seek freedom and become captive of your desires, seek discipline and find your liberty.
FRANK HERBERT (1920–1986), *Dune*

It is seldom that liberty of any kind is lost all at once.
DAVID HUME (1711–1776)

One of the qualities of liberty is that, as long as it is being striven after, it goes on expanding. Therefore, the man who stands in the midst of the struggle and says, "I have it," merely shows by doing so that he has just lost it.
HENRIK IBSEN (1828–1906)

Law is order in liberty, and without order liberty is social chaos.
ARCHBISHOP JOHN IRELAND (1838–1918)

Whenever any form of government becomes destructive of these ends [life, liberty, and the pursuit of happiness] it is the right of the people to alter or abolish it, and to institute new government….
THOMAS JEFFERSON (1743–1826), *The Declaration of Independence*

Educate and inform the whole mass of the people.... They are the only sure reliance for the preservation of our liberty.
THOMAS JEFFERSON (1743–1826)

I would rather be exposed to the inconveniences attending too much liberty than to those attending too small a degree of it.
THOMAS JEFFERSON (1743–1826)

Liberty is the great parent of science and of virtue; and a nation will be great in both always in proportion as it is free.
THOMAS JEFFERSON (1762–1826)

The natural progress of things is for liberty to yield and government to gain ground.
THOMAS JEFFERSON (1762–1826)

The tree of liberty must be refreshed from time to time with the blood of patriots and tyrants.
THOMAS JEFFERSON (1743–1826)

Let every nation know, whether it wishes us well or ill, we shall pay any price, bear any burden, meet any hardship, support any friend, oppose any foe, to assure the survival and success of liberty.
JOHN F. KENNEDY (1917–1963)

Liberty without learning is always in peril; learning without liberty is always in vain.
JOHN F. KENNEDY (1917–1963)

Our defense is in the preservation of the spirit which prizes liberty as a heritage of all men, in all lands, everywhere. Destroy this spirit and you have planted the seeds of despotism around your own doors.
ABRAHAM LINCOLN (1809–1865)

The shepherd drives the wolf from the sheep's throat, for which the sheep thanks the shepherd as his liberator, while the wolf denounces him for the same act as the destroyer of liberty.
ABRAHAM LINCOLN (1809–1865)

A useful definition of liberty is obtained only by seeking the principle of liberty in the main business of human life, that is to say, in the process by which men educate their responses and learn to control their environment.
WALTER LIPPMAN (1889–1974)

The only thing that saves us from the bureaucracy is inefficiency. An efficient bureaucracy is the greatest threat to liberty.
EUGENE MCCARTHY (1916–2005)

The only freedom which deserves the name is that of pursuing our own good in our own way, so long as we do not attempt to deprive others of theirs, or impede their efforts to obtain it. Each is the proper guardian of his own health, whether bodily, or mental or spiritual. Mankind are greater gainers by suffering each other to live as seems good to themselves, than by compelling each to live as seems good to the rest.
JOHN STUART MILL (1806–1873), *On Liberty*

Give me the liberty to know, to utter, and to argue freely according to conscience, above all liberties.
JOHN MILTON (1608–1674)

Discipline must come through liberty.... We do not consider an individual disciplined only when he has been rendered as artificially silent as a mute and as immovable as a paralytic. He is an individual annihilated, not disciplined.
MARIA MONTESSORI (1870–1952)

I sometimes think that the price of liberty is not so much eternal vigilance as eternal dirt.
GEORGE ORWELL (1903–1950)

He that would make his own liberty secure, must guard even his enemy from oppression; for if he violates this duty, he establishes a precedent that will reach to himself.
THOMAS PAINE (1737–1809)

Such is the irresistible nature of truth that all it asks, and all it wants, is the liberty of appearing.
THOMAS PAINE (1737–1809)

Eternal vigilance is the price of liberty; power is ever stealing from the many for the few.
WENDELL PHILLIPS (1811–1884)

The sovereignty of one's self over one's self is called Liberty.
ALBERT PIKE (1809–1891)

The principle of liberty and equality, if coupled with mere selfishness, will make men only devils, each trying to be independent that he may fight only for his own interest. And here is the need of religion and its power, to bring in the principle of benevolence and love to men.
JOHN RANDOLPH (1773–1833)

Where there is no law, but every man does what is right in his own eyes, there is the least of real liberty.
HENRY M. ROBERT (1837–1923)

Order without liberty and liberty without order are equally destructive.
THEODORE ROOSEVELT (1858–1919)

Free people, remember this maxim: We may acquire liberty, but it is never recovered if it is once lost.
JEAN-JACQUES ROUSSEAU (1712–1778)

To renounce liberty is to renounce being a man, to surrender the rights of humanity and even its duties. For he who renounces everything, no indemnity is possible. Such a renunciation is incompatible with man's nature; to remove all liberty from his will is to remove all morality from his acts.
JEAN-JACQUES ROUSSEAU (1712–1778)

Too little liberty brings stagnation and too much brings chaos.
BERTRAND RUSSELL (1872–1970)

Few men desire liberty: The majority are satisfied with a just master.
SALLUST (86–34 BC)

The higher your station, the less your liberty.
SALLUST (86–34 BC)

If you want to be free, there is but one way; it is to guarantee an equally full measure of liberty to all your neighbors. There is no other.
CARL SCHURZ (1829–1906)

Liberty means responsibility. That is why most men dread it.
GEORGE BERNARD SHAW (1856–1950)

Liberty is the possibility of doubting, the possibility of making a mistake, the possibility of searching and experimenting, the possibility of saying No to any authority—literary, artistic, philosophic, religious, social and even political.
IGNAZIO SILONE (1900–1978), *The God That Failed*

What more felicity can fall to creature, than to enjoy delight with liberty.
EDMUND SPENSER (1552–1599), *The Fate of the Butterfly*

Too much liberty corrupts us all.
TERENCE (185–159 BC)

Liberty, then, about which so many volumes have been written is, when accurately defined, only the power of acting.
VOLTAIRE (1694–1778)

The preservation of the sacred fire of liberty and the destiny of the republican model of government are justly considered … deeply, … finally, staked on the experiment entrusted to the hands of the American people.
GEORGE WASHINGTON (1732–1799)

God grants liberty only to those who love it and are always ready to guard and defend it.
DANIEL WEBSTER (1782–1852)

Liberty is the proper end and object of authority, and cannot subsist without it; and it is liberty to that which is good, just, and honest.
JOHN WINTHROP (1588–1649)

No nation ancient or modern ever lost the liberty of freely speaking, writing, or publishing their sentiments, but forthwith lost their liberty in general and became slaves.
JOHN PETER ZENGER (1697–1746)

A library is an arsenal of liberty.
ANONYMOUS

Liberty is the right to choose. Freedom is the result of the right choice.
ANONYMOUS

To him that you tell your secret you resign your liberty.
ANONYMOUS

Libraries

Here is where people,
One frequently finds,
Lower their voices
And raise their minds.
RICHARD ARMOUR (1906–1989), "Library"

I love the place; the magnificent books; I require books as I require air.
SHOLEM ASCH (1880–1957)

Libraries are as the shrines where all the relics of the ancient saints, full of true virtue, and that without delusion or imposture, are preserved and reposed.
SIR FRANCIS BACON (1561–1626)

A library is but the soul's burial ground. It is the land of shadows.
HENRY WARD BEECHER (1813–1887)

A library is not a luxury but one of the necessities of life.
HENRY WARD BEECHER (1813–1887)

A little library growing each year is an honorable part of a man's history.
HENRY WARD BEECHER (1813–1887)

Libraries are not made, they grow.
AUGUSTINE BIRRELL (1850–1933)

As a child, my number one best friend was the librarian in my grade school. I actually believed all those books belonged to her.
ERMA BOMBECK (1927–1996)

I have always imagined that Paradise will be a kind of library.
JORGE LUIS BORGES (1899–1986)

Without libraries what have we? We have no past and no future.
RAY BRADBURY (1920–)

Libraries allow children to ask questions about the world and find the answers. And the wonderful thing is that once a child learns to use a library, the doors to learning are always open.
LAURA BUSH (1946–)

The true university of these days is a collection of books.
THOMAS CARLYLE (1795–1881)

There is not such a cradle of democracy upon the earth as the Free Public Library, this republic of letters, where neither rank, office, nor wealth receives the slightest consideration.
ANDREW CARNEGIE (1835–1919)

If you have a garden and a library, you have everything you need.
CICERO (106–43 BC)

A library is not a shrine for the worship of books. It is not a temple where literary incense must be burned or where one's devotion to the bound book is expressed in ritual. A library, to modify the famous metaphor of Socrates, should be the delivery room for the birth of ideas—a place where history comes to life.
NORMAN COUSINS (1915–1990)

A great library contains the diary of the human race.
GEORGE MERCER DAWSON (1849–1901)

Libraries are where it all begins.
RITA DOVE (1952–)

Libraries are the wardrobes of literature, whence men, properly informed may bring forth something for ornament, much for curiosity, and more for use.
William Dyer (1881–1933)

A man's library is a sort of harem.
Ralph Waldo Emerson (1803–1882)

Be a little careful about your library. Do you foresee what you will do with it? Very little to be sure. But the real question is, What it will do with you? You will come here and get books that will open your eyes, and your ears, and your curiosity, and turn you inside out or outside in.
Ralph Waldo Emerson (1803–1882)

Consider what you have in the smallest chosen library. A company of the wisest and wittiest men that could be picked out of all civil countries, in a thousand years, have set in best order the results of their learning and wisdom. The men themselves were hid and inaccessible, solitary, impatient of interruption, fenced by etiquette; but the thought which they did not uncover to their bosom friend is here written out in transparent words to us, the strangers of another age.
Ralph Waldo Emerson (1803–1882)

The richest person in the world—in fact all the riches in the world—couldn't provide you with anything like the endless, incredible loot available at your local library.
Malcolm S. Forbes (1919–1990)

To those with ears to hear, libraries are really very noisy places. On their shelves we hear the captured voices of the centuries-old conversation that makes up our civilization.
Timothy Healy (1855–1931)

My experience with public libraries is that the first volume of the book I inquire for is out, unless I happen to want the second, when that is out.
Oliver Wendell Holmes Sr. (1809–1894)

My books are very few, but then the world is before me—a library open to all—from which poverty of purse cannot exclude me—in which the meanest and most paltry volume is sure to furnish something to amuse, if not to instruct and improve.
Joseph Howe (1804–1873)

Perhaps no place in any community is so totally democratic as the town library. The only entrance requirement is interest.
Lady Bird Johnson (1912–2007)

No place affords a more striking conviction of the vanity of human hopes than a public library.
Samuel Johnson (1709–1784)

Libraries are the one American institution you shouldn't rip off.
Barbara Kingsolver (1955–)

It is almost everywhere the case that soon after it is begotten the greater part of human wisdom is laid to rest in repositories.
Georg C. Lichtenberg (1742–1799)

What is more important in a library than anything else—than everything else—is the fact that it exists.
Archibald MacLeish (1892–1982)

A good library is a place, a palace where the lofty spirits of all nations and generations meet.
Samuel Niger (1883–1956)

A library represents the mind of its collector, his fancies and foibles, his strength and weakness, his prejudices and preferences. Particularly is this the case if to the character of a collector he adds—or tries to add—the qualities of a student who wishes to know the books and the lives of the men who wrote them. The friendships of his life, the phases of his growth, the vagaries of his mind, all are represented.
Sir William Osler (1849–1919)

Our libraries are valuable centers of education, learning and enrichment for people of all ages. In recent years, libraries have taken on an increasingly important role. Today's libraries are about much more than books.
Jodi Rell (1946–)

What do we, as a nation, care about books? How much do you think we spend altogether on our libraries, public or private, as compared with what we spend on our horses?
JOHN RUSKIN (1819–1900)

A library is thought in cold storage.
HERBERT SAMUEL (1870–1963)

My library was dukedom large enough.
WILLIAM SHAKESPEARE (1564–1616), *The Tempest*

To a historian, libraries are food, shelter, and even muse.
BARBARA W. TUCHMAN (1912–1989)

A library is an arsenal of liberty.
ANONYMOUS

An hour spent in the library is worth a month in the laboratory.
ANONYMOUS

Lies

I apologize for lying to you. I promise I won't deceive you except in matters of this sort.
SPIRO T. AGNEW (1918–1986)

Men are liars. We'll lie about lying if we have to. I'm an algebra liar. I figure two good lies make a positive.
TIM ALLEN (1953–)

The trouble with lying and deceiving is that their efficiency depends entirely upon a clear notion of the truth that the liar and deceiver wishes to hide.
HANNAH ARENDT (1906–1975)

Liars when they speak the truth are not believed.
ARISTOTLE (384–322 BC)

The least initial deviation from the truth is multiplied later a thousandfold.
ARISTOTLE (384–322 BC)

He who observes etiquette but objects to lying is like someone who dresses fashionably but wears no vest.
WALTER BENJAMIN (1892–1940)

Heaven lies about us in our infancy and the world begins lying about us pretty soon afterward.
AMBROSE BIERCE (1842–1914)

The hardest tumble a man can make is to fall over his own bluff.
AMBROSE BIERCE (1842–1914)

There are some people so addicted to exaggeration that they can't tell the truth without lying.
JOSH BILLINGS (1818–1885)

It's essential to tell the truth at all times. This will reduce life's pain. Lying distorts reality. All forms of distorted thinking must be corrected.
JOHN BRADSHAW (1933–)

Any fool can tell the truth, but it requires a man of some sense to know how to lie well.
SAMUEL BUTLER (1835–1902)

I do not mind lying, but I hate inaccuracy.
SAMUEL BUTLER (1835–1902)

Lying has a kind of respect and reverence with it. We pay a person the compliment of acknowledging his superiority whenever we lie to him.
SAMUEL BUTLER (1835–1902)

The best liar is he who makes the smallest amount of lying go the longest way.
SAMUEL BUTLER (1835–1902)

Remember that it is not enough to abstain from lying by word of mouth; for the worst lies are often conveyed by a false look, smile, or act.
ABRAHAM CAHAN (1860–1951)

Truth, like light, blinds. Falsehood, on the contrary, is a beautiful twilight that enhances every object.
ALBERT CAMUS (1913–1960)

Autobiography is probably the most respectable form of lying.
HUMPHREY CARPENTER (1946–2005)

I have always loved truth so passionately that I have often resorted to lying as a way of introducing it into the minds which were ignorant of its charms.
GIACOMO CASANOVA (1725–1798)

Truth is a pain which will not stop. And the truth of this world is to die. You must choose: either dying or lying. Personally, I have never been able to kill myself.
LOUIS-FERDINAND CELINE (1894–1961)

A lie gets halfway around the world before the truth has a chance to get its pants on.
SIR WINSTON CHURCHILL (1874–1965)

Lying just for the fun of it is either art or pathology.
MASON COOLEY (1927–2002)

The power of lying is much less than the power of what is not to be discussed.
MASON COOLEY (1927–2002)

When you stretch the truth, watch out for the snapback.
BILL COPELAND (1929–)

A liar is always lavish of oaths.
PIERRE CORNEILLE (1606–1684)

Lying to ourselves is more deeply ingrained than lying to others.
FYODOR DOSTOEVSKY (1821–1881)

Truth is beautiful, without doubt; but so are lies.
RALPH WALDO EMERSON (1803–1882)

We tell lies, yet it is easy to show that lying is immoral.
EPICTETUS (AD 55–135)

Lying is an indispensable part of making life tolerable.
BERGEN EVANS (1904–1978)

Lying rides upon debt's back
BENJAMIN FRANKLIN (1706–1790)

Euphemism is a euphemism for lying.
BOBBIE GENTRY (1944–)

Lying can never save us from another lie.
VACLAV HAVEL (1936–)

By means of shrewd lies, unremittingly repeated, it is possible to make people believe that heaven is hell—and hell heaven. The greater the lie, the more readily it will be believed.
ADOLPH HITLER (1889–1945), *Mein Kampf*

The foundation of morality is to have done, once and for all, with lying.
THOMAS H. HUXLEY (1825–1895)

It is always the best policy to speak the truth—unless, of course, you are an exceptionally good liar.
JEROME K. JEROME (1859–1927)

It is more from carelessness about truth than from intentionally lying that there is so much falsehood in the world.
SAMUEL JOHNSON (1709–1784)

Our aversion to lying is commonly a secret ambition to make what we say considerable, and have every word received with a religious respect.
FRANÇOIS DE LA ROCHEFOUCAULD (1613–1680)

A lie told often enough becomes the truth.
VLADIMIR I. LENIN (1870–1924)

A degree of lying—you know, white lies—seems to be inherent in all languages and all forms of communication.
MATTHEW LESKO (1943–)

No man has a good enough memory to make a successful liar.
ABRAHAM LINCOLN (1809–1865)

Lying increases the creative faculties, expands the ego, and lessens the frictions of social contacts.
CLARE BOOTH LUCE (1903–1987)

Fishing is a delusion entirely surrounded by liars in old clothes.
DON MARQUIS (1878–1937)

If you're lying, you're lying.
JOHN C. MAXWELL (1947–)

It is hard to believe that a man is telling the truth when you know that you would lie if you were in his place.
H. L. MENCKEN (1880–1956), *A Little Book in C Major*

All men are frauds. The only difference between them is that some admit it. I myself deny it.
H. L. MENCKEN (1880–1956)

Lying is not only excusable; it is not only innocent; it is, above all, necessary and unavoidable. Without the ameliorations that it offers, life would become a mere syllogism and hence too metallic to be borne.
H. L. MENCKEN (1880–1956)

It's silly to go on pretending that under the skin we are all brothers. The truth is more likely that under the skin we are all cannibals, assassins, traitors, liars, hypocrites, poltroons.
HENRY MILLER (1891–1980)

He who is not very strong in memory should not meddle with lying.
MICHEL DE MONTAIGNE (1533–1592)

I do myself a greater injury in lying than I do him of whom I tell a lie.
MICHEL DE MONTAIGNE (1533–1592)

The most common lie is that which one lies to himself; lying to others is relatively an exception.
FRIEDRICH NIETZSCHE (1844–1900)

The visionary lies to himself, the liar only to others.
FRIEDRICH NIETZSCHE (1844–1900)

Those who think it is permissible to tell white lies soon grow color-blind.
AUSTIN O'MALLEY (1858–1932)

Equivocation is half-way to lying, and lying the whole way to hell.
WILLIAM PENN (1644–1718)

False words are not only evil in themselves, but they infect the soul with evil.
PLATO (C. 428–348 BC), *Dialogues*

The rulers of the state are the only persons who ought to have the privilege of lying, either at home or abroad; they may be allowed to lie for the good of the state.
PLATO (C. 428–348 BC)

A liar should have a good memory.
QUINTILIAN (C. AD 35–100), *De Institutione Oratoria*

The gain of lying is, not to be trusted of any, nor to be believed when we speak the truth.
SIR WALTER RALEIGH (C. 1552–1618)

Lying is done with words and also with silence.
ADRIENNE RICH (1929–)

Repetition does not transform a lie into a truth.
FRANKLIN D. ROOSEVELT (1882–1945)

The essence of lying is in deception, not in words.
JOHN RUSKIN (1819–1900)

Ambition drove many men to become false; to have one thought locked in the breast, another ready on the tongue.
SALLUST (86–34 BC), *The War with Catiline*

It is the nature of ambition to make men liars and cheats, to hide the truth in their breasts, and show, like jugglers, another thing in their mouths, to cut all friendships and enmities to the measure of their own interest, and to make a good countenance without the help of good will.
SALLUST (86–34 BC)

Oh what a tangled web we weave,
When first we practise to deceive!
SIR WALTER SCOTT (1771–1832), "Marmion"

If an ordinary person is silent, it may be a tactical maneuver. If a writer is silent, he is lying.
JAROSLAV SEIFERT (1901–1986)

No one can be happy who has been thrust outside the pale of truth. And there are two ways that one can be removed from this realm: by lying, or by being lied to.
SENECA (5 BC–AD 65)

Lord, Lord, how subject we old men are to this vice of lying!
WILLIAM SHAKESPEARE (1564–1616), *Henry IV*

I propose a Constitutional Amendment providing that, if any public official, elected or appointed, at any level of government, is caught lying to any member of the public for any reason, the punishment shall be death by public hanging.
L. NEIL SMITH (1946–)

Lying is like alcoholism. You are always recovering.
STEVEN SODERBERGH (1963–)

Lying is the most simple form of self-defence.
SUSAN SONTAG (1933–2004)

Truly, to tell lies is not honorable;
But when the truth entails tremendous ruin,
To speak dishonorably is pardonable.
SOPHOCLES (496–406 BC), *Creusa*

The cruelest lies are often told in silence.
ROBERT LOUIS STEVENSON (1850–1894)

Every government is run by liars. Nothing they say should be believed.
I. F. STONE (1907–1989)

The history of our race, and each individual's experience, are sown thick with evidence that a truth is not hard to kill and that a lie told well is immortal.
MARK TWAIN (1835–1910), *Advice to Youth*

A lie can travel halfway around the world while the truth is putting on its shoes.
MARK TWAIN (1835–1910)

What we have to do, what at any rate it is our duty to do, is to revive the old art of Lying.
OSCAR WILDE (1854–1900)

We tell lies when we are afraid… afraid of what we don't know, afraid of what others will think, afraid of what will be found out about us. But every time we tell a lie, the thing that we fear grows stronger.
TAD WILLIAMS (1957–)

There's hostility to lying, and there should be.
BOB WOODWARD (1943–)

Clever liars give details, but the cleverest don't.
ANONYMOUS

If lying were a capital crime, the hangman would work overtime.
ANONYMOUS

Who lies for you will lie against you.
BOSNIAN PROVERB

With lies you may get ahead in the world—but you can never go back.
RUSSIAN PROVERB

A half truth is a whole lie.
YIDDISH PROVERB

Life

I don't want to get to the end of my life and find that I have just lived the length of it. I want to have lived the width of it as well.
DIANE ACKERMAN (1948–)

Life is a dream for the wise, a game for the fool, a comedy for the rich, a tragedy for the poor.
SHOLOM ALEICHEM (1859–1916)

Life, in my estimation, is a biological misadventure that we terminate on the shoulders of six strange men whose only objective is to make a hole in one with you.
FRED ALLEN (1894–1956)

Health, happiness, and success depend upon the fighting spirit of each person. The big thing is not what happens to us in life—but what we do about what happens to us.
GEORGE ALLEN (1952–)

Life is just a mirror, and what you see out there, you must first see inside of you.
WALLY "FAMOUS" AMOS (1936–)

Every man's life is a fairy-tale written by God's fingers.
HANS CHRISTIAN ANDERSEN (1805–1875)

Life is pleasant. Death is peaceful. It's the transition that's troublesome.
ISAAC ASIMOV (1920–1992)

You don't get to choose how you're going to die. Or when. You can only decide how you're going to live. Now.
JOAN BAEZ (1941–)

I can't feel anything but gratitude for every single moment of my stupid little life.
ALAN BALL (1957–), *American Beauty*

Life is a long lesson in humility.
JAMES M. BARRIE (1860–1937)

The art of living lies less in eliminating our troubles than in growing with them.
BERNARD M. BARUCH (1870–1965)

Life itself is hazardous. There are sharp rocks everywhere. What changes from years of practice is coming to know something you didn't know before: that there are no sharp rocks—the road is covered with diamonds.
CHARLOTTE JOKO BECK (1917–)

Life is all one piece. Men err when they think they can be inhuman exploiters in their business life, and loving husbands and fathers at home. For achievement without love is a cold and tight-lipped murderer of human happiness everywhere.
SMILEY BLANTON (1882–1966)

If life doesn't offer a game worth playing, then invent a new one.
ASHLEIGH BRILLIANT (1933–)

I finally figured out the only reason to be alive is to enjoy it.
RITA MAE BROWN (1944–)

Life is a pure flame, and we live by an invisible sun within us.
SIR THOMAS BROWNE (1605–1682)

On life's journey faith is nourishment, virtuous deeds are a shelter, wisdom is the light by day and right mindfulness is the protection by night. If a man lives a pure life, nothing can destroy him.
THE BUDDHA (563–483 BC)

Life is a struggle, but not a warfare.
JOHN BURROUGHS (1837–1921)

Life is like playing a violin in public and learning the instrument as one goes on.
SAMUEL BUTLER (1835–1902)

To live is like to love—all reason is against it, and all healthy instinct for it.
SAMUEL BUTLER (1835–1902)

I see many people die because they judge that life is not worth living. I see others paradoxically getting killed for the ideas or illusions that give them a reason for living (what is called a reason for living is also an excellent reason for dying). I therefore conclude that the meaning of life is the most urgent of questions.
ALBERT CAMUS (1913–1960), *The Myth of Sisyphus*

Life is a moderately good play with a badly written third act.
TRUMAN CAPOTE (1924–1984)

She used to drag her mattress beside her low window and lie awake for a long while, vibrating with excitement, as a machine vibrates from speed. Life rushed in upon her through that window—or so it seemed. In reality, of course, life rushes from within, not from without. There is no work of art so big or so beautiful that is was not once all contained

in some youthful body, like this one which lay on the floor in the moonlight, pulsing with ardor and anticipation.
WILLA CATHER (1873–1947), *The Song of the Lark*

We are the living links in a life force that moves and plays around and through us, binding the deepest soils with the farthest stars.
ALAN CHADWICK (1909–1981)

No more duty can be urged upon those who are entering the great theater of life than simple loyalty to their best convictions.
EDWIN HUBBEL CHAPIN (1814–1880)

I like living. I have sometimes been wildly, despairingly, acutely miserable, racked with sorrow, but through it all I still know quite certainly that just to be alive is a grand thing.
AGATHA CHRISTIE (1890–1976)

We make a living by what we get, we make a life by what we give.
SIR WINSTON CHURCHILL (1874–1965)

Everyone is trying to accomplish something big, not realizing that life is made up of little things.
FRANK A. CLARK (1915–2003)

How small a portion of our life it is that we really enjoy! In youth we are looking forward to things that are to come; in old age we are looking backward to things that are gone past; in manhood, although we appear indeed to be more occupied in things that are present, yet even that is too often absorbed in vague determinations to be vastly happy on some future day when we have time.
CHARLES CALEB COLTON (1780–1832)

It's extraordinary how we go through life with eyes half shut, with dull ears, with dormant thoughts. Perhaps it's just as well; and it may be that it is this very dullness that makes life to the incalculable majority so supportable and so welcome.
JOSEPH CONRAD (1857–1924), *Lord Jim*

Life is just a bowl of pits.
RODNEY DANGERFIELD (1921–2004)

A man who dares to waste one hour of life has not discovered the value of life.
CHARLES DARWIN (1809–1882)

People worry too much. Life is good, just the way it is.
GEORGE DAWSON (1898–2001)

Dream as if you'll live forever. Live as if you'll die today.
JAMES DEAN (1931–1955)

Life is a zoo in a jungle.
PETER DE VRIES (1910–1993)

Life is a B Movie: it's stupid and it's strange, it's a directionless story, the dialogue is lame, but in the "he said she said" sometimes there's some poetry, if you turn your back long enough and let it happen naturally.
ANI DIFRANCO (1970–)

Life is like a B-picture script. It is that corny. If I had my life story offered to me to film, I'd turn it down.
KIRK DOUGLAS (1916–)

The state of your life is nothing more than a reflection of your state of mind.
WAYNE D. DYER (1940–)

Only a life lived for others is worth living.
ALBERT EINSTEIN (1879–1955)

Strange is our situation here upon Earth. Each of us comes for a short visit, not knowing why, yet sometimes seeming to divine a purpose. From the standpoint of daily life, however, there is one thing we do know: that man is here for the sake of other men.
ALBERT EINSTEIN (1879–1955)

There are only two ways to live your life. One is as though nothing is a miracle. The other is as if everything is.
ALBERT EINSTEIN (1879–1955)

If a person were to try stripping the disguises from actors while they play a scene upon stage, showing

to the audience their real looks and the faces they were born with, would not such a one spoil the whole play? And would not the spectators think he deserved to be driven out of the theatre with brickbats, as a drunken disturber? Now what else is the whole life of mortals but a sort of comedy, in which the various actors, disguised by various costumes and masks, walk on and play each one his part, until the manager waves them off the stage? Moreover, this manager frequently bids the same actor to go back in a different costume, so that he who has but lately played the king in scarlet now acts the flunkey in patched clothes. Thus all things are presented by shadows.
DESIDERIUS ERASMUS (1469–1536), *The Praise of Folly*

I shall not waste my days in trying to prolong them.
IAN L. FLEMING (1908–1964)

Dost thou love life? Then do not squander time, for that is the stuff life is made of.
BENJAMIN FRANKLIN (1706–1790)

In three words I can sum up everything I've learned about life. It goes on.
ROBERT FROST (1874–1963)

Live as you will have wished to have lived when you are dying.
CHRISTIAN FÜRCHTEGOTT GELLERT (1715–1769)

Life without liberty is like a body without spirit.
KAHLIL GIBRAN (1883–1931)

Not a shred of evidence exists in favor of the idea that life is serious.
BRENDAN GILL (1914–1997)

Plunge boldly into the thick of life, and seize it where you will. It is always interesting.
JOHANN WOLFGANG VON GOETHE (1749–1832)

Life isn't fair. It's just fairer than death, that's all.
WILLIAM GOLDMAN (1931–), *The Princess Bride*

Life is pain.... Anyone who says differently is selling something.
WILLIAM GOLDMAN (1931–), *The Princess Bride*

It has begun to occur to me that life is a stage I'm going through.
ELLEN GOODMAN (1941–)

You're alive. Do something. The directive in life, the moral imperative was so uncomplicated. It could be expressed in single words, not complete sentences. It sounded like this: Look. Listen. Choose. Act.
BARBARA HALL (1946–)

The hardest years in life are those between ten and seventy.
HELEN HAYES (1900–1993)

The supreme irony of life is that hardly anyone gets out of it alive.
ROBERT A. HEINLEIN (1907–1988), *Job*

Life is hard. After all, it kills you.
KATHARINE HEPBURN (1907–2003)

Whether one is twenty, forty, or sixty; whether one has succeeded, failed, or just muddled along; whether yesterday was full of sun or storm, or one of those dull days with no weather at all, life begins each morning!
LEIGH MITCHELL HODGES (1876–1954)

Life is a fatal complaint, and an eminently contagious one.
OLIVER WENDELL HOLMES SR. (1809–1894)

Life is ten percent what happens to you, and ninety percent how you respond to it.
LOU HOLTZ (1937–)

Life is largely a matter of expectation.
HORACE (65–8 BC)

Life is just one damned thing after another.
ELBERT HUBBARD (1856–1915)

Life moves pretty fast. If you don't stop and look around once in awhile, you could miss it.
JOHN HUGHES (1950–), *Ferris Bueller's Day Off*

Have courage for the great sorrows of life and patience for the small ones; and when you have

laboriously accomplished your daily task, go to sleep in peace. God is awake.
VICTOR HUGO (1802–1885)

When making your choice in life, do not neglect to live.
SAMUEL JOHNSON (1709–1784)

Life's splendor forever lies in wait about each one of us in all its fullness, but veiled from view, deep down, invisible, far off. It is there, though, not hostile, not reluctant, not deaf. If you summon it by the right word, by its right name, it will come.
FRANZ KAFKA (1883–1924)

Live daringly, boldly, fearlessly. Taste the relish to be found in competition—in having put forth the best within you.
HENRY J. KAISER (1882–1967)

The art of life lies in a constant readjustment to our surroundings.
OKAKURA KAKUZO (1863–1913)

Life is either a daring adventure or nothing.
HELEN KELLER (1880–1968)

Life can only be understood backwards, but it must be lived forward.
SØREN KIERKEGAARD (1813–1855)

Life is not a problem to be solved, but a reality to be experienced.
SØREN KIERKEGAARD (1813–1855)

It is only when we truly know and understand that we have a limited time on Earth and that we have no way of knowing when our time is up that we will begin to live each day to the fullest, as if it were the only one we had.
ELIZABETH KÜBLER-ROSS (1926–2004)

Life is a sexually transmitted disease.
R. D. LAING (1927–1989)

Life is something that happens when you can't get to sleep.
FRAN LEBOWITZ (1950–)

Life is always a struggle with eternal forces.
EINO LEINO (1878–1926)

Life is what happens to you while you're busy making other plans.
JOHN LENNON (1940–1980)

And in the end, it's not the years in your life that count. It's the life in your years.
ABRAHAM LINCOLN (1809–1865)

There is an ecstasy that marks the summit of life, and beyond which life cannot rise. And such is the paradox of living, this ecstasy comes when one is most alive, and it comes as a complete forgetfulness that one is alive.
JACK LONDON (1876–1916), *The Call of the Wild*

How is one to live a moral and compassionate existence when one is fully aware of the blood, the horror inherent in life, when one finds darkness not only in one's culture but within oneself? If there is a stage at which an individual life becomes truly adult, it must be when one grasps the irony in its unfolding and accepts responsibility for a life lived in the midst of such paradox. One must live in the middle of contradiction, because if all contradiction were eliminated at once life would collapse. There are simply no answers to some of the great pressing questions. You continue to live them out, making your life a worthy expression of leaning into the light.
BARRY LOPEZ (1945–), *Arctic Dreams*

Life is one long struggle in the dark.
LUCRETIUS (C. 99–55 BC)

Life is a tragedy full of joy.
BERNARD MALAMUD (1914–1986)

Laugh and your life will be lengthened, for this is the great secret of long life.
OG MANDINO (1923–1996)

The thing that is incredible is life itself. Why should we be here in this sun-illuminated universe? Why should there be green earth under our feet?
EDWIN MARKHAM (1852–1940)

A difficult time can be more readily endured if we retain the conviction that our existence holds a purpose—a cause to pursue, a person to love, a goal to achieve.
JOHN MAXWELL (1586–1647)

It's not true that life is one damn thing after another; it is one damn thing over and over.
EDNA ST. VINCENT MILLAY (1892–1950)

Develop interest in life as you see it; in people, things, literature, music—the world is so rich, simply throbbing with rich treasures, beautiful souls and interesting people. Forget yourself.
HENRY MILLER (1891–1980)

Our attitude toward life determines life's attitude towards us.
JOHN N. MITCHELL (1913–1988)

Life is a foreign language; all men mispronounce it.
CHRISTOPHER MORLEY (1890–1957)

Life is like a game of cards. The hand that is dealt you represents determinism; the way you play it is free will.
JAWAHARLAL NEHRU (1889–1964)

For believe me: the secret for harvesting from existence the greatest fruitfulness and greatest enjoyment is—to live dangerously.
FRIEDRICH NIETZSCHE (1844–1900), *The Gay Science*

He who has a why to live can bear almost any how.
FRIEDRICH NIETZSCHE (1844–1900)

Our attitude toward life determines life's attitude toward us.
EARL NIGHTINGALE (1921–1989)

You only get out of it what you put into it. If you are a sheep in this world, you're not going to get much out of it.
GREG NORMAN (1955–)

To have striven, to have made an effort, to have been true to certain ideals—this alone is worth the struggle. We are here to add what we can to, not to get what we can from, life.
SIR WILLIAM OSLER (1849–1919)

On a long enough timeline, the survival rate for everyone drops to zero.
CHUCK PALAHNIUK (1962–), *Fight Club*

In this theater of man's life, it is reserved only for God and angels to be lookers-on.
PYTHAGORAS (C. 582–500 BC)

Think of life as a terminal illness, because, if you do, you will live it with joy and passion, as it ought to be lived.
ANNA QUINDLEN (1953–), *A Short Guide to a Happy Life*

As I grow to understand life less and less, I learn to love it more and more.
JULES RENARD (1864–1910)

There are no classes in life for beginners: right away you are always asked to deal with what is most difficult.
RAINER MARIA RILKE (1875–1926)

If life were predictable it would cease to be life, and be without flavor.
ELEANOR ROOSEVELT (1884–1962)

Life is a banquet, and most poor suckers are starving to death.
ROSALIND RUSSELL (1908–1976)

Life resembles a novel more often than novels resemble life.
GEORGE SAND (1804–1876)

Everything has been figured out, except how to live.
JEAN-PAUL SARTRE (1905–1980)

[Y]ou wanna hear my philosophy of life? Do it to him before he does it to you.
BUDD SCHULBERG (1914–), *On the Waterfront*

One should count each day a separate life.
SENECA (5 BC–AD 65)

To-morrow, and to-morrow, and to-morrow,
Creeps in this petty pace from day to day
To the last syllable of recorded time,
And all our yesterdays have lighted fools
The way to dusty death. Out, out, brief candle!
Life's but a walking shadow, a poor player
That struts and frets his hour upon the stage
And then is heard no more: it is a tale
Told by an idiot, full of sound and fury,
Signifying nothing.
WILLIAM SHAKESPEARE (1564–1616), *Macbeth*

I want to be thoroughly used up when I die, for the harder I work the more I love. I rejoice in life for its own sake. Life is no brief candle to me; it is a sort of splendid torch which I've got a hold of for the moment and I want to make it burn as brightly as possible before handing it on to future generations.
GEORGE BERNARD SHAW (1856–1950)

Life does not cease to be funny when people die any more than it ceases to be serious when people laugh.
GEORGE BERNARD SHAW (1856–1950)

I love living. I have some problems with my life, but living is the best thing they've come up with so far.
NEIL SIMON (1927–)

The unexamined life is not worth living.
SOCRATES (469–399 BC)

Do not pursue what is illusory—property and position: all that is gained at the expense of your nerves decade after decade and can be confiscated in one fell night. Live with a steady superiority over life—don't be afraid of misfortune, and do not yearn after happiness; it is after all, all the same: the bitter doesn't last forever, and the sweet never fills the cup to overflowing.
ALEXANDER SOLZHENITSYN (1918–)

The first step to getting the things you want out of life is this: Decide what you want.
BEN STEIN (1944–)

The best things in life are nearest: Breath in your nostrils, light in your eyes, flowers at your feet, duties at your hand, the path of right just before you. Then do not grasp at the stars, but do life's plain, common work as it comes.
ROBERT LOUIS STEVENSON (1850–1894)

Unless life is lived for others, it is not worthwhile.
MOTHER TERESA (1910–1997)

The secret of a good life is to have the right loyalties and hold them in the right scale of values.
NORMAN THOMAS (1884–1968)

However mean your life is, meet it and live it: do not shun it and call it hard names. Cultivate poverty like a garden herb, like sage. Do not trouble yourself much to get new things, whether clothes or friends. Things do not change, we change. Sell your clothes and keep your thoughts.
HENRY DAVID THOREAU (1817–1862)

Our truest life is when we are in our dreams awake.
HENRY DAVID THOREAU (1817–1862)

Life is like unto a long journey with a heavy burden. Let thy step be slow and steady, that thou stumble not. Persuade thyself that imperfection and inconvenience are the natural lot of mortals, and there will be no room for discontent, neither for despair. When ambitious desires arise in thy heart, recall the days of extremity thou has passed through. Forbearance is the root of quietness and assurance forever. Look upon the wrath of the enemy. If thou knowest only what it is to conquer, and knowest not what it is to be defeated, woe unto thee; it will fare ill with thee. Find fault with thyself rather than with others.
IEYASU TOKUGAWA (1543–1616)

To offer no resistance to life is to be in a state of grace, ease, and lightness.
ECKHART TOLLE (1948–)

I have reached the conclusion that the only purpose in the life of every man is to strengthen love within himself, and by strengthening it within himself, to infect other people with it.
LEO TOLSTOY (1828–1910)

The trouble with the rat race is that even if you win, you're still a rat.
LILY TOMLIN (1939–)

Twenty years from now you will be more disappointed by the things you didn't do than by the ones you did do. So throw off the bowlines. Sail away from the safe harbor. Catch the trade winds in your sails. Explore. Dream. Discover.
MARK TWAIN (1835–1910)

Be glad of life because it gives you the chance to love and to work and to play and to look up at the stars.
HENRY VAN DYKE (1852–1933)

Each player must accept the cards life deals him or her: but once they are in hand, he or she alone must decide how to play the cards in order to win the game.
VOLTAIRE (1694–1778)

We never live; we are always in the expectation of living.
VOLTAIRE (1694–1778)

Here we are, trapped in the amber of the moment. There is no why.
KURT VONNEGUT JR. (1922–2007)

Every man dies, not every man really lives.
RANDALL WALLACE (1949–), *Braveheart*

Being on the tightrope is living; everything else is waiting.
KARL WALLENDA (1905–1978)

Life ought to be a struggle of desire toward adventures whose nobility will fertilize the soul.
REBECCA WEST (1892–1983)

We turn our lives into stories, and, in doing so, we can stop them where we choose. Our stories do in a small way what memoirs and autobiographies do on a grander scale: they allow a self-fashioning that gives remembered lives a coherence that the day-to-day lives of actual experience lack.
RICHARD WHITE (1947–), *Remembering Ahanagran: Storytelling in a Family's Past*

Our obligation is to give meaning to life and in doing so to overcome the passive, indifferent life.
ELIE WIESEL (1928–)

Life is far too important a thing ever to talk seriously about.
OSCAR WILDE (1854–1900), *Lady Windermere's Fan*

Life is a pilgrimage. The wise man does not rest by the roadside inns. He marches direct to the illimitable domain of eternal bliss, his ultimate destination.
OSCAR WILDE (1854–1900)

Life is an unbroken succession of false situations.
THORNTON WILDER (1897–1975)

I don't know why we are here, but I'm pretty sure that it is not in order to enjoy ourselves.
LUDWIG WITTGENSTEIN (1889–1951)

Learn from yesterday, live for today, hope for tomorrow.
ANONYMOUS

Live for those who love me,
For those who know me true,
For the Heaven that smiles above me,
And awaits my coming too;
For the cause that lacks resistance,
For the future and the distance,
And the good that I can do.
ANONYMOUS

One day your life will flash before your eyes. Make sure it's worth watching.
ANONYMOUS

Light

In the beginning there was nothing. God said, "Let there be light!" And there was light. There was still nothing, but you could see it a whole lot better.
ELLEN DEGENERES (1958–)

What I give form to in daylight is only one per cent of what I have seen in darkness.
M. C. ESCHER (1898–1972)

You can't have a light without a dark to stick it in.
ARLO GUTHRIE (1947–)

Darkness is only driven out with light, not more darkness.
MARTIN LUTHER KING JR. (1929–1968)

Any one who has common sense will remember that the bewilderments of the eyes are of two kinds, and arise from two causes, either from coming out of the light or from going into the light, which is true of the mind's eye, quite as much as of the bodily eye; and he who remembers this when he sees any one whose vision is perplexed and weak, will not be too ready to laugh; he will first ask whether that soul of man has come out of the brighter light, and is unable to see because unaccustomed to the dark, or having turned from darkness to the day is dazzled by excess of light.
PLATO (C. 428–348 BC), *The Republic*

Light thinks it travels faster than anything but it is wrong. No matter how fast light travels, it finds the darkness has always got there first, and is waiting for it.
TERRY PRATCHETT (1948–)

In the right light, at the right time, everything is extraordinary.
AARON ROSE (1940–)

There are two kinds of light—the glow that illuminates, and the glare that obscures.
JAMES THURBER (1894–1961)

Listening

As I get older, I've learned to listen to people rather than accuse them of things.
PO BRONSON (1964–)

Listening, not imitation, may be the sincerest form of flattery.
DR. JOYCE BROTHERS (1928–)

No man ever listened himself out of a job.
CALVIN COOLIDGE (1872–1933)

There are people who, instead of listening to what is being said to them, are already listening to what they are going to say themselves.
ALBERT GUINON (1863–1923)

When people talk, listen completely. Most people never listen.
ERNEST HEMINGWAY (1899–1961)

It is the province of knowledge to speak, and it is the privilege of wisdom to listen.
OLIVER WENDELL HOLMES SR. (1809–1894)

A good listener is usually thinking about something else.
KIN HUBBARD (1868–1930)

To listen closely and reply well is the highest perfection we are able to attain in the art of conversation.
FRANÇOIS DE LA ROCHEFOUCAULD (1613–1680)

No one really listens to anyone else, and if you try it for a while you'll see why.
MIGNON MCLAUGHLIN (1913–1983)

Listening is a magnetic and strange thing, a creative force. The friends who listen to us are the ones we move toward. When we are listened to, it creates us, makes us unfold and expand.
DR. KARL A. MENNINGER (1893–1990)

A good listener is not only popular everywhere, but after a while he gets to know something.
WILSON MIZNER (1876–1933)

Know how to listen, and you will profit even from those who talk badly.
PLUTARCH (AD 46–120)

Make sure you have finished speaking before your audience has finished listening.
DOROTHY SARNOFF (1914–)

The first duty of love is to listen.
PAUL TILLICH (1886–1965)

A good listener is a good talker with a sore throat.
KATHARINE WHITEHORN (1928–)

Literacy

You teach a child to read, and he or her will be able to pass a literacy test.
GEORGE W. BUSH (1947–)

If we talk about literacy, we have to talk about how to enhance our children's mastery over the tools needed to live intelligent, creative, and involved lives.
DANNY GLOVER (1947–)

Through literacy you can begin to see the universe. Through music you can reach anybody. Between the two there is you, unstoppable.
GRACE SLICK (1939–)

Literature

Bad literature is a form of treason.
JOSEPH BRODSKY (1940–1996)

The tendinous part of the mind, so to speak, is more developed in winter; the fleshy, in summer. I should say winter had given the bone and sinew to literature, summer the tissues and the blood.
JOHN BURROUGHS (1837–1921), *The Snow-Walkers*

Literature is a luxury; fiction is a necessity.
G. K. CHESTERTON (1874–1936), *Defendant*

Literature is the art of writing something that will be read twice; journalism what will be read once.
CYRIL CONNOLLY (1903–1974), *Enemies of Promise*

In a real sense, people who have read good literature have lived more than people who cannot or will not read. It is not true that we have only one life to live; if we can read, we can live as many more lives and as many kinds of lives as we wish.
SAMUEL ICHIYE HAYAKAWA (1906–1992)

It takes a great deal of history to produce a little literature.
HENRY JAMES (1843–1916)

Literature is my Utopia. Here I am not disenfranchised. No barrier of the senses shuts me out from the sweet, gracious discourses of my book friends. They talk to me without embarrassment or awkwardness.
HELEN KELLER (1880–1968)

Even in literature and art, no man who bothers about originality will ever be original: whereas if you simply try to tell the truth (without caring twopence how often it has been told before) you will, nine times out of ten, become original without ever having noticed it.
C. S. LEWIS (1898–1963)

Our American professors like their literature clear, cold, pure and very dead.
SINCLAIR LEWIS (1885–1951)

In literature as in love, we are astonished at what is chosen by others.
ANDRÉ MAUROIS (1885–1967)

Develop interest in life as you see it; in people, things, literature, music—the world is so rich, simply throbbing with rich treasures, beautiful souls and interesting people. Forget yourself.
HENRY MILLER (1891–1980)

Literature is the most noble of professions. In fact, it is about the only one fit for a man. For my own part, there is no seducing me from the path.
EDGAR ALLAN POE (1809–1849)

Literature is news that stays news.
EZRA POUND (1885–1972), *ABC of Reading*

Literature is an occupation in which you have to keep proving your talent to people who have none.
JULES RENARD (1864–1910)

My main reason for adopting literature as a profession was that, as the author is never seen by his clients, he need not dress respectably.
GEORGE BERNARD SHAW (1856–1950)

The very essence of literature is the war between emotion and intellect, between life and death. When literature becomes too intellectual—when it begins to ignore the passions, the emotions—it becomes sterile, silly, and actually without substance.
ISAAC BASHEVIS SINGER (1904–1991)

But what is the difference between literature and journalism? Journalism is unreadable and literature is not read. That is all.
OSCAR WILDE (1854–1900), *The Critic as Artist*

Literature is strewn with the wreckage of men who have minded beyond reason the opinions of others.
VIRGINIA WOOLF (1882–1941), *A Room of One's Own*

Loans

Speculations and loans in foreign fields are likely to bring us into war.... The war-for-profit group has counterfeited patriotism.
CHARLES LINDBERG (1859–1924)

Applications for loans would be judged on a nation's social justice record as well as its economic efficiency.
LEWIS THOMPSON PRESTON (1926–1995)

The bankers made loans to business so that the volume of money increased faster than the increase in goods. The result was inflation.
CARROLL QUIGLEY (1910–1977)

Logic

I hope you become comfortable with the use of logic without being deceived into concluding that logic will inevitably lead you to the correct conclusion.
NEIL ARMSTRONG (1930–)

Logic, n.: The art of thinking and reasoning in strict accordance with the limitations and incapacities of the human misunderstanding.
AMBROSE BIERCE (1842–1914), *The Devil's Dictionary*

If scientific reasoning were limited to the logical processes of arithmetic, we should not get very far in our understanding of the physical world. One might as well attempt to grasp the game of poker entirely by the use of the mathematics of probability.
VANNEVAR BUSH (1890–1974)

Logic is like the sword—those who appeal to it shall perish by it.
SAMUEL BUTLER (1835–1902)

When dealing with people, let us remember we are not dealing with creatures of logic. We are dealing with creatures of emotion, creatures bustling with prejudices and motivated by pride and vanity.
DALE CARNEGIE (1888–1955)

The poet only asks to get his head into the heavens. It is the logician who seeks to get the heavens into his head. And it is his head that splits.
G. K. CHESTERTON (1874–1936), *Orthodoxy*

You can only find truth with logic if you have already found truth without it.
G. K. CHESTERTON (1874–1936)

If I have learnt anything, it is that life forms no logical patterns. It is haphazard and full of beauties which I try to catch as they fly by, for who knows whether any of them will ever return?
MARGOT FONTEYN (1919–1991)

Deep in the human unconscious is a pervasive need for a logical universe that makes sense. But the real universe is always one step beyond logic.
FRANK HERBERT (1920–1986), *Dune*

The Army has carried the American ideal to its logical conclusion. Not only do they prohibit discrimination on the grounds of race, creed and color, but also on ability.
TOM LEHRER (1928–)

Against logic there is no armor like ignorance.
DR. LAURENCE J. PETER (1919–1990)

Grammar and logic free language from being at the mercy of the tone of voice. Grammar protects us against misunderstanding the sound of an uttered name; logic protects us against what we say having double meaning.
EUGEN ROSENSTOCK-HUESSY (1888–1973)

Somebody who thinks logically is a nice contrast to the real world.
THE LAW OF THUMB

Loneliness

Inside myself is a place where I live all alone, and that's where you renew your springs that never dry up.
PEARL S. BUCK (1892–1973)

Isolation is the sum total of wretchedness to a man.
THOMAS CARLYLE (1795–1881)

Who knows what true loneliness is—not the conventional word, but the naked terror? To the lonely themselves it wears a mask. The most miserable outcast hugs some memory or some illusion. Now and then a fatal conjunction of events may lift the veil for an instant. For an instant only. No human being could bear a steady view of moral solitude without going mad.
JOSEPH CONRAD (1857–1924)

When you close your doors, and make darkness within, remember never to say that you are alone, for you are not alone; nay, God is within, and your genius is within. And what need have they of light to see what you are doing?
EPICTETUS (AD 55–135), *Discourses*

Pray that your loneliness may spur you into finding something to live for, great enough to die for.
DAG HAMMARSKJÖLD (1905–1961)

All men's misfortunes spring from their hatred of being alone.
JEAN DE LA BRUYÈRE (1645–1696)

To be an adult is to be alone.
JEAN ROSTAND (1894–1977), *Thoughts of a Biologist*

If you are lonely when you are alone, you are in bad company.
JEAN-PAUL SARTRE (1905–1980)

To live alone is the fate of all great souls.
ARTHUR SCHOPENHAUER (1788–1860)

Loneliness has been following me my whole life.
PAUL SCHRADER (1946–), *Taxi Driver*

They are never alone that are accompanied with noble thoughts.
SIR PHILIP SIDNEY (1554–1586)

Be good and you will be lonely.
MARK TWAIN (1835–1910)

The worst loneliness is not to be comfortable with yourself.
MARK TWAIN (1835–1910)

What should young people do with their lives today? Many things, obviously. But the most daring thing is to create stable communities in which the terrible disease of loneliness can be cured.
KURT VONNEGUT JR. (1922–2007)

No matter how lonely you get or how many birth announcements you receive, the trick is not to get frightened. There's nothing wrong with being alone.
WENDY WASSERSTEIN (1950–2005), *Isn't It Romantic*

I celebrate myself, and sing myself.
WALT WHITMAN (1819–1892)

We are all sentenced to solitary confinement inside our own skins, for life.
TENNESSEE WILLIAMS (1911–1983)

When so many are lonely as seem to be lonely, it would be inexcusably selfish to be lonely alone.
TENNESSEE WILLIAMS (1911–1983)

The surest cure for vanity is loneliness.
TOM WOLFE (1931–)

We are most of us very lonely in this world; you who have any who love you, cling to them and thank God.
ANONYMOUS

Longevity

If you ask what is the single most important key to longevity, I would have to say it is avoiding worry, stress and tension. And if you didn't ask me, I'd still have to say it.
GEORGE BURNS (1896–1996)

[M]y longevity is due to my good timing.
TONY CURTIS (1925–)

Mere longevity is a good thing for those who watch Life from the side lines. For those who play the game, an hour may be a year, a single day's work an achievement for eternity.
HELEN HAYES (1900–1993)

The quality, not the longevity, of one's life is what is important.
MARTIN LUTHER KING JR. (1929–1968)

To sustain longevity, you have to evolve.
ARIES SPEARS (1975–)

I think my longevity has a lot to do with where I come from—a blue-collar town in Ohio—and how I was raised: to work hard and respect other folks.
ROBERT URICH (1946–2002)

Losing

I try to do the right thing at the right time. They may just be little things, but usually they make the difference between winning and losing.
KAREEM ABDUL-JABBAR (1947–)

I never thought of losing, but now that it's happened, the only thing is to do it right. That's my obligation to all the people who believe in me. We all have to take defeats in life.
MUHAMMAD ALI (1942–)

The sad events that occur in my life are the sad events that happen to everybody, with losing friends and family, but that is a natural occurrence, as natural as being born.
SERGIO ARAGONES (1937–)

Two things scare me. The first is getting hurt. But that's not nearly as scary as the second, which is losing.
LANCE ARMSTRONG (1971–)

Always have the situation under control, even if losing. Never betray an inward sense of defeat.
ARTHUR ASHE (1943–1993)

Every time you win, it diminishes the fear a little bit. You never really cancel the fear of losing; you keep challenging it.
ARTHUR ASHE (1943–1993)

That's what learning is, after all; not whether we lose the game, but how we lose and how we've changed because of it and what we take away from it that we never had before, to apply to other games. Losing, in a curious way, is winning.
RICHARD BACH (1936–)

There is no comparison between that which is lost by not succeeding and that lost by not trying.
SIR FRANCIS BACON (1561–1626)

I love the winning, I can take the losing, but most of all I love to play.
BORIS BECKER (1967–)

The art of losing isn't hard to master; so many things seem filled with the intent to be lost that their loss is no disaster.
ELIZABETH BISHOP (1911–1979)

If you're afraid of losing, then you daren't win.
BJÖRN BORG (1956–)

Losing an illusion makes you wiser than finding a truth.
LUDWIG BORNE (1786–1837)

If a tie is like kissing your sister, losing is like kissing your grandmother with her teeth out.
GEORGE BRETT (1953–)

I never expect to lose. Even when I'm the underdog, I still prepare a victory speech.
H. JACKSON BROWN JR. (1948–)

When you win, say nothing. When you lose, say less.
PAUL BROWN (1908–1991)

Losing doesn't make me want to quit. It makes me want to fight that much harder.
PAUL "BEAR" BRYANT (1913–1983)

If you're losing your soul and you know it, then you've still got a soul left to lose.
CHARLES BUKOWSKI (1920–1994)

Every human being must find his own way to cope with severe loss, and the only job of a true friend is to facilitate whatever method he chooses.
CALEB CARR (1955–)

The way to love anything is to realize that it might be lost.
G. K. CHESTERTON (1874–1936)

Victory has a hundred fathers but defeat is an orphan.
GALEAZZO CIANO (1903–1944)

Only when you are lost can love find itself in you without losing its way.
HÉLÈNE CIXOUS (1937–)

I never could stand losing. Second place didn't interest me. I had a fire in my belly.
TY COBB (1886–1961)

Sport and life is about losing. It's about understanding how to lose.
LYNN DAVIES (1942–)

Win as if you were used to it, lose as if you enjoyed it for a change.
RALPH WALDO EMERSON (1803–1882)

If you can react the same way to winning and losing, that is a big accomplishment. That quality is important because it stays with you the rest of your life.
CHRIS EVERT (1954–)

Because no battle is ever won, he said. They are not even fought. The field only reveals to man his own folly and despair, and victory is an illusion of philosophers and fools.
WILLIAM FAULKNER (1897–1962), *The Sound and the Fury*

Winning may not be everything, but losing has little to recommend it.
DIANNE FEINSTEIN (1933–)

Sometimes when you start losing detail, whether it's in music or in life, something as small as failing to be polite, you start to lose substance.
BENNY GOODMAN (1909–1986)

When wealth is lost, nothing is lost; when health is lost, something is lost; when character is lost, all is lost.
BILLY GRAHAM (1918–1995)

If you are losing a tug of war with a tiger, give him the rope before he gets to your arm. You can always buy a new rope.
MAX GUNTHER (1934–1974)

You know what makes a good loser? Practice.
ERNEST HEMINGWAY (1899–1961)

Loss means losing what was. We want to change but we don't want to lose. Without time for loss, we don't have time for soul.
JAMES HILLMAN (1926–)

It's a funny thing, the less people have to live for, the less nerve they have to risk losing nothing.
ZORA NEALE HURSTON (1891–1960)

I'm afraid of losing my obscurity. Genuineness only thrives in the dark. Like celery.
ALDOUS HUXLEY (1894–1963)

The greatest test of courage on earth is to bear defeat without losing heart.
Robert Green Ingersoll (1833–1899)

While you're saving your face, you're losing your ass.
Lyndon B. Johnson (1908–1973)

The goal of winning is not losing two times in a row.
Rosabeth Moss Kanter (1943–)

I don't think you can be a success at anything if you think about losing, whether it's in sports or in politics.
Edward M. Kennedy (1932–)

I have always believed that one should not be scared of losing, I think that really is the key.
Imran Khan (1952–)

A champion is afraid of losing. Everyone else is afraid of winning.
Billie Jean King (1943–)

Victory is fleeting. Losing is forever.
Billie Jean King (1943–)

If you can accept losing you can't win.
Vince Lombardi (1913–1970)

Show me a good loser, and I'll show you a loser.
Vince Lombardi (1913–1970)

Winning is habit. Unfortunately, so is losing.
Vince Lombardi (1913–1970)

Losing streaks are funny. If you lose at the beginning you got off to a bad start. If you lose in the middle of the season, you're in a slump. If you lose at the end, you're choking.
Gene Mauch (1925–2002)

When I was losing, they called me nuts. When I was winning they called me eccentric.
Al McGuire (1931–2001)

Why are we so full of restraint? Why do we not give in all directions? Is it fear of losing ourselves? Until we do lose ourselves there is no hope of finding ourselves.
Henry Miller (1891–1980)

Southerners can never resist a losing cause.
Margaret Mitchell (1900–1949)

Whoever said, "It's not whether you win or lose that counts," probably lost.
Martina Navratilova (1956–)

Losing is not in my vocabulary.
Ruud van Nistelrooy (1976–)

A man who has never lost himself in a cause bigger than himself has missed one of life's mountaintop experiences. Only in losing himself does he find himself. Only then does he discover all the latent strengths he never knew he had and which otherwise would have remained dormant.
Richard M. Nixon (1913–1994)

You must never be satisfied with losing. You must get angry, terribly angry, about losing. But the mark of the good loser is that he takes his anger out on himself and not his victorious opponents or on his teammates.
Richard M. Nixon (1913–1994)

And I don't think it makes sense to talk about winning or losing now, in a strategic sense we lost when we started the war.
William Odom (1909–)

Losing is no disgrace if you've given your best.
Jim Palmer (1945–)

Losing a game is heartbreaking. Losing your sense of excellence or worth is a tragedy.
Joe Paterno (1924–)

Here's a very good rule of thumb in politics: losing begets losing.
John Podhoretz (1961–)

Above anything else, I hate to lose.
Jackie Robinson (1919–1972)

And if we're losing, we're gonna deserve losing.
KNUTE ROCKNE (1888–1931)

Losing feels worse than winning feels good.
VIN SCULLY (1927–)

If you are losing your leisure, look out; you may be losing your soul.
LOGAN PEARSALL SMITH (1865–1946)

No one wants to quit when he's losing and no one wants to quit when he's winning.
RICHARD STRAUSS (1864–1949)

The difference between winning and losing is always a mental one.
PETER THOMSON (1929–)

For myself, losing is not coming second. It's getting out of the water knowing you could have done better. For myself, I have won every race I've been in.
IAN THORPE (1982–)

We lost because we told ourselves we lost.
LEO TOLSTOY (1828–1910)

There's such a thin line between winning and losing.
JOHN R. TUNIS (1889–1975)

The eruption of lived pleasure is such that in losing myself I find myself; forgetting that I exist, I realize myself.
RAOUL VANEIGEM (1934–)

I don't mind losing, but I don't like losing to cheats.
PETE WATERMAN (1947–)

I'm in competition with myself and I'm losing.
ROGER WATERS (1943–)

If you are explaining, you are losing.
J. C. WATTS (1957–)

About the only time losing is more fun than winning is when you're fighting temptation.
TOM WILSON (1931–1978)

The disappointment of losing is huge.
JACK YOUNGBLOOD (1950–)

Losing comes of winning money.
CHINESE PROVERB

Better lose the anchor than the whole ship.
DUTCH PROVERB

Loss

You don't know about real loss, 'cause it only occurs when you've loved something more than you love yourself. And I doubt you've ever dared to love anybody that much.
BEN AFFLECK (1972–) and MATT DAMON (1970–), *Good Will Hunting*

Seek ye first the good things of the mind, and the rest will either be supplied or its loss will not be felt.
SIR FRANCIS BACON (1561–1626)

Do not measure your loss by itself; if you do, it will seem intolerable; but if you will take all human affairs into account you will find that some comfort is to be derived from them.
SAINT BASIL (329–379)

If you can't sleep, then get up and do something instead of lying there and worrying. It's the worry that gets you, not the loss of sleep.
DALE CARNEGIE (1888–1955)

What greater grief than the loss of one's native land.
EURIPIDES (C. 480–406 BC), *Medea*

Every time you don't follow your inner guidance, you feel a loss of energy, loss of power, a sense of spiritual deadness.
SHAKTI GAWAIN (1948–)

Riches do not delight us so much with their possession, as torment us with their loss.
DICK GREGORY (1932–)

He who blinded by ambition, raises himself to a position whence he cannot mount higher, must thereafter fall with the greatest loss.
NICCOLÒ MACHIAVELLI (1469–1527)

[T]he day came when the risk to remain tight in a bud was more painful than the risk it took to blossom.
ANAÏS NIN (1903–1977)

The loss which is unknown is no loss at all.
PUBLILIUS SYRUS (C. 100 BC), *Maxims*

There are occasions when it is undoubtedly better to incur loss than to make gain.
TITUS MACCIUS PLAUTUS (254–184 BC), *Captivi*

Love

Sure I've thought about [being in love]. Who hasn't? If I could ever meet the right sort of girl. Aw, where you gonna find her? Somebody that's real. Somebody that's alive. They don't come that way anymore. Have I ever thought about it? I've even been sucker enough to make plans. You know, I saw an island in the Pacific once. I've never been able to forget it. That's where I'd like to take her. She'd have to be the sort of a girl who'd... well, who'd jump in the surf with me and love it as much as I did. You know, nights when you and the moon and the water all become one. You feel you're part of something big and marvelous. That's the only place to live... where the stars are so close over your head you feel you could reach up and stir them around. Certainly, I've been thinking about it. Boy, if I could ever find a girl who was hungry for those things...
SAMUEL HOPKINS ADAMS (1871–1958) and ROBERT RISKIN (1897–1955), *It Happened One Night*

You don't know about real loss, 'cause it only occurs when you've loved something more than you love yourself. And I doubt you've ever dared to love anybody that much.
BEN AFFLECK (1972–) and MATT DAMON (1970–), *Good Will Hunting*

The wise man will love; all others will desire.
AFRANIUS (C. 90 BC)

To love is to suffer. To avoid suffering, one must not love; but then one suffers from not loving. Therefore, to love is to suffer, not to love is to suffer, to suffer is to suffer. To be happy is to love; to be happy then is to suffer, but suffering makes one unhappy; therefore to be unhappy one must love or love to suffer or suffer from too much happiness. I hope you're getting this down.
WOODY ALLEN (1935–), *Love and Death*

Sex alleviates tension. Love causes it.
WOODY ALLEN (1935–)

Love is, above all else, the gift of oneself.
JEAN ANOUILH (1910–1987)

The enthusiasm of a woman's love is even beyond the biographer's.
JANE AUSTEN (1775–1817), *Mansfield Park*

Friendship is certainly the finest balm for the pangs of disappointed love.
JANE AUSTEN (1775–1817), *Northanger Abbey*

When we love anyone with our whole hearts, life begins when we are with that person; it is only in their company that we are really and truly alive.
WILLIAM BARCLAY (1907–1978)

Love is an exploding cigar we willingly smoke.
LYNDA BARRY (1956–)

Love is the delightful interval between meeting a beautiful girl and discovering that she looks like a haddock.
JOHN BARRYMORE (1882–1942)

Love is a dress that you made long to hide your knees.
SAM BEAM (1974–), "Love and Some Verses"

Sensuality without love is a sin; love without sensuality is worse than a sin.
JOSÉ BERGAMIN (1897–1983)

And we are put on Earth a little space, that we may learn to bear the beams of love.
WILLIAM BLAKE (1757–1827)

Love seeketh not itself to please,
Nor for itself hath any care,
But for another gives its ease,
And builds a Heaven in Hell's despair.
WILLIAM BLAKE (1757–1827)

Life is all one piece. Men err when they think they can be inhuman exploiters in their business life, and loving husbands and fathers at home. For achievement without love is a cold and tight-lipped murderer of human happiness everywhere.
SMILEY BLANTON (1882–1966)

The mind has a thousand eyes.
And the heart but one;
Yet the life of a whole life dies
When love is done.
FRANCIS WILLIAM BOURDILLON (1852–1921)

A good friend can tell you what is the matter with you in a minute. He may not seem such a good friend after telling.
ARTHUR BRISBANE (1864–1936)

Love comes when manipulation stops; when you think more about the other person than about his or her reactions to you. When you dare to reveal yourself fully. When you dare to be vulnerable.
DR. JOYCE BROTHERS (1928–)

To live is like to love—all reason is against it, and all healthy instinct for it.
SAMUEL BUTLER (1835–1902)

Love is the kind of illness that does not spare the intelligent or the dull.
ALBERT CAMUS (1913–1960), *Caligula*

Love is more pleasant than marriage for the same reason that novels are more amusing than history.
NICOLAS CHAMFORT (1741–1794)

Perhaps the feelings that we experience when we are in love represent a normal state. Being in love shows a person who he should be.
ANTON CHEKHOV (1860–1904)

The way to love anything is to realize that it might be lost.
G. K. CHESTERTON (1874–1936)

For centuries now we've tried everything else; the power of wealth, of mighty armies and navies, machinations of diplomats. All have failed. Before it's too late, and time is running out, let us turn from trust in the chain reactions of exploding atoms to faith of the chain reaction of God's love. Love—love of God and fellow men. That is God's formula for peace. Peace on earth to men of good will.
RICHARD CARDINAL CUSHING (1895–1970)

Love is not enough. It must be the foundation, the cornerstone—but not the complete structure. It is much too pliable, too yielding.
BETTE DAVIS (1908–1989)

In love, as in everything else, experience is a physician who never comes until after the disorder is cured.
FRANCES DE LA TOUR (1944–)

It is easy to hate and it is difficult to love. This is how the whole scheme of things works. All good things are difficult to achieve; and bad things are very easy to get.
RENÉ DESCARTES (1596–1650)

A loving heart is the truest wisdom.
CHARLES DICKENS (1812–1870)

You will find as you look back upon your life that the moments when you have truly lived are the moments when you have done things in the spirit of love.
HENRY DRUMMOND (1851–1897)

Pure love and suspicion cannot dwell together: at the door where the latter enters, the former makes its exit.
ALEXANDRE DUMAS (1802–1870)

Blessed is the influence of one true, loving human soul on another.
GEORGE ELIOT (1819–1880)

When love is suppressed hate takes its place.
HENRY HAVELOCK ELLIS (1859–1939)

He who is in love is wise and is becoming wiser, sees newly every time he looks at the object beloved, drawing from it with his eyes and his mind those virtues which it possesses.
RALPH WALDO EMERSON (1803–1882), *Address on the Method of Nature*

When love is in excess it brings a man no honor nor worthiness.
EURIPIDES (C. 480–406 BC), *Medea*

Nobody has ever measured, not even poets, how much the heart can hold.
ZELDA FITZGERALD (1900–1948)

Love and respect are the most important aspects of parenting, and of all relationships.
JODIE FOSTER (1962–)

There is no difficulty that enough love will not conquer; no disease that enough love will not heal; no door that enough love will not open.
EMMET FOX (1886–1951)

The salvation of man is through love and in love.
VIKTOR FRANKL (1905–1997), *Man's Search for Meaning*

Love is an irresistible desire to be irresistibly desired.
ROBERT FROST (1874–1963)

Money is the sinew of love as well as war.
THOMAS FULLER (1608–1661), *Gnomologia*

A coward is incapable of exhibiting love; it is the prerogative of the brave.
MAHATMA GANDHI (1869–1948)

When I despair, I remember that all through history the ways of truth and love have always won. There have been tyrants, and murderers, and for a time they can seem invincible, but in the end they always fall. Think of it—always.
MAHATMA GANDHI (1869–1948)

Where there is love there is life.
MAHATMA GANDHI (1869–1948)

It is better to be hated for what you are than to be loved for what you are not.
ANDRÉ GIDE (1869–1951)

The weight of the world is love. Under the burden of solitude, under the burden of dissatisfaction.
ALLEN GINSBERG (1926–1997)

Death cannot stop true love. All it can do is delay it for a while.
WILLIAM GOLDMAN (1931–), *The Princess Bride*

Today I begin to understand what love must be, if it exists. When we are parted, we each feel the lack of the other half of ourselves. We are incomplete like a book in two volumes of which the first has been lost. That is what I imagine love to be: incompleteness in absence.
EDMOND DE GONCOURT (1822–1896)

There is only one terminal dignity—love.
HELEN HAYES (1900–1993)

When the power of love overcomes the love of power, the world will know peace.
JIMI HENDRIX (1942–1970)

When all is said and done, the weather and love are the two elements about which one can never be sure.
ALICE HOFFMAN (1952–), *Here on Earth*

The love we give away is the only love we keep.
ELBERT HUBBARD (1856–1915)

Life's greatest happiness is to be convinced we are loved.
VICTOR HUGO (1802–1885), *Les Miserables*

Passion makes the world go round. Love just makes it a safer place.
ICE T (1958–), *The Ice Opinion*

The meeting of two personalities is like the contact of two chemical substances: if there is any reaction, both are transformed.
CARL JUNG (1875–1961)

Never cease loving a person, and never give up hope for him, for even the prodigal son who had fallen most low could still be saved; the bitterest enemy and also he who was your friend could again be your friend; love that has grown cold can kindle.
SØREN KIERKEGAARD (1813–1855)

Hatred paralyses life; love releases it. Hatred confuses life; love harmonizes it. Hatred darkens life; love illuminates it.
MARTIN LUTHER KING JR. (1929–1968)

He who is devoid of the power to forgive, is devoid of the power to love.
MARTIN LUTHER KING JR. (1929–1968)

I believe that unarmed truth and unconditional love will have the final word in reality. That is why right, temporarily defeated, is stronger than evil triumphant.
MARTIN LUTHER KING JR. (1929–1968)

Love is the only force capable of transforming an enemy into friend.

MARTIN LUTHER KING JR. (1929–1968)
Kindness in words creates confidence. Kindness in thinking creates profoundness. Kindness in giving creates love.
LAO-TZU (C. 600 BC)

Loving a child is a circular business…the more you give, the more you get, the more you get, the more you give.
PENELOPE LEACH (1937–)

Discovering that with every child, your heart grows bigger and stronger—that there is no limit to how much or how many people you can love, even though at times you feel as though you could burst—you don't—you just love even more.
YASMIN LE BON (1964–)

Romantic love is mental illness. But it's a pleasurable one. It's a drug. It distorts reality, and that's the point of it. It would be impossible to fall in love with someone that you really saw.
FRAN LEBOWITZ (1950–)

Love never dies of starvation, but often of indigestion.
NINON DE LENCLOS (1620–1705)

We've got this gift of love, but love is like a precious plant. You can't just accept it and leave it in the cupboard or just think it's going to get on by itself. You've got to keep watering it. You've got to really look after it and nurture it.
JOHN LENNON (1940–1980)

Mortal lovers must not try to remain at the first step; for lasting passion is the dream of a harlot and from it we wake in despair.
C. S. LEWIS (1898–1963), *The Pilgrim's Regress*

Only love can be divided endlessly and still not diminish.
ANNE MORROW LINDBERGH (1906–2001)

Treasure the love you have received above all. It will survive long after your gold and good health have vanished.
OG MANDINO (1923–1996)

Accept the things to which fate binds you, and love the people with whom fate brings you together, but do so with all your heart.
MARCUS AURELIUS ANTONINUS (121–180)

Why is it that we don't always recognize the moment when love begins but we always know when it ends?
STEVE MARTIN (1945–), *L.A. Story*

Love is only the dirty trick played on us to achieve continuation of the species.
W. SOMERSET MAUGHAM (1874–1965)

There is no love without forgiveness, and there is no forgiveness without love.
BRYANT H. MCGILL (1969–)

Love is the delusion that one woman differs from another
H. L. MENCKEN (1880–1956)

Love is the triumph of imagination over intelligence.
H. L. MENCKEN (1880–1956)

Age does not protect you from love. But love, to some extent, protects you from age.
JEANNE MOREAU (1928–)

Love is or it ain't. Thin love ain't love at all.
TONI MORRISON (1931–), *Beloved*

Love, love, love, that is the soul of genius.
WOLFGANG AMADEUS MOZART (1756–1791)

To forgive is the highest, most beautiful form of love. In return, you will receive untold peace and happiness.
ROBERT MULLER (1944–)

Love is the difficult realization that something other than oneself is real.
IRIS MURDOCH (1919–1999)

There is always some madness in love. But there is also always some reason in madness.
FRIEDRICH NIETZSCHE (1844–1900), *On Reading and Writing*

What else is love but understanding and rejoicing in the fact that another person lives, acts, and experiences otherwise than we do?
FRIEDRICH NIETZSCHE (1844–1900)

Dignity and love do not blend well, nor do they continue long together.
OVID (43 BC–AD 17)

Oh, life is a glorious cycle of song,
A medley of extemporanea;
And love is a thing that can never go wrong;
And I am Marie of Romania.
DOROTHY PARKER (1893–1967), "Comment"

Clarity of mind means clarity of passion, too; this is why a great and clear mind loves ardently and sees distinctly what it loves.
BLAISE PASCAL (1623–1662)

Beyond happiness or unhappiness, though it is both things, love is intensity; it does not give us eternity but life, that second in which the doors of time and space open just a crack: here is there and now is always.
OCTAVIO PAZ (1914–)

Nirvana or lasting enlightenment or true spiritual growth can be achieved only through persistent exercise of real love.
M. SCOTT PECK (1936–2005)

Love is the greatest refreshment in life.
PABLO PICASSO (1881–1973)

Life is the first gift, love is the second, and understanding the third.
MARGE PIERCY (1936–)

We often settle for sex when we want love. And we often want love when we need something else, like a good job or a chance to go back to school.
MARGE PIERCY (1936–)

Love is a reciprocal torture.
MARCEL PROUST (1871–1922)

When you have seen as much of life as I have, you will not underestimate the power of obsessive love.
J. K. ROWLING (1965–), *Harry Potter and the Half-Blood Prince*

I have found that if you love life, life will love you back.
ARTHUR RUBINSTEIN (1886–1982)

Three passions, simple but overwhelmingly strong, have governed my life: the longing for love, the search for knowledge, and unbearable pity for the suffering of mankind.
BERTRAND RUSSELL (1872–1970), *Autobiography*

To fear love is to fear life, and those who fear life are already three parts dead.
BERTRAND RUSSELL (1872–1970), *Marriage and Morals*

How is individual transformation to be achieved? There are some bad habits among individuals such as smoking, drinking liquor, meat eating and

gambling. These bad habits not only degrade the individuals but also inflict hardships on their families. These bad habits have to be given up for the individual to manifest his inherent goodness.
SRI SATHYA SAI BABA (1926–)

Only through Love transformation of the so-called wicked ones is possible.
SRI SATHYA SAI BABA (1926–)

Nothing takes the taste out of peanut butter quite like unrequited love.
CHARLES M. SCHULZ (1922–2000)

Love all, trust a few, do wrong to none.
WILLIAM SHAKESPEARE (1564–1616), *All's Well That Ends Well*

But love is blind and lovers cannot see
The pretty follies that themselves commit;
For if they could, Cupid himself would blush
To see me thus transformed to a boy.
WILLIAM SHAKESPEARE (1564–1616), *The Merchant of Venice*

Love looks not with the eyes, but with the mind.
WILLIAM SHAKESPEARE (1564–1616), *A Midsummer Night's Dream*

There is no sincerer love than the love of food.
GEORGE BERNARD SHAW (1856–1950)

Love is the outreach of self toward completion.
RALPH W. SOCKMAN (1889–1970)

One word frees us of all the weight and pain of life:
That word is love.
SOPHOCLES (496–406 BC)

The main source of good discipline is growing up in a loving family, being loved, and learning to love in return.
BENJAMIN SPOCK (1903–1998)

So long as we love, we serve; so long as we are loved by others, I would almost say that we are indispensable.
ROBERT LOUIS STEVENSON (1850–1894)

To love deeply in one direction makes us more loving in all others.
ANNE-SOPHIE SWETCHINE (1782–1857)

We have just enough religion to make us hate, but not enough to make us love one another.
JONATHAN SWIFT (1667–1745)

I have found the paradox that if I love until it hurts, then there is no hurt, but only more love.
MOTHER TERESA (1910–1997)

There is more hunger for love and appreciation in this world than for bread.
MOTHER TERESA (1910–1997)

Love flies, runs, and rejoices; it is free and nothing can hold it back.
THOMAS À KEMPIS (1380–1471)

There is no remedy for love but to love more.
HENRY DAVID THOREAU (1817–1862), *Journal*

The first duty of love is to listen.
PAUL TILLICH (1886–1965)

I have reached the conclusion that the only purpose in the life of every man is to strengthen love within himself, and by strengthening it within himself, to infect other people with it.
LEO TOLSTOY (1828–1910)

Love is an act of endless forgiveness, a tender look which becomes a habit.
PETER USTINOV (1921–2004)

Love many things, for therein lies the true strength, and whosoever loves much performs much, and can accomplish much, and what is done in love is done well.
VINCENT VAN GOGH (1853–1890)

To love and be loved is to feel the sun from both sides.
DAVID VISCOTT (1938–1996), *How to Live with Another Person*

They say, when you meet the love of your life, time stops, and that's true. What they don't tell you is

that when it starts again, it moves extra fast to catch up.
DANIEL WALLACE (1959–), *Big Fish*

Never pretend to a love which you do not actually feel, for love is not ours to command.
ALAN W. WATTS (1915–1973)

To love oneself is the beginning of a lifelong romance
OSCAR WILDE (1854–1900)

Who, being loved, is poor?
OSCAR WILDE (1854–1900)

Yet each man kills the thing he loves,
By each let this be heard,
Some do it with a bitter look,
Some with a flattering word.
The coward does it with a kiss,
The brave man with a sword!
OSCAR WILDE (1854–1900)

Love isn't something you find. Love is something that finds you.
LORETTA YOUNG (1913–2000)

Follow love and it will flee, flee love and it will follow.
ANONYMOUS

If you begin the day with love in your heart, peace in your nerves, and truth in your mind, you not only benefit by their presence but also bring them to others, to your family and friends, and to all those whose destiny draws across your path that day.
ANONYMOUS

Love is like a puzzle. When you're in love, all the pieces fit but when your heart gets broken, it takes a while to get everything back together.
ANONYMOUS

The heart that loves is always young.
ANONYMOUS

When love is lost, do not bow your head in sadness; instead keep your head up high and gaze into heaven for that is where your broken heart has been sent to heal.
ANONYMOUS

Love is patient, love is kind. It does not envy, it does not boast, it is not proud. It does not dishonor others, it is not self-seeking, it is not easily angered, it keeps no record of wrongs. Love does not delight in evil but rejoices with the truth. It always protects, always trusts, always hopes, always perseveres.
THE BIBLE, 1 Corinthians 13:4-7

A man loves his sweetheart the most, his wife the best, but his mother the longest.
IRISH PROVERB

Loyalty

A boy can learn a lot from a dog: obedience, loyalty, and the importance of turning around three times before lying down.
ROBERT BENCHLEY (1889–1945)

When you're part of a team, you stand up for your teammates. Your loyalty is to them. You protect them through good and bad, because they'd do the same for you.
YOGI BERRA (1925–), *When You Come to a Fork in the Road, Take It*

An ounce of loyalty is worth a pound of cleverness.
ELBERT HUBBARD (1856–1915)

The greater the loyalty of a group toward the group, the greater is the motivation among the members to achieve the goals of the group, and the greater the probability that the group will achieve its goals.
RENSIS LIKERT (1903–1981)

So much of what is best in us is bound up in our love of family, that it remains the measure of our stability because it measures our sense of loyalty. All other pacts of love or fear derive from it and are modeled upon it.
HANIEL LONG (1888–1956)

Loyalty to petrified opinion never yet broke a chain or freed a human soul.
MARK TWAIN (1835–1910)

Luck

We must believe in luck. For how else can we explain the success of those we don't like?
JEAN COCTEAU (1889–1963)

Shallow men believe in luck. Strong men believe in cause and effect.
RALPH WALDO EMERSON (1803–1882)

A pound of pluck is worth a ton of luck.
JAMES A. GARFIELD (1831–1881)

The only thing that overcomes hard luck is hard work.
HARRY GOLDEN (1902–1981)

It is a great piece of skill to know how to guide your luck, even while waiting for it.
BALTASAR GRACIAN (1601–1658)

True luck consists not in holding the best of the cards at the table; luckiest is he who knows just when to rise and go home.
JOHN HAY (1838–1905), *Distichs*

I'm a great believer in luck, and I find the harder I work the more I have of it.
THOMAS JEFFERSON (1743–1826)

Luck affects everything. Let your hook always be cast; in the stream where you least expect it there will be a fish.
OVID (43 BC–AD 17)

Luck favors the mind that is prepared.
LOUIS PASTEUR (1822–1895)

People always call it luck when you've acted more sensibly than they have.
ANNE TYLER (1941–), *Celestial Navigation*

Lunch

Time is an illusion. Lunchtime doubly so.
DOUGLAS ADAMS (1952–2001)

Eat breakfast like a king, lunch like a prince, and dinner like a pauper.
ADELLE DAVIS (1904–1974)

Some weasel took the cork out of my lunch.
W. C. FIELDS (1880–1946)

There is no free lunch.
MILTON FRIEDMAN (1912–)

There ain't no free lunches in this country.
LEE IACOCCA (1924–)

No matter how much spin, effort, lunch or dinner you give the media, they will not fail to notice whether you have won or lost.
ROBIN RENWICK (1937–)

Ask not what you can do for your country. Ask what's for lunch.
ORSON WELLES (1915–1985)

Lust

The most violent appetites in all creatures are lust and hunger; the first is a perpetual call upon them to propagate their kind, the latter to preserve themselves.
JOSEPH ADDISON (1672–1719)

If one wants another only for some self-satisfaction, usually in the form of sensual pleasure, that wrong desire takes the form of lust rather than love.
MORTIMER ADLER (1902–2001)

There are three things which the superior man guards against. In youth, lust. When he is strong, quarrelsomeness. When he is old, covetousness.
CONFUCIUS (551–479 BC), *The Confucian Analects*

Lust and greed are more gullible than innocence.
MASON COOLEY (1927–2002)

Christian morality prefers remorse to precede lust, and then lust not to follow.
KARL KRAUS (1874–1936)

Lust is to the other passions what the nervous fluid is to life; it supports them all, lends strength to them all. Ambition, cruelty, avarice, revenge, are all founded on lust.
MARQUIS DE SADE (1740–1814)

Though lust do masque in ne'er so strange disguise,
She's oft found witty, but is never wise.
JOHN WEBSTER (1578–1634)

Machines

For man is not the creature and product of Mechanism; but, in a far truer sense, its creator and producer.
THOMAS CARLYLE (1795–1881)

The fathers of the field had been pretty confusing: John von Neumann speculated about computers and the human brain in analogies sufficiently wild to be worthy of a medieval thinker, and Alan Turing thought about criteria to settle the question of whether machines can think, a question of which we now know that it is about as relevant as the question of whether submarines can swim.
EDSGER W. DIJKSTRA (1930–2002)

Ours is the age that is proud of machines that think and suspicious of men who try to.
HOWARD MUMFORD JONES (1892–1980)

Machines were, it may be said, the weapon employed by the capitalists to quell the revolt of specialized labor.
KARL MARX (1818–1883)

Thus, be it understood, to demonstrate a theorem, it is neither necessary nor even advantageous to know what it means.... [A] machine might be imagined where the assumptions were put in at one end, while the theorems came out at the other, like the legendary Chicago machine where the pigs go in alive and come out transformed into hams and sausages. No more than these machines need the mathematician know what he does.
HENRI POINCARÉ (1854–1912)

Machines are worshipped because they are beautiful and valued because they confer power; they are hated because they are hideous and loathed because they impose slavery.
BERTRAND RUSSELL (1872–1970)

The machine does not isolate man from the great problems of nature but plunges him more deeply into them.
ANTOINE DE SAINT-EXUPÉRY (1900–1944)

The real problem is not whether machines think but whether men do.
B. F. SKINNER (1904–1990)

Machines take me by surprise with great frequency.
ALAN TURING (1912–1954)

Man has made some machines that can answer questions provided the facts are profusely stored in them, but we will never be able to make a machine that will ask questions. The ability to ask the right question is more than half the battle of finding the answer.
THOMAS J. WATSON (1874–1956)

Nothing is less instructive than a machine.
SIMONE WEIL (1910–1943)

Madness

No great genius has ever existed without some touch of madness.
ARISTOTLE (384–322 BC)

He may be mad, but there's method in his madness. There nearly always is method in madness. It's what drives men mad, being methodical.
G. K. CHESTERTON (1874–1936), *The Fad of the Fisherman*

There is only one difference between a madman and me. I am not mad.
SALVADOR DALÍ (1904–1989)

A little Madness in the Spring
Is wholesome even for the King.
EMILY DICKINSON (1830–1886), "No. 1333"

Great wits are sure to madness near allied
And thin partitions do their bounds divide.
JOHN DRYDEN (1631–1700)

It is madness for sheep to talk peace with a wolf.
THOMAS FULLER (1608–1661)

In a mad world only the mad are sane.
AKIRA KUROSAWA (1910–1998)

Howard Hughes was able to afford the luxury of madness, like a man who not only thinks he is Napoleon but hires an army to prove it.
TED MORGAN (1932–)

There is always some madness in love. But there is also always some reason in madness.
FRIEDRICH NIETZSCHE (1844–1900), *On Reading and Writing*

Correct me if I'm wrong, but hasn't the fine line between sanity and madness gotten finer?
GEORGE PRICE (1901–1995)

Sanity calms, but madness is more interesting.
JOHN RUSSELL (1792–1878)

Sanity is a madness put to good use.
GEORGE SANTAYANA (1863–1952)

There is no great genius without some touch of madness.
SENECA (5 BC–AD 65), *Epistles*

Afflicted by love's madness, all are blind.
SEXTUS PROPERTIUS (C. 50–2 BC)

Though this be madness, yet there is method in 't.
WILLIAM SHAKESPEARE (1564–1616), *Hamlet*

Oh, that way madness lies; let me shun that.
WILLIAM SHAKESPEARE (1564–1616), *King Lear*

Eccentricity is not, as dull people would have us believe, a form of madness. It is often a kind of innocent pride, and the man of genius and the aristocrat are frequently regarded as eccentrics because genius and aristocrat are entirely unafraid of and uninfluenced by the opinions and vagaries of the crowd.
EDITH SITWELL (1887–1964)

Truly great madness cannot be achieved without significant intelligence.
HENRIK TIKKANEN (1924–1984)

Anger is a momentary madness, so control your passion or it will control you.
G. M. TREVELYAN (1876–1962)

You're only given a little spark of madness. You mustn't lose it.
ROBIN WILLIAMS (1951–)

Magazines

Magazines and advertising are flogging the idea that you have to keep changing things and get something new. I think that's evil. But obviously that's your livelihood.
ROBIN DAY (1923–2000)

Men's magazines often feature pictures of naked ladies. Women's magazines also often feature pictures of naked ladies. This is because the female body is a beautiful work of art, while the male body is hairy and lumpy and should not be seen by the light of day.
RICHARD ROEPER (1960–)

The many magazines, ranging from pulp to slick, that used to serve as both farm teams for writers and lures to readers, with hundreds of short stories every month, don't exist. Most of the doors for new people have been sealed.
DONALD E. WESTLAKE (1933–)

Majorities

It is bad to be oppressed by a minority, but it is worse to be oppressed by a majority. For there is a reserve of latent power in the masses which, if it is called into play, the minority can seldom resist. But from the absolute will of an entire people there is no appeal, no redemption, no refuge but treason.
LORD ACTON (1834–1902)

The majority of people perform well in a crisis and when the spotlight is on them; it's on the Sunday afternoons of this life, when nobody is looking, that the spirit falters.
ALAN BENNETT (1934–)

It's extraordinary how we go through life with eyes half shut, with dull ears, with dormant thoughts. Perhaps it's just as well; and it may be that it is this very dullness that makes life to the incalculable majority so supportable and so welcome.
JOSEPH CONRAD (1857–1924), *Lord Jim*

A majority is always better than the best repartee.
BENJAMIN DISRAELI (1804–1881)

In matters of conscience, the law of majority has no place.
MAHATMA GANDHI (1869–1948)

It is not worth an intelligent man's time to be in the majority. By definition, there are already enough people to do that.
G. H. HARDY (1877–1947)

Our test of truth is a reference to either a present or imagined future majority in favour of our view.
OLIVER WENDELL HOLMES JR. (1841–1935)

One man with courage makes a majority.
ANDREW JACKSON (1767–1845)

All, too, will bear in mind this sacred principle, that though the will of the majority is in all cases to prevail, that will, to be rightful, must be reasonable; that the minority possess their equal rights, which equal laws must protect, and to violate would be oppression.
THOMAS JEFFERSON (1762–1826)

We in America do not have government by the majority. We have government by the majority who participate.
THOMAS JEFFERSON (1743–1826)

In Republics, the great danger is, that the majority may not sufficiently respect the rights of the minority.
JAMES MADISON (1751–1836)

The object in life is not to be on the side of the majority, but to escape finding oneself in the ranks of the insane.
MARCUS AURELIUS ANTONINUS (121–180)

The third-rate mind is only happy when it is thinking with the majority. The second-rate mind is only happy when it is thinking with the minority. The first-rate mind is only happy when it is thinking.
A. A. MILNE (1882–1956)

The great majority of us are required to live a life of constant, systematic duplicity. Your health is bound to be affected if, day after day, you say the opposite of what you feel, if you grovel before what you dislike and rejoice at what bring you nothing but misfortune. Our nervous system isn't just a fiction, it's part of our physical body, and our soul exists in space and is inside us, like teeth in our mouth. It can't be forever violated with impunity.
BORIS PASTERNAK (1890–1960), *Doctor Zhivago*

The right to vote is a consequence, not a primary cause, of a free social system—and its value depends on the constitutional structure implementing and strictly delimiting the voters' power; unlimited majority rule is an instance of the principle of tyranny.
AYN RAND (1905–1982)

I sometimes think that the saving grace of America lies in the fact that the overwhelming majority of Americans are possessed of two great qualities—a sense of humor and a sense of proportion.
FRANKLIN D. ROOSEVELT (1882–1945)

The fact that an opinion has been widely held is no evidence whatever that it is not utterly absurd; indeed in view of the silliness of the majority of mankind, a widespread belief is more likely to be foolish than sensible.
BERTRAND RUSSELL (1872–1970), *Marriage and Morals*

There is no nonsense so errant that it cannot be made the creed of the vast majority by adequate governmental action.
BERTRAND RUSSELL (1872–1970)

Few men desire liberty: The majority are satisfied with a just master.
SALLUST (86–34 BC)

It does not prove a thing to be right because the majority say it is so.
FRIEDRICH VON SCHILLER (1759–1805)

Democracy encourages the majority to decide things about which the majority is blissfully ignorant.
JOHN SIMON (1873–1954)

The test of courage comes when we are in the minority. The test of tolerance comes when we are in the majority.
RALPH W. SOCKMAN (1889–1970)

[G]overnment in which the majority rule in all cases can not be based on justice, even as far as men understand it.
HENRY DAVID THOREAU (1817–1862), *Civil Disobedience*

Whenever you find that you are on the side of the majority, it is time to reform.
MARK TWAIN (1835–1910)

What is morality in any given time or place? It is what the majority then and there happen to like, and immorality is what they dislike.
ALFRED NORTH WHITEHEAD (1861–1947)

The deadliest contagion is majority opinion.
ANONYMOUS

Malevolence

The evil that is in the world almost always comes of ignorance, and good intentions may do as much harm as malevolence if they lack understanding.
ALBERT CAMUS (1913–1960)

To excite opposition and inflame malevolence is the unhappy privilege of courage made arrogant by consciousness of strength.
SAMUEL JOHNSON (1709–1784)

We should never have any kind of malevolence towards our friends.
THE ATHARVA VEDA

Lack of faith, treachery, arguments and animosity only breed malevolence. It is in the best interest of all to avoid this and tread on the path of progress.
THE RIG VEDA

Malice

Forcible ways make not an end of evil, but leave hatred and malice behind them.
SIR THOMAS BROWNE (1605–1682)

At least two-thirds of our miseries spring from human stupidity, human malice and those great motivators and justifiers of malice and stupidity: idealism, dogmatism and proselytizing zeal on behalf of religious or political ideas.
ALDOUS HUXLEY (1894–1963)

Folly is often more cruel in the consequences than malice can be in the intent.
ALDOUS HUXLEY (1894–1963)

With malice toward none, with charity for all, … let us strive on to finish the work we are in, … to do all which may achieve and cherish a just and lasting peace among ourselves and with all nations.
ABRAHAM LINCOLN (1809–1865)

Malice sucks up the greater part of her own venom, and poisons herself.
MICHEL DE MONTAIGNE (1533–1592)

Of all the creatures that were made, man is the most detestable. Of the entire brood he is the only one—the solitary one—that possesses malice. That is the basest of all instincts, passions, vices—the most hateful. He is the only creature that has pain for sport, knowing it to be pain. Also—in all the list he is the only creature that has a nasty mind.
MARK TWAIN (1835–1910), *Mark Twain's Autobiography*

Never attribute to malice what can be adequately explained by stupidity.
ANONYMOUS

Managers

If the Earth could be made to rotate twice as fast, managers would get twice as much done. If the Earth could be made to rotate twenty times as fast, everyone else would get twice as much done since all the managers would fly off.
NORMAN R. AUGUSTINE (1935–)

Effective leadership is putting first things first. Effective management is discipline, carrying it out.
STEPHEN R. COVEY (1932–)

A manager is responsible for the application and performance of knowledge.
PETER F. DRUCKER (1909–2005)

Management by objective works—if you know the objectives. Ninety percent of the time you don't.
PETER F. DRUCKER (1909–2005)

There is an enormous number of managers who have retired on the job.
PETER F. DRUCKER (1909–2005)

In order to become a big-league manager you have to be in the right place at the right time. That's rule number one.
LEO DUROCHER (1905–1991)

Managers in all too many American companies do not achieve the desired results because nobody makes them do it.
HAROLD S. GENEEN (1910–1997)

They recruit their managers from the factory floor; we get ours out of law schools.
JOHN GIBBONS (1962–)

A manager has his cards dealt to him and he must play them.
MILLER HUGGINS (1879–1929)

If I had to sum up in a word what makes a good manager, I'd say decisiveness. You can use the fanciest computers to gather the numbers, but in the end you have to set a timetable and act.
LEE IACOCCA (1924–)

I'm not the manager because I'm always right, but I'm always right because I'm the manager.
GENE MAUCH (1925–2002)

Strong managers who make tough decisions to cut jobs provide the only true job security in today's world. Weak managers are the problem. Weak managers destroy jobs.
JACK WELCH (1935–)

Manipulation

It's so easy to manipulate an audience, but it's nearly always clear that you are being manipulated. I think even people that are not critically attuned are aware of cynical manipulation in film.
JOHN BOORMAN (1933–)

Love comes when manipulation stops; when you think more about the other person than about his or her reactions to you. When you dare to reveal yourself fully. When you dare to be vulnerable.
DR. JOYCE BROTHERS (1928–)

The basic tool for the manipulation of reality is the manipulation of words. If you can control the meaning of words, you can control the people who must use the words.
PHILIP K. DICK (1928–1982), *How to Build a Universe That Doesn't Fall Apart Two Days Later*

For manipulation to be most effective, evidence of its presence should be nonexistent.... It is essential, therefore, that people who are manipulated believe

in the neutrality of their key social institutions.
HERBERT SCHILLER (1919–2000)

Mankind

The avarice of mankind is insatiable.
ARISTOTLE (384–322 BC)

I hate mankind, for I think myself one of the best of them, and I know how bad I am.
JOSEPH BARETTI (1716–1789)

Man is an animal, which, alone among the animals, refuses to be satisfied by the fulfilment of animal desires.
ALEXANDER GRAHAM BELL (1847–1922)

Man is the only animal that laughs and has a state legislature.
SAMUEL BUTLER (1835–1902)

We must, however, acknowledge, as it seems to me, that man with all his noble qualities … still bears in his bodily frame the indelible stamp of his lowly origin.
CHARLES DARWIN (1809–1882)

A human being is part of a whole, called by us the Universe, a part limited in time and space. He experiences himself, his thoughts and feelings, as something separated from the rest, a kind of optical delusion of his consciousness. This delusion is a kind of prison for us, restricting us to our personal desires and to affection for a few persons nearest us. Our task must be to free ourselves from this prison by widening our circles of compassion to embrace all living creatures and the whole of nature in its beauty.
ALBERT EINSTEIN (1879–1955)

Mankind is becoming a single unit, and that for a unit to fight against itself is suicide.
HENRY HAVELOCK ELLIS (1859–1939)

I decline to accept the end of man. It is easy enough to say that man is immortal simply because he will endure: that when the last dingdong of doom has clanged and faded from the last worthless rock hanging tideless in the last red and dying evening, that even then there will still be one more sound: that of his puny inexhaustible voice, still talking. I refuse to accept this. I believe that man will not merely endure: he will prevail. He is immortal, not because he alone among creatures has an inexhaustible voice, but because he has a soul, a spirit capable of compassion and sacrifice and endurance.
WILLIAM FAULKNER (1897–1962)

The poet's voice need not merely be the record of man, it can be one of the props, the pillars to help him endure and prevail.
WILLIAM FAULKNER (1897–1962)

Man is the only animal whose desires increase as they are fed; the only animal that is never satisfied.
HENRY GEORGE (1839–1897)

So long as we live among men, let us cherish humanity.
ANDRÉ GIDE (1869–1951)

Thought is the wind, knowledge the sail, and mankind the vessel.
AUGUST HARE (1792–1834)

The fates have given mankind a patient soul.
HOMER (800–700 BC), *The Iliad*

As I know more of mankind I expect less of them, and am ready now to call a man a good man upon easier terms than I was formerly.
SAMUEL JOHNSON (1709–1784)

Which is it, is man one of God's blunders or is God one of man's?
FRIEDRICH NIETZSCHE (1844–1900)

The world is my country, all mankind are my brethren, and to do good is my religion.
THOMAS PAINE (1737–1809)

I have discovered that all human evil comes from this, man's being unable to sit still in a room.
BLAISE PASCAL (1623–1662)

Man … is a tame or civilized animal; never-the-less, he requires proper instruction and a fortunate nature, and then of all animals he becomes the most divine and most civilized; but if he be insufficiently or ill-educated he is the most savage of earthly creatures.
PLATO (C. 428–348 BC)

It has been said that man is a rational animal. All my life I have been searching for evidence which could support this.
BERTRAND RUSSELL (1872–1970)

It was enough to make a body ashamed of the human race.
MARK TWAIN (1835–1910), *The Adventures of Huckleberry Finn*

Man is the only animal that blushes. Or needs to.
MARK TWAIN (1835–1910), *Following the Equator*

I think that God in creating Man somewhat overestimated his ability.
OSCAR WILDE (1854–1900)

Manners

Manners are the hypocrisy of a nation.
HONORÉ DE BALZAC (1799–1850)

Good manners and good morals are sworn friends and fast allies.
C. A. BARTOL (1813–1900)

One of the greatest victories you can gain over someone is to beat him at politeness.
JOSH BILLINGS (1818–1885)

You can't be truly rude until you understand good manners.
RITA MAE BROWN (1944–)

Manners are of more importance than laws. Manners are what vex or soothe, corrupt or purify, exalt or debase, barbarize or refine us, by a constant, steady, uniform, insensible operation, like that of the air we breathe in.
EDMUND BURKE (1729–1797)

A man's own good breeding is the best security against other people's ill manners.
LORD CHESTERFIELD (1694–1773)

Ceremony is necessary as the outwork and defense of manners.
LORD CHESTERFIELD (1694–1773)

Manners must adorn knowledge, and smooth its way through the world.
LORD CHESTERFIELD (1694–1773)

Prepare yourself for the world, as the athletes used to do for their exercise; oil your mind and your manners, to give them the necessary suppleness and flexibility; strength alone will not do.
LORD CHESTERFIELD (1694–1773)

We are justified in enforcing good morals, for they belong to all mankind; but we are not justified in enforcing good manners, for good manners always mean our own manners.
G. K. CHESTERTON (1874–1936)

A man's own manner and character is what most becomes him.
CICERO (106–43 BC)

Consideration for others is the basis of a good life, a good society.
CONFUCIUS (551–479 BC)

Nowadays, manners are easy and life is hard.
BENJAMIN DISRAELI (1804–1881)

Good manners are made up of petty sacrifices.
RALPH WALDO EMERSON (1803–1882)

Manners require time, and nothing is more vulgar than haste.
RALPH WALDO EMERSON (1803–1882)

The basis of good manners is self-reliance.
RALPH WALDO EMERSON (1803–1882)

Savages we call them because their manners differ from ours.
BENJAMIN FRANKLIN (1706–1790)

Teach your child to hold his tongue; he'll learn fast enough to speak.
BENJAMIN FRANKLIN (1706–1790)

The society of women is the element of good manners.
JOHANN WOLFGANG VON GOETHE (1749–1832)

Rudeness is a weak imitation of strength.
ERIC HOFFER (1902–1983)

Children are guilty of unpardonable rudeness when they spit in the face of a companion; neither are they excusable who spit from windows or on walls or furniture.
SAINT JEAN-BAPTISTE DE LA SALLE (1651–1719), *The Rules of Christian Manners and Civility*

In truth, politeness is artificial good humor, it covers the natural want of it, and ends by rendering habitual a substitute nearly equivalent to the real virtue.
THOMAS JEFFERSON (1762–1826)

I seek constantly to improve my manners and graces, for they are the sugar to which all are attracted.
OG MANDINO (1923–1996)

We are all born charming, fresh and spontaneous and must be civilized before we are fit to participate in society.
JUDITH MARTIN (1938–)

What once were vices are manners now.
SENECA (5 BC–AD 65)

Promptitude is not only a duty, but is also a part of good manners; it is favorable to fortune, reputation, influence, and usefulness; a little attention and energy will form the habit, so as to make it easy and delightful.
CHARLES SIMMONS (1924–)

Those that are good manners at the court are as ridiculous in the country, as the behavior of the country is most mockable at the court.
WILLIAM SHAKESPEARE (1564–1616), *As You Like It*

We don't bother much about dress and manners in England, because as a nation we don't dress well and we've no manners.
GEORGE BERNARD SHAW (1856–1950), *You Never Can Tell*

To have respect for ourselves guides our morals; and to have a deference for others governs our manners.
LAWRENCE STERNE (1713–1768)

Good manners will open doors that the best education cannot.
CLARENCE THOMAS (1948–)

Don't reserve your best behavior for special occasions. You can't have two sets of manners, two social codes—one for those you admire and want to impress, another for those whom you consider unimportant. You must be the same to all people.
LILLIAN EICHLER WATSON (1902–)

Manners are especially the need of the plain. The pretty can get away with anything.
EVELYN WAUGH (1903–1966)

To be always thinking about your manners is not the way to make them good; the very perfection of manners is not to think about yourself.
RICHARD WHATELY (1787–1853)

To the real artist in humanity, what are called bad manners are often the most picturesque and significant of all.
WALT WHITMAN (1819–1892)

Manners maketh man.
WILLIAM OF WYKEHAM (1324–1404)

Children are natural mimics; they act like their parents in spite of every effort to teach them good manners.
ANONYMOUS

Do not be misled: "Bad company corrupts good character."
THE BIBLE, 1 Corinthians 15:33

Marriage

My husband and I fell in love at first sight… maybe I should have taken a second look.
WOODY ALLEN (1935–), *Crimes and Misdemeanors*

I tended to place my wife under a pedestal.
WOODY ALLEN (1935–)

My toughest fight was with my first wife.
MUHAMMAD ALI (1942–)

I pay very little regard … to what any young person says on the subject of marriage. If they profess a disinclination for it, I only set it down that they have not yet seen the right person.
JANE AUSTEN (1775–1817), *Mansfield Park*

I used to believe that marriage would diminish me, reduce my options. That you had to be someone less to live with someone else when, of course, you have to be someone more.
CANDICE BERGEN (1946–)

The world has suffered more from the ravages of ill-advised marriages than from virginity.
AMBROSE BIERCE (1842–1914)

A good marriage is one which allows for change and growth in the individuals and in the way they express their love.
PEARL S. BUCK (1892–1973)

I have great hopes that we shall love each other all our lives as much as if we had never married at all.
LORD BYRON (1788–1824)

The difficulty with marriage is that we fall in love with a personality, but must live with a character.
PETER DE VRIES (1910–1993)

There's only one way to have a happy marriage and as soon as I learn what it is I'll get married again.
CLINT EASTWOOD (1930–)

Never say that marriage has more of joy than pain.
EURIPIDES (C. 480–406 BC), *Alcestis*

Man's best possession is a sympathetic wife.
EURIPIDES (C. 480–406 BC), *Antigone*

We were happily married for eight months. Unfortunately, we were married for four and a half years.
NICK FALDO (1957–)

Keep your eyes wide open before marriage, and half-shut afterwards.
BENJAMIN FRANKLIN (1706–1790)

I know nothing about sex because I was always married.
ZSA ZSA GABOR (1919–)

On rare occasions one does hear of a miraculous case of a married couple falling in love after marriage, but on close examination it will be found that it is a mere adjustment to the inevitable.
EMMA GOLDMAN (1869–1940)

The conception of two people living together for twenty-five years without having a cross word suggests a lack of spirit only to be admired in sheep.
ALAN PATRICK HERBERT (1890–1971)

There is no observation more frequently made by such as employ themselves in surveying the conduct of mankind, than that marriage, though the dictate of nature, and the institution of Providence, is yet very often the cause of misery, and that those who enter into that state can seldom forbear to express their repentance, and their envy of those whom either chance or caution hath withheld from it.
SAMUEL JOHNSON (1709–1784), *Rambler*, No. 18

Such is the common process of marriage. A youth and maiden exchange meeting by chance, or brought together by artifice, exchange glances,

reciprocate civilities, go home, and dream of one another. Having little to divert attention, or diversify thought, they find themselves uneasy when they are apart, and therefore conclude that they shall be happy together. They marry, and discover what nothing but voluntary blindness had before concealed; they wear out life in altercations, and charge nature with cruelty.
SAMUEL JOHNSON (1709–1784), *Rasselas*

All married couples should learn the art of battle as they should learn the art of making love. Good battle is objective and honest—never vicious or cruel. Good battle is healthy and constructive, and brings to a marriage the principle of equal partnership.
ANN LANDERS (1918–2002)

Well, first you must be temperamentally suited, and there must be constant adjustment and give and take. I mean no marriages are made in heaven.
LEE KUAN YEW (1923–)

A simple enough pleasure, surely, to have breakfast alone with one's husband, but how seldom married people in the midst of life achieve it.
ANNE MORROW LINDBERGH (1906–2001)

Let the wife make the husband glad to come home, and let him make her sorry to see him leave.
MARTIN LUTHER (1483–1546)

A successful marriage is an edifice that must be rebuilt every day.
ANDRÉ MAUROIS (1885–1967)

A successful marriage requires falling in love many times, always with the same person.
MIGNON MCLAUGHLIN (1913–1983)

[M]arriage is punishment for shoplifting in some countries!
MIKE MYERS (1963–), *Wayne's World*

The best friend is likely to acquire the best wife, because a good marriage is based on the talent for friendship.
FRIEDRICH NIETZSCHE (1844–1900)

Intimacy is what makes a marriage, not a ceremony, not a piece of paper from the state.
KATHLEEN NORRIS (1880–1966)

If you would marry suitably, marry your equal.
OVID (43 BC–AD 17)

Never marry but for love; but see that thou lovest what is lovely.
WILLIAM PENN (1644–1718)

Marriage is really tough because you have to deal with feelings...and lawyers.
RICHARD PRYOR (1940–2005)

Remember, that if thou marry for beauty, thou bindest thyself all thy life for that which perchance will neither last nor please thee one year; and when thou hast it, it will be to thee of no price at all; for the desire dieth when it is attained, and the affection perisheth when it is satisfied.
SIR WALTER RALEIGH (C. 1552–1618)

I'm not a real movie star. I've still got the same wife I started out with twenty-eight years ago.
WILL ROGERS (1879–1935)

Always get married early in the morning. That way, if it doesn't work out, you haven't wasted a whole day.
MICKEY ROONEY (1920–)

One man's folly is another man's wife.
HELEN ROWLAND (1876–1950)

I love being married. It's so great to find that one special person you want to annoy for the rest of your life.
RITA RUDNER (1956–)

In Hollywood a marriage is a success if it outlasts milk.
RITA RUDNER (1956–)

When I meet a man I ask myself, "Is this the man I want my children to spend their weekends with?"
RITA RUDNER (1956–)

If there be no great love in the beginning, yet heaven may decrease it upon better acquaintance, when we are married and have more occasion to know one another: I hope, upon familiarity will grow more contempt.
WILLIAM SHAKESPEARE (1564–1616), *The Merry Wives of Windsor*

By all means marry. If you get a good wife, you'll be happy. If you get a bad one, you'll become a philosopher.
SOCRATES (469–399 BC)

Nearly all marriages, even happy ones, are mistakes: in the sense that almost certainly (in a more perfect world, or even with a little more care in this very imperfect one) both partners might be found more suitable mates. But the real soul-mate is the one you are actually married to.
J. R. R. TOLKIEN (1892–1973)

That is what marriage really means: helping one another to reach the full status of being persons, responsible and autonomous beings who do not run away from life.
PAUL TOURNIER (1898–1961)

Both marriage and death ought to be welcome: The one promises happiness, doubtless the other assures it.
MARK TWAIN (1835–1910)

Marriage is the only adventure open to the cowardly.
VOLTAIRE (1694–1778)

Marriage is a great institution, but I'm not ready for an institution yet.
MAE WEST (1892–1980)

I wonder, among all the tangles of this mortal coil, which one contains tighter knots to undo, and consequently suggests more tugging, and pain, and diversified elements of misery, than the marriage tie.
EDITH WHARTON (1862–1937)

Long engagements give people the opportunity of finding out each other's character before marriage, which is never advisable.
OSCAR WILDE (1854–1900)

The proper basis for marriage is mutual misunderstanding.
OSCAR WILDE (1854–1900)

One of society's biggest problems today is that we've allowed relationships to be accepted as impermanent, particularly marriage.
ANONYMOUS

The man who says his wife can't take a joke forgets that she took him.
ANONYMOUS

Martyrs

It is often pleasant to stone a martyr, no matter how much we admire him.
JOHN BARTH (1930–)

Although prepared for martyrdom, I preferred that it be postponed.
SIR WINSTON CHURCHILL (1874–1965)

Men reject their prophets and slay them, but they love their martyrs and honor those whom they have slain.
FYODOR DOSTOEVSKY (1821–1881)

Christ died for our sins. Dare we make his martyrdom meaningless by not committing them?
JULES FEIFFER (1929–)

It requires greater courage to preserve inner freedom, to move on in one's inward journey into new realms, than to stand defiantly for outer freedom. It is often easier to play the martyr, as it is to be rash in battle.
ROLLO MAY (1909–1994)

It is the cause, not the death, that makes the martyr.
NAPOLÉON I (1769–1821)

The only difference between suicide and martyrdom is press coverage.
CHUCK PALAHNIUK (1962–)

For some not to be martyrs is martyrdom indeed.
LEO ROSTEN (1908–1997)

Martyrdom … is the only way in which a man can become famous without ability.
GEORGE BERNARD SHAW (1856–1950), *The Devil's Disciple*

The ink of the scholar and the blood of a martyr are of equal value in heaven.
THE KORAN

Masochism

A spirit of national masochism prevails, encouraged by an effete corps of impudent snobs who characterize themselves as intellectuals.
SPIRO T. AGNEW (1918–1996)

Masochism is a valuable job skill.
CHUCK PALAHNIUK (1962–), *Choke*

Masturbation

Don't knock masturbation; it's sex with someone I love.
WOODY ALLEN (1935–)

I used to think masturbation was not really sex because it only involved me. That's a very limited view of human sexuality, and it isn't going to work for women.
BETTY DODSON (1929–)

If only it was as easy to banish hunger by rubbing the belly as it is to masturbate.
DIOGENES LAERTIUS (C. 200)

Intercourse with a woman is sometimes a satisfactory substitute for masturbation. But it takes a lot of imagination to make it work.
KARL KRAUS (1874–1936)

Philosophy is to the real world as masturbation is to sex.
KARL MARX (1818–1883)

We have reason to believe that man first walked upright to free his hands for masturbation.
LILY TOMLIN (1939–)

Materialism

Materialism coarsens and petrifies everything, making everything vulgar, and every truth false.
HENRI-FRÉDÉRIC AMIEL (1821–1881)

The son will run away from the family not at eighteen but at twelve, emancipated by his gluttonous precocity; he will fly not to seek heroic adventures, not to deliver a beautiful prisoner from a tower, not to immortalize a garret with sublime thoughts, but to found a business, to enrich himself and to compete with his infamous papa.
CHARLES BAUDELAIRE (1821–1867)

Not what I have, but what I do is my kingdom.
THOMAS CARLYLE (1795–1881)

Materialism has never been so ominous as now in North America, as management takes over.
ARTHUR ERICKSON (1924–)

Increase of material comforts, it may be generally laid down, does not in any way whatsoever conduce to moral growth.
MAHATMA GANDHI (1869–1948)

We are the slaves of objects around us, and appear little or important according as these contract or give us room to expand.
JOHANN WOLFGANG VON GOETHE (1749–1832)

When we of the so–called better classes are scared as men were never scared in history at material ugliness and hardship; when we put off marriage until our house can be artistic, and quake at the thought of having a child without a bank-account and doomed to manual labor, it is time for thinking men to protest against so unmanly and irreligious a state of opinion.
WILLIAM JAMES (1842–1910)

The things you own end up owning you.
CHUCK PALAHNIUK (1962–), *Fight Club*

Happiness will come from materialism, not from meaning.
ANDREI PLATONOV (1899–1951)

It is preoccupation with possessions, more than anything else, that prevents men from living freely and nobly.
BERTRAND RUSSELL (1872–1970)

Freedom comes only to those who no longer ask of life that it shall yield them any of those personal goods that are subject to the mutations of time.
BERTRAND RUSSELL (1872–1970)

A cold atheistical materialism is the tendency of the so-called material philosophy of the present day.
ADAM SEDGWICK (1785–1873)

Any so-called material thing that you want is merely a symbol: you want it not for itself, but because it will content your spirit for the moment.
MARK TWAIN (1835–1910)

Many wealthy people are little more than janitors of their possessions.
FRANK LLOYD WRIGHT (1868–1959)

Once one is caught up into the material world not one person in ten thousand finds the time to form literary taste, to examine the validity of philosophic concepts for himself, or to form what, for lack of a better phrase, I might call the wise and tragic sense of life.
ANONYMOUS

Mathematics

1. Mathematics is the language of nature. 2. Everything around us can be represented and understood through numbers. 3. If you graph these numbers, patterns emerge. Therefore, there are patterns everywhere in nature.
DARREN ARONOFSKY (1969–), *Pi*

If scientific reasoning were limited to the logical processes of arithmetic, we should not get very far in our understanding of the physical world. One might as well attempt to grasp the game of poker entirely by the use of the mathematics of probability.
VANNEVAR BUSH (1890–1974)

We used to think that if we knew one, we knew two, because one and one are two. We are finding that we must learn a great deal more about "and."
SIR ARTHUR EDDINGTON (1882–1944), *The Harvest of a Quiet Eye*

Proof is the idol before whom the pure mathematician tortures himself.
SIR ARTHUR EDDINGTON (1882–1944), *The Nature of the Physical World*

The mathematics is not there till we put it there.
SIR ARTHUR EDDINGTON (1882–1944), *The Philosophy of Physical Science*

As far as the laws of mathematics refer to reality, they are not certain; and as far as they are certain, they do not refer to reality.
ALBERT EINSTEIN (1879–1955), *Geometry and Experience*

Do not worry about your difficulties in Mathematics. I can assure you mine are still greater.
ALBERT EINSTEIN (1879–1955)

[T]he creative principle resides in mathematics. In a certain sense, therefore, I hold true that pure thought can grasp reality, as the ancients dreamed.
ALBERT EINSTEIN (1879–1955)

Mathematics is the queen of the sciences.
CARL FRIEDRICH GAUSS (1777–1855)

In mathematics you don't understand things. You just get used to them.
JOHANN VON NEUMANN (1903–1957)

I have hardly ever known a mathematician who was capable of reasoning.
PLATO (C. 428–348 BC), *The Republic*

Mathematics may be defined as the subject in which we never know what we are talking about, nor whether what we are saying is true.
BERTRAND RUSSELL (1872–1970), *Mysticism and Logic*

Mathematics, rightly viewed, possesses not only truth, but supreme beauty—a beauty cold and austere, like that of sculpture.
BERTRAND RUSSELL (1872–1970)

Today's scientists have substituted mathematics for experiments, and they wander off through equation after equation, and eventually build a structure which has no relation to reality.
NIKOLA TESLA (1857–1943), *Modern Mechanics and Inventions*

I went off to college planning to major in math or philosophy—of course, both those ideas are really the same idea.
FRANK WILCZEK (1951–)

Maturity

By the time I'd grown up, I naturally supposed that I'd be grown up.
EVE BABITZ (1943–)

What I look forward to is continued immaturity followed by death.
DAVE BARRY (1947–)

I live in that solitude which is painful in youth, but delicious in the years of maturity.
ALBERT EINSTEIN (1879–1955)

The rate at which a person can mature is directly proportional to the embarrassment he can tolerate.
DOUGLAS ENGELBART (1925–)

Maturity is only a short break in adolescence.
JULES FEIFFER (1929–)

Every human being on this earth is born with a tragedy, and it isn't original sin. He's born with the tragedy that he has to grow up. That he has to leave the nest, the security, and go out to do battle. He has to lose everything that is lovely and fight for a new loveliness of his own making, and it's a tragedy. A lot of people don't have the courage to do it.
HELEN HAYES (1900–1993)

To be mature means to face, and not evade, every fresh crisis that comes.
FRITZ KUNKEL (1889–1956)

When we were children, we used to think that when we were grown-up we would no longer be vulnerable. But to grow up is to accept vulnerability.... To be alive is to be vulnerable.
MADELEINE L'ENGLE (1918–), *Walking on Water: Reflections on Faith and Art*

A mature person is one who does not think only in absolutes, who is able to be objective even when deeply stirred emotionally, who has learned that there is both good and bad in all people and all things, and who walks humbly and deals charitably.
ELEANOR ROOSEVELT (1884–1962)

The mark of the immature man is that he wants to die nobly for a cause, while the mark of a mature man is that he wants to live humbly for one.
WILHELM STEKEL (1868–1940)

Age is a very high price to pay for maturity.
TOM STOPPARD (1937–)

Maturity is: the ability to stick with a job until it's finished; the ability to do a job without being supervised; the ability to carry money without spending it; and the ability to bear an injustice without wanting to get even.
ABIGAIL VAN BUREN (1918–)

Maturity is a bitter disappointment for which no remedy exists, unless laughter could be said to remedy anything.
KURT VONNEGUT JR. (1922–2007)

To make mistakes is human; to stumble is commonplace; to be able to laugh at yourself is maturity.
WILLIAM ARTHUR WARD (1921–1994)

Maxims

It is unbecoming for young men to utter maxims.
ARISTOTLE (384–322 BC)

Maxims are like lawyers who must need to see but one side of the case.
FRANK GELETT BURGESS (1866–1951)

Know thyself! A maxim as pernicious as it is ugly. Whoever observes himself arrests his own development. A caterpillar who wanted to know itself well would never become a butterfly.
ANDRÉ GIDE (1869–1951)

A collection of anecdotes and maxims is the greatest of treasures for the man of the world, for he knows how to intersperse conversation with the former in fit places, and to recollect the latter on proper occasions.
JOHANN WOLFGANG VON GOETHE (1749–1832)

Maxims are the condensed good sense of nations.
JAMES MACKINTOSH (1765–1832)

It is more trouble to make a maxim than it is to do right.
MARK TWAIN (1835–1910)

Meals

If you knew what I know about the power of giving, you would not let a single meal pass without sharing it in some way.
THE BUDDHA (563–483 BC)

In all recorded history there has not been one economist who has had to worry about where the next meal would come from.
PETER F. DRUCKER (1909–2005)

To lengthen thy life, lessen thy meals.
BENJAMIN FRANKLIN (1706–1790)

The act of nutrition is not a purely physiological event.... The family meal is a formality that cultivates in us ... capacity for sharing, generosity, thoughtfulness, a talent for civilized conversation.
FRANCINE DU PLESSIX GRAY (1930–)

People who go broke in a big way never miss any meals. It is the poor jerk who is shy a half slug who must tighten his belt.
ROBERT A. HEINLEIN (1907–1988)

Sham Harga had run a succesful eatery for many years by always smiling, never extending credit, and realizing that most of his customers wanted meals properly balanced between the four food groups: sugar, starch, grease, and burnt crunchy bits.
TERRY PRATCHETT (1948–), *Men at Arms*

Thanksgiving is a typically American holiday.... The lavish meal is a symbol of the fact that abundant consumption is the result and reward of production.
AYN RAND (1905–1982)

The most remarkable thing about my mother is that for thirty years she served the family nothing but leftovers. The original meal has never been found.
CALVIN TRILLIN (1935–)

A smiling face is half the meal.
LATVIAN PROVERB

Meaning

No one means all he says, and yet very few say all they mean.
HENRY ADAMS (1838–1918)

Meanings are not determined by situations, but we determine ourselves by the meanings we give to situations.
ALFRED ADLER (1870–1937)

Old friends pass away, new friends appear. It is just like the days. An old day passes, a new day arrives. The important thing is to make it meaningful: a meaningful friend—or a meaningful day.
THE DALAI LAMA (1935–)

A man who uses a great many words to express his meaning is like a bad marksman who, instead of aiming a single stone at an object, takes up a handful and throws at it in hopes he may hit.
SAMUEL JOHNSON (1709–1784)

Weigh the meaning and look not at the words.
BEN JONSON (1572–1637)

Our obligation is to give meaning to life and in doing so to overcome the passive, indifferent life.
ELIE WIESEL (1928–)

Media

The media's power is frail. Without the people's support, it can be shut off with the ease of turning a light switch.
CORAZON AQUINO (1933–)

All of us who professionally use the mass media are the shapers of society. We can vulgerize that society. We can brutalize it. Or we can help lift it onto a higher level.
WILLIAM BERNBACH (1911–1982)

People without an internalized symbolic system can all too easily become captives of the media.
MIHALY CSIKSZENTMIHALYI (1934–), *Flow: The Psychology of Optimal Experience*

The biases the media has are much bigger than conservative or liberal. They're about getting ratings, about making money, about doing stories that are easy to cover.
AL FRANKEN (1951–), *Lies and the Lying Liars Who Tell Them*

The media's the most powerful entity on earth. They have the power to make the innocent guilty and to make the guilty innocent, and that's power. Because they control the minds of the masses.
MALCOLM X (1925–1965)

Times have not become more violent. They have just become more televised.
MARILYN MANSON (1969–)

All media exist to invest our lives with artificial perceptions and arbitrary values.
MARSHALL MCLUHAN (1911–1980)

If you don't know what to do, call the media and at least give the appearance of doing something.
DAVID PETERSON (1943–)

For a politician to complain about the press is like a ship's captain complaining about the sea.
ENOCH POWELL (1827–1956)

No matter how much spin, effort, lunch, or dinner you give the media, they will not fail to notice whether you have won or lost.
ROBIN RENWICK (1937–)

Medicine

One has a greater sense of intellectual degradation after an interview with a doctor than from any human experience.
ALICE JAMES (1848–1892)

[Medicine is] a collection of uncertain prescriptions the results of which, taken collectively, are more fatal than useful to mankind.
NAPOLÉON I (1769–1821)

One of the first duties of the physician is to educate the masses not to take medicine.
SIR WILLIAM OSLER (1849–1919), *Aphorisms from His Bedside Teachings*

The desire to take medicine is perhaps the greatest feature which distinguishes man from animals.
SIR WILLIAM OSLER (1849–1919)

Medicine sometimes snatches away health, sometimes gives it.
OVID (43 BC–AD 17)

Some remedies are worse than the disease.
PUBLILIUS SYRUS (C. 100 BC)

Formerly, when religion was strong and science weak, men mistook magic for medicine; now, when science is strong and religion weak, men mistake medicine for magic.
THOMAS SZASZ (1920–), *The Second Sin*

Doctors are men who prescribe medicines of which they know little, to cure diseases of which they know less, in human beings of whom they know nothing.
VOLTAIRE (1694–1778)

The art of medicine consists in amusing the patient while nature cures the disease.
VOLTAIRE (1694–1778)

Laughter is the best medicine.
ANONYMOUS

Don't live in a town where there are no doctors.
JEWISH PROVERB

Mediocrity

Radio is a bag of mediocrity where little men with carbon minds wallow in sluice of their own making.
FRED ALLEN (1894–1956)

It's a sign of mediocrity when you demonstrate gratitude with moderation.
ROBERTO BENIGNI (1952–)

Mediocrity knows nothing higher than itself, but talent instantly recognizes genius.
SIR ARTHUR CONAN DOYLE (1859–1930), *Valley of Fear*

Great spirits have always encountered opposition from mediocre minds. The mediocre mind is incapable of understanding the man who refuses to bow blindly to conventional prejudices and chooses instead to express his opinions courageously and honestly.
ALBERT EINSTEIN (1879–1955)

Solitude, the safeguard of mediocrity.
RALPH WALDO EMERSON (1803–1882)

Some men are born mediocre, some men achieve mediocrity, and some men have mediocrity thrust upon them.
JOSEPH HELLER (1923–1999), *Catch-22*

The essential element of successful strategy is that it derives its success from the differences between competitors with a consequent difference in their behavior. Ordinarily, this means that any corporate policy and plan which is typical of the industry is doomed to mediocrity. Where this is not so, it should be possible to demonstrate that all other competitors are at a distinct disadvantage.
BRUCE HENDERSON (1915–1992)

Mediocrity is not allowed to poets, either by the gods or man.
HORACE (65–8 BC)

In the republic of mediocrity genius is dangerous.
ROBERT GREEN INGERSOLL (1833–1899)

Awards are merely the badges of mediocrity.
CHARLES IVES (1874–1954)

Anybody who accepts mediocrity—in school, on the job, in life—is a person who compromises, and when the leader compromises, the whole organization compromises.
CHARLES KNIGHT (1874–1953)

It is cruel to discover one's mediocrity only when it is too late.
W. SOMERSET MAUGHAM (1874–1965), *Of Human Bondage*

There is real magic in enthusiasm. It spells the difference between mediocrity and accomplishment.
NORMAN VINCENT PEALE (1898–1993)

Jealousy is the tribute mediocrity pays to genius.
BISHOP FULTON J. SHEEN (1895–1975)

Meditation

Meditation brings wisdom; lack of meditation leaves ignorance. Know well what leads you forward and what holds you back, and choose the path that leads to wisdom.
THE BUDDHA (563–483 BC)

Meditation is the soul's perspective glass.
OWEN FELTHAM (1602–1668)

Reading makes a full man, meditation a profound man, discourse a clear man.
BENJAMIN FRANKLIN (1706–1790)

The execution of anything considerable implies in the first place previous persevering meditation.
WILLIAM GODWIN (1756–1836)

The affairs of the world will go on forever. Do not delay the practice of meditation.
MILAREPA (C. 1052–1135)

Those who eat too much or eat too little, who sleep too much or sleep too little, will not succeed in meditation. But those who are temperate in eating and sleeping, work and recreation, will come to the end of sorrow through meditation.
THE BHAGAVAD GITA

When meditation is mastered, the mind is unwavering like the flame of a lamp in a windless place.
THE BHAGAVAD GITA

See how they lie in wait for me! Powerful people conspire against me for no offense or sin of mine, LORD.
THE BIBLE, Psalm 59:3

Meetings

Here's my theory about meetings and life; the three things you can't fake are erections, competence and creativity. That's why meetings become toxic—they put uncreative people in a situation in which they have to be something they can never be. And the more effort they put into concealing their inabilities, the more toxic the meeting becomes. One of the most common creativity-faking tactics is when someone puts their hands in prayer position and conceals their mouth while they nod at you and say, "Mmmmmm. Interesting." If pressed, they'll add, "I'll have to get back to you on that." Then they don't say anything else.
DOUGLAS COUPLAND (1961–)

Melancholy

Great men are always of a nature originally melancholy.
ARISTOTLE (384–322 BC)

Many men are melancholy by hearing music, but it is a pleasing melancholy that it causeth; and therefore to such as are discontent, in woe, fear, sorrow, or dejected, it is a most present remedy.
ROBERT BURTON (1577–1640)

Melancholy is a fearful gift. What is it but the telescope of truth!
LORD BYRON (1788–1824)

Melancholy is sadness that has taken on lightness.
ITALO CALVINO (1923–1985)

I have often thought what a melancholy world this would be without children, and what an inhuman world without the aged.
SAMUEL TAYLOR COLERIDGE (1772–1834)

Melancholy is the pleasure of being sad.
VICTOR HUGO (1802–1885)

Memory

If any one faculty of our nature may be called more wonderful than the rest, I do think it is memory. There seems something more speakingly incomprehensible in the powers, the failures, the inequalities of memory, than in any other of our intelligences. The memory is sometimes so retentive, so serviceable, so obedient; at others, so bewildered

and so weak; and at others again, so tyrannic, so beyond control! We are, to be sure, a miracle every way; but our powers of recollecting and of forgetting do seem peculiarly past finding out.
JANE AUSTEN (1775–1817), *Mansfield Park*

There is not any memory with less satisfaction than the memory of some temptation we resisted.
JAMES BRANCH CABELL (1879–1958)

It's a poor sort of memory that only works backward.
LEWIS CARROLL (1832–1898)

[T]he sense of smell, almost more than any other, has the power to recall memories and it is a pity that you use it so little.
RACHEL CARSON (1907–1964)

A good storyteller is a person with a good memory and hopes other people haven't.
IRVIN S. COBB (1876–1944)

We do not know the true value of our moments until they have undergone the test of memory.
GEORGES DUHAMEL (1884–1966)

The secret of a good memory is attention, and attention to a subject depends upon our interest in it. We rarely forget that which has made a deep impression on our minds.
TYRON EDWARDS (1809–1894)

Memory believes before knowing remembers. Believes longer than recollects, longer than knowing even wonders.
WILLIAM FAULKNER (1897–1962), *Light in August*

Memory tempers prosperity, mitigates adversity, controls youth, and delights old age.
FIRMIANUS LACTANTIUS (C. 240–320)

Creditors have better memories than debtors.
BENJAMIN FRANKLIN (1706–1790), *Poor Richard's Almanac*

Nothing is so admirable in politics as a short memory.
JOHN KENNETH GALBRAITH (1908–2006)

It was one of those perfect English autumnal days which occur more frequently in memory than in life.
P. D. JAMES (1920–)

Why is it that our memory is good enough to retain the least triviality that happens to us, and yet not good enough to recollect how often we have told it to the same person?
FRANÇOIS DE LA ROCHEFOUCAULD (1613–1680)

A fellow will remember a lot of things you wouldn't think he'd remember. You take me. One day, back in 1896, I was crossing over to Jersey on the ferry, and as we pulled out, there was another ferry pulling in, and on it there was a girl waiting to get off. A white dress she had on. She was carrying a white parasol. I only saw her for one second. She didn't see me at all, but I'll bet a month hasn't gone by since that I haven't thought of that girl.
HERMAN J. MAKIEWICZ (1897–1953) and ORSON WELLES (1915–1985), *Citizen Kane*

He who is not very strong in memory should not meddle with lying.
MICHEL DE MONTAIGNE (1533–1592)

Nothing fixes a thing so intensely in the memory as the wish to forget it.
MICHEL DE MONTAIGNE (1533–1592)

One must have a good memory to be able to keep the promises one makes.
FRIEDRICH NIETZSCHE (1844–1900)

The advantage of a bad memory is that one enjoys several times the same good things for the first time.
FRIEDRICH NIETZSCHE (1844–1900)

The memory should be specially taxed in youth, since it is then that it is strongest and most tenacious. But in choosing the things that should be committed to memory the utmost care and forethought must be exercised; as lessons well learnt in youth are never forgotten.
ARTHUR SCHOPENHAUER (1788–1860)

A man's real possession is his memory. In nothing else is he rich, in nothing else is he poor.
ALEXANDER SMITH (1830–1867)

Own only what you can carry with you; know language, know countries, know people. Let your memory be your travel bag.
ALEXANDER SOLZHENITSYN (1918–)

Memory feeds imagination.
AMY TAN (1952–)

When I was younger, I could remember anything, whether it had happened or not.
MARK TWAIN (1835–1910)

The palest ink is better than the best memory.
CHINESE PROVERB

Men

Men live in a fantasy world. I know this because I am one, and I actually receive my mail there.
SCOTT ADAMS (1957–)

Men are what their mothers made them.
RALPH WALDO EMERSON (1803–1882)

That is the great distinction between the sexes. Men see objects, women see the relationships between objects.
JOHN FOWLES (1926–2005)

The little man is still a man.
JOHANN WOLFGANG VON GOETHE (1749–1832)

Men have as exaggerated an idea of their rights as women have of their wrongs.
EDGAR WATSON HOWE (1853–1937)

It is easier to know men in general, than men in particular.
FRANÇOIS DE LA ROCHEFOUCAULD (1613–1680)

There are three classes of men; the retrograde, the stationary and the progressive.
JOHANN KASPAR LAVATER (1741–1801)

How beautiful maleness is, if it finds its right expression.
D. H. LAWRENCE (1885–1930)

Women who seek to be equal with men lack ambition.
TIMOTHY LEARY (1920–1996)

Women cannot complain about men anymore until they start getting better taste in them.
BILL MAHER (1956–)

Masculinity is not something given to you, but something you gain. And you gain it by winning small battles with honor.
NORMAN MAILER (1923–2007)

It is much more easy to accuse the one sex than to excuse the other.
MICHEL DE MONTAIGNE (1533–1592)

The most unhappy and frail creatures are men and yet they are the proudest.
MICHEL DE MONTAIGNE (1533–1592)

Don't accept rides from strange men, and remember that all men are strange.
ROBIN MORGAN (1941–)

The true man wants two things: danger and play. For that reason he wants woman, as the most dangerous plaything.
FRIEDRICH NIETZSCHE (1844–1900)

I require three things in a man. He must be handsome, ruthless, and stupid.
DOROTHY PARKER (1893–1967)

There are three classes of men; lovers of wisdom, lovers of honor, and lovers of gain.
PLATO (C. 428–348 BC)

Men dream of courtship, but in wedlock wake.
ALEXANDER POPE (1688–1744)

Reading, solitude, idleness, a soft and sedentary life, intercourse with women and young people, these are perilous paths for a young man, and these lead him constantly into danger.
JEAN-JACQUES ROUSSEAU (1712–1778)

There are only two kinds of men; the dead and the deadly.
HELEN ROWLAND (1875–1950)

There's so much saint in the worst of them, and so much devil in the best of them, that a woman who's married to one of them, has nothing to learn of the rest of them.
HELEN ROWLAND (1875–1950)

Man is the only animal of which I am thoroughly and cravenly afraid.
GEORGE BERNARD SHAW (1856–1950)

What is most beautiful in virile men is something feminine; what is most beautiful in feminine women is something masculine.
SUSAN SONTAG (1933–2004), *Against Interpretation*

Women might be able to fake orgasms. But men can fake a whole relationship.
SHARON STONE (1958–)

Men are happy to be laughed at for their humor, but not for their folly.
JONATHAN SWIFT (1667–1745)

One of the things being in politics has taught me is that men are not a reasoned or reasonable sex.
MARGARET THATCHER (1925–)

Silent men, like still waters, are deep and dangerous.
ANONYMOUS

Prudent men woo thrifty women.
GERMAN PROVERB

Mental Illness

People often write me and ask how I keep my wood floors so clean when I live with a child and a dog, and my answer is that I use a technique called Suffering From a Mental Illness.
HEATHER ARMSTRONG (1975–)

The statistics on sanity are that one out of every four Americans is suffering from some form of mental illness. Think of your three best friends. If they're okay, then it's you.
RITA MAE BROWN (1944–)

Mental illness is nothing to be ashamed of, but stigma and bias shame us all.
BILL CLINTON (1946–)

Psychoanalysis is the mental illness it purports to cure.
KARL KRAUS (1874–1936)

Romantic love is mental illness. But it's a pleasurable one. It's a drug. It distorts reality, and that's the point of it. It would be impossible to fall in love with someone that you really saw.
FRAN LEBOWITZ (1950–)

No further evidence is needed to show that "mental illness" is not the name of a biological condition whose nature awaits to be elucidated, but is the name of a concept whose purpose is to obscure the obvious.
THOMAS S. SZASZ (1920–)

You must always be puzzled by mental illness. The thing I would dread most, if I became mentally ill, would be your adopting a common sense attitude; that you could take it for granted that I was deluded.
LUDWIG WITTGENSTEIN (1889–1951)

Mercy

Too much mercy … often resulted in further crimes which were fatal to innocent victims who need not have been victims if justice had been put first and mercy second.
AGATHA CHRISTIE (1890–1976)

We shall show mercy, but we shall not ask for it.
SIR WINSTON CHURCHILL (1874–1965)

Cowards are cruel, but the brave
Love mercy, and delight to save.
JOHN GAY (1685–1732)

I have always found that mercy bears richer fruits than strict justice.
ABRAHAM LINCOLN (1809–1865)

The most merciful thing in the world, I think, is the inability of the human mind to correlate all its contents.
H. P. LOVECRAFT (1890–1937), *The Call of Cthulhu*

The quality of mercy is not strain'd,
It droppeth as the gentle rain from heaven
Upon the place beneath. It is twice blest:
It blesseth him that gives and him that takes.
'Tis mightiest in the mightiest: it becomes
The throned monarch better than his crown;
His sceptre shows the force of temporal power,
The attribute to awe and majesty,
Wherein doth sit the dread and fear of kings;
But mercy is above this sceptred sway,
It is enthroned in the hearts of kings,
It is an attribute to God himself;
And earthly power doth then show likest God's,
When mercy seasons justice. Therefore, Jew,
Though justice be thy plea, consider this,
That in the course of justice none of us
Should see salvation: we do pray for mercy;
And that same prayer doth teach us all to render
The deeds of mercy…
WILLIAM SHAKESPEARE (1564–1616), *The Merchant of Venice*

Nothing emboldens sin so much as mercy.
WILLIAM SHAKESPEARE (1564–1616), *Timon of Athens*

Sweet mercy is nobility's true badge.
WILLIAM SHAKESPEARE (1564–1616), *Titus Andronicus*

Do not stand on a high pedestal and take 5 cents in your hand and say, "here, my poor man," but be grateful that the poor man is there, so by making a gift to him you are able to help yourself. It is not the receiver that is blessed, but it is the giver. Be thankful that you are allowed to exercise your power of benevolence and mercy in the world, and thus become pure and perfect.
SWAMI VIVEKANANDA (1863–1902)

Middle Age

Middle age is youth without levity, and age without decay.
DORIS DAY (1924–)

The really frightening thing about middle age is that you know you'll grow out of it.
DORIS DAY (1924–)

Setting a good example for children takes all the fun out of middle age.
WILLIAM FEATHER (1908–1976)

Middle age is when your age starts to show around your middle.
BOB HOPE (1903–2003)

Middle age is the time when a man is always thinking that in a week or two he will feel as good as ever.
DON MARQUIS (1878–1937)

Middle age is when you've met so many people that every new person you meet reminds you of someone else.
OGDEN NASH (1902–1971)

The Middle Ages

What progress we are making. In the Middle Ages they would have burned me. Now they are content with burning my books.
SIGMUND FREUD (1856–1939)

Generals think war should be waged like the tourneys of the Middle Ages. I have no use for knights; I need revolutionaries.
ADOLF HITLER (1889–1945)

In the middle ages, people took potions for their ailments. In the 19th century they took snake oil. Citizens of today's shiny, technological age are too modern for that. They take antioxidants and extract of cactus instead.
CHARLES KRAUTHAMMER (1950–)

We owe to the Middle Ages the two worst inventions of humanity—romantic love and gunpowder.
ANDRÉ MAUROIS (1885–1967)

The philosophers of the Middle Ages demonstrated both that the Earth did not exist and also that it was flat. Today they are still arguing about whether the world exists, but they no longer dispute about whether it is flat.
VILHJALMUR STEFANSSON (1879–1962)

Mind

Words are the physicians of the mind diseased.
AESCHYLUS (C. 525–456 BC), *Prometheus Bound*

The smaller the mind the greater the conceit.
AESOP (620–560 BC)

All paid jobs absorb and degrade the mind.
ARISTOTLE (384–322 BC)

Seek ye first the good things of the mind, and the rest will either be supplied or its loss will not be felt.
SIR FRANCIS BACON (1561–1626)

Irony is the hygiene of the mind.
ELIZABETH BIBESCO (1897–1945)

The most potent weapon in the hands of the oppressor is the mind of the oppressed.
STEPHEN BANTU BIKO (1946–1977)

A belief is not merely an idea the mind possesses; it is an idea that possesses the mind.
ROBERT OXTON BOLTON (1924–1995)

To resist the frigidity of old age one must combine the body, the mind and the heart—and to keep them in parallel vigor one must exercise, study and love.
KARL VON BONSTETTEN (1745–1832)

No passion so effectually robs the mind of all its powers of acting and reasoning as fear.
EDMUND BURKE (1729–1797), *A Philosophical Inquiry into the Origin of Our Ideas of the Sublime and Beautiful*

The tendinous part of the mind, so to speak, is more developed in winter; the fleshy, in summer. I should say winter had given the bone and sinew to literature, summer the tissues and the blood.
JOHN BURROUGHS (1837–1921), *The Snow-Walkers*

Anger so clouds the mind, that it cannot perceive the truth.
CATO THE ELDER (234–149 BC)

Prepare yourself for the world, as the athletes used to do for their exercise; oil your mind and your manners, to give them the necessary suppleness and flexibility; strength alone will not do.
LORD CHESTERFIELD (1694–1773)

The empires of the future are the empires of the mind.
SIR WINSTON CHURCHILL (1874–1965)

All action is of the mind and the mirror of the mind is the face, its index the eyes.
CICERO (106–43 BC)

A mind without instruction can no more bear fruit than can a field, however fertile, without cultivation.
CICERO (106–43 BC)

In so far as the mind is stronger than the body, so are the ills contracted by the mind more severe than those contracted by the body.
CICERO (106–43 BC)

Advice is like snow—the softer it falls, the longer it dwells upon, and the deeper it sinks into the mind.
SAMUEL TAYLOR COLERIDGE (1772–1834)

Ignorance is the night of the mind, but a night without moon and star.
CONFUCIUS (551–479 BC)

Once you have traveled, the voyage never ends, but is played out over and over again in the quietest chambers, that the mind can never break off from the journey.
PAT CONROY (1945–), *The Prince of Tides*

To read a newspaper is to refrain from reading something worthwhile. The first discipline of

education must therefore be to refuse resolutely to feed the mind with canned chatter.
ALEISTER CROWLEY (1875–1947)

Without the capacity to provide its own information, the mind drifts into randomness.
MIHALY CSIKSZENTMIHALYI (1934–), *Flow: The Psychology of Optimal Experience*

In order to improve the mind, we ought less to learn, than to contemplate.
RENÉ DESCARTES (1596–1650)

How hard it is, sometimes, to trust the evidence of one's senses! How reluctantly the mind consents to reality.
NORMAN DOUGLAS (1868–1952)

The state of your life is nothing more than a reflection of your state of mind.
WAYNE D. DYER (1940–)

Reading, after a certain age, diverts the mind too much from its creative pursuits. Any man who reads too much and uses his own brain too little falls into lazy habits of thinking.
ALBERT EINSTEIN (1879–1955)

He that can heroically endure adversity will bear prosperity with equal greatness of the soul; for the mind that cannot be dejected by the former is not likely to be transported without the latter.
HENRY FIELDING (1707–1754)

The test of a first-rate intelligence is the ability to hold two opposed ideas in the mind at the same time, and still retain the ability to function.
F. SCOTT FITZGERALD (1896–1940), *The Crack-Up*

Judge of thine improvement, not by what thou speakest or writest, but by the firmness of thy mind, and the government of thy passions and affections.
THOMAS FULLER (1608–1661)

It is the mind which creates the world about us, and even though we stand side by side in the same meadow, my eyes will never see what is beheld by yours, my heart will never stir to the emotions with which yours is touched.
GEORGE GISSING (1857–1903)

Any ideas, plan, or purpose may be placed in the mind through repetition of thought.
NAPOLEON HILL (1883–1970)

There are no limitations to the mind except those we acknowledge.
NAPOLEON HILL (1883–1970)

The mind of a bigot is like the pupil of the eye. The more light you shine on it, the more it will contract.
OLIVER WENDELL HOLMES JR. (1841–1935)

A man's mind, stretched by a new idea, can never go back to its original dimension.
OLIVER WENDELL HOLMES SR. (1809–1894)

The minds of the everlasting gods are not changed suddenly.
HOMER (800–700 BC), *The Odyssey*

Beauty is no quality in things themselves: it exists merely in the mind which contemplates them.
DAVID HUME (1711–1776)

Anger is a wind which blows out the lamp of the mind.
ROBERT GREEN INGERSOLL (1833–1899)

Any doctrine that will not bear investigation is not a fit tenant for the mind of an honest man.
ROBERT GREEN INGERSOLL (1833–1899)

Great minds have purposes, others have wishes. Little minds are tamed and subdued by misfortune; but great minds rise above them.
WASHINGTON IRVING (1783–1859)

What we truly and earnestly aspire to be, that in some sense, we are. The mere aspiration, by changing the frame of the mind, for the moment realizes itself.
ANNA JAMESON (1794–1860)

I have sworn upon the altar of God, eternal hostility against every form of tyranny over the mind of man.
THOMAS JEFFERSON (1743–1826)

The face is the mirror of the mind, and eyes without speaking confess the secrets of the heart.
SAINT JEROME (C. 342–420)

You should pray for a sound mind in a sound body.
JUVENAL (AD 55–127), *Satires*

A healthy mind in a healthy body.
JUVENAL (AD 55–127)

It has been said, "time heals all wounds." I do not agree. The wounds remain. In time, the mind, protecting its sanity, covers them with scar tissue and the pain lessens. But it is never gone.
ROSE F. KENNEDY (1890–1995)

The absence of alternatives clears the mind marvelously.
HENRY KISSINGER (1923–)

Without freedom from the past, there is no freedom at all, because the mind is never new, fresh, innocent.
JIDDU KRISHNAMURTI (1895–1986)

When the heart speaks, the mind finds it indecent to object.
MILAN KUNDERA (1929–), *The Unbearable Lightness of Being*

The defects and faults in the mind are like wounds in the body. After all imaginable care has been taken to heal them up, still there will be a scar left behind.
FRANÇOIS DE LA ROCHEFOUCAULD (1613–1680)

Iron rusts from disuse; stagnant water loses its purity and in cold weather becomes frozen; even so does inaction sap the vigor of the mind.
LEONARDO DA VINCI (1452–1519), *The Notebooks*

In the province of the mind, what one believes to be true either is true or becomes true.
JOHN LILLY (1915–2001)

A sound mind in a sound body is a short but full description of a happy state in this world.
JOHN LOCKE (1632–1704)

The most merciful thing in the world, I think, is the inability of the human mind to correlate all its contents.
H. P. LOVECRAFT (1890–1937), *The Call of Cthulhu*

Let your mind go and your body will follow.
STEVE MARTIN (1945–), *L.A. Story*

The quality of an organization can never exceed the quality of the minds that make it up.
HAROLD R. MCALINDON (1940–)

The sword the body wounds, sharp words the mind.
MENANDER (342–292 BC)

The mind is its own place, and in itself can make a Heaven of Hell, a Hell of Heaven.
JOHN MILTON (1608–1674)

Read, every day, something no one else is reading. Think, every day, something no one else is thinking. Do, every day, something no one else would be silly enough to do. It is bad for the mind to be always part of unanimity.
CHRISTOPHER MORLEY (1890–1957)

If both the past and the external world exist only in the mind, and if the mind itself is controllable—what then?
GEORGE ORWELL (1903–1950), *1984*

True silence is the rest of the mind; it is to the spirit what sleep is to the body, nourishment and refreshment.
WILLIAM PENN (1644–1718)

The mind ought sometimes to be diverted that it may return the better to thinking.
PHAEDRUS (15 BC–AD 50)

Any one who has common sense will remember that the bewilderments of the eyes are of two kinds, and arise from two causes, either from coming out of the light or from going into the light, which is true of the mind's eye, quite as much as of the bodily eye; and he who remembers this when he sees any one whose vision is perplexed and weak, will not be too ready to laugh; he will first ask whether that soul of man has come out of the brighter light, and

is unable to see because unaccustomed to the dark, or having turned from darkness to the day is dazzled by excess of light.
PLATO (C. 428–348 BC), *The Republic*

Bodily exercise, when compulsory, does no harm to the body; but knowledge which is acquired under compulsion obtains no hold on the mind.
PLATO (C. 428–348 BC), *The Republic*

The mind is not a vessel to be filled, but a fire to be ignited.
PLUTARCH (AD 46–120)

Could we have entered into the mind of Sir Isaac Newton, and have traced all the steps by which he produced his great works, we might see nothing very extraordinary in the process.
JOSEPH PRIESTLEY (1733–1804)

I know but one freedom and that is the freedom of the mind.
ANTOINE DE SAINT-EXUPÉRY (1900–1944)

Progress, far from consisting in change, depends on retentiveness. When change is absolute there remains no being to improve and no direction is set for possible improvement: and when experience is not retained, as among savages, infancy is perpetual. Those who cannot remember the past are condemned to repeat it. In the first stage of life the mind is frivolous and easily distracted, it misses progress by failing in consecutiveness and persistence. This is the condition of children and barbarians, in which instinct has learned nothing from experience.
GEORGE SANTAYANA (1863–1952), *The Life of Reason*

The body is an instrument, the mind its function, the witness and reward of its operation.
GEORGE SANTAYANA (1863–1952)

Difficulties strengthen the mind, as labor does the body.
SENECA (5 BC–AD 65)

I do not distinguish by the eye, but by the mind, which is the proper judge.
SENECA (5 BC–AD 65)

Speech is the mirror of the mind.
SENECA (5 BC–AD 65)

The mind is slow to unlearn what it learnt early.
SENECA (5 BC–AD 65)

Where the speech is corrupted, the mind is also.
SENECA (5 BC–AD 65)

To be, or not to be: that is the question:
Whether 'tis nobler in the mind to suffer
The slings and arrows of outrageous fortune,
Or to take arms against a sea of troubles,
And by opposing end them? To die: to sleep:
No more; and by a sleep to say we end
The heartache and the thousand natural shocks
That flesh is heir to,—'tis a consummation
Devoutly to be wish'd. To die, to sleep;
To sleep: perchance to dream: ay, there's the rub:
For in that sleep of death what dreams may come,
When we have shuffled off this mortal coil,
Must give us pause: there's the respect
That makes calamity of so long life;
For who would bear the whips and scorns of time,
The oppressor's wrong, the proud man's contumely,
The pangs of despised love, the law's delay,
The insolence of office and the spurns
That patient merit of the unworthy takes,
When he himself might his quietus make
With a bare bodkin? who would fardels bear,
To grunt and sweat under a weary life,
But that the dread of something after death,
The undiscover'd country from whose bourn
No traveller returns, puzzles the will
And makes us rather bear those ills we have
Than fly to others that we know not of?
Thus conscience does make cowards of us all;
And thus the native hue of resolution
Is sicklied o'er with the pale cast of thought,
And enterprises of great pith and moment
With this regard their currents turn awry,
And lose the name of action.
WILLIAM SHAKESPEARE (1564–1616), *Hamlet*

Is this a dagger which I see before me,
The handle toward my hand? Come, let me clutch thee.
I have thee not, and yet I see thee still.
Art thou not, fatal vision, sensible

To feeling as to sight? or art thou but
A dagger of the mind, a false creation,
Proceeding from the heat-oppressed brain?
WILLIAM SHAKESPEARE (1564–1616), *Macbeth*

Love looks not with the eyes, but with the mind.
WILLIAM SHAKESPEARE (1564–1616), *A Midsummer Night's Dream*

When griping grief the heart doth wound,
And doleful dumps the mind oppress,
Then music, with her silver sound,
With speedy help doth lend redress.
WILLIAM SHAKESPEARE (1564–1616), *Romeo and Juliet*

The mind's first step to self-awareness must be through the body.
GEORGE SHEEHAN (1918–1993)

Nothing contributes so much to tranquilizing the mind as a steady purpose—a point on which the soul may fix its intellectual eye.
MARY SHELLEY (1797–1851)

Reading is to the mind what exercise is to the body.
SIR RICHARD STEELE (1672–1729)

Extensive traveling induces a feeling of encapsulation, and travel, so broadening at first, contracts the mind.
PAUL THEROUX (1941–)

The most powerful factors in the world are clear ideas in the minds of energetic men of good will.
J. ARTHUR THOMSON (1861–1933)

The Earth is the Cradle of the Mind, but one cannot eternally live in a cradle.
KONSTANTIN E. TSIOLKOVSKY (1857–1935)

God conceals himself from the mind of man, but reveals himself to his heart.
AFRICAN PROVERB

Beware of too much laughter, for it deadens the mind and produces oblivion.
THE TALMUD

Minorities

It is bad to be oppressed by a minority, but it is worse to be oppressed by a majority. For there is a reserve of latent power in the masses which, if it is called into play, the minority can seldom resist. But from the absolute will of an entire people there is no appeal, no redemption, no refuge but treason.
LORD ACTON (1834–1902)

The most certain test by which we judge whether a country is really free is the amount of security enjoyed by minorities.
LORD ACTON (1834–1902)

All, too, will bear in mind this sacred principle, that though the will of the majority is in all cases to prevail, that will, to be rightful, must be reasonable; that the minority possess their equal rights, which equal laws must protect, and to violate would be oppression.
THOMAS JEFFERSON (1762–1826)

In Republics, the great danger is, that the majority may not sufficiently respect the rights of the minority.
JAMES MADISON (1751–1836)

The third-rate mind is only happy when it is thinking with the majority. The second-rate mind is only happy when it is thinking with the minority. The first-rate mind is only happy when it is thinking.
A. A. MILNE (1882–1956)

The test of courage comes when we are in the minority. The test of tolerance comes when we are in the majority.
RALPH W. SOCKMAN (1889–1970)

Civilization is a slow process of adopting the ideas of minorities.
ANONYMOUS

Miracles

In order to be a realist you must believe in miracles.
HENRY CHRISTOPHER BAILEY (1878–1961)

Miracles happen to those who believe in them.
BERNHARD BERENSON (1865–1959)

I am the miracle.
THE BUDDHA (563–483 BC)

If we could see the miracle of a single flower clearly, our whole life would change.
THE BUDDHA (563–483 BC)

The most astonishing thing about miracles is that they happen.
G. K. CHESTERTON (1874–1936)

There are two ways to live: you can live as if nothing is a miracle; you can live as if everything is a miracle.
ALBERT EINSTEIN (1879–1955)

A strong positive mental attitude will create more miracles than any wonder drug.
PATRICIA NEAL (1926–)

Hope is the companion of power, and mother of success; for who so hopes strongly has within him the gift of miracles.
SAMUEL SMILES (1812–1904)

The miracle is not that we do this work, but that we are happy to do it.
MOTHER TERESA (1910–1997)

Could a greater miracle take place than for us to look through each other's eyes for an instant?
HENRY DAVID THOREAU (1817–1862)

If it is a Miracle, any sort of evidence will answer, but if it is a Fact, proof is necessary.
MARK TWAIN (1835–1910)

Mirrors

Look in the mirror. The face that pins you with its double gaze reveals a chastening secret.
DIANE ACKERMAN (1948–)

All action is of the mind and the mirror of the mind is the face, its index the eyes.
CICERO (106–43 BC)

The face is the mirror of the mind, and eyes without speaking confess the secrets of the heart.
SAINT JEROME (C. 342–420)

Speech is the mirror of the mind.
SENECA (5 BC–AD 65)

There are two ways of spreading light: to be the candle or the mirror that reflects it.
EDITH WHARTON (1862–1937), *Vesalius in Zante*

And thou shalt smite thine enemy even unto the wall, gnashing thy teeth, and he shall grow small in thy mirrors.
JEFF ZURSCHMEIDE (1964–)

Misers

To be a book-collector is to combine the worst characteristics of a dope fiend with those of a miser.
ROBERTSON DAVIES (1913–1995), *The Table Talk of Samuel Marchbanks*

Every man serves a useful purpose: A miser, for example, makes a wonderful ancestor.
DR. LAURENCE J. PETER (1919–1990)

Misery

A misery is not to be measured from the nature of the evil, but from the temper of the sufferer.
JOSEPH ADDISON (1672–1719)

Friendship improves happiness, and abates misery, by doubling our joys, and dividing our grief.
JOSEPH ADDISON (1672–1719)

Life is full of misery, loneliness, and suffering—and it's all over much too soon.
WOODY ALLEN (1935–)

Resolve to be thyself: and know, that he who finds himself, loses his misery.
MATTHEW ARNOLD (1822–1888), *Self-Dependence*

Misery no longer loves company. Nowadays it insists on it.
RUSSELL BAKER (1925–)

Happiness, n.: An agreeable sensation arising from contemplating the misery of another.
AMBROSE BIERCE (1842–1914), *The Devil's Dictionary*

The Baptists believe in The Right to Life before you're born. They also believe in Life After Death, but that is a privilege and you have to earn it by spending the interim in guilt-ridden misery. At an early age I decided that living a life of pious misery in the hope of going to heaven when it's over is a lot like keeping your eyes shut all through a movie in the hope of getting your money back at the end.
A. WHITNEY BROWN (1952–), *The Big Picture*

There is no credulity so eager and blind as the credulity of covetousness, which, in its universal extent, measures the moral misery and the intellectual destitution of mankind.
JOSEPH CONRAD (1857–1924), *Nostromo*

Annual income twenty pounds, annual expenditure nineteen six, result happiness. Annual income twenty pounds, annual expenditure twenty pound ought and six, result misery.
CHARLES DICKENS (1812–1870), *David Copperfield*

Educate your children to self-control, to the habit of holding passion and prejudice and evil tendencies subject to an upright and reasoning will, and you have done much to abolish misery from their future and crimes from society.
BENJAMIN FRANKLIN (1706–1790)

I conceive that the great part of the miseries of mankind are brought upon them by false estimates they have made of the value of things.
BENJAMIN FRANKLIN (1706–1790)

There is always more misery among the lower classes than there is humanity in the higher.
VICTOR HUGO (1802–1885), *Les Miserables*

There is no observation more frequently made by such as employ themselves in surveying the conduct of mankind, than that marriage, though the dictate of nature, and the institution of Providence, is yet very often the cause of misery, and that those who enter into that state can seldom forbear to express their repentance, and their envy of those whom either chance or caution hath withheld from it.
SAMUEL JOHNSON (1709–1784), *Rambler*, No. 18

Puritanism ... helps us enjoy our misery while we are inflicting it on others.
MARCEL OPHULS (1927–)

Philosophers should consider the fact that the greatest happiness principle can easily be made an excuse for a benevolent dictatorship. We should replace it by a more modest and more realistic principle—the principle that the fight against avoidable misery should be a recognized aim of public policy, while the increase of happiness should be left, in the main, to private initiative.
KARL POPPER (1902–1994)

It is a consolation to the wretched to have companions in misery.
PUBLILIUS SYRUS (C. 100 BC), *Maxims*

Misery acquaints a man with strange bedfellows.
WILLIAM SHAKESPEARE (1564–1616), *The Tempest*

Chastity is a monkish and evangelical superstition, a greater foe to natural temperance even than unintellectual sensuality; it strikes at the root of all domestic happiness, and consigns more than half of the human race to misery.
PERCY BYSSHE SHELLEY (1792–1822)

I am still determined to be cheerful and happy, in whatever situation I may be; for I have also learned from experience that the greater part of our happiness or misery depends upon our dispositions, and not upon our circumstances.
MARTHA WASHINGTON (1732–1802)

If I was more complacent and I let things slide, my life would be easier, but you all wouldn't be as entertained. My misery is your pleasure.
KANYE WEST (1977–)

A man's subconscious self is not the ideal companion. It lurks for the greater part of his life in some dark den of its own, hidden away, and emerges only to taunt and deride and increase the misery of a miserable hour.
P. G. WODEHOUSE (1881–1975), *Uneasy Money*

Hope is the nurse of misery.
AMERICAN PROVERB

If one speaks or acts with a cruel mind, misery follows, as the cart follows the horse.... If one speaks or acts with a pure mind, happiness follows, as a shadow follows its source.
THE DHAMMAPADA

Misfortune

Better be wise by the misfortunes of others than by your own.
AESOP (620–560 BC)

Misfortune shows those who are not really friends.
ARISTOTLE (384–322 BC), *Eudemian Ethics*

A man's mother is his misfortune, but his wife is his fault.
WALTER BAGEHOT (1826–1877)

Calamities are of two kinds: misfortunes to ourselves, and good fortune to others.
AMBROSE BIERCE (1842–1914), *The Devil's Dictionary*

It is how people respond to stress that determines whether they will profit from misfortune or be miserable.
MIHALY CSIKSZENTMIHALYI (1934–), *Flow: The Psychology of Optimal Experience*

Physical deformity, calls forth our charity. But the infinite misfortune of moral deformity calls forth nothing but hatred and vengeance.
CLARENCE DARROW (1857–1938)

Reflect on your present blessings, of which every man has many; not on your past misfortunes, of which all men have some.
CHARLES DICKENS (1812–1870)

History is indeed little more than the register of the crimes, follies and misfortunes of mankind.
EDWARD GIBBON (1737–1794)

A bad neighbor is a misfortune, as much as a good one is a great blessing.
HESIOD (C. 800 BC), *Works and Days*

Little minds attain and are subdued by misfortunes, but great minds rise above them.
WASHINGTON IRVING (1783–1859)

All men's misfortunes spring from their hatred of being alone.
JEAN DE LA BRUYÈRE (1645–1696)

We all have strength enough to endure the misfortunes of others.
FRANÇOIS DE LA ROCHEFOUCAULD (1613–1680)

Indeed, wretched the man whose fame makes his misfortunes famous.
LUCIUS ACCIUS (170–86 BC), *Telephus*

Much talking is the cause of danger. Silence is the means of avoiding misfortune. The talkative parrot is shut up in a cage. Other birds, without speech, fly freely about.
SASKYA PANDITA (1182–1251)

Fortune knocks but once, but misfortune has much more patience.
DR. LAURENCE J. PETER (1919–1990)

Ignorance of all things is an evil neither terrible nor excessive, nor yet the greatest of all; but great cleverness and much learning, if they be accompanied by a bad training, are a much greater misfortune.
PLATO (C. 428–348 BC)

Never find your delight in another's misfortunc.
PUBLILIUS SYRUS (C. 100 BC), *Maxims*

Love is an attachment to another self. Humor is a form of self-detachment—a way of looking at one's existence, one's misfortune, or one's discomfort. If you really love, if you really know how to laugh, the result is the same: you forget yourself.
CLAUDE ROY (1915–1997)

Not to feel one's misfortunes is not human, not to bear them is not manly.
SENECA (5 BC–AD 65)

Men are slower to recognize blessings than misfortunes.
TITUS LIVIUS (59 BC–AD 17)

[H]istory is nothing more than a tableau of crimes and misfortunes.
VOLTAIRE (1694–1778)

Philosophy teaches us to bear with equanimity the misfortunes of others.
OSCAR WILDE (1854–1900)

A great fortune in the hands of a fool is a great misfortune.
ANONYMOUS

One should go invited to a friend in good fortune, and uninvited in misfortune.
SWEDISH PROVERB

Misogyny

Feminism is hated because women are hated. Anti-feminism is a direct expression of misogyny; it is the political defense of women hating.
ANDREA DWORKIN (1946–2005)

The misogyny that shapes every aspect of our civilization is the institutionalized form of male fear and hatred of what they have denied and therefore cannot know, cannot share: that wild country, the being of women.
URSULA K. LE GUIN (1929–)

Mistakes

Creativity is allowing yourself to make mistakes. Art is knowing which ones to keep.
SCOTT ADAMS (1957–), *The Dilbert Principle*

The greatest mistake is trying to be more agreeable than you can be.
WALTER BAGEHOT (1826–1877)

If I had to live my life again, I'd make the same mistakes, only sooner.
TALLULAH BANKHEAD (1903–1968)

An expert is a person who has made all the mistakes that can be made in a very narrow field.
NIELS BOHR (1885–1962)

Every great mistake has a halfway moment, a split second when it can be recalled and perhaps remedied.
PEARL S. BUCK (1892–1973)

Wise men profit more from fools than fools from wise men; for the wise men shun the mistakes of fools, but fools do not imitate the successes of the wise.
CATO THE ELDER (234–149 BC)

We must not say every mistake is a foolish one.
CICERO (106–43 BC)

Be not ashamed of mistakes and thus make them crimes.
CONFUCIUS (551–479 BC)

Anyone who has never made a mistake has never tried anything new.
ALBERT EINSTEIN (1879–1955)

No one who cannot rejoice in the discovery of his own mistakes deserves to be called a scholar.
DONALD FOSTER (1950–)

Mistakes are a part of being human. Appreciate your mistakes for what they are: precious life lessons that can only be learned the hard way. Unless it's a fatal mistake, which, at least, others can learn from.
AL FRANKEN (1951–), *Oh, the Things I Know*

Experience teaches slowly and at the cost of mistakes.
JAMES A. FROUDE (1818–1894)

Freedom is not worth having if it does not include the freedom to make mistakes.
MAHATMA GANDHI (1869–1948)

The greatest mistake you can make in life is to be continually fearing you will make one.
ELBERT HUBBARD (1856–1915)

She had an unequalled gift … of squeezing big mistakes into small opportunities.
HENRY JAMES (1843–1916)

Experience is that marvelous thing that enables you to recognize a mistake when you make it again.
FRANKLIN P. JONES (1887–1929)

Mistakes are the portals of discovery.
JAMES JOYCE (1882–1941)

Mistakes are part of the dues one pays for a full life.
SOPHIA LOREN (1934–)

It's always helpful to learn from your mistakes because then your mistakes seem worthwhile.
GARRY MARSHALL (1934–), *Wake Me When It's Funny*

I have learned the novice can often see things that the expert overlooks. All that is necessary is not to be afraid of making mistakes, or of appearing naive.
ABRAHAM MASLOW (1908–1970)

I daresay one profits more by the mistakes one makes off one's own bat than by doing the right thing on somebody's else advice.
W. SOMERSET MAUGHAM (1874–1965), *Of Human Bondage*

Never interrupt your enemy when he is making a mistake.
NAPOLÉON I (1769–1821)

If you have made mistakes, even serious ones, there is always another chance for you. What we call failure is not the falling down but the staying down.
MARY PICKFORD (1893–1979)

We're all capable of mistakes, but I do not care to enlighten you on the mistakes we may or may not have made.
DAN QUAYLE (1947–)

I believe in recovery, and I believe that as a role model I have the responsibility to let young people know that you can make a mistake and come back from it.
ANN RICHARDS (1933–2006)

A life spent making mistakes is not only more honorable, but more useful than a life spent doing nothing.
GEORGE BERNARD SHAW (1856–1950)

It is the greatest of all mistakes to do nothing because you can do only a little. Do what you can.
SYDNEY SMITH (1771–1845)

If I had my life to live over … I'd dare to make more mistakes next time.
NADINE STAIR (1906–)

I have learned throughout my life as a composer chiefly through my mistakes and pursuits of false assumptions, not by my exposure to founts of wisdom and knowledge.
IGOR STRAVINSKY (1882–1971)

When you make a mistake, don't look back at it long. Take the reason of the thing into your mind and then look forward. Mistakes are lessons of wisdom. The past cannot be changed. The future is yet in your power.
HUGH WHITE (1773–1840)

Experience is the name everyone gives to their mistakes.
OSCAR WILDE (1854–1900), *Lady Windermere's Fan*

Nowadays most people die of a sort of creeping common sense, and discover when it is too late that the only things one never regrets are one's mistakes.
OSCAR WILDE (1854–1900), *The Picture of Dorian Gray*

Never make the same mistake twice, or you'll never get around to all of them.
ANONYMOUS

Only those who do nothing make no mistakes.
ANONYMOUS

A wise man learns by the mistakes of others, a fool by his own.
LATIN PROVERB

Misunderstanding

It is by universal misunderstanding that all agree. For if, by ill luck, people understood each other, they would never agree.
CHARLES BAUDELAIRE (1821–1867)

The world only goes round by misunderstanding.
CHARLES BAUDELAIRE (1821–1867)

Logic, n.: The art of thinking and reasoning in strict accordance with the limitations and incapacities of the human misunderstanding.
AMBROSE BIERCE (1842–1914), *The Devil's Dictionary*

Shallow understanding from people of good will is more frustrating than absolute misunderstanding from people of ill will.
MARTIN LUTHER KING JR. (1929–1968)

Living is easy with eyes closed, misunderstanding all you see.
JOHN LENNON (1940–1980), "Strawberry Fields"

The same passions in man and woman nonetheless differ in tempo; hence man and woman do not cease misunderstanding one another.
FRIEDRICH NIETZSCHE (1844–1900)

I have been misunderstood perhaps more than anyone else ever, but it has not affected me, for the simple reason that there is no desire to be understood. It is their problem if they don't understand, it is not my problem. If they misunderstand, it is their problem and their misery. I am not going to waste my sleep because millions of people are misunderstanding me.
BHAGWAN SHREE RAJNEESH (1931–1990)

Grammar and logic free language from being at the mercy of the tone of voice. Grammar protects us against misunderstanding the sound of an uttered name; logic protects us against what we say having double meaning.
EUGEN ROSENSTOCK-HUESSY (1888–1973)

Language is the source of misunderstandings.
ANTOINE DE SAINT-EXUPÉRY (1900–1944)

In human intercourse the tragedy begins, not when there is misunderstanding about words, but when silence is not understood.
HENRY DAVID THOREAU (1817–1862)

The proper basis for marriage is mutual misunderstanding.
OSCAR WILDE (1854–1900)

Mobs

Only the mob and the elite can be attracted by the momentum of totalitarianism itself. The masses have to be won by propaganda.
HANNAH ARENDT (1906–1975)

A mob is the method by which good citizens turn over the law and the government to the criminal or irresponsible classes.
RAY STANNARD BAKER (1870–1946)

Mob law is the most forcible expression of an abnormal public opinion; it shows that society is rotten to the core.
TIMOTHY THOMAS FORTUNE (1856–1928)

The nose of a mob is its imagination. By this, at any time, it can be quietly led.
EDGAR ALLAN POE (1809–1849)

The mob is a sort of bear; while your ring is through its nose, it will even dance under your cudgel; but should the ring slip, and you lose your hold, the brute will turn and rend you.
JANE PORTER (1776–1850)

Moderation

Total abstinence is easier than perfect moderation.
SAINT AUGUSTINE (354–430) *On the Good of Marriage*

It's a sign of mediocrity when you demonstrate gratitude with moderation.
ROBERTO BENIGNI (1952–)

A really great man is known by three signs … generosity in the design, humanity in the execution, moderation in success.
OTTO VON BISMARCK (1815–1898)

There is nothing wrong with sobriety in moderation.
JOHN CIARDI (1916–1986)

Never go to excess, but let moderation be your guide.
CICERO (106–43 BC)

I would remind you that extremism in the defense of liberty is no vice! And let me remind you also that moderation in the pursuit of justice is no virtue.
BARRY GOLDWATER (1909–1998)

Everything in excess! To enjoy the flavor of life, take big bites. Moderation is for monks.
ROBERT A. HEINLEIN (1907–1988)

Abstinence is as easy to me, as temperance would be difficult.
SAMUEL JOHNSON (1709–1784)

Moderation is a virtue only in those who are thought to have an alternative.
HENRY KISSINGER (1923–)

Excess on occasion is exhilarating. It prevents moderation from acquiring the deadening effect of a habit.
W. SOMERSET MAUGHAM (1874–1965)

Moderation? It's mediocrity, fear, and confusion in disguise. It's the devil's dilemma. It's neither doing nor not doing. It's the wobbling compromise that makes no one happy. Moderation is for the bland, the apologetic, for the fence-sitters of the world afraid to take a stand. It's for those afraid to laugh or cry, for those afraid to live or die. Moderation … is lukewarm tea, the devil's own brew.
DAN MILLMAN (1946–), *The Way of the Peaceful Warrior*

A thing moderately good is not so good as it ought to be. Moderation in temper is always a virtue, but moderation in principle is always a vice.
THOMAS PAINE (1737–1809), *The Rights of Man*

Only actions give life strength; only moderation gives it a charm.
JEAN PAUL RICHTER (1763–1825)

Moderation in all things.
TERENCE (185–159 BC), *Andria*

A little more moderation would be good. Of course, my life hasn't exactly been one of moderation.
DONALD TRUMP (1946–)

Water, taken in moderation, cannot hurt anybody.
MARK TWAIN (1835–1910)

Use, do not abuse; neither abstinence nor excess ever renders man happy.
VOLTAIRE (1694–1778)

Moderation is a fatal thing. Nothing succeeds like excess.
OSCAR WILDE (1854–1900)

Modesty

Modesty is not only an ornament, but also a guard to virtue.
JOSEPH ADDISON (1672–1719)

Modesty is the conscience of the body.
HONORÉ DE BALZAC (1799–1850)

Modesty is my best quality.
JACK BENNY (1894–1974)

At least I have the modesty to admit that lack of modesty is one of my failings.
LOUIS-HECTOR BERLIOZ (1803–1869)

Modesty is the only sure bait when you angle for praise.
LORD CHESTERFIELD (1694–1773)

He who speaks without modesty will find it difficult to make his words good.
CONFUCIUS (551–479 BC), *The Confucian Analects*

Modesty is the citadel of beauty.
DEMADES (C. 380–318 BC)

Modesty is a vastly overrated virtue.
JOHN KENNETH GALBRAITH (1908–2006)

Modesty in an actor is as fake as passion in a call girl.
JACKIE GLEASON (1916–1987)

Modesty is a shining light; it prepares the mind to receive knowledge, and the heart for truth.
MADAM GUIZOT (1773–1827)

Modesty and unselfishness: These are the virtues which men praise, and pass by.
ANDRÉ MAUROIS (1885–1967)

Modesty is a quality in a lover more praised by the women than liked.
RICHARD BRINSLEY SHERIDAN (1751–1816)

I have often wished I had time to cultivate modesty.... But I am too busy thinking about myself.
EDITH SITWELL (1887–1964)

Monarchs

For righteous monarchs,
Justly to judge, with their own eyes should see;
To rule o'er freemen, should themselves be free.
HENRY BROOKE (1564–1618)

The state is nothing but an instrument of oppression of one class by another—no less so in a democratic republic than in a monarchy.
FRIEDRICH ENGELS (1820–1895)

A free life cannot acquire many possessions, because this is not easy to do without servility to mobs or monarchs.
EPICURUS (341–271 BC)

The quality of mercy is not strain'd,
It droppeth as the gentle rain from heaven
Upon the place beneath. It is twice blest:
It blesseth him that gives and him that takes.
'Tis mightiest in the mightiest: it becomes
The throned monarch better than his crown;
His sceptre shows the force of temporal power,
The attribute to awe and majesty,
Wherein doth sit the dread and fear of kings;
But mercy is above this sceptred sway,
It is enthroned in the hearts of kings,
It is an attribute to God himself;
And earthly power doth then show likest God's,
When mercy seasons justice. Therefore, Jew,
Though justice be thy plea, consider this,
That in the course of justice none of us
Should see salvation: we do pray for mercy;
And that same prayer doth teach us all to render
The deeds of mercy.
WILLIAM SHAKESPEARE (1564–1616), *The Merchant of Venice*

Slavery to monarchs and ministers, which the world will be long freeing itself from, and whose deadly grasp stops the progress of the human mind, is not yet abolished.
MARY WOLLSTONECRAFT (1759–1797)

Money

Money is better than poverty, if only for financial reasons.
WOODY ALLEN (1935–)

Money doesn't mind if we say it's evil, it goes from strength to strength. It's a fiction, an addiction, and a tacit conspiracy.
MARTIN AMIS (1949–)

Weapons are like money; no one knows the meaning of enough.
MARTIN AMIS (1949–)

A large income is the best recipe for happiness I ever heard of.
JANE AUSTEN (1775–1817), *Mansfield Park*

Nothing amuses me more than the easy manner with which everybody settles the abundance of those who have a great deal less than themselves.
JANE AUSTEN (1775–1817), *Mansfield Park*

No one can earn a million dollars honestly.
WILLIAM JENNINGS BRYAN (1860–1925)

It has been said that the love of money is the root of all evil. The want of money is so quite as truly.
SAMUEL BUTLER (1835–1902), *Erewhon*

The rich are the scum of the earth in every country.
G. K. CHESTERTON (1874–1936), *Flying Inn*

Endless money forms the sinews of war.
CICERO (106–43 BC), *Philippics*

Be you in what line of life you may, it will be amongst your misfortunes if you have not time properly to attend to pecuniary matters. Want of attention to these matters has impeded the progress of science and of genius itself.
WILLIAM COBBETT (1763–1835)

Riches may enable us to confer favours, but to confer them with propriety and grace requires a something that riches cannot give.
CHARLES CALEB COLTON (1780–1832), *Lacon*

I'm living so far beyond my income that we may almost be said to be living apart.
E. E. CUMMINGS (1894–1962)

Money cannot buy peace of mind. It cannot heal ruptured relationships, or build meaning into a life that has none.
RICHARD M. DEVOS (1926–)

Annual income twenty pounds, annual expenditure nineteen six, result happiness. Annual income twenty pounds, annual expenditure twenty pound ought and six, result misery.
CHARLES DICKENS (1812–1870), *David Copperfield*

A billion here, a billion there, pretty soon it adds up to real money.
SENATOR EVERETT DIRKSEN (1896–1969)

One must be poor to know the luxury of giving.
GEORGE ELIOT (1819–1880)

The mint makes it first, it is up to you to make it last.
EVAN ESAR (1899–1995)

Make money your god and it will plague you like the devil.
HENRY FIELDING (1707–1754)

My problem lies in reconciling my gross habits with my net income.
ERROL FLYNN (1909–1959)

He that is of the opinion money will do everything may well be suspected of doing everything for money.
BENJAMIN FRANKLIN (1706–1790)

If you would be wealthy, think of saving as well as getting.
BENJAMIN FRANKLIN (1706–1790)

Who is rich? He that is content. Who is that? Nobody.
BENJAMIN FRANKLIN (1706–1790)

Money is the sinew of love as well as war.
THOMAS FULLER (1608–1661), *Gnomologia*

If you can count your money, you don't have a billion dollars.
J. PAUL GETTY (1892–1976)

Lack of money is no obstacle. Lack of an idea is an obstacle.
KEN HAKUTA (1950–)

The man of power is ruined by power, the man of money by money, the submissive man by subservience, the pleasure seeker by pleasure.
HERMANN HESSE (1877–1962)

Make money, by fair means if you can, if not, by any means.
HORACE (65–8 BC), *Epistles*

It is pretty hard to tell what does bring happiness; poverty and wealth have both failed.
KIN HUBBARD (1868–1930)

The safest way to double your money is to fold it over and put it in your pocket.
KIN HUBBARD (1868–1930)

Never spend your money before you have it.
THOMAS JEFFERSON (1743–1826)

It is not easy for men to rise whose qualities are thwarted by poverty.
JUVENAL (AD 55–127), *Satires*

Be rich to yourself and poor to your friends.
JUVENAL (AD 55–127)

It's good to have money and the things that money can buy, but it's good, too, to make sure you haven't lost the things that money can't buy.
GEORGE HORACE LORIMER (1867–1937)

Money frees you from doing things you dislike. Since I dislike doing nearly everything, money is handy.
GROUCHO MARX (1890–1977)

I have enough money to last me the rest of my life, unless I buy something.
JACKIE MASON (1934–)

He had heard people speak contemptuously of money: he wondered if they had ever tried to do without it.
W. SOMERSET MAUGHAM (1874–1965), *Of Human Bondage*

Money is like a sixth sense without which you cannot make a complete use of the other five.
W. SOMERSET MAUGHAM (1874–1965), *Of Human Bondage*

Riches cover a multitude of woes.
MENANDER (342–292 BC), *Lady of Andros*

The chief value of money lies in the fact that one lives in a world in which it is overestimated.
H. L. MENCKEN (1880–1956)

Money can't buy friends, but it can get you a better class of enemy.
SPIKE MILLIGAN (1918–2002)

A little wanton money, which burned out the bottom of his purse.
SIR THOMAS MORE (1478–1535), *Works*

If women didn't exist, all the money in the world would have no meaning.
ARISTOTLE ONASSIS (1906–1975)

If you want to know what God thinks of money, just look at the people he gave it to.
DOROTHY PARKER (1893–1967)

Wealth is the parent of luxury and indolence, and poverty of meanness and viciousness, and both of discontent.
PLATO (C. 428–348 BC), *The Republic*

Money alone sets all the world in motion.
PUBLILIUS SYRUS (C. 100 BC), *Maxims*

Do not be fooled into believing that because a man is rich he is necessarily smart. There is ample proof to the contrary.
JULIUS ROSENWALD (1862–1932)

Money can't buy happiness, but neither can poverty.
LEO ROSTEN (1908–1997)

Someday I want to be rich. Some people get so rich they lose all respect for humanity. That's how rich I want to be.
RITA RUDNER (1956–)

Finance is the art of passing money from hand to hand until it finally disappears.
ROBERT W. SARNOFF (1918–1997)

Lack of money is the root of all evil.
GEORGE BERNARD SHAW (1856–1950)

It is the wretchedness of being rich that you have to live with rich people.
LOGAN PEARSALL SMITH (1865–1946), *Afterthoughts*

Money: There's nothing in the world so demoralizing as money.
SOPHOCLES (496–406 BC), *Antigone*

If all the rich people in the world divided up their money among themselves there wouldn't be enough to go around.
CHRISTINA STEAD (1903–1983), *House of All Nations*

A wise man should have money in his head, but not in his heart.
JONATHAN SWIFT (1667–1745)

The art of living easily as to money is to pitch your scale of living one degree below your means.
SIR HENRY TAYLOR (1800–1886)

I choose the likely man in preference to the rich man; I want a man without money rather than money without a man.
THEMISTOCLES (527–460 BC)

Money was never a big motivation for me, except as a way to keep score. The real excitement is playing the game.
DONALD TRUMP (1946–), *Trump: Art of the Deal*

The only way not to think about money is to have a great deal of it.
EDITH WHARTON (1862–1937)

The easiest way for your children to learn about money is for you not to have any.
KATHARINE WHITEHORN (1928–)

It is better to have a permanent income than to be fascinating.
OSCAR WILDE (1854–1900), *The Model Millionaire*

Money will buy you a bed, but not a good night's sleep; a house but not a home; a companion but not a friend.
ZIG ZIGLAR (1926–)

The Moon

That's one small step for [a] man, one giant leap for mankind.
NEIL ARMSTRONG (1930–)

Language exerts hidden power, like a moon on the tides.
RITA MAE BROWN (1944–), *Starting from Scratch*

There are nights when the wolves are silent and only the moon howls.
GEORGE CARLIN (1937–)

She used to drag her mattress beside her low window and lie awake for a long while, vibrating with excitement, as a machine vibrates from speed. Life rushed in upon her through that window—or so it seemed. In reality, of course, life rushes from within, not from without. There is no work of art so big or so beautiful that is was not once all contained in some youthful body, like this one which lay on the floor in the moonlight, pulsing with ardor and anticipation.
WILLA CATHER (1873–1947), *The Song of the Lark*

I'm sure we would not have had men on the Moon if it had not been for Wells and Verne and the people who write about this and made people think about it. I'm rather proud of the fact that I know several astronauts who became astronauts through reading my books.
ARTHUR C. CLARKE (1917–)

Ignorance is the night of the mind, but a night without moon and star.
CONFUCIUS (551–479 BC)

We may go to the moon, but that's not very far. The greatest distance we have to cover still lies within us.
CHARLES DE GAULLE (1890–1970)

The sun, the moon and the stars would have disappeared long ago, had they happened to be within reach of predatory human hands.
HENRY HAVELOCK ELLIS (1859–1939), *The Dance of Life*

Moonlight is sculpture.
NATHANIEL HAWTHORNE (1804–1864)

It's the opinion of some that crops could be grown on the moon. Which raises the fear that it may not be long before we're paying somebody not to.
FRANKLIN P. JONES (1887–1929)

Tis the witching hour of night,
Or bed is the moon and bright,
And the stars they glisten, glisten,
Seeming with bright eyes to listen
For what listen they?
JOHN KEATS (1795–1821)

Upon the clothes behind the tenement,
That hang like ghosts suspended from the lines,
Linking each flat, but to each indifferent,
Incongruous and strange the moonlight shines.
CLAUDE MCKAY (1889–1948)

Music is moonlight in the gloomy night of life.
JEAN PAUL RICHTER (1763–1825)

A dreamer is one who can only find his way by moonlight, and his punishment is that he sees the dawn before the rest of the world.
OSCAR WILDE (1854–1900)

Morality

Good laws have their origins in bad morals.
AMBROSIUS MACROBIUS (395–423)

Truth is the secret of eloquence and of virtue, the basis of moral authority; it is the highest summit of art and life.
HENRI-FRÉDÉRIC AMIEL (1821–1881)

The true meaning of religion is thus not simply morality, but morality touched by emotion.
MATTHEW ARNOLD (1822–1888), *Literature and Dogma*

Never let your sense of morals get in the way of doing what's right.
ISAAC ASIMOV (1920–1992), *Foundation*

No moral system can rest solely on authority.
A. J. AYER (1910–1989), *Humanist Outlook*

Morality is the custom of one's country and the current feeling of one's peers.
SAMUEL BUTLER (1835–1902)

I say that a man must be certain of his morality for the simple reason that he has to suffer for it.
G. K. CHESTERTON (1874–1936)

The greatest tragedy in mankind's entire history may be the hijacking of morality by religion.
ARTHUR C. CLARKE (1917–)

As for the charges against me, I am unconcerned; I am above their timid, lying morality and so I am beyond caring.
FRANCIS FORD COPPOLA (1939–) and
JOHN MILIUS (1944–), *Apocalypse Now*

The higher the buildings, the lower the morals.
NOËL COWARD (1899–1973)

The ability to see beauty is the beginning of our moral sensibility. What we believe is beautiful we will not wantonly destroy.
EAN PARKER DENNISON (1979–)

There is no moral precept that does not have something inconvenient about it.
DENIS DIDEROT (1713–1784)

History is a voice forever sounding across the centuries the laws of right and wrong. Opinions alter, manners change, creeds rise and fall, but the moral law is written on the tablets of eternity.
JAMES A. FROUDE (1818–1894)

A man does what he must—in spite of personal consequences, in spite of obstacles and dangers and pressures—and that is the basis of all human morality.
JOHN F. KENNEDY (1917–1963)

The difference between a moral man and a man of honor is that the latter regrets a discreditable act, even when it has worked and he has not been caught.
H. L. MENCKEN (1880–1956), *Prejudices: Fourth Series*

Perhaps misguided moral passion is better than confused indifference.
IRIS MURDOCH (1919–1999)

Morality is herd instinct in the individual.
FRIEDRICH NIETZSCHE (1844–1900), *The Gay Science*

Morality is a test of our conformity rather than our integrity.
JANE RULE (1931–)

Taste is not only a part and index of morality, it is the only morality. The first, and last, and closest trial question to any living creature is "What do you like?" Tell me what you like, I'll tell you what you are.
JOHN RUSKIN (1819–1900)

We have, in fact, two kinds of morality side by side: one which we preach but do not practice, and another which we practice but seldom preach.
BERTRAND RUSSELL (1872–1970), *Sceptical Essays*

The people who are regarded as moral luminaries are those who forego ordinary pleasures themselves and find compensation in interfering with the pleasures of others.
BERTRAND RUSSELL (1872–1970)

The soul is the captain and ruler of the life of morals.
SALLUST (86–34 BC)

Compassion is the basis of all morality.
ARTHUR SCHOPENHAUER (1788–1860)

An Englishman thinks he is moral when he is only uncomfortable.
GEORGE BERNARD SHAW (1856–1950), *Man and Superman*

If your morals make you dreary, depend on it, they are wrong.
ROBERT LOUIS STEVENSON (1850–1894)

Perfection of moral virtue does not wholly take away the passions, but regulates them.
SAINT THOMAS AQUINAS (1225–1274)

Do not be too moral. You may cheat yourself out of much life. Aim above morality. Be not simply good; be good for something.
HENRY DAVID THOREAU (1817–1862)

All sects are different, because they come from men; morality is everywhere the same, because it comes from God.
VOLTAIRE (1694–1778)

Scandal is gossip made tedious by morality.
OSCAR WILDE (1854–1900), *Lady Windermere's Fan*

His morality is all sympathy, just what morality should be.
OSCAR WILDE (1854–1900)

Morality, like art, means drawing a line someplace.
OSCAR WILDE (1854–1900)

Mothers

Mothers have as powerful an influence over the welfare of future generations as all other earthly causes combined.
JOHN S. C. ABBOTT (1805–1877)

All that I am, my mother made me.
JOHN QUINCY ADAMS (1767–1848)

A mother never realizes that her children are no longer children.
JAMES AGEE (1909–1955)

Where there is a mother in the home, matters go well.
AMOS BRONSON ALCOTT (1799–1888)

To describe my mother would be to write about a hurricane in its perfect power.
MAYA ANGELOU (1928–)

Mothers are fonder than fathers of their children because they are more certain they are their own.
ARISTOTLE (384–322 BC)

Their mothers had finally caught up to them and been proven right. There were consequences after all but they were the consequences to things you didn't even know you'd done.
MARGARET ATWOOD (1939–)

A man's mother is his misfortune, but his wife is his fault.
WALTER BAGEHOT (1826–1877)

Education commences at the mother's knee, and every word spoken within the hearing of little children tends towards the formation of character.
HOSEA BALLOU (1771–1852)

A mother's happiness is like a beacon, lighting up the future but reflected also on the past in the guise of fond memories.
HONORÉ DE BALZAC (1799–1850)

The heart of a mother is a deep abyss at the bottom of which you will always find forgiveness.
HONORÉ DE BALZAC (1799–1850)

She never quite leaves her children at home, even when she doesn't take them along.
MARGARET CULKIN BANNING (1891–1982)

I know how to do anything—I'm a mom.
ROSEANNE BARR (1952–)

Mothers—especially single mothers—are heroic in their efforts to raise our nation's children, but men must also take responsibility for their children and recognize the impact they have on their families' well-being.
EVAN BAYH (1955–)

A mother has, perhaps, the hardest earthly lot; and yet no mother worthy of the name ever gave herself thoroughly for her child who did not feel that, after all, she reaped what she had sown.
HENRY WARD BEECHER (1813–1887)

The babe at first feeds upon the mother's bosom, but it is always on her heart.
HENRY WARD BEECHER (1813–1887)

The mother's heart is the child's schoolroom.
HENRY WARD BEECHER (1813–1887)

When God thought of mother, He must have laughed with satisfaction, and framed it quickly—so rich, so deep, so divine, so full of soul, power, and beauty, was the conception.
HENRY WARD BEECHER (1813–1887)

If evolution really works, how come mothers only have two hands?
MILTON BERLE (1908–2002)

Mother's words of wisdom: "Answer me! Don't talk with food in your mouth!"
ERMA BOMBECK (1927–1996)

Who in their infinite wisdom decreed that Little League uniforms be white? Certainly not a mother.
ERMA BOMBECK (1927–1996)

[M]y opinion is that the future good or bad conduct of a child depends on its mother.
MARIA LETIZIA BONAPARTE (1750–1836)

Mothers are the pivot on which the family spins.
PAM BROWN (1948–)

You never realize how much your mother loves you till you explore the attic—and find every letter you ever sent her, every finger painting, clay pot, bead necklace, Easter chicken, cardboard Santa Claus, paperlace Mother's Day card and school report since day one.
PAM BROWN (1948–)

Women know the way to rear up children (to be just). They know a simple, merry, tender knack of tying sashes, fitting baby shoes, and stringing pretty words that make no sense.
ELIZABETH BARRETT BROWNING (1806–1861)

Motherhood: All love begins and ends there.
ROBERT BROWNING (1812–1889)

Mother is the heartbeat in the home; and without her, there seems to be no heart throb.
LEROY BROWNLOW (1914–2002)

My first vivid memory is ... when first I looked into her face and she looked into mine. That I do remember, and that exchanging look I have carried with me all of my life. We recognized each other. I was her child and she was my mother.
PEARL S. BUCK (1892–1973)

Some are kissing mothers and some are scolding mothers, but it is love just the same, and most mothers kiss and scold together.
PEARL S. BUCK (1892–1973)

Being a mother has made my life complete.
DARCY BUSSELL (1969–)

She was the best of all mothers, to whom I owe endless gratitude.
THOMAS CARLYLE (1795–1881)

Who is it that loves me and will love me for ever with an affection which no chance, no misery, no crime of mine can do away? It is you, my mother.
THOMAS CARLYLE (1795–1881)

It seems to me that my mother was the most splendid woman I ever knew..... I have met a lot of people knocking around the world since, but I have never met a more thoroughly refined woman than my mother. If I have amounted to anything, it will be due to her.
CHARLIE CHAPLIN (1889–1977)

I never thought that you should be rewarded for the greatest privilege of life.
MARY ROPER COKER (1908–1975)

A mother is a mother still, the holiest thing alive.
SAMUEL TAYLOR COLERIDGE (1772–1834)

So for the mother's sake the child was dear, and dearer was the mother for the child.
SAMUEL TAYLOR COLERIDGE (1772–1834)

There is a religion in all deep love, but the love of a mother is the veil of a softer light between the heart and the heavenly Father.
SAMUEL TAYLOR COLERIDGE (1772–1834)

I miss thee, my Mother! Thy image is still the deepest impressed on my heart.
ELIZA COOK (1818–1889)

A suburban mother's role is to deliver children obstetrically once, and by car forever after.
PETER DE VRIES (1910–1993)

My mother is a walking miracle.
LEONARDO DICAPRIO (1974–)

A mother is one to whom you hurry when you are troubled.
EMILY DICKINSON (1830–1886)

Mothers don't let your daughters grow up to be models unless you're present.
JANICE DICKINSON (1953–)

Becoming a mother makes you a grown-up. You're all they have. They trust you, they need you. That's all they want. They want to be loved, protected, and supported.
CELINE DION (1968–)

My mother was the making of me. She was so true and so sure of me, I felt that I had someone to live for—someone I must not disappoint. The memory of my mother will always be a blessing to me.
THOMAS A. EDISON (1847–1931)

Life began with waking up and loving my mother's face.
GEORGE ELIOT (1819–1880)

I love my mother dearly, but it wouldn't be suitable for me to live with her all the time.
KEITH EMERSON (1944–)

Men are what their mothers made them.
RALPH WALDO EMERSON (1803–1882)

There never was a child so lovely but his mother was glad to get him asleep.
RALPH WALDO EMERSON (1803–1882)

If pregnancy were a book, they would cut the last two chapters.
NORA EPHRON (1941–)

Oh what a power is mother, possessing a potent spell.
EURIPIDES (C. 480–406 BC)

I affirm my profound belief that God's greatest creation is womanhood. I also believe that there is no greater good in all the world than motherhood. The influence of a mother in the lives of her children is beyond calculation.
JAMES E. FAUST (1920–2007)

God's interest in the human race is nowhere better evinced than in obstetrics.
MARTIN H. FISCHER (1879–1962)

A mother is not a person to lean on, but a person to make leaning unnecessary.
DOROTHY CANFIELD FISHER (1879–1958)

Blaming mother is just a negative way of clinging to her still.
NANCY FRIDAY (1933–)

When I stopped seeing my mother with the eyes of a child, I saw the woman who helped me give birth to myself.
NANCY FRIDAY (1933–)

Strange new problems are being reported in the growing generations of children whose mothers were always there, driving them around, helping them with their homework—an inability to endure pain or discipline or pursue any self-sustained goal of any sort, a devastating boredom with life.
BETTY FRIEDAN (1921–2006)

Mother's love is peace. It need not be acquired, it need not be deserved.
ERICH FROMM (1900–1980)

The mother-child relationship is very paradoxical. It requires the most intense love on the mother's side, yet this very love must help the child grow away from the mother and become fully independent.
ERICH FROMM (1900–1980)

A mother takes twenty years to make a man of her boy, and another woman makes a fool of him in twenty minutes.
ROBERT FROST (1874–1963)

Mothers are the people who love us for no good reason. And those of us who are mothers know it's the most exquisite love of all.
MAGGIE GALLAGHER (1960–)

A mother's love is the fuel that enables a normal human being to do the impossible.
MARION C. GARRETTY

All the earth, though it were full of kind hearts, is but a desolation and a desert place to a mother when her only child is absent.
ELIZABETH GASKELL (1810–1865)

Mother: the most beautiful word on the lips of mankind.
KAHLIL GIBRAN (1883–1931)

It was my mother who gave me my voice. She did this, I know now, by clearing a space where my words could fall, grow, then find their way to others.
PAULA GIDDINGS (1947–)

You may have tangible wealth untold;
Caskets of jewels and coffers of gold.
Richer than I you can never be—
I had a mother who read to me.
STRICKLAND GILLILAN (1869–1954)

My mother's great. She has the major looks. She could stop you from doing anything, through a closed door even, with a single look. Without saying a word, she has that power to rip out your tonsils.
WHOOPI GOLDBERG (1955–)

Only mothers can think of the future—because they give birth to it in their children.
MAXIM GORKY (1868–1936)

As a mother, my job is to take care of what is possible and trust God with the impossible.
RUTH BELL GRAHAM (1920–2007)

There is no influence so powerful as that of the mother.
SARAH J. HALE (1788–1879)

There is none, in all this cold and hollow world, no fount of deep, strong, deathless love, save that within a mother's heart.
FELICIA D. HERMANS (1793–1835)

What are Raphael's Madonnas but the shadow of a mother's love, fixed in a permanent outline forever.
THOMAS WENTWORTH HIGGINSON (1823–1911)

There came a moment quite suddenly a mother realized that a child was no longer hers... without bothering to ask or even give notice, her daughter had just grown up.
ALICE HOFFMAN (1952–)

Youth fades; love droops, the leaves of friendship fall; a mother's secret hope outlives them all.
OLIVER WENDELL HOLMES SR. (1809–1894)

If there were no schools to take the children away from home part of the time, the insane asylums would be filled with mothers.
EDGAR WATSON HOWE (1853–1937)

The worst feature of a new baby is its mother's singing.
KIN HUBBARD (1868–1930)

A mother's arms are made of tenderness and children sleep soundly in them.
VICTOR HUGO (1802–1885)

A mother is the truest friend we have.
WASHINGTON IRVING (1783–1859)

The tie which links mother and child is of such pure and immaculate strength as to never be violated.
WASHINGTON IRVING (1783–1859)

There never was a woman like her. She was gentle as a dove and brave as a lioness.... The memory of my mother and her teachings were, after all, the only capital I had to start life with, and on that capital I have made my way.
ANDREW JACKSON (1767–1845)

Motherhood is priced of God, at price no man may dare to lessen or misunderstand.
HELEN HUNT JACKSON (1830–1885)

Mother's Day is in honor of the best Mother who ever lived—the Mother of your heart.
ANNA JARVIS (1832–1905)

My mother wanted me to be her wings, to fly as she never quite had the courage to do. I love her for that. I love the fact that she wanted to give birth to her own wings.
ERICA JONG (1942–)

I shall never forget my mother, for it was she who planted and nurtured the first seeds of good within me. She opened my heart to the lasting impressions of nature; she awakened my understanding and extended my horizon and her percepts exerted an everlasting influence upon the course of my life.
IMMANUEL KANT (1724–1804)

The mother is the most precious possession of the nation, so precious that society advances its highest well-being when it protects the functions of the mother.
ELLEN KEY (1849–1926)

To be a mother is a woman's greatest vocation in life. She is a partner with God. No being has a position of such power and influence. She holds in her hands the destiny of nations, for to her comes the responsibility and opportunity of molding the nation's citizens.
SPENCER W. KIMBALL (1895–1973)

The strength of motherhood is greater than natural laws.
BARBARA KINGSOLVER (1955–)

If I were hanged on the highest hill,
Mother o' mine, O mother o' mine!
I know whose love would follow me still...
RUDYARD KIPLING (1865–1936)

She was a genius, my mother.
SALLY KIRKLAND (1944–)

Mothers love you to the end, and she didn't want to hold me back from my livelihood. So I left for a month and called her every couple of days. I came home and she died 24 hours later.
LENNY KRAVITZ (1964–)

There is a woman at the beginning of all great things.
ALPHONSE DE LAMARTINE (1790–1869)

Mother's love grows by giving.
CHARLES LAMB (1775–1834)

So mothers everywhere take heart. The indoctrination you administer now may have unanticipated positive effects years later.
ROBERT B. LAUGHLIN (1950–)

She is my first, great love.
D. H. LAWRENCE (1885–1930)

I love being a mother... I am more aware. I feel things on a deeper level. I have a kind of understanding about my body, about being a woman.
SHELLEY LONG (1949–)

A mother always has to think twice, once for herself and once for her child.
SOPHIA LOREN (1934–)

She is my Mother, with a capital "M"; she's something sacred to me.
SOPHIA LOREN (1934–)

That best academy, a mother's knee.
JAMES RUSSELL LOWELL (1819–1891)

All mothers are rich when they love their children. Their love is always the most beautiful of joys.
MAURICE MAETERLINCK (1862–1949)

My mother loved children—she would have given anything if I had been one.
GROUCHO MARX (1890–1977)

Her caress first awakens in the child a sense of security; her kiss the first realization of affection; her sympathy and tenderness, the first assurance that there is love in the world.
DAVID O. MCKAY (1873–1970)

Motherhood is the greatest potential influence in human society.
DAVID O. MCKAY (1873–1970)

The noblest calling in the world is that of mother. True motherhood is the most beautiful of all arts, the greatest of all professions.
DAVID O. MCKAY (1873–1970)

A mother is she who can take the place of all others but whose place no one else can take.
CARDINAL GASPARD MERMILLOD (1824–1892)

Grown don't mean nothing to a mother. A child is a child. They get bigger, older, but grown? What's that suppose to mean? In my heart it don't mean a thing.
TONI MORRISON (1931–)

One must still have chaos in oneself to be able to give birth to a dancing star.
FRIEDRICH NIETZSCHE (1844–1900)

Women as the guardians of children possess a great power. They are the molders of their children's personalities and the arbiters of their development.
ANN OAKLEY (1944–)

Every mother is like Moses. She does not enter the promised land. She prepares a world she will not see.
POPE PAUL VI (1897–1978)

Because I feel that in the heavens above the angels, whispering one to another, can find among their burning tears of love, none so devotional as that of "Mother."
EDGAR ALLAN POE (1809–1849)

You don't appreciate your mother until you're a mother yourself.
CATHERINE PULSIFER (1957–)

A mother's love is patient and forgiving when all others are forsaking, and it never fails or falters, even though the heart is breaking.
HELEN STEINER RICE (1900–1981)

I always wanted children, but not until they were actually part of my life did I realize that I could love that fiercely, or get that angry.
COKIE ROBERTS (1943–)

I think, at a child's birth, if a mother could ask a fairy godmother to endow it with the most useful gift, that gift should be curiosity.
ELEANOR ROOSEVELT (1884–1962)

Her dignity consists in being Anonymous to the world; her glory is in the esteem of her husband; her pleasures in the happiness of her family.
JEAN-JACQUES ROUSSEAU (1712–1778)

When motherhood becomes the fruit of a deep yearning, not the result of ignorance or accident, its children will become the foundation of a new race.
MARGARET SANGER (1879–1966)

There was never a great man who had not a great mother.
OLIVE SCHREINER (1855–1920)

Love still has something of the sea
From whence his mother rose.
SIR CHARLES SEDLEY (1639–1701)

Thou art thy mother's glass, and she in thee
Calls back the lovely April of her prime.
WILLIAM SHAKESPEARE (1564–1616), "Sonnet 3"

And say to mothers what a holy charge is theirs—with what a kingly power their love might rule the fountains of the new-born mind.
LYDIA SIGOURNEY (1791–1865)

For the mother is and must be, whether she knows it or not, the greatest, strongest and most lasting teacher her children have.
HANNAH W. SMITH (1832–1911)

Children are the anchors that hold a mother to life.
SOPHOCLES (496–406 BC)

Women are aristocrats, and it is always the mother who makes us feel that we belong to the better sort.
BISHOP JOHN LANCASTER SPALDING (1840–1916)

Motherhood is not for the fainthearted. Frogs, skinned knees, and the insult of teenage girls are not meant for the wimpy.
DANIELLE STEELE (1947–)

Motherhood has a very humanizing effect. Everything gets reduced to essentials.
MERYL STREEP (1949–)

Mother—that was the bank where we deposited all our hurts and worries.
THOMAS DEWITT TALMAGE (1832–1902)

Who ran to help me when I fell, and would some pretty story tell, or kiss the place to make it well? My mother.
ANN TAYLOR (1782–1866)

Happy he with such a mother! Faith in womankind beats with his blood.
ALFRED, LORD TENNYSON (1809–1892)

The bearing and the training of a child is woman's wisdom.
ALFRED, LORD TENNYSON (1809–1892)

Mother is the name of God in the lips and hearts of children.
WILLIAM MAKEPEACE THACKERAY (1811–1863)

Some things I never learned to like. I didn't like to kiss babies, though I didn't mind kissing their mothers.
PIERRE TRUDEAU (1919–2000)

No one in the world can take the place of your mother.
HARRY S TRUMAN (1884–1972)

A baby is an inestimable blessing and bother.
MARK TWAIN (1835–1910)

My mother had a great deal of trouble with me but I think she enjoyed it.
MARK TWAIN (1835–1910)

My mother had a slender, small body, but a large heart—a heart so large that everybody's joys found welcome in it, and hospitable accommodation.
MARK TWAIN (1835–1910)

And it came to me, and I knew what I had to have before my soul would rest. I wanted to belong—to

belong to my mother. And in return—I wanted my mother to belong to me.
GLORIA VANDERBILT (1924–)

And so our mothers and grandmothers have, more often than not anonymously, handed on the creative spark, the seed of the flower they themselves never hoped to see—or like a sealed letter they could not plainly read.
ALICE WALKER (1944–)

The hand that rocks the cradle is the hand that rules the world.
WILLIAM ROSS WALLACE (1819–1881), "What Rules the World"

In all my efforts to learn to read, my mother shared fully my ambition and sympathized with me and aided me in every way she could. If I have done anything in life worth attention, I feel sure that I inherited the disposition from my mother.
BOOKER T. WASHINGTON (1856–1915)

My mother was the most beautiful woman I ever saw.
GEORGE WASHINGTON (1732–1799)

Mothers are the necessity of invention.
BILL WATTERSON (1958–)

Some women are great mothers at 20 and others are great at 50. If I had done it sooner I wouldn't be doing what I'm doing now.
RUBY WAX (1953–)

She tried in every way to understand me, and she succeeded. It was this deep, loving understanding as long as she lived that more than anything else helped and sustained me on my way to success.
MAE WEST (1892–1980)

Most of all the other beautiful things in life come by twos and threes, by dozens and hundreds. Plenty of roses, stars, sunsets, rainbows, brothers and sisters, aunts and cousins, comrades and friends—but only one mother in the whole world.
KATE DOUGLAS WIGGIN (1856–1923)

All women become like their mothers. That is their tragedy. No man does. That is his.
OSCAR WILDE (1854–1900)

One lamp—thy mother's love—amid the stars
Shall lift its pure flame changeless, and before
The throne of God, burn through eternity—
Holy—as it was lit and lent thee here.
NATHANIEL PARKER WILLIS (1806–1867)

Biology is the least of what makes someone a mother.
OPRAH WINFREY (1954–)

Mama was my greatest teacher, a teacher of compassion, love, and fearlessness. If love is sweet as a flower, then my mother is that sweet flower of love.
STEVIE WONDER (1950–)

Of all the rights of women, the greatest is to be a mother.
LIN YUTANG (1895–1976)

A mother is a person who if she is not there when you get home from school, you wouldn't know how to get your dinner, and you wouldn't feel like eating it anyway.
ANONYMOUS

A mother is someone who dreams great dreams for you, but then she lets you chase the dreams you have for yourself and loves you just the same.
ANONYMOUS

A mother is the one who is still there when everyone else has deserted you.
ANONYMOUS

A mother's children are portraits of herself.
ANONYMOUS

A mother's work is never done.
ANONYMOUS

Children are the sum of what mothers contribute to their lives.
ANONYMOUS

I know you've been the best there is—a mother beyond all compare.
ANONYMOUS

Motherhood ... What a glorious career!
ANONYMOUS

No painter's brush, nor poet's pen in justice to her name, has ever reached half high enough to write a mother's name.
ANONYMOUS

Once upon a memory someone wiped away a tear, held me close and loved me. Thank you, Mother dear.
ANONYMOUS

The best medicine in the world is a mother's kiss.
ANONYMOUS

The joys of motherhood are never fully experienced until the children are in bed.
ANONYMOUS

The mother is queen of that realm and sways a scepter more potent than that of kings or priests.
ANONYMOUS

When it comes to love, Mom's the word.
ANONYMOUS

There is only one pretty child in the world, and every mother has it.
CHINESE PROVERB

A rich child often sits in a poor mother's lap.
DANISH PROVERB

Who takes the child by the hand takes the mother by the heart.
GERMAN PROVERB

A man loves his sweetheart the most, his wife the best, but his mother the longest.
IRISH PROVERB

A mother understands what a child does not say.
JEWISH PROVERB

God could not be everywhere, so He created mothers.
JEWISH PROVERB

An ounce of mother is worth a ton of priest.
SPANISH PROVERB

Motivation

Desire is the key to motivation, but it's determination and commitment to an unrelenting pursuit of your goal—a commitment to excellence—that will enable you to attain the success you seek.
MARIO ANDRETTI (1940–)

Motivation will almost always beat mere talent.
NORMAN R. AUGUSTINE (1935–)

God made man to go by motives, and he will not go without them, any more than a boat without steam or a balloon without gas.
HENRY WARD BEECHER (1813–1887)

One very important aspect of motivation is the willingness to stop and to look at things that no one else has bothered to look at. This simple process of focusing on things that are normally taken for granted is a powerful source of creativity.
EDWARD DE BONO (1933–)

Wanting something is not enough. You must hunger for it. Your motivation must be absolutely compelling in order to overcome the obstacles that will invariably come your way.
LES BROWN (1945–)

If you do not wish a man to do a thing, you had better get him to talk about it; for the more men talk, the more likely they are to do nothing else.
THOMAS CARLYLE (1795–1881)

People who are unable to motivate themselves must be content with mediocrity, no matter how impressive their other talents.
ANDREW CARNEGIE (1835–1919)

There is only one way ... to get anybody to do anything. And that is by making the other person want to do it.
DALE CARNEGIE (1888–1955)

People need motivation to do anything. I don't think human beings learn anything without desperation.
JIM CARREY (1962–)

If you must have motivation, think of your paycheck on Friday.
NOËL COWARD (1899–1973)

Motivation is the art of getting people to do what you want them to do because they want to do it.
DWIGHT D. EISENHOWER (1890–1969)

Who is sure of their own motives can in confidence advance or retreat.
JOHANN WOLFGANG VON GOETHE (1749–1832)

Motivation is simple. You eliminate those who are not motivated.
LOU HOLTZ (1937–)

Motivation is everything. You can do the work of two people, but you can't be two people. Instead, you have to inspire the next guy down the line and get him to inspire his people.
LEE IACOCCA (1924–)

We would frequently be ashamed of our good deeds if people saw all of the motives that produced them.
FRANÇOIS DE LA ROCHEFOUCAULD (1613–1680)

The whole idea of motivation is a trap. Forget motivation. Just do it. Exercise, lose weight, test your blood sugar, or whatever. Do it without motivation. And then, guess what? After you start doing the thing, that's when the motivation comes and makes it easy for you to keep on doing it.
JOHN C. MAXWELL (1947–)

There are two levers for moving men—interest and fear.
NAPOLÉON I (1769–1821)

Motivation is what gets you started. Habit is what keeps you going.
JIM RYUN (1947–)

People often say that motivation doesn't last. Well, neither does bathing—that's why we recommend it daily.
ZIG ZIGLAR (1927–)

Mourning

Mourning is not forgetting.... It is an undoing. Every minute tie has to be untied and something permanent and valuable recovered and assimilated from the dust.
MARGERY ALLINGHAM (1904–1966)

Arms are instruments of ill omen.... When one is compelled to use them, it is best to do so without relish. There is no glory in victory, and to glorify it despite this is to exult in the killing of men.... When great numbers of people are killed, one should weep over them with sorrow. When victorious in war, one should observe mourning rites.
LAO-TZU (C. 600 BC)

Public display of mourning is no longer made by people of fashion, although some flashier kinds of widows may insist on sleeping with only black men during the first year after the death.
P. J. O'ROURKE (1947–)

It is better to go to a house of mourning than to go to a house of feasting, for death is the destiny of everyone; the living should take this to heart.
THE BIBLE, *Ecclesiastes* 7:2

Murder

Murder is unique in that it abolishes the party it injures, so that society has to take the place of the victim and on his behalf demand atonement or grant forgiveness; it is the one crime in which society has a direct interest.
W. H. AUDEN (1907–1973)

The slanderer and the assassin differ only in the weapon they use; with the one it is the dagger, with the other the tongue. The former is worse than the latter, for the last only kills the body, while the other murders the reputation.
TYRON EDWARDS (1809–1894)

He who joyfully marches to music rank and file, has already earned my contempt. He has been given a large brain by mistake, since for him the spinal cord would surely suffice. This disgrace to civilization should be done away with at once. Heroism at command, how violently I hate all this, how despicable and ignoble war is; I would rather be torn to shreds than be a part of so base an action. It is my conviction that killing under the cloak of war is nothing but an act of murder.
ALBERT EINSTEIN (1879–1955)

In films murders are always very clean. I show how difficult it is and what a messy thing it is to kill a man.
ALFRED HITCHCOCK (1899–1980)

Seeing a murder on television ... can help work off one's antagonisms. And if you haven't any antagonisms, the commercials will give you some.
ALFRED HITCHCOCK (1899–1980)

There is nothing more dread and more shameless than a woman who plans such deeds in her heart as the foul deed which she plotted when she contrived her husband's murder.
HOMER (800–700 BC), *The Odyssey*

I count religion but a childish toy,
And hold there is no sin but ignorance.
Birds of the air will tell of murders past.
I am asham'd to hear such fooleries!
CHRISTOPHER MARLOWE (1564–1593), *The Jew of Malta*

One murder makes a villain, millions a hero.
BEILBY PORTEUS (1731–1808)

Kill one man, and you are a murderer. Kill millions of men, and you are a conqueror. Kill them all, and you are a god.
JEAN ROSTAND (1894–1977), *Thoughts of a Biologist*

O, my offence is rank, it smells to heaven;
It hath the primal eldest curse upon 't,
A brother's murder...
WILLIAM SHAKESPEARE (1564–1616), *Hamlet*

Gold is worse poison to a man's soul, doing more murders in this loathsome world, than any mortal drug.
WILLIAM SHAKESPEARE (1564–1616), *Romeo and Juliet*

When a man wants to murder a tiger he calls it sport; when a tiger wants to murder him he calls it ferocity.
GEORGE BERNARD SHAW (1856–1950)

It's just murder. All God's creatures do it. You look in the forests and you see species killing other species, our species killing all species including the forests, and we just call it industry, not murder.
OLIVER STONE (1946–) and
QUENTIN TARANTINO (1963–), *Natural Born Killers*

Civilizations die from suicide, not by murder.
ARNOLD J. TOYNBEE (1889–1975)

It is forbidden to kill; therefore all murderers are punished unless they kill in large numbers and to the sound of trumpets.
VOLTAIRE (1694–1778)

Music

Every composer knows the anguish and despair occasioned by forgetting ideas which one had no time to write down.
LOUIS-HECTOR BERLIOZ (1803–1869)

Many men are melancholy by hearing music, but it is a pleasing melancholy that it causeth; and therefore to such as are discontent, in woe, fear, sorrow, or dejected, it is a most present remedy.
ROBERT BURTON (1577–1640)

If you develop an ear for sounds that are musical it is like developing an ego. You begin to refuse sounds that are not musical and that way cut yourself off from a good deal of experience.
JOHN CAGE (1912–1992)

Music is well said to be the speech of angels.
THOMAS CARLYLE (1795–1881)

Music with dinner is an insult both to the cook and the violinist.
G. K. CHESTERTON (1874–1936)

Music is the refuge of souls ulcerated by happiness.
E. M. CIORAN (1911–1995)

The whole problem can be stated quite simply by asking, "Is there a meaning to music?" My answer would be, "Yes." And "Can you state in so many words what the meaning is?" My answer to that would be, "No."
AARON COPLAND (1900–1990)

I hate music, especially when it's played.
JIMMY DURANTE (1893–1980)

There is no feeling, except the extremes of fear and grief, that does not find relief in music.
GEORGE ELIOT (1819–1880), *The Mill on the Floss*

I think I should have no other mortal wants, if I could always have plenty of music. It seems to infuse strength into my limbs and ideas into my brain. Life seems to go on without effort, when I am filled with music.
GEORGE ELIOT (1819–1880)

Music is the only language in which you cannot say a mean or sarcastic thing.
JOHN ERSKINE (1879–1951)

Opera is when a guy gets stabbed in the back and, instead of bleeding, he sings.
ED GARDNER (1901–1963)

Take a music bath once or twice a week for a few seasons, and you will find that it is to the soul what the water bath is to the body.
OLIVER WENDELL HOLMES SR. (1809–1894)

Among all men on the earth bards have a share of honor and reverence, because the muse has taught them songs and loves the race of bards.
HOMER (800–700 BC), *The Odyssey*

Classical music is the kind we keep thinking will turn into a tune.
KIN HUBBARD (1868–1930)

After silence, that which comes nearest to expressing the inexpressible is music.
ALDOUS HUXLEY (1894–1963), *Music at Night*

Of all noises, I think music is the least disagreeable.
SAMUEL JOHNSON (1709–1784)

Beautiful music is the art of the prophets that can calm the agitations of the soul; it is one of the most magnificent and delightful presents God has given us.
MARTIN LUTHER (1483–1546)

Music is a discipline, and a mistress of order and good manners, she makes the people milder and gentler, more moral and more reasonable.
MARTIN LUTHER (1483–1546)

Music is the art of the prophets and the gift of God.
MARTIN LUTHER (1483–1546)

My heart, which is so full to overflowing, has often been solaced and refreshed by music when sick and weary.
MARTIN LUTHER (1483–1546)

Next to theology I give to music the highest place and honor. And we see how David and all the saints have wrought their godly thoughts into verse, rhyme, and song.
MARTIN LUTHER (1483–1546)

Who has skill in the art of music is of good temperament and fitted for all things.
MARTIN LUTHER (1483–1546)

One good thing about music, when it hits you, you feel no pain.
BOB MARLEY (1945–1981)

Military justice is to justice what military music is to music.
GROUCHO MARX (1890–1977)

Music like religion, unconditionally brings in its train all the moral virtues to the heart it enters, even though that heart is not in the least worthy.
JEAN-BAPTISTE MONTEGUT (1825–1895)

Music inflames temperament.
JIM MORRISON (1943–1971)

Only sick music makes money today.
FRIEDRICH NIETZSCHE (1844–1900), *Der Fall Wagner*

Without music, life would be a mistake.... I would only believe in a God who knew how to dance.
FRIEDRICH NIETZSCHE (1844–1900)

Wagner's music is better than it sounds.
EDGAR WILSON NYE (1850–1896)

I don't know anything about music. In my line you don't have to.
ELVIS PRESLEY (1935–1977)

Music is moonlight in the gloomy night of life.
JEAN PAUL RICHTER (1763–1825)

Ah, music. A magic beyond all we do here!
J. K. ROWLING (1965–), *Harry Potter and the Sorcerer's Stone*

Music is essentially useless, as life is: but both have an ideal extension which lends utility to its conditions.
GEORGE SANTAYANA (1863–1952), *Life of Reason*

On the page it looked nothing. The beginning simple...almost comic. Just a pulse—bassoons and basset horns—like a rusty squeezebox. Then suddenly—high above it—an oboe, a single note, hanging there unwavering, till a clarinet took over and sweetened it into a phrase of such delight! This was no composition by a performing monkey! This was a music I'd never heard. Filled with such longing, such unfulfillable longing, it had me trembling. It seemed to me that I was hearing a voice of God.
PETER SHAFFER (1926–), *Amadeus*

Hell is full of musical amateurs: music is the brandy of the damned.
GEORGE BERNARD SHAW (1856–1950), *Man and Superman*

My music is best understood by children and animals.
IGOR STRAVINSKY (1882–1971)

Music exists for the purpose of growing an admirable heart.
SHINICHI SUZUKI (1898–1998)

We are a spectacular, splendid manifestation of life. We have language. We have affection. We have genes for usefulness, and usefulness is about as close to a "common goal" of nature as I can guess at. And finally, and perhaps best of all, we have music.
LEWIS THOMAS (1913–1993), *The Medusa and the Snail*

Ray Charles' revolutionary approach to music was also reflected in his politics and his deep and abiding commitment to Martin Luther King and the plight of African-Americans. Ray Charles may not have been on the front lines, but he put his money where his mouth was.
DIANE WATSON (1933–)

Mystery

Now comes the mystery.
HENRY WARD BEECHER (1813–1887), last words

At least half the mystery novels published violate the law that the solution, once revealed, must seem to be inevitable.
RAYMOND CHANDLER (1888–1959)

To me there is something thrilling and exalting in the thought that we are drifting forward into a splendid mystery—into something that no mortal eye hath yet seen, and no intelligence has yet declared.
EDWARD CHAPIN (1831–1863)

The important thing is not to stop questioning. Curiosity has its own reason for existing. One cannot help but be in awe when he contemplates the mysteries of eternity, of life, of the marvelous structure of reality. It is enough if one tries merely to comprehend a little of this mystery every day. Never lose a holy curiosity.
ALBERT EINSTEIN (1879–1955)

The mystery of life isn't a problem to solve, but a reality to experience.
FRANK HERBERT (1920–1986), *Dune*

The good man is the teacher of the bad,
And the bad is the material from which the good
may learn.
He who does not value the teacher,
Or greatly care for the material,
Is greatly deluded although he may be learned.
Such is the essential mystery.
LAO-TZU (C. 600 BC)

It is curious to note the old sea-margins of human thought. Each subsiding century reveals some new mystery; we build where monsters used to hide themselves.
HENRY WADSWORTH LONGFELLOW (1807–1882)

The greatest mystery is not that we have been flung at random between the profusion of matter and of the stars, but that within this prison we can draw from ourselves images powerful enough to deny our nothingness.
ANDRÉ MALRAUX (1901–1976)

Any genuine philosophy leads to action and from action back again to wonder, to enduring fact of mystery.
HENRY MILLER (1891–1980)

We must not allow the clock and the calendar to blind us to the fact that each moment of life is a miracle and mystery.
H. G. WELLS (1866–1946)

The true mystery of the world is the visible, not the invisible.
OSCAR WILDE (1854–1900)

Mythology

Myths and creeds are heroic struggles to comprehend the truth in the world.
ANSEL ADAMS (1902–1984)

In every age "the good old days" were a myth. No one ever thought they were good at the time. For every age has consisted of crises that seemed intolerable to the people who lived through them.
BROOKS ATKINSON (1894–1984), *Once Around the Sun*

Myths can't be translated as they did in their ancient soil. We can only find our own meaning in our own time.
MARGARET ATWOOD (1939–)

Mythology, n.: The body of a primitive people's beliefs, concerning its origin, early history, heroes, deities and so forth, as distinguished from the true accounts which it invents later.
AMBROSE BIERCE (1842–1914), *The Devil's Dictionary*

A one sentence definition of mythology? "Mythology" is what we call someone else's religion.
JOSEPH CAMPBELL (1904–1987)

Myths are public dreams, dreams are private myths.
JOSEPH CAMPBELL (1904–1987)

A myth is a religion in which no one any longer believes.
JAMES FEIBLEMAN (1904–1987)

We must not be hampered by yesterday's myths in concentrating on today's needs.
HAROLD S. GENEEN (1910–1997)

I have recently been examining all the known superstitions of the world, and do not find in our particular superstition [Christianity] one redeeming feature. They are all alike founded on fables and mythology.
THOMAS JEFFERSON (1762–1826)

Men do not invent Myths. They only invent fables, and tell lies. True Myths create themselves, and find

their expression in the men who serve their purpose.
DENIS JOHNSTON (1901–1984)

We can keep from a child all knowledge of earlier myths, but we cannot take from him the need for mythology.
CARL JUNG (1875–1961)

The great enemy of the truth is very often not the lie—deliberate, contrived and dishonest—but the myth—persistent, persuasive, and unrealistic. Belief in myths allows the comfort of opinion without the discomfort of thought.
JOHN F. KENNEDY (1917–1963)

The depth of your mythology is the extent of your effectiveness.
JOHN C. MAXWELL (1947–)

If a man is offered a fact which goes against his instincts, he will scrutinize it closely, and unless the evidence is overwhelming, he will refuse to believe it. If, on the other hand, he is offered something which affords a reason for acting in accordance to his instincts, he will accept it even on the slightest evidence. The origin of myths is explained in this way.
BERTRAND RUSSELL (1872–1970)

The myths connected with individual sanctuaries and ceremonies were merely part of the apparatus of the worship; they served to excite the fancy and sustain the interest of the worshipper … no one cared what he believed about its origin.
WILLIAM ROBERTSON SMITH (1846–1894)

Myths are a waste of time. They prevent progression.
BARBRA STREISAND (1942–)

The Bible is a mass of fables and traditions, mere mythology.
MARK TWAIN (1835–1910)

The myths underlying our culture and underlying our common sense have not taught us to feel identical with the universe, but only parts of it, only in it, only confronting it—aliens.
ALAN W. WATTS (1915–1973)

Nakedness

Nakedness is uncomely, as well in mind as body, and it addeth no small reverence to men's manners and actions if they be not altogether open. Therefore set it down: That a habit of secrecy is both politic and moral.
SIR FRANCIS BACON (1909–1992)

Nakedness reveals itself. Nudity is placed on display. The nude is condemned to never being naked. Nudity is a form of dress.
JOHN BERGER (1926–)

The nakedness of woman is the work of God.
WILLIAM BLAKE (1757–1827)

It's only when the tide goes out that you discover who's been swimming naked.
WARREN BUFFETT (1930–)

Nudity is the uniform of the other side … nudity is a shroud.
MILAN KUNDERA (1929–)

Eros will have naked bodies; friendship naked personalities.
C. S. LEWIS (1898–1963)

Clothes make the man. Naked people have little or no influence on society.
MARK TWAIN (1835–1910)

Names

We do what we must, and call it by the best names.
RALPH WALDO EMERSON (1803–1882)

Do not ask the name of the person who seeks a bed for the night. He who is reluctant to give his name is the one who most needs shelter.
VICTOR HUGO (1802–1885)

Forgive your enemies, but never forget their names.
JOHN F. KENNEDY (1917–1963)

They certainly give very strange names to diseases.
PLATO (C. 428–348 BC)

What's in a name? That which we call a rose
By any other name would smell as sweet.
WILLIAM SHAKESPEARE (1564–1616), *Romeo and Juliet*

A name pronounced is the recognition of the individual to whom it belongs. He who can pronounce my name aright, he can call me, and is entitled to my love and service.
HENRY DAVID THOREAU (1817–1862)

Good men must die, but death cannot kill their names.
ANONYMOUS

Nation

There is no legitimacy on earth but in a government which is the choice of the nation.
CHARLES JOSEPH BONAPARTE (1768–1844)

God grant that not only the love of liberty but a thorough knowledge of the rights of man may pervade all the nations of the earth, so that a philosopher may set his foot anywhere on its surface and say: "This is my country."
BENJAMIN FRANKLIN (1706–1790)

With malice toward none, with charity for all, with firmness in the right as God gives us to see the right, let us strive on to finish the work we are in, to bind up the nation's wounds.
ABRAHAM LINCOLN (1809–1865)

A statesman is a politician who places himself at the service of the nation. A politician is a statesman who places the nation at his service.
GEORGES POMPIDOU (1911–1974)

I like to think of us as Clearasil on the face of the nation. Jim Morrison would have said that if he was smart, but he's dead.
LOU REED (1942–)

Big nations are like chickens. They like to make big noises, but very often it is no more than squabbling.
DR. ALBERT SCHWEITZER (1875–1965)

The state has no business in the bedrooms of the nation.
PIERRE TRUDEAU (1919–2000)

Did you know that every two hours the nations of this world spend as much on armaments as they spend on the children of this world every year?
PETER USTINOV (1921–2004)

Surely the nations are like a drop in a bucket; they are regarded as dust on the scales; he weighs the islands as though they were fine dust.
THE BIBLE, Isaiah 40:15

Nationalism

Nationalism is a silly cock crowing on his own dunghill.
RICHARD ALDINGTON (1892–1962)

Traditional nationalism cannot survive the fissioning of the atom. One world or none.
STUART CHASE (1888–1985)

It is not easy to see how the more extreme forms of nationalism can long survive when men have seen the Earth in its true perspective as a single small globe against the stars.
ARTHUR C. CLARKE (1917–)

Patriotism is when love of your own people comes first; nationalism, when hate for people other than your own comes first.
CHARLES DE GAULLE (1890–1970)

Nationalism is an infantile disease. It is the measles of mankind.
ALBERT EINSTEIN (1879–1955)

Nationalism is our form of incest, our idolatry, our insanity. "Patriotism" is its cult. It should hardly be necessary to say, that by "patriotism" I mean that attitude which puts the own nation above humanity,

above the principles of truth and justice; not the loving interest in one's own nation, which is the concern with the nation's spiritual as much as with its material welfare—never with its power over other nations. Just as love for one individual which excludes the love for others is not love, love for one's country which is not part of one's love for humanity is not love, but idolatrous worship.
ERICH FROMM (1900–1980)

Patriotism is proud of a country's virtues and eager to correct its deficiencies; it also acknowledges the legitimate patriotism of other countries, with their own specific virtues. The pride of nationalism, however, trumpets its country's virtues and denies its deficiencies, while it is contemptuous toward the virtues of other countries. It wants to be, and proclaims itself to be, "the greatest," but greatness is not required of a country; only goodness is.
SYDNEY J. HARRIS (1917–1986)

Of the many unforeseen consequences of typography, the emergence of nationalism is, perhaps, the most familiar.
MARSHALL MCLUHAN (1911–1980)

Nationalism is power hunger tempered by self-deception.
GEORGE ORWELL (1903–1950)

Born in iniquity and conceived in sin, the spirit of nationalism has never ceased to bend human institutions to the service of dissension and distress.
THORSTEIN VEBLEN (1857–1929)

[Nationalism is] a set of beliefs taught to each generation in which the Motherland or the Fatherland is an object of veneration and becomes a burning cause for which one becomes willing to kill the children of other Motherlands or Fatherlands.
HOWARD ZINN (1922–)

Native Americans

As to the Indians, the guiding principle was, promise them anything just so long as they get out of the way.
STEPHEN AMBROSE (1936–2002)

Native Americans are the original inhabitants of the land that now constitutes the United States. They have helped develop the fundamental principles of freedom of speech and separation of powers that form the foundation of the United States Government.
JOE BACA (1947–)

During our travels, the Indians entertained me well; and their affection for me was so great, that they utterly refused to leave me there with the others, although the Governor offered them one hundred pounds sterling for me, on purpose to give me a parole to go home.
DANIEL BOONE (1734–1820)

The Indians knew that life was equated with the earth and its resources, that America was a paradise, and they could not comprehend why the intruders from the East were determined to destroy all that was Indian as well as America itself.
DEE BROWN (1908–2002)

Native Americans had only stone and wooden weapons and no animals that could be ridden. Those military advantages repeatedly enabled troops of a few dozen mounted Spaniards to defeat Indian armies numbering in the thousands.
JARED DIAMOND (1937–)

The Native American has been generally despised by his white conquerors for his poverty and simplicity.
CHARLES EASTMAN (1858–1939)

It could probably be shown by facts and figures that there is no distinctively Native American criminal class except Congress.
MARK TWAIN (1835–1910)

A brave man dies but once, a coward many times.
NATIVE AMERICAN PROVERB

Never criticize a man until you've walked a mile in his moccasins.
NATIVE AMERICAN PROVERB

Nature

Nature never makes any blunders, when she makes a fool she means it.
ARCHIBALD ALEXANDER (1772–1871)

In all things of nature there is something of the marvelous.
ARISTOTLE (384–322 BC), *Parts of Animals*

Nature does nothing uselessly.
ARISTOTLE (384–322 BC), *Politics*

One cannot fix one's eyes on the commonest natural production without finding food for a rambling fancy.
JANE AUSTEN (1775–1817), *Mansfield Park*

The subtlety of nature is greater many times over than the subtlety of the senses and understanding.
SIR FRANCIS BACON (1561–1626)

Nature is just enough; but men and women must comprehend and accept her suggestions.
ANTOINETTE BROWN BLACKWELL (1825–1921)

Art is born of the observation and investigation of nature.
CICERO (106–43 BC)

I will go further, and assert that nature without culture can often do more to deserve praise than culture without nature.
CICERO (106–43 BC)

Having had to encounter single-handed during his period of eclipse many physical dangers, he was well aware of the most dangerous element common to them all: of the crushing, paralysing sense of human littleness, which is what really defeats a human struggling with natural forces, alone, far from the eyes of his fellows.
JOSEPH CONRAD (1857–1924)

Nature gives to every time and season some beauties of its own; and from morning to night, as from the cradle to the grave, it is but a succession of changes so gentle and easy that we can scarcely mark their progress.
CHARLES DICKENS (1812–1870)

Nature and Books belong to the eyes that see them.
RALPH WALDO EMERSON (1803–1882)

Nature magically suits a man to his fortunes, by making them the fruit of his character.
RALPH WALDO EMERSON (1803–1882)

To speak truly, few adult persons can see nature. Most persons do not see the sun. At least they have a very superficial seeing. The sun illuminates only the eye of the man, but shines into the eye and heart of the child.
RALPH WALDO EMERSON (1803–1882)

The best remedy for those who are afraid, lonely, or unhappy is to go outside, somewhere where they can be quiet, alone with the heavens, nature, and God. Because only then does one feel that all is as it should be and that God wishes to see people happy, amidst the simple beauty of nature.
ANNE FRANK (1929–1945)

Nature is wont to hide herself.
HERACLITUS (C. 535–475 BC), *On the Universe*

Art may make a suit of clothes: but nature must produce a man.
DAVID HUME (1711–1776)

Human subtlety will never devise an invention more beautiful, more simple or more direct than does nature because in her inventions nothing is lacking, and nothing is superfluous.
LEONARDO DA VINCI (1452–1519)

The mountain teaches stability and grandeur; the ocean immensity and change. Forests, lakes, and rivers, clouds and winds, stars and flowers, stupendous glaciers and crystal snowflakes—every form of animate or inanimate existence leaves its impress upon the world.
ORISON SWETT MARDEN (1850–1924)

If you can't be in awe of Mother Nature, there's something wrong with you.
ALEX TREBEK (1940–)

It is not true that equality is a law of nature. Nature has no equality. Its sovereign law is subordination and dependence.
MARQUIS DE VAUVENARGUES (1715–1747)

If people think nature is their friend, then they sure don't need an enemy.
KURT VONNEGUT JR. (1922–2007)

Adapt or perish, now as ever, is nature's inexorable imperative.
H. G. WELLS (1866–1946)

It's amazing how quickly nature consumes human places after we turn our backs on them. Life is a hungry thing.
SCOTT WESTERFELD (1963–), *Peeps*

I would feel more optimistic about a bright future for man if he spent less time proving that he can outwit Nature and more time tasting her sweetness and respecting her seniority.
E. B. WHITE (1899–1985)

After you have exhausted what there is in business, politics, conviviality, and so on—have found that none of these finally satisfy, or permanently wear—what remains? Nature remains.
WALT WHITMAN (1819–1892)

A vacuum is a hell of a lot better than some of the stuff that nature replaces it with.
TENNESSEE WILLIAMS (1911–1983), *Cat on a Hot Tin Roof*

I believe in God, only I spell it Nature.
FRANK LLOYD WRIGHT (1869–1959)

The goal of life is living in agreement with nature.
ZENO (335–264 BC)

Necessity

If necessity is the mother of invention, it's the father of cooperation. And we're cooperating like never before.
JOHN ASHCROFT (1942–)

The wise are instructed by reason; ordinary minds by experience; the stupid, by necessity; and brutes by instinct.
CICERO (106–43 BC)

Necessity has no law.
OLIVER CROMWELL (1599–1658)

Necessity makes an honest man a knave.
DANIEL DEFOE (1660–1731)

Discontent is the first necessity of progress.
THOMAS A. EDISON (1847–1931)

Necessity never made a good bargain.
BENJAMIN FRANKLIN (1706–1790)

Necessity has no law.
WILLIAM LANGLAND (1332–1400)

Necessity is the plea for every infringement of human freedom. It is the argument of tyrants; it is the creed of slaves.
WILLIAM PITT (1708–1778)

Necessity is the mother of invention.
PLATO (C. 428–348 BC)

Not even the gods fight against necessity.
SIMONIDES (556–468 BC)

Neglect

People are always neglecting something they can do in trying to do something they can't do.
EDGAR WATSON HOWE (1853–1937)

No man is well pleased to have his all neglected, be it ever so little.
SAMUEL JOHNSON (1709–1784)

When making your choice in life, do not neglect to live.
SAMUEL JOHNSON (1709–1784)

More business is lost every year through neglect than through any other cause.
ROSE F. KENNEDY (1890–1995)

It is no profit to have learned well, if you neglect to do well.
PUBLILIUS SYRUS (C. 100 BC)

Indifference and neglect often do much more damage than outright dislike.
J. K. ROWLING (1965–), *Harry Potter and the Order of the Phoenix*

I, thus neglecting worldly ends, all dedicated
To closeness and the bettering of my mind.
WILLIAM SHAKESPEARE (1564–1616), *The Tempest*

Perpetual devotion to what a man calls his business is only to be sustained by perpetual neglect of many other things.
ROBERT LOUIS STEVENSON (1850–1894)

Neglect will sooner kill an injury than revenge.
LATIN PROVERB

Negotiation

Negotiation in the classic diplomatic sense assumes parties more anxious to agree than to disagree.
DEAN ACHESON (1893–1971)

Let us never negotiate out of fear. But, let us never fear to negotiate.
JOHN F. KENNEDY (1917–1963)

The freedom of the city is not negotiable. We cannot negotiate with those who say, "What's mine is mine and what's yours is negotiable."
JOHN F. KENNEDY (1917–1963)

Given a fair wind, we will negotiate our way into the Common Market, head held high, not crawling in. Negotiations? Yes. Unconditional acceptance of whatever terms are offered us? No.
HAROLD WILSON (1916–1995)

Neurosis

Neurosis is the natural, logical development of an individual who is comparatively inactive, filled with a personal, egocentric striving for superiority, and is therefore retarded in the development of his social interest…
ALFRED ADLER (1870–1937)

Neurosis is the inability to tolerate ambiguity.
SIGMUND FREUD (1856–1939)

National isolation breeds national neurosis.
HUBERT H. HUMPHREY (1911–1978)

Neurosis is always a substitute for legitimate suffering.
CARL JUNG (1875–1961)

Neurosis is the way of avoiding non-being by avoiding being.
PAUL TILLICH (1886–1965)

Every neurosis is a primitive form of legal proceeding in which the accused carries on the prosecution, imposes judgment and executes the sentence: all to the end that someone else should not perform the same process.
LIONEL TRILLING (1905–1975)

A neurosis is a secret that you don't know you are keeping.
KENNETH TYNAN (1927–1980)

Neutrality

The darkest places in hell are reserved for those who maintain their neutrality in times of moral crisis.
DANTE ALIGHIERI (1265–1321)

Washing one's hands of the conflict between the powerful and the powerless means to side with the powerful, not to be neutral.
PAULO FREIRE (1921–1997)

When once a man has made celebrity necessary to his happiness, he has put it in the power of the weakest and most timorous malignity, if not to take away his satisfaction, at least to withhold it. His enemies may indulge their pride by airy negligence

and gratify their malice by quiet neutrality.
SAMUEL JOHNSON (1709–1784)

Sometimes I get the feeling the whole world is against me, but deep down I know that's not true. Some smaller countries are neutral.
ROBERT ORBEN (1927–)

For manipulation to be most effective, evidence of its presence should be nonexistent.... It is essential, therefore, that people who are manipulated believe in the neutrality of their key social institutions.
HERBERT SCHILLER (1919–2000)

The News

The one function that TV news performs very well is that when there is no news we give it to you with the same emphasis as if there were.
DAVID BRINKLEY (1920–2003)

Television news is like a lightning flash. It makes a loud noise, lights up everything around it, leaves everything else in darkness and then is suddenly gone.
HODDING CARTER JR. (1907–1972)

It is better to be making the news than taking it; to be an actor rather than a critic.
SIR WINSTON CHURCHILL (1874–1965)

News is that which comes from the North, East, West and South, and if it comes from only one point on the compass, then it is a class publication and not news.
BENJAMIN DISRAELI (1804–1881)

Everyone has inside of him a piece of good news. The good news is that you don't know how great you can be! How much you can love! What you can accomplish! And what your potential is!
ANNE FRANK (1929–1945)

Nowadays truth is the greatest news.
THOMAS FULLER (1608–1661)

If it's far away, it's news, but if it's close at home, it's sociology.
JAMES RESTON (1909–1995)

To a philosopher all news, as it is called, is gossip, and they who edit it and read it are old women over their tea.
HENRY DAVID THOREAU (1817–1862)

When we hear news we should always wait for the sacrament of confirmation.
VOLTAIRE (1694–1778)

Bad news travels fast.
AMERICAN PROVERB

Newspapers

I never did like the idea of sitting on newspapers. I did it once, and all the headlines came off on my white pants. On the level! It actually happened. Nobody bought a paper that day. They just followed me around over town and read the news on the seat of my pants.
SAMUEL HOPKINS ADAMS (1871–1958) and ROBERT RISKIN (1897–1955), *It Happened One Night*

Trying to be a first-rate reporter on the average American newspaper is like trying to play Bach's "St. Matthew's Passion" on a ukulele.
BEN BAGDIKIAN (1920–)

Rage is the only quality which has kept me, or anybody I have ever studied, writing columns for newspapers.
JIMMY BRESLIN (1930–)

You must have a room, or a certain hour or so a day, where you don't know what was in the newspapers that morning ... a place where you can simply experience and bring forth what you are and what you might be.
JOSEPH CAMPBELL (1904–1987)

To read a newspaper is to refrain from reading something worthwhile. The first discipline of education must therefore be to refuse resolutely to

feed the mind with canned chatter.
ALEISTER CROWLEY (1875–1947)

A newspaper consists of just the same number of words, whether there be any news in it or not.
HENRY FIELDING (1707–1754)

Being a newspaper columnist is like marrying a nymphomaniac—it's great for the first two weeks.
LEWIS GRIZZARD (1946–1994)

Trying to determine what is going on in the world by reading newspapers is like trying to tell the time by watching the second hand of a clock.
BEN HECHT (1893–1964)

Editor: a person employed by a newspaper, whose business it is to separate the wheat from the chaff, and to see that the chaff is printed.
ELBERT HUBBARD (1856–1915)

Advertisements … contain the only truths to be relied on in a newspaper.
THOMAS JEFFERSON (1743–1826)

I do not take a single newspaper, nor read one a month, and I feel myself infinitely the happier for it.
THOMAS JEFFERSON (1743–1826)

The man who reads nothing at all is better educated than the man who reads nothing but newspapers.
THOMAS JEFFERSON (1743–1826)

There are … people in this world who seldom pick up a newspaper, people who, when watching television, sneer in displeasure and change channels at the first glimpse of an anchorperson. While such willfully uninformed citizens are rare, emerging from seclusion only to serve on juries in trials of great national significance, they do exist.
JOE KEENAN (1896–1984)

Newspapermen learn to call a murderer "an alleged murderer" and the King of England "the alleged King of England" to avoid libel suits.
STEPHEN LEACOCK (1869–1944)

People everywhere confuse what they read in newspapers with news.
A. J. LIEBLING (1904–1963)

Once a newspaper touches a story, the facts are lost forever, even to the protagonists.
NORMAN MAILER (1923–2007)

All successful newspapers are ceaselessly querulous and bellicose. They never defend anyone or anything if they can help it; if the job is forced on them, they tackle it by denouncing someone or something else.
H. L. MENCKEN (1880–1956)

Newspapers should have no friends.
JOSEPH PULITZER (1847–1911)

It's amazing that the amount of news that happens in the world every day always just exactly fits the newspaper.
JERRY SEINFELD (1954–)

Half of the American people have never read a newspaper. Half never voted for president. One hopes it is the same half.
GORE VIDAL (1925–)

Nihilism

Liberal capitalism is not at all the good of humanity. Quite the contrary; it is the vehicle of savage, destructive nihilism.
ALAIN BADIOU (1937–)

The modern mind is in complete disarray. Knowledge has stretched itself to the point where neither the world nor our intelligence can find any foot-hold. It is a fact that we are suffering from nihilism.
ALBERT CAMUS (1913–1960)

The way I devolved, moved out from, this position of strict cognitive nihilism, was with the idea of building a new culture.
HENRY FLYNT (1909–)

Nihilism is best done by professionals.
IGGY POP (1947–)

Nobility

No one can build his security upon the nobleness of another person.
WILLA CATHER (1873–1947)

I too shall lie in the dust when I am dead, but now let me win noble renown.
HOMER (800–700 BC), *The Iliad*

It is nobler to declare oneself wrong than to insist on being right—especially when one is right.
FRIEDRICH NIETZSCHE (1844–1900), *Thus Spoke Zarathustra*

Sweet mercy is nobility's true badge.
WILLIAM SHAKESPEARE (1564–1616), *Titus Andronicus*

They are never alone that are accompanied with noble thoughts.
SIR PHILIP SIDNEY (1554–1586)

Put more trust in nobility of character than in an oath.
SOLON (638-559 BC)

Life ought to be a struggle of desire toward adventures whose nobility will fertilize the soul.
REBECCA WEST (1892–1983)

Whenever a man does a thoroughly stupid thing, it is always from the noblest motives.
OSCAR WILDE (1854–1900), *The Picture of Dorian Gray*

Noble life demands a noble architecture for noble uses of noble men. Lack of culture means what it has always meant: ignoble civilization and therefore imminent downfall.
FRANK LLOYD WRIGHT (1869–1959)

The truth is that there is nothing noble in being superior to somebody else. The only real nobility is in being superior to your former self.
WHITNEY YOUNG (1921–1971)

Noise

Man is a great blunderer going about in the woods, and there is no other except the bear makes so much noise.
MARY AUSTIN (1868–1934)

Movie music is noise … even more painful than my sciatica.
THOMAS BEECHAM (1879–1961)

Phonograph, n.: An irritating toy that restores life to dead noises.
AMBROSE BIERCE (1842–1914), *The Devil's Dictionary*

Television news is like a lightning flash. It makes a loud noise, lights up everything around it, leaves everything else in darkness and then is suddenly gone.
HODDING CARTER JR. (1907–1972)

Noise is an easy thing to hide behind. If you make a lot of noise and shout behind that, nobody can tell what you're singing.
JARVIS COCKER (1963–)

Nonsense and noise will oft prevail, when honour and affection fail.
WILLIAM LLOYD GARRISON (1805–1879)

Of all noises, I think music is the least disagreeable.
SAMUEL JOHNSON (1709–1784)

Accustomed to the veneer of noise, to the shibboleths of promotion, public relations, and market research, society is suspicious of those who value silence.
JOHN LAHR (1941–)

He who establishes his argument by noise and command, shows that his reason is weak.
MICHEL DE MONTAIGNE (1533–1592)

Ten people who speak make more noise than ten thousand who are silent.
NAPOLÉON I (1769–1821)

Love is two minutes fifty-two seconds of squishing noises. It shows your mind isn't clicking right.
JOHNNY ROTTEN (1956–)

How about a little noise. How do you expect a man to putt?
GEORGE HERMAN "BABE" RUTH JR. (1895–1948)

Noise is the most impertinent of all forms of interruption. It is not only an interruption, but is also a disruption of thought.
ARTHUR SCHOPENHAUER (1788–1860)

The amount of noise which anyone can bear undisturbed stands in inverse proportion to his mental capacity.
ARTHUR SCHOPENHAUER (1788–1860)

In lieu whereof, I pray you, bear me hence
From forth the noise and rumour of the field,
Where I may think the remnant of my thoughts
In peace, and part this body and my soul
With contemplation and devout desires.
WILLIAM SHAKESPEARE (1564–1616), *King John*

To refuse awards is another way of accepting them with more noise than is normal.
PETER USTINOV (1921–2004)

Nonconformity

It gives me great pleasure indeed to see the stubbornness of an incorrigible nonconformist warmly acclaimed.
ALBERT EINSTEIN (1879–1955)

Nonconformists travel as a rule in bunches. You rarely find a nonconformist who goes it alone. And woe to him inside a nonconformist clique who does not conform with nonconformity
ERIC HOFFER (1902–1983)

The hope of a secure and livable world lies with disciplined nonconformists who are dedicated to justice, peace, and brotherhood.
MARTIN LUTHER KING JR. (1929–1968)

Yes, I see the Church as the body of Christ. But, oh! How we have blemished and scarred that body through social neglect and through fear of being nonconformists.
MARTIN LUTHER KING JR. (1929–1968)

Read, every day, something no one else is reading. Think, every day, something no one else is thinking. Do, every day, something no one else would be silly enough to do. It is bad for the mind to be always part of unanimity.
CHRISTOPHER MORLEY (1890–1957)

Why do you have to be a nonconformist like everybody else?
JAMES THURBER (1894–1961)

If there is anything the nonconformist hates worse than a conformist it's another nonconformist who doesn't conform to the prevailing standard of nonconformity.
BILL VAUGHAN (1915–1977)

Nonsense

All philosophies, if you ride them home, are nonsense, but some are greater nonsense than others.
SAMUEL BUTLER (1835–1902)

A little nonsense now and then, is relished by the wisest men.
ROALD DAHL (1916–1990)

There is no nonsense so gross that society will not, at some time, make a doctrine of it and defend it with every weapon of communal stupidity.
ROBERTSON DAVIES (1913–1995)

Finish each day and be done with it. You have done what you could. Some blunders and absurdities no doubt crept in; forget them as soon as you can. Tomorrow is a new day; begin it well and serenely and with too high a spirit to be encumbered with your old nonsense.
RALPH WALDO EMERSON (1803–1882)

Forgive me my nonsense as I also forgive the nonsense of those who think they talk sense.
ROBERT FROST (1874–1963)

It is a far, far better thing to have a firm anchor in nonsense than to put out on the troubled sea of thought.
JOHN KENNETH GALBRAITH (1908–2006)

Creationist critics often charge that evolution cannot be tested, and therefore cannot be viewed as a properly scientific subject at all. This claim is rhetorical nonsense.
STEPHEN JAY GOULD (1941 – 2002)

'Tis the privilege of friendship to talk nonsense, and have her nonsense respected.
CHARLES LAMB (1775–1834)

Can a mortal ask questions which God finds unanswerable? Quite easily, I should think. All nonsense questions are unanswerable.
C. S. LEWIS (1898–1963)

There is no nonsense so errant that it cannot be made the creed of the vast majority by adequate governmental action.
BERTRAND RUSSELL (1872–1970)

Skeptical scrutiny is the means, in both science and religion, by which deep insights can be winnowed from deep nonsense.
CARL SAGAN (1934–1996)

I like nonsense, it wakes up the brain cells. Fantasy is a necessary ingredient in living. It's a way of looking at life through the wrong end of a telescope. Which is what I do, and that enables you to laugh at life's realities.
THEODOR SEUSS GEISEL (1904–1991)

Wherever you come near the human race there's layers and layers of nonsense.
THORNTON WILDER (1897–1975), *Our Town*

Confidence in nonsense is a requirement for the creative process.
ANONYMOUS

Nonviolence

The only thing that's been a worse flop than the organization of non-violence has been the organization of violence.
JOAN BAEZ (1941–)

It is better to be violent, if there is violence in our hearts, than to put on the cloak of nonviolence to cover impotence.
MAHATMA GANDHI (1869–1948)

Nonviolence is the answer to the crucial political and moral questions of our time; the need for mankind to overcome oppression and violence without resorting to oppression and violence. Mankind must evolve for all human conflict a method which rejects revenge, aggression, and retaliation. The foundation of such a method is love.
MARTIN LUTHER KING JR. (1929–1968)

Normalcy

I am very abnormal.... But it wasn't very long ago that I wasn't so abnormal. I was very normal and headed for a lifetime of paying medical bills as proof of my normalcy.
DIRK BENEDICT (1945–)

If you say city to people, people have no problem thinking of the city as rife with problematic, screwed-up people, but if you say suburbs—and I'm not the first person to say this, it's been said over and over again in literature—there's a sense of normalcy.
ERIC BOGOSIAN (1953–)

I love the normalcy of Cleveland. There's regular people there.
DREW CAREY (1961–)

Normal is getting dressed in clothes that you buy for work and driving through traffic in a car that you are still paying for—in order to get to the job you need to pay for the clothes and the car, and the house you leave vacant all day so you can afford to live in it.
ELLEN GOODMAN (1941–)

The adjuration to be "normal" seems shockingly repellent to me; I see neither hope nor comfort in sinking to that low level. I think it is ignorance that makes people think of abnormality only with horror and allows them to remain undismayed at the proximity of "normal" to average and mediocre. For surely anyone who achieves anything is, essentially, abnormal.
DR. KARL A. MENNINGER (1893–1990)

Novels

The best part of the fiction in many novels is the notice that the characters are purely imaginary.
FRANKLIN P. ADAMS (1881–1960)

Love is more pleasant than marriage for the same reason that novels are more amusing than history.
NICOLAS CHAMFORT (1741–1794)

At least half the mystery novels published violate the law that the solution, once revealed, must seem to be inevitable.
RAYMOND CHANDLER (1888–1959)

It's with bad sentiments that one makes good novels.
ALDOUS HUXLEY (1894–1963)

The light that radiates from the great novels time can never dim, for human existence is perpetually being forgotten by man, and thus the novelists' discoveries, however old they may be, will never cease to astonish.
MILAN KUNDERA (1929–)

Life resembles a novel more often than novels resemble life.
GEORGE SAND (1804–1876)

I think that novels that leave out technology misrepresent life as badly as Victorians misrepresented life by leaving out sex.
KURT VONNEGUT JR. (1922–2007), *A Man Without a Country*

One should not be too severe on English novels; they are the only relaxation of the intellectually unemployed.
OSCAR WILDE (1854–1900)

Numbers

The creator of the universe works in mysterious ways. But he uses a base ten counting system and likes round numbers.
SCOTT ADAMS (1957–)

There are 10^{11} stars in the galaxy. That used to be a huge number. But it's only a hundred billion. It's less than the national deficit! We used to call them astronomical numbers. Now we should call them economical numbers.
RICHARD FEYNMAN (1918–1988)

Beyond a critical point within a finite space, freedom diminishes as numbers increase. ...The human question is not how many can possibly survive within the system, but what kind of existence is possible for those who do survive.
FRANK HERBERT (1920–1986), *Dune*

To grow old is to grow common. Old age equalizes—we are aware that what is happening to us has happened to untold numbers from the beginning of time. When we are young we act as if we were the first young people in the world.
ERIC HOFFER (1902–1983)

The teacher pretended that algebra was a perfectly natural affair, to be taken for granted, whereas I didn't even know what numbers were. Mathematics classes became sheer terror and torture to me. I was so intimidated by my incomprehension that I did not dare to ask any questions.
CARL JUNG (1875–1961)

Why is it that we entertain the belief that for every purpose odd numbers are the most effectual?
PLINY THE ELDER (AD 23–79)

This is the third time; I hope good luck lies in odd numbers.... There is divinity in odd numbers, either in nativity, chance, or death.
WILLIAM SHAKESPEARE (1564–1616), *The Merry Wives of Windsor*

There is no safety in numbers, or in anything else.
JAMES THURBER (1894–1961), *The Fairly Intelligent Fly*

Statistics show that we lose more fools on this day than on all other days of the year put together. This proves, by the numbers left in stock, that one Fourth of July per year is now inadequate, the country has grown so.
MARK TWAIN (1835–1910)

Economists are people who work with numbers but who don't have the personality to be accountants.
ANONYMOUS

Oaths

Oaths are but words, and words are but wind.
SAMUEL BUTLER (1835–1902)

A liar is always lavish of oaths.
PIERRE CORNEILLE (1606–1684)

Oaths are the fossils of piety.
GEORGE SANTAYANA (1863–1952)

Put more trust in nobility of character than in an oath.
SOLON (638–559 BC)

Obedience

A boy can learn a lot from a dog: obedience, loyalty, and the importance of turning around three times before lying down.
ROBERT BENCHLEY (1889–1945)

There was a time when we expected nothing of our children but obedience, as opposed to the present, when we expect everything of them but obedience.
ANATOLE BROYARD (1920–1990)

In a republic the first rule for the guidance of the citizen is obedience of the law.
CALVIN COOLIDGE (1872–1933)

He that cannot obey, cannot command.
BENJAMIN FRANKLIN (1706–1790)

Rebellion against tyrants is obedience to God.
BENJAMIN FRANKLIN (1706–1790) and THOMAS JEFFERSON (1743–1826)

Wherever there is authority, there is a natural inclination to disobedience.
THOMAS C. HALIBURTON (1796–1865)

The strongest is never strong enough to be always the master, unless he transforms strength into right, and obedience into duty.
JEAN-JACQUES ROUSSEAU (1712–1778), *The Social Contract*

When you think of the long and gloomy history of man, you will find more hideous crimes have been committed in the name of obedience than have ever been committed in the name of rebellion.
C. P. SNOW (1905–1980)

Disobedience, in the eyes of anyone who has read history, is man's original virtue. It is through disobedience and rebellion that progress has been made.
OSCAR WILDE (1854–1900), *The Soul of Man Under Socialism*

Obesity

The number of kids affected by obesity has tripled since 1980, and this can be traced in large part to lack of exercise and a healthy diet.
VIRGINIA FOXX (1943–)

Exercise is one of the best ways in preventing the rapid growth of obesity in America.
LEE HANEY (1959–)

The correlation between poverty and obesity can be traced to agricultural policies and subsidies.
MICHAEL POLLAN (1955–)

I couldn't open up a magazine, you couldn't read a newspaper, you couldn't turn on the TV without hearing about the obesity epidemic in America.
MORGAN SPURLOCK (1970–)

Objectives

We succeed only as we identify in life, or in war, or in anything else, a single overriding objective, and make all other considerations bend to that one objective.
DWIGHT D. EISENHOWER (1890–1969)

A straight path never leads anywhere except to the objective.
ANDRÉ GIDE (1869–1951)

In a balanced organization, working towards a common objective, there is success.
SIR ARTHUR HELPS (1813–1875)

Failure comes only when we forget our ideals and objectives and principles.
JAWAHARLAL NEHRU (1889–1964)

Plan backwards as well as forward. Set objectives and trace back to see how to achieve them. You may find that no path can get you there. Plan forward to see where your steps will take you, which may not be clear or intuitive.
DONALD H. RUMSFELD (1932–)

You are a product of your environment. So choose the environment that will best develop you toward your objective. Analyze your life in terms of its environment. Are the things around you helping you toward success—or are they holding you back?
CLEMENT STONE (1902–2002)

Objectivity

It is impossible to experience one's death objectively and still carry a tune.
WOODY ALLEN (1935–)

We journalists make it a point to know very little about an extremely wide variety of topics; this is how we stay objective.
DAVE BARRY (1947–)

Diplomacy is a disguised war, in which states seek to gain by barter and intrigue, by the cleverness of arts, the objectives which they would have to gain more clumsily by means of war.
RANDOLPH BOURNE (1886–1918)

A creation needs not only subjectivity, but also objectivity.
STEPHEN CHOW (1962–)

The director comes in, and he's supposed to take all of this subjectivity and hone it down into some sense of objectivity.
RICHARD DONNER (1930–)

[O]ne of the strongest motives that lead men to art and science is escape from everyday life with its painful crudity and hopeless dreariness, from the fetters of one's own ever-shifting desires. A finely tempered nature longs to escape from the personal life into the world of objective perception and thought.
ALBERT EINSTEIN (1879–1955)

An objective truth and individual reason are feared above all.
JIMMY JOHNSON (1943–)

Show me a man who claims he is objective and I'll show you a man with illusions.
HENRY R. LUCE (1898–1967)

Dispassionate objectivity is itself a passion, for the real and for the truth.
ABRAHAM MASLOW (1908–1970)

Oblivion

The stream of thought flows on; but most of its segments fall into the bottomless abyss of oblivion. Of some, no memory survives the instant of their passage. Of others, it is confined to a few moments,

hours, or days. Others, again, leave vestiges which are indestructible, and by means of which they may be recalled as long as life endures.
WILLIAM JAMES (1842–1910)

Life is a warfare and a stranger's sojourn, and after fame is oblivion.
MARCUS AURELIUS ANTONIUS (121–180)

How frequently are the honesty and integrity of a man disposed of by a smile or a shrug. How many good and generous actions have been sunk into oblivion by a distrustful look, or stamped with the imputation of bad motives, by a mysterious and seasonable whisper!
LAWRENCE STERNE (1713–1768)

Fame is a vapor; popularity an accident; the only earthly certainty is oblivion.
MARK TWAIN (1835–1910)

Ignorance is not bliss, it is oblivion.
PHILIP WYLIE (1902–1971)

Beware of too much laughter, for it deadens the mind and produces oblivion.
THE TALMUD

Obscenity

It is only the great men who are truly obscene. If they had not dared to be obscene, they could never have dared to be great.
HENRY HAVELOCK ELLIS (1859–1939)

Women should be obscene and not heard.
GROUCHO MARX (1890–1977)

Obscenity is what happens to shock some elderly and ignorant magistrate.
BERTRAND RUSSELL (1872–1970)

Obscurity

It is folly for an eminent person to think of escaping censure, and a weakness to be affected by it. All the illustrious persons of antiquity, and indeed of every age, have passed through this fiery persecution. There is no defense against reproach but obscurity; it is a kind of concomitant to greatness, as satires and invectives were an essential part of a Roman triumph.
JOSEPH ADDISON (1672–1719)

Ten thousand fools proclaim themselves into obscurity, while one wise man forgets himself into immortality.
MARTIN LUTHER KING JR. (1929–1968)

Glory is fleeting, but obscurity is forever.
NAPOLÉON I (1769–1821)

Learn to be pleased with everything; with wealth, so far as it makes us beneficial to others; with poverty, for not having much to care for; and with obscurity, for being unenvied.
PLUTARCH (AD 46–120)

Observation

Do not believe in anything simply because you have heard it. Do not believe in anything simply because it is spoken and rumored by many. Do not believe in anything simply because it is found written in your religious books. Do not believe in anything merely on the authority of your teachers and elders. Do not believe in traditions because they have been handed down for many generations. But after observation and analysis, when you find that anything agrees with reason and is conducive to the good and benefit of one and all, then accept it and live up to it.
THE BUDDHA (563–483 BC)

Our observation of nature must be diligent, our reflection profound, and our experiments exact. We rarely see these three means combined; and for this reason, creative geniuses are not common.
DENIS DIDEROT (1713–1784)

There are three principal means of acquiring knowledge ... observation of nature, reflection, and experimentation. Observation collects facts;

reflection combines them; experimentation verifies the result of that combination.
DENIS DIDEROT (1713–1784)

For the truth of the conclusions of physical science, observation is the supreme Court of Appeal. It does not follow that every item which we confidently accept as physical knowledge has actually been certified by the Court; our confidence is that it would be certified by the Court if it were submitted. But it does follow that every item of physical knowledge is of a form which might be submitted to the Court. It must be such that we can specify (although it may be impracticable to carry out) an observational procedure which would decide whether it is true or not. Clearly a statement cannot be tested by observation unless it is an assertion about the results of observation. Every item of physical knowledge must therefore be an assertion of what has been or would be the result of carrying out a specified observational procedure.
SIR ARTHUR EDDINGTON (1882–1944),
The Philosophy of Physical Science

In the field of observation, chance favors only the prepared mind.
LOUIS PASTEUR (1822–1895)

The power of accurate observation is commonly called cynicism by those who have not got it.
GEORGE BERNARD SHAW (1856–1950)

Practical observation commonly consists of collecting a few facts and loading them with guesses.
ANONYMOUS

Obsession

People can get obsessed with romance; they can get obsessed with political paranoia; they can get obsessed with horror. It isn't the fault of the subject matter that creates the obsession, I don't think.
ADAM ARKIN (1956–)

Obsession is a young man's game, and my only excuse is that I never grew old.
MICHAEL CAINE (1933–)

Without obsession, life is nothing.
JOHN WATERS (1946–)

Obstacles

Courage and perseverance have a magical talisman, before which difficulties disappear and obstacles vanish into air.
JOHN QUINCY ADAMS (1767–1848)

A good intention but fixed and resolute, bent on high and holy ends, we shall find means to them on every side and at every moment; and even obstacles and opposition will but make us "like the fabled specter-ships," which sail the fastest in the very teeth of the wind.
RALPH WALDO EMERSON (1803–1882)

[O]bstacles do not exist to be surrendered to, but only to be broken.
ADOLF HITLER (1889–1945), *Mein Kampf*

It still holds true that man is most uniquely human when he turns obstacles into opportunities.
ERIC HOFFER (1902–1983)

Obstacles cannot crush me. Every obstacle yields to stern resolve. He who is fixed to a star does not change his mind.
LEONARDO DA VINCI (1452–1519)

We find no real satisfaction or happiness in life without obstacles to conquer and goals to achieve.
MAXWELL MALTZ (1899–1975)

Most of our obstacles would melt away if, instead of cowering before them, we should make up our minds to walk boldly through them.
ORISON SWETT MARDEN (1850–1924)

Obstacles are those frightful things you see when you take your eyes off the goal.
HANNAH MORE (1745–1833)

Formulate and stamp indelibly on your mind a mental picture of yourself as succeeding. Hold this picture tenaciously. Never permit it to fade. Your

mind will seek to develop the picture.... Do not build up obstacles in your imagination.
NORMAN VINCENT PEALE (1898–1993)

I think a hero is an ordinary individual who finds strength to persevere and endure in spite of overwhelming obstacles.
CHRISTOPHER REEVE (1952–2004)

Everyone who achieves success in a great venture, solved each problem as they came to it. They helped themselves. And they were helped through powers known and unknown to them at the time they set out on their voyage. They kept going regardless of the obstacles they met.
CLEMENT STONE (1902–2002)

My freedom will be so much the greater and more meaningful the more narrowly I limit my field of action and the more I surround myself with obstacles. Whatever diminishes constraint diminishes strength. The more constraints one imposes, the more one frees one's self of the chains that shackle the spirit.
IGOR STRAVINSKY (1882–1971), *Poetics of Music*

Success is to be measured not so much by the position that one has reached in life as by the obstacles which he has overcome.
BOOKER T. WASHINGTON (1856–1915)

Only the curious will learn and only the resolute overcome the obstacles to learning. The quest quotient has always excited me more than the intelligence quotient.
EUGENE S. WILSON (1900–1981)

Occupation

Blessed is the man who has some congenial work, some occupation in which he can put his heart, and which affords a complete outlet to all the forces there are in him.
JOHN BURROUGHS (1837–1921)

It is necessary to try to surpass oneself always; this occupation ought to last as long as life.
QUEEN CHRISTINA OF SWEDEN (1626–1689)

Idleness and lack of occupation tend—nay are dragged—towards evil.
HIPPOCRATES (460–377 BC), *Decorum*

It is neither wealth nor splendor, but tranquility and occupation which give happiness.
THOMAS JEFFERSON (1743–1826)

Winter is not a season, it's an occupation.
SINCLAIR LEWIS (1885–1951)

The most common of all follies is to believe passionately in the palpably not true. It is the chief occupation of mankind.
H. L. MENCKEN (1880–1956)

Whenever it is in any way possible, every boy and girl should choose as his life work some occupation which he should like to do anyhow, even if he did not need the money.
WILLIAM LYON PHELPS (1865–1943)

A human being must have occupation if he or she is not to become a nuisance to the world.
DOROTHY L. SAYERS (1893–1957)

To give an accurate description of what has never occurred is not merely the proper occupation of the historian, but the inalienable privilege of any man of parts and culture.
OSCAR WILDE (1854–1900), *The Critic as Artist*

Ocean

The ocean is a body of water occupying about two-thirds of a world made for man—who has no gills.
AMBROSE BIERCE (1842–1914), *The Devil's Dictionary*

All of us have in our veins the exact same percentage of salt in our blood that exists in the ocean, and, therefore, we have salt in our blood, in our sweat, in our tears. We are tied to the ocean. And when we go back to the sea—whether it is to sail or to watch it—we are going back from whence we came.
JOHN F. KENNEDY (1917–1963)

We are opening up an enormous new era in archaeology. Time capsules in the deep oceans.
JOHN LEHMAN (1942–)

Nothing is wrong with California that a rise in the ocean level wouldn't cure.
ROSS MACDONALD (1915–1983)

When beholding the tranquil beauty and brilliancy of the ocean's skin, one forgets the tiger heart that pants beneath it; and would not willingly remember that this velvet paw but conceals a remorseless fang.
HERMAN MELVILLE (1819–1891), *Moby Dick*

Either you decide to stay in the shallow end of the pool or you go out in the ocean.
CHRISTOPHER REEVE (1952–2004)

There are treasures beyond compare in the ocean. If you seek safety, stay ashore.
SUFI PROVERB

Old Age

To keep the heart unwrinkled, to be hopeful, kindly, cheerful, reverent—that is to triumph over old age.
AMOS BRONSON ALCOTT (1799–1888)

Education is the best provision for old age.
ARISTOTLE (384–322 BC)

To me, old age is always 15 years older than I am.
BERNARD M. BARUCH (1870–1965)

To resist the frigidity of old age one must combine the body, the mind, and the heart—and to keep them in parallel vigor one must exercise, study, and love.
KARL VON BONSTETTEN (1745–1832)

The failure of the mind in old age is often less the results of natural decay, than of disuse. Ambition has ceased to operate; contentment brings indolence, and indolence decay of mental power, ennui, and sometimes death. Men have been known to die, literally speaking, of disease induced by intellectual vacancy.
SIR BENJAMIN COLLINS BRODIE (1783–1862)

Old age is not so bad when you consider the alternatives.
MAURICE CHEVALIER (1888–1972)

A life of peace, purity, and refinement leads to a calm and untroubled old age.
CICERO (106–43 BC)

A truly great book should be read in youth, again in maturity and once more in old age, as a fine building should be seen by morning light, at noon, and by moonlight.
ROBERTSON DAVIES (1913–1995)

Old age ain't no place for sissies.
BETTE DAVIS (1908–1989)

The pride of youth is in strength and beauty, the pride of old age is in discretion.
DEMOCRITUS (460–370 BC)

Old age means realizing you will never own all the dogs you wanted to.
JOE GORES (1931–)

To grow old is to grow common. Old age equalizes—we are aware that what is happening to us has happened to untold numbers from the beginning of time. When we are young we act as if we were the first young people in the world.
ERIC HOFFER (1902–1983)

The heads of strong old age are beautiful beyond all grace of youth.
ROBINSON JEFFERS (1887–1962)

There is no old age. There is, as there always was, just you.
CAROL MATTHAU (1925–)

When I was young I was amazed at Plutarch's statement that the elder Cato began at the age of eighty to learn Greek. I am amazed no longer. Old age is ready to undertake tasks that youth shirked because they would take too long.
W. SOMERSET MAUGHAM (1874–1965)

Cherish all your happy moments: they make a fine cushion for old age.
CHRISTOPHER MORLEY (1890–1957)

A graceful and honorable old age is the childhood of immortality.
PINDAR (522–443 BC)

There is no happiness where there is no wisdom;
No wisdom but in submission to the gods.
Big words are always punished,
And proud men in old age learn to be wise.
SOPHOCLES (496–406 BC), *Antigone*

Do not go gentle into that good night,
Old age should burn and rave at close of day;
Rage, rage against the dying of the light.
DYLAN THOMAS (1914–1953)

Old age is the most unexpected of things that can happen to a man.
LEON TROTSKY (1879–1940), *Diary in Exile*

Wisdom doesn't automatically come with old age. Nothing does—except wrinkles. It's true, some wines improve with age. But only if the grapes were good in the first place.
ABIGAIL VAN BUREN (1918–)

Old age, calm, expanded, broad with the haughty breadth of the universe, old age flowing free with the delicious near-by freedom of death.
EDITH WHARTON (1862–1937)

Old age may seem a long way off. But on the day it doesn't, it will be too late to do anything about it.
ANONYMOUS

Opinions

I have opinions of my own—strong opinions—but I don't always agree with them.
GEORGE H. W. BUSH (1924–)

Fight for your opinions, but do not believe that they contain the whole truth, or the only truth.
CHARLES A. DANA (1819–1897)

When men exercise their reason coolly and freely on a variety of distinct questions, they inevitably fall into different opinions on some of them. When they are governed by a common passion, their opinions, if they are to be called, will be the same.
ALEXANDER HAMILTON (1755–1804)

The recipe for perpetual ignorance is: be satisfied with your opinions and content with your knowledge.
ELBERT HUBBARD (1856–1915)

There is no greater mistake than the hasty conclusion that opinions are worthless because they are badly argued.
THOMAS H. HUXLEY (1825–1895)

It takes in reality only one to make a quarrel. It is useless for the sheep to pass resolutions in favour of vegetarianism while the wolf remains of a different opinion.
WILLIAM RALPH INGE (1860–1954), *Outspoken Essays*

Opinions founded on prejudice are always sustained with the greatest of violence.
LORD FRANCIS JEFFREY (1773–1850)

Too often we … enjoy the comfort of opinion without the discomfort of thought.
JOHN F. KENNEDY (1917–1963)

You get fifteen Democrats in a room, and you get twenty opinions.
PATRICK LEAHY (1940–)

Don't judge a man by his opinions, but what his opinions have made of him.
GEORG C. LICHTENBERG (1742–1799)

Nothing is more conducive to peace of mind than not having any opinions at all.
GEORG C. LICHTENBERG (1742–1799)

When men are brought face to face with their opponents, forced to listen and learn and mend their ideas, they cease to be children and savages and begin to live like civilized men. Then only is freedom a reality, when men may voice their opinions because they must examine their opinions.
WALTER LIPPMANN (1889–1974)

Risk! Risk anything! Care no more for the opinions of others, for those voices. Do the hardest thing on earth for you. Act for yourself. Face the truth.
KATHERINE MANSFIELD (1888–1923)

Everything we hear is an opinion, not a fact. Everything we see is a perspective, not the truth.
MARCUS AURELIUS ANTONINUS (121–180)

Where there is much desire to learn, there of necessity will be much arguing, much writing, many opinions; for opinions in good men is but knowledge in the making.
JOHN MILTON (1608–1674)

It is hard enough to remember my opinions, without also remembering my reasons for them!
FRIEDRICH NIETZSCHE (1844–1900)

What we have to do is to be forever curiously testing new opinions and courting new impressions.
WALTER PATER (1839–1894)

[A]s the years go by, time will change and even reverse many of your present opinions. Refrain therefore awhile from setting yourself up as a judge of the highest matters.
PLATO (C. 428–348 BC)

It is not advisable … to venture unsolicited opinions. You should spare yourself the embarrassing discovery of their exact value to your listener.
AYN RAND (1905–1982), *Atlas Shrugged*

I think we ought always to entertain our opinions with some measure of doubt. I shouldn't wish people dogmatically to believe any philosophy, not even mine.
BERTRAND RUSSELL (1872–1970)

The moment we begin to fear the opinions of others and hesitate to tell the truth that is in us, and from motives of policy are silent when we should speak, the divine floods of light and life no longer flow into our souls.
ELIZABETH CADY STANTON (1815–1902)

I am not one of those who in expressing opinions confine themselves to facts.
MARK TWAIN (1835–1910)

Our opinions do not really blossom into fruition until we have expressed them to someone else.
MARK TWAIN (1835–1910)

Sane and intelligent human beings are like all other human beings, and carefully and cautiously and diligently conceal their private real opinions from the world and give out fictitious ones in their stead for general consumption.
MARK TWAIN (1835–1910)

Prejudice is opinion without judgment.
VOLTAIRE (1694–1778)

Opportunity

In this life, it's not what you hope for, it's not what you deserve—it's what you take.
PAUL THOMAS ANDERSON (1970–), *Magnolia*

A wise man will make more opportunities than he finds.
SIR FRANCIS BACON (1561–1626)

Nothing is more expensive than a missed opportunity.
H. JACKSON BROWN JR. (1948–)

Opportunity dances with those who are already on the dance floor.
H. JACKSON BROWN JR. (1948–)

If you view all the things that happen to you, both good and bad, as opportunities, then you operate out of a higher level of consciousness.
LES BROWN (1912–2001)

The pessimist sees difficulty in every opportunity. The optimist sees the opportunity in every difficulty.
SIR WINSTON CHURCHILL (1874–1965)

Great minds must be ready not only to take opportunities, but to make them.
CHARLES CALEB COLTON (1780–1832)

Subtract from the great man all that he owes to opportunity, all that he owes to chance, and all that he gained by the wisdom of his friends and the folly of his enemies, and the giant will often be seen to be a pygmy.
CHARLES CALEB COLTON (1780–1832)

Small opportunities are often the beginning of great enterprises.
DEMOSTHENES (384–322 BC)

Not knowing when the dawn will come, I open every door.
EMILY DICKINSON (1830–1886)

Next to knowing when to seize an opportunity, the most important thing in life is to know when to forego an advantage.
BENJAMIN DISRAELI (1804–1881)

Thou strong seducer, Opportunity!
JOHN DRYDEN (1631–1700)

Opportunity is missed by most people because it comes dressed in overalls and looks like work.
THOMAS A. EDISON (1847–1931)

There is far more opportunity than there is ability.
THOMAS A. EDISON (1847–1931)

In the middle of difficulty lies opportunity.
ALBERT EINSTEIN (1879–1955)

Be an opener of doors.
RALPH WALDO EMERSON (1803–1882)

Every wall is a door.
RALPH WALDO EMERSON (1803–1882)

If a man can write a better book, preach a better sermon, or make a better mousetrap, than his neighbor, though he build his house in the woods, the world will make a beaten path to his door.
RALPH WALDO EMERSON (1803–1882)

Never lose an opportunity of seeing anything that is beautiful; for beauty is God's handwriting—a wayside sacrament. Welcome it in every fair face, in every fair sky, in every fair flower, and thank God for it as a cup of blessing.
RALPH WALDO EMERSON (1803–1882)

Opportunity rarely knocks on your door. Knock rather on opportunity's door if you ardently wish to enter.
B. C. FORBES (1880–1954)

Plough deep while sluggards sleep.
BENJAMIN FRANKLIN (1706–1790)

The right man is the one that seizes the moment.
JOHANN WOLFGANG VON GOETHE (1749–1832)

Opportunity often comes disguised in the form of misfortune, or temporary defeat.
NAPOLEON HILL (1883–1970)

Your big opportunity may be right where you are now.
NAPOLEON HILL (1883–1970)

It sometimes seems that intense desire creates not only its own opportunities, but its own talents.
ERIC HOFFER (1902–1983)

It still holds true that man is most uniquely human when he turns obstacles into opportunities.
ERIC HOFFER (1902–1983)

I despise making the most of one's time. Half of the pleasures of life consist of the opportunities one has neglected.
OLIVER WENDELL HOLMES JR. (1841–1935)

Let us my friends snatch our opportunity from the passing day.
HORACE (65–8 BC)

It's when ordinary people rise above the expectations and seize the opportunity that milestones truly are reached.
MIKE HUCKABEE (1955–)

Trouble is only opportunity in work clothes.
HENRY J. KAISER (1882–1967)

The Chinese use two brush strokes to write the word "crisis." One brush stroke stands for danger; the other for opportunity. In a crisis, be aware of the danger—but recognize the opportunity.
JOHN F. KENNEDY (1917–1963)

Procrastination is opportunity's assassin.
VICTOR KIAM (1926–2001)

Opportunities are usually disguised as hard work, so most people don't recognize them.
ANN LANDERS (1918–2002)

Who makes quick use of the moment is a genius of prudence.
JOHANN KASPAR LAVATER (1741–1801)

There is no security on this earth, there is only opportunity.
GENERAL DOUGLAS MACARTHUR (1880–1964)

Don't wait for extraordinary opportunities. Seize common occasions and make them great. Weak men wait for opportunities; strong men make them.
ORISON SWETT MARDEN (1850–1924)

It is the youth who sees a great opportunity hidden in just these simple services, who sees a very uncommon situation, a humble position, who gets on in the world.
ORISON SWETT MARDEN (1850–1924)

The golden opportunity you are seeking is in yourself. It is not in your environment; it is not in luck or chance, or the help of others; it is in yourself alone.
ORISON SWETT MARDEN (1850–1924)

The lack of opportunity is ever the excuse of a weak, vacillating mind. Opportunities! Every life is full of them. Every newspaper article is an opportunity. Every client is an opportunity. Every sermon is an opportunity. Every business transaction is an opportunity—an opportunity to be polite, an opportunity to be manly, an opportunity to be honest, an opportunity to make friends.
ORISON SWETT MARDEN (1850–1924)

Catch a man a fish, and you can sell it to him. Teach a man to fish, and you ruin a wonderful business opportunity.
KARL MARX (1818–1883)

Grasp your opportunities, no matter how poor your health; nothing is worse for your health than boredom.
MIGNON MCLAUGHLIN (1913–1983)

Problems are only opportunities with thorns on them.
HUGH MILLER (1802–1856), *Snow on the Wind*

Wherever there is danger, there lurks opportunity; whenever there is opportunity, there lurks danger. The two are inseparable. They go together.
EARL NIGHTINGALE (1921–1989)

Always have your hook baited, in the pool you least think, there will be a fish.
OVID (43 BC–AD 17)

While we stop to think, we often miss our opportunity.
PUBLILIUS SYRUS (C. 100 BC), *Maxims*

We see the brightness of a new page where everything yet can happen.
RAINER MARIA RILKE (1875–1926)

I always tried to turn every disaster into an opportunity.
JOHN D. ROCKEFELLER (1839–1937)

The follies which a man regrets most in his life, are those which he didn't commit when he had the opportunity.
HELEN ROWLAND (1875–1950)

Opportunities multiply as they are seized.
SUN-TZU (C. 544–496 BC)

A clash of doctrines is not a disaster—it is an opportunity.
ALFRED NORTH WHITEHEAD (1861–1947)

Opportunities neglected can never be recovered.
ANONYMOUS

Opportunity seems to have an uncanny habit of favoring those who have paid the price of years of preparation.
ANONYMOUS

Some people not only expect opportunity to knock, they expect it to beat down the door.
ANONYMOUS

The back of one door is the face of another.
ANONYMOUS

Four things come not back. The spoken word, the sped arrow, the past life, and the neglected opportunity.
ARABIAN PROVERB

Seize opportunity by the beard, for it is bald behind.
BULGARIAN PROVERB

Some men go through a forest and see no firewood.
ENGLISH PROVERB

When fortune knocks open the door.
GERMAN PROVERB

Men never moan over the opportunities lost to do good, only the opportunities to be bad.
GREEK PROVERB

Opposites

Light is meaningful only in relation to darkness, and truth presupposes error. It is these mingled opposites which people our life, which make it pungent, intoxicating. We only exist in terms of this conflict, in the zone where black and white clash.
LOUIS ARAGON (1897–1982)

Power and violence are opposites; where the one rules absolutely, the other is absent. Violence appears where power is in jeopardy, but left to its own course it ends in power's disappearance.
HANNAH ARENDT (1906–1975)

Our mind is capable of passing beyond the dividing line we have drawn for it. Beyond the pairs of opposites of which the world consists, other, new insights begin.
HERMANN HESSE (1877–1962)

Force and mind are opposites; morality ends where a gun begins.
AYN RAND (1905–1982)

The most exciting attractions are between two opposites that never meet.
ANDY WARHOL (1927–1987)

Opposition

Many a man's strength is in opposition, and when he faileth, he grows out of use.
SIR FRANCIS BACON (1561–1626)

Opposition is true friendship.
WILLIAM BLAKE (1757–1827)

He that wrestles with us strengthens our nerves, and sharpens our skill. Our antagonist is our helper. This amicable conflict with difficulty helps us to an intimate acquaintance with our object, and compels us to consider it in all its relations. It will not suffer us to be superficial.
EDMUND BURKE (1729–1797)

No government can be long secure without a formidable opposition. It reduces their supporters to that tractable number which can be managed by the joint influences of fruition and hope. It offers vengeance to the discontented, and distinction to the ambitious; and employs the energies of aspiring spirits, who otherwise may prove traitors in a division or assassins in a debate.
BENJAMIN DISRAELI (1804–1881)

Great spirits have always found violent opposition from mediocrities. The latter cannot understand it when a man does not thoughtlessly submit to hereditary prejudices, but honestly and courageously uses his intelligence.
ALBERT EINSTEIN (1879–1955)

But most of us are apt to settle within ourselves that the man who blocks our way is odious, and not to mind causing him a little of the disgust which his personality excites in ourselves.
GEORGE ELIOT (1819–1880)

Opposition is not necessarily enmity; it is merely misused and made an occasion for enmity.
SIGMUND FREUD (1856–1939)

Opposition brings concord. Out of discord comes the fairest harmony.
HERACLITUS (C. 535–475 BC)

I have spent many years of my life in opposition and I like the role.
ELEANOR ROOSEVELT (1884–1962)

Opposition always enflames the enthusiast, never converts him.
FRIEDRICH VON SCHILLER (1759–1805)

Oppression

It is bad to be oppressed by a minority, but it is worse to be oppressed by a majority. For there is a reserve of latent power in the masses which, if it is called into play, the minority can seldom resist. But from the absolute will of an entire people there is no appeal, no redemption, no refuge but treason.
LORD ACTON (1834–1902)

Fascism is fascism. Terrorism is terrorism. Oppression is oppression.
HARRY BELAFONTE (1927–)

A belief is not merely an idea the mind possesses; it is an idea that possesses the mind.
ROBERT OXTON BOLTON (1924–1995)

For too long, many nations, including my own, tolerated, even excused, oppression in the Middle East in the name of stability. Oppression became common, but stability never arrived. We must take a different approach. We must help the reformers of the Middle East as they work for freedom, and strive to build a community of peaceful, democratic nations.
GEORGE W. BUSH (1946–)

The state is nothing but an instrument of oppression of one class by another—no less so in a democratic republic than in a monarchy.
FRIEDRICH ENGELS (1820–1895)

They have exiled me now from their society and I am pleased, because humanity does not exile except the one whose noble spirit rebels against despotism and oppression. He who does not prefer exile to slavery is not free by any measure of freedom, truth and duty.
KAHIL GIBRAN (1883–1931), *Spirits Rebellious*

Enlighten the people, generally, and tyranny and oppressions of body and mind will vanish like spirits at the dawn of day.
THOMAS JEFFERSON (1743–1826)

It is from numberless diverse acts of courage and belief that human history is shaped. Each time a man stands up for an ideal, or acts to improve the lot of others, or strikes out against injustice, he sends forth a tiny ripple of hope, and crossing each other from a million different centers of energy and daring, those ripples build a current that can sweep down the mightiest walls of oppression and resistance.
ROBERT F. KENNEDY (1925–1968)

Freedom is never voluntarily given by the oppressor; it must be demanded by the oppressed.
MARTIN LUTHER KING JR. (1929–1968)

Nonviolence is the answer to the crucial political and moral questions of our time; the need for mankind to overcome oppression and violence without resorting to oppression and violence. Mankind must evolve for all human conflict a method which rejects revenge, aggression, and retaliation. The foundation of such a method is love.
MARTIN LUTHER KING JR. (1929–1968)

The ultimate tragedy is not the oppression and cruelty by the bad people but the silence over that by the good people.
MARTIN LUTHER KING JR. (1929–1968)

The provision of the Constitution giving the war-making power to Congress was dictated, as I understand it, by the following reasons. Kings had always been involving and impoverishing their people in wars, pretending generally, if not always, that the good of the people was the object. This, our Convention understood to be the most oppressive of all Kingly oppressions; and they resolved to so frame the Constitution that no one man should hold the power of bringing this oppression upon us.
ABRAHAM LINCOLN (1809–1865)

The trouble with fighting for human freedom is that one spends most of one's time defending scoundrels. For it is against scoundrels that oppressive laws are first aimed, and oppression must be stopped at the beginning if it is to be stopped at all.
H. L. MENCKEN (1880–1956)

My loathings are simple: stupidity, oppression, crime, cruelty, soft music.
VLADIMIR NABOKOV (1899–1977)

He that would make his own liberty secure, must guard even his enemy from oppression; for if he violates this duty, he establishes a precedent that will reach to himself.
THOMAS PAINE (1737–1809)

We must remember that any oppression, any injustice, any hatred, is a wedge designed to attack our civilization.
FRANKLIN D. ROOSEVELT (1882–1945)

Optimism

Many an optimist has become rich by buying out a pessimist.
ROBERT G. ALLEN (1902–1963)

The optimist proclaims that we live in the best of all possible worlds; and the pessimist fears this is true.
JAMES BRANCH CABELL (1879–1958), *The Silver Stallion*

A pessimist sees the difficulty in every opportunity; an optimist sees the opportunity in every difficulty.
SIR WINSTON CHURCHILL (1874–1965)

For myself I am an optimist—it does not seem to be much use being anything else.
SIR WINSTON CHURCHILL (1874–1965)

The place where optimism most flourishes is the lunatic asylum.
HENRY HAVELOCK ELLIS (1859–1939)

I find nothing more depressing than optimism.
PAUL FUSSELL (1924–)

The optimist sees the rose and not its thorns; the pessimist stares at the thorns, oblivious to the rose.
KAHLIL GIBRAN (1883–1931)

Pessimism of the spirit; optimism of the will.
ANTONIO GRAMSCI (1891–1937)

Don't ever become a pessimist … a pessimist is correct oftener than an optimist, but an optimist has more fun—and neither can stop the march of events.
ROBERT A. HEINLEIN (1907–1988)

No pessimist ever discovered the secret of the stars or sailed an uncharted land, or opened a new doorway for the human spirit.
HELEN KELLER (1880–1968)

I do the very best I can to look upon life with optimism and hope and looking forward to a better day, but I don't think there is anything such as complete happiness. It pains me that there is still a lot of Klan activity and racism. I think when you say you're happy, you have everything that you need and everything that you want, and nothing more to wish for. I haven't reached that stage yet.
ROSA PARKS (1913–2005)

Perpetual optimism is a force multiplier.
COLIN POWELL (1937–)

My pessimism extends to the point of even suspecting the sincerity of the pessimists.
JEAN ROSTAND (1894–1977), *Journal of a Character*

An optimist may see a light where there is none, but why must the pessimist always run to blow it out?
MICHEL DE SAINT-PIERRE (1916–1987)

An optimist is a person who sees a green light everywhere, while a pessimist sees only the red stoplight.... The truly wise person is colorblind.
DR. ALBERT SCHWEITZER (1875–1965)

Both optimists and pessimists contribute to our society. The optimist invents the airplane and the pessimist the parachute.
G. B. STERN (1890–1973)

A pessimist is one who makes difficulties of his opportunities, and an optimist is one who makes opportunities of his difficulties.
HARRY S TRUMAN (1884–1972)

The man who is a pessimist before forty-eight knows too much; if he is an optimist after it he knows too little.
MARK TWAIN (1835–1910)

The point of living and of being an optimist, is to be foolish enough to believe the best is yet to come.
PETER USTINOV (1921–2004)

The reason we all like to think so well of others is that we are all afraid for ourselves. The basis of optimism is sheer terror.
OSCAR WILDE (1854–1900), *The Picture of Dorian Gray*

Few cases of eyestrain have been developed by looking on the bright side of things.
ANONYMOUS

Order

Order is power.
HENRI-FRÉDÉRIC AMIEL (1821–1881)

Good order is the foundation of all things.
EDMUND BURKE (1729–1797)

Set all things in their own peculiar place, and know that order is the greatest grace.
JOHN DRYDEN (1631–1700)

Law is order in liberty, and without order liberty is social chaos.
ARCHBISHOP JOHN IRELAND (1838–1918)

As order exponentially increases, time exponentially speeds up.
RAY KURZWEIL (1948–)

The more laws and order are made prominent,
The more thieves and robbers there will be.
LAO-TZU (C. 600 BC), *The Way of Lao-tzu*

Order without liberty and liberty without order are equally destructive.
THEODORE ROOSEVELT (1858–1919)

Order, unity, and continuity are human inventions, just as truly as catalogues and encyclopedias.
BERTRAND RUSSELL (1872–1970)

Organization

Equality ... is the result of human organization. We are not born equal.
HANNAH ARENDT (1906–1975)

From each according to his abilities, to each according to his needs.
LOUIS BLANC (1811–1882), *The Organization of Work*

An empowered organization is one in which individuals have the knowledge, skill, desire, and opportunity to personally succeed in a way that leads to collective organizational success.
STEPHEN R. COVEY (1932–)

Quality is the result of a carefully constructed cultural environment. It has to be the fabric of the organization, not part of the fabric.
PHILIP CROSBY (1926–2001), *Reflections on Quality*

You will find that the State is the kind of organization which, though it does big things badly, does small things badly, too.
JOHN KENNETH GALBRAITH (1908–2006)

First comes thought; then organization of that thought into ideas and plans; then transformation of those plans into reality. The beginning, as you will observe, is in your imagination.
NAPOLEON HILL (1883–1970)

Create the kind of climate in your organization where personal growth is expected, recognized, and rewarded.
ANONYMOUS

Originality

About the most originality that any writer can hope to achieve honestly is to steal with good judgment.
JOSH BILLINGS (1818–1885)

Next to the originator of a good sentence is the first quoter of it.
RALPH WALDO EMERSON (1803–1882), *Letters and Social Aims*

Originality is simply a pair of fresh eyes.
THOMAS WENTWORTH HIGGINSON (1823–1911)

Even in literature and art, no man who bothers about originality will ever be original: whereas if you simply try to tell the truth (without caring twopence how often it has been told before) you will, nine times out of ten, become original without ever having noticed it.
C. S. LEWIS (1898–1963)

Creativity can solve almost any problem. The creative act, the defeat of habit by originality, overcomes everything.
GEORGE LOIS (1937–)

It is better to fail in originality than to succeed in imitation.
HERMAN MELVILLE (1819–1891)

Originality is the fine art of remembering what you hear but forgetting where you heard it.
DR. LAURENCE J. PETER (1919–1990)

Originality is not seen in single words or even sentences. Originality is the sum total of a man's thinking or his writing.
ISAAC BASHEVIS SINGER (1904–1991)

True originality consists not in a new manner but in a new vision.
EDITH WHARTON (1862–1937)

Orthodoxy

To overturn orthodoxy is no easier in science than in philosophy, religion, economics, or any of the other disciplines through which we try to comprehend the world and the society in which we live.
RUTH HUBBARD (1924–)

Orthodoxy is the diehard of the world of thought. It learns not, neither can it forget.
ALDOUS HUXLEY (1894–1963)

Universal orthodoxy is enriched by every new discovery of truth: what at first appeared universal, by wishing to stand still, sooner or later becomes a sect.
EDGAR QUINET (1803–1875)

Biblical orthodoxy without compassion is surely the ugliest thing in the world.
FRANCIS SCHAEFFER (1912–1984)

Pacifism

The pacifist's task today is to find a method of helping and healing which provides a revolutionary constructive substitute for war.
VERA BRITTAIN (1893–1970)

The people can always be brought to the bidding of their leaders. All you have to do is tell them that they are in danger of being attacked and denounce the pacifists for lack of patriotism and exposing the country to danger.
HERMAN GOERING (1893–1946)

Santa Claus wears a Red Suit,
He must be a communist.
And a beard and long hair,
Must be a pacifist.
What's in that pipe that he's smoking?
ARLO GUTHRIE (1947–)

Even a pacifist should admire the military virtues.
JOHN KEEGAN (1934–)

Everyone's a pacifist between wars. It's like being a vegetarian between meals.
COLMAN MCCARTHY (1938–)

We pacifists have not ceased to point to the grave danger of armaments and to insist on their curtailment.
LUDWIG QUIDDE (1858–1941)

The absolute pacifist is a bad citizen; times come when force must be used to uphold right, justice and ideals.
ALFRED NORTH WHITEHEAD (1861–1947)

Pain

One of the greatest pains to human nature is the pain of a new idea.
WALTER BAGEHOT (1826–1877)

The world is so constructed, that if you wish to enjoy its pleasures, you must also endure its pains. Whether you like it or not, you cannot have one without the other.
SWAMI BRAHNMANANDA (1863–1922)

But pain … seems to me an insufficient reason not to embrace life. Being dead is quite painless. Pain, like time, is going to come on regardless. Question is, what glorious moments can you win from life in addition to the pain?
LOIS MCMASTER BUJOLD (1949–), *Barrayar*

The same refinement which brings us new pleasures, exposes us to new pains.
SIR EDWARD G. BULWER-LYTTON (1803–1873)

What we call pleasure, and rightly so, is the absence of all pain.
CICERO (106–43 BC)

Time cancels young pain.
EURIPIDES (C. 480–406 BC), *Alcestis*

Do not consider painful what is good for you.
EURIPIDES (C. 480–406 BC)

Sometimes it is harder to deprive oneself of a pain than of a pleasure.
F. SCOTT FITZGERALD (1896–1940), *Tender Is the Night*

It's very easy to feel someone's pain when you love them.
SALMA HAYEK (1966–)

It's odd that you can get so anesthetized by your own pain or your own problem that you don't quite fully share the hell of someone close to you.
LADY BIRD JOHNSON (1912–2007)

The trick is not how much pain you feel—but how much joy you feel. Any idiot can feel pain. Life is full of excuses to feel pain, excuses not to live, excuses, excuses, excuses.
ERICA JONG (1942–)

I drank to drown my pain, but the damned pain learned how to swim, and now I am overwhelmed by this decent and good behavior.
FRIDA KAHLO (1907–1954)

If you are distressed by anything external, the pain is not due to the thing itself, but to your estimate of it; and this you have the power to revoke at any moment.
MARCUS AURELIUS ANTONINUS (121–180)

One good thing about music, when it hits you, you feel no pain.
BOB MARLEY (1945–1981)

Pain (any pain—emotional, physical, mental) has a message. The information it has about our life can be remarkably specific, but it usually falls into one of two categories: "We would be more alive if we did more of this," and, "Life would be more lovely if we did less of that." Once we get the pain's message, and follow its advice, the pain goes away.
PETER MCWILLIAMS (1949–2000)

If you don't get what you want, you suffer; if you get what you don't want, you suffer; even when you get exactly what you want, you still suffer because you can't hold on to it forever. Your mind is your predicament. It wants to be free of change. Free of pain, free of the obligations of life and death. But change is a law, and no amount of pretending will alter that reality.
DAN MILLMAN (1946–), *The Way of the Peaceful Warrior*

We must embrace pain and burn it as fuel for our journey.
KENJI MIYAZAWA (1896–1933)

Take chances. Make mistakes. That's how you grow. Pain nourishes your courage. You have to fail in order to practice being brave.
MARY TYLER MOORE (1936–)

And the day came when the risk to remain tight in a bud was more painful than the risk it took to blossom.
ANAÏS NIN (1903–1977)

Pain makes man think. Thought makes man wise. Wisdom makes life endurable.
JOHN PATRICK (1905–1995)

Scorching my seared heart with a pain, not hell shall make me fear again.
EDGAR ALLAN POE (1809–1849), "Tamerlane"

The happiest is the person who suffers the least pain; the most miserable who enjoys the least pleasure.
JEAN-JACQUES ROUSSEAU (1712–1778), *Émile*

Numbing the pain for a while will make it worse when you finally feel it.
J. K. ROWLING (1965–), *Harry Potter and the Goblet of Fire*

A wretched soul, bruised with adversity,
We bid be quiet when we hear it cry;
But were we burdened with like weight of pain,
As much or more we should ourselves complain.
WILLIAM SHAKESPEARE (1564–1616), *The Comedy of Errors*

The longer I live the more I see that I am never wrong about anything, and that all the pains I have so humbly taken to verify my notions have only wasted my time.
GEORGE BERNARD SHAW (1856–1950)

One word
Frees us of all the weight and pain of life:
That word is love.
SOPHOCLES (496–406 BC), *Oedipus at Colonus*

Sometimes you feel other people's pain worse than your own. We're armored against our own troubles. We can't afford to give in to despair. Then you see someone else struggling, and it breaks your … heart.
SEAN STEWART (1965–), *Perfect Circle*

Of all the animals, man is the only one that is cruel. He is the only one that inflicts pain for the pleasure of doing it.
MARK TWAIN (1835–1910), *The Lowest Animal*

Do something every day that you don't want to do; this is the golden rule for acquiring the habit of doing your duty without pain.
MARK TWAIN (1835–1910)

It was as if all the pain in the world had found a voice. Yet had I known such pain was in the next room, and had it been dumb, I believe—I have thought since—I could have stood it well enough. It is when suffering finds a voice and sets our nerves quivering that this pity comes troubling us.
H. G. WELLS (1866–1946), *The Island of Dr. Moreau*

Pain is inevitable; suffering is optional.
ANONYMOUS

Not to have felt pain is not to have been human.
JEWISH PROVERB

Painting

Each painting has its own way of evolving…. When the painting is finished, the subject reveals itself.
WILLIAM BAZIOTES (1912–1963)

Every artist dips his brush in his own soul, and paints his own nature into his pictures.
HENRY WARD BEECHER (1813–1887), *Proverbs from Plymouth Pulpit*

Painting, n.: The art of protecting flat surfaces from the weather and exposing them to the critic.
AMBROSE BIERCE (1842–1914), *The Devil's Dictionary*

I say that good painters imitated nature; but that bad ones vomited it.
MIGUEL DE CERVANTES (1547–1616), *Exemplary Novels*

A painting in a museum hears more ridiculous opinions than anything else in the world.
EDMOND DE GONCOURT (1822–1896)

I do believe it is possible to create, even without ever writing a word or painting a picture, by simply molding one's inner life. And that too is a deed.
ETTY HILLESUM (1914–1943)

I paint my own reality. The only thing I know is that I paint because I need to, and I paint whatever passes through my head without any other consideration.
FRIDA KAHLO (1907–1954)

I am not sick. I am broken. But I am happy as long as I can paint.
FRIDA KAHLO (1907–1954)

I paint self-portraits because I am so often alone, because I am the person I know best.
FRIDA KAHLO (1907–1954)

A man paints with his brains and not with his hands.
MICHELANGELO (1475–1564)

Painting is just another way of keeping a diary.
PABLO PICASSO (1881–1973)

There are painters who transform the sun to a yellow spot, but there are others who with the help of their art and their intelligence, transform a yellow spot into the sun.
PABLO PICASSO (1881–1973)

The world today doesn't make sense, so why should I paint pictures that do?
PABLO PICASSO (1881–1973)

The painting has a life of its own. I try to let it come through.
JACKSON POLLOCK (1912–1956)

Every time I paint a portrait I lose a friend.
JOHN SINGER SARGENT (1856–1925)

Painting is silent poetry, and poetry is painting with the gift of speech.
SIMONIDES (556–468 BC)

Painting is an attempt to come to terms with life. There are as many solutions as there are human beings.
GEORGE TOOKER (1920–)

Every portrait that is painted with feeling is a portrait of the artist, not of the sitter.
OSCAR WILDE (1854–1900)

It's a small world, but I wouldn't want to paint it.
STEVEN WRIGHT (1955–)

Paradise

Paradise is exactly like where you are right now … only much, much better.
LAURIE ANDERSON (1947–), *Language Is a Virus*

I have always imagined that Paradise will be a kind of library.
JORGE LUIS BORGES (1899–1986)

Be such a man, and live such a life, that if every man were such as you, and every life a life like yours, this earth would be God's Paradise.
PHILLIPS BROOKS (1835–1893)

How high must we build these walls
Around the fields of paradise?
RICARDO PINTO (1961–), *The Chosen*

The only paradise is paradise lost.
MARCEL PROUST (1871–1922)

If there were in the world today any large number of people who desired their own happiness more than they desired the unhappiness of others, we could have paradise in a few years.
BERTRAND RUSSELL (1872–1970)

It is a curious thing ... that every creed promises a paradise which will be absolutely uninhabitable for anyone of civilized taste.
EVELYN WAUGH (1903–1966)

He deserves Paradise who makes his companions laugh.
THE KORAN

Paradox

I see many people die because they judge that life is not worth living. I see others paradoxically getting killed for the ideas or illusions that give them a reason for living (what is called a reason for living is also an excellent reason for dying). I therefore conclude that the meaning of life is the most urgent of questions.
ALBERT CAMUS (1913–1960), *The Myth of Sisyphus*

So they [the Government] go on in strange paradox, decided only to be undecided, resolved to be irresolute, adamant for drift, solid for fluidity, all-powerful to be impotent.
SIR WINSTON CHURCHILL (1874–1965), *Hansard*

There is this paradox in pride—it makes some men ridiculous, but prevents others from becoming so.
CHARLES CALEB COLTON (1780–1832)

The paradox is really the pathos of intellectual life, and just as only great souls are exposed to passions, it is only the great thinker who is exposed to what I call paradoxes, which are nothing else than grandiose thoughts in embryo.
SØREN KIERKEGAARD (1813–1855)

There is an ecstasy that marks the summit of life, and beyond which life cannot rise. And such is the paradox of living, this ecstasy comes when one is most alive, and it comes as a complete forgetfulness that one is alive.
JACK LONDON (1876–1916), *The Call of the Wild*

How is one to live a moral and compassionate existence when one is fully aware of the blood, the horror inherent in life, when one finds darkness not only in one's culture but within oneself? If there is a stage at which an individual life becomes truly adult, it must be when one grasps the irony in its unfolding and accepts responsibility for a life lived in the midst of such paradox. One must live in the middle of contradiction, because if all contradiction were eliminated at once life would collapse. There are simply no answers to some of the great pressing questions. You continue to live them out, making your life a worthy expression of leaning into the light.
BARRY LOPEZ (1945–), *Arctic Dreams*

Two paradoxes are better than one; they may even suggest a solution.
EDWARD TELLER (1908–2003)

I have found the paradox that if I love until it hurts, then there is no hurt, but only more love.
MOTHER TERESA (1910–1997)

The folly of mistaking a paradox for a discovery, a metaphor for a proof, a torrent of verbiage for a spring of capital truths, and oneself for an oracle, is inborn in us.
PAUL VALÉRY (1871–1945)

Paradoxically though it may seem, it is none the less true that life imitates art far more than art imitates life.
OSCAR WILDE (1854–1900)

The greatest paradox of them all is to speak of "civilized warfare."
ANONYMOUS

Paranoia

A paranoid is someone who knows a little of what's going on.
WILLIAM S. BURROUGHS (1914–1997)

I've always found paranoia to be a perfectly defensible position.
PAT CONROY (1945–)

My husband gave me a necklace. It's fake. I requested fake. Maybe I'm paranoid, but in this day and age, I don't want something around my neck that's worth more than my head.
RITA RUDNER (1956–)

I am a kind of paranoiac in reverse. I suspect people of plotting to make me happy.
J. D. SALINGER (1919–)

Even paranoids have real enemies.
DELMORE SCHWARTZ (1913–1966)

Parenthood

That's sort of a cliché about parents. We all believe that our children are the most beautiful children in the world. But the thing is, what no one really talks about is the fact that we all really believe it.
HEATHER ARMSTRONG (1975–)

It's frightening to think that you mark your children merely by being yourself. It seems unfair. You can't assume the responsibility for everything you do—or don't do.
SIMONE DE BEAUVOIR (1908–1986)

There is no friendship, no love, like that of the parent for the child.
HENRY WARD BEECHER (1813–1887)

Loving a child doesn't mean giving in to all his whims; to love him is to bring out the best in him, to teach him to love what is difficult.
NADIA BOULANGER (1887–1979)

Some are kissing mothers and some are scolding mothers, but it is love just the same.
PEARL S. BUCK (1892–1973)

Some men just aren't cut out for paternity. Better they should realize it before and not after they become responsible for a son.
LOIS MCMASTER BUJOLD (1949–), *Ethan of Athos*

If a child is to keep alive his inborn sense of wonder, he needs the companionship of at least one adult who can share it, rediscovering with him the joy, excitement and mystery of the world we live in.
RACHEL CARSON (1907–1964)

There are only two lasting bequests we can hope to give our children. One is roots; the other, wings.
HODDING CARTER JR. (1907–1972)

If your parents never had children, chances are you won't, either.
DICK CAVETT (1936–)

A mother's love for her child is like nothing else in the world. It knows no law, no pity, it dares all things and crushes down remorselessly all that stands in its path.
AGATHA CHRISTIE (1890–1976)

The most important thing she'd learned over the years was that there was no way to be a perfect mother and a million ways to be a good one.
JILL CHURCHILL (1943–)

Cherishing children is the mark of a civilized society.
JOAN GANZ COONEY (1929–)

The first half of our lives is ruined by our parents, and the second half by our children.
CLARENCE DARROW (1857–1938)

There are times when parenthood seems nothing but feeding the mouth that bites you.
PETER DE VRIES (1910–1993)

The trouble with children is that they are not returnable.
FYODOR DOSTOEVSKY (1821–1881)

It is easier to build strong children than to repair broken men.
FREDERICK DOUGLASS (1818–1895)

If you as parents cut corners, your children will too. If you lie, they will too. If you spend all your money on yourselves and tithe no portion of it for charities, colleges, churches, synagogues, and civic causes, your children won't either. And if parents snicker at racial and gender jokes, another generation will pass on the poison adults still have not had the courage to snuff out.
MARIAN WRIGHT EDELMAN (1939–)

The thing that impresses me most about America is the way parents obey their children.
KING EDWARD VIII (1894–1972)

The gods visit the sins of the fathers upon the children.
EURIPIDES (C. 480–406 BC), *Phrixus*

A mother is not a person to lean on but a person to make leaning unnecessary.
DOROTHY CANFIELD FISHER (1879–1958)

When a child enters the world through you it alters everything on a psychic, psychological and purely practical level.
JANE FONDA (1937–)

Love and respect are the most important aspects of parenting, and of all relationships.
JODIE FOSTER (1962–)

Parents can only give good advice or put them on the right paths, but the final forming of a person's character lies in their own hands.
ANNE FRANK (1929–1945)

As a parent you try to maintain a certain amount of control and so you have this tug-of-war.... You have to learn when to let go. And that's not easy.
ARETHA FRANKLIN (1942–)

Parents often talk about the younger generation as if they didn't have anything to do with it.
HAIM GINOTT (1922–1973)

Bitter are the tears of a child: sweeten them. Deep are the thoughts of a child: quiet them. Sharp is the grief of a child: take it from him. Soft is the heart of a child: do not harden it.
PAMELA GLENCONNER (1871–1928)

The central struggle of parenthood is to let our hopes for our children outweigh our fears.
ELLEN GOODMAN (1941–)

The beauty of "spacing" children many years apart lies in the fact that parents have time to learn the mistakes that were made with the older ones—which permits them to make exactly the opposite mistakes with the younger ones.
SYDNEY J. HARRIS (1917–1986)

For rarely are sons similar to their fathers: most are worse, and a few are better than their fathers.
HOMER (800–700 BC), *The Odyssey*

Your children need your presence more than your presents.
JESSE JACKSON (1941–)

You can learn many things from children. How much patience you have, for instance.
FRANKLIN P. JONES (1887–1929)

It kills you to see them grow up. But I guess it would kill you quicker if they didn't.
BARBARA KINGSOLVER (1955–)

It is not what you do for your children but what you have taught them to do for themselves that will make them successful human beings.
ANN LANDERS (1918–2002)

Discovering that with every child, your heart grows bigger and stronger—that there is no limit to how

much or how many people you can love, even though at times you feel as though you could burst—you don't—you just love even more.
YASMIN LE BON (1964–)

The reason grandparents and grandchildren get along so well is that they have a common enemy.
SAM LEVENSON (1911–1980)

This would be a better world for children if parents had to eat the spinach.
GROUCHO MARX (1890–1977)

Grown don't mean nothing to a mother. A child is a child. They get bigger, older, but grown? What's that supposed to mean? In my heart it don't mean a thing.
TONI MORRISON (1931–)

Children aren't happy with nothing to ignore, and that's what parents were created for.
OGDEN NASH (1902–1971)

If you bungle raising your children, I don't think whatever else you do matters very much.
JACQUELINE KENNEDY ONASSIS (1929–1994)

Getting down on all fours and imitating a rhinoceros stops babies from crying.… I don't know why parents don't do this more often. Usually it makes the kid laugh. Sometimes it sends him into shock. Either way it quiets him down. If you're a parent, acting like a rhino has another advantage. Keep it up until the kid is a teenager and he definitely won't have his friends hanging around your house all the time.
P. J. O'ROURKE (1947–)

Your parents, they give you your life, but then they try to give you their life.
CHUCK PALAHNIUK (1962–), *Invisible Monsters*

Life is the first gift, love is the second, and understanding the third.
MARGE PIERCY (1936–)

Let parents bequeath to their children not riches, but the spirit of reverence.
PLATO (C. 428–348 BC)

Furnish an example, stop preaching, stop shielding, don't prevent self-reliance and initiative, allow your children to develop along their own lines.
ELEANOR ROOSEVELT (1884–1962)

Romance fails us and so do friendships, but the relationship of parent and child, less noisy than all the others, remains indelible and indestructible, the strongest relationship on earth.
THEODORE REIK (1888–1969)

Having a baby is definitely a labor of love.
JOAN RIVERS (1933–)

I always wanted children, but not until they were actually part of my life did I realize that I could love that fiercely, or get that angry.
COKIE ROBERTS (1943–)

Neurotics build castles in the air, psychotics live in them. My mother cleans them.
RITA RUDNER (1956–)

The place of the father in the modern suburban family is a very small one, particularly if he plays golf.
BERTRAND RUSSELL (1872–1970)

Children reinvent your world for you.
SUSAN SARANDON (1946–)

It is a wise father that knows his own child.
WILLIAM SHAKESPEARE (1564–1616), *The Merchant of Venice*

Perhaps the greatest social service that can be rendered by anybody to the country and to mankind is to bring up a family.
GEORGE BERNARD SHAW (1856–1950)

Nothing has a better effect upon children than praise.
SIR PHILIP SIDNEY (1554–1586)

Mothers are instinctive philosophers.
HARRIET BEECHER STOWE (1811–1896)

Children require guidance and sympathy far more than instruction.
ANNIE SULLIVAN (1866–1936)

Children learn to smile from their parents.
SHINICHI SUZUKI (1898–1998)

If you raise your children to feel that they can accomplish any goal or task they decide upon, you will have succeeded as a parent and you will have given your children the greatest of all blessings.
BRIAN TRACY (1944–)

The most remarkable thing about my mother is that for thirty years she served the family nothing but leftovers. The original meal has never been found.
CALVIN TRILLIN (1935–)

I have found the best way to give advice to your children is to find out what they want and then advise them to do it.
HARRY S TRUMAN (1884–1972)

My mother had a great deal of trouble with me, but I think she enjoyed it.
MARK TWAIN (1835–1910)

I stood in the hospital corridor the night after she was born. Through a window I could see all the small, crying newborn infants, and somewhere among them slept the one who was mine. I stood there for hours filled with happiness until the night nurse sent me to bed.
LIV ULLMAN (1938–)

If you want children to keep their feet on the ground, put some responsibility on their shoulders.
ABIGAIL VAN BUREN (1918–)

How simple a thing it seems to me that to know ourselves as we are, we must know our mothers' names.
ALICE WALKER (1944–)

The hand that rocks the cradle is the hand that rules the world.
WILLIAM ROSS WALLACE (1819–1881)

My hope for my children must be that they respond to the still, small voice of God in their own hearts.
ANDREW YOUNG (1932–)

When you put faith, hope, and love together, you can raise positive kids in a negative world.
ZIG ZIGLAR (1926–)

It takes a village to raise a child.
AFRICAN PROVERB

A mother holds her children's hands for a while, their hearts forever.
ANONYMOUS

Don't limit a child to your own learning, for he was born in another time.
ANONYMOUS

The trouble with being a parent is that by the time you are experienced, you are unemployed.
ANONYMOUS

Govern a family as you would cook a small fish, very gently.
CHINESE PROVERB

When you have children yourself, you begin to understand what you owe your parents.
JAPANESE PROVERB

An ounce of mother is worth a ton of priest.
SPANISH PROVERB

Passion

Passion cuts everything else, it blocks all, it's what psychologists call unhealthy. It's what one calls total alienation.
ISABELLE ADJANI (1955–)

When the habitually even-tempered suddenly fly into a passion, that explosion is apt to be more impressive than the outburst of the most violent amongst us.
MARGERY ALLINGHAM (1904–1966), *Death of a Ghost*

All humanity is passion; without passion, religion, history, novels, art would be ineffectual.
HONORÉ DE BALZAC (1799–1850)

There was a disturbance in my heart, a voice that spoke there and said, I want, I want, I want! It happened every afternoon, and when I tried to suppress it, it got even stronger.
SAUL BELLOW (1915–2005)

I had learnt to seek intensity… more of life, a concentrated sense of life.
NINA BERBEROVA (1901–1993)

He only employs his passion who can make no use of his reason.
CICERO (106–43 BC)

My passions were all gathered together like fingers that made a fist. Drive is considered aggression today; I knew it then as purpose.
BETTE DAVIS (1908–1989), *The Lonely Life*

Only passions, great passions, can elevate the soul to great things.
DENIS DIDEROT (1713–1784)

Judgment, not passion should prevail.
EPICHARMUS (C. 540–450 BC)

Passion makes the world go round. Love just makes it a safer place.
ICE T (1958–), *The Ice Opinion*

Be still when you have nothing to say; when genuine passion moves you, say what you've got to say, and say it hot.
D. H. LAWRENCE (1885–1930)

Waste no more time talking about great souls and how they should be. Become one yourself!
MARCUS AURELIUS ANTONINUS (121–180)

The worst sin—perhaps the only sin—passion can commit, is to be joyless.
DOROTHY L. SAYERS (1893–1957), *Gaudy Night*

It is easier to exclude harmful passions than to rule them, and to deny them admittance than to control them after they have been admitted.
SENECA (5 BC–AD 65)

Blaze with the fire that is never extinguished.
LUISA SIGEA (1522–1560)

Passion is the quickest to develop, and the quickest to fade. Intimacy develops more slowly, and commitment more gradually still.
ROBERT STERNBERG (1949–)

The happiness of a man in this life does not consist in the absence but in the mastery of his passions.
ALFRED, LORD TENNYSON (1809–1892)

It's the soul's duty to be loyal to its own desires. It must abandon itself to its master passion.
REBECCA WEST (1892–1983)

Nothing great in the world has been accomplished without passion.
GEORG WILHELM (1770–1831)

The Past

By a series of violent shocks, the nations in succession have struggled to shake off the Past, to reverse the action of Time and the verdict of success, and to rescue the world from the reign of the dead.
LORD ACTON (1834–1902)

This only is denied to God: the power to undo the past.
AGATHON (448–400 BC)

The past is a source of knowledge, and the future is a source of hope. Love of the past implies faith in the future.
STEPHEN AMBROSE (1936–2002)

The book says, we might be through with the past, but the past ain't through with us.
PAUL THOMAS ANDERSON (1970–), *Magnolia*

One must always maintain one's connection to the past and yet ceaselessly pull away from it. To remain in touch with the past requires a love of memory. To remain in touch with the past requires a constant imaginative effort.
GASTON BACHELARD (1884–1962)

Antiquities are history defaced, or some remnants of history which have casually escaped the shipwreck of time.
SIR FRANCIS BACON (1561–1626)

The present contains nothing more than the past, and what is found in the effect was already in the cause.
HENRI BERGSON (1859–1941)

I tend to live in the past because most of my life is there.
HERB CAEN (1916–1997)

The past is all holy to us; the dead are all holy; even they that were wicked when alive.
THOMAS CARLYLE (1795–1881)

All the king's horses and all the king's men can't put the past together again. So let's remember: Don't try to saw sawdust.
DALE CARNEGIE (1888–1955)

To look back to antiquity is one thing, to go back to it is another.
CHARLES CALEB COLTON (1780–1832)

Study the past if you would divine the future.
CONFUCIUS (551–479 BC)

Stop acting as if life is a rehearsal. Live this day as if it were your last. The past is over and gone. The future is not guaranteed.
WAYNE D. DYER (1940–)

The farther behind I leave the past, the closer I am to forging my own character.
ISABELLE EBERHARDT (1877–1904)

The distinction between the past, present and future is only a stubbornly persistent illusion.
ALBERT EINSTEIN (1879–1955)

With memory set smarting like a reopened wound, a man's past is not simply a dead history, an outworn preparation of the present: it is not a repented error shaken loose from the life: it is a still quivering part of himself, bringing shudders and bitter flavors and the tinglings of a merited shame.
GEORGE ELIOT (1819–1880)

Only by acceptance of the past, can you alter it.
T. S. ELIOT (1888–1965)

There is no past that we can bring back by longing for it. There is only an eternally new now that builds and creates itself out of the Best as the past withdraws.
JOHANN WOLFGANG VON GOETHE (1749–1832)

The past is a foreign country; they do things differently there.
LESLIE POLES HARTLEY (1895–1972)

Clogged with yesterday's excess, the body drags the mind down with it.
HORACE (65–8 BC)

Events in the past may be roughly divided into those which probably never happened and those which do not matter.
WILLIAM RALPH INGE (1860–1954)

We can draw lessons from the past, but we cannot live in it.
LYNDON B. JOHNSON (1908–1973)

The past is prophetic in that it asserts loudly that wars are poor chisels for carving out peaceful tomorrows.
MARTIN LUTHER KING JR. (1929–1968)

Without freedom from the past, there is no freedom at all, because the mind is never new, fresh, innocent.
JIDDU KRISHNAMURTI (1895–1986)

Look not mournfully into the past. It comes not back again. Wisely improve the present. It is thine. Go forth to meet the shadowy future, without fear.
HENRY WADSWORTH LONGFELLOW (1807–1882)

I don't think of the past. The only thing that matters is the everlasting present.
W. SOMERSET MAUGHAM (1874–1965), *The Moon and Sixpence*

Because men really respect only that which was founded of old and has developed slowly, he who wants to live on after his death must take care not only of his posterity but even more of his past.
FRIEDRICH NIETZSCHE (1844–1900)

Man … cannot learn to forget, but hangs on the past: however far or fast he runs, that chain runs with him.
FRIEDRICH NIETZSCHE (1844–1900)

Who controls the past controls the future: who controls the present controls the past.
GEORGE ORWELL (1903–1950)

Live neither in the past nor in the future, but let each day's work absorb your entire energies, and satisfy your widest ambition.
SIR WILLIAM OSLER (1849–1919)

The good of other times let people state; I think it lucky I was born so late.
OVID (43 BC–AD 17)

The present is never our goal: the past and present are our means: the future alone is our goal. Thus, we never live but we hope to live; and always hoping to be happy, it is inevitable that we will never be so.
BLAISE PASCAL (1623–1662)

Some are so very studious of learning what was done by the ancients that they know not how to live with the moderns.
WILLIAM PENN (1644–1718)

You have to know the past to understand the present.
CARL SAGAN (1934–1996)

I tell you the past is a bucket of ashes, so live not in your yesterdays, not just for tomorrow, but in the here and now. Keep moving and forget the post mortems; and remember, no one can get the jump on the future.
CARL SANDBURG (1878–1967)

Those who cannot remember the past are condemned to repeat it.
GEORGE SANTAYANA (1863–1952), *The Life of Reason*

Things without all remedy should be without regard: what's done, is done.
WILLIAM SHAKESPEARE (1564–1616), *Macbeth*

We cannot change our past. We cannot change the fact that people act in a certain way. We cannot change the inevitable. The only thing we can do is play on the one string we have, and that is our attitude.
CHARLES R. SWINDOLL (1934–)

The past has to inform the present.
JOHN TURTURRO (1957–)

The destruction of the past is perhaps the greatest of all crimes.
SIMONE WEIL (1910–1943)

The past is but the past of a beginning.
H. G. WELLS (1866–1946)

The Past—the dark unfathomed retrospect! The teeming gulf—the sleepers and the shadows! The past! the infinite greatness of the past! For what is the present after all but a growth out of the past?
WALT WHITMAN (1819–1892)

One's past is what one is. It is the only way by which people should be judged.
OSCAR WILDE (1854–1900)

If you look back too much, you will soon be headed that way.
ANONYMOUS

If you must cry over spilled milk then please try to condense it.
ANONYMOUS

It is sadder to find the past again and find it inadequate to the present than it is to have it elude you and remain forever a harmonious conception of memory.
ANONYMOUS

The rewards in life go to those who are willing to give up the past.
ANONYMOUS

Nothing is as new as something which has been long forgotten.
GERMAN PROVERB

Patience

Learn the art of patience. Apply discipline to your thoughts when they become anxious over the outcome of a goal. Impatience breeds anxiety, fear, discouragement and failure. Patience creates confidence, decisiveness, and a rational outlook, which eventually leads to success.
BRIAN ADAMS (1959–)

Patience is bitter, but its fruit is sweet.
ARISTOTLE (384–322 BC)

Patience is the companion of wisdom.
SAINT AUGUSTINE (354–430)

Never think that God's delays are God's denials. Hold on; hold fast; hold out. Patience is genius.
GEORGE-LOUIS DE BUFFON (1707–1788)

Our patience will achieve more than our force.
EDMUND BURKE (1729–1797)

Endurance is patience concentrated.
THOMAS CARLYLE (1795–1881)

Patience is the greatest of all virtues.
CATO THE ELDER (234–149 BC)

Patience is the support of weakness; impatience the ruin of strength.
CHARLES CALEB COLTON (1780–1832)

Have patience with all things, but chiefly have patience with yourself. Do not lose courage in considering your own imperfections but instantly set about remedying them—every day begin the task anew.
SAINT FRANCIS DE SALES (1567–1622)

Patience, persistence, and perspiration make an unbeatable combination for success.
NAPOLEON HILL (1883–1970)

The fates have given mankind a patient soul.
HOMER (800–700 BC), *The Iliad*

Have courage for the great sorrows of life and patience for the small ones; and when you have laboriously accomplished your daily task, go to sleep in peace. God is awake.
VICTOR HUGO (1802–1885)

Patience has its limits. Take it too far, and it's cowardice.
GEORGE JACKSON (1941–1971)

There art two cardinal sins from which all others spring: Impatience and Laziness.
FRANZ KAFKA (1883–1924)

We could never learn to be brave and patient, if there were only joy in the world.
HELEN KELLER (1880–1968)

Do you have the patience to wait until your mud settles and the water is clear? Can you remain unmoving until the right action arises by itself?
LAO-TZU (C. 600 BC)

You must first have a lot of patience to learn to have patience.
STANISLAW LEC (1909–1966), *Unkempt Thoughts*

Patience serves as a protection against wrongs as clothes do against cold. For if you put on more clothes as the cold increases, it will have no power to hurt you. So in like manner you must grow in patience when you meet with great wrongs, and they will then be powerless to vex your mind.
LEONARDO DA VINCI (1452–1519)

Endurance is the crowning quality, and patience all the passion of great hearts.
JAMES RUSSELL LOWELL (1819–1891)

If I have ever made any valuable discoveries, it has been owing more to patient attention, than to any other talent.
SIR ISAAC NEWTON (1642–1727)

Endurance is nobler than strength and patience than beauty.
JOHN RUSKIN (1819–1900)

How poor are they who have not patience!
What wound did ever heal but by degrees.
WILLIAM SHAKESPEARE (1564–1616), *Othello*

It is very strange that the years teach us patience—that the shorter our time, the greater our capacity for waiting.
ELIZABETH TAYLOR (1932–), *A Wreath of Roses*

I am extraordinarily patient, provided I get my own way in the end.
MARGARET THATCHER (1925–)

Patience is the best remedy for every trouble.
TITUS MACCIUS PLAUTUS (254–184 BC), *Rudens*

A handful of patience is worth more than a bushel of brains.
DUTCH PROVERB

Patients

The doctor of the future will give no medicine, but will interest her or his patients in the care of the human frame, in a proper diet, and in the cause and prevention of disease.
THOMAS A. EDISON (1847–1931)

I was once thrown out of a mental hospital for depressing the other patients.
OSCAR LEVANT (1906–1972)

To study the phenomenon of disease without books is to sail an uncharted sea, while to study books without patients is not to go to sea at all.
SIR WILLIAM OSLER (1849–1919)

The best doctor in the world is the veterinarian. He can't ask his patients what is the matter—he's got to just know.
WILL ROGERS (1879–1935)

Patriotism

Our obligations to our country never cease but with our lives.
JOHN ADAMS (1735–1826)

How beautiful is death, when earn'd by virtue!
Who would not be that youth? What pity is it
That we can die but once to serve our country!
JOSEPH ADDISON (1672–1719), *Cato*

Nationalism is a silly cock crowing on his own dunghill.
RICHARD ALDINGTON (1892–1962)

"My country, right or wrong," is a thing that no patriot would think of saying except in a desperate case. It is like saying, "My mother, drunk or sober."
G. K. CHESTERTON (1874–1936)

When I am abroad, I always make it a rule never to criticize or attack the government of my own country. I make up for lost time when I come home.
SIR WINSTON CHURCHILL (1874–1965)

Patriotism is easy to understand in America. It means looking out for yourself by looking out for your country.
CALVIN COOLIDGE (1872–1933)

Patriotism is when love of your own people comes first; nationalism, when hate for people other than your own comes first.
CHARLES DE GAULLE (1890–1970)

Heroism on command, senseless violence, and all the loathsome nonsense that goes by the name of patriotism—how passionately I hate them!
ALBERT EINSTEIN (1879–1955)

When a whole nation is roaring Patriotism at the top of its voice, I am fain to explore the cleanness of its hands and purity of its heart.
RALPH WALDO EMERSON (1803–1882)

I only regret that I have but one life to lose for my country.
NATHAN HALE (1755–1776), last words

Patriotism is proud of a country's virtues and eager to correct its deficiencies; it also acknowledges the legitimate patriotism of other countries, with their own specific virtues. The pride of nationalism, however, trumpets its country's virtues and denies its deficiencies, while it is contemptuous toward the virtues of other countries. It wants to be, and proclaims itself to be, "the greatest," but greatness is not required of a country; only goodness is.
SYDNEY J. HARRIS (1917–1986)

It is not unseemly for a man to die fighting in defense of his country.
HOMER (800–700 BC), *The Iliad*

The single best augury is to fight for one's country.
HOMER (800–700 BC), *The Iliad*

Patriotism is the last refuge of a scoundrel.
SAMUEL JOHNSON (1709–1784)

And so, my fellow Americans: ask not what your country can do for you, ask what you can do for your country. My fellow citizens of the world: ask not what America will do for you, but what together we can do for the freedom of man.
JOHN F. KENNEDY (1917–1963)

You're not to be so blind with patriotism that you can't face reality. Wrong is wrong, no matter who does it or says it.
MALCOLM X (1925–1965)

Patriotism is a kind of religion; it is the egg from which wars are hatched.
GUY DE MAUPASSANT (1850–1893)

War is an ugly thing, but not the ugliest of things. The decayed and degraded state of moral and patriotic feeling which thinks that nothing is worth war is much worse. The person who has nothing for which he is willing to fight, nothing which is more important than his own personal safety, is a miserable creature and has no chance of being free unless made and kept so by the exertions of better men than himself.
JOHN STUART MILL (1806–1873)

Patriotism is often an arbitrary veneration of real estate above principles.
GEORGE JEAN NATHAN (1882–1958)

Patriotism is the willingness to kill and be killed for trivial reasons.
BERTRAND RUSSELL (1872–1970)

You'll never have a quiet world till you knock the patriotism out of the human race.
GEORGE BERNARD SHAW (1856–1950), *Misalliance*

Patriotism is your conviction that this country is superior to all other countries because you were born in it.
GEORGE BERNARD SHAW (1856–1950)

Patriotism is not short, frenzied outbursts of emotion, but the tranquil and steady dedication of a lifetime.
ADLAI E. STEVENSON II (1900–1965)

The flag is the embodiment, not of sentiment, but of history.
WOODROW WILSON (1856–1924)

Patriots

True patriots all; for be it understood,
We left our country for our country's good.
GEORGE BARRINGTON (1755–1804)

For what were all these country patriots born?
To hunt, and vote, and raise the price of corn?
LORD BYRON (1788–1824)

No matter that patriotism is too often the refuge of scoundrels. Dissent, rebellion, and all-around hell-raising remain the true duty of patriots.
BARBARA EHRENREICH (1941–)

Patriots try to solve real problems and not seek out remedies to perceived problems.
ALCÉE HASTINGS (1936–)

I've seen a lot of patriots and they all died just like anybody else if it hurt bad enough and once they

were dead their patriotism was only good for legends; it was bad for their prose and made them write bad poetry. If you are going to be a great patriot, i.e. loyal to any existing order of government (not one who wishes to destroy the existing for something better), you want to be killed early if your life and works won't stink.
ERNEST HEMINGWAY (1899–1961)

The tree of liberty must be refreshed from time to time with the blood of patriots and tyrants.
THOMAS JEFFERSON (1743–1826)

When a nation is filled with strife, then do patriots flourish.
LAO-TZU (C. 600 BC)

The American patriots of today continue the tradition of the long line of patriots before them, by helping to promote liberty and freedom around the world.
JOHN LINDER (1942–)

The military caste did not originate as a party of patriots, but as a party of bandits.
H. L. MENCKEN (1880–1956)

There are patriots who opposed the war in Iraq and there are patriots who supported the war in Iraq. We are one people, all of us pledging allegiance to the stars and stripes, all of us defending the United States of America.
BARACK OBAMA (1961–)

From death springs life and from the graves of great patriots springs a great nation.
PATRICK HENRY PEARSE (1879–1916)

Patriots always talk of dying for their country, but never of killing for their country.
BERTRAND RUSSELL (1872–1970)

When a nation is filled with strife, then do patriots flourish.
ADLAI E. STEVENSON II (1900–1965)

Peace

We make war that we may live in peace.
ARISTOTLE (384–322 BC), *Nichomachean Ethics*

Better than a thousand hollow words, is one word that brings peace.
THE BUDDHA (563–483 BC)

One of the most basic principles for making and keeping peace within and between nations … is that in political, military, moral, and spiritual confrontations, there should be an honest attempt at the reconciliation of differences before resorting to combat.
JIMMY CARTER (1924–)

We shall find peace. We shall hear the angels, we shall see the sky sparkling with diamonds.
ANTON CHEKHOV (1860–1904)

The name of peace is sweet, and the thing itself is beneficial, but there is a great difference between peace and servitude. Peace is freedom in tranquillity, servitude is the worst of all evils, to be resisted not only by war, but even by death.
CICERO (106–43 BC)

If you want to make peace, you don't talk to your friends. You talk to your enemies.
MOSHE DAYAN (1915–1981)

That doctrine of peace at any price has done more mischief than any I can well recall that have been afloat in this country. It has occasioned more wars than any of the most ruthless conquerors. It has disturbed and nearly destroyed that political equilibrium so necessary to the liberties and the welfare of the world.
BENJAMIN DISRAELI (1804–1881)

I like to believe that people in the long run are going to do more to promote peace than our governments. Indeed, I think that people want peace so much that one of these days governments had better get out of the way and let them have it.
DWIGHT D. EISENHOWER (1890–1969)

Nothing can bring you peace but yourself.
RALPH WALDO EMERSON (1803–1882)

Peace is its own reward.
MAHATMA GANDHI (1869–1948)

If you wish to experience peace, provide peace for another.
TENZIN GYATSO (1935–)

When the power of love overcomes the love of power, the world will know peace.
JIMI HENDRIX (1942–1970)

Has not peace honours and glories of her own unattended by the dangers of war?
HERMOCRATES (C. 407 BC)

Among the individuals, as well as among nations, respecting the other people's rights leads to peace.
BENITO JUÁREZ (1806–1872)

I do not want the peace which passeth understanding, I want the understanding which bringeth peace.
HELEN KELLER (1880–1968)

[P]eace does not rest in the charters and covenants alone. It lies in the hearts and minds of all people. So let us not rest all our hopes on parchment and on paper, let us strive to build peace, a desire for peace, a willingness to work for peace in the hearts and minds of all of our people. I believe that we can. I believe the problems of human destiny are not beyond the reach of human beings.
JOHN F. KENNEDY (1917–1963)

Those who make peaceful revolution impossible will make violent revolution inevitable.
JOHN F. KENNEDY (1917–1963)

Peace is not merely a distant goal that we seek, but a means by which we arrive at that goal.
MARTIN LUTHER KING JR. (1929–1968)

If war is ever lawful, then peace is sometimes sinful.
C. S. LEWIS (1898–1963)

With malice toward none, with charity for all, ... let us strive on to finish the work we are in, ... to do all which may achieve and cherish a just and lasting peace among ourselves and with all nations.
ABRAHAM LINCOLN (1809–1865)

You can't separate peace from freedom because no one can be at peace unless he has his freedom.
MALCOLM X (1925–1965), *Malcolm X Speaks*

If man does find the solution for world peace it will be the most revolutionary reversal of his record we have ever known.
GEORGE C. MARSHALL (1880–1959)

If you want peace, stop fighting. If you want peace of mind, stop fighting with your thoughts.
PETER MCWILLIAMS (1949–2000)

Peace is not a relationship of nations. It is a condition of mind brought about by a serenity of soul. Peace is not merely the absence of war. It is also a state of mind. Lasting peace can come only to peaceful people.
JAWAHARLAL NEHRU (1889–1964)

The only alternative to coexistence is codestruction.
JAWAHARLAL NEHRU (1889–1964)

When you find peace within yourself, you become the kind of person who can live at peace with others.
PEACE PILGRIM (1908–1981)

Peace has never come from dropping bombs. Real peace comes from enlightenment and educating people to behave more in a divine manner.
CARLOS SANTANA (1947–)

The peace of heaven is theirs that lift their swords,
In such a just and charitable war.
WILLIAM SHAKESPEARE (1564–1616), *King John*

Peace is not only better than war, but infinitely more arduous.
GEORGE BERNARD SHAW (1856–1950)

Peace is not an absence of war, it is a virtue, a

state of mind, a disposition for benevolence, confidence, justice.
BENEDICT DE SPINOZA (1632–1677)

Let us forgive each other—only then will we live in peace.
LEO TOLSTOY (1828–1910)

Let him who desires peace prepare for war.
FLAVIUS RENATUS VEGETIUS (C. 400), *De Rei Militari*

Peace won by the compromise of principles is a short-lived achievement.
ANONYMOUS

The more you sweat in peacetime, the less you bleed during war.
CHINESE PROVERB

Peace of Mind

Peace comes from within. Do not seek it without.
THE BUDDHA (563–483 BC)

Those who seek consolation in existing churches often pay for their peace of mind with a tacit agreement to ignore a great deal of what is known about the way the world works.
MIHALY CSIKSZENTMIHALYI (1934–), *Flow: The Psychology of Optimal Experience*

Money cannot buy peace of mind. It cannot heal ruptured relationships, or build meaning into a life that has none.
RICHARD M. DEVOS (1926–)

Nothing can bring you peace but yourself.
RALPH WALDO EMERSON (1803–1882)

Each one has to find his peace from within. And peace to be real must be unaffected by outside circumstances.
MAHATMA GANDHI (1869–1948)

If we are aware of our life, our way of looking at things, we will know how to make peace right in the moment, we are alive.
THICH NHAT HAHN (1926–)

Success in highest and noblest form calls for peace of mind and enjoyment and happiness which comes only to the man who has found the work he likes best.
NAPOLEON HILL (1883–1970)

I do not want the peace which passeth understanding, I want the understanding which bringeth peace.
HELEN KELLER (1880–1968)

When we are unable to find tranquility within ourselves, it is useless to seek it elsewhere.
FRANÇOIS DE LA ROCHEFOUCAULD (1613–1680)

Nothing is more conducive to peace of mind than not having any opinion at all.
GEORG C. LICHTENBERG (1742–1799)

If you want peace, stop fighting. If you want peace of mind, stop fighting with your thoughts.
PETER MCWILLIAMS (1949–2000)

Peace is not a relationship of nations. It is a condition of mind brought about by a serenity of soul. Peace is not merely the absence of war. It is also a state of mind. Lasting peace can come only to peaceful people.
JAWAHARLAL NEHRU (1889–1964)

When you find peace within yourself, you become the kind of person who can live at peace with others.
PEACE PILGRIM (1908–1981)

To be feared is to fear: no one has been able to strike terror into others and at the same time enjoy peace of mind.
SENECA (5 BC–AD 65)

Peace is not an absence of war, it is a virtue, a state of mind, a disposition for benevolence, confidence, justice.
BENEDICT DE SPINOZA (1632–1677)

First keep the peace within yourself, then you can also bring peace to others.
THOMAS À KEMPIS (1380–1471)

Peace of mind is that mental condition in which you have accepted the worst.
LIN YUTANG (1895–1976)

People

It seemed the world was divided into good and bad people. The good ones slept better … while the bad ones seemed to enjoy the waking hours much more.
WOODY ALLEN (1935–)

There are two kinds of people, those who finish what they start and so on.
ROBERT BYRNE (1928–)

As long as people will accept crap, it will be financially profitable to dispense it.
DICK CAVETT (1936–)

Horse sense is the thing a horse has which keeps it from betting on people.
W. C. FIELDS (1880–1946)

I know that there are people who do not love their fellow man, and I hate people like that!
TOM LEHRER (1928–)

Most people ignore most poetry
because most poetry ignores most people.
ADRIAN MITCHELL (1932–)

Many people would sooner die than think; in fact, they do so.
BERTRAND RUSSELL (1872–1970)

You can fool too many of the people too much of the time.
JAMES THURBER (1894–1961)

Clothes make the man. Naked people have little or no influence on society.
MARK TWAIN (1835–1910)

Perception

No man has the right to dictate what other men should perceive, create or produce, but all should be encouraged to reveal themselves, their perceptions and emotions, and to build confidence in the creative spirit.
ANSEL ADAMS (1902–1984)

If the doors of perception were cleansed, everything would appear to man as it is, infinite. For man has closed himself up, till he sees all things thru' chinks of his cavern.
WILLIAM BLAKE (1757–1827)

We have learned that terrorist attacks are not caused by the use of strength; they are invited by the perception of weakness. And the surest way to avoid attacks on our own people is to engage the enemy where he lives and plans. We are fighting that enemy in Iraq and Afghanistan today so that we do not meet him again on our own streets, in our own cities.
GEORGE W. BUSH (1946–)

[O]ne of the strongest motives that lead men to art and science is escape from everyday life with its painful crudity and hopeless dreariness, from the fetters of one's own ever-shifting desires. A finely tempered nature longs to escape from the personal life into the world of objective perception and thought.
ALBERT EINSTEIN (1879–1955)

Do what you know and perception is converted into character.
RALPH WALDO EMERSON (1803–1882)

Only in quiet waters do things mirror themselves undistorted. Only in a quiet mind is adequate perception of the world.
HANS MARGOLIUS (1902–1984)

Perception is strong and sight weak. In strategy it is important to see distant things as if they were close and to take a distanced view of close things.
MIYAMOTO MUSASHI (1584–1645)

I don't believe in intuition. When you get sudden flashes of perception, it is just the brain working faster than usual. But you've been getting ready to know it for a long time, and when it comes, you feel you've known it always.
KATHERINE ANNE PORTER (1894–1980)

Science is nothing but developed perception, interpreted intent, common sense rounded out and minutely articulated.
GEORGE SANTAYANA (1863–1952)

All perception of truth is the detection of an analogy.
HENRY DAVID THOREAU (1817–1862)

The poet, the artist, the sleuth—whoever sharpens our perception tends to be antisocial … he cannot go along with currents and trends.
ALFRED NORTH WHITEHEAD (1861–1947)

Perfection

This is the very perfection of a man, to find out his own imperfection.
SAINT AUGUSTINE (354–430)

There is such a thing as perfection … and our purpose for living is to find that perfection and show it forth.… Each of us is in truth an unlimited idea of freedom. Everything that limits us we have to put aside.
RICHARD BACH (1936–)

I don't confuse greatness with perfection. To be great anyhow is … the higher achievement.
LOIS MCMASTER BUJOLD (1949–), *Mirror Dance*

Out of perfection nothing can be made. Every process involves breaking something up.
JOSEPH CAMPBELL (1904–1987)

Try as hard as we may for perfection, the net result of our labors is an amazing variety of imperfectness. We are surprised at our own versatility in being able to fail in so many different ways.
SAMUEL MCCHORD CROTHERS (1857–1927)

Have no fear of perfection—you'll never reach it.
SALVADOR DALÍ (1904–1989)

Artists who seek perfection in everything are those who cannot attain it in anything.
EUGÈNE DELACROIX (1798–1863)

I am careful not to confuse excellence with perfection. Excellence, I can reach for; perfection is God's business.
MICHAEL J. FOX (1961–)

Practice means to perform, over and over again in the face of all obstacles, some act of vision, of faith, of desire. Practice is a means of inviting the perfection desired.
MARTHA GRAHAM (1894–1991)

Trifles make perfection, but perfection is no trifle.
MICHELANGELO (1475–1564)

The fact of storytelling hints at a fundamental human unease, hints at human imperfection. Where there is perfection there is no story to tell.
BEN OKRI (1959–)

The thing that is really hard, and really amazing, is giving up on being perfect and beginning the work of becoming yourself.
ANNA QUINDLEN (1953–)

Perfection is achieved, not when there is nothing more to add, but when there is nothing left to take away.
ANTOINE DE SAINT-EXUPÉRY (1900–1944)

It is through Art, and through Art only, that we can realize our perfection.
OSCAR WILDE (1854–1900)

Performance

It is an immutable law in business that words are words, explanations are explanations, promises are promises but only performance is reality.
HAROLD S. GENEEN (1910–1997)

Performance stands out like a ton of diamonds. Non-performance can almost always be explained away.
HAROLD S. GENEEN (1910–1997)

Remember that there is a proper dignity and proportion to be observed in the performance of every act of life.
MARCUS AURELIUS ANTONINUS (121–180)

Life has no rehearsals, only performances.
ANONYMOUS

Persecution

It is folly for an eminent person to think of escaping censure, and a weakness to be affected by it. All the illustrious persons of antiquity, and indeed of every age, have passed through this fiery persecution. There is no defense against reproach but obscurity; it is a kind of concomitant to greatness, as satires and invectives were an essential part of a Roman triumph.
JOSEPH ADDISON (1672–1719)

A religion which requires persecution to sustain it is of the devil's propagation.
HOSEA BALLOU (1771–1852)

Cruel persecutions and intolerance are not accidents, but grow out of the very essence of religion, namely, its absolute claims.
MORRIS COHEN (1880–1947)

Persecution was at least a sign of personal interest. Tolerance is composed of nine parts of apathy to one of brotherly love.
FRANK MOORE COLBY (1865–1925)

Persecution is the first law of society because it is always easier to suppress criticism than to meet it.
HOWARD MUMFORD JONES (1892–1980)

Indeed the dictum that truth always triumphs over persecution, is one of those pleasant falsehoods which men repeat after one another till they pass into common places, but which all experience refutes.
JOHN STUART MILL (1806–1873)

Persecution is not an original feature in any religion; but it is always the strongly marked feature of all religions established by law.
THOMAS PAINE (1737–1809)

Perseverance

Courage and perseverance have a magical talisman, before which difficulties disappear and obstacles vanish into air.
JOHN QUINCY ADAMS (1767–1848)

If you wish success in life, make perseverance your bosom friend, experience your wise counselor, caution your elder brother and hope your guardian genius.
JOSEPH ADDISON (1672–1719)

The surest method against scandal is to live it down by perseverance in well doing.
HERMANN BOERHAAVE (1668–1738)

Studies indicate that the one quality all successful people have is persistence. They're willing to spend more time accomplishing a task and to persevere in the face of many difficult odds. There's a very positive relationship between people's ability to accomplish any task and the time they're willing to spend on it.
DR. JOYCE BROTHERS (1928–)

In the confrontation between the stream and the rock, the stream always wins—not through strength but by perseverance.
H. JACKSON BROWN JR. (1948–)

Most of the important things in the world have been accomplished by people who have kept on trying when there seemed to be no hope at all.
DALE CARNEGIE (1888–1955)

Perseverance is not a long race; it is many short races one after the other.
WALTER ELLIOT (1842–1928)

Edison failed 10,000 times before he made the electric light. Do not be discouraged if you fail a few times.
NAPOLEON HILL (1883–1970)

I'm convinced that about half of what separates the successful entrepreneurs from the non-successful ones is pure perseverance.
STEVE JOBS (1955–)

Few things are impossible to diligence and skill. Great works are performed not by strength, but perseverance.
SAMUEL JOHNSON (1709–1784)

Perseverance is a great element of success. If you only knock long enough and loud enough at the gate, you are sure to wake up somebody.
HENRY WADSWORTH LONGFELLOW (1807–1882)

In general, any form of exercise, if pursued continuously, will help train us in perseverance. Long-distance running is particularly good training in perseverance.
MAO TSE-TUNG (1893–1976)

Perseverance is more prevailing than violence; and many things which cannot be overcome when they are together, yield themselves up when taken little by little.
PLUTARCH (AD 46–120), *Lives*

When you get to the end of your rope, tie a knot and hang on.
FRANKLIN D. ROOSEVELT (1882–1945)

By perseverance the snail reached the ark.
CHARLES H. SPURGEON (1834–1892)

The miracle, or the power, that elevates the few is to be found in their industry, application, and perseverance under the prompting of a brave, determined spirit.
MARK TWAIN (1835–1910)

Persistence

Persistence pays and so does a willingness to follow directions.
LYNN ABBEY (1948–)

You must keep sending work out; you must never let a manuscript do nothing but eat its head off in a drawer. You send that work out again and again, while you're working on another one. If you have talent, you will receive some measure of success—but only if you persist.
ISAAC ASIMOV (1920–1992)

Persistence and self-education are the keys. Nobody can teach you how to write—you have to teach yourself, using the examples of others for inspiration.
GREG BEAR (1951–)

Nothing in the world can take the place of Persistence. Talent will not; nothing is more common than unsuccessful men with talent. Genius will not; unrewarded genius is almost a proverb. Education will not; the world is full of educated derelicts. Persistence and determination alone are omnipotent. The slogan "Press On" has solved and always will solve the problems of the human race.
CALVIN COOLIDGE (1872–1933)

That which we persist in doing becomes easier, not that the task itself has become easier, but that our ability to perform it has improved.
RALPH WALDO EMERSON (1803–1882)

Energy and persistence conquer all things.
BENJAMIN FRANKLIN (1706–1790)

Paralyze resistance with persistence.
WOODY HAYES (1913–1987)

Patience, persistence, and perspiration make an unbeatable combination for success.
NAPOLEON HILL (1883–1970)

Persistence is to the character of man as carbon is to steel.
NAPOLEON HILL (1883–1970)

The most interesting thing about a postage stamp is the persistence with which it sticks to its job.
NAPOLEON HILL (1883–1970)

They who lack talent expect things to happen without effort. They ascribe failure to a lack of inspiration or ability, or to misfortune, rather than to insufficient application. At the core of every true talent there is an awareness of the difficulties inherent in any achievement, and the confidence that by persistence and patience something worthwhile will be realized. Thus talent is a species of vigor.
ERIC HOFFER (1902–1983)

A little more persistence, a little more effort, and what seemed hopeless failure may turn to glorious success.
ELBERT HUBBARD (1856–1915)

Success is almost totally dependent upon drive and persistence. The extra energy required to make another effort or try another approach is the secret of winning.
DENIS WAITLEY (1933–)

We are made to persist. That's how we find out who we are.
TOBIAS WOLFF (1945–), *In Pharaoh's Army*

Personality

Intolerance of ambiguity is the mark of an authoritarian personality.
THEODOR W. ADORNO (1903–1969)

Poetry is not a turning loose of emotion, but an escape from emotion; it is not the expression of personality, but an escape from personality. But, of course, only those who have personality and emotions know what it means to want to escape from these things.
T. S. ELIOT (1888–1965), *Tradition and the Individual Talent*

I want freedom for the full expression of my personality.
MAHATMA GANDHI (1869–1948)

The meeting of two personalities is like the contact of two chemical substances: if there is any reaction, both are transformed.
CARL JUNG (1875–1961)

Like an unchecked cancer, hate corrodes the personality and eats away its vital unity. Hate destroys a man's sense of values and his objectivity. It causes him to describe the beautiful as ugly and the ugly as beautiful, and to confuse the true with the false and the false with the true.
MARTIN LUTHER KING JR. (1929–1968)

Humility is no substitute for a good personality.
FRAN LEBOWITZ (1950–), *Metropolitan Life*

Art is the desire of a man to express himself, to record the reactions of his personality to the world he lives in.
AMY LOWELL (1874–1925)

Knowledge and personality make doubt possible, but knowledge is also the cure of doubt; and when we get a full and adequate sense of personality we are lifted into a region where doubt is almost impossible, for no man can know himself as he is, and all fullness of his nature, without also knowing God.
T. T. MUNGER (1883–1975)

The peculiar striations that define someone's personality are too numerous to know, no matter how close the observer. A person we think we know can suddenly become someone else when previously hidden strands of his character are called to the fore by circumstance.
ELLIOT PERLMAN (1964–), *Seven Types of Ambiguity*

While one should always study the method of a great artist, one should never imitate his manner. The manner of an artist is essentially individual, the method of an artist is absolutely universal. The first is personality, which no one should copy; the second is perfection, which all should aim at.
OSCAR WILDE (1854–1900)

Economists are people who work with numbers but who don't have the personality to be accountants.
ANONYMOUS

If it weren't for caffeine I'd have no personality whatsoever!
ANONYMOUS

Perspective

I never saw an ugly thing in my life: for let the form of an object be what it may—light, shade, and perspective will always make it beautiful.
JOHN CONSTABLE (1776–1837)

Wisdom is your perspective on life, your sense of balance, your understanding of how the various parts and principles apply and relate to each other. It embraces judgment, discernment, comprehension. It is a gestalt or oneness, an integrated wholeness.
STEPHEN R. COVEY (1932–)

Meditation is the soul's perspective glass.
OWEN FELLTHAM (1602–1668)

Never write about a place until you're away from it, because that gives you perspective.
ERNEST HEMINGWAY (1899–1961)

Our loyalties must transcend our race, our tribe, our class, and our nation; and this means we must develop a world perspective.
MARTIN LUTHER KING JR. (1929–1968)

Everything we hear is an opinion, not a fact. Everything we see is a perspective, not the truth.
MARCUS AURELIUS ANTONINUS (121–180)

You must look within for value, but must look beyond for perspective.
DENIS WAITLEY (1933–)

Perspiration

Genius is one per cent inspiration, ninety-nine per cent perspiration.
THOMAS A. EDISON (1847–1931)

Patience, persistence, and perspiration make an unbeatable combination for success.
NAPOLEON HILL (1883–1970)

Give the laborer his wage before his perspiration be dry.
MUHAMMAD (C. 570–632)

Persuasion

Persuasion is often more effectual than force.
AESOP (620–560 BC)

Character may almost be called the most effective means of persuasion.
ARISTOTLE (384–322 BC)

Advertising is fundamentally persuasion, and persuasion happens to be not a science, but an art.
WILLIAM BERNBACH (1911–1982)

If you would persuade, you must appeal to interest rather than intellect.
BENJAMIN FRANKLIN (1706–1790)

Would you persuade, speak of interest, not of reason.
BENJAMIN FRANKLIN (1706–1790)

Oral delivery aims at persuasion and making the listener believe they are converted. Few persons are capable of being convinced; the majority allow themselves to be persuaded.
JOHANN WOLFGANG VON GOETHE (1749–1832)

People have a peculiar pleasure in making converts, that is, in causing others to enjoy what they enjoy, thus finding their own likeness represented and reflected back to them.
JOHANN WOLFGANG VON GOETHE (1749–1832)

Secrecy has many advantages, for when you tell someone the purpose of any object right away, they often think there is nothing to it.
JOHANN WOLFGANG VON GOETHE (1749–1832)

To make converts is the natural ambition of everyone.
JOHANN WOLFGANG VON GOETHE (1749–1832)

The art of pleasing consists in being pleased.
WILLIAM HAZLITT (1778–1830)

The real persuaders are our appetites, our fears and above all our vanity. The skillful propagandist stirs and coaches these internal persuaders.
ERIC HOFFER (1902–1983)

A companion's words of persuasion are effective.
HOMER (800–700 BC), *The Iliad*

Why harass with eternal purposes a mind too weak to grasp them?
HORACE (65–8 BC)

As there is no worse lie than a truth misunderstood by those who hear it, so reasonable arguments, challenges to magnanimity, and appeals to sympathy or justice, are folly when we are dealing with human crocodiles and boa-constrictors.
WILLIAM JAMES (1842–1910)

In a republican nation, whose citizens are to be led by reason and persuasion and not by force, the art of reasoning becomes of first importance
THOMAS JEFFERSON (1762–1826)

If economists could manage to get themselves thought of as humble, competent people on a level with dentists, that would be splendid.
JOHN MAYNARD KEYNES (1883–1946), *The Future*

If you wish to win a man over to your ideas, first make him your friend.
ABRAHAM LINCOLN (1809–1865)

When the conduct of men is designed to be influenced, persuasion, kind unassuming persuasion, should ever be adopted. It is an old and true maxim that "a drop of honey catches more flies than a gallon of gall." So with men. If you would win a man to your cause, first convince him that you are his sincere friend. Therein is a drop of honey that catches his heart, which, say what he will, is the great highroad to his reason, and which, once gained, you will find but little trouble in convincing him of the justice of your cause, if indeed that cause is really a good one.
ABRAHAM LINCOLN (1809–1865)

You may fool all the people some of the time, you can even fool some of the people all of the time, but you cannot fool all of the people all the time.
ABRAHAM LINCOLN (1809–1865)

The object of oratory alone is not truth, but persuasion.
LORD THOMAS BABINGTON MACAULAY (1800–1859)

People are usually more convinced by reasons they discovered themselves than by those found out by others.
BLAISE PASCAL (1623–1662)

I have with me two gods, Persuasion and Compulsion.
THEMISTOCLES (527–460 BC)

At the end of reasons comes persuasion.
LUDWIG WITTGENSTEIN (1889–1951)

The most important persuasion tool you have in your entire arsenal is integrity.
ZIG ZIGLAR (1926–)

If you can't get people to listen to you any other way, tell them it's confidential.
ANONYMOUS

Persuasion is better than force.
ANONYMOUS

That which proves too much, proves nothing!
ANONYMOUS

When a heart is on fire, sparks always fly out of the mouth.
ANONYMOUS

The tongue can paint what the eye can't see.
CHINESE PROVERB

Those that will not hear must be made to feel.
GERMAN PROVERB

Pessimism

Pessimists are the people who have no hope for themselves or for others. Pessimists are also people who think the human race is beneath their notice, that they're better than other human beings.
JAMES ARTHUR BALDWIN (1924–1987)

Pessimism, when you get used to it, is just as agreeable as optimism.
ARNOLD BENNETT (1867–1931)

The optimist proclaims that we live in the best of all possible worlds; and the pessimist fears this is true.
JAMES BRANCH CABELL (1879–1958), *The Silver Stallion*

Pessimism is only the name that men of weak nerves give to wisdom.
BERNARD DEVOTO (1897–1955)

I don't believe in pessimism. If something doesn't come up the way you want, forge ahead. If you think it's going to rain, it will.
CLINT EASTWOOD (1930–)

Pessimism never won any battle.
DWIGHT D. EISENHOWER (1890–1969)

The optimist sees the rose and not its thorns; the pessimist stares at the thorns, oblivious to the rose.
KAHLIL GIBRAN (1883–1931)

Pessimism of the spirit; optimism of the will.
ANTONIO GRAMSCI (1891–1937)

Don't ever become a pessimist ... a pessimist is correct oftener than an optimist, but an optimist has more fun—and neither can stop the march of events.
ROBERT A. HEINLEIN (1907–1988)

No pessimist ever discovered the secret of the stars or sailed an uncharted land, or opened a new doorway for the human spirit.
HELEN KELLER (1880–1968)

My pessimism extends to the point of even suspecting the sincerity of the pessimists.
JEAN ROSTAND (1894–1977), *Journal of a Character*

An optimist may see a light where there is none, but why must the pessimist always run to blow it out?
MICHEL DE SAINT-PIERRE (1916–1987)

An optimist is a person who sees a green light everywhere, while a pessimist sees only the red stoplight.... The truly wise person is colorblind.
DR. ALBERT SCHWEITZER (1875–1965)

Both optimists and pessimists contribute to our society. The optimist invents the airplane and the pessimist the parachute.
G. B. STERN (1890–1973)

A pessimist is one who makes difficulties of his opportunities, and an optimist is one who makes opportunities of his difficulties.
HARRY S TRUMAN (1884–1972)

The man who is a pessimist before forty-eight knows too much; if he is an optimist after it he knows too little.
MARK TWAIN (1835–1910)

There is no sadder sight than a young pessimist.
MARK TWAIN (1835–1910)

Pessimist: One who, when he has the choice of two evils, chooses both.
OSCAR WILDE (1854–1900)

Pessimism is as American as apple pie—frozen apple pie with a slice of processed cheese.
GEORGE F. WILL (1941–)

The nice part about being a pessimist is that you are constantly being either proven right or pleasantly surprised.
GEORGE F. WILL (1941–)

Pessimism only describes an attitude, and not facts, and hence is entirely subjective.
FRANCIS P. YOCKEY (1917–1960)

Pets

A boy can learn a lot from a dog: obedience, loyalty, and the importance of turning around three times before lying down.
ROBERT BENCHLEY (1889–1945)

I like pigs. Dogs look up to us. Cats look down on us. Pigs treat us as equals.
SIR WINSTON CHURCHILL (1874–1965)

Animals are such agreeable friends—they ask no questions, they pass no criticisms.
GEORGE ELIOT (1819–1880)

Old age means realizing you will never own all the dogs you wanted to.
JOE GORES (1931–)

If you are a dog and your owner suggests that you wear a sweater, suggest that he wear a tail.
FRAN LEBOWITZ (1950–)

No animal should ever jump up on the dining-room furniture unless absolutely certain that he can hold his own in the conversation.
FRAN LEBOWITZ (1950–)

We are alone, absolutely alone on this chance planet: and, amid all the forms of life that surround us, not one, excepting the dog, has made an alliance with us.
MAURICE MAETERLINCK (1862–1949)

Cats regard people as warm-blooded furniture.
JACQUELYN MITCHARD (1955–), *The Deep End of the Ocean*

A door is what a dog is perpetually on the wrong side of.
OGDEN NASH (1902–1971)

It's funny how dogs and cats know the inside of folks better than other folks do, isn't it?
ELEANOR H. PORTER (1868–1920), *Pollyanna*

I wonder if other dogs think poodles are members of a weird religious cult.
RITA RUDNER (1956–)

Yesterday I was a dog. Today I'm a dog. Tomorrow I'll probably still be a dog. Sigh! There's so little hope for advancement.
CHARLES M. SCHULZ (1922–2000), as Snoopy

We call them dumb animals, and so they are, for they cannot tell us how they feel, but they do not suffer less because they have no words.
ANNA SEWELL (1820–1878), *Black Beauty*

I loathe people who keep dogs. They are cowards who haven't got the guts to bite people themselves.
AUGUST STRINDBERG (1849–1912), *A Madman's Diary*

If you pick up a starving dog and make him prosperous, he will not bite you. This is the principal difference between a dog and a man.
MARK TWAIN (1835–1910)

My dog is worried about the economy because Alpo is up to 99 cents a can. That's almost $7.00 in dog money.
JOE WEINSTEIN (1953–)

If a dog jumps in your lap, it is because he is fond of you; but if a cat does the same thing, it is because your lap is warmer.
ALFRED NORTH WHITEHEAD (1861–1947)

Cats are intended to teach us that not everything in nature has a function.
ANONYMOUS

Philosophy

When the philosopher's argument becomes tedious, complicated, and opaque, it is usually a sign that he is attempting to prove as true to the intellect what is plainly false to common sense.
EDWARD ABBEY (1927–1989)

Philosophy is the science which considers truth.
ARISTOTLE (384–322 BC)

All are lunatics, but he who can analyze his delusion is called a philosopher.
AMBROSE BIERCE (1842–1914)

All philosophies, if you ride them home, are nonsense, but some are greater nonsense than others.
SAMUEL BUTLER (1835–1902)

There is nothing so absurd but some philosopher has said it.
CICERO (106–43 BC), *De Divinatione*

True philosophy invents nothing; it merely establishes and describes what is.
VICTOR COUSIN (1792–1867)

One cannot conceive anything so strange and so implausible that it has not already been said by one philosopher or another.
RENÉ DESCARTES (1596–1650), *Le discours de la methode*

The man of science is a poor philosopher.
ALBERT EINSTEIN (1879–1955)

Let no one delay the study of philosophy while young nor weary of it when old.
EPICURUS (341–270 BC)

Philosophers say a great deal about what is absolutely necessary for science, and it is always, so far as one can see, rather naive, and probably wrong.
RICHARD FEYNMAN (1918–1988)

God grant that not only the love of liberty but a thorough knowledge of the rights of man may pervade all the nations of the earth, so that a philosopher may set his foot anywhere on its surface and say: "This is my country."
BENJAMIN FRANKLIN (1706–1790)

Making itself intelligible is suicide for philosophy.
MARTIN HEIDEGGER (1889–1976)

So it's clear from whence the history of philosophy is the inner movement of the course of spirit, that is, of absolute subjectivity, towards itself.
MARTIN HEIDEGGER (1889–1976)

Leisure is the mother of philosophy.
THOMAS HOBBES (1588–1679)

Be a philosopher but, amid all your philosophy, be still a man.
DAVID HUME (1711–1776)

There is only one thing a philosopher can be relied upon to do, and that is to contradict other philosophers.
WILLIAM JAMES (1842–1910)

I have a simple philosophy. Fill what's empty. Empty what's full. And scratch where it itches.
ALICE ROOSEVELT LONGWORTH (1884–1980)

Philosophy is to the real world as masturbation is to sex.
KARL MARX (1818–1883)

Philosophy consists very largely of one philosopher arguing that all others are jackasses. He usually proves it, and I should add that he also usually proves that he is one himself.
H. L. MENCKEN (1880–1956)

Any genuine philosophy leads to action and from action back again to wonder, to enduring fact of mystery.
HENRY MILLER (1891–1980)

One's philosophy is not best expressed in words; it is expressed in the choices one makes … and the choices we make are ultimately our responsibility.
ELEANOR ROOSEVELT (1884–1962)

The point of philosophy is to start with something so simple as not to seem worth stating, and to end with something so paradoxical that no one will believe it.
BERTRAND RUSSELL (1872–1970), *The Philosophy of Logical Atomism*

I think we ought always to entertain our opinions with some measure of doubt. I shouldn't wish people dogmatically to believe any philosophy, not even mine.
BERTRAND RUSSELL (1872–1970)

This is patently absurd; but whoever wishes to become a philosopher must learn not to be frightened by absurdities.
BERTRAND RUSSELL (1872–1970)

Love makes us poets, and the approach of death makes us philosophers.
GEORGE SANTAYANA (1863–1952)

If I became a philosopher, if I have so keenly sought this fame for which I'm still waiting, it's all been to seduce women basically.
JEAN-PAUL SARTRE (1905–1980)

I have a new philosophy. I'm only going to dread one day at a time.
CHARLES M. SCHULZ (1922–2000)

There's a difference between a philosophy and a bumper sticker.
CHARLES M. SCHULZ (1922–2000)

There are more things in heaven and earth
Horatio,
Than are dreamt of in your philosophy.
WILLIAM SHAKESPEARE (1564–1616), *Hamlet*

A fool's brain digests philosophy into folly, science into superstition, and art into pedantry. Hence University education.
GEORGE BERNARD SHAW (1856–1950)

To be a philosopher is not merely to have subtle thoughts, not even to found a school, but so to love wisdom as to live according to its dictates, a life of simplicity, independence, magnanimity, and trust.
HENRY DAVID THOREAU (1817–1862)

When he who hears does not know what he who speaks means, and when he who speaks does not know what he himself means, that is philosophy.
VOLTAIRE (1694–1778)

The guiding motto in the life of every natural philosopher should be, Seek simplicity and distrust it.
ALFRED NORTH WHITEHEAD (1861–1947)

I went off to college planning to major in math or philosophy—of course, both those ideas are really the same idea.
FRANK WILCZEK (1951–)

My philosophy is that not only are you responsible for your life, but doing the best at this moment puts you in the best place for the next moment.
OPRAH WINFREY (1954–)

Philosophy is a battle against the bewitchment of our intelligence by means of language.
LUDWIG WITTGENSTEIN (1889–1951)

Philosophy is like trying to open a safe with a combination lock: each little adjustment of the dials seems to achieve nothing, only when everything is in place does the door open.
LUDWIG WITTGENSTEIN (1889–1951)

Photography

Photography helps people to see.
BERENICE ABBOTT (1898–1991)

I have often thought that if photography were difficult in the true sense of the term—meaning that the creation of a simple photograph would entail as much time and effort as the production of a good watercolor or etching—there would be a vast improvement in total output. The sheer ease with which we can produce a superficial image often leads to creative disaster.
ANSEL ADAMS (1902–1984)

To the complaint, "There are no people in these photographs," I respond, "There are always two people: the photographer and the viewer."
ANSEL ADAMS (1902–1984)

A photograph is a secret about a secret. The more it tells you the less you know.
DIANE ARBUS (1923–1971)

They used to photograph Shirley Temple through gauze. They should photograph me through linoleum.
TALLULAH BANKHEAD (1903–1968)

Photographers deal in things which are continually vanishing, and when they have vanished there is no contrivance on earth which can make them come back again.
HENRI CARTIER BRESSON (1908–2004)

Best wide-angle lens? Two steps backward. Look for the "ah-ha."
ERNST HAAS (1921–1986)

The camera doesn't make a bit of difference. All of them can record what you are seeing. But, you have to SEE.
ERNST HAAS (1921–1986)

Photography, fortunately, to me has not only been a profession but also a contact between people—to understand human nature and record, if possible, the best in each individual.
NICKOLAS MURAY (1892–1965)

Your photography is a record of your living, for anyone who really sees.
PAUL STRAND (1890–1976)

No matter how slow the film, spirit always stands still long enough for the photographer it has chosen.
MINOR WHITE (1908–1976)

Physics

If anybody says he can think about quantum physics without getting giddy, that only shows he has not understood the first thing about them.
NIELS BOHR (1885–1962)

It is wrong to think that the task of physics is to find out how Nature is. Physics concerns what we say about Nature.
NIELS BOHR (1885–1962)

I am now convinced that theoretical physics is actually philosophy.
MAX BORN (1882–1970)

It is impossible to trap modern physics into predicting anything with perfect determinism because it deals with probabilities from the outset.
SIR ARTHUR EDDINGTON (1882–1944)

Politics is far more complicated than physics.
ALBERT EINSTEIN (1879–1955)

We must be physicists in order to be creative since so far codes of values and ideals have been constructed in ignorance of physics or even in contradiction to physics.
FRIEDRICH NIETZSCHE (1844–1900)

Nothing is accidental in the universe—this is one of my Laws of Physics—except the entire universe itself, which is pure accident, pure divinity.
JOYCE CAROL OATES (1938–)

Physics is, hopefully, simple. Physicists are not.
EDWARD TELLER (1908–)

In science there is only physics; all the rest is stamp collecting.
WILLIAM THOMSON, LORD KELVIN (1824–1907)

In physics, your solution should convince a reasonable person. In math, you have to convince a person who's trying to make trouble. Ultimately, in physics, you're hoping to convince Nature. And I've found Nature to be pretty reasonable.
FRANK WILCZEK (1951–)

Pilgrimage

Pilgrim, n.: A traveler that is taken seriously. A Pilgrim Father was one who, leaving Europe in 1620 because not permitted to sing psalms through his nose, followed it to Massachusetts, where he could personate God according to the dictates of his conscience.
AMBROSE BIERCE (1842–1914), *The Devil's Dictionary*

A pilgrim is a wanderer with purpose.
PEACE PILGRIM (1908–1981)

When the road ends, and the goal is gained, the pilgrim finds that he has traveled only from himself to himself.
SRI SATHYA SAI BABA (1926–)

Life is a pilgrimage. The wise man does not rest by the roadside inns. He marches direct to the illimitable domain of eternal bliss, his ultimate destination.
SWAMI SIVANANDA (1887–1963)

The Pilgrim Fathers landed on the shores of America and fell upon their knees. Then they fell upon the aborigines.
ANONYMOUS

The merits of pilgrimages, fasts and hundreds of thousands of techniques of austere self-discipline are found in the dust of the feet of the Holy.
THE SRI GURU GRANTH SAHIB

Pity

How beautiful is death, when earn'd by virtue!
Who would not be that youth? What pity is it
That we can die but once to serve our country!
JOSEPH ADDISON (1672–1719), *Cato*

What a pity, when Christopher Columbus discovered America, that he ever mentioned it.
MARGOT ASQUITH (1864–1945)

Never feel self-pity, the most destructive emotion there is. How awful to be caught up in the terrible squirrel cage of self.
MILLICENT FENWICK (1910–1992)

Rebellion against your handicaps gets you nowhere. Self-pity gets you nowhere. One must have the adventurous daring to accept oneself as a bundle of possibilities and undertake the most interesting game in the world—making the most of one's best.
HARRY EMERSON FOSDICK (1878–1969)

Ah, sweet pity. Where would my love life be without it?
MATT GROENING (1954–)

Self-pity is our worst enemy, and if we yield to it, we can never do anything good in the world.
HELEN KELLER (1880–1968)

Pity the meek, for they shall inherit the earth.
DON MARQUIS (1878–1937)

Three passions, simple but overwhelmingly strong, have governed my life: the longing for love, the search for knowledge, and unbearable pity for the suffering of mankind.
BERTRAND RUSSELL (1872–1970), *Autobiography*

Pity is the virtue of the law, and none but tyrants use it cruelly.
WILLIAM SHAKESPEARE (1564–1616), *Timon of Athens*

A pity beyond all telling is hid in the heart of love.
WILLIAM BUTLER YEATS (1865–1939)

Plagiarism

About the most originality that any writer can hope to achieve honestly is to steal with good judgment.
JOSH BILLINGS (1818–1885)

If we steal thoughts from the moderns, it will be cried down as plagiarism; if from the ancients, it will be cried up as erudition.
CHARLES CALEB COLTON (1780–1832)

I don't like composers who think. It gets in the way of their plagiarism.
HOWARD DIETZ (1896–1983)

The secret to creativity is knowing how to hide your sources.
ALBERT EINSTEIN (1879–1955)

Art is either plagiarism or revolution.
PAUL GAUGUIN (1848–1903)

Self-plagiarism is style.
ALFRED HITCHCOCK (1899–1980)

Originality is undetected plagiarism.
WILLIAM RALPH INGE (1860–1954)

Copy from one, it's plagiarism; copy from two, it's research.
WILSON MIZNER (1876–1933)

Taking something from one man and making it worse is plagiarism.
GEORGE MOORE (1873–1958)

I suppose that now if I ever wrote a play about myself I'd be sued for plagiarism.
DOROTHY PARKER (1893–1967)

Planning

Make no little plans; they have no magic to stir men's blood.... Make big plans, aim high in hope and work.
DANIEL H. BURNHAM (1846–1912)

We must be willing to get rid of the life we've planned, so as to have the life that is waiting for us.
JOSEPH CAMPBELL (1904–1987)

Plans are only good intentions unless they immediately degenerate into hard work.
PETER F. DRUCKER (1909–2005)

Just because something doesn't do what you planned it to do doesn't mean it's useless.
THOMAS A. EDISON (1847–1931)

In preparing for battle I have always found that plans are useless, but planning is indispensable.
DWIGHT D. EISENHOWER (1890–1969)

Create a definite plan for carrying out your desire and begin at once, whether you are ready or not, to put this plan into action.
NAPOLEON HILL (1883–1970)

Zeus does not bring all men's plans to fulfillment.
HOMER (800–700 BC), *The Iliad*

He who every morning plans the transaction of the day and follows out that plan, carries a thread that will guide him through the maze of the most busy life. But where no plan is laid, where the disposal of time is surrendered merely to the chance of incidence, chaos will soon reign.
VICTOR HUGO (1802–1885)

When we are planning for posterity, we ought to remember that virtue is not hereditary.
THOMAS PAINE (1737–1809)

A good plan, violently executed now, is better than a perfect plan next week.
GEORGE S. PATTON (1885–1945)

It is a bad plan that admits of no modification.
PUBLILIUS SYRUS (C. 100 BC), *Maxims*

Plan backwards as well as forward. Set objectives and trace back to see how to achieve them. You may find that no path can get you there. Plan forward to see where your steps will take you, which may not be clear or intuitive.
DONALD H. RUMSFELD (1932–)

A goal without a plan is just a wish.
ANTOINE DE SAINT-EXUPÉRY (1900–1944)

Bite off more than you can chew, then chew it. Plan more than you can do, then do it.
ANONYMOUS

Plants

Natural abilities are like natural plants; they need pruning by study.
SIR FRANCIS BACON (1561–1626)

I'm not a vegetarian because I love animals. I'm a vegetarian because I hate plants.
A. WHITNEY BROWN (1952–)

If you think in terms of a year, plant a seed; if in terms of ten years, plant trees; if in terms of 100 years, teach the people.
CONFUCIUS (551–479 BC)

He that plants trees loves others beside himself.
THOMAS FULLER (1608–1661), *Gnomologia*

Always do your best. What you plant now, you will harvest later.
OG MANDINO (1923–1996)

We have been God-like in our planned breeding of our domesticated plants and animals, but we have been rabbit-like in our unplanned breeding of ourselves.
ARNOLD J. TOYNBEE (1889–1975)

A society grows great when old men plant trees whose shade they know they shall never sit in.
GREEK PROVERB

The best time to plant a tree is twenty years ago. The second best time is now.
ANONYMOUS

Pleasure

The friendships of the world are oft confederacies in vice, or leagues of pleasures.
JOSEPH ADDISON (1672–1719)

Pleasure in the job puts perfection in the work.
ARISTOTLE (384–322 BC)

One half of the world cannot understand the pleasures of the other.
JANE AUSTEN (1775–1817), *Emma*

The greatest pleasure in life is doing what people say you cannot do.
WALTER BAGEHOT (1826–1877)

People seem to enjoy things more when they know a lot of other people have been left out of the pleasure.
RUSSELL BAKER (1925–)

We are weighed down, every moment, by the conception and the sensation of Time. And there are but two means of escaping and forgetting this nightmare: pleasure and work. Pleasure consumes us. Work strengthens us. Let us choose.
CHARLES BAUDELAIRE (1821–1867)

Variety is the soul of pleasure.
APHRA BEHN (1640–1689)

Pleasure, n.: The least hateful form of dejection.
AMBROSE BIERCE (1842–1914), *The Devil's Dictionary*

Reading well is one of the great pleasures that solitude can afford you.
HAROLD BLOOM (1930–)

Of all the riches that we hug, of all the pleasures we enjoy, we can carry no more out of this world than out of a dream.
JAMES BONNELL (1653–1699)

The world is so constructed, that if you wish to enjoy its pleasures, you must also endure its pains. Whether you like it or not, you cannot have one without the other.
SWAMI BRAHNMANANDA (1863–1922)

A life of pleasure makes even the strongest mind frivolous at last.
SIR EDWARD G. BULWER-LYTTON (1803–1873)

The same refinement which brings us new pleasures, exposes us to new pains.
SIR EDWARD G. BULWER-LYTTON (1803–1873)

I consider being ill as one of the great pleasures of life, provided one is not too ill.
SAMUEL BUTLER (1835–1902)

To make pleasures pleasant, shorten them.
CHARLES BUXTON (1856–1934)

Now hatred is by far the longest pleasure;
Men love in haste, but they detest at leisure.
LORD BYRON (1788–1824)

Choose your pleasures for yourself, and do not let them be imposed upon you.
LORD CHESTERFIELD (1694–1773)

You find yourself refreshed by the presence of cheerful people. Why not make an honest effort to confer that pleasure on others? Half the battle is gained if you never allow yourself to say anything gloomy.
LYDIA M. CHILD (1802–1880)

What we call pleasure, and rightly so, is the absence of all pain.
CICERO (106–43 BC)

The best way to realize the pleasure of feeling rich is to live in a smaller house than your means would entitle you to have.
EDWARD CLARKE (1769–1822)

We may lay in a stock of pleasures, as we would lay in a stock of wine; but if we defer tasting them too long, we shall find that both are soured by age.
CHARLES CALEB COLTON (1780–1832)

Pleasure is an important component of the quality of life, but by itself it does not bring happiness. Pleasure helps to maintain order, but by itself cannot create a new order in consciousness.
MIHALY CSIKSZENTMIHALYI (1934–), *Flow: The Psychology of Optimal Experience*

Sinful and forbidden pleasures are like poisoned bread; they may satisfy appetite for the moment, but there is death in them at the end.
TYRON EDWARDS (1809–1894)

All pleasures contain an element of sadness.
JONATHAN EIBESCHUTZ (1690–1764)

One should guard against preaching to young people success in the customary form as the main aim in life. The most important motive for work in school and in life is pleasure in work, pleasure in its result, and the knowledge of the value of the result to the community.
ALBERT EINSTEIN (1879–1955), *On Education*

Pleasure is the beginning and the end of living happily.
EPICURUS (341–270 BC)

The pleasures which we most rarely experience give us the greatest delight.
DESIDERIUS ERASMUS (1469–1536)

Short is the joy that guilty pleasure brings.
EURIPIDES (C. 480–406 BC)

Sometimes it is harder to deprive oneself of a pain than of a pleasure.
F. SCOTT FITZGERALD (1896–1940), *Tender Is the Night*

Pleasure and love are the pinions of great deeds.
CHARLES FOX (1749–1806)

Whoever feels pain in hearing a good character of his neighbor, will feel a pleasure in the reverse. And those who despair to rise in distinction by their virtues, are happy if others can be depressed to a level of themselves.
BENJAMIN FRANKLIN (1706–1790)

The greatest and noblest pleasure which men can have in this world is to discover new truths; and the next is to shake off old prejudices.
FREDERICK THE GREAT (1712–1786)

None has more frequent conversations with a disagreeable self than the man of pleasure; his enthusiasms are but few and transient; his appetites, like angry creditors, are continually making fruitless demands for what he is unable to pay; and the greater his former pleasures, the more strong his regret, the more impatient his expectations. A life of pleasure is, therefore, the most unpleasing life.
JAMES GOLDSMITH (1933–1997)

It never pays to deal with the flyweights of the world. They take far too much pleasure in thwarting you at every turn.
SUE GRAFTON (1940–), *'H' Is for Homicide*

The man of power is ruined by power, the man of money by money, the submissive man by subservience, the pleasure seeker by pleasure.
HERMANN HESSE (1877–1962)

I despise making the most of one's time. Half of the pleasures of life consist of the opportunities one has neglected.
OLIVER WENDELL HOLMES JR. (1841–1935)

He wins every hand who mingles profit with pleasure.
HORACE (65–8 BC), *Epistles*

Get pleasure out of life … as much as you can. Nobody ever died from pleasure.
SOL HUROK (1888–1974)

Do not bite at the bait of pleasure till you know there is no hook beneath it.
THOMAS JEFFERSON (1743–1826)

No man is a hypocrite in his pleasures.
SAMUEL JOHNSON (1709–1784)

Fortune can, for her pleasure, fools advance,
And toss them on the wheels of Chance.
JUVENAL (AD 55–127)

If I were to wish for anything, I should not wish for wealth and power, but for the passionate sense of potential—for the eye which, ever young and ardent, sees the possible. Pleasure disappoints; possibility never.
SØREN KIERKEGAARD (1813–1855)

Most men pursue pleasure with such breathless haste that they hurry past it.
SØREN KIERKEGAARD (1813–1855)

Your chances of success are directly proportional to the degree of pleasure you desire from what you do. If you are in a job you hate, face the fact squarely and get out.
MICHAEL KORDA (1933–)

The pleasures of the world are deceitful; they promise more than they give. They trouble us in seeking them, they do not satisfy us when possessing them and they make us despair in losing them.
MADAME DE LAMBERT (1647–1733)

If we had no faults of our own, we would not take so much pleasure in noticing those of others.
FRANÇOIS DE LA ROCHEFOUCAULD (1613–1680)

The pleasure of love is in loving.
FRANÇOIS DE LA ROCHEFOUCAULD (1613–1680)

Pleasure is a by-product of doing something that is worth doing. Therefore, do not seek pleasure as such. Pleasure comes of seeking something else, and comes by the way.
LAWRENCE LOWELL (1856–1943)

The Puritan hated bear-baiting, not because it gave pain to the bear, but because it gave pleasure to the spectators.
LORD THOMAS BABINGTON MACAULAY (1800–1859)

Poor is the man whose pleasures depend on the permission of another.
MADONNA (1958–)

It is one of man's curious idiosyncrasies to create difficulties for the pleasure of resolving them.
JOSEPH DE MAISTRE (1753–1821)

Even pleasure itself is a toil.
MANILIUS (C. 1 BC)

Virtue extends our days: he lives two lives who relives his past with pleasure.
MARCUS VALERIUS MARTIALIS (AD 40–103), *Epigrams*

Men seek but one thing in life, their pleasure.
W. SOMERSET MAUGHAM (1874–1965), *Of Human Bondage*

What we learn with pleasure we never forget.
ALFRED MERCIER (1816–1894)

I despise the pleasure of pleasing people that I despise.
LADY MARY WORTLEY MONTAGU (1689–1762)

Virtue is its own reward, and brings with it the truest and highest pleasure; but if we cultivate it only for pleasure's sake, we are selfish, not religious, and will never gain the pleasure, because we can never have the virtue.
CARDINAL JOHN NEWMAN (1801–1890)

There is no such thing as pure pleasure; some anxiety always goes with it.
OVID (43 BC–AD 17)

It is in his pleasure that a man really lives; it is from his leisure that he constructs the true fabric of self.
AGNES REPPLIER (1855–1950)

I can think of nothing less pleasurable than a life devoted to pleasure.
JOHN D. ROCKEFELLER (1839–1937)

The happiest is the person who suffers the least pain; the most miserable who enjoys the least pleasure.
JEAN-JACQUES ROUSSEAU (1712–1778), *Émile*

The people who are regarded as moral luminaries are those who forego ordinary pleasures themselves

and find compensation in interfering with the pleasures of others.
BERTRAND RUSSELL (1872–1970)

There is much pleasure to be gained from useless knowledge.
BERTRAND RUSSELL (1872–1970)

Work is not man's punishment. It is his reward and his strength and his pleasure.
GEORGE SAND (1804–1876)

Enjoy present pleasures in such a way as not to injure future ones.
SENECA (5 BC–AD 65)

No profit grows where is no pleasure ta'en,
In brief, sir, study what you most affect.
WILLIAM SHAKESPEARE (1564–1616), *The Taming of the Shrew*

Happiness is different from pleasure. Happiness has something to do with struggling and enduring and accomplishing.
GEORGE SHEEHAN (1918–1993)

To name an object is to deprive a poem of three-fourths of its pleasure, which consists in a little-by-little guessing game; the ideal is to suggest.
WALLACE STEVENS (1879–1955)

Mistake not. Those pleasures are not pleasures that trouble the quiet and tranquillity of thy life.
JEREMY TAYLOR (1613–1667)

That man is the richest whose pleasures are the cheapest.
HENRY DAVID THOREAU (1817–1862)

When we are unhurried and wise, we perceive that only great and worthy things have any permanent and absolute existence, that petty fears and petty pleasures are but the shadow of the reality.
HENRY DAVID THOREAU (1817–1862), *Walden*

Of all the animals, man is the only one that is cruel. He is the only one that inflicts pain for the pleasure of doing it.
MARK TWAIN (1835–1910), *The Lowest Animal*

Virtue is its own reward. There's a pleasure in doing good which sufficiently pays itself.
SIR JOHN VANBRUGH (1664–1726), *The Relapse*

If I was more complacent and I let things slide, my life would be easier, but you all wouldn't be as entertained. My misery is your pleasure.
KANYE WEST (1977–)

I adore simple pleasures. They are the last refuge of the complex.
OSCAR WILDE (1854–1900), *The Picture of Dorian Gray*

Illusion is the first of all pleasures.
OSCAR WILDE (1854–1900)

Never let the demands of tomorrow interfere with the pleasures and excitement of today.
MEREDITH WILLSON (1902–1984), *The Music Man*

It is a pleasure to give advice, humiliating to need it, normal to ignore it.
ANONYMOUS

Bygone troubles are a pleasure to talk about.
YIDDISH PROVERB

Poetry

A poem records emotions and moods that lie beyond normal language, that can only be patched together and hinted at metaphorically.
DIANE ACKERMAN (1948–)

Talent is like a faucet; while it is open, you have to write. Inspiration—a hoax fabricated by poets for their self-importance.
JEAN ANOUILH (1910–1987)

Homer has taught all other poets the art of telling lies skillfully.
ARISTOTLE (384–322 BC)

Poetry is finer and more philosophical than history; for poetry expresses the universal, and history only the particular.
ARISTOTLE (384–322 BC)

A poet's hope: to be,
like some valley cheese,
local, but prized elsewhere.
W. H. AUDEN (1907–1973)

As a poet there is only one political duty, and that is to defend one's language against corruption. When it is corrupted, people lose faith in what they hear and this leads to violence.
W. H. AUDEN (1907–1973)

I cannot accept the doctrine that in poetry there is a "suspension of belief." A poet must never make a statement simply because it sounds poetically exciting; he must also believe it to be true.
W. H. AUDEN (1907–1973)

It is a sad fact about our culture that a poet can earn much more money writing or talking about his art than he can by practicing it.
W. H. AUDEN (1907–1973)

Poetry makes nothing happen. It survives in the valley of its saying.
W. H. AUDEN (1907–1973)

Rhymes, meters, stanza forms, etc., are like servants. If the master is fair enough to win their affection and firm enough to command their respect, the result is an orderly happy household. If he is too tyrannical, they give notice; if he lacks authority, they become slovenly, impertinent, drunk and dishonest.
W. H. AUDEN (1907–1973)

There exist only three beings worthy of respect: the priest, the soldier, the poet. To know, to kill, to create.
CHARLES BAUDELAIRE (1821–1867), *Mon coeur mis à nu*

Any healthy man can go without food for two days—but not without poetry.
CHARLES BAUDELAIRE (1821–1867)

Poetry and progress are like two ambitious men who hate one another with an instinctive hatred, and when they meet upon the same road, one of them has to give place.
CHARLES BAUDELAIRE (1821–1867)

Who among us has not, in moments of ambition, dreamt of the miracle of a form of poetic prose, musical but without rhythm and rhyme, both supple and staccato enough to adapt itself to the lyrical movements of our souls, the undulating movements of our reveries, and the convulsive movements of our consciences? This obsessive ideal springs above all from frequent contact with enormous cities, from the junction of their innumerable connections.
CHARLES BAUDELAIRE (1821–1867)

The very idea of a bird is a symbol and a suggestion to the poet. A bird seems to be at the top of the scale, so vehement and intense his life.... The beautiful vagabonds, endowed with every grace, masters of all climes, and knowing no bounds—how many human aspirations are realized in their free, holiday-lives—and how many suggestions to the poet in their flight and song!
JOHN BURROUGHS (1837–1921), *Birds and Poets*

Poetry reveals to us the loveliness of nature, brings back the freshness of youthful feelings, reviews the relish of simple pleasures, keeps unquenched the enthusiasm which warmed the springtime of our being, refines youthful love, strengthens our interest in human nature, by vivid delineations of its tenderest and softest feelings, and through the brightness of its prophetic visions, helps faith to lay hold on the future life.
WILLIAM E. CHANNING (1780–1842)

All slang is a metaphor, and all metaphor is poetry.
G. K. CHESTERTON (1874–1936), *Defendant*

Poets have been mysteriously silent on the subject of cheese.
G. K. CHESTERTON (1874–1936)

You don't have to suffer to be a poet; adolescence is enough suffering for anyone.
JOHN CIARDI (1916–1986)

The freedom of poetic license.
CICERO (106–43 BC), *Pro Publio Sestio*

The worst tragedy for a poet is to be admired through being misunderstood.
JEAN COCTEAU (1889–1963)

A poet ought not to pick nature's pocket. Let him borrow, and so borrow as to repay by the very act of borrowing. Examine nature accurately, but write from recollection, and trust more to the imagination than the memory.
SAMUEL TAYLOR COLERIDGE (1772–1834)

To a poet, silence is an acceptable response, even a flattering one.
SIDONIE GABRIELLE COLETTE (1873–1954)

A prose writer gets tired of writing prose, and wants to be a poet. So he begins every line with a capital letter, and keeps on writing prose.
SAMUEL MCCHORD CROTHERS (1857–1927)

You campaign in poetry. You govern in prose.
MARIO CUOMO (1932–)

In science one tries to tell people, in such a way as to be understood by everyone, something that no one ever knew before. But in poetry, it's the exact opposite.
PAUL DIRAC (1902–1984)

Poetry is not a turning loose of emotion, but an escape from emotion; it is not the expression of personality, but an escape from personality. But, of course, only those who have personality and emotions know what it means to want to escape from these things.
T. S. ELIOT (1888–1965), *Tradition and the Individual Talent*

Immature poets imitate; mature poets steal.
T. S. ELIOT (1888–1965)

The bad poet is usually unconscious where he ought to be conscious, and conscious where he ought to be unconscious.
T. S. ELIOT (1888–1965)

There are two classes of poets—the poets by education and practice, these we respect; and poets by nature, these we love.
RALPH WALDO EMERSON (1803–1882)

The poet's voice need not merely be the record of man, it can be one of the props, the pillars to help him endure and prevail.
WILLIAM FAULKNER (1897–1962)

Poetry is what gets lost in translation.
ROBERT FROST (1874–1963)

Writing a poem is discovering.
ROBERT FROST (1874–1963)

Poetry is a deal of joy and pain and wonder, with a dash of the dictionary.
KAHLIL GIBRAN (1883–1931)

One ought, every day at least, to hear a little song, read a good poem, see a fine picture, and if it were possible, to speak a few reasonable words.
JOHANN WOLFGANG VON GOETHE (1749–1832)

Every English poet should master the rules of grammar before he attempts to bend or break them.
ROBERT GRAVES (1895–1985)

Translation is an interestingly different way to be involved both with poetry and with the language that I've found myself living in much of the time. I think the two feed each other.
MARILYN HACKER (1942–)

A poet who reads his verse in public may have other nasty habits.
ROBERT A. HEINLEIN (1907–1988), *Time Enough for Love*

Many brave men lived before Agamemnon; but all are overwhelmed in eternal night, unwept, unknown, because they lack a sacred poet.
HORACE (65–8 BC), *Odes*

Mediocrity is not allowed to poets, either by the gods or man.
HORACE (65–8 BC)

A poem is no place for an idea.
EDGAR WATSON HOWE (1853–1937), *Country Town Sayings*

Poetry cannot be translated; and, therefore, it is the poets that preserve the languages; for we would not be at the trouble to learn a language if we could

have all that is written in it just as well in a translation. But as the beauties of poetry cannot be preserved in any language except that in which it was originally written, we learn the language.
SAMUEL JOHNSON (1709–1784)

Poetry should please by a fine excess and not by singularity. It should strike the reader as a wording of his own highest thoughts, and appear almost as a remembrance.
JOHN KEATS (1795–1821)

Painting is poetry that is seen rather than felt, and poetry is painting that is felt rather than seen.
LEONARDO DA VINCI (1452–1519)

The writer of prose can only step aside when the poet passes.
W. SOMERSET MAUGHAM (1874–1965)

A poet more than thirty years old is simply an overgrown child.
H. L. MENCKEN (1880–1956)

Poetry has done enough when it charms, but prose must also convince.
H. L. MENCKEN (1880–1956)

Most people ignore most poetry because most poetry ignores most people.
ADRIAN MITCHELL (1932–)

Poets are shameless with their experiences: they exploit them.
FRIEDRICH NIETZSCHE (1844–1900), *Beyond Good and Evil*

Poetry is adolescence fermented, and thus preserved.
JOSÉ ORTEGA Y GASSET (1883–1955)

Poetry is nearer to vital truth than history.
PLATO (C. 428–348 BC)

Poetry often enters through the window of irrelevance.
M. C. RICHARDS (1916–1999)

Poetry is an echo, asking a shadow to dance.
CARL SANDBURG (1878–1967)

Love makes us poets, and the approach of death makes us philosophers.
GEORGE SANTAYANA (1863–1952)

We don't read and write poetry because it's cute. We read and write poetry because we are members of the human race. And the human race is filled with passion. And medicine, law, business, engineering—these are noble pursuits and necessary to sustain life. But poetry, beauty, romance, love—these are what we stay alive for.
TOM SCHULMAN (1951–), *Dead Poets Society*

Poetry is an orphan of silence. The words never quite equal the experience behind them.
CHARLES SIMIC (1938–)

Painting is silent poetry, and poetry is painting with the gift of speech.
SIMONIDES (556–468 BC)

My poems are hymns of praise to the glory of life.
EDITH SITWELL (1887–1964)

Poetry is the deification of reality.
EDITH SITWELL (1887–1964)

I decided that it was not wisdom that enabled [poets] to write their poetry, but a kind of instinct or inspiration, such as you find in seers and prophets who deliver all their sublime messages without knowing in the least what they mean.
SOCRATES (469–399 BC), *Apology*

[The] most important tribute any human being can pay to a poem or a piece of prose he or she really loves is to learn it by heart. Not by brain, by heart; the expression is vital.
GEORGE STEINER (1929–)

To name an object is to deprive a poem of three-fourths of its pleasure, which consists in a little-by-little guessing game; the ideal is to suggest.
WALLACE STEVENS (1879–1955)

A translation is no translation … unless it will give you the music of a poem along with the words of it.
JOHN MILLINGTON SYNGE (1871–1909)

Good poetry seems too simple and natural a thing that when we meet it we wonder that all men are not always poets. Poetry is nothing but healthy speech.
HENRY DAVID THOREAU (1817–1862)

A poem is never finished, only abandoned.
PAUL VALÉRY (1871–1945)

Poetry is the music of the soul, and, above all, of great and feeling souls.
VOLTAIRE (1694–1778)

Still, language is resilient, and poetry when it is pressured simply goes underground.
DIANE WAKOSKI (1937–)

Poets, we know, are terribly sensitive people, and in my observation one of the things they are most sensitive about is money.
ROBERT PENN WARREN (1905–1989)

Nature gets credit which should in truth be reserved for ourselves: the rose for its scent; the nightingale for its song; and the sun for its radiance. The poets are entirely mistaken. They should address their lyrics to themselves and should turn them into odes of self-congratulation on the excellence of the human mind.
ALFRED NORTH WHITEHEAD (1861–1947)

The poet judges not as a judge judges but as the sun falling around a helpless thing.
WALT WHITMAN (1819–1892)

At twilight, nature is not without loveliness, though perhaps its chief use is to illustrate quotations from the poets.
OSCAR WILDE (1854–1900)

I was working on the proof of one of my poems all the morning, and took out a comma. In the afternoon I put it back again.
OSCAR WILDE (1854–1900)

But all art is sensual and poetry particularly so. It is directly, that is, of the senses, and since the senses do not exist without an object for their employment all art is necessarily objective. It doesn't declaim or explain, it presents.
WILLIAM CARLOS WILLIAMS (1883–1963)

By listening to his language of his locality the poet begins to learn his craft. It is his function to lift, by use of imagination and the language he hears, the material conditions and appearances of his environment to the sphere of the intelligence where they will have new currency.
WILLIAM CARLOS WILLIAMS (1883–1963)

There is something about poetry beyond prose logic, there is mystery in it, not to be explained but admired.
EDWARD YOUNG (1683–1765)

Police

No tyranny is so irksome as petty tyranny: the officious demands of policemen, government clerks, and electromechanical gadgets.
EDWARD ABBEY (1927–1989)

Any community's arm of force—military, police, security—needs people in it who can do necessary evil, and yet not be made evil by it. To do only the necessary and no more. To constantly question the assumptions, to stop the slide into atrocity.
LOIS MCMASTER BUJOLD (1949–), *Barrayar*

A functioning police state needs no police.
WILLIAM S. BURROUGHS (1914–1997)

All I need to make a comedy is a park, a policeman and a pretty girl.
CHARLIE CHAPLIN (1889–1977), *My Autobiography*

As repressed sadists are supposed to become policemen or butchers so those with irrational fear of life become publishers.
CYRIL CONNOLLY (1903–1974)

Gentlemen, get this thing straight for once and for all. The policeman isn't there to create disorder; the policeman is there to preserve disorder.
RICHARD M. DALEY (1902–1976)

Every kind of peaceful cooperation among men is primarily based on mutual trust and only secondarily on institutions such as courts of justice and police.
ALBERT EINSTEIN (1879–1955)

Follow your inclinations with due regard to the policeman round the corner.
W. SOMERSET MAUGHAM (1874–1965), *Of Human Bondage*

Capital Punishment is a silly excuse for fear. The police fear the guy so they say, "Off with his head!" Not only is it morally wrong, but it's medieval!
WALT WHITMAN (1819–1892)

Policy

The worst policy is one made in secrecy by the experts.
JOHN KENNETH GALBRAITH (1908–2006)

The first Principle of Policy is for a State to preserve itself.
JAMES HOWELL (1593–1666)

Policy should be tested out on those who will be affected by it, and the details worked out by those who will have to implement it.
ANTHONY JAY (1930–)

It is always good policy to tell the truth unless of course you are an exceptionally good liar.
JEROME K. JEROME (1859–1927)

Domestic policy can only defeat us; foreign policy can kill us.
JOHN F. KENNEDY (1917–1963)

Effective policy depends not only on the skill of individual moves, but even more importantly on their relationship to each other.
HENRY KISSINGER (1923–), *The Necessity for Choice: Prospects of American Foreign Policy*

My policy is to have no policy.
ABRAHAM LINCOLN (1809–1865)

The severest justice may not always be the best policy.
ABRAHAM LINCOLN (1809–1865)

The really basic thing in government is policy. Bad administration can destroy good policy, but good administration can never save bad policy.
ADLAI E. STEVENSON II (1900–1965)

Political Correctness

Political correctness does not legislate tolerance; it only organizes hatred.
JACQUES BARZUN (1907–)

The notion of political correctness declares certain topics, certain expressions, even certain gestures, off-limits. What began as a crusade for civility has soured into a cause of conflict and even censorship.
GEORGE H. W. BUSH (1924–)

Political Correctness is a killer, and so is the fact that on papers like the Globe, only the Beautiful People need apply for jobs.
HOWIE CARR (1952–)

I think you have to judge everything based on your personal taste. And if that means being critical, so be it. I hate political correctness. I absolutely loathe it.
SIMON COWELL (1959–)

Transcend political correctness and strive for human righteousness.
ANTHONY J. D'ANGELO (1972–)

It is silly to call fat people gravitationally challenged—a self-righteous fetishism of language which is no more than a symptom of political frustration.
TERRY EAGLETON (1943–)

I am absolutely opposed to political correctness. You cannot confront hate speech until you've experienced it. You need to hear every side of the issue instead of just one.
JANE ELLIOTT (1933–)

I worry that we are approaching a time when that which is shocking is squeezed out by the Stalinism of political correctness.
JOE ESZTERHAS (1944–)

If all printers were determined not to print anything till they were sure it would offend nobody, there would be very little printed.
BENJAMIN FRANKLIN (1706–1790)

Nothing that is morally wrong can be politically right.
WILLIAM GLADSTONE (1809–1898)

We now have a situation where a type of reverse racism is applied to mainstream Australians by those who promote political correctness.
PAULINE HANSON (1954–)

Political correctness is tyranny with manners.
CHARLTON HESTON (1924–)

I got a feeling about political correctness. I hate it. It causes us to lie silently instead of saying what we think.
HAL HOLBROOK (1925–)

When you get into corporate decision-making, especially in these days of political correctness, you are in jail.
HAL HOLBROOK (1925–)

I believe that political correctness can be a form of linguistic fascism, and it sends shivers down the spine of my generation who went to war against fascism.
P. D. JAMES (1920–)

We have needed to define ourselves by reclaiming the words that define us. They have used language as weapons. When we open ourselves to what they say and how they say it, our narrow prejudices evaporate and we are nourished and armed.
SELMA JAMES (1930–)

Political correctness is the natural continuum from the party line. What we are seeing once again is a self-appointed group of vigilantes imposing their views on others. It is a heritage of communism, but they don't seem to see this.
DORIS LESSING (1919–)

The two pillars of "political correctness" are:
a) willful ignorance
b) a steadfast refusal to face the truth.
GEORGE MACDONALD (1824–1905)

We live in oppressive times. We have, as a nation, become our own thought police; but instead of calling the process by which we limit our expression of dissent and wonder "censorship," we call it "concern for commercial viability."
DAVID MAMET (1947–)

When you're writing these things, you're in a room making each other laugh, you really have very little sense of political correctness or incorrectness. This is a question that Europe tends to ask and America doesn't.
MIKE MYERS (1963–)

Being Politically Correct means always having to say you're sorry.
CHARLES OSGOOD (1933–)

National Standards was not a narrative of past events but was leftwing revisionism and Political Correctness.
PHYLLIS SCHLAFLY (1924–)

The cornerstone of the political correctness that dominates campus culture is radical feminism.
PHYLLIS SCHLAFLY (1924–)

Political correctness allows for two basic types of complaint: that people who behave the same are treated differently, and that people who behave differently are treated the same.
ANONYMOUS

Political correctness is simply a speed bump in the traffic of truth, free thought and speech.
ANONYMOUS

Political Parties

All political parties die at last of swallowing their own lies.
JOHN ARBUTHNOT (1667–1735)

Ignorance makes most men go into a political party, and shame keeps them from getting out of it.
EDWARD FREDERICK HALIFAX (1881–1959)

People who live in the post-totalitarian system know only too well that the question of whether one or several political parties are in power, and how these parties define and label themselves, is of far less importance than the question of whether or not it is possible to live like a human being.
VACLAV HAVEL (1936–)

No one party can fool all of the people all of the time; that's why we have two parties.
BOB HOPE (1903–2003)

Political language—and with variations this is true of all political parties, from Conservatives to Anarchists—is designed to make lies sound truthful and murder respectable, and to give an appearance of solidity to pure wind.
GEORGE ORWELL (1903–1950), *Politics and the English Language*

If the Soviet Union let another political party come into existence, they would still be a one-party state, because everybody would join the other party.
RONALD REAGAN (1911–2004)

Both political parties have their good times and bad times, only they have them at different times.
WILL ROGERS (1879–1935)

No, I'm not a part of any organized political party—I'm a Democrat.
WILL ROGERS (1879–1935)

There's no way in the world you're going to make a political party respectable unless you keep it out of office.
WILL ROGERS (1879–1935)

The President cannot make clouds to rain and cannot make the corn to grow, he cannot make business good; although when these things occur, political parties do claim some credit for the good things that have happened in this way.
WILLIAM HOWARD TAFT (1857–1930)

Politics is the gizzard of society, full of grit and gravel, and the two political parties are its opposite halves—sometimes split into quarters—which grind on each other. Not only individuals but states have thus a confirmed dyspepsia.
HENRY DAVID THOREAU (1817–1862)

Men think they think upon the great political questions, and they do; but they think with their party, not independently; they read its literature, but not that of the other side.
MARK TWAIN (1835–1910)

The two real political parties in America are the Winners and the Losers. The people don't acknowledge this. They claim membership in two imaginary parties, the Republicans and the Democrats, instead.
KURT VONNEGUT JR. (1922–2007)

I adore political parties. They are the only place left to us where people don't talk politics.
OSCAR WILDE (1854–1900)

In his farewell address, George Washington warned the people about political parties. Now we see how both Democrats and Republicans have conspired to reduce democratic participation. If this is the best the Democrats and Republicans have to offer, it's time to look elsewhere.... Politics should be the prism for our most noble intentions.
MARIANNE WILLIAMSON (1952–)

Politicians

You have all the characteristics of a popular politician: a horrible voice, bad breeding, and a vulgar manner.
ARISTOPHANES (C. 448–380 BC), *Knights*

Under every stone lurks a politician.
ARISTOPHANES (C. 448–380 BC), *Thesmophoriazusae*

Anyone who is capable of getting themselves made President should on no account be allowed to do the job.
DOUGLAS ADAMS (1952–2001), *The Hitchhiker's Guide to the Galaxy*

Government is too big and too important to be left to the politicians.
CHESTER BOWLES (1901–1986)

An honest politician is one who, when he is bought, will stay bought.
SIMON CAMERON (1799–1889)

A politician needs the ability to foretell what is going to happen tomorrow, next week, next month, and next year. And to have the ability afterwards to explain why it didn't happen.
SIR WINSTON CHURCHILL (1874–1965)

Get all the fools on your side and you can be elected to anything.
FRANK DANE (1981–)

I have come to the conclusion that politics are too serious a matter to be left to the politicians.
CHARLES DE GAULLE (1890–1970)

Since a politician never believes what he says, he is quite surprised to be taken at his word.
CHARLES DE GAULLE (1890–1970)

Now I know what a statesman is; he's a dead politician. We need more statesmen.
BOB EDWARDS (1947–)

Men say I am a saint losing himself in politics. The fact is that I am a politician trying my hardest to become a saint.
MAHATMA GANDHI (1869–1948)

A politician is a person with whose politics you don't agree; if you agree with him he's a statesman.
DAVID LLOYD GEORGE (1863–1945)

You've got to vote for someone. It's a shame, but it's got to be done.
WHOOPI GOLDBERG (1955–)

Priests are no more necessary to religion than politicians to patriotism.
JOHN HAYNES HOLMES (1879–1964)

There is one sure way of telling when politicians aren't telling the truth—their lips move.
FELICITY KENDALL (1946–)

I'm always rather nervous about how you talk about women who are active in politics, whether they want to be talked about as women or as politicians.
JOHN F. KENNEDY (1917–1963)

Politicians are the same all over. They promise to build a bridge even where there is no river.
NIKITA KHRUSHCHEV (1894–1971)

Ninety percent of the politicians give the other ten percent a bad reputation.
HENRY KISSINGER (1923–)

If God had wanted us to vote, he would have given us candidates.
JAY LENO (1950–)

I once said cynically of a politician, "He'll double-cross that bridge when he comes to it."
OSCAR LEVANT (1906–1972)

At home, you always have to be a politician; when you're abroad, you almost feel yourself a statesman.
HAROLD MACMILLAN (1894–1986)

A man who is a politician at forty is a statesman at three score and ten. It is at this age, when he would be too old to be a clerk or a gardener or a police-court magistrate, that he is ripe to govern a country.
W. SOMERSET MAUGHAM (1874–1965)

A good politician is quite as unthinkable as an honest burglar.
H. L. MENCKEN (1880–1956)

The reason there are so few female politicians is that it is too much trouble to put makeup on two faces.
MAUREEN MURPHY (1952–)

The magician and the politician have much in common: they both have to draw our attention away from what they are really doing.
BEN OKRI (1959–)

The statesman shears the sheep; the politician skins them.
AUSTIN O'MALLEY (1858–1932)

Washington is a place where politicians don't know which way is up and taxes don't know which way is down.
ROBERT ORBEN (1927–)

Political language … is designed to make lies sound truthful and murder respectable, and to give an appearance of solidity to pure wind.
GEORGE ORWELL (1903–1950)

That politician who curries favor with the citizens and indulges them and fawns upon them and has a presentiment of their wishes, and is skillful in gratifying them, he is esteemed a great statesman.
PLATO (428-348 BC)

A statesman is a politician who places himself at the service of the nation. A politician is a statesman who places the nation at his service.
GEORGES POMPIDOU (1911–1974)

A politician will do anything to keep his job—even become a patriot.
WILLIAM RANDOLPH (1650–1711)

Everything is changing. People are taking their comedians seriously and the politicians as a joke.
WILL ROGERS (1879–1935)

Politicians can do more funny things naturally than I can think of to do purposely.
WILL ROGERS (1879–1935)

The short memories of American voters is what keeps our politicians in office.
WILL ROGERS (1879–1935)

The most successful politician is he who says what the people are thinking most often in the loudest voice.
THEODORE ROOSEVELT (1858–1919)

I was really too honest a man to be a politician and live.
SOCRATES (469–399 BC)

Whoever makes two ears of corn, or two blades of grass to grow where only one grew before, deserves better of mankind, and does more essential service to his country than the whole race of politicians put together.
JONATHAN SWIFT (1667–1745)

Ninety eight percent of the adults in this country are decent, hardworking, honest Americans. It's the other lousy two percent that get all the publicity. But then, we elected them.
LILY TOMLIN (1939–)

A politician is a man who understands government. A statesman is a politician who's been dead for 15 years.
HARRY S TRUMAN (1884–1972)

My choice early in life was either to be a piano-player in a whorehouse or a politician. And to tell the truth, there's hardly any difference.
HARRY S TRUMAN (1884–1972)

A recent survey was said to prove that the people we Americans most admire are our politicians and doctors. I don't believe it. They are simply the people we are most afraid of. And with the most reason.
ANONYMOUS

Politics

When the political columnists say "Every thinking man" they mean themselves, and when candidates appeal to "Every intelligent voter" they mean everybody who is going to vote for them.
FRANKLIN P. ADAMS (1881–1960), *Nods and Becks*

Politics … [has] always been the systematic organization of hatreds.
HENRY ADAMS (1838–1918)

Politics is the gentle art of getting votes from the poor and campaign funds from the rich by promising to protect each from the other.
OSCAR AMERINGER (1870–1943)

Man is by nature a political animal.
ARISTOTLE (384–322 BC), *Politics*

Politics is the art of looking for trouble, finding it whether it exists or not, diagnosing it incorrectly, and applying the wrong remedy.
ERNEST BENN (1875–1954)

Politics, n.: Strife of interests masquerading as a contest of principles.
AMBROSE BIERCE (1842–1914), *The Devil's Dictionary*

Politics is the art of the possible.
OTTO VON BISMARCK (1815–1898)

In politics you must always keep running with the pack. The moment that you falter and they sense that you are injured, the rest will turn on you like wolves.
R. A. BUTLER (1902–1982)

Politics is largely a matter of heart.
R. A. BUTLER (1902–1982)

Politics is made up largely of irrelevancies.
DALTON CAMP (1920–2002)

Nothing can so alienate a voter from the political system as backing a winning candidate.
MARK B. COHEN (1949–)

I have come to the conclusion that politics are too serious a matter to be left to the politicians.
CHARLES DE GAULLE (1890–1970)

Political history is largely an account of mass violence and of the expenditure of vast resources to cope with mythical fears and hopes.
MURRAY EDELMAN (1919–2001), *Politics as Symbolic Action*

It is the duty of every citizen according to his best capacities to give validity to his convictions in political affairs.
ALBERT EINSTEIN (1879–1955), *Treasury for the Free World*

Politics is far more complicated than physics.
ALBERT EINSTEIN (1879–1955)

The only justifiable purpose of political institutions is to ensure the unhindered development of the individual.
ALBERT EINSTEIN (1879–1955)

Politics ought to be the part-time profession of every citizen who would protect the rights and privileges of free people and who would preserve what is good and fruitful in our national heritage
DWIGHT D. EISENHOWER (1890–1969)

A man known to us only as a celebrity in politics or in trade, gains largely in our esteem if we discover that he has some intellectual taste or skill.
RALPH WALDO EMERSON (1803–1882)

Concentration is the secret of strength in politics, in war, in trade, in short in all management of human affairs.
RALPH WALDO EMERSON (1803–1882)

Nothing is so admirable in politics as a short memory.
JOHN KENNETH GALBRAITH (1908–2006)

Politics is not the art of the possible. It consists in choosing between the disastrous and the unpalatable.
JOHN KENNETH GALBRAITH (1908–2006)

Statesmanship is harder than politics. Politics is the art of getting along with people, whereas statesmanship is the art of getting along with politicians.
FLETCHER KNEBEL (1911–1993)

Politics is war without bloodshed while war is politics with bloodshed.
MAO TSE-TUNG (1893–1976)

Being in politics is like being a football coach. You have to be smart enough to understand the game, and dumb enough to think it's important.
EUGENE MCCARTHY (1916–2005)

The whole aim of practical politics is to keep the populace alarmed (and hence clamorous to be led to safety) by menacing it with an endless series of hobgoblins, all of them imaginary.
H. L. MENCKEN (1880–1956)

Without alienation, there can be no politics.
ARTHUR MILLER (1915–2005)

Political language, and with variations this is true of all political parties, from Conservatives to Anarchists, is designed to make lies sound truthful and murder respectable, and to give an appearance of solidity to pure wind.
GEORGE ORWELL (1903–1950), *Politics and the English Language*

Assuming either the Left Wing or the Right Wing gained control of the country, it would probably fly around in circles.
PAT PAULSEN (1927–1997)

Politics is the skilled use of blunt objects.
LESTER B. PEARSON (1897–1972)

Politics is not a bad profession. If you succeed there are many rewards, if you disgrace yourself you can always write a book.
RONALD REAGAN (1911–2004)

Politics is supposed to be the second oldest profession. I have come to realize that it bears a very close resemblance to the first.
RONALD REAGAN (1911–2004)

Politics is applesauce.
WILL ROGERS (1879–1935)

The more you read and observe about this Politics thing, you got to admit that each party is worse than the other. The one that's out always looks the best.
WILL ROGERS (1879–1935)

Politics is perhaps the only profession for which no preparation is thought necessary.
ROBERT LOUIS STEVENSON (1850–1894)

Ninety-eight percent of the adults in this country are decent, hard-working, honest Americans. It's the other lousy two percent that get all the publicity. But then, we elected them.
LILY TOMLIN (1939–)

In religion and politics, people's beliefs and convictions are in almost every case gotten at second hand, and without examination.
MARK TWAIN (1835–1910)

Politics is the art of preventing people from taking part in affairs which properly concern them.
PAUL VALÉRY (1871–1945), *Tel Quel 2*

Most people assume the fights are going to be the left versus the right, but it always is the reasonable versus the jerks.
JIMMY WALES (1966–)

Pollution

The sharp rise in environmental pollution in the 20 years following World War II could be traced to such new technologies of production: new ways of producing electric power, transportation and food that, while they generated these valuable goods, now violently assaulted the environment as well.
BARRY COMMONER (1917–)

Water and air, the two essential fluids on which all life depends, have become global garbage cans.
JACQUES COUSTEAU (1910–1997)

Pollution is nothing but the resources we are not harvesting. We allow them to disperse because we've been ignorant of their value.
R. BUCKMINSTER FULLER (1895–1983)

Racism, pollution and the rest of it are themselves very close to extinction.
R. BUCKMINSTER FULLER (1895–1983)

There's so much pollution in the air now that if it weren't for our lungs there'd be no place to put it all.
ROBERT ORBEN (1927–)

It isn't pollution that's harming the environment. It's the impurities in our air and water that are doing it.
DAN QUAYLE (1947–)

If ever we had proof that our nation's pollution laws aren't working, it's reading the list of industrial chemicals in the bodies of babies who have not yet lived outside the womb.
LOUISE SLAUGHTER (1929–)

The Poor

The rich swell up with pride, the poor from hunger.
SHOLOM ALEICHEM (1859–1916)

You cannot strengthen the weak by weakening the strong.
You cannot help small men by tearing down big men.
You cannot help the poor by destroying the rich.
You cannot lift the wage earner by pulling down the wage payer.
You cannot keep out of trouble by spending more than your income.
You cannot further the brotherhood of man by inciting class hatreds.
You cannot establish security on borrowed money.
You cannot build character and courage by taking away a man's initiative and independence.
You cannot help men permanently by doing for them what they could and should do for themselves.
WILLIAM J. H. BOETCKER (1873–1962)

When I feed the poor, they call me a saint, but when I ask why the poor are hungry, they call me a communist.
HELDER CAMARA (1909–1999)

If the misery of the poor be caused not by the laws of nature, but by our institutions, great is our sin.
CHARLES DARWIN (1809–1882)

The petty economies of the rich are just as amazing as the silly extravagances of the poor.
WILLIAM FEATHER (1908–1976)

The law, in its majestic equality, forbids the rich as well as the poor to sleep under bridges, to beg in the streets, and to steal bread.
ANATOLE FRANCE (1844–1924), *The Red Lily*

The endurance of the inequalities of life by the poor is the marvel of human society.
JAMES A. FROUDE (1818–1894)

I believe, and I say it is true Democratic feeling, that all the measures of the government are directed to the purpose of making the rich richer and the poor poorer.
WILLIAM HENRY HARRISON (1773–1841)

Indignation boils my blood at the thought of the heritage we are throwing away; at the thought that, with few exceptions, the fight for freedom is left to the poor, forlorn and defenseless, and to the few radicals and revolutionaries who would make use of liberty to destroy, rather than to maintain, American institutions.
ARTHUR GARFIELD HAYS (1881–1954)

People who go broke in a big way never miss any meals. It is the poor jerk who is shy a half slug who must tighten his belt.
ROBERT A. HEINLEIN (1907–1988)

Hope is the poor man's bread.
GEORGE HERBERT (1593–1633)

The poor on the borderline of starvation live purposeful lives. To be engaged in a desperate struggle for food and shelter is to be wholly free from a sense of futility.
ERIC HOFFER (1902–1983), *The True Believer*

The great can protect themselves, but the poor and humble require the arm and shield of the law.
ANDREW JACKSON (1767–1845)

The poor wish to be rich, the rich wish to be happy, the single wish to be married, and the married wish to be dead.
ANN LANDERS (1918–2002)

God has always been hard on the poor.
JEAN-PAUL MARAT (1743–1793)

Of all the preposterous assumptions of humanity over humanity, nothing exceeds most of the criticisms made on the habits of the poor by the well-housed, well-warmed, and well-fed.
HERMAN MELVILLE (1819–1891)

To someone seeking power, the poorest man is the most useful.
SALLUST (86–34 BC)

When the rich wage war it's the poor who die.
JEAN-PAUL SARTRE (1905–1980), *The Devil and the Good Lord*

Gambling promises the poor what property performs for the rich—something for nothing.
GEORGE BERNARD SHAW (1856–1950)

I am a gentleman: I live by robbing the poor.
GEORGE BERNARD SHAW (1856–1950)

What is the matter with the poor is poverty; what is the matter with the rich is uselessness.
GEORGE BERNARD SHAW (1856–1950)

The fields were fruitful and starving men moved on the roads. The granaries were full and the children of the poor grew up rachitic.
JOHN STEINBECK (1902–1968)

If the rich could hire the poor to die for them, the poor would make a very nice living.
JEWISH PROVERB

If you disclose your alms, even then it is well done, but if you keep them secret, and give them to the poor, then that is better still for you; and this wipes off from you some of your evil deeds.
THE KORAN

Humor the sons of the poor, for they give science its splendor.
THE TALMUD

If rich people could hire other people to die for them, the poor could make a wonderful living.
YIDDISH PROVERB

Popularity

Popularity, next to virtue and wisdom, ought to be aimed at; for it is the dictate of wisdom, and is necessary to the practice of virtue inmost.
JOHN ADAMS (1735–1826)

Popular opinion is the greatest lie in the world.
THOMAS CARLYLE (1795–1881)

Applause waits on success.
BENJAMIN FRANKLIN (1706–1790)

Popularity? It is glory's small change.
VICTOR HUGO (1802–1885)

To his dog, every man is Napoleon; hence the constant popularity of dogs.
ALDOUS HUXLEY (1894–1963)

Seek not the favor of the multitude; it is seldom got by honest and lawful means. But seek the testimony of few; and number not voices, but weigh them.
IMMANUEL KANT (1724–1804)

I would jump down Etna for any public good—but I hate a mawkish popularity.
JOHN KEATS (1795–1821)

Avoid popularity if you would have peace.
ABRAHAM LINCOLN (1809–1865)

True popularity is not the popularity which is followed after, but the popularity which follows after.
WILLIAM MURRAY, LORD MANSFIELD (1705–1793)

Avoid popularity; it has many snares, and no real benefit.
WILLIAM PENN (1644–1718)

There are few cases in which mere popularity should be considered a proper test of merit; but the case of song writing is, I think, one of the few.
EDGAR ALLAN POE (1809–1849)

Popularity is the easiest thing in the world to gain and it is the hardest thing to hold.
WILL ROGERS (1879–1935)

Popularity is a crime from the moment it is sought; it is only a virtue where men have it whether they will or no.
GEORGE SAVILE (1633–1695)

By common consent of all the nations and all the ages the most valuable thing in this world is the homage of men, whether deserved or undeserved.
MARK TWAIN (1835–1910)

Everybody's private motto: It's better to be popular than right.
MARK TWAIN (1835–1910)

Fame is a vapor; popularity an accident; the only earthly certainty is oblivion.
MARK TWAIN (1835–1910)

Popularity is the crown of laurel which the world puts on bad art. Everything popular is wrong.
OSCAR WILDE (1854–1900)

Popularity is the one insult I have never suffered.
OSCAR WILDE (1854–1900)

The one who pleased everybody died before they were born.
ANONYMOUS

Pornography

A widespread taste for pornography means that nature is alerting us to some threat of extinction.
J. G. BALLARD (1930–)

At the heart of pornography is sexuality haunted by its own disappearance.
JEAN BAUDRILLARD (1929–2007)

Pornography exists for the lonesome, the ugly, the fearful—it's made for the losers.
RITA MAE BROWN (1944–)

Pornography is a satire on human pretensions.
ANGELA CARTER (1940–1992)

Pornography is rather like trying to find out about a Beethoven symphony by having somebody tell you about it and perhaps hum a few bars.
ROBERTSON DAVIES (1913–1995)

Pornography is the attempt to insult sex, to do dirt on it.
D. H. LAWRENCE (1885–1930)

Pornography is human imagination in tense theatrical action; its violations are a protest against the violations of our freedom by nature.
CAMILLE PAGLIA (1947–)

Pornography is pornography, what is there to see? Movies are attempting to destroy something that's supposed to be the most beautiful thing a man and a woman can have by making it cheap and common. It's what you don't see that's attractive.
NANCY REAGAN (1921–)

Possessions

Why grab possessions like thieves, or divide them like socialists, when you can ignore them like wise men?
NATALIE CLIFFORD BARNEY (1876–1972)

Of all our possessions, wisdom alone is immortal.
ISOCRATES (436–338 BC)

One watches them on the seashore, all the people, and there is something pathetic, almost wistful in them, as if they wished their lives did not add up to this scaly nullity of possession, but as if they could not escape. It is a dragon that has devoured us all: these obscene, scaly houses, this insatiable struggle and desire to possess, to possess always and in spite of everything, this need to be an owner, lest one be owned. It is too hideous and nauseating. Owners

and owned, they are like the two sides of a ghastly disease. One feels a sort of madness come over one, as if the world had become hell. But it is only superimposed: it is only a temporary disease. It can be cleaned away.
D. H. LAWRENCE (1885–1930)

My most treasured possessions are not things, they are only things, my friends, family and animals are what counts.
OLIVIA NEWTON-JOHN (1948–)

Unnecessary possessions are unnecessary burdens. If you have them, you have to take care of them! There is great freedom in simplicity of living. It is those who have enough but not too much who are the happiest.
PEACE PILGRIM (1908–1981)

It is preoccupation with possessions, more than anything else, that prevents us from living freely and nobly.
BERTRAND RUSSELL (1872–1970)

Many possessions, if they do not make a man better, are at least expected to make his children happier; and this pathetic hope is behind many exertions.
GEORGE SANTAYANA (1863–1952)

Your most precious, valued possessions and your greatest powers are invisible and intangible. No one can take them. You, and you alone, can give them. You will receive abundance for your giving.
W. CLEMENT STONE (1902–2002)

Possibilities

We have more possibilities available in each moment than we realize.
THICH NHAT HAHN (1926–)

Our aspirations are our possibilities.
SAMUEL JOHNSON (1709–1784)

If I were to wish for anything, I should not wish for wealth and power, but for the passionate sense of potential—for the eye which, ever young and ardent, sees the possible. Pleasure disappoints; possibility never.
SØREN KIERKEGAARD (1813–1855)

Become a possibilitarian. No matter how dark things seem to be or actually are, raise your sights and see possibilities—always see them for they're always there.
NORMAN VINCENT PEALE (1898–1993)

The possibilities are numerous once we decide to act and not react.
GEORGE BERNARD SHAW (1856–1950)

Fiction is obliged to stick to possibilities. Truth isn't.
MARK TWAIN (1835–1910)

Positivity

A positive attitude can really make dreams come true—it did for me.
DAVID BAILEY (1938–)

Having a positive mental attitude is asking how something can be done rather than saying it can't be done.
BO BENNETT (1972–)

A positive attitude causes a chain reaction of positive thoughts, events, and outcomes. It is a catalyst and it sparks extraordinary results.
WADE BOGGS (1958–)

Positive anything is better than negative nothing.
ELBERT HUBBARD (1856–1915)

Positive thinking is the key to success in business, education, pro football, anything that you can mention. I go out there thinking that I'm going to complete every pass.
RON JAWORSKI (1951–)

A positive attitude is something everyone can work on, and everyone can learn how to employ it.
JOAN LUNDEN (1950–)

A strong positive mental attitude will create more miracles than any wonder drug.
PATRICIA NEAL (1926–)

Choosing to be positive and having a grateful attitude is going to determine how you're going to live your life.
JOEL OSTEEN (1963–)

The person who sends out positive thoughts activates the world around him positively and draws back to himself positive results.
NORMAN VINCENT PEALE (1898–1993)

Positive thinking will let you do everything better than negative thinking will.
ZIG ZIGLAR (1926–)

Poverty

Poverty is the schoolmaster of character.
ANTIPHANES (408–334 BC)

Poverty is the parent of revolution and crime.
ARISTOTLE (384–322 BC)

Where justice is denied, where poverty is enforced, where ignorance prevails, and where any one class is made to feel that society is in an organized conspiracy to oppress, rob, and degrade them, neither persons nor property will be safe.
FREDERICK DOUGLASS (1817–1895)

There is no scandal like rags, nor any crime so shameful as poverty.
GEORGE FARQUHAR (1678–1707)

It is not the rich man you should properly call happy, but him who knows how to use with wisdom the blessings of the gods, to endure hard poverty, and who fears dishonor worse than death, and is not afraid to die for cherished friends or fatherland.
HORACE (65–8 BC), *Odes*

It is pretty hard to tell what does bring happiness; poverty and wealth have both failed.
KIN HUBBARD (1868–1930)

A propensity to hope and joy is real riches; one to fear and sorrow real poverty.
DAVID HUME (1711–1776)

It is not easy for men to rise whose qualities are thwarted by poverty.
JUVENAL (AD 55–127), *Satires*

Wealth is the parent of luxury and indolence, and poverty of meanness and viciousness, and both of discontent.
PLATO (C. 428–348 BC), *The Republic*

Learn to be pleased with everything; with wealth, so far as it makes us beneficial to others; with poverty, for not having much to care for; and with obscurity, for being unenvied.
PLUTARCH (AD 46–120)

The correlation between poverty and obesity can be traced to agricultural policies and subsidies.
MICHAEL POLLAN (1955–)

What is the matter with the poor is poverty; what is the matter with the rich is uselessness.
GEORGE BERNARD SHAW (1856–1950)

You are going to let the fear of poverty govern your life and your reward will be that you will eat, but you will not live.
GEORGE BERNARD SHAW (1856–1950)

However mean your life is, meet it and live it: do not shun it and call it hard names. Cultivate poverty like a garden herb, like sage. Do not trouble yourself much to get new things, whether clothes or friends. Things do not change, we change. Sell your clothes and keep your thoughts. God will see that you do not want society.
HENRY DAVID THOREAU (1817–1862)

Power

Power tends to corrupt, and absolute power corrupts absolutely.
LORD ACTON (1834–1902)

Knowledge is power.
SIR FRANCIS BACON (1561–1626), *Religious Meditations*

A man's true state of power and riches is to be in himself.
HENRY WARD BEECHER (1813–1887)

We thought, because we had power, we had wisdom.
STEPHEN VINCENT BENET (1898–1943), *Litany for Dictatorships*

It is said that power corrupts, but actually it's more true that power attracts the corruptible. The sane are usually attracted by other things than power.
DAVID BRIN (1950–)

If power was an illusion, wasn't weakness necessarily one also?
LOIS MCMASTER BUJOLD (1949–), *A Civil Campaign*

To know the pains of power, we must go to those who have it; to know its pleasures, we must go to those who are seeking it.
CHARLES CALEB COLTON (1780–1832), *Lacon*

The power may come from outside us, but the order we impose on it must come from within.
C. S. FRIEDMAN (1957–), *Black Sun Rising*

Let not thy will roar, when thy power can but whisper.
THOMAS FULLER (1608–1661), *Gnomologia*

Be fit for more than the thing you are now doing. Let everyone know that you have a reserve in yourself; that you have more power than you are now using. If you are not too large for the place you occupy, you are too small for it.
JAMES A. GARFIELD (1831–1881)

Far better to think historically, to remember the lessons of the past. Thus, far better to conceive of power as consisting in part of the knowledge of when not to use all the power you have. Far better to be one who knows that if you reserve the power not to use all your power, you will lead others far more successfully and well.
BARTLETT GIAMATTI (1938–1989)

The sole advantage of power is that you can do more good.
BALTASAR GRACIAN (1601–1658), *The Art of Worldly Wisdom*

The love of liberty is the love of others; the love of power is the love of ourselves.
WILLIAM HAZLITT (1778–1830)

This is the bitterest pain among men, to have much knowledge but no power.
HERODOTUS (484–430 BC), *The Histories of Herodotus*

The man of power is ruined by power, the man of money by money, the submissive man by subservience, the pleasure seeker by pleasure.
HERMANN HESSE (1877–1962)

It is when power is wedded to chronic fear that it becomes formidable.
ERIC HOFFER (1902–1983), *The Passionate State of Mind*

The great secret of power is never to will to do more than you can accomplish.
HENRIK IBSEN (1828–1906)

An honest man can feel no pleasure in the exercise of power over his fellow citizens.
THOMAS JEFFERSON (1743–1826)

The men who create power make an indispensable contribution to the nation's greatness, but the men who question power make a contribution just as indispensable, especially when that questioning is disinterested, for they determine whether we use power or power uses us.
JOHN F. KENNEDY (1917–1963)

The problem of power is how to achieve its responsible use rather than its irresponsible and indulgent use—of how to get men of power to live for the public rather than off the public.
ROBERT F. KENNEDY (1925–1968)

Power corrupts. Absolute power is kind of neat.
JOHN LEHMAN (1942–)

Nearly all men can stand adversity, but if you want to test a man's character, give him power.
ABRAHAM LINCOLN (1809–1865)

The highest proof of virtue is to possess boundless power without abusing it.
LORD THOMAS BABINGTON MACAULAY (1800–1859)

Power never takes a back step—only in the face of more power.
MALCOLM X (1925–1965), *Malcolm X Speaks*

One person with a belief is equal to a force of 99 who have only interests.
JOHN STUART MILL (1806–1873)

The powerful don't make revolutions.
MARGE PIERCY (1936–)

Most powerful is he who has himself in his own power.
SENECA (5 BC–AD 65)

If absolute power corrupts absolutely, does absolute powerlessness make you pure?
HARRY SHEARER (1943–)

You see what power is, holding someone else's fear in your hand and showing it to them!
AMY TAN (1952–)

We have, I fear, confused power with greatness.
STEWART L. UDALL (1920–)

Ultimately, the only power to which man should aspire is that which he exercises over himself.
ELIE WIESEL (1928–)

Power consists in one's capacity to link his will with the purpose of others, to lead by reason and a gift of cooperation.
WOODROW WILSON (1856–1924)

Praise

Praise from the common people is generally false, and rather follows the vain than the virtuous.
SIR FRANCIS BACON (1561–1626)

The praise that comes from love does not make us vain, but more humble.
JAMES M. BARRIE (1860–1937)

The meanest, most contemptible kind of praise is that which first speaks well of a man, and then qualifies it with a "but."
HENRY WARD BEECHER (1813–1887)

Falsehood often lurks upon the tongue of him, who, by self-praise, seeks to enhance his value in the eyes of others.
ARNOLD BENNETT (1867–1931)

Modesty is the only sure bait when you angle for praise.
LORD CHESTERFIELD (1694–1773)

Such praise coming from so degraded a source, was degrading to me, its recipient.
CICERO (106–43 BC)

We are all motivated by a keen desire for praise, and the better a man is, the more he is inspired to glory.
CICERO (106–43 BC)

Praise the bridge that carried you over.
GEORGE COLMAN (1762–1836), *The Younger*

There are two modes of establishing our reputation: to be praised by honest men, and to be abused by rogues. It is best, however, to secure the former, because it will invariably be accompanied by the latter.
CHARLES CALEB COLTON (1780–1832)

Most of our censure of others is only oblique praise of self, uttered to show the wisdom and superiority of the speaker. It has all the insidiousness of self-praise, and all the ill-desert of falsehood.
TYRON EDWARDS (1809–1894)

Praise in the beginning is agreeable enough; and we receive it as a favor; but when it comes in great quantities, we regard it only as a debt, which nothing but our merit could extort.
JAMES GOLDSMITH (1933–1997)

He only profits from praise who values criticism.
HEINRICH HEINE (1797–1856)

Praise, like gold and diamonds, owes its value only to its scarcity.
SAMUEL JOHNSON (1709–1784)

The real satisfaction which praise can afford, is when what is repeated aloud agrees with the whispers of conscience, by showing us that we have not endeavored to deserve well in vain.
SAMUEL JOHNSON (1709–1784)

You do ill if you praise, but worse if you censure, what you do not understand.
LEONARDO DA VINCI (1452–1519)

He who praises you for what you lack wishes to take from you what you have.
DON JUAN MANUEL (1282–1349)

Whatever is in any way beautiful hath its source of beauty in itself, and is complete in itself; praise forms no part of it. So it is none the worse nor the better for being praised.
MARCUS AURELIUS ANTONINUS (121–180), *Meditations*

I do not confer praise or blame: I accept. I am the measure of all things. I am the centre of the world.
W. SOMERSET MAUGHAM (1874–1965), *Of Human Bondage*

People ask for criticism, but they only want praise.
W. SOMERSET MAUGHAM (1874–1965)

There's no praise to beat the sort you can put in your pocket.
MOLIÈRE (1622–1673)

Don't discuss yourself, for you are bound to lose; if you belittle yourself, you are believed; if you praise yourself, you are disbelieved.
MICHEL DE MONTAIGNE (1533–1592)

When all is summed up, a man never speaks of himself without loss; his accusations of himself are always believed; his praises never.
MICHEL DE MONTAIGNE (1533–1592)

I pay no attention whatever to anybody's praise or blame. I simply follow my own feelings.
WOLFGANG AMADEUS MOZART (1756–1791)

I cannot believe in a God who wants to be praised all the time.
FRIEDRICH NIETZSCHE (1844–1900)

Undeserved praise causes more pangs of conscience later than undeserved blame, but probably only for this reason, that our powers of judgment are more completely exposed by being over praised than by being unjustly underestimated.
FRIEDRICH NIETZSCHE (1844–1900)

Be thou the first true merit to befriend,
His praise is lost who stays till all commend.
ALEXANDER POPE (1688–1744)

Admonish thy friends in secret, praise them openly.
PUBLILIUS SYRUS (C. 100 BC)

You can tell the character of every man when you see how he receives praise.
SENECA (5 BC–AD 65), *Epistles*

If a man is proud of his wealth, he should not be praised until it is known how he employs it.
SOCRATES (469–399 BC)

Think not those faithful who praise all thy words and actions; but those who kindly reprove thy faults.
SOCRATES (469–399 BC)

I don't mind a little praise—as long as it's fulsome.
ADLAI E. STEVENSON II (1900–1965)

Their silence is sufficient praise.
TERENCE (185–159 BC)

We are always more anxious to be distinguished for a talent which we do not possess, than to be praised for the fifteen which we do possess.
MARK TWAIN (1835–1910), *Mark Twain's Autobiography*

Having the critics praise you is like having the hangman say you've got a pretty neck.
ELI WALLACH (1915–)

A man desires praise that he may be reassured, that he may be quit of his doubting of himself; he is indifferent to applause when he is confident of success.
ALEC WAUGH (1898–1981)

It is usually best to be generous with praise, but cautious with criticism.
ANONYMOUS

The test of any man's character is how he takes praise.
ANONYMOUS

Praise youth and it will prosper.
IRISH PROVERB

Prayer

Courage is just fear, plus prayers, plus understanding.
EDWARD ALBERT (1951–)

The time to pray is not when we are in a tight spot but just as soon as we get out of it.
JOSH BILLINGS (1818–1885)

Do not pray for easy lives. Pray to be stronger men. Do not pray for tasks equal to your powers. Pray for powers equal to your tasks. Then the doing of your work shall be no miracle, but you shall be the miracle.
PHILLIPS BROOKS (1835–1893)

You must pray that the way be long, full of adventures and experiences.
CONSTANTINE PETER CAVAFY (1863–1933)

If the only prayer you ever say in your whole life is "thank you," that would suffice.
MEISTER ECKHART (C. 1260–1328)

Prayer indeed is good, but while calling on the gods a man should himself lend a hand.
HIPPOCRATES (460–377 BC), *Regimen*

You should pray for a sound mind in a sound body.
JUVENAL (AD 55–127), *Satires*

One single grateful thought raised to heaven is the most perfect prayer.
G. E. LESSING (1729–1781)

Prayer may not change things for you, but it for sure changes you for things.
SAM SHOEMAKER (1893–1963)

Our prayers should be for blessings in general, for God knows best what is good for us.
SOCRATES (469–399 BC)

Pray as if everything depended upon God, and work as if everything depended upon man.
CARDINAL FRANCIS SPELLMAN (1889–1967)

There are more tears shed over answered prayers than over unanswered prayers.
SAINT THERESA OF JESUS (1515–1582)

I have never made but one prayer to God, a very short one: "O Lord, make my enemies ridiculous." And God granted it.
VOLTAIRE (1694–1778)

When the gods wish to punish us, they answer our prayers.
OSCAR WILDE (1854–1900), *An Ideal Husband*

Preachers

The business of an orthodox preacher is about as successful as that of a celluloid dog chasing an asbestos cat through hell.
ELBERT HUBBARD (1856–1915)

A preacher must be both soldier and shepherd. He must nourish, defend, and teach; he must have teeth in his mouth, and be able to bite and fight.
MARTIN LUTHER (1483–1546)

We do not condemn the preachers as [individuals] but we condemn what they teach. We urge that the preachers teach the truth, to teach our people the

one important guiding rule of conduct—unity of purpose.
MALCOLM X (1925–1965)

I think there ought to be a club in which preachers and journalists could come together and have the sentimentalism of the one matched with the cynicism of the other. That ought to bring them pretty close to the truth.
REINHOLD NIEBUHR (1892–1971)

All criminals turn preachers under the gallows.
ANONYMOUS

Prediction

No one can possibly know what is about to happen: it is happening, each time, for the first time, for the only time.
JAMES ARTHUR BALDWIN (1924–1987)

It's tough to make predictions, especially about the future.
YOGI BERRA (1925–)

The unpredictability inherent in human affairs is due largely to the fact that the by-products of a human process are more fateful than the product.
ERIC HOFFER (1902–1983)

The groundhog is like most other prophets; it delivers its prediction and then disappears.
BILL VAUGHAN (1915–1977)

Prejudice

If we were to wake up some morning and find that everyone was the same race, creed and color, we would find some other cause for prejudice by noon.
GEORGE D. AIKEN (1892–1984)

Common sense is the collection of prejudices acquired by age eighteen.
ALBERT EINSTEIN (1879–1955)

I am free of all prejudice. I hate everyone equally.
W. C. FIELDS (1880–1946)

Without the aid of prejudice and custom I should not be able to find my way across the room.
WILLIAM HAZLITT (1778–1830)

Nobody outside of a baby carriage or a judge's chamber believes in an unprejudiced point of view.
LILLIAN HELLMAN (1905–1984)

A great many people think they are thinking when they are really rearranging their prejudices.
WILLIAM JAMES (1842–1910)

Opinions founded on prejudice are always sustained with the greatest of violence.
LORD FRANCIS JEFFREY (1773–1850)

There are, in every age, new errors to be rectified and new prejudices to be opposed.
SAMUEL JOHNSON (1709–1784)

Criticism is prejudice made plausible.
H. L. MENCKEN (1880–1956)

Everyone is a prisoner of his own experiences. No one can eliminate prejudices—just recognize them.
EDWARD R. MURROW (1908–1965)

When the judgement's weak,
The prejudice is strong.
KANE O'HARA (1711–1782)

Education is a method whereby one acquires a higher grade of prejudices.
DR. LAURENCE J. PETER (1919–1990)

Errors to be dangerous must have a great deal of truth mingled with them. It is only from this alliance that they can ever obtain an extensive circulation.
SYDNEY SMITH (1771–1845)

Never try to reason the prejudice out of a man. It was not reasoned into him, and cannot be reasoned out.
SYDNEY SMITH (1771–1845)

It is never too late to give up our prejudices.
HENRY DAVID THOREAU (1817–1862), *Walden*

Prejudice is opinion without judgment.
VOLTAIRE (1694–1778)

The Present

Write down the thoughts of the moment. Those that come unsought for are commonly the most valuable.
SIR FRANCIS BACON (1561–1626)

There is never a time in the future in which we will work out our salvation. The challenge is in the moment; the time is always now.
JAMES ARTHUR BALDWIN (1924–1987)

The pleasure we derive from the representation of the present is due, not only to the beauty it can be clothed in, but also to its essential quality of being the present.
CHARLES BAUDELAIRE (1821–1867)

No matter what looms ahead, if you can eat today, enjoy the sunlight today, mix good cheer with friends today, enjoy it and bless God for it. Do not look back on happiness—or dream of it in the future. You are only sure of today; do not let yourself be cheated out of it.
HENRY WARD BEECHER (1813–1887)

The secret of health for both mind and body is not to mourn for the past, not to worry about the future, or not to anticipate troubles, but to live in the present moment wisely and earnestly.
THE BUDDHA (563–483 BC)

Our main business is not to see what lies dimly at a distance, but to do what clearly lies at hand.
THOMAS CARLYLE (1795–1881)

Remember, today is the tomorrow you worried about yesterday.
DALE CARNEGIE (1888–1955)

Today is life—the only life you are sure of. Make the most of today. Get interested in something. Shake yourself awake. Develop a hobby. Let the winds of enthusiasm sweep through you. Live today with gusto.
DALE CARNEGIE (1888–1955)

To live is so starlting it leaves little time for anything else.
EMILY DICKINSON (1830–1886)

Equations are more important to me, because politics is for the present, but an equation is something for eternity.
ALBERT EINSTEIN (1879–1955)

The art of life is to live in the present moment, and to make that moment as perfect as we can by the realization that we are the instruments and expression of God Himself.
EMMET FOX (1886–1951)

The future depends on what we do in the present.
MAHATMA GANDHI (1869–1948)

Children have neither a past nor a future. Thus they enjoy the present—which seldom happens to us.
JEAN DE LA BRUYÈRE (1645–1696)

In rivers, the water that you touch is the last of what has passed and the first of that which comes; so with present time.
LEONARDO DA VINCI (1452–1519)

He who controls the present, controls the past. He who controls the past, controls the future.
GEORGE ORWELL (1903–1950)

The present is never our goal: the past and present are our means: the future alone is our goal. Thus, we never live but we hope to live; and always hoping to be happy, it is inevitable that we will never be so.
BLAISE PASCAL (1623–1662)

Yesterday is history, tomorrow is a mystery, today is God's gift, that's why we call it the present.
JOAN RIVERS (1935–)

I'm not interested in what should be, could be, was. I'm interested in what is, what we control.
NICK SABAN (1951–)

The true felicity of life is to be free from anxieties and perturbations; to understand and do our duties to God and man, and to enjoy the present without any serious dependence on the future.
SENECA (5 BC–AD 65)

You must live in the present, launch yourself on every wave, find your eternity in each moment. Fools stand on their island opportunities and look toward another land. There is no other land, there is no other life but this.
HENRY DAVID THOREAU (1817–1862)

Presents

I'm not materialistic. I believe in presents from the heart, like a drawing that a child does.
VICTORIA BECKHAM (1974–)

A friend that you buy with presents will be bought from you.
THOMAS FULLER (1608–1661)

Your children need your presence more than your presents.
JESSE JACKSON (1941–)

Beautiful music is the art of the prophets that can calm the agitations of the soul; it is one of the most magnificent and delightful presents God has given us.
MARTIN LUTHER (1483–1546)

Preservation

This is Preservation Month. I appreciate preservation. It's what you do when you run for president. You gotta preserve.
GEORGE W. BUSH (1946–)

We stand now where two roads diverge. But unlike the roads in Robert Frost's familiar poem, they are not equally fair. The road we have long been traveling is deceptively easy, a smooth superhighway on which we progress with great speed, but at its end lies disaster. The other fork of the road—the one less traveled by—offers our last, our only chance to reach a destination that assures the preservation of the earth.
RACHEL CARSON (1907–1964)

Conservation is the foresighted utilization, preservation and/or renewal of forests, waters, lands and minerals, for the greatest good of the greatest number for the longest time.
GIFFORD PINCHOT (1865–1946)

Presidents

The progress of evolution from President Washington to President Grant was alone evidence enough to upset Darwin.
HENRY ADAMS (1838–1918)

If presidents can't do it to their wives, they do it to their country.
MEL BROOKS (1926–)

I would rather be right than President.
HENRY CLAY (1777–1852)

And still the question, "What shall be done with our ex-Presidents?" is not laid at rest; and I sometimes think Watterson's solution of it, "Take them out and shoot them," is worthy of attention.
GROVER CLEVELAND (1837–1908)

One of the first things a President learns is that everything he says weighs a ton.
CALVIN COOLIDGE (1872–1933)

When I was a boy I was told that anybody could become President; I'm beginning to believe it.
CLARENCE DARROW (1857–1938)

We need a president who's fluent in at least one language.
BUCK HENRY (1930–)

A president's hardest task is not to do what is right but to know what is right.
LYNDON B. JOHNSON (1908–1973)

If one morning I walked on top of the water across the Potomac River, the headline that afternoon would read "President Can't Swim."
LYNDON B. JOHNSON (1908–1973)

My most fervent prayer is to be a President who can make it possible for every boy in this land to grow to manhood by loving his country—instead of dying for it.
LYNDON B. JOHNSON (1908–1973)

It is my ambition and desire to so administer the affairs of the government while I remain President that if at the end, I have lost every other Friend on earth, I shall at least have one friend remaining, and that one shall be down inside me.
ABRAHAM LINCOLN (1809–1865)

Only events and not a man's exertions in his own behalf, can make a President.
ABRAHAM LINCOLN (1809–1865)

Presidents do make mistakes, but the immortal Dante tells us that divine justice weighs the sins of the cold-blooded and the sins of the warm-hearted in different scales.
FRANKLIN D. ROOSEVELT (1882–1945)

In America, any boy may become president, and I suppose that's just one of the risks he takes.
ADLAI E. STEVENSON II (1900–1965)

I would rather have peace in the world than be president.
HARRY S TRUMAN (1884–1972)

When you see how the President makes political or policy decisions, you see who he is. The essence of the Presidency is decision-making.
BOB WOODWARD (1943–)

Pride

Pride goes before destruction and a haughty spirit before a fall.
JOSEPH ADDISON (1672–1719)

Vanity and pride are different things, though the words are often used synonymously. A person may be proud without being vain. Pride relates more to our opinion of ourselves; vanity, to what we would have others think of us.
JANE AUSTEN (1775–1817)

Pampered vanity is a better thing perhaps than starved pride.
JOANNA BAILLIE (1762–1851)

How sweet I roamed from field to field, and tasted all the summer's pride.
WILLIAM BLAKE (1757–1827)

Shame is pride's cloak.
WILLIAM BLAKE (1757–1827)

The pride of the peacock is the glory of God.
WILLIAM BLAKE (1757–1827)

Show class, have pride, and display character. If you do, winning takes care of itself.
PAUL "BEAR" BRYANT (1913–1983)

The truest characters of ignorance are vanity, and pride and arrogance.
SAMUEL BUTLER (1835–1902)

And the Devil did grin, for his darling sin is pride that apes humility.
SAMUEL TAYLOR COLERIDGE (1772–1834)

There is this paradox in pride—it makes some men ridiculous, but prevents others from becoming so.
CHARLES CALEB COLTON (1780–1832)

Generosity is giving more than you can, and pride is taking less than you need.
KAHLIL GIBRAN (1883–1931)

Pride is seldom delicate; it will please itself with very mean advantages.
SAMUEL JOHNSON (1709–1784)

Pride attaches undue importance to the superiority of one's status in the eyes of others; and shame is fear of humiliation at one's inferior status in the estimation of others. When one sets his heart on being highly esteemed, and achieves such rating, then he is automatically involved in fear of losing his status
LAO-TZU (C. 600 BC)

Pride does not wish to owe and vanity does not wish to pay.
FRANÇOIS DE LA ROCHEFOUCAULD (1613–1680)

A proud man is always looking down on things and people; and, of course, as long as you're looking down, you can't see something that's above you.
C. S. LEWIS (1898–1963)

Pride makes us artificial and humility makes us real.
THOMAS MERTON (1915–1968)

Our vanity is hardest to wound precisely when our pride has just been wounded.
FRIEDRICH NIETZSCHE (1844–1900)

In general, pride is at the bottom of all great mistakes.
JOHN RUSKIN (1819–1900)

The passions grafted on wounded pride are the most inveterate; they are green and vigorous in old age.
GEORGE SANTAYANA (1863–1952)

We are rarely proud when we are alone.
VOLTAIRE (1694–1778)

You can't give people pride, but you can provide the kind of understanding that makes people look to their inner strengths and find their own sense of pride.
CHARLESZETTA WADDLES (1912–2001)

No one ever choked to death swallowing his pride.
ANONYMOUS

Pride is a personal commitment. It is an attitude which separates excellence from mediocrity.
ANONYMOUS

Temper gets you into trouble. Pride keeps you there.
ANONYMOUS

When pride comes, then comes disgrace, but with humility comes wisdom.
THE BIBLE, Proverbs 11:2

It is a beggar's pride that he is not a thief.
JAPANESE PROVERB

Priests

The question before the human race is whether the God of nature shall govern the world by His own laws, or whether priests and kings shall rule it by fictitious miracles.
JOHN ADAMS (1735–1826)

There exist only three beings worthy of respect: the priest, the soldier, the poet. To know, to kill, to create.
CHARLES BAUDELAIRE (1821–1867), *Mon coeur mis à nu*

They said this mystery never shall cease: the priest promotes war, and the soldier peace.
WILLIAM BLAKE (1757–1827)

In pious times 'ere priest craft did begin,
Before polygamy was made a sin:
When man, on many, multiply'd his kind
Ere one to one was, cursedly, confined;
When Nature prompted, and no law deny'd
Promiscuous use of concubine and bride.
JOHN DRYDEN (1631–1700)

Priests are no more necessary to religion than politicians to patriotism
JOHN HAYNES HOLMES (1879–1964)

This crime called blasphemy was invented by priests for the purpose of defending doctrines not able to take care of themselves.
ROBERT GREEN INGERSOLL (1833–1899)

If anybody thinks that kings, nobles, priests are good conservators of the public happiness, send him [to Europe].
THOMAS JEFFERSON (1762–1826)

In every country and in every age the priest has been hostile to liberty; he is always in allegiance to the despot, abetting his abuses in return for protection of his own.
THOMAS JEFFERSON (1762–1826)

I shall always be a priest of love.
D. H. LAWRENCE (1885–1930)

I am surrounded by priests who repeat incessantly that their kingdom is not of this world, and yet they lay their hands on everything they can get.
NAPOLÉON I (1769–1821)

I did not see why the schoolmaster should be taxed to support the priest, and not the priest the schoolmaster.
HENRY DAVID THOREAU (1817–1862)

Man is a free agent; were it otherwise, the priests could not damn him.
VOLTAIRE (1694–1778)

The first priest was the first rogue who met the first fool.
VOLTAIRE (1694–1778)

Civilization will not attain to its perfection until the last stone from the last church falls on the last priest.
ÉMILE ZOLA (1840–1902)

An ounce of mother is worth a ton of priest.
SPANISH PROVERB

Principles

The highest principles for our aspirations and judgments are given to us in the Jewish-Christian religious tradition. It is a very high goal which, with our weak powers, we can reach only very inadequately, but which gives a sure foundation to our aspirations and valuations.
ALBERT EINSTEIN (1879–1955)

By denying scientific principles, one may maintain any paradox.
GALILEO GALILEI (1564–1642)

Where ambition can cover its enterprises, even to the person himself, under the appearance of principle, it is the most incurable and inflexible of passions.
DAVID HUME (1711–1776)

The deepest principle in human nature is the craving to be appreciated.
WILLIAM JAMES (1842–1910)

Peace won by the compromise of principles is a short-lived achievement.
ANONYMOUS

Prison

Stone walls do not a prison make.
AMBROSE BIERCE (1842–1914)

America is the land of the second chance—and when the gates of the prison open, the path ahead should lead to a better life.
GEORGE W. BUSH (1946–)

Prison life consists of routine, and then more routine.
FRANK DARABONT (1959–) and STEPHEN KING (1947–), *The Shawshank Redemption*

The degree of civilization in a society can be judged by entering its prisons
FYODOR DOSTOEVSKY (1821–1881)

Wherever any one is against his will, that is to him a prison.
EPICTETUS (AD 55–135)

Let us reform our schools, and we shall find little reform needed in our prisons.
JOHN RUSKIN (1819–1900), *Unto This Last*

A pedestal is as much a prison as any small, confined space.
Gloria Steinem (1934–)

Under a government which imprisons any unjustly, the true place for a just man is also a prison.
Henry David Thoreau (1817–1862)

The White House is the finest prison in the world.
Harry S Truman (1884–1972)

One of the many lessons that one learns in prison is, that things are what they are and will be what they will be.
Oscar Wilde (1854–1900)

Privacy

Privacy is not something that I'm merely entitled to, it's an absolute prerequisite.
Marlon Brando (1924–2004)

When it comes to privacy and accountability, people always demand the former for themselves and the latter for everyone else.
David Brin (1950–)

The personal life of every individual is based on secrecy, and perhaps it is partly for that reason that civilised man is so nervously anxious that personal privacy should be respected.
Anton Chekhov (1860–1904)

Nor has he spent his life badly who has passed it in privacy.
Cicero (106–43 BC)

There is no private life which has not been determined by a wider public life.
George Eliot (1819–1880)

I've never looked through a keyhole without finding someone was looking back.
Judy Garland (1922–1969)

Privacy was in sufficient danger before TV appeared, and TV has given it its death blow.
Louis Kronenberger (1904–1980)

Publication is a self-invasion of privacy.
Marshall McLuhan (1911–1980)

Civilization is the progress toward a society of privacy. The savage's whole existence is public, ruled by the laws of his tribe. Civilization is the process of setting man free from men.
Ayn Rand (1905–1982)

There is nothing new in the realization that the Constitution sometimes insulates the criminality of a few in order to protect the privacy of us all.
Antonin Scalia (1936–)

Privilege

Privilege is the greatest enemy of right.
Marie Von Ebner-Eschenbach (1830–1916)

Equal rights for all, special privileges for none.
Thomas Jefferson (1743–1826)

What men prize most is a privilege, even if it be that of chief mourner at a funeral.
James Russell Lowell (1819–1891)

What men value in this world is not rights but privileges.
H. L. Mencken (880–1956)

Problems

Problems are only opportunities with thorns on them.
Hugh Miller (1802–1856), *Snow on the Wind*

Life's problems wouldn't be called "hurdles" if there wasn't a way to get over them.
Anonymous

Procrastination

We shall never have more time. We have, and always had, all the time there is. No object is served in waiting until next week or even until tomorrow. Keep going.... Concentrate on something useful.
ARNOLD BENNETT (1867–1931)

No idleness, no laziness, no procrastination; never put off till tomorrow what you can do today.
LORD CHESTERFIELD (1694–1773)

Procrastination is one of the most common and deadliest of diseases and its toll on success and happiness is heavy.
WAYNE GRETZKY (1961–)

Procrastination is the bad habit off putting of until the day after tomorrow what should have been done the day before yesterday.
NAPOLEON HILL (1883–1970)

This is the last hair in the tail of procrastination.
LLOYD KENYON (1805–1869)

Procrastination is opportunity's assassin.
VICTOR KIAM (1926–2001)

How soon "not now" becomes "never."
MARTIN LUTHER (1483–1546)

Procrastination is the art of keeping up with yesterday.
DON MARQUIS (1878–1937)

Procrastination is like a credit card: it's a lot of fun until you get the bill.
CHRISTOPHER PARKER (1983–)

If once a man indulges himself in murder, very soon he comes to think little of robbing; and from robbing he next comes to drinking and Sabbath-breaking, and from that to incivility and procrastination.
THOMAS DE QUINCEY (1785–1859)

Procrastination is the thief of time:
Year after year it steals, till all are fled,
And to the mercies of a moment leaves
The vast concerns of an eternal scene.
EDWARD YOUNG (1683–1765)

Profit

Remind people that profit is the difference between revenue and expense. This makes you look smart.
SCOTT ADAMS (1957–)

We have to choose between a global market driven only by calculations of short-term profit, and one which has a human face.
KOFI ANNAN (1938–)

Madness is badness of spirit, when one seeks profit from all sources.
ARISTOTLE (384–322 BC)

I hold every man a debtor to his profession; from the which as men of course do seek to receive countenance and profit, so ought they of duty to endeavour themselves by way of amends to be a help and ornament thereunto.
SIR FRANCIS BACON (1561–1626)

If you mean to profit, learn to please.
SIR WINSTON CHURCHILL (1874–1965)

Civilization and profit go hand in hand.
CALVIN COOLIDGE (1872–1933)

Drop the question what tomorrow may bring, and count as profit every day that fate allows you.
HORACE (65–8 BC)

He wins every hand who mingles profit with pleasure.
HORACE (65–8 BC)

It takes nearly as much ability to know how to profit by good advice as to know how to act for one's self.
FRANÇOIS DE LA ROCHEFOUCAULD (1613–1680)

It is more profitable for your congressman to support the tobacco industry than your life.
JACKIE MASON (1931–)

Don't be seduced into thinking that that which does not make a profit is without value.
ARTHUR MILLER (1915–2005)

Profit is the ignition system of our economic engine.
CHARLES SAWYER (1868–1954)

The fact is that one side thinks that the profits to be won outweigh the risks to be incurred, and the other side would rather avoid danger than accept an immediate loss.
THUCYDIDES (C. 460–395 BC)

Profits, like sausages … are esteemed most by those who know least about what goes into them.
ALVIN TOFFLER (1928–)

Take every gain without showing remorse about missed profits, because an eel may escape sooner than you think.
LOPE DE VEGA (1562–1635)

Progress

Progress would not have been the rarity it is if the early food had not been the late poison.
WALTER BAGEHOT (1826–1877)

Poetry and progress are like two ambitious men who hate one another with an instinctive hatred, and when they meet upon the same road, one of them has to give place.
CHARLES BAUDELAIRE (1821–1867)

Every day you may make progress. Every step may be fruitful. Yet there will stretch out before you an ever-lengthening, ever-ascending, ever-improving path. You know you will never get to the end of the journey. But this, so far from discouraging, only adds to the joy and glory of the climb.
SIR WINSTON CHURCHILL (1874–1965)

The perfecting of one's self is the fundamental base of all progress and all moral development.
CONFUCIUS (551–479 BC)

Little progress can be made by merely attempting to repress what is evil. Our great hope lies in developing what is good.
CALVIN COOLIDGE (1872–1933)

I was taught that the way of progress was neither swift nor easy.
MARIE CURIE (1867–1934)

My own experience and development deepen every day my conviction that our moral progress may be measured by the degree in which we sympathize with individual suffering and individual joy.
T. S. ELIOT (1888–1965)

The progress of an artist is a continual self-sacrifice, a continual extinction of personality.
T. S. ELIOT (1888–1965)

All our progress is an unfolding, like a vegetable bud. You have first an instinct, then an opinion, then a knowledge as the plant has root, bud, and fruit. Trust the instinct to the end, though you can render no reason.
RALPH WALDO EMERSON (1803–1882)

Coming together is a beginning. Keeping together is progress. Working together is success.
HENRY FORD (1863–1947)

Without continual growth and progress, such words as improvement, achievement, and success have no meaning.
BENJAMIN FRANKLIN (1706–1790)

Progress comes from the intelligent use of experience.
ELBERT HUBBARD (1856–1915)

The reason men oppose progress is not that they hate progress, but that they love inertia.
ELBERT HUBBARD (1856–1915)

Emergencies have always been necessary to progress. It was darkness which produced the lamp. It was fog that produced the compass. It was hunger that drove us to exploration. And it took a depression to teach us the real value of a job.
VICTOR HUGO (1802–1885)

Progress is the life-style of man. The general life of the human race is called Progress, and so is its collective march. Progress advances, it makes the great human and earthly journey towards what is heavenly and divine…
VICTOR HUGO (1802–1885)

Progress is the stride of God.
VICTOR HUGO (1802–1885)

The natural progress of things is for liberty to yield and government to gain ground.
THOMAS JEFFERSON (1762–1826)

All progress is precarious, and the solution of one problem brings us face to face with another problem.
MARTIN LUTHER KING JR. (1929–1968)

A process which led from the amoebae to man appeared to the philosophers to be obviously a progress—though whether the amoebae would agree with this opinion is not known.
BERTRAND RUSSELL (1872–1970)

All progress has resulted from people who took unpopular positions.
ADLAI E. STEVENSON II (1900–1965)

Fundamental progress has to do with the reinterpretation of basic ideas.
ALFRED NORTH WHITEHEAD (1861–1947)

Promises

Never before in history has innovation offered promise of so much to so many in so short a time.
BILL GATES (1955–)

Girls we love for what they are; young men for what they promise to be.
JOHANN WOLFGANG VON GOETHE (1749–1832)

The longer we live, and the more we think, the higher value we learn to put on the friendship and tenderness of parents and friends. Parents we can have but once; and he promises himself too much, who enters life with the expectation of finding many.
SAMUEL JOHNSON (1709–1784)

We promise according to our hopes and perform according to our fears.
FRANÇOIS DE LA ROCHEFOUCAULD (1613–1680)

Promises that you make to yourself are often like the Japanese plum tree—they bear no fruit.
FRANCIS MARION (1732–1795)

My strong point, if I have a strong point, is performance. I always do more than I say. I always produce more than I promise.
RICHARD M. NIXON (1913–1994)

Nature is as wasteful of promising young men as she is of fish spawn.
RICHARD M. NIXON (1913–1994)

Never promise more than you can perform.
PUBLILIUS SYRUS (C. 100 BC)

He who is slowest in making a promise is most faithful in its performance.
JEAN-JACQUES ROUSSEAU (1712–1778)

Propaganda

Propaganda is a soft weapon; hold it in your hands too long, and it will move about like a snake, and strike the other way.
JEAN ANOUILH (1910–1987)

Only the mob and the elite can be attracted by the momentum of totalitarianism itself. The masses have to be won by propaganda.
HANNAH ARENDT (1906–1975)

Art is moral passion married to entertainment. Moral passion without entertainment is propaganda, and entertainment without moral passion is television.
RITA MAE BROWN (1944–)

Propaganda is to a democracy what the bludgeon is to a totalitarian state.
NOAM CHOMSKY (1928–)

With a new familiarity and a flesh-creeping "homeliness" entirely of this unreal, materialistic world, where all "sentiment" is coarsely manufactured and advertised in colossal sickly captions, disguised for the sweet tooth of a monstrous baby called "the Public," the family as it is, broken up on all hands by the agency of feminist and economic propaganda, reconstitutes itself in the image of the state.
WYNDHAM LEWIS (1882–1957)

You must not kill your neighbor, whom perhaps you genuinely hate, but by a little propaganda this hate can be transferred to some foreign nation, against whom all your murderous impulses become patriotic heroism.
BERTRAND RUSSELL (1872–1970)

In Russia we only had two TV channels. Channel One was propaganda. Channel Two consisted of a KGB officer telling you: Turn back at once to Channel One.
YAKOV SMIRNOFF (1951–)

Property

The moment the idea is admitted into society that property is not as sacred as the laws of God, and there is not a force of law and public justice to protect it, anarchy and tyranny commence.
JOHN ADAMS (1735–1826)

A lawyer's dream of heaven: every man reclaimed his property at the resurrection, and each tried to recover it from all his forefathers.
SAMUEL BUTLER (1835–1902)

Upon the sacredness of property, civilization itself depends—the right of the laborer to his hundred dollars in the savings bank, and equally the legal right of the millionaire to his millions.
ANDREW CARNEGIE (1835–1919)

Some people talk of morality, and some of religion, but give me a little snug property.
MARIA EDGEWORTH (1767–1849)

We are under a Constitution, but the Constitution is what the judges say it is, and the judiciary is the safeguard of our property and our liberty and our property under the Constitution.
CHARLES EVANS HUGHES (1862–1948)

So long as the great majority of men are not deprived of either property or honor, they are satisfied.
NICCOLÒ MACHIAVELLI (1469–1527)

As a man is said to have a right to his property, he may be equally said to have a property in his rights.
JAMES MADISON (1751–1836)

The earth is the general and equal possession of all humanity and therefore cannot be the property of individuals.
LEO TOLSTOY (1828–1910)

Property is robbery.
LATIN PROVERB

Prophets

Dream manfully and nobly, and thy dreams shall be prophets.
SIR EDWARD G. BULWER-LYTTON (1803–1873)

Men reject their prophets and slay them, but they love their martyrs and honor those whom they have slain.
FYODOR DOSTOEVSKY (1821–1881)

Music is the art of the prophets and the gift of God.
MARTIN LUTHER (1483–1546)

There is no rustic so rude but that, if he dreams or fancies anything, it must be the whisper of the Holy Ghost, and he himself a prophet.
MARTIN LUTHER (1483–1546)

We have decided to follow the example of the prophets and the fathers of the church and write German hymns for the German people.
MARTIN LUTHER (1483–1546)

It is far better that we admitted a thousand devils to roam at large than that we permitted one such impostor and monster as Moses, Joshua, Samuel, and the Bible prophets, to come with the pretended word of God and have credit among us.
THOMAS PAINE (1737–1809)

Think of how many religions attempt to validate themselves with prophecy. Think of how many people rely on these prophecies, however vague, however unfulfilled, to support or prop up their beliefs. Yet has there ever been a religion with the prophetic accuracy and reliability of science?
CARL SAGAN (1934–1996)

Jesters do oft prove prophets.
WILLIAM SHAKESPEARE (1564–1616), *King Lear*

I have done some indiscreet things in my day, but this thing of playing myself for a prophet was the worst. Still, it had its ameliorations. A prophet doesn't have to have any brains. They are good to have, of course, for the ordinary exigencies of life, but they are no use in professional work. It is the restfulest vocation there is. When the spirit of prophecy comes upon you, you merely take your intellect and lay it off somewhere in a cool place for a rest, and unship your jaw and leave it alone; it will work itself. The result is prophecy.
MARK TWAIN (1835–1910), *A Connecticut Yankee in King Arthur's Court*

A prophet is not recognized in his own land.
ANONYMOUS

Prose

He had written much blank verse, and blanker prose.
LORD BYRON (1788–1824)

The simple Wordsworth…
Who, both by precept and example, shows
That prose is verse, and verse is merely prose.
LORD BYRON (1788–1824)

You campaign in poetry. You govern in prose.
MARIO CUOMO (1932–)

Prose books are the show dogs I breed and sell to support my cat.
ROBERT GRAVES (1895–1985)

The writer of prose can only step aside when the poet passes.
W. SOMERSET MAUGHAM (1874–1965)

It is also true that one can write nothing readable unless one constantly struggles to efface one's own personality. Good prose is like a windowpane.
GEORGE ORWELL (1903–1950)

[The] most important tribute any human being can pay to a poem or a piece of prose he or she really loves is to learn it by heart. Not by brain, by heart; the expression is vital.
GEORGE STEINER (1929–)

This is not at all bad, except as prose.
GORE VIDAL (1925–)

There is something about poetry beyond prose logic, there is mystery in it, not to be explained but admired.
EDWARD YOUNG (1683–1765)

Prosperity

It is easy when we are in prosperity to give advice to the afflicted.
AESCHYLUS (C. 525–456 BC)

Prosperity is the blessing of the Old Testament; adversity is the blessing of the New.
SIR FRANCIS BACON (1561–1626)

A helping word to one in trouble is often like a switch on a railroad track … an inch between wreck and smooth, rolling prosperity.
HENRY WARD BEECHER (1813–1887)

If we had no winter, the spring would not be so pleasant: if we did not sometimes taste of adversity, prosperity would not be so welcome.
ANNE BRADSTREET (1612–1672), *Meditations Divine and Moral*

He that can heroically endure adversity will bear prosperity with equal greatness of the soul; for the mind that cannot be dejected by the former is not likely to be transported without the latter.
HENRY FIELDING (1707–1754)

Prosperity is a great teacher; adversity a greater.
WILLIAM HAZLITT (1778–1830)

Adversity reveals genius, prosperity conceals it.
HORACE (65–8 BC)

Adversity makes men, and prosperity makes monsters.
VICTOR HUGO (1802–1885)

Nothing is harder to direct than a man in prosperity; nothing more easily managed than one in adversity.
PLUTARCH (AD 46–120)

Prosperity is no just scale; adversity is the only balance to weigh friends.
PLUTARCH (AD 46–120)

Adversity is sometimes hard upon a man; but for one man who can stand prosperity, there are a hundred that will stand adversity.
ELVIS PRESLEY (1935–1977)

Prosperity makes friends, adversity tries them.
PUBLILIUS SYRUS (C. 100 BC), *Maxims*

The point in history at which we stand is full of promise and danger. The world will either move forward toward unity and widely shared prosperity—or it will move apart.
FRANKLIN D. ROOSEVELT (1882–1945)

The good things which belong to prosperity are to be wished, but the good things that belong to adversity are to be admired.
SENECA (5 BC–AD 65)

Remember that there is nothing stable in human affairs; therefore avoid undue elation in prosperity, or undue depression in adversity.
SOCRATES (469–399 BC)

Prostitution

What it comes down to is this: the grocer, the butcher, the baker, the merchant, the landlord, the druggist, the liquor dealer, the policeman, the doctor, the city father and the politician—these are the people who make money out of prostitution, these are the real reapers of the wages of sin.
POLLY ADLER (1900–1962)

I think it's unfair that men put laws on a woman's body…. I think a woman has a right to choose with her own body. I mean, I don't think prostitution is a career … but maybe a little steppingstone.
HEIDI FLEISS (1965–)

It's sort of like the difference between love and prostitution…. You don't pay people to like you.
PHIL GRAMM (1942–)

Writing is like prostitution. First you do it for love, and then for a few close friends, and then for money.
MOLIÈRE (1622–1673)

The need for prostitution arises from the fact that many men are either unmarried or away from their wives on journeys, that such men are not content to remain continent, and that in a conventionally virtuous community they do not find respectable women.
BERTRAND RUSSELL (1872–1970)

Protestantism

The religion most prevalent in our northern colonies is a refinement on the principles of resistance: it is the dissidence of dissent, and the Protestantism of the Protestant religion.
EDMUND BURKE (1729–1797)

The three great elements of modern civilization: Gunpowder, Printing, and the Protestant Religion.
THOMAS CARLYLE (1795–1881)

Before that we had thought of ourselves in large part as being defined religiously, 98 percent of Americans were Protestant.
SAMUEL P. HUNTINGTON (1821–1900)

When Catholicism goes bad it becomes the religion of amulets and holy places and priestcraft: Protestantism, in its corresponding decay, becomes a vague mist of ethical platitudes.
C. S. LEWIS (1898–1963)

The feeling of a direct responsibility of the individual to God is almost wholly a creation of Protestantism.
JOHN STUART MILL (1806–1873)

Prudence

Affairs are easier of entrance than of exit; and it is but common prudence to see our way out before we venture in.
AESOP (620–560 BC)

If we continue to develop our technology without wisdom or prudence, our servant may prove to be our executioner.
OMAR BRADLEY (1893–1981)

There is nothing more imprudent than excessive prudence.
CHARLES CALEB COLTON (1780–1832)

Often a certain abdication of prudence and foresight is an element of success.
RALPH WALDO EMERSON (1803–1882)

There are goods so opposed that we cannot seize both, but, by too much prudence, may pass between them at too great a distance to reach either.
SAMUEL JOHNSON (1709–1784)

Genius always gives its best at first; prudence, at last.
SENECA (5 BC–AD 65)

It is by the goodness of God that in our country we have those three unspeakably precious things: freedom of speech, freedom of conscience, and the prudence never to practice either.
MARK TWAIN (1835–1910)

Psychiatry

Television has done much for psychiatry by spreading information about it, as well as contributing to the need for it.
ALFRED HITCHCOCK (1899–1980)

I maintained that psychiatry, in the broadest sense, is a dialogue between the sick psyche and the psyche of the doctor, which is presumed to be "normal." It is a coming to terms between the sick personality and that of the therapist, both in principle equally subjective.
CARL JUNG (1875–1961)

It had become clear to me, in a flash of illumination, that for me the only possible goal was psychiatry. Here alone the two currents of my interest could flow together and in a united stream dig their own bed. Here was the empirical field common to biological and spiritual facts, which I had everywhere sought and nowhere found. Here at last was the place where the collision of nature and spirit became a reality.
CARL JUNG (1875–1961)

Psychiatry enables us to correct our faults by confessing our parents' shortcomings.
LAURENCE J. PETER (1919–1990)

Psychology

Psychology is the Science of Mental Life, both of its phenomena and their conditions.
WILLIAM JAMES (1842–1910)

We have lost the art of living, and in the most important science of all, the science of daily life, the science of behavior, we are complete ignoramuses. We have psychology instead.
D. H. LAWRENCE (1885–1930)

Psychology often becomes the disease of which it should be the cure.
BERTRAND RUSSELL (1872–1970)

I maintain that today many an inventor, many a diplomat, many a financier is a sounder philosopher than all those who practice the dull craft of experimental psychology.
OSWALD SPENGLER (1880–1936)

The Public

No greater nor more affectionate honor can be conferred on an American than to have a public school named after him.
HERBERT HOOVER (1874–1964)

I have the consolation of having added nothing to my private fortune during my public service, and of retiring with hands clean as they are empty.
THOMAS JEFFERSON (1762–1826)

Civilization is the progress toward a society of privacy. The savage's whole existence is public, ruled by the laws of his tribe. Civilization is the process of setting man free from men.
AYN RAND (1905–1982)

Public life is regarded as the crown of a career, and to young men it is the worthiest ambition. Politics is still the greatest and the most honorable adventure.
PAT RILEY (1945–)

One should respect public opinion in so far as is necessary to avoid starvation and to keep out of prison, but anything that goes beyond this is voluntary submission to an unnecessary tyranny.
BERTRAND RUSSELL (1872–1970)

People of the same trade seldom meet together, even for merriment and diversion, but the conversation ends in a conspiracy against the public, or in some contrivance to raise prices.
ADAM SMITH (1723–1790)

Publicity

Live by publicity, you'll probably die by publicity.
RUSSELL BAKER (1925–)

Publicity is justly commended as a remedy for social and industrial diseases. Sunlight is said to be the best of disinfectants; electric light the most efficient policeman.
LOUIS D. BRANDEIS (1856–1941)

The government being the people's business, it necessarily follows that its operations should be at all times open to the public view. Publicity is therefore as essential to honest administration as freedom of speech is to representative government. "Equal rights to all and special privileges to none" is the maxim which should control in all departments of government.
WILLIAM JENNINGS BRYAN (1860–1925)

Publicity is like poison; it doesn't hurt unless you swallow it.
JOE PATERNO (1924–)

Publicity, publicity, publicity is the greatest moral factor and force in our public life.
JOSEPH PULITZER (1847–1911)

My activities are not for publicity or propaganda or even to confer joy on others! They are for conferring joy primarily on Me!
SRI SATHYA SAI BABA (1926–)

Any publicity is good publicity.
ANONYMOUS

Punctuality

Punctuality is the stern virtue of men of business, and the graceful courtesy of princess.
SIR EDWARD G. BULWER-LYTTON (1803–1873)

I never could have done what I have done without the habits of punctuality, order, and diligence, without the determination to concentrate myself on one subject at a time.
CHARLES DICKENS (1812–1870)

Punctuality is the soul of business.
THOMAS C. HALIBURTON (1796–1865)

Few things tend more to alienate friendship than a want of punctuality in our engagements. I have known the breach of a promise to dine or sup to break up more than one intimacy.
WILLIAM HAZLITT (1778–1830)

Punctuality is one of the cardinal business virtues: always insist on it in your subordinates.
DON MARQUIS (1878–1937)

Punctuality is the virtue of the bored.
EVELYN WAUGH (1903–1966)

He was always late on principle, his principle being that punctuality is the thief of time.
OSCAR WILDE (1854–1900)

Punishment

God preordained, for his own glory and the display of His attributes of mercy and justice, a part of the human race, without any merit of their own, to eternal salvation, and another part, in just punishment of their sin, to eternal damnation.
JOHN CALVIN (1509–1564)

A man's ethical behavior should be based effectually on sympathy, education, and social ties; no religious basis is necessary. Man would indeed be in a poor way if he had to be restrained by fear of punishment and hope of reward after death.
ALBERT EINSTEIN (1879–1955)

If people are good only because they fear punishment, and hope for reward, then we are a sorry lot indeed.
ALBERT EINSTEIN (1879–1955)

Men are not punished for their sins, but by them.
ELBERT HUBBARD (1856–1915)

Punishment—The justice that the guilty deal out to those that are caught.
ELBERT HUBBARD (1856–1915)

He who does not punish evil commands it to be done.
LEONARDO DA VINCI (1452–1519)

Whatever punishment does to a nation, it does not induce a sense of guilt.
ANNE O'HARE MCCORMICK (1882–1954)

All in all, punishment hardens and renders people more insensible; it concentrates; it increases the feeling of estrangement; it strengthens the power of resistance.
FRIEDRICH NIETZSCHE (1844–1900)

The punishment which the wise suffer, who refuse to take part in government, is to live under the government of worse men.
PLATO (C. 428–348 BC)

Shame is a fitter and generally a more effectual punishment for a child than beating.
SAMUEL RICHARDSON (1689–1761)

Punishment is the last and the least effective instrument in the hands of the legislator for the prevention of crime.
JOHN RUSKIN (1819–1900)

Every guilty person is his own hangman.
SENECA (5 BC–AD 65)

The first and greatest punishment of the sinner is the conscience of sin.
SENECA (5 BC–AD 65)

There is no person so severely punished, as those who subject themselves to the whip of their own remorse.
SENECA (5 BC–AD 65)

And where the offence is, let the great axe fall.
WILLIAM SHAKESPEARE (1564–1616), *Hamlet*

Whipping and abuse are like laudanum: you have to double the dose as the sensibilities decline.
HARRIET BEECHER STOWE (1811–1896)

Men are rewarded or punished not for what they do but for how their acts are defined. That is why men are more interested in better justifying themselves than in better behaving themselves.
THOMAS S. SZASZ (1920–)

Fear follows crime, and is its punishment.
VOLTAIRE (1694–1778)

The punishment of criminals should serve a purpose. When a man is hanged he is useless.
VOLTAIRE (1694–1778)

When the gods wish to punish us, they answer our prayers.
OSCAR WILDE (1854–1900)

Let the punishment fit the crime.
ANONYMOUS

Next to the prosperity of a good person, I am best pleased with the confusion of a rascal.
ANONYMOUS

No punishment of the unrighteous has ever been too severe in the eyes of the righteous.
ANONYMOUS

When God punishes a land, he deprives its leaders of wisdom.
ITALIAN PROVERB

Purity

To insist on purity is to baptize instinct, to humanize art, and to deify personality.
GUILLAUME APOLLINAIRE (1880–1918)

No one is more dangerous than he who imagines himself pure in heart: for his purity, by definition, is unassailable.
JAMES ARTHUR BALDWIN (1924–1987)

When I was five years old I saw an insect that had been eaten by ants and of which nothing remained except the shell. Through the holes in its anatomy one could see the sky. Every time I wish to attain purity I look at the sky through flesh.
SALVADOR DALÍ (1904–1989)

Purity of heart is to will one thing.
SØREN KIERKEGAARD (1813–1855)

Throughout human history, the apostles of purity, those who have claimed to possess a total explanation, have wrought havoc among mere mixed-up human beings.
SALMAN RUSHDIE(1947–)

Purity of the heart is the gateway to God.
SWAMI SIVANANDA (1887–1963)

The purity men love is like the mists which envelope the earth, and not like the azure ether beyond.
HENRY DAVID THOREAU (1817–1862)

Life does not need to mutilate itself in order to be pure.
SIMONE WEIL (1910–1943)

Purpose

Your work is to discover your work and then with all your heart to give yourself to it.
THE BUDDHA (563–483 BC)

What mankind wants is not talent; it is purpose.
EDWARD G. BULWER-LYTTON (1803–1873)

The purpose of man is in action not thought.
THOMAS CARLYLE (1795–1881)

The man without a purpose is like a ship without a rudder—waif, a nothing, a no man. Have a purpose in life, and, having it, throw such strength of mind

and muscle into your work as God has given you.
THOMAS CARLYLE (1795–1881)

Your purpose is to make your audience see what you saw, hear what you heard, feel what you felt. Relevant detail, couched in concrete, colorful language, is the best way to recreate the incident as it happened and to picture it for the audience.
DALE CARNEGIE (1888–1955)

Nothing can resist the human will that will stake even its existence on its stated purpose.
BENJAMIN DISRAELI (1804–1881)

The secret to success is constancy to purpose.
BENJAMIN DISRAELI (1804–1881)

Everything in the universe has a purpose. Indeed, the invisible intelligence that flows through everything in a purposeful fashion is also flowing through you.
WAYNE D. DYER (1940–)

The only failure a man ought to fear is failure in cleaving to the purpose he sees to be best.
GEORGE ELIOT (1819–1880)

What makes life dreary is the want of a motive.
GEORGE ELIOT (1819–1880)

I know of no such unquestionable badge and ensign of a sovereign mind as that of tenacity of purpose…
RALPH WALDO EMERSON (1803–1882)

Men achieve a certain greatness unawares, when working to another aim.
RALPH WALDO EMERSON (1803–1882)

Be the business never so painful, you may have it done for money.
THOMAS FULLER (1608–1661)

A purpose you impart is no longer your own.
JOHANN WOLFGANG VON GOETHE (1749–1832)

Be above it! Make the world serve your purpose, but do not serve it.
JOHANN WOLFGANG VON GOETHE (1749–1832)

Every person above the ordinary has a certain mission that they are called to fulfill.
JOHANN WOLFGANG VON GOETHE (1749–1832)

To the person with a firm purpose all men and things are servants.
JOHANN WOLFGANG VON GOETHE (1749–1832)

What is my life if I am no longer useful to others?
JOHANN WOLFGANG VON GOETHE (1749–1832)

It is good to have an end to journey toward; but it is the journey that matters, in the end
ERNEST HEMINGWAY (1898–1961)

We need not only a purpose in life to give meaning to our existence but also something to give meaning to our suffering. We need as much something to suffer for as something to live for.
ERIC HOFFER (1902–1983)

Nothing contributes so much to tranquilize the mind as a steady purpose—a point on which the soul may fix its intellectual eye.
MARY SHELLEY (1797–1851)

Quality

Quality is the result of a carefully constructed cultural environment. It has to be the fabric of the organization, not part of the fabric.
PHILIP CROSBY (1926–2001), *Reflections on Quality*

People who learn to control inner experience will be able to determine the quality of their lives, which is as close as any of us can come to being happy.
MIHALY CSIKSZENTMIHALYI, (1934–) *Flow: The Psychology of Optimal Experience*

There are two main strategies we can adopt to improve the quality of life. The first is to try making external conditions match our goals. The second is to change how we experience external conditions to make them fit our goals better.
MIHALY CSIKSZENTMIHALYI (1934–), *Flow: The Psychology of Optimal Experience*

Quality in a product or service is not what the supplier puts in. It is what the customer gets out and is willing to pay for. A product is not quality because it is hard to make and costs a lot of money, as manufacturers typically believe. This is incompetence. Customers pay only for what is of use to them and gives them value. Nothing else constitutes quality.
Peter F. Drucker (1909–2005)

The more I give myself permission to live in the moment and enjoy it without feeling guilty or judgmental about any other time, the better I feel about the quality of my work.
Wayne D. Dyer (1940–)

It is the quality of our work which will please God and not the quantity.
Mahatma Gandhi (1869–1948)

The world has to learn that the actual pleasure derived from material things is of rather low quality on the whole and less even in quantity than it looks to those who have not tried it.
Oliver Wendell Holmes Sr. (1809–1894)

The quantity of civilization is measured by the quality of imagination.
Victor Hugo (1802–1885), *Les Miserables*

Quality is more important than quantity. One home run is much better than two doubles.
Steve Jobs (1955–)

The great society is a place where men are more concerned with the quality of their goods than with the quantity of their goods.
Lyndon B. Johnson (1908–1973)

The quality of American life must keep pace with the quantity of American goods. This country cannot afford to be materially rich and spiritually poor.
John F. Kennedy (1917–1963)

Those who speak most of progress measure it by quantity and not by quality.
George Santayana (1863–1952)

It is quality rather than quantity that matters.
Seneca (5 BC–AD 65), *Epistles*

Consistency is the quality of a stagnant mind.
John Sloan (1871–1951)

It is not much for its beauty that makes a claim upon men's hearts, as for that subtle something, that quality of air that emanates from old trees, that so wonderfully changes and renews a weary spirit.
Robert Louis Stevenson (1850–1894)

Time is that quality of nature which keeps events from happening all at once. Lately it doesn't seem to be working.
Anonymous

A country can be judged by the quality of its proverbs.
German Proverb

Quantity

Who, for false quantities, was whipped at school.
John Dryden (1631–1700)

Youth, Age, and Sick require a different Quantity.
Benjamin Franklin (1706–1790)

It is the quality of our work which will please God and not the quantity.
Mahatma Gandhi (1869–1948)

The world has to learn that the actual pleasure derived from material things is of rather low quality on the whole and less even in quantity than it looks to those who have not tried it.
Oliver Wendell Holmes Sr. (1809–1894)

The quantity of civilization is measured by the quality of imagination.
Victor Hugo (1802–1885), *Les Miserables*

Quality is more important than quantity. One home run is much better than two doubles.
Steve Jobs (1955–)

The great society is a place where men are more concerned with the quality of their goods than with the quantity of their goods.
LYNDON B. JOHNSON (1908–1973)

The quality of American life must keep pace with the quantity of American goods. This country cannot afford to be materially rich and spiritually poor.
JOHN F. KENNEDY (1917–1963)

All things will be produced in superior quantity and quality, and with greater ease, when each man works at a single occupation, in accordance with his natural gifts, and at the right moment, without meddling with anything else.
PLATO (C. 428–348 BC)

Talent is a matter of quantity. Talent does not write one page, it writes three hundred.
JULES RENARD (1864–1910)

Those who speak most of progress measure it by quantity and not by quality.
GEORGE SANTAYANA (1863–1952)

It is quality rather than quantity that matters.
SENECA (5 BC–AD 65), *Epistles*

Value denotes a relation reciprocally existing between two objects, and the precise relation which it denotes is the quantity of the one which can be obtained in exchange for a given quantity of the other.
NASSAU WILLIAM SENIOR (1790–1864)

I must have a prodigious quantity of mind; it takes me as much as a week sometimes to make it up.
MARK TWAIN (1835–1910)

Through and through the world is infested with quantity. To talk sense is to talk quantities. It is no use saying the nation is large—how large? It is no use saying that radium is scarce—how scarce? You cannot evade quantity. You may fly to poetry and music, and quantity and number will face you in your rhythms and your octaves.
ALFRED NORTH WHITEHEAD (1861–1947)

Quarrels

Two things, well considered, would prevent many quarrels; first to have it well ascertained whether we are not disputing about terms rather than things; and secondly, to examine whether that on which we differ is worth contending about.
CHARLES CALEB COLTON (1780–1832)

There are three things which the superior man guards against. In youth, lust. When he is strong, quarrelsomeness. When he is old, covetousness.
CONFUCIUS (551–479 BC), *The Confucian Analects*

He that blows the coals in quarrels that he has nothing to do with, has no right to complain if the sparks fly in his face.
BENJAMIN FRANKLIN (1706–1790)

It takes in reality only one to make a quarrel. It is useless for the sheep to pass resolutions in favour of vegetarianism while the wolf remains of a different opinion.
WILLIAM RALPH INGE (1860–1954), *Outspoken Essays*

Quarrels would not last long if the fault were only on one side.
FRANÇOIS DE LA ROCHEFOUCAULD (1613–1680)

In false quarrels there is no true valor.
WILLIAM SHAKESPEARE (1564–1616), *Much Ado About Nothing*

Queens

Women have been called queens for a long time, but the kingdom given them isn't worth ruling.
LOUISA MAY ALCOTT (1832–1888)

The monarchy is so extraordinarily useful. When Britain wins a battle she shouts, "God save the Queen"; when she loses, she votes down the prime minister.
SIR WINSTON CHURCHILL (1874–1965)

I'd like to be a queen in people's hearts but I don't see myself being queen of this country.
PRINCESS DIANA (1961–1997)

Boy George is all England needs—another queen who can't dress.
JOAN RIVERS (1935–)

The Queen is most anxious to enlist everyone in checking this mad, wicked folly of "Women's Rights." It is a subject which makes the Queen so furious that she cannot contain herself.
QUEEN VICTORIA (1819–1901)

There are more queens crowned in one night in Dallas than in 400 years in Westminster Abbey.
MIKE WALLACE (1918–)

Think like a queen. A queen is not afraid to fail. Failure is another steppingstone to greatness.
OPRAH WINFREY (1954–)

Questions

A psychiatrist is a fellow who asks you a lot of expensive questions your wife asks for nothing.
JOEY ADAMS (1968–)

If there are no stupid questions, then what kind of questions do stupid people ask? Do they get smart just in time to ask questions?
SCOTT ADAMS (1957–)

The purpose of art is to lay bare the questions which have been hidden by the answers.
JAMES ARTHUR BALDWIN (1924–1987)

The real questions are the ones that obtrude upon your consciousness whether you like it or not, the ones that make your mind start vibrating like a jackhammer, the ones that you "come to terms with" only to discover that they are still there. The real questions refuse to be placated. They barge into your life at the times when it seems most important for them to stay away. They are the questions asked most frequently and answered most inadequately, the ones that reveal their true natures slowly, reluctantly, most often against your will.
INGRID BENGIS (1944–)

As soon as questions of will or decision or reason or choice of action arise, human science is at a loss.
NOAM CHOMSKY (1928–)

We must not let go manifest truths because we cannot answer all questions about them.
JEREMY COLLIER (1650–1726)

The real object of education is to have a man in the condition of continually asking questions.
BISHOP MANDELL CREIGHTON (1843–1901)

Sometimes the questions are complicated and the answers are simple.
THEODOR SEUSS GEISEL (1904–1991)

When men exercise their reason coolly and freely on a variety of distinct questions, they inevitably fall into different opinions on some of them. When they are governed by a common passion, their opinions, if they are to be called, will be the same.
ALEXANDER HAMILTON (1755–1804)

There was no telling what people might find out once they felt free to ask whatever questions they wanted to.
JOSEPH HELLER (1923–1999), *Catch–22*

The wise man doesn't give the right answers, he poses the right questions.
CLAUDE LEVI-STRAUSS (1908–)

Can a mortal ask questions which God finds unanswerable? Quite easily, I should think. All nonsense questions are unanswerable.
C. S. LEWIS (1898–1963)

Take the attitude of a student, never be too big to ask questions, never know too much to learn something new.
OG MANDINO (1923–1996)

A thinker sees his own actions as experiments and questions—as attempts to find out something. Success and failure are for him answers above all.
FRIEDRICH NIETZSCHE (1844–1900), *The Gay Science*

Live your questions now, and perhaps even without knowing it, you will live along some distant day into your answers.
RAINER MARIA RILKE (1875–1926)

Good questions outrank easy answers.
PAUL A. SAMUELSON (1915–)

So many men, so many questions.
TERENCE (185–159 BC)

It is better to know some of the questions than all of the answers.
JAMES THURBER (1894–1961)

Historians are like deaf people who go on answering questions that no one has asked them.
LEO TOLSTOY (1828–1910)

The outcome of any serious research can only be to make two questions grow where only one grew before.
THORSTEIN VEBLEN (1857–1929)

Judge a man by his questions rather than by his answers.
VOLTAIRE (1694–1778)

Every scientific fulfillment raises new questions; it asks to be surpassed and outdated.
MAX WEBER (1864–1920)

An expert knows all the answers—if you ask the right questions.
ANONYMOUS

Truth fears no questions.
ANONYMOUS

Ask questions from your heart and you will be answered from the heart.
NATIVE AMERICAN PROVERB

Quiet

A quiet mind cureth all.
ROBERT BURTON (1577–1640)

I lived in solitude in the country and noticed how the monotony of a quiet life stimulates the creative mind.
ALBERT EINSTEIN (1879–1955)

The good and the wise lead quiet lives.
EURIPIDES (480-406 BC)

You do not need to leave your room. Remain sitting at your table and listen. Do not even listen, simply wait, be quiet, still and solitary. The world will freely offer itself to you to be unmasked, it has no choice, it will roll in ecstasy at your feet.
FRANZ KAFKA (1883–1924)

Arranging a bowl of flowers in the morning can give a sense of quiet in a crowded day—like writing a poem, or saying a prayer.
ANNE MORROW LINDBERGH (1906–2001)

Only in quiet waters do things mirror themselves undistorted. Only in a quiet mind is adequate perception of the world.
HANS MARGOLIUS (1902–1984)

Are you going to come quietly, or do I have to use earplugs?
SPIKE MILLIGAN (1918–2002)

Religion is excellent stuff for keeping common people quiet.
NAPOLÉON I (1769–1821)

A happy life must be to a great extent a quiet life, for it is only in an atmosphere of quiet that true joy dare live.
BERTRAND RUSSELL (1872–1970)

I know myself now; and I feel within me
A peace above all earthly dignities,
A still and quiet conscience.
WILLIAM SHAKESPEARE (1564–1616), *Henry VIII*

You'll never have a quiet world till you knock the patriotism out of the human race.
GEORGE BERNARD SHAW (1856–1950), *Misalliance*

In quiet places, reason abounds.
ADLAI E. STEVENSON II (1900–1965)

Mistake not. Those pleasures are not pleasures that trouble the quiet and tranquillity of thy life.
JEREMY TAYLOR (1613–1667)

We need quiet time to examine our lives openly and honestly…spending quiet time alone gives your mind an opportunity to renew itself and create order.
SUSAN TAYLOR (1827–1860)

Quiet people are well able to look after themselves.
IRISH PROVERB

Quotations

A quotation in a speech, article, or book is like a rifle in the hands of an infantryman. It speaks with authority.
BRENDAN FRANCIS BEHAN (1923–1964)

I pick my favourite quotations and store them in my mind as ready armour, offensive or defensive, amid the struggle of this turbulent existence.
ROBERT BURNS (1759–1796)

It is a good thing for an uneducated man to read books of quotations.
SIR WINSTON CHURCHILL (1874–1965), *My Early Life*

The point of quotations is that one can use another's words to be insulting.
AMANDA CROSS (1926–)

I love quotations because it is a joy to find thoughts one might have, beautifully expressed with much authority by someone recognized wiser than oneself.
MARLENE DIETRICH (1901–1992)

Next to the originator of a good sentence is the first quoter of it. I hate quotations. Tell me what you know.
RALPH WALDO EMERSON (1803–1882)

The wisdom of the wise and the experience of the ages is preserved into perpetuity by a nation's proverbs, fables, folk sayings and quotations.
WILLIAM FEATHER (1908–1976)

A writer expresses himself in words that have been used before because they give his meaning better than he can give it himself, or because they are beautiful or witty, or because he expects them to touch a cord of association in his reader, or because he wishes to show that he is learned and well read. Quotations due to the last motive are invariably ill-advised; the discerning reader detects it and is contemptuous; the undiscerning is perhaps impressed, but even then is at the same time repelled, pretentious quotations being the surest road to tedium.
HENRY W. FOWLER (1858–1933), *A Dictionary of Modern English Usage*

Quotations (such as have point and lack triteness) from the great old authors are an act of reverence on the part of the quoter, and a blessing to a public grown superficial and external.
LOUISE GUINEY (1861–1920)

He wrapped himself in quotations—as a beggar would enfold himself in the purple of Emperors.
RUDYARD KIPLING (1865–1936)

Be careful—with quotations, you can damn anything.
ANDRÉ MALRAUX (1901–1976)

To be amused by what you read—that is the great spring of happy quotations.
C. E. MONTAGUE (1867–1928), *A Writer's Notes on His Trade*

Wise men make proverbs, but fools repeat them.
SAMUEL PALMER (1805–1880)

I might repeat to myself slowly and soothingly, a list of quotations beautiful from minds profound—if I can remember any of the damn things.
DOROTHY PARKER (1893–1967)

Misquotations are the only quotations that are never misquoted.
HESKETH PEARSON (1887–1964)

I often quote myself. It adds spice to my conversation.
GEORGE BERNARD SHAW (1856–1950)

It is better to be quotable than to be honest.
TOM STOPPARD (1937–)

Now we sit through Shakespeare in order to recognize the quotations.
ORSON WELLES (1915–1985)

At twilight, nature is not without loveliness, though perhaps its chief use is to illustrate quotations from the poets.
OSCAR WILDE (1854–1900)

Quotation is a serviceable substitute for wit.
OSCAR WILDE (1854–1900)

Racism

Racism tears down your insides so that no matter what you achieve, you're not quite up to snuff.
ALVIN AILEY (1931–1989)

Racism is a refuge for the ignorant. It seeks to divide and to destroy. It is the enemy of freedom, and deserves to be met head-on and stamped out.
PIERRE BERTON (1920–)

Most African Americans, especially the men and women from my generation, would accept the nationalist gambit that says only European Americans can be racists, which is an interesting gambit.
ANTHONY BRAXTON (1945–)

The modern definition of "racist" is someone who is winning an argument with a liberal.
PETER BRIMELOW (1947–)

Racism is always there underneath, but usually it is exploited in these times of economic crisis, and it's hard to find out when one slides into another.
IRIS CHANG (1968–2004)

Racism is really skinism. Dark skin is an adaptation to the natural environment. It has nothing to do with being God's chosen people.
JANE ELLIOT (1947–)

Racism, pollution and the rest of it are themselves very close to extinction.
R. BUCKMINSTER FULLER (1895–1983)

Racism may be as systemic as it always was. It is the great problem of America. It's the one stumbling block that I don't believe was ever smoothed over.
ROBERT GUILLAUME (1927–)

Racism is taught in our society, it is not automatic. It is learned behavior toward persons with dissimilar physical characteristics.
ALEX HALEY (1921–2002)

I think that people have to be able to see two sides of the coin to survive, because it is a racist society and yet you're being raised by racists.
BETH HENLEY (1952–)

Racism is man's gravest threat to man—the maximum of hatred for a minimum of reason.
ABRAHAM J. HESCHEL (1907–1972)

Racism is a scholarly pursuit. It's all over the world, I am convinced.
TONI MORRISON (1931–)

I do the very best I can to look upon life with optimism and hope and looking forward to a better day, but I don't think there is anything such as complete happiness. It pains me that there is still a lot of Klan activity and racism. I think when you say you're happy, you have everything that you need and everything that you want, and nothing more to wish for. I haven't reached that stage yet.
ROSA PARKS (1913–2005)

Racism is still with us. But it is up to us to prepare our children for what they have to meet, and, hopefully, we shall overcome.
ROSA PARKS (1913–2005)

Unfortunately, the people of Louisiana are not racists.
DAN QUAYLE (1947–)

I couldn't join a party that, frankly, tolerates members who are bigots for one thing, homophobes, racists.
RON REAGAN (1958–)

Racists are irrational and illogical in their attempts to justify their prejudices.
SARGENT SHRIVER (1915–)

The roots of racism lie deep in man's nature, wounded and bruised by original sin.
SARGENT SHRIVER (1915–)

No human race is superior; no religious faith is inferior. All collective judgments are wrong. Only racists make them.
ELIE WIESEL (1928–)

Radio

Radio is a bag of mediocrity where little men with carbon minds wallow in sluice of their own making.
FRED ALLEN (1894–1956)

If it weren't for Philo T. Farnsworth, inventor of television, we'd still be eating frozen radio dinners.
JOHNNY CARSON (1925–2005)

My father hated radio and could not wait for television to be invented so he could hate that too.
PETER DE VRIES (1910–1993)

You see, wire telegraph is a kind of a very, very long cat. You pull his tail in New York and his head is meowing in Los Angeles. Do you understand this? And radio operates exactly the same way: you send signals here, they receive them there. The only difference is that there is no cat.
ALBERT EINSTEIN (1879–1955)

Rain

I think fish is nice, but then I think that rain is wet, so who am I to judge?
DOUGLAS ADAMS (1952–2001)

If the rain spoils our picnic, but saves a farmer's crop, who are we to say it shouldn't rain?
TOM BARRETT (1953–)

Many a man curses the rain that falls upon his head, and knows not that it brings abundance to drive away the hunger.
SAINT BASIL (329–379)

Rain! whose soft architectural hands have power to cut stones, and chisel to shapes of grandeur the very mountains.
HENRY WARD BEECHER (1813–1887)

The rain it raineth on the just
And also on the unjust fella,
But chiefly on the just, because
The unjust steals the just's umbrella.
CHARLES BOWEN (1835–1894)

The drops of rain make a hole in the stone, not by violence, but by oft falling.
LUCRETIUS (C. 99–55 BC)

Rain is grace; rain is the sky condescending to the earth; without rain, there would be no life.
JOHN UPDIKE (1932–)

You pray for rain, you gotta deal with the mud too. That's a part of it.
DENZEL WASHINGTON (1954–)

Rainbows

Let no one who loves be unhappy; even love unreturned has its rainbow.
JAMES M. BARRIE (1860–1937)

It was the rainbow gave thee birth, and left thee all her lovely hues.
W. H. DAVIES (1871–1940)

I loved Mississippi and do to this day. The rainbows that stretch from horizon to horizon after a summer rain are the most spectacular I have ever seen.
CHARLEY PRIDE (1938–)

Rape

Abolition of a woman's right to abortion, when and if she wants it, amounts to compulsory maternity: a form of rape by the State.
EDWARD ABBEY (1927–1989)

People out there must be told about the self-loathing that follows rape and how it's the greatest breakage in divine law to mutilate themselves, as I have done.
TORI AMOS (1963–)

As long as there is rape … there is not going to be any peace or justice or equality or freedom. You are not going to become what you want to become or who you want to become. You are not going to live in the world you want to live in.
ANDREA DWORKIN (1946–2005)

Seduction is often difficult to distinguish from rape. In seduction, the rapist often bothers to buy a bottle of wine.
ANDREA DWORKIN (1946–2005)

I think when a person has been found guilty of rape he should be castrated. That would stop him pretty quick.
BILLY GRAHAM (1918–)

The principle of procrastinated rape is said to be the ruling one in all the great best-sellers.
VICTOR SAWDON PRITCHETT (1900–1997)

Rape is highly reprehensible, both in a moral sense and in its almost total contempt for the personal integrity and autonomy of the female victim and for the latter's privilege of choosing those with whom intimate relations are to be established.
BYRON R. WHITE (1917–2002)

Rationalism

I prefer rationalism to atheism. The question of God and other objects-of-faith are outside reason and play no part in rationalism, thus you don't have to waste your time in either attacking or defending.
ISAAC ASIMOV (1920–1992)

Rationalists are admirable beings, rationalism is a hideous monster when it claims for itself omnipotence. Attribution of omnipotence to reason is as bad a piece of idolatry as is worship of stock and stone believing it to be God. I plead not for the suppression of reason, but for a due recognition of that in us which sanctifies reason.
MAHATMA GANDHI (1869–1948)

If people would forget about utopia! When rationalism destroyed heaven and decided to set it up here on earth, that most terrible of all goals entered human ambition. It was clear there'd be no end to what people would be made to suffer for it.
NADINE GORDIMER (1923–)

While rationalism at the individual level is a plea for more personal autonomy from cultural norms, at the social level it is often a claim—or arrogation—of power to stifle the autonomy of others.
THOMAS SOWELL (1930–)

Reading

Learn as much by writing as by reading.
LORD ACTON (1834–1902)

I took a speed reading course and read *War and Peace* in twenty minutes. It involves Russia.
WOODY ALLEN (1935–)

Reading maketh a full man, conference a ready man, and writing an exact man.
SIR FRANCIS BACON (1561–1626)

Reading well is one of the great pleasures that solitude can afford you.
HAROLD BLOOM (1930–)

I'm sure we would not have had men on the Moon if it had not been for Wells and Verne and the people who write about this and made people think about it. I'm rather proud of the fact that I know several astronauts who became astronauts through reading my books.
ARTHUR C. CLARKE (1917–)

The reading of all good books is indeed like a conversation with the noblest men of past centuries who were the authors of them, nay a carefully studied conversation, in which they reveal to us none but the best of their thoughts.
RENÉ DESCARTES (1596–1650)

Reading, after a certain age, diverts the mind too much from its creative pursuits. Any man who reads too much and uses his own brain too little falls into lazy habits of thinking.
ALBERT EINSTEIN (1879–1955)

If the riches of the Indies, or the crowns of all the kingdom of Europe, were laid at my feet in exchange for my love of reading, I would spurn them all.
FRANÇOIS DE FÉNELON (1651–1715)

If you would not be forgotten
As soon as you are rotten,
Either write things worth reading
Or do things worth the writing.
BENJAMIN FRANKLIN (1706–1790)

Reading makes a full man, meditation a profound man, discourse a clear man.
BENJAMIN FRANKLIN (1706–1790)

Trying to determine what is going on in the world by reading newspapers is like trying to tell the time by watching the second hand of a clock.
BEN HECHT (1893–1964)

Reading is sometimes an ingenious device for avoiding thought.
SIR ARTHUR HELPS (1813–1875)

A book burrows into your life in a very profound way because the experience of reading is not passive.
ERICA JONG (1942–)

Resolve to edge in a little reading every day, if it is but a single sentence. If you gain fifteen minutes a day, it will make itself felt at the end of the year.
HORACE MANN (1796–1859)

The pleasure of all reading is doubled when one lives with another who shares the same books.
KATHERINE MANSFIELD (1888–1923)

Readers are plentiful; thinkers are rare.
HARRIET MARTINEAU (1802–1876)

From the moment I picked up your book until I laid it down, I was convulsed with laughter. Some day I intend reading it.
GROUCHO MARX (1890–1977)

No entertainment is so cheap as reading, nor any pleasure so lasting. She will not want new fashions nor regret the loss of expensive diversions or variety of company if she can be amused with an author in her closet.
LADY MARY WORTLEY MONTAGU (1689–1762)

The books that help you most are those which make you think the most. The hardest way of learning is that of easy reading; but a great book that comes from a great thinker is a ship of thought, deep freighted with truth and beauty.
THEODORE PARKER (1810–1860)

Much reading is an oppression of the mind, and extinguishes the natural candle, which is the reason of so many senseless scholars in the world.
WILLIAM PENN (1644–1718)

Properly, we should read for power. Man reading should be man intensely alive. The book should be a ball of light in one's hand.
EZRA POUND (1885–1972)

We've always been here and we'll always be here. We are a specific arrangement of particles and this instant is infinite. Did we luck out, or didn't we? The odds against this sentence having ever being typed, much less the odds against you reading it were inconceivable. Smile, because the fact that you're able to is almost impossible to comprehend.
JEFFREY ROWLAND (1974–)

There are two motives for reading a book: one, that you enjoy it; the other, that you can boast about it.
BERTRAND RUSSELL (1872–1970)

I've never known any trouble that an hour's reading didn't assuage.
CHARLES DE SECONDAT (1689–1755)

Desultory reading is delightful, but to be beneficial, our reading must be carefully directed.
SENECA (5 BC–AD 65)

Reading made Don Quixote a gentleman. Believing what he read made him mad.
GEORGE BERNARD SHAW (1856–1950)

My personal hobbies are reading, listening to music, and silence.
EDITH SITWELL (1887–1964)

People say that life is the thing, but I prefer reading.
LOGAN PEARSALL SMITH (1865–1946), *Afterthoughts*

Reading is to the mind what exercise is to the body.
SIR RICHARD STEELE (1672–1729)

How many a man has dated a new era in his life from the reading of a book.
HENRY DAVID THOREAU (1817–1862), *Walden*

Education … has produced a vast population able to read but unable to distinguish what is worth reading.
G. M. TREVELYAN (1876–1962), *English Social History*

Be careful about reading health books. You may die of a misprint.
MARK TWAIN (1835–1910)

Let us read and let us dance—two amusements that will never do any harm to the world.
VOLTAIRE (1694–1778)

There are two ways of spreading light: to be the candle or the mirror that reflects it.
EDITH WHARTON (1862–1937), *Vesalius in Zante*

When I read about the evils of drinking, I gave up reading.
HENNY YOUNGMAN (1906–1998)

Drink nothing without seeing it; sign nothing without reading it.
SPANISH PROVERB

Real Estate

A strong economy causes an increase in the demand for housing; the increased demand for housing drives real-estate prices and rentals through the roof. And then affordable housing becomes completely inaccessible.
WILLIAM BALDWIN (1963–)

What we call real estate—the solid ground to build a house on—is the broad foundation on which nearly all the guilt of this world rests.
NATHANIEL HAWTHORNE (1804–1864), *The House of Seven Gables*

Babbitt spoke well—and often—at these orgies of commercial righteousness about the "realtor's function as a seer of the future development of the community, and as a prophetic engineer clearing the pathway for inevitable changes"—which meant that a real estate broker could make money by guessing which way the town would grow. This guessing he called Vision.
SINCLAIR LEWIS (1885–1951), *Babbitt*

Patriotism is often an arbitrary veneration of real estate above principles.
GEORGE JEAN NATHAN (1882–1958)

It is a comfortable feeling to know that you stand on your own ground. Land is about the only thing that can't fly away.
ANTHONY TROLLOPE (1815–1882), *The Last Chronicle of Barset*

No real estate is permanently valuable but the grave.
MARK TWAIN (1835–1910)

Realism

Realism … has no more to do with reality than anything else.
HOB BROUN (1950–1987)

True realism consists in revealing the surprising things which habit keeps covered and prevents us from seeing.
JEAN COCTEAU (1889–1963)

Realism is a bad word. In a sense everything is realistic. I see no line between the imaginary and the real.
FEDERICO FELLINI (1920–1993)

Realism is not a matter of any fidelity to an empirical reality, but of the discursive conventions by which and for which a sense of reality is constructed.
JOHN FISKE (1842–1901)

Realism is always subjective in film. There's no such thing as cinema verité.
CRISPIN GLOVER (1964–)

I believed in realism, as summarized by John McCarthy's comment to the effect that if we worked really hard, we'd have an intelligent system in from four to four hundred years.
MARVIN MINSKY (1927–)

I only understand realism.
MANUEL PUIG (1932–1990)

We need realism to deal with reality.
RICHARD "SLICK RICK" WALTERS (1965–)

Reality

The adjustment of reality to the masses and of the masses to reality is a process of unlimited scope, as much for thinking as for perception.
WALTER BENJAMIN (1892–1940)

Men decide far more problems by hate, love, lust, rage, sorrow, joy, hope, fear, illusion, or some other inward emotion, than by reality, authority, any legal standard, judicial precedent, or statute.
CICERO (106–43 BC)

Reality has become a commodity.
STEPHEN COLBERT (1964–)

We know that polls are just a collection of statistics that reflect what people are thinking in "reality." And reality has a well-known liberal bias.
STEPHEN COLBERT (1964–)

Everything is a dangerous drug except reality, which is unendurable.
CYRIL CONNOLLY (1903–1974), *The Unquiet Grave*

Reality is that which, when you stop believing in it, doesn't go away.
PHILIP K. DICK (1928–1982), *Do Androids Dream of Electric Sheep?*

Sometimes the appropriate response to reality is to go insane.
PHILIP K. DICK (1928–1982), *Valis*

How hard it is, sometimes, to trust the evidence of one's senses! How reluctantly the mind consents to reality.
NORMAN DOUGLAS (1868–1952)

The real hero is always a hero by mistake; he dreams of being an honest coward like everybody else.
UMBERTO ECO (1932–), *Travels in Hyperreality*

As far as the laws of mathematics refer to reality, they are not certain; and as far as they are certain, they do not refer to reality.
ALBERT EINSTEIN (1879–1955), *Geometry and Experience*

Reality is merely an illusion, albeit a very persistent one.
ALBERT EINSTEIN (1879–1955)

Humankind cannot stand very much reality.
T. S. ELIOT (1888–1965)

There are some people who live in a dream world, and there are some who face reality; and then there are those who turn one into the other.
DOUGLAS EVERETT (1927–)

For a successful technology, reality must take precedence over public relations, for Nature cannot be fooled.
RICHARD FEYNMAN (1918–1988)

Imagination is the one weapon in the war against reality.
THÉOPHILE GAUTIER (1811–1872)

It is difficult to say what is impossible, for the dream of yesterday is the hope of today and the reality of tomorrow.
ROBERT H. GODDARD (1882–1945)

Maybe entertainment is not supposed to be reality.
VICTORIA JACKSON (1959–)

I believe in looking reality straight in the eye and denying it.
GARRISON KEILLOR (1942–)

The real distinction is between those who adapt their purposes to reality and those who seek to mold reality in the light of their purposes.
HENRY KISSINGER (1923–)

A dream will always triumph over reality, once it is given the chance.
STANISLAW LEM (1921–2006)

When men are brought face to face with their opponents, forced to listen and learn and mend their ideas, they cease to be children and savages and begin to live like civilized men. Then only is freedom a reality, when men may voice their opinions because they must examine their opinions.
WALTER LIPPMANN (1889–1974)

You're not to be so blind with patriotism that you can't face reality. Wrong is wrong, no matter who does it or says it.
MALCOLM X (1925–1965)

Set up as an ideal the facing of reality as honestly and as cheerfully as possible.
DR. KARL A. MENNINGER (1893–1990)

Reality is something you rise above.
LIZA MINNELLI (1946–)

Let's just say I was testing the bounds of reality. I was curious to see what would happen. That's all it was: curiosity.
JIM MORRISON (1943–1971)

Consider that which exists to exist and that which does not exist to not exist, and recognize things just as they are. With such a frame of mind, one will have divine protection even though he does not pray.
HÔJÔ NAGAUJI (1432–1519)

There is only one admirable form of the imagination: the imagination that is so intense that it creates a new reality, that it makes things happen.
SEAN O'FAOLAIN (1900–1991)

There is no abstract art. You must always start with something. Afterward you can remove all traces of reality.
PABLO PICASSO (1881–1973)

Without art, the crudeness of reality would make the world unbearable.
GEORGE BERNARD SHAW (1856–1950)

The shortest and surest way to live with honour in the world, is to be in reality what we would appear to be; and if we observe, we shall find, that all human virtues increase and strengthen themselves by the practice of them.
SOCRATES (469–399 BC)

The camera makes everyone a tourist in other people's reality, and eventually in one's own.
SUSAN SONTAG (1933–2004)

When we are unhurried and wise, we perceive that only great and worthy things have any permanent and absolute existence, that petty fears and petty pleasures are but the shadow of the reality.
HENRY DAVID THOREAU (1817–1862), *Walden*

Reality is a crutch for people who can't cope with drugs.
LILY TOMLIN (1939–)

Reality continues to ruin my life.
BILL WATTERSON (1958–)

Realization

With realization of one's own potential and self-confidence in one's ability, one can build a better world.
THE DALAI LAMA (1935–)

[A] moment of realization is worth a thousand prayers.
OLIVER STONE (1946–) and QUENTIN TARANTINO (1963–), *Natural Born Killers*

At that moment of realization I knew that I had been blind because I had wished not to see; it was only then that I realized, at last, that all these dead men, French and Germans, were brothers, and I was the brother of them all.
ERNST TOLLER (1893–1939)

The realization of ignorance is the first act of knowing.
JEAN TOOMER (1894–1967)

Reason

Reason itself is fallible, and this fallibility must find a place in our logic.
NICOLA ABBAGNANO (1901–1990)

Why does man kill? He kills for food. And not only food: frequently there must be a beverage.
WOODY ALLEN (1935–)

O reason, reason, abstract phantom of the waking state, I had already expelled you from my dreams, now I have reached a point where those dreams are about to become fused with apparent realities: now there is only room here for myself.
LOUIS ARAGON (1897–1982)

There are strange flowers of reason to match each error of the senses.
LOUIS ARAGON (1897–1982)

Everything that is beautiful and noble is the product of reason and calculation.
CHARLES BAUDELAIRE (1821–1867)

If scientific reasoning were limited to the logical processes of arithmetic, we should not get very far in our understanding of the physical world. One might as well attempt to grasp the game of poker entirely by the use of the mathematics of probability.
VANNEVAR BUSH (1890–1974)

If you follow reason far enough it always leads to conclusions that are contrary to reason.
SAMUEL BUTLER (1835–1902)

A person usually has two reasons for doing something: a good reason and the real reason.
THOMAS CARLYLE (1795–1881)

The more you reason the less you create.
RAYMOND CHANDLER (1888–1959)

He only employs his passion who can make no use of his reason.
CICERO (106–43 BC)

Let your desires be ruled by reason.
CICERO (106–43 BC)

The wise are instructed by reason; ordinary minds by experience; the stupid, by necessity; and brutes by instinct.
CICERO (106–43 BC)

The very essence of instinct is that it's followed independently of reason.
CHARLES DARWIN (1809–1882)

He who will not reason is a bigot; he who cannot is a fool; and he who dares not is a slave.
SIR WILLIAM DRUMMOND (1585–1649)

The intuitive mind is a sacred gift and the rational mind is a faithful servant. We have created a society that honors the servant and has forgotten the gift.
ALBERT EINSTEIN (1879–1955)

Fragile as reason is and limited as law is as the institutionalized medium of reason, that's all we have between us and the tyranny of mere will and the cruelty of unbridled, undisciplined feelings.
FELIX FRANKFURTER (1882–1965)

I do not feel obliged to believe that the same God who has endowed us with sense, reason, and intellect has intended us to forgo their use.
GALILEO GALILEI (1564–1642)

In a republican nation, whose citizens are to be led by reason and persuasion and not by force, the art of reasoning becomes of first importance.
THOMAS JEFFERSON (1762–1826)

First there is a time when we believe everything, then for a little while we believe with discrimination, then we believe nothing whatever, and then we believe everything again—and, moreover, give reasons why we believe.
GEORG C. LICHTENBERG (1742–1799)

The sign of an intelligent people is their ability to control emotions by the application of reason.
MARYA MANNES (1904–1990)

Reason has always existed, but not always in a reasonable form.
KARL MARX (1818–1883)

It's asking a great deal that things should appeal to your reason as well as your sense of the aesthetic.
W. SOMERSET MAUGHAM (1874–1965), *Of Human Bondage*

I prefer the company of peasants because they have not been educated sufficiently to reason incorrectly.
MICHEL DE MONTAIGNE (1533–1592)

There is always some madness in love. But there is also always some reason in madness.
FRIEDRICH NIETZSCHE (1844–1900), *On Reading and Writing*

Reason clears and plants the wilderness of the imagination to harvest the wheat of art.
AUSTIN O'MALLEY (1858–1932)

He that rebels against reason is a real rebel, but he that in defence of reason rebels against tyranny has a better title to Defender of the Faith, than George the Third.
THOMAS PAINE (1737–1809)

We are generally the better persuaded by the reasons we discover ourselves than by those given to us by others.
BLAISE PASCAL (1623–1662)

There is an evil tendency underlying all our technology—the tendency to do what is reasonable even when it isn't any good.
ROBERT M. PIRSIG (1928–), *Zen and the Art of Motorcycle Maintenance*

The reasonable man adapts himself to the world; the unreasonable one persists in trying to adapt the world to himself. Therefore all progress depends on the unreasonable man.
GEORGE BERNARD SHAW (1856–1950), *Man and Superman*

Never try to reason the prejudice out of a man. It was not reasoned into him, and cannot be reasoned out.
SYDNEY SMITH (1771–1845)

A man has free choice to the extent that he is rational.
SAINT THOMAS AQUINAS (1225–1274)

Most men seem to live according to sense rather than reason.
SAINT THOMAS AQUINAS (1225–1274)

Reason is the test of ridicule, not ridicule the test of truth.
WILLIAM WARBURTON (1698–1779)

An epigram often flashes light into regions where reason shines but dimly.
EDWIN P. WHIPPLE (1819–1886)

One is tempted to define man as a rational animal who always loses his temper when he is called upon to act in accordance with the dictates of reason.
OSCAR WILDE (1854–1900), *The Critic as Artist*

Imagination is the pontoon bridge making way for the timid feet of reason.
ANONYMOUS

Rebellion

Kings will be tyrants from policy, when subjects are rebels from principle.
EDMUND BURKE (1729–1797)

Every act of rebellion expresses a nostalgia for innocence and an appeal to the essence of being.
ALBERT CAMUS (1913–1960)

The only way to deal with an unfree world is to become so absolutely free that your very existence is an act of rebellion.
ALBERT CAMUS (1913–1960)

What is a rebel? A man who says no.
ALBERT CAMUS (1913–1960)

Real rebels are rarely anything but second rate outside their rebellion; the drain of time and temper is ruinous to any other accomplishment.
JAMES GOULD COZZENS (1903–1978)

Rebellion is the only thing that keeps you alive!
MARIANNE FAITHFULL (1946–)

Rebellion against tyrants is obedience to God.
BENJAMIN FRANKLIN (1706–1790) and THOMAS JEFFERSON (1743–1826)

Rebellion without truth is like spring in a bleak, arid desert.
KAHLIL GIBRAN (1883–1931)

The Earth needs rebels!
DAVID ICKE (1952–)

He that rebels against reason is a real rebel, but he that in defence of reason rebels against tyranny has a better title to Defender of the Faith, than George the Third.
THOMAS PAINE (1737–1809)

When you think of the long and gloomy history of man, you will find more hideous crimes have been committed in the name of obedience than have ever been committed in the name of rebellion.
C. P. SNOW (1905–1980)

Repression will provoke rebellion.
HUGH WILLIAMSON (1735–1819)

Reconciliation

Reconciliation should be accompanied by justice, otherwise it will not last. While we all hope for peace it shouldn't be peace at any cost but peace based on principle, on justice.
CORAZON AQUINO (1933–)

One of the most basic principles for making and keeping peace within and between nations … is that in political, military, moral, and spiritual confrontations, there should be an honest attempt at the reconciliation of differences before resorting to combat.
JIMMY CARTER (1924–)

Reconciliation requires changes of heart and spirit, as well as social and economic change. It requires symbolic as well as practical action.
MALCOLM FRASER (1930–)

Reconciliation is everyone recognising and treating each other as equals, and everyone must be responsible for their own actions.
PAULINE HANSON (1954–)

Moments of kindness and reconciliation are worth having, even if the parting has to come sooner or later.
ALICE MUNRO (1931–)

Recovery

Courage consists in the power of self-recovery.
RALPH WALDO EMERSON (1803–1882)

The hardest thing you can do is smile when you are ill, in pain, or depressed. But this no-cost remedy is a necessary first half-step if you are to start on the road to recovery.
ALLEN KLEIN (1931–)

I believe in recovery, and I believe that as a role model I have the responsibility to let young people know that you can make a mistake and come back from it.
ANN RICHARDS (1933–2006)

Genius is the recovery of childhood at will.
ARTHUR RIMBAUD (1854–1891)

Understanding is the first step to acceptance, and only with acceptance can there be recovery.
J. K. ROWLING (1965–)

The goal of spiritual practice is full recovery, and the only thing you need to recover from is a fractured sense of self.
MARIANNE WILLIAMSON (1952–)

Redemption

The Spirit is Love expressed towards man as redeeming love, and the Spirit is truth, and the Spirit is the Holy Spirit. Redemption is inconceivable without truth and holiness.
ROLAND ALLEN (1868–1947)

I don't feel any need for redemption. I'm satisfied with what I did in the Senate. I don't look back. I look forward.
ALAN CRANSTON (1914–2000)

There is no redemption from hell.
POPE PAUL III (1468–1549)

Most action is based on redemption and revenge, and that's a formula. *Moby Dick* was formula. It's how you get to the conclusion that makes it interesting.
SYLVESTER STALLONE (1946–)

I believe in the forgiveness of sin and the redemption of ignorance.
ADLAI E. STEVENSON II (1900–1965)

Hell is yourself and the only redemption is when a person puts himself aside to feel deeply for another person.
TENNESSEE WILLIAMS (1911–1983)

Reflection

By three methods we may learn wisdom: First, by reflection, which is noblest; Second, by imitation, which is easiest; and Third by experience, which is the bitterest.
CONFUCIUS (551–479 BC)

There is an art of which every man should be a master—the art of reflection. If you are not a thinking man, to what purpose are you a man at all?
WILLIAM HART COLERIDGE (1789–1842)

Our observation of nature must be diligent, our reflection profound, and our experiments exact. We rarely see these three means combined; and for this reason, creative geniuses are not common.
DENIS DIDEROT (1713–1784)

There are three principal means of acquiring knowledge…observation of nature, reflection, and experimentation. Observation collects facts; reflection combines them; experimentation verifies the result of that combination.
DENIS DIDEROT (1713–1784)

It is a most mortifying reflection for a man to consider what he has done, compared to what he might have done.
SAMUEL JOHNSON (1709–1784), *Boswell's Life*

The real man smiles in trouble, gathers strength from distress, and grows brave by reflection.
THOMAS PAINE (1737–1809)

We learn our virtues from our friends who love us; our faults from the enemy who hates us. We cannot easily discover our real character from a friend. He is a mirror, on which the warmth of our breath impedes the clearness of the reflection.
JEAN PAUL RICHTER (1763–1825)

And since you know you cannot see yourself,
so well as by reflection, I, your glass,
will modestly discover to yourself,
that of yourself which you yet know not of.
WILLIAM SHAKESPEARE (1564–1616), *The Tragedy of Julius Caeser*

Reform

We were married by a reformed rabbi in Long Island. A very reformed rabbi. A Nazi.
WOODY ALLEN (1935–)

Repentance may begin instantly, but reformation often requires a sphere of years.
HENRY WARD BEECHER (1813–1887)

To reform a world, to reform a nation, no wise man will undertake; and all but foolish men know, that the only solid, though a far slower reformation, is what each begins and perfects on himself.
THOMAS CARLYLE (1795–1881)

At twenty a man is full of fight and hope. He wants to reform the world. When he is seventy he still wants to reform the world, but he knows he can't.
CLARENCE DARROW (1857–1938)

The key to every man is his thought. Sturdy and defying though he look, he has a helm which he obeys, which is the idea after which all his facts are classified. He can only be reformed by showing him a new idea which commands his own.
RALPH WALDO EMERSON (1803–1882)

The outward freedom that we shall attain will only be in exact proportion to the inward freedom to which we may have grown at a given moment. And if this is a correct view of freedom, our chief energy must be concentrated on achieving reform from within.
MAHATMA GANDHI (1869–1948)

Reformation ends not in contemplation, but in action.
GEORGE GILLESPIE (1613–1648)

The only way to reform some people is to chloroform them.
THOMAS C. HALIBURTON (1796–1865)

To give up the task of reforming society is to give up one's responsibility as a free man.
ALAN PATON (1903–1988)

Let us reform our schools, and we shall find little reform needed in our prisons.
JOHN RUSKIN (1819–1900), *Unto This Last*

All Reformers, however strict their social conscience, live in houses just as big as they can pay for.
LOGAN PEARSALL SMITH (1865–1946), *Afterthoughts*

Whenever you find that you are on the side of the majority, it is time to reform.
MARK TWAIN (1835–1910)

Missionaries are going to reform the world whether it wants to or not.
OSCAR WILDE (1854–1900)

I used to be a lawyer, but now I am a reformed character.
WOODROW WILSON (1856–1924)

Refuge

Violence is the last refuge of the incompetent.
ISAAC ASIMOV (1920–1992)

If I take refuge in ambiguity, I can assure you that it's quite conscious.
FRANK BOYDEN (1879–1972)

A technical objection is the first refuge of a scoundrel.
HEYWOOD BROUN (1888–1939)

Therefore, be ye lamps unto yourselves, be a refuge to yourselves. Hold fast to Truth as a lamp; hold fast to the truth as a refuge. Look not for a refuge in anyone beside yourselves. And those, who shall be a lamp unto themselves, shall betake themselves to no external refuge, but holding fast to the Truth as their lamp, and holding fast to the Truth as their refuge, they shall reach the topmost height.
THE BUDDHA (563–483 BC)

Music is the refuge of souls ulcerated by happiness.
E. M. CIORAN (1911–1995)

Historically, the claim of consensus has been the first refuge of scoundrels; it is a way to avoid debate by claiming that the matter is already settled.
MICHAEL CRICHTON (1942–)

Castles in the air—they are so easy to take refuge in. And so easy to build, too.
HENRIK IBSEN (1828–1906), *The Master Builder*

Patriotism is the last refuge of a scoundrel.
SAMUEL JOHNSON (1709–1784)

Art is merely the refuge which the ingenious have invented, when they were supplied with food and women, to escape the tediousness of life.
W. SOMERSET MAUGHAM (1874–1965), *Of Human Bondage*

Oh, how one wishes sometimes to escape from the meaningless dullness of human eloquence, from all those sublime phrases, to take refuge in nature, apparently so inarticulate, or in the wordlessness of long grinding labor, of sound sleep, of true music, or of a human understanding, rendered speechless by emotion!
BORIS PASTERNAK (1890–1960), *Dr. Zhivago*

I adore simple pleasures. They are the last refuge of the complex.
OSCAR WILDE (1854–1900), *The Picture of Dorian Gray*

Consistency is the last refuge of the unimaginative.
OSCAR WILDE (1854–1900)

Seriousness is the only refuge of the shallow.
OSCAR WILDE (1854–1900)

Regret

My one regret in life is that I am not someone else.
WOODY ALLEN (1935–)

When one door closes another door opens; but we often look so long and so regretfully upon the closed door, that we do not see the ones which open for us.
ALEXANDER GRAHAM BELL (1847–1922)

Regret for wasted time is more wasted time.
MASON COOLEY (1927–2002)

I want to live my life so that my nights are full of regrets.
ZELDA FITZGERALD (1900–1948)

I only regret that I have but one life to lose for my country.
NATHAN HALE (1755–1776), last words

Regret for the things we did can be tempered by time; it is regret for the things we did not do that is inconsolable.
SYDNEY J. HARRIS (1917–1986)

It is better to look ahead and prepare than to look back and regret.
JACKIE JOYNER-KERSEE (1962–)

Make it a rule of life never to regret and never to look back. Regret is an appalling waste of energy; you can't build on it; it's only for wallowing in.
KATHERINE MANSFIELD (1888–1923)

Speak when you are angry—and you will make the best speech you'll ever regret.
DR. LAURENCE J. PETER (1919–1990)

The follies which a man regrets most, in his life, are those which he didn't commit when he had the opportunity.
HELEN ROWLAND (1876–1950), *A Guide to Men*

As you grow older, you'll find the only things you regret are the things you didn't do.
ZACHARY SCOTT (1914–1965)

Happiness is essentially a state of going somewhere, wholeheartedly, one-directionally, without regret or reservation.
WILLIAM H. SHELDON (1898–1977)

To regret deeply is to live afresh.
HENRY DAVID THOREAU (1817–1862)

I have often regretted my speech, never my silence.
XENOCRATES (396–314 BC)

Rejection

Look up the definition of rejection in the dictionary, get really comfortable with it, and then maybe you can go into acting.
LONI ANDERSON (1946–)

A rejection is nothing more than a necessary step in the pursuit of success.
BO BENNETT (1972–)

You have to know how to accept rejection and reject acceptance.
RAY BRADBURY (1920–)

There's nothing like rejection to make you do an inventory of yourself.
JAMES BURKE (1936–)

Actors search for rejection. If they don't get it they reject themselves.
CHARLIE CHAPLIN (1889–1977)

Don't waste yourself in rejection, nor bark against the bad, but chant the beauty of the good.
RALPH WALDO EMERSON (1803–1882)

In life we don't get what we want, we get in life what we are. If we want more we have to be able to be more, in order to be more you have to face rejection.
FARRAH GRAY (1984–)

Every great advance in natural knowledge has involved the absolute rejection of authority.
THOMAS H. HUXLEY (1825–1895)

I take rejection as someone blowing a bugle in my ear to wake me up and get going, rather than retreat.
SYLVESTER STALLONE (1946–)

Rejoice

The artist, depicting man disdainful of the storm and stress of life, is no less reconciling and healing than the poet who, while endowing Nature and Humanity, rejoices in its measureless superiority to human passions and human sorrows.
BERNARD BERENSON (1865–1959)

I cannot pretend to feel impartial about colours. I rejoice with the brilliant ones and am genuinely sorry for the poor browns.
SIR WINSTON CHURCHILL (1874–1965)

He is a wise man who does not grieve for the things which he has not, but rejoices for those which he has.
EPICURUS (341–270 BC)

No one who cannot rejoice in the discovery of his own mistakes deserves to be called a scholar.
DONALD FOSTER (1950–)

Do not rejoice over what has not yet happened.
EGYPTIAN PROVERB

When you were born, you cried and the world rejoiced. Live your life so that when you die, the world cries and you rejoice.
INDIAN PROVERB

Rejoice not at thine enemy's fall—but don't rush to pick him up either.
JEWISH PROVERB

Relationships

Let's face it … most relationships you have in life don't work out.
ALEX BENNETT (1939–)

Our relationships, relationships between adults, how all those pieces fit together—that's the most complicated thing we all face.
BILL CONDON (1955–)

Relationships based on obligation lack dignity.
WAYNE D. DYER (1940–)

Relationships of trust depend on our willingness to look not only to our own interests, but also the interests of others.
PETER FARQUHARSON (1832–1869)

Broken relationships are a source of heavy heartbreak that seem to affect every family.
JERRY B. JENKINS (1949–)

Relationships in general make people a bit nervous. It's about trust. Do I trust you enough to go there?
NEIL LABUTE (1963–)

Relationships do not preclude issues of morality.
JHUMPA LAHIRI (1909–)

Intimate relationships cannot substitute for a life plan. But to have any meaning or viability at all, a life plan must include intimate relationships.
HARRIET LERNER (1944–)

Relationships are so much a rerun of our parental relationships. We're rerunning the relationship they were in together, and we're rerunning the relationship we had with them with our lover.
KENNY LOGGINS (1948–)

Most relationships where two people have the same motivation, needs, desires and requirements ... there's usually a butting of heads at one point.
JOHN OATES (1948–)

Assumptions are the termites of relationships.
HENRY WINKLER (1945–)

Relatives

Friends are relatives you make for yourself.
EUSTACHE DESCHAMPS (1346–1406)

Some people are your relatives but others are your ancestors, and you choose the ones you want to have as ancestors. You create yourself out of those values.
RALPH ELLISON (1914–1994)

Blood relatives often have nothing to do with family, and similarly, family is about who you choose to make your life with.
OLIVER HUDSON (1976–)

It isn't necessary to have relatives in Kansas City in order to be unhappy.
GROUCHO MARX (1890–1977)

God gives us relatives; thank God we can choose our friends.
ETHEL MUMFORD (1878–1940)

Eat and drink with your relatives; do business with strangers.
GREEK PROVERB

Man has three friends on whose company he relies. First, wealth which goes with him only while good fortune lasts. Second, his relatives; they go only as far as the grave and leave him there. The third friend, his good deeds, go with him beyond the grave.
THE TALMUD

Relativity

In relativity, movement is continuous, causally determinate and well defined, while in quantum mechanics it is discontinuous, not causally determinate and not well defined.
DAVID BOHM (1917–1992)

Relativity must replace absolutism in the realm of morals as well as in the spheres of physics and biology.
THOMAS COCHRANE (1775–1860)

In Einstein's theory of relativity the observer is a man who sets out in quest of truth armed with a measuring-rod. In quantum theory he sets out with a sieve.
SIR ARTHUR EDDINGTON (1882–1944)

Gravitation cannot be held responsible for people falling in love. How on earth can you explain in terms of chemistry and physics so important a biological phenomenon as first love? Put your hand on a stove for a minute and it seems like an hour. Sit with that special girl for an hour and it seems like a minute. That's relativity.
ALBERT EINSTEIN (1879–1955)

The theory of relativity worked out by Mr. Einstein, which is in the domain of natural science, I believe can also be applied to the political field. Both democracy and human rights are relative concepts—and not absolute and general.
JIANG ZEMIN (1917–)

In Einstein's general relativity the structure of space can change but not its topology. Topology is the property of something that doesn't change when you bend it or stretch it as long as you don't break anything.
EDWARD WITTEN (1951–)

Relaxation

To sit in the shade on a fine day, and look upon verdure is the most perfect refreshment.
JANE AUSTEN (1775–1817)

No matter how much pressure you feel at work, if you could find ways to relax for at least five minutes every hour, you'd be more productive.
DR. JOYCE BROTHERS (1928–)

During [these] periods of relaxation after concentrated intellectual activity, the intuitive mind seems to take over and can produce the sudden clarifying insights which give so much joy and delight.
FRITJOF CAPRA (1939–)

I take it that what all men are really after is some form or perhaps only some formula of peace.
JOSEPH CONRAD (1857–1924)

Man is so made that he can only find relaxation from one kind of labor by taking up another.
ANATOLE FRANCE (1844–1924), *The Crime of Sylvestre Bonnard*

This art of resting the mind and the power of dismissing from it all care and worry is probably one of the secrets of energy in our great men.
J. A. HADFIELD (1883–1967)

If a man insisted always on being serious, and never allowed himself a bit of fun and relaxation, he would go mad or become unstable without knowing it.
HERODOTUS (484–430 BC), *The Histories of Herodotus*

True relaxation, which would do me the world of good, does not exist for me.
GUSTAV KLIMT (1862–1918)

There is no need to go to India or anywhere else to find peace. You will find that deep place of silence right in your room, your garden or even your bathtub.
ELISABETH KÜBLER-ROSS (1926–2004)

When we are unable to find tranquillity within ourselves, it is useless to seek it elsewhere.
FRANÇOIS DE LA ROCHEFOUCAULD (1613–1680)

Every now and then go away, have a little relaxation, for when you come back to your work your judgment will be surer. Go some distance away because then the work appears smaller and more of it can be taken in at a glance, and a lack of harmony and proportion is more readily seen.
LEONARDO DA VINCI (1452–1519)

Take rest; a field that has rested gives a bountiful crop.
OVID (43 BC–AD 17)

Sometimes I sits and thinks, and sometimes I just sits.
LEROY "SATCHEL" PAIGE(1906–1982)

To be able to fill leisure intelligently is the last product of civilization, and at present very few people have reached this level.
BERTRAND RUSSELL (1872–1970), *Conquest of Happiness*

Learning to ignore things is one of the great paths to inner peace.
ROBERT J. SAWYER (1960–), *Calculating God*

Working in the garden … gives me a profound feeling of inner peace.
RUTH STOUT (1884–1980)

It is requisite for the relaxation of the mind that we make use, from time to time, of playful deeds and jokes.
SAINT THOMAS AQUINAS (1225–1274)

He enjoys true leisure who has time to improve his soul's estate.
HENRY DAVID THOREAU (1817–1862)

Walking has a very good effect in that you're in this state of relaxation, but at the same time you're allowing the sub-conscious to work on you.
ANDREW WILES (1953–)

Never lose sight of this important truth, that no one can be truly great until he has gained a knowledge of himself, a knowledge which can only be acquired by occasional retirement.
JOHANN GEORG VON ZIMMERMANN (1728–1795)

Reliability

The shifts of Fortune test the reliability of friends.
CICERO (106–43 BC), *De Amicitia*

Simplicity is prerequisite for reliability.
EDSGER W. DIJKSTRA (1930–2002)

Facts from paper are not the same as facts from people. The reliability of the people giving you the facts is as important as the facts themselves.
HAROLD S. GENEEN (1910–1997)

Religion

Nothing defines humans better than their willingness to do irrational things in the pursuit of phenomenally unlikely payoffs. This is the principle behind lotteries, dating, and religion.
SCOTT ADAMS (1957–)

Of all possible sexual perversions, religion is the only one to have ever been scientifically systematized.
LOUIS ARAGON (1897–1982)

The true meaning of religion is thus not simply morality, but morality touched by emotion.
MATTHEW ARNOLD (1822–1888), *Literature and Dogma*

Everybody likes to go their own way—to choose their own time and manner of devotion.
JANE AUSTEN (1775–1817), *Mansfield Park*

A religion which requires persecution to sustain it is of the devil's propagation.
HOSEA BALLOU (1771–1852)

Art and Religion are, then, two roads by which men escape from circumstance to ecstasy. Between aesthetic and religious rapture there is a family alliance. Art and Religion are means to similar states of mind.
CLIVE BELL (1881–1964)

Religion, n.: A daughter of Hope and Fear, explaining to Ignorance the nature of the Unknowable.
AMBROSE BIERCE (1842–1914), *The Devil's Dictionary*

Nothing is so fatal to religion as indifference.
EDMUND BURKE (1729–1797)

The secret of a good sermon is to have a good beginning and a good ending, then having the two as close together as possible.
GEORGE BURNS (1896–1996)

The more I study religions the more I am convinced that man never worshipped anything but himself.
SIR RICHARD FRANCIS BURTON (1821–1890)

I am always most religious upon a sunshiny day…
LORD BYRON (1788–1824)

A cosmic philosophy is not constructed to fit a man; a cosmic philosophy is constructed to fit a cosmos. A man can no more possess a private religion than he can possess a private sun and moon.
G. K. CHESTERTON (1874–1936)

Cruel persecutions and intolerance are not accidents, but grow out of the very essence of religion, namely, its absolute claims.
MORRIS COHEN (1880–1947)

Those who seek consolation in existing churches often pay for their peace of mind with a tacit agreement to ignore a great deal of what is known about the way the world works.
MIHALY CSIKSZENTMIHALYI (1934–), *Flow: The Psychology of Optimal Experience*

Man is made to adore and to obey: but if you will not command him, if you give him nothing to worship, he will fashion his own divinities, and find a chieftain in his own passions.
BENJAMIN DISRAELI (1804–1881)

Science without religion is lame, religion without science is blind.
ALBERT EINSTEIN (1879–1955), *Science, Philosophy and Religion: a Symposium*

It was the experience of mystery—even if mixed with fear—that engendered religion.
ALBERT EINSTEIN (1879–1955)

My religion consists of a humble admiration of the illimitable superior spirit who reveals himself in the slight details we are able to perceive with our frail and feeble mind.
ALBERT EINSTEIN (1879–1955)

The reliance on authority measures the decline of religion, the withdrawal of the soul.
RALPH WALDO EMERSON (1803–1882)

The religion that is afraid of science dishonors God and commits suicide.
RALPH WALDO EMERSON (1803–1882)

The more the fruits of knowledge become accessible to men, the more widespread is the decline of religious belief.
SIGMUND FREUD (1856–1939), *The Future of an Illusion*

For it is with the mysteries of our religion, as with wholesome pills for the sick, which swallowed whole, have the virtue to cure; but chewed, are for the most part cast up again without effect.
THOMAS HOBBES (1588–1679)

The opposite of the religious fanatic is not the fanatical atheist but the gentle cynic who cares not whether there is a god or not.
ERIC HOFFER (1902–1983)

There is no religion in which everyday life is not considered a prison; there is no philosophy or ideology that does not think that we live in alienation.
EUGÈNE IONESCO (1909–1994)

Religion is a monumental chapter in the history of human egotism.
WILLIAM JAMES (1842–1910)

Say nothing of my religion. It is known to God and myself alone. Its evidence before the world is to be sought in my life: if it has been honest and dutiful to society, the religion which has regulated it cannot be a bad one.
THOMAS JEFFERSON (1743–1826)

Everyone ought to worship God according to his own inclinations, and not to be constrained by force.
JOSEPHUS (AD 37–100), *Life*

When a culture feels that its end has come, it sends for a priest.
KARL KRAUS (1874–1936)

I am determined that my children shall be brought up in their father's religion, if they can find out what it is.
CHARLES LAMB (1775–1834)

It is a fine thing to establish one's own religion in one's heart, not to be dependent on tradition and second-hand ideals. Life will seem to you, later, not a lesser, but a greater thing.
D. H. LAWRENCE (1885–1930)

When I do good, I feel good; when I do bad, I feel bad, and that is my religion.
ABRAHAM LINCOLN (1809–1865)

Such evil deeds could religion prompt.
LUCRETIUS (C. 99–55 BC), *De Rerum Natura*

A church is disaffected when it is persecuted, quiet when it is tolerated, and actively loyal when it is favored and cherished.
THOMAS B. MACAULAY (1800–1859)

I've often thought the Bible should have a disclaimer in the front saying this is fiction.
IAN MCKELLEN (1939–)

For centuries, theologians have been explaining the unknowable in terms of the not-worth-knowing.
H. L. MENCKEN (1880–1956)

Religion is excellent stuff for keeping common people quiet.
NAPOLÉON I (1769–1821)

Persecution is not an original feature in any religion; but it is always the strongly marked feature of all religions established by law.
THOMAS PAINE (1737–1809)

Men never do evil so completely and cheerfully as when they do it from a religious conviction.
BLAISE PASCAL (1623–1662)

[T]o emph asize the afterlife is to deny life. To concentrate on Heaven is to create hell. In their desperate longing to transcend the disorderliness, friction, and unpredictability that pesters life; in their desire for a fresh start in a tidy habitat, germ-free and secured by angels, religious multitudes are gambling the only life they may ever have on a dark horse in a race that has no finish line.
TOM ROBBINS (1936–), *Skinny Legs and All*

Think of how many religions attempt to validate themselves with prophecy. Think of how many people rely on these prophecies, however vague, however unfulfilled, to support or prop up their beliefs. Yet has there ever been a religion with the prophetic accuracy and reliability of science?
CARL SAGAN (1934–1996)

I won't take my religion from any man who never works except with his mouth.
CARL SANDBURG (1878–1967)

I am convinced that the teaching of the church is in theory a crafty and evil lie, and in practice a concoction of gross superstition and witchcraft.
LEO TOLSTOY (1828–1910)

In religion and politics, people's beliefs and convictions are in almost every case gotten at second hand, and without examination.
MARK TWAIN (1835–1910)

With or without religion, you would have good people doing good things and evil people doing evil things. But for good people to do evil things, that takes religion.
STEVEN WEINBERG (1933–)

A cult is a religion with no political power.
TOM WOLFE (1931–)

Slavery to monarchs and ministers, which the world will be long freeing itself from, and whose deadly grasp stops the progress of the human mind, is not yet abolished.
MARY WOLLSTONECRAFT (1759–1797)

Remedies

He that will not apply new remedies must expect new evils; for time is the greatest innovator.
SIR FRANCIS BACON (1561–1626)

Nothing is more despicable than a professional talker who uses his words as a quack uses his remedies.
FRANÇOIS DE FÉNELON (1651–1715)

There is no difficulty that enough love will not conquer; no disease that enough love will not heal; no door that enough love will not open.
EMMET FOX (1886–1951)

We should manage our fortunes as we do our health—enjoy it when good, be patient when it is

bad, and never apply violent remedies except in an extreme necessity.
FRANÇOIS DE LA ROCHEFOUCAULD (1613–1680)

To extraordinary circumstance we must apply extraordinary remedies.
NAPOLÉON I (1769–1821)

Focus on remedies, not faults.
JACK NICKLAUS (1940–)

Learn the fundamentals of the game and stick to them. Band-Aid remedies never last.
JACK NICKLAUS (1940–)

There are some remedies worse than the disease.
PUBLILIUS SYRUS (C. 100 BC), *Maxims*

Our remedies oft in ourselves do lie.
WILLIAM SHAKESPEARE (1564–1616), *All's Well That Ends Well*

Remembrance

[P]raising what is lost
Makes the remembrance dear…
WILLIAM SHAKESPEARE (1564–1616), *All's Well that Ends Well*

When to the sessions of sweet silent thought
I summon up remembrance of things past,
I sigh the lack of many a thing I sought,
And with old woes new wail my dear time's waste.
WILLIAM SHAKESPEARE (1564–1616), "Sonnet 30"

Sow good services; sweet remembrances will grow them.
MADAME DE STAËL (1766–1817)

Remorse

I do not feel remorse. Everybody makes mistakes in war.
ABU ABBAS (1948–2004)

Childhood, n.: The period of human life intermediate between the idiocy of infancy and the folly of youth—two removes from the sin of manhood and three from the remorse of age.
AMBROSE BIERCE (1842–1914), *The Devil's Dictionary*

Remorse is virtue's root; its fair increase are fruits of innocence and blessedness.
WILLIAM C. BRYANT (1794 –1878)

Remorse is the echo of a lost virtue.
SIR EDWARD G. BULWER-LYTTON (1803–1873)

Remorse, the fatal egg that pleasure laid.
WILLIAM COWPER (1731–1800)

Christian morality prefers remorse to precede lust, and then lust not to follow.
KARL KRAUS (1874–1936)

Remorse for what? You people have done everything in the world to me. Doesn't that give me equal right?
CHARLES MANSON (1934–)

One man's remorse is another man's reminiscence.
OGDEN NASH (1902–1971)

The gaudy, blabbing, and remorseful day
Is crept into the bosom of the sea.
WILLIAM SHAKESPEARE (1564–1616), *King Henry VI*

Who feels no ills, should, therefore, fear them; and when fortune smiles, be doubly cautious, lest destruction come remorseless on him, and he fall unpitied.
SOPHOCLES (496–406 BC)

The Renaissance

The Renaissance is studded by the names of the artists and architects, with their creations recorded as great historical events.
ARTHUR ERICKSON (1924–)

In essence the Renaissance was simply the green end of one of civilization's hardest winters.
JOHN FOWLES (1926–2005)

No account of the Renaissance can be complete without some notice of the attempt made by certain Italian scholars of the fifteenth century to reconcile Christianity with the religion of ancient Greece.
WALTER PATER (1839–1894)

The mind of the Renaissance was not a pilgrim mind, but a sedentary city mind, like that of the ancients.
GEORGE SANTAYANA (1863–1952)

Repartee

Repartee, n.: Prudent insult in retort. Practiced by gentlemen with a constitutional aversion to violence, but a strong disposition to offend. In a war of words, the tactics of the North American Indian.
AMBROSE BIERCE (1842–1914), *The Devil's Dictionary*

Repartee is what you wish you'd said.
HEYWOOD BROUN (1888–1939)

Repartee is perfect when it effects its purpose with a double edge. It is the highest order of wit, as it indicates the coolest yet quickest exercise of genius, at a moment when the passions are roused.
CHARLES CALEB COLTON (1780–1832)

A man renowned for repartee will seldom scruple to make free with friendship's finest feeling, will thrust a dagger at your breast, and say he wounded you in jest, by way of balm for healing.
WILLIAM COWPER (1731–1800)

A majority is always better than the best repartee.
BENJAMIN DISRAELI (1804–1881)

Repartee is something we think of twenty-four hours too late.
MARK TWAIN (1835–1910)

Repentance

Bad men are full of repentance.
ARISTOTLE (384–322 BC)

Repentance may begin instantly, but reformation often requires a sphere of years.
HENRY WARD BEECHER (1813–1887)

Repentance is but want of power to sin.
JOHN DRYDEN (1631–1700)

Nothing spoils a confession like repentance.
ANATOLE FRANCE (1844–1924)

Our repentance is not so much regret for the ill we have done as fear of the ill that may happen to us in consequence.
FRANÇOIS DE LA ROCHEFOUCAULD (1613–1680)

He who carries out one good deed acquires one advocate in his own behalf, and he who commits one transgression acquires one accuser against himself. Repentance and good works are like a shield against calamity.
THE TALMUD

Repression

Repression is not the way to virtue. When people restrain themselves out of fear, their lives are by necessity diminished. Only through freely chosen discipline can life be enjoyed and still kept within the bounds of reason.
MIHALY CSIKSZENTMIHALYI (1934–), *Flow: The Psychology of Optimal Experience*

If repression has indeed been the fundamental link between power, knowledge, and sexuality since the classical age, it stands to reason that we will not be able to free ourselves from it except at a considerable cost.
MICHEL FOUCAULT (1926–1984)

When decorum is repression, the only dignity free men have is to speak out.
ABBIE HOFFMAN (1936–1989)

Severity and repression of the old type, however, almost certainly carried with it in adolescence, disturbance, confusion and the necessity of revolt.
DORA RUSSELL (1894–1986)

Repression will provoke rebellion.
HUGH WILLIAMSON (1735–1819)

The seed of revolution is repression.
WOODROW WILSON (1856–1924)

Republicans

The rise in the Republican Party in the former Confederacy has brought about major changes in politics.
STEPHEN AMBROSE (1936–2002)

The Republicans would like to take us back to a darker time, when corporations ruled and the underserved had no rights.
JOE BACA (1947–)

Republicans have nothing but bad ideas, and Democrats have no ideas.
LEWIS BLACK (1948–)

As a Republican, I am all for competition.
MICHAEL BURGESS (1950–)

Republicans are men of narrow vision, who are afraid of the future.
JIMMY CARTER (1924–)

Opportunity for all means making taxes fair. I'm not out to soak the rich. But I do believe the rich should pay their fair share. For twelve years, the Republicans have raised taxes on the middle class. It's time to give the middle class tax relief.
BILL CLINTON (1946–)

Republicans believe largely in the market working, Democrats believe stereotypically that you've got to give people something. So why not give people a chance to let the market work for them.
HAROLD FORD (1970–)

All along, House Republicans have had faith in the American people's ability to grow our economy and are looking to the future with confidence.
VIRGINIA FOXX (1943–)

Simply put, Republican economic policies let Americans keep more of their own money to spend, save and invest, while Democrats want to take it away.
J. D. HAYWORTH (1958–)

The Republican Party is committed to the basic principle that everyone deserves a chance to achieve the American Dream.
ALPHONSO JACKSON (1945–)

The only difference between the Democrats and the Republicans is that the Democrats allow the poor to be corrupt, too.
OSCAR LEVANT (1906–1972)

In this world of sin and sorrow there is always something to be thankful for; as for me, I rejoice that I am not a Republican.
H. L. MENCKEN (1880–1956)

Republicans understand the importance of bondage between a mother and child.
DAN QUAYLE (1947–)

I have been thinking that I would make a proposition to my Republican friends… that if they will stop telling lies about the Democrats, we will stop telling the truth about them.
ADLAI E. STEVENSON II (1900–1965)

I came from a disadvantaged home. They were Republicans.
PAUL TSONGAS (1941–1997)

Reputation

Reputation is what other people know about you. Honor is what you know about yourself.
LOIS MCMASTER BUJOLD (1949–), *A Civil Campaign*

There are two modes of establishing our reputation: to be praised by honest men, and to be abused by rogues. It is best, however, to secure the former, because it will invariably be accompanied by the latter.
CHARLES CALEB COLTON (1780–1832)

You can't build a reputation on what you are going to do.
HENRY FORD (1863–1947)

A man is what he is, not what men say he is. His character no man can touch. His character is what he is before his God and his Judge; and only he himself can damage that. His reputation's what men say he is. That can be damaged; but reputation is for time, character is for eternity
JOHN BALLANTINE GOUGH (1817–1886)

A good name, like good will, is got by many actions and lost by one.
LORD FRANCIS JEFFERY (1773–1850)

Character is like a tree and reputation like its shadow. The shadow is what we think of it; the tree is the real thing.
ABRAHAM LINCOLN (1809–1865)

Reputation is only a candle of wavering and uncertain flame and easily blown out, but it is the light by which the world looks for and finds merit.
JAMES RUSSELL LOWELL (1819–1891)

Until you've lost your reputation, you never realize what a burden it was.
MARGARET MITCHELL (1900–1949)

Reputation is what men and women think of us; character is what God and angels know of us.
THOMAS PAINE (1737–1809)

A good reputation is more valuable than money.
PUBLILIUS SYRUS (C. 100 BC), *Maxims*

Good name in man and woman, dear my lord,
Is the immediate jewel of their souls:
Who steals my purse steals trash; 'tis something
  nothing;
'Twas mine, 'tis his, and has been slave to
  thousands;
But he that filches from me my good name
Robs me of that which not enriches him
And makes me poor indeed...
WILLIAM SHAKESPEARE (1564–1616), *Othello*

Regard your good name as the richest jewel you can possibly be possessed of—for credit is like fire; when once you have kindled it you may easily preserve it, but if you once extinguish it, you will find it an arduous task to rekindle it again. The way to gain a good reputation is to endeavor to be what you desire to appear.
SOCRATES (469–399 BC)

One can survive everything, nowadays, except death, and live down everything except a good reputation.
OSCAR WILDE (1854–1900)

A bad wound may be cured, bad repute kills.
SPANISH PROVERB

Research

Research is the process of going up alleys to see if they are blind.
MARSTON BATES (1906–1974)

Basic research is what I am doing when I don't know what I am doing.
WERNHER VON BRAUN (1912–1977)

I do a great deal of research, particularly in the apartments of tall blondes.
RAYMOND CHANDLER (1888–1959)

If all people are unique, and if they are constantly changing each and every day, then all one can say about any social research finding is that it applied to that group of people on that given day, and given the propensity of humans to be different and to change, then it is unlikely that one would get the same results if one were to repeat the study.
WAYNE D. DYER (1940–)

If we knew what it was we were doing, it would not be called research, would it?
ALBERT EINSTEIN (1879–1955)

The great question that has never been answered, and which I have not yet been able to answer, despite my thirty years of research into the feminine soul, is "What does a woman want?"
SIGMUND FREUD (1856–1939)

Many of our research projects will fail.
BILL GATES (1955 –)

What is research but a blind date with knowledge?
WILL HARVEY (1967–)

Research is formalized curiosity. It is poking and prying with a purpose.
ZORA NEALE HURSTON (1903–1960)

The trouble with research is that it tells you what people were thinking about yesterday, not tomorrow. It's like driving a car using a rearview mirror.
BERNARD LOOMIS (1923–2006)

It is a good morning exercise for a research scientist to discard a pet hypothesis every day before breakfast. It keeps him young.
KONRAD LORENZ (1903–1989)

Copy from one, it's plagiarism; copy from two, it's research.
WILSON MIZNER (1876–1933)

Research is usually a policeman stopping a novel from progressing.
BRIAN MOORE (1921–1999)

I notice increasing reluctance on the part of marketing executives to use judgment; they are coming to rely too much on research, and they use it as a drunkard uses a lamp post for support, rather than for illumination.
DAVID OGILVY (1911–1999)

The valid research for the future is on the inner side, on the spiritual side.
PEACE PILGRIM (1908–1981)

On a sofa upholstered in panther skin
Mona did researches in original sin.
WILLIAM PLOMER (1903–1973)

The outcome of any serious research can only be to make two questions grow where only one grew before.
THORSTEIN VEBLEN (1857–1929)

We don't devote enough scientific research to finding a cure for jerks.
BILL WATTERSON (1958–)

Fools make researches and wise men exploit them.
H. G. WELLS (1866–1946)

Lost in a gloom of uninspired research.
WILLIAM WORDSWORTH (1770–1850)

Resistance

The duration of passion is proportionate with the original resistance of the woman.
HONORÉ DE BALZAC (1799–1850)

When I'm not doing something that comes deeply from me, I get bored. When I get bored I get distracted and when I get distracted, I become depressed. It's a natural resistance, and it insures your integrity.
MARIA IRENE FORNES (1930–)

Adaptability is not imitation. It means power of resistance and assimilation.
MAHATMA GANDHI (1869–1948)

The spirit of resistance to government is so valuable on certain occasions, that I wish it always to be kept alive.
THOMAS JEFFERSON (1743–1826)

It is from numberless diverse acts of courage and belief that human history is shaped. Each time a man stands up for an ideal, or acts to improve the lot of others, or strikes out against injustice, he sends forth a tiny ripple of hope, and crossing each other from a million different centers of energy and daring, those ripples build a current that can sweep down the mightiest walls of oppression and resistance.
ROBERT F. KENNEDY (1925–1968)

To fly we have to have resistance.
MAYA LIN (1959–)

To fight and conquer in all your battles is not supreme excellence; supreme excellence consists in breaking the enemy's resistance without fighting.
SUN-TZU (C. 544–496 BC)

Courage is resistance to fear, mastery of fear—not absence of fear.
MARK TWAIN (1835–1910)

A little tact and wise management may often evade resistance, and carry a point, where direct force might be in vain.
ANONYMOUS

Resolution

Tenderness and kindness are not signs of weakness and despair, but manifestations of strength and resolutions.
KAHLIL GIBRAN (1883–1931)

The reason of a resolution is more to be considered than the resolution itself.
SIR JOHN HOLT (1642–1710)

It takes in reality only one to make a quarrel. It is useless for the sheep to pass resolutions in favour of vegetarianism while the wolf remains of a different opinion.
WILLIAM RALPH INGE (1860–1954), *Outspoken Essays*

Always bear in mind that your own resolution to succeed is more important than any one thing.
ABRAHAM LINCOLN (1809–1865)

The Christian resolution to find the world ugly and bad has made the world ugly and bad.
FRIEDRICH NIETZSCHE (1844–1900), *The Gay Science*

"Where there is a will there is a way," is an old and true saying. He who resolves upon doing a thing, by that very resolution often scales the barriers to it, and secures its achievement. To think we are able, is almost to be so—to determine upon attainment is frequently attainment itself.
SAMUEL SMILES (1812–1904)

Good resolutions are simply checks that men draw on a bank where they have no account.
OSCAR WILDE (1854–1900)

A good resolution is like an old horse, which is often saddled but rarely ridden.
MEXICAN PROVERB

Respect

Civilization is a method of living, an attitude of equal respect for all men.
JANE ADDAMS (1860–1935)

He removes the greatest ornament of friendship, who takes away from it respect.
CICERO (106–43 BC)

Respect yourself and others will respect you.
CONFUCIUS (551–479 BC)

The way to procure insults is to submit to them: a man meets with no more respect than he exacts.
WILLIAM HAZLITT (1778–1830)

Respect a man, he will do the more.
JAMES HOWELL (1594–1666)

[Y]ou can't respect somebody who kisses your ass. It just doesn't work.
JOHN HUGHES (1950–), *Ferris Bueller's Day Off*

The more things a man is ashamed of, the more respectable he is.
GEORGE BERNARD SHAW (1856–1950), *Man and Superman*

To have respect for ourselves guides our morals; and to have a deference for others governs our manners.
LAWRENCE STERNE (1713–1768)

If you want to be respected, you must respect yourself.
SPANISH PROVERB

Respectability

God has been replaced, as he has all over the West, with respectability and air conditioning.
IMAMU AMIRI BARAKA (1934–)

Income, n.: The natural and rational gauge and measure of respectability.
AMBROSE BIERCE (1842–1914), *The Devil's Dictionary*

Respectability, n.: The offspring of a liaison between a bald head and a bank account.
AMBROSE BIERCE (1842–1914), *The Devil's Dictionary*

There exists, at the bottom of all abasement and misfortune, a last extreme which rebels and joins battle with the forces of law and respectability in a desperate struggle, waged partly by cunning and partly by violence, at once sick and ferocious, in which it attacks the prevailing social order with the pin-pricks of vice and the hammer-blows of crime.
VICTOR HUGO (1802–1885)

I shall be glad when you have strangled the invincible respectability that dogs your steps.
D. H. LAWRENCE (1885–1930)

It is also, I would guess, a universal that in all societies people value respectability granted to them.
KENNETH L. PIKE (1912–)

Men have to do some awfully mean things to keep up their respectability.
GEORGE BERNARD SHAW (1856–1950)

To be good, according to the vulgar standard of goodness, is obviously quite easy. It merely requires a certain amount of sordid terror, a certain low passion for middle-class respectability.
OSCAR WILDE (1854–1900)

Responsibility

In every child who is born under no matter what circumstances and of no matter what parents, the potentiality of the human race is born again, and in him, too, once more, and each of us, our terrific responsibility toward human life: toward the utmost idea of goodness, of the horror of terrorism, and of God.
JAMES AGEE (1909–1955), *Let Us Now Praise Famous Men*

The perfect bureaucrat everywhere is the man who manages to make no decisions and escape all responsibility.
BROOKS ATKINSON (1894–1984), *Once Around the Sun*

Action springs not from thought, but from a readiness for responsibility.
DIETRICH BONHOEFFER (1906–1945)

Forming characters! Whose? Our own or others? Both. And in that momentous fact lies the peril and responsibility of our existence.
ELIHU BURRITT (1810–1879)

One can pass on responsibility, but not the discretion that goes with it.
BENVENUTO CELLINI (1500–1571)

The price of greatness is responsibility.
SIR WINSTON CHURCHILL (1874–1965)

You can delegate authority, but not responsibility.
STEPHEN W. COMISKEY (1947–)

You cannot hope to build a better world without improving the individuals. To that end each of us must work for his own improvement, and at the same time share a general responsibility for all humanity, our particular duty being to aid those to whom we think we can be most useful.
MARIE CURIE (1867–1934)

Character—the willingness to accept responsibility for one's own life—is the source from which self respect springs.
JOAN DIDION (1934–), *Slouching Towards Bethlehem*

I think of a hero as someone who understands the degree of responsibility that comes with his freedom.
BOB DYLAN (1941–)

We are at the very beginning of time for the human race. It is not unreasonable that we grapple with problems. But there are tens of thousands of years in the future. Our responsibility is to do what we can, learn what we can, improve the solutions, and pass them on.
RICHARD FEYNMAN (1918–1988)

If we want unity, we must all be unifiers. If we want accountability, each of us must be accountable for all we do.
CHRISTINE GREGOIRE (1947–)

So many new ideas are at first strange and horrible, though ultimately valuable, that a very heavy responsibility rests upon those who would prevent their dissemination.
J. B. S. HALDANE (1892–1964)

You cannot escape the responsibility of tomorrow by evading it today.
ABRAHAM LINCOLN (1809–1865)

If you don't accept responsibility for your own actions, then you are forever chained to a position of defense.
HOLLY LISLE (1960–), *Fire in the Mist*

We've gotten to the point where everybody's got a right and nobody's got a responsibility.
NEWTON MINOW (1926–)

To give up the task of reforming society is to give up one's responsibility as a free man.
ALAN PATON (1903–1988)

I believe that every right implies a responsibility; every opportunity an obligation; every possession a duty.
JOHN D. ROCKEFELLER JR. (1874–1960)

The more freedom we enjoy, the greater the responsibility we bear, toward others as well as ourselves.
OSCAR ARIAS SANCHEZ (1941–)

Liberty means responsibility. That is why most men dread it.
GEORGE BERNARD SHAW (1856–1950)

Action springs not from thought, but from a readiness for responsibility.
G. M. TREVELYAN (1876–1962)

Man has responsibility, not power.
NATIVE AMERICAN PROVERB

Restaurants

The murals in restaurants are on par with the food in museums.
PETER DE VRIES (1910–1993)

In restaurants, you never have enough money, you're taking a very diverse group of people and building them into a team with a common purpose.
JOHN HICKENLOOPER (1952–)

Restaurants are a wonderful escape for me. And are for a lot of people.
GAY TALESE (1932–)

I never eat in a restaurant that's over a hundred feet off the ground and won't stand still.
CALVIN TRILLIN (1935–)

Retirement

Wisdom and penetration are the fruit of experience, not the lessons of retirement and leisure. Great necessities call out great virtues.
ABIGAIL ADAMS (1744–1818)

There are more pleasant things to do than beat up people.
MUHAMMAD ALI (1942–)

Retirement may be looked upon either as a prolonged holiday or as a rejection, a being thrown on to the scrap-heap.
SIMONE DE BEAUVOIR (1908–1986)

Retirement will become evident to me at the time.
PETER BROCK (1945–)

Retirement at sixty-five is ridiculous. When I was sixty-five I still had pimples.
GEORGE BURNS (1896–1996)

The current institutionally provided retirement plans will not cover people's needs upon retirement.
SCOTT COOK (1952–)

O Winter! ruler of the inverted year...
I crown thee king of intimate delights,
Fireside enjoyments, home-born happiness,
And all the comforts that the lowly roof
Of undisturb'd Retirement, and the hours
Of long uninterrupted evening, know.
WILLIAM COWPER (1731–1800), *Task*

Who knows whether in retirement I shall be tempted to the last infirmity of mundane minds, which is to write a book.
GEOFFREY FISHER (1887–1972)

Retirement kills more people than hard work ever did.
MALCOLM S. FORBES (1919–1990)

Faithful servants never retire. You can retire from your career, but you will never retire from serving God.
RICK WARREN (1909–)

Never lose sight of this important truth, that no one can be truly great until he has gained a knowledge of himself, a knowledge which can only be acquired by occasional retirement.
JOHANN GEORG VON ZIMMERMANN (1728–1795)

Retreat

A tactical retreat is not a bad response to a surprise assault, you know. First you survive. Then you choose your own ground. Then you counterattack.
LOIS MCMASTER BUJOLD, *A Civil Campaign*

Knowledge is a comfortable and necessary retreat and shelter for us in advanced age, and if we do not plant it while young, it will give us no shade when we grow old.
LORD CHESTERFIELD (1694–1773)

I am in earnest; I will not equivocate; I will not excuse; I will not retreat a single inch; and I will be heard.
WILLIAM LLOYD GARRISON (1805–1879)

No retreat. No retreat. They must conquer or die who've no retreat.
JOHN GAY (1685–1732)

Every moment of one's existence one is growing into more or retreating into less.
NORMAN MAILER (1923–2007)

In politics, it seems, retreat is honorable if dictated by military considerations and shameful if even suggested for ethical reasons.
MARY MCCARTHY (1912–1989)

Above all things, never be afraid. The enemy who forces you to retreat is himself afraid of you at that very moment.
ANDRÉ MAUROIS (1885–1967)

Honorable retreats are no ways inferior to brave charges, as having less fortune, more of discipline, and as much valor.
SIR WILLIAM NAPIER (1785–1860), *Peninsular War*

In politics ... never retreat, never retract ... never admit a mistake.
NAPOLÉON I (1769–1821)

Revelation

Faith in God's revelation has nothing to do with an ideology which glorifies the status quo.
KARL BARTH (1886–1968)

Experience is a revelation in the light of which we renounce our errors of youth for those of age.
AMBROSE BIERCE (1842–1914)

The revelation of thought takes men out of servitude into freedom.
RALPH WALDO EMERSON (1803–1882)

There is one evident, indubitable manifestation of the Divinity, and that is the laws of right which are made known to the world through Revelation.
LEO TOLSTOY (1828–1910)

The events in our lives happen in a sequence in time, but in their significance to ourselves they find their own order: the continuous thread of revelation.
EUDORA WELTY (1909–2001)

Revenge

Nothing inspires forgiveness quite like revenge.
SCOTT ADAMS (1957–)

In taking revenge, a man is but even with his enemy; but in passing it over, he is superior.
SIR FRANCIS BACON (1561–1626)

Revenge is a kind of wild justice, which the more man's nature runs to, the more ought law to weed it out.
SIR FRANCIS BACON (1561–1626)

There is no revenge so complete as forgiveness.
JOSH BILLINGS (1818–1885)

People don't remember. Revenge is sweet.
TRACEY EMIN (1963–)

Men are more prone to revenge injuries than to requite kindness.
THOMAS FULLER (1608–1661)

An eye for an eye makes the whole world blind.
MAHATMA GANDHI (1869–1948)

Life being what it is, one dreams of revenge.
PAUL GAUGUIN (1848–1903)

Revenge is sweet and not fattening.
ALFRED HITCHCOCK (1899–1980)

If an injury has to be done to a man it should be so severe that his vengeance need not be feared.
NICCOLÒ MACHIAVELLI (1469–1527)

The best revenge is to be unlike him who performed the injury.
MARCUS AURELIUS ANTONINUS (121–180)

Neglect will sooner kill an injury than revenge.
LATIN PROVERB

Live well. It is the greatest revenge.
THE TALMUD

Reverence

Impiety, n.: Your irreverence toward my deity.
AMBROSE BIERCE (1842–1914), *The Devil's Dictionary*

Reverence, n.: the spiritual attitude of a man to a god and a dog to a man.
AMBROSE BIERCE (1842–1914), *The Devil's Dictionary*

Pride defeats its own end, by bringing the man who seeks esteem and reverence into contempt.
KING HENRY IV (1367–1413)

Among all men on the earth bards have a share of honor and reverence, because the muse has taught them songs and loves the race of bards.
HOMER (800–700 BC), *The Odyssey*

Above all things, reverence yourself.
PYTHAGORAS (C. 582–500 BC)

Self-reverence, self-knowledge, self-control. These three alone lead life to sovereign power.
ALFRED, LORD TENNYSON (1809–1892)

Living in the moment brings you a sense of reverence for all of life's blessings.
OPRAH WINFREY (1954–)

Revolution

The most radical revolutionary will become a conservative the day after the revolution.
HANNAH ARENDT (1906–1975)

Poverty is the parent of revolution and crime.
ARISTOTLE (384–322 BC)

Revolution begins with the self, in the self.
TONI CADE BAMBARA (1939–1995)

It is a revolution, and it can no more be checked by human effort … than a prairie fire by a gardener's watering pot.
JUDAH PHILIP BENJAMIN (1811–1884)

Revolution, n.: A bursting of the boilers which usually takes place when the safety valve of public discussion is closed.
AMBROSE BIERCE (1842–1914), *The Devil's Dictionary*

The Revolution is like Saturn—it eats its own children.
GEORG BUCHNER (1813–1837)

A revolution is an act of violence whereby one class shatters the authority of another.
JAMES MACGREGOR BURNS (1918–)

A revolution is a struggle to the death between the future and the past.
FIDEL CASTRO (1926–)

The revolution is a dictatorship of the exploited against the exploiters.
FIDEL CASTRO (1926–)

Every revolutionary idea seems to evoke three stages of reaction. They may be summed up by the phrases: 1.) It's completely impossible. 2.) It's possible, but it's not worth doing. 3.) I said it was a good idea all along.
ARTHUR C. CLARKE (1917–)

Revolution is a serious thing, the most serious thing about a revolutionary's life. When one commits oneself to the struggle, it must be for a lifetime.
ANGELA DAVIS (1944–)

I am a Conservative to preserve all that is good in our constitution, a Radical to remove all that is bad. I seek to preserve property and to respect order, and I equally decry the appeal to the passions of the many or the prejudices of the few.
BENJAMIN DISRAELI (1804–1881)

Normal life cannot sustain revolutionary attitudes for long.
MILOVAN DJILAS (1911–1995)

To be a revolutionary you have to be a human being. You have to care about people who have no power.
JANE FONDA (1937–)

You can kill a revolutionary but you can never kill the revolution.
FRED HAMPTON (1948–1969)

Indignation boils my blood at the thought of the heritage we are throwing away; at the thought that, with few exceptions, the fight for freedom is left to the poor, forlorn and defenseless, and to the few radicals and revolutionaries who would make use of liberty to destroy, rather than to maintain, American institutions.
ARTHUR GARFIELD HAYS (1881–1954)

A modern revolutionary group heads for the television station.
ABBIE HOFFMAN (1936–1989)

The first duty of a revolutionary is to get away with it.
ABBIE HOFFMAN (1936–1989)

Every revolution evaporates and leaves behind only the slime of a new bureaucracy.
FRANZ KAFKA (1883–1924)

Those who make peaceful revolution impossible will make violent revolution inevitable.
JOHN F. KENNEDY (1917–1963)

Revolution is not a onetime event.
AUDRE LORDE (1934–1992)

A revolution is an idea which has found its bayonets.
NAPOLÉON I (1769–1821)

Any revolution has to start with the transformation of the individual, otherwise individuals are corrupted by the power they get if their revolution succeeds.
WES NISKER (1942—)

Repression will provoke rebellion.
HUGH WILLIAMSON (1735–1819)

The seed of revolution is repression.
WOODROW WILSON (1856–1924)

Reward

[I] learned that hard work in stable surroundings could yield rewards, even if only in infinitesimally small increments.
SIDNEY ALTMAN (1939–)

Dogs and philosophers do the greatest good and get the fewest rewards.
DIOGENES LAERTIUS (C. 200)

If people are good only because they fear punishment, and hope for reward, then we are a sorry lot indeed.
ALBERT EINSTEIN (1879–1955)

The reward of a thing well done is to have done it.
RALPH WALDO EMERSON (1803–1882), *The Conduct of Life*

The rewards for those who persevere far exceed the pain that must precede the victory.
TED W. ENGSTROM (1916–2006)

There are no rewards or punishments—only consequences.
WILLIAM RALPH INGE (1860–1954)

Believe me, the reward is not so great without the struggle.
WILMA RUDOLPH (1940–1994)

The rewards of virtue alone abide secure.
SOPHOCLES (496–406 BC)

Men are rewarded or punished not for what they do but for how their acts are defined. That is why men are more interested in better justifying themselves than in better behaving themselves.
THOMAS S. SZASZ (1920–)

Rewards and punishments are the lowest form of education.
ZHUANG ZI (369–286 BC)

Rhetoric

It is not empty rhetoric to talk of the Free World.
BARBARA AMIEL (1940–)

Rhetoric is cheap, evidence comes more dearly.
JOHN FUND (1957–)

Rhetoric and dialectics can't change what I have learned from observation and experience.
PAUL GETTY (1932–2003)

Rhetoric is the art of ruling the minds of men.
PLATO (C. 428–348 BC)

Rhetoric is a poor substitute for action, and we have trusted only to rhetoric. If we are really to be a great nation, we must not merely talk; we must act big.
THEODORE ROOSEVELT (1858–1919)

Rhythm

Well, I think writing is basically about time and rhythm. Like with jazz. You have your basic melody and then you just riff off of it. And the riffs are about timing.
KATHY ACKER (1947–1997)

A scene has to have a rhythm of its own, a structure of its own.
MICHELANGELO ANTONIONI (1912–2007)

Life is about rhythm. We vibrate, our hearts are pumping blood, we are a rhythm machine, that's what we are.
MICKEY HART (1943–)

The best way to express rhythm is music.
JOHN HARTFORD (1937–2001)

Sometimes I just hit the keyboard in a way I'd like the rhythm of the tracks to sound.
RICHARD D. JAMES (1971–)

Jazz is rhythm and meaning.
HENRI MATISSE (1869–1954)

The mathematics of rhythm are universal. They don't belong to any particular culture.
JOHN MCLAUGHLIN (1942–)

To me, rhythm and what you do with it is everything. Right after rhythm is melody.
PAT METHENY (1954–)

Rhythm is something you either have or don't have, but when you have it, you have it all over.
ELVIS PRESLEY (1935–1977)

Rhythm and sounds are born with syllables.
JEAN-PHILIPPE RAMEAU (1683–1764)

[R]hythm is 90 percent of the interpretation.
RUGGIERO RICCI (1918–)

Rhythm is the basis of life, not steady forward progress. The forces of creation, destruction, and preservation have a whirling, dynamic interaction.
THE KABBALAH

Rich and Poor

Politics is the gentle art of getting votes from the poor and campaign funds from the rich by promising to protect each from the other.
OSCAR AMERINGER (1870–1943)

It is better to be rich and healthy than poor and sick.
DAVE BARRY (1947–)

No man can tell whether he is rich or poor by turning to his ledger. It is the heart that makes a man rich. He is rich or poor according to what he is, not according to what he has.
HENRY WARD BEECHER (1813–1887)

They say it is better to be poor and happy than rich and miserable, but how about a compromise like moderately rich and just moody?
PRINCESS DIANA (1961–1997)

The petty economies of the rich are just as amazing as the silly extravagances of the poor.
WILLIAM FEATHER (1908–1976)

The law, in its majestic equality, forbids the rich as well as the poor to sleep under bridges, to beg in the streets, and to steal bread.
ANATOLE FRANCE (1844–1924)

Let him who expects one class of society to prosper into highest degree, while the other is in distress, try whether one side of his face can smile while the other is pinched. Try whether.
THOMAS FULLER (1608–1661)

I believe, and I say it is true Democratic feeling, that all the measures of the government are directed to the purpose of making the rich richer and the poor poorer.
WILLIAM HENRY HARRISON (1773–1841)

It is not the rich man you should properly call happy, but him who knows how to use with wisdom the blessings of the gods, to endure hard poverty, and who fears dishonor worse than death, and is not afraid to die for cherished friends or fatherland.
HORACE (65–8 BC), *Odes*

Over and above that we let them get rich on our sweat and blood, while we remain poor and they suck the marrow from our bones.
MARTIN LUTHER (1483–1546)

Education … beyond all other devices of human origin, is a great equalizer of conditions of men—the balance wheel of the social machinery…. It does better than to disarm the poor of their hostility toward the rich; it prevents being poor.
HORACE MANN (1796–1859)

You may send poetry to the rich; to poor men give substantial presents.
MARCUS AURELIUS ANTONINUS (121–180)

The rich will do anything for the poor but get off their backs.
KARL MARX (1818–1883)

Of all the preposterous assumptions of humanity over humanity, nothing exceeds most of the criticisms made on the habits of the poor by the well-housed, well-warmed, and well-fed.
HERMAN MELVILLE (1819–1891)

The forces in a capitalist society, if left unchecked, tend to make the rich richer and the poor poorer.
JAWAHARLAL NEHRU (1889–1964)

When the rich wage war it's the poor who die.
JEAN-PAUL SARTRE (1905–1980), *The Devil and the Good Lord*

Rich gifts wax poor when givers prove unkind.
WILLIAM SHAKESPEARE (1564–1616), *Hamlet*

Gambling promises the poor what property performs for the rich—something for nothing.
GEORGE BERNARD SHAW (1856–1950)

What is the matter with the poor is poverty; what is the matter with the rich is uselessness.
GEORGE BERNARD SHAW (1856–1950)

A miser grows rich by seeming poor; an extravagant man grows poor by seeming rich.
WILLIAM SHENSTONE (1714–1763)

The observances of the church concerning feasts and fasts are tolerably well-kept, since the rich keep the feasts and the poor keep the fasts.
SYDNEY SMITH (1771–1845)

Mankind is divided into rich and poor, into property owners and exploited. To abstract oneself from this fundamental division and from the antagonism between poor and rich means abstracting oneself from fundamental facts.
JOSEPH STALIN (1879–1953)

The best thing a man can do for his culture when he is rich is to endeavor to carry out those schemes which he entertained when he was poor.
HENRY DAVID THOREAU (1817–1862)

If all men were rich, all men would be poor.
MARK TWAIN (1835–1910)

Extravagance is the luxury of the poor; penury is the luxury of the rich.
OSCAR WILDE (1854–1900)

Unless one is wealthy there is no use in being a charming fellow. Romance is the privilege of the rich, not the profession of the unemployed. The poor should be practical and prosaic. It is better to have a permanent income than to be fascinating.
OSCAR WILDE (1854–1900)

Fools live poor to die rich.
ANONYMOUS

It is better to be poor and live long than rich and die young.
ANONYMOUS

Wishing does not make a poor man rich.
ARABIAN PROVERB

It is harder to be poor without complaining than to be rich without boasting.
CHINESE PROVERB

Poor men take to the sea; the rich to the mountains.
IRISH PROVERB

If the rich could hire the poor to die for them, the poor would make a very nice living.
JEWISH PROVERB

Riches

Riches are a good handmaid, but the worst mistress.
SIR FRANCIS BACON (1561–1626)

A man's true state of power and riches is to be in himself.
HENRY WARD BEECHER (1813–1887)

Riches are not an end of life, but an instrument of life.
HENRY WARD BEECHER (1813–1887)

Riches without law are more dangerous than is poverty without law.
HENRY WARD BEECHER (1813–1887)

Since all the riches of this world
May be gifts from the Devil and earthly kings,
I should suspect that I worshipp'd the Devil
If I thank'd my God for worldly things.
WILLIAM BLAKE (1757–1827)

Great abundance of riches cannot be gathered and kept by any man without sin.
DESIDERIUS ERASMUS (1469–1536)

I care for riches, to make gifts
To friends, or lead a sick man back to health
With ease and plenty. Else small aid is wealth
For daily gladness; once a man be done
With hunger, rich and poor are all as one.
EURIPIDES (C. 480–406 BC), *Electra*

He who multiplies riches multiplies cares.
BENJAMIN FRANKLIN (1706–1790)

He is not fit for riches who is afraid to use them.
THOMAS FULLER (1608–1661)

Riches have made more covetous men than covetousness hath made rich men.
THOMAS FULLER (1608–1661)

I have no riches but my thoughts, yet these are wealth enough for me.
SARAH J. HALE (1788–1879)

The real "haves" are they who can acquire freedom, self-confidence, and even riches without depriving others of them.
ERIC HOFFER (1902–1983)

A propensity to hope and joy is real riches; one to fear and sorrow real poverty.
DAVID HUME (1711–1776)

To have what we want is riches; but to be able to do without is power.
GEORGE MACDONALD (1824–1905)

Worldly riches are like nuts; many a tooth is broke in cracking them, but never is the stomach filled with eating them.
RABBI NACHMAN (1772–1810)

We may see the small value God has for riches by the people He gives them to.
ALEXANDER POPE (1688–1744)

Sleep, riches, and health, to be truly enjoyed, must be interrupted.
JEAN PAUL RICHTER (1763–1825)

A good name is rather to be chosen than riches.
KING SOLOMON (C. 1000–929 BC)

The desire of knowledge, like the thirst for riches, increases ever with the acquisition of it.
LAURENCE STERNE (1713–1768)

Nothing is so hard for those who abound in riches to conceive how others can be in want.
JONATHAN SWIFT (1667–1745)

Ordinary riches can be stolen: real riches cannot. In your soul are infinitely precious things that cannot be taken from you.
OSCAR WILDE (1854–1900)

Moreover, when God gives people wealth and possessions, and the ability to enjoy them, to accept their lot and be happy in their toil—this is a gift of God.
THE BIBLE, Ecclesiastes 5:19

Children are poor men's riches.
ENGLISH PROVERB

Ridicule

Ridicule is generally made use of to laugh men out of virtue and good sense, by attacking everything praiseworthy in human life.
JOSEPH ADDISON (1672–1719)

Fashion, n.: A despot whom the wise ridicule and obey.
AMBROSE BIERCE (1842–1914), *The Devil's Dictionary*

Honest error is to be pitied, not ridiculed.
LORD CHESTERFIELD (1694–1773)

I prefer to be true to myself, even at the hazard of incurring the ridicule of others, rather than to be false, and to incur my own abhorrence.
FREDERICK DOUGLASS (1817–1895)

It is curious how there seems to be an instinctive disgust in Man for his nearest ancestors and relations. If only Darwin could conscientiously have traced man back to the Elephant or the Lion or the Antelope, how much ridicule and prejudice would have been spared to the doctrine of Evolution.
HENRY HAVELOCK ELLIS (1859–1939)

Ridicule has always been the enemy of enthusiasm, and the only worthy opponent to ridicule is success.
OLIVER GOLDSMITH (1730–1774)

We grow tired of everything but turning others into ridicule, and congratulating ourselves on their defects.
WILLIAM HAZLITT (1778–1830)

Society is a republic. When [individuals try] to lift themselves above others, they are dragged down by the mass, either by ridicule or slander.
VICTOR HUGO (1802–1885)

Ridicule is a kind of gangrene, which if it seizes one part of a character corrupts all the rest.
SAMUEL JOHNSON (1709–1784)

Mysticism and exaggeration go together. A mystic must not fear ridicule if he is to push all the way to the limits of humility or the limits of delight.
MILAN KUNDERA (1929–)

I know that there are things that never have been funny, and never will be. And I know that ridicule may be a shield, but it is not a weapon.
DOROTHY PARKER (1893–1967)

Every nation ridicules other nations—and all are right.
ARTHUR SCHOPENHAUER (1788–1860)

Ridicule often checks what is absurd, and fully as often smothers that which is noble.
SIR WALTER SCOTT (1771–1832)

No God and no religion can survive ridicule. No political church, no nobility, no royalty or other fraud, can face ridicule in a fair field, and live.
MARK TWAIN (1835–1910)

I avoid talking before the youth of the age as I would dancing before them: for if one's tongue doesn't move in the steps of the day, and thinks to please by its old graces, it is only an object of ridicule.
HORACE WALPOLE (1717–1797)

Reason is the test of ridicule, not ridicule the test of truth.
WILLIAM WARBURTON (1698–1779)

Right

Perhaps it is better to be irresponsible and right, than to be responsible and wrong.
SIR WINSTON CHURCHILL (1874–1965)

No amount of experimentation can ever prove me right; a single experiment can prove me wrong.
ALBERT EINSTEIN (1879–1955)

Success is the sole earthly judge of right and wrong.
ADOLF HITLER (1889–1945)

It often requires more courage to dare to do right than to fear to do wrong.
ABRAHAM LINCOLN (1809–1865)

Right is right, even if everyone is against it; and wrong is wrong, even if everyone is for it.
WILLIAM PENN (1644–1718)

A child becomes an adult when he realizes that he has a right not only to be right but also to be wrong.
THOMAS S. SZASZ (1920–)

The fact that man knows right from wrong proves his intellectual superiority to other creatures; but the fact that he can do wrong proves his moral inferiority to any creature that cannot.
MARK TWAIN (1835–1910)

The proper office of a friend is to side with you when you are wrong. Nearly anybody will side with you when you are right.
MARK TWAIN (1835–1910)

It is dangerous to be right when the government is wrong.
VOLTAIRE (1694–1778)

Two wrongs do not make a right.
ENGLISH PROVERB

Rights

Men, their rights, and nothing more; women, their rights, and nothing less.
SUSAN B. ANTHONY (1820–1906)

Privilege is the greatest enemy of right.
MARIE VON EBNER-ESCHENBACH (1830–1916)

The strength of the Constitution lies entirely in the determination of each citizen to defend it. Only if every single citizen feels duty bound to do his share in this defense are the constitutional rights secure.
ALBERT EINSTEIN (1879–1955)

Safeguarding the rights of others is the most noble and beautiful end of a human being.
KAHLIL GIBRAN (1883–1931)

The rights that we have under the Constitution [cover] anything we want to do, as long as it's not harmful. I can't see any way in the world that being a gay can cause damage to somebody else.
BARRY GOLDWATER (1909–1998)

Freedom from fear could be said to sum up the whole philosophy of human rights.
DAG HAMMARSKJÖLD (1905–1961)

Men have as exaggerated an idea of their rights as women have of their wrongs.
EDGAR WATSON HOWE (1853–1937)

All, too, will bear in mind this sacred principle, that though the will of the majority is in all cases to prevail, that will, to be rightful, must be reasonable; that the minority possess their equal rights, which equal laws must protect, and to violate would be oppression.
THOMAS JEFFERSON (1762–1826)

What is true of every member of the society, individually, is true of them all collectively; since the rights of the whole can be no more than the sum of the rights of the individuals.
THOMAS JEFFERSON (1762–1826)

Among individuals as among nations, the respect to other people's rights is peace.
BENITO JUÁREZ (1806–1972)

The ultimate tragedy is not the oppression and cruelty by the bad people but the silence over that by the good people.
MARTIN LUTHER KING JR. (1929–1968)

I believe that every individual is naturally entitled to do as he pleases with himself and the fruits of his labor, so far as it in no way interferes with any other men's rights.
ABRAHAM LINCOLN (1809–1865)

In Republics, the great danger is, that the majority may not sufficiently respect the rights of the minority.
JAMES MADISON (1751–1836)

A man will fight harder for his interests than for his rights.
NAPOLÉON I (1769–1821)

I never doubted that equal rights was the right direction. Most reforms, most problems are complicated. But to me there is nothing complicated about ordinary equality.
ALICE PAUL (1885–1977)

The battle for women's rights has largely been won.
MARGARET THATCHER (1925–)

Risk

It seems to me that people have vast potential. Most people can do extraordinary things if they have the confidence or take the risks. Yet most people don't. They sit in front of the telly and treat life as if it goes on forever.
PHILIP ADAMS (1939–)

He who is not courageous enough to take risks will accomplish nothing in life.
MUHAMMED ALI (1942–)

In order for people to be happy, sometimes they have to take risks. It's true these risks can put them in danger of being hurt.
MEG CABOT (1967–), *The Boy Next Door*

I don't think about risks much. I just do what I want to do. If you gotta go, you gotta go.
LILLIAN CARTER (1898–1983)

To win without risk is to triumph without glory.
PIERRE CORNEILLE (1606–1684), *The Cid*

Only those who will risk going too far can possibly find out how far one can go.
T. S. ELIOT (1888–1965)

Security is not the meaning of my life. Great opportunities are worth the risk.
SHIRLEY HUFSTEDLER (1925–)

The universe will reward you for taking risks on its behalf.
SHAKTI GAWAIN (1948–)

Great deeds are usually wrought at great risks.
HERODOTUS (484–430 BC), *The Histories of Herodotus*

If you don't risk anything, you risk even more.
ERICA JONG (1942–)

There are risks and costs to a program of action. But they are far less than the long-range risks and costs of comfortable inaction.
JOHN F. KENNEDY (1917–1963)

Any time you take a chance you better be sure the rewards are worth the risk because they can put you away just as fast for a ten dollar heist as they can for a million dollar job.
STANLEY KUBRICK (1928–1999)

Risk! Risk anything! Care no more for the opinions of others, for those voices. Do the hardest thing on earth for you. Act for yourself. Face the truth.
KATHERINE MANSFIELD (1888–1923)

First weigh the considerations, then take the risks.
HELMUTH VON MOLTKE (1800–1891)

The policy of being too cautious is the greatest risk of all.
JAWAHARLAL NEHRU (1889–1964)

And the day came when the risk to remain tight in a bud was more painful than the risk it took to blossom.
ANAÏS NIN (1903–1977)

Take calculated risks. That is quite different from being rash.
GEORGE S. PATTON (1885–1945)

One hour of life, crowded to the full with glorious action, and filled with noble risks, is worth whole years of those mean observances of paltry decorum.
SIR WALTER SCOTT (1771–1832)

Life is a risk.
DIANE VON FURSTENBERG (1945–)

What you risk reveals what you value.
JEANETTE WINTERSON (1959–)

Rivalry

The essence of a free government consists in an effectual control of rivalries.
JOHN ADAMS (1735–1826)

However fragmented the world, however intense the national rivalries, it is an inexorable fact that we become more interdependent every day.
JACQUES COUSTEAU (1910–1997)

Such seems to be the disposition of man, that whatever makes a distinction produces rivalry.
SAMUEL JOHNSON (1709–1784)

Sometimes the worst rivalries, in private life as well as in communal life, are precisely the conflict between two victims of the same oppressor.
AMOS OZ (1939–)

The ruling classes today nourish the conviction that national hatreds and rivalries are inevitable.
CHARLES E. TREVELYAN (1807–1886)

Rivers

The deepest rivers make least din,
The silent soul doth most abound in care.
WILLIAM ALEXANDER (1915–1997)

You could not step twice into the same rivers; for other waters are ever flowing on to you.
HERACLITUS (C. 535–475 BC)

In rivers and bad governments, the lightest things swim at the top.
BENJAMIN FRANKLIN (1706–1790)

Never give up; for even rivers someday wash dams away.
ARTHUR GOLDEN (1956–)

In rivers, the water that you touch is the last of what has passed and the first of that which comes; so with present time.
LEONARDO DA VINCI (1452–1519)

Ideas, like large rivers, never have just one source.
WILLY LEY (1906–1969)

All the rivers run into the sea; yet the sea is not full.
KING SOLOMON (C. 1000–929 BC)

It is with rivers as it is with people: the greatest are not always the most agreeable nor the best to live with.
HENRY VAN DYKE (1852–1933)

Roads

Philosophy, n.: A route of many roads leading from nowhere to nothing.
AMBROSE BIERCE (1842–1914), *The Devil's Dictionary*

Many roads lead to the Path, but basically there are only two: reason and practice.
BODHIDHARMA (470–543)

Two roads diverged in a wood, and I—
I took the one less traveled by,
And that has made all the difference.
ROBERT FROST (1874–1963), "The Road Not Taken"

All roads lead to Rome.
ANCIENT ROMAN PROVERB

There are many roads to hate, but envy is the shortest of them all.
ANONYMOUS

Rogues

For every inch that is not fool is rogue.
JOHN DRYDEN (1631–1700)

As there is a use in medicine for poisons, so the world cannot move without rogues.
RALPH WALDO EMERSON (1803–1882)

There is no den in the wide world to hide a rogue. Commit a crime and the earth is made of glass. Commit a crime, and it seems as if a coat of snow fell on the ground, such as reveals in the woods the track of every partridge, and fox, and squirrel.
RALPH WALDO EMERSON (1803–1882)

Commend a fool for his wit, or a rogue for his honesty and he will receive you into his favor.
HENRY FIELDING (1707–1754)

No one likes a fellow who is all rogue, but we'll forgive him almost anything if there is warmth of human sympathy underneath his rogueries. The immortal types of comedy are just such men.
W. C. FIELDS (1880–1946)

A rich rogue nowadays is fit company for any gentleman; and the world, my dear, hath not such a contempt for roguery as you imagine.
JOHN GAY (1685–1732)

The political arena leaves one no alternative, one must either be a dunce or a rogue.
EMMA GOLDMAN (1869–1940)

We do not wish to lose life; we do wish to gain glory, and this makes brave men show more tact and address in avoiding death, than rogues show in preserving their fortunes.
FRANÇOIS DE LA ROCHEFOUCAULD (1613–1680)

What is commonly called friendship is only a little more honor among rogues.
HENRY DAVID THOREAU (1817–1862)

O what fine thought we had because we thought that the worst rogues and rascals had died out.
WILLIAM BUTLER YEATS (1865–1939)

Roots

There are two lasting bequests we can give our children. One is roots. The other is wings.
HODDING CARTER JR. (1907–1972)

Love is like a tree, it grows of its own accord, it puts down deep roots into our whole being.
VICTOR HUGO (1802–1885), *Notre-Dame de Paris*

The roots of true achievement lie in the will to become the best that you can become.
HAROLD TAYLOR (1914–1993)

Roses

God gave us memory so that we might have roses in December.
JAMES M. BARRIE (1860–1937)

All of us tend to put off living. We are all dreaming of some magical rose garden over the horizon—instead of enjoying the roses that are blooming outside our windows today.
DALE CARNEGIE (1888–1955)

It matters not what goal you seek
Its secret here reposes:
You've got to dig from week to week
To get Results or Roses.
EDGAR GUEST (1881–1955)

You can complain because roses have thorns, or you can rejoice because thorns have roses.
TOM WILSON (1931–1978)

Ruin

What is a ruin but time easing itself of endurance?
DJUNA BARNES (1892–1982)

Resolved to ruin or to rule the state.
JOHN DRYDEN (1631–1700)

Truly, to tell lies is not honorable;
But when the truth entails tremendous ruin,

To speak dishonorably is pardonable.
SOPHOCLES (496–406 BC), *Creusa*

Reality continues to ruin my life.
BILL WATTERSON (1958–)

Rulers

Rulers do not reduce taxes to be kind. Expediency and greed create high taxation, and normally it takes an impending catastrophe to bring it down.
CHARLES ADAMS (1930–)

The object of government in peace and in war is not the glory of rulers or of races, but the happiness of the common man.
LORD WILLIAM BEVERIDGE (1879–1963)

History, n.: An account mostly false, of events unimportant, which are brought about by rulers mostly knaves, and soldiers mostly fools.
AMBROSE BIERCE (1842–1914), *The Devil's Dictionary*

Rulers who want to unleash war know very well that they must procure or invent a first victim.
ELIAS CANETTI (1905–1994)

What luck for rulers that men do not think.
ADOLF HITLER (1889–1945)

A multitude of rulers is not a good thing. Let there be one ruler, one king.
HOMER (800–700 BC), *The Iliad*

Dictators are rulers who always look good until the last ten minutes.
JAN MASARYK (1886–1948)

They [who] seek to establish systems of government based on the regimentation of all human beings by a handful of individual rulers … call this a new order. It is not new and it is not order.
FRANKLIN D. ROOSEVELT (1882–1945)

Rumors

Do not believe in anything simply because you have heard it. Do not believe in anything simply because it is spoken and rumored by many. Do not believe in anything simply because it is found written in your religious books. Do not believe in anything merely on the authority of your teachers and elders. Do not believe in traditions because they have been handed down for many generations. But after observation and analysis, when you find that anything agrees with reason and is conducive to the good and benefit of one and all, then accept it and live up to it.
THE BUDDHA (563–483 BC)

We must set up a strong present tense against all rumors of wrath, past and to come.
RALPH WALDO EMERSON (1803–1882)

Rumor: Weapons of mass hypnosis are found in the USA.
LOESJE (1983–), *Active and International Girl*

Rumor grows as it goes.
VIRGIL (C. 70–19 BC)

Rust

Sunday clears away the rust of the whole week.
JOSEPH ADDISON (1672–1719)

As iron is eaten by rust, so are the envious consumed by envy.
ANTISTHENES (444–371 BC)

If you rest, you rust.
HELEN HAYES (1900–1993)

It is better to rust out than wear out.
EDWIN MARKHAM (1852–1940)

The soul is made for action, and cannot rest till it be employed. Idleness is its rust. Unless it will up and think and taste and see, all is in vain.
ROBERT TOWNSEND (1957–)

Sacrifice

In this life we get only those things for which we hunt, for which we strive, and for which we are willing to sacrifice.
GEORGE MATTHEW ADAMS (1878–1962)

Sacrifice still exists everywhere, and everywhere the elect of each generation suffers for the salvation of the rest.
HENRI-FRÉDÉRIC AMIEL (1821–1881)

Sacrifice is nothing other than the production of sacred things.
GEORGES BATAILLE (1897–1962)

In this world it is not what we take up, but what we give up, that makes us rich.
HENRY WARD BEECHER (1813–1887)

For you to be successful, sacrifices must be made. It's better that they are made by others, but failing that, you'll have to make them yourself.
RITA MAE BROWN (1944–)

They never fail who die in a great cause.
LORD BYRON (1788–1824)

The important thing is this: to be able at any moment to sacrifice what we are for what we could become.
CHARLES DU BOS (1882–1939)

The mice which helplessly find themselves between the cat's teeth acquire no merit from their enforced sacrifice.
MAHATMA GANDHI (1869–1948)

The stern hand of fate has scourged us to an elevation where we can see the great everlasting things which matter for a nation—the great peaks we had forgotten, of Honor, Duty, Patriotism, and clad in glittering white, the great pinnacle of Sacrifice pointing like a rugged finger to Heaven.
DAVID LLOYD GEORGE (1863–1945)

Great achievement is usually born of great sacrifice, and is never the result of selfishness.
NAPOLEON HILL (1883–1970)

The remarkable thing is that we really love our neighbor as ourselves: we do unto others as we do unto ourselves. We hate others when we hate ourselves. We are tolerant toward others when we tolerate ourselves. We forgive others when we forgive ourselves. We are prone to sacrifice others when we are ready to sacrifice ourselves.
ERIC HOFFER (1902–1983)

There's only one effectively redemptive sacrifice, the sacrifice of self–will to make room for the knowledge of God.
ALDOUS HUXLEY (1894–1963)

Don't sacrifice your political convictions for the convenience of the hour.
EDWARD M. KENNEDY (1932–)

If anyone is crazy enough to want to kill a president of the United States, he can do it. All he must be prepared to do is give his life for the president's.
JOHN F. KENNEDY (1917–1963)

A woman can forgive a man for the harm he does her … but she can never forgive him for the sacrifices he makes on her account.
W. SOMERSET MAUGHAM (1874–1965), *The Moon and Sixpence*

In olden times, sacrifices were made at the altar, a practice which is still very much practiced.
HELEN ROWLAND (1875–1950)

Only he can understand what a farm is, what a country is, who shall have sacrificed part of himself to his farm or country, fought to save it, struggled to make it beautiful. Only then will the love of farm or country fill his heart.
ANTOINE DE SAINT–EXUPÉRY (1900–1944)

Nothing so much enhances a good as to make sacrifices for it.
GEORGE SANTAYANA (1863–1952)

It is a clear gain to sacrifice pleasure in order to avoid pain.
ARTHUR SCHOPENHAUER (1788–1860)

Humanitarianism consists in never sacrificing a human being to a purpose.
DR. ALBERT SCHWEITZER (1875–1965)

Self-development is a higher duty than self-sacrifice.
ELIZABETH CADY STANTON (1815–1902)

Sadness

Sadness is also a kind of defense.
IVO ANDRIC (1892–1975)

When sadness happens in the middle of work, I separate my personal grief from my train of thought.
SERGIO ARAGONES (1913–)

Melancholy is sadness that has taken on lightness.
ITALO CALVINO (1923–1985)

The sadness of our existence should not leave us blunted, on the contrary—how to remain thin-skinned, vulnerable and stay alive?
MONTGOMERY CLIFT (1920–1966)

We ask God to forgive us for our evil thoughts and evil temper, but rarely, if ever, ask Him to forgive us for our sadness.
R. W. DALE (1829–1895)

Sadness does not inhere in things; it does not reach us from the world and through mere contemplation of the world. It is a product of our own thought. We create it out of whole cloth.
ÉMILE DURKHEIM (1858–1917)

All pleasures contain an element of sadness.
JONATHAN EIBESCHUTZ (1690–1764)

We all have sadness in our life and things that we can draw upon.
SHERILYN FENN (1965–)

Lord, make me an instrument of Your peace!
Where there is hatred let me sow love;
Where there is injury, pardon;
Where there is doubt, faith;
Where there is despair, hope;
Where there is darkness, light;
Where there is sadness, joy.
SAINT FRANCIS OF ASSISI (1181–1226)

An ounce of cheerfulness is worth a pound of sadness to serve God with.
THOMAS FULLER (1608–1661)

Sadness is but a wall between two gardens.
KAHLIL GIBRAN (1883–1931)

Melancholy is the pleasure of being sad.
VICTOR HUGO (1802–1885)

Even a happy life cannot be without a measure of darkness, and the word happy would lose its meaning if it were not balanced by sadness. It is far better to take things as they come along with patience and equanimity.
CARL JUNG (1875–1961)

Sadness flies away on the wings of time.
JEAN DE LA FONTAINE (1621–1695)

Melancholy and sadness are the start of doubt … doubt is the beginning of despair; despair is the cruel beginning of the differing degrees of wickedness.
ISIDORE DUCASSE LAUTREAMONT (1846–1870)

The greatness comes not when things go always good for you. But the greatness comes when you're really tested, when you take some knocks, some disappointments, when sadness comes. Because only if you've been in the deepest valley can you ever know how magnificent it is to be on the highest mountain.
RICHARD M. NIXON (1913–1994)

Half of the secular unrest and dismal, profane sadness of modern society comes from the vain ideas that every man is bound to be a critic for life.
HENRY VAN DYKE (1852–1933)

Safety

Obedience is the mother of success and is wedded to safety.
AESCHYLUS (C. 525–456 BC)

The superior man, when resting in safety, does not forget that danger may come. When in a state of security he does not forget the possibility of ruin. When all is orderly, he does not forget that disorder may come. Thus his person is not endangered, and his States and all their clans are preserved.
CONFUCIUS (551–479 BC)

There is no right to strike against the public safety by anybody, anywhere, any time.
CALVIN COOLIDGE (1872–1933)

Safety is something that happens between your ears, not something you hold in your hands.
JEFF COOPER (1920–2006)

Where duty is plain, delay is both foolish and hazardous; where it is not, delay may provide both wisdom and safety.
TYRON EDWARDS (1809–1894)

Those who would give up essential liberty to purchase a little temporary safety deserve neither liberty nor safety.
BENJAMIN FRANKLIN (1706–1790), *Historical Review of Pennsylvania*

The free expression of the hopes and aspirations of a people is the greatest and only safety in a sane society.
EMMA GOLDMAN (1869–1940), *Living My Life*

Through danger safety comes—through trouble rest.
JOHN MARSTON (1576–1634)

You will either step forward into growth or you will step back into safety.
ABRAHAM MASLOW (1908–1970)

War is an ugly thing, but not the ugliest of things. The decayed and degraded state of moral and patriotic feeling which thinks that nothing is worth war is much worse. The person who has nothing for which he is willing to fight, nothing which is more important than his own personal safety, is a miserable creature and has no chance of being free unless made and kept so by the exertions of better men than himself.
JOHN STUART MILL (1806–1873)

As if there were safety in stupidity alone.
HENRY DAVID THOREAU (1817–1862)

There is no safety in numbers, or in anything else.
JAMES THURBER (1894–1961)

Many that live deserve death. And some die that deserve life. Can you give it to them? Then be not too eager to deal out death in the name of justice, fearing for your own safety. Even the wise cannot see all ends.
J. R. R. TOLKIEN (1892–1973), *The Lord of the Rings*

Confidence cannot find a place wherein to rest in safety.
VIRGIL (C. 70–19 BC)

For lack of guidance a nation falls, but victory is won through many advisers.
THE BIBLE, Proverbs 11:14

Saints

Knee-jerk liberals and all the certified saints of sanctified humanism are quick to condemn this great and much-maligned Transylvanian statesman.
WILLIAM F. BUCKLEY JR. (1925–), *The Wit and Wisdom of Vlad the Impaler*

Colleges hate geniuses, just as convents hate saints.
RALPH WALDO EMERSON (1803–1882)

I'd rather laugh with the sinners than cry with the
saints,
Sinners are much more fun.
BILLY JOEL (1949–), "Only the Good Die Young"

Next to theology I give to music the highest place and honor. And we see how David and all the saints have wrought their godly thoughts into verse, rhyme, and song.
MARTIN LUTHER (1483–1546)

The history of saints is mainly the history of insane people.
BENITO MUSSOLINI (1883–1945)

Saints should always be judged guilty until they are proved innocent.
GEORGE ORWELL (1903–1950)

There are but few saints amongst scientists, as among other men, but truth itself is a goal comparable with sanctity.
GEORGE SARTON (1884–1956), *History of Science*

That the saints may enjoy their beatitude and the grace of God more abundantly, they are permitted to see the punishment of the damned in hell.
SAINT THOMAS AQUINAS (1225–1274)

Saints need sinners.
ALAN W. WATTS (1915–1973)

Salesmen

No salesman can ever guarantee you a grant from any government or non-profit organization.
MATTHEW LESKO (1943–)

Sales are contingent upon the attitude of the salesman—not the attitude of the prospect.
W. CLEMENT STONE (1902–2002)

The salesman knows nothing of what he is selling save that he is charging a great deal too much for it.
OSCAR WILDE (1854–1900)

Salvation

Work out your own salvation. Do not depend on others.
THE BUDDHA (563–483 BC)

God preordained, for his own glory and the display of His attributes of mercy and justice, a part of the human race, without any merit of their own, to eternal salvation, and another part, in just punishment of their sin, to eternal damnation.
JOHN CALVIN (1509–1564)

Acquire inner peace and a multitude will find their salvation near you.
CATHERINE DE HUECK DOHERTY (1896–1985)

I grasped the meaning of the greatest secret that human poetry and human thought and belief have to impart: The salvation of man is through love and in love.
VIKTOR FRANKL (1905–1997), *Man's Search for Meaning*

Every year, if not every day, we have to wager our salvation upon some prophecy based upon imperfect knowledge.
OLIVER WENDELL HOLMES JR. (1841–1935)

Human salvation lies in the hands of the creatively maladjusted.
MARTIN LUTHER KING JR. (1929–1968)

There is no salvation in becoming adapted to a world which is crazy.
HENRY MILLER (1891–1980), *The Colossus of Maroussi*

Three things are necessary for the salvation of man: to know what he ought to believe; to know what he ought to desire; and to know what he ought to do.
SAINT THOMAS AQUINAS (1225–1274), *Two Precepts of Charity*

An idea is salvation by imagination.
FRANK LLOYD WRIGHT (1869–1959)

Sanity

I don't really trust a sane person.
LYLE ALZADO (1949–1992)

The statistics on sanity are that one out of every four Americans is suffering from some form of

mental illness. Think of your three best friends. If they're okay, then it's you.
RITA MAE BROWN (1944–)

Ordinarily he was insane, but he had lucid moments when he was merely stupid.
HEINRICH HEINE (1797–1856)

When dealing with the insane, the best method is to pretend to be sane.
HERMANN HESSE (1877–1962)

It is no measure of health to be well adjusted to a profoundly sick society.
JIDDU KRISHNAMURTI (1895–1986)

In a mad world only the mad are sane.
AKIRA KUROSAWA (1910–1998)

All sanity depends on this: that it should be a delight to feel heat strike the skin, a delight to stand upright, knowing the bones are moving easily under the flesh.
DORIS LESSING (1919–)

Correct me if I'm wrong, but hasn't the fine line between sanity and madness gotten finer?
GEORGE PRICE (1870–1963)

Sanity calms, but madness is more interesting.
JOHN RUSSELL (1921–)

Sanity is a madness put to good uses.
GEORGE SANTAYANA (1863–1952)

Sarcasm

Neither irony or sarcasm is argument.
SAMUEL BUTLER (1835–1902)

Sarcasm I now see to be, in general, the language of the devil; for which reason I have long since as good as renounced it.
THOMAS CARLYLE (1795–1881)

Sarcasm: the last refuge of modest and chaste-souled people when the privacy of their soul is coarsely and intrusively invaded.
FYODOR DOSTOEVSKY (1821–1881)

Avoid sarcasm. Don't insist on the last word.
FORD FRICK (1894–1978)

A sarcastic person has a superiority complex that can be cured only by the honesty of humility.
LAWRENCE G. LOVASIK (1913–)

We are suffering from too much sarcasm.
MARIANNE MOORE (1887–1972)

Satan

Even Satan might get another chance.
PAT BUCKLEY (1952–)

We must remember that Satan has his miracles, too.
JOHN CALVIN (1509–1564)

God is the Creator; Satan is the counterfeiter.
EDWIN LOUIS COLE (1922–2002)

Satan trembles when he sees the weakest saints upon their knees.
WILLIAM COWPER (1731–1800)

Satan, really, is the romantic youth of Jesus re-appearing for a moment.
JAMES JOYCE (1882–1941)

The greatest trick the devil ever pulled was convincing the world he didn't exist.
CHRISTOPHER MCQUARRIE (1968–), *The Usual Suspects*

But Satan now is wiser than of yore,
And tempts by making rich, not making poor.
ALEXANDER POPE (1688–1744)

I do not fear Satan half so much as I fear those who fear him.
SAINT TERESA OF AVILA (1515–1582)

But who prays for Satan? Who, in eighteen centuries, has had the common humanity to pray

for the one sinner that needed it most?
MARK TWAIN (1835–1910)

For Satan always finds some mischief still for idle hands to do.
ISAAC WATTS (1674–1748)

The LORD said to Satan, "Where have you come from?" Satan answered the LORD, "From roaming through the earth and going back and forth in it."
THE BIBLE, Job 1:7

And if Satan opposes himself and is divided, he cannot stand; his end has come.
THE BIBLE, Mark 3:26

Jesus turned and said to Peter, "Get behind me, Satan! You are a stumbling block to me; you do not have in mind the concerns of God, but merely human concerns."
THE BIBLE, Matthew 16:23

The great dragon was hurled down—that ancient serpent called the devil, or Satan, who leads the whole world astray. He was hurled to the earth, and his angels with him.
THE BIBLE, Revelation 12:9

Satire

All satire is blind to the forces liberated by decay. Which is why total decay has absorbed the forces of satire.
THEODOR W. ADORNO (1913–1969)

Satire is tragedy plus time. You give it enough time, the public, the reviewers will allow you to satirize it. Which is rather ridiculous, when you think about it.
LENNY BRUCE (1925–1966)

Fools are my theme, let satire be my song.
LORD BYRON (1788–1824)

The purpose of satire has been rightly stated as to strip off the veneer of comforting illusion and cozy half-truth, and our job, as I see it, is to put it back again!
MICHAEL FLANDERS (1922 –1975)

Satirists gain the applause of others through fear, not through love.
WILLIAM HAZLITT (1778–1830)

Satire is traditionally the weapon of the powerless against the powerful.
MOLLY IVINS (1944–2002)

Satire is what closes on Saturday night.
GEORGE S. KAUFMAN (1889–1961)

It is said that truth comes from the mouths of fools and children: I wish every good mind which feels an inclination for satire would reflect that the finest satirist always has something of both in him.
GEORG C. LICHTENBERG (1742–1799)

Satire is a lesson, parody is a game.
VLADIMIR NABOKOV (1899–1977)

Praise undeserved, is satire in disguise.
ALEXANDER POPE (1688–1744)

Satire's my weapon, but I'm too discreet
To run amuck, and tilt at all I meet.
ALEXANDER POPE (1688–1744)

Satire is focused bitterness.
LEO ROSTEN (1908–1997)

Satire is a sort of glass, wherein beholders do generally discover everybody's face but their own.
JONATHAN SWIFT (1667–1745)

The satirist who writes nothing but satire should write but little or it will seem that his satire springs rather from his own caustic nature than from the sins of the world in which he lives.
ANTHONY TROLLOPE (1815–1882)

Satire lies about literary men while they live and eulogy lies about them when they die.
VOLTAIRE (1694–1778)

People say satire is dead. It's not dead; it's alive and living in the White House.
ROBIN WILLIAMS (1952–)

Tomorrow is a satire on today,
And shows its weakness.
EDWARD YOUNG (1683–1765)

Satisfaction

What we call happiness in the strictest sense comes from the (preferably sudden) satisfaction of needs, which have been dammed up to a high degree.
SIGMUND FREUD (1856–1939)

A complacent satisfaction with present knowledge is the chief bar to the pursuit of knowledge.
B. H. LIDDELL HART (1895–1970)

My attitude is never to be satisfied, never enough, never.
BÉLA KÁROLYI (1942–)

Curiosity killed the cat, but satisfaction brought it back.
EUGENE O'NEILL (1888–1953)

Your best shot at happiness, self-worth and personal satisfaction—the things that constitute real success—is not in earning as much as you can but in performing as well as you can something that you consider worthwhile.
WILLIAM RASPBERRY (1935–)

Saviors

If you were not a sinful, polluted, helpless, and miserable creature, this Savior would not be suited to you, and you would not be comprehended in his gracious invitations to the children of men.
ARCHIBALD ALEXANDER (1772–1851)

God may be a matter of indifference to the evolutionists, and a life beyond may have no charm for them, but the mass of mankind will continue to worship their creator and continue to find comfort in the promise of their Savior that he has gone to prepare a place for them.
WILLIAM JENNINGS BRYAN (1860–1925)

The great Savior has not his highest glory from his atoning and redeeming acts, but from the manifestation of his saving power.
ADAM CLARKE (1760–1832)

In each individual the spirit is made flesh, in each one the whole of creation suffers, in each one a Savior is crucified.
HERMANN HESSE (1877–1962)

The savior who wants to turn men into angels is as much a hater of human nature as the totalitarian despot who wants to turn them into puppets.
ERIC HOFFER (1902–1983)

Scandals

Mistakes, scandals, and failures no longer signal catastrophe. The crucial thing is that they be made credible, and that the public be made aware of the efforts being expended in that direction. The "marketing" immunity of governments is similar to that of the major brands of washing powder.
JEAN BAUDRILLARD (1929–2007)

The surest method against scandal is to live it down by perseverance in well doing.
HERMANN BOERHAAVE (1668–1738)

There is no scandal like rags, nor any crime so shameful as poverty.
GEORGE FARQUHAR (1678–1707)

Love and scandal are the best sweeteners of tea.
HENRY FIELDING (1707–1754)

Scandal begins when the police put a stop to it.
KARL KRAUS (1874–1936)

Scandal dies sooner of itself, than we could kill it.
BENJAMIN RUSH (1745–1813)

You talk about scandals and the Americans put theirs right in the store window for everyone to look at.
GORDON SINCLAIR (1900–1984)

Absent scandal, a federal judge can serve for decades on the bench, underscoring the importance of appointing judges who have a proper understanding of their constitutional role.
PAUL WEYRICH (1942–)

Sometimes voters will replace a political leader at the top just to make a point or because of scandals or whatever.
PAUL WEYRICH (1942–)

Scandal is gossip made tedious by morality.
OSCAR WILDE (1854–1900), *Lady Windermere's Fan*

Scholars

A mere scholar, a mere ass.
ROBERT BURTON (1577–1640)

The minute you try to talk business with him he takes the attitude that he is a gentleman and a scholar, and the moment you try to approach him on the level of his moral integrity he starts to talk business.
RAYMOND CHANDLER (1888–1959)

The greatest scholars are not usually the wisest people.
GEOFFREY CHAUCER (1343–1400)

I am an old scholar, better-looking now than when I was young. That's what sitting on your ass does to your face.
LEONARD COHEN (1934–)

Iron sharpens iron; scholar, the scholar.
SIR WILLIAM DRUMMOND (1585–1649)

I cannot forgive a scholar his homeless despondency.
RALPH WALDO EMERSON (1803–1882)

The land of scholars, and the nurse of arms.
OLIVER GOLDSMITH (1730–1774)

A scholar is like a book written in a dead language. It is not every one that can read in it.
WILLIAM HAZLITT (1778–1830)

The world's great men have not commonly been scholars, nor its great scholars great men.
OLIVER WENDELL HOLMES SR. (1809–1894)

Scholars will argue with each other about everything.
PETER JENNINGS (1938–2005)

A scholar who cherishes the love of comfort is not fit to be deemed a scholar.
LAO-TZU (C. 600 BC)

Much reading is an oppression of the mind, and extinguishes the natural candle, which is the reason of so many senseless scholars in the world.
WILLIAM PENN (1644–1718)

The scholars and poets of an earlier time can be read only with a dictionary to help.
CARL SANDBURG (1878–1967)

It is the unknown that excites the ardor of scholars, who, in the known alone, would shrivel up with boredom.
WALLACE STEVENS (1879–1955)

The success of great scholars and thinkers is commonly a courtier-like success, not kingly, not manly.
HENRY DAVID THOREAU (1817–1862)

The ink of the scholar and the blood of a martyr are of equal value in heaven.
THE KORAN

A nation's treasure is its scholars.
YIDDISH PROVERB

Schools

Mr. Speaker, less than 10 percent of our Nation's children walk or ride their bicycles to school, and too many schools continue to invite fast-food vendors into their cafeterias.
LOIS CAPPS (1938–)

Good schools underpin not only our economy, but the social fabric of our lives.
DONALD L. CARCIERI (1942–)

Schools are successful only insofar as they reduce the dependence of a child's opportunities upon his social origins.
JAMES S. COLEMAN (1926–)

Schools that are to cater for the whole population must offer courses that are as rich and varied as are the needs and abilities of the children who enter them.
PETER FRASER (1884–1950)

Schools in general are being asked to do an enormous number of things they never had to do, with a much more complex population than they ever had to do it with.
CLIFFORD GEERTZ (1926–2006)

Unhappiness in a child accumulates because he sees no end to the dark tunnel. The thirteen weeks of a term might just as well be thirteen years.
GRAHAM GREENE (1904–1991)

When schools flourish, all flourishes.
MARTIN LUTHER (1483–1546)

Public schools have not traditionally had a mission to train young people to go into technical, professional or academic careers. Public schools were instead mass institutions set up to get young people to read and write and perform various basic activities in the context of industrial employment.
MAJOR OWENS (1936–)

Let us reform our schools, and we shall find little reform needed in our prisons.
JOHN RUSKIN (1819–1900), *Unto This Last*

Science

[N]othing's wrong with science. You know, between air conditioning and the Pope, I'll take air conditioning.
WOODY ALLEN (1935–), *Deconstructing Harry*

The most exciting phrase to hear in science, the one that heralds new discoveries, is not "Eureka!" but "that's funny!"
ISAAC ASIMOV (1920–1992)

The important thing in science is not so much to obtain new facts as to discover new ways of thinking about them.
SIR WILLIAM BRAGG (1862–1942)

Science knows only one commandment—contribute to science.
BERTOLT BRECHT (1898–1956)

If scientific reasoning were limited to the logical processes of arithmetic, we should not get very far in our understanding of the physical world. One might as well attempt to grasp the game of poker entirely by the use of the mathematics of probability.
VANNEVAR BUSH (1890–1974)

Science, after all, is only an expression for our ignorance of our own ignorance.
SAMUEL BUTLER (1835–1902)

Science is but the exchange of ignorance for that which is another kind of ignorance.
LORD BYRON (1788–1824)

Science must have originated in the feeling that something was wrong.
THOMAS CARLYLE (1795–1881)

There are two kinds of truth; the truth that lights the way and the truth that warms the heart. The first of these is science, and the second is art. Without art science would be as useless as a pair of high forceps in the hands of a plumber. Without science art would become a crude mess of folklore and emotional quackery.
RAYMOND CHANDLER (1888–1959)

Science in the modern world has many uses; its chief use, however, is to provide long words to cover the errors of the rich.
G. K. CHESTERTON (1874–1936)

The ordinary scientific man is strictly a sentimentalist. He is a sentimentalist in this essential sense, that he is soaked and swept away by mere associations.
G. K. CHESTERTON (1874–1936)

As soon as questions of will or decision or reason or choice of action arise, human science is at a loss.
NOAM CHOMSKY (1928–)

When a distinguished but elderly scientist states that something is possible, he is almost certainly right. When he states that something is impossible, he is very probably wrong.
ARTHUR C. CLARKE (1917–)

I am among those who think that science has great beauty. A scientist in his laboratory is not only a technician: he is also a child placed before natural phenomena, which impress him, like a fairy tale.
MARIE CURIE (1867–1934)

We must not forget that when radium was discovered no one knew that it would prove useful in hospitals. The work was one of pure science. And this is a proof that scientific work must not be considered from the point of view of the direct usefulness of it. It must be done for itself, for the beauty of science, and then there is always the chance that a scientific discovery may become, like the radium, a benefit for humanity.
MARIE CURIE (1867–1934)

Ignorance more frequently begets confidence than does knowledge: it is those who know little, and not those who know much, who so positively assert that this or that problem will never be solved by science.
CHARLES DARWIN (1809–1882)

In science the credit goes to the man who convinces the world, not the man to whom the idea first occurs.
SIR FRANCIS DARWIN (1848–1925)

In science, one tries to tell people, in such a way as to be understood by everyone, something that no one ever knew before. But in poetry, it's the exact opposite.
PAUL DIRAC (1902–1984)

Science is one thing, wisdom is another. Science is an edged tool, with which men play like children, and cut their own fingers.
SIR ARTHUR EDDINGTON (1882–1944)

Science without religion is lame, religion without science is blind.
ALBERT EINSTEIN (1879–1955)

I believe that a scientist looking at nonscientific problems is just as dumb as the next guy.
RICHARD FEYNMAN (1918–1988)

Philosophers say a great deal about what is absolutely necessary for science, and it is always, so far as one can see, rather naive, and probably wrong.
RICHARD FEYNMAN (1918–1988)

The pace of science forces the pace of technique. Theoretical physics forces atomic energy on us; the successful production of the fission bomb forces upon us the manufacture of the hydrogen bomb. We do not choose our problems, we do not choose our products; we are pushed, we are forced … by a system which has no purpose and goal transcending it, and which makes man its appendix.
ERICH FROMM (1900–1980)

In science, "fact" can only mean "confirmed to such a degree that it would be perverse to withhold provisional assent." I suppose that apples might start to rise tomorrow, but the possibility does not merit equal time in physics classrooms.
STEPHEN JAY GOULD (1941–2002)

The most important scientific revolutions all include, as their only common feature, the dethronement of human arrogance from one pedestal after another of previous convictions about our centrality in the cosmos.
STEPHEN JAY GOULD (1941–2002)

Well: what we gain by science is, after all, sadness, as the Preacher saith. The more we know of the laws and nature of the Universe the more ghastly a business we perceive it all to be—and the non-necessity of it.
THOMAS HARDY (1840–1928)

There are in fact two things, science and opinion; the former begets knowledge, the latter ignorance.
HIPPOCRATES (460–377 BC)

Equipped with his five senses, man explores the universe around him and calls the adventure Science.
EDWIN POWELL HUBBLE (1889–1953)

Science is nothing but trained and organized common sense, differing from the latter only as a veteran may differ from a raw recruit: and its methods differ from those of common sense only as far as the guardsman's cut and thrust differ from the manner in which a savage wields his club.
THOMAS H. HUXLEY (1825–1895)

The great tragedy of Science—the slaying of a beautiful hypothesis by an ugly fact.
THOMAS H. HUXLEY (1825–1895)

We are living now, not in the delicious intoxication induced by the early successes of science, but in a rather grisly morning-after, when it has become apparent that what triumphant science has done hitherto is to improve the means for achieving unimproved or actually deteriorated ends.
ALDOUS HUXLEY (1894–1963)

Science is organized knowledge. Wisdom is organized life.
IMMANUEL KANT (1724–1804)

Our scientific power has outrun our spiritual power. We have guided missiles and misguided men.
MARTIN LUTHER KING JR. (1929–1968), *Strength to Love*

Einstein's space is no closer to reality than Van Gogh's sky. The glory of science is not in a truth more absolute than the truth of Bach or Tolstoy, but in the act of creation itself. The scientist's discoveries impose his own order on chaos, as the composer or painter imposes his; an order that always refers to limited aspects of reality, and is based on the observer's frame of reference, which differs from period to period as a Rembrandt nude differs from a nude by Manet.
ARTHUR KOESTLER (1905–1983), *The Act of Creation*

There is no greater impediment to progress in the sciences than the desire to see it take place too quickly.
GEORG C. LICHTENBERG (1742–1799)

It is a good morning exercise for a research scientist to discard a pet hypothesis every day before breakfast. It keeps him young.
KONRAD LORENZ (1903–1989)

Natural science will in time incorporate into itself the science of man, just as the science of man will incorporate into itself natural science: there will be one science.
KARL MARX (1818–1883)

The product of mental labor—science—always stands far below its value, because the labor-time necessary to reproduce it has no relation at all to the labor-time required for its original production.
KARL MARX (1818–1883)

Science has proof without any certainty. Creationists have certainty without any proof.
ASHLEY MONTAGU (1905–1999)

Oh, how much is today hidden by science! Oh, how much it is expected to hide!
FRIEDRICH NIETZSCHE (1844–1900)

Vanity of science. Knowledge of physical science will not console me for ignorance of morality in time of affliction, but knowledge of morality will always console me for ignorance of physical science.
BLAISE PASCAL (1623–1662)

There are no such things as applied sciences, only applications of science.
LOUIS PASTEUR (1822–1895)

Perfect as the wing of a bird may be, it will never enable the bird to fly if unsupported by the air. Facts are the air of science. Without them a man of science can never rise.
IVAN PAVLOV (1849–1936)

If the study of all these sciences which we have enumerated, should ever bring us to their mutual

association and relationship, and teach us the nature of the ties which bind them together, I believe that the diligent treatment of them will forward the objects which we have in view, and that the labor, which otherwise would be fruitless, will be well bestowed.
PLATO (C. 428–348 BC)

Science is nothing but perception.
PLATO (C. 428–348 BC)

I have hardly ever known a mathematician who was capable of reasoning.
PLATO (C. 428–348 BC)

Science is facts; just as houses are made of stones, so is science made of facts; but a pile of stones is not a house and a collection of facts is not necessarily science.
HENRI POINCARÉ (1854–1912)

One science only will one genius fit; so vast is art, so narrow human wit.
ALEXANDER POPE (1688–1744)

Science may set limits to knowledge, but should not set limits to imagination.
BERTRAND RUSSELL (1872–1970)

Whereas in art nothing worth doing can be done without genius, in science even a very moderate capacity can contribute to a supreme achievement.
BERTRAND RUSSELL (1872–1970)

I maintain there is much more wonder in science than in pseudoscience. And in addition, to whatever measure this term has any meaning, science has the additional virtue, and it is not an inconsiderable one, of being true.
CARL SAGAN (1934–1996)

Think of how many religions attempt to validate themselves with prophecy. Think of how many people rely on these prophecies, however vague, however unfulfilled, to support or prop up their beliefs. Yet has there ever been a religion with the prophetic accuracy and reliability of science?
CARL SAGAN (1934–1996)

Science is nothing but developed perception, interpreted intent, common sense rounded out and minutely articulated.
GEORGE SANTAYANA (1863–1952)

The cloning of humans is on most of the lists of things to worry about from Science, along with behavior control, genetic engineering, transplanted heads, computer poetry and the unrestrained growth of plastic flowers.
LEWIS THOMAS (1913–1993)

There is something fascinating about science. One gets such wholesale returns of conjecture out of such a trifling investment of fact.
MARK TWAIN (1835–1910)

Scripture

A dream is a scripture, and many scriptures are nothing but dreams.
UMBERTO ECO (1932–)

Scripture nowhere divides worship up into a series of independent "elements," each requiring independent scriptural justification. Scripture nowhere tells us that the regulative principle demands that particular level of specificity, rather than some other.
JOHN FRAME (1939–)

To substitute Scripture for the self-revealing Spirit is to put the dead letter in the place of the living Word.
SEBASTIAN FRANCK (1499–1543)

But every great scripture, whether Hebrew, Indian, Persian, or Chinese, apart from its religious value will be found to have some rare and special beauty of its own; and in this respect the original Bible stands very high as a monument of sublime poetry and of artistic prose.
LAFCADIO HEARN (1850–1904)

Compare Scripture with Scripture. False doctrines, like false witnesses, agree not among themselves.
WILLIAM GURNALL (1617–1679)

Scripture suggests that the elements in space were created for the benefit of earth, while evolution suggests that earth is an insignificant speck in vast space.
WALTER LANG (1896–1972)

The devil can cite Scripture for his purpose.
WILLIAM SHAKESPEARE (1564–1616), *The Merchant of Venice*

Scripture makes it clear to me that there is an obligation to speak out on behalf of those being persecuted.
FRANK R. WOLF (1939–)

Sculpture

What sculpture is to a block of marble, education is to the soul.
JOSEPH ADDISON (1672–1719)

Architecture is inhabited sculpture.
CONSTANTIN BRANCUSI (1876–1957)

Sculpture occupies real space like we do … you walk around it and relate to it almost as another person or another object.
CHUCK CLOSE (1940–)

Sculpture occupies the same space as your body.
ANISH KAPOOR (1954–)

Sculpture is the art of the intelligence.
PABLO PICASSO (1881–1973)

Sculpture is the best comment that a painter can make on painting.
PABLO PICASSO (1881–1973)

Sculpture is the art of the hole and the lump.
AUGUSTE RODIN (1840–1917)

Sculpture is made with two instruments and some supports and pretty air.
GERTRUDE STEIN (1874–1946)

A sculpture is just a painting cut out and stood up somewhere.
FRANK STELLA (1936–)

The Sea

The sea hath fish for every man.
WILLIAM CAMDEN (1551–1623)

The sea has neither meaning nor pity.
ANTON CHEKHOV (1860–1904)

The voice of the sea speaks to the soul. The touch of the sea is sensuous, enfolding the body in its soft, close embrace.
KATE CHOPIN (1850–1904)

The sea has never been friendly to man. At most it has been the accomplice of human restlessness.
JOSEPH CONRAD (1857–1924)

The sea, once it casts its spell, holds one in its net of wonder forever.
JACQUES COUSTEAU (1910–1997)

Praise the sea, on shore remain.
JOHN FLORIO (1553–1625)

Why do we love the sea? It is because it has some potent power to make us think things we like to think.
ROBERT HENRI (1865–1929)

The sea does not reward those who are too anxious, too greedy, or too impatient. One should lie empty, open, choiceless as a beach—waiting for a gift from the sea.
ANNE MORROW LINDBERGH (1906–2001)

The sea speaks a language polite people never repeat. It is a colossal scavenger slang and has no respect.
CARL SANDBURG (1878–1967)

The sea complains upon a thousand shores.
ALEXANDER SMITH (1830 –1867)

Seasons

Good seasons start with good beginnings.
SPARKY ANDERSON (1934–)

The flowers anew, returning seasons bring;
But beauty faded has no second spring.
AMBROSE PHILIPS (1675–1749)

The seasons come up undisturbed by crime and war.
GEORGE A. SMITH (1817–1875)

Secrets

Look in the mirror. The face that pins you with its double gaze reveals a chastening secret.
DIANE ACKERMAN (1948–)

Everything secret degenerates, even the administration of justice; nothing is safe that does not show how it can bear discussion and publicity.
LORD ACTON (1834–1902)

Our true history is scarcely ever deciphered by others. The chief part of the drama is a monologue, or rather an intimate debate between God, our conscience, and ourselves. Tears, grief, depressions, disappointments, irritations, good and evil thoughts, decisions, uncertainties, deliberations—all these belong to our secret, and are almost all incommunicable and intransmissible, even when we try to speak of them, and even when we write them down.
HENRI-FRÉDÉRIC AMIEL (1821–1881)

You know there are no secrets in America. It's quite different in England, where people think of a secret as a shared relation between two people.
W. H. AUDEN (1907–1973)

To know that one has a secret is to know half the secret itself.
HENRY WARD BEECHER (1813–1887)

A man's most open actions have a secret side to them.
JOSEPH CONRAD (1857–1924)

A wonderful fact to reflect upon, that every human creature is constituted to be that profound secret and mystery to every other.
CHARLES DICKENS (1812–1870)

His mind of man, a secret makes
I meet him with a start
He carries a circumference
In which I have no part --
EMILY DICKINSON (1830–1886) "No. 1663"

Three can keep a secret if two are dead.
BENJAMIN FRANKLIN (1706–1790)

He that has eyes to see and ears to hear may convince himself that o mortal can keep a secret. If his lips are silent, he chatters with his fingertips; betrayal oozes out of him at every pore.
SIGMUND FREUD (1856–1939)

We dance round in a ring and suppose, but the secret sits in the middle and knows.
ROBERT FROST (1874–1963)

If you reveal your secrets to the wind, you should not blame the wind for revealing them to the trees.
KAHLIL GIBRAN (1883–1931)

Whoever wishes to keep a secret must hide the fact that he possesses one.
JOHANN WOLFGANG VON GOETHE (1749–1832)

The secret thoughts of a man run over all things, holy, profane, clean, obscene, grave, and light, without shame or blame.
THOMAS HOBBES (1588–1679)

Youth fades; love droops, the leaves of friendship
 fall;
A mother's secret hope outlives them all.
OLIVER WENDELL HOLMES SR. (1809–1894)

No one ever keeps a secret so well as a child.
VICTOR HUGO (1802–1885)

The face is the mirror of the mind, and eyes without speaking confess the secrets of the heart.
SAINT JEROME (C. 342–420)

The vanity of being known to be trusted with a secret is generally one of the chief motives to disclose it.
SAMUEL JOHNSON (1709–1784)

To keep your secret is wisdom; but to expect others to keep it is folly.
SAMUEL JOHNSON (1709–1784)

Where secrecy or mystery begins, vice or roguery is not far off.
SAMUEL JOHNSON (1709–1784)

A man can keep a secret better than his own. A woman her own better than others.
JEAN DE LA BRUYÈRE (1645–1696)

Nothing weighs on us so heavily as a secret.
JEAN DE LA FONTAINE (1621–1695)

How can we accept another to keep our secret if we have been unable to keep it ourselves.
FRANÇOIS DE LA ROCHEFOUCAULD (1613–1680)

Trust him not with your secrets, who, when left alone in your room, turns over your papers.
JOHANN KASPAR LAVATER (1741–1801)

Secrets travel fast in Paris.
NAPOLÉON I (1769–1821)

The first step towards vice is to shroud innocent actions in mystery, and whoever likes to conceal something sooner or later has reason to conceal it.
JEAN-JACQUES ROUSSEAU (1712–1778)

No one gossips about other people's secret virtues.
BERTRAND RUSSELL (1872–1970)

It is wise to disclose what cannot be concealed.
FRIEDRICH VON SCHILLER (1759–1805)

There are no secrets better kept than the secrets that everybody guesses.
GEORGE BERNARD SHAW (1856–1950), *Mrs. Warren's Profession*

Everyone is like a moon, and has a dark side which he never shows to anybody.
MARK TWAIN (1835–1910)

What is told into the ear of a man is often heard a hundred miles away.
CHINESE PROVERB

A secret between two is God's secret, between three is all men's.
SPANISH PROVERB

Secularism

It seems true that the growth of science and secularism made organized Christianity feel under threat.
MARY DOUGLAS (1921–)

Our vision of secularism isn't anti-religious, but is one of the State's neutrality and the spirit of tolerance.
JEAN-PIERRE RAFFARIN (1948–)

I believe that pluralistic secularism, in the long run, is a more deadly poison than straightforward persecution.
FRANCIS SCHAEFFER (1912 1984)

Unity and secularism will be the motto of the government. We can't afford divisive polity in India.
MANMOHAN SINGH (1932–)

A neurosis is a secret that you don't know you are keeping.
KENNETH TYNAN (1927–1980)

To him that you tell your secret you resign your liberty.
ANONYMOUS

Security

The most certain test by which we judge whether a country is really free is the amount of security enjoyed by minorities.
LORD ACTON (1834–1902)

Better be despised for too anxious apprehensions, than ruined by too confident security.
EDMUND BURKE (1729–1797)

Too many people are thinking of security instead of opportunity. They seem more afraid of life than death.
JAMES F. BYRNES (1879–1972)

No one can build his security upon the nobleness of another person.
WILLA CATHER (1873–1947)

The superior man, when resting in safety, does not forget that danger may come. When in a state of security he does not forget the possibility of ruin. When all is orderly, he does not forget that disorder may come. Thus his person is not endangered, and his States and all their clans are preserved.
CONFUCIUS (554–479 BC)

Security is mostly a superstition. It does not exist in nature.... Life is either a daring adventure or nothing.
HELEN KELLER (1880–1968), *The Open Door*

There is no security on this earth, there is only opportunity.
GENERAL DOUGLAS MACARTHUR (1880–1964)

Security is a kind of death.
TENNESSEE WILLIAMS (1911–1983)

Seduction

Seduction is always more singular and sublime than sex and it commands the higher price.
JEAN BAUDRILLARD (1929–2007)

Seduction is often difficult to distinguish from rape. In seduction, the rapist often bothers to buy a bottle of wine.
ANDREA DWORKIN (1946–2005)

All great lovers are articulate, and verbal seduction is the surest road to actual seduction.
MARYA MANNES (1904–1990)

I don't mind seducing as long as at the end of the seduction there's an idea or a shock.
ALAN RICKMAN (1946–)

Segregation

The grand irony ... is that Southern segregation was not brought to an end, nor redneck violence dramatically reduced, by violence.
STANLEY CROUCH (1945–)

The legal battle against segregation is won, but the community battle goes on.
DOROTHY DAY (1897–1980)

From slavery to segregation, we remember that America did not always live up to its ideals. In fact, we often fell far short of them. But we also learned that fundamental to our national character is the drive to live out the true meaning of our creed.
BILL FRIST (1952–)

Segregation never brought anyone anything except trouble.
PAUL HARRIS (1868–1947)

Segregation is the adultery of an illicit intercourse between injustice and immorality.
MARTIN LUTHER KING JR. (1929–1968)

Segregation in education was a social ill that involved a number of states and had existed for at least 60 years.
CONSTANCE BAKER MOTLEY (1921–2005)

Segregation now, segregation tomorrow, and segregation forever!
GEORGE C. WALLACE (1919–1998)

And thus goes segregation, which is the most far-reaching development in the history of the Negro since the enslavement of the race.
CARTER G. WOODSON (1875–1950)

Self

Self-conceit may lead to self-destruction.
AESOP (620–560 BC)

I count him braver who overcomes his desires than him who conquers his enemies; for the hardest victory is over self.
ARISTOTLE (384–322 BC)

And whatsoever Self has in it a mental form is an essence, other than a body, and not within a body, and standing of itself.
AVICENNA (980–1037)

There is as much difference between the counsel that a friend giveth, and that a man giveth himself, as there is between the counsel of a friend and of a flatterer. For there is no such flatterer as is a man's self.
SIR FRANCIS BACON (1561–1621)

It's not only the most difficult thing to know one's self, but the most inconvenient.
JOSH BILLINGS (1818–1885)

Worship means reverence and humility; it means revering your real self and humbling delusions.
BODHIDHARMA (470–543)

Ego is to the true self what a flashlight is to a spotlight.
JOHN BRADSHAW (1933–)

Self esteem is the reputation we acquire with ourselves.
NATHANIEL BRANDEN (1930–)

He who experiences the unity of life sees his own Self in all beings, and all beings in his own Self, and looks on everything with an impartial eye.
THE BUDDHA (563–483 BC)

The self is just not a worthy enough vehicle to worship.
PETER COYOTE (1941–)

The self is not something ready-made, but something in continuous formation through choice of action.
JOHN DEWEY (1859–1952)

It is a peculiar sensation, this double-consciousness, this sense of always looking at one's self through the eyes of others, of measuring one's soul by the tape of a world that looks on in amused contempt and pity.
W. E. B. DU BOIS (1868–1963)

Tears shed for self are tears of weakness, but tears shed for others are a sign of strength.
BILLY GRAHAM (1918–)

Without self knowledge, without understanding the working and functions of his machine, man cannot be free, he cannot govern himself and he will always remain a slave.
G. I. GURDJIEFF (1872–1949)

The reason man does not experience his true cultural self is that until he experiences another self as valid he has little basis for validating his own self.
EDWARD T. HALL (1914–)

Self-knowledge begins with the neighbor, the mirror, and just the same with true self-love; that goes from the mirror to the matter.
JOHANN G. HAMANN (1730–1788)

If you do not conquer self, you will be conquered by self.
NAPOLEON HILL (1883–1970)

Self is the root, the tree, and the branches of all the evils of our fallen state.
WILLIAM LAW (1686–1761)

A self does not amount to much, but no self is an island; each exists in a fabric of relations that is now more complex and mobile than ever before.
JEAN-FRANÇOIS LYOTARD (1924–1998)

The self is something which has a development; it is not initially there, at birth, but arises in the process of social experience and activity, that is, develops in the given individual as a result of his relations to

that process as a whole and to other individuals within that process.
GEORGE H. MEAD (1863–1931)

The self is hateful.
BLAISE PASCAL (1623–1662)

The self thus becomes aware of itself, at least in its practical action, and discovers itself as a cause among other causes and as an object subject to the same laws as other objects.
JEAN PIAGET (1896–1980)

The sovereignty of one's self over one's self is called Liberty.
ALBERT PIKE (1809–1891)

Friendship with one's self is all important, because without it one cannot be friends with anyone else in the world.
ELEANOR ROOSEVELT (1884–1962)

[T]o thine own self be true,
And it must follow, as the night the day,
Thou canst not then be false to any man.
WILLIAM SHAKESPEARE (1564–1616), *Hamlet*

Love is the outreach of self toward completion.
RALPH W. SOCKMAN (1889–1970)

Know thy self, know thy enemy. A thousand battles, a thousand victories.
SUN-TZU (C. 544–496 BC)

To be one's self, and unafraid whether right or wrong, is more admirable than the easy cowardice of surrender to conformity.
IRVING WALLACE (1916–1990)

The denial of the self has come, as is natural, to mean in general the making of the self thoroughly uncomfortable.
CHARLES WILLIAMS (1886–1945)

But when the self speaks to the self, who is speaking?—the entombed soul, the spirit driven in, in, in to the central catacomb; the self that took the veil and left the world—a coward perhaps, yet somehow beautiful, as it flits with its lantern restlessly up and down the dark corridors.
VIRGINIA WOOLF (1882–1941)

Self-Confidence

One important key to success is self-confidence. An important key to self-confidence is preparation.
ARTHUR ASHE (1943–1993)

Self-confidence is either a petty pride in our own narrowness, or the realization of our duty and privilege as God's children.
PHILLIPS BROOKS (1835–1893)

Humor comes from self-confidence.
RITA MAE BROWN (1944–)

It is only necessary to have courage, for strength without self-confidence is useless.
GIACOMO CASANOVA (1725–1798)

If I have lost confidence in myself, I have the universe against me.
RALPH WALDO EMERSON (1803–1882)

Self-confidence is the first requisite to great undertakings.
SAMUEL JOHNSON (1709–1784)

Smile, for everyone lacks self-confidence and more than any other one thing a smile reassures them.
ANDRÉ MAUROIS (1885–1967)

Calm self-confidence is as far from conceit as the desire to earn a decent living is remote from greed.
CHANNING POLLOCK (1880–1946)

Giving people self-confidence is by far the most important thing that I can do. Because then they will act.
JACK WELCH (1935–)

Self-Control

Any fool can criticize, condemn, and complain, but it takes character and self-control to be

understanding and forgiving.
DALE CARNEGIE (1888–1955)

Educate your children to self-control, to the habit of holding passion and prejudice and evil tendencies subject to an upright and reasoning will, and you have done much to abolish misery from their future and crimes from society.
BENJAMIN FRANKLIN (1706–1790)

By constant self-discipline and self-control you can develop greatness of character.
GRENVILLE KLEISER (1868–1953)

Self-help and self-control are the essence of the American tradition.
FRANKLIN D. ROOSEVELT (1882–1945)

Confirm thy soul in self-control.
GEORGE WASHINGTON (1732–1799)

Self-Esteem

Self-esteem is the greatest sickness known to man or woman because it's conditional.
ALBERT ELLIS (1913–2007)

Low self-esteem comes from who you assess yourself to be. It's about who you are, and I didn't think I was anything or anybody.
GLORIA GAYNOR (1949–)

Every new adjustment is a crisis in self-esteem.
ERIC HOFFER (1902–1983)

Low self-esteem is like driving through life with your hand-break on.
MAXWELL MALTZ (1899–1975)

Self-Respect

That you may retain your self-respect, it is better to displease the people by doing what you know is right, than to temporarily please them by doing what you know is wrong.
WILLIAM J. H. BOETCKER (1873–1962)

In order to preserve your self-respect, it is sometimes necessary to lie and cheat.
ROBERT BYRNE (1928–)

Self-respect permeates every aspect of your life.
JOE CLARK (1939–)

Character—the willingness to accept responsibility for one's own life—is the source from which self-respect springs.
JOAN DIDION (1934–), *Slouching Towards Bethlehem*

Self-respect is a question of recognizing that anything worth having has a price.
JOAN DIDION (1934–)

Self-respect knows no considerations.
MAHATMA GANDHI (1869–1948)

Self-respect is the cornerstone of all virtue.
JOHN HERSCHEL (1792–1871)

Self-respect is the fruit of discipline; the sense of dignity grows with the ability to say no to oneself.
ABRAHAM J. HESCHEL (1907–1972)

Self-respect: the secure feeling that no one, as yet, is suspicious.
H. L. MENCKEN (1880–1956)

I have no right, by anything I do or say, to demean a human being in his own eyes. What matters is not what I think of him; it is what he thinks of himself. To undermine a man's self-respect is a sin.
ANTOINE DE SAINT-EXUPÉRY (1900–1944)

If you want to be respected, you must respect yourself.
SPANISH PROVERB

Selfishness

Glory built on selfish principles is shame and guilt.
WILLIAM COWPER (1731–1800)

To be stupid, selfish, and have good health are three requirements for happiness, though if stupidity is

lacking, all is lost.
GUSTAVE FLAUBERT (1821–1880)

Manifest plainness,
Embrace simplicity,
Reduce selfishness,
Have few desires.
LAO-TZU (C. 600 BC), *The Way of Lao-tzu*

Selfishness is not living as one wishes to live, it is asking others to live as one wishes to live.
OSCAR WILDE (1854–1900)

Senses

There is no way in which to understand the world without first detecting it through the radar-net of our senses.
DIANE ACKERMAN (1948–)

Nothing we use or hear or touch can be expressed in words that equal what is given by the senses.
HANNAH ARENDT (1906–1975)

Man has no Body distinct from his Soul; for that called Body is a portion of Soul discerned by the five Senses, the chief inlets of Soul in this age.
WILLIAM BLAKE (1757–1827)

Whoever realizes that the six senses aren't real, that the five aggregates are fictions, that no such things can be located anywhere in the body, understands the language of Buddhas.
BODHIDHARMA (470–543)

The senses are the organs by which man places himself in connection with exterior objects.
JEAN ANTHELME BRILLAT-SAVARIN (1755–1826)

Both our senses and our passions are a supply to the imperfection of our nature; thus they show that we are such sort of creatures as to stand in need of those helps which higher orders of creatures do not.
JOSEPH BUTLER (1692–1752)

The wise man should restrain his senses like the crane and accomplish his purpose with due knowledge of his place, time and ability.
CHANAKYA (350–275 BC)

Where the senses fail us, reason must step in.
GALILEO GALILEI (1564–1642)

Equipped with his five senses, man explores the universe around him and calls the adventure Science.
EDWIN POWELL HUBBLE (1889–1953)

We know that our senses are subject to decay, that from our middle years they are decaying all the time; but happily it is as if we didn't know and didn't believe.
WILLIAM H. HUDSON (1841–1922)

Of all the senses, sight must be the most delightful.
HELEN KELLER (1880–1968)

The strong man is the one who is able to intercept at will the communication between the senses and the mind.
NAPOLÉON I (1769–1821)

Terrible is the fight put up by the senses. Fight bravely! Conquer them you must.
SWAMI SIVANANDA (1887–1963)

Nothing can cure the soul but the senses, just as nothing can cure the senses but the soul.
OSCAR WILDE (1854–1900)

Sensitivity

Exaggerated sensitiveness is an expression of the feeling of inferiority.
ALFRED ADLER (1870–1937)

There's a sensitivity chip that's missing.
JENNIFER ANISTON (1969–)

Wallow too much in sensitivity and you can't deal with life, or the truth.
NEAL BOORTZ (1945–)

Beauty of whatever kind, in its supreme development, invariably excites the sensitive soul to tears.
EDGAR ALLAN POE (1809–1849)

Idle youth, enslaved to everything; by being too sensitive I have wasted my life.
ARTHUR RIMBAUD (1854–1891)

Thinking is not enough. Sensitivity is not enough. People want to be accepted for sensitivity, for tender thoughts, for high ideals. That's not enough.
SHEL SILVERSTEIN (1930–1999)

Poets, we know, are terribly sensitive people, and in my observation one of the things they are most sensitive about is money.
ROBERT PENN WARREN (1905–1989)

Sensuality

Sensuality without love is a sin; love without sensuality is worse than a sin.
JOSÉ BERGAMIN (1897–1983)

I am acquainted with no immaterial sensuality so delightful as good acting.
LORD BYRON (1788–1824)

Intellectual passion drives out sensuality.
LEONARDO DA VINCI (1452–1519)

Sensuality often makes love grow too quickly, so that the root remains weak and is easy to pull out.
FRIEDRICH NIETZSCHE (1844–1900)

The spiritualization of sensuality is called love: it is a great triumph over Christianity.
FRIEDRICH NIETZSCHE (1844–1900)

If sensuality were happiness, beasts were happier than men; but human felicity is lodged in the soul, not in the flesh.
SENECA (5 BC–AD 65)

Any nobleness begins at once to refine a man's features, any meanness or sensuality to imbrute them.
HENRY DAVID THOREAU (1817–1862)

Sentimentality

In deep sadness there is no place for sentimentality.
WILLIAM S. BURROUGHS (1914–1997)

Sentimentality is a form of fatigue.
LEONORA CARRINGTON (1917–)

Only a struggle twists sentimentality and lust together into love.
E. M. FORSTER (1879–1970)

Sentimentality—that's what we call the sentiment we don't share.
GRAHAM GREENE (1904–1991)

Sentimentality is the emotional promiscuity of those who have no sentiment.
NORMAN MAILER (1923–2007)

Sentimentality is only sentiment that rubs you the wrong way.
W. SOMERSET MAUGHAM (1874–1965)

In dread fear of sentimentality, another thing true is not said—that for its staff [*New York Times*] is a source of pride and, I do believe, an object of affection and—yes, love.
ARTHUR OCHS SULZBERGER (1926–)

Serenity

Mirth is like a flash of lightning, that breaks through a gloom of clouds, and glitters for a moment; cheerfulness keeps up a kind of daylight in the mind, and fills it with a steady and perpetual serenity.
JOSEPH ADDISON (1672–1719)

Supreme serenity still remains the Ideal of great Art. The shapes and transitory forms of life are but stages toward this Ideal, which Christ's religion illuminates with His divine light.
FRANZ LISZT (1811–1886)

Serenity is knowing that your worst shot is still pretty good.
JOHNNY MILLER (1947–)

God grant me the serenity
to accept the things I cannot change;
courage to change the things I can;
and wisdom to know the difference.
Living one day at a time;
Enjoying one moment at a time;
Accepting hardships as the pathway to peace;
Taking, as He did, this sinful world
as it is, not as I would have it;
Trusting that He will make all things right
if I surrender to His Will;
That I may be reasonably happy in this life
and supremely happy with Him
Forever in the next.
Amen.
REINHOLD NIEBUHR (1892–1971)

Only nature has a right to grieve perpetually, for she only is innocent. Soon the ice will melt, and the blackbirds sing along the river which he frequented, as pleasantly as ever. The same everlasting serenity will appear in this face of God, and we will not be sorrowful, if he is not.
HENRY DAVID THOREAU (1817–1862)

Serenity isn't freedom from the storm, but peace within the storm.
ANONYMOUS

Seriousness

Men are convinced of your arguments, your sincerity, and the seriousness of your efforts only by your death.
ALBERT CAMUS (1913–1960)

Man is most nearly himself when he achieves the seriousness of a child at play.
HERACLITUS (C. 535–475 BC)

Seriousness is stupidity sent to college.
P. J. O'ROURKE (1947–)

Seriousness is the only refuge of the shallow.
OSCAR WILDE (1854–1900)

Servants

Good servants frequently make good masters.
JUPITER HAMMON (1711–1806)

The best servants of the people, like the best valets, must whisper unpleasant truths in the master's ear. It is the court fool, not the foolish courtier, whom the king can least afford to lose.
WALTER LIPPMANN (1889–1974)

Faithful servants never retire. You can retire from your career, but you will never retire from serving God.
RICK WARREN (1909–)

Service

To give real service you must add something which cannot be bought or measured with money, and that is sincerity and integrity.
DOUGLAS ADAMS (1952–2001)

Service to others is the rent you pay for your room here on earth.
MUHAMMAD ALI (1942–)

While you are not able to serve men, how can you serve spirits [of the dead]? … While you do not know life, how can you know about death?
CONFUCIUS (551–479 BC), *The Confucian Analects*

Great services are not canceled by one act or by one single error.
BENJAMIN DISRAELI (1804–1881)

Service is what life is all about.
MARIAN WRIGHT EDELMAN (1939–)

Help others and give something back. I guarantee you will discover that while public service improves the lives and the world around you, its greatest reward is the enrichment and new meaning it will bring your own life.
ARNOLD SCHWARZENEGGER (1947–)

Be silent as to services you have rendered, but speak of favours you have received.
SENECA (5 BC–AD 65)

Sow good services; sweet remembrances will grow them.
MADAME DE STAËL (1766–1817)

We serve God by serving others. The world defines greatness in terms of power, possessions, prestige, and position. If you can demand service from others, you've arrived. In our self-serving culture with its me-first mentality, acting like a servant is not a popular concept.
RICK WARREN (1909–)

I've come to believe that each of us has a personal calling that's as unique as a fingerprint—and that the best way to succeed is to discover what you love and then find a way to offer it to others in the form of service, working hard, and also allowing the energy of the universe to lead you.
OPRAH WINFREY (1954–)

Be alert to give service. What counts a great deal in life is what we do for others.
ANONYMOUS

Sex

I think the real obscenity comes from raising our youth to believe that sex is bad and ugly and dirty. And yet, it is heroic to go spill guts and blood in the most ghastly manner in the name of humanity. With all the taboos attached to sex, it's no wonder we have the problems we have. It's no wonder we're angry and violent and genocidal. But ask yourself the question, what is more obscene: sex or war?
SCOTT ALEXANDER (1963–) and LARRY KARASZEWSKI (1961–), *The People vs. Larry Flynt*

I can remember when the air was clean and sex was dirty.
GEORGE BURNS (1896–1996)

Women need a reason to have sex. Men just need a place.
BILLY CRYSTAL (1947–)

In America sex is an obsession; in other parts of the world it is a fact.
MARLENE DIETRICH (1901–1992)

Instead of fulfilling the promise of infinite orgasmic bliss, sex in the America of the feminine mystique is becoming a strangely joyless national compulsion, if not a contemptuous mockery.
BETTY FRIEDAN (1921– 2006)

I know nothing about sex because I was always married.
ZSA ZSA GABOR (1919–)

Life is a sexually transmitted disease.
R. D. LAING (1927–1989)

Mortal lovers must not try to remain at the first step; for lasting passion is the dream of a harlot and from it we wake in despair.
C. S. LEWIS (1898–1963), *The Pilgrim's Regress*

One thing I've learned in all these years is not to make love when you really don't feel it; there's probably nothing worse you can do to yourself than that.
NORMAN MAILER (1923–2007)

A man can sleep around, no questions asked, but if a woman makes nineteen or twenty mistakes she's a tramp.
JOAN RIVERS (1935–)

I'm too shy to express my sexual needs except over the phone to people I don't know.
GARRY SHANDLING (1949–)

The happiness of a man in this life does not consist in the absence but in the mastery of his passions.
ALFRED, LORD TENNYSON (1809–1892)

Sexism

Sexism is the foundation on which all tyranny is built. Every social form of hierarchy and abuse is modeled on male-over-female domination.
ANDREA DWORKIN (1946–2005)

Sexism is not the fault of women—kill your fathers, not your mothers.
ROBIN MORGAN (1941–)

Sexism, like racism, goes with us into the next century. I see class warfare as overshadowing both.
CONSTANCE BAKER MOTLEY (1921–2005)

Sexuality

Sexuality is the lyricism of the masses.
CHARLES BAUDELAIRE (1821–1867)

A part of sexuality may go to research, and a much larger part must lead to aesthetic creation. The art of the future will, because of the very opportunities and materials it will have at its command, need an infinitely stronger formative impulse than it does now.
JOHN DESMOND BERNAL (1901–1971)

Human sexuality has been regulated and shaped by men to serve men's needs.
ANA CASTILLO (1953–)

There is no sexuality that is greater or lesser than another.
JASMINE GUY (1964–)

Understand that sexuality is as wide as the sea. Understand that your morality is not law. Understand that we are you. Understand that if we decide to have sex whether safe, safer, or unsafe, it is our decision and you have no rights in our lovemaking.
DEREK JARMAN (1942–1994)

Sexuality itself means mortality—equally for both man and woman.
LEON KASS (1939–)

I think one's sexuality can be the center of life, and coming out and discovering your sexuality is something that really can define your existence.
MIA KIRSHNER (1975–)

Sexuality poorly repressed unsettles some families; well repressed, it unsettles the whole world.
KARL KRAUS (1874–1936)

I've always felt that sexuality is a really slippery thing. In this day and age, it tends to get categorized and labeled, and I think labels are for food. Canned food.
MICHAEL STIPE (1960–)

Shadows

There are dark shadows on the earth, but its lights are stronger in the contrast.
CHARLES DICKENS (1812–1870)

Manipulating shadows and tonality is like writing music or a poem.
CONRAD HALL (1926–2003)

Thoughts are the shadows of our sensation—always darker, emptier, simpler than these.
FRIEDRICH NIETZSCHE (1844–1900)

Keep your face always toward the sunshine—and shadows will fall behind you.
WALT WHITMAN (1819–1892)

Most people think that shadows follow, precede or surround beings or objects. The truth is that they also surround words, ideas, desires, deeds, impulses and memories.
ELIE WIESEL (1928–)

The light of lights looks always on the motive, not the deed; the shadow of shadows on the deed alone.
WILLIAM BUTLER YEATS (1865–1939)

Shakespeare

This was Shakespeare's form; who walked in every path of human life, felt every passion; and to all mankind doth now, will ever, that experience yield which his own genius only could acquire.
MARK AKENSIDE (1721–1770)

Shakespeare is the true multicultural author. He exists in all languages. He is put on the stage everywhere. Everyone feels that they are represented by him on the stage.
HAROLD BLOOM (1930–)

The elasticity of Shakespeare is extraordinary.
KENNETH BRANAGH (1960–)

Shakespeare, who is probably the greatest writer and poet of the English language, lived in a time that was politically very conservative and it's reflected in his writings.
ALEX COX (1954–)

I have tried lately to read Shakespeare, and found it so intolerably dull that it nauseated me.
CHARLES DARWIN (1809–1882)

I think reading Shakespeare's plays when I was young was extremely important. He had the ability to make utter strangers come alive.
RITA DOVE (1952–)

First of all, Shakespeare is about pleasure and interest. He was from the first moment he actually wrote something for the stage, and he remains so.
STEPHEN GREENBLATT (1943–)

Shakespeare was the great one before us. His place was between God and despair.
EUGÈNE IONESCO (1912–1994)

When Shakespeare was writing, he wasn't writing for stuff to lie on the page; it was supposed to get up and move around.
KEN KESEY (1935–2001)

Now we sit through Shakespeare in order to recognize the quotations.
ORSON WELLES (1915–1985)

Shame

Shame is pride's cloak.
WILLIAM BLAKE (1757–1827)

Girls blush, sometimes, because they are alive, half wishing they were dead to save the shame. The sudden blush devours them, neck and brow; They have drawn too near the fire of life, like gnats, and flare up bodily, wings and all. What then? Who's sorry for a gnat or girl?
ELIZABETH BARRETT BROWNING (1806–1861)

Shame is an unhappy emotion invented by pietists in order to exploit the human race.
BLAKE EDWARDS (1922–)

Whatever is begun in anger ends in shame.
BENJAMIN FRANKLIN (1706–1790)

False shame accompanies a man that is poor, shame that either harms a man greatly or profits him; shame is with poverty, but confidence with wealth.
HESIOD (C. 800 BC)

Pride attaches undue importance to the superiority of one's status in the eyes of others; and shame is fear of humiliation at one's inferior status in the estimation of others. When one sets his heart on being highly esteemed, and achieves such rating, then he is automatically involved in fear of losing his status.
LAO-TZU (C. 600 BC)

What do you regard as most humane? To spare someone shame.
FRIEDRICH NIETZSCHE (1844–1900)

Shame is a fitter and generally a more effectual punishment for a child than beating.
SAMUEL RICHARDSON (1689–1761)

Shame may restrain what law does not prohibit.
SENECA (5 BC–AD 65)

Where there is no shame, there is no honor.
AFRICAN PROVERB

Sharing

Sharing is sometimes more demanding than giving.
MARY CATHERINE BATESON (1939–)

The inherent vice of capitalism is the unequal sharing of blessings; the inherent virtue of socialism is the equal sharing of miseries.
SIR WINSTON CHURCHILL (1874–1965)

Happiness seems made to be shared.
PIERRE CORNEILLE (1606–1684)

There is no joy in possession without sharing.
DESIDERIUS ERASMUS (1469–1536)

Life has taught me that respect, caring and love must be shared, for it's only through sharing that friendships are born.
DONNA A. FAVORS (1955–)

When we share—that is poetry in the prose of life.
SIGMUND FREUD (1856–1939)

A bone to the dog is not charity. Charity is the bone shared with the dog, when you are just as hungry as the dog.
JACK LONDON (1876–1916)

I am treating you as my friend, asking you to share my present minuses in the hope that I can ask you to share my future pluses.
KATHERINE MANSFIELD (1888–1923)

The miracle is this—the more we share, the more we have.
LEONARD NIMOY (1931–)

It is the nature of the ego to take, and the nature of the spirit to share.
ANONYMOUS

Shelter

Houses mean a creation, something new, a shelter freed from the idea of a cave.
STEPHEN GARDINER (1497–1555)

All architecture is shelter, all great architecture is the design of space that contains, cuddles, exalts, or stimulates the persons in that space.
PHILIP JOHNSON (1906–2005)

A sheltered life can be a daring life as well. For all serious daring starts from within.
EUDORA WELTY (1909–2001)

For you have been my refuge, a strong tower against the foe.
THE BIBLE, Psalm 61:3

It is in the shelter of each other that the people live.
IRISH PROVERB

Shepherds

We are like ignorant shepherds living on a site where great civilizations once flourished. The shepherds play with the fragments that pop up to the surface, having no notion of the beautiful structures of which they were once a part.
ALLAN BLOOM (1930–1992)

The shepherd drives the wolf from the sheep's throat, for which the sheep thanks the shepherd as his liberator, while the wolf denounces him for the same act as the destroyer of liberty.
ABRAHAM LINCOLN (1809–1865)

It is the part of a good shepherd to shear his flock, not to skin it.
LATIN PROVERB

Showbiz

The payoffs in showbiz seemed as random as a slot machine.
KATHIE LEE GIFFORD (1953–)

In showbiz, you've gotta surround yourself with real, down-home people. They'll keep you straight.
JOHN RATZENBERGER (1947–)

Everyone in showbiz is driven by ego, so how do you go from having loads of fame to working at 7–11? You can't do it!
RYAN SEACREST (1974–)

Shyness

Shyness has a strange element of narcissism…. [It is] a belief that how we look, how we perform, is truly important to other people.
ANDRE DUBUS (1936–1999)

Shyness is just egoism out of its depth.
PENELOPE KEITH (1940–)

Many a man is praised for his reserve and so-called shyness when he is simply too proud to risk making a fool of himself.
J. B. PRIESTLEY (1894–1984)

The level of shyness has gone up dramatically in the last decade. I think shyness is an index of social pathology rather than a pathology of the individual.
PHILIP ZIMBARDO (1933–)

What troubles me is the Internet and the electronic technology revolution. Shyness is fueled in part by so many people spending huge amounts of time alone, isolated on e-mail, in chat rooms, which reduces their face-to-face contact with other people.
PHILIP ZIMBARDO (1933–)

Siblings

I do not believe that the accident of birth makes people sisters and brothers. It makes them siblings. Gives them mutuality of parentage. Sisterhood and brotherhood are conditions people have to work at. It's a serious matter. You compromise, you give, you take, you stand firm, and you're relentless…
MAYA ANGELOU (1928–)

Being pretty on the inside means you don't hit your brother and you eat all your peas, that's what my grandma taught me.
LORD CHESTERFIELD (1694–1773)

I've come to realize that people don't tell everything. As much as you love your siblings, there are things you just don't share.
TERRY MCMILLAN (1951–)

I've got three brothers, and I think relationships between siblings are very interesting and not examined very much in film.
COLM MEANEY (1953–)

Friends are the siblings God never gave us.
MENCIUS (371–289 BC)

Help your brother's boat across, and your own will reach the shore.
HINDU PROVERB

Brothers and sisters are as close as hands and feet.
VIETNAMESE PROVERB

Sickness

Exuberant health is always, as such, sickness also.
THEODOR W. ADORNO (1903–1969)

There is no sickness worse for me than words that to be kind must lie.
AESCHYLUS (C. 525–456 BC)

Sickness and healing are in every heart; death and deliverance in every hand.
ORSON SCOTT CARD (1951–), *Speaker for the Dead*

Living is a sickness to which sleep provides relief every sixteen hours. It's a palliative. The remedy is death.
NICOLAS CHAMFORT (1741–1794)

Old age and sickness bring out the essential characteristics of a man.
FELIX FRANKFURTER (1882–1965)

Sickness sensitizes man for observation, like a photographic plate.
EDMOND DE GONCOURT (1822–1896)

Sickness is mankind's greatest defect.
GEORG C. LICHTENBERG (1742–1799)

Three-quarters of the sicknesses of intelligent people come from their intelligence. They need at least a doctor who can understand this sickness
MARCEL PROUST (1871–1922)

Now, this sickness and this death and all these things that happen here on earth are not necessary. It's totally out of harmony, coordination, precision, and discipline.
SUN RA (1914–1993)

His sickness increases from the remedies applied to cure it.
VIRGIL (C. 70–19 BC)

Silence

Since long I've held silence a remedy for harm.
AESCHYLUS (C. 525–456 BC)

Deep vengeance is the daughter of deep silence.
VITTORIO ALFIERI (1749–1803)

Silence is golden when you can't think of a good answer.
MUHAMMAD ALI (1942–)

Only silence perfects silence.
ARCHIE R. AMMONS (1926–2001)

Soon silence will have passed into legend. Man has turned his back on silence. Day after day he invents machines and devices that increase noise and distract humanity from the essence of life, contemplation, meditation.
JEAN ARP (1886–1966)

He who does not know how to be silent will not know how to speak.
AUSONIUS (C. 310–395)

No man pleases by silence; many I please by speaking briefly.
AUSONIUS (C. 310–395)

Silence is the sleep that nourishes wisdom.
SIR FRANCIS BACON (1561–1626)

Silence is the virtue of fools.
SIR FRANCIS BACON (1561–1626)

It is more noble by silence to avoid an injury than by argument to overcome it.
FRANCIS BEAUMONT (1584–1616)

Silence is one of the hardest arguments to refute.
JOSH BILLINGS (1818–1885)

To listen to your own silence is the key to comedy.
ELAYNE BOOSLER (1952–)

Silence is only frightening to people who are compulsively verbalizing.
WILLIAM S. BURROUGHS (1914–1997)

Silence and tact may or may not be the same thing.
SAMUEL BUTLER (1835–1902)

Silence is sometimes the severest criticism.
CHARLES BUXTON (1823–1871)

Under all speech that is good for anything there lies a silence that is better. Silence is deep as Eternity; speech is shallow as Time.
THOMAS CARLYLE (1795–1881)

I think the first virtue is to restrain the tongue; he approaches nearest to gods who knows how to be silent, even though he is in the right.
CATO THE ELDER (234–149 BC)

Silence moves faster when it's going backward.
JEAN COCTEAU (1889–1963)

To a poet, silence is an acceptable response, even a flattering one.
SIDONIE GABRIELLE COLETTE (1873–1954)

Silence is a true friend who never betrays.
CONFUCIUS (551– 479 BC)

A fair request should be followed by the deed in silence.
DANTE ALIGHIERI (1265–1321), *The Divine Comedy*

Silence is the ultimate weapon of power.
CHARLES DE GAULLE (1890–1970)

Who tells a finer tale than any of us? Silence does.
ISAK DINESEN (1885–1962)

Silence is the mother of truth.
BENJAMIN DISRAELI (1804–1881)

Silence is safer than speech.
EPICTETUS (AD 55–135)

Silence is the wit of fools.
ANATOLE FRANCE (1844–1924)

In the attitude of silence the soul finds the path in a clearer light, and what is elusive and deceptive resolves itself into crystal clearness. Our life is a long and arduous quest after Truth.
MAHATMA GANDHI (1869–1948)

I have learnt silence from the talkative, toleration from the intolerant, and kindness from the unkind; yet strange, I am ungrateful to these teachers.
KAHLIL GIBRAN (1883–1931)

Silence is argument carried out by other means.
CHE GUEVARA (1928–1967)

A man's silence is wonderful to listen to.
THOMAS HARDY (1840–1928)

Well-timed silence is the most commanding expression.
MARK HELPRIN (1947–)

With silence favor me.
HORACE (65–8 BC)

Silence propagates itself, and the longer talk has been suspended, the more difficult it is to find anything to say.
SAMUEL JOHNSON (1709–1784)

The most profound statements are often said in silence.
LYNN JOHNSTON (1947–)

Everything has its wonders, even darkness and silence, and I learn whatever state I am in, therein to be content.
HELEN KELLER (1880–1968)

In the end, we will remember not the words of our enemies, but the silence of our friends.
MARTIN LUTHER KING JR. (1929–1968)

Our lives begin to end the day we become silent about things that matter.
MARTIN LUTHER KING JR. (1929–1968)

Silence is the safest course for any man to adopt who distrust himself.
FRANÇOIS DE LA ROCHEFOUCAULD (1613–1680)

There are grammatical errors even in his silence.
STANISLAW LEC (1909–1966), *Unkempt Thoughts*

Better to remain silent and be thought a fool than to speak out and remove all doubt.
ABRAHAM LINCOLN (1809–1865)

Silence is the element in which great things fashion themselves.
MAURICE MAETERLINCK (1862–1949)

Much talking is the cause of danger. Silence is the means of avoiding misfortune. The talkative parrot is shut up in a cage. Other birds, without speech, fly freely about.
SASKYA PANDITA (1182–1251)

The eternal silence of these infinite spaces fills me with dread.
BLAISE PASCAL (1623–1662)

True silence is the rest of the mind; it is to the spirit what sleep is to the body, nourishment and refreshment.
WILLIAM PENN (1644–1718)

Not every truth is the better for showing its face undisguised; and often silence is the wisest thing for a man to heed.
PINDAR (522–433 BC)

Silence at the proper season is wisdom, and better than any speech.
PLUTARCH (AD 46–120)

I have often regretted my speech, never my silence.
PUBLILIUS SYRUS (C. 100 BC), *Maxims*

It is better wither to be silent, or to say things of more value than silence. Sooner throw a pearl at hazard than an idle or useless word; and do not say a little in many words, but a great deal in a few.
PYTHAGORAS (C. 582–500 BC)

Silence is better than unmeaning words.
PYTHAGORAS (C. 582–500 BC)

Silence is more musical than any song.
CHRISTINA G. ROSSETTI (1830–1894)

Absolute silence leads to sadness. It is the image of death.
JEAN-JACQUES ROUSSEAU (1712–1778)

Nothing is so good for an ignorant man as silence; and if he was sensible of this he would not be ignorant.
SAADI (1184–1291)

It is a great thing to know the season for speech and the season for silence.
SENECA (5 BC–AD 65)

Silence is the most perfect expression of scorn.
GEORGE BERNARD SHAW (1856–1950), *Back to Methuselah*

My personal hobbies are reading, listening to music, and silence.
EDITH SITWELL (1887–1964)

The cruelest lies are often told in silence.
ROBERT LOUIS STEVENSON (1850–1894)

Silence will save me from being wrong (and foolish), but it will also deprive me of the possibility of being right.
IGOR STRAVINSKY (1882–1971)

Their silence is sufficient praise.
TERENCE (185–159 BC)

In human intercourse the tragedy begins, not when there is misunderstanding about words, but when silence is not understood.
HENRY DAVID THOREAU (1817–1862)

A good word is an easy obligation; but not to speak ill, requires only our silence, which costs nothing.
JOHN TILLOTSON (1630–1694)

Well-timed silence hath more eloquence than speech.
MARTIN FARQUHAR TUPPER (1810–1889)

The right word may be effective, but no word was ever as effective as a rightly timed pause.
MARK TWAIN (1835–1910)

There is a wide difference between speaking to deceive, and being silent to be impenetrable.
VOLTAIRE (1694–1778)

Silence may be as variously shaded as speech.
EDITH WHARTON (1862–1937)

Simplicity

Simplicity is the most deceitful mistress that ever betrayed man.
HENRY ADAMS (1838–1918)

Simplicity may indeed be empty but, on the other hand, may be pregnant with meanings that ritual cannot express or can express only incompletely.
FELIX ADLER (1855–1931)

It is simplicity that makes the uneducated more effective than the educated when addressing popular audiences.
ARISTOTLE (384–322 BC), *Rhetoric*

Simplicity is nature's first step, and the last of art.
PHILIP JAMES BAILEY (1816–1902)

Simplicity is not an objective in art, but one achieves simplicity despite one's self by entering into the real sense of things.
CONSTANTIN BRANCUSI (1876–1957)

A taste for simplicity cannot endure for long.
EUGENE DELACROIX (1798–1863)

Simplicity is prerequisite for reliability.
EDSGER W. DIJKSTRA (1930–2002)

Everything should be made as simple as possible, but not one bit simpler.
ALBERT EINSTEIN (1879–1955)

Manifest plainness,
Embrace simplicity,
Reduce selfishness,
Have few desires.
LAO-TZU (604– 531 BC), *The Way of Lao-tzu*

Simplicity is the ultimate sophistication.
LEONARDO DA VINCI (1452–1519)

Simplicity in character, in manners, in style; in all things the supreme excellence is simplicity.
HENRY WADSWORTH LONGFELLOW (1807–1882)

Simplicity does not precede complexity, but follows it.
ALAN PERLIS (1922–1990)

Unnecessary possessions are unnecessary burdens. If you have them, you have to take care of them! There is great freedom in simplicity of living. It is those who have enough but not too much who are the happiest.
PEACE PILGRIM (1908–1981)

There is a certain majesty in simplicity which is far above all the quaintness of wit.
ALEXANDER POPE (1688–1744)

Simplicity is not the goal. It is the by-product of a good idea and modest expectations.
PAUL RAND (1914–1996)

Go confidently in the direction of your dreams! Live the life you've imagined. As you simplify your life, the laws of the universe will be simpler.
HENRY DAVID THOREAU (1817–1862)

Seek simplicity, and distrust it.
ALFRED NORTH WHITEHEAD (1861–1947)

The art of art, the glory of expression and the sunshine of the light of letters, is simplicity.
WALT WHITMAN (1819–1892)

I adore simple pleasures. They are the last refuge of the complex.
OSCAR WILDE (1854–1900), *The Picture of Dorian Gray*

Simplicity and repose are qualities that measure the true value of any work of art.
FRANK LLOYD WRIGHT (1867–1959)

Sin

All sins tend to be addictive, and the terminal point of addiction is what is called damnation.
W. H. AUDEN (1907–1973)

To abstain from sin when one can no longer sin is to be forsaken by sin, not to forsake it.
SAINT AUGUSTINE (354–430)

Sin is the dare of God's justice, the rape of His mercy, the jeer of His patience, the slight of His power, and the contempt of His love.
JOHN BUNYAN (1628–1688)

Sinners have to have the right to sin, up to the point, obviously, where it doesn't produce damage, at which point the law intervenes. The law doesn't touch upon the morality of our behaviour, but it touches upon the defence of the rights of the other. It's an old distinction that remains valid.
ROCCO BUTTIGLIONE (1948–)

For if there is a sin against life, it consists perhaps not so much in despairing of life as in hoping for another life and in eluding the implacable grandeur of this life.
ALBERT CAMUS (1913–1960)

It is the grace of God, that shows and condemns the sin that humbles us.
ADAM CLARKE (1760–1832)

Sin is basically a denial of God's right of possession.
EDWIN LOUIS COLE (1922–2002)

And the Devil did grin, for his darling sin is pride that apes humility.
SAMUEL TAYLOR COLERIDGE (1772–1834)

If the misery of the poor be caused not by the laws of nature, but by our institutions, great is our sin.
CHARLES DARWIN (1809–1882)

'Tis no sin to cheat the devil.
DANIEL DEFOE (1660–1731)

Great abundance of riches cannot be gathered and kept by any man without sin.
DESIDERIUS ERASMUS (1469–1536)

Sin is whatever obscures the soul.
ANDRÉ GIDE (1869–1951)

A "sin" is something which is not necessary.
G. I. GURDJIEFF (1872–1949)

I would rather die than do something, which I know to be a sin, or to be against God's will.
JOAN OF ARC (1412–1431)

Be a sinner and sin strongly, but more strongly have faith and rejoice in Christ.
MARTIN LUTHER (1483–1546)

There is no sin but ignorance.
CHRISTOPHER MARLOWE (1564–1593)

Humanity is the sin of God.
THEODORE PARKER (1810–1860)

Sin is geographical.
BERTRAND RUSSELL (1872–1970)

Every sin is the result of a collaboration.
SENECA (5 BC–AD 65)

Some rise by sin, and some by virtue fall.
WILLIAM SHAKESPEARE (1564–1616), *Measure for Measure*

The seven deadly sins … food, clothing, firing, rent, taxes, respectability and children. Nothing can lift those seven millstones from man's neck but money; and the spirit cannot soar until the millstones are lifted.
GEORGE BERNARD SHAW (1856–1950)

Sin cannot be conceived in a natural state, but only in a civil state, where it is decreed by common consent what is good or bad.
BENEDICT DE SPINOZA (1632–1677)

Sin is too stupid to see beyond itself.
ALFRED, LORD TENNYSON (1809–1892)

Three conditions are necessary for Penance: contrition, which is sorrow for sin, together with a purpose of amendment; confession of sins without any omission; and satisfaction by means of good works.
SAINT THOMAS AQUINAS (1225–1274)

There is no sin except stupidity.
OSCAR WILDE (1854–1900)

Sincerity

Hold faithfulness and sincerity as first principles.
CONFUCIUS (551–479 BC), *The Confucian Analects*

Sincerity and truth are the basis of every virtue.
CONFUCIUS (551–479 BC)

Truth of a modest sort I can promise you, and also sincerity. That complete, praiseworthy sincerity which, while it delivers one into the hands of one's enemies, is as likely as not to embroil one with one's friends.
JOSEPH CONRAD (1857–1924)

What is earnest is not always true; on the contrary, error is often more earnest than truth.
BENJAMIN DISRAELI (1804–1881)

Every man alone is sincere. At the entrance of a second person, hypocrisy begins.
RALPH WALDO EMERSON (1803–1882)

Sincerity is the luxury allowed, like diadems and authority, only to the highest rank. Every man alone is sincere. At the entrance of a second person, hypocrisy begins.
RALPH WALDO EMERSON (1803–1882)

The secret of success is sincerity. Once you can fake that you've got it made.
JEAN GIRAUDOUX (1882–1944)

Judge thyself with the judgment of sincerity, and thou will judge others with the judgment of charity.
JOHN MITCHELL MASON (1770–1829)

Sincerity is the way of Heaven.
MENCIUS (371–289 BC), *Works*

I am not sincere, even when I say I am not.
JULES RENARD (1864–1910)

It is dangerous to be sincere unless you are also stupid.
GEORGE BERNARD SHAW (1856–1950), *Man and Superman*

A little sincerity is a dangerous thing, and a great deal of it is absolutely fatal.
OSCAR WILDE (1854–1900), *The Critic as Artist*

Sisters

Sisterhood means if you happen to be in Burma and I happen to be in San Diego and I'm married to someone who is very jealous and you're married to somebody who is very possessive, if you call me in the middle of the night, I have to come.
MAYA ANGELOU (1928–)

Women are a sisterhood. They make common cause in behalf of the sex; and, indeed, this is natural enough, when we consider the vast power that the law gives us over them.
WILLIAM COBBETT (1763–1835)

A sister is both your mirror—and your opposite.
ELIZABETH FISHEL (1950–)

We are sisters. We will always be sisters. Our differences may never go away, but neither, for me, will our song.
ELIZABETH FISHEL (1950–)

Sister is probably the most competitive relationship within the family, but once the sisters are grown, it becomes the strongest relationship.
MARGARET MEAD (1901–1978)

There can be no situation in life in which the conversation of my dear sister will not administer some comfort to me.
LADY MARY WORTLEY MONTAGU (1689–1762)

For there is no friend like a sister, in calm or stormy weather, to cheer one on the tedious way, to fetch one if one goes astray, to lift one if one totters down, to strengthen whilst one stands.
CHRISTINA G. ROSSETTI (1830–1894)

Big sisters are the crab grass in the lawn of life.
CHARLES M. SCHULZ (1922–2000)

Is solace anywhere more comforting than that in the arms of a sister?
ALICE WALKER (1944–)

For the younger sisters, we always look up to the older sisters because they're always ahead of us and they always win.
SERENA WILLIAMS (1981–)

Skepticism

It is evident that skepticism, while it makes no actual change in man, always makes him feel better.
AMBROSE BIERCE (1842–1914)

Skepticism is the sadism of embittered souls.
E. M. CIORAN (1911–1995)

A thing is not proved just because no one has ever questioned it. What has never been gone into impartially has never been properly gone into. Hence skepticism is the first step toward truth. It must be applied generally, because it is the touchstone.
Denis Diderot (1713–1784)

Skepticism is slow suicide.
Ralph Waldo Emerson (1803–1882)

To believe in luck is skepticism.
Ralph Waldo Emerson (1803–1882)

All in all, I am not surprised that the people who want to unravel the social contract start with young adults. Those who are urged to feel afraid, very afraid, have both the greatest sense of independence and the most finely honed skepticism about government.
Ellen Goodman (1941–)

Modern cynics and skeptics … see no harm in paying those to whom they entrust the minds of their children a smaller wage than is paid to those to whom they entrust the care of their plumbing.
John F. Kennedy (1917–1963)

Skepticism is a virtue in history as well as in philosophy.
Napoléon I (1769–1821)

Skeptical scrutiny is the means, in both science and religion, by which deep insights can be winnowed from deep nonsense.
Carl Sagan (1934–1996)

Skepticism is the chastity of the intellect, and it is shameful to surrender it too soon or to the first comer: there is nobility in preserving it coolly and proudly through long youth, until at last, in the ripeness of instinct and discretion, it can be safely exchanged for fidelity and happiness.
George Santayana (1863–1952)

Skepticism, like chastity, should not be relinquished too readily.
George Santayana (1863–1952)

The three main sources of skepticism are, first, that not every people desires freedom; second, that democracy in certain parts of the world would be dangerous; and third, that there is little the world's democracies can do to advance freedom outside their countries.
Natan Sharansky (1948–)

There's a certain kind of skepticism that can't bear uncertainty.
Rupert Sheldrake (1942–)

Education has failed in a very serious way to convey the most important lesson science can teach: skepticism.
David Suzuki (1936–)

The skeptic does not mean him who doubts, but him who investigates or researches, as opposed to him who asserts and thinks that he has found.
Miguel de Unamuno (1864–1936)

In the end we shall have had enough of cynicism and skepticism and humbug and we shall want to live more musically.
Vincent Van Gogh (1853–1890)

Skeptics

For the skeptic there remains only one consolation: if there should be such a thing as superhuman law it is administered with subhuman inefficiency.
Eric Ambler (1909–1998)

I am the skeptic of skeptics.
Taylor Caldwell (1900–1985)

[T]he wonder is that there are so few skeptics.
Norman Finkelstein (1953–)

Modern cynics and skeptics … see no harm in paying those to whom they entrust the minds of their children a smaller wage than is paid to those to whom they entrust the care of their plumbing.
John F. Kennedy (1917–1963)

The problems of the world cannot possibly be solved by skeptics or cynics whose horizons are limited by the obvious realities. We need men who can dream of things that never were.
JOHN F. KENNEDY (1917–1963)

No actual skeptic, so far as I know, has claimed to disbelieve in an objective world. Skepticism is not a denial of belief, but rather a denial of rational grounds for belief.
WILLIAM PEPPERELL MONTAGUE (1873–1953)

The fact that a believer is happier than a skeptic is no more to the point than the fact that a drunken man is happier than a sober one.
GEORGE BERNARD SHAW (1856–1950)

The skeptic does not mean him who doubts, but him who investigates or researches, as opposed to him who asserts and thinks that he has found.
MIGUEL DE UNAMUNO (1864–1936)

Skill

If I had more skill in what I'm attempting, I wouldn't need so much courage.
ASHLEIGH BRILLIANT (1933–)

'Tis God gives skill, but not without men's hand: He could not make Antonio Stradivarius's violins without Antonio.
GEORGE ELIOT (1819–1880)

Skill to do comes of doing.
RALPH WALDO EMERSON (1803–1882)

'Tis skill, not strength, that governs a ship.
THOMAS FULLER (1608–1661)

It is a great piece of skill to know how to guide your luck, even while waiting for it.
BALTASAR GRACIAN (1601–1658)

Skill and confidence are an unconquered army.
GEORGE HERBERT (1593–1633)

Where there is the necessary technical skill to move mountains, there is no need for the faith that moves mountains.
ERIC HOFFER (1902–1983)

Wisdom is knowing what to do next; Skill is knowing how to do it, and Virtue is doing it.
DAVID STARR JORDAN (1851–1931)

Education can give you a skill, but a liberal education can give you dignity.
ELLEN KEY (1849–1926)

Tricks and treachery are merely proofs of lack of skill.
FRANÇOIS DE LA ROCHEFOUCAULD (1613–1680)

A handsome person, with perverted will, is a fine craft that's handled without skill.
MENANDER (342–292 BC)

Old age and treachery will overcome youth and skill.
ANONYMOUS

Try your skill in gilt first, then in gold.
ENGLISH PROVERB

Slander

Setting too good an example is a kind of slander seldom forgiven.
BENJAMIN FRANKLIN (1706–1790)

A generous confession disarms slander.
THOMAS FULLER (1608–1661)

No one is safe from slander. The best way is to pay no attention to it, but live in innocence and let the world talk.
MOLIÈRE (1622–1673)

You cannot slander human nature; it is worse than words can paint it.
CHARLES H. SPURGEON (1834–1892)

I'm tired of malicious articles slandering me.
BARBRA STREISAND (1942–)

Slander expires at a good woman's door.
DANISH PROVERB

Slang

The downtrodden are the great creators of slang.
ANTHONY BURGESS (1917–1993)

All slang is metaphor, and all metaphor is poetry.
G. K. CHESTERTON (1874–1936)

I know only two words of American slang, "swell" and "lousy." I think "swell" is lousy, but "lousy" is swell.
J. B. PRIESTLEY (1894–1984)

Slang is a language that rolls up its sleeves, spits on its hands and goes to work.
CARL SANDBURG (1878–1967)

Slavery

Consenting to slavery is a sacrilegious breach of trust, as offensive in the sight of God as it is derogatory from our own honor or interest of happiness.
JOHN ADAMS (1735–1826)

Better to starve free than be a fat slave.
AESOP (620–560 BC)

Before complaining that you are a slave to another, be sure that you are not a slave to self. Look within.... You will find there, perchance, slavish thoughts, slavish desires, and in your daily life and conduct slavish habits. Conquer these; cease to be a slave to self, and no man will have the power to enslave you.
JAMES ALLEN (1864–1912)

What a curious phenomenon it is that you can get men to die for the liberty of the world who will not make the little sacrifice that is needed to free themselves from their own individual bondage.
BRUCE BARTON (1886–1967)

When we abolish the slavery of half of humanity, together with the whole system of hypocrisy it implies, then the "division" of humanity will reveal its genuine significance and the human couple will find its true form.
SIMONE DE BEAUVOIR (1908–1986), *The Second Sex*

Enjoy things which are pleasant; that is not the evil: it is the reducing of our moral self to slavery by them that is.
THOMAS CARLYLE (1795–1881)

Should slavery be abolished there, (and it is an event, which, from these circumstances, we may reasonably expect to be produced in time) let it be remembered, that the Quakers will have had the merit of its abolition.
THOMAS CLARKSON (1760–1846)

I didn't know I was a slave until I found out I couldn't do the things I wanted.
FREDERICK DOUGLASS (1817–1895)

In thinking of America, I sometimes find myself admiring her bright blue sky—her grand old woods—her fertile fields—her beautiful rivers—her mighty lakes and star-crowned mountains. But my rapture is soon checked when I remember that all is cursed with the infernal spirit of slave-holding and wrong; when I remember that with the waters of her noblest rivers, the tears of my brethren are borne to the ocean, disregarded and forgotten; that her most fertile fields drink daily of the warm blood of my outraged sisters, I am filled with unutterable loathing.
FREDERICK DOUGLASS (1817–1895)

A strict belief, fate is the worst kind of slavery; on the other hand there is comfort in the thought that God will be moved by our prayers.
EPICURUS (341–270 BC)

From slavery to segregation, we remember that America did not always live up to its ideals. In fact, we often fell far short of them. But we also learned that fundamental to our national character is the

drive to live out the true meaning of our creed.
BILL FRIST (1952–)

The moment the slave resolves that he will no longer be a slave, his fetters fall. Freedom and slavery are mental states.
MAHATMA GANDHI (1869–1948)

They have exiled me now from their society and I am pleased, because humanity does not exile except the one whose noble spirit rebels against despotism and oppression. He who does not prefer exile to slavery is not free by any measure of freedom, truth and duty.
KAHLIL GIBRAN (1883–1931), *Spirits Rebellious*

Is life so dear, or peace so sweet, as to be purchased at the price of chains or slavery? Forbid it, Almighty God! I know not what course others may take; but as for me, give me liberty or give me death!
PATRICK HENRY (1736–1799)

Wide-sounding Zeus takes away half a man's worth on the day when slavery comes upon him.
HOMER (800–700 BC), *The Odyssey*

There is no slavery but ignorance.
ROBERT GREEN INGERSOLL (1833–1899), *The Philosophy of Ingersoll*

Until the late abolition movement, the spiritual interests of the slaves were about as little regarded as their physical necessities.
FANNY KEMBLE (1809–1863)

If the cruelties of slavery could not stop us, the opposition we now face will surely fail. Because the goal of America is freedom, abused and scorned tho' we may be, our destiny is tied up with America's destiny.
MARTIN LUTHER KING JR. (1929–1968)

We must free the slaves or be ourselves subdued. The slaves were undeniably an element of strength to those who had their service, and we must decide whether that element should be with us or "against us." Emancipation will strike at the heart of the rebellion.
ABRAHAM LINCOLN (1809–1865)

Whenever I hear anyone arguing for slavery, I feel a strong impulse to see it tried on him personally.
ABRAHAM LINCOLN (1809–1865)

Emancipate yourselves from mental slavery,
None but ourselves can free our minds.
BOB MARLEY (1945–1981)

Life without the courage for death is slavery.
SENECA (5 BC–AD 65)

The most onerous slavery is to be a slave to oneself.
SENECA (5 BC–AD 65)

The slave of fear: the worst of slaveries.
GEORGE BERNARD SHAW (1856–1950)

For in reason, all government without the consent of the governed is the very definition of slavery.
JONATHAN SWIFT (1667–1745)

Money is a new form of slavery, and distinguishable from the old simply by the fact that it is impersonal—that there is no human relation between master and slave.
LEO TOLSTOY (1828–1910)

That man over there says that women need to be helped into carriages, and lifted over ditches, and to have the best place everywhere. Nobody ever helps me into carriages, or over mud-puddles, or gives me any best place! And ain't I a woman? Look at me! Look at my arm! I have ploughed and planted, and gathered into barns, and no man could head me! And ain't I a woman? I could work as much and eat as much as a man—when I could get it—and bear the lash as well! And ain't I a woman? I have borne thirteen children, and seen most all sold off to slavery, and when I cried out with my mother's grief, none but Jesus heard me! And ain't I a woman?
SOJOURNER TRUTH (1797–1883)

The blunting effects of slavery upon the slaveholder's moral perceptions are known and conceded the world over; and a privileged class, an aristocracy, is but a band of slaveholders under another name.
MARK TWAIN (1835–1910)

Slavery to monarchs and ministers, which the world will be long freeing itself from, and whose deadly grasp stops the progress of the human mind, is not yet abolished.
MARY WOLLSTONECRAFT (1759 –1797)

And thus goes segregation, which is the most far-reaching development in the history of the Negro since the enslavement of the race.
CARTER G. WOODSON (1875–1950)

Sleep

Laugh and the world laughs with you, snore and you sleep alone.
ANTHONY BURGESS (1917–1993)

If you can't sleep, then get up and do something instead of lying there and worrying. It's the worry that gets you, not the loss of sleep.
DALE CARNEGIE (1888–1955)

Oh sleep! It is a gentle thing,
Beloved from pole to pole.
SAMUEL TAYLOR COLERIDGE (1772–1834)

[Sleep is] the golden chain that ties health and our bodies together.
THOMAS DEKKER (1572–1632)

Early to bed and early to rise makes a man healthy, wealthy, and wise.
BENJAMIN FRANKLIN (1706–1790)

It is better to sleep on things beforehand than lie awake about them afterward.
BALTASAR GRACIAN (1601–1658)

There is a time for many words, and there is also a time for sleep.
HOMER (800–700 BC), *The Odyssey*

Not being able to sleep is terrible. You have the misery of having partied all night … without the satisfaction.
LYNN JOHNSTON (1947–)

Life is something that happens when you can't get to sleep.
FRAN LEBOWITZ (1950–)

I have never taken any exercise except sleeping and resting.
MARK TWAIN (1835–1910)

Death's brother, Sleep.
VIRGIL (C. 70–19 BC), *Aeneid*

When I woke up this morning my girlfriend asked me, "Did you sleep good?" I said "No, I made a few mistakes."
STEVEN WRIGHT (1955–)

The best bridge between despair and hope is a good night's sleep.
ANONYMOUS

Smiles

What sunshine is to flowers, smiles are to humanity. These are but trifles, to be sure; but scattered along life's pathway, the good they do is inconceivable.
JOSEPH ADDISON (1672–1719)

Smiles form the channels of a future tear.
LORD BYRON (1788–1824)

Most smiles are started by another smile.
FRANK A. CLARK (1915–2003)

Youth smiles without any reason. It is one of its chiefest charms.
THOMAS GRAY (1716–1771)

Sometimes your joy is the source of your smile, but sometimes your smile can be the source of your joy.
THICH NHAT HAHN (1926–)

Smiles are the language of love.
DAVID HARE (1947–)

There are many kinds of smiles, each having a distinct character. Some announce goodness, and sweetness, others betray sarcasm, bitterness, and

pride; some soften the countenance by their languishing tenderness, others brighten by their spiritual vivacity.
JOHANN KASPAR LAVATER (1741–1801)

The real man smiles in trouble, gathers strength from distress, and grows brave by reflection.
THOMAS PAINE (1737–1809)

Smile. It increases your face value.
DOLLY PARTON (1946–)

Give a smile to everyone you meet (smile with your eyes) and you'll smile and receive smiles.
W. CLEMENT STONE (1902–2002)

A smile is the light in your window that tells others that there is a caring, sharing person inside.
DENIS WAITLEY (1933–)

Let my soul smile through my heart and my heart smile through my eyes, that I may scatter rich smiles in sad hearts.
PARAMAHANSA YOGANANDA (1893–1952)

It takes seventy-two muscles to frown, but only thirteen to smile.
ANONYMOUS

Smoking

Smoking is related to practically every terrible thing that can happen to you.
LONI ANDERSON (1946–)

Smoking has a sedative effect upon the nerves, and enables a man to bear the sorrows of this life (of which every one has his share) not only decently, but dignifiedly.
GEORGE BORROW (1803–1881)

The true face of smoking is disease, death and horror—not the glamour and sophistication the pushers in the tobacco industry try to portray.
DAVID BYRNE (1952–)

So smoking is the perfect way to commit suicide without actually dying. I smoke because it's bad, it's really simple.
DAMIEN HIRST (1909–)

Smoking is hateful to the nose, harmful to the brain, and dangerous to the lungs.
KING JAMES I (1566–1625)

Smoking is one of the leading causes of statistics.
FLETCHER KNEBEL (1911–1993)

Much smoking kills live men and cures dead swine.
GEORGE DENNISON PRENTICE(1802–1870)

Giving up smoking is the easiest thing in the world. I know because I've done it thousands of times.
MARK TWAIN (1835–1910)

Snow

He who ascends to mountain tops, shall find,
The loftiest peaks most wrapt in clouds and snow;
He who surpasses or subdues mankind,
Must look down on the hate of those below.
LORD BYRON (1788–1824)

Advice is like snow—the softer it falls, the longer it dwells upon, and the deeper it sinks into the mind.
SAMUEL TAYLOR COLERIDGE (1772–1834)

This is the Hour of Lead—
Remembered, if outlived,
As Freezing persons recollect the Snow—
First—Chill—then Stupor—then the letting go—
EMILY DICKINSON (1830–1886), "No. 342"

Sunshine cannot bleach the snow,
Nor time unmake what poets know.
RALPH WALDO EMERSON (1803–1882)

Whose woods these are I think I know.
His house is in the village though;
He will not see me stopping here
To watch his woods fill up with snow.
ROBERT FROST (1874–1963), "Stopping by Woods on a Snowy Evening"

If you walk on snow you cannot hide your footprints.
GEORGE HERBERT (1593–1633)

The aging process has you firmly in its grasp if you never get the urge to throw a snowball.
DOUG LARSON (1902–1981)

A lot of people like snow. I find it to be an unnecessary freezing of water.
CARL REINER (1922–)

In the bleak midwinter
Frosty wind made moan,
Earth stood hard as iron,
Water like a stone;
Snow had fallen, snow on snow,
Snow on snow,
In the bleak midwinter,
Long ago.
CHRISTINA G. ROSSETTI (1830–1894), "A Christmas Carol"

We build statues out of snow, and weep to see them melt.
SIR WALTER SCOTT (1771–1832)

Snow and adolescence are the only problems that disappear if you ignore them long enough.
EARL WILSON (1934–2005)

Sobriety

Always do sober what you said you'd do drunk. That will teach you to keep your mouth shut.
ERNEST HEMINGWAY (1899–1961)

Perfect reason flees all extremity, and leads one to be wise with sobriety.
MOLIÈRE (1622–1673)

Strength of mind rests in sobriety; for this keeps your reason unclouded by passion.
PYTHAGORAS (C. 582–500 BC)

In sobriety they teach you to think the drink through. Think through to the next morning, how it's going to influence you, the shame, how it's going to trigger the domino effect.
CHARLIE SHEEN (1965–)

The worst thing about some men is that when they are not drunk they are sober.
WILLIAM BUTLER YEATS (1865–1939)

Socialism

Socialism is nothing more nor less than the social, political and ideological system which breaks the fetters upon economic growth created under capitalism and opens the way to a new period of economic and social expansion on a much larger scale.
EARL BROWDER (1891–1973)

I recognise that Socialism has ended its purely theoretical course, and that the hour to construct has come.
JOHN BURNS (1858–1943)

Socialism is good when it comes to wages, but it tells me nothing when it comes to other questions in life that are more private and painful, for which I must seek answers elsewhere.
KAREL CAPEK (1890–1938)

Socialism is like a dream. Sooner or later you wake up to reality.
SIR WINSTON CHURCHILL (1874–1965)

The inherent vice of capitalism is the unequal sharing of blessings; the inherent virtue of socialism is the equal sharing of miseries.
SIR WINSTON CHURCHILL (1874–1965)

Socialism appeals to better classes and has far more strength. Attack the state and you excite feelings of loyalty even among the disaffected classes; but attack the industrial system and appeal to the state, and you may have loyalty in your favor.
JOHN BATES CLARK (1847–1938)

There is nothing in socialism that a little age or a little money will not cure.
WILL DURANT (1885–1981)

International socialism recognizes the right of free independent nations, with equal rights.
KARL LIEBKNECHT (1871–1919)

Democracy is the road to socialism.
KARL MARX (1818–1883)

Socialism is… not only a way of life, but a certain scientific approach to social and economic problems.
JAWAHARLAL NEHRU (1889–1964)

The historical experience of socialist countries has sadly demonstrated that collectivism does not do away with alienation but rather increases it, adding to it a lack of basic necessities and economic inefficiency.
POPE JOHN PAUL II (1920–2005)

The only hope of socialism resides in those who have already brought about in themselves, as far as is possible in the society of today, that union between manual and intellectual labor which characterizes the society we are aiming at.
SIMONE WEIL (1909–1943)

Society

The test of one's behavior pattern is [one's] relationship to society, relationship to work and relationship to sex.
ALFRED ADLER (1870–1937)

If we all said to people's faces what we say behind one another's backs, society would be impossible.
HONORÉ DE BALZAC (1799–1850)

Society cannot share a common communication system so long as it is split into warring factions.
BERTOLT BRECHT (1898–1956)

Solitude shows us what we should be; society shows us what we are.
ROBERT CECIL (1563–1612)

I don't have to tell you things are bad. Everybody knows things are bad. It's a depression. Everybody's out of work or scared of losing their job. The dollar buys a nickel's worth, banks are going bust, shopkeepers keep a gun under the counter. Punks are running wild in the street and there's nobody anywhere who seems to know what to do, and there's no end to it. We know the air is unfit to breathe and our food is unfit to eat, and we sit watching our TV's while some local newscaster tells us that today we had fifteen homicides and sixty-three violent crimes, as if that's the way it's supposed to be.

We know things are bad—worse than bad. They're crazy. It's like everything everywhere is going crazy, so we don't go out anymore. We sit in the house, and slowly the world we are living in is getting smaller, and all we say is, "Please, at least leave us alone in our living rooms. Let me have my toaster and my TV and my steel-belted radials and I won't say anything. Just leave us alone."

Well, I'm not gonna leave you alone. I want you to get mad! I don't want you to protest. I don't want you to riot—I don't want you to write to your congressman because I wouldn't know what to tell you to write. I don't know what to do about the depression and the inflation and the Russians and the crime in the street. All I know is that first you've got to get mad. You've got to say, "I'm a human being, goddamnit! My life has value!" So I want you to get up now. I want all of you to get up out of your chairs. I want you to get up right now and go to the window. Open it, and stick your head out, and yell, "I'm mad as hell, and I'm not going to take this anymore!" Things have got to change. But first, you've gotta get mad!… Then we'll figure out what to do about the depression and the inflation and the oil crisis. But first get up out of your chairs, open the window, stick your head out, and yell, and say it: "I'm mad as hell, and I'm not going to take this anymore."
PADDY CHAYEFSKY (1923–1981), *Network*

We must beware of trying to build a society in which nobody counts for anything except a politician or an official, a society where enterprise gains no reward and thrift no privileges.
SIR WINSTON CHURCHILL (1874–1965)

Knowledge of what is does not open the door directly to what should be. If one asks whence derives the authority of fundamental ends, since they cannot be stated and justified merely by reason, one can only answer: they exist in a healthy society.
ALBERT EINSTEIN (1879–1955)

The intuitive mind is a sacred gift and the rational mind is a faithful servant. We have created a society that honors the servant and has forgotten the gift.
ALBERT EINSTEIN (1879–1955)

Society everywhere is in conspiracy against the manhood of every one of its members. The virtue in most request is conformity. Self-reliance is its aversion. It loves not realities and creators, but names and customs.
RALPH WALDO EMERSON (1803–1882)

The endurance of the inequalities of life by the poor is the marvel of human society.
JAMES A. FROUDE (1818–1894)

Let him who expects one class of society to prosper into highest degree, while the other is in distress, try whether one side of his face can smile while the other is pinched. Try whether.
THOMAS FULLER (1608–1661)

There will be "two societies" in the future: high-paid knowledge workers and low-paid service workers.
BILL GATES (1955–)

Society is a republic. When [individuals try] to lift themselves above others, they are dragged down by the mass, either by ridicule or slander.
VICTOR HUGO (1802–1885)

The reason why men enter into society is the preservation of their property.
JOHN LOCKE (1632–1704)

Individual commitment to a group effort—that is what makes a team work, a company work, a society work, a civilization work.
VINCE LOMBARDI (1913–1970)

If you have no friends to share or rejoice in your success in life—if you cannot look back to those whom you owe gratitude, or forward to those to whom you ought to afford protection, still it is no less incumbent on you to move steadily in the path of duty; for your active excretions are due not only to society; but in humble gratitude to the Being who made you a member of it, with powers to save yourself and others.
SIR WALTER SCOTT (1771–1832)

Society is no comfort to one not sociable.
WILLIAM SHAKESPEARE (1564–1616), *Cymbeline*

A well ordered society would be one where the State only had a negative action, comparable to that of a rudder: a light pressure at the right moment to counteract the first suggestion of any loss of equilibrium.
MARGARET THATCHER (1925–)

We pass the word around; we ponder how the case is put by different people, we read the poetry; we meditate over the literature; we play the music; we change our minds; we reach an understanding. Society evolves this way, not by shouting each other down, but by the unique capacity of unique, individual human beings to comprehend each other.
LEWIS THOMAS (1913–1993), *The Medusa and the Snail*

Soldiers

There exist only three beings worthy of respect:
The priest, the soldier, the poet.
To know, to kill, to create.
CHARLES BAUDELAIRE (1821–1867), *Mon coeur mis à nu*

History, n.: An account mostly false, of events unimportant, which are brought about by rulers mostly knaves, and soldiers mostly fools.
AMBROSE BIERCE (1842–1914), *The Devil's Dictionary*

They said this mystery never shall cease:
The priest promotes war, and the soldier peace.
WILLIAM BLAKE (1757–1827)

A man is not necessarily intelligent because he has plenty of ideas any more than he is a good general because he has plenty of soldiers.
NICOLAS CHAMFORT (1741–1794)

Why, you may take the most gallant sailor, the most intrepid airman or the most audacious soldier, put them at a table together, what do you get? The sum of their fears.
SIR WINSTON CHURCHILL (1874–1965)

Christians, like slaves and soldiers, ask no questions.
JERRY FALWELL (1933–)

It is a tragic mix-up when the United States spends $500,000 for every enemy soldier killed, and only $53 annually on the victims of poverty.
MARTIN LUTHER KING JR. (1929–1968)

When you're left wounded on Afghanistan's plains
And the women come out to cut up what remains,
Just roll to your rifle and blow out your brains,
And go to your God like a soldier.
RUDYARD KIPLING (1865–1936)

By profession I am a Soldier and take pride in that fact, but I am prouder to be a father.
GENERAL DOUGLAS MACARTHUR (1880–1964)

Soldiers generally win battles; generals get credit for them.
NAPOLÉON I (1769–1821)

If a soldier or laborer complains of the hardships of his lot, set him to do nothing.
BLAISE PASCAL (1623–1662)

War then, is a relation—not between man and man: but between state and state; and individuals are enemies only accidentally: not as men, nor even as citizens: but as soldiers; not as members of their country, but as its defenders.
JEAN-JACQUES ROUSSEAU (1712–1778)

Then a soldier, Full of strange oaths and bearded like the bard, Jealous in honor, sudden and quick in quarrel, Seeking the bubble reputation Even in the cannon's mouth.
WILLIAM SHAKESPEARE (1564–1616), *As You Like It*

He was wont to speak plain and to the purpose, like an honest man and a soldier.
WILLIAM SHAKESPEARE (1564–1616), *Much Ado About Nothing*

By and by when each nation has 20,000 battleships and 5,000,000 soldiers we shall all be safe and the wisdom of statesmanship will stand confirmed.
MARK TWAIN (1835–1910)

Too much zeal is a bad soldier who fires before the word of command.
ANONYMOUS

The best soldiers are not warlike.
CHINESE PROVERBS

The common soldier's blood makes the general great.
ITALIAN PROVERB

The soldiers fight, and the kings are heroes.
YIDDISH PROVERB

Solitude

Whosoever is delighted in solitude is either a wild beast or a god.
ARISTOTLE (384–322 BC)

Solitude is better than the society of evil persons.
ABU BAKR (C. 573–634)

Solitude is fine, but you need someone to tell you that solitude is fine.
HONORÉ DE BALZAC (1799–1850)

But in the end, in the end one is alone. We are all of us alone. I mean I'm told these days we have to consider ourselves as being in society… but in the end one knows one is alone, that one lives at the heart of a solitude.
HAROLD BLOOM (1930–)

In solitude, where we are least alone.
LORD BYRON (1788–1824)

Solitude shows us what we should be; society shows us what we are.
ROBERT CECIL (1563–1612)

I live in that solitude which is painful in youth, but delicious in the years of maturity.
ALBERT EINSTEIN (1879–1955)

I lived in solitude in the country and noticed how the monotony of a quiet life stimulates the creative mind.
ALBERT EINSTEIN (1879–1955)

The weight of the world is love. Under the burden of solitude, under the burden of dissatisfaction.
ALLEN GINSBERG (1926–1997)

True solitude is a din of birdsong, seething leaves, whirling colors, or a clamor of tracks in the snow.
EDWARD HOAGLAND (1932–)

O Solitude! If I must with thee dwell,
Let it not be among the jumbled heap of murky buildings.
JOHN KEATS (1795–1821)

Solitude would be ideal if you could pick the people to avoid.
KARL KRAUS (1874–1936)

The whole value of solitude depends upon one's self; it may be a sanctuary or a prison, a haven of repose or a place of punishment, a heaven or a hell, as we ourselves make it.
JOHN LUBBOCK (1834–1913)

Solitude terrifies the soul at twenty.
MOLIÈRE (1622–1673)

One of the greatest necessities in America is to discover creative solitude.
CARL SANDBURG (1878–1967)

Solitude cherishes great virtues and destroys little ones.
SYDNEY SMITH (1771–1845)

I have never found a companion that was so companionable as solitude. We are for the most part more lonely when we go abroad among men than when we stay in our chambers. A man thinking or working is always alone, let him be where he will.
HENRY DAVID THOREAU (1817–1862)

Only in solitude do we find ourselves; and in finding ourselves, we find in ourselves all our brothers in solitude.
MIGUEL DE UNAMUNO (1864–1936)

Songs

There are quite a few honest songwriters out there writing about relationships and their own personality traits. But for some reason, once they step out of the bedroom, their honesty doesn't seem to come with them.
BILLY BRAGG (1957–)

You know, a song is like a kid. You bring it up. And sometimes something you thought was going to be fantastic, by the time it's finished, is a bit of a disappointment.
PHIL COLLINS (1951–)

I've never written a political song. Songs can't save the world. I've gone through all that.
BOB DYLAN (1941–)

A song is anything that can walk by itself.
BOB DYLAN (1941–)

Each song is a lifetime, it begins and ends, and there's a journey taken within the songs.
LEIF GARRETT (1961–)

Without a song, each day would be a century.
MAHALIA JACKSON (1911–1972)

My songs are like my kids.
BILLY JOEL (1949–)

I've never written a song in my life. It's all a big hoax.
ELVIS PRESLEY (1935–1977)

A song has to become as much a part of you as a tailored suit.
MARTHA REEVES (1941–)

I always try to write a song, I never just want to write a record.
SMOKEY ROBINSON (1940–)

Silence is more musical than any song.
CHRISTINA G. ROSSETTI (1830–1894)

So many good songs get written fast, because you know exactly what has to work.
STEPHEN SONDHEIM (1930–)

Sons

As a single withered tree, if set aflame, causes a whole forest to burn, so does a rascal son destroy a whole family.
CHANAKYA (350–275 BC)

I live for my sons. I would be lost without them.
PRINCESS DIANA (1961–1997)

Grieve not, then, if your sons seem to desert you, but rejoice, rather, seeing the will of God done gladly.
JIM ELLIOT (1927–1956)

I love you when you bow in your mosque, kneel in your temple, pray in your church. For you and I are sons of one religion, and it is the spirit.
KAHLIL GIBRAN (1883–1931)

He only half dies who leaves an image of himself in his sons.
CARLO GOLDONI (1707–1793)

Rich men's sons are seldom rich men's fathers.
HERBERT KAUFMAN (1878–1947)

I have a dream that one day on the red hills of Georgia, the sons of former slaves and the sons of former slave owners will be able to sit together at the table of brotherhood.
MARTIN LUTHER KING JR. (1929–1968)

Sophistication

There is more sophistication and less sense in New York than anywhere else on the globe.
DON HEROLD (1889–1966)

Simplicity is the ultimate sophistication.
LEONARDO DA VINCI (1452–1519)

Hip is the sophistication of the wise primitive in a giant jungle.
NORMAN MAILER (1923–2007)

Sophistication might be described as the ability to cope gracefully with a situation involving the presence of a formidable menace to one's poise and prestige (such as the butler, or the man under the bed—but never the husband).
JAMES THURBER (1894–1961)

Sorrow

Sorrow makes men sincere.
HENRY WARD BEECHER (1813–1887)

Can I see another's woe, and not be in sorrow, too?
Can I see another's grief, and not seek for kind relief?
WILLIAM BLAKE (1757–1827)

Excess of sorrow laughs, excess of joy weeps.
WILLIAM BLAKE (1757–1827)

Joys impregnate, sorrows bring forth.
WILLIAM BLAKE (1757–1827)

The busy bee has no time for sorrow.
WILLIAM BLAKE (1757–1827)

Proud people breed sad sorrows for themselves.
EMILY BRONTË (1818–1848)

There is an alchemy in sorrow. It can be transmuted into wisdom, which, if it does not bring joy, can yet bring happiness.
PEARL S. BUCK (1892–1973)

Partying is such sweet sorrow.
ROBERT BYRNE (1928–)

All sorrows are good (or are less) with bread.
MIGUEL DE CERVANTES (1547–1616)

There is no greater sorrow than to be mindful of the happy time in misery.
DANTE ALIGHIERI (1265–1321)

We choose our joys and sorrows long before we experience them.
KAHLIL GIBRAN (1883–1931)

The natural effect of sorrow over the dead is to refine and elevate the mind.
WASHINGTON IRVING (1783–1859)

Sorrow is the mere rust of the soul. Activity will cleanse and brighten it.
SAMUEL JOHNSON (1709–1784)

Sorrow and silence are strong, and patient endurance is godlike.
HENRY WADSWORTH LONGFELLOW (1807–1882)

Earth hath no sorrow that heaven cannot heal.
SIR THOMAS MORE (1478–1535)

Sorrow is tranquillity remembered in emotion.
DOROTHY PARKER (1893–1967)

When sorrows come, they come not single spies, but in battalions!
WILLIAM SHAKESPEARE (1564–1616), *Hamlet*

Give sorrow words. The grief that does not speak whispers the o'er-fraught heart, and bids it break.
WILLIAM SHAKESPEARE (1564–1616), *Macbeth*

He that loves not his wife and children feeds a lioness at home, and broods a nest of sorrows.
JEREMY TAYLOR (1613–1667)

If you are patient in one moment of anger, you will escape a hundred days of sorrow.
CHINESE PROVERB

You cannot prevent the birds of sorrow from flying over your head, but you can prevent them from building nests in your hair.
CHINESE PROVERB

Soul

Flowers are the sweetest things God ever made and forgot to put a soul into.
HENRY WARD BEECHER (1813–1887)

Man has no Body distinct from his Soul; for that called Body is a portion of Soul discerned by the five Senses, the chief inlets of Soul in this age.
WILLIAM BLAKE (1757–1827)

Safeguard the health both of body and soul.
CLEOBULUS (C. 500 BC)

Happiness resides not in possessions, and not in gold, happiness dwells in the soul.
DEMOCRITUS (460–370 BC)

Oh, heart, if one should say to you that the soul perishes like the body, answer that the flower withers, but the seed remains.
KAHLIL GIBRAN (1883–1931)

What the soul knows is often unknown to the man who has a soul. We are infinitely more than we think.
KAHLIL GIBRAN (1883–1931)

This is what I believe: That I am I. That my soul is a dark forest. That my known self will never be more than a little clearing in the forest. That gods, strange gods, come forth from the forest into the clearing of my known self, and then go back. That I must have the courage to let them come and go. That I will never let mankind put anything over me, but that I will try always to recognize and submit to the gods in me and the gods in other men and women. There is my creed.
D. H. LAWRENCE (1885–1930)

Years wrinkle the skin, but to give up enthusiasm wrinkles the soul.
GENERAL DOUGLAS MACARTHUR (1880–1964)

The soul becomes dyed with the color of its thoughts.
MARCUS AURELIUS ANTONINUS (121–180)

Loyalty to petrified opinion never yet broke a chain or freed a human soul.
MARK TWAIN (1835–1910)

I will permit no man to narrow and degrade my soul by making me hate him.
BOOKER T. WASHINGTON (1856–1915)

There are victories of the soul and spirit. Sometimes, even if you lose, you win.
ELIE WIESEL (1928–)

Nothing can cure the soul but the senses, just as nothing can cure the senses but the soul.
OSCAR WILDE (1854–1900)

Space

Somewhere, behind space and time,
Is wetter water, slimier slime.
RUPERT BROOKE (1887–1915)

We will never be an advanced civilization as long as rain showers can delay the launching of a space rocket.
GEORGE CARLIN (1937–)

Boundaries are actually the main factor in space, just as the present, another boundary, is the main factor in time.
EDUARDO CHILLIDA (1924–2002)

Nothing exists except atoms and empty space; everything else is opinion.
DEMOCRITUS (460-370 BC)

Space by itself, and time by itself, are doomed to fade away into mere shadows, and only a kind union of the two will preserve an independent reality.
ALBERT EINSTEIN (1879–1955)

Every true man is a cause, a country, and an age; requires infinite spaces and numbers and time fully to accomplish his design;—and posterity seem to follow his steps as a train of clients.
RALPH WALDO EMERSON (1803–1882)

Put three grains of sand inside a vast cathedral, and the cathedral will be more closely packed with sand than space is with stars.
JAMES JEANS (1877–1946)

Nothing puzzles me more than time and space; and yet nothing troubles me less.
CHARLES LAMB (1775–1834)

Through space the universe encompasses and swallows me up like an atom; through thought I comprehend the world.
BLAISE PASCAL (1623–1662)

God has no intention of setting a limit to the efforts of man to conquer space.
POPE PIUS XII (1876–1958)

I wouldn't know a space-time continuum or warp core breach if they got into bed with me.
PATRICK STEWART (1940–)

Speaking

He who does not know how to be silent will not know how to speak.
AUSONIUS (C. 310–395)

No man pleases by silence; many I please by speaking briefly.
AUSONIUS (C. 310–395)

Silence is only frightening to people who are compulsively verbalizing.
WILLIAM S. BURROUGHS (1914–1997)

Under all speech that is good for anything there lies a silence that is better. Silence is deep as Eternity; speech is shallow as Time.
THOMAS CARLYLE (1795–1881)

Who you are speaks so loudly I can't hear what you're saying.
RALPH WALDO EMERSON (1803–1882)

Silence is safer than speech.
EPICTETUS (AD 55–135)

Remember not only to say the right thing in the right place, but far more difficult still, to leave unsaid the wrong thing at the tempting moment.
BENJAMIN FRANKLIN (1706–1790)

The liberty of speaking and writing guards our other liberties.
THOMAS JEFFERSON (1762–1826)

When angry, count ten before you speak; if very angry, an hundred.
THOMAS JEFFERSON (1762–1826)

In order that all men may be taught to speak the truth, it is necessary that all likewise should learn to hear it.
SAMUEL JOHNSON (1709–1784)

Better to remain silent and be thought a fool than to speak out and remove all doubt.
ABRAHAM LINCOLN (1809–1865)

The object of oratory alone is not truth, but persuasion.
LORD THOMAS BABINGTON MACAULAY (1800–1859)

Don't appear so scholarly, pray. Humanize your talk, and speak to be understood.
MOLIÈRE (1622–1673)

Silence at the proper season is wisdom, and better than any speech.
PLUTARCH (AD 46–120)

I have often regretted my speech, never my silence.
PUBLILIUS SYRUS (C. 100 BC), *Maxims*

It is better wither to be silent, or to say things of more value than silence. Sooner throw a pearl at hazard than an idle or useless word; and do not say a little in many words, but a great deal in a few.
PYTHAGORAS (C. 582–500 BC)

It is a great thing to know the season for speech and the season for silence.
SENECA (5 BC–AD 65)

The silence often of pure innocence persuades when speaking fails.
WILLIAM SHAKESPEARE (1564–1616), *The Winter's Tale*

Never say more than is necessary.
RICHARD BRINSLEY SHERIDAN (1751–1816)

All speech, written or spoken, is a dead language, until it finds a willing and prepared hearer.
ROBERT LOUIS STEVENSON (1850–1894)

Trees are Earth's endless effort to speak to the listening heaven.
RABINDRANATH TAGORE (1861–1941)

Kind words can be short and easy to speak, but their echoes are truly endless.
MOTHER TERESA (1910–1997)

A good word is an easy obligation; but not to speak ill, requires only our silence, which costs nothing.
JOHN TILLOTSON (1630–1694)

Anything that is too stupid to be spoken is sung.
VOLTAIRE (1694–1778)

There is a wide difference between speaking to deceive, and being silent to be impenetrable.
VOLTAIRE (1694–1778)

People have to talk about something just to keep their voice boxes in working order so they'll have good voice boxes in case there's ever anything really meaningful to say.
KURT VONNEGUT JR. (1922–2007)

I speak two languages, Body and English.
MAE WEST (1892–1980)

Silence may be as variously shaded as speech.
EDITH WHARTON (1862–1937)

Spirit

The majority of people perform well in a crisis and when the spotlight is on them; it's on the Sunday

afternoons of this life, when nobody is looking, that the spirit falters.
ALAN BENNETT (1934–)

If a man possesses a repentant spirit his sins will disappear, but if he has an unrepentant spirit his sins will continue and condemn him for their sake forever.
THE BUDDHA (563–483 BC)

Great spirits have always found violent opposition from mediocrities. The latter cannot understand it when a man does not thoughtlessly submit to hereditary prejudices but honestly and courageously uses his intelligence.
ALBERT EINSTEIN (1879–1955)

My religion consists of a humble admiration of the illimitable superior spirit who reveals himself in the slight details we are able to perceive with our frail and feeble mind.
ALBERT EINSTEIN (1879–1955)

Life is either a daring adventure or nothing. To keep our faces toward change and behave like free spirits in the presence of fate is strength undefeatable.
HELEN KELLER (1880–1968)

A child's spirit is like a child, you can never catch it by running after it; you must stand still, and, for love, it will soon itself come back.
ARTHUR MILLER (1915–2005)

How much truth can a spirit bear, how much truth can a spirit dare? … that became for me more and more the real measure of value.
FRIEDRICH NIETZSCHE (1844–1900)

In everyone's life, at some time, our inner fire goes out. It is then burst into flame by an encounter with another human being. We should all be thankful for those people who rekindle the inner spirit.
DR. ALBERT SCHWEITZER (1875–1965)

It is inevitable that some defeat will enter even the most victorious life. The human spirit is never finished when it is defeated … it is finished when it surrenders.
BEN STEIN (1944–)

You can kill the body but not the spirit.
ROBERT LOUIS STEVENSON (1850–1894)

It is better to be high-spirited even though one makes more mistakes, than to be narrow-minded and all too prudent.
VINCENT VAN GOGH (1853–1890)

There are victories of the soul and spirit. Sometimes, even if you lose, you win.
ELIE WIESEL (1928–)

You are not here merely to make a living. You are here in order to enable the world to live more amply, with greater vision, with a finer spirit of hope and achievement. You are here to enrich the world, and you impoverish yourself if you forget the errand.
WOODROW WILSON (1856–1924)

Spirituality

The spiritual is the parent of the practical.
THOMAS CARLYLE (1795–1881)

I believe deeply that we must find, all of us together, a new spirituality.
THE DALAI LAMA (1935–)

All earthly delights are sweeter in expectation than in enjoyment; but all spiritual pleasures more in fruition than in expectation.
FRANÇOIS DE FÉNELON (1651–1715)

Our scientific power has outrun our spiritual power. We have guided missiles and misguided men.
MARTIN LUTHER KING JR. (1929–1968), *Strength to Love*

I think it's a wonderful idea.… The fact that not everybody is religious doesn't mean that we can't recognize the fact that most people are. The idea of having spirituality doesn't fly in the face of the nation.
MUHAMMAD (C. 570–632)

Science is not only compatible with spirituality; it is a profound source of spirituality.
CARL SAGAN (1934–1996)

Sports

Anybody who watches three games of football in a row should be declared brain dead.
ERMA BOMBECK (1927–1996)

Sports is the toy department of human life.
HOWARD COSELL (1918–1995)

I went to a fight the other night, and a hockey game broke out.
RODNEY DANGERFIELD (1921– 2004)

If it weren't for baseball, many kids wouldn't know what a millionaire looked like.
PHYLLIS DILLER (1917–)

A good hockey player plays where the puck is. A great hockey player plays where the puck is going to be.
WAYNE GRETZKY (1961–)

I am a member of a team, and I rely on the team, I defer to it and sacrifice for it, because the team, not the individual, is the ultimate champion.
MIA HAMM (1972–)

Talent wins games, but teamwork and intelligence win championships.
MICHAEL JORDAN (1963–)

In order to excel, you must be completely dedicated to your chosen sport. You must also be prepared to work hard and be willing to accept destructive criticism. Without 100% dedication, you won't be able to do this.
WILSON MIZNER (1876–1933)

I don't know anything that builds the will to win better than competitive sports.
RICHARD M. NIXON (1913–1994)

Serious sport has nothing to do with fair play. It is bound up with hatred, jealousy, boastfulness, disregard of all rules and sadistic pleasure in witnessing violence. In other words, it is war minus the shooting.
GEORGE ORWELL (1903–1950)

For when the One Great Scorer comes
To write against your name,
He marks—not that you won or lost—
But how you played the game.
GRANTLAND RICE (1880–1954), "Alumnus Football"

The way a team plays as a whole determines its success. You may have the greatest bunch of individual stars in the world, but if they don't play together, the club won't be worth a dime.
GEORGE HERMAN "BABE" RUTH (1895–1948)

If all the year were playing holidays;
To sport would be as tedious as to work.
WILLIAM SHAKESPEARE (1564–1616), *King Henry IV*

Some people think football is a matter of life and death. I don't like that attitude. I can assure them it is much more serious than that.
BILL SHANKLY (1913–1981)

Desire is the most important factor in the success of any athlete.
WILLIE SHOEMAKER (1931–2003)

Sport is imposing order on what was chaos.
ANTHONY STARR (1975–)

In response to the challenge of strangers, sport arose as a sublimated representation of a community's armed might as well as its pride of place and clan.
JOHN THORN (1947–)

Not every age is fit for childish sports.
TITUS MACCIUS PLAUTUS (254–184 BC)

Football is a mistake. It combines the two worst elements of American life. Violence and committee meetings.
GEORGE F. WILL (1941–)

Sports serve society by providing vivid examples of excellence.
GEORGE F. WILL (1941–)

It's not so important who starts the game but who finishes it.
JOHN WOODEN (1910–)

Sports do not build character. They reveal it.
JOHN WOODEN (1910–)

Spring

If we had no winter, the spring would not be so pleasant: if we did not sometimes taste of adversity, prosperity would not be so welcome.
ANNE BRADSTREET (1612–1672), *Meditations Divine and Moral*

I trust in nature for the stable laws of beauty and utility. Spring shall plant and autumn garner to the end of time.
ROBERT BROWNING (1812–1889)

If there comes a little thaw,
Still the air is chill and raw,
Here and there a patch of snow,
Dirtier than the ground below,
Dribbles down a marshy flood,
Ankle-deep you stick in mud
In the meadows while you sing,
"This is Spring."
CHRISTOPHER PEARCE CRANCH (1813–1892), "A Spring Growl"

A little Madness in the Spring
Is wholesome even for the King…
EMILY DICKINSON (1830–1886), "No. 1333"

Winter is on my head, but eternal spring is in my heart.
VICTOR HUGO (1802–1885)

Spring is when you feel like whistling even with a shoe full of slush.
DOUG LARSON (1902–1981)

[Spring is] when life's alive in everything.
CHRISTINA G. ROSSETTI (1830–1894)

To be interested in the changing seasons is a happier state of mind than to be hopelessly in love with spring.
GEORGE SANTAYANA (1863–1952)

O, how this spring of love resembleth
The uncertain glory of an April day!
WILLIAM SHAKESPEARE (1564–1616), *The Two Gentlemen of Verona*

If winter comes, can spring be far behind?
PERCY BYSSHE SHELLEY (1792–1822)

[Spring is] a true reconstructionist.
HENRY TIMROD (1828–1867)

It's spring fever.… You don't quite know what it is you DO want, but it just fairly makes your heart ache, you want it so!
MARK TWAIN (1835–1910)

Stars

When it is dark enough, you can see the stars.
CHARLES AUSTIN BEARD (1874–1948)

Watch the stars, and from them learn.
To the Master's honor all must turn,
Each in its track, without a sound,
Forever tracing Newton's ground.
ALBERT EINSTEIN (1879–1955)

When it is darkest, men see the stars.
RALPH WALDO EMERSON (1803–1882)

The Milky Way is nothing else but a mass of innumerable stars planted together in clusters.
GALILEO GALILEI (1564–1642)

What we need is Star Peace and not Star Wars.
MIKHAIL GORBACHEV (1931–)

I am glad we do not have to try to kill the stars. Imagine if each day a man must try to kill the

moon. The moon runs away. But imagine if a man each day should have to try to kill the sun? We are born lucky. Yes, we are born lucky.
ERNEST HEMINGWAY (1899–1961)

Go for the moon. If you don't get it, you'll still be heading for a star.
WILLIS REED (1942–)

Keep your eyes on the stars, and your feet on the ground.
THEODORE ROOSEVELT (1858–1919)

Wait for a time, exactly under the star. Then, if a little man appears who laughs, who has golden hair and who refuses to answer questions, you will know who he is. If this should happen, please comfort me. Send me word that he has come back.
ANTOINE DE SAINT-EXUPÉRY (1900–1944)

The fault, dear Brutus, lies not in our stars,
But in ourselves if we are underlings.
WILLIAM SHAKESPEARE (1564–1616), *The Tragedy of Julius Caesar*

Starvation

Death by starvation is slow.
MARY AUSTIN (1868–1934)

To deprive a man of his natural liberty and to deny to him the ordinary amenities of life is worse than starving the body; it is starvation of the soul…
MAHATMA GANDHI (1869–1948)

Love never dies of starvation, but often of indigestion.
NINON DE LENCLOS (1620–1705)

And who is any of us, that without starvation he can go through the kingdoms of starvation?
HANIEL LONG (1888–1956)

Where is there beauty when you see deprivation and starvation?
ROSALIND RUSSELL (1908–1976)

Who wants a world in which the guarantee that we shall not die of starvation entails the risk of dying of boredom?
RAOUL VANEIGEM (1934–)

Starvation, not sin, is the parent of modern crime.
OSCAR WILDE (1854–1900)

Man has only a thin layer of soil between himself and starvation.
ANONYMOUS

Statesmen

The first requirement of a statesman is that he be dull. This is not always easy to achieve.
DEAN ACHESON (1893–1971)

The national defense is one of the cardinal duties of a statesman.
JOHN ADAMS (1735–1826)

What the statesman is most anxious to produce is a certain moral character in his fellow citizens, namely a disposition to virtue and the performance of virtuous actions.
ARISTOTLE (384–322 BC)

A constitutional statesman is in general a man of common opinions and uncommon abilities.
WALTER BAGEHOT (1826–1877)

A statesman wants courage and a statesman wants vision; but believe me, after six months' experience, he wants first, second, third and all the time—patience.
STANLEY BALDWIN (1867–1947)

A statesman … must wait until he hears the steps of God sounding through events, then leap up and grasp the hem of His garment.
OTTO VON BISMARCK (1815–1898)

A disposition to preserve, and an ability to improve, taken together, would be my standard of a statesman.
EDMUND BURKE (1729–1797)

A witty statesman said, you might prove anything by figures.
THOMAS CARLYLE (1795–1881)

The three great ends which a statesman ought to propose to himself in the government of a nation, are 1. Security to possessors; 2. Facility to acquirers; and, 3. Hope to all.
SAMUEL TAYLOR COLERIDGE (1772–1834)

The true statesman is the one who is willing to take risks.
CHARLES DE GAULLE (1890–1970)

An insular country, subject to fogs, and with a powerful middle class, requires grave statesmen.
BENJAMIN DISRAELI (1804–1881)

The world is weary of statesmen whom democracy has degraded into politicians.
BENJAMIN DISRAELI (1804–1881)

A statesman cannot afford to be a moralist.
WILL DURANT (1885–1981)

A statesman who keeps his ear permanently glued to the ground will have neither elegance of posture nor flexibility of movement.
ABBA EBAN (1915–)

A foolish consistency is the hobgoblin of little minds, adored by little statesmen and philosophers and divines.
RALPH WALDO EMERSON (1803–1882)

One man's opportunism is another man's statesmanship.
MILTON FRIEDMAN (1912–2006)

The successful revolutionary is a statesman, the unsuccessful one a criminal.
ERICH FROMM (1900–1980)

To be a statesman, you must first get elected.
J. WILLIAM FULBRIGHT (1905–1995)

My father was a statesman, I am a political woman. My father was a saint. I am not.
INDIRA GANDHI (1917–1984)

A politician is a person with whose politics you don't agree; if you agree with him he's a statesman.
DAVID LLOYD GEORGE (1863–1945)

The less a statesman amounts to, the more he loves the flag.
KIN HUBBARD (1868–1930)

The essence of statesmanship is not a rigid adherence to the past, but a prudent and probing concern for the future.
HUBERT H. HUMPHREY (1911–1978)

The man who is dishonest as a statesman would be a dishonest man in any station.
THOMAS JEFFERSON (1762–1826)

The statesman's duty is to bridge the gap between his nation's experience and his vision.
HENRY KISSINGER (1923–)

Statesmanship is harder than politics. Politics is the art of getting along with people, whereas statesmanship is the art of getting along with politicians.
FLETCHER KNEBEL (1911–1993)

The opposition is indispensable. A good statesman, like any other sensible human being, always learns more from his opponents than from his fervent supporters.
WALTER LIPPMANN (1889–1974)

At home, you always have to be a politician; when you're abroad, you almost feel yourself a statesman.
HAROLD MACMILLAN (1894–1986)

A man who is a politician at forty is a statesman at three score and ten. It is at this age, when he would be too old to be a clerk or a gardener or a police-court magistrate, that he is ripe to govern a country.
W. SOMERSET MAUGHAM (1874–1965)

The art of statesmanship is to foresee the inevitable and to expedite its occurrence.
CHARLES MAURICE DE TALLEYRAND (1754–1838)

A great statesman is he who knows when to depart from traditions, as well as when to adhere to them.
JOHN STUART MILL (1806–1873)

Great Socialist statesmen aren't made, they're stillborn.
H. H. MUNRO (1870–1916)

The heart of a statesman must be in his head.
NAPOLÉON I (1769–1821)

The statesman shears the sheep; the politician skins them.
AUSTIN O'MALLEY (1858–1932)

You can always get the truth from an American statesman after he has turned seventy, or given up all hope of the Presidency.
WENDELL PHILLIPS (1811–1884)

That politician who curries favor with the citizens and indulges them and fawns upon them and has a presentiment of their wishes, and is skillful in gratifying them, he is esteemed a great statesman.
PLATO (C. 428–348 BC)

When all is said and done, and statesmen discuss the future of the world, the fact remains that people fight these wars.
ELEANOR ROOSEVELT (1884–1962)

The statesman cannot govern without stability of belief, true or false.
GEORGE BERNARD SHAW (1856–1950)

A wise man who stands firm is a statesman, a foolish man who stands firm is a catastrophe.
ADLAI E. STEVENSON II (1900–1965)

A politician is a man who understands government. A statesman is a politician who's been dead for 15 years.
HARRY S TRUMAN (1884–1972)

I always considered statesmen to be more expendable than soldiers.
HARRY S TRUMAN (1884–1972)

Statesmen will invent cheap lies, putting blame upon the nation that is attacked, and every man will be glad of those conscience-soothing falsities, and will diligently study them, and refuse to examine any refutations of them.
MARK TWAIN (1835–1910)

Statesmen have to bend to the collective will of their peoples or be broken.
WOODROW WILSON (1856–1924)

Statistics

There are three kinds of lies: lies, damned lies, and statistics.
BENJAMIN DISRAELI (1804–1881)

Statistician: A man who believes figures don't lie, but admits that under analysis some of them won't stand up either.
EVAN ESAR (1899–1995), *Esar's Comic Dictionary*

Statistics: The only science that enables different experts using the same figures to draw different conclusions.
EVAN ESAR (1899–1995), *Esar's Comic Dictionary*

I could prove God statistically.
GEORGE GALLUP (1901–1984)

Smoking is one of the leading causes of statistics.
FLETCHER KNEBEL (1911–1993)

USA Today has come out with a new survey—apparently, three out of every four people make up 75% of the population.
DAVID LETTERMAN (1947–)

A single death is a tragedy; a million deaths is a statistic.
JOSEPH STALIN (1879–1953)

Status

I love to utilize my celebrity status in a responsible and constructive and substantive manner. I like to get my hands dirty rather than a photo op.
WILLIAM BALDWIN (1963–)

Remember, social progress only happens when those in society's privileged classes choose to give up their status.
TAMMY BRUCE (1962–)

For no continuity of social act is possible without a corresponding social status and the many different kinds of act required in an industrial state, with its high degree of specialization, make for corresponding classification of status.
KENNETH BURKE (1897–1993)

Never make friends with people who are above or below you in status. Such friendships will never give you any happiness.
CHANAKYA (350–275 BC)

I consider it important, indeed urgently necessary, for intellectual workers to get together, both to protect their own economic status and, also, generally speaking, to secure their influence in the political field.
ALBERT EINSTEIN (1879–1955)

Americans are the only people in the world known to me whose status anxiety prompts them to advertise their college and university affiliations in the rear window of their automobiles.
PAUL FUSSELL (1924–)

As the rich consume more and more, they are clearly not going to want to downgrade their own status.
SUSAN GEORGE (1950–)

In love as in sport, the amateur status must be strictly maintained.
ROBERT GRAVES (1895–1985)

Attention is the way social primates measure status. It is highly rewarding because it causes the release of brain chemicals such as dopamine and endorphins.
KEITH HENSON (1942–)

Humans have evolved to be exquisitely sensitive to changes in status.
KEITH HENSON (1942–)

Pride attaches undue importance to the superiority of one's status in the eyes of others; And shame is fear of humiliation at one's inferior status in the estimation of others. When one sets his heart on being highly esteemed, and achieves such rating, then he is automatically involved in fear of losing his status.
LAO-TZU (C. 600 BC)

A society person who is enthusiastic about modern painting or Truman Capote is already half a traitor to his class. It is middle-class people who, quite mistakenly, imagine that a lively pursuit of the latest in reading and painting will advance their status in the world.
MARY MCCARTHY (1912–1989)

Status symbols are medals you buy yourself.
BERNHARD WICKI (1919–2000)

Status Quo

Faith in God's revelation has nothing to do with an ideology which glorifies the status quo.
KARL BARTH (1886–1968)

Everything is in a state of flux, including the status quo.
ROBERT BYRNE (1928–)

The status quo sucks.
GEORGE CARLIN (1937–)

I have news for the forces of greed and the defenders of the status quo; your time has come and gone. It's time for change in America.
BILL CLINTON (1946–)

People who demand neutrality in any situation are usually not neutral but in favor of the status quo.
MAX EASTMAN (1883–1969)

If there is dissatisfaction with the status quo, good. If there is ferment, so much the better. If there is restlessness, I am pleased. Then let there be ideas, and hard thought, and hard work. If man feels small, let man make himself bigger.
HUBERT H. HUMPHREY (1911–1978)

I'm not interested in preserving the status quo; I want to overthrow it.
NICCOLÒ MACHIAVELLI (1469–1527)

Bureaucracy defends the status quo long past the time when the quo has lost its status.
DR. LAURENCE J. PETER (1919–1990)

Status quo, you know, that is Latin for "the mess we're in."
RONALD REAGAN (1911–2004)

We emphasize that we believe in change because we were born of it, we have lived by it, we prospered and grew great by it. So the status quo has never been our god, and we ask no one else to bow down before it.
CARL T. ROWAN (1925–2000)

Any woman who chooses to behave like a full human being should be warned that the armies of the status quo will treat her as something of a dirty joke. That's their natural and first weapon. She will need her sisterhood.
GLORIA STEINEM (1934–)

[A] businessman's candidate, hovering around the status quo like a sick kitten around a hot brick.
WILLIAM ALLEN WHITE (1868–1944)

Stock Market

If stock market experts were so expert, they would be buying stock, not selling advice.
NORMAN R. AUGUSTINE (1935–)

Most people get interested in stocks when everyone else is. The time to get interested is when no one else is. You can't buy what is popular and do well.
WARREN BUFFETT (1930–)

Neither an assembly line nor a stock market nor an oil well did it, simply what came from one small skull and that one right hand.
ILKA CHASE (1903–1978)

Glamour is what I sell, it's my stock in trade.
MARLENE DIETRICH (1901–1992)

Bob Dole revealed he is one of the test subjects for Viagra. He said on Larry King, "I wish I had bought stock in it." Only a Republican would think the best part of Viagra is the fact that you could make money off of it.
JAY LENO (1950–)

The key to making money in stocks is not to get scared out of them.
PETER LYNCH (1944–)

Don't gamble; take all your savings and buy some good stock and hold it till it goes up, then sell it. If it don't go up, don't buy it.
WILL ROGERS (1879–1935)

October: This is one of the peculiarly dangerous months to speculate in stocks. The others are July, January, September, April, November, May, March, June, December, August, and February.
MARK TWAIN (1835–1910)

Stories

People create stories create people; or rather stories create people create stories.
CHINUA ACHEBE (1930–)

A good storyteller never lets the facts get in the way.
DAVE ALLEN (1936–2005)

Every man's life is a fairy tale written by God's fingers.
HANS CHRISTIAN ANDERSEN (1805–1875)

There is no greater agony than bearing an untold story inside you.
MAYA ANGELOU (1928–)

The life of every man is a diary in which he means to write one story, and writes another.
JAMES M. BARRIE (1860–1937)

Wherever a story comes from, whether it is a familiar myth or a private memory, the retelling exemplifies the making of a connection from one pattern to another: a potential translation in which narrative becomes parable and the once upon a time comes to stand for some renascent truth. This approach applies to all the incidents of everyday life: the phrase in the newspaper, the endearing or infuriating game of a toddler, the misunderstanding at the office. Our species thinks in metaphors and learns through stories.
MARY CATHERINE BATESON (1939–)

Storytellers, by the very act of telling, communicate a radical learning that changes lives and the world: telling stories is a universally accessible means through which people make meaning.
CHRIS CAVANAUGH (1962–)

A good storyteller is a person with a good memory and hopes other people haven't.
IRVIN S. COBB (1876–1944)

Who tells a finer tale than any of us? Silence does.
ISAK DINESEN (1885–1962)

The most erroneous stories are those we think we know best—and therefore never scrutinize or question.
STEPHEN JAY GOULD (1941–2002)

If a nation loses its storytellers, it loses its childhood.
PETER HANDKE (1942–)

No storyteller has ever been able to dream up anything as fantastically unlikely as what really does happen in this mad Universe.
ROBERT A. HEINLEIN (1907–1988), *The Notebooks of Lazarus Long*

Madame, all stories, if continued far enough, end in death, and he is no true-story teller who would keep that from you.
ERNEST HEMINGWAY (1899–1961)

Man is eminently a storyteller. His search for a purpose, a cause, an ideal, a mission and the like is largely a search for a plot and a pattern in the development of his life story—a story that is basically without meaning or pattern.
ERIC HOFFER (1902–1983)

It is tedious to tell again tales already plainly told.
HOMER (800–700 BC), *The Odyssey*

Trust the tale, not the teller.
DAVID KNOPFLER (1952–)

Your life story would not make a good book. Don't even try.
FRAN LEBOWITZ (1950–)

The story—from *Rumplestiltskin* to *War and Peace*—is one of the basic tools invented by the human mind, for the purpose of gaining understanding. There have been great societies that did not use the wheel, but there have been no societies that did not tell stories.
URSULA K. LE GUIN (1929–)

The universe is made of stories, not of atoms.
MURIEL RUKEYSER (1913–1980)

As is a tale, so is life: not how long it is, but how good it is, is what matters.
SENECA (5 BC–AD 65)

People are hungry for stories. It's part of our very being. Storytelling is a form of history, of immortality too. It goes from one generation to another.
LOUIS "STUDS" TERKEL (1912–)

Do not tell fish stories where the people know you; but particularly, don't tell them where they know the fish.
MARK TWAIN (1835–1910)

We turn our lives into stories, and, in doing so, we can stop them where we choose. Our stories do in a small way what memoirs and autobiographies do on a grander scale: they allow a self-fashioning that gives remembered lives a coherence that the day-to-day lives of actual experience lack.
RICHARD WHITE (1947–), *Remembering Ahanagran: Storytelling in a Family's Past*

God made man because He loves stories.
ELIE WIESEL (1928–)

Their story, yours and mine—it's what we all carry with us on this trip we take, and we owe it to each other to respect our stories and learn from them.
WILLIAM CARLOS WILLIAMS (1883–1963)

Of course that is not the whole story, but that is the way with stories; we make them what we will. It's a way of explaining the universe while leaving the universe unexplained, it's a way of keeping it all alive, not boxing it into time.
JEANETTE WINTERSON (1959–)

Strangers

If two friends ask you to judge a dispute, don't accept, because you will lose one friend; on the other hand, if two strangers come with the same request, accept because you will gain one friend.
SAINT AUGUSTINE (354-430)

If a man be gracious and courteous to strangers, it shows he is a citizen of the world.
SIR FRANCIS BACON (1561–1626)

I don't go to bed with strangers.
BORIS BECKER (1967–)

All you'll get from strangers is surface pleasantry or indifference. Only someone who loves you will criticize you.
JUDITH CRIST (1922–)

Strangers are exciting,
Their mystery never ends.
But there's nothing like looking at your own history
In the faces of your friends.
ANI DIFRANCO (1970–), "Good, Bad, Ugly"

We sometimes encounter people, even perfect strangers, who begin to interest us at first sight, somehow suddenly, all at once, before a word has been spoken.
FYODOR DOSTOEVSKY (1821–1881)

It is my fate to be constantly dependent upon the generosity of strangers.
CASS ELLIOT (1941–)

And if strangers come to supper they shall be served with more according as they have need.
ROBERT GROSSETESTE (1175–1253)

Ninety percent of the world's woe comes from people not knowing themselves, their abilities, their frailties, and even their real virtues. Most of us go almost all the way through life as complete strangers to ourselves.
SYDNEY J. HARRIS (1917–1986)

All strangers and beggars are from Zeus, and a gift, though small, is precious.
HOMER (800–700 BC)

Great perils have this beauty, that they bring to light the fraternity of strangers.
VICTOR HUGO (1802–1885)

At the bottom of enmity between strangers lies indifference.
SØREN KIERKEGAARD (1813–1855)

Marriage is nature's way of keeping us from fighting with strangers.
ALAN KING (1927–2004)

Strangers still leave me self-conscious.
ALAN LADD (1913–1964)

Good things happen when you meet strangers.
YO-YO MA (1955–)

The more I traveled the more I realized that fear makes strangers of people who would be friends.
SHIRLEY MACLAINE (1934–)

Borders are scratched across the hearts of men, by strangers with a calm, judicial pen, and when the borders bleed we watch with dread the lines of ink along the map turn red.
MARYA MANNES (1904–1990)

Sometimes you have to get to know someone really well to realize you're really strangers.
MARY TYLER MOORE (1936–)

Our very lives depend on the ethics of strangers, and most of us are always strangers to other people.
BILL MOYERS (1934–)

Soon the child learns that there are strangers, and ceases to be a child.
MAX MULLER (1823–1900)

When strangers start acting like neighbors … communities are reinvigorated.
RALPH NADER (1934–)

One would be in less danger from the wiles of the stranger if one's own kin and kith were more fun to be with.
OGDEN NASH (1902–1971)

It is rash to intrude upon the piety of others: both the depth and the grace of it elude the stranger.
GEORGE SANTAYANA (1863–1952)

I do desire we be better strangers.
WILLIAM SHAKESPEARE (1564–1616), *As You Like It*

For this reason, strangers are not really conceived as individuals, but as strangers of a particular type: the element of distance is no less general in regard to them than the element of nearness.
GEORG SIMMEL (1858–1918)

And every stranger's face I see
Reminds me that I long to be,
Homeward bound.
PAUL SIMON (1941–), "Homeward Bound"

On this shrunken globe, men can no longer live as strangers.
ADLAI E. STEVENSON II (1900–1965)

I have heard of a dog that barked at every stranger who approached his master's premises with clothes on, but was easily quieted by a naked thief.
HENRY DAVID THOREAU (1817–1862)

All war must be just the killing of strangers against whom you feel no personal animosity; strangers whom, in other circumstances, you would help if you found them in trouble, and who would help you if you needed it.
MARK TWAIN (1835–1910)

Only strangers eat tamarinds—but they only eat them once.
MARK TWAIN (1835–1910)

I have always depended on the kindness of strangers.
TENNESSEE WILLIAMS (1911–1983, *A Streetcar Named Desire*

There are no strangers here;
Only friends you haven't yet met.
WILLIAM BUTLER YEATS (1865–1939)

Live together like brothers and do business like strangers.
ARABIAN PROVERB

Do not forget to show hospitality to strangers, for by so doing some people have shown hospitality to angels without knowing it.
THE BIBLE, Hebrews 13:2

Strategy

However beautiful the strategy, you should occasionally look at the results.
SIR WINSTON CHURCHILL (1874–1965)

If you believe in a security strategy, a strategy of more friends and fewer enemies, a strategy of greater cooperation and a strategy of keeping America better at home as we grow more diverse, we have to build the minds and hearts to build this kind of world.
BILL CLINTON (1946–)

You have to be fast on your feet and adaptive or else a strategy is useless.
CHARLES DE GAULLE (1890–1970)

I figured out Karl Rove's political strategy—make gas so expensive, no Democrats can afford to go to the polls.
JOHN KERRY (1943–)

If the enemy thinks of the mountains, attack like the sea; and if he thinks of the sea, attack like the mountains.
MIYAMOTO MUSASHI (1584–1645)

If we watch men of other schools discussing theory, and concentrating on techniques with the hands, even though they seem skillfull to watch, they have not the slightest true spirit.
MIYAMOTO MUSASHI (1584–1645)

In strategy your spiritual bearing must not be any different from normal. Both in fighting and in everday life you should be determined though calm. Meet the situation without tenseness yet not recklessly, your spirit settled yet unbiased.
MIYAMOTO MUSASHI (1584–1645)

Strategy is the craft of the warrior. Commanders must enact the craft, and troopers should know this Way. There is no warrior in the world today who really understands the Way of strategy.... It is said the warrior's is the twofold Way of pen and sword, and he should have a taste for both Ways.
MIYAMOTO MUSASHI (1584–1645)

Students of the Ichi school Way of strategy should train from the start with the sword and long sword in either hand. This is a truth: when you sacrifice your life, you must make fullest use of your weaponry. It is false not to do so, and to die with a weapon yet undrawn.
MIYAMOTO MUSASHI (1584–1645)

Study strategy over the years and achieve the spirit of the warrior. Today is victory over yourself of yesterday; tomorrow is your victory over lesser men.
MIYAMOTO MUSASHI (1584–1645)

In marketing I've seen only one strategy that can't miss—and that is to market to your best customers first, your best prospects second and the rest of the world last.
JOHN ROMERO (1967–)

Leadership is a potent combination of strategy and character. But if you must be without one, be without the strategy.
NORMAN SCHWARZKOPF (1934–)

All men can see these tactics whereby I conquer, but what none can see is the strategy out of which victory is evolved.
SUN-TZU (C. 544–496 BC)

Strategy without tactics is the slowest route to victory. Tactics without strategy is the noise before defeat.
SUN-TZU (C. 544–496 BC)

[W]hat is of supreme importance in war is to attack the enemy's strategy.
SUN-TZU (C. 544–496 BC)

You may not be interested in strategy, but strategy is interested in you.
LEON TROTSKY (1879–1940)

Who asks whether the enemy were defeated by strategy or valor?
VIRGIL (C. 70–19 BC)

Perception is strong and sight weak. In strategy it is important to see distant things as if they were close and to take a distanced view of close things.
ANONYMOUS

When you're prepared, you're more confident. When you have a strategy, you're more comfortable.
ANONYMOUS

Strength

When strength is yoked with justice, where is a mightier pair than they?
AESCHYLUS (C. 525–456 BC)

Strengthen me by sympathizing with my strength, not my weakness.
AMOS BRONSON ALCOTT (1799–1888)

You're only given as much as you can handle at any given time. Whether it's true or not, it gives you the strength.
GILLIAN ANDERSON (1968–)

God grant you the strength to fight off the temptations of surrender.
WALTER ANNENBERG (1902–2002)

Our passion is our strength.
BILLIE JOE ARMSTRONG (1972–)

Strength instead of being the lusty child of passion, grows by grappling with and subduing them.
JAMES M. BARRIE (1860–1937)

Greatness lies, not in being strong, but in the right using of strength; and strength is not used rightly when it serves only to carry a man above his fellows for his own solitary glory. He is the greatest whose strength carries up the most hearts by the attraction of his own.
HENRY WARD BEECHER (1813–1887)

You really have to look inside yourself and find your own inner strength, and say, "I'm proud of what I am and who I am, and I'm just going to be myself."
MARIAH CAREY (1970–)

Only one who devotes himself to a cause with his whole strength and soul can be a true master. For this reason mastery demands all of a person.
ALBERT EINSTEIN (1879–1955)

Only strength can cooperate. Weakness can only beg.
DWIGHT D. EISENHOWER (1890–1969)

Our real problem, then, is not our strength today; it is rather the vital necessity of action today to ensure our strength tomorrow.
DWIGHT D. EISENHOWER (1890–1969)

If you haven't the strength to impose your own terms upon life, you must accept the terms it offers you.
T. S. ELIOT (1888–1965)

We acquire the strength we have overcome.
RALPH WALDO EMERSON (1803–1882)

Strength does not come from physical capacity. It comes from an indomitable will.
MAHATMA GANDHI (1869–1948)

Tenderness and kindness are not signs of weakness and despair, but manifestations of strength and resolutions.
KAHLIL GIBRAN (1883–1931)

Tears shed for self are tears of weakness, but tears shed for others are a sign of strength.
BILLY GRAHAM (1918–)

People do not lack strength; they lack will.
VICTOR HUGO (1802–1885)

We confide in our strength, without boasting of it; we respect that of others, without fearing it.
THOMAS JEFFERSON (1762–1826)

Life is either a daring adventure or nothing. To keep our faces toward change and behave like free spirits in the presence of fate is strength undefeatable.
HELEN KELLER (1880–1968)

Credulity is the man's weakness, but the child's strength.
CHARLES LAMB (1775–1834)

Mastering others is strength; mastering yourself is true power.
LAO-TZU (600-531 BC)

You have power over your mind—not outside events. Realize this, and you will find strength.
MARCUS AURELIUS ANTONINUS (121–180)

Good actions give strength to ourselves and inspire good actions in others.
PLATO (C. 428–348 BC)

A powerful idea communicates some of its strength to him who challenges it.
MARCEL PROUST (1871–1922)

The strongest is never strong enough to be always the master, unless he transforms strength into right, and obedience into duty.
JEAN-JACQUES ROUSSEAU (1712–1778), *The Social Contract*

Strength does not come from winning. Your struggles develop your strengths. When you go through hardships and decide not to surrender, that is strength.
ARNOLD SCHWARZENEGGER (1947–)

Strength alone knows conflict, weakness is born vanquished.
ANNE SOPHIE SWETCHINE (1782–1857)

My strength is the strength of ten,
Because my heart is pure.
ALFRED, LORD TENNYSON (1809–1892), "Sir Galahad"

Be faithful in small things because it is in them that your strength lies.
MOTHER TERESA (1910–1997)

Love many things, for therein lies the true strength, and whosoever loves much performs much, and can accomplish much, and what is done in love is done well.
VINCENT VAN GOGH (1853–1890)

The man who is swimming against the stream knows the strength of it.
WOODROW WILSON (1856–1924)

Anyone can give up; it's the easiest thing in the world to do. But to hold it together when everyone would understand if you fell apart, that's true strength.
ANONYMOUS

There is no substitute for strength, and no excuse for the lack of it.
ANONYMOUS

You don't realize how strong a person really is until you see them at their weakest moment.
ANONYMOUS

Dwell not upon thy weariness, thy strength shall be according to the measure of thy desire.
ARAB PROVERB

Distance tests a horse's strength. Time reveals a person's character.
CHINESE PROVERB

Struggle

When good people in any country cease their vigilance and struggle, then evil men prevail.
PEARL S. BUCK (1892–1973)

Life is a struggle, but not a warfare.
JOHN BURROUGHS (1837–1921)

A revolution is a struggle to the death between the future and the past.
FIDEL CASTRO (1926–)

The important thing in life is not the triumph but the struggle.
PIERRE DE COUBERTIN (1863–1937)

Struggle is strengthening. Battling with evil gives us the power to battle evil even more.
OSSIE DAVIS (1917–2005)

Life is a continued struggle to be what we are not, and to do what we cannot.
WILLIAM HAZLITT (1778–1830)

Struggle is the father of all things. It is not by the principles of humanity that man lives or is able to preserve himself above the animal world, but solely by means of the most brutal struggle.
ADOLF HITLER (1889–1945)

Strength is happiness. Strength is itself victory. In weakness and cowardice there is no happiness. When you wage a struggle, you might win or you might lose. But regardless of the short-term outcome, the very fact of your continuing to struggle is proof of your victory as a human being.
DAISAKU IKEDA (1928–)

Need and struggle are what excite and inspire us; our hour of triumph is what brings the void.
WILLIAM JAMES (1842–1910)

The way I see things, the way I see life, I see it as a struggle. And there's a great deal of reward I have gained coming to that understanding—that existence is a struggle.
HARVEY KEITEL (1942–)

Life is always struggle with eternal forces.
EINO LEINO (1878–1926)

The probability that we may fail in the struggle ought not to deter us from the support of a cause we believe to be just.
ABRAHAM LINCOLN (1809–1865)

Life is one long struggle in the dark.
LUCRETIUS (C. 99–55 BC)

Once all struggle is grasped, miracles are possible.
MAO TSE-TUNG (1893–1976)

Every day sees humanity more victorious in the struggle with space and time.
GUGLIELMO MARCONI (1874–1937)

The class struggle necessarily leads to the dictatorship of the proletariat.
KARL MARX (1818–1883)

The battles that count aren't the ones for gold medals. The struggles within yourself—the invisible, inevitable battles inside all of us—that's where it's at.
JESSE OWENS (1913–1980)

To have striven, to have made the effort, to have been true to certain ideals—this alone is worth the struggle.
WILLIAM PENN (1644–1718)

Believe me, the reward is not so great without the struggle.
WILMA RUDOLPH (1940–1994)

Life has meaning only in the struggle. Triumph or defeat is in the hands of the gods. So let us celebrate the struggle!
SWAMI SIVANANDA (1887–1963)

In a serious struggle there is no worse cruelty than to be magnanimous at an inopportune time.
LEON TROTSKY (1879–1940)

Some struggle is healthy. If you can embrace it rather than be angry, you can use it as your pilot light.
DAMON WAYANS (1960–)

He who would live must fight, he who will not fight in this world where eternal struggle is the law of life, has not the right to exist.
ANONYMOUS

Sometimes, struggles are exactly what we need in our life. If we were to go through our life without any obstacles, we would be crippled. We would not be as strong as what we could have been. Give every opportunity a chance, leave no room for regrets.
ANONYMOUS

Students

That is the difference between good teachers and great teachers: good teachers make the best of a pupil's means; great teachers foresee a pupil's ends.
MARIA CALLAS (1923–1977)

Students must have initiative; they should not be mere imitators. They must learn to think and act for themselves—and be free.
CESAR CHAVEZ (1927–1993

Don't try to fix the students, fix ourselves first. The good teacher makes the poor student good and the good student superior. When our students fail, we, as teachers, too, have failed.
MARVA COLLINS (1936–)

Teaching is useless unless you can learn from your students.
MARTIN DANSKY (1952–)

Students today are a pretty solemn lot. One of the really notable achievements of the twentieth century has been to make the young old before their time.
ROBERTSON DAVIES (1913–1995)

Today's students can put dope in their veins or hope in their brains. If they can conceive it and believe it, they can achieve it. They must know it is not their aptitude but their attitude that will determine their altitude.
JESSE JACKSON (1941–)

To be a teacher in the right sense is to be a learner. I am not a teacher, only a fellow student.
SØREN KIERKEGAARD (1813–1855)

Take the attitude of a student, never be too big to ask questions, never know too much to learn something new.
OG MANDINO (1923–1996)

Responsibility for learning belongs to the student, regardless of age.
ROBERT MARTIN (1947–)

A student never forgets an encouraging private word, when it is given with sincere respect and admiration.
WILLIAM LYON PHELPS (1865–1943)

I believe that the testing of the student's achievements in order to see if he meets some criterion held by the teacher, is directly contrary to the implications of therapy for significant learning.
CARL ROGERS (1902–1987)

Passive acceptance of the teacher's wisdom is easy to most boys and girls. It involves no effort of independent thought, and seems rational because the teacher knows more than his pupils; it is moreover the way to win the favour of the teacher unless he is a very exceptional man. Yet the habit of passive acceptance is a disastrous one in later life. It causes man to seek and to accept a leader, and to accept as a leader whoever is established in that position.
BERTRAND RUSSELL (1872–1970)

No student knows his subject: the most he knows is where and how to find out the things he does not know.
WOODROW WILSON (1856–1924)

The world is run by C students.
ANONYMOUS

Studying

Our delight in any particular study, art, or science rises and improves in proportion to the application which we bestow upon it. Thus, what was at first an exercise becomes at length an entertainment.
JOSEPH ADDISON (1672–1719)

I would live to study, and not study to live.
SIR FRANCIS BACON (1561–1626)

Excellence is a better teacher than mediocrity. The lessons of the ordinary are everywhere. Truly profound and original insights are to be found only in studying the exemplary.
WARREN G. BENNIS (1925–)

There are more men ennobled by study than by nature.
CICERO (106–43 BC)

Some men grow mad by studying much to know,
But who grows mad by studying good to grow.
BENJAMIN FRANKLIN (1706–1790)

We all learn best in our own ways. Some people do better studying one subject at a time, while some do better studying three things at once. Some people do best studying in a structured, linear way, while others do best jumping around, "surrounding" a subject rather than traversing it. Some people prefer to learn by manipulating models, and others by reading.
BILL GATES (1955–)

The world's great men have not commonly been great scholars, nor its great scholars great men.
OLIVER WENDELL HOLMES SR. (1809–1894)

There is nothing too little for so little a creature as man. It is by studying little things that we attain the great art of having as little misery and as much happiness as possible.
SAMUEL JOHNSON (1709–1784)

The mind of the scholar, if he would leave it large and liberal, should come in contact with other minds.
HENRY WADSWORTH LONGFELLOW (1807–1882)

Too much attention to health is a hindrance to learning, to invention, and to studies of any kind, for we are always feeling suspicious shootings and swimmings in our heads, and we are prone to blame studies for them.
PLATO (C. 428–348 BC)

I have been studying how I may compare
The prison where I live unto the world.
WILLIAM SHAKESPEARE (1564–1616), *King Richard II*

No student knows his subject: the most he knows is where and how to find out the things he does not know.
WOODROW WILSON (1856–1924)

Studying history warns against making it.
ANONYMOUS

The bitterness of studying is preferable to the bitterness of ignorance.
ANONYMOUS

Those who do not study are only cattle dressed up in men's clothes.
CHINESE PROVERB

Stupidity

If there are no stupid questions, then what kind of questions do stupid people ask? Do they get smart just in time to ask questions?
SCOTT ADAMS (1957–)

Only two things are infinite, the universe and human stupidity, and I'm not sure about the former.
ALBERT EINSTEIN (1879–1955)

The two most common elements in the universe are hydrogen and stupidity.
HARLAN ELLISON (1934–)

Talk sense to a fool and he calls you foolish.
EURIPIDES (C. 484–406 BC), *The Bacchae*

To be stupid, selfish, and have good health are three requirements for happiness, though if stupidity is lacking, all is lost.
GUSTAVE FLAUBERT (1821–1880)

There is nothing worse than aggressive stupidity.
JOHANN WOLFGANG VON GOETHE (1749–1832)

Ordinarily he was insane, but he had lucid moments when he was merely stupid.
HEINRICH HEINE (1797–1856)

There are more fools in the world than there are people.
HEINRICH HEINE (1797–1856)

Stupidity talks, vanity acts.
VICTOR HUGO (1802–1885)

At least two-thirds of our miseries spring from human stupidity, human malice and those great motivators and justifiers of malice and stupidity: idealism, dogmatism and proselytizing zeal on behalf of religious or political ideas.
ALDOUS HUXLEY (1894–1963)

Genius may have its limitations, but stupidity is not thus handicapped.
ELBERT HUBBARD (1856–1915)

Nothing in all the world is more dangerous than sincere ignorance and conscientious stupidity.
MARTIN LUTHER KING JR. (1929–1968), *Strength to Love*

My loathings are simple: stupidity, oppression, crime, cruelty, soft music.
VLADIMIR NABOKOV (1899–1977)

To forget one's purpose is the commonest form of stupidity.
FRIEDRICH NIETZSCHE (1844–1900)

Against stupidity, the gods themselves contend in vain.
FRIEDRICH VON SCHILLER (1759–1805)

Lord, what fools these mortals be!
WILLIAM SHAKESPEARE (1564–1616), *A Midsummer Night's Dream*

It is dangerous to be sincere unless you are also stupid.
GEORGE BERNARD SHAW (1856–1950), *Man and Superman*

As if there were safety in stupidity alone.
HENRY DAVID THOREAU (1817–1862)

Strange as it seems, no amount of learning can cure stupidity, and higher education positively fortifies it.
STEPHEN VIZINCZEY (1933–), *An Innocent Millionaire*

Anything that is too stupid to be spoken is sung.
VOLTAIRE (1694–1778)

To succeed in the world it is not enough to be stupid, you must also be well-mannered.
VOLTAIRE (1694–1778)

There is more stupidity than hydrogen in the universe, and it has a longer shelf life.
FRANK ZAPPA (1940–1993)

Artificial intelligence is no match for natural stupidity.
ANONYMOUS

Everyone is entitled to be stupid, but some abuse the privilege.
ANONYMOUS

Fools rush in where fools have been before.
ANONYMOUS

Never attribute to malice what can be adequately explained by stupidity.
ANONYMOUS

Style

The difference between style and fashion is quality.
GIORGIO ARMANI (1934–)

To speak as the common people do, to think as wise men do is style.
ROGER ASCHAM (1515–1568)

Style is a reflection of your attitude and your personality.
SHAWN ASHMORE (1979–)

Style is primarily a matter of instinct.
BILL BLASS (1922–2002)

The style is the man himself.
GEORGE-LOUIS DE BUFFON (1707–1788)

Joan of Arc had style. Jesus had style.
CHARLES BUKOWSKI (1920–1994)

Style, like sheer silk, too often hides eczema.
ALBERT CAMUS (1913–1960)

Fashion fades, only style remains the same.
COCO CHANEL (1883–1971)

Style is the dress of thoughts.
LORD CHESTERFIELD (1694–1773)

Style is a simple way of saying complicated things.
JEAN COCTEAU (1889–1963)

What I think of as style—and I've gotten to this over years of really thinking about it—is that style is the unconscious choices I make.
JOHN CORIGLIANO (1938–)

Growing up, I was the plain one. I had no style. I was the tough kid with the comb in the back pocket and the feathered hair.
CAMERON DIAZ (1972–)

And, after all, it is style alone by which posterity will judge of a great work, for an author can have nothing truly his own but his style.
ISAAC D'ISRAELI (1766–1848)

Style! Style! Why, all writers will tell you that it is the very thing which can least of all be changed. A man's style is nearly as much a part of him as his physiognomy, his figure, the throbbing of his pulse…
ISAAC D'ISRAELI (1766–1848)

Style is the perfection of a point of view.
RICHARD EBERHART (1904–2005)

Styles, like everything else, change. Style doesn't.
LINDA ELLERBEE (1944–)

I discovered that what's really important for a creator isn't what we vaguely define as inspiration or even what it is we want to say, recall, regret, or rebel against. No, what's important is the way we say it. Art is all about craftsmanship. Others can interpret craftsmanship as style if they wish. Style is what unites memory or recollection, ideology, sentiment, nostalgia, presentiment, to the way we express all that. It's not what we say but how we say it that matters.
FEDERICO FELLINI (1920–1993)

One arrives at style only with atrocious effort, with fanatical and devoted stubbornness.
GUSTAVE FLAUBERT (1821–1880)

Style is as much under the words as in the words. It is as much the soul as it is the flesh of a work.
GUSTAVE FLAUBERT (1821–1880)

A feel-good style can be a symptom of unawareness or lack of caring.
FERNANDO FLORES (1943–)

Style is something that's extremely important, but it must grow naturally out of who and what you are and what the material calls for. It cannot be superimposed.
WILLIAM FRIEDKIN (1939–)

Style is the mind skating circles around itself as it moves forward.
ROBERT FROST (1874–1963)

Style is the image of character.
EDWARD GIBBON (1737–1794)

To me style is just the outside of content, and content the inside of style, like the outside and the inside of the human body. Both go together, they can't be separated.
JEAN-LUC GODARD (1930–)

Style's not something that you decide on Monday and photograph on Thursday. You've been developing that for your whole life.
SIMON LE BON (1958–)

Style is the hallmark of a temperament stamped upon the material at hand.
ANDRÉ MAUROIS (1885–1967)

Fashions fade, style is eternal.
YVES SAINT-LAURENT (1940–)

Style is a magic wand, and turns everything to gold that it touches.
LOGAN PEARSALL SMITH (1865–1946)

I've come up with another formulation about style: that it's essentially a manifestation of a certain habitual set of limitations. It's what a composer does not do that defines a style.
JAMES TENNEY (1934–)

He never chooses an opinion; he just wears whatever happens to be in style
LEO TOLSTOY (1828 1910)

Style is knowing who you are, what you want to say, and not giving a damn.
GORE VIDAL (1925–)

All styles are good except the tiresome kind.
VOLTAIRE (1694–1778)

Create your own visual style … let it be unique for yourself and yet identifiable for others.
ORSON WELLES (1915–1985)

Style is the dress of thought; a modest dress, neat, but not gaudy, will true critics please.
SAMUEL WESLEY (1766–1837)

One forges one's style on the terrible anvil of daily deadlines.
ÉMILE ZOLA (1840–1902)

Subjectivity

A creation needs not only subjectivity, but also objectivity.
STEPHEN CHOW (1962–)

The director comes in, and he's supposed to take all of this subjectivity and hone it down into some sense of objectivity.
RICHARD DONNER (1930–)

The focus of subjectivity is a distorting mirror.
HANS-GEORG GADAMER (1900–2002)

As the ego cogito, subjectivity is the consciousness that represents something, relates this representation back to itself, and so gathers with itself.
MARTIN HEIDEGGER (1889–1976)

So it's clear from whence the history of philosophy is the inner movement of the course of spirit, that is, of absolute subjectivity, towards itself.
MARTIN HEIDEGGER (1889–1976)

It's all about people. It's all about the subjectivity of what people love.
JOE PANTOLIANO (1951–)

Where conscious subjectivity is concerned, there is no distinction between the observation and the thing observed.
JOHN SEARLE (1932–)

We can escape the commonplace only by manipulating it, controlling it, thrusting it into our dreams or surrendering it to the free play of our subjectivity.
RAOUL VANEIGEM (1934–)

Subtlety

It pays to be obvious, especially if you have a reputation for subtlety.
ISAAC ASIMOV (1920–1992)

The subtlety of nature is greater many times over than the subtlety of the senses and understanding.
SIR FRANCIS BACON (1561–1626)

Subtlety may deceive you; integrity never will.
OLIVER CROMWELL (1599–1658)

I appreciate subtlety. I have never enjoyed a kiss in front of the camera. There's nothing to it except not getting your lipstick smeared.
HEDY LAMARR (1913–2000)

Human subtlety will never devise an invention more beautiful, more simple or more direct than does nature because in her inventions nothing is lacking, and nothing is superfluous.
LEONARDO DA VINCI (1452–1519)

The powers of subtlety have been weakened by the fact that you can say anything.
PAT OLIPHANT (1935–)

The difference between stupid and intelligent people—and this is true whether or not they are well-educated—is that intelligent people can handle subtlety.
NEAL STEPHENSON (1959–)

O divine art of subtlety and secrecy! Through you we learn to be invisible, through you inaudible and hence we can hold the enemy's fate in our hands.
SUN-TZU (C. 544–496 BC)

Subtlety is the art of saying what you think and getting out of the way before it is understood.
ANONYMOUS

Success

If you wish success in life, make perseverance your bosom friend, experience your wise counselor,

caution your elder brother and hope your guardian genius.
JOSEPH ADDISON (1672–1719)

People of mediocre ability sometimes achieve outstanding success because they don't know when to quit. Most men succeed because they are determined to.
GEORGE HERBERT ALLEN (1918–1990)

Eighty percent of success is showing up.
WOODY ALLEN (1935–)

It is possible to fail in many ways … while to succeed is possible only in one way.
ARISTOTLE (384–322 BC), *Nichomachean Ethics*

Pretend that every single person you meet has a sign around his or her neck that says, "Make Me Feel Important." You will succeed in life.
MARY KAY ASH (1918–2001)

To succeed, planning alone is insufficient. One must improvise as well.
ISAAC ASIMOV (1920–1992), *Foundation*

A rejection is nothing more than a necessary step in the pursuit of success.
BO BENNETT (1972–)

The toughest thing about success is that you've got to keep on being a success. Talent is only a starting point in this business. You've got to keep on working that talent. Someday I'll reach for it and it won't be there.
IRVING BERLIN (1888–1989)

Your success depends mainly upon what you think of yourself and whether you believe in yourself.
WILLIAM J. H. BOETCKER (1873–1962)

Why be a man when you can be a success?
BERTOLT BRECHT (1898–1956)

A successful man is one who can lay a firm foundation with the bricks others throw at him.
DAVID BRINKLEY (1920–2003)

A minute's success pays the failure of years.
ROBERT BROWNING (1812–1889)

The important thing to recognize is that it takes a team, and the team ought to get credit for the wins and the losses. Successes have many fathers, failures have none.
PHILIP CALDWELL (1920–)

People rarely succeed unless they have fun in what they are doing.
DALE CARNEGIE (1888–1955)

I owe my success to having listened respectfully to the very best advice, and then going away and doing the exact opposite.
G. K. CHESTERTON (1874–1936)

Success is the ability to go from one failure to another with no loss of enthusiasm.
SIR WINSTON CHURCHILL (1874–1965)

The man of virtue makes the difficulty to be overcome his first business, and success only a subsequent consideration.
CONFUCIUS (551–479 BC), *The Confucian Analects*

I don't know the key to success, but the key to failure is trying to please everybody.
BILL COSBY (1937–)

The person who makes a success of living is the one who sees his goal steadily and aims for it unswervingly. That is dedication.
CECIL B. DEMILLE (1881–1959)

Success is counted sweetest
By those who ne'er succeed.
EMILY DICKINSON (1830–1886), "No. 67"

Success isn't permanent, and failure isn't fatal.
MIKE DITKA (1939–)

What's money? A man is a success if he gets up in the morning and goes to bed at night and in between does what he wants to do.
BOB DYLAN (1941–)

Many of life's failures are people who did not realize how close they were to success when they gave up.
THOMAS A. EDISON (1847–1931)

If A is success in life, then A equals x plus y plus z. Work is x; y is play; and z is keeping your mouth shut.
ALBERT EINSTEIN (1879–1955)

Try not to become a man of success but rather to become a man of value.
ALBERT EINSTEIN (1879–1955)

We succeed only as we identify in life, or in war, or in anything else, a single overriding objective, and make all other considerations bend to that one objective.
DWIGHT D. EISENHOWER (1890–1969)

Often a certain abdication of prudence and foresight is an element of success.
RALPH WALDO EMERSON (1803–1882)

Success is the good fortune that comes from aspiration, desperation, perspiration, and inspiration.
EVAN ESAR (1899–1995)

Along with success comes a reputation for wisdom.
EURIPIDES (C. 480–406 BC)

It's how you deal with failure that determines how you achieve success.
DAVID FEHERTY (1958–)

Coming together is a beginning. Keeping together is progress. Working together is success.
HENRY FORD (1863–1947)

Without continual growth and progress, such words as improvement, achievement, and success have no meaning.
BENJAMIN FRANKLIN (1706–1790)

The secret of success is sincerity. Once you can fake that you've got it made.
JEAN GIRAUDOUX (1882–1944)

My mother drew a distinction between achievement and success. She said that "achievement is the knowledge that you have studied and worked hard and done the best that is in you. Success is being praised by others, and that's nice, too, but not as important or satisfying. Always aim for achievement and forget about success."
HELEN HAYES (1900–1993)

It is literally true that you can succeed best and quickest by helping others to succeed.
NAPOLEON HILL (1883–1970)

Patience, persistence, and perspiration make an unbeatable combination for success.
NAPOLEON HILL (1883–1970)

Success is the sole earthly judge of right and wrong.
ADOLF HITLER (1889–1945)

A little more persistence, a little more effort, and what seemed hopeless failure may turn to glorious success.
ELBERT HUBBARD (1856–1915)

He who has achieved success has worked well, laughed often, and loved much.
ELBERT HUBBARD (1856–1915)

There's no secret about success. Did you ever know a successful man who didn't tell you about it?
KIN HUBBARD (1868–1930)

I'm convinced that about half of what separates the successful entrepreneurs from the non-successful ones is pure perseverance.
STEVE JOBS (1955–)

Each success only buys an admission ticket to a more difficult problem.
HENRY KISSINGER (1923–)

Your chances of success are directly proportional to the degree of pleasure you desire from what you do. If you are in a job you hate, face the fact squarely and get out.
MICHAEL KORDA (1933–)

Nothing succeeds like the appearance of success.
CHRISTOPHER LASCH (1932–1994)

Success didn't spoil me, I've always been insufferable.
FRAN LEBOWITZ (1950–)

A successful individual typically sets his next goal somewhat but not too much above his last achievement. In this way he steadily raises his level of aspiration.
KURT LEWIN (1890–1947)

Always bear in mind that your own resolution to succeed is more important than any one thing.
ABRAHAM LINCOLN (1809–1865)

Once you agree upon the price you and your family must pay for success, it enables you to ignore the minor hurts, the opponent's pressure, and the temporary failures.
VINCE LOMBARDI (1913–1970)

Perseverance is a great element of success. If you only knock long enough and loud enough at the gate, you are sure to wake up somebody.
HENRY WADSWORTH LONGFELLOW (1807–1882)

The victory of success is half won when one gains the habit of setting goals and achieving them. Even the most tedious chore will become endurable as you parade through each day convinced that every task, no matter how menial or boring, brings you closer to fulfilling your dreams.
OG MANDINO (1923–1996)

Real success is finding your lifework in the work that you love.
DAVID MCCULLOUGH (1933–)

There is only one success—to be able to spend your life in your own way.
CHRISTOPHER MORLEY (1890–1957)

If you wish to be a success in the world, promise everything, deliver nothing.
NAPOLÉON I (1769–1821)

To follow, without halt, one aim: There's the secret of success.
ANNA PAVLOVA (1885–1931)

Formulate and stamp indelibly on your mind a mental picture of yourself as succeeding. Hold this picture tenaciously. Never permit it to fade. Your mind will seek to develop the picture.... Do not build up obstacles in your imagination.
NORMAN VINCENT PEALE (1898–1993)

Success is the result of perfection, hard work, learning from failure, loyalty, and persistence.
COLIN POWELL (1937–)

If your success is not on your own terms, if it looks good to the world but does not feel good in your heart, it is not success at all.
ANNA QUINDLEN (1953–)

Your best shot at happiness, self-worth and personal satisfaction—the things that constitute real success—is not in earning as much as you can, but in performing as well as you can … something that you consider worthwhile.
WILLIAM RASPBERRY (1935–)

Success in business requires training and discipline and hard work. But if you're not frightened by these things, the opportunities are just as great today as they ever were.
DAVID ROCKEFELLER (1915–)

You always pass failure on the way to success.
MICKEY ROONEY (1920–)

Of course there is no formula for success except perhaps an unconditional acceptance of life and what it brings.
ARTHUR RUBINSTEIN (1886–1982)

A great secret of success is to go through life as a man who never gets used up.
DR. ALBERT SCHWEITZER (1875–1965)

I can't give you a sure-fire formula for success, but I can give you a formula for failure: try to please everybody all the time.
HERBERT BAYARD SWOPE (1882–1958)

A discovery is said to be an accident meeting a prepared mind.
ALBERT SZENT-GYORGYI (1893–1986)

If one advances confidently in the direction of his dreams and endeavors to live the life which he has imagined, he will meet with a success unexpected in common hours.
HENRY DAVID THOREAU (1817–1862)

Men are born to succeed, not fail.
HENRY DAVID THOREAU (1817–1862)

Success usually comes to those who are too busy to be looking for it.
HENRY DAVID THOREAU (1817–1862)

All you need in this life is ignorance and confidence; then success is sure.
MARK TWAIN (1835–1910)

Success is almost totally dependent upon drive and persistence. The extra energy required to make another effort or try another approach is the secret of winning.
DENIS WAITLEY (1933–)

Success is to be measured not so much by the position that one has reached in life as by the obstacles which he has overcome.
BOOKER T. WASHINGTON (1856–1915)

A man desires praise that he may be reassured, that he may be quit of his doubting of himself; he is indifferent to applause when he is confident of success.
ALEC WAUGH (1898–1981)

Some people dream of success … while others wake up and work hard at it.
ANONYMOUS

Suckers

There's a sucker born every minute.
P. T. BARNUM (1810–1891)

It's morally wrong to allow a sucker to keep his money.
W. C. FIELDS (1880–1946)

Never give a sucker an even break.
W. C. FIELDS (1880–1946)

If you're playing a poker game and you look around the table and can't tell who the sucker is, it's you.
PAUL NEWMAN (1925–)

Life is a banquet, and most poor suckers are starving to death.
ROSALIND RUSSELL (1908–1976)

Suffering

A misery is not to be measured from the nature of the evil, but from the temper of the sufferer.
JOSEPH ADDISON (1672–1719)

You desire to know the art of living, my friend? It is contained in one phrase: make use of suffering.
HENRI-FRÉDÉRIC AMIEL (1821–1881)

To perceive is to suffer.
ARISTOTLE (384–322 BC)

I cannot believe that the inscrutable universe turns on an axis of suffering; surely the strange beauty of the world must somewhere rest on pure joy!
LOUISE BOGAN (1897–1970)

But a somewhat more liberal and sympathetic examination of mankind will convince us that the cross is even older than the gibbet, that voluntary suffering was before and independent of compulsory; and in short that in most important matters a man has always been free to ruin himself if he chose.
G. K. CHESTERTON (1874–1936), *What's Wrong with the World*

We shall draw from the heart of suffering itself the means of inspiration and survival.
SIR WINSTON CHURCHILL (1874–1965)

But penance need not be paid in suffering.... It can be paid in forward motion. Correcting the mistake is a positive move, a nurturing move.
BARBARA HALL (1946–)

People have a hard time letting go of their suffering. Out of a fear of the unknown, they prefer suffering that is familiar.
THICH NHAT HAHN (1926–)

If suffer we must, let's suffer on the heights.
VICTOR HUGO (1802–1885), *Les Malheureux*

Whenever evil befalls us, we ought to ask ourselves, after the first suffering, how we can turn it into good. So shall we take occasion, from one bitter root, to raise perhaps many flowers.
LEIGH HUNT (1784–1859)

Neurosis is always a substitute for legitimate suffering.
CARL JUNG (1875–1961)

Although the world is full of suffering, it is full also of the overcoming of it.
HELEN KELLER (1880–1968)

Character cannot be developed in ease and quiet. Only through experience of trial and suffering can the soul be strengthened, ambition inspired, and success achieved.
HELEN KELLER (1880–1968)

Man has to suffer. When he has no real afflictions, he invents some.
JOSE MARTI (1853–1895)

The truth that many people never understand, until it is too late, is that the more you try to avoid suffering the more you suffer because smaller and more insignificant things begin to torture you in proportion to your fear of being hurt.
THOMAS MERTON (1915–1968)

Never to suffer would never to have been blessed.
EDGAR ALLAN POE (1809–1849)

In the part of this universe that we know there is great injustice, and often the good suffer, and often the wicked prosper, and one hardly knows which of those is the more annoying.
BERTRAND RUSSELL (1872–1970)

The sufferings that fate inflicts on us should be borne with patience, what enemies inflict with manly courage.
THUCYDIDES (C. 460–395 BC)

Pain is inevitable, suffering is optional.
ANONYMOUS

Suicide

Some day science may have the existence of mankind in power, and the human race can commit suicide by blowing up the world.
HENRY ADAMS (1838–1918)

Democracy never lasts long. It soon wastes, exhausts and murders itself. There was never a democracy that did not commit suicide.
JOHN ADAMS (1735–1826)

The joke of our time is the suicide of intention.
THEODOR W. ADORNO (1903–1969)

If you don't do it my way, I suggest you commit suicide.
JOSEF ALBERS (1888–1976)

To run away from trouble is a form of cowardice and, while it is true that the suicide braves death, he does it not for some noble object but to escape some ill.
ARISTOTLE (384–322 BC)

There is something great and terrible about suicide.
HONORÉ DE BALZAC (1799–1850)

Two armies that fight each other is like one large army that commits suicide.
HENRI BARBUSSE (1873–1935)

My husband and I didn't sign a pre-nuptial agreement. We signed a mutual suicide pact.
ROSEANNE BARR (1952–)

The destructive character lives from the feeling, not that life is worth living, but that suicide is not worth the trouble.
WALTER BENJAMIN (1892–1940)

I tried to commit suicide by sticking my head in the oven, but there was a cake in it.
LESLEY BOONE (1968–)

One said of suicide, As long as one has brains one should not blow them out. And another answered, But when one has ceased to have them, too often one cannot.
F. H. BRADLEY (1846–1924)

I'm not that clever to do a suicide. I wouldn't know how to tie a rope in the first place, you know what I mean?
FRANK BRUNO (1961–)

No one ever committed suicide while reading a good book, but many have tried while trying to write one.
ROBERT BYRNE (1928–)

There is but one truly serious philosophical problem and that is suicide.
ALBERT CAMUS (1913–1960)

I look upon indolence as a sort of suicide; for the man is effectually destroyed, though the appetites of the brute may survive.
LORD CHESTERFIELD (1694–1773)

The obsession with suicide is characteristic of the man who can neither live nor die, and whose attention never swerves from this double impossibility.
E. M. CIORAN (1911–1995)

For many centuries, suicides were treated like criminals by the society. That is part of the terrible legacy that has come down into society's method of handling suicide recovery. Now we have to fight off the demons that have been hanging around suicide for centuries.
JUDY COLLINS (1939–)

I think suicide is sort of like cancer was 50 years ago. People don't want to talk about it, they don't want to know about it. People are frightened of it, and they don't understand, when actually these issues are medically treatable.
JUDY COLLINS (1939–)

Suicide sometimes proceeds from cowardice, but not always; for cowardice sometimes prevents it; since as many live because they are afraid to die, as die because they are afraid to live.
CHARLES CALEB COLTON (1780–1832)

That's the thing about suicide. Try as you might to remember how a person lived his life, you always end up thinking about how he ended it.
ANDERSON COOPER (1967–)

Killing yourself is a major commitment, it takes a kind of courage. Most people just lead lives of cowardly desperation. It's kinda half suicide where you just dull yourself with substances.
ROBERT CRUMB (1943–)

When one realizes that his life is worthless he either commits suicide or travels.
EDWARD DAHLBERG (1900–1977)

Suicide is a permanent solution to a temporary problem.
PHIL DONAHUE (1935–)

Each victim of suicide gives his act a personal stamp which expresses his temperament, the special conditions in which he is involved, and which, consequently, cannot be explained by the social and general causes of the phenomenon.
ÉMILE DURKHEIM (1858–1917)

Mankind is becoming a single unit, and that for a unit to fight against itself is suicide.
HENRY HAVELOCK ELLIS (1859–1939)

The prevalence of suicide, without doubt, is a test of height in civilization; it means that the population is winding up its nervous and intellectual system to the utmost point of tension and that sometimes it snaps.
HENRY HAVELOCK ELLIS (1859–1939)

Skepticism is slow suicide.
RALPH WALDO EMERSON (1803–1882)

The great thing about suicide is that it's not one of those things you have to do now or you lose your chance. I mean, you can always do it later.
HARVEY FIERSTEIN (1954–)

Depression is close to me, but suicide hasn't been.
CLAIRE FORLANI (1972–)

If I had no sense of humor, I would long ago have committed suicide.
MAHATMA GANDHI (1869–1948)

Suicide is not a remedy.
JAMES A. GARFIELD (1831–1881)

Would Hamlet have felt the delicious fascination of suicide if he hadn't had an audience, and lines to speak?
JEAN GENET (1910–1986)

I think about death a lot, like I think we all do. I don't think of suicide as an option, but as fun. It's an interesting idea that you can control how you go. It's this thing that's looming, and you can control it.
RYAN GOSLING (1980–)

I was darkly convinced that at age 52 I would kill myself because my mother committed suicide at that age. I was fantasizing that she was waiting for me on the other side of the grave.
SPALDING GRAY (1941–2004)

As anyone who has been close to someone that has committed suicide knows, there is no other pain like that felt after the incident.
PETER GREENE (1965–)

What makes life worth living? Better surely, to yield to the stain of suicide blood in me and seek forgetfulness in the embrace of cold dark death.
ZANE GREY (1872–1939)

I think suicide is the most perfect thing you can do in life.
DAMIEN HIRST (1909–)

When God desires to destroy a thing, he entrusts its destruction to the thing itself. Every bad institution of this world ends by suicide.
VICTOR HUGO (1802–1885)

I don't persuade to suicide.
JACK KEVORKIAN (1928–)

Anybody who has listened to certain kinds of music, or read certain kinds of poetry, or heard certain kinds of performances on the concertina, will admit that even suicide has its brighter aspects.
STEPHEN LEACOCK (1869–1944)

If you are of the opinion that the contemplation of suicide is sufficient evidence of a poetic nature, do not forget that actions speak louder than words.
FRAN LEBOWITZ (1950–)

Life is only a long and bitter suicide, and faith alone can transform this suicide into a sacrifice.
FRANZ LISZT (1811–1886)

I would be going until I went over the bounds of reality and was then caught up in a profound wish to be dead without having to go through the shaming defeat of suicide.
JOSHUA LOGAN (1908–)

Suicide is man's way of telling God, "You can't fire me—I quit."
BILL MAHER (1956–)

We can consciously end our life almost anytime we choose. This ability is an endowment, like laughing and blushing, given to no other animal ... in any given moment, by not exercising the option of suicide, we are choosing to live.
PETER MCWILLIAMS (1949–2000)

Suicide is belated acquiescence in the opinion of one's wife's relatives.
H. L. MENCKEN (1880–1956)

Hope is a necessity for normal life and the major weapon against the suicide impulse.
DR. KARL A. MENNINGER (1893–1990)

Is it hard for the reader to believe that suicides are sometimes committed to forestall the committing of murder? There is no doubt of it. Nor is there any doubt that murder is sometimes committed to avert suicide.
DR. KARL A. MENNINGER (1893–1990)

A suicide kills two people … that's what it's for!
ARTHUR MILLER (1915–2005)

It is always consoling to think of suicide: in that way one gets through many a bad night.
FRIEDRICH NIETZSCHE (1844–1900)

The only difference between suicide and martyrdom is press coverage.
CHUCK PALAHNIUK (1962–)

No one ever lacks a good reason for suicide.
CESARE PAVESE (1908–1950)

Allow me to say that I would long since have committed suicide had desisting made me a professor of Latin.
EZRA POUND (1885–1972)

I have always thought the suicide should bump off at least one swine before taking off for parts unknown.
EZRA POUND (1885–1972)

Anyone who thinks must think of the next war as they would of suicide.
ELEANOR ROOSEVELT (1884–1962)

Every man has the right to risk his own life in order to preserve it. Has it ever been said that a man who throws himself out the window to escape from a fire is guilty of suicide?
JEAN-JACQUES ROUSSEAU (1712–1778)

Drunkenness is temporary suicide.
BERTRAND RUSSELL (1872–1970)

They tell us that suicide is the greatest piece of cowardice … that suicide is wrong; when it is quite obvious that there is nothing in the world to which every man has a more unassailable title than to his own life and person.
ARTHUR SCHOPENHAUER (1788–1860)

To be, or not to be: that is the question:
Whether 'tis nobler in the mind to suffer
The slings and arrows of outrageous fortune,
Or to take arms against a sea of troubles,
And by opposing end them? To die: to sleep:
No more; and by a sleep to say we end
The heartache and the thousand natural shocks
That flesh is heir to,—'tis a consummation
Devoutly to be wish'd. To die, to sleep;
To sleep: perchance to dream: ay, there's the rub:
For in that sleep of death what dreams may come,
When we have shuffled off this mortal coil,
Must give us pause: there's the respect
That makes calamity of so long life;
For who would bear the whips and scorns of time,
The oppressor's wrong, the proud man's contumely,
The pangs of despised love, the law's delay,
The insolence of office and the spurns
That patient merit of the unworthy takes,
When he himself might his quietus make
With a bare bodkin? who would fardels bear,
To grunt and sweat under a weary life,
But that the dread of something after death,
The undiscover'd country from whose bourn
No traveller returns, puzzles the will
And makes us rather bear those ills we have
Than fly to others that we know not of?
Thus conscience does make cowards of us all;
And thus the native hue of resolution
Is sicklied o'er with the pale cast of thought,
And enterprises of great pith and moment
With this regard their currents turn awry,
And lose the name of action.
WILLIAM SHAKESPEARE (1564–1616), *Hamlet*

Civilizations die from suicide, not by murder.
ARNOLD J. TOYNBEE (1889–1975)

The suicide arrives at the conclusion that what he is seeking does not exist; the seeker concludes that he has not yet looked in the right place.
PAUL WATZLAWICK (1921–)

There is no refuge from confession but suicide; and suicide is confession.
DANIEL WEBSTER (1782–1852)

Never attempt to murder a man who is committing suicide.
WOODROW WILSON (1856–1924)

Summer

Even in America, the Indian summer of life should be a little sunny and a little sad, like the season, and infinite in wealth and depth of tone—but never hustled.
HENRY ADAMS (1838–1918)

The activity of happiness must occupy an entire lifetime; for one swallow does not a summer make.
ARISTOTLE (384–322 BC), *Nichomachean Ethics*

The tendinous part of the mind, so to speak, is more developed in winter; the fleshy, in summer. I should say winter had given the bone and sinew to literature, summer the tissues and the blood.
JOHN BURROUGHS (1837–1921), *The Snow-Walkers*

In the depth of winter, I finally learned that within me there lay an invincible summer.
ALBERT CAMUS (1913–1960)

Long stormy spring-time, wet contentious April, winter chilling the lap of very May; but at length the season of summer does come.
THOMAS CARLYLE (1795–1881)

Our fear of death is like our fear that summer will be short, but when we have had our swing of pleasure, our fill of fruit and our swelter of heat, we say we have had our day.
RALPH WALDO EMERSON (1803–1882)

For him in vain the envious seasons roll,
Who bears eternal summer in his soul.
OLIVER WENDELL HOLMES SR. (1809–1894)

Summer afternoon ... the two most beautiful words in the English language.
HENRY JAMES (1843–1916)

The summer night is like a perfection of thought.
WALLACE STEVENS (1879–1955)

There shall be eternal summer in the grateful heart.
CELIA THAXTER (1835–1894)

In summer, the song sings itself.
WILLIAM CARLOS WILLIAMS (1883–1963)

A life without love is like a year without summer.
SWEDISH PROVERB

The Sun

The higher the sun ariseth, the less shadow doth he cast; even so the greater is the goodness, the less doth it covet praise; yet cannot avoid its rewards in honors.
AKHENATON (C. 1400 BC)

To speak truly, few adult persons can see nature. Most persons do not see the sun. At least they have a very superficial seeing. The sun illuminates only the eye of the man, but shines into the eye and heart of the child.
RALPH WALDO EMERSON (1803–1882)

A single sunbeam is enough to drive away many shadows.
SAINT FRANCIS OF ASSISI (1181–1226)

Spots are on the surface of the solar body where they are produced and also dissolved, some in shorter and others in longer periods. They are carried around the Sun: an important occurrence in itself.
GALILEO GALILEI (1564–1642)

The Sun, with all the planets revolving around it, and depending on it, can still ripen a bunch of grapes as though it had nothing else in the Universe to do.
GALILEO GALILEI (1564–1642)

The time to repair the roof is when the sun is shining.
JOHN F. KENNEDY (1917–1963)

Some painters transform the sun into a yellow spot; others transform a yellow spot into the sun.
PABLO PICASSO (1881–1973)

A good heart is the sun and the moon; or, rather, the sun and not the moon, for it shines bright and never changes.
WILLIAM SHAKESPEARE (1564–1616), *Henry V*

Superiority

The difference of race is one of the reasons why I fear war may always exist; because race implies difference, difference implies superiority, and superiority leads to predominance.
BENJAMIN DISRAELI (1804–1881)

Whoever envies another confesses his superiority.
SAMUEL JOHNSON (1709–1784)

Great men never make bad use of their superiority. They see it and feel it and are not less modest. The more they have, the more they know their own deficiencies.
JEAN-JACQUES ROUSSEAU (1712–1778)

Ideas of superiority and inferiority arise only in a heart corrupted by egoism. If someone argues that he is higher or his religion is holier, it proves that he has missed the significance of his faith.
SRI SATHYA SAI BABA (1926–)

If you wish to make a man look noble, your best course is to kill him. What superiority he may have inherited from his race, what superiority nature may have personally gifted him with, comes out in death.
ALEXANDER SMITH (1830–1867)

The fact that man knows right from wrong proves his intellectual superiority to other creatures; but the fact that he can do wrong proves his moral inferiority to any creature that cannot.
MARK TWAIN (1835–1910)

The Supernatural

Belief in the supernatural reflects a failure of the imagination.
EDWARD ABBEY (1927–1989)

Whatever the scientists may say, if we take the supernatural out of life, we leave only the unnatural.
AMELIA BARR (1831–1919)

The belief in a supernatural source of evil is not necessary; men alone are quite capable of every wickedness.
JOSEPH CONRAD (1857–1924)

Man can know his world without falling back on revelation; he can live his life without feeling his utter dependence on supernatural powers.
CHRISTOPHER DAWSON (1889–1970)

In every religion there is an element of the supernatural, varying with the influence of pure reason over its devotees.
CHARLES EASTMAN (1858–1939)

The supernatural is the natural not yet understood.
ELBERT HUBBARD (1856–1915)

I think the supernatural is a catch-all for everything we don't understand about the vast other parts of life that we cannot perceive.
WILLIAM SHATNER (1931–)

Superstition

Superstition is the religion of feeble minds.
EDMUND BURKE (1729–1797)

Man's mind is like a store of idolatry and superstition; so much so that if a man believes his own mind it is certain that he will forsake God and forge some idol in his own brain.
JOHN CALVIN (1509–1564)

Superstition is an unreasoning fear of God.
CICERO (106–43 BC)

We do not destroy religion by destroying superstition.
CICERO (106–43 BC)

When superstition is allowed to perform the task of old age in dulling the human temperament, we can

say goodbye to all excellence in poetry, in painting, and in music.
DENIS DIDEROT (1713–1784)

Superstition is the weakness of the human mind; it is inherent in that mind; it has always been, and always will be.
FREDERICK THE GREAT (1712–1786)

Superstition is the poetry of life.
JOHANN WOLFGANG VON GOETHE (1749–1832)

Count Hermann Keyserling once said truly that the greatest American superstition was belief in facts.
JOHN GUNTHER (1901–1970)

Mankind are an incorrigible race. Give them but bugbears and idols—it is all that they ask; the distinctions of right and wrong, of truth and falsehood, of good and evil, are worse than indifferent to them.
WILLIAM HAZLITT (1778–1830)

Faith must have adequate evidence, else it is mere superstition.
ALEXANDER HODGE (1823–1886)

Security is mostly a superstition. It does not exist in nature.... Life is either a daring adventure or nothing.
HELEN KELLER (1880–1968), *The Open Door*

Fear is the main source of superstition, and one of the main sources of cruelty. To conquer fear is the beginning of wisdom.
BERTRAND RUSSELL (1872–1970), *Unpopular Essays*

I have only one superstition. I touch all the bases when I hit a home run.
GEORGE HERMAN "BABE" RUTH, JR. (1895–1948)

A fool's brain digests philosophy into folly, science into superstition, and art into pedantry. Hence University education.
GEORGE BERNARD SHAW (1856–1950)

When the human race has once acquired a superstition, nothing short of death is ever likely to remove it.
MARK TWAIN (1835–1910)

Superstition is to religion what astrology is to astronomy: the mad daughter of a wise mother.
VOLTAIRE (1694–1778)

Surprise

The secret to humor is surprise.
ARISTOTLE (384–322 BC)

Surprises are foolish things. The pleasure is not enhanced, and the inconvenience is often considerable.
JANE AUSTEN (1775–1817)

The backbone of surprise is fusing speed with secrecy.
KARL VON CLAUSEWITZ (1780–1831)

Surprise is the greatest gift which life can grant us.
BORIS PASTERNAK (1890–1960)

That I exist is a perpetual surprise which is life.
RABINDRANATH TAGORE (1861–1941)

Survival

Self-interest is but the survival of the animal in us. Humanity only begins for man with self-surrender.
HENRI-FREDÉRIC AMIEL (1821–1881)

Man's survival, from the time of Adam and Eve until the invention of agriculture, must have been precarious because of his inability to ensure his food supply.
NORMAN BORLAUG (1914–)

The planet's survival has become so uncertain that any effort, any thought that presupposes an assured future amounts to a mad gamble.
ELIAS CANETTI (1905–1994)

We shall draw from the heart of suffering itself the means of inspiration and survival.
SIR WINSTON CHURCHILL (1874–1965)

It has yet to be proven that intelligence has any survival value.
ARTHUR C. CLARKE (1917–)

Survival is triumph enough.
HARRY CREWS (1935–)

Learning is not compulsory ... neither is survival.
W. EDWARDS DEMING (1900–1993)

In the name of Hypocrites, doctors have invented the most exquisite form of torture ever known to man: survival.
EDWARD EVERETT HALE (1822–1909)

On a long enough timeline, the survival rate for everyone drops to zero.
CHUCK PALAHNIUK (1962–), *Fight Club*

Survival is a privilege which entails obligations. I am forever asking myself what I can do for those who have not survived.
SIMON WIESENTHAL (1908–2005)

Suspicion

Suspicion is not less an enemy to virtue than to happiness; he that is already corrupt is naturally suspicious, and he that becomes suspicious will quickly be corrupt.
JOSEPH ADDISON (1672–1719)

Suspicions amongst thoughts are like bats amongst birds, they ever fly by twilight.
SIR FRANCIS BACON (1561–1626)

Suspicions that the mind, of itself, gathers, are but buzzes; but suspicions that are artificially nourished and put into men's heads by the tales and whisperings of others, have stings.
SIR FRANCIS BACON (1561–1626)

Suspicion is far more to be wrong than right; more often unjust than just. It is no friend to virtue, and always an enemy to happiness.
HOSEA BALLOU (1771–1852)

Suspicion is a heavy armor, and with its weight it impedes more than it protects.
ROBERT BURNS (1759–1796)

Caesar's wife must be above suspicion.
JULIUS CAESAR (100–44 BC)

There is one safeguard known generally to the wise, which is an advantage and security to all, but especially to democracies as against despots—suspicion.
DEMOSTHENES (384–322 BC)

Pure love and suspicion cannot dwell together: at the door where the latter enters, the former makes its exit.
ALEXANDRE DUMAS (1802–1870)

What we won when all of our people united must not be lost in suspicion and distrust and selfishness and politics. Accordingly, I shall not seek, and I will not accept, the nomination of my party for another term as president.
LYNDON B. JOHNSON (1908–1973)

Suspicion is most often useless pain.
SAMUEL JOHNSON (1709–1784)

Let me remind you of the old maxim: people under suspicion are better moving than at rest, since at rest they may be sitting in the balance without knowing it, being weighed together with their sins.
FRANZ KAFKA (1883–1924)

Let us resolve to be masters, not the victims, of our history, controlling our own destiny without giving way to blind suspicions and emotions.
JOHN F. KENNEDY (1917–1963)

Suspicion of happiness is in our blood.
E. V. LUCAS (1868–1938)

A fellow who is always declaring he's no fool usually has his suspicions.
WILSON MIZNER (1876–1933)

Suspicion is the companion of mean souls, and the bane of all good society.
THOMAS PAINE (1737–1809)

Suspicion is the cancer of friendship.
PETRARCH (1304–1374)

We can gain no lasting peace if we approach it with suspicion and mistrust or with fear. We can gain it only if we proceed with the understanding, the confidence, and the courage which flows from conviction.
FRANKLIN D. ROOSEVELT (1882–1945)

Suspicion is one of the morbid reactions by which an organism defends itself and seeks another equilibrium.
NATHALIE SARRAUTE (1900–1999)

Suspicion always haunts the guilty mind.
WILLIAM SHAKESPEARE (1564–1616), *King Henry VI*

Suspicion and doubt lead to animosity and hatred.
RALPH STEADMAN (1936–)

We are always paid for our suspicion by finding what we suspect.
HENRY DAVID THOREAU (1817–1862)

Her own mother lived the latter years of her life in the horrible suspicion that electricity was dripping invisibly all over the house.
JAMES THURBER (1894–1961)

A lock is better than suspicion.
IRISH PROVERB

Sympathy

Sympathy is the first condition of criticism.
HENRI-FREDÉRIC AMIEL (1821–1881)

The writer must be universal in sympathy and an outcast by nature; only then can he see clearly.
JULIAN BARNES (1946–)

You will find that the woman who is really kind to dogs is always one who has failed to inspire sympathy in men.
MAX BEERBOHM (1872–1956)

Next to love, sympathy is the divinest passion of the human heart.
EDMUND BURKE (1729–1797)

To be in one's own heart in kindly sympathy with all things; this is the nature of righteousness.
CONFUCIUS (551–479 BC)

All sympathy not consistent with acknowledged virtue is but disguised selfishness.
SAMUEL TAYLOR COLERIDGE (1772–1834)

The more sympathy you give, the less you need.
MALCOLM S. FORBES (1919–1990)

One is led astray alike by sympathy and coldness, by praise and by blame.
JOHANN WOLFGANG VON GOETHE (1749–1832)

There are sufferings which sympathy may not make lighter.
LAMENNAIS (1782–1854)

Women have no sympathy, and my experience of women is almost as large as Europe.
FLORENCE NIGHTINGALE (1820–1910)

I have a deep sympathy with war, it so apes the gait and bearing of the soul.
HENRY DAVID THOREAU (1817–1862)

It appears to be a law that you cannot have a deep sympathy with both man and nature.
HENRY DAVID THOREAU (1817–1862)

Let your secret sympathies and your compassion be always with the under dog in the fight—this is magnanimity; but bet on the other one—this is business.
MARK TWAIN (1835–1910)

His morality is all sympathy, just what morality should be.
OSCAR WILDE (1854–1900)

If there was less sympathy in the world, there would be less trouble in the world.
OSCAR WILDE (1854–1900)

Taboos

There are no taboos in bed, and there shouldn't be any taboos in bed.
FRANK LANGELLA (1940–)

The taboo subjects have become fewer and fewer with television. These were never touched in the '70s.
BOB NEWHART (1929–)

Let us overthrow the totems, break the taboos. Or better, let us consider them cancelled. Coldly, let us be intelligent.
PIERRE TRUDEAU (1919–2000)

Tact

Tact is the discrimination of differences. It consists in conscious deviations.
THEODOR W. ADORNO (1903–1969)

Silence is not always tact, but it is tact that is golden, not silence.
SAMUEL BUTLER (1835–1902)

One shouldn't talk of halters in the hanged man's house.
MIGUEL DE CERVANTES (1547–1616)

Tact in audacity is knowing how far you can go without going too far.
JEAN COCTEAU (1889–1963)

Without tact you can learn nothing.
BENJAMIN DISRAELI (1804–1881)

Tact and diplomacy are fine in international relations, in politics, perhaps even in business; in science only one thing matters, and that is the facts.
HANS EYSENCK (1916–1997)

A spoonful of honey will catch more flies than a gallon of vinegar.
BENJAMIN FRANKLIN (1706–1790)

Tact is to lie about others as you would have them lie about you.
OLIVER HERFORD (1863–1935)

Experience was to be taken as showing that one might get a five-pound note as one got a light for a cigarette; but one had to check the friendly impulse to ask for it in the same way.
HENRY JAMES (1843–1916)

Tact is, after all, a kind of mind reading.
SARAH ORNE JEWETT (1849–1909)

Tact is the ability to describe others as they see themselves.
ABRAHAM LINCOLN (1809–1865)

Tact is the knack of making a point without making an enemy.
SIR ISAAC NEWTON (1642–1727)

Give thy thoughts no tongue, nor any unproportioned thought his act. Be thou familiar but by no means vulgar.
WILLIAM SHAKESPEARE (1564–1616), *Hamlet*

Tact is one of the first mental virtues, the absence of it is fatal to the best talent.
WILLIAM GILMORE SIMMS (1806–1870)

To have the reputation of possessing the most perfect social tact, talk to every woman as if you loved her, and to every man as if he bored you.
OSCAR WILDE (1854–1900)

A little tact and wise management may often evade resistance and carry a point, where direct force might be in vain.
ANONYMOUS

Tact is ability to see others as they wish to be seen.
ANONYMOUS

Tact is the intelligence of the heart.
ANONYMOUS

Talent

Work while you have the light. You are responsible for the talent that has been entrusted to you.
HENRI-FRÉDÉRIC AMIEL (1821–1881)

There are two kinds of talents, man-made talent and God-given talent. With man-made talent you have to work very hard. With God-given talent, you just touch it up once in a while.
PEARL BAILEY (1918–1990)

If you have a talent, use it in every which way possible. Don't hoard it. Don't dole it out like a miser. Spend it lavishly like a millionaire intent on going broke.
BRENDAN FRANCIS BEHAN (1923–1964)

The toughest thing about success is that you've got to keep on being a success. Talent is only a starting point in this business. You've got to keep on working that talent. Someday I'll reach for it and it won't be there.
IRVING BERLIN (1888–1989)

You have to have confidence in your ability, and then be tough enough to follow through.
ROSALYNN CARTER (1927–)

Natural ability without education has more often attained to glory and virtue than education without natural ability.
CICERO (106–43 BC)

Mediocrity knows nothing higher than itself, but talent instantly recognizes genius.
SIR ARTHUR CONAN DOYLE (1859–1930), *Valley of Fear*

The peril of every fine faculty is the delight of playing with it for pride. Talent is commonly developed at the expense of character, and the greater it grows, the more is the mischief. Talent is mistaken for genius, a dogma or system for truth, ambition for greatest, ingenuity for poetry, sensuality for art.
RALPH WALDO EMERSON (1803–1882)

Hide not your talents, they for use were made.
What's a sun-dial in the shade?
BENJAMIN FRANKLIN (1706–1790)

The person born with a talent they are meant to use will find their greatest happiness in using it.
JOHANN WOLFGANG VON GOETHE (1749–1832)

Great ability develops and reveals itself increasingly with every new assignment.
BALTASAR GRACIAN (1601–1658)

Put yourself on view. This brings your talents to light.
BALTASAR GRACIAN (1601–1658)

They who lack talent expect things to happen without effort. They ascribe failure to a lack of inspiration or ability, or to misfortune, rather than to insufficient application. At the core of every true talent there is an awareness of the difficulties inherent in any achievement, and the confidence that by persistence and patience something worthwhile will be realized. Thus talent is a species of vigor.
ERIC HOFFER (1902–1983)

Adversity has the effect of eliciting talents, which in prosperous circumstances would have lain dormant.
HORACE (65–8 BC)

Everyone has talent. What is rare is the courage to follow the talent to the dark place where it leads.
SIR WILLIAM ALTON JONES (1746–1794)

Everyone has talent. What is rare is the courage to follow the talent to the dark place where it leads.
ERICA JONG (1942–)

Getting ahead in a difficult profession requires avid faith in yourself. That is why some people with mediocre talent, but with great inner drive, go much further than people with vastly superior talent.
SOPHIA LOREN (1934–)

If I have ever made any valuable discoveries, it has been owing more to patient attention, than to any other talent.
SIR ISAAC NEWTON (1643–1727)

Talent is a matter of quantity. Talent does not write one page, it writes three hundred.
JULES RENARD (1864–1910)

Toil to make yourself remarkable by some talent or other.
SENECA (5 BC–AD 65)

Looks don't concern me.... Only talent interests a woman of taste.
PETER SHAFFER (1926–), *Amadeus*

A great deal of talent is lost to the world for the want of a little courage.
SYDNEY SMITH (1771–1845)

Whatever you are by nature, keep to it; never desert your line of talent. Be what nature intended you for and you will succeed.
SYDNEY SMITH (1771–1845)

More men fail through lack of purpose than lack of talent.
WILLIAM ASHLEY SUNDAY (1862–1935)

Talent is no accident of birth. In today's society a good many people seem to have the idea that if one is born without talent, there is nothing he can do about it; they simply resign themselves to what they consider to be their fate.
SHINICHI SUZUKI (1898–1998)

We are always more anxious to be distinguished for a talent which we do not possess, than to be praised for the fifteen which we do possess.
MARK TWAIN (1835–1910), *Mark Twain's Autobiography*

Use what talents you possess: the woods would be very silent if no birds sang there except those that sang best.
HENRY VAN DYKE (1852–1933)

If a man has a talent and cannot use it, he has failed. If he has a talent and uses only half of it, he has partly failed. If he has a talent and learns somehow to use the whole of it, he has gloriously succeeded and has a satisfaction and a triumph few men ever know.
THOMAS WOLFE (1900–1938)

There is nothing worse in this world then wasted talent.
ANONYMOUS

Talk

Why talk when you can paint?
MILTON AVERY (1885–1965)

Talk that does not end in any kind of action is better suppressed altogether.
THOMAS CARLYLE (1795–1881)

I prefer tongue-tied knowledge to ignorant loquacity.
CICERO (106–43 BC)

Talk about yourself as much as you like, but do not expect others to listen.
MASON COOLEY (1927–2002)

What you do speaks so loud that I cannot hear what you say.
RALPH WALDO EMERSON (1803–1882)

We never say so much as when we do not quite know what we want to say. We need few words when we have something to say, but all the words in all the dictionaries will not suffice when we have nothing to say and want desperately to say it.
ERIC HOFFER (1902–1983)

Don't talk about what you have done or what you are going to do.
THOMAS JEFFERSON (1743–1826)

Don't talk—keep it in your heart.
DUKE KAHANAMOKU (1890–1968)

How ironical that it is by means of speech that man can degrade himself below the level of dumb creation—for a chatterbox is truly of a lower category than a dumb creature.
SØREN KIERKEGAARD (1813–1855)

Wise men talk because they have something to say; fools, because they have to say something.
PLATO (C. 428–348 BC)

They talk most who have the least to say.
MATTHEW PRIOR (1664–1721)

A good old man, sir. He will be talking. As they say, when the age is in, the wit is out.
WILLIAM SHAKESPEARE (1564–1616), *Much Ado About Nothing*

I don't mind how much my ministers talk—as long as they do what I say.
MARGARET THATCHER (1925–)

I like to do all the talking myself. It saves time, and prevents arguments.
OSCAR WILDE (1854–1900)

I talk by playing, not by words.
BERNIE WORRELL (1944–)

To talk without thinking is to shoot without aiming.
ENGLISH PROVERB

Taste

Everyone carries his own inch rule of taste, and amuses himself by applying it, triumphantly, wherever he travels.
HENRY ADAMS (1838–1918)

I think I may define taste to be that faculty of the soul which discerns the beauties of an author with pleasure, and the imperfections with dislike.
JOSEPH ADDISON (1672–1719)

Bad taste is simply saying the truth before it should be said.
MEL BROOKS (1926–)

It is good taste, and good taste alone, that possesses the power to sterilize and is always the first handicap to any creative functioning.
SALVADOR DALÍ (1904–1989)

It is a wretched taste to be gratified with mediocrity when the excellent lies before us.
ISAAC D'ISRAELI (1766–1848)

A truly elegant taste is generally accompanied with excellency of heart.
HENRY FIELDING (1707–1754)

There is nothing more dreadful than imagination without taste.
JOHANN WOLFGANG VON GOETHE (1749–1842)

Taste is nothing but an enlarged capacity for receiving pleasure from works of imagination.
WILLIAM HAZLITT (1778–1830)

Taste cannot be controlled by law.
THOMAS JEFFERSON (1743–1826)

Between good sense and good taste there lies the difference between a cause and its effect.
JEAN DE LA BRUYÈRE (1645–1696)

Taste may change, but inclination never.
FRANÇOIS DE LA ROCHEFOUCAULD (1613–1680)

It's bad taste to be wise all the time, like being at a perpetual funeral.
D. H. LAWRENCE (1885–1930)

All of life is a dispute over taste and tasting.
FRIEDRICH NIETZSCHE (1844–1900)

A little bad taste is like a nice dash of paprika.
DOROTHY PARKER (1893–1967)

Ah, good taste—What a dreadful thing! Taste is the enemy of creativeness.
PABLO PICASSO (1881–1973)

Taste is not only a part and index of morality, it is the only morality. The first, and last, and closest trial question to any living creature is "What do you like?" Tell me what you like, I'll tell you what you are.
JOHN RUSKIN (1819–1900)

Good taste is the worst vice ever invented.
EDITH SITWELL (1887–1964)

I think "taste" is a social concept and not an artistic one. I'm willing to show good taste, if I can, in somebody else's living room, but our reading life is

too short for a writer to be in any way polite. Since his words enter into another's brain in silence and intimacy, he should be as honest and explicit as we are with ourselves.
JOHN UPDIKE (1932–)

Good taste is the excuse I've always given for leading such a bad life.
OSCAR WILDE (1854–1900)

Taxes

Rulers do not reduce taxes to be kind. Expediency and greed create high taxation, and normally it takes an impending catastrophe to bring it down.
CHARLES ADAMS (1930–)

Taxing is an easy business. Any projector can contrive new compositions, any bungler can add to the old.
EDMUND BURKE (1729–1797)

To tax and to please, no more than to love and to be wise, is not given to men.
EDMUND BURKE (1729–1797)

Opportunity for all means making taxes fair. I'm not out to soak the rich. But I do believe the rich should pay their fair share. For twelve years, the Republicans have raised taxes on the middle class. It's time to give the middle class tax relief.
BILL CLINTON (1946–)

The hardest thing in the world to understand is the income tax.
ALBERT EINSTEIN (1879–1955)

Every advantage has its tax.
RALPH WALDO EMERSON (1803–1882)

We are taxed twice as much by our idleness, three times as much by our pride and four times as much by our foolishness.
BENJAMIN FRANKLIN (1706–1790)

The avoidance of taxes is the only intellectual pursuit that carries any reward.
JOHN MAYNARD KEYNES (1883–1946)

Tax reform means "Don't tax you, don't tax me, tax that fellow behind the tree."
RUSSELL LONG (1918–)

Unquestionably, there is progress. The average American now pays out twice as much in taxes as he formerly got in wages.
H. L. MENCKEN (1880–1956)

When there is an income tax, the just man will pay more and the unjust less on the same amount of income.
PLATO (C. 428–348 BC), *The Republic*

The income tax has made more liars out of the American people than golf has.
WILL ROGERS (1879–1935)

Taxes, after all, are the dues that we pay for the privileges of membership in an organized society.
FRANKLIN D. ROOSEVELT (1882–1945)

I did not see why the schoolmaster should be taxed to support the priest, and not the priest the schoolmaster.
HENRY DAVID THOREAU (1817–1862)

Income tax returns are the most imaginative fiction being written today.
HERMAN WOUK (1915–)

Teachers

A teacher affects eternity; he can never tell where his influence stops.
HENRY ADAMS (1838–1918)

The true teacher defends his pupils against his own personal influence. He inspires self-distrust. He guides their eyes from himself to the spirit that quickens him. He will have no disciple.
AMOS BRONSON ALCOTT (1799–1888)

I am indebted to my father for living, but to my teacher for living well.
ALEXANDER THE GREAT (356–323 BC)

A courage which looks easy and yet is rare; the courage of a teacher repeating day after day the same lessons—the least rewarded of all forms of courage.
HONORÉ DE BALZAC (1799–1850)

Very often we developed a better grasp of the subjects than the overworked teachers.
ALBERT BANDURA (1925–)

In teaching you cannot see the fruit of a day's work. It is invisible and remains so, maybe for twenty years.
JACQUES BARZUN (1907–)

The parents have a right to say that no teacher paid by their money shall rob their children of faith in God and send them back to their homes skeptical, or infidels, or agnostics, or atheists.
WILLIAM JENNINGS BRYAN (1860–1925)

The best teacher is the one who suggests rather than dogmatizes, and inspires his listener with the wish to teach himself.
SIR EDWARD G. BULWER-LYTTON (1803–1873)

That is the difference between good teachers and great teachers: good teachers make the best of a pupil's means; great teachers foresee a pupil's ends.
MARIA CALLAS (1923–1977)

A teacher is one who makes himself progressively unnecessary.
THOMAS CARRUTHERS (1841–1924)

Benevolence alone will not make a teacher, nor will learning alone do it. The gift of teaching is a peculiar talent, and implies a need and a craving in the teacher himself.
JOHN JAY CHAPMAN (1862–1933)

What nobler employment, or more valuable to the state, than that of the man who instructs the rising generation?
CICERO (106–43 BC)

Don't try to fix the students, fix ourselves first. The good teacher makes the poor student good and the good student superior. When our students fail, we, as teachers, too, have failed.
MARVA COLLINS (1936–)

If I am walking with two other men, each of them I will serve as my teacher. I will pick out the good points of the one and imitate them, and the bad points of the other and correct them in myself.
CONFUCIUS (551–479 BC)

If you think in terms of a year, plant a seed; if in terms of ten years, plant trees; if in terms of 100 years, teach the people.
CONFUCIUS (551–479 BC)

A wisely chosen illustration is almost essential to fasten the truth upon the ordinary mind, and no teacher can afford to neglect this part of his preparation.
HOWARD CROSBY (1826–1891)

Who dares to teach must never cease to learn.
JOHN COTTON DANA (1856–1929)

Teaching is useless unless you can learn from your students.
MARTIN DANSKY (1952–)

Give the pupils something to do, not something to learn; and the doing is of such a nature as to demand thinking; learning naturally results.
JOHN DEWEY (1859–1952)

Teaching is the only major occupation of man for which we have not yet developed tools that make an average person capable of competence and performance. In teaching we rely on the "naturals," the ones who somehow know how to teach.
PETER F. DRUCKER (1909–2005)

If you would thoroughly know anything, teach it to others.
TYRON EDWARDS (1809–1894)

It is the supreme art of the teacher to awaken joy in creative expression and knowledge.
ALBERT EINSTEIN (1879–1955)

The whole art of teaching is only the art of awakening the natural curiosity of young minds for the purpose of satisfying it afterwards.
ANATOLE FRANCE (1844–1924), *The Crime of Sylvestre Bonnard*

Wise teachers create an environment that encourages students to teach themselves.
LEONARD ROY FRANK (1932—)

Those who know how to think need no teachers.
MAHATMA GANDHI (1869–1948)

If you think your teacher is tough, wait until you get a boss. He doesn't have tenure.
BILL GATES (1955–)

The teacher who is indeed wise does not bid you to enter the house of his wisdom but rather leads you to the threshold of your mind.
KAHLIL GIBRAN (1883–1931)

Teachers are expected to reach unattainable goals with inadequate tools. The miracle is that at times they accomplish this impossible task.
HAIM G. GINOTT (1922–1973)

Good teaching is one-fourth preparation and three-fourths theater.
GAIL GODWIN (1937–)

It's a very ancient saying,
But a true and honest thought,
That if you become a teacher,
By your pupils you'll be taught.
OSCAR HAMMERSTEIN II (1895–1960)

Experience teaches only the teachable.
ALDOUS HUXLEY (1894–1963)

Be not too hasty to trust or to admire the teachers of morality: they discourse like angels, but they live like men.
SAMUEL JOHNSON (1709–1784)

My teachers treated me as a diamond in the rough, someone who needed smoothing.
MOTHER JONES (1830–1930)

To teach is to learn twice.
JOSEPH JOUBERT (1754–1824)

An understanding heart is everything in a teacher, and cannot be esteemed highly enough. One looks back with appreciation to the brilliant teachers, but with gratitude to those who touched our human feeling. The curriculum is so much necessary raw material, but warmth is the vital element for the growing plant and for the soul of the child.
CARL JUNG (1875–1961)

Most teachers have little control over school policy or curriculum or choice of texts or special placement of students, but most have a great deal of autonomy inside the classroom. To a degree shared by only a few other occupations, such as police work, public education rests precariously on the skill and virtue of the people at the bottom of the institutional pyramid.
TRACY KIDDER (1945–)

To be a teacher in the right sense is to be a learner. I am not a teacher, only a fellow student.
SØREN KIERKEGAARD (1813–1855)

A teacher who is attempting to teach without inspiring the pupil with a desire to learn is hammering on a cold iron.
HORACE MANN (1796–1859)

Teachers teach because they care. Teaching young people is what they do best. It requires long hours, patience, and care.
HORACE MANN (1796–1859)

There are three things to remember when teaching: know your stuff; know whom you are stuffing; and then stuff them elegantly.
LOLA MAY (1923–2007)

We teachers can only help the work going on, as servants wait upon a master.
MARIA MONTESSORI (1870–1952)

A master can tell you what he expects of you. A teacher, though, awakens your own expectation.
PATRICIA NEAL (1926–)

No bubble is so iridescent or floats longer than that blown by the successful teacher.
SIR WILLIAM OSLER (1849–1919)

Quite frankly, teachers are the only profession that teach our children.
DAN QUAYLE (1947–)

The dream begins with a teacher who believes in you, who tugs and pushes and leads you to the next plateau, sometimes poking you with a sharp stick called truth.
DAN RATHER (1931–)

The test of a good teacher is not how many questions he can ask his pupils that they will answer readily, but how many questions he inspires them to ask him which he finds it hard to answer.
ALICE WELLINGTON ROLLINS (1847–1897)

Passive acceptance of the teacher's wisdom is easy to most boys and girls. It involves no effort of independent thought, and seems rational because the teacher knows more than his pupils; it is moreover the way to win the favour of the teacher unless he is a very exceptional man. Yet the habit of passive acceptance is a disastrous one in later life. It causes man to seek and to accept a leader, and to accept as a leader whoever is established in that position.
BERTRAND RUSSELL (1872–1970)

The teacher, like the artist and the philosopher, can perform his work adequately only if he feels himself to be an individual directed by an inner creative impulse, not dominated and fettered by an outside authority.
BERTRAND RUSSELL (1872–1970)

We expect teachers to handle teenage pregnancy, substance abuse, and the failings of the family. Then we expect them to educate our children.
JOHN SCULLEY (1939–)

He who can, does. He who cannot, teaches.
GEORGE BERNARD SHAW (1856–1950), *Man and Superman*

As a teacher of Greek I gave the intellectual man weapons against the common man. I now want to give the common man weapons against the intellectual man.
GEORGE BERNARD SHAW (1856–1950)

I cannot teach anybody anything. I can only make them think.
SOCRATES (469–399 BC)

I am almost overwhelmed by the courage and dedication of teachers.
SYLVIA SOLOMON (1949–)

I did not see why the schoolmaster should be taxed to support the priest, and not the priest the schoolmaster.
HENRY DAVID THOREAU (1817–1862)

The art of teaching is the art of assisting discovery.
MARK VAN DOREN (1894–1972)

The mediocre teacher tells. The good teacher explains. The superior teacher demonstrates. The great teacher inspires.
WILLIAM ARTHUR WARD (1921–1994)

Come forth into the light of things;
Let nature be your Teacher.
WILLIAM WORDSWORTH (1770–1850)

A good teacher is like a candle—it consumes itself to light the way for others.
ANONYMOUS

A teacher's purpose is not to create students in his own image, but to develop students who can create their own image.
ANONYMOUS

Teachers who inspire know that teaching is like cultivating a garden, and those who would have nothing to do with thorns must never attempt to gather flowers.
ANONYMOUS

Teaching is the profession that teaches all the other professions.
ANONYMOUS

Teaching should be full of ideas instead of stuffed with facts.
ANONYMOUS

The best teachers teach from the heart, not from the book.
ANONYMOUS

The secret of teaching is to appear to have known all your life what you just learned this morning.
ANONYMOUS

To teach well, we need not say all that we know, only what is useful for the pupil to hear.
ANONYMOUS

Teachers open the door. You enter by yourself.
CHINESE PROVERB

Better than a thousand days of diligent study is one day with a great teacher.
JAPANESE PROVERB

Teamwork

One man alone can be pretty dumb sometimes, but for real bona fide stupidity, there ain't nothin' can beat teamwork.
EDWARD ABBEY (1927–1989)

One man can be a crucial ingredient on a team, but one man cannot make a team.
KAREEM ABDUL–JABBAR (1947–)

The important thing to recognize is that it takes a team, and the team ought to get credit for the wins and the losses. Successes have many fathers, failures have none.
PHILIP CALDWELL (1920–)

Coming together is a beginning, staying together is progress, and working together is success.
HENRY FORD (1863–1947)

It is literally true that you can succeed best and quickest by helping others to succeed.
NAPOLEON HILL (1883–1970)

Talent wins games, but teamwork and intelligence wins championships.
MICHAEL JORDAN (1963–)

To me, teamwork is the beauty of our sport, where you have five acting as one. You become selfless.
MIKE KRZYZEWSKI (1947–)

The best teamwork comes from men who are working independently toward one goal in unison.
JAMES CASH PENNEY (1875–1971)

Unity is strength … when there is teamwork and collaboration, wonderful things can be achieved.
MATTIE STEPANEK (1990–2004)

A job worth doing is worth doing together.
ANONYMOUS

Tears

Repentant tears wash out the stain of guilt.
SAINT AURELIUS (C. 391–430)

Tears are the summer showers to the soul.
ALFRED AUSTIN (1835–1913)

Tears of joy are like the summer rain drops pierced by sunbeams.
HOSEA BALLOU (1771–1852)

The tears of the world are a constant quality. For each one who begins to weep, somewhere else another stops. The same is true of the laugh.
SAMUEL BECKETT (1906–1989)

The busy have no time for tears.
LORD BYRON (1788–1824)

The tears that you spill, the sorrowful, are sweeter than the laughter of snobs and the guffaws of scoffers.
KAHLIL GIBRAN (1883–1931)

Tears shed for self are tears of weakness, but tears shed for others are a sign of strength.
BILLY GRAHAM (1918–)

Tears are the noble language of the eye.
ROBERT HERRICK (1591–1674)

Joy's smile is much closer to tears than laughter.
VICTOR HUGO (1802–1885)

Tears at times have the weight of speech.
OVID (43 BC–AD 17)

Tears are the natural penalties of pleasure. It is a law that we should pay for all that we enjoy.
WILLIAM GILMORE SIMMS (1806–1870)

More tears are shed over answered prayers than unanswered ones.
SAINT TERESA OF ÁVILA (1515–1582)

Tears are due to human misery, and human sufferings touch the mind.
VIRGIL (C. 70–19 BC)

Tears are the silent language of grief.
VOLTAIRE (1694–1778)

Laughter and tears are both responses to frustration and exhaustion. I myself prefer to laugh, since there is less cleaning up to do afterward.
KURT VONNEGUT JR. (1922–2007)

Technology

When we can drain the Ocean into mill-ponds, and bottle up the Force of Gravity, to be sold by retail, in gas jars; then may we hope to comprehend the infinitudes of man's soul under formulas of Profit and Loss; and rule over this too, as over a patent engine, by checks, and valves, and balances.
THOMAS CARLYLE (1795–1881)

Any sufficiently advanced technology is indistinguishable from magic.
ARTHUR C. CLARKE (1917–)

For a successful technology, reality must take precedence over public relations, for Nature cannot be fooled.
RICHARD FEYNMAN (1918–1988)

Technology is a way of organizing the universe so that man doesn't have to experience it.
MAX FRISCH (1911–1991)

Humanity is acquiring all the right technology for all the wrong reasons.
R. BUCKMINSTER FULLER (1895–1983)

For a list of all the ways technology has failed to improve the quality of life, please press three.
ALICE KAHN (1943–)

Men are only as good as their technical development allows them to be.
GEORGE ORWELL (1903–1950)

There is an evil tendency underlying all our technology—the tendency to do what is reasonable even when it isn't any good.
ROBERT M. PIRSIG (1928–), *Zen and the Art of Motorcycle Maintenance*

In health of mind and body, men should see with their own eyes, hear and speak without trumpets, walk on their feet, not on wheels, and work and war with their arms, not with engine–beams, nor rifles warranted to kill twenty men at a shot before you can see them.
JOHN RUSKIN (1819–1900)

Teenagers

All teenagers have this desire to somehow run away.
JOAN CHEN (1961–)

What teens will realize is always a mystery to me. I'm still realizing so many things myself, very belatedly, that it seems unwise to think I have any right to be showing people things in hopes that they'll realize them.
DIANE DUANE (1952–)

Teenagers are still teenagers and adults are adults, but the two worlds are no longer totally incomprehensible to either.
BOB GELDOF (1954–)

We teach teens what we think they ought to know, and we never tell them what they want to know.
SUE JOHANSON (1946–)

Teenagers today are more free to be themselves and to accept themselves.
JOHN KNOWLES (1926–2001)

Teens are dealing with the same problems now in the '90s as they did back in the '70s, the only real difference is the clothes we wear!
MILA KUNIS (1983–)

Ask me if I believe teenagers can really be in love and I'll say yes emphatically.
KENT MCCORD (1942–)

I think the hardest part about being a teenager is dealing with other teenagers—the criticism and the ridicule, the gossip and rumors.
BEVERLY MITCHELL (1981–)

Researchers try to "establish a dialogue" to "understand teenage frustrations," but don't these researchers remember that they were teenagers, too?
CHRIS WARE (1967–)

Telephones

The telephone book is full of facts, but it doesn't contain a single idea.
MORTIMER ADLER (1902–2001)

Gossip is nature's telephone.
SHOLOM ALEICHEM (1859–1916)

I've suffered from all of the hang-ups known, and none is as bad as the telephone.
RICHARD ARMOUR (1906–1989)

Tell me about yourself—your struggles, your dreams, your telephone number.
PETER ARNO (1904–1968)

Telephone, n.: An invention of the devil which abrogates some of the advantages of making a disagreeable person keep his distance.
AMBROSE BIERCE (1842–1914), *The Devil's Dictionary*

America's best buy is a telephone call to the right man.
ILKA CHASE (1903–1978)

Telephones are a virtual necessity—not a luxury…
MIKE FITZPATRICK (1963–)

If we discovered that we only had five minutes left to say all that we wanted to say, every telephone booth would be occupied by people calling other people to stammer that they loved them.
CHRISTOPHER MORLEY (1890–1957)

People used what they called a telephone because they hated being close together and they were scared of being alone.
CHUCK PALAHNIUK (1962–)

Excuse me, everybody, I have to go to the bathroom. I really have to telephone, but I'm too embarrassed to say so.
DOROTHY PARKER (1893–1967)

Television

Imitation is the sincerest form of television.
FRED ALLEN (1894–1956)

Television is a new medium. It's called a medium because nothing is well-done.
FRED ALLEN (1894–1956)

[Television is] the triumph of machine over people.
FRED ALLEN (1894–1956)

Television is the first truly democratic culture—the first culture available to everybody and entirely governed by what the people want. The most terrifying thing is what people do want.
CLIVE BARNES (1927–)

If there's anything unsettling to the stomach, it's watching actors on television talk about their personal lives.
MARLON BRANDO (1924–2004)

The one function TV news performs very well is that when there is no news we give it to you with the same emphasis as if there were.
DAVID BRINKLEY (1920–2003)

If it weren't for Philo T. Farnsworth, inventor of television, we'd still be eating frozen radio dinners.
JOHNNY CARSON (1925–2005)

Television news is like a lightning flash. It makes a loud noise, lights up everything around it, leaves everything else in darkness and then is suddenly gone.
HODDING CARTER JR. (1907–1972)

Television is for appearing on—not for looking at.
NOËL COWARD (1899–1973)

My father hated radio and could not wait for television to be invented so he could hate that too.
PETER DE VRIES (1910–1993)

I can think of nothing more boring for the American people than to have to sit in their living rooms for a whole half hour looking at my face on their television screens.
DWIGHT D. EISENHOWER (1890–1969)

Television enables you to be entertained in your home by people you wouldn't have in your home.
DAVID FROST (1939–)

Don't you wish there were a knob on the TV to turn up the intelligence? There's one marked "Brightness," but it doesn't work.
GALLAGHER (1947–)

Television has raised writing to a new low.
SAMUEL GOLDWYN (1882–1974)

Seeing a murder on television … can help work off one's antagonisms. And if you haven't any antagonisms, the commercials will give you some.
ALFRED HITCHCOCK (1899–1980)

Television has done much for psychiatry by spreading information about it, as well as contributing to the need for it.
ALFRED HITCHCOCK (1899–1980)

Today we have, in a sense, the transmission of sight for the first time in the world's history. Human genius has now destroyed the impediment of distance in a new respect, and in a manner hitherto unknown.
HERBERT HOOVER (1874–1964)

There are … people in this world who seldom pick up a newspaper, people who, when watching television, sneer in displeasure and change channels at the first glimpse of an anchorperson. While such willfully uninformed citizens are rare, emerging from seclusion only to serve on juries in trials of great national significance, they do exist.
JOE KEENAN (1896–1984)

Privacy was in sufficient danger before TV appeared, and TV has given it its death blow.
LOUIS KRONENBERGER (1904–1980)

Television has proved that people will look at anything rather than each other.
ANN LANDERS (1918–2002)

I find television very educating. Every time somebody turns on the set, I go into the other room and read a book.
GROUCHO MARX (1890–1977)

Imagine what it would be like if TV actually were good. It would be the end of everything we know.
MARVIN MINSKY (1927–)

Dealing with network executives is like being nibbled to death by ducks.
ERIC SEVAREID (1912–1992)

It is difficult to produce a television documentary that is both incisive and probing when every twelve minutes one is interrupted by twelve dancing rabbits singing about toilet paper.
ROD SERLING (1924–1975)

In Russia we only had two TV channels. Channel One was propaganda. Channel Two consisted of a KGB officer telling you: Turn back at once to Channel One.
YAKOV SMIRNOFF (1951–)

One of the few good things about modern times: If you die horribly on television, you will not have died in vain. You will have entertained us.
KURT VONNEGUT JR. (1922–2007)

Thanks to TV and for the convenience of TV, you can only be one of two kinds of human beings, either a liberal or a conservative.
KURT VONNEGUT JR. (1922–2007)

TV is chewing gum for the eyes.
FRANK LLOYD WRIGHT (1869–1959)

The human race is faced with a cruel choice: work or daytime television.
ANONYMOUS

Temperament

Temperament lies behind mood; behind will lies the fate of character. Then behind both, the influence of family; the tyranny of culture; and finally the power of climate and environment; and we are free, only to the extent we rise above these.
JOHN BURROUGHS (1837–1921)

The artistic temperament is a disease that affects amateurs. Artists of a large and wholesome vitality get rid of their art easily, as they breathe easily or perspire easily.
G. K. CHESTERTON (1874–1936)

When superstition is allowed to perform the task of old age in dulling the human temperament, we can say goodbye to all excellence in poetry, in painting, and in music.
DENIS DIDEROT (1713–1784)

Bodily temperaments have a common course and rule which imperceptibly affect our will. They advance in combination, and successively exercise a secret empire over us, so that, without our perceiving it, they become a great part of all our actions.
FRANÇOIS DE LA ROCHEFOUCAULD (1613–1680)

Who has skill in the art of music is of good temperament and fitted for all things.
MARTIN LUTHER (1483–1546)

Music inflames temperament.
JIM MORRISON (1943–1971)

He had that curious love of green, which in individuals is always the sign of a subtle artistic temperament, and in nations is said to denote a laxity, if not a decadence of morals.
OSCAR WILDE (1854–1900)

Nobody of any real culture … ever talks nowadays about the beauty of sunset. Sunsets are quite old fashioned. To admire them is a distinct sign of provincialism of temperament. Upon the other hand they go on.
OSCAR WILDE (1854–1900)

Temptation

It is good to be without vices, but it is not good to be without temptations.
WALTER BAGEHOT (1826–1877), *Biographical Studies*

Why comes temptation, but for man to meet and master and crouch beneath his foot, and so be pedestaled in triumph?
ROBERT BROWNING (1812–1889)

There is not any memory with less satisfaction than the memory of some temptation we resisted.
JAMES BRANCH CABELL (1879–1958)

The last temptation is the greatest treason: to do the right deed for the wrong reason.
T. S. ELIOT (1888–1965)

Every normal man must be tempted at times to spit upon his hands, hoist the black flag, and begin slitting throats.
H. L. MENCKEN (1880–1956)

Most people would like to be delivered from temptation but would like it to keep in touch.
ROBERT ORBEN (1927–)

I never resist temptation because I have found that things that are bad for me do not tempt me.
GEORGE BERNARD SHAW (1856–1950), *The Apple Cart*

There are several good protections against temptations, but the surest is cowardice.
MARK TWAIN (1835–1910), *Following the Equator*

I generally avoid temptation unless I can't resist it.
MAE WEST (1892–1980)

I can resist anything but temptation.
OSCAR WILDE (1854–1900), *Lady Windermere's Fan*

The only way to get rid of a temptation is to yield to it. Resist it, and your soul grows sick with longing for the things it has forbidden to itself.
OSCAR WILDE (1854–1900), *The Picture of Dorian Gray*

Good habits result from resisting temptation.
ANONYMOUS

Our Father in heaven, hallowed be your name, your kingdom come, your will be done, on earth as it is in heaven. Give us today our daily bread. And forgive us our debts, as we also have forgiven our debtors. And lead us not into temptation, but deliver us from the evil one.
THE BIBLE, Matthew 6:9–13

No temptation has overtaken you except what is common to us all. And God is faithful; he will not let you be tempted beyond what you can bear. But when you are tempted, he will also provide a way out so that you can endure it.
THE BIBLE, 1 Corinthians 10:13

Tennis

Tennis belongs to the individualistic past—a hero, or at most a pair of friends or lovers, against the world.
JACQUES BARZUN (1907–)

The fifth set is not about tennis, it's about nerves.
BORIS BECKER (1967–)

In tennis the addict moves about a hard rectangle and seeks to ambush a fuzzy ball with a modified snowshoe.
ELLIOT CHAZE (1915–1990)

Good shot, bad luck and hell are the five basic words to be used in a game of tennis, though these, of course, can be slightly amplified.
VIRGINIA GRAHAM (1912–1998)

Tennis and golf are best played, not watched.
ROGER KAHN (1927–)

In the complete overall history of tennis, I figure I'll be worth a sentence or two.... That's why my place in the all-time rankings means so very little to me, because I know I won't be anybody's number one, and it's that same old thing: if you're not number one, then what does it really matter?
BILLIE JEAN KING (1943–)

I think that tennis is a lady's sport, so we should look like ladies out there.
ANNA KOURNIKOVA (1981–)

Tennis is an addiction that once it has truly hooked a man will not let him go.
RUSSELL LYNES (1910–1991)

I have always considered tennis as a combat in an arena between two gladiators who have their racquets and their courage as their weapons.
YANNICK NOAH (1960–)

Men hate to lose. I beat my husband once at tennis. I asked him, "Will we ever make love again?" He said, "Yes.... but not with each other."
RITA RUDNER (1955–)

Terrorism

As the war on terrorism spreads and prolongs, the fruits of ending the threat of terrorism around the world will be tempered with a whole new series of problems to be addressed and resolved.
CHARLES FOSTER BASS (1952–)

You cannot make peace with terrorists. The normal dividing lines between war and peace do not apply.
ULRICH BECK (1944–)

Fascism is fascism. Terrorism is terrorism. Oppression is oppression.
HARRY BELAFONTE (1927–)

Most terrorists are people deeply concerned by what they see as social, political, or religious injustice and hypocrisy, and the immediate grounds for their terrorism is often retaliation for an action of the United States.
WILLIAM BLUM (1933–)

Terrorism is contempt for human dignity.
KJELL MAGNE BONDEVIK (1947–)

Everybody's worried about stopping terrorism. Well, there's a really easy way: stop participating in it.
NOAM CHOMSKY (1928–)

Democracy is stronger than terrorism, and we will not cower to the terrorists' campaign of fear.
JOHN DOOLITTLE (1950–)

They call them terrorists, I call them freedom fighters.
LOUIS FARRAKHAN (1933–)

The threat of terrorism is not stronger than the will of the American people.
CHAKA FATTAH (1956–)

In the face of terrorism, a united front is one of the strongest weapons.
VIRGINIA FOXX (1943–)

Historically, terrorism falls in a category different from crimes that concern a criminal court judge.
JURGEN HABERMAS (1929–)

Fighting terrorism is not unlike fighting a deadly cancer. It can't be treated just where it's visible—every diseased cell in the body must be destroyed.
DAVID HACKWORTH (1930–2005)

The war against terrorism is terrorism.
WOODY HARRELSON (1961–)

Terrorism is the tactic of demanding the impossible, and demanding it at gunpoint.
CHRISTOPHER HITCHENS (1949–)

Terrorism as a force is gone. As individuals they are all around, and we will continue to look for them.
HAMID KARZAI (1957–)

Terrorism can never be accepted. We must fight it together, with methods that do not compromise our respect for the rule of law and human rights, or are used as an excuse for others to do so.
ANNA LINDH (1957–2003)

Terrorism cannot be linked with any religion or nation, as such approach will inevitably lead to further escalation of tenseness in the world.
NURSULTAN NAZARBAYEV (1940–)

The terrorists, whatever slogans they use, have nothing in common with Islam.
NURSULTAN NAZARBAYEV (1940–)

Terrorism has once again shown it is prepared deliberately to stop at nothing in creating human victims. An end must be put to this. As never before, it is vital to unite forces of the entire world community against terror.
VLADIMIR PUTIN (1952–)

Throughout the world, terrorists are actively seeking their next recruit. Alarmingly, terrorist organizations are increasingly targeting school-age children as the next generation of terrorists.
PAT ROBERTS (1936–)

Terrorists are going to find us facing them and that together we are going to win.
JOSE LUIS RODRIGUEZ ZAPATERO (1960–)

Within terrorism, we now discover that there are factions who operate at a level of savagery where you can't even begin to understand it.
DIANE SAWYER (1945–)

What terrorism finally winds up saying to us is that you can't live in a world that bends some people so totally out of shape that they want to destroy

themselves and anybody who gets in their way.
JOHN SHELBY SPONG (1931–)

Terrorists always have the advantage of surprise.
GIJS DE VRIES (1956–)

The terrible thing about terrorism is that ultimately it destroys those who practice it. Slowly but surely, as they try to extinguish life in others, the light within them dies.
TERRY WAITE (1939–)

Fighting terrorism is like being a goalkeeper. You can make a hundred brilliant saves but the only shot that people remember is the one that gets past you.
PAUL WILKINSON (1937–)

Thankfulness

Thankfulness is the beginning of gratitude. Gratitude is the completion of thankfulness. Thankfulness may consist merely of words. Gratitude is shown in acts.
HENRI-FRÉDÉRIC AMIEL (1821–1881)

Sometimes we need to remind ourselves that thankfulness is indeed a virtue.
WILLIAM BENNETT (1943–)

All our discontents about what we want appeared to spring from the want of thankfulness for what we have.
DANIEL DEFOE (1660–1731)

It is another's fault if he be ungrateful, but it is mine if I do not give. To find one thankful man, I will oblige a great many that are not so.
SENECA (5 BC–AD 65)

Theater

The theatre is a spiritual and social X-ray of its time.
STELLA ADLER (1901–1992)

What people really want in the theater is fantasy involvement and not reality involvement.
EDWARD ALBEE (1928–)

The theatre is a gross art, built in sweeps and over-emphasis. Compromise is its second name.
ENID BAGNOLD (1889–1981)

The theatre is the involuntary reflex of the ideas of the crowd.
SARAH BERNHARDT (1845–1921)

The theatre only knows what it's doing next week, not like the opera, where they say: What are we going to do in five years' time? A completely different attitude.
HARRISON BIRTWISTLE (1934–)

The theatre, our theatre, comes from the Greeks.
EDWARD BOND (1934–)

The most difficult character in comedy is that of a fool, and he must be no simpleton who plays the part.
MIGUEL DE CERVANTES (1547–1616)

I adore the theater and I am a painter. I think the two are made for a marriage of love. I will give all my soul to prove this once more.
MARC CHAGALL (1887–1985)

The drama may be called that part of theatrical art which lends itself most readily to intellectual discussion: what is left is theater.
ROBERTSON DAVIES (1913–1995)

If a person were to try stripping the disguises from actors while they play a scene upon stage, showing to the audience their real looks and the faces they were born with, would not such a one spoil the whole play? And would not the spectators think he deserved to be driven out of the theatre with brickbats, as a drunken disturber? Now what else is the whole life of mortals but a sort of comedy, in which the various actors, disguised by various costumes and masks, walk on and play each one his part, until the manager waves them off the stage? Moreover, this manager frequently bids the same actor to go back in a different costume, so that he who has but lately played the king in scarlet now acts the flunkey in patched clothes. Thus all things are presented by shadows.
DESIDERIUS ERASMUS (1469–1536), *The Praise of Folly*

The truth is you don't like the theater except the times when you're in a room by yourself putting the play on paper.
DASHIELL HAMMETT (1894–1961)

I think theatre should always be somewhat suspect.
VACLAV HAVEL (1936–)

Theatre is more exciting in the sense that you can actually see the audience in the eye. You know there are no takes and retakes. You have one chance to do your job... and you better do it well!
CHRISTINE LAHTI (1950–)

Every person on the streets of New York is a type. The city is one big theater where everyone is on display.
JERRY RUBIN (1938–1994)

No theater could sanely flourish until there was an umbilical connection between what was happening on the stage and what was happening in the world.
KENNETH TYNAN (1927–1980)

The theater needs continual reminders that there is nothing more debasing than the work of those who do well what is not worth doing at all.
GORE VIDAL (1925–)

I regard the theatre as the greatest of all art forms, the most immediate way in which a human being can share with another the sense of what it is to be a human being.
OSCAR WILDE (1854–1900)

Theft

Identity theft is one of the fastest-growing crimes in the nation, especially in the suburbs.
MELISSA BEAN (1962–)

Every gun that is made, every warship launched, every rocket fired, signifies in the final sense a theft from those who hunger and are not fed, those who are cold and are not clothed.
DWIGHT D. EISENHOWER (1890–1969)

For the theft of agricultural implements, of arms and of medicines, let the king award punishment, taking into account the time, of the offence and the use, of the object.
GURU NANAK (1469–1539)

Gambling and betting amount to open theft, the king shall always exert himself in suppressing both of them.
GURU NANAK (1469–1539)

The king shall cut off the hands of those robbers who, breaking into houses, commit thefts at night, and cause them to be impaled on a pointed stake.
GURU NANAK (1469–1539)

Property is theft.
PIERRE-JOSEPH PROUDHON (1809–1865)

Even a thief takes ten years to learn his trade.
JAPANESE PROVERB

Theology

The best theology would need no advocates; it would prove itself.
KARL BARTH (1886–1968)

Theology is a science of mind applied to God.
HENRY WARD BEECHER (1813–1887)

Our theology is still in a time of crisis, and I think this will last for some years more.
GODFRIED DANNEELS (1933–)

What has "theology" ever said that is of the smallest use to anybody? When has "theology" ever said anything that is demonstrably true and is not obvious? What makes you think that "theology" is a subject at all?
RICHARD DAWKINS (1941–)

One man's theology is another man's belly laugh.
ROBERT A. HEINLEIN (1907–1988)

Theology is the effort to explain the unknowable in terms of the not worth knowing.
H. L. MENCKEN (1880–1956)

The function of theology? The recitation of the incomprehensible by the unspeakable to pick the pockets of the unthinking.
ROBERT ANTON WILSON (1932–)

Theories

There is a theory which states that if ever for any reason anyone discovers what exactly the Universe is for and why it is here it will instantly disappear and be replaced by something even more bizarre and inexplicable. There is another that states that this has already happened.
DOUGLAS ADAMS (1952–2001)

It's not so much what you have to learn if you accept weird theories, it's what you have to unlearn.
ISAAC ASIMOV (1920–1992)

Our theories of the eternal are as valuable as are those which a chick which has not broken its way through its shell might form of the outside world.
THE BUDDHA (563–483 BC)

If the facts don't fit the theory, change the facts.
ALBERT EINSTEIN (1879–1955)

It is the theory that decides what can be observed.
ALBERT EINSTEIN (1879–1955)

Relativity applies to physics, not ethics
ALBERT EINSTEIN (1879–1955)

The truth of a theory is in your mind, not in your eyes.
ALBERT EINSTEIN (1879–1955)

An ounce of action is worth a ton of theory.
FRIEDRICH ENGELS (1820–1895)

First, you know, a new theory is attacked as absurd; then it is admitted to be true, but obvious and insignificant; finally it is seen to be so important that its adversaries claim that they themselves discovered it.
WILLIAM JAMES (1842–1910)

All theory is against the freedom of the will; all experience for it.
SAMUEL JOHNSON (1709–1784)

He who loves practice without theory is like the sailor who boards ship without a rudder and compass and never knows where he may cast.
LEONARDO DA VINCI (1452–1519)

The theory seems to be that as long as a man is a failure he is one of God's children, but that as soon as he succeeds he is taken over by the Devil.
H. L. MENCKEN (1880–1956)

Scientific theory is a contrived foothold in the chaos of living phenomena.
WILHELM REICH (1897–1957)

Theory helps us to bear our ignorance of facts.
GEORGE SANTAYANA (1863–1952)

The theory that can absorb the greatest number of facts, and persist in doing so, generation after generation, through all changes of opinion and detail, is the one that must rule all observation.
ADAM SMITH (1723–1790)

When a torrent sweeps a man against a boulder, you must expect him to scream, and you need not be surprised if the scream is sometimes a theory.
ROBERT LOUIS STEVENSON (1850–1894)

I cannot help fearing that men may reach a point where they look on every new theory as a danger, every innovation as a toilsome trouble, every social advance as a first step toward revolution, and that they may absolutely refuse to move at all.
ALEXIS DE TOCQUEVILLE (1805–1859)

How empty is theory in the presence of fact.
MARK TWAIN (1835–1910)

Thought and theory must precede all salutary action; yet action is nobler in itself than either thought or theory.
WILLIAM WORDSWORTH (1770–1850)

Thieves

We hang the petty thieves and appoint the great ones to public office.
AESOP (620–560 BC)

The number one rule of thieves is that nothing is too small to steal.
JIMMY BRESLIN (1930–)

Thieves respect property. They merely wish the property to become their property that they may more perfectly respect it.
G. K. CHESTERTON (1874–1936)

The great thieves lead away the little thief.
DIOGENES LAERTIUS (C. 200)

A thief believes everybody steals.
EDGAR WATSON HOWE (1853–1937)

The more laws and order are made prominent, the more thieves and robbers there will be.
LAO-TZU (C. 600 BC)

Honor among thieves is the ancestor of all honor.
JOHN MCCARTHY (1815–1893)

In a closed society where everybody's guilty, the only crime is getting caught. In a world of thieves, the only final sin is stupidity.
HUNTER S. THOMPSON (1937–2005)

Set a thief to catch a thief.
ANONYMOUS

There is honor among thieves.
ANONYMOUS

The big thieves hang the little ones
CZECH PROVERB

Thoughts

The thinker dies, but his thoughts are beyond the reach of destruction. Men are mortal; but ideas are immortal.
RICHARD ADAMS (1626–1698)

True thoughts are those alone which do not understand themselves.
THEODOR W. ADORNO (1903–1969)

To be free from evil thoughts is God's best gift.
AESCHYLUS (425–456 BC)

Good thoughts bear good fruit, bad thoughts bear bad fruit.
JAMES ALLEN (1864–1912)

You are today where your thoughts have brought you; you will be tomorrow where your thoughts take you.
JAMES ALLEN (1864–1912)

Thought is a kind of opium; it can intoxicate us, while still broad awake; it can make transparent the mountains and everything that exists.
HENRI-FRÉDÉRIC AMIEL (1821–1881)

He was my North, my South, my East and West,
My working week and Sunday rest,
My noon, my midnight, my talk, my song;
I thought that love would last forever: I was wrong.
W. H. AUDEN (1907–1973)

Concentrate all your thoughts upon the work at hand. The sun's rays do not burn until brought to a focus.
ALEXANDER GRAHAM BELL (1847–1922)

Action springs not from thought, but from a readiness for responsibility.
DIETRICH BONHOEFFER (1906–1945)

All that we are is the result of what we have thought.
THE BUDDHA (563–483 BC)

We are shaped by our thoughts; we become what we think. When the mind is pure, joy follows like a shadow that never leaves.
THE BUDDHA (563–483 BC)

We are what we think. All that we are arises with our thoughts. With our thoughts, we make the world.
THE BUDDHA (563–483 BC)

What we are today comes from our thoughts of yesterday, and our present thoughts build our life of tomorrow: Our life is the creation of our mind.
THE BUDDHA (563–483 BC)

I still find each day too short for all the thoughts I want to think, all the walks I want to take, all the books I want to read, and all the friends I want to see.
JOHN BURROUGHS (1837–1921)

All great deeds and all great thoughts have a ridiculous beginning. Great works are often born on a street corner or in a restaurant's revolving door.
ALBERT CAMUS (1913–1960)

How you think when you lose determines how long it will be until you win.
G. K. CHESTERTON (1874–1936)

Learning without thought is labor lost; thought without learning is perilous.
CONFUCIUS (551–479 BC), *The Confucian Analects*

If a man take no thought about what is distant, he will find sorrow near at hand.
CONFUCIUS (551–479 BC)

In the information society, nobody thinks. We expect to banish paper, but we actually banish thought.
MICHAEL CRICHTON (1942–), *Jurassic Park*

I doubt, therefore I think; I think, therefore I am.
RENÉ DESCARTES (1596–1650)

Nurture your minds with great thoughts. To believe in the heroic makes heroes.
BENJAMIN DISRAELI (1804–1881)

Far more numerous are those as such; who think to little and talk too much.
JOHN DRYDEN (1631–1700)

[O]ne of the strongest motives that lead men to art and science is escape from everyday life with its painful crudity and hopeless dreariness, from the fetters of one's own ever-shifting desires. A finely tempered nature longs to escape from the personal life into the world of objective perception and thought.
ALBERT EINSTEIN (1879–1955)

These thoughts did not come in any verbal formulation. I rarely think in words at all. A thought comes, and I may try to express it in words afterward.
ALBERT EINSTEIN (1879–1955)

When I examine myself and my methods of thought, I come to the conclusion that the gift of fantasy has meant more to me than any talent for abstract, positive thinking.
ALBERT EINSTEIN (1879–1955)

All the thoughts of a turtle are turtle.
RALPH WALDO EMERSON (1803–1882)

A man is what he thinks about all day long.
RALPH WALDO EMERSON (1803–1882)

Our best thoughts come from others.
RALPH WALDO EMERSON (1803–1882)

The ancestor of every action is a thought.
RALPH WALDO EMERSON (1803–1882)

The revelation of thought takes men out of servitude into freedom.
RALPH WALDO EMERSON (1803–1882)

The soul of God is poured into the world through the thoughts of men.
RALPH WALDO EMERSON (1803–1882)

We are ashamed of our thoughts and often see them brought forth by others.
RALPH WALDO EMERSON (1803–1882)

Freedom of speech and freedom of action are meaningless without freedom to think. And there is no freedom of thought without doubt.
BERGEN EVANS (1904–1978)

Kind thoughts are rarer than either kind words or deeds. They imply a great deal of thinking about others. This in itself is rare. But they also imply a great deal of thinking about others without the thoughts being criticisms. This is rarer still.
FREDERICK WILLIAM FABER (1814–1863)

Either you think—or else others have to think for you and take power from you, pervert and discipline your natural tastes, civilize and sterilize you.
F. SCOTT FITZGERALD (1896–1940)

Thinking is not to agree or disagree. That is voting.
ROBERT FROST (1875–1963)

We must dare to think "unthinkable" thoughts. We must learn to explore all the options and possibilities that confront us in a complex and rapidly changing world. We must learn to welcome and not to fear the voices of dissent. We must dare to think about "unthinkable things" because when things become unthinkable, thinking stops and action becomes mindless.
J. WILLIAM FULBRIGHT (1905–1995)

Always aim at complete harmony of thought and word and deed. Always aim at purifying your thoughts and everything will be well.
MAHATMA GANDHI (1869–1948)

A man is but the product of his thoughts. What he thinks, he becomes.
MAHATMA GANDHI (1869–1948)

All intelligent thoughts have already been thought; what is necessary is only to try to think them again.
JOHANN WOLFGANG VON GOETHE (1749–1832)

Thinking is easy, acting is difficult, and to put one's thoughts into action is the most difficult thing in the world.
JOHANN WOLFGANG VON GOETHE (1749–1832)

Thought expands, but paralyzes; action animates, but narrows.
JOHANN WOLFGANG VON GOETHE (1749–1832)

Ideas are not thoughts; the thought respects the boundaries that the idea ignores, thereby failing to realize itself.
FRANZ GRILLPARZER (1791–1872)

As I grow older, I regret to say that a detestable habit of thinking seems to be getting a hold of me.
H. RIDER HAGGARD (1856–1925), *King Solomon's Mines*

To be able to be caught up into the world of thought—that is being educated.
EDITH HAMILTON (1867–1963)

Thought is the wind, knowledge the sail, and mankind the vessel.
AUGUST HARE (1792–1834)

Great thoughts reduced to practice become great acts.
WILLIAM HAZLITT (1778–1830)

Beware thoughts that come in the night.
WILLIAM LEAST HEAT-MOON (1940–)

Reading is sometimes an ingenious device for avoiding thought.
SIR ARTHUR HELPS (1813–1875)

A thought is often original, though you have uttered it a hundred times.
OLIVER WENDELL HOLMES SR. (1809–1894), *The Autocrat of the Breakfast-Table*

Every event that a man would master must be mounted on the run, and no man ever caught the reins of a thought except as it galloped past him.
OLIVER WENDELL HOLMES SR. (1809–1894)

Certain thoughts are prayers. There are moments when, whatever be the attitude of the body, the soul is on its knees.
VICTOR HUGO (1802–1885)

Thought is the labor of the intellect, reverie is its pleasure.
VICTOR HUGO (1802–1885)

Thought must be divided against itself before it can come to any knowledge of itself.
ALDOUS HUXLEY (1894–1963)

The glow of one warm thought is to me worth more than money.
THOMAS JEFFERSON (1762–1826)

Thoughts without content are empty, intuitions without concepts are blind.
IMMANUEL KANT (1724–1804)

Too often we … enjoy the comfort of opinion without the discomfort of thought.
JOHN F. KENNEDY (1917–1963)

[I]t is only the great thinker who is exposed to what I call paradoxes, which are nothing else than grandiose thoughts in embryo.
SØREN KIERKEGAARD (1813–1855)

My thoughts are my company; I can bring them together, select them, detain them, dismiss them.
WALTER SAVAGE LANDOR (1775–1864)

Thoughts, like fleas, jump from man to man, but they don't bite everybody.
STANISLAW LEC (1909–1966)

All my life I have tried to pluck a thistle and plant a flower wherever the flower would grow in thought and mind.
ABRAHAM LINCOLN (1809–1865)

Books serve to show a man that those original thoughts of his aren't very new after all.
ABRAHAM LINCOLN (1809–1865)

Where all think alike, no one thinks very much.
WALTER LIPPMANN (1889–1974)

The actions of men are the best interpreters of their thoughts.
JOHN LOCKE (1632–1704)

Our life is what our thoughts make it.
MARCUS AURELIUS ANTONINUS (121–180)

Such as are your habitual thoughts, such also will be the character of your mind; for the soul is dyed by the thoughts.
MARCUS AURELIUS ANTONINUS (121–180)

The soul becomes dyed with the color of its thoughts.
MARCUS AURELIUS ANTONINUS (121–180)

Our thoughts and imagination are the only real limits to our possibilities.
ORISON SWETT MARDEN (1850–1924)

Our thoughts create our reality—where we put our focus is the direction we tend to go.
PETER MCWILLIAMS (1949–2000)

Once you replace negative thoughts with positive ones, you'll start having positive results.
WILLIE NELSON (1933–)

All truly great thoughts are conceived by walking.
FRIEDRICH NIETZSCHE (1844–1900)

Thoughts are the shadows of our sensations—always darker, emptier, simpler than these.
FRIEDRICH NIETZSCHE (1844–1900)

The mind moves in the direction of our currently dominant thoughts.
EARL NIGHTINGALE (1921–1989)

Thoughts give birth to a creative force that is neither elemental nor sidereal. Thoughts create a new heaven, a new firmament, a new source of energy, from which new arts flow. When a man undertakes to create something, he establishes a new heaven, as it were, and from it the work that he desires to create flows into him. For such is the immensity of man that he is greater than heaven and earth.
PARACELSUS (1493–1541)

Be not a traitor in your thoughts. Be sincere; act according to your thoughts; and you shall surely succeed. Pray with a sincere and simple heart, and

your prayers will be heard.
Sri Ramakrishna Paramahamsa (1836–1886)

If we examine our thoughts, we shall find them always occupied with the past and the future.
Blaise Pascal (1623–1662)

Man's greatness lies in his power of thought.
Blaise Pascal (1623–1662)

Pain makes man think. Thought makes man wise. Wisdom makes life endurable.
John Patrick (1905–1995)

Change your thoughts, and you change your world.
Norman Vincent Peale (1898–1993)

The fingers of your thoughts are molding your face ceaselessly.
Charles Reznikoff (1894–1976)

Great thoughts speak only to the thoughtful mind, but great actions speak to all mankind.
Theodore Roosevelt (1858–1919)

Men fear thought as they fear nothing else on earth—more than ruin—more even than death.... Thought is subversive and revolutionary, destructive and terrible, thought is merciless to privilege, established institutions, and comfortable habit. Thought looks into the pit of hell and is not afraid. Thought is great and swift and free, the light of the world, and the chief glory of man.
Bertrand Russell (1872–1970)

Skeptical scrutiny is the means, in both science and religion, by which deep thoughts can be winnowed from deep nonsense.
Carl Sagan (1934–1996)

Ideas are infinite, original, and lively divine thoughts.
Friedrich von Schlegel (1772–1829)

Wicked thoughts and worthless efforts gradually set their mark on the face, especially the eyes.
Arthur Schopenhauer (1788–1860)

It takes but one positive thought, when given a chance to survive and thrive, to overpower an entire army of negative thoughts.
Robert H. Schuller(1926–)

The future of civilization depends on our overcoming the meaninglessness and hopelessness that characterizes the thoughts of men today.
Dr. Albert Schweitzer (1875–1965)

Words without thoughts never to heaven go.
William Shakespeare (1564–1616), *Hamlet*

Our sweetest songs are those that tell of saddest thoughts.
Percy Bysshe Shelley (1792–1822)

Thinking is not enough. Sensitivity is not enough. People want to be accepted for sensitivity, for tender thoughts, for high ideals. That's not enough.
Shel Silverstein (1930–1999)

A mountain is composed of tiny grains of earth. The ocean is made up of tiny drops of water. Even so, life is but an endless series of little details, actions, speeches, and thoughts. And the consequences whether good or bad of even the least of them are far-reaching.
Swami Sivananda (1887–1963)

It is divinity that shapes, not only your ends, but also your acts, your words and thoughts.
Swami Sivananda (1887–1963)

To find yourself, think for yourself.
Socrates (469–399 BC)

The quality of our thoughts is bordered on all sides by our facility with language.
J. Michael Straczynski (1954–)

Discovery consists in seeing what everyone else has seen and thinking what no one else has thought.
Albert Szent-Gyorgyi (1893–1986)

Do not trouble yourself much to get new things, whether clothes or friends.... Sell your clothes and keep your thoughts.
Henry David Thoreau (1817–1862)

Thought is the sculptor who can create the person you want to be.
HENRY DAVID THOREAU (1817–1862)

Beware thoughts that come in the night. They aren't turned properly; they come in askew, free of sense and restriction, deriving from the most remote of sources.
WILLIAM TROGDON (1939–)

Drag your thoughts away from your troubles … by the ears, by the heels, or any other way you can manage it.
MARK TWAIN (1835–1910)

Great thoughts come from the heart.
MARQUIS DE VAUVENARGUES (1715–1747)

We are what our thoughts have made us; so take care about what you think. Words are secondary. Thoughts live; they travel far.
SWAMI VIVEKANANDA (1863–1902)

Men use thought only to justify their wrong doings, and employ speech only to conceal their thoughts.
VOLTAIRE (1694–1778)

One great use of words is to hide our thoughts.
VOLTAIRE (1694–1778)

The thoughts and opinions of one human being, if they are sincere, must always have an interest for some other human beings.
MARY A. WARD (1851–1920)

You cannot plough a field by turning it over in your mind.
ANONYMOUS

Time

Time is an illusion. Lunchtime doubly so.
DOUGLAS ADAMS (1952–2001)

Oh! Do not attack me with your watch. A watch is always too fast or too slow. I cannot be dictated to by a watch.
JANE AUSTEN (1775–1817), *Mansfield Park*

Nothing is as far away as one minute ago.
JIM BISHOP (1907–1987)

Doing a thing well is often a waste of time.
ROBERT BYRNE (1928–)

Under all speech that is good for anything there lies a silence that is better. Silence is deep as Eternity; speech is shallow as Time.
THOMAS CARLYLE (1795–1881)

The greatest friend of Truth is Time, her greatest enemy is Prejudice, and her constant companion Humility.
CHARLES CALEB COLTON (1780–1832)

Regret for wasted time is more wasted time.
MASON COOLEY (1927–2002)

If we take care of the moments, the years will take care of themselves.
MARIA EDGEWORTH (1767–1849)

There is time for everything.
THOMAS A. EDISON (1847–1931)

All my possessions for a moment of time.
QUEEN ELIZABETH I (1533–1603)

This time, like all times, is a very good one, if we but know what to do with it.
RALPH WALDO EMERSON (1803–1882)

There is never enough time, unless you're serving it.
MALCOLM S. FORBES (1919–1990)

Dost thou love life? Then do not squander time, for that is the stuff life is made of.
BENJAMIN FRANKLIN (1706–1790)

Time does not change us. It just unfolds us.
MAX FRISCH (1911–1991)

All that really belongs to us is time; even he who has nothing else has that.
BALTASAR GRACIAN (1601–1658)

Time is a cruel thief to rob us of our former selves. We lose as much to life as we do to death.
ELIZABETH FORSYTHE HAILEY (1938–)

The great French Marshall Lyautey once asked his gardener to plant a tree. The gardener objected that the tree was slow growing and would not reach maturity for 100 years. The Marshall replied, "In that case, there is no time to lose; plant it this afternoon!"
JOHN F. KENNEDY (1917–1963)

We must use time as a tool, not as a crutch.
JOHN F. KENNEDY (1917–1963)

A single day is enough to make us a little larger.
PAUL KLEE (1879–1940)

As order exponentially increases, time exponentially speeds up.
RAY KURZWEIL (1948–)

People find life entirely too time-consuming.
STANISLAW LEC (1909–1966), *Unkempt Thoughts*

So little time and so little to do.
OSCAR LEVANT (1906–1972)

Eventually, all things merge into one, and a river runs through it. The river was cut by the world's great flood and runs over rocks from the basement of time. On some of the rocks are timeless raindrops. Under the rocks are the words, and some of the words are theirs. I am haunted by waters.
NORMAN MACLEAN (1902–1990), *A River Runs Through It*

I don't think of the past. The only thing that matters is the everlasting present.
W. SOMERSET MAUGHAM (1874–1965), *The Moon and Sixpence*

The whole life of man is but a point of time; let us enjoy it.
PLUTARCH (AD 46–120)

Nothing is a waste of time if you use the experience wisely.
AUGUSTE RODIN (1840–1917)

Half our life is spent trying to find something to do with the time we have rushed through life trying to save.
WILL ROGERS (1879–1935)

Time is the coin of your life. It is the only coin you have, and only you can determine how it will be spent. Be careful lest you let other people spend it for you.
CARL SANDBURG (1878–1967)

The greatest loss of time is delay and expectation, which depend upon the future. We let go the present, which we have in our power, and look forward to that which depends upon chance, and so relinquish a certainty for an uncertainty.
SENECA (5 BC–AD 65)

Lost wealth may be replaced by industry, lost knowledge by study, lost health by temperance or medicine, but lost time is gone forever.
SAMUEL SMILES (1812–1904)

Time is the most valuable thing a man can spend.
THEOPHRASTUS (372–287 BC)

As if you could kill time without injuring eternity.
HENRY DAVID THOREAU (1817–1862)

Time is but the stream I go a-fishing in. I drink at it; but while I drink, I see the sandy bottom and detect how shallow it is. Its thin current slides away, but eternity remains. I would drink deeper; fish fill the sky, whose bottom is pebbly with stars. I cannot count one. I know not the first letter of the alphabet. I have always been regretting that I was not as wise as the day I was born.
HENRY DAVID THOREAU (1817–1862)

All we have to do is decide what to do with the time that is given to us.
J. R. R. TOLKIEN (1892–1973)

Time cools, time clarifies; no mood can be maintained quite unaltered through the course of hours.
MARK TWAIN (1835–1910)

An inch of time cannot be bought with an inch of gold.
CHINESE PROVERB

What may be done at any time will be done at no time.
SCOTTISH PROVERB

Timidity

In talking, shyness and timidity distort the very meaning of my words. I don't pretend to know anybody well. People are like shadows to me, and I am like a shadow.
GWEN JOHN (1876–1939)

Timidity is a fault for which it is dangerous to reprove persons whom we wish to correct of it.
FRANÇOIS DE LA ROCHEFOUCAULD (1613–1680)

Like timidity, bravery is also contagious.
MUNSHI PREMCHAND (1880–1936)

A great deal of talent is lost to the world for want of a little courage. Every day sends to their graves obscure men whose timidity prevented them from making a first effort.
SYDNEY SMITH (1771–1845)

Tobacco

The true face of smoking is disease, death and horror—not the glamour and sophistication the pushers in the tobacco industry try to portray.
DAVID BYRNE (1952–)

The believing we do something when we do nothing is the first illusion of tobacco.
RALPH WALDO EMERSON (1803–1882)

The tools I need for my work are paper, tobacco, food, and a little whiskey.
WILLIAM FAULKNER (1897–1962)

For thy sake, tobacco, I would do anything but die.
CHARLES LAMB (1775–1834)

Because tobacco is responsible for an impressive one-third of cancers, prevention efforts naturally begin with it.
BERNARD LEVIN (1928–2004)

Never slap a man who chews tobacco.
WILLARD SCOTT (1934–)

I wish we could do something useful with tobacco—like making fertilizer out of it.
PAUL D. WHITE (1886–1973)

Today

Look well to this day. Yesterday is but a dream, and tomorrow is only a vision. But today well-lived makes every yesterday a dream of happiness and every tomorrow a vision of hope. Look well therefore to this day.
FRANCIS GRAY (1884–1962)

All the flowers of tomorrow are in the seeds of today.
ANONYMOUS

Live life today. Yesterday is gone, and tomorrow may never come.
ANONYMOUS

Today is the tomorrow we worried about yesterday.
ANONYMOUS

Togetherness

Constant togetherness is fine—but only for Siamese twins.
VICTORIA BILLINGS (1945–)

I think togetherness is a very important ingredient to family life.
BARBARA BUSH (1925–)

But let there be spaces in your togetherness and let the winds of the heavens dance between you. Love one another but make not a bond of love: let it rather be a moving sea between the shores of your souls.
KAHLIL GIBRAN (1883–1931)

I will, from this day, strive to forge togetherness out of our differences.
JOSEFA ILOILO (1920–)

Perhaps only those people who are capable of real togetherness have that look of being alone in the world.
D. H. LAWRENCE (1885–1930)

Everyone has this sense of togetherness right now. For example, one guy on the subway today, he wanted to share my pants.
DAVID LETTERMAN (1947–)

Tolerance

If men would consider not so much where they differ, as wherein they agree, there would be far less of uncharitableness and angry feeling in the world.
JOSEPH ADDISON (1672–1719)

Not the power to remember, but its very opposite, the power to forget, is a necessary condition for our existence.
SHOLEM ASCH (1880–1957)

You must look into people, as well as at them.
LORD CHESTERFIELD (1745–1846)

I have seen gross intolerance shown in support of tolerance.
SAMUEL TAYLOR COLERIDGE (1772–1834)

Laws alone can not secure freedom of expression; in order that every man present his views without penalty there must be spirit of tolerance in the entire population.
ALBERT EINSTEIN (1879–1955)

The responsibility of tolerance lies in those who have the wider vision.
GEORGE ELIOT (1819–1880)

Judge a tree from its fruit, not from its leaves.
EURIPIDES (C. 480–406 BC)

I have learnt silence from the talkative, toleration from the intolerant, and kindness from the unkind; yet strange, I am ungrateful to these teachers.
KAHLIL GIBRAN (1883–1931)

If we are to live together in peace, we must come to know each other better.
LYNDON B. JOHNSON (1908–1973)

If we cannot end our differences, at least we can help make the world safe for diversity.
JOHN F. KENNEDY (1961–1963)

Be entirely tolerant or not at all; follow the good path or the evil one. To stand at the crossroads requires more strength than you possess.
HEINRICH HEINE (1797–1856)

The highest result of education is tolerance.
HELEN KELLER (1880–1968)

To say the least, a town life makes one more tolerant and liberal in one's judgement of others.
HENRY WADSWORTH LONGFELLOW (1807–1882)

Tolerance is another word for indifference.
W. SOMERSET MAUGHAM (1874–1965)

The test of courage comes when we are in the minority. The test of tolerance comes when we are in the majority.
RALPH W. SOCKMAN (1889–1970)

Once lead this people into war and they will forget there ever was such a thing as tolerance.
WOODROW WILSON (1856–1924)

When you meet a man, you judge him by his clothes; when you leave, you judge him by his heart.
RUSSIAN PROVERB

Tomorrow

If today were half as good as tomorrow is supposed to be, it would probably be twice as good as yesterday was.
NORMAN R. AUGUSTINE (1935–)

What we are today comes from our thoughts of yesterday, and our present thoughts build our life of tomorrow: Our life is the creation of our mind.
THE BUDDHA (563–483 BC)

Life lived for tomorrow will always be just a day away from being realized.
LEO F. BUSCAGLIA (1924–1998)

Worry never robs tomorrow of its sorrow, it only saps today of its joy.
LEO F. BUSCAGLIA (1924–1998)

Yesterday, we can't do anything; tomorrow, we don't know. Today.
CELINE DION (1968–)

Yesterday's just a memory, tomorrow is never what it's supposed to be.
BOB DYLAN (1941–)

Learn from yesterday, live for today, hope for tomorrow.
ALBERT EINSTEIN (1879–1955)

Finish each day and be done with it. You have done what you could. Some blunders and absurdities no doubt crept in, forget them as soon as you can. Tomorrow is a new day, you shall begin it well and serenely…
RALPH WALDO EMERSON (1803–1882)

Live as if you were to die tomorrow. Learn as if you were to live forever.
MAHATMA GANDHI (1869–1948)

Yesterday is but today's memory, tomorrow is today's dream.
KAHLIL GIBRAN (1883–1931)

Yesterday's tomorrow is today.
SIMS HATCHER (1983–)

The idol of today pushes the hero of yesterday out of our recollection; and will, in turn, be supplanted by his successor of tomorrow.
WASHINGTON IRVING (1783–1859)

You can't have a better tomorrow if you are thinking about yesterday all the time.
CHARLES KETTERING (1876–1958)

You cannot escape the responsibility of tomorrow by evading it today.
ABRAHAM LINCOLN (1809–1865)

Tomorrow is nothing, today is too late; the good lived yesterday.
MARCUS AURELIUS ANTONINUS (121–180)

Only put off until tomorrow what you are willing to die having left undone.
PABLO PICASSO (1881–1973)

Yesterday's gone forever and tomorrow may never come, which leaves the present moment.
WILLIAM SHOCKLEY (1910–1989)

Tomorrow is the most important thing in life. Comes into us at midnight very clean. It's perfect when it arrives and puts itself in our hands. It hopes we've learned something from yesterday.
JOHN WAYNE (1907–1979)

Today's greatest labor-saving device is tomorrow.
WOODROW WILSON (1856–1924)

All the flowers of tomorrow are in the seeds of today.
ANONYMOUS

The lazier a man is, the more he plans to do tomorrow.
NORWEGIAN PROVERB

Tomorrow is often the busiest day of the week.
SPANISH PROVERB

Torture

War is organized murder and torture against our brothers.
ALFRED ADLER (1870–1937)

Torture is banned, but in two-thirds of the world's countries it is still being committed in secret. Too many governments still allow wrongful imprisonment, murder or "disappearance" to be carried out by their officials with impunity.
PETER BENENSON (1921–2005)

Anyone will say anything under torture.
GEORGE GALLOWAY (1954–)

You can chain me, you can torture me, you can even destroy this body, but you will never imprison my mind.
MAHATMA GANDHI (1869–1948)

To torture a man you have to know his pleasures.
STANISLAW LEC (1909–1966)

It is as absurd to argue men, as to torture them, into believing.
JOHN HENRY NEWMAN (1801–1890)

Love is a reciprocal torture.
MARCEL PROUST (1871–1922)

Congress's definition of torture in those laws—the infliction of severe mental or physical pain—leaves room for interrogation methods that go beyond polite conversation.
JOHN YOO (1967–)

Totalitarianism

Totalitarianism is patriotism institutionalized.
STEVE ALLEN (1921–2000)

Totalitarianism is feudalism in the twelfth-century sense of the word.
BARBARA AMIEL (1940–)

Only the mob and the elite can be attracted by the momentum of totalitarianism itself. The masses have to be won by propaganda.
HANNAH ARENDT (1906–1975)

Totalitarianism is never content to rule by external means, namely, through the state and a machinery of violence; thanks to its peculiar ideology and the role assigned to it in this apparatus of coercion, totalitarianism has discovered a means of dominating and terrorizing human beings from within.
HANNAH ARENDT (1906–1975)

The new soft totalitarianism that is advancing on the left wants to have a state religion. It is an atheist, nihilistic religion—but it is a religion that is obligatory for all.
ROCCO BUTTIGLIONE (1948–)

Propaganda is to a democracy what the bludgeon is to a totalitarian state.
NOAM CHOMSKY (1928–)

What difference does it make to the dead, the orphans, and the homeless, whether the mad destruction is wrought under the name of totalitarianism or the holy name of liberty or democracy?
MAHATMA GANDHI (1869–1948)

Corporate nationalism to me is a little bit like what would have happened if Hitler had won. It's scary stuff. It's totalitarianism in a different form, under a different flavour.
LANCE HENRIKSEN (1940–)

A civilization in which there is not a continuous controversy about important issues is on the way to totalitarianism and death.
ROBERT M. HUTCHINS (1899–1977)

Russia needs a strong state power and must have it. But I am not calling for totalitarianism.
VLADIMIR PUTIN (1952–)

Liberalism is totalitarianism with a human face.
THOMAS SOWELL (1930–)

Democracy's a very fragile thing. You have to take care of democracy. As soon as you stop being responsible to it and allow it to turn into scare tactics, it's no longer democracy, is it? It's something else. It may be an inch away from totalitarianism.
SAM SHEPARD (1943–)

Toughness

Brave men are all vertebrates; they have their softness on the surface and their toughness in the middle.
G. K. CHESTERTON (1874–1936)

You become a champion by fighting one more round. When things are tough, you fight one more round.
JAMES J. CORBETT (1866–1933)

Toughness doesn't have to come in a pinstripe suit.
DIANNE FEINSTEIN (1933–)

Anyone who has a continuous smile on his face conceals a toughness that is almost frightening.
GRETA GARBO (1905–1990)

Toughness is in the soul and spirit, not in muscles.
ALEX KARRAS (1935–)

We must combine the toughness of the serpent with the softness of the dove, a tough mind and a tender heart.
MARTIN LUTHER KING JR. (1929–1968)

A lot of people are afraid to tell the truth, to say no. That's where toughness comes into play. Toughness is not being a bully. It's having backbone.
ROBERT KIYOSAKI (1947–)

Mental toughness is to physical as four is to one.
BOBBY KNIGHT (1940–)

Concentration and mental toughness are the margins of victory.
BILL RUSSELL (1934–)

Tough times never last, but tough people do.
ROBERT H. SCHULLER(1926–)

Tourism

What an odd thing tourism is. You fly off to a strange land, eagerly abandoning all the comforts of home, and then expend vast quantities of time and money in a largely futile attempt to recapture the comforts that you wouldn't have lost if you hadn't left home in the first place.
BILL BRYSON (1946–)

The traveler sees what he sees, the tourist sees what he has come to see.
G. K. CHESTERTON (1874–1936)

The whole object of travel is not to set foot on foreign land; it is at last to set foot on one's own country as a foreign land.
G. K. CHESTERTON (1874–1936)

The routines of tourism are even more monotonous than those of daily life.
MASON COOLEY (1927–2002)

Tourism, human circulation considered as consumption, is fundamentally nothing more than the leisure of going to see what has become banal.
GUY DEBORD (1931–1994)

Traveling makes a man wiser, but less happy.
THOMAS JEFFERSON (1762–1826)

The tourist may complain of other tourists, but he would be lost without them.
AGNES REPPLIER (1855–1950)

In the Middle Ages people were tourists because of their religion, whereas now they are tourists because tourism is their religion.
ROBERT RUNCIE (1921–)

Toys

Of all the toys available, none is better designed than the owner himself. A large multipurpose plaything, its parts can be made to move in almost any direction. It comes completely assembled, and it makes a sound when you jump on it.
STEPHEN BAKER (1964–)

If there is a species which is more maltreated than children, then it must be their toys, which they handle in an incredibly off-hand manner. Toys are thus the end point in that long chain in which all

the conditions of despotic high-handedness are in play which enchain beings one to another, from one species to another—cruel divinities to their sacrificial victims, from masters to slaves, from adults to children, and from children to their objects.
JEAN BAUDRILLARD (1929–2007)

Don't take your toys inside just because it's raining.
CHER (1946–)

Sports is the toy department of human life.
HOWARD COSELL (1918–1995)

As men get older, the toys get more expensive.
MARVIN DAVIS (1925–2004)

The simplest toy, one which even the youngest child can operate, is called a grandparent.
SAM LEVENSON (1911–1980)

Some parents say it is toy guns that make boys warlike. But give a boy a rubber duck and he will seize its neck like the butt of a pistol and shout "Bang!"
GEORGE F. WILL (1941–)

Trade

By virtue of exchange, one man's prosperity is beneficial to all others.
FREDERIC BASTIAT (1801–1850)

Free trade is not based on utility but on justice.
EDMUND BURKE (1729–1797)

Concentration is the secret of strength in politics, in war, in trade, in short in all management of human affairs.
RALPH WALDO EMERSON (1803–1882)

We rail at trade, but the historian of the world will see that it was the principle of liberty; that it settled America, and destroyed feudalism, and made peace and keeps peace; that it will abolish slavery.
RALPH WALDO EMERSON (1803–1882)

No nation was ever ruined by trade.
BENJAMIN FRANKLIN (1706–1790)

Rivalry is the life of trade, and the death of the trader.
ELBERT HUBBARD (1856–1915)

A day will come when markets, open to trade, and minds, open to ideas, will become the sole battlefield.
VICTOR HUGO (1802–1885)

Free trade, one of the greatest blessings which a government can confer on a people, is in almost every country unpopular.
LORD THOMAS BABINGTON MACAULAY (1800–1859)

For whosoever commands the sea commands the trade; whosoever commands the trade of the world commands the riches of the world, and consequently the world itself.
SIR WALTER RALEIGH (C. 1552–1618)

Where others fear trade and economic growth, we see opportunities for creting new wealth and undreamed-of opportunities for millions in our own land and beyond. Where others seek to throw up barriers, we seek to bring them down; where others take counsel of their fears, we follow our hopes.
RONALD REAGAN (1911–2004)

A crowded police court docket is the surest of all signs that trade is brisk and money plenty.
MARK TWAIN (1835–1910)

Trade knows neither friends or kindred.
ANONYMOUS

Tradition

Tradition is an important help to history, but its statements should be carefully scrutinized before we rely on them.
JOSEPH ADDISON (1672–1719)

Tradition is the illusion of permanence.
WOODY ALLEN (1935–)

In America nothing dies easier than tradition.
RUSSELL BAKER (1925–)

Tradition demands that we not speak poorly of the dead.
DANIEL BARENBOIM (1942–)

Tradition simply means that we need to end what began well and continue what is worth continuing.
JOSÉ BERGAMIN (1895–1983)

As soon as tradition has come to be recognized as tradition, it is dead.
ALLAN BLOOM (1930–1992)

What an enormous magnifier is tradition! How a thing grows in the human memory and in the human imagination, when love, worship, and all that lies in the human heart, is there to encourage it.
THOMAS CARLYLE (1795–1881)

Tradition means giving votes to the most obscure of all classes, our ancestors. It is the democracy of the dead. Tradition refuses to submit to that arrogant oligarchy who merely happen to be walking around.
G. K. CHESTERTON (1874–1936)

A love for tradition has never weakened a nation, indeed it has strengthened nations in their hour of peril.
SIR WINSTON CHURCHILL (1874–1965)

Thou shalt not covet, but tradition approves of all forms of competition.
ARTHUR HUGH CLOUGH (1819–1861)

Preserving tradition has become a nice hobby, like stamp collecting.
MASON COOLEY (1927–2002)

We don't want tradition. We want to live in the present, and the only history that is worth a tinker's dam is the history we make today.
HENRY FORD (1863–1947)

God has graced every tradition with insight into the divine mystery, from the most primitive to the most sophisticated—each has a gift to bring to the world.
BEDE GRIFFITHS (1906–1993)

It's my guess that those cutting-edge artists who attack tradition secretly believe tradition will survive to enshrine them as the wild and crazy geniuses who destroyed it.
BRAD HOLLAND (1943–)

It takes an endless amount of history to make even a little tradition.
HENRY JAMES (1843–1916)

To keep up even a worthwhile tradition means vitiating the idea behind it which must necessarily be in a constant state of evolution: it is mad to try to express new feelings in a mummified form.
ALFRED JARRY (1873–1907)

Tradition becomes our security, and when the mind is secure it is in decay.
JIDDU KRISHNAMURTI (1895–1986)

Tradition does not mean that the living are dead, it means that the dead are living.
HAROLD MACMILLAN (1894–1986)

Tradition is a guide and not a jailer.
W. SOMERSET MAUGHAM (1874–1965)

A great statesman is he who knows when to depart from traditions, as well as when to adhere to them.
JOHN STUART MILL (1806–1873)

Self-help and self-control are the essence of the American tradition.
FRANKLIN D. ROOSEVELT (1882–1945)

The role of tradition is that of a catalyst which furthers a chemical reaction, but is no longer detectable in the end result.
KENZO TANGE (1913–2005)

Tradition wears a snowy beard, romance is always young.
JOHN GREENLEAF WHITTIER (1807–1892)

Traffic

Traffic is only one of the side effects of growth.
ROY BARNES (1948–)

Outside of traffic, there is nothing that has held this country back as much as committees.
WILL ROGERS (1879–1935)

The only way to solve the traffic problems of the country is to pass a law that only paid-for cars are allowed to use the highways. That would make traffic so scarce, we could use our boulevards for children's playgrounds.
WILL ROGERS (1879–1935)

Tragedy

The difference between tragedy and comedy: Tragedy is something awful happening to somebody else, while comedy is something awful happening to somebody else.
AARON ALLSTON (1960–)

Tragedy is thus a representation of an action that is worth serious attention, complete in itself and of some amplitude … by means of pity and fear, bringing about the purgation of such emotions.
ARISTOTLE (384–322 BC)

Tragedy on the stage is no longer enough for me, I shall bring it into my own life.
ANTONIN ARTAUD (1896–1948)

The real tragedy is the tragedy of the man who never in his life braces himself for his one supreme effort, who never stretches to his full capacity, never stands up to his full stature.
ARNOLD BENNETT (1867–1931)

Tragedy is when I cut my finger. Comedy is when you fall into an open sewer and die.
MEL BROOKS (1926–)

Comedy is tragedy plus time.
CAROL BURNETT (1933–)

History is moving, and it will tend toward hope, or tend toward tragedy.
GEORGE W. BUSH (1946–)

That there should one man die ignorant who had capacity for knowledge, this I call a tragedy.
THOMAS CARLYLE (1795–1881)

The greatest tragedy in mankind's entire history may be the hijacking of morality by religion.
ARTHUR C. CLARKE (1917–)

The tragedy of life is in what dies inside a man while he lives—the death of genuine feeling, the death of inspired response, the awareness that makes it possible to feel the pain or the glory of other men in yourself.
NORMAN COUSINS (1915–1990)

Our tragedy is a general and universal physical fear so long sustained by now that we can even bear it … the basest of all things is to be afraid.
WILLIAM FAULKNER (1897–1962)

Show me a hero and I will write you a tragedy.
F. SCOTT FITZGERALD (1896–1940)

Life's Tragedy is that we get old too soon and wise too late.
BENJAMIN FRANKLIN (1706–1790)

In tragedy, every moment is eternity; in comedy, eternity is a moment.
CHRISTOPHER FRY (1907–2005)

The tragedy of modern man is not that he knows less and less about the meaning of his own life, but that it bothers him less and less.
VACLAV HAVEL (1936–)

Forget your personal tragedy. We are all bitched from the start and you especially have to be hurt like hell before you can write seriously. But when you get the damned hurt, use it—don't cheat with it.
ERNEST HEMINGWAY (1899–1961)

Tragedy is a tool for the living to gain wisdom, not a guide by which to live.
ROBERT F. KENNEDY (1925–1968)

The ultimate tragedy is not the oppression and cruelty by the bad people but the silence over that by the good people.
MARTIN LUTHER KING JR. (1929–1968)

Life is a tragedy full of joy.
BERNARD MALAMUD (1914–1986)

We can easily forgive a child who is afraid of the dark; the real tragedy of life is when men are afraid of the light.
PLATO (C. 428–348 BC)

The basis of tragedy is man's helplessness against disease, war and death; the basis of comedy is man's helplessness against vanity (the vanity of love, greed, lust, power).
DAWN POWELL (1896–1965)

Tragedy, for me, is not a conflict between right and wrong, but between two different kinds of right.
PETER SHAFFER (1926–)

The tragedy of human life consists in our vain attempts to stretch the limits of things which can never become unlimited, to reach the infinite by absurdly adding to the rungs of the ladder of the finite.
RABINDRANATH TAGORE (1861–1941)

In human intercourse the tragedy begins, not when there is misunderstanding about words, but when silence is not understood.
HENRY DAVID THOREAU (1817–1862)

Life is a tragedy for those who feel, but a comedy to those who think.
HORACE WALPOLE (1717–1797)

There are only two tragedies in life: one is not getting what one wants, and the other is getting it.
OSCAR WILDE (1854–1900)

Traitors

I have learned to hate all traitors, and there is no disease that I spit on more than treachery.
AESCHYLUS (C. 525–456 BC)

Among famous traitors of history one might mention the weather.
ILKA CHASE (1903–1978)

This principle is old, but true as fate,
Kings may love treason, but the traitor hate.
THOMAS DEKKER (1570–1632)

A traitor is everyone who does not agree with me.
KING GEORGE III (1738–1820)

For while the treason I detest,
The traitor still I love.
JOHN HOOLE (1727–1803), *Metastatio*

Be not a traitor in your thoughts. Be sincere; act according to your thoughts; and you shall surely succeed. Pray with a sincere and simple heart, and your prayers will be heard.
SRI RAMAKRISHNA PARAMAHAMSA (1836–1886)

'Tis not seasonable to call a man a traitor that has an army at his heels.
JOHN SELDEN (1584–1654)

Our doubts are traitors and make us lose the good we oft might win by fearing to attempt.
WILLIAM SHAKESPEARE (1564–1616), *Measure for Measure*

Transcendentalism

The Transcendentalist adopts the whole connection of spiritual doctrine. He believes in miracle, in the perpetual openness of the human mind to new influx of light and power; he believes in inspiration, and in ecstasy. He wishes that the spiritual principle should be suffered to demonstrate itself to the end, in all possible applications to the state of man, without the admission of anything unspiritual; that is, anything positive, dogmatic, personal. Thus, the spiritual measure of inspiration is the depth of the thought, and never, who said it? And so he resists all attempts to palm other rules and measures on the spirit than its own…
RALPH WALDO EMERSON (1803–1882)

Especially the transcendental philosophy needs the leaven of humor to render it light and digestible.
HENRY DAVID THOREAU (1817–1862)

Even as empiricism is winning the mind, transcendentalism continues to win the heart.
EDWARD O. WILSON (1929–)

Transformation

When we quit thinking primarily about ourselves and our own self-preservation, we undergo a truly heroic transformation of consciousness.
JOSEPH CAMPBELL (1904–1987)

Transformation literally means going beyond your form.
WAYNE D. DYER (1940–)

Sometimes a breakdown can be the beginning of a kind of breakthrough, a way of living in advance through a trauma that prepares you for a future of radical transformation.
CHERRIE MORAGA (1952–)

Any revolution has to start with the transformation of the individual, otherwise individuals are corrupted by the power they get if their revolution succeeds.
WES NISKER (1942–)

The way of the Creative works through change and transformation, so that each thing receives its true nature and destiny and comes into permanent accord with the Great Harmony: this is what furthers and what perseveres.
ALEXANDER POPE (1688–1744)

Whoever undertakes to create soon finds himself engaged in creating himself. Self-transformation and the transformation of others have constituted the radical interest of our century, whether in painting, psychiatry, or political action.
HAROLD ROSENBERG (190–1978)

A human body is associated with six stages of transformation: birth, growth, change, evolution, death and destruction.
SRI SATHYA SAI BABA (1926–)

How is individual transformation to be achieved? There are some bad habits among individuals such as smoking, drinking liquor, meat eating and gambling. These bad habits not only degrade the individuals but also inflict hardships on their families. These bad habits have to be given up for the individual to manifest his inherent goodness.
SRI SATHYA SAI BABA (1926—)

Only through Love transformation of the so-called wicked ones is possible.
SRI SATHYA SAI BABA (1926–)

Personal transformation can and does have global effects. As we go, so goes the world, for the world is us. The revolution that will save the world is ultimately a personal one.
MARIANNE WILLIAMSON (1952–)

Translation

Translation is at best an echo.
GEORGE BORROW (1803–1881)

Translation is the art of failure.
UMBERTO ECO (1932–)

Poetry is what gets lost in translation.
ROBERT FROST (1874–1963)

Translation is an interestingly different way to be involved both with poetry and with the language that I've found myself living in much of the time. I think the two feed each other.
MARILYN HACKER (1942–)

A translation is no translation … unless it will give you the music of a poem along with the words of it.
JOHN MILLINGTON SYNGE (1871–1909)

Translation is like a woman. If it is beautiful, it is not faithful. If it is faithful, it is most certainly not beautiful.
YEVGENY YEVTUSHENKO (1933–)

Travel

The true traveler is he who goes on foot, and even then, he sits down a lot of the time.
SIDONIE GABRIELLE COLETTE (1873–1954), *Paris from My Window*

Once you have traveled, the voyage never ends, but is played out over and over again in the quietest chambers, that the mind can never break off from the journey.
PAT CONROY (1945–), *The Prince of Tides*

When one realizes that his life is worthless he either commits suicide or travels.
EDWARD DAHLBERG (1900–1977)

When you travel, remember that a foreign country is not designed to make you comfortable. It is designed to make its own people comfortable.
CLIFTON FADIMAN (1904–1999)

Everywhere I go I find a poet has been there before me.
SIGMUND FREUD (1856–1939)

Thanks to the Interstate Highway System, it is now possible to travel from coast to coast without seeing anything.
CHARLES KURALT (1934–1997)

He who would travel happily must travel light.
ANTOINE DE SAINT-EXUPÉRY (1900–1944)

Before he sets out, the traveler must possess fixed interests and facilities to be served by travel.
GEORGE SANTAYANA (1863–1952)

To travel hopefully is a better thing than to arrive.
ROBERT LOUIS STEVENSON (1850–1894)

Travel is only glamorous in retrospect.
PAUL THEROUX (1941–)

No one travelling on a business trip would be missed if he failed to arrive.
THORSTEIN VEBLEN (1857–1929)

Travel only with thy equals or thy betters; if there are none, travel alone.
THE DHAMMAPADA

Treason

Bad literature is a form of treason.
JOSEPH BRODSKY (1940–1996)

No wise man ever thought that a traitor should be trusted.
CICERO (106–43 BC), *Orationes in verrem*

Treason is not own'd when 'tis descried; Successful crimes alone are justified.
JOHN DRYDEN (1631–1700), *Medals*

Treason doth never prosper: what's the reason? For if it prosper, none dare call it treason.
JOHN HARRINGTON (1561–1612)

For while the treason I detest, The traitor still I love.
JOHN HOOLE (1727–1803), *Metastatio*

Treason is like diamonds; there is nothing to be made by the small trader.
DOUGLAS JERROLD (1803–1857)

More men are guilty of treason through weakness than any studied design to betray.
FRANÇOIS DE LA ROCHEFOUCAULD (1613–1680)

Ingratitude is treason to mankind.
JAMES THOMSON (1700–1748)

Trees

As the poet said, "Only God can make a tree"—probably because it's so hard to figure out how to get the bark on.
WOODY ALLEN (1935–)

You will find something more in woods than in books. Trees and stones will teach you that which you can never learn from masters.
SAINT BERNARD OF CLAIRVAUX (1090–1153), *Epistle*

He plants trees to benefit another generation.
CAECILIUS STATIUS (220–168 BC), *Synephebi*

I like trees because they seem more resigned to the way they have to live than other things do.
WILLA CATHER (1873–1947), *O Pioneers!*

Train up a fig tree in the way it should go, and when you are old sit under the shade of it.
CHARLES DICKENS (1812–1870)

He that plants trees loves others besides himself.
THOMAS FULLER (1608–1661), *Gnomologia*

There's nothing that keeps its youth,
So far as I know, but a tree and truth.
OLIVER WENDELL HOLMES SR. (1809–1894), *The Deacon's Masterpiece*

I think that I shall never see
A poem lovely as a tree.
JOYCE KILMER (1886–1918), "Trees"

The trees that are slow to grow bear the best fruit.
MOLIÈRE (1622–1673)

I think that I shall never see
A billboard lovely as a tree.
Perhaps, unless the billboards fall,
I'll never see a tree at all.
OGDEN NASH (1902–1971)

Trees, though they are cut and lopped, grow up again quickly, but if men are destroyed, it is not easy to get them again.
PERICLES (490–429 BC)

You should go to a pear tree for pears, not to an elm.
PUBLILIUS SYRUS (C. 100 BC), *Maxims*

He that climbs the tall tree has won right to the fruit.
SIR WALTER SCOTT (1771–1832)

Triumph

To keep the heart unwrinkled, to be hopeful, kindly, cheerful, reverent—that is to triumph over old age.
AMOS BRONSON ALCOTT (1799–1888)

We triumph without glory when we conquer without danger.
PIERRE CORNEILLE (1606–1684)

Survival is triumph enough.
HARRY CREWS (1935–)

Conquer, but don't triumph.
MARIE VON EBNER-ESCHENBACH (1830–1916)

The harder the conflict, the more glorious the triumph.
THOMAS PAINE (1737–1809)

For every moment of triumph, for every instance of beauty, many souls must be trampled.
HUNTER S. THOMPSON (1937–2005)

Trouble

To be satisfied with a little is the greatest wisdom; and he that increaseth his riches, increaseth his cares; but a contented mind is a hidden treasure, and trouble findeth it not.
AKHENATON (C. 1400 BC)

Entrepreneurship is the last refuge of the trouble making individual.
NATALIE CLIFFORD BARNEY (1876–1972)

Difficulties exist to be surmounted.
RALPH WALDO EMERSON (1803–1882)

Trouble is a sieve through which we sift our acquaintances. Those too big to pass through are our friends.
ARLENE FRANCIS (1907–2001)

Do not anticipate trouble or worry about what may never happen. Keep in the sunlight.
BENJAMIN FRANKLIN (1706–1790)

Troubles are like babies—they only grow by nursing.
DOUGLAS JERROLD (1803–1857)

I know the world is filled with troubles and many injustices. But reality is as beautiful as it is ugly. I think it is just as important to sing about beautiful mornings as it is to talk about slums. I just couldn't write anything without hope in it.
OSCAR HAMMERSTEIN II (1895–1960)

Happiness is not being pained in body or troubled in mind.
THOMAS JEFFERSON (1762–1826)

Trouble is only opportunity in work clothes.
HENRY J. KAISER (1882–1967)

Trouble is the common denominator of living. It is the great equalizer.
SØREN KIERKEGAARD (1813–1855)

Borrow trouble for yourself, if that's your nature, but don't lend it to your neighbours.
RUDYARD KIPLING (1865–1936)

Expect trouble as an inevitable part of life and when it comes, hold your head high, look it squarely in the eye and say, "I will be bigger than you. You cannot defeat me."
ANN LANDERS (1918–2002)

I believe that a man is converted when first he hears the low, vast murmur of life, of human life, troubling his hitherto unconscious self.
D. H. LAWRENCE (1885–1930)

If there must be trouble, let it be in my day, that my child may have peace.
THOMAS PAINE (1737–1809)

The trouble is that everyone talks about reforming others and no one thinks about reforming himself.
SAINT PETER OF ALCANTARA (1499–1562)

The biggest cause of trouble in the world today is that the stupid people are so sure about things and the intelligent folks are so full of doubts.
BERTRAND RUSSELL (1872–1970)

Trouble is part of your life— if you don't share it, you don't give the person who loves you a chance to love you enough.
DINAH SHORE (1916–1994)

The trouble with our times is that the future is not what it used to be.
PAUL VALÉRY (1871–1945)

It takes two to get one in trouble.
MAE WEST (1892–1980)

If there was less sympathy in the world, there would be less trouble in the world.
OSCAR WILDE (1854–1900)

Trust

[T]his is tyranny's disease, to trust no friends.
AESCHYLUS (C. 525–456 BC), *Prometheus Bound*

The man who trusts men will make fewer mistakes than he who distrusts them.
CAMILLO BENSO, CONTE DI CAVOUR (1810–1861)

He who trusts no one should never be trusted
AUGUSTUS DURANT (1982–)

Do not trust all men, but trust men of worth; the former course is silly, the latter a mark of prudence.
DEMOCRITUS (460–370 BC)

Trust men and they will be true to you; treat them greatly, and they will show themselves great.
RALPH WALDO EMERSON (1803–1882)

Relationships of trust depend on our willingness to look not only to our own interests, but also the interests of others.
PETER FARQUHARSON (1832–1869)

If we are bound to forgive an enemy, we are not bound to trust him.
THOMAS FULLER (1608–1661)

Trust thyself only, and another shall not betray thee.
THOMAS FULLER (1608–1661)

When I'm trusting and being myself ... everything in my life reflects this by falling into place easily, often miraculously.
SHAKTI GAWAIN (1948–)

As soon as you trust yourself, you will know how to live.
JOHANN WOLFGANG VON GOETHE (1749–1832), *Faust*

A man who doesn't trust himself can never truly trust anyone else.
JEAN-FRANÇOIS-PAUL DE GONDI (1614–1679), *Memoires*

The people I distrust most are those who want to improve our lives but have only one course of action.
FRANK HERBERT (1920–1986)

It is better to suffer wrong than to do it, and happier to be sometimes cheated than not to trust.
SAMUEL JOHNSON (1709–1784)

Relationships in general make people a bit nervous. It's about trust. Do I trust you enough to go there?
NEIL LABUTE (1963–)

Mistrust the man who finds everything good, the man who finds everything evil and still more the man who is indifferent to everything.
JOHANN KASPAR LAVATER (1741–1801)

For it is mutual trust, even more than mutual interest, that holds human associations together. Our friends seldom profit us but they make us feel safe.... Marriage is a scheme to accomplish exactly that same end.
H. L. MENCKEN (1880–1956)

But the life that no longer trusts another human being and no longer forms ties to the political community is not a human life any longer.
MARTHA NUSSBAUM (1947–)

Never trust anything that can think for itself if you can't see where it keeps its brain.
J. K. ROWLING (1965–), *Harry Potter and The Chamber of Secrets*

Love looks not with the eyes, but with the mind.
WILLIAM SHAKESPEARE (1564–1616), *A Midsummer Night's Dream*

The chief lesson I have learned in a long life is that the only way to make a man trustworthy is to trust him; and the surest way to make him untrustworthy is to distrust him and show your distrust.
HENRY L. STIMSON (1867–1950)

A human being is only interesting if he's in contact with himself. I learned you have to trust yourself, be what you are, and do what you ought to do the way you should do it. You have got to discover you, what you do, and trust it.
BARBRA STREISAND (1942–)

Trust one who has gone through it.
VIRGIL (C. 70–19 BC), *Aeneid*

Truth

The truth that makes men free is for the most part the truth which men prefer not to hear.
HERBERT AGAR (1897–1980)

All people know the same truth, our lives consist of how we choose to distort it.
WOODY ALLEN (1935–), *Deconstructing Harry*

Truth is the secret of eloquence and of virtue, the basis of moral authority; it is the highest summit of art and life.
HENRI-FRÉDÉRIC AMIEL (1821–1881)

Truth sits upon the lips of dying men.
MATTHEW ARNOLD (1822–1888), *Sohrab and Rustum*

As scarce as truth is, the supply has always been in excess of the demand.
JOSH BILLINGS (1818–1885)

The opposite of a correct statement is a false statement. But the opposite of a profound truth may well be another profound truth.
NIELS BOHR (1885–1962)

Getting rid of a delusion makes us wiser than getting hold of a truth.
LUDWIG BORNE (1786–1837)

Truth, like light, blinds. Falsehood, on the contrary, is a beautiful twilight that enhances every object.
ALBERT CAMUS (1913–1960)

You can only find truth with logic if you have already found truth without it.
G. K. CHESTERTON (1874–1936)

Walk with those seeking truth. Run from those who think they've found it.
DEEPAK CHOPRA (1946–)

Men occasionally stumble over the truth, but most of them pick themselves up and hurry off as if nothing ever happened.
SIR WINSTON CHURCHILL (1874–1965)

In everything truth surpasses the imitation and copy.
CICERO (106–43 BC)

Chase after truth like hell and you'll free yourself, even though you never touch its coat-tails.
CLARENCE DARROW (1857–1938)

Time is precious, but truth is more precious than time.
BENJAMIN DISRAELI (1804–1881)

How often have I said to you that when you have eliminated the impossible, whatever remains, however improbable, must be the truth?
SIR ARTHUR CONAN DOYLE (1859–1930), *The Sign of Four*

I have come to believe that the whole world is an enigma, a harmless enigma that is made terrible by our own mad attempt to interpret it as though it had an underlying truth.
UMBERTO ECO (1932–)

The pursuit of truth and beauty is a sphere of activity in which we are permitted to remain children all our lives.
ALBERT EINSTEIN (1879–1955)

Truth is beautiful, without doubt; but so are lies.
RALPH WALDO EMERSON (1803–1882)

All truths are easy to understand once they are discovered; the point is to discover them.
GALILEO GALILEI (1564–1642)

When I despair, I remember that all through history the ways of truth and love have always won. There have been tyrants, and murderers, and for a time they can seem invincible, but in the end they always fall. Think of it—always.
MAHATMA GANDHI (1869–1948)

Rebellion without truth is like spring in a bleak, arid desert.
KAHLIL GIBRAN (1883–1931)

Say not, "I have found the truth," but rather, "I have found a truth."
KAHLIL GIBRAN (1883–1931)

Believe those who are seeking the truth. Doubt those who find it.
ANDRÉ GIDE (1869–1951)

There are times when we must sink to the bottom of our misery to understand truth, just as we must descend to the bottom of a well to see the stars in broad daylight.
VACLAV HAVEL (1936–)

Truth is tough. It will not break, like a bubble, at a touch; nay, you may kick it about all day like a football, and it will be round and full at evening.
OLIVER WENDELL HOLMES SR. (1809–1894)

Often the truth spoken with a smile will penetrate the mind and reach the heart; the lesson strikes home without wounding because of the wit in the saying.
HORACE (65–8 BC)

Irrationally held truths may be more harmful than reasoned errors.
THOMAS H. HUXLEY (1825–1895)

For here we are not afraid to follow truth wherever it may lead…
THOMAS JEFFERSON (1743–1826)

Beauty is truth, truth beauty.
JOHN KEATS (1795–1821), "Ode on a Grecian Urn"

The enemy of the truth is very often not the lie—deliberate, contrived, and dishonest—but the myth—persistent, persuasive, and unrealistic.
JOHN F. KENNEDY (1917–1963)

I believe that unarmed truth and unconditional love will have the final word in reality. That is why right, temporarily defeated, is stronger than evil triumphant.
MARTIN LUTHER KING JR. (1929–1968)

A lie told often enough becomes the truth.
VLADIMIR I. LENIN (1870–1924)

Truth is generally the best vindication against slander.
ABRAHAM LINCOLN (1809–1865)

Peace if possible, but truth at any rate.
MARTIN LUTHER (1483–1546)

I do not know what I may appear to the world; but to myself I seem to have been only like a boy playing on the seashore, and diverting myself in now and then finding a smoother pebble or a prettier shell than ordinary, whilst the great ocean of truth lay all undiscovered before me.
SIR ISAAC NEWTON (1642–1727)

Hope is nature's veil for hiding truth's nakedness.
ALFRED BERNHARD NOBEL (1833–1896)

Truth is its own reward.
PLATO (C. 428–348 BC)

Truth is like the sun. You can shut it out for a time, but it ain't goin' away.
ELVIS PRESLEY (1935–1977)

Truth persuades by teaching, but does not teach by persuading.
QUINTUS SEPTIMIUS TERTULLIANUS (160–230)

The dream begins with a teacher who believes in you, who tugs and pushes and leads you to the next plateau, sometimes poking you with a sharp stick called "truth."
DAN RATHER (1931–)

There are few nudities so objectionable as the naked truth.
AGNES REPPLIER (1855–1950)

The truth. It is a beautiful and terrible thing, and should therefore be treated with great caution.
J. K. ROWLING (1965–), *Harry Potter and the Sorcerer's Stone*

Think of how many religions attempt to validate themselves with prophecy. Think of how many people rely on these prophecies, however vague, however unfulfilled, to support or prop up their beliefs. Yet has there ever been a religion with the prophetic accuracy and reliability of science?
CARL SAGAN (1934–1996)

All truth passes through three stages. First, it is ridiculed. Second, it is violently opposed. Third, it is accepted as being self-evident.
ARTHUR SCHOPENHAUER (1788–1860)

Truth is truth
To the end of reckoning…
WILLIAM SHAKESPEARE (1564–1616), *Measure for Measure*

The public will believe anything, so long as it is not founded on truth.
EDITH SITWELL (1887–1964)

The moment we begin to fear the opinions of others and hesitate to tell the truth that is in us, and from motives of policy are silent when we should speak, the divine floods of light and life no longer flow into our souls.
ELIZABETH CADY STANTON (1815–1902)

Truth is the only safe ground to stand on.
ELIZABETH CADY STANTON (1815–1902)

The truth is always a compound of two half-truths, and you never reach it, because there is always something more to say.
TOM STOPPARD (1937–)

The truth is the kindest thing we can give people in the end.
HARRIET BEECHER STOWE (1811–1896)

All perception of truth is the detection of an analogy.
HENRY DAVID THOREAU (1817–1862)

Rather than love, than money, than fame, give me truth.
HENRY DAVID THOREAU (1817–1862)

Truth, like gold, is to be obtained not by its growth, but by washing away from it all that is not gold.
LEO TOLSTOY (1828–1910)

The best mind-altering drug is truth.
LILY TOMLIN (1939–)

The history of our race, and each individual's experience, are sown thick with evidence that a truth is not hard to kill and that a lie told well is immortal.
MARK TWAIN (1835–1910), *Advice to Youth*

A lie can travel halfway around the world while the truth is putting on its shoes.
MARK TWAIN (1835–1910)

Fiction is obliged to stick to possibilities. Truth isn't.
MARK TWAIN (1835–1910)

If you tell the truth, you don't have to remember anything.
MARK TWAIN (1835–1910)

Truth is more of a stranger than fiction.
MARK TWAIN (1835–1910)

Why shouldn't truth be stranger than fiction? Fiction, after all, has to make sense.
MARK TWAIN (1835–1910)

Love truth, and pardon error.
VOLTAIRE (1694–1778)

To announce truths is an infallible receipt for being persecuted.
VOLTAIRE (1694–1778)

A thing is not necessarily true because a man dies for it.
OSCAR WILDE (1854–1900)

The truth is rarely pure and never simple.
OSCAR WILDE (1854–1900), *The Importance of Being Earnest*

The truth is more important than the facts.
FRANK LLOYD WRIGHT (1869–1959)

If we all worked on the assumption that what is accepted as true were really true, there would be little hope of advance.
ORVILLE WRIGHT (1871–1948)

Tell the truth and then run.
ANONYMOUS

Then you will know the truth, and the truth will set you free.
THE BIBLE, John 8:32

Twilight

Twilight is about getting older and relationships—not about a murder mystery. It's about love when you reach a certain age; nothing is in primary colors.
ROBERT BENTON (1932–)

Love prefers twilight to daylight.
OLIVER WENDELL HOLMES SR. (1809–1894)

Twilight, a timid fawn, went glimmering by, and Night, the dark-blue hunter, followed fast.
GEORGE WILLIAM RUSSELL (1867–1935)

Tyranny

The distrust of wit is the beginning of tyranny.
EDWARD ABBEY (1927–1989)

No tyranny is so irksome as petty tyranny: the officious demands of policemen, government clerks, and electromechanical gadgets.
EDWARD ABBEY (1927–1989)

[T]his is tyranny's disease, to trust no friends.
AESCHYLUS (C. 525–456 BC), *Prometheus Bound*

Death is better, a milder fate than tyranny.
AESCHYLUS (C. 525–456 BC)

Political tyranny is nothing compared to the social tyranny, and a reformer who defies society is a more courageous man than a politician who defies Government.
B. R. AMBEDKAR (1891–1956)

Under conditions of tyranny it is far easier to act than to think.
HANNAH ARENDT (1906–1975)

You may talk of the tyranny of Nero and Tiberius; but the real tyranny is the tyranny of your next-door neighbor.
WALTER BAGEHOT (1826–1877)

Tyranny and anarchy are never far apart.
JEREMY BENTHAM (1748–1832)

Tyranny absolves all faith; and who invades our rights, however his own commence, can never be but an usurper.
HENRY BROOKE (1703–1783)

Kings will be tyrants from policy, when subjects are rebels from principle.
EDMUND BURKE (1729–1797)

Tyrants have not yet discovered any chains that can fetter the mind.
CHARLES CALEB COLTON (1780–1832)

All men would be tyrants if they could.
DANIEL DEFOE (1660–1731)

Excessive dealings with tyrants are not good for the security of free states.
DEMOSTHENES (384–322 BC)

The limits of tyrants are prescribed by the endurance of those whom they oppose.
FREDERICK DOUGLASS (1817–1895)

Rebellion against tyrants is obedience to God.
BENJAMIN FRANKLIN (1706–1790) and THOMAS JEFFERSON (1743–1826)

The evils of tyranny are rarely seen but by him who resists it.
JOHN HAY (1838–1905)

All tyranny needs to gain a foothold is for people of good conscience to remain silent.
THOMAS JEFFERSON (1743–1826)

I have sworn upon the altar of God, eternal hostility against every form of tyranny over the mind of man.
THOMAS JEFFERSON (1743–1826)

Tyranny and despotism can be exercised by many, more rigourously, more vigourously, and more severely, than by one.
ANDREW JOHNSON (1808–1875)

There is no crueler tyranny than that which is perpetuated under the shield of law and in the name of justice.
CHARLES DE MONTESQUIEU (1689–1755)

Tyranny is always better organized than freedom.
CHARLES PEGUY (1873–1914)

Tyranny naturally arises out of democracy.
PLATO (C. 428–348 BC)

There can be no tyrants where there are no slaves.
JOSE RIZAL (1861–1896)

Tyrants are seldom free; the cares and the instruments of their tyranny enslave them.
GEORGE SANTAYANA (1863–1952)

Clever tyrants are never punished.
VOLTAIRE (1694–1778)

Tyrants have always some slight shade of virtue; they support the laws before destroying them.
VOLTAIRE (1694–1778)

Peace without justice is tyranny.
WILLIAM ALLEN WHITE (1868–1944)

Ugliness

I seated ugliness on my knee, and almost immediately grew tired of it.
SALVADOR DALÍ (1904–1989)

The secret of ugliness consists not in irregularity, but in being uninteresting.
RALPH WALDO EMERSON (1803–1882)

Ugliness is in a way superior to beauty because it lasts.
SERGE GAINSBOURG (1928–1991)

I love it when ugliness is beautiful. I love character flaws.
MARCIA GAY HARDEN (1959–)

Once you can laugh at your own weaknesses, you can move forward. Comedy breaks down walls. It opens up people. If you're good, you can fill up those openings with something positive. Maybe … combat some of the ugliness in the world.
GOLDIE HAWN (1945–)

When the people of the world all know beauty as beauty, There arises the recognition of ugliness. When they all know the good as good, There arises the recognition of evil.
LAO-TZU (C. 600 BC), *The Way of Lao-tzu*

Time takes the ugliness and horror out of death and turns it into beauty.
DODIE SMITH (1896–1990)

Fashion is a form of ugliness so intolerable that we have to alter it every six months.
OSCAR WILDE (1854–1900)

Uncertainty

Uncertainty is the refuge of hope.
HENRI-FRÉDÉRIC AMIEL (1821–1881)

I have known uncertainty: a state unknown to the Greeks.
JORGE LUIS BORGES (1899–1986)

Certainty is the mother of quiet and repose, and uncertainty the cause of variance and contentions.
EDWARD COKE (1552–1634)

Uncertainty will always be part of the taking charge process.
HAROLD S. GENEEN (1910–1997)

Without the element of uncertainty, the bringing off of even the greatest business triumph would be dull, routine, and eminently unsatisfying.
J. PAUL GETTY (1892–1976)

When there's uncertainty they always think there's another shoe to fall. There is no other shoe to fall.
KENNETH LAY (1942–2006)

The only thing that makes life possible is permanent, intolerable uncertainty; not knowing what comes next.
URSULA K. LE GUIN (1929–)

Uncertainty! fell demon of our fears! The human soul that can support despair, supports not thee.
DAVID MALLET (1705–1765)

In these matters the only certainty is that nothing is certain.
PLINY THE ELDER (AD 23–79)

Not to be absolutely certain is, I think, one of the essential things in rationality.
BERTRAND RUSSELL (1872–1970), *Am I an Atheist or an Agnostic?*

When one admits that nothing is certain one must, I think, also admit that some things are much more nearly certain than others.
BERTRAND RUSSELL (1872–1970), *Am I an Atheist or an Agnostic?*

Uncertainty is a sign of humility, and humility is just the ability or the willingness to learn.
CHARLIE SHEEN (1965–)

Doubt is not a pleasant condition, but certainty is absurd.
VOLTAIRE (1694–1778)

The Unconscious

Our unconscious is not more animal than our conscious, it is often even more human.
EDWARD BOND (1934–)

An unconscious consciousness is no more a contradiction in terms than an unseen case of seeing.
FRANZ CLEMENS BRENTANO (1838–1917)

The unconscious mind has a habit of asserting itself in the afternoon.
ANTHONY BURGESS (1917–1993)

The unconscious is the ocean of the unsayable, of what has been expelled from the land of language, removed as a result of ancient prohibitions.
ITALO CALVINO (1923–1985)

Every extension of knowledge arises from making the conscious the unconscious.
FRIEDRICH NIETZSCHE (1844–1900)

Our life is composed greatly from dreams, from the unconscious, and they must be brought into connection with action. They must be woven together.
ANAÏS NIN (1903–1977)

I paint what cannot be photographed, that which comes from the imagination or from dreams, or from an unconscious drive.
MAN RAY (1890–1976)

Underground

What was once underground is now coming to the surface.
GAVIN BRYARS (1943–)

I don't think anything's underground anymore. And I think that's a good thing. Everything is up for grabs.
COLIN GREENWOOD (1969–)

Underground literature only began in the '70s, when technical developments made it possible. Before that, we were involved in a game with the censors. That was our struggle.
RYSZARD KAPUSCINSKI (1932–)

So it's like the underground world no longer exists economically, 'cause they're not giving money back to their supporting artists.
KOOL KEITH (1964–)

There's a lot more hypocrisy than before. Racism has gone back underground.
RICHARD PRYOR (1940–2005)

Understanding

Courage is just fear, plus prayers, plus understanding.
EDWARD ALBERT (1951–)

Seek not to understand that you may believe, but believe that you may understand.
SAINT AUGUSTINE (354–430)

It is by universal misunderstanding that all agree. For if, by ill luck, people understood each other, they would never agree.
CHARLES BAUDELAIRE (1821–1867)

The world only goes round by misunderstanding.
CHARLES BAUDELAIRE (1821–1867)

To seek understanding before taking action, yet to trust my instincts when action is called for. Never to avoid danger from fear, never to seek out danger for its own sake. Never to conform to fashion from fear of eccentricity, never to be eccentric from fear of conformity.
STEVEN BRUST (1955–)

If scientific reasoning were limited to the logical processes of arithmetic, we should not get very far in our understanding of the physical world. One might as well attempt to grasp the game of poker entirely by the use of the mathematics of probability.
VANNEVAR BUSH (1890–1974)

A blind man knows he cannot see, and is glad to be led, though it be by a dog; but he that is blind in his understanding, which is the worst blindness of all, believes he sees as the best, and scorns a guide.
SAMUEL BUTLER (1835–1902)

Imagination is a poor matter when it has to part company with understanding.
THOMAS CARLYLE (1795–1881)

No person was ever rightly understood until they had been first regarded with a certain feeling, not of tolerance, but of sympathy.
THOMAS CARLYLE (1795–1881)

If you do not understand a man you cannot crush him. And if you do understand him, very probably you will not.
G. K. CHESTERTON (1874–1936)

People in high life are hardened to the wants and distresses of mankind as surgeons are to their bodily pains.
G. K. CHESTERTON (1874–1936)

We obviously need more love in the world. And we obviously need more compassion and understanding. Our leaders need to really address these issues properly now.
DAVE DAVIES (1947–)

Our understanding is correlative to our perception.
ROBERT DELAUNAY (1885–1941)

The fact that you are willing to say, "I do not understand, and it is fine," is the greatest understanding you could exhibit.
WAYNE D. DYER (1940–)

Great spirits have always encountered opposition from mediocre minds. The mediocre mind is incapable of understanding the man who refuses to bow blindly to conventional prejudices and chooses instead to express his opinions courageously and honestly.
ALBERT EINSTEIN (1879–1955)

The most incomprehensible thing about the world is that it is comprehensible.
ALBERT EINSTEIN (1879–1955)

The qualities of a great man are vision, integrity, courage, understanding, the power of articulation, and profundity of character.
DWIGHT D. EISENHOWER (1890–1969)

It is better to understand a little than to misunderstand a lot.
ANATOLE FRANCE (1844–1924)

It is well to give when asked but it is better to give unasked, through understanding.
KAHLIL GIBRAN (1883–1931)

So long as you live and work, you will be misunderstood; to that you must resign yourself once and for all. Be silent!
JOHANN WOLFGANG VON GOETHE (1749–1832)

The man of understanding finds everything laughable.
JOHANN WOLFGANG VON GOETHE (1749–1832)

To know someone here or there with whom you can feel there is understanding in spite of distances or thoughts expressed—That can make life a garden.
JOHANN WOLFGANG VON GOETHE (1749–1832)

Whatever you cannot understand, you cannot possess.
JOHANN WOLFGANG VON GOETHE (1749–1832)

The thing is plain. All that men really understand, is confined to a very small compass; to their daily affairs and experience; to what they have an opportunity to know, and motives to study or practice. The rest is affectation and imposture.
WILLIAM HAZLITT (1778–1830)

Much learning does not teach understanding.
HERACLITUS (C. 535–475 BC)

Understanding is nothing else than conception caused by speech.
THOMAS HOBBES (1588–1679)

A man who pretends to understand women is bad manners. For him to really to understand them is bad morals.
HENRY JAMES (1843–1916)

Sir, I have found you an argument; but I am not obliged to find you an understanding.
SAMUEL JOHNSON (1709–1784)

Everything that irritates us about others can lead us to an understanding of ourselves.
CARL JUNG (1875–1961)

I do not want the peace which passeth understanding, I want the understanding which bringeth peace.
HELEN KELLER (1880–1968)

Nothing can be loved or hated unless it is first known.
LEONARDO DA VINCI (1452–1519)

The noblest pleasure is the joy of understanding.
LEONARDO DA VINCI (1452–1519)

What else is love but understanding and rejoicing in the fact that another person lives, acts, and experiences otherwise than we do…?
FRIEDRICH NIETZSCHE (1844–1900)

Language is the source of misunderstandings.
ANTOINE DE SAINT-EXUPÉRY (1900–1944)

It is difficult to get a man to understand something when his job depends on not understanding it.
UPTON SINCLAIR (1878–1968)

Do not weep; do not wax indignant. Understand.
BENEDICT DE SPINOZA (1632–1677)

We pass the word around; we ponder how the case is put by different people, we read the poetry; we meditate over the literature; we play the music; we change our minds; we reach an understanding. Society evolves this way, not by shouting each other down, but by the unique capacity of unique, individual human beings to comprehend each other.
LEWIS THOMAS (1913–1993), *The Medusa and the Snail*

Unemployment

Unemployment is capitalism's way of getting you to plant a garden.
ORSON SCOTT CARD (1951–)

If you've got unemployment, low pay, that was just too bad. But that was the system. That was the sort of economy and philosophy against which I was fighting in the 1930s.
BARBARA CASTLE (1910–2002)

More people out of work leads to higher unemployment.`
CALVIN COOLIDGE (1872–1933)

Unemployment is of vital importance, particularly to the unemployed.
EDWARD HEATH (1916–2005)

Any degree of unemployment worries me.
GERHARD SCHRODER (1944–)

The effects of unemployment are particularly harmful when it is concentrated on a small percentage of the labor force, with consequent increases in crime and delinquency and disruptions of family life, rather than expressing itself as, say, an extra three weeks vacation for everybody.
WILLIAM VICKREY (1914–1996)

Unhappiness

Happiness is always a by-product. It is probably a matter of temperament, and for anything I know it may be glandular. But it is not something that can be demanded from life, and if you are not happy you had better stop worrying about it and see what treasures you can pluck from your own brand of unhappiness.
ROBERTSON DAVIES (1913–1995)

Unhappiness in a child accumulates because he sees no end to the dark tunnel. The thirteen weeks of a term might just as well be thirteen years.
GRAHAM GREENE (1904–1991)

I am more and more convinced that our happiness or unhappiness depends more on the way we meet the events of life than on the nature of those events themselves.
ALEXANDER VON HUMBOLDT (1769–1859)

Happiness is the interval between periods of unhappiness.
DON MARQUIS (1878–1937)

If there were in the world today any large number of people who desired their own happiness more than they desired the unhappiness of others, we could have paradise in a few years.
BERTRAND RUSSELL (1872–1970)

There is nothing in the world so much admired as a man who knows how to bear unhappiness with courage.
SENECA (5 BC–AD 65)

Uniqueness

I want all my senses engaged. Let me absorb the world's variety and uniqueness.
MAYA ANGELOU (1928–)

Mom always tells me to celebrate everyone's uniqueness.
HILARY DUFF (1987–)

The Paleolithic hunters who painted the unsurpassed animal murals on the ceiling of the cave at Altamira had only rudimentary tools. Art is older than production for use, and play older than work. Man was shaped less by what he had to do than by what he did in playful moments. It is the child in man that is the source of his uniqueness and creativeness, and the playground is the optimal milieu for the unfolding of his capacities.
ERIC HOFFER (1902–1983)

While we have the gift of life, it seems to me that the only tragedy is to allow part of us to die—whether it is our spirit, our creativity, or our glorious uniqueness.
GILDA RADNER (1946–1989)

Unity

We are totally committed to ending partition and to creating the conditions for unity and independence [of Ireland].
GERRY ADAMS (1948–)

United we stand; divided we fall.
AESOP (620–560 BC)

The human mind, if it is to keep its sanity, must maintain the nicest balance between unity and plurality.
IRVING BABBITT (1865–1933)

So powerful is the light of unity that it can illuminate the whole earth.
BAHA'U'LLAH (1817–1892)

Unity in things Necessary, Liberty in things Unnecessary, and Charity in all.
RICHARD BAXTER (1615–1691)

He who experiences the unity of life sees his own Self in all beings, and all beings in his own Self, and looks on everything with an impartial eye.
THE BUDDHA (563–483 BC)

Unity can only be manifested by the Binary. Unity itself and the idea of Unity are already two.
THE BUDDHA (563–483 BC)

What ever disunites man from God, also disunites man from man.
EDMUND BURKE (1729–1797)

We now know that unity, the cornerstone of Canada's greatness and prosperity, is above all a matter of emotion and reason for every citizen.
KIM CAMPBELL (1947–)

Men's hearts ought not to be set against one another, but set with one another, and all against evil only.
THOMAS CARLYLE (1795–1881)

The great unity which true science seeks is found only by beginning with our knowledge of God, and

coming down from Him along the stream of causation to every fact and event that affects us.
HOWARD CROSBY (1826–1891)

Damn your principals. Stick to your Party!
BENJAMIN DISRAELI (1804–1881)

Do not follow the ideas of others, but learn to listen to the voice within yourself. Your body and mind will become clear and you will realize the unity of all things.
DOGEN (1200–1253)

We must all hang together, or assuredly we shall all hang separately.
BENJAMIN FRANKLIN (1706–1790)

Unity to be real must stand the severest strain without breaking.
MAHATMA GANDHI (1869–1948)

If we want unity, we must all be unifiers. If we want accountability, each of us must be accountable for all we do.
CHRISTINE GREGOIRE (1947–)

For the strength of the Pack is the Wolf, and the strength of the Wolf is the Pack.
RUDYARD KIPLING (1865–1936)

A house divided against itself cannot stand—I believe this government cannot endure permanently half slave and half free.
ABRAHAM LINCOLN (1809–1865)

The workers of the world have nothing to lose, but their chains. Workers of the world unite.
KARL MARX (1818–1883)

The essence of the beautiful is unity in variety.
W. SOMERSET MAUGHAM (1874–1965)

At bottom every man knows well enough that he is a unique being, only once on this earth; and by no extraordinary chance will such a marvelously picturesque piece of diversity in unity as he is, ever be put together a second time.
FRIEDRICH NIETZSCHE (1844–1900)

Any unity which doesn't have its origin in the multitudes is tyranny.
BLAISE PASCAL (1623–1662)

The multitude which is not brought to act as a unity, is confusion. That unity which has not its origin in the multitude is tyranny.
BLAISE PASCAL (1623–1662)

I know that my unity with all people cannot be destroyed by national boundaries and government orders.
LEO TOLSTOY (1828–1910)

Unity of the different forces and particles is achieved because they all come from different kinds of vibrations of the same basic string.
EDWARD WITTEN (1951–)

The Universe

In the beginning the Universe was created. This has made a lot of people very angry and has been widely regarded as a bad move.
DOUGLAS ADAMS (1952–2001)

There is a theory which states that if ever anybody discovers exactly what the Universe is for and why it is here, it will instantly disappear and be replaced by something even more bizarre and inexplicable. There is another theory which states that this has already happened.
DOUGLAS ADAMS (1952–2001)

The creator of the universe works in mysterious ways. But he uses a base-ten counting system and likes round numbers.
SCOTT ADAMS (1957–)

I'm astounded by people who want to "know" the universe when it's hard enough to find your way around Chinatown.
WOODY ALLEN (1935–)

I cannot believe that the inscrutable universe turns on an axis of suffering; surely the strange beauty of the world must somewhere rest on pure joy!
LOUISE BOGAN (1897–1970)

Wonder is what sets us apart from other life forms. No other species wonders about the meaning of existence or the complexity of the universe or themselves.
HERBERT W. BOYER (1936–)

We are an impossibility in an impossible universe.
RAY BRADBURY (1920–)

Humor is just another defense against the universe.
MEL BROOKS (1926–)

It's important that someone celebrate our existence.... People are the only mirror we have to see ourselves in. The domain of all meaning. All virtue, all evil, are contained only in people. There is none in the universe at large. Solitary confinement is a punishment in every human culture.
LOIS MCMASTER BUJOLD (1949–), *Mirror Dance*

If it's true that our species is alone in the universe, then I'd have to say that the universe aimed rather low and settled for very little.
GEORGE CARLIN (1937–)

Programming today is a race between software engineers striving to build bigger and better idiot-proof programs, and the Universe trying to produce bigger and better idiots. So far, the Universe is winning.
RICK COOK (1944–), *The Wizardry Compiled*

The universe we observe has precisely the properties we should expect if there is, at bottom, no design, no purpose, no evil, no good, nothing but blind, pitiless indifference.
CHARLES DARWIN (1809–1882)

Not only is the universe stranger than we imagine, it is stranger than we can imagine.
SIR ARTHUR EDDINGTON (1882–1944)

A human being is part of a whole, called by us the Universe, a part limited in time and space. He experiences himself, his thoughts and feelings, as something separated from the rest, a kind of optical delusion of his consciousness. This delusion is a kind of prison for us, restricting us to our personal desires and to affection for a few persons nearest us. Our task must be to free ourselves from this prison by widening our circles of compassion to embrace all living creatures and the whole of nature in its beauty.
ALBERT EINSTEIN (1879–1955)

Only two things are infinite, the universe and human stupidity, and I'm not sure about the former.
ALBERT EINSTEIN (1879–1955)

The two most common elements in the universe are hydrogen and stupidity.
HARLAN ELLISON (1934–)

If I have lost confidence in myself, I have the universe against me.
RALPH WALDO EMERSON (1803–1882)

Technology is a way of organizing the universe so that man doesn't have to experience it.
MAX FRISCH (1911–1991)

Everything you've learned in school as "obvious" becomes less and less obvious as you begin to study the universe. For example, there are no solids in the universe. There's not even a suggestion of a solid. There are no absolute continuums. There are no surfaces. There are no straight lines.
R. BUCKMINSTER FULLER (1895–1983)

The universe will reward you for taking risks on its behalf.
SHAKTI GAWAIN (1948–)

Well: what we gain by science is, after all, sadness, as the Preacher saith. The more we know of the laws and nature of the Universe the more ghastly a business we perceive it all to be—and the non-necessity of it.
THOMAS HARDY (1840–1928)

No storyteller has ever been able to dream up anything as fantastically unlikely as what really does happen in this mad Universe.
ROBERT A. HEINLEIN (1907–1988), *The Notebooks of Lazarus Long*

At the height of laughter, the universe is flung into a kaleidoscope of new possibilities.
JEAN HOUSTON (1939–)

There is a coherent plan in the universe, though I don't know what it's a plan for.
FRED HOYLE (1915–2001)

There's only one corner of the universe you can be certain of improving, and that's your own self.
ALDOUS HUXLEY (1894–1963)

My theology, briefly, is that the universe was dictated but not signed.
CHRISTOPHER MORLEY (1890–1957)

There is but one temple in the universe and that is the body of man.
NOVALIS (1772–1801)

The universe, they said, depended for its operation on the balance of four forces, which they identified as charm, persuasion, uncertainty and bloody-mindedness.
TERRY PRATCHETT (1948–)

The universe is made of stories, not of atoms.
MURIEL RUKEYSER (1913–1980)

In the part of this universe that we know, there is great injustice, and often the good suffer, and often the wicked prosper, and one hardly knows which of those is the more annoying.
BERTRAND RUSSELL (1872–1970)

The universe may have a purpose, but nothing we know suggests that, if so, this purpose has any similarity to ours.
BERTRAND RUSSELL (1872–1970)

If you want to make an apple pie from scratch, you must first create the universe.
CARL SAGAN (1934–1996)

It is far better to grasp the Universe as it really is than to persist in delusion, however satisfying and reassuring.
CARL SAGAN (1934–1996)

Go confidently in the direction of your dreams! Live the life you've imagined. As you simplify your life, the laws of the universe will be simpler.
HENRY DAVID THOREAU (1817–1862)

In answer to the question of why it happened, I offer the modest proposal that our Universe is simply one of those things which happens from time to time.
EDWARD P. TYRON (1809–1894)

The universe is a big place, perhaps the biggest.
KURT VONNEGUT JR. (1922–2007)

Sometimes I think the surest sign that intelligent life exists elsewhere in the universe is that none of it has tried to contact us.
BILL WATTERSON (1958–)

The effort to understand the universe is one of the very few things that lifts human life a little above the level of farce, and gives it some of the grace of tragedy.
STEVEN WEINBERG (1933–)

Universities

In places like universities, where everyone talks too rationally, it is necessary for a kind of enchanter to appear.
JOSEPH BEUYS (1921–1986)

Criticism in the universities, I'll have to admit, has entered a phase where I am totally out of sympathy with 95% of what goes on. It's Stalinism without Stalin.
HAROLD BLOOM (1930–)

During the days of segregation, there was not a place of higher learning for African Americans. They were simply not welcome in many of the traditional schools. And from this backward policy grew the network of historical black colleges and universities.
MICHAEL N. CASTLE (1939–)

Let's not burn the universities yet. After all, the damage they do might be worse.
H. L. MENCKEN (1880–1956)

They teach anything in universities today. You can major in mud pies.
ORSON WELLES (1915–1985)

Uselessness

Natural amiableness is too often seen in company with sloth, with uselessness, with the vanity of fashionable life.
SAMUEL BUTLER (1835–1902)

Most of our assumptions have outlived their uselessness.
MARSHALL MCLUHAN (1911–1980)

What is the matter with the poor is poverty; what is the matter with the rich is uselessness.
GEORGE BERNARD SHAW (1856–1950)

Utilitarianism

[N]aive utilitarianism can do considerable social damage; and moral rules are required under a variety of circumstances.
HERMAN KAHN (1922–1983)

I'm a Utilitarian, so I don't see the rule against lying as absolute; it's always subject to some overriding utility which may prevent its exercise.
PETER SINGER (1946–)

Utility

The pain of dispute exceeds, by much, its utility. All disputation makes the mind deaf, and when people are deaf I am dumb.
JOSEPH JOUBERT (1754–1824)

Utility is when you have one telephone, luxury is when you have two, opulence is when you have three—and paradise is when you have none.
DOUG LARSON (1902–1981)

Nothing can have value without being an object of utility.
KARL MARX (1818–1883)

Utility is the great idol of the age, to which all powers must do service and all talents swear allegiance.
FRIEDRICH VON SCHILLER (1759–1805)

The difference between utility and utility plus beauty is the difference between telephone wires and the spider web.
EDWIN TEALE (1899–1980)

The architect should strive continually to simplify; the ensemble of the rooms should then be carefully considered that comfort and utility may go hand in hand with beauty.
FRANK LLOYD WRIGHT (1869–1959)

Utopia

In the modern world, in which thousands of people are dying every hour as a consequence of politics, no writing anywhere can begin to be credible unless it is informed by political awareness and principles. Writers who have neither produce utopian trash.
JOHN BERGER (1926–)

There is nothing like dream to create the future. Utopia today, flesh and blood tomorrow.
VICTOR HUGO (1802–1885), *Les Miserables*

Utopia would seem to offer the spectacle of one of those rare phenomena whose concept is indistinguishable from its reality, whose ontology coincides with its representation.
FREDRIC JAMESON (1934–)

Literature is my Utopia. Here I am not disenfranchised. No barrier of the senses shuts me out from the sweet, gracious discourses of my book friends. They talk to me without embarrassment or awkwardness.
HELEN KELLER (1880–1968)

Human beings will be happier—not when they cure cancer or get to Mars or eliminate racial prejudice or flush Lake Erie, but when they find ways to inhabit primitive communities again. That's my utopia.
KURT VONNEGUT JR. (1922–2007)

A map of the world that does not include Utopia is not worth even glancing at, for it leaves out the one country at which Humanity is always landing.
OSCAR WILDE (1854–1900)

Vacations

On vacations: We hit the sunny beaches where we occupy ourselves keeping the sun off our skin, the saltwater off our bodies, and the sand out of our belongings.
ERMA BOMBECK (1927–1996)

Your kids inevitably want to move where they had their vacations when they were younger.
JIM HARRISON (1937–)

I hate vacations. If you can build buildings, why sit on the beach?
PHILIP JOHNSON (1906–2005)

Vacation used to be a luxury, however, in today's world, it has become a necessity.
ANONYMOUS

Valor

Valor lies just halfway between rashness and cowardice.
MIGUEL DE CERVANTES (1547–1616)

Perfect Valor is to do, without a witness, all that we could do before the whole world.
FRANÇOIS DE LA ROCHEFOUCAULD (1613–1680)

Valor is stability, not of legs and arms, but of courage and the soul.
MICHEL DE MONTAIGNE (1533–1592)

Valor grows by daring, fear by holding back.
PUBLILIUS SYRUS (C. 100 BC)

Valor is a gift. Those having it never know for sure whether they have it till the test comes. And those having it in one test never know for sure if they will have it when the next test comes.
CARL SANDBURG (1878–1967)

Valor is common but great souls are rare.
BERNARD JOSEPH SAURIN (1706–1781)

Valor is superior to number.
FLAVIUS RENATUS VEGETIUS (C. 375)

Value

Men value things in three ways: as useful, as pleasant or sources of pleasure, and as excellent, or as intrinsically admirable or honorable.
MORTIMER ADLER (1902–2001)

Believe nothing, no matter where you read it, or who said it, no matter if I have said it, unless it agrees with your own reason and your own common sense.
THE BUDDHA (563–483 BC)

The three most important things a man has are, briefly, his private parts, his money, and his religious opinions.
SAMUEL BUTLER (1835–1902)

That which costs little is less valued.
MIGUEL DE CERVANTES (1547–1616)

You will be as much value to others as you have been to yourself.
CICERO (106–43 BC)

Teach us that wealth is not elegance, that profusion is not magnificence, that splendor is not beauty.
BENJAMIN DISRAELI (1804–1881)

We do not know the true value of our moments until they have undergone the test of memory.
GEORGES DUHAMEL (1884–1966)

All that is valuable in human society depends upon the opportunity for development accorded the individual.
ALBERT EINSTEIN (1879–1955)

Not everything that can be counted counts, and not everything that counts can be counted.
ALBERT EINSTEIN (1879–1955)

Try not to become a man of success but rather try to become a man of value.
ALBERT EINSTEIN (1879–1955)

The value of a principle is the number of things it will explain; and there is no good theory of disease which does not at once suggest a cure.
RALPH WALDO EMERSON (1803–1882)

Too many people overvalue what they are not and undervalue what they are.
MALCOLM S. FORBES (1919–1990)

I conceive that the great part of the miseries of mankind are brought upon them by false estimates they have made of the value of things.
BENJAMIN FRANKLIN (1706–1790)

One man's compost is another man's potpourri.
THEODOR SUESS GEISEL (1904–1991), *How the Grinch Stole Christmas*

The least pain in our little finger gives us more concern and uneasiness than the destruction of millions of our fellow-beings.
WILLIAM HAZLITT (1778–1830)

The longer we live the more we think and the higher the value we put on friendship and tenderness towards parents and friends.
SAMUEL JOHNSON (1709–1784)

Every time a value is born, existence takes on a new meaning; every time one dies, some part of that meaning passes away
JOSEPH WOOD KRUTCH (1893–1970)

Nothing can have value without being an object of utility.
KARL MARX (1818–1883)

We may define therapy as a search for value.
ABRAHAM MASLOW (1908–1970)

What we obtain too cheap we esteem too little; it is dearness only that gives everything value.
THOMAS PAINE (1737–1809)

People exaggerate the value of things they haven't got: everybody worships truth and unselfishness because they have no experience with them.
GEORGE BERNARD SHAW (1856–1950)

The real price of everything, what everything really costs to the man who wants to acquire it, is the toil and trouble of acquiring it.
ADAM SMITH (1723–1790)

What you risk reveals what you value.
JEANETTE WINTERSON (1959–)

Values

Don't let your special character and values, the secret that you know and no one else does, the truth—don't let that get swallowed up by the great chewing complacency.
AESOP (620–560 BC)

Authentic values are those by which a life can be lived, which can form a people that produces great deeds and thoughts.
ALLAN BLOOM (1930–1992)

The values by which we are to survive are not rules for just and unjust conduct, but are those deeper illuminations in whose light justice and injustice, good and evil, means and ends are seen in fearful sharpness of outline.
JACOB BRONOWSKI (1908–1974)

Some values are like sugar on the doughnut, legitimate, desirable, but insufficient, apart from the doughnut itself. We need substance as well as frosting.
RALPH T. FLEWELLING (1871–1960)

The resulting corruption of values is far advanced, but to fathom its hold, we have to understand that people have surrendered for the sake of their own benefits—not in order to line the pockets of the moguls, though there is no massive objection to lining those pockets in the process.
TODD GITLIN (1943–)

Values are not trendy items that are casually traded in.
ELLEN GOODMAN (1941–)

Humanistic values of equality and equal rights for all nations and individuals as crystallized in the principles of the United Nations Charter are mankind's great achievements in the 20th century.
TRAN DUC LUONG (1937–)

Values are principles and ideas that bring meaning to the seemingly mundane experience of life. A meaningful life that ultimately brings happiness and pride requires you to respond to temptations as well as challenges with honor, dignity, and courage.
LAURA SCHLESSINGER (1947–)

Moral values, and a culture and a religion, maintaining these values are far better than laws and regulations.
SWAMI SIVANANDA (1887–1963)

Some values must be universal, like human rights and the equal worth of every human being.
BJÖRN ULVAEUS (1945–)

Vampires

There are two levels of vampirism: one is the regular vampire, which is just like it has always been; and then there's the super vampires, which are a new breed we've created.
GUILLERMO DEL TORO (1964–)

Vampires to me have always been very sexy.
STEPHEN DORFF (1973–)

Vampires are sexy to a woman perhaps because the fantasy is similar to that of the man on the white horse sweeping her off to paradise.
FRANK LANGELLA (1940–)

The vampires have always been metaphors for me. They've always been vehicles through which I can express things I have felt very, very deeply.
ANNE RICE (1941–)

There are such beings as vampires, some of us have evidence that they exist. Even had we not the proof of our own unhappy experience, the teachings and the records of the past give proof enough for sane peoples.
BRAM STOKER (1847–1912)

Vanity

Vanity and pride are different things, though the words are often used synonymously. A person may be proud without being vain. Pride relates more to our opinion of ourselves; vanity, to what we would have others think of us.
JANE AUSTEN (1775–1817)

Pampered vanity is a better thing perhaps than starved pride.
JOANNA BAILLIE (1762–1851)

The only cure for vanity is laughter, and the only fault that is laughable is vanity.
HENRI BERGSON (1859–1941)

The truest characters of ignorance are vanity, and pride and arrogance.
SAMUEL BUTLER (1835–1902)

Vanity is as ill at ease under indifference as tenderness is under a love which it cannot return.
GEORGE ELIOT (1819–1880)

Stupidity talks, vanity acts.
VICTOR HUGO (1802–1885)

Pride does not wish to owe and vanity does not wish to pay.
FRANÇOIS DE LA ROCHEFOUCAULD (1613–1680)

Virtue would go far if vanity did not keep it company.
FRANÇOIS DE LA ROCHEFOUCAULD (1613–1680)

Our vanity is hardest to wound precisely when our pride has just been wounded.
FRIEDRICH NIETZSCHE (1844–1900)

Vanity dies hard; in some obstinate cases it outlives the man.
ROBERT LOUIS STEVENSON (1850–1894)

Our vanity is the constant enemy of our dignity.
ANNE SOPHIE SWETCHINE (1782–1857)

The surest cure for vanity is loneliness.
TOM WOLFE (1931–)

Vegetarianism

When I meet vegetarians who might have diabetes, pre-diabetes or massive obesity, I tell them they would be better off if they gave up their vegetarianism.
ROBERT ATKINS (1930–2003)

[V]egetarianism alone can give us the quality of compassion, which distinguishes man from the rest of the animal world.
MORARJI DESAI (1896–1995)

Most vegetarians look so much like the food they eat that they can be classified as cannibals.
FINLEY PETER DUNNE (1867–1936)

Nothing will benefit human health and increase the chances for survival of life on Earth as much as the evolution to a vegetarian diet.
ALBERT EINSTEIN (1879–1955)

Vegetarianism is a link to perfection and peace.
RIVER PHOENIX (1970–1993)

Vengeance

Deep vengeance is the daughter of deep silence.
VITTORIO ALFIERI (1749–1803)

Vengeance is not the point; change is. But the trouble is that in most people's minds the thought of victory and the thought of punishing the enemy coincide.
BARBARA DEMING (1917–1984)

Revenge is an act of passion; vengeance of justice. Injuries are revenged; crimes are avenged.
SAMUEL JOHNSON (1709–1784)

On wrongs swift vengeance waits.
ALEXANDER POPE (1688–1744)

Vice

Prosperity discovers vice, adversity discovers virtue.
SIR FRANCIS BACON (1561–1626)

It is good to be without vices, but it is not good to be without temptations.
WALTER BAGEHOT (1826–1877), *Biographical Studies*

Here's a rule I recommend: Never practice two vices at once.
TALLULAH BANKHEAD (1903–1968)

Alas, human vices, however horrible one might imagine them to be, contain the proof (were it only in their infinite expansion) of man's longing for the infinite; but it is a longing that often takes the wrong route. It is my belief that the reason behind all culpable excesses lies in this depravation of the sense of the infinite.
CHARLES BAUDELAIRE (1821–1867)

Half the vices which the world condemns most loudly have seeds of good in them and require moderated use rather than total abstinence.
SAMUEL BUTLER (1835–1902)

The function of vice is to keep virtue within reasonable bounds.
SAMUEL BUTLER (1835–1902)

Every day confirms my opinion on the superiority of a vicious life—and if Virtue is not its own reward I don't know any other stipend annexed to it.
LORD BYRON (1788–1824)

Let them show me a cottage where there are not the same vices of which they accuse the courts.
LORD CHESTERFIELD (1694–1773)

Vice, in its true light, is so deformed, that it shocks us at first sight; and would hardly ever seduce us, if it did not at first wear the mask of some virtue.
LORD CHESTERFIELD (1694–1773)

It is a great thing to know our vices.
CICERO (106–43 BC)

Think no vice so small that you may commit it, and no virtue so small that you may over look it.
CONFUCIUS (551–479 BC)

The greatest minds are capable of the greatest vices as well as of the greatest virtues.
RENÉ DESCARTES (1596–1650), *Le discours de la methode*

Vices are sometimes only virtues carried to excess!
CHARLES DICKENS (1812–1870)

As far as I'm concerned, I prefer silent vice to ostentatious virtue.
ALBERT EINSTEIN (1879–1955)

What's vice today may be virtue tomorrow.
HENRY FIELDING (1707–1754)

Search others for their virtues, thyself for thy vices.
BENJAMIN FRANKLIN (1706–1790)

Vice knows that she is ugly, so she puts on her mask.
BENJAMIN FRANKLIN (1706–1790)

A portion of mankind take pride in their vices and pursue their purpose; many more waver between doing what is right and complying with what is wrong.
HORACE (65–8 BC)

The disgrace of others often keeps tender minds from vice.
HORACE (65–8 BC)

Most vices demand considerable self-sacrifices. There is no greater mistake than to suppose that a vicious life is a life of uninterrupted pleasure. It is a life almost as wearisome and painful—if strenuously led—as Christian's in *The Pilgrim's Progress*.
ALDOUS HUXLEY (1894–1963)

Most virtues when carried beyond certain bonds degenerate into vices.
THOMAS JEFFERSON (1762–1826)

If he really thinks there is no distinction between vice and virtue, when he leaves our houses let us count our spoons.
SAMUEL JOHNSON (1709–1784)

We do not despise all those who have vices, but we do despise those that have no virtue.
FRANÇOIS DE LA ROCHEFOUCAULD (1613–1680)

It has been my experience that folks who have no vices have very few virtues.
ABRAHAM LINCOLN (1809–1865)

A prince must be prudent enough to know how to escape the bad reputation of those vices that would lose the state for him, and must protect himself from those that will not lose it for him, if this is possible; but if he cannot, he need not concern himself unduly if he ignores these less serious vices.
NICCOLÒ MACHIAVELLI (1469–1527)

I prefer an interesting vice to a virtue that bores.
MOLIÈRE (1622–1673)

Nothing is as certain as that the vices of leisure are gotten rid of by being busy.
SENECA (5 BC–AD 65)

What were once vices are the fashion of the day.
SENECA (5 BC–AD 65)

Why do people not confess vices? It is because they have not yet laid them aside. It is a waking person only who can tell their dreams.
SENECA (5 BC–AD 65)

The gods are just, and of our pleasant vices
Make instruments to plague us…
WILLIAM SHAKESPEARE (1564–1616), *King Lear*

The problem with people who have no vices is that generally you can be pretty sure they're going to have some pretty annoying virtues.
ELIZABETH TAYLOR (1932–)

I have not a particle of confidence in a man who has no redeeming vices.
MARK TWAIN (1835–1910)

Time, which alone makes the reputation of men, ends by making their defects respectable.
VOLTAIRE (1694–1778)

Victimization

It is a very rare man who does not victimize the helpless.
JAMES ARTHUR BALDWIN (1924–1987)

We live in a society of victimization, where people are much more comfortable being victimized than actually standing up for themselves.
MARILYN MANSON (1969–)

Victory

One of the greatest victories you can gain over someone is to beat him at politeness.
JOSH BILLINGS (1818–1885)

If you believe in yourself and have dedication and pride, and never quit, you'll be a winner. The price of victory is high but so are the rewards.
PAUL "BEAR" BRYANT (1913–1983)

Endurance is one of the most difficult disciplines, but it is to the one who endures that the final victory comes.
THE BUDDHA (563–483 BC)

Exile, for no other motive than ease, would be the last defeat, with no seed of future victory in it.
LOIS MCMASTER BUJOLD (1949–)

There are always survivors at a massacre. Among the victors, if nowhere else.
LOIS MCMASTER BUJOLD (1949–)

Any coward can fight a battle when he's sure of winning, but give me the man who has pluck to fight when he's sure of losing. That's my way, sir; and there are many victories worse than a defeat.
GEORGE ELIOT (1819–1880)

Victory attained by violence is tantamount to a defeat, for it is momentary.
MAHATMA GANDHI (1869–1948)

We improve ourselves by victories over ourself. There must be contests, and you must win.
EDWARD GIBBON (1737–1794)

A mind troubled by doubt cannot focus on the course to victory.
ARTHUR GOLDEN (1956–)

Arms are instruments of ill omen.... When one is compelled to use them, it is best to do so without relish. There is no glory in victory, and to glorify it despite this is to exult in the killing of men.... When great numbers of people are killed, one should weep over them with sorrow. When victorious in war, one should observe mourning rites.
LAO-TZU (C. 600 BC)

Beware of rashness, but with energy, and sleepless vigilance, go forward and give us victories.
ABRAHAM LINCOLN (1809–1865)

Force is all-conquering, but its victories are short-lived.
ABRAHAM LINCOLN (1809–1865)

Be ashamed to die until you have won some victory for humanity.
HORACE MANN (1796–1859)

The secret of all victory lies in the organization of the non-obvious.
MARCUS AURELIUS ANTONINUS (121–180)

Victory belongs to the most persevering.
NAPOLÉON I (1769–1821)

The moment of victory is much too short to live for that and nothing else.
MARTINA NAVRATILOVA (1956–)

Accept challenges, so that you may feel the exhilaration of victory.
GEORGE S. PATTON (1885–1945)

Those who know how to win are much more numerous than those who know how to make proper use of their victories.
POLYBIUS (205–118 BC), *History*

Another such victory over the Romans, and we are undone.
PYRRHUS (319–272 BC)

Far better it is to dare mighty things, to win glorious triumphs even though checkered by failure, than to rank with those poor spirits who neither enjoy nor suffer much because they live in the gray twilight that knows neither victory nor defeat.
THEODORE ROOSEVELT (1858–1919)

Be careful that victories do not carry the seed of future defeats.
RALPH W. SOCKMAN (1889–1970)

The best victory is when the opponent surrenders of its own accord before there are any actual hostilities.... It is best to win without fighting.
SUN-TZU (C. 544–496 BC), *The Art of War*

Victorious warriors win first and then go to war, while defeated warriors go to war first and then seek to win.
SUN-TZU (C. 544–496 BC), *The Art of War*

Victory goes to the player who makes the next-to-last mistake.
SAVIELLY GRIGORIEVITCH TARTAKOWER (1887–1956)

Vigilance

When good people in any country cease their vigilance and struggle, then evil men prevail.
PEARL S. BUCK (1892–1973)

Eternal vigilance is the price of liberty.
JOHN PHILPOT CURRAN (1750–1817)

To prevent evil is the great end of government, the end for which vigilance and severity are properly employed.
SAMUEL JOHNSON (1709–1784)

I sometimes think that the price of liberty is not so much eternal vigilance as eternal dirt.
GEORGE ORWELL (1903–1950)

Eternal vigilance is the price of liberty; power is ever stealing from the many to give to the few.
WENDELL PHILLIPS (1811–1884)

In the stress of modern life, how little room is left for that most comfortable vanity that whispers in our ears that failures are not faults! Now we are taught from infancy that we must rise or fall upon our own merits; that vigilance wins success, and incapacity means ruin.
AGNES REPPLIER (1855–1950)

Villains

Villains are very, very boring to do. They're so much easier than heroes.
JEREMY BRETT (1933–1995)

I like villains because there's something so attractive about a committed person—they have a plan, an ideology, no matter how twisted. They're motivated.
RUSSELL CROWE (1964–)

The world needs heroes, and it's better they be harmless men like me than villains like Hitler.
ALBERT EINSTEIN (1879–1955)

Villains never know they are villains in a picture, so I play this like I'm the nicest guy in the world.
WAYNE ROGERS (1933–)

One may smile, and smile, and be a villain.
WILLIAM SHAKESPEARE (1564–1616), *Hamlet*

Violence

There are more pleasant things to do than beat up people.
MUHAMMAD ALI (1942–)

Power and violence are opposites; where the one rules absolutely, the other is absent. Violence appears where power is in jeopardy, but left to its own course it ends in power's disappearance.
HANNAH ARENDT (1906–1975)

Violence is the last refuge of the incompetent.
ISAAC ASIMOV (1920–1992)

The only thing that's been a worse flop than the organization of non-violence has been the organization of violence.
JOAN BAEZ (1941–)

Hungry people cannot be good at learning or producing anything, except perhaps violence.
PEARL BAILEY (1918–1990)

Violence does even justice unjustly.
THOMAS ENGLISH CARLYLE (1795–1881)

Violence has no constitutional sanction; and every government from the beginning has moved against it. But where grievances pile high and most of the elected spokesmen represent the Establishment, violence may be the only effective response.
WILLIAM ORVILLE DOUGLAS (1898–1980)

Degeneracy follows every autocratic system of violence, for violence inevitably attracts moral inferiors. Time has proven that illustrious tyrants are succeeded by scoundrels.
ALBERT EINSTEIN (1879–1955)

It is better to be violent, if there is violence in our hearts, than to put on the cloak of nonviolence to cover impotence.
MAHATMA GANDHI (1869–1948)

Victory attained by violence is tantamount to a defeat, for it is momentary.
MAHATMA GANDHI (1869–1948)

The most violent element in society is ignorance.
EMMA GOLDMAN (1869–1940)

Opinions founded on prejudice are always sustained with the greatest of violence.
LORD FRANCIS JEFFREY (1773–1850)

Those who make peaceful revolution impossible will make violent revolution inevitable.
JOHN F. KENNEDY (1917–1963)

Nonviolence is the answer to the crucial political and moral questions of our time; the need for mankind to overcome oppression and violence without resorting to oppression and violence. Mankind must evolve for all human conflict a method which rejects revenge, aggression, and retaliation. The foundation of such a method is love.
MARTIN LUTHER KING JR. (1929–1968)

Returning violence for violence multiplies violence, adding deeper darkness to a night already devoid of stars.... Hate cannot drive out hate: only love can do that.
MARTIN LUTHER KING JR. (1929–1968)

Nothing good ever comes of violence.
MARTIN LUTHER (1483–1546)

Perseverance is more prevailing than violence; and many things which cannot be overcome when they are together, yield themselves up when taken little by little.
PLUTARCH (AD 46–120)

The right things to do are those that keep our violence in abeyance; the wrong things are those that bring it to the fore.
ROBERT J. SAWYER (1960–), *Calculating God*

Virginity

I didn't lose my virginity until I was 18. The first time was a nightmare. Who shows you how to use a condom?
ADAM ANT (1954–)

The world has suffered more from the ravages of ill-advised marriages than from virginity.
AMBROSE BIERCE (1842–1914)

Fighting for peace is like screwing for virginity.
GEORGE CARLIN (1937–)

Virginity can be lost by a thought.
SAINT JEROME (C. 342–420)

Virginity is the ideal of those who want to deflower.
KARL KRAUS (1874–1936)

It is difficult to believe in a religion that places such a high premium on chastity and virginity.
MADONNA (1958–)

Ladies, just a little more virginity, if you don't mind.
HERBERT BEERBOHM TREE (1853–1917)

It is an infantile superstition of the human spirit that virginity would be thought a virtue and not the barrier that separates ignorance from knowledge.
VOLTAIRE (1694–1778)

Virtue

Great necessities call out great virtues.
ABIGAIL ADAMS (1744–1818)

Some virtues are only seen in affliction and others only in prosperity.
JOSEPH ADDISON (1672–1719)

All virtue is summed up in dealing justly.
ARISTOTLE (384–322 BC)

Of all the varieties of virtues, liberalism is the most beloved.
ARISTOTLE (384–322 BC)

The greatest virtues are those which are most useful to other persons.
ARISTOTLE (384–322 BC)

Virtue is more clearly shown in the performance of fine actions than in the nonperformance of base ones.
ARISTOTLE (384–322 BC)

What the statesman is most anxious to produce is a certain moral character in his fellow citizens, namely a disposition to virtue and the performance of virtuous actions.
ARISTOTLE (384–322 BC)

As in nature, things move violently to their place and calmly in their place, so virtue in ambition is violent, in authority settled and calm.
SIR FRANCIS BACON (1561–1626)

Certainly virtue is like precious odors, most fragrant when they are incensed, or crushed: for prosperity doth best discover vice, but adversity doth best discover virtue.
SIR FRANCIS BACON (1561–1626)

Prosperity discovers vice, adversity discovers virtue.
SIR FRANCIS BACON (1561–1626)

Virtue is like a rich stone, best plain set.
SIR FRANCIS BACON (1561–1626)

There are in every man, always, two simultaneous allegiances, one to God, the other to Satan. Invocation of God, or Spirituality, is a desire to climb higher; that of Satan, or animality, is delight in descent.
CHARLES BAUDELAIRE (1821–1867)

A medal is a small metal disk given as a reward for virtues, attainments or services more or less authentic.
AMBROSE BIERCE (1842–1914)

Remorse is virtue's root; its fair increase are fruits of innocence and blessedness.
WILLIAM C. BRYANT (1794 –1878)

The virtues, like the Muses, are always seen in groups. A good principle was never found solitary in any breast.
THE BUDDHA (563–483 BC)

Remorse is the echo of a lost virtue.
SIR EDWARD G. BULWER-LYTTON (1803–1873)

But what is liberty without wisdom, and without virtue? It is the greatest of all possible evils; for it is folly, vice, and madness, without tuition or restraint.
EDMUND BURKE (1729–1797)

If you can be well without health, you may be happy without virtue.
EDMUND BURKE (1729–1797)

A virtue to be serviceable must, like gold, be alloyed with some commoner, but more durable alloy.
SAMUEL BUTLER (1612–1680)

Rare virtues are like rare plants or animals, things that have not been able to hold their own in the world. A virtue to be serviceable must, like gold, be alloyed with some commoner but more durable metal.
SAMUEL BUTLER (1612–1680)

The function of vice is to keep virtue within reasonable bounds.
SAMUEL BUTLER (1835–1902)

If prosperity is regarded as the reward of virtue, it will be regarded as the symptom of virtue.
G. K. CHESTERTON (1874–1936)

He has all the virtues I dislike and none of the vices I admire.
SIR WINSTON CHURCHILL (1874–1965)

Virtue is a habit of the mind, consistent with nature and moderation and reason.
CICERO (106–43 BC)

The man of virtue makes the difficulty to be overcome his first business, and success only a subsequent consideration.
CONFUCIUS (551–479 BC), *The Confucian Analects*

To be able to practice five things everywhere under heaven constitutes perfect virtue.... [They are] gravity, generosity of soul, sincerity, earnestness, and kindness.
CONFUCIUS (551–479 BC), *The Confucian Analects*

Virtue is not left to stand alone. He who practices it will have neighbors.
CONFUCIUS (551–479 BC)

The greatest minds are capable of the greatest vices as well as of the greatest virtues.
RENÉ DESCARTES (1596–1650), *Le discours de la methode*

As far as I'm concerned, I prefer silent vice to ostentatious virtue.
ALBERT EINSTEIN (1879–1955)

The only reward of virtue is virtue; the only way to have a friend is to be one.
RALPH WALDO EMERSON (1803–1882)

What is a weed? A plant whose virtues have never been discovered.
RALPH WALDO EMERSON (1803–1882)

Innocence most often is a good fortune and not a virtue.
ANATOLE FRANCE (1844–1924)

Search others for their virtues, thyself for thy vices.
BENJAMIN FRANKLIN (1706–1790)

Sell not virtue to purchase wealth, nor liberty to purchase power.
BENJAMIN FRANKLIN (1706–1790)

Dependence begets subservience and venality, suffocates the germ of virtue, and prepares fit tools for the designs of ambition.
THOMAS JEFFERSON (1762–1826)

Liberty is the great parent of science and of virtue; and a nation will be great in both always in proportion as it is free.
THOMAS JEFFERSON (1762–1826)

Most virtues when carried beyond certain bonds degenerate into vices.
THOMAS JEFFERSON (1762–1826)

The order of nature is that individual happiness shall be inseparable from the practice of virtue.
THOMAS JEFFERSON (1762–1826)

Wisdom is knowing what to do next; virtue is doing it.
DAVID STARR JORDAN (1851–1931), *The Philosophy of Despair*

Virtue would go far if vanity did not keep it company.
FRANÇOIS DE LA ROCHEFOUCAULD (1613–1680)

It has been my experience that folks who have no vices have very few virtues.
ABRAHAM LINCOLN (1809–1865)

The highest proof of virtue is to possess boundless power without abusing it.
LORD THOMAS BABINGTON MACAULAY (1800–1859)

Waste no more time arguing about what a good man should be. Be one.
MARCUS AURELIUS ANTONINUS (121–180)

If everyone were clothed with integrity, if every heart were just, frank, kindly, the other virtues would be well-nigh useless, since their chief purpose is to make us bear with patience the injustice of our fellows.
MOLIÈRE (1622–1673)

I prefer an interesting vice to a virtue that bores.
MOLIÈRE (1622–1673)

Glory is fleeting, but obscurity is forever.
NAPOLÉON I (1769–1821)

Virtue is its own reward, and brings with it the truest and highest pleasure; but if we cultivate it only for pleasure's sake, we are selfish, not religious, and will never gain the pleasure, because we can never have the virtue.
JOHN HENRY NEWMAN (1801–1890)

When we are planning for posterity, we ought to remember that virtue is not hereditary.
THOMAS PAINE (1737–1809)

The power of a man's virtue should not be measured by his special efforts, but by his ordinary doing.
BLAISE PASCAL (1623–1662)

Virtue is a state of war, and to live in it we have always to combat with ourselves.
JEAN-JACQUES ROUSSEAU (1712–1778)

Assume a virtue if you have it not.
WILLIAM SHAKESPEARE (1564–1616), *Hamlet*

Virtue is bold, and goodness never fearful.
WILLIAM SHAKESPEARE (1564–1616), *Measure for Measure*

The shortest and surest way to live with honour in the world, is to be in reality what we would appear to be; and if we observe, we shall find, that all human virtues increase and strengthen themselves by the practice of them.
SOCRATES (469–399 BC)

Virtue does not come from wealth, but ... wealth, and every other good thing which men have ... comes from virtue.
SOCRATES (469–399 BC)

The problem with people who have no vices is that generally you can be pretty sure they're going to have some pretty annoying virtues.
ELIZABETH TAYLOR (1932–)

Philanthropy is almost the only virtue which is sufficiently appreciated by mankind.
HENRY DAVID THOREAU (1817–1862)

Virtue is its own reward. There's a pleasure in doing good which sufficiently pays itself.
SIR JOHN VANBRUGH (1664–1726), *The Relapse*

Virtue has its own reward, but has no sale at the box office.
MAE WEST (1892–1980)

True courage is not the brutal force of vulgar heroes, but the firm resolve of virtue and reason.
ALFRED NORTH WHITEHEAD (1861–1947)

Vision

Far away there in the sunshine are my highest aspirations. I may not reach them, but I can look up and see their beauty, believe in them, and try to follow where they lead.
LOUISA MAY ALCOTT (1832–1888)

Visions are worth fighting for. Why spend your life making someone else's dreams?
SCOTT ALEXANDER (1963–) and LARRY KARASZEWSKI (1961–), *Ed Wood*

As a man is, so he sees. As the eye is formed, such are its powers.
WILLIAM BLAKE (1757–1827)

"When the sun rises, do you not see a round disc of fire somewhat like a guinea?" O no, no, I see an innumerable company of the heavenly host crying "Holy, Holy, Holy is the Lord God Almighty."
WILLIAM BLAKE (1757–1827)

I have seen gleams in the face and eyes of the man that have let you look into a higher country.
THOMAS CARLYLE (1795–1881)

No man sees far, most see no farther than their noses.
THOMAS CARLYLE (1795–1881)

The farther backward you can look, the farther forward you are likely to see.
SIR WINSTON CHURCHILL (1874–1965)

The qualities of a great man are vision, integrity, courage, understanding, the power of articulation, and profundity of character.
DWIGHT D. EISENHOWER (1890–1969)

Commerce is of trivial import; love, faith, truth of character, the aspiration of man, these are sacred.
RALPH WALDO EMERSON (1803–1882)

Hitch your wagon to a star. Let us not fag in paltry works which serve our pot and bag alone.
RALPH WALDO EMERSON (1803–1882)

I have nothing new to teach the world. Truth and Non-violence are as old as the hills. All I have done is to try experiments in both on as vast a scale as I could.
MAHATMA GANDHI (1869–1948)

Art arises when the secret vision of the artist and the manifestation of nature agree to find new shapes.
KAHLIL GIBRAN (1883–1931)

They consider me to have sharp and penetrating vision because I see them through the mesh of a sieve.
KAHLIL GIBRAN (1883–1931)

Cherish your visions and your dreams as they are the children of your soul; the blueprints of your ultimate achievements.
NAPOLEON HILL (1883–1970)

The great thing in the world is not so much where we stand, as in what direction we are moving.
OLIVER WENDELL HOLMES SR. (1809–1894)

The business of a seer is to see; and if he involves himself in the kind of God-eclipsing activities which make seeing impossible, he betrays the trust which his fellows have tacitly placed in him.
ALDOUS HUXLEY (1894–1963)

Your vision will become clear only when you can look into your own heart. Who looks outside, dreams; who looks inside, awakens.
CARL JUNG (1875–1961)

A vision is not just a picture of what could be; it is an appeal to our better selves, a call to become something more.
ROSABETH MOSS KANTER (1943–)

The most pathetic person in the world is someone who has sight, but has no vision.
HELEN KELLER (1880–1968)

The energy, the faith, the devotion which we bring this endeavor will light our bounty and all who serve it, and the glow from that fire can truly light the world.
JOHN F. KENNEDY (1917–1963)

I just want to do God's will. And He's allowed me to go up to the mountain. And I've looked over, and I've seen the Promised Land.
MARTIN LUTHER KING JR. (1929–1968)

Leaders must invoke an alchemy of great vision.
HENRY KISSINGER (1923–)

Every civilization when it loses its inner vision and its cleaner energy, falls into a new sort of sordidness, more vast and more stupendous than the old savage sort. An Augean stable of metallic filth.
D. H. LAWRENCE (1885–1930)

If you would hit the mark, you must aim a little above it; Every arrow that flies feels the attraction of earth.
HENRY WADSWORTH LONGFELLOW (1807–1882)

The hand cannot reach higher than does the heart.
ORISON SWETT MARDEN (1850–1924)

We lift ourselves by our thought. We climb upon our vision of ourselves. If you want to enlarge your life, you must first enlarge your thought of it and of yourself. Hold the ideal of yourself as you long to be, always everywhere.
ORISON SWETT MARDEN (1850–1924)

I would like to recapture that freshness of vision which is characteristic of extreme youth when all the world is new to it.
HENRI MATISSE (1869–1954)

Anything new, anything worth doing, can't be recognized. People just don't have that much vision.
PABLO PICASSO (1881–1973)

Vision is the art of seeing things invisible.
JONATHAN SWIFT (1667–1745)

I would give all the wealth of the world, and all the deeds of all the heroes, for one true vision.
HENRY DAVID THOREAU (1817–1862)

Yesterday is but a dream, tomorrow but a vision. But today well lived makes every yesterday a dream of happiness, and every tomorrow a vision of hope. Look well, therefore, to this day. Such is the salutation to the dawn.
SANSKRIT PROVERB

Vocation

The price one pays for pursuing any profession, or calling, is an immediate knowledge of its ugly side.
JAMES ARTHUR BALDWIN (1924–1987)

Vocations which we wanted to pursue, but didn't, bleed, like colors, on the whole of our existence.
HONORÉ DE BALZAC (1799–1850)

It is the first of all problems for a man to find out what kind of work he is to do in this universe.
THOMAS CARLYLE (1795–1881)

Look around the inhabited world; how few know their own good, or knowing it, pursue.
JOHN DRYDEN (1631–1700)

For most men life is a search for the proper manila envelope in which to get themselves filed.
CLIFTON FADIMAN (1904–1999)

People of genius do not excel in any profession because they work in it, they work in it because they excel.
WILLIAM HAZLITT (1778–1830)

The player envies only the player, the poet envies only the poet.
WILLIAM HAZLITT (1778–1830)

The world judge of men by their ability in their profession, and we judge of ourselves by the same test: for it is on that on which our success in life depends.
WILLIAM HAZLITT (1778–1830)

Many people mistake our work for our vocation. Our vocation is the love of Jesus.
MOTHER TERESA (1910–1997)

Sweetest Lord, make me appreciative of the dignity of my high vocation, and its many responsibilities. Never permit me to disgrace it by giving way to coldness, unkindness, or impatience.
MOTHER TERESA (1910–1997)

Voting

Every citizen of this country should be guaranteed that their vote matters, that their vote is counted, and that in the voting booth, their vote has as much weight as that of any CEO, any member of Congress, or any President.
BARBARA BOXER (1940–)

We need to make voting more accessible.
DONNA BRAZILE (1959–)

Of course voting is useful. But then again, I don't put a big glow to it. Voting is about as essential as washing yourself. It's something you're supposed to do. Now, you can't go around bragging, expecting to get props because you voted. That's stupid.
CHUCK D (1960–)

Voting is the most precious right of every citizen, and we have a moral obligation to ensure the integrity of our voting process.
HILLARY CLINTON (1947–)

If voting changed anything, they'd make it illegal.
EMMA GOLDMAN (1869–1940)

Voting is a civic sacrament.
THEODORE HESBURGH (1917–)

Voting is a right best exercised by people who have taken time to learn about the issues.
TONY SNOW (1955–)

Voting is fundamental in our democracy. It has yielded enormous returns.
ARLEN SPECTER (1930–)

Half of the American people have never read a newspaper. Half never voted for president. One hopes it is the same half.
GORE VIDAL (1925–)

Vulgarity

The vulgar man is always the most distinguished, for the very desire to be distinguished is vulgar.
G. K. CHESTERTON (1874–1936)

Vulgarity is the garlic in the salad of life.
CYRIL CONNOLLY (1903–1974)

Vulgarity begins when imagination succumbs to the explicit.
DORIS DAY (1924–)

To endeavor to work upon the vulgar with fine sense is like attempting to hew blocks with a razor.
ALEXANDER POPE (1688–1744)

The higher a man stands, the more the word "vulgar" becomes unintelligible to him.
JOHN RUSKIN (1819–1900)

Vulgarity is, in reality, nothing but a modern, chic, pert descendant of the goddess Dullness.
EDITH SITWELL (1887–1964)

There are no people who are quite so vulgar as the over-refined.
MARK TWAIN (1835–1910)

Vulgarity is the conduct of other people, just as falsehoods are the truths of other people.
OSCAR WILDE (1854–1900)

Whatever harsh criticisms may be passed on the construction of her sentences, she at least possesses that one touch of vulgarity that makes the whole world kin.
OSCAR WILDE (1854–1900)

Honest vulgarity is in the central tradition of English humour—the humour of the music-hall. Uninhibitedness is the essence of comedy.
KENNETH WILLIAMS (1926–1988)

Vulgarity is the rich man's modest contribution to democracy.
ANONYMOUS

Think with the wise, but talk with the vulgar.
GREEK PROVERB

Vulnerability

When we were children, we used to think that when we were grown-up we would no longer be vulnerable. But to grow up is to accept vulnerability.... To be alive is to be vulnerable.
MADELEINE L'ENGLE (1918–), *Walking on Water: Reflections on Faith and Art*

There can be no vulnerability without risk; there can be no community without vulnerability; there can be no peace, and ultimately no life, without community.
M. SCOTT PECK (1936–2005)

You show your vulnerability through relationships, and those feelings are your soft spot. You need to have a soft spot.
VICTORIA PRATT (1970–)

I think sexy is vulnerability, and there's no way you can act vulnerable. It just has to be there.
MICHAEL ZASLOW (1944–1998)

Wages

I don't pay good wages because I have a lot of money; I have a lot of money because I pay good wages.
ROBERT BOSCH (1861–1942)

A fair day's wages for a fair day's work.
THOMAS CARLYLE (1795–1881)

If we see to it that wages conform to the final productivity of social labor, we should see to it that trusts do not lower that standard.
JOHN BATES CLARK (1847–1938)

It is not the employer who pays the wages. Employers only handle the money. It is the customer who pays the wages.
HENRY FORD (1863–1947)

There is one rule for industrialists and that is: Make the best quality of goods possible at the lowest cost possible, paying the highest wages possible.
HENRY FORD (1863–1947)

Poorly paid labor is inefficient labor, the world over.
HENRY GEORGE (1839–1897)

Modern cynics and skeptics ... see no harm in paying those to whom they entrust the minds of their children a smaller wage than is paid to those to whom they entrust the care of their plumbing.
JOHN F. KENNEDY (1917–1963)

The more the division of labor and the application of machinery extend, the more does competition extend among the workers, the more do their wages shrink together.
KARL MARX (1818–1883)

Unquestionably, there is progress. The average American now pays out twice as much in taxes as he formerly got in wages.
H. L. MENCKEN (1880–1956)

The wages of sin are death, but by the time taxes are taken out, it's just sort of a tired feeling.
PAULA POUNDSTONE (1959–)

Only in our dreams are we free. The rest of the time we need wages.
TERRY PRATCHETT (1948–)

Most men would feel insulted if it were proposed to employ them in throwing stones over a wall, and then in throwing them back, merely that they might earn their wages. But many are no more worthily employed now.
HENRY DAVID THOREAU (1817–1862)

One man's wage increase is another man's price increase.
HAROLD WILSON (1916–1995)

War

I do not feel remorse. Everybody makes mistakes in war.
ABU ABBAS (1948–2004)

War is organized murder and torture against our brothers.
ALFRED ADLER (1870–1937)

I think the real obscenity comes from raising our youth to believe that sex is bad and ugly and dirty. And yet, it is heroic to go spill guts and blood in the most ghastly manner in the name of humanity. With all the taboos attached to sex, it's no wonder we have the problems we have. It's no wonder we're angry and violent and genocidal. But ask yourself the question, what is more obscene: sex or war?
SCOTT ALEXANDER (1963–) and LARRY KARASZEWSKI (1961–), *The People vs. Larry Flynt*

We make war that we may live in peace.
ARISTOTLE (384–322 BC), *Nichomachean Ethics*

The way to win an atomic war is to make certain it never starts.
OMAR BRADLEY (1893–1981)

War is not its own end, except in some catastrophic slide into absolute damnation. It's peace that's wanted. Some better peace than the one you started with.
LOIS MCMASTER BUJOLD (1949–), *The Vor Game*

War is not nice.
BARBARA BUSH (1925–)

Rulers who want to unleash war know very well that they must procure or invent a first victim.
ELIAS CANETTI (1905–1994)

War may sometimes be a necessary evil. But no matter how necessary, it is always an evil, never a good. We will not learn how to live together in peace by killing each other's children.
JIMMY CARTER (1924–)

One is left with the horrible feeling now that war settles nothing; that to win a war is as disastrous as to lose one.
AGATHA CHRISTIE (1890–1976), *Autobiography*

Never, never, never believe any war will be smooth and easy, or that anyone who embarks on the strange voyage can measure the tides and hurricanes he will encounter. The statesman who yields to war fever must realize that once the signal is given, he is no longer the master of policy but the slave of unforeseeable and uncontrollable events.
SIR WINSTON CHURCHILL (1874–1965)

Endless money forms the sinews of war.
CICERO (106–43 BC), *Philippics*

The name of peace is sweet, and the thing itself is beneficial, but there is a great difference between peace and servitude. Peace is freedom in tranquillity; servitude is the worst of all evils, to be resisted not only by war, but even by death.
CICERO (106–43 BC)

War is a series of catastrophes that results in a victory.
GEORGES CLEMENCEAU (1841–1929)

War is much too serious a matter to be entrusted to the military.
GEORGES CLEMENCEAU (1841–1929)

If you want to make peace, you don't talk to your friends. You talk to your enemies.
MOSHE DAYAN (1915–1981)

He who joyfully marches to music rank and file, has already earned my contempt. He has been given a large brain by mistake, since for him the spinal cord would surely suffice. This disgrace to civilization should be done away with at once. Heroism at command, how violently I hate all this, how

despicable and ignoble war is; I would rather be torn to shreds than be a part of so base an action. It is my conviction that killing under the cloak of war is nothing but an act of murder.
ALBERT EINSTEIN (1879–1955)

I know not with what weapons World War III will be fought, but World War IV will be fought with sticks and stones.
ALBERT EINSTEIN (1879–1955)

You cannot simultaneously prevent and prepare for war.
ALBERT EINSTEIN (1879–1955)

Every gun that is made, every warship launched, every rocket fired signifies, in the final sense, a theft from those who hunger and are not fed, those who are cold and not clothed. This world in arms is not spending money alone. It is spending the sweat of its laborers, the genius of its scientists, the hopes of its children. This is not a way of life at all in any true sense. Under the cloud of threatening war, it is humanity hanging from a cross of iron.
DWIGHT D. EISENHOWER (1890–1969)

Because no battle is ever won, he said. They are not even fought. The field only reveals to man his own folly and despair, and victory is an illusion of philosophers and fools.
WILLIAM FAULKNER (1897–1962), *The Sound and the Fury*

I hate war … for the dictatorships it puts in the place of democracies, and for the starvation that stalks after it.
HARRY EMERSON FOSDICK (1878–1969)

Either war is obsolete or men are.
R. BUCKMINSTER FULLER (1895–1983)

Wars teach us not to love our enemies, but to hate our allies.
W. L. GEORGE (1882–1926)

The idea of all-out nuclear war is unsettling.
WALTER GOODMAN (1838–1912)

The art of war is simple enough. Find out where your enemy is. Get at him as soon as you can. Strike him as hard as you can, and keep moving on.
ULYSSES S. GRANT (1822–1885)

Has not peace honours and glories of her own unattended by the dangers of war?
HERMOCRATES (C. 407 BC)

Demoralize the enemy from within by surprise, terror, sabotage, assassination. This is the war of the future.
ADOLF HITLER (1889–1945)

It is entirely seemly for a young man killed in battle to lie mangled by the bronze spear. In his death all things appear fair. But when dogs shame the gray head and gray chin and nakedness of an old man killed, it is the most piteous thing that happens among wretched mortals.
HOMER (800–700 BC), *The Iliad*

The outcome of the war is in our hands; the outcome of words is in the council.
HOMER (800–700 BC), *The Iliad*

My views and feelings [are] in favor of the abolition of war—and I hope it is practicable, by improving the mind and morals of society, to lessen the disposition to war; but of its abolition I despair.
THOMAS JEFFERSON (1743–1826)

One day it's going to dawn on the human race that war is as barbaric a means of resolving conflict as cannibalism is as a means of coping with diet deficiencies.
BRUCE KENT (1929–)

Arms are instruments of ill omen…. When one is compelled to use them, it is best to do so without relish. There is no glory in victory, and to glorify it despite this is to exult in the killing of men…. When great numbers of people are killed, one should weep over them with sorrow. When victorious in war, one should observe mourning rites.
LAO-TZU (C. 600 BC)

It is well that war is so terrible—otherwise we would grow too fond of it.
ROBERT E. LEE (1807–1870)

If war is ever lawful, then peace is sometimes sinful.
C. S. LEWIS (1898–1963)

A prince should therefore have no other aim or thought, nor take up any other thing for his study but war and its organization and discipline, for that is the only art that is necessary to one who commands.
NICCOLÒ MACHIAVELLI (1469–1527), *The Prince*

War is a cowardly escape from the problems of peace.
THOMAS MANN (1875–1955)

Politics is war without bloodshed while war is politics with bloodshed.
MAO TSE-TUNG (1893–1976)

War is an ugly thing, but not the ugliest of things. The decayed and degraded state of moral and patriotic feeling which thinks that nothing is worth war is much worse. The person who has nothing for which he is willing to fight, nothing which is more important than his own personal safety, is a miserable creature and has no chance of being free unless made and kept so by the exertions of better men than himself.
JOHN STUART MILL (1806–1873)

Peace is not a relationship of nations. It is a condition of mind brought about by a serenity of soul. Peace is not merely the absence of war. It is also a state of mind. Lasting peace can come only to peaceful people.
JAWAHARLAL NEHRU (1889–1964)

The quickest way of ending a war is to lose it.
GEORGE ORWELL (1903–1950)

War is war. The only good human being is a dead one.
GEORGE ORWELL (1903–1950)

It is only necessary to make war with five things, with the maladies of the body, the ignorances of the mind, with the passions of the body, with the seditions of the city and the discords of families.
PYTHAGORAS (C. 582–500 BC)

You can no more win a war than you can win an earthquake.
JEANNETTE RANKIN (1880–1973)

Take the diplomacy out of war and the thing would fall flat in a week.
WILL ROGERS (1879–1935)

You can't say that civilization don't advance, however, for in every war they kill you in a new way.
WILL ROGERS (1879–1935)

Anyone who thinks must think of the next war as they would of suicide.
ELEANOR ROOSEVELT (1884–1962)

Sometime they'll give a war and nobody will come.
CARL SANDBURG (1878–1967), "The People, Yes"

Peace has never come from dropping bombs. Real peace comes from enlightenment and educating people to behave more in a divine manner.
CARLOS SANTANA (1947–)

The peace of heaven is theirs that lift their swords,
In such a just and charitable war.
WILLIAM SHAKESPEARE (1564–1616), *King John*

[O], now, for ever
Farewell the tranquil mind! farewell content!
Farewell the plumed troop and the big wars
That make ambition virtue! O, farewell!
Farewell the neighing steed and the shrill trump,
The spirit-stirring drum, the ear-piercing fife,
The royal banner, and all quality,
Pride, pomp, and circumstance of glorious war!
And, O you mortal engines, whose rude throats
The immortal Jove's dread clamours counterfeit,
Farewell! Othello's occupation's gone!
WILLIAM SHAKESPEARE (1564–1616), *Othello*

Peace is not only better than war, but infinitely more arduous.
GEORGE BERNARD SHAW (1856–1950)

War is cruelty. There's no use trying to reform it, the crueler it is the sooner it will be over.
WILLIAM TECUMSEH SHERMAN (1820–1891)

War is hell.
WILLIAM TECUMSEH SHERMAN (1820–1891)

Son, we live in a world that has walls and those walls need to be guarded by men with guns. Who's gonna do it? You? You, Lieutenant Weinberg? I have a greater responsibility than you can possibly fathom. You weep for Santiago and curse the Marines; you have that luxury. You have the luxury of not knowing what I know: that Santiago's death, while tragic, probably saved lives and that my existence, while grotesque and incomprehensible to you, saves lives.

You don't want the truth because deep down in places you don't talk about at parties you want me on that wall, you need me on that wall. We use words like honor, code, loyalty. We use them as the backbone of a life trying to defend something. You use them as a punch line. I have neither the time nor the inclination to explain myself to a man who rises and sleeps under the blanket of the very freedom I provide and then questions the manner in which I provide it. I would rather you just said "thank you," and went on your way. Otherwise, I suggest that you pick up a weapon and stand a post. Either way, I don't give a damn what you think you are entitled to.
AARON SORKIN (1961–), *A Few Good Men*

Peace is not an absence of war, it is a virtue, a state of mind, a disposition for benevolence, confidence, justice.
BENEDICT DE SPINOZA (1632–1677)

[W]hat is of supreme importance in war is to attack the enemy's strategy.
SUN-TZU (C. 544–496 BC)

All war must be just the killing of strangers against whom you feel no personal animosity; strangers whom, in other circumstances, you would help if you found them in trouble, and who would help you if you needed it.
MARK TWAIN (1835–1910)

Did you know that every two hours the nations of this world spend as much on armaments as they spend on the children of this world every year?
PETER USTINOV (1921–2004)

Let him who desires peace prepare for war.
FLAVIUS RENATUS VEGETIUS (C. 375), *De rei militari*

During my three years in Vietnam, I certainly heard plenty of last words by dying American footsoldiers. Not one of them, however, had illusions that he had somehow accomplished something worthwhile in the process of making the Supreme Sacrifice.
KURT VONNEGUT JR. (1922–2007), *Hocus Pocus*

The more you sweat in peacetime, the less you bleed during war.
CHINESE PROVERB

Warriors

The warrior's approach is to say "yes" to life: "yea" to it all.
JOSEPH CAMPBELL (1904–1987)

A warrior never worries about his fear.
CARLOS CASTANEDA (1925–1998)

Only as a warrior can one withstand the path of knowledge. A warrior cannot complain or regret anything. His life is an endless challenge, and challenges cannot possibly be good or bad. Challenges are simply challenges.
CARLOS CASTANEDA (1925–1998)

The basic difference between an ordinary man and a warrior is that a warrior takes everything as a challenge while an ordinary man takes everything either as a blessing or a curse.
CARLOS CASTENEDA (1925–1998)

Courage, above all things, is the first quality of a warrior.
KARL VON CLAUSEWITZ (1780–1831)

Ideas are the great warriors of the world, and a war that has no idea behind it, is simply a brutality.
JAMES A. GARFIELD (1831–1881)

Mankind must put an end to war, or war will put an end to mankind.... War will exist until that distant day when the conscientious objector enjoys the same reputation and prestige that the warrior does today.
JOHN F. KENNEDY (1917–1963)

Generally speaking, the Way of the warrior is resolute acceptance of death.
MIYAMOTO MUSASHI (1584–1645)

Victorious warriors win first and then go to war, while defeated warriors go to war first and then seek to win.
SUN-TZU (C. 544–496 BC)

I do not love the bright sword for its sharpness, nor the arrow for its swiftness, nor the warrior for his glory. I love only that which they defend.
J. R. R. TOLKIEN (1892–1973)

The two most powerful warriors are patience and time.
LEO TOLSTOY (1828–1910)

Who is the happy Warrior? Who is he
That every man in arms should wish to be?
WILLIAM WORDSWORTH (1770–1850)

Waste

Waste is worse than loss. The time is coming when every person who lays claim to ability will keep the question of waste before him constantly. The scope of thrift is limitless.
THOMAS A. EDISON (1847–1931)

Willful waste brings woeful want.
THOMAS FULLER (1608–1661)

Waste cannot be accurately told, though we are sensible how destructive it is. Economy, on the one hand, by which a certain income is made to maintain a man genteelly; and waste, on the other, by which on the same income another man lives shabbily, cannot be defined. It is a very nice thing; as one man wears his coat out much sooner than another, we cannot tell how.
SAMUEL JOHNSON (1709–1784)

The waste of plenty is the resource of scarcity.
THOMAS LOVE PEACOCK (1785–1866)

Haste makes waste, no less in life than in housekeeping.
HENRY DAVID THOREAU (1817–1862)

Water

Water and air, the two essential fluids on which all life depends, have become global garbage cans.
JACQUES COUSTEAU (1910–1997)

Water, like religion and ideology, has the power to move millions of people. Since the very birth of human civilization, people have moved to settle close to it. People move when there is too little of it. People move when there is too much of it. People journey down it. People write, sing, and dance about it. People fight over it. And all people, everywhere and every day, need it.
MIKHAIL GORBACHEV (1931–)

Water is also one of the four elements, the most beautiful of God's creations. It is both wet and cold, heavy, and with a tendency to descend, and flows with great readiness. It is this the Holy Scripture has in view when it says, "And the darkness was upon the face of the deep. And the Spirit of God moved upon the face of the waters." Water, then, is the most beautiful element and rich in usefulness, and purifies from all filth, and not only from the filth of the body but from that of the soul, if it should have received the grace of the Spirit.
JOHN OF DAMASCUS (C. 676–749), *Exposition of the Orthodox Faith*

Nothing in the world is more flexible and yielding than water. Yet when it attacks the firm and the strong, none can withstand it, because they have no way to change it. So the flexible overcome the adamant, the yielding overcome the forceful. Everyone knows this, but no one can do it.
LAO-TZU (C. 600 BC)

There is nothing softer and weaker than water,
And yet there is nothing better for attacking hard and strong things. For this reason there is no substitute for it.
LAO-TZU (C. 600 BC)

Water is life's mater and matrix, mother and medium. There is no life without water.
ALBERT SZENT-GYORGYI (1893–1986)

Water is the only drink for a wise man.
HENRY DAVID THOREAU (1817–1862)

Weakness

It is the bodily weakness and my own sense of ignorance that form the pit of blackness and fill me with impatient dread.
HAROLD BRODKEY (1930–1996)

Solitude is strength; to depend on the presence of the crowd is weakness. The man who needs a mob to nerve him is much more alone than he imagines.
PAUL BRUNTON (1898–1981)

Our greatest weakness lies in giving up. The most certain way to succeed is always to try just one more time.
THOMAS A. EDISON (1847–1931)

Weakness of attitude becomes weakness of character.
ALBERT EINSTEIN (1879–1955)

Only strength can cooperate. Weakness can only beg.
DWIGHT D. EISENHOWER (1890–1969)

Weakness of character is the only defect which cannot be amended.
FRANÇOIS DE LA ROCHEFOUCAULD (1613–1680)

Credulity is the man's weakness, but the child's strength.
CHARLES LAMB (1775–1834)

Strength alone knows conflict, weakness is born vanquished.
ANNE SOPHIE SWETCHINE (1782–1857)

It is from weakness that people reach for dictators and concentrated government power. Only the strong can be free. And only the productive can be strong.
WENDELL WILLKIE (1892–1944)

Wealth

The rich swell up with pride, the poor from hunger.
SHOLOM ALEICHEM (1859–1916)

Now, for some of you it doesn't matter. You were born rich and you're going to stay rich. But here's my advice to the rest of you: Take dead aim on the rich boys. Get them in the crosshairs and take them down. Just remember, they can buy anything but they can't buy backbone. Don't let them forget it.
WES ANDERSON (1969–) and OWEN WILSON (1968–), *Rushmore*

The fact remains that the overwhelming majority of people who have become wealthy have become so thanks to work they found profoundly absorbing. The long term study of people who eventually became wealthy clearly reveals that their "luck" arose from accidental dedication they had to an arena they enjoyed.
SRULLY D. BLOTNICK (1941–2004)

Being rich is having money; being wealthy is having time.
MARGARET BONNANO (1950–)

You aren't wealthy until you have something money can't buy.
GARTH BROOKS (1956–)

Be charitable before wealth makes thee covetous.
SIR THOMAS BROWNE (1605–1682)

The life of the wealthy is one long Sunday.
GEORG BUCHNER (1813–1837)

Early to bed and early to rise makes a man healthy, wealthy, and wise.
BENJAMIN FRANKLIN (1706–1790)

If you would be wealthy, think of saving as well as getting.
BENJAMIN FRANKLIN (1706–1790)

The conspicuously wealthy turn up urging the character building values of the privation of the poor.
JOHN KENNETH GALBRAITH (1908–2006)

It is pretty hard to tell what does bring happiness; poverty and wealth have both failed.
KIN HUBBARD (1868–1930)

Wealth is the parent of luxury and indolence, and poverty of meanness and viciousness, and both of discontent.
PLATO (C. 428–348 BC), *The Republic*

Learn to be pleased with everything; with wealth, so far as it makes us beneficial to others; with poverty, for not having much to care for; and with obscurity, for being unenvied.
PLUTARCH (AD 46–120)

If thou desire to purchase honor with thy wealth, consider first how that wealth became thine; if thy labor got it, let thy wisdom keep it; if oppression found it, let repentance restore it; if thy parent left it, let thy virtues deserve it; so shall thy honor be safer, better and cheaper.
FRANCIS QUARLES (1592–1644)

It is the sign of a weak mind to be unable to bear wealth.
SENECA (5 BC–AD 65)

Wealth is the slave of a wise man. The master of a fool.
SENECA (5 BC–AD 65)

Virtue does not come from wealth, but … wealth, and every other good thing which men have … comes from virtue.
SOCRATES (469–399 BC)

Wisdom outweighs any wealth.
SOPHOCLES (496–406 BC), *Antigone*

If all the rich people in the world divided up their money among themselves there wouldn't be enough to go around.
CHRISTINA STEAD (1903–1983)

Nothing is more admirable than the fortitude with which millionaires tolerate the disadvantages of their wealth.
REX STOUT (1886–1975)

I am opposed to millionaires, but it would be dangerous to offer me the position.
MARK TWAIN (1835–1910)

The offspring of riches: Pride, vanity, ostentation, arrogance, tyranny.
MARK TWAIN (1835–1910)

Unless one is wealthy there is no use in being a charming fellow. Romance is the privilege of the rich, not the profession of the unemployed. The poor should be practical and prosaic. It is better to have a permanent income than to be fascinating.
OSCAR WILDE (1854–1900)

I have about concluded that wealth is a state of mind, and that anyone can acquire a wealthy state of mind by thinking rich thoughts.
ANDREW YOUNG (1932–)

Man has three friends on whose company he relies. First, wealth which goes with him only while good fortune lasts. Second, his relatives; they go only as far as the grave and leave him there. The third friend, his good deeds, go with him beyond the grave.
THE TALMUD

Weapons

Weapons are like money; no one knows the meaning of enough.
MARTIN AMIS (1949–)

I know not with what weapons World War III will be fought, but World War IV will be fought with sticks and stones.
ALBERT EINSTEIN (1879–1955)

Once weapons are allowed to become widely diffused, it becomes much more difficult to work out methods of arms control.
HERMAN KAHN (1922–1983)

Weapons are an important factor in war, but not the decisive one; it is man and not materials that counts.
MAO TSE-TUNG (1893–1976)

There are weapons that are simply thoughts. For the record, prejudices can kill and suspicion can destroy.
ROD SERLING (1924–1975)

Weapons are created to be used. There's no place for the weak on this earth.
CURTIS SIODMAK (1902–2000)

Weather

Barometer, n.: An ingenious instrument which indicates what kind of weather we are having.
AMBROSE BIERCE (1842–1914), *The Devil's Dictionary*

Weather forecast for tonight: dark. Continued dark overnight, with widely scattered light by morning.
GEORGE CARLIN (1937–)

When all is said and done, the weather and love are the two elements about which one can never be sure.
ALICE HOFFMAN (1952–), *Here on Earth*

Don't knock the weather. If it didn't change once in a while, nine out of ten people couldn't start a conversation.
KIN HUBBARD (1868–1930)

Sunshine is delicious, rain is refreshing, wind braces us up, snow is exhilarating; there is really no such thing as bad weather, only different kinds of good weather.
JOHN RUSKIN (1819–1900)

Climate is what we expect, weather is what we get.
MARK TWAIN (1835–1910)

Weather is a literary specialty, and no untrained hand can turn out a good article on it.
MARK TWAIN (1835–1910)

Conversation about the weather is the last refuge of the unimaginative.
OSCAR WILDE (1854–1900)

When the goose honks high, fair weather; when the goose honks low, foul weather.
ANONYMOUS

Weddings

A wedding is a ceremony at which two persons undertake to become one, one undertakes to become nothing, and nothing undertakes to become supportable.
AMBROSE BIERCE (1842–1914)

Weddings are for women, I tell you.
ERIC BRAEDEN (1941–)

When the wedding march sounds the resolute approach, the clock no longer ticks, it tolls the hour. The figures in the aisle are no longer individuals, they symbolize the human race.
ANNE MORROW LINDBERGH (1906–2001)

All weddings, except those with shotguns in evidence, are wonderful.
LIZ SMITH (1923–)

I think that weddings have probably been crashed since the beginning of time. Cavemen crashed them. You go to meet girls. It makes sense.
CHRISTOPHER WALKEN (1943–)

Welfare

And having looked to government for bread, on the very first scarcity they will turn and bite the hand that fed them. To avoid that evil, government will

redouble the causes of it; and then it will become inveterate and incurable.
EDMUND BURKE (1729–1797)

Anyone who can walk to the welfare office can walk to work.
AL CAPP (1909–1979)

Power has only one duty—to secure the social welfare of the People.
BENJAMIN DISRAELI (1804–1881)

That doctrine of peace at any price has done more mischief than any I can well recall that have been afloat in this country. It has occasioned more wars than any of the most ruthless conquerors. It has disturbed and nearly destroyed that political equilibrium so necessary to the liberties and the welfare of the world.
BENJAMIN DISRAELI (1804–1881)

A decent provision for the poor is the true test of civilization.
SAMUEL JOHNSON (1709–1784)

Normal fear protects us; abnormal fear paralyses us. Normal fear motivates us to improve our individual and collective welfare; abnormal fear constantly poisons and distorts our inner lives. Our problem is not to be rid of fear but, rather, to harness and master it.
MARTIN LUTHER KING JR. (1929–1968)

The effect of violent dislike between groups has always created an indifference to the welfare and honor of the state.
LORD THOMAS BABINGTON MACAULAY (1800–1859)

Welfare's purpose should be to eliminate, as far as possible, the need for its own existence.
RONALD REAGAN (1911–2004)

We should measure welfare's success by how many people leave welfare, not by how many are added.
RONALD REAGAN (1911–2004)

Your duty is to pray for the welfare of the world and to work for it as far as it lies in your power.
SRI SATHYA SAI BABA (1926–)

The welfare state is not really about the welfare of the masses. It is about the egos of the elites.
THOMAS SOWELL (1930–)

As the Republican platforms says, the welfare of the farmer is vital to that of the whole country.
WILLIAM HOWARD TAFT (1857–1930)

To desire and strive to be of some service to the world, to aim at doing something which shall really increase the happiness and welfare and virtue of mankind—this is a choice which is possible for all of us; and surely it is a good haven to sail for.
HENRY VAN DYKE (1852–1933)

Wilderness

The idea of wilderness needs no defense, it only needs defenders.
EDWARD ABBEY (1927–1989)

The Promised Land always lies on the other side of a Wilderness.
HENRY HAVELOCK ELLIS (1859–1939)

When it comes to wilderness animals, we have to make an effort to preserve what areas we can that they can be themselves in. It's come to a point though, clearly, where some species have to be cared for by humans, if they are not going to disappear altogether.
MATTHEW FOX (1966–)

In wilderness I sense the miracle of life, and behind it our scientific accomplishments fade to trivia.
CHARLES LINDBERGH (1902–1974)

Wilderness is not defined by the absence of certain activities, but rather by the presence of certain unique and invaluable characteristics.
NICK RAHALL (1949–)

In wilderness is the preservation of the world.
HENRY DAVID THOREAU (1817–1862)

Wine

Wine is a peephole on a man.
ALCAEUS (C. 600 BC)

Quickly, bring me a beaker of wine, so that I may wet my mind and say something clever.
ARISTOPHANES (C. 448–380 BC)

Wine is a treacherous friend who you must always be on guard for.
CHRISTIAN NESTELL BOVÉE (1820–1904)

Tis pity wine should be so deleterious,
For tea and coffee leave us much more serious.
LORD BYRON (1788–1824)

What grape to keep its place in the sun, taught our ancestors to make wine?
CYRIL CONNOLLY (1903–1974)

I cook with wine, sometimes I even add it to the food.
W. C. FIELDS (1880–1946)

Behold the rain which descends from heaven upon our vineyards, and which incorporates itself with the grapes, to be changed into wine; a constant proof that God loves us, and loves to see us happy.
BENJAMIN FRANKLIN (1706–1790)

It is better to hide ignorance, but it is hard to do this when we relax over wine.
HERACLITUS (C. 535–475 BC)

The wine urges me on, the bewitching wine, which sets even a wise man to singing and to laughing gently and rouses him up to dance and brings forth words which were better unspoken.
HOMER (800–700 BC), *The Odyssey*

Wine can of their wits the wise beguile,
Make the sage frolic, and the serious smile.
HOMER (800–700 BC)

Wine makes a man more pleased with himself; I do not say it makes him more pleasing to others.
SAMUEL JOHNSON (1709–1784)

O thou invisible spirit of wine, if thou hast no name to be known by, let us call thee devil.
WILLIAM SHAKESPEARE (1564–1616), *Othello*

Wine moistens the soul and lulls our grief to sleep while it also wakens kindly feelings.
SOCRATES (469–399 BC)

Wine is bottled poetry.
ROBERT LOUIS STEVENSON (1850–1894)

The first duty of a wine is to be red, the second that it should be Burgundy.
ALEC WAUGH (1898–1981)

Wine improves with age. The older I get, the better I like it.
ANONYMOUS

Winning

Only a man who knows what it is like to be defeated can reach down to the bottom of his soul and come up with the extra ounce of power it takes to win when the match is even.
MUHAMMAD ALI (1942–)

Sooner or later, those who win are those who think they can.
RICHARD BACH (1936–)

That's what learning is, after all; not whether we lose the game, but how we lose and how we've changed because of it and what we take away from it that we never had before, to apply to other games. Losing, in a curious way, is winning.
RICHARD BACH (1936–)

If you believe in yourself and have dedication and pride, and never quit, you'll be a winner. The price of victory is high but so are the rewards.
PAUL "BEAR" BRYANT (1913–1983)

Show class, have pride, and display character. If you do, winning takes care of itself.
PAUL "BEAR" BRYANT (1913–1983)

All that's necessary for the forces of evil to win in the world is for enough good men to do nothing.
EDMUND BURKE (1729–1797)

To win without risk is to triumph without glory.
PIERRE CORNEILLE (1606–1684)

If winning isn't everything, why do they keep score?
VINCE LOMBARDI (1913–1970)

It's easy to have faith in yourself and have discipline when you're a winner, when you're number one. What you got to have is faith and discipline when you're not a winner.
VINCE LOMBARDI (1913–1970)

Winning is a habit. Unfortunately, so is losing.
VINCE LOMBARDI (1913–1970)

Remember, always give your best. Never get discouraged. Never be petty. Always remember, others may hate you. But those who hate you don't win unless you hate them. And then you destroy yourself.
RICHARD M. NIXON (1913–1994)

You must play boldly to win.
ARNOLD PALMER (1929–)

Winning is great, sure, but if you are really going to do something in life, the secret is learning how to lose. Nobody goes undefeated all the time. If you can pick up after a crushing defeat, and go on to win again, you are going to be a champion someday.
WILMA RUDOLPH (1940–1994)

Our doubts are traitors and make us lose the good we oft might win, by fearing to attempt.
WILLIAM SHAKESPEARE (1564–1616), *Measure for Measure*

Winners make a habit of manufacturing their own positive expectations in advance of the event.
BRIAN TRACY (1944–)

Part of being a winner is knowing when enough is enough. Sometimes you have to give up the fight and walk away, and move on to something that's more productive.
DONALD TRUMP (1946–)

The reason most people never reach their goals is that they don't define them, learn about them, or even seriously consider them as believable or achievable. Winners can tell you where they are going, what they plan to do along the way, and who will.
DENIS WAITLEY (1933–)

The winner's edge is not in a gifted birth, a high IQ, or in talent. The winner's edge is all in the attitude, not aptitude. Attitude is the criterion for success.
DENIS WAITLEY (1933–)

Winners are people with definite purpose in life.
DENIS WAITLEY (1933–)

Winners take time to relish their work, knowing that scaling the mountain is what makes the view from the top so exhilarating.
DENIS WAITLEY (1933–)

There are victories of the soul and spirit. Sometimes, even if you lose, you win.
ELIE WIESEL (1928–)

I would rather lose in a cause that will some day win, than win in a cause that will some day lose.
WOODROW WILSON (1856–1924)

You were born to win, but to be a winner, you must plan to win, prepare to win, and expect to win.
ZIG ZIGLAR (1926–)

Winter

And for the season it was winter, and they that know the winters of that country know them to be sharp and violent, and subject to cruel and fierce storms.
WILLIAM BRADFORD (1590–1657), *Of Plymouth Plantation*

If we had no winter, the spring would not be so pleasant: if we did not sometimes taste of adversity, prosperity would not be so welcome.
ANNE BRADSTREET (1612–1672), *Meditations Divine and Moral*

The tendinous part of the mind, so to speak, is more developed in winter; the fleshy, in summer. I should say winter had given the bone and sinew to literature, summer the tissues and the blood.
JOHN BURROUGHS (1837–1921), *The Snow-Walkers*

In the depth of winter, I finally learned that within me there lay an invincible summer.
ALBERT CAMUS (1913–1960)

Winter lies too long in country towns; hangs on until it is stale and shabby, old and sullen.
WILLA CATHER (1873–1947), *My Antonia*

O Winter! ruler of the inverted year, …
I crown thee king of intimate delights,
Fireside enjoyments, home-born happiness,
And all the comforts that the lowly roof
Of undisturb'd Retirement, and the hours
Of long uninterrupted evening, know.
WILLIAM COWPER (1731–1800), *Task*

There's a certain Slant of light,
Winter Afternoons --
That oppresses, like the Heft
Of Cathedral Tunes --
EMILY DICKINSON (1830–1886), "No. 258"

Every mile is two in winter.
GEORGE HERBERT (1593–1633), *Jacula prudentum*

Winter is on my head, but eternal spring is in my heart.
VICTOR HUGO (1802–1885)

Every winter,
When the great sun has turned his face away,
The earth goes down into a vale of grief,
And fasts, and weeps, and shrouds herself in sables,
Leaving her wedding-garlands to decay—
Then leaps in spring to his returning kisses.
CHARLES KINGSLEY (1819–1875), "Saint's Tragedy"

Perhaps I am a bear, or some hibernating animal underneath, for the instinct to be half asleep all winter is so strong in me.
ANNE MORROW LINDBERGH (1906–2001)

When you live in Texas, every single time you see snow it's magical.
PAMELA RIBON (1975–), *Why Girls Are Weird*

In the bleak midwinter
Frosty wind made moan,
Earth stood hard as iron,
Water like a stone;
Snow had fallen, snow on snow,
Snow on snow,
In the bleak midwinter,
Long ago.
CHRISTINA G. ROSSETTI (1830–1894), "A Christmas Carol"

Blow, blow, thou winter wind
Thou art not so unkind,
As man's ingratitude.
WILLIAM SHAKESPEARE (1564–1616), "Blow, Blow, Thou Winter Wind"

Wisdom

It is unbecoming for young men to utter maxims.
ARISTOTLE (384–322 BC)

To wisdom belongs the intellectual apprehension of things eternal; to knowledge, the rational apprehension of things temporal.
SAINT AUGUSTINE (354–430)

History makes people wise.
SIR FRANCIS BACON (1561–1626)

We thought, because we had power, we had wisdom.
STEPHEN VINCENT BENET (1898–1943), *Litany for Dictatorships*

Men are wise in proportion, not to their experience, but to their capacity for experience.
JAMES BOSWELL (1740–1795), *Life of Samuel Johnson*

If we continue to develop our technology without wisdom or prudence, our servant may prove to be our executioner.
OMAR BRADLEY (1893–1981)

Meditation brings wisdom; lack of meditation leaves ignorance. Know well what leads you forward and what holds you back, and choose the path that leads to wisdom.
THE BUDDHA (563–483 BC)

On life's journey faith is nourishment, virtuous deeds are a shelter, wisdom is the light by day and right mindfulness is the protection by night. If a man lives a pure life, nothing can destroy him.
THE BUDDHA (563–483 BC)

But what is liberty without wisdom, and without virtue? It is the greatest of all possible evils; for it is folly, vice, and madness, without tuition or restraint.
EDMUND BURKE (1729–1797)

Wisdom is your perspective on life, your sense of balance, your understanding of how the various parts and principles apply and relate to each other. It embraces judgment, discernment, comprehension. It is a gestalt or oneness, an integrated wholeness.
STEPHEN R. COVEY (1932–)

Men and nations behave wisely once they have exhausted all the other alternatives.
ABBA EBAN (1915–2002)

The invariable mark of wisdom is to see the miraculous in the common.
RALPH WALDO EMERSON (1803–1882)

Along with success comes a reputation for wisdom.
EURIPIDES (C. 480–406 BC)

In seeking wisdom, the first step is silence, the second listening, the third remembering, the fourth practicing, the fifth—teaching others.
SOLOMON IBN GABIROL (C. 1021–1058)

It is unwise to be too sure of one's own wisdom. It is healthy to be reminded that the strongest might weaken and the wisest might err.
MAHATMA GANDHI (1869–1948)

Knowledge speaks, but wisdom listens.
JIMI HENDRIX (1942–1970)

How prone to doubt, how cautious are the wise!
HOMER (800–700 BC)

Force without wisdom falls of its own weight.
HORACE (65–8 BC), *Odes*

Of all our possessions, wisdom alone is immortal.
ISOCRATES (436–338 BC)

The art of being wise is knowing what to overlook.
WILLIAM JAMES (1842–1910)

Wisdom is knowing what to do next; virtue is doing it.
DAVID STARR JORDAN (1851–1931), *The Philosophy of Despair*

Science is organized knowledge. Wisdom is organized life.
IMMANUEL KANT (1724–1804)

Ten thousand fools proclaim themselves into obscurity, while one wise man forgets himself into immortality.
MARTIN LUTHER KING JR. (1929–1968)

One's first step in wisdom is to question everything—and one's last is to come to terms with everything.
GEORG C. LICHTENBERG (1742–1799)

Don't gain the world and lose your soul,
Wisdom is better than silver or gold.
BOB MARLEY (1945–1981), "Zion Train"

It is not white hair that engenders wisdom.
MENANDER (342–292 BC)

The older I grow, the more I distrust the familiar doctrine that age brings wisdom.
H. L. MENCKEN (1880–1956)

And let that day be lost to us on which we did not dance once! And let that wisdom be false to us that brought no laughter with it!
FRIEDRICH NIETZSCHE (1844–1900)

Wisdom sets bounds even to knowledge.
FRIEDRICH NIETZSCHE (1844–1900)

Pain makes man think. Thought makes man wise. Wisdom makes life endurable.
JOHN PATRICK (1905–1995)

Discipline is wisdom and vice versa.
M. SCOTT PECK (1936–2005)

We don't receive wisdom; we must discover it for ourselves after a journey that no one can take for us or spare us.
MARCEL PROUST (1871–1922)

Those who wish to appear wise among fools, among the wise seem foolish.
QUINTILIAN (C. AD 35–100), *De institutione oratoria*

The whole problem with the world is that fools and fanatics are always so certain of themselves, but wiser people so full of doubts.
BERTRAND RUSSELL (1872–1970)

The wisest mind has something yet to learn.
GEORGE SANTAYANA (1863–1952)

Good people are good because they've come to wisdom through failure.
WILLIAM SAROYAN (1908–1981)

To acquire knowledge, one must study; but to acquire wisdom, one must observe.
MARILYN VOS SAVANT (1946–)

No man was ever wise by chance.
SENECA (5 BC–AD 65)

The fool doth think he is wise, but the wise man knows himself to be a fool.
WILLIAM SHAKESPEARE (1564–1616), *As You Like It*

Wisdom outweighs any wealth.
SOPHOCLES (496–406 BC), *Antigone*

Wisdom is the right use of knowledge. To know is not to be wise. Many men know a great deal, and are all the greater fools for it. There is no fool so great a fool as a knowing fool. But to know how to use knowledge is to have wisdom.
CHARLES H. SPURGEON (1834–1892)

No man is wise enough by himself.
TITUS MACCIUS PLAUTUS (254–184 BC), *Miles gloriosus*

Not by age but by capacity is wisdom acquired.
TITUS MACCIUS PLAUTUS (254–184 BC), *Trinummus*

Wisdom doesn't automatically come with old age. Nothing does—except wrinkles. It's true, some wines improve with age. But only if the grapes were good in the first place.
ABIGAIL VAN BUREN (1918–)

Wisdom is not finally tested in the schools,
Wisdom cannot be pass'd from one having it to
another not having it,
Wisdom is of the soul, is not susceptible of proof, is
its own proof.
WALT WHITMAN (1819–1892)

I am not young enough to know everything.
OSCAR WILDE (1854–1900)

A wise man can see more from the bottom of a well than a fool can from a mountain top .
ANONYMOUS

Wishes

You are never given a wish without also being given the power to make it come true.
RICHARD BACH (1936–)

Where there is great love, there are always wishes.
WILLA CATHER (1873–1947)

Stop the habit of wishful thinking and start the habit of thoughtful wishes.
MARY MARTIN (1913–1990)

When all of your wishes are granted, many of your dreams will be destroyed.
MARILYN MANSON (1969–)

Work will win when wishy washy wishing won't.
THOMAS S. MONSON (1927–)

Wishing does not make a poor man rich.
ARABIAN PROVERB

Great souls have wills; feeble ones have only wishes.
CHINESE PROVERB

Wit

The distrust of wit is the beginning of tyranny.
EDWARD ABBEY (1927–1989)

Good nature is more agreeable in conversation than wit, and gives a certain air to the countenance which is more amiable than beauty.
JOSEPH ADDISON (1672–1719)

Wit is the fetching of congruity out of incongruity.
JOSEPH ADDISON (1672–1719)

Wit is cultured insolence.
ARISTOTLE (384–322 BC)

This delivering of knowledge in distinct and disjointed aphorisms doth leave the wit of man more free to turn and toss, and to make use of that which is so delivered to more several purposes and applications.
SIR FRANCIS BACON (1561–1626)

For daring nonsense seldom fails to hit, Like scattered shot, and pass with some for wit.
SAMUEL BUTLER (1835–1902)

Don't put too fine a point to your wit for fear it should get blunted.
MIGUEL DE CERVANTES (1547–1616)

It is by vivacity and wit that man shines in company; but trite jokes and loud laughter reduce him to a buffoon.
LORD CHESTERFIELD (1694–1773)

Wit is so shining a quality that everybody admires it; most people aim at it, all people fear it, and few love it unless in themselves.
LORD CHESTERFIELD (1694–1773)

Wit is a sword; it is meant to make people feel the point as well as see it.
G. K. CHESTERTON (1874–1936)

Manner is all in all whatever is writ, the substitute for genius sense and wit.
WILLIAM COWPER (1731–1800)

Nor sequent centuries could hit
Orbit and sum of Shakespeare's wit.
RALPH WALDO EMERSON (1803–1882)

A clever man commits no minor blunders.
JOHANN WOLFGANG VON GOETHE (1749–1832)

You can pretend to be serious; you can't pretend to be witty.
SACHA GUITRY (1885–1957)

Wit is the salt of conversation, not the food.
WILLIAM HAZLITT (1778–1830)

No task's too steep for human wit.
HORACE (65–8 BC)

Often the truth spoken with a smile will penetrate the mind and reach the heart; the lesson strikes home without wounding because of the wit in the saying.
HORACE (65–8 BC)

It is a great misfortune not to possess sufficient wit to speak well, nor sufficient judgment to keep silent.
JEAN DE LA BRUYÈRE (1645–1696)

A wit would often be embarrassed without the company of fools.
FRANÇOIS DE LA ROCHEFOUCAULD (1613–1680)

Wit is a dangerous weapon, even to the possessor, if he knows not how to use it discreetly.
MICHEL DE MONTAIGNE (1533–1592)

Wit is the epitaph of an emotion.
FRIEDRICH NIETZSCHE (1844–1900)

So vast is art, so narrow human wit.
ALEXANDER POPE (1688–1744)

There is a certain majesty in simplicity which is far above all the quaintness of wit.
ALEXANDER POPE (1688–1744)

Wit is the lowest form of humor.
ALEXANDER POPE (1688–1744)

Better a witty fool than a foolish wit.
WILLIAM SHAKESPEARE (1564–1616), *Twelfth Night*

Wit consists in seeing the resemblance between things which differ, and the difference between things which are alike.
MADAME DE STAËL (1766–1817)

The wit makes fun of other persons; the satirist makes fun of the world; the humorist makes fun of himself.
JAMES THURBER (1894–1961)

Wit is the sudden marriage of ideas which before their union were not perceived to have any relation.
MARK TWAIN (1835–1910)

Wit is the only wall between us and the dark.
MARK VAN DOREN (1894–1972)

Quotation is a serviceable substitute for wit.
OSCAR WILDE (1854–1900)

Witchcraft

It is the want to know the end that makes us believe in God, or witchcraft, believe, at least, in something.
TRUMAN CAPOTE (1924–1984)

Polygraph tests are 20th-century witchcraft.
SAM ERVIN (1896–1985)

With color one obtains an energy that seems to stem from witchcraft.
HENRI MATISSE (1869–1954)

All magic, all witchcraft, depends on the Devil, and is fundamentally evil.
MONTAGUE SUMMERS (1880–1948), *Witchcraft and Black Magic*

I am convinced that the teaching of the church is in theory a crafty and evil lie, and in practice a concoction of gross superstition and witchcraft.
LEO TOLSTOY (1828–1910)

Giving up witchcraft is, in effect, giving up the Bible.
JOHN WESLEY (1703–1791)

Wives

Wives are young men's mistresses, companions for middle age, and old men's nurses.
SIR FRANCIS BACON (1561–1626)

A man's mother is his misfortune, but his wife is his fault.
WALTER BAGEHOT (1826–1877)

The fact is that my wife if she had common sense would have more power over me than any other whatsoever, for my heart always alights upon the nearest perch.
LORD BYRON (1788–1824)

Wives in their husbands' absences grow subtler,
And daughters sometimes run off with the butler.
LORD BYRON (1788–1824)

Variability is one of the virtues of a woman. It avoids the crude requirement of polygamy. So long as you have one good wife you are sure to have a spiritual harem.
G. K. CHESTERTON (1874–1936)

If I was your wife Sir, I'd poison you! Madam, if you were my wife, I'd let you!
SIR WINSTON CHURCHILL (1874–1965)

Pride is the chief cause in the decline in the number of husbands and wives.
NEIL DIAMOND (1941–), *Husbands and Wives*

It's my old girl that advises. She has the head. But I never own to it before her. Discipline must be maintained.
CHARLES DICKENS (1812–1870)

Nature meant me a wife, a silly harmless household Dove, fond without art; and kind without deceit.
JOHN DRYDEN (1631–1700)

That's what a man wants in a wife, mostly; he wants to make sure one fool tells him he's wise.
GEORGE ELIOT (1819–1880)

A man's wife has more power over him than the state has.
RALPH WALDO EMERSON (1803–1882)

Man's best possession is a sympathetic wife.
EURIPIDES (C. 480–406 BC), *Antigone*

Never take a wife till thou hast a house (and a fire) to put her in.
BENJAMIN FRANKLIN (1706–1790)

Choose a wife by your ear than your eye.
THOMAS FULLER (1608–1661)

He knows little, who will tell his wife all he knows.
THOMAS FULLER (1608–1661)

There are women whose infidelities are the only link they still have with their husbands.
SACHA GUITRY (1885–1957)

When you consider what a chance women have to poison their husbands, it's a wonder there isn't more of it done.
KIN HUBBARD (1868–1930)

A man is in general better pleased when he has a good dinner upon his table than when his wife talks Greek.
SAMUEL JOHNSON (1709–1784)

Wives are people who feel they don't dance enough.
GROUCHO MARX (1890–1977)

American women expect to find in their husbands a perfection that English women only hope to find in their butlers.
W. SOMERSET MAUGHAM (1874–1965)

What makes men indifferent to their wives is that they can see them when they please.
OVID (43 BC–AD 17)

No girl who is going to marry need bother to win a college degree; she just naturally becomes a "Master of Arts" and a "Doctor of Philosophy" after catering to an ordinary man for a few years.
HELEN ROWLAND (1875–1950)

One man's folly is another man's wife.
HELEN ROWLAND (1876–1950)

The philosophy of the common man is an old wife that gives him no pleasure, yet he cannot live without her, and resents any aspersions that strangers may cast on her character.
GEORGE SANTAYANA (1863–1952)

To suckle fools, and chronicle small beer.
WILLIAM SHAKESPEARE (1564–1616), *Othello*

This comes of James teaching me to think for myself, and never to hold back out of fear of what other people may think of me. It works beautifully as long as I think the same things as he does.
GEORGE BERNARD SHAW (1856–1950)

A good wife and health is a man's best wealth.
ANONYMOUS

Women

Feminine weaknesses and fainting spells are the direct result of our confining young girls to the house, bent over their needlework, and restrictive corsets.
LOUISA MAY ALCOTT (1832–1888), *Little Women*

Woman is the salvation or the destruction of the family. She carries its destiny in the folds of her mantle.
HENRI-FRÉDÉRIC AMIEL (1821–1881)

That's the nature of women, not to love when we love them, and to love when we love them not.
MIGUEL DE CERVANTES (1547–1616)

A woman is the most fiendish instrument of torture ever devised to bedevil the days of man.
ETHAN COEN (1957–) AND JOEL COEN (1954–), *Oh Brother, Where Art Thou?*

Women want love to be a novel, men a short story.
DAPHNE DU MAURIER (1907–1989)

Women, like men, should try to do the impossible. And when they fail, their failure should be a challenge to others.
AMELIA EARHART (1898–1937)

Women rule our lives, don't they?
JUAN MANUEL FANGIO (1911–1995)

That is the great distinction between the sexes. Men see objects, women see the relationships between objects.
JOHN FOWLES (1926–2005)

The great question that has never been answered, and which I have not yet been able to answer, despite my thirty years of research into the feminine soul, is "What does a woman want?"
SIGMUND FREUD (1856–1939)

The society of women is the element of good manners.
JOHANN WOLFGANG VON GOETHE (1749–1832)

There are women whose infidelities are the only link they still have with their husbands.
SACHA GUITRY (1885–1957)

How fickle is woman.
SIDNEY HOWARD (1891–1939) and MARGARET MITCHELL (1900–1949), *Gone with the Wind*

Men have as exaggerated an idea of their rights as women have of their wrongs.
EDGAR WATSON HOWE (1853–1937)

When you consider what a chance women have to poison their husbands, it's a wonder there isn't more of it done.
KIN HUBBARD (1868–1930)

A woman's whole life is a history of the affections.
WASHINGTON IRVING (1783–1859)

Kindness in women, not their beauteous looks, shall win my love.
WASHINGTON IRVING (1783–1859)

Women cannot complain about men anymore until they start getting better taste in them.
BILL MAHER (1956–)

Women are afraid of mice and of murder and of very little in between.
MIGNON MCLAUGHLIN (1913–1983)

No matter how happily a woman may be married, it always pleases her to discover that there is a nice man who wishes that she were not.
H. L. MENCKEN (1880–1956)

Women have simple tastes. They get pleasure out of the conversation of children in arms and men in love.
H. L. MENCKEN (1880–1956)

Women are considered deep—why? Because one can never discover any bottom to them. Women are not even shallow.
FRIEDRICH NIETZSCHE (1844–1900)

Woman was God's second mistake.
FRIEDRICH NIETZSCHE (1844–1900)

If women didn't exist, all the money in the world would have no meaning.
ARISTOTLE ONASSIS (1906–1975)

Whether they give or refuse, it delights women just the same to have been asked.
OVID (43 BC–AD 17)

When an actress takes off her clothes onscreen but a nursing mother is told to leave, what message do we send about the roles of women? In some ways we're as committed to the old madonna-whore dichotomy as ever. And the madonna stays home, feeding the baby behind the blinds, a vestige of those days when for a lady to venture out was a flagrant act of public exposure.
ANNA QUINDLEN (1953–)

A woman is like a teabag. It's only when she's in hot water that you realize how strong she is.
ELEANOR ROOSEVELT (1884–1962)

Ever since Eve started it all by offering Adam the apple, woman's punishment has been to supply a man with food then suffer the consequences when it disagrees with him.
HELEN ROWLAND (1876–1950)

Women—always in trouble with them, but can't live without them.
AYRTON SENNA (1960–1994)

Do you not know I am a woman? When I think, I must speak.
WILLIAM SHAKESPEARE (1564–1616), *As You Like It*

Women may fall when there's no strength in men.
WILLIAM SHAKESPEARE (1564–1616), *Romeo and Juliet*

What is most beautiful in virile men is something feminine; what is most beautiful in feminine women is something masculine.
SUSAN SONTAG (1933–2004), *Against Interpretation*

A woman without a man is like a fish without a bicycle.
GLORIA STEINEM (1934–)

That man over there says that women need to be helped into carriages, and lifted over ditches, and to have the best place everywhere. Nobody ever helps me into carriages, or over mud-puddles, or gives me any best place! And ain't I a woman? Look at me! Look at my arm! I have ploughed and planted, and gathered into barns, and no man could head me! And ain't I a woman? I could work as much and eat as much as a man—when I could get it—and bear the lash as well! And ain't I a woman? I have borne thirteen children, and seen most all sold off to slavery, and when I cried out with my mother's grief, none but Jesus heard me! And ain't I a woman?
SOJOURNER TRUTH (1797–1883)

Women are responsible for creating their own roles.
KATHLEEN TURNER (1954–)

Well-behaved women rarely make history.
LAUREL THATCHER ULRICH (1938–)

Women are never stronger than when they arm themselves with their weakness.
MARIE ANNE DE VICHY-CHAMROND (1697–1780)

The strength of women comes from the fact that psychology cannot explain us. Men can be analyzed, women merely adored.
OSCAR WILDE (1854–1900), *An Ideal Husband*

To be born woman is to know—although they do not speak of it at school—women must labor to be beautiful.
WILLIAM BUTLER YEATS (1865–1939)

Words

We have too many high sounding words, and too few actions that correspond with them.
ABIGAIL ADAMS (1744–1818)

No man means all he says, and yet very few say all they mean, for words are slippery and thought is viscous.
HENRY ADAMS (1838–1918)

Words are the physicians of the mind diseased.
AESCHYLUS (525–456 BC), *Prometheus Bound*

Words mean more than what is set down on paper. It takes the human voice to infuse them with shades of deeper meaning.
MAYA ANGELOU (1928–)

A synonym is a word you use when you can't spell the word you first thought of.
BURT BACHARACH (1928–)

[E]very tongue that gets bit always has another word to say.
SAM BEAM (1974–), "Innocent Bones"

For me, words are a form of action, capable of influencing change.
INGRID BENGIS (1944–)

Freeing oneself from words is liberation.
BODHIDHARMA (470–543)

Words are as recalcitrant as circus animals, and the unskilled trainer can crack his whip at them in vain.
GERALD BRENAN (1894–1987)

All I want is a warm bed and a kind word and unlimited power.
ASHLEIGH BRILLIANT (1933–)

Better than a thousand hollow words, is one word that brings peace.
THE BUDDHA (563–483 BC)

Words are like planets, each with its own gravitational pull.
KENNETH BURKE (1897–1993)

Grasp the subject, the words will follow.
CATO THE ELDER (234–149 BC)

Broadly speaking, the short words are the best, and the old words best of all.
SIR WINSTON CHURCHILL (1874–1965)

Words are the voice of the heart.
CONFUCIUS (551–479 BC)

Deeds, not words, shall speak me.
JOHN FLETCHER (1579–1625)

Words are the leaves of the tree of language, of which, if some fall away, a new succession takes their place.
JOHN FRENCH (1949–)

When ideas fail, words come in very handy.
JOHANN WOLFGANG VON GOETHE (1749–1832)

He who does not understand your silence will probably not understand your words.
ELBERT HUBBARD (1856–1915)

Words form the thread on which we string our experiences.
ALDOUS HUXLEY (1894–1963)

A man who uses a great many words to express his meaning is like a bad marksman who, instead of aiming a single stone at an object, takes up a handful and throws at it in hopes he may hit.
SAMUEL JOHNSON (1709–1784)

Do not accustom yourself to use big words for little matters.
SAMUEL JOHNSON (1709–1784)

Always and never are two words you should always remember never to use.
WENDELL JOHNSON (1906–1965)

Once I knew only darkness and stillness … my life was without past or future … but a little word from the fingers of another fell into my hand that clutched at emptiness, and my heart leaped to the rapture of living.
HELEN KELLER (1880–1968)

He can compress the most words into the smallest ideas of any man I ever met.
ABRAHAM LINCOLN (1809–1865)

Eventually, all things merge into one, and a river runs through it. The river was cut by the world's great flood and runs over rocks from the basement of time. On some of the rocks are timeless raindrops. Under the rocks are the words, and some of the words are theirs. I am haunted by waters.
NORMAN MACLEAN (1902–1990), *A River Runs Through It*

A man thinks that by mouthing hard words he understands hard things.
HERMAN MELVILLE (1819–1891)

Speak properly, and in as few words as you can, but always plainly, for the end of speech is not ostentation, but to be understood.
WILLIAM PENN (1644–1718)

Words have a longer life than deeds.
PINDAR (522–443 BC), *Nemean Ode*

Words have no power to impress the mind without the exquisite horror of their reality.
EDGAR ALLAN POE (1809–1849)s

Free speech is intended to protect the controversial and even outrageous word; and not just comforting platitudes too mundane to need protection.
COLIN POWELL (1937–)

It is better wither to be silent, or to say things of more value than silence. Sooner throw a pearl at hazard than an idle or useless word; and do not say a little in many words, but a great deal in a few.
PYTHAGORAS (C. 582–500 BC)

Silence is better than unmeaning words.
PYTHAGORAS (C. 582–500 BC)

Never part without loving words to think of during your absence. It may be that you will not meet again in this life.
JEAN PAUL RICHTER (1763–1825)

Words are easy, like the wind;
Faithful friends are hard to find.
WILLIAM SHAKESPEARE (1564–1616), "As It Fell Upon a Day"

My words fly up, my thoughts remain below.
Words without thoughts never to heaven go.
WILLIAM SHAKESPEARE (1564–1616), *Hamlet*

I understand a fury in your words,
But not the words…
WILLIAM SHAKESPEARE (1564–1616), *Othello*

Words are only postage stamps delivering the object for you to unwrap.
GEORGE BERNARD SHAW (1856–1950)

A mountain is composed of tiny grains of earth. The ocean is made up of tiny drops of water. Even so, life is but an endless series of little details, actions, speeches, and thoughts. And the consequences whether good or bad of even the least of them are far-reaching.
SWAMI SIVANANDA (1887–1963)

Words calculated to catch everyone may catch no one.
ADLAI E. STEVENSON II (1900–1965)

The bitterest tears shed over graves are for words left unsaid and deeds left undone.
HARRIET BEECHER STOWE (1811–1896)

Kind words can be short and easy to speak, but their echoes are truly endless.
MOTHER TERESA (1910–1997)

The difference between the right word and the almost right word is the difference between lightning and the lightning bug.
MARK TWAIN (1835–1910)

The right word may be effective, but no word was ever as effective as a rightly timed pause.
MARK TWAIN (1835–1910)

Words are only painted fire; a look is the fire itself.
MARK TWAIN (1835–1910)

County library? Reference desk, please. Hello? Yes, I need a word definition. Well, that's the problem. I don't know how to spell it and I'm not allowed to say it. Could you just rattle off all the swear words you know and I'll stop you when … Hello?
BILL WATTERSON (1958–)

Words are some of the most powerful and important things I know.… Language is the tool of love and the weapon of hatred. It's the bright red warning flag of danger—and the stone foundation of diplomacy and peace.
ANONYMOUS

Words lead to deeds.… They prepare the soul, make it ready, and move it to tenderness.
ANONYMOUS

Use soft words and hard arguments.
ENGLISH PROVERB

Do not be wise in words—be wise in deeds.
JEWISH PROVERB

Work

Work while you have the light. You are responsible for the talent that has been entrusted to you.
HENRI-FRÉDÉRIC AMIEL (1821–1881)

All paid jobs absorb and degrade the mind.
ARISTOTLE (384–322 BC)

Pleasure in the job puts perfection in the work.
ARISTOTLE (384–322 BC)

The more I want to get something done, the less I call it work.
RICHARD BACH (1936–)

Nothing is really work unless you would rather be doing something else.
JAMES M. BARRIE (1860–1937)

It is necessary to work, if not from inclination, at least from despair. Everything considered, work is less boring than amusing oneself.
CHARLES BAUDELAIRE (1821–1867)

Anyone can do any amount of work provided it isn't the work he is supposed to be doing at the moment.
ROBERT BENCHLEY (1889–1945)

Hard work never killed anybody, but why take a chance?
EDGAR BERGEN (1903–1978)

Measure not the work until the day's out and the labor done.
ELIZABETH BARRETT BROWNING (1806–1861)

Blessed is he who has found his work; let him ask no other blessedness.
THOMAS CARLYLE (1795–1881), *Past and Present*

Every noble work is at first impossible.
THOMAS CARLYLE (1795–1881)

Never continue in a job you don't enjoy. If you're happy in what you're doing, you'll like yourself, you'll have inner peace. And if you have that, along with physical health, you will have had more success than you could possibly have imagined.
JOHNNY CARSON (1925–2005)

It does not seem to be true that work necessarily needs to be unpleasant. It may always have to be hard, or at least harder than doing nothing at all. But there is ample evidence that work can be enjoyable, and that indeed, it is often the most enjoyable part of life.
MIHALY CSIKSZENTMIHALYI (1934–), *Flow: The Psychology of Optimal Experience*

It has been my experience that one cannot, in any shape or form, depend on human relations for lasting reward. It is only work that truly satisfies.
BETTE DAVIS (1908–1989), *The Lonely Life*

Plans are only good intentions unless they immediately degenerate into hard work.
PETER F. DRUCKER (1909–2005)

Genius is one per cent inspiration, ninety-nine per cent perspiration.
THOMAS A. EDISON (1847–1931)

My work is a game, a very serious game.
M. C. ESCHER (1898–1972)

Hard work spotlights the character of people: some turn up their sleeves, some turn up their noses, and some don't turn up at all.
SAM EWING (1921–)

It's not the hours you put in your work that counts, it's the work you put in the hours.
SAM EWING (1921–)

Man is so made that he can only find relaxation from one kind of labor by taking up another.
ANATOLE FRANCE (1844–1924), *The Crime of Sylvestre Bonnard*

There are two kinds of people: those who do the work and those who take the credit. Try to be in the first group; there is less competition there.
INDIRA GANDHI (1917–1984)

Normal is getting dressed in clothes that you buy for work and driving through traffic in a car that you are still paying for—in order to get to the job you need to pay for the clothes and the car, and the house you leave vacant all day so you can afford to live in it.
ELLEN GOODMAN (1941–)

Life grants nothing to us mortals without hard work.
HORACE (65–8 BC), *Satires*

Get happiness out of your work or you may never know what happiness is.
ELBERT HUBBARD (1856–1915)

I'm a great believer in luck, and I find the harder I work the more I have of it.
THOMAS JEFFERSON (1743–1826)

When your work speaks for itself, don't interrupt.
HENRY J. KAISER (1882–1967)

What's really important in life? Sitting on a beach? Looking at television eight hours a day? I think we have to appreciate that we're alive for only a limited period of time, and we'll spend most of our lives working. That being the case, I believe one of the most important priorities is to do whatever we do as well as we can. We should take pride in that.
VICTOR KIAM (1926–2001)

The sweat of hard work is not to be displayed. It is much more graceful to appear favored by the gods.
MAXINE HONG KINGSTON (1940–), *The Woman Warrior*

By the work one knows the workmen.
JEAN DE LA FONTAINE (1621–1695)

When a man tells you that he got rich through hard work, ask him: "Whose?"
DON MARQUIS (1878–1937)

Derive happiness in oneself from a good day's work, from illuminating the fog that surrounds us.
HENRI MATISSE (1869–1954)

Real success is finding your lifework in the work that you love.
DAVID MCCULLOUGH (1933–)

He who labors diligently need never despair; for all things are accomplished by diligence and labor.
MENANDER (342–292 BC)

Work will win when wishy washy wishing won't.
THOMAS S. MONSON (1927–)

Anyone who works is a fool. I don't work—I merely inflict myself upon the public.
ROBERT MORLEY (1908–1992)

People who work sitting down get paid more than people who work standing up.
OGDEN NASH (1902–1971)

Remember the generational battles twenty years ago? Remember all the screaming at the dinner table about haircuts, getting jobs and the American dream? Well, our parents won. They're out living the American dream on some damned golf course in Vero Beach, and we're stuck with the jobs and haircuts.
P. J. O'ROURKE (1947–)

Live neither in the past nor in the future, but let each day's work absorb your entire energies, and satisfy your widest ambition.
SIR WILLIAM OSLER (1849–1919)

Think enthusiastically about everything; but especially about your job. If you do, you'll put a touch of glory in your life. If you love your job with enthusiasm, you'll shake it to pieces. You'll love it into greatness.
NORMAN VINCENT PEALE (1898–1993)

Whenever it is in any way possible, every boy and girl should choose as his life work some occupation which he should like to do anyhow, even if he did not need the money.
WILLIAM LYON PHELPS (1865–1943)

Far and away the best prize that life offers is the chance to work hard at work worth doing.
THEODORE ROOSEVELT (1858–1919)

[I]n order that a man may be happy, it is necessary that he should not only be capable of his work, but a good judge of his work.
JOHN RUSKIN (1819–1900)

One of the symptoms of an approaching nervous breakdown is the belief that one's work is terribly important.
BERTRAND RUSSELL (1872–1970), *Conquest of Happiness*

Work is not man's punishment. It is his reward and his strength and his pleasure.
GEORGE SAND (1804–1876)

A human being must have occupation if he or she is not to become a nuisance to the world.
DOROTHY L. SAYERS (1893–1957)

Perpetual devotion to what a man calls his business is only to be sustained by perpetual neglect of many other things.
ROBERT LOUIS STEVENSON (1850–1894)

Do not hire a man who does your work for money, but him who does it for love of it.
HENRY DAVID THOREAU (1817–1862)

Work saves us from three great evils: boredom, vice and need.
VOLTAIRE (1694–1778), *Candide*

If you can do a half-assed job of anything, you're a one-eyed man in a kingdom of the blind.
KURT VONNEGUT JR. (1922–2007)

Whoever does not love his work cannot hope that it will please others.
ANONYMOUS

The World

Surely the world we live in is but the world that lives in us.
DAISY BATES (1863–1951)

The world is so constructed, that if you wish to enjoy its pleasures, you must also endure its pains. Whether you like it or not, you cannot have one without the other.
SWAMI BRAHNMANANDA (1863–1922)

The most incomprehensible thing about the world is that it is at all comprehensible.
ALBERT EINSTEIN (1879–1955)

The world is a dangerous place. Not because of the people who are evil; but because of the people who don't do anything about it.
ALBERT EINSTEIN (1879–1955)

What really interests me is whether God had any choice in the creation of the world.
ALBERT EINSTEIN (1879–1955)

Life is a series of experiences, each of which makes us bigger, even though it is hard to realize this. For the world was built to develop character, and we must learn that the setbacks and griefs which we endure help us in our marching onward.
HENRY FORD (1863–1947)

I would rather live in a world where my life is surrounded by mystery than live in a world so small that my mind could comprehend it.
HARRY EMERSON FOSDICK (1878–1969)

The world is full of willing people; some willing to work, the rest willing to let them.
ROBERT FROST (1874–1963)

The world is so empty if one thinks only of mountains, rivers and cities; but to know someone here and there who thinks and feels with us, and though distant, is close to us in spirit—this makes the earth for us an inhabited garden.
JOHANN WOLFGANG VON GOETHE (1749–1832)

Maybe this world is another planet's Hell.
ALDOUS HUXLEY (1894–1963)

You do not need to leave your room. Remain sitting at your table and listen. Do not even listen, simply wait, be quiet, still and solitary. The world will freely offer itself to you to be unmasked, it has no choice, it will roll in ecstasy at your feet.
FRANZ KAFKA (1883–1924)

An unfortunate thing about this world is that the good habits are much easier to give up than the bad ones.
W. SOMERSET MAUGHAM (1874–1965)

Develop an interest in life as you see it; the people, things, literature, music—the world is so rich, simply throbbing with rich treasures, beautiful souls and interesting people. Forget yourself.
HENRY MILLER (1891–1980)

The Christian resolution to find the world ugly and bad has made the world ugly and bad.
FRIEDRICH NIETZSCHE (1844–1900)

The world today doesn't make sense, so why should I paint pictures that do?
PABLO PICASSO (1881–1973)

A man's feet should be planted in his country, but his eyes should survey the world.
GEORGE SANTAYANA (1863–1952)

To do anything in this world worth doing, we must not stand back shivering and thinking of the cold and danger, but jump in, and scramble through as well as we can.
SYDNEY SMITH (1771–1845)

What's the use of a fine house if you haven't got a tolerable planet to put it on?
HENRY DAVID THOREAU (1817–1862)

The wide world is all about you; you can fence yourselves in, but you cannot forever fence it out.
J. R. R. TOLKIEN (1892–1973)

Don't go around saying the world owes you a living; the world owes you nothing; it was here first.
MARK TWAIN (1835–1910)

Worries

It is not work that kills men; it is worry. Work is healthy; you can hardly put more upon a man than he can bear. Worry is the rust upon the blade. It is not the revolution which destroys the machinery but the friction. Fear secretes acids; but love and trust are sweet juices
HENRY WARD BEECHER (1813–1887)

As a cure for worrying, work is better than whiskey.
THOMAS A. EDISON (1847–1931)

Little minds have little worries, big minds have no time for worries.
RALPH WALDO EMERSON (1803–1882)

Do not anticipate trouble, or worry about what may never happen. Keep in the sunlight.
BENJAMIN FRANKLIN (1706–1790)

The reason why worry kills more people than work is that more people worry than work.
ROBERT FROST (1874–1963)

Worry a little bit every day and in a lifetime you will lose a couple of years. If something is wrong, fix it if you can. But train yourself not to worry. Worry never fixes anything.
MARY HEMINGWAY (1908–1984)

If you believe that feeling bad or worrying long enough will change a past or future event, then you are residing on another planet with a different reality system.
WILLIAM JAMES (1842–1910)

The sovereign cure for worry is prayer.
WILLIAM JAMES (1842–1910)

If you can solve your problem, then what is the need of worrying? If you cannot solve it, then what is the use of worrying?
SHANTIDEVA (C. 800)

That's the secret to life … replace one worry with another….
CHARLES M. SCHULZ (1922–2000)

Worries go down better with soup than without.
JEWISH PROVERB

Worship

Natural worship is that which depends upon the nature of God. Even though there were no law revealed and set forth by God, if we rightly perceived and knew the nature of God by proper contemplation, with the grace of God helping, we might know all those things which pertain to our duty.
WILLIAM AMES (1576–1633)

He who desires to worship God must harbor no childish illusions about the matter but bravely renounce his liberty and humanity.
MIKHAIL BAKUNIN (1814–1876)

Worship means reverence and humility; it means revering your real self and humbling delusions.
BODHIDHARMA (470–543)

Worship is transcendent wonder.
THOMAS CARLYLE (1795–1881)

It may be that our role on this planet is not to worship God, but to create him.
ARTHUR C. CLARKE (1917–)

So long as man remains free he strives for nothing so incessantly and painfully as to find someone to worship.
FYODOR DOSTOEVSKY (1821–1881)

A person will worship something, have no doubt about that. We may think our tribute is paid in secret in the dark recesses of our hearts, but it will out. That which dominates our imaginations and our thoughts will determine our lives, and our character. Therefore, it behooves us to be careful what we worship, for what we are worshipping we are becoming.
RALPH WALDO EMERSON (1803–1882)

When I admire the wonder of a sunset or the beauty of the moon, my soul expands in worship of the Creator.
MAHATMA GANDHI (1869–1948)

Worship is a way of seeing the world in the light of God.
ABRAHAM J. HESCHEL (1907–1972)

A man can no more diminish God's glory by refusing to worship Him than a lunatic can put out the sun by scribbling the word, "darkness" on the walls of his cell.
C. S. LEWIS (1898–1963)

Let's face it; God has a big ego problem. Why do we always have to worship him?
BILL MAHER (1956–)

Democracy is also a form of worship. It is the worship of Jackals by Jackasses.
H. L. MENCKEN (1880–1956)

I think worship is a lifestyle, first of all.
MICHAEL W. SMITH (1957–)

To worship God even for the sake of salvation or any other reward is equally degenerate. Love knows no reward. Give your love unto God, but do not ask anything in return even from Him through prayer.
SWAMI VIVEKANANDA (1863–1902)

People fashion their God after their own understanding. They make their God first and worship him afterwards.
OSCAR WILDE (1854–1900)

No man can worship God or love his neighbor on an empty stomach.
WOODROW WILSON (1856–1924)

He will never worship well the image on the altar who knew it when it was a trunk of wood in the garden.
SPANISH PROVERB

Wounds

Some people are afraid of what they might find if they try to analyze themselves too much, but you have to crawl into your wounds to discover where your fears are. Once the bleeding starts, the cleansing can begin.
TORI AMOS (1963–)

Incurable wounds are those inflicted by tongue and eye, by mockery and disdain.
HONORÉ DE BALZAC (1799–1850)

God who sends the wound sends the medicine.
MIGUEL DE CERVANTES (1547–1616)

I'm a little wounded but I'm not slain;
I will lay me down for to bleed awhile,
Then I'll rise and fight with you again.
JOHN DRYDEN (1631–1700)

Fools, through false shame, conceal their open wounds.
HORACE (65–8 BC)

Often the truth spoken with a smile will penetrate the mind and reach the heart; the lesson strikes home without wounding because of the wit in the saying.
HORACE (65–8 BC)

The difference between coarse and refined abuse is the difference between being bruised by a club and wounded by a poisoned arrow.
SAMUEL JOHNSON (1709–1784)

We shall heal our wounds, collect our dead and continue fighting.
MAO TSE-TUNG (1893–1976)

Here bring your wounded hearts, here tell your anguish;
Earth has no sorrow that Heaven cannot heal.
SIR THOMAS MORE (1478–1535)

He jests at scars that never felt a wound.
WILLIAM SHAKESPEARE (1564–1616), *Romeo and Juliet*

There's no wound deeper than a pen can give,
It makes men living dead, and dead men live.
JOHN TAYLOR (1753–1824)

A broken bone can heal, but the wound a word opens can fester forever.
JESSAMYN WEST (1902–1984)

A knife wound heals; a wound caused by words does not.
ANONYMOUS

Wounds from a friend can be trusted, but an enemy multiplies kisses.
THE BIBLE, Proverbs 27:6

All the hours wound you, the last one kills.
LATIN PROVERB

A bad wound may be cured, bad repute kills.
SPANISH PROVERB

Writing

Well, I think writing is basically about time and rhythm. Like with jazz. You have your basic melody and then you just riff off of it. And the riffs are about timing.
KATHY ACKER (1947–1997)

Learn as much by writing as by reading.
LORD ACTON (1834–1902)

Good writers define reality; bad ones merely restate it. A good writer turns fact into truth; a bad writer will, more often than not, accomplish the opposite.
EDWARD ALBEE (1928–)

A writer should say to himself, not, How can I get more money?, but How can I reach more readers (without lowering standards)?
BRIAN W. ALDISS (1925–)

There are two kinds of writer: those that make you think, and those that make you wonder.
BRIAN W. ALDISS (1925–)

All that writers can do is keep trying to say what is deepest in their hearts.
LLOYD ALEXANDER (1924–)

Writers want to summarize: What does this mean? What did we learn from this? That's a very 19th-century way of thinking about art, because it assumes that it should make our lives better or teach us something.
LAURIE ANDERSON (1947–)

A scene has to have a rhythm of its own, a structure of its own.
MICHELANGELO ANTONIONI (1912–2007)

Keep writing. Keep doing it and doing it. Even in the moments when it's so hurtful to think about writing.
HEATHER ARMSTRONG (1975–)

Rejection slips, or form letters, however tactfully phrased, are lacerations of the soul, if not quite inventions of the devil—but there is no way around them.
ISAAC ASIMOV (1920–1992)

You must keep sending work out; you must never let a manuscript do nothing but eat its head off in a drawer. You send that work out again and again, while you're working on another one. If you have talent, you will receive some measure of success—but only if you persist.
ISAAC ASIMOV (1920–1992)

Some writers confuse authenticity, which they ought always to aim at, with originality, which they should never bother about.
W. H. AUDEN (1907–1973)

Reading maketh a full man, conference a ready man, and writing an exact man.
SIR FRANCIS BACON (1561–1626)

The only thing I was fit for was to be a writer, and this notion rested solely on my suspicion that I would never be fit for real work, and that writing didn't require any.
RUSSELL BAKER (1925–)

Unless a writer is extremely old when he dies, in which case he has probably become a neglected institution, his death must always be seen as untimely. This is because a real writer is always shifting and changing and searching. The world has many labels for him, of which the most treacherous is the label of Success.
JAMES ARTHUR BALDWIN (1924–1987)

I am a galley slave to pen and ink.
HONORÉ DE BALZAC (1799–1850)

The writer must be universal in sympathy and an outcast by nature; only then can he see clearly.
JULIAN BARNES (1946–)

There is only one way to defeat the enemy, and that is to write as well as one can. The best argument is an undeniably good book.
SAUL BELLOW (1915–2005)

It took me fifteen years to discover I had no talent for writing, but I couldn't give it up because by that time I was too famous.
ROBERT BENCHLEY (1889–1945)

Why do writers write? Because it isn't there.
THOMAS BERGER (1924–)

Inspiration is wonderful when it happens, but the writer must develop an approach for the rest of the time.... The wait is simply too long.
LEONARD BERNSTEIN (1918–1990)

About the most originality that any writer can hope to achieve honestly is to steal with good judgment.
JOSH BILLINGS (1818–1885)

If you believe you can make a living as a writer, you already have enough ego.
DAVID BRIN (1950–)

If you have other things in your life—family, friends, good productive day work—these can interact with your writing and the sum will be all the richer.
DAVID BRIN (1950–)

The writer is important only by dint of the territory he colonizes.
VAN WYCK BROOKS (1886–1963)

Writers will happen in the best of families.
RITA MAE BROWN (1944–)

Either a writer doesn't want to talk about his work, or he talks about it more than you want.
ANATOLE BROYARD (1920–1990)

Beneath the rule of men entirely great,
The pen is mightier than the sword.
SIR EDWARD G. BULWER-LYTTON (1803–1873), *Richelieu*

Words, once they are printed, have a life of their own.
CAROL BURNETT (1933–)

It's not enough to create magic. You have to create a price for magic, too. You have to create rules.
ERIC A. BURNS (1968–)

This is the sixth book I've written, which isn't bad for a guy who's only read two.
GEORGE BURNS (1896–1996)

No one ever committed suicide while reading a good book, but many have tried while trying to write one.
ROBERT BYRNE (1928–)

I believe more in the scissors than I do in the pencil.
TRUMAN CAPOTE (1924–1984)

Writers are either putter-inners or taker-outers. I'm a taker-outer, because I can't write a book longer than 300 pages. Too many books are wordy and pedantic.
JONATHAN CARROLL (1949–)

I've always believed in writing without a collaborator, because where two people are writing the same book, each believes he gets all the worries and only half the royalties.
AGATHA CHRISTIE (1890–1976)

Writers never feel comfortable having labels attached to them, however accurate they are.
JONATHAN COE (1961–)

It is not a bad idea to get in the habit of writing down one's thoughts. It saves one having to bother anyone else with them.
ISABEL COLEGATE (1931–)

Many books require no thought from those who read them, and for a very simple reason; they made no such demand upon those who wrote them.
CHARLES CALEB COLTON (1780–1832)

Better to write for yourself and have no public, than to write for the public and have no self.
CYRIL CONNOLLY (1903–1974)

The writer is the man or woman who automatically takes a stance against his or her government. There are so many temptations for American writers to become part of the system and part of the structure that now, more than ever, we have to resist.
DON DELILLO (1936–)

And, after all, it is style alone by which posterity will judge of a great work, for an author can have nothing truly his own but his style.
ISAAC D'ISRAELI (1766–1848)

Style! Style! Why, all writers will tell you that it is the very thing which can least of all be changed. A man's style is nearly as much a part of him as his physiognomy, his figure, the throbbing of his pulse.
ISAAC D'ISRAELI (1766–1848)

The best way to become acquainted with a subject is to write a book about it.
BENJAMIN DISRAELI (1804–1881)

Planning to write is not writing. Outlining, researching, talking to people about what you're doing, none of that is writing. Writing is writing.
E. L. DOCTOROW (1931–)

Writers are not just people who sit down and write. They hazard themselves. Every time you compose a book your composition of yourself is at stake.
E. L. DOCTOROW (1931–)

Writing a novel is like driving a car at night. You can only see as far as your headlights, but you can make the whole trip that way.
E. L. DOCTOROW (1931–)

Writing is turning one's worst moments into money.
J. P. DONLEAVY (1926–)

Writers should be read, but neither seen nor heard.
DAPHNE DU MAURIER (1907–1989)

Some editors are failed writers, but so are most writers.
T. S. ELIOT (1888–1965)

Next to the originator of a good sentence is the first quoter of it.
RALPH WALDO EMERSON (1803–1882), *Letters and Social Aims*

A writer expresses himself in words that have been used before because they give his meaning better than he can give it himself, or because they are beautiful or witty, or because he expects them to touch a cord of association in his reader, or because he wishes to show that he is learned and well read. Quotations due to the last motive are invariably ill-advised; the discerning reader detects it and is contemptuous; the undiscerning is perhaps impressed, but even then is at the same time repelled, pretentious quotations being the surest road to tedium.
HENRY W. FOWLER (1858–1933), *A Dictionary of Modern English Usage*

Unprovided with original learning, unformed in the habits of thinking, unskilled in the arts of composition, I resolved to write a book.
EDWARD GIBBON (1737–1794)

If any man wish to write in a clear style, let him be first clear in his thoughts; and if any would write in a noble style, let him first possess a noble soul.
JOHANN WOLFGANG VON GOETHE (1749–1832)

Please write again soon. Though my own life is filled with activity, letters encourage momentary escape into others' lives, and I come back to my own with greater contentment.
ELIZABETH FORSYTHE HAILEY (1938–), *A Woman of Independent Means*

Writing is not necessarily something to be ashamed of, but do it in private and wash your hands afterwards.
ROBERT A. HEINLEIN (1907–1988)

[S]ometimes when I was started on a new story and I could not get going, I would sit in front of the fire and squeeze the peel of the little oranges into the edge of the flame and watch the sputter of blue that they made. I would stand and look out over the roofs of Paris and think, "Do not worry. You have always written before and you will write now. All you have to do is write one true sentence. Write the truest sentence you know."
ERNEST HEMINGWAY (1899–1961), *A Moveable Feast*

Forget your personal tragedy. We are all bitched from the start and you especially have to be hurt like hell before you can write seriously. But when you get the damned hurt, use it—don't cheat with it.
ERNEST HEMINGWAY (1899–1961)

Never write about a place until you're away from it, because that gives you perspective.
ERNEST HEMINGWAY (1899–1961)

Writing, at its best, is a lonely life. Organizations for writers palliate the writer's loneliness but I doubt if they improve his writing. He grows in public stature as he sheds his loneliness and often his work deteriorates. For he does his work alone and if he is a good enough writer he must face eternity, or the lack of it, each day.
ERNEST HEMINGWAY (1899–1961)

Manuscript: something submitted in haste and returned at leisure.
OLIVER HERFORD (1863–1935)

The way you define yourself as a writer is that you write every time you have a free minute. If you didn't behave that way you would never do anything.
JOHN IRVING (1942–)

Be generous, be delicate, and always pursue the prize.
HENRY JAMES (1843–1916)

What is written without effort is in general read without pleasure.
SAMUEL JOHNSON (1709–1784)

If you don't have the time to read, you don't have the time or the tools to write.
STEPHEN KING (1947–), *On Writing*

All of us learn to write in the second grade. Most of us go on to greater things.
BOBBY KNIGHT (1940–)

Your life story would not make a good book. Don't even try.
FRAN LEBOWITZ (1950–)

Advice to writers: Sometimes you just have to stop writing. Even before you begin.
STANISLAW LEC (1909–1966), *Unkempt Thoughts*

Don't use words too big for the subject. Don't say "infinitely" when you mean "very"; otherwise you'll have no word left when you want to talk about something really infinite.
C. S. LEWIS (1898–1963)

Even in literature and art, no man who bothers about originality will ever be original: whereas if you simply try to tell the truth (without caring twopence how often it has been told before) you will, nine times out of ten, become original without ever having noticed it.
C. S. LEWIS (1898–1963)

I can write better than anybody who can write faster, and I can write faster than anybody who can write better.
A. J. LIEBLING (1904–1963)

A writer is a person for whom writing is more difficult than it is for other people.
THOMAS MANN (1875–1955)

The writer of prose can only step aside when the poet passes.
W. SOMERSET MAUGHAM (1874–1965)

Copy from one, it's plagiarism; copy from two, it's research.
WILSON MIZNER (1876–1933)

Writing is like prostitution. First you do it for love, and then for a few close friends, and then for money.
MOLIÈRE (1622–1673)

An author is a fool who, not content with boring those he lives with, insists on boring future generations.
CHARLES DE MONTESQUIEU (1689–1755)

Research is usually a policeman stopping a novel from progressing.
BRIAN MOORE (1921–1999)

I take the view, and always have, that if you cannot say what you are going to say in twenty minutes you ought to go away and write a book about it.
LORD JOHN MOORE-BRABAZON (1884–1964)

You ask me why I do not write something.... I think one's feelings waste themselves in words, they ought all to be distilled into actions and into actions which bring results.
FLORENCE NIGHTINGALE (1820–1910)

Everywhere I go I'm asked if I think the university stifles writers. My opinion is that they don't stifle enough of them.
FLANNERY O'CONNOR (1925–1964)

There's many a bestseller that could have been prevented by a good teacher.
FLANNERY O'CONNOR (1925–1964)

A scrupulous writer, in every sentence that he writes, will ask himself at least four questions, thus: 1. What am I trying to say? 2. What words will express it? 3. What image or idiom will make it clearer? 4. Is this image fresh enough to have an effect?
GEORGE ORWELL (1903–1950), *Politics and the English Language*

In certain kinds of writing, particularly in art criticism and literary criticism, it is normal to come

across long passages which are almost completely lacking in meaning.
GEORGE ORWELL (1903–1950), *Politics and the English Language*

It is also true that one can write nothing readable unless one constantly struggles to efface one's own personality. Good prose is like a windowpane.
GEORGE ORWELL (1903–1950)

I have made this [letter] longer, because I have not had the time to make it shorter.
BLAISE PASCAL (1623–1662)

There is nothing to write about, you say. Well then, write and let me know just this—that there is nothing to write about; or tell me in the good old style if you are well. That's right. I am quite well.
PLINY THE YOUNGER (AD 62–114)

To achieve lasting literature, fictional or factual, a writer needs perceptive vision, absorptive capacity, and creative strength.
LAWRENCE CLARK POWELL (1906–2001)

Literature is an occupation in which you have to keep proving your talent to people who have none.
JULES RENARD (1864–1910)

Writing is the only profession where no one considers you ridiculous if you earn no money.
JULES RENARD (1864–1910)

The only reason for being a professional writer is that you can't help it.
LEO ROSTEN (1908–1997)

Say all you have to say in the fewest possible words, or your reader will be sure to skip them; and in the plainest possible words or he will certainly misunderstand them.
JOHN RUSKIN (1819–1900)

Writing gives you the illusion of control, and then you realize it's just an illusion, that people are going to bring their own stuff into it.
DAVID SEDARIS (1956–)

The man who writes about himself and his own time is the only man who writes about all people and all time.
GEORGE BERNARD SHAW (1856–1950)

Originality is not seen in single words or even sentences. Originality is the sum total of a man's thinking or his writing.
ISAAC BASHEVIS SINGER (1904–1991)

The wastepaper basket is the writer's best friend.
ISAAC BASHEVIS SINGER (1811–1875)

Writing for me is just like building a chair, making an artifact. The idea is that you build, create a story and cobble it together. If it stands up, that's good. If it stands up, it's comfortable, it's a good story, a good chair.
SCOTT SMITH (1965–)

A writer must always try to have a philosophy and he should also have a psychology and a philology and many other things. Without a philosophy and a psychology and all these various other things he is not really worthy of being called a writer.
GERTRUDE STEIN (1874–1946)

The discipline of the written word punishes both stupidity and dishonesty.
JOHN STEINBECK (1902–1968)

Vigorous writing is concise.
WILLIAM STRUNK JR. (1869–1946), *The Elements of Style*

Write something to suit yourself and many people will like it; write something to suit everybody and scarcely anyone will care for it.
JESSE STUART (1906–1984)

I'm never going to be shy about anything, what I write about is what I know; it's more about my version of the truth as I know it. That's part of my talent, really—putting the way people really speak into the things I write. My only obligation is to my characters. And they came from where I have been.
QUENTIN TARANTINO (1963–)

How vain it is to sit down to write when you have not stood up to live.
HENRY DAVID THOREAU (1817–1862)

Who is more to be pitied, a writer bound and gagged by policemen or one living in perfect freedom who has nothing more to say?
KURT VONNEGUT JR. (1922–2007)

No passion in the world is equal to the passion to alter someone else's draft.
H. G. WELLS (1866–1946)

A classic is classic not because it conforms to certain structural rules, or fits certain definitions (of which its author had quite probably never heard). It is classic because of a certain eternal and irrepressible freshness.
EDITH WHARTON (1862–1937)

I was working on the proof of one of my poems all the morning, and took out a comma. In the afternoon I put it back again.
OSCAR WILDE (1854–1900)

I'm all in favor of keeping dangerous weapons out of the hands of fools. Let's start with typewriters.
FRANK LLOYD WRIGHT (1868–1959)

Wrong

Where so many hours have been spent in convincing myself that I am right, is there not some reason to fear I may be wrong?
JANE AUSTEN (1775–1817)

Take Courage! Whatever you decide to do, it will probably be the wrong thing.
ASHLEIGH BRILLIANT (1933–)

Life appears to me too short to be spent in nursing animosity, or registering wrongs.
CHARLOTTE BRONTË (1816–1855)

Perhaps it is better to be irresponsible and right, than to be responsible and wrong.
SIR WINSTON CHURCHILL (1874–1965)

As long as the world shall last there will be wrongs, and if no man objected and no man rebelled, those wrongs would last forever.
CLARENCE DARROW (1857–1938)

One of the hardest things in this world is to admit you are wrong. And nothing is more helpful in resolving a situation than its frank admission.
BENJAMIN DISRAELI (1804–1881)

No amount of experimentation can ever prove me right; a single experiment can prove me wrong.
ALBERT EINSTEIN (1879–1955)

Don't take the wrong side of an argument just because your opponent has taken the right side.
BALTASAR GRACIAN (1601–1658)

Success is the sole earthly judge of right and wrong.
ADOLF HITLER (1889–1945)

You do not examine legislation in the light of the benefits it will convey if properly administered, but in the light of the wrongs it would do and the harms it would cause if improperly administered.
LYNDON B. JOHNSON (1908–1973)

It is better to suffer wrong than to do it, and happier to be sometimes cheated than not to trust.
SAMUEL JOHNSON (1709–1784)

I am not bound to win, but I am bound to be true. I am not bound to succeed, but I am bound to live by the light that I have. I must stand with anybody that stands right, and stand with him while he is right, and part with him when he goes wrong.
ABRAHAM LINCOLN (1809–1865)

It often requires more courage to dare to do right than to fear to do wrong.
ABRAHAM LINCOLN (1809–1865)

Nothing is wrong with California that a rise in the ocean level wouldn't cure.
ROSS MACDONALD (1915–1983)

There is always an easy solution to every human problem; neat, plausible, and wrong.
H. L. MENCKEN (1880–1956)

The worst-tempered people I've ever met were the people who knew they were wrong.
WILSON MIZNER (1876–1933)

Right is right, even if everyone is against it; and wrong is wrong, even if everyone is for it.
WILLIAM PENN (1644–1718)

I would never die for my beliefs because I might be wrong.
BERTRAND RUSSELL (1872–1970)

Love all, trust a few, do wrong to none.
WILLIAM SHAKESPEARE (1564–1616), *All's Well That Ends Well*

A child becomes an adult when he realizes that he has a right not only to be right but also to be wrong.
THOMAS S. SZASZ (1920–)

The fact that man knows right from wrong proves his intellectual superiority to other creatures; but the fact that he can do wrong proves his moral inferiority to any creature that cannot.
MARK TWAIN (1835–1910)

The proper office of a friend is to side with you when you are wrong. Nearly anybody will side with you when you are right.
MARK TWAIN (1835–1910)

It is dangerous to be right when the government is wrong.
VOLTAIRE (1694–1778)

Everything popular is wrong.
OSCAR WILDE (1854–1900)

Whenever people agree with me I always feel I must be wrong.
OSCAR WILDE (1854–1900)

Two wrongs do not make a right.
ENGLISH PROVERB

Submission to one wrong brings on another.
LATIN PROVERB

Yankees

The Yankee is one who, if he once gets his teeth set on a thing, all creation can't make him let go.
RALPH WALDO EMERSON (1803–1882)

True Yankees are born, not made.
JAY MOHR (1970–)

Yesterday

If today were half as good as tomorrow is supposed to be, it would probably be twice as good as yesterday was.
NORMAN R. AUGUSTINE (1935–)

What we are today comes from our thoughts of yesterday, and our present thoughts build our life of tomorrow: Our life is the creation of our mind.
THE BUDDHA (563–483 BC)

I can't go back to yesterday—because I was a different person then.
LEWIS CARROLL (1832–1898)

Yesterday, we can't do anything; tomorrow, we don't know. Today.
CELINE DION (1968–)

Yesterday's just a memory, tomorrow is never what it's supposed to be.
BOB DYLAN (1941–)

Learn from yesterday, live for today, hope for tomorrow.
ALBERT EINSTEIN (1879–1955)

Every day is a new opportunity. You can build on yesterday's success or put its failures behind and start over again. That's the way life is, with a new game every day, and that's the way baseball is.
BOB FELLER (1918–)

Today is yesterday's pupil.
THOMAS FULLER (1608–1661)

Yesterday is but today's memory, tomorrow is today's dream.
KAHLIL GIBRAN (1883–1931)

Yesterday we obeyed kings and bent our necks before emperors. But today we kneel only to truth, follow only beauty, and obey only love.
KAHLIL GIBRAN (1883–1931)

Yesterday's tomorrow is today.
SIMS HATCHER (1983–)

Clogged with yesterday's excess, the body drags the mind down with it.
HORACE (65–8 BC)

The idol of today pushes the hero of yesterday out of our recollection; and will, in turn, be supplanted by his successor of tomorrow.
WASHINGTON IRVING (1783–1859)

You can't have a better tomorrow if you are thinking about yesterday all the time.
CHARLES F. KETTERING (1876–1958)

Tomorrow is nothing, today is too late; the good lived yesterday.
MARCUS AURELIUS ANTONINUS (121–180)

I can't live off of yesterday—that's in the past.
JUICE NEWTON (1952–)

Yesterday's gone forever and tomorrow may never come, which leaves the present moment.
WILLIAM SHOCKLEY (1910–1989)

Yoga

Yoga teaches us to cure what need not be endured and endure what cannot be cured.
B. K. S. IYENGAR (1918–)

My mat is a safe place. I'll go into Child's pose or I'll simply sit on it and cry. It's my rock. I haven't been depressed in a while, but it's something I know how to look for in my life. Yoga has made a big difference there…
ASHLEY JUDD (1968–)

The way to true yoga is found by dwelling in God and remaining detached in the midst of worldly attachments.
GURU NANAK (1469–1539)

The meaning of our self is not to be found in its separateness from God and others, but in the ceaseless realization of yoga, of union.
RABINDRANATH TAGORE (1861–1941)

Youth

In case you're worried about what's going to become of the younger generation, it's going to grow up and start worrying about the younger generation.
ROGER ALLEN (1957–)

Young people are in a condition like permanent intoxication, because youth is sweet and they are growing.
ARISTOTLE (384–322 BC), *Nicomachean Ethics*

Youth would be an ideal state if it came a little later in life.
HERBERT HENRY ASQUITH (1852–1928)

I'm youth, I'm joy, I'm a little bird that has broken out of the egg.
JAMES M. BARRIE (1860–1937)

You can only be young once. But you can always be immature.
DAVE BARRY (1947–)

Childhood, n.: The period of human life intermediate between the idiocy of infancy and the folly of youth—two removes from the sin of manhood and three from the remorse of age.
AMBROSE BIERCE (1842–1914), *The Devil's Dictionary*

When I was a boy of fourteen, my father was so ignorant I could hardly stand to have the old man around. But when I got to be twenty-one, I was astonished at how much the old man had learned in seven years.
JOSH BILLINGS (1818–1885)

What Youth deemed crystal, Age finds out was dew.
ROBERT BROWNING (1812–1889)

What a mistake to suppose that the passions are strongest in youth! The passions are not stronger, but the control over them is weaker! They are more easily excited, they are more violent and apparent; but they have less energy, less durability, less intense and concentrated power than in the maturer life.
SIR EDWARD G. BULWER-LYTTON (1803–1873)

The arrogance of age must submit to be taught by youth.
EDMUND BURKE (1729–1797)

If you want to recapture your youth, just cut off his allowance.
RED BUTTONS (1919–2006)

Youth is to all the glad season of life; but often only by what it hopes, not by what it attains, or what it escapes.
THOMAS CARLYLE (1795–1881)

Youth is something very new: twenty years ago no one mentioned it.
COCO CHANEL (1883–1971)

Young men are apt to think themselves wise enough, as drunken men are apt to think themselves sober enough.
LORD CHESTERFIELD (1694–1773)

No man knows he is young while he is young.
G. K. CHESTERTON (1874–1936)

A sensual and intemperate youth translates into an old worn-out body.
CICERO (106–43 BC)

As I approve of a youth that has something of the old man in him, so I am no less pleased with an old man that has something of the youth. He that follows this rule may be old in body, but can never be so in mind.
CICERO (106–43 BC)

The pride of youth is in strength and beauty, the pride of old age is in discretion.
DEMOCRITUS (460–370 BC)

A boy's story is the best that is ever told.
CHARLES DICKENS (1812–1870)

We live in an age when to be young and to be indifferent can be no longer synonymous. We must prepare for the coming hour. The claims of the Future are represented by suffering millions; and the Youth of a Nation are the trustees of Posterity.
BENJAMIN DISRAELI (1804–1881)

The foundation of every state is the education of its youth.
DIOGENES LAERTIUS (C. 200)

In youth we learn; in age we understand.
MARIE VON EBNER-ESCHENBACH (1830–1916)

The young feel tired at the end of an action, the old at the beginning.
T. S. ELIOT (1888–1965)

If youth only knew: if age only could.
HENRI ESTIENNE (1470–1520)

Youth holds no society with grief.
EURIPIDES (C. 480–406 BC)

Youth is the best time to be rich, and the best time to be poor.
EURIPIDES (C. 480–406 BC)

Young men wish; love, money and health. One day, they'll say; health, money and love.
PAUL GÉRALDY (1885–1983)

Great endowments often announce themselves in youth in the form of singularity and awkwardness.
JOHANN WOLFGANG VON GOETHE (1749–1832)

Nothing can be so amusingly arrogant as a young man who has just discovered an old idea and thinks it is his own.
SYDNEY J. HARRIS (1917–1986)

Never suffer youth to be an excuse for inadequacy, nor age and fame to be an excuse for indolence.
BENJAMIN HAYDON (1786–1846)

Youth itself is a talent, a perishable talent.
ERIC HOFFER (1902–1983)

There's nothing that keeps its youth,
So far as I know, but a tree and truth.
OLIVER WENDELL HOLMES SR. (1809–1894), *The Deacon's Masterpiece*

Through our great good fortune, in our youth our hearts were touched with fire. It was given to us to learn at the outset that life is a profound and passionate thing.
OLIVER WENDELL HOLMES SR. (1809–1894)

Youth is unduly busy with pampering the outer person.
HORACE (65–8 BC)

The heads of strong old age are beautiful beyond all grace of youth.
ROBINSON JEFFERS (1887–1962)

So different are the colors of life, as we look forward to the future, or backward to the past; and so different the opinions and sentiments which this contrariety of appearance naturally produces, that the conversation of the old and young ends generally with contempt or pity on either side.
SAMUEL JOHNSON (1709–1784)

Youth enters the world with very happy prejudices in her own favor. She imagines herself not only certain of accomplishing every adventure, but of obtaining those rewards which the accomplishment may deserve. She is not easily persuaded to believe that the force of merit can be resisted by obstinacy and avarice, or its luster darkened by envy and malignity.
SAMUEL JOHNSON (1709–1784)

Ask the young. They know everything.
JOSEPH JOUBERT (1754–1824)

Youth is happy because it has the ability to see beauty. Anyone who keeps the ability to see beauty never grows old.
FRANZ KAFKA (1883–1924)

Enjoy the Spring of Love and Youth, to some good angel leave the rest; For Time will teach thee soon the truth, there are no birds in last year's nest!
HENRY WADSWORTH LONGFELLOW (1807–1882)

How beautiful is youth! how bright it gleams with its illusions, aspirations, dreams! Book of Beginnings, Story without End, Each maid a heroine, and each man a friend!
HENRY WADSWORTH LONGFELLOW (1807–1882)

Youth comes but once in a lifetime.
HENRY WADSWORTH LONGFELLOW (1807–1882)

The secret of eternal youth is arrested development.
ALICE ROOSEVELT LONGWORTH (1884–1980)

If youth be a defect, it is one that we outgrow only too soon.
JAMES RUSSELL LOWELL (1819–1891)

Every youth owes it to himself and to the world to make the most possible out of the stuff that is in him…
ORISON SWETT MARDEN (1850–1924)

It is the youth who sees a great opportunity hidden in just these simple services, who sees a very uncommon situation, a humble position, who gets on in the world.
ORISON SWETT MARDEN (1850–1924)

I would like to recapture that freshness of vision which is characteristic of extreme youth when all the world is new to it.
HENRI MATISSE (1869–1954)

It is an illusion that youth is happy, an illusion of those who have lost it; but the young know they are wretched, for they are full of the truthless ideals, which have been instilled into them, and each time they come in contact with the real, they are bruised and wounded.
W. SOMERSET MAUGHAM (1874–1965), *Of Human Bondage*

The American ideal is youth—handsome, empty youth.
HENRY MILLER (1891–1980)

Young alienation, disappointment, and heartache is all a part of the first real growing up that we do.
JUDD NELSON (1959–)

The surest way to corrupt a youth is to instruct him to hold in higher esteem those who think alike than those who think differently.
FRIEDRICH NIETZSCHE (1844–1900), *The Dawn*

Youth has no age.
PABLO PICASSO (1881–1973)

The young know how truly difficult and dreadful youth can be. Their youth is wasted on everyone else, that's the horror. The young have no authority, no respect.
ANNE RICE (1941–), *Tale of the Body Thief*

Idle youth, enslaved to everything; by being too sensitive I have wasted my life.
ARTHUR RIMBAUD (1854–1891)

We cannot always build the future for our youth, but we can build our youth for the future.
FRANKLIN D. ROOSEVELT (1882–1945)

Age is foolish and forgetful when it underestimates youth.
J. K. ROWLING (1965–), *Harry Potter and the Half-Blood Prince*

Youth cannot know how age thinks and feels. But old men are guilty if they forget what it was to be young.
J. K. ROWLING (1965–), *Harry Potter and the Order of the Phoenix*

Keep true to the dreams of thy youth.
FRIEDRICH VON SCHILLER (1759–1805)

Youth covets; let not this covetousness seduce you.
FRIEDRICH VON SCHILLER (1759–1805)

It is the failing of youth not to be able to restrain its own violence.
SENECA (5 BC–AD 65)

Do you set down your name in the scroll of youth, that are written down old with all the characters of age?
WILLIAM SHAKESPEARE (1564–1616), *King Henry IV*

We have some salt of our youth in us.
WILLIAM SHAKESPEARE (1564–1616), *The Merry Wives of Windsor*

A man loves the meat in his youth that he cannot endure in his age.
WILLIAM SHAKESPEARE (1564–1616), *Much Ado About Nothing*

Youth, which is forgiven everything, forgives itself nothing: age, which forgives itself everything, is forgiven nothing.
GEORGE BERNARD SHAW (1856–1950) *Man and Superman*

It is all that the young can do for the old, to shock them and keep them up to date.
GEORGE BERNARD SHAW (1856–1950)

Youth is a wonderful thing. What a crime to waste it on children.
GEORGE BERNARD SHAW (1856–1950)

Don't laugh at a youth for his affectations; he is only trying on one face after another to find his own.
LOGAN PEARSALL SMITH (1865–1946)

Youth is the time to go flashing from one end of the world to the other… to try the manners of different nations; to hear the chimes at midnight; to see the sunrise in town and country; to be converted at a revival; to circumnavigate the metaphysics, write halting verses, run a mile to see a fire, and wait all day long in the theatre to applaud Hernani.
ROBERT LOUIS STEVENSON (1850–1894)

For God's sake give me the young man who has brains enough to make a fool of himself!
ROBERT LOUIS STEVENSON (1850–1894)

No wise man ever wished to be younger.
JONATHAN SWIFT (1667–1745)

Youth gets together with their materials to build a bridge to the moon or maybe a palace on earth; then in middle age they decide to build a woodshed with them instead.
HENRY DAVID THOREAU (1817–1862)

It is better to be a young June-bug than an old bird of paradise.
MARK TWAIN (1835–1910)

What is youth except a man or a woman before it is ready or fit to be seen?
EVELYN WAUGH (1903–1966)

The deepest definition of youth is life as yet untouched by tragedy.
ALFRED NORTH WHITEHEAD (1861–1947)

Youth, large, lusty, loving—Youth, full of grace, force, fascination. Do you know that Old Age may come after you with equal grace, force, fascination?
WALT WHITMAN (1819–1892)

To get back my youth I would do anything in the world, except take exercise, get up early, or be respectable.
OSCAR WILDE (1854–1900), *The Picture of Dorian Gray*

I am not young enough to know everything.
OSCAR WILDE (1854–1900)

In America the young are always ready to give to those who are older than themselves the full benefits of their inexperience.
OSCAR WILDE (1854–1900)

Those whom the gods love grow young.
OSCAR WILDE (1854–1900)

Youth! There is nothing like youth. The middle-aged are mortgaged to Life. The old are in Life's lumber-room. But youth is the Lord of Life. Youth has a kingdom waiting for it. Every one is born a king, and most people die in exile.
OSCAR WILDE (1854–1900)

The most conservative persons I ever met are college undergraduates. The radicals are the men past middle life.
WOODROW WILSON (1856–1924)

Boyhood, like measles, is one of those complaints which a man should catch young and have done with, for when it comes in middle life it is apt to be serious.
P. G. WODEHOUSE (1881–1975), *Uneasy Money*

Youth is a quality, not a matter of circumstances.
FRANK LLOYD WRIGHT (1867–1959)

After all, life hasn't much to offer except youth and I suppose for older people the love of youth in others.
ANONYMOUS

Everybody's youth is a dream, a form of chemical madness.
ANONYMOUS

The good thing about being young is that you are not experienced enough to know you cannot possibly do the things you are doing.
ANONYMOUS

Praise youth and it will prosper.
IRISH PROVERB

Zeal

Never let your zeal outrun your charity. The former is but human, the latter is divine.
HOSEA BALLOU (1771–1852)

Zeal without humanity is like a ship without a rudder, liable to be stranded at any moment.
OWEN FELTHAM (1602–1668)

Zeal without knowledge is fire without light.
THOMAS FULLER (1608–1661)

Zeal is a volcano, the peak of which the grass of indecisiveness does not grow.
KAHLIL GIBRAN (1883–1931)

Zeal will do more than knowledge.
WILLIAM HAZLITT (1778–1830)

Zeal is very blind, or badly regulated, when it encroaches upon the rights of others.
PASQUIER QUESNEL (1634–1719)

The warmth of zeal is not perhaps the most dangerous rock that we have to avoid; but rather that languour which ease produces and a distrust of our own courage.
MAXIMILIEN ROBESPIERRE (1758–1794)

Zeal is fit for wise men, but flourishes chiefly among fools.
JOHN TILLOTSON (1630–1694)

Zealots

To attempt the destruction of our passions is the height of folly. What a noble aim is that of the zealot who tortures himself like a madman in order to desire nothing, love nothing, feel nothing, and who, if he succeeded, would end up a complete monster!
DENIS DIDEROT (1713–1784)

Zealots often carry the day.
BOBBY R. INMAN (1931–)

In the fevered state of our country, no good can ever result from any attempt to set one of these fiery zealots to rights, either in fact or principle. They are determined as to the facts they will believe, and the opinions on which they will act. Get by them, therefore, as you would by an angry bull; it is not for a man of sense to dispute the road with such an animal.
THOMAS JEFFERSON (1762–1826)

Slavery is now no where more patiently endured, than in countries once inhabited by the zealots of liberty.
SAMUEL JOHNSON (1709–1784)

For modes of faith let graceless zealots fight,
His can't be wrong whose life is in the right.
ALEXANDER POPE (1688–1744)

Zen

Zen, per se, is not just an art, it's not just a religion, it's a realization.
GENE CLARK (1944–1991)

Reverence for all life is the formula of Zen Buddhism, and in this is hidden the secret of Zen.
EUGEN HERRIGEL (1885–1955)

Zen teaches that once we can open up to the inevitability of our demise, we can begin to transform that situation and lighten up about it.
ALLEN KLEIN (1931–)

The only Zen you can find on the tops of mountains is the Zen you bring up there.
ROBERT M. PIRSIG (1928–), *Zen and the Art of Motorcycle Maintenence*

Zen is not some kind of excitement, but concentration on our usual everyday routine.
SHUNRYU SUZUKI (1904–1971)

Zen Buddhism is a discipline where belief isn't necessary.
DAVID SYLVIAN (1958–)

Zen does not confuse spirituality with thinking about God while one is peeling potatoes. Zen spirituality is just to peel the potatoes.
ALAN W. WATTS (1915–1973)

Zionism

Zionism demands a publicly recognized and legally secured homeland in Palestine for the Jewish people. This platform is unchangeable.
THEODOR HERZL (1860–1904)

One of the dreams of Zionism was to be a bridge. Instead, we are creating exclusion between the East and the West instead of creating bridges; we are contributing to the conflict between East and West by our stupid desire to have more.
A. B. YEHOSHUA (1936–)

Index by Author or Source

A

Aalto, Alvar (1898–1976)
Architecture 60
Abbagnano, Nicola (1901–1990)
Reason 678
Abbas, Abu (1948–2004)
Remorse 690
War 859
Abbey, Edward (1927–1989)
Abortion 13
Anarchy 50
Cancer 114
Ideology 416
Philosophy 618
Police 631
Rape 673
The Supernatural 788
Teamwork 800
Tyranny 833
Wilderness 867
Wit 873
Abbey, Lynn (1948–)
Persistence 613
Abbott, Berenice (1898–1991)
Photography 620
Abbott, John S. C. (1805–1877)
Mothers 552
Abdul, Paula (1962–)
Chance 128
Abdul-Jabbar, Kareem (1947–)
Losing 501
Teamwork 800
Abraham, F. Murray (1939–)
Creativity 189
Abraham, Spencer (1952–)
The Cold War 154
Achebe, Chinua (1930–)
Stories 766
Acheson, Dean (1893–1971)
Bureaucracy 107
Ego 263
Endurance 269
Negotiation 571
Statesmen 762
Acker, Kathy (1947–1997)
Rhythm 701
Writing 885
Ackerman, Diane (1948–)
Life 489
Mirrors 540
Poetry 627
Secrets 724
Senses 730
Acton, Lord (1834–1902)
Artists 65
Authority 72
Books 97
The Dead 207
Elections 265
History 398
Liberty 479, 480
Majorities 515
Minorities 539
Oppression 589
The Past 601
Power 643
Reading 673
Secrets 724
Security 725
Writing 885
Adams, Abigail (1744–1818)
Chance 128
Daughters 206
Feminism 315
Learning 474
Retirement 697
Virtue 852
Words 877
Adams, Ansel (1902–1984)
Creativity 189

Adams, Ansel (cont.)
Emotions 267
Mythology 565
Anxiety 56
Patience 604
Adams, Brian (1964–)
Anxiety 56
Adams, Charles (1930–)
Rulers 710
Taxes 796
Adams, Douglas (1952–2001)
Ancestors 51
Breakfast 105
Cats 115
Common Sense 158
The Dead 207
Disability 238
Discovery 240
Dreams 249
Ego 263
Enemies 270
Experience 291
Fools 326
Fruit 351
Illusion 421
Learning 474
Lunch 512
Politicians 635
Rain 672
Service 732
Theories 809
Time 815
The Universe 840
Adams, Franklin P. (1881–1960)
Elections 265
Fiction 316
Forgiveness 331
Information 432
Novels 577
Politics 636
Adams, George Matthew (1878–1962)
Sacrifice 711
Adams, Gerry (1948–)
Unity 839
Adams, Henry (1838–1918)
Eternity 281
Friendship 340
Intelligence 437
Meaning 527
Politics 636
Presidents 650
Simplicity 740
Suicide 783
Summer 787
Taste 795
Teachers 796
Words 877
Adams, Joey (1968–)
Questions 668
Adams, John (1735–1826)
America 47
Avarice 74
Defiance 216
Democracy 220
Education 259
Facts 295
Freedom 336
God 367
Government 371
Horses 404
Juries 450
Kings 456
Liberty 480
Patriotism 605
Popularity 640
Priests 652
Property 658
Rivalry 708
Slavery 746
Statesmen 762
Suicide 783
Adams, John Quincy (1767–1848)
Courage 186
Elections 265
Immorality 426

Adams, John Quincy (cont.)
- Independence 428
- Leadership 470
- Mothers 552
- Obstacles 581

Adams, Philip (1939–)
- Confidence 165
- Risk 707

Adams, Richard (1626–1698)
- Ideas 413
- Thoughts 810

Adams, Samuel Hopkins (1871–1958)
- Love 505
- Newspapers 572

Adams, Scott (1957–)
- Atheism 70
- Creativity 189
- Dating 206
- Decisions 213
- Fantasy 304
- Men 532
- Mistakes 543
- Numbers 577
- Profit 655
- Questions 668
- Religion 687
- Revenge 699
- Stupidity 775
- The Universe 840

Adams, William (1706–1789)
- Achievement 19

Addams, Jane (1860–1935)
- Adults 29
- Civilization 150
- Respect 695

Addis, Don (1964–)
- Cats 115

Addison, Joseph (1672–1719)
- Admiration 26
- Arguments 60
- Birds 91
- Books 97
- Censure 126
- Conversation 176
- Daughters 206
- Devotion 233
- Education 259
- Epitaphs 279
- Exercise 289
- Fame 300
- Faults 310
- Flowers 322
- Friendship 340
- Fruit 351
- Happiness 383
- Humanity 406
- Hunger 411
- Laughter 463
- Lust 512
- Misery 540
- Modesty 546
- Obscurity 580
- Patriotism 605
- Persecution 612
- Perseverance 612
- Pity 622
- Pleasure 624
- Pride 651
- Ridicule 705
- Sculpture 723
- Serenity 731
- Smiles 748
- Studying 774
- Success 779
- Suffering 782
- Suspicion 790
- Taste 795
- Tolerance 818
- Tradition 522
- Virtue 852
- Wit 873

Adie, Kate (1945–)
- Journalists 443

Adjani, Isabelle (1955–)
- Alienation 43
- Cruelty 198

Adjani, Isabelle (cont.)
Passion 600
Adler, Alfred (1870–1937)
Inferiority 431
Meaning 527
Neurosis 571
Sensitivity 730
Society 751
Torture 819
War 859
Adler, Felix (1855–1931)
Church 145
Family 302
Simplicity 740
Adler, Mortimer (1902–2001)
Friendship 340
Leisure 476
Lust 512
Telephones 802
Valor 844
Adler, Polly (1900–1962)
Prostitution 660
Adler, Stella (1901–1992)
Theater 807
Adorno, Theodor W. (1903–1969)
Anti-Semitism 56
Dehumanization 218
Fascism 305
Health 388
Ideology 416
Intolerance 438
Personality 614
Satire 716
Sickness 737
Suicide 783
Tact 792
Thoughts 810
Aethelred, Saint, of Rievaulx (c. 1110–1167)
Friendship 340
Aeschylus (525–456 BC)
Anarchy 50
Death 207
Decency 211
Despair 226
Destiny 228
Disease 240
Dreams 249
Envy 278
Hope 403
Mind 535
Prosperity 659
Safety 713
Sickness 737
Silence 738
Strength 771
Thoughts 810
Traitors 825
Trust 829
Tyranny 833, 834
Words 877
Aesop (620–560 BC)
Adultery 28
Advice 33
Anxiety 56
Appearances 58
Birds 91
Conceit 164
Enemies 270
Friendship 340
Kindness 453
Mind 535
Misfortune 542
Persuasion 615
Prudence 661
Self 727
Slavery 746
Thieves 810
Unity 839
Values 845
Affleck, Ben (1972–)
Loss 504
Love 505
Afranius (c. 900 BC)
Desire 224
Love 505

Agar, Herbert (1897–1980)
Truth 830
Agathon (448-400 BC)
Change 128
God 367
The Past 601
Agee, James (1909–1955)
Humanity 406
Mothers 552
Responsibility 696
Agesilaus II (c. 444–360 BC)
Courage 186
Justice 451
Agnew, Spiro T. (1918–1986)
Lies 486
Masochism 524
Aiken, George D. (1892–1984)
Conflict 167
Conservation 174
Prejudice 648
Aiken, John (1747–1822)
Censorship 122
Aiken, Howard (1900–1973)
Ideas 413
Ailey, Alvin (1931–1989)
Racism 671
Aimee, Anouk (1932–)
Age 36
Beauty 80
Akaka, Daniel (1923–)
Crisis 192
Akenside, Mark (1721–1770)
Shakespeare 735
Akhenaton (c. 1400 BC)
Cowardice 188
The Sun 787
Trouble 828
Akin, Todd (1947–)
Crisis 192
Alba, Jessica (1981–)
Celebrities 122
Fame 300
Albee, Edward (1928–)
Courage 185
Democracy 220
Theater 807
Writing 885
Albers, Josef (1888–1976)
Artists 65
Suicide 783
Albert, Edward (1951–)
Courage 186
Crisis 192
Fear 311
Prayer 647
Understanding 836
Alberti, Leon Battista (1404–1472)
Beauty 80
Albini, Steve (1962–) ....
Artists 65
Albom, Mitch (1959–)
Beginnings 85
Endings 269
Albright, Herm (1876–1944)....
Effort 262
Alcaeus (c. 600 BC) ....
Wine 869
Alcott, Amos Bronson (1799–1888)
Civilization 150
Corruption 184
Debate 210
Dreams 249
Expectations 290
The Garden of Eden 355
Mothers 552
Strength 771
Teachers 796
Triumph 828
Alcott, Louisa May (1832–1888)
Babies 75
Cats 115
Conceit 164
Kingdoms 454
Old Age 583
Queens 667

Alcott, Louisa May (cont.)
Vision 855
Women 875
Alda, Alan (1936–)
Heaven 392
Intuition 439
Aldington, Richard (1892–1962)
Nationalism 567
Patriotism 605
Aldiss, Brian W. (1925–)
Childhood 136
Creativity 189
Writing 885
Aldrich, Thomas Bailey (1836–1907)
Age 36
Aldrin, Buzz (1930–)
Exercise 289
Heart 390
Aleichem, Sholom (1859–1916)
Life 489
The Poor 639
Telephones 802
Wealth 864
Alexander the Great (356–323 BC)
Teachers 796
Alexander, Archibald (1772–1851)
Blunders 94
Nature 569
Saviors 717
Alexander, J. W. (1888–1971)
Ideas 413
Alexander, Lloyd (1924–)
Achievement 19
Cats 115
Learning 474
Writing 886
Alexander, Samuel (1859–1938)
Curiosity 200
Alexander, Scott (1963–)
Sex 733
Vision 855
War 859
Alexander, Shana (1925–2005)
Excellence 286
Alexander, William (1915–1997)
Rivers 708
Alfieri, Vittorio (1749–1803)
Silence 738
Vengeance 847
Ali Ibn Abi Talib (c. 599–661)
Abstinence 14
Enemies 270
Friendship 340
Ali, Muhammad (1942–)
Boxing 102
Challenges 127
Champions 127
Faith 299
Gold 369
Losing 501
Marriage 521
Retirement 697
Risk 707
Service 732
Silence 738
Violence 851
Winning 868
Allen, Dave (1936–2005)
Stories 766
Allen, David (1945–)
Creativity 190
Allen, Fred (1894–1956)
Alliances 44
California 113
Celebrities 122
Hollywood 400
Imitaion 425
Life 489
Mediocrity 529
Radio 672
Television 802
Allen, George (1952–)
Appeasement 59
Determination 230

Allen, George (cont.)
Life 490
Allen, George Herbert (1918–1990)
Success 779
Allen, Gracie (1906–1964)
Birds 92
Birth 92
Allen, Hervey (1889–1949)
Beer 84
Legends 476
Allen, James (1864–1912)
Adjustment 25
Dreams 249
Slavery 746
Thoughts 810
Allen, Marty (1922–)
Economics 256
Allen, Richard V. (1936–)
Bureaucracy 107
Allen, Robert G. (1902–1963)
Optimism 590
Allen, Roger (1957–)
Age 36
Youth 893
Allen, Roland (1868–1947)
Redemption 681
Allen, Steve (1921–2000)
Totalitarianism 820
Allen, Tim (1953–)
Lies 486
Allen, Tom (1945–)
Conservation 174
Allen, Woody (1935–)
Atheism 70, 71
Cheating 136
Cinema 146
College 155
Crime 191
Dating 206
Days 206
Death 207
Despair 226
Dessert 228
Divorce 243
Dreams 249
Famine 304
Illusion 421
Immorality 426
Love 505
Marriage 521
Masturbation 524
Misery 540
Money 547
Objectivity 579
People 610
Reading 673
Reason 678
Reform 682
Regret 683
Science 719
Success 779
Tradition 522
Trees 827
Truth 830
The Universe 840
Allende, Isabel (1942–)
Giving 363
Allison, Dorothy (1949–)
Fiction 316
Allingham, Margery (1904–1966)
Mourning 561
Passion 600
Allred, Gloria (1941–)
Dogs 245
Allston, Aaron (1960–)
Comedy 155
Tragedy 824
Almodovar, Pedro (1951–)
Cinema 146
Alther, Lisa (1944–)
Intelligence 437
Althusser, Louis (1918–1990)
Ideology 416
Altman, Sidney (1939–)
Reward 701

Alzado, Lyle (1949–1992)
Sanity 714
Amanpour, Christiane (1958–)
The Cold War 154
Journalists 443
Ambedkar, B. R. (1891–1956)
Tyranny 834
Ambler, Eric (1909–1998)
Skeptics 744
Ambrose, Stephen (1936–2002)
Blunders 95
Coorporations 179
The Future 353
Hope 403
Native Americans 568
The Past 601
Republicans 692
Ambrosius Macrobius (c. 400 BC)
Laws 465
Morality 551
Ameringer, Oscar (1870–1943)
Politics 637
Rich and Poor 702
Ames, Aldrich (1941–)
Confessions 165
Ames, Fisher (1758–1808)
The Bible 88
Ames, William (1576–1633)
Church 146
Worship 884
Amherst, Jeffrey, Baron (1717–1797)
Farming 305
Amiel, Barbara (1940–)
Rhetoric 701
Amiel, Henri-Frédéric (1821–1881)
Authority 72
Charm 135
Childhood 136
Common Sense 158
Criticism 196
Difficulty 235
Energy 271
Error 280
Family 302
Fate 306
Gratitude 376
Greatness 377
Hope 403
Humanity 406
Ideology 416
Individualism 429
Justice 451
Materialism 524
Morality 551
Order 591
Sacrifice 711
Secrets 724
Suffering 782
Survival 789
Sympathy 791
Talent 793
Thankfulness 807
Thoughts 810
Totalitarianism 820
Truth 830
Uncertainty 835
Women 876
Work 880
Amis, Kingsley (1922–1995)
Censorship 122
Amis, Martin (1949–)
Money 547
Weapons 865
Ammons, Archie R. (1926–2001)
Silence 738
Amory, Cleveland (1917–1998)
Cats 116
Amos, Tori (1963–)
Change 128
Rape 673
Wounds 885
Amos, Wally "Famous" (1936–)
Life 490
Andersen, Hans Christian (1805–1875)
Life 490
Stories 766

Anderson, Gillian (1968–)
Strength 771
Anderson, Laurie (1947–)
Artists 66
Eyes 293
Paradise 595
Writing 886
Anderson, Loni (1946–)
Acting 21
Rejection 684
Smoking 749
Anderson, Marian (1897–1993)
Dreams 249
Anderson, Paul Thomas (1970–)
Opportunity 585
The Past 601
Anderson, Sparky (1934–)
Seasons 724
Anderson, Wes (1969–)
Wealth 864
Ando, Tadao (1941–)
Architects 59
Computers 163
Creativity 190
Economics 256
Andretti, Mario (1940–)
Determination 230
Motivation 560
Andrews, Julie (1935–)
Bathrooms 80
Discipline 238
Andric, Ivo (1892–1975)
Sadness 712
Angelou, Maya (1928–)
Bigotry 89
Cancer 114
Consistency 175
Courage 186
Ethics 282
Forgetfulness 331
Friendship, ...340
History 398
Ignorance 418
Mothers 552
Siblings 737
Sisters 743
Stories 766
Uniqueness 839
Words 877
Aniston, Jennifer (1969–)
Sensitivity 730
Annan, Kofi (1938–)
Choice 144
Conflict 167
Profit 655
Annaud, Jean-Jacques
Cinema 146
Annenberg, Walter (1902–2002)
Strength 771
Annis, Francesca (1945–)
Bureaucracy 107
Anouilh, Jean (1910–1987)
Love 505
Poetry 627
Propaganda 657
Ansberry, Clare (1957–)
Flowers 322
Ant, Adam (1954–)
Virginity 852
Anthony, Susan B. (1820–1906)
Rights 706
Antiphanes (408-334 BC)
Poverty 643
Antisthenes (444–371 BC)
Character 131
Enemies 270
Envy 278
Rust 710
Antonioni, Michelangelo (1912–2007)
Rhythm 701
Writing 886
Aoun, Michel (1935–)
Freedom 336
Apple, R. W., Jr. (1934–)
Journalists 443

Apocrypha
Language 463
Apollinaire, Guillaume (1880–1918)
Happiness 383
Purity 664
Appianus (c. 200)
Forgetfulness 331
Apuleius (124–170)
Admiration 26
Aquino, Corazon (1933–)
Bedrooms 83
Media 528
Reconciliation 680
Aragon, Louis (1897–1982)
Fallibility 300
Genius 360
Opposites 588
Reason 678
Religion 687
Aragones, Sergio (1937–)
Losing 501
Sadness 712
Arbus, Diane (1923–1971)
Aristocracy 61
The Garden of Eden 355
Photography 620
Arbuthnot, John (1667–1735)
Political Parties 634
Arcesilaus (c. 316–241 BC)
Injustice 432
Laws 466
Arendt, Hannah (1906–1975)
Confessions 165
Conservatives 174
Defiance 216
Equality 279
Hypocrisy 412
Ideology 416
Liberals 477
Lies 486
Mobs 545
Opposites 588
Organization 591
Propaganda 657
Revolution 700
Senses 730
Totalitarianism 820
Tyranny 834
Violence 851
Aretino, Pietro (1492–1556)
Cowardice 188
Friendship 340
Arguello, Alexis (1952–)
Boxing 102, 103
Arinze, Francis (1932–)
Church 146
Ariosto, Ludovico (1471–1533)
Heresy 396
Aristippus (c. 435–366)
Humanity 406
Ignorance 418
Aristophanes (c. 448–380 BC)
Art 63
Home 400
Jokes 441
Language 462
Polilticians 634, 635
Wine 869
Aristotle (384–322 BC)
Accidents 18
Actions 22
Age 36
Anger 53
Animals 55
Avarice 74
Birds 91
Bravery 104
Chance 128
Character 131
Community 161
Conflict 167
Consciousness 172
Cowardice 188
Crime 191
Crisis 192
Democracy 220

Aristotle (cont.)
Desire 224
Dignity 236
Dreams 249
Education 259
Equality 279
Evil 284
Excellence 286
Failure 296
Fathers 309
Friendship 340
Fruit 351
Genius 360
Goals 366
God 367
Habits 382
Happiness 383
Heroes 398
Hope 403
Humor 410
Intoxication 438
Justice 451
Knowledge 459
Laws 466
Leadership 470
Learning 474
Leisure 476
Liberals 477
Liberty 480
Lies 486
Madness 513
Mankind 518
Maxims 527
Melancholy 530
Mind 535
Misfortune 542
Mothers 552
Nature 569
Old Age 583
Patience 604
Peace 607
Persuasion 615
Philosophy 618
Pleasure 624
Poetry 627
Politics 637
Poverty 643
Profit 655
Repentance 691
Revolution 700
Self 727
Simplicity 740
Solitude 753
Statesmen 762
Success 779
Suffering 782
Suicide 783
Summer 787
Surprise 789
Tragedy 824
Virtue 852
War 859
Wisdom 870
Wit 873
Work 880
Youth 893
Arkin, Adam (1956–)
Obsession 581
Arledge, Roone (1931–)
Crisis 192
Armani, Giorgio (1934–)
Style 777
Armour, Richard (1906–1989)
Libraries 484
Telephones 802
Armstrong, Billie Joe (1972–)
Strength 771
Armstrong, Heather (1975–)
Mental Illness 533
Parenthood 597
Writing 886
Armstrong, Lance (1971–)
Losing 501
Armstrong, Neil (1930–)
Logic 499
The Moon 550

Arno, Peter (1904–1968)
- Telephones 802

Arnold, Matthew (1822–1888)
- Catholicism 115
- Common Sense 158
- Crowds 198
- Emotions 267
- Misery 541
- Morality 551
- Religion 687
- Truth 830

Arnold, Thomas (1795–1842)
- Ability 9

Aronofsky, Darren (1969–)
- Mathematics 525

Arp, Jean (1886–1966)
- Silence 738

Artaud, Antonin (1896–1948)
- Death 207
- Tragedy 824

Arthur, Owen 1949–)
- Journalists 443

Asch, Sholem (1880–1957)
- Libraries 484
- Tolerance 818

Ascham, Roger (1515–1568)
- Style 777

Ash, Mary Kay (1918–2001)
- Appreciation 59
- Banks 78
- Enthusiasm 275
- Success 779

Ashcroft, John (1942–)
- Necessity 570

Ashe, Arthur (1943–1993)
- Losing 501
- Self-Confidence 728

Ashmore, Shawn (1979–)
- Style 777

Asimov, Isaac (1920–1992)
- Boredom 100
- Computers 163
- Cruelty 198
- Death 207
- Discovery 240
- Ethics 282
- Faith 299
- The Great Depression 379
- Humanity 406
- Ignorance 418
- Knowledge 459
- Life 490
- Morality 551
- Persistence 613
- Rationalism 673
- Refuge 682
- Science 719
- Subtlety 778
- Success 779
- Theories 809
- Violence 851
- Writing 886

Askin, Leon (1907–2005)
- Anti-Semitism 56

Asquith, Herbert Henry (1852–1928)
- Youth 893

Asquith, Margot (1864–1945)
- America 47
- Journalists 443
- Pity 622

Assante, Armand (1949–)
- Economics 256

Astin, Mackenzie (1973–)
- Guns 381

Astor, Nancy (1879–1964)
- Alcohol 40
- Boredom 100
- Chance 128
- Humanity 406

Atharva Veda, The
- Malevolence 516

Atkins, Robert (1930–2003)
- Vegetarianism 847

Atkinson, Brooks (1894–1984)
- Adults 29

Atkinson, Brooks (cont.)
Bureaucracy 107
College 155
Mythology 565
Responsibility 696
Atlee, Clement (1883–1967)
Democracy 220
Attenborough, David (1926–)
Biology 91
Atwood, Margaret (1939–)
Adults 29
Catholicism 115
Conflict 167
Gardens 356
Mothers 553
Mythology 565
Auden, W. H. (1907–1973)
Addiction 24
Aristocracy 61
Artists 66
Books 97
Class 152
Crime 191
Criticism 196
Earth 254
Faces 295
Genius 360
Laughter 463
Murder 561
Poetry 628
Secrets 724
Sin 741
Thoughts 810
Writing 886
Auerbach, Berthold (1812–1882)
Contempt 176
Judaism 447
Auerbach, Frank (1931–)
Crisis 193
Auerback, Red (1917–2006)
Ability 9
Basketball 80
Aughey, John (1828–1911)
Encouragement 268
Augustine, Norman R. (1935–)
Executives 288
Managers 517
Motivation 560
Stock Market 766
Tomorrow 818
Yesterday 892
Augustine, Saint (354–430)
Abstinence 14
Admiration, ...26
Adultery 28
Belief 86
Conscience 170
Custom 202
Forgiveness 332
Friendship 340
Imperfection 427
Knowledge 459
Moderation 545
Patience 604
Perfection 611
Sin 741
Strangers 768
Understanding 836
Wisdom 870
Auletta, Ken (1942–)
Journalists 443
Aurelius, Saint (c. 391–430)
Tears 800
Ausonius (c. 310–395)
Forgiveness 332
Silence 738
Speaking 757
Austen, Jane (1775–1817)
Artists 66
Beauty 81
Chance 128
Clergy 152
Cooperation 179
Enthusiasm 275
Excellence 286

Austen, Jane (cont.)
Friendship 340
Human Nature 405
Love 505
Marriage 521
Memory 530, 531
Money 547, 548
Nature 569
Pleasure 624
Pride 651
Relaxation 686
Religion 687
Surprise 789
Time 815
Vanity 846
Wrong 891
Austin, Alfred (1835–1913)
Gardens 356
Tears 800
Austin, Mary (1868–1934)
Death 207
Noise 574
Starvation 762
Avery, Milton (1885–1965)
Talk 794
Avicenna (980–1037)
Self 727
Ayer, A. J. (1910–1989)
Morality 551
Ayers, Roy (1940–)
Artists 66

B

Babitz, Eve (1943–)
Maturity 526
Babbitt, Irving (1865–1933)
Adjustment 25
Imperialism 427
Unity 839
Babangida, Ibrahim (1941–)
Debate 210
Babbitt, Irving (1865–1933)
Adjustment 25
Baca, Joe (1947–)
Coorporations 179
Native Americans 568
Republicans 692
Bach, John (1946–)
Idols 418
Bach, Richard (1936–)
Choice 144
Family 302
Friendship 340
Hell 394
Humanity 406
Losing 501
Perfection 611
Winning 868
Wishes 872
Work 880
Bach, Sebastian (1968–)
Artists 66
Bacharach, Burt (1928–)
Words 878
Bachelard, Gaston (1884–1962)
Imagination 422
The Past 601
Bacon, Sir Francis (1561–1626)
Ability 9
Adversity 30
Artists 66
Beauty 81
The Bible 88
Books 97
Charity 134
Crowds 198
Cunning 200
Eloquence 266
Excess 287
Experience 291
Fate 306
Fear 311
Fiction 316
Fools 326

Bacon, Sir Francis (cont.)
Forgiveness 332
Fortune 334
Friendship 340
History 398
Ideas 413
Judges 447
Knowledge 459
Laws 466
Libraries 484
Losing 501
Loss 504
Mind 535
Nakedness 566
Nature 569
Opportunity 585
Opposition 588
The Past 602
Plants 623
Power 644
Praise 645
The Present 649
Profit 655
Prosperity 659
Reading 673
Remedies 689
Revenge 699
Riches 704
Self 727
Silence 738
Strangers 768
Studying 774
Subtlety 778
Suspicion 790
Vice 847
Virtue 852
Wisdom 870
Wit 873
Wives 874
Writing 886
Badnarik, Michael (1954–)
Guns 381
Badiou, Alain (1937–)
Capitalism 114
Nihilism 573
Baez, Joan (1941–)
Actions 22
Despair 226
Life 490
Nonviolence 576
Violence 851
Bagdikian, Ben (1920–)
Newspapers 572
Bagehot, Walter (1826–1877)
Ambassadors 45
Bureaucracy 107
The Dead 207
Human Nature 405
Ideas 413
Misfortune 542
Mistakes 543
Mothers 553
Pain 593
Pleasure 624
Progress 656
Statesmen 762
Temptation 804
Tyranny 834
Vice 847
Wives 874
Bagnold, Enid (1889–1981)
Judges 447
Theater 807
Baha'u'llah (1817–1892)
Unity 839
Bailey, David (1938–)
Positivity 642
Bailey, Henry Christopher (1878–1916)
Miracles 539
Bailey, Liberty Hyde (1858–1954)
Gardens 356
Bailey, Pearl (1918–1990)
Ambition 45
The Dead 207
Kitchens 458

Bailey, Pearl (cont.)
- Talent 793
- Violence 851

Bailey, Philip James (1816–1902)
- Art 63
- Fraud 335
- Simplicity 740

Baillie, Joanna (1762–1851)
- Pride 651
- Vanity 846

Baily, Bernard (1916–1996)
- Ego 263

Baily, Pearl (1918–1990)
- Bureaucracy 108

Baker, Ginger (1939–)
- Abortion 13

Baker, Ray Stannard (1870–1946)
- Mobs 545

Baker, Russell (1925–)
- Age 36
- Cooking 177
- Journalists 443
- Misery 541
- Pleasure 624
- Publicity 662
- Tradition 822
- Writing 886

Baker, Stephen (1964–)
- Cats 116
- Toys 821

Baker, Tom (1934–)
- Decency 211

Bakr, Abu (573–634)
- Greed 379
- Solitude 753

Bakunin, Mikhail (1814–1876)
- Censure 126
- Worship 884

Balanchine, George (1904–1983)
- Dance 202

Baldwin, James Arthur (1924–1987)
- Biology 91
- Change 128
- Enthusiasm 275
- Freedom 336
- Gender 358
- Pessimism 617
- Prediction 648
- The Present 649
- Purity 664
- Questions 668
- Identity 415
- Victimization 849
- Vocation 856
- Writing 886

Baldwin, Roger (1884–1981)
- Communism 159

Baldwin, Stanley (1867–1947)
- The Dead 207
- Statesmen 762

Baldwin, Stephen (1966–)
- The Bible 88

Baldwin, William (1963–)
- Economics 256
- Real Estate 675
- Status 764

Balfour, Arthur James (1848–1930)
- Ability 9

Balfour, Francis Maitland (1851–1882)
- Charity 134

Ball, Alan (1957–)
- Beauty 81
- Life 490

Ball, Lucille (1911–1989)
- Ability 9
- Age 36

Ballard, J. G. (1930–)
- Pornography 641

Ballard, M. Russell (1928–)
- Church 146

Ballou, Hosea (1771–1852)
- Mothers 553
- Persecution 612
- Religion 687
- Suspicion 790
- Tears 800

Ballou, Hosea (cont.)
Zeal 897
Balzac, Honoré de (1799–1850)
Bureaucracy 108
Cheating 136
Coffee 154
Crime 191
Devotion 233
Fools 326
Forgiveness 332
Fortune 334
Humanity 406
Manners 519
Modesty 546
Mothers 553
Passion 600
Resistance 694
Society 751
Solitude 753
Suicide 783
Teachers 797
Vocation 856
Wounds 885
Writing 886
Bambara, Toni Cade (1939–1995)
Revolution 700
Bancroft, George (1800–1891)
Authority 72
Class 152
Dishonesty 241
Government 371
Bandura, Albert (1925–)
Teachers 797
Bangs, Lester (1948–1982)
Coorporations 179
Bankhead, Tallulah (1903–1968)
Mistakes 543
Photography 620
Vice 847
Banks, Dennis (1932–)
Coorporations 179
Banning, Margaret Culkin (1891–1982)
Mothers 553
Banting, Sir Frederick G. (1891–1941)
Ideas 413
Baraka, Imamu Amiri (1934–)
God 367
Respectability 696
Barbera, Joseph (1911–)
Boxing 103
Barbusse, Henri (1873–1935)
Suicide 783
Barclay, William (1907–1978)
Endurance 269
Love 505
Barenboim, Daniel (1942–)
Anti-Semitism 56
Tradition 822
Bareti, Joseph (1716–1789)
Mankind 518
Barham, Richard Harris (1788–1845)
Ghosts 362
Baring, Maurice (1874–1945)
Artists 66
Barker, Dan (1949–)
Faith 299
Barkley, Charles (1963–)
Basketball 80
Barnes, Albert (1798–1870)
The Bible 88
Barnes, Clive (1927–)
Culture 199
Television 802
Barnes, Djuna (1892–1982)
Ruin 709
Barnes, Julian (1946–)
Sympathy 791
Writing 886
Barnes, Roy (1948–)
Traffic 823
Barney, Natalie Clifford (1876–1972)
Possessions 641
Trouble 828
Barnum, P. T. (1810–1891)
Suckers 782

Barr, Amelia (1831–1919)
The Supernatural 788
Barr, Roseanne (1952–)
Mothers 553
Suicide 783
Barrett, Tom (1953–)
Rain 672
Barrie, James M. (1860–1937)
Ambition 45
Babies 75
Humility 409
Life 490
Praise 645
Rainbows 672
Roses 709
Stories 766
Strength 771
Work 880
Youth 893
Barrington, George (1755–1804)
Patriots 606
Barrows, Sydney Biddle (1952–)
Business 111
Integrity 436
Barry, Dave (1947–)
Adults 29
Alcohol 40
Arguments 60
Babies 75
Beer 84
Camping 114
College 155
Dance 202
Democrats 223
Electricity 266
Fishing 319
Golf 370
Journalists 443
Maturity 526
Objectivity 579
Rich and Poor 702
Youth 893
Barry, Lynda (1956–)
Class 152
Love 505
Barrymore, Drew (1975–)
Kisses 456
Barrymore, Ethel (1879–1959)
Friendship 341
Laughter 463
Barrymore, John (1882–1942)
Brides 105
Love 506
Barth, John (1930–)
Heroes 396
Martyrs 523
Revelation 698
Barth, Karl (1886–1968)
Church 146
Conscience 171
Ideology 416
Status Quo 765
Theology 808
Bartol, C. A. (1813–1900)
Manners 519
Barthelmess, Richard (1895–1963)
Banks 78
Barton, Bruce (1886–1967)
Achievement 19
Children 138
Conceit 164
Enthusiasm 275
Slavery 746
Baruch, Bernard M. (1870–1965)
Age 36
Encouragement 268
Life 490
Old Age 583
Baryshnikov, Mikhail (1948–)
Addiction 24
Barzun, Jacques (1907–)
Artists 66
Political Correctness 632

Barzun, Jacques (cont.)
Teachers 797
Tennis 805
Basil, Saint (329–379)
Loss 504
Rain 672
Basinger, Kim (1953–)
Cinema 147
Bass, Charles Foster (1952–)
Terrorism 805
Bass, Ronald (1942–)
Hell 394
Bastiat, Frederic (1801–1850)
Commerce 156
Trade 822
Bataille, Georges (1897–1962)
Sacrifice 711
Bates, Daisy (1863–1951)
The World 882
Bates, Marston (1906–1974)
Research 693
Bateson, Mary Catherine (1939–)
Sharing 736
Stories 767
Baudelaire, Charles (1821–1867)
Aristocracy 61
Cats 116
Despair 226
Fantasy 304
Fashion 305
Genius 360
Heresy 396
Materialism 524
Misunderstanding 545
Pleasure 624
Poetry 628
The Present 649
Priests 652
Progress 656
Reason 678
Sexuality 734
Soldiers 752
Understanding 836
Vice 847
Virtue 852
Work 880
Baudrillard, Jean (1929–2007)
Cities 149
Cowardice 188
Difficulty 235
Infidelity 431
Pornography 641
Scandals 717
Seduction 726
Toys 821, 822
Bauer, Gary (1946–)
Bureaucracy 108
Bax, Sir Arnold (1883–1953)
Dance 202
Baxter, Anne (1923–1985)
Idleness 417
Baxter, Richard (1615–1691)
Liberty 480
Unity 839
Bayh, Birch (1928–)
Abortion 13
Bayh, Evan (1955–)
Children 138
Fathers 309
Mothers 553
Bayle, Pierre (1647–1706)
Acceptance 17
Bayley, Stephen (1951–)
Architects 59
Baylor, Elgin (1934–)
Basketball 80
Bazin, Andre (1918–1958)
Cinema 147
Baziotes, William (1912–1963)
Painting 595
Beagle, Peter S. (1939–)
Burdens 107
Beam, Sam (1974–)
Grace 374
Love 506

Beam, Sam (cont.)
Words 878
Bean, Melissa (1962–)
Theft 808
Bear, Greg (1951–)
Silence 738
Beard, Charles Austin (1874–1948)
Censorship 123
Darkness 205
Independence 428
Stars 761
Beard, James (1903–1985)
Cannibalism 114
Food 324
Beaumarchais, Pierre-Augustin (1732–1799)
Censorship 123
Beaumont, Francis (1584–1616)
Heart 390
Beauvoir, Simone de (1908–1986)
Arrogance 62
Change 128
Feminism 315
Generosity 359
Genius 360
Homosexuality 401
Hypocrisy 412
Parenthood 597
Retirement 697
Slavery 746
Becerra, Xavier (1958–)
Alcohol 40
Beck, Charlotte Joko (1917–)
Life 490
Beck, Martha (1962–)
Admiration 27
Adolescence 27
Change 128
Crisis 193
Heartbreak 392
Beck, Ulrich (1944–)
Terrorism 806
Becker, Boris (1967–)
Losing 501
Strangers 768
Tennis 805
Beckett, Samuel (1906–1989)
Bliss 94
Tears 800
Beckham, Victoria (1974–)
Presents 650
Beecham, Thomas (1879–1961)
Noise 574
Beecher, Henry Ward (1813–1887)
Ability 9
Ambition 45
Anarchy 50
Anger 53
Art 63
Artists 66
Blessings 93
Books 97
Charity 134
Children 138
Church 146
Common Sense 158
Debt 210
Determination 230
Difficulty 235
Dogs 245
Encouragement 268
Enthusiasm 275
Fear 312
Feelings 314
Flowers 322
Forgiveness 332
Gambling 354
The Garden of Eden 355
Genius 360
Government 371
Gratitude 376
Heart 390
Heaven 392
Heroes 396
Human Nature 405
Imagination 422

Beecher, Henry Ward (cont.)
Judges 448
Kisses 456
Laughter 463
Libraries 484
Mothers 553
Motivation 560
Mystery 564
Painting 595
Parenthood 597
Power 644
Praise 645
The Present 649
Prosperity 660
Rain 672
Reform 682
Repentance 691
Rich and Poor 702
Riches 704
Sacrifice 711
Secrets 724
Sorrow 755
Soul 756
Strength 771
Theology 808
Worries 883
Beerbohm, Max (1872–1956)
Sympathy 791
Beethoven, Ludwig van (1770–1827)
Comedy 155
Gold 369
Beeton, Isabella (1836–1865)
Kitchens 458
Behan, Brendan Francis (1923–1964)
Advice 33
Authority 72
Criticism 196
Desire 224
England 272
Quotations 670
Talent 793
Behe, Michael (1952–)
Biology 91
Behn, Aphra (1640–1689)
Pleasure 624
Belafonte, Harry (1927–)
Censorship 123
Fascism 305
Oppression 589
Terrorism 806
Bell, Alexander Graham (1847–1922)
Animals 55
Cooperation 179
Desire 224
Mankind 518
Regret 683
Thoughts 810
Bell, Clive (1881–1964)
Art 63
Religion 687
Bell, Daniel (1919–)
Cults 199
Bellay, Joachim du (1522–1560)
France 335
Belloc, Hilaire (1870–1953)
Courtesy 187
Bellow, Saul (1915–2005)
California 113
Ignorance 418
Illusion 422
Passion 601
Writing 886
Belushi, John (1949–1982)
Alcohol 40
Chocolate 143
Drugs 252
Benchley, Robert (1889–1945)
Age 36
Alcohol 41
Dogs 245
Fools 326
Humor 410
Language 462
Loyalty 511

Benchley, Robert (cont.)
Obedience 578
Pets 618
Work 880
Writing 886
Benedict, Dirk (1945–)
Difficulty 235
Normalcy 576
Benenson, Peter (1921–2005)
Torture 820
Benet, Stephen Vincent (1898–1943)
Power 644
Wisdom 870
Bengis, Ingrid (1944–)
Consciousness 172
Censorship 123
Questions 668
Words 878
Benigni, Roberto (1952–)
Gratitude 376
Mediocrity 529
Moderation 546
Benjamin, Judah Philip (1811–1884)
Revolution 700
Benjamin, Walter (1892–1940)
Adjustment 25
Lies 486
Reality 676
Suicide 784
Benn, Ernest (1875–1954)
Politics 637
Bennett, Alan (1934–)
Afternoon 35
Cancer 114
Majorities 515
Spirit 759
Bennett, Alex (1939–)
Relationships 684
Bennett, Arnold (1867–1931)
Accidents 18
Confidence 165
Depression 224
Human Nature 405
Journalists 443
Pessimism 617
Praise 645
Procrastination 655
Tragedy 824
Bennett, Bo (1972–)
Excitement 288
Positivity 642
Rejection 684
Success 779
Bennett, Robert F. (1927–2000)
Choice 144
Bennett, William (1943–)
Admiration 26
Attitude 71
Difficulty, ...235
Thankfulness 807
Bennis, Warren G. (1925–)
Achievement 19
Dogs 245
Excellence 286
Leadership 470
Studying 774
Benny, Jack (1894–1974)
Conflict 167
Modesty 546
Benoit, Jehane (1904–1987)
Cooking 177
Benserade, Isaac de (1613–1691)
Beds 83
Benson, E. F. (1867–1940)
Fatigue 310
Benson, Robert Hugh (1871–1914)
Intolerance 438
Bent, Charles (1799–1847)
Conformity 168
Bentham, George (1800–1884)
Botany 102
Bentham, Jeremy (1748–1832)
Anarchy 50
Censorship 123
Community 161
Flowers 322

Bentham, Jeremy (cont.)
Lawyers 468
Liberty 480
Tyranny 834
Bentley, Nicolas (1907–1978)
Journalists 443
Benton, Robert (1932–)
Twilight 833
Berberova, Nina (1901–1993)
Passion 601
Berenson, Bernard (1865–1959)
Consistency 175
Ignorance 418
Miracles 540
Rejoice 684
Berg, Paul (1926–)
Biology 91
Bergamin, José (1895–1983)
Love 506
Sensuality 731
Tradition 823
Bergen, Candice (1946–)
Marriage 521
Bergen, Edgar (1903–1978)
Ambition, ...45
Laziness 469
Work 880
Berger, John (1926–)
Nakedness 566
Utopia 843
Berger, Thomas (1924–)
Writing 886
Bergerac, Cyrano de (1619–1655)
Arrogance 62
Bergman, Ingrid (1915–1982)
Kisses 456
Bergson, Henri (1859–1941)
Change 128
Laughter 463
The Past 602
Vanity 846
Berle, Milton (1908–2002)
Mothers 553
Berlin, Irving (1888–1989)
Success 779
Talent 793
Berlioz, Louis-Hector (1803–1869)
Ideas 413
Modesty 546
Music 562
Bernal, John Desmond (1901–1971)
Aristocracy 61
Bureaucracy 108
Coorporations 179
Sexuality 734
Bernanos, Georges (1888–1948)
Beggars 84
Corruption 184
Bernard, Dorothy (1890–1955)
Courage 186
Fear 312
Bernard of Clairvaux, Saint (1090–1153)
Humility 409
Trees 827
Bernbach, William (1911–1982)
Advertising 32
Media 528
Persuasion 615
Berne, Eric (1910–1970)
Birds 91
Berners-Lee, Tim (1955–)
Bureaucracy 108
Bernhardt, Sarah (1845–1921)
Energy 271
Theater 807
Bernstein, Andrew (1949–)
Conflict 167
Bernstein, Elmer (1922–2004)
Alienation 43
Bernstein, Leonard (1918–1990)
Inspiration 435
Writing 886
Berra, Yogi (1925–)
Baseball 79

Berra, Yogi (cont.)
The Future 353
Loyalty 511
Prediction 648
Berry, Wendell (1934–)
Gardens 356
Bertolucci, Bernardo (1940–)
Censorship 123
Berton, Pierre (1920–)
Rascism 671
Besant, Annie (1847–1933)
Atheism 71
Beston, Henry (1888–1968)
Autumn 74
Beuys, Joseph (1921–1986)
Artists 66
Universities 842
Bevan, Aneurin (1897–1960)
Fascism 305
Beveridge, Lord William (1879–1963)
Glory 364
Rulers 710
Beyle, Marie Henri (1783–1842)
Character 131
The Bhagavad Gita
Death 210
Delusion 220
Devotion 234
Fruit 352
Meditation 530
Biafra, Jello (1958–)
Coorporations 180
Bibesco, Elizabeth (1879–1945)
Fashion 305
Irony 440
Mind 535
The Bible
Angels 53
Beauty 83
Disaster 238
Envy 279
Fools 329
Forgetfulness 331
Friendship, ...351
Fruit 352
The Garden of Eden 356
Glory 366
Hair 383
Healing 388
Humility 410
Hunger 411
Kisses 458
Love 511
Manners 521
Meditation 530
Mourning 561
Nation 567
Pride 652
Riches 704
Safety 713
Satan 716
Shelter 736
Strangers 769
Temptation 805
Truth 833
Wounds 885
Bierce, Ambrose (1842–1914)
Absurdity 16
Admiration, ...26
Age 36
Amnesty 49
Ancestry 52
Art 63
Beggars 84
Books 97
Boredom 100
Botany 102
Business 111
Censorship 123
Clergy 152
Cowardice 188
Debt 210
Delusion 219
Democrats 223
Diplomacy 237
Dogs 245

Bierce, Ambrose (cont.)
Eccentricity 255
Enthusiasm 275
Epitaphs 279
Etiquette 283
Fashion 305
Fidelity 317
Fishing 319
Forgiveness 332
Funerals 352
Gambling 354
Happiness 383
History 398
Hypocrisy 412
Ignorance 418
Independence 428
Insanity 434
Knowledge 459
Learning 474
Lies 486
Logic 499
Marriage 521
Misery 541
Misfortune 542
Misunderstanding 545
Mythology 565
Noise 574
Ocean 582
Painting 595
Philosophy 618
Pilgrimage 621
Pleasure 624
Politics 637
Prison 653
Religion 687
Remorse 690
Repartee 691
Respectability 696
Revelation 698
Reverence 699
Revolution 700
Ridicule 705
Roads 708
Rulers 710
Skepticism 743
Soldiers 752
Telephones 802
Virginity 852
Virtue 852
Weather 866
Weddings 866
Youth 893
Bigelow, Jacob (1787–1879)
Cause and Effect 120
Bikel, Theodore (1924–)
Arrogance 62
Biko, Stephen Bantu (1946–1977)
The Dead 207
Mind 535
Billings, Josh (1818–1885)
Arguments 60
Common Sense 158
Confessions 165
Debt 210
Dogs 245
Envy 278
Etiquette 283
Excess 287
Flattery 320
Fools 326
Forgiveness 332
Happiness 383
Heaven 392
Lies 486
Manners 519
Originality 592
Plagiarism 622
Prayer 647
Revenge 699
Self 727
Silence 738
Truth 830
Victory 849
Writing 886
Youth 893

Billings, Victoria (1945–)
Today 817
Binoche, Juliette (1964–)
Chocolate 143
Cinema 147
Binstock, Louis (1896–1974)
Happiness 383
Birrell, Augustine (1850–1887)
Books 97
Libraries 484
Birtwistle, Harrison (1934–)
Theater 807
Bishop, Elizabeth (1911–1979)
Losing 501
Bishop, Jim (1907–1987)
Dating 206
The Future 353
Journalists 443
Time 815
Bismarck, Otto von (1815–1898)
Alliances 44
Consciousness 172
Journalists 445
Laws 466
Moderation 546
Politics 637
Statesmen 762
Bisset, Jacqueline (1964–)
Cinema 147
Bizet, Georges (1838–1875)
Adultery 28
Black, Conrad (1944–)
Journalists 443
Black, Hugo L. (1886–1971)
Censorship 123
Judges 448
Black, Lewis (1948–)
Democrats 223
Republicans 692
Blackburn, Simon (1944–)
Free Will 339
Black Elk (1863–1950)
Clouds 154
Grandfathers 376
Blackmun, Justice Harry A. (1908–1999)
Abortion 13
Blackwell, Antoinette Brown (1825–1921)
Nature 569
Blagojevich, Rod (1956–)
Alcohol 41
Blair, Tony (1953–)
Abortion 13
America 47
Leadership 470
Blake, William (1757–1827)
Abstinence 15
Admiration 26
Angels 52
The Bible 88
Birds 91
Desire 225
Despair 226
Enemies 270
Energy 271
Eternity 281
Flowers 322
Fools 326
Forgiveness 332
Friendship 341
Fun 352
Generalizations 358
Heaven 392
Ignorance 418
Imagination 422, 423
Innocence 433
Insanity 434
Love 506
Nakedness 566
Opposition 588
Perception 610
Pride 651
Priests 652

Blake, William (cont.)
Riches 704
Senses 730
Shame 735
Soldiers 752
Sorrow 755
Soul 756
Vision 855
Blanc, Louis (1811–1882)
Organization 591
Blanchard, Kenneth (1939–)
Leadership 470
Blanton, Smiley (1882–1966)
Achievement 19
Fathers 309
Life 490
Love 506
Blass, Bill (1922–2002)
Style 777
Bloch, Robert (1917–1994)
Heart 390
Bloom, Allan (1930–1992)
Addiction 24
Education 259
Shepherds 736
Tradition 823
Values 845
Bloom, Harold (1930–)
Books 97
Pleasure 624
Reading 673
Shakespeare 735
Solitude 753
Universities 842
Bloomberg, Michael (1942–)
Elections 265
Bloomfield, Robert (1766–1823)
Benevolence 88
Blotnick, Srully D. (1941–2004)
Achievement 19
Wealth 864
Blount, Roy, Jr. (1941–)
Drugs 252
Blue, Lionel (1930–)
Anti-Semitism 56
Kingdoms 454
Blum, William (1933–)
Censorship 123
Terrorism 806
Bly, Mary (1962–)
Dogs 245
Boas, Franz (1858–1942)
Bureaucracy 108
Bodhidharma (470–543)
Delusion 219
Enlightenment 274
Liberation 478
Roads 708
Self 727
Senses 730
Words 878
Worship 884
Boehlert, Sherwood (1936–)
Addiction 24
Boerhaave, Hermann (1668–1738)
Perseverance 612
Scandals 717
Boetcker, William J. H. (1873–1962)
Determination 230
The Poor 639
Self-Respect 729
Success 779
Bogan, Louise (1897–1970)
Happiness 384
Joy 446
Suffering 782
The Universe 840
Bogart, John B. (1848–1921)
Dogs 245
Boggs, Wade (1958–)
Positivity 642
Bohm, David (1917–1992)
Relativity 685
Bohn, H. G. (1796–1884)
Boldness 96

Bohr, Niels (1885–1962)
Difficulty 235
Experience 291
Experts 292
The Future 353
Mistakes 543
Physics 621
Truth 830
Boileau-Despréaux, Nicolas (1636–1711)
Fools 326
Boiste, Pierre-Claude-Victor (1765–1824)
Confidence 166
Bolger, Jim (1935–)
Campaigns 113
Bolívar, Simon (1783–1830)
Experience 291
Judgment 450
Bolton, Robert Oxton (1924–1995)
Mind 535
Oppression 589
Bombeck, Erma (1927–1996)
Beds 83
Children 138
Dessert 228
Dogs 246
Feminism 315
Football 330
Libraries 484
Mothers 553
Sports 760
Vacations 844
Bonaduce, Danny (1959–)
Adolescence 27
Bonaparte, Charles Joseph (1851–1921)
Government 371
Nation 567
Bonaparte, Maria Letizia (1750–1836)
Children 138
Mothers 553
Bond, Christopher (1939–)
Bureaucracy 108
Bond, Edward (1934–)
Consciousness 172
Consumerism 175
Theater 807
The Unconcious 836
Bondevik, Kjell Magne (1947–)
Terrorism 806
Bonhoeffer, Dietrich (1906–1945)
Children 138
Responsibility 696
Thoughts 810
Bonino, Emma (1948–)
Chauvinism 136
Bonnano, Margaret (1950–)
Wealth 864
Bonnell, James (1653–1699)
Pleasure 624
Bono (1960–)
America 47
Encouragement 268
Famine 304
Bono, Edward de (1933–)
Creativity 190
Humor 410
Motivation 560
Bonstetten, Karl von (1745–1832)
Age 36
Mind 535
Old Age 583
Boom, Corrie ten (1892–1983)
The Future 353
Boone, Daniel (1734–1820)
Commerce 156
Native Americans 568
Boone, Lesley (1968–)
Suicide 784
Boorman, John (1933–)
Cinema 147
Legends 476
Manipulation 517

Boorstin, Daniel J. (1914–)
Celebrities 122
Discovery 240
Illusion 422
Knowledge 459
Boortz, Neal (1945–)
Sensitivity 730
Boosler, Elayne (1952–)
Silence 738
Booth, Shirley (1907–1992)
Crisis 193
Borah, William E. (1865–1940)
Censorship 123
Government 371
Borenstein, Nathaniel (1957–)
Accidents 18
Computers 163
Borg, Björn (1956–)
Losing 501
Borge, Victor (1909–2000)
Happiness 384
Laughter 463
Borges, Jorge Luis (1899–1986)
Ethics 282
Libraries 484
Paradise 595
Uncertainty 835
Bogosian, Eric (1953–)
Normalcy 576
Bork, Robert (1927–)
Judges 448
Borland, Hal (1900–1978)
Beginnings 85
Forests 330
Borlaug, Norman (1914–)
Survival 789
Born, Max (1882–1970)
Physics 621
Borne, Ludwig (1786–1837)
Delusion 219
Losing 501
Truth 831
Borrow, George (1803–1881)
Smoking 749
Translation 826
Bosley, Tom (1927–)
Depression 224
Botton, Alain de (1969–)
Architects 59
Bosch, Robert (1861–1942)
Wages 858
Bossuet, Jacques (1627–1704)
Belief 86
Boswell, James (1740–1795)
Experience 291
Friendship 341
Journals 446
Wisdom 870
Botton, Alain de (1969–)
Architects 59
Boulanger, Nadia (1887–1979)
Children 138
Parenthood 597
Bourdillon, Francis William (1852–1921)
Eyes 293
Love 506
Bourne, Randolph (1886–1918)
Objectivity 579
Bovée, Christian Nestell (1820–1904)
Artists 66
Cowardice 188
Delusion 219
Wine 869
Bowen, Charles (1835–1894)
Rain 672
Bowen, Elizabeth (1899–1973)
Art 63
Illusion 422
Bowles, Chester (1901–1986)
Economics 256
Government 371
Politicians 635
Boxer, Barbara (1940–)
Voting 857

Boyden, Frank (1879–1972)
Refuge 682
Boyer, Herbert W. (1936–)
The Universe 841
Boynton, Sandra (1953–)
Chocolate 143
Bradbury, Ray (1920–)
Acceptance 17
Censorship 123
Libraries 484
Rejection 684
The Universe 841
Bradford, William (1590–1657)
Winter 869
Bradlaugh, Charles (1833–1891)
Censorship 123
Bradley, Bill (1943–)
Basketball 80
Bradley, F. H. (1846–1924)
Suicide 784
Bradley, Omar (1893–1981)
Bravery 104
Prudence 661
War 859
Wisdom 871
Bradshaw, John (1933–)
Lies 486
Self 727
Bradshaw, Terry (1948–)
Challenges 127
Bradstreet, Anne (1612–1672)
Adversity 30
Prosperity 660
Spring 761
Winter 870
Braeden, Eric (1941–)
Coorporations 180
Weddings 866
Bragg, Billy (1957–)
Bedrooms 83
Songs 754
Bragg, Sir William (1862–1942)
Science 719
Brahimi, Lakhdar (1934–)
Anarchy 50
Brahnmananda, Swami (1863–1922)
Pain 593
Pleasure 624
The World 882
Brainard, J. G. C. (1796–1828)
Hate 387
Branagh, Kenneth (1960–)
Shakespeare 735
Brancusi, Constantin (1876–1957)
Architecture 60
Art 63
Sculpture 723
Simplicity 741
Brand, Jo (1957–)
Chocolate 143
Brande, Dorothea (1893–1948)
Failure 296
Brandeis, Louis D. (1856–1941)
America 47
Anarchy 50
Censorship 123
Liberty 480
Publicity 662
Branden, Nathaniel (1930–)
Acceptance 17
Self 727
Brando, Marlon (1924–2004)
Actors 23
Privacy 654
Television 802
Braun, Wernher von (1912–1977)
Bureaucracy 108
Research 693
Braxton, Anthony (1945–)
Racism 671
Brazile, Donna (1959–)
Church 146
Voting 857

Brecht, Bertolt (1898–1956)
Brothers 106
Death 207
Ethics 282
Faces 295
Science 719
Society 751
Success 779
Brenan, Gerald (1894–1987)
Words 878
Brentano, Franz Clemens (1838–1917)
Consciousness 172
The Unconcious 836
Breslin, Jimmy (1930–)
Architects 59
Journalism 442
Newspapers 572
Thieves 810
Bresson, Henri Cartier (1908–2004)
Photography 620
Brett, George (1953–)
Losing 502
Brett, Jeremy (1933–1995)
Villains 850
Brewster, Kingman, Jr. (1919–1988)
Ambassadors 45
Brewster, William (1566–1644)
The Bible 88
Breyer, Stephen (1938–)
Judges 448
Bridges, Robert (1844–1930)
Clouds 154
Bridges, William (1797–1872)
Beginnings 85
Brillat-Savarin, Jean Anthelme (1755–1826)
Cooking 177
Food 324
Happiness 384
Senses 730
Brilliant, Ashleigh (1933–)
Crisis 193
Life 490
Skill 745
Words 878
Wrong 891
Brimelow, Peter (1947–)
Racism 671
Brin, David (1950–)
Corruption 184
Power 644
Privacy 654
Writing 886
Brink, Andre P. (1935–)
Censorship 123
Brinkley, David (1920–2003)
The News 572
Success 779
Television 803
Brisbane, Arthur (1864–1936)
Friendship 341
Love 506
Bristol, Claude M. (1891–1951)
Determination 230
Brittain, Vera (1893–1970)
Pacifism 592
Brittany, Morgan (1951–)
Addiction 24
Brock, Alice May (1941–)
Food 324
Brock, Peter (1945–)
Retirement 697
Broderick, Matthew (1962–)
Babies 75
Brodie, Sir Benjamin Collins (1783–1862)
Old Age 583
Brodkey, Harold (1930–1996)
Adolescence 27
Weakness 864
Brodsky, Joseph (1940–1996)
Cities 149
Eccentricity 255
Friendship 341
Literature 498
Treason 827

Brokaw, Tom (1940–)
Fishing 319
Bronowski, Jacob (1908–1974)
Conformity 169
Values 845
Bronson, Charles (1921–2003)
Beer 84
Bronson, Po (1964–)
Listening 497
Brontë, Charlotte (1816–1855)
Conscience 171
Friendship 341
Guilt 381
Wrong, ...891
Brontë, Emily (1818–1848)
Cowardice 188
Sorrow 755
Brooke, Henry (1703–1783)
Monarchs 547
Tyranny 834
Brooke, Rupert (1887–1915)
Cities 149
Space 757
Brookner, Anita (1938–)
Commerce 156
Brooks, Garth (1956–)
Conflict 167
Wealth 864
Brooks, Gwendolyn (1917–)
Body 95
Brooks, James L. (1940–)
Decency 211
Brooks, Mel (1926–)
Comedy 155
Humor 410
Presidents 650
Taste 795
Tragedy 824
The Universe 841
Brooks, Meredith (1958–)
Alcohol 41
Brooks, Paul (1959–)
Environment 277
Brooks, Phillips (1835–1893)
Blunders 95
Deeds 214
Devotion 233
Greatness 377
Paradise 596
Prayer 647
Self-Confidence 728
Brooks, Van Wyck (1886–1963)
Writing 887
Brothers, Dr. Joyce (1928–)
Anger 53
Flattery 320
Listening 497
Love 506
Manipulation 517
Perseverance 612
Relaxation 686
Brougham, Henry (1778–1868)
Laws 466
Broun, Heywood (1888–1939)
Atheism 71
Broun, Hob (1950–1987)
Realism 675
Browder, Earl (1891–1973)
Socialism 750
Brown, A. Whitney (1952–)
Animals 55
Humor 410
Misery 541
Plants 623
Brown, Dean Gordon (1908–1996)
Engineering 272
Brown, Dee (1908–2002)
Native Americans 568
Brown, H. Jackson, Jr. (1948–)
Character 131
Determination 230
Excellence 286
Losing 502
Opportunity 585

Brown, H. Jackson, Jr. (cont.)
Perseverance 612
Brown, Jerry (1938–)
Bureaucracy 108
Corporations 180
Brown, John (1800–1859)
Dignity 237
Brown, John Mason (1900–1969)
Education 259
Brown, Les (1912–2001)
Motivation 560
Opportunity 585
Brown, Les (1945–)
Commerce 157
Brown, Lester R. (1934–)
Capitalism 114
Economics 256
Brown, Pam (1948–)
Children 138
Family 302
Friendship 341
Mothers 553
Brown, Paul (1908–1991)
Losing 502
Brown, Rita Mae (1944–)
Art 63
Conformity 169
Creativity 190
Dating 206
Decency 211
Entertainment 274
Happiness 384
Impatience 426
Instinct 435
Language 462
Life 490
Manners 519
Mental Illness 533
The Moon 550
Pornography 641
Propaganda 657
Sacrifice 711
Sanity 715
Self-Confidence 728
Writing 887
Browne, Sylvia (1943–)
Ghosts 362
Browne, Sir Thomas (1605–1682)
Charity 134
Life 490
Malice 516
Wealth 864
Browne, William, of Tavistock (1591–1643)
Gardens 356
Browning, Elizabeth Barrett (1806–1861)
Mothers 553
Shame 735
Work 880
Browning, Robert (1812–1889)
Doubt 248
Earth 254
Failure 296
Fiction 316
Heaven 392
Ignorance 418
Innocence 433
Mothers 553
Spring 761
Success 779
Temptation 804
Youth 894
Brownlow, Leroy (1914–2002)
Mothers 553
Broyard, Anatole (1920–1990)
Children 138
Friendship 341
Obedience 578
Writing 887
Bruce, Lenny (1925–1966)
Communism 159
Learning 474
Liberals 477
Satire 716
Bruce, Tammy (1962–)
Judges 448
Status 765

Bruckheimer, Jerry (1945–)
Crisis 193
Bruno, Frank (1961–)
Blood 94
Boxing 103
Suicide 784
Brunton, Paul (1898–1981)
Weakness 864
Brust, Steven (1955–)
Conformity 169
Danger 204
Eccentricity 255
Understanding 836
Bryan, William Jennings (1860–1925)
The Bible 88
Destiny 228
Determination 231
Evolution 285
Money 548
Publicity 662
Saviors 717
Teachers 797
Bryant, Paul "Bear" (1913–1983)
Character 131
Crisis 193
Horses 404
Losing 502
Pride 651
Victory 849
Winning 868
Bryant, William C. (1794 –1878)
Difficulty 235
Remorse 690
Virtue 852
Bryars, Gavin (1943–)
Underground 836
Bryson, Bill (1946–)
Consumerism 175
Tourism 821
Buber, Martin (1878–1965)
Dogs 246
Buchan, James (1954–)
Bankers 78
Buchan, John (1875–1940)
Atheism 71
Fishing 319
Leadership 470
Buchanan, James (1791–1868)
Alliances 44
Buchner, Georg (1813–1837)
Revolution 700
Wealth 864
Buck, Pearl S. (1892–1973)
Beauty 81
Excellence 286
Food 324
Individuals 430
Joy 446
Kisses 456
Loneliness 500
Marriage 521
Mistakes 543
Mothers 554
Parenthood 597
Sorrow 755
Struggle 772
Vigilance 850
Buckley, James L. (1923–)
Campaigns 113
Buckley, Pat (1952–)
Environment 277
Satan 715
Buckley, William F., Jr. (1925–)
The Garden of Eden 355
Learning 474
Saints 713
Buckminster, J. S. (1797–1812)
Charity 134
The Buddha (563–483 BC)
Anger 53
Belief 86
Change 128
Endurance 269
Enjoyment 273
Enlightenment 274
Evil 284

The Buddha (cont.)
Faith 299
Fear 312
Friendship 341
Heart 390
Liberation 478
Life 490
Meals 527
Meditation 530
Miracles 540
Observation 580
Peace 607
Peace of Mind 609
The Present 649
Purpose 664
Refuge 682
Rumors 710
Salvation 714
Self 727
Spirit 759
Theories 809
Thoughts 810, 811
Tomorrow 819
Unity 839
Value 844
Victory 849
Virtue 853
Wisdom 871
Words 878
Yesterday 892

Budgell, Eustace (1686–1737)
Friendship 341

Buffett, Jimmy (1946–)
Fun 352
Indecision 427
Laughter 463
Nakedness 566

Buffett, Warren (1930–)
Business 111
Journalists 443
Stock Market 766

Buffon, George-Louis de (1707–1788)
Delay 218
Patience 604
Style 777

Bujold, Lois McMaster (1949–)
Achievement 19
Adversity 30
Children 138
The Dead 207
Death 207
Debt 210
Defeat 216
Desire 225
Duty 253
Friendship 341
Gardens 356
Giving 363
Glory 364
Heart 390
Home 400
Honesty 401
Honor 402
Humanity 406
Humility 409
Illusion 422
Justice 451
Pain 593
Parenthood 597
Perfection 611
Police 631
Power 644
Reputation 692
Retreat 698
The Universe 841
Victory 849
War 859

Bukowski, Charles (1920–1994)
Losing 502
Style 777

Bulfinch, Thomas (1796–1867)
Knights 458, 459

Bulwer-Lytton, Sir Edward (1803–1873)
Aging 38
Common Sense 158
Conscience 171

Bulwer-Lytton, Sir Edward (cont.)
Destiny 228
Dogma 244
Dreams 249
Eccentricity 255
Enemies 270
Enthusiasm 275
Error 280
Fate 306, 307
Flattery 320
Genius 360
Gifts 362
Illness 421
Pain 593
Pleasure 624
Prophets 658
Punctuality 663
Purpose 664
Remorse 690
Teachers 797
Virtue 853
Writing 887
Youth 894
Bulwer-Lytton, Robert (1831–1891)
Cause and Effect 120
Buñuel, Luis (1900–1983)
Atheism 71
Bunyan, John (1628–1688)
Sin 741
Burchill, Julie (1959–)
Abortion 13
Burger, Warren E. (1907–1955)
Judges 448
Burgess, Anthony (1917–1993)
Slang 746
Sleep 748
The Unconcious 836
Burgess, Frank Gelett (1866–1951)
Maxims 527
Burgess, Michael (1950–)
Crisis 193
Republicans 692
Burgh, James (1714–1775)
Adversity 30
Change 128
Burke, Arleigh (1901–1996)
Commanders 155
Burke, Edmund (1729–1797)
Arrogance 62
Cause and Effect 120
Change 129
Curiosity 200
Custom 202
Delusion 219
Despair 226
Dogs 246
Evil 284
Fear 312
Finance 318
Flattery 320
Force 330
Fraud 335
Government 371
Greatness 377
Hypocrisy 412
Imitation 425
Indifference 428
Injustice 433
Judges 448
Kings 456
Liberty 480
Manners 519
Mind 535
Opposition 588
Order 591
Patience 604
Protestantism 661
Rebellion 680
Religion 687
Security 726
Statesmen 762
Superstition 788
Sympathy 791
Taxes 796

Burke, Edmund (cont.)
Trade 822
Unity 839
Virtue 853
Welfare 867
Winning 869
Wisdom 871
Youth 894
Burke, James (1936–)
Abstinence 15
Rejection 684
Burke, Kenneth (1897–1993)
Status 765
Words 878
Burke, Leo J. (1911–1980)
Babies 75
Children 138
Burke, Thomas (1910–1973)
Friendship 341
Burleigh, William Cecil (1520–1598)
Heart 390
Burnett, Carol (1933–)
Adolescence 27
Change 129
Comedy 156
Tragedy 824
Writing 887
Burnett, Leo (1891–1971)
Creativity 190
Curiosity 200
Burnham, Daniel H. (1846–1912)
Planning 623
Burnham, George P. (1868–1939)
Achievement 19
Burnham, Sophy (1936–)
Faith 299
Burns, Eric A. (1968–)
Humanity 406
Writing 887
Burns, George (1896–1996)
Acting 21
Age 36
Death 208
Effort 262
Family 302
Government 371
Hair 383
Happiness 384
Longevity 501
Religion 687
Retirement 698
Sex 733
Writing 887
Burns, Horace (1915–2000)
Friendship 341
Burns, James MacGregor (1918–)
Revolution 700
Burns, John (1858–1943)
Socialism 750
Burns, Ken (1953–)
Artists 66
Burns, Robert (1759–1796)
Quotations 670
Suspicion 790
Burr, Aaron (1756–1836)
Delay 218
Burritt, Elihu (1810–1879)
Character 131
Responsibility 696
Burroughs, Augusten (1909–)
Alcohol 41
Burroughs, John (1837–1921)
Birds 91
Books 97
Character 131
Friendship 341
Kindness 454
Life 490
Literature 498
Mind 535
Occupation 582
Poetry 628
Struggle 772

Burroughs, John (cont.)
Summer 787
Temperament 804
Thoughts 811
Winter 870
Burroughs, William S. (1914–1997)
Addiction 24
Alcohol 41
Conformity 169
Desperation 227
Intellectuals 437
Paranoia 597
Police 631
Sentimentality 731
Silence 738
Speaking 757
Burstyn, Ellen (1932–)
Addiction 24
Burton, Richard (1925–1984)
Friendship 341
Gold 369
Burton, Robert (1577–1640)
Ambition 45
Anxiety 57
Charm 135
Kindness 454
Melancholy 530
Music 562
Quiet 669
Scholars 718
Burton, Sir Richard Francis (1821–1890)
Religion 687
Burwell, Carter (1955–)
Bliss 94
Ignorance 418
Buscaglia, Leo F. (1924–1998)
Earthquakes 254
Friendship 342
Tomorrow 819
Bush, Barbara (1925–)
Kisses 457
Togetherness 817
War 859
Bush, George H. W. (1924–)
Charisma 133
Political Correctness 632
Bush, George W. (1946–)
America 47
Authority 72
Diplomacy 237
Glory 364
Government 371
History 398
Hope 403
Liberty 480
Literacy 498
Opinions 584
Oppression 589
Perception 610
Preservation 650
Prison 653
Tragedy 824
Bush, Laura (1946–)
Children 138
Libraries 484
Bush, Vannevar (1890–1974)
Logic 499
Mathematics 525
Reason 678
Science 719
Understanding 836
Bussell, Darcy (1969–)
Mothers 554
Butler, Brett (1958–)
Dreams 249
Butler, Edward B. (1853–1928)
Enthusiasm 275
Butler, Joseph (1692–1752)
Benevolence 88
Senses 730
Butler, Nicholas (1862–1947)
Conviction 177
Butler, R. A. (1902–1982)
Politics 637

Butler, Samuel (1835–1902)
Abstinence 15
Adultery 28
Alcohol 41
Arrogance 62
The Bible 88
Conflict 167
Dogma 244
Dogs 246
Enjoyment 273
Experience 291
Fools 326
Forgiveness 332
Friendship 342
Fun 352
Genius 360
Honesty 401
Ignorance 418
Intoxication 439
Irony 440
Laws 466
Lawyers 468
Lies 486
Life 490
Logic 499
Love 506
Mankind 518
Money 548
Morality 551
Nonsense 575
Oaths 578
Philosophy 619
Pleasure 624
Pride 651
Reason 678
Sarcasm 715
Science 719
Silence 738
Tact 792
Understanding 837
Uselessness 843
Value 844
Vanity 846
Vice 847
Virtue 853
Wit 873

Butros-Ghali, Butros (1922–)
Bureaucracy 108

Butterworth, Eric (1916–2003)
Achievement 19

Buttiglione, Rocco (1948–)
Laws 466
Sin 741
Totalitarianism 820

Buttons, Red (1919–2006)
Youth 894

Buxton, Charles (1823–1871)
Criticism 196
Pleasure 624
Silence 738

Byrne, David (1952–)
Smoking 749
Tobacco 817

Byrne, Jane (1934–)
Commerce 157

Byrne, Rhonda (1955–)
Encouragement 268

Byrne, Robert (1928–)
Cheating 136
Children 138
Democracy 220
People 610
Self-Respect 729
Invention 440
Sorrow 756
Status Quo 765
Suicide 784
Time 815
Writing 887

Byrnes, James F. (1879–1972)
Security 726

Byron, Lord (1788–1824)
Absurdity 16
Adultery 28
Circumstances 149

Byron, Lord (cont.)
Debt 210
Fantasy 304
Fate 307
Fiction 316
Fidelity 317
Flattery 320
Fools 326
Friendship 342
Gambling 354
Glory 364
Greatness 377
Hate 387
Hell 394
Intoxication 439
Laughter 463
Leisure 476
Marriage 521
Melancholy 530
Patriots 606
Pleasure 624
Prose 659
Religion 687
Sacrifice 711
Satire 716
Science 719
Sensuality 731
Smiles 748
Snow 749
Solitude 753
Tears 800
Vice 847
Wine 869
Wives 874

C

Cabell, James Branch (1879–1958)
Memory 531
Optimism 590
Pessimism 617
Temptaion 804
Cabot, Meg (1967–)
Happiness 384
Rights 707
Caddy, Eileen (1917–2006)
Joy 446
Laughter 463
Caecilius Statius (220–168 BC)
Delay 218
Caen, Herb (1916–1997)
Immortality 426
The Past 602
Caesar, Julius (100–44 BC)
Belief 86
Suspicion 790
Cage, John (1912–1992)
Beauty 81
Ego 263
Ideas 413
Music 562
Cahan, Abraham (1860–1951)
Lies 486
Cahill, Tim (1979–)
Editors 258
Journals 446
Cahn, Sammy (1913–1999)
Ambassadors 45
Caine, Michael (1933–)
Obsession 581
Calderón de la Barca, Pedro (1600–1681)
Illusion 422
Caldwell, Philip (1920–)
Failure 296
Fathers 309
Success 779
Teamwork 800
Caldwell, Sarah (1924–2006)
Learning 474
Caldwell, Taylor (1900–1985)
Skeptics 744
Calhoun, John (1782–1850)
Liberty 480

Calisher, Hortense (1911–)
Ideas 413
Callaghan, James (1912–2005)
Leadership 470
Callas, Maria (1923–1977)
Artists 66
Students 773
Teachers 797
Calvin, John (1509–1564)
Punishment 663
Salvation 714
Satan 715
Superstition 788
Calvino, Italo (1923–1985)
Gluttony 366
Melancholy 530
Sadness 712
The Unconcious 836
Camara, Helder (1909–1999)
The Poor 639
Camden, William (1551–1623)
The Sea 723
Cameron, Julia (1948–)
Creativity 190
Cameron, Simon (1799–1889)
Politicians 635
Camillo Benso, Conte di Cavour (1810–1861)
Distrust 242
Trust 829
Campbell, Anne (1940–)
Elections 265
Campbell, Beatrix (1947–)
Crisis 193
Campbell, David (1948–)
Discipline 239
Campbell, Joseph (1904–1987)
Bliss 94
Consciousness 172
Enthusiasm 275
Eternity 281
Journalism 442
Mythology 565
Newspapers 572
Perfection 611
Planning 623
Transformation 826
Unity 839
Warriors 862
Campbell, Kim (1947–)
Unity 839
Campbell, Mrs. Patrick (1865–1940)
Affection 34
Campbell, Thomas (1777–1844)
Hope 403
Joy 446
Camus, Albert (1913–1960)
Absurdity 16
Autumn 74
Beauty 81
Beginnings 85
Censorship 123
Charity 134
Charm 135
Choice 144
Cowardice 188
Deeds 214
Despair 226
Ethics 282
Evil 284
Experience 291
Faces 295
Fallibility 300
Fate 307
Fools 326
Forgiveness 332
Freedom 336
Free Will 339
Generosity 359
Government 371
Greatness 377
Heartbreak 392
Hope 403
Ignorance 419
Illusion 422
Lies 486

Camus, Albert (cont.)
Life 490
Love 506
Malevolence 516
Nihilism 573
Paradox 596
Rebellion 680
Seriousness 732
Sin 741
Style 777
Suicide 784
Summer 787
Thoughts 811
Truth 831
Winter 870
Camuti, Dr. Louis J. (1894–1981)
Cats 116
Canetti, Elias (1905–1994)
Rulers 710
Survival 789
War 859
Canning, George (1770–1827)
Commerce 157
Cannon, Dyan (1937–)
The Bible 88
Cannon, Jimmy (1910–1973)
Fishing 319
Cantona, Eric (1966–)
Cinema 147
Cantor, Eddie (1892–1964)
Enemies 270
Happiness 384
Capek, Karel (1890–1938)
Cats 116
Socialism 750
Capote, Truman (1924–1984)
California 113
Chocolate 143
Life 490
Witchcraft 874
Writing 887
Capp, Al (1909–1979)
Art 63
Welfare 867
Capper, Arthur (1865–1951)
Bureaucracy 108
Capps, Lois (1938–)
Addiction 24
Capps, Lois (cont.)
Schools 718
Capra, Frank (1897–1991)
Creativity 190
Capra, Fritjof (1939–)
Activity 23
Joy 446
Relaxation 686
Caras, Roger A. (1929–2001)
Cats 116
Dogs 246
Carcieri, Donald L. (1942–)
Debate 210
Schools 719
Card, Orson Scott (1951–)
Healing 388
Sickness 737
Unemployment 838
Carême, Marie-Antoine (1784–1933)
Cooking 177
Carey, Drew (1961–)
Normalcy 576
Carey, Mariah (1970–)
Strength 771
Carleton, William (1794–1869)
Character 131
Carlin, George (1937–)
Addiction 24
Camping 114
Clergy 152
Comedy 156
Dishonesty 241
Duty 253
Hell 394
Lawyers 468
The Moon 550
Status Quo 765
The Universe 841

Carlin, George (cont.)
Virginity 851
Weather 866
Carlisle, Ruth (1908–)
Adults 29
Carlyle, Thomas (1795–1881)
Ability 9
Adversity 30
Angels 52
Brothers 106
Censorship 124
Change 129
Civilization 150
Conceit 164
Cunning 200
Debt 210
Delay 218
Despair 226
Endurance 269
Enemies, ...270
Enthusiasm 275
Eternity 281
Fashion 305, 306
Faults 310
Fear 312
Forests 330
Genius 360
Ghosts 362
Goals 366
Government 372
Greatness 377
Heroes 396
Idleness 417
Ignorance 419
Imagination 423
Jesus 441
Justice 451
Kingdoms 454
Knowledge 459
Libraries 484
Loneliness 500
Machines 513
Materialism 524
Mothers 554
Motivation 560
Music 563
The Past 602
Patience 604
Popularity 640
The Present 649
Protestantism 661
Purpose 665
Reason 678
Reform 682
Sarcasm 715
Science 719
Silence 738
Slavery 746
Space 757
Speaking 757
Spirituality 759
Statesmen 763
Summer 787
Talk 794
Technology 801
Time 815
Tradition 823
Tragedy 824
Understanding 837
Unity 839
Violence 851
Vision 855
Vocation 856
Wages 858
Work 880
Worship 884
Youth 894
Carmack, John (1970–)
Art 63
Entertainment 274
Carman, Bliss (1861–1929)
Apathy 57
Carmichael, Stokely (1941–1998)
Grandfathers 375
Carnegie, Andrew (1835–1919)
Ability 9

Carnegie, Andrew (cont.)
- Charity 134
- Honesty 401
- Industry 430
- Lawyers 468
- Libraries 484
- Motivation 560

Carnegie, Dale (1888–1955)
- Achievement 19
- Arguments 60
- Character 131
- Criticism 196
- Determination 231
- Emotions 267
- Enjoyment 273
- Enthusiasm 275
- Fatigue 310
- Fear 312
- Fools 326
- Friendship 342
- Fun 352
- Heart 390
- Hope 403
- Horses 404
- Logic 499
- Loss 504
- Motivation 561
- The Past 602
- Perseverance 612
- The Present 649
- Property 658
- Purpose 665
- Roses 709
- Self-Control 729
- Sleep 748
- Success 779

Caron, Leslie (1931–)
- Cinema 147

Carpenter, Humphrey (1946–2005)
- Lies 487

Carpentier, Georges (1894–1975)
- Boxing 103

Carr, Allan (1937–1999)
- Addiction 24

Carr, Caleb (1955–)
- Losing 502

Carr, Howie (1952–)
- Political Correctness 632

Carrel, Alexis (1873–1944)
- Destiny 229
- Intuition 439

Carreras, Jose (1946–)
- Bathrooms 80

Carrere, Tia (1966–)
- Adolescence 27

Carrey, Jim (1962–)
- Alcohol 41
- Motivation 561

Carrington, Leonora (1917–)
- Sentimentality 731

Carroll, Jonathan (1949–)
- Writing 887

Carroll, Lewis (1832–1898)
- Belief 86
- Breakfast 105
- Dance 202
- Memory 531
- Yesterday 892

Carruthers, Thomas (1841–1924)
- Teachers 797

Carson, Johnny (1925–2005)
- Death 208
- Hair 383
- Radio 672
- Television 803
- Work 880

Carson, Rachel (1907–1964)
- Children 139
- Meemory 531
- Parenthood 597
- Preservation 650

Carter, Angela (1940–1992)
- Cinema 147
- Liberation 478

Carter, Angela (cont.)
Pornography 641
Carter, Billy (1937–1988)
Beer 84
Carter, Hodding, Jr. (1907–1972)
Beer 84
The News 572
Noise 574
Parenthood 597
Roots 709
Television 803
Carter, Jimmy (1924–)
Achievement 19
Adultery 28
Afternoon 35
America 47
Crisis 193
Killing 453
Peace 607
Reconciliation 680
Republicans 692
War 859
Carter, Lillian (1898–1983)
Age 36
Risk 707
Carter, Rosalynn (1927–)
Ability 9
Confidence 166
Leadership 470
Talent 793
Cartwright, Wiliam (1611–1645)
Fools 326
Carvel, Paul (1964–)
Astrology 70
Carver, George Washington (1864–1943)
Compassion 162
Excuses 288
Carville, James (1944–)
Economics 256
Casals, Pablo (1876–1973)
Age 36
Children 139
Decency 211
Casanova, Giacomo (1725–1798)
Bliss 94
Lies 487
Self-Confidence 728
Casey, Robert (1932–2000)
Crisis 193
Castellaneta, Dan (1957–)
Beer 84
Casteneda, Carlos (1925–1998)
Warriors 862
Castillo, Ana (1953–)
Sexuality 734
Castle, Barbara (1910–2002)
Unemployment 838
Castle, Michael N. (1939–)
Universities 842
Castro, Fidel (1926–)
Imperialism 427
Revolution 700
Struggle 772
Cather, Willa (1873–1947)
Forests 330
Heart 390
Life 490, 491
The Moon 550
Nobility 574
Security 726
Trees 828
Winter 870
Wishes 872
Catherine the Great (1729–1796)
Forgiveness 332
Cato the Elder (234–149 BC)
Farming 305
Fools 326
Gossip 370
Mind 535
Mistakes 543
Patience 604
Silence 738
Words 878

Catt, Carrie Chapman (1859–1947)
Adjustment 25
Cattrall, Kim (1956–)
Bedrooms 83
Catullus (84–54 BC)
Kisses 457
Cavafy, Constantine Peter (1863–1933)
Prayer 647
Cavanaugh, Chris (1962–)
Stories 767
Cavendish, Margaret (1623–1673)
Decency 211
Cavett, Dick (1936–)
Censorship 124
Children 139
Comedy 156
Parenthood 597
People 610
Cayce, Edgar (1877–1945)
Ego 263
Cecil, Robert (1563–1612)
Horses 404
Society 751
Solitude 754
Celine, Louis-Ferdinand (1894–1961)
Lies 487
Cellini, Benvenuto (1500–1571)
Responsibility 696
Centlivre, Susannah (1669–1723)
Cheating 136
Honesty 401
Cerf, Bennett (1898–1971)
Laughter 463
Cerf, Vinton (1943–)
Ideology 416
Cerutty, Percy (1895–1975)
Destiny 229
Cervantes, Miguel de (1547–1616)
Acting 22
Caution 121
Comedy 156
Delay 218
Enemies 270
Faces 295
Fear 312
Fools 326
Government 372
Hunger 411
Judges 448
Painting 595
Sorrow 756
Tact 792
Theater 807
Valor 844
Value 844
Wit 873
Women 876
Wounds 885
Cezanne, Paul (1839–1906)
Artists 66
Chadwick, Alan (1909–1981)
Life 491
Chagall, Marc (1887–1985)
Theater 807
Chalmers, Allan K. (1915–1990)
Crisis 193
Chamberlain, Wilt (1936–)
Basketball 80
Chambers, Oswald
Ability 9
Chambers, Whittaker (1901–1961)
Communism 159
Crisis 193
Chamfort, Nicolas (1741–1794)
Love 506
Novels 577
Sickness 737
Soldiers 753
Champfleury, Jules (1820–1889)
Cats 116
Chanakya (350–275 BC)
Forests 330
Idols 418
Senses 730
Sons 755

Chanakya (cont.)
Status 765
Chandler, Raymond (1888–1959)
Advertising 32
Alcohol 41
California 113
Economics 256
Floods 322
Mystery 564
Novels 577
Reason 678
Research 693
Scholars 718
Science 719
Chanel, Coco (1883–1971)
Adolescence 27
Fashion 306
Style 777
Youth 894
Chang, Iris (1968–2004)
Acceptance 17
Crisis 193
Racism 671
Chang-tzu (369–286 BC)
Fame 300
Channing, William Ellery (1780–1842)
Conflict 167
Difficulty 235
Discipline 239
Poetry 628
Chapin, Edward (1831–1863)
Appearances 58
Bigotry 89
Eternity 281
Mystery 564
Chapin, Edwin Hubbel (1814–1880)
Cowardice 188
Life 491
Chaplin, Charlie (1889–1977)
Actors 23
Comedy 156
Humor 410
Laughter 463
Mothers 554
Police 631
Rejection 684
Chapman, Arthur (1873–1935)
Envy 278
Chapman, George (1559–1634)
Admiration 26
Ignorance 419
Chapman, Graham (1941–1989)
Cannibalism 114
Chapman, John Jay (1862–1933)
Benevolence 88
Commerce 157
Teachers 797
Charron, Pierre (1541–1603)
Advice 33
Friendship 342
Chartier, Émile-Auguste (1868–1951)
Cats 116
Ideas 413
Chase, Ilka (1903–1978)
Stock Market 766
Telephones 802
Traitors 825
Chase, Samuel (1741–1811)
Juries 451
Chase, Stuart (1888–1985)
Nationalism 567
Chateaubriand, de Vicomte (1768–1848)
Killing 453
Chaucer, Geoffrey (1343–1400)
Fashion 306
Scholars 718
Chavez, Cesar (1927–1993
Corporations 180
Students 773
Chavez, Linda (1947–)
Journalists 443
Chayefsky, Paddy (1923–1981)
Society 751
Chazal (1956–)
Eyes 293

Chaze, Elliot (1915–1990)
Tennis 805
Cheever, John (1912–1982)
Adultery 28
Chekhov, Anton (1860–1904)
Angels 52
Belief 86
Crisis 193
Doctors 243
Electricity 266
Lawyers 468
Love 506
Peace 607
Privacy 654
The Sea 723
Chen, Joan (1961–)
Teenagers 801
Cheney, Dick (1941–)
Defiance 217
Cheney, John Vance (1848–1922)
Encouragement 268
Cher (1946–)
Architects 59
Toys 822
Chernow, Ron (1949–)
Corporations 180
Inflation 431-432
Chesterfield, Lord (1694–1773)
Ancestry 52
Common Sense 158
Dance 203
Enemies 270
Fashion 306
Flattery 320
Forgiveness 332
Fun 352
Greatness 377
Idleness 417
Inferiority 431
Knowledge 459
Learning 474
Manners 519
Mind 535
Modesty 546
Pleasure 624
Praise 645
Procrastination 655
Retreat 698
Ridicule 705
Siblings 737
Style 777
Suicide 784
Tolerance 818
Vice 848
Wit 873
Youth 894
Chesterton, G. K. (1874–1936)
Absurdity 16
Adventure 30
Advice 33
Ancestors 51
Architecture 60
Aristocracy 61
Art 63
Artists 66
Atheism 71
The Bible 88
Bigotry 90
Books 97
Bravery 104
Childhood 136
Consistency 175
Criticism 196
Cruelty 198
Democracy 220
Education 259
Experience 291
Fear 312
Fiction 316
Fighting 318
Food 324
Greatness 377
Heaven 392
Journalism 442
Literature 498

Chesterton, G. K. (cont.)
Logic 499
Losing 502
Love 506
Madness 513
Miracles 540
Money 548
Morality 551
Music 563
Patriotism 605
Poetry 628
Religion 687
Science 719, 720
Slang 746
Success 779
Suffering 782
Temperament 804
Thieves 810
Thoughts 811
Toughness 821
Tourism 821
Tradition 823
Truth 831
Understanding 837
Virtue 853
Vulgarity 857
Wit 873
Wives 874
Youth 894
Chevalier, Maurice (1888–1972)
Age 36
Artists 66
Old Age 583
Chiat, Jay (1931–2002)
Architecture 60
Chicago, Judy (1939–)
Artists 66
Child, Julia (1912–2004)
Cooking 178
Food 324
Child, Lydia M. (1802–1880)
Earth 254
Fathers 309
Genius 360
Pleasure 624
Chillida, Eduardo (1924–2002)
Space 757
Chilo (c. 620–550 BC)
Adversity 30
Chisholm, Shirley (1924–2005)
Achievement 19
America 47
Chittister, Joan (1936–)
Anger 53
Chocola, Chris (1962–)
Bureaucracy 108
Chodron, Pema (1936–)
Body 95
Cholmondeley, Mary (1859–1925)
Childhood 137
Chomsky, Noam (1928 –)
Censorship 124
Conformity 169
Culture 199
Democracy 220
Propaganda 658
Questions 668
Science 720
Terrorism 806
Totalitarianism 820
Chopin, Kate (1850–1904)
Artists 66
The Sea 723
Chopra, Deepak (1946–)
Babies 76
Bliss 94
Chaos 130
Childhood 137
Truth 831
Chow, Stephen (1962–)
Objectivity 579
Subjectivity 778
Christie, Agatha (1890–1976)
Ability 9
Age 36
Children 139

Christie, Agatha (cont.)
- Despair 226
- Emotions 267
- Encouragement 268
- Habits 382
- Idleness 417
- Invention 440
- Justice 451
- Laziness 469
- Life 491
- Mercy 533
- Parenthood 597
- War 859
- Writing 887

Christina of Sweden (1626–1689)
- Dignity 237
- Occupation 582

Christo (1935–)
- Artists 66

Chrysler, Walter (1875–1940)
- Enthusiasm 275

Chubais, Anatoly (1955–)
- Ideology 416

Chuck D. (1960–)
- Voting 857

Churchill, Charles (1731–1764)
- Fools 326
- Genius 360

Churchill, Jennie Jerome (1854–1921)
- Friendship 342

Churchill, Jill (1943–)
- Parenthood 597

Churchill, Sir Winston (1874–1965)
- Alcohol 41
- Anger 53
- Babies 76
- Capitalism 115
- Cats 116
- Censorship 124
- Change 129
- Class 152
- Communism 159
- Community 161
- Conflict 167
- Countries 185
- Days 206
- Defiance 217
- Democracy 220, 221
- Destiny 229
- Determination 231
- Difficulty 235
- Dogs 246
- Ego 263
- Encouragement 268
- Enthusiasm 275
- Excellence 286
- Excess 287
- Failure 296
- Fear 312
- Fools 326
- The Future 353
- Genius 361
- Giving 363
- Glory 364
- Golf 370
- Government 372
- Grammar 375
- Greatness 377
- Hell 394
- History 398, 399
- Jokes 441
- Liberals 477
- Lies 487
- Life 491
- Martyrs 523
- Mercy 533
- Mind 535
- The News 572
- Opportunity 585
- Optimism 590
- Paradox 596
- Patriotism 605
- Pets 618
- Politicians 635
- Profit 655
- Progress 656

Churchill, Sir Winston (cont.)
Queens 667
Quotations 670
Rejoice 684
Responsibility 696
Right 705
Sharing 736
Socialism 750
Society 751
Soldiers 753
Strategy 769
Success 779
Suffering 782
Survival 789
Tradition 823
Truth 831
Vision 855
War 859
Wives 874
Words 878
Wrong 891
Ciano, Galeazzo (1903–1944)
Losing 502
Ciardi, John (1916–1986)
Adolescence 27
Ancestors 51
Cats 116
College 155
Liberation 478
Moderation 546
Poetry 628
Genius 361
Cicero (106–43 BC)
Ability 9
Admiration 26
Adversity 30
Agriculture 40
Art 63
Authority 72
Avarice 74
Blame 93
Body 95
Books 98
Bureaucracy 108
Character 131
Charm 135
Courage 186
Culture 199
Decency 212
Decisions 213
Desire 225
Difficulty 235
Dignity 237
Doctors 243
Education 259
Emotions 267
Excess 287
Experience 291
Eyes 293
Fidelity 317
Fools 326
Freedom 336
Friendship 342
Fruit 351
Glory 365
Gratitude 376
Habits 382
History 399
Honesty 401
Hope 403
Ignorance 419
Instinct 435
Judges 448
Kindness 453
Laws 466
Leisure 476
Liberty 480
Libraries 484
Manners 519
Mind 535
Mirrors 540
Mistakes 543
Moderation 546
Money 548
Nature 569
Necessity 570

Cicero (cont.)
Old Age 583
Pain 593
Passion 601
Peace 607
Philosophy 619
Pleasure 624
Poetry 628
Praise 645
Privacy 654
Reality 676
Reason 678
Reliability 687
Respect 695
Studying 774
Superstition 788
Talent 793
Talk 794
Teachers 797
Treason 827
Truth 831
Value 844
Vice 848
Virtue 853
War 859
Youth 894
Cioran, E. M. (1911–1995)
Intellectuals 437
Music 563
Refuge 682
Skepticism 743
Suicide 784
Cisneros, Sandra (1954–)
Homelessness 401
Liberation 478
Cixous, Hélène (1937–)
Losing 502
Claiborne, Craig (1920–2000)
Cooking 178
Clare, John (1793–1864)
Difficulty 235
Clark, Dick (1929–)
Babies 76
Humor 410
Clark, Frank A. (1915–2003)
Life 491
Smiles 748
Clark, Gene (1944–1991)
Zen 898
Clark, Joe (1939–)
Self-Respect 729
Clark, John Bates (1847–1938)
Socialism 750
Wages 858
Clark, Ramsay (1927–)
Change 129
Clark, Richard (1951–)
Achievement 19
Clarke, Adam (1760–1832)
Saviors 717
Sin 742
Clarke, Arthur C. (1917–)
Astrology 70
Fiction 316
Honesty 401
Intelligence 437
Judges 448
The Moon 550
Morality 551
Nationalism 567
Reading 673
Revolution 700
Science 720
Survival 790
Technology 801
Tragedy 824
Worship 884
Clarke, Edward (1769–1822)
Pleasure 624
Clarkson, Thomas (1760–1846)
Slavery 746
Clary, Julian (1959–)
Eccentricity 255
Claudianus (c. 350 BC)
Desire 225

Clausewitz, Karl von (1780–1831)
Surprise 789
Warriors 862
Clay, Henry (1777–1852)
Presidents 650
Clayton, Powell (1833–1914)
Adjustment 25
Freedom 336
Cleese, John (1939–)
Business 111
Clemenceau, Georges (1841–1929)
War 859
Clement of Alexandria (c. 150–211)
Hope 403
Cleobulus (c. 500 BC)
Body 95
Health 388
Soul 756
Cleveland, Grover (1872–1933)
Presidents 650
Cleveland, Harlan (1918–)
Leadership 470
Clift, Montgomery (1920–1966)
Sadness 712
Clinton, Bill (1946–)
America 47
Bigotry 90
Elections 265
The Internet 438
Mental Illness 533
Republicans 692
Status Quo 765
Strategy 769
Taxes 796
Clinton, Hillary (1947–)
Abstinence 15
Voting 857
Clooney, George (1961–)
Endings 269
Clooney, Nick (1934–)
Corporations 180
Close, Chuck (1940–)
Artists 66
Sculpture 723
Clough, Arthur Hugh (1819–1861)
Tradition 823
Clough, Brian (1935–2004)
Epitaphs 279
Clyburn, Jim (1940–)
Environment 277
Cobain, Kurt (1967–1994)
Apathy 57
The Dead 207
Cobb, Irvin S. (1876–1944)
Epitaphs 279
Memory 531
Stories 767
Cobb, Ty (1886–1961)
Losing 502
Cobbett, William (1763–1835)
Money 548
Sisters 743
Cobden, Richard (1804–1865)
Commerce 157
Coble, Howard (1931–)
Corporations 180
Cochran, Johnnie (1937–2005)
Crisis 193
Cochrane, Thomas (1775–1860)
Relativity 685
Cocker, Jarvis (1963–)
Noise 574
Cockran, Bourke (1854–1923)
Civilization 150
Cocks, Sir Barnett (1907–1989)
Ideas 414
Cocteau, Jean (1889–1963)
Admiration 26
Alcohol 41
Artists 67
Dreams 249
Journals 446
Luck 512
Poetry 628
Realism 676

Cocteau, Jean (cont.)
- Silence 738
- Tact 792

Coe, Jonathan (1961–)
- Writing 887

Coen, Ethan (1957–)
- Heart 390
- Women 876

Coen, Joel (1954–)
- Heart 390
- Women 876

Cohen, Leonard (1934–)
- Depression 224
- Judges, ...448
- Scholars 718

Cohnen, Andrew (1955–)
- Liberation 478, 479

Cohen, Mark B. (1949–)
- Politics 637

Cohen, Morris (1880–1947)
- Persecution 612
- Religion 688

Coke, Edward (1552–1634)
- Cause and Effect 120
- Certainty 126
- Corporations 180
- Persecution 612
- Religion, ...688
- Uncertainty 835

Coker, Mary Roper (1908–1975)
- Mothers 554

Colbert, Stephen (1964–)
- America 47
- Atheism 71
- Beauty 81
- Facts 295
- Ignorance 419
- Reality 676

Colby, Frank Moore (1865–1925)
- Anger 53
- Boredom 100
- Communication 158
- Persecution 612

Cole, Edwin Louis (1922–2002)
- Crisis 193
- Satan 715
- Sin 742

Colegate, Isabel (1931–)
- Writing 887

Coleman, James S. (1926–)
- Education 259
- Schools 719

Coleridge, Samuel Taylor (1772–1834)
- Ability 9
- Admiration 26
- Advice 33
- The Bible 89
- Heart 390
- Intolerance 438
- Knights 459
- Language 462
- Melancholy 530
- Mind 535
- Mothers 554
- Poetry 629
- Pride 651
- Sin 742
- Sleep 748
- Snow 749
- Statesmen 763
- Sympathy 791
- Tolerance 818

Coleridge, William Hart (1789–1842)
- Reflection 681

Coles, Abraham (1813–1891)
- Cause and Effect 120

Colette, Sidonie Gabrielle (1873–1954)
- Cats 116
- Dogs 246
- Enthusiasm 275
- Etiquette 283
- Friendship 342
- Humor 410
- Laughter 463
- Travel 827
- Poetry 629

Colette, Sidonie Gabrielle (cont.)
Silence 738
Collier, Jeremy (1650–1726)
Difficulty 235
Idleness 417
Questions 668
Collins, John Churton (1848–1908)
Adversity 30
Flattery 320
Friendship 342
Collins, Judy (1939–)
Journals 446
Suicide 784
Collins, Marva (1936)
Determination 231
Excellence 286
Imitation 425
Individualism 429
Students 773
Teachers 797
Collins, Phil (1951–)
Songs 754
Collins, Susan (1952–)
Corporations 180
Colman, George (1762–1836)
Praise 645
Colton, Charles Caleb (1780–1832)
Ability 9
Adversity 31
Aging 38
Avarice 74
Bigotry 90
Books 97
Cause and Effect 120
Commerce 157
Corruption 184
Difficulty 235
Doubt 248
Employment 268
Envy 278
Eyes 293
Flattery 320
Fraud 335
Friendship 342
Hate 387
Imitation 425
Impatience 426
Impotence 427
Liberty 480
Life 491
Money 548
Opportunity 586
Paradox 596
The Past 602
Patience 604
Plagiarism 622
Pleasure 625
Power 644
Praise 645
Pride 651
Prudence 661
Quarrels 667
Repartee 691
Reputation 692
Suicide 784
Time 815
Tyranny 834
Writing 887
Colwin, Laurie (1944–1992)
Cooking 178
Comfort, Alex (1920–2000)
Charm 135
Comiskey, Stephen W. (1947–)
Authority 72
Responsibility 696
Commager, Henry Steele (1902–1998)
Censorship 124
Dissent 242
Commoner, Barry (1917–)
Corporations 180
Environment 277
Pollution 638
Comte, Auguste (1798–1857)
The Dead 207

Condon, Bill (1955–)
Earthquakes 254
Confucius (551–479 BC)
Actions 22
Anger 53
Beauty 81
Boredom 100
Caution 121
Character 131
Dance 203
Destiny 229
Difficulty 235
Envy 278
Faith 299
Family 302
Fate 307
Faults 310
Fools 326
Forgiveness 332
Friendship 342
Generosity 359
Heart 390
Humility 409
Ignorance 419
Imitation 425
Kindness 453
Kisses 457
Knowledge 460
Learning 474
Lust 512
Manners 519
Mind 535
Mistakes 543
Modesty 547
The Moon 550
The Past 602
Plants 623
Progress 656
Quarrels 667
Reflection 681
Respect 695
Safety 713
Security 726
Service 732
Silence 738
Sincerity 742
Success 779
Sympathy 791
Teachers 797
Thoughts 811
Vice 848
Virtue 854
Words 878
Congreve, William (1670–1729)
Ambition 45
Deeds 214
Heaven 392
Connolly, Billy (1942–)
Hypocrisy 412
Connolly, Cyril (1903–1974)
Age 36
Charm 135
The Dead 207
Journalism 442
Literature 498
Police 631
Reality 676
Vulgarity 857
Wine 869
Writing 887
Conrad, Joseph (1857–1924)
America 47
Conscience 171
Cruelty 198
Despair 226
Effort 262
Enemies 270
Envy 278
Evil 284
Eyes 293
Fiction 316
Fidelity 318
Gossip 370
Government 372
Greed 379

Conrad, Joseph (cont.)
Imagination 423
Kitchens 458
Life 491
Loneliness 500
Majorities 515
Misery 541
Nature 569
Relaxation 686
The Sea 723
Secrets 724
Sincerity 742
The Supernatural 788
Conroy, Pat (1945–)
Mind 535
Paranoia 597
Travel 827
Constable, John (1776–1837)
Beauty 81
Perspective 615
Cook, Barbara (1927–)
Addiction 24
Cook, Dane (1972–)
Alcohol 41
Cook, Eliza (1818–1889)
Mothers, ...554
Cook, Rick (1944–)
Computers 163
The Universe 841
Cook, Scott (1952–)
Retirement 698
Cooley, Charles Horton (1864–1929)
Greed 380
Cooley, Mason (1927–2002)
Acceptance 17
Ideology 416
Insults 436
Kitchens 458
Lies 487
Lust 512
Regret 683
Talk 794
Time 815
Tourism 821
Tradition 823
Coolidge, Calvin (1872–1933)
Business 112
Civilization 150
Determination 231
Effort 262
Emotions 268
Honor 402
Listening 497
Obedience 578
Patriotism 605
Persistence 613
Presidents 650
Profit 655
Progress 656
Safety 713
Unemployment 838
Cooney, Gerry (1956–)
Boxing 103
Cooney, Joan Ganz (1929–)
Parenthood 597
Cooper, Anderson (1967–)
Suicide 784
Cooper, Tommy (1921–1984)
Dreams 250
Cooper, Jeff (1920–2006)
Safety 713
Copeland, Bill (1929–)
Lies 487
Copland, Aaron (1900–1980)
Consciousness 172
Inspiration 435
Music 563
Coppola, Francis Ford (1939–)
Cinema 147
Morality 551
Cora, Tom (1909–1998)
Difficulty 236
Corbett, James J. (1866–1933)
Toughness 821

Corgan, Billy (1967–)
Devotion 233
Corigliano, John (1938–)
Style 777
Cormier, Robert (1925–2000)
Adolescence 27
Corneille, Pierre (1606–1684)
Ambassadors 45
Glory 365
Lies 487
Oaths 578
Risk 707
Sharing 736
Triumph 828
Winning 869
Cornelius Tacitus (AD 55–117)
Excess 287
Fame 300
Generosity 359
Health 388
History 399
Human Nature 405
Laws 466
Leadership 470
Cortazar, Julio (1914–1984)
Kingdoms 455
Cosby, Bill (1937–)
Advertising 32
Childhood 137
Children 139
Hair 383
Laughter 463
Success 779
Cosell, Howard (1918–1995)
Sports 760
Toys 822
Coubertin, Pierre de (1863–1937)
Struggle 772
Coupland, Douglas (1961–)
Business 112
Meetings 530
Courbet, Gustave (1819–1877)
Artists 67
Courteline, Georges (1858–1929)
Babies 76
Cousin, Victor (1792–1867)
Philosophy 619
Cousins, Norman (1915–1990)
Crisis 193
Forgiveness 332
Laughter 463
Libraries 484
Tragedy 824
Cousteau, Jacques (1910–1997)
Abortion 13
Farming 305
Pollution 638
Rivalry 708
The Sea 723
Water 863
Coventry, Thomas (1578–1640)
Kingdoms 455
Covey, Stephen R. (1932–)
Character 131
Choice 144
Determination 231
Freedom 336
Habits 382
Leadership 470
Managers 517
Organization 591
Perspective 615
Wisdom 871
Coward, Noël (1899–1973)
Morality 551
Motivation 561
Television 803
Cowell, Simon (1959–)
Political Correctness 632
Cowley, Abraham (1618–1667)
Curiosity 200
Cowper, William (1731–1800)
Blessings 93
Cats 116

Cowper, William (cont.)
Gardens 356
Glory 365
Guilt 381
Happiness 384
Hell 394
Remorse 690
Repartee 691
Retirement 698
Satan 715
Selfishness 729
Winter 870
Wit 873
Cox, Alex (1954–)
Corporations 180
Shakespeare 735
Coyote, Peter (1941–)
Self 727
Cozzens, James Gould (1903–1978)
Rebellion 680
Crabbe, George (1754–1832)
Deception 213
Cranch, Christopher Pearce (1813–1892)
Spring 761
Crane, Frank (1861–1928)
Friendship 342
Cranston, Alan (1914–2000)
Redemption 681
Creighton, Bishop Mandell (1843–1901)
Questions 668
Crescenzo, Luciano de (1928–)
Angels 53
Crews, Harry (1935–)
Survival 790
Triumph 828
Crichton, Michael (1942–)
Certainty 127
Change 129
Debate 210
Refuge 683
Thoughts 811
Crisp, Quentin (1908–1999)
Decency 212
Disaster 238
Disease 240
Failure 296
Flowers 322
Health 388
Crist, Judith (1922–)
Strangers 768
Cromwell, Oliver (1599–1658)
Doctors 243
Integrity 436
Necessity 570
Subtlety 778
Cronauer, Adrian (1938–)
Apathy 57
Cronenberg, David (1943–)
Art 64
Cronkite, Walter (1916–)
Censorship 124
Freedom 336
Crosby, Howard (1826–1891)
Teachers 797
Unity 840
Crosby, Norm (1927–)
Fate 307
Juries 451
Crosby, Philip (1926–2001)
Organization 592
Quality 665
Croseus of Lydia (595–546)
Fathers 309
Cross, Amanda (1926–)
Quotations 670
Cross, David (1964–)
Corporations 180
Crothers, Samuel McChord (1857–1927)
Facts 295
Failure 296
Crouch, Stanley (1945–)
Segregation 726

Crowe, Russell (1964–)
Villains 850
Crowley, Aleister (1875–1947)
Authority 72
Independence 428
Journalism 442
Mind 535-536
Newspapers 572-573
Crumb, George (1929–)
Crisis 193
Crumb, Robert (1943–)
Suicide 784
Crystal, Billy (1947–)
Sex 733
Csikszentmihalyi, Mihaly (1934–)
Conformity 169
Consciousness 172
Discipline 239
Ego 263
Individualism 429
Media 528
Mind 536
Misfortune 542
Peace of Mind 609
Pleasure 625
Quality 665
Religion 688
Repression 691
Work 880
Cummings, E.E. (1894–1962)
Censorship 124
Error 280
Eyes 293
Kisses 457
Laughter 464
Money 548
Cuomo, Mario (1932–)
Poetry 629
Prose 659
Cuppy, Will (1884–1949)
Blood 94
Curie, Marie (1867–1934)
Curiosity 200
Error 280
Ideas 414
Individuals 430
Progress 656
Responsibility 696
Science 720
Curran, John Philpot (1750–1817)
Liberty 480
Vigilance 850
Cushing, Richard Cardinal (1895–1970)
Love 506
Curtis, Charles (1860–1936)
Fraud 335
Curtis, George William (1824–1892)
Crisis 193
Curtis, Tony (1925–)
Longevity 501
Cusack, John (1966–)
Crisis 193

D

Dahl, Roald (1916–1990)
Chocolate 143
Nonsense 575
Dahlberg, Edward (1900–1977)
Suicide 784
Travel 827
The Dalai Lama (1935–)
Belief 86
Compassion 162
Delusion 219
Friendship 342
Meaning 527
Realization 678
Spirituality 759
Dale, R. W. (1829–1895)
Sadness 712
Daley, Richard M. (1902–1976)
Corporations 180
Police 631
Dalí, Salvador (1904–1989)
Art 64

Dalí, Salvador (cont.)
Madness 514
Perfection 611
Purity 664
Taste 795
Ugliness 835
Dall, Caroline (1822–1912)
Character 131
Dalton, Timothy (1946–)
Crisis 194
Daly, Mary (1928–)
God 367
Damon, Matt (1970–)
Loss 504
Love 505
Dana, Charles A. (1819–1897)
Opinions 584
Dana, John Cotton (1856–1929)
Teachers 797
Dane, Frank (1981–)
Fools 326
Politicians 635
D'Angelo, Anthony J. (1972–)
Political Correctness 632
Dangerfield, Rodney (1921– 2004)
Birth Control 92
Life 491
Sports 760
Danneels, Godfried (1933–)
Theology 808
Dansky, Martin (1952–)
Students 773
Teachers 797
Dante Alighieri (1265–1321)
Avarice 74
Conflict 167
Crisis 194
Envy 278
Hell 394
Liberty 480
Neutrality 571
Silence 738
Sorrow 756
Darabont, Frank (1959–)
Hope 403
Prison 653
Dark, Alvin (1922–)
Baseball 79
Darman, Richard (1943–)
Bureaucracy 108
Darrow, Clarence (1857–1938)
Agnosticism 39
Children 139
Decency 212
Doubt 248
English 272
Ignorance 419
Laws 466
Misfortune 542
Parenthood 597
Presidents 650
Reform 682
Truth 831
Wrong 891
Darwin, Charles (1809–1882)
Agnosticism 39
Alcohol 41
Change 129
Culture 199
Evolution 285
Friendship 342
History 399
Ignorance 419
Indifference 428
Instinct 435
Life 491
Mankind 518
The Poor 639
Reason 678
Science 720
Shakespeare 735
Sin 742
The Universe 841
Darwin, Erasmus (1731–1802)
Cats 116

Darwin, Sir Francis (1848–1925)
Science 721
Daschle, Tom (1947–)
Acceptance 17
David, Jacques-Louis (1748–1825)
Artists 67
Davies, Arthur Powell (1902–1957)
Brotherhood 105
Davies, Dave (1947–)
Understanding 837
Davies, Lynn (1942–)
Losing 502
Davies, Robertson (1913–1995)
Books 98
Cats 117
Effort 262
The Future 353
Genius 361
Happiness 384
Misers 540
Nonsense 575
Old Age 583
Pornography 641
Students 774
Theater 807
Unhappiness 838
Davies, W. H. (1871–1940)
Leisure 476
Rainbows 672
Davies, William M. (1850–1934)
Gardens 356
Davis, Adelle (1904–1974)
Breakfast 105
Disease 240
Food 324
Health 388
Lunch 512
Davis, Angela (1944–)
Revolution 700
Davis, Bette (1908–1989)
Actors 23
Children 139
Discipline 239
Enemies 270
Goals 366
Heroes 396
Liberation 479
Love 506
Old Age 583
Passion 601
Work 880
Davis, Kristin (1965–)
Dating 206
Davis, Marvin (1925–2004)
Toys 822
Davis, Ossie (1917–2005)
Struggle 772
Dawkins, Richard (1941–)
Atheism 71
Evolution 285
Theology 808
Dawson, Christopher (1889–1970)
Humanism 406
The Supernatural 788
Dawson, George (1989–2001)
Life 491
Dawson, George Mercer (1849–1901)
Libraries 484
Day, Clarence (1874–1935)
Addiction 24
Curiosity 200
Day, Doris (1924–)
Middle Age 534
Vulgarity 857
Day, Dorothy (1897–1980)
Actions 22
Individualism 429
Segregation 726
Day, Robin (1923–2000)
Advertising 32
Commerce 157
Magazines 514
Day, Stockwell (1950–)
Judges 448
Dayan, Moshe (1915–1981)
Enemies 270

Dayan, Moshe (cont.)
Peace 607
War 859
Dean, Howard (1948–)
Abortion 13
Dean, James (1931–1955)
Dreams 250
Life 491
Debord, Guy (1931–1994)
Tourism 821
Debreu, Gerard (1921–2004)
Economics 256
Debs, Eugene V. (1855–1926)
Leadership 470, 471
Dees, Morris (1936–)
African-Americans 34
Corporations 180
Defoe, Daniel (1660–1731)
Necessity 570
Sin 742
Thankfulness 807
Tyranny 834
de Gaulle, Charles (1890–1970)
Achievement 19
Countries 185
Crisis 194
Difficulty 236
Ego 263
France 335
Glory 365
Statesmen 763
Strategy 769
DeGeneres, Ellen (1958–)
Childhood 137
Grandmothers 376
Light 496
de Jesus, Carolina Maria
Children 139
Dekker, Thomas (1570–1632)
Sleep 748
Traitors 825
Delacroix, Eugène (1798–1863)
Artists 67
Body 95
Perfection 611
Simplicity 741
Deland, Margaret (1857–1945)
Desire 225
De La Tour, Frances (1944–)
Love 506
Delaunay, Robert (1885–1941)
Understanding 837
DeLauro, Rosa (1943–)
Abortion 13
Delille, Jacques (1738–1813)
Family 302
Fate 307
Friendship 343
DeLillo, Don (1936–)
California 113
Writing 887
Dell, Floyd (1887–1969)
Idleness 417
Laziness 469
Delors, Jacques (1925–)
Cinema 147
Del Toro, Guillermo (1964–)
Vampires 846
Demades (c. 380–318 BC)
Humanity 409
Modesty 547
Demaret, Jimmy (1910–1983)
Golf 370
Dement, William (1928–)
Dreams 250
DeMille, Cecil B. (1881–1959)
Determination 231
Goals 366
Success 779
Deming, Barbara (1917–1984)
Vengeance 847
Deming, W. Edwards (1900–1993)
Consistency 175
Learning 474
Survival 790

Democritus (460–370 BC)
Criticism 196
Happiness 384
Old Age 583
Soul 756
Space 757
Trust 829
Youth 894
Demosthenes (384–322 BC)
Actions 22
Anxiety 57
Beginnings 85
Censure 126
Opportunity 586
Suspicion 790
Tyranny 834
Dempsey, Jack (1895–1983)
Champions 127
Denham, John (1953–)
Beginnings 85
De Niro, Robert (1943–)
Anarchy 50
Dennison, Reverend Sean Parker (1979–)
Morality 551
Dennett, Daniel (1942–)
Free Will 339
De Palma, Brian (1940–)
Corporations 180
Depew, Chauncey (1834–1928)
Conformity 169
Derrida, Jacques (1930–2004)
Ghosts 362
Dershowitz, Alan M. (1938–)
The Bible 89
Judges 448
Desai, Morarji (1896–1995)
Cruelty 198
Vegetarianism 847
Descartes, René (1596–1650)
Desire 225
Difficulty 236
Doubt 248
Dreams 250
Hate 387
Love 506
Mind 536
Philosophy 619
Reading 674
Thoughts 811
Vice 848
Virtue 854
Deschamps, Eustache (1346–1406)
Friendship 343
Relatives 685
Deval, Jacques (1745–1794)
Birds 91
DeVos, Richard M. (1926–)
Money 548
Peace of Mind 609
Devlin, Lord Patrick (1905–1992)
Judges 448
DeVoto, Bernard (1897–1955)
Pessimism 617
De Vries, Peter (1910–1993)
Atheism 71
Celibacy 122
Confessions 165
Gluttony 366
Life 491
Marriage 521
Mothers 554
Parenthood 598
Radio 672
Restaurants 697
Television 803
Dewey, John (1859–1952)
Conflict 167
Decisions 213
Facts 295
Self 727
Teachers 797
The Dhammapada
Happiness 387
Misery 542
Travel 827

Diamond, Jared (1937–)
Biology 91
Elections 265
Native Americans 568
Diamond, Neil (1941–)
Husbands 412
Wives 875
Diana, Princess (1961–1997)
Expectations 290
Kindness 453
Queens 668
Rich and Poor 702
Sons 755
Diaz, Cameron (1972–)
Style 776
DiCaprio, Leonardo (1974–)
Mothers 554
Dick, Philip K. (1928–1982)
Manipulation 517
Reality 676
Dickens, Charles (1812–1870)
Accidents 18
Affection 34
Babies 76
Blessings 93
Charity 134
Debt 210
Excess 288
Greatness 377
Heart 390
Human Nature 405
Love 507
Misery 541
Misfortune 542
Money 548
Nature 569
Punctuality 663
Secrets 724
Shadows 734
Trees 828
Vice 848
Wives 875
Youth 894
Dickinson, Emily (1830–1886)
Afternoon 35
Anger 54
Beauty 81
Birds 91
Doctors 243
Dogs 246
Fear 312
Fog 323
God 367
Heaven 392, 393
Hell 394
Hope 403
Madness 514
Mothers 554
Opportunity 586
The Present 649
Secrets 724
Snow 749
Spring 761
Success 779
Winter 870
Dickinson, Janice (1953–)
Daughters 206
Mothers 554
Dickson, Gordon R. (1923–2001)
Advice 33
Diderot, Denis (1713–1784)
Admiration 26
Doctors 243
Education 259
Flattery 320
Gambling 354
Genius 361
Knowledge 460
Morality 551
Observation 580, 581
Passion 601
Reflection 681
Skepticism 744
Superstition 789
Temperament 804
Zealots 898

Didion, Joan (1934–)
Responsibility 696
Self-Respect 729
Dietrich, Marlene (1901–1992)
Authority 72
Courage 186
Friendship 343
Grace 374
Quotations 670
Sex 733
Stock Market 766
Dietz, Howard (1896–1983)
Plagiarism 622
Difranco, Ani (1970–)
Bedrooms 83
Life 491
Strangers 768
Dijkstra, Edsger (1930–2002)
Computers 163
Machines 513
Reliability 687
Simplicity 741
Dijlas, Milovan (1911–1995)
Ideology 416
Dillard, Annie (1945–)
Chaos 130
Diller, Phyllis (1917–)
Baseball 79
Children 139
Sports 760
Dillinger, John (1903–1934)
Banks 78
Dinesen, Isak (1885–1962)
Artists 67
Silence 739
Stories 767
Diogenes Laertius (412–323 BC)
Education 259
Ego 263
Enemies 270
Friendship 343
Hunger 411
Masturbation 524
Reward 701
Thieves 810
Youth 894
Dion, Celine (1968–)
Mothers 554
Poetry 629
Science 720
Tomorrow 819
Yesterday 892
Dirac, Paul (1902–1984)
Poetry 629
Dirksen, Senator Everett (1896–1969)
Money 548
Disney, Walt (1901–1966)
Adults 29
Cinema 147
Curiosity 200
Gardens 356
Disraeli, Benjamin (1804–1881)
Assassination 69
Christianity 144
Circumstances 149
Civilization 150
Conservatives 174
Criticism 196
Desperation 227
Enthusiasm 275
Error 280
Etiquette 283
Fate 307
Faults 310
Frankness 335
Gardens 356
Genius 361
Greatness 377
Grief 381
Heroes 396
Hypocrisy 412
Ignorance 419
Individuals 430
Inspiration 435
Knowledge 460
Laws 466

Disraeli, Benjamin (cont.)
Liberals 477
Majorities 515
Manners 519
The News 572
Opportunity 586
Opposition 588
Peace 607
Purpose 665
Religion 688
Repartee 691
Revolution 700
Service 732
Silence 739
Sincerity 742
Statesmen 763
Statistics 764
Superiority 788
Thoughts 811
Tact 792
Truth 831
Unity 840
Value 844
Welfare 867
Writing 887
Wrong 891
Youth 894
D'Israeli, Isaac (1766–1848)
Style 776, 777
Taste 795
Writing 887
Ditka, Mike (1939–)
Beer 84
Failure 296
Success 779
Djilas, Milovan (1911–1995)
Communism 159
Revolution 700
Dixon, Donna (1957–)
Dessert 228
Dobson, James (1936–)
Children 139
Dobzhansky, Theodosius (1900–1975)
Biology 91
Doctorow, E. L. (1931–)
Writing 887, 888
Dodson, Betty (1929–)
Masturbation 524
Dogen (1200–1253)
Unity 840
Doherty, Catherine de Hueck (1896–1985)
Salvation 714
Dokken, Don (1953–)
Alcohol 41
Dole, Elizabeth (1936–)
Leadership 471
Donahue, Phil (1935–)
Suicide 784
Donleavy, J. P. (1926–)
Writing 888
Donne, John (1572–1631)
Grace 374
Donner, Richard (1930–)
Objectivity 579
Subjectivity 778
Doolittle, John (1950–)
Terrorism 806
Dorff, Stephen (1973–)
Vampires 846
Dorfsman, Lou (1918–)
Creativity 190
Dorgan, Byron (1942–)
Decency 212
Dostoevsky, Fyodor (1821–1881)
Anxiety 57
Cannibalism 114
Children 139
Evil 284
Freedom 336
Immortality 426
Laughter 464
Lies 487
Martyrs 523
Parenthood 598
Prison 653

Dostoevsky, Fyodor (cont.)
- Prophets 658
- Sarcasm 715
- Strangers 768
- Worship 884

Douglas, Kirk (1916–)
- Life 491

Douglas, Kyan (1970–)
- Alcohol 41

Douglas, Mary (1921–)
- Corporations 180
- Cults 199
- Individualism 429
- Secularism 725

Douglas, Norman (1868–1952)
- Advertising 32
- Children 139
- Education 259
- Mind 536
- Reality 676

Douglas, William Orville (1898–1980)
- Acceptance 967
- Bureaucracy 108
- Censorship 124
- Ideas 414
- Laws 466
- Violence 851

Douglas, T. C. (1904–1986)
- Learning 474

Douglass, Frederick (1817–1895)
- Ignorance 419
- Justice 452
- Parenthood 598
- Poverty 643
- Ridicule 705
- Slavery 746
- Tyranny 834

Dove, Rita (1952–)
- Bureaucracy 108
- Complaints 163
- Libraries 484
- Shakespeare 735

Doyle, Sir Arthur Conan (1859–1930)
- Abstinence 15
- Death 208
- Genius 361
- Mediocrity 529
- Talent 793
- Truth 831

Dr. Dre (1965–)
- Alcohol 41

Drew, Elizabeth (1935–)
- Conversation 176

Drucker, Peter F. (1909–2005)
- Business, ...112
- Computers 164
- Cooperation 179
- Economics 256
- Efficiency 262
- Executives 289
- Industry 430
- Information 432
- Leadership 471
- Managers 517
- Meals 527
- Planning 623
- Quality 666
- Teachers 797
- Work 880

Drummond, Henry (1851–1897)
- Friendship 343
- Love 507

Drummond, Sir William (1585–1649)
- Reason 678
- Scholars 718

Dryden, John (1631–1700)
- Affection 34
- Conscience 171
- Democracy 221
- Familiarity 302
- Fate 307
- Fortune 334
- Genius 361
- Grace 374
- Intoxication 439

Dryden, John (cont.)
Leisure 476
Madness 514
Opportunity 586
Order 591
Priests 652
Quantity 666
Repentance 691
Rogues 709
Ruin 709
Thoughts 811
Treason 827
Vocation 856
Wives 875
Wounds 885
D'Souza, Dinesh (1961–)
America 47
Du Bois, W. E. B. (1868–1963)
Self 727
Du Bos, Charles (1882–1939)
Sacrifice 711
Duane, Diane (1952–)
Teenagers 801
Dubus, Andre (1936–1999)
Shyness 737
Duff, Hilary (1987–)
Uniqueness 839
Duhamel, Georges (1884–1966)
Atheism 71
Memory 531
Value 845
Dumas, Alexandre (1802–1870)
Danger 204
Daughters 206
Friendship 343
Love 507
Suspicion 790
Du Maurier, Daphne (1907–1989)
Women 876
Writing 888
Duncan, Isadora (1877–1927)
Children 139
Dunne, Finley Peter (1867–1936)
Alcohol 41
Bachelors 77
Contempt 176
Vegetarianism 847
Du Plassix Gray, Francine (1830–)
Generosity 359
Meals 527
Du Pont, Pete (1935–)
Corporations 180
Durant, Ariel (1898–1981)
Family 302
Durant, Augustus (1982–)
Dreams 250
Trust 829
Durant, Will (1885–1981)
Anarchy 50
Chaos 130
Civilization 150
Education 259
Family 302
Friendship 343
Ignorance 419
Liberty 480
Socialism 751
Statesmen 763
Durante, Jimmy (1893–1980)
Music 563
Duras, Marguerite (1914–1996)
Alcohol 41
Journalists 444
Durkheim, Émile (1858–1917)
Sadness 712
Suicide 784
Durocher, Leo (1905–1991)
Baseball 79
Managers 517
Durst, Will (1952–)
Defiance 217
Duvall, Robert (1931–)
Economics 256
Dvorak, John C. (1952–)
Corporations 180

Dworkin, Andrea (1946–2005)
Feminism 315
Misogyny 435
Rape 673
Dworkin, Andrea (cont.)
Seduction 726
Sexism 734
Dyer, Sir Edward (1543–1607)
Beggars 84
Joy 446
Dyer, Wayne D. (1940–)
Abundance 16, 17
Acceptance 17
Enthusiasm 275
Ignorance 419
Kingdoms 455
Laughter 464
Life 491
Mind 536
The Past 602
Purpose 665
Quality 666
Relationships 684
Research 693
Transformation 826
Understanding 837
Dyer, William (1881–1933)
Libraries 485
Dyke, Henry Van (1852–1933)
Rivers 708
Sadness 712
Dykes, John (1823–1876)
Deeds 214
Dylan, Bob (1941–)
Birth 92
Death 208
Freedom 336
Heroes 397
Responsibility 696
Songs 754
Success 779
Tomorrow 819
Yesterday 892
Dyson, Esther (1951–)
The Internet 438

E

Eagleton, Terry (1943–)
Political Correctness 632
Earhart, Amelia (1898–1937)
Adventure 30
Courage 186
Women 876
Eastman, Charles (1858–1939)
Native Americans 568
The Supernatural 788
Eastman, Max (1883–1969)
Consciousness 173
Dogs 246
Status Quo 765
Easton, Sheena (1959–)
Biological Clock 90
Eastwood, Clint (1930–)
Marriage 521
Pessimism 617
Easwaran, Eknath (1910–1999)
Crisis 194
Eban, Abba (1915–) ....
Ignorance 419
Statesmen 763
Wisdom 871
Eberhardt, Isabelle (1877–1904)
The Past 602
Eberhart, Richard (1904–2005)
Style 777
Ebner-Eschenbach, Marie Von (1830–1916)
Fear 312
Privilege 654
Rights 706
Triumph 828
Youth 894
Eckhart, Meister (c. 1260–1328)
Integrity 436
Prayer 647

Eco, Umberto (1932–)
Cowardice 188
Dreams 250
Heroes 397
Ideology 416
Reality 676
Scripture 722
Translation 826
Truth 831
Eddington, Sir Arthur (1882–1944)
Mathematics 525
Observations 581
Physics 621
Relativity 685
Science 720
The Universe 841
Edelman, Marian Wright (1939–)
Liberals 477
Parenthood 598
Service 732
Edelman, Murray (1919–2001)
Children 139
Conflict 167
Politics 637
Eden, Anthony (1897–1977)
Appeasement 59
Corruption 184
Edgeworth, Maria (1767–1849)
Property 658
Time 815
Edison, Thomas A. (1847–1931)
Ability 9
Disease 241
Ethics 282
Evolution 285
Failure 296
Faith 299
Genius 361
Inspiration 435
Invention 440
Mothers 554
Necessity 570
Opportunity 586
Patients 605
Perspiration 615
Planning 623
Success 780
Time 815
Waste 863
Weakness 864
Work 880
Worries 883
Edmonds, Kenneth (1958–)
African-Americans 34
Edward III, King (1312–1377)
Evil 284
Edward VIII, King (1894–1972)
America 47
Children 140
Parenthood 598
Edwards, Anthony (1962–)
Cats 117
Edwards, Bob (1947–)
Politicians 635
Edward, Tyron (1809–1894)
Anxiety 57
Brotherhood 106
Delay 218
Destiny 229
Duty 253
Memory 531
Murder 562
Pleasure 625
Praise 645
Safety 713
Teachers 797
The Universe 842
Edwards, Blake (1922–)
Shame 735
Edwards, Bob (1947–)
Ignorance 419
Edwards, Edwin (1927–)
Judges 448
Effinger, George Alec
Adolescence 27

Ega, Greg (1961–)
Caffeine 112
Ehrenreich, Barbara (1941–)
Liberation 479
Ehrenreich, Barbara (cont.)
Patriots 606
Eibeschutz, Jonathan (1690–1764)
Pleasure 625
Sadness 712
Einstein, Albert (1879–1955)
Ability 9
Admiration 26
Ambition 45
Anger 54
Artists 67
Attitude 71
Authority 72
Books 98
Bureaucracy 109
Cause and Effect 120
Character 131
Common Sense 158
Communism 159
Conflict 167
Consciousness 173
Cooperation 179
Corruption 184
Countries 185
Creativity 190
Curiosity 200
Dance 203
Dehumanization 218
Delusion 219
Devotion 233
Difficulty 236
Duty 253
Education 259
Environment 278
Equality 279
Eternity 281
Ethics 282
Evolution 285
Experience 291
Facts 295
Fantasy 304
Fate 307
Food 324
Forgetfulness 331
Freedom 336
The Future 353
Gambling 354
Goals 366
God 367
Heroes 397
Humanity 406, 407
Illusion 422
Imagination 423
Insanity 434
Intellectualism 436
Intuition 439
Killing 453
Kindness 453
Knowledge 460
Laws 466
Learning 474
Liberation 479
Life 491
Mankind 518
Mathematics 525
Maturity 526
Mediocrity 529
Mind 536
Miracles 540
Mistakes 543
Murder 562
Mystery 565
Nationalism 567
Nonconformity 575
Objectivity 579
Opportunity 586
Opposition 588
The Past 602
Patriotism 605
Perception 610
Philosophy 619
Physics 621

Einstein, Albert (cont.)
Plagiarism 622
Pleasure 625
Police 632
Politics 637
Prejudice 648
The Present 649
Principles 653
Punishment 663
Quiet 669
Radio 672
Reading 674
Reality 676
Reason 678
Relativity 685
Religion 688
Research 693
Reward 701
Right 705
Rights 706
Science 720
Simplicity 741
Society 752
Solitude 754
Space 757
Spirit 759
Stars 761
Status 765
Strength 771
Stupidity 775
Success 780
Taxes 796
Teachers 797
Theories 809
Thoughts 811
Tolerance 818
Tomorrow 819
Truth 831
Understanding 837
The Universe 841
Value 845
Vegetarianism 847
Vice 848
Villains 850
Violence 851
Virtue 854
War 860
Weakness 864
Weapons 866
The World 882
Wrong 891
Yesterday 892

Eisenhower, Dwight D. (1890–1969)
America 47
Books, ...98
Courage 186
Defiance 217
Determination 231
Economics 257
Farming 305
Humanity 407
Humor 410
Integrity 436
Leadership 471
Motivation 561
Objectives 579
Peace 607
Pessimism 617
Planning 623
Politics 637
Strength 771
Success 780
Television 803
Theft 808
Understanding 837
Vision 855
War 860
Weakness 864

Eisenstein, Sergei (1898–1948)
Cinema 147

Eldridge Paul (1888–1982)
Epitaphs 279

Eliot, Charles W. (1834–1926)
Books 98

Eliot, George (1819–1880)
Ancestry 52
Angels 53
Animals 55
Children 140
Cowardice 188
Cruelty 198
Decisions 213
Deeds 215
Defeat 216
Despair 226
Devotion 233
Dogs 246
Dreams 250
Duty 253
Ego 263
Experience 291
Feelings 314
Fiction 316
Fools 326
Forgiveness 332
Friendship 343
Funerals 352
Genius 361
Giving 363
Gossip 370
Happiness 384
Hope 403
Ignorance 419
Love 507
Money 548
Mothers 554
Music 563
Opposition 589
The Past 602
Pets 618
Privacy 654
Purpose 665
Skill 745
Tolerance 818
Vanity 846
Victory 849
Wives 875

Eliot, T. S. (1888–1965)
Acceptance 17
The Bible 89
Cats 117
Conformity 169
Editors 258
Emotions 267
Failure 296
Hell 394
Home 400
Humor 410
The Past 602
Personality 614
Poetry 629
Progress 656
Reality 676
Risk 707
Strength 771
Temptation 804
Writing 888
Youth 894

Elizabeth I, Queen (1533–1603)
Anger 54
Beggars 84
Time 815

Ellerbee, Linda (1944–)
Style 777

Elliot, Cass (1941–)
Strangers 768

Elliot, Jane (1947–)
Racism 671

Elliot, Jim (1927–1956)
Sons 755

Elliot, Walter (1842–1928)
Crowds 198
Perseverance 612

Elliott, Ebenezer (1781–1849)
Communism 159

Elliott, Jane (1933–)
Political Correctness 632

Ellis, Albert (1913–2007)
Acceptance 17
Depression 224

Ellis, Albert (cont.)
Destiny 229
Self-Esteem 729
Ellis, Bret Easton (1964–)
Crisis 194
Ellis, Henry Havelock (1859–1939)
Abstinence 15
Beauty 81
Civilization 151
Evolution 285
Hate 387
Love 507
Mankind 518
The Moon 550
Obscenity 580
Optimism 590
Ridicule 705
Suicide 784
Wilderness 867
Ellison, Harlan (1934–)
Stupidity 775
The Universe 841
Ellison, Ralph (1914–1994)
Ancestors 51
The Cold War 154
Relatives 685
Elliston, George Sampson (1875–1954)
Kindness 454
Elmer-DeWitt, Philip (1949–)
History 399
Emecheta, Buchi (1944–)
Liberation 479
Emerson, Keith (1944–)
Mothers 554
Emerson, Ralph Waldo (1803–1882)
Ability 9
Achievement 19
Actions 22
Admiration 26
Age 36
Agriculture 40
Ambition 45
Ancestry 52
Anger 54
Aristocracy 62
Art 64
Authority 72
Avarice 74
Beauty 81
Beggars 84
Blunders 95
Boldness 96
Books 98
Boredom 100
Bosses 102
Botany 102
Brains 104
Cause and Effect 120
Censorship 124
Chance 128
Chaos 130
Character 132
Children 140
Civilization 151
College 155
Comedy 156
Commerce 157
Common Sense 158
Confidence 166
Conformity 169
Conservatives 174
Consistency 175
Courage 186
Crime 192
Crowds 198
Curiosity 201
Danger 204
Debt 211
Destiny 229
Diet 235
Difficulty 236
Dignity 237
Earthquakes 254
Editors 258
Ego 263
Encouragement 268

Emerson, Ralph Waldo (cont.)
Enthusiasm 275
Evening 283
Evil 284
Experience 291
Eyes 293
Faces 295
Faith 299
Fame 300
Familiarity 302
Fate 307
Faults 310
Fiction 316
Finance 318
Flowers 322
Fortune 334
Friendship 343
Fruit 351
Funerals 352
Generosity 359
Genius 361
Gifts 362
Government 372
Grace 374
Gratitude 376
Greatness 377, 378
Happiness 384
Heart 390
Heroes 397
Honor 402
Humanity 407
Humor 410
Ideas 414
Identity 415
Ignorance 419
Imagination 423
Immortality 426
Independence 428
Individualism 430
Intelligence 437
Intuition 439
Jokes 441
Judges 448
Kindness 454
Laughter 464
Leadership 471
Learning 474
Libraries 485
Lies 487
Losing 502
Love 507
Luck 512
Manners 519
Mediocrity 529
Men 532
Mothers 554
Names 566
Nature 569
Nonsense 575
Obstacles 581
Opportunity 586
Originality 592
Patriotism 605
Peace 608
Peace of Mind 609
Perception 610
Persistence 613
Poetry 629
Politics 637
Progress 656
Prudence 661
Purpose 665
Quotations 670
Recovery 680
Reform 682
Rejection 684
Religion 688
Revelation 699
Reward 701
Rogues 709
Rumors 710
Saints 713
Scholars 718
Self-Confidence 728
Sincerity 743
Skepticism 744

Emerson, Ralph Waldo (cont.)
Skill 745
Snow 749
Society 752
Space 757
Speaking 757
Stars 761
Statesmen 763
Strength 771
Success 780
Suicide 785
Summer 787
The Sun 787
Talent 793
Talk 794
Taxes 796
Thoughts 811, 812
Time 815
Tobacco 817
Tomorrow 819
Trade 822
Transcendentalism 825
Trouble 828
Trust 829
Truth 831
Ugliness 835
The Universe 841
Value 845
Virtue 853
Vision 855
Wisdom 871
Wit 873
Wives 875
Worries 883
Worship 884
Writing 888
Yankees 892
Emin, Tracey (1963–)
Revenge 699
Engel, Eliot (1947–)
African-Americans 34
Anti-Semitism 56
Bigotry 90
Engelbart, Douglas (1925–)
Maturity 526
Engels, Friedrich (1820–1895)
Class 152
Monarchs 547
Oppression 589
Theories 809
Engstrom, Ted W. (1916–2006)
Reward 701
Eno, Brian (1948–)
Activity 23
Ephron, Nora (1941–)
Adolescence 27
Bachelors 77
Cooking 178
Mothers 554
Epicharmus (c. 540–450 BC)
Judgment 450
Passion 601
Epictetus (AD 55–135)
Anger 54
Darkness 205
Desire 225
Difficulty 236
Education 259
Food 324
Freedom 336
Greatness 377
Lies 487
Loneliness 500
Prison 653
Silence 739
Speaking 758
Epicurus (341–270 BC)
Death 208
Fate 307
Friendship 343
Glory 365
Grief 381
Hope 403
Justice 452
Monarchs 547
Philosophy 619

Epicurus (cont.)
- Pleasure 625
- Rejoice 684
- Slavery 746

Epstein, Joseph (1911–1944)
- Anti-Semitism 56

Erasmus, Desiderius (1469–1536)
- Ability 9
- Doctors 243
- Fools 326
- Genius 361
- Kingdoms 455
- Life 492
- Pleasure 625
- Riches 704
- Sharing 736
- Sin 742
- Theater 807

Erdogan, Recep Tayyip (1959–)
- Anti-Semitism 56

Erdrich, Louise (1954–)
- Belief 86

Erickson, Arthur (1924–)
- Bankers 78
- Entertainment 274
- Materialism 524
- The Renaissance 690

Erskine, John (1879–1951)
- Music 563

Ertz, Susan (1894–1985)
- Afternoon 35
- Immortality 426

Ervin, Sam (1896–1985)
- Witchcraft 874

Erving, Julius (1950–)
- Basketball 80

Esar, Evan (1899–1995)
- Books 98
- Cats 117
- Conscience 171
- Education 259
- Housework 405
- Money 548
- Statistics 764
- Success 780

Eschenbach, Marie Ebner von (1830–1916)
- Conflict 167

Escher, M. C. (1898–1972)
- Artists 67
- Chaos 130
- Light 496
- Work 880

Estienne, Henri (1470–1520)
- Youth 894

Eszterhas, Joe (1944–)
- Political Correctness 633

Euripides (c. 480–406 BC)
- Chance 128
- Conscience 171
- Courage 186
- Enemies 270
- Evil 284
- Excess 288
- Fate 307
- Fathers 309
- Food 324
- Forgiveness 332
- Fortune 334
- Friendship 343
- Generosity 359
- Gifts 362
- Giving 364
- God 367
- Grief 381
- Guilt 381
- Honesty 401
- Ignorance 419
- Joy 446
- Learning 475
- Loss 504
- Love 507
- Marriage 521
- Mothers 555
- Pain 593
- Parenthood 598
- Pleasure 625

Euripides (cont.)
Quiet 669
Riches 704
Stupidity 775
Success 780
Tolerance 818
Wisdom 871
Wives 875
Youth 894
Evans, Bergen (1904–1978)
Doubt 248
Lies 487
Thoughts 812
Evans, Greg (1947–)
Anger 54
Everage, Dame Edna (1934–)
Friendship 343
Everett, Douglas (1927–)
Dreams 250
Reality 676
Everett, Edward (1794–1865)
Liberty 480
Evert, Chris (1954–)
Cats 117
Excellence 287
Losing 502
Evslin, Dorothy (1923–)
Children 140
Ewing, Sam (1921–)
Character 132
Determination 231
Experts 292
Inflation 432
Work 880
Eysenck, Hans (1916–1997)
Tact 792

F

Faber, Frederick William (1814–1863)
Thoughts 812
Fabricius, Georg (1516–1571)
Achievement 19
Death 208
Fadiman, Clifton (1904–1999)
Travel 827
Vocation 856
Fahey, Albert (1913–)
Depression 224
Fairchild, Henry P. (1880–1956)
Individuals 430
Faithfull, Marianne (1946–)
Rebellion 680
Faldo, Nick (1957–)
Marriage 521
Falkland, Lord (1610–1643)
Decisions 214
Fallici, Oriana (1929–2006)
Anti-Semitism 56
Fallon, Jimmy (1974–)
Guns 381
Falwell, Jerry (1933–)
Adultery 28
Alcohol 42
The Bible 89
Soldiers 753
Fane, Violet (1843–1905)
Gardens 356
Fangio, Juan Manuel (1911–1995)
Billiards 90
Women 876
Farmer, Frances (1913–1970)
Friendship 343
Farmer, Paul (1909–)
Corporations 181
Farouk, King, of Egypt (1920–1965)
Kings 456
Farquhar, George (1678–1707)
Poverty 643
Scandals 717
Farquharson, Peter (1832–1869)
Relationships 684
Trust 829
Farrakhan, Louis (1933–)
Anarchy 50
Terrorism 806

Farrina, Dennis (1944–)
- Addiction ... 24

Fattah, Chaka (1956–)
- Terrorism ... 806

Faulkner, William (1897–1962)
- Artists ... 67
- Criticism ... 196
- Decency ... 212
- Dreams ... 250
- Encouragement ... 269
- Epitaphs ... 279
- Fear ... 312
- Gratitude ... 376
- Losing ... 502
- Mankind ... 518
- Memory ... 531
- Poetry ... 629
- Tobacco ... 817
- Tragedy ... 824
- War ... 860

Faunce, Corporal John (1897–1962)
- Ability ... 9

Faust, James E. (1920–2007)
- Mothers ... 555

Favors, Donna A. (1955–)
- Deception ... 213
- Friendship ... 344
- Sharing ... 736

Feather, William (1908–1976)
- Adventure ... 30
- Civilization ... 151
- Fathers ... 309
- Godfathers ... 376
- Middle Age ... 534
- The Poor ... 639
- Quotations ... 670
- Rich and Poor ... 702

Feather, William (1908–1976)
- Adventure ... 30
- Civilization ... 151
- Fathers ... 309
- Godfathers ... 376

Feherty, David (1958–)
- Failure ... 297
- Success ... 780

Feibleman, James (1904–1987)
- Mythology ... 565

Feifer, Jules (1929–)
- Adolescence ... 28
- Artists ... 67
- Fathers ... 309
- Martyrs ... 523
- Maturity ... 526

Feinstein, Dianne (1933–)
- Guns ... 381
- Losing ... 502
- Toughness ... 821

Feldman, Morton (1926–1987)
- Crisis ... 194

Feldstein, Martin (1939–)
- Inflation ... 432

Feller, Bob (1918–)
- Baseball ... 79
- Yesterday ... 892

Fellini, Federico (1920–1993)
- Art ... 64
- Censorship ... 124
- Cinema ... 147
- Realism ... 676
- Style ... 777

Feltham, Owen (1602–1668)
- Perspective ... 615
- Zeal ... 897

Fénelon, François de (1651–1715)
- Civil War ... 150
- Despair ... 226
- Imperfection ... 427
- Reading ... 674
- Remedies ... 690
- Spirituality ... 759

Fenn, Sherilyn (1965–)
- Sadness ... 712

Fenwick, Millicent (1910–1992)
- Emotions ... 267
- Pity ... 622

Ferguson, Marilyn (1938–)
- Age 36
- Body 95
- Culture 199
- Fear 312

Ferlinghetti, Lawrence (1919–)
- Automobiles 73
- Editors 258

Fermi, Enrico (1901–1954)
- Ignorance 419
- Knowledge 460

Ferraro, Geraldine (1935–)
- Economics 257

Feuerbach, Ludwig (1804–1872)
- Food 324

Feyerabend, Paul (1924–1994)
- Consciousness 173
- Knowledge 460

Feynman, Richard (1918–1988)
- Awe 75
- Discovery 240
- Economics 257
- Humanity 407
- Journalism 442
- Knowledge 460
- Numbers 577
- Philosophy 619
- Reality 676
- Responsibility 697
- Science 720
- Technology 801

Fichte, Immanuel Hermann (1797–1879)
- Happiness 384

Field, David Dudley (1805–1894)
- Judges 448

Field, Stephen J. (1816–1899)
- Judges 448

Fiedler, Arthur (1894–1979)
- Dessert 228

Fielding, Henry (1707–1754)
- Adversity 31
- Criticism 196
- Faces 295
- Fashion 306
- Flattery 320
- Mind 536
- Money, ...548
- Newspapers 573
- Prosperity 660
- Rogues 709
- Scandals 717
- Taste 795
- Vice 848

Fields, Suzanne (1950–)
- Bureaucracy 109

Fields, Totie (1930–1978)
- Food 324

Fields, W. C. (1880–1946)
- Alcohol 42
- Babies 76
- California 113
- Cheating 136
- Decency 212
- Drugs 252
- Earthquakes 255
- Horses 404
- Illness 421
- Laziness 469
- Lunch 512
- People 610
- Prejudice 648
- Rogues 709
- Suckers 782
- Wine 869

Fierstein, Harvey (1954–)
- Suicide 785

Fillmore, Charles (1854–1948)
- Kingdoms 455

Finkelstein, Louis (1895–1991)
- Judaism 447

Finkelstein, Norman (1953–)
- Skeptics 744

Finley, Guy (1949–)
- Crisis 194

Firestone, Harvey S. (1868–1938)
- Circumstances 149

Firmianus Lactantius (c. 240–320)
Adversity 31
Memory 531
Fischer, Martin H. (1879–1962)
Mothers 555
Fishel, Elizabeth (1950–)
Sisters 743
Fisher, Carrie (1956–)
Hollywood 400
Fisher, Dorothy Canfield (1879–1958)
Mothers 555
Parenthood 598
Fisher, Geoffrey (1887–1972)
Cities 150
Retirement 698
Fisk, Robert (1909–)
Journalists 444
Fiske, John (1842–1901)
Realism 676
Fitzgerald, F. Scott (1896–1940)
Ability 10
Conviction 177
Friendship 344
Intelligence 437
Mind 536
Pain 593
Pleasure 625
Thoughts 812
Tragedy 824
Fitzgerald, Zelda (1900–1948)
Boredom 100
Love 507
Regret 683
Fitzpatrick, Mike (1963–)
Telephones 802
Flanders, Michael (1922 –1975)
Satire 716
Flaubert, Gustave (1821–1880)
Artists 67
Democracy 221
Happiness 384
Selfishness 730
Style 777
Stupidity 775
Fleishman, Jerome (1922–)
Encouragement 269
Fleiss, Heidi (1965–)
Prostitution 660
Fleming, Ian L. (1908–1964)
Life 492
Fletcher, John (1579–1625)
Deeds 215
Fate 307
Words 878
Flewelling, Ralph T. (1871–1960)
Values 845
Flint, Jerry (1931–)
Competition 162
Flores, Fernando (1943–)
Style 777
Florio, John (1553–1625)
The Sea 723
Floyd, Keith (1943–)
Cooking 178
Flynn, Errol (1909–1959)
Habits 382
Money 548
Flynn, John T. (1882–1964)
Fascism 305
Flynt, Henry (1909–)
Nihilism 573
Fo, Dario (1926–)
Ideology 416
Foch, Marshal Ferdinand (1851–1929)
Airplanes 40
Fear 312
Foley, Elisabeth (1965–)
Friendship 344
Follett, Mary Parker (1942–)
Apathy 57
Conflict 167
Fonda, Jane (1937–)
Birth Control 92
Parenthood 598
Revolution 700

Fontenelle (1657–1757)
Expectations 290
Happiness 384
Fonteyn, Margot (1919–1991)
Logic 499
Foran, Thomas (1924–2000)
Intellectualism 436
Forbes, B. C. (1880–1954)
Children 140
Dessert 228
Opportunity 586
Forbes, Malcolm S. (1919–1990)
Ability 10
Education, ...259
Ego 264
Executives 289
Libraries 485
Retirement 698
Sympathy 791
Time 815
Value 845
Forbes, Randy (1952–)
Crisis 194
Ford, Harold (1970–)
Bureaucracy 109
Democrats 223
Ford, Harrison (1942–)
Change 129
Ford, Henry (1863–1947)
Ability 10
Achievement 19
Airplanes 40
Attitude 71
Competition 162
Determination 231
Experience 291
Faults 310
Fools 326
Friendship 344
History 399
Idealism 413
Independence 428
Individualism 430
Progress 656
Republicans 692
Reputation 693
Success 780
Teamwork 800
Tradition 823
Wages 858
The World 882
Ford, Henry, II (1917–1987)
America 47
Foreman, George (1949–)
Boxing 103
Forlani, Claire (1972–)
Depression 224
Suicide 785
Fornes, Maria Irene (1930–)
Resistance 694
Forster, E. M. (1879–1970)
Art 64
Body 95
Courage 186
Curiosity 201
Friendship 344
Sentimentality 731
Fortas, Abe (1910–1982)
Judges 449
Fort, Charles (1874–1932)
Adjustment 25
Fortune, Timothy Thomas (1856–1928)
Mobs 545
Forude, James A. (1818–1894)
Eternity 281
History 399
Morality 551
Fosdick, Harry Emerson (1878–1969)
Pity 622
War 860
The World 882
Foss, Lukas (1922–)
Charisma 133
Foster, Alan Dean (1946–)
Chaos 130
Freedom 336

Foster, Donald (1950–)
Mistakes 543
Rejoice 684
Foster, Jodie (1962–)
Love 507
Parenthood 598
Foucault, Michel (1926–1984)
Repression 691
Fowler, Henry W. (1858–1933)
Quotations 670
Writing 888
Fowler, Jim (1932–)
Economics 257
Fowles, John (1926–2005)
Men 532
The Renaissance 690
Women 876
Fox, Charles (1749–1806)
Deeds 215
Pleasure 625
Fox, Emmet (1886–1951)
Consciousness 173
Destiny 229
Disease 241
Love 507
The Present 649
Remedies 689
Fox, Matthew (1966–)
Wilderness 867
Fox, Michael J. (1961–)
Dignity 237
Excellence 287
Perfection 611
Foxworthy, Jeff (1958–)
Family 302
Ignorance 419
Foxx, Redd (1922–1991)
Health 388
Foxx, Virginia (1943–)
Obesity 578
Republicans 692
Terrorism 806
Frame, Janet (1924–2004)
Fiction 316
Irrelevance 440
France, Anatole (1844–1924)
Achievement 20
Curiosity 201
Dreams 250
Education 259
Enthusiasm 276
Fashion 306
Growth 380
Happiness 384
Human Nature 405
Ignorance 419
Immortality 426
Impotence 427
Innocence 433
Laws 466
The Poor 639
Relaxation 686
Repentance 691
Rich and Poor 702
Silence 739
Teachers 798
Understanding 837
Virtue 853
Work 880
Francis, Arlene (1907–2001)
Friendship 344
Trouble 828
Francis de Sales, Saint (1567–1622)
Imperfection 427
Patience 604
Francis of Assisi, Saint (1181–1226)
Despair 226
Joy 446
Sadness 712
The Sun 787
Franck, Sebastian (1499–1543)
Scripture 722
Frank, Anne (1929–1945)
Beauty 81
Happiness 384

Frank, Anne (cont.)
Idealism 413
Nature 569
The News 572
Parenthood 598
Frank, Leonard Roy (1932–)
Teachers 798
Frankel, Marvin E. (1921–2002)
Advertising 32
Franken, Al (1951–)
Media 528
Mistakes 543
Frankfurter, Felix (1882–1965)
Laws 466
Lawyers 468
Reason 678
Sickness 737
Frankl, Viktor (1905–1997)
Love 507
Salvation 714
Franklin, Aretha (1942–)
Parenthood 598
Franklin, Benjamin (1706–1790)
Abstinence 15
Admiration 26
Age 36
Anger 54
Beggars 84
Boldness 96
Business 112
Childhood 137
Christianity 144
Circumstances 149
Conversation 176
Debt 211
Delay 219
Despair 226
Discipline 239
Dishonesty 241
Doctors 243
Education 259
Effort 262
Ego 263
Energy 271
Error 280
Excuses 288
Experience 291
Fashion 306
Faults 310
Fish 318
Fools 326
Fortune 334
Friendship 344
Genius 361
Government 372
Greatness 378
Habits 382
Holidays 400
Hope 403
Horses 404
Ignorance 419, 420
Industry 430, 431
Kitchens 458
Lawyers 468
Laziness 469
Learning 475
Leisure 476
Liberty 480, 481
Lies 487
Life 492
Manners 519, 520
Marriage 521
Meals 527
Meditation 530
Memory 531
Misery 541
Money 548
Nation 567
Necessity 570
Obedience 578
Opportunity 586
Persistence 613
Persuasion 615
Philosophy 619
Pleasure 625
Political Correctness 633

Franklin, Benjamin (cont.)
Popularity 640
Progress 656
Quantity 666
Quarrels 667
Reading 674
Rebellion 680
Riches 704
Rivers 708
Safety, ...713
Secrets 724
Self-Control 729
Shame 735
Slander 745
Sleep 748
Speaking 758
Studying 774
Success 780
Tact 792
Talent 793
Taxes 796
Time 815
Trade 822
Tragedy 824
Trouble 829
Unity 840
Value 845
Vice 848
Virtue 853
Wealth 865
Wine 869
Wives 875
Worries 883
Fraser, Malcolm (1930–)
Acceptance 17
Reconciliation 680
Fraser, Peter (1884–1950)
Schools 719
Frazier, Joe (1944–)
Boxing 103
Frederick the Great (1712–1786)
Diplomacy 237
Pleasure 625
Superstition 789
Freeman, Morgan (1937–)
Alcohol 42
Freire, Paulo (1921–1997)
Neutrality 571
French, John (1949–)
Words 878
French, Marilyn (1929–)
Children 140
Freud, Anna (1895–1982)
Confidence 166
Freud, Sigmund (1856–1939)
Adults 29
America 47
Anxiety 57
Censorship 124
Childhood 137
Civilization 151
Destiny 229
Doctors 243
Flowers 322
Knowledge 460
The Middle Ages 534
Neurosis 571
Opposition 589
Religion 688
Research 694
Satisfaction, ...717
Secrets 724
Sharing 736
Travel 827
Women 876
Frick, Ford (1894–1978)
Sarcasm 715
Friday, Nancy (1933–)
Clothes 153
Mothers 555
Friedan, Betty (1921– 2006)
Age 36
Children 140
Dissatisfaction 241
Divorce 243
Feminism 315

Friedan, Betty (cont.)
- Glory 365
- Mothers 555
- Sex 733

Friedkin, William (1939–)
- Style 777

Friedman, Edwin H. (1948–)
- Leadership 471
- Power 644

Friedman, Kinky (1944–)
- Beauty 81

Friedman, Milton (1912–2006)
- Bureaucracy 109
- The Great Depression 379
- Hell 394
- Lunch 512
- Statesmen 763

Frisch, Max (1911–1991)
- Technology 801
- Time 815
- The Universe 841

Frist, Bill (1952–)
- America 48
- Segregation 726
- Slavery 747

Fromm, Erich (1900–1980)
- Charity 134
- Creativity 190
- Education 260
- Greed 380
- Human Nature 405
- Identity 416
- Integrity 436
- Mothers 555
- Nationalism 567, 568
- Science 720
- Statesmen 763

Frost, David (1939–)
- Bosses 102
- Complaints 163
- Cooking 178
- Freedom 336
- Television 803

Frost, Robert (1874–1963)
- Conservatives 174
- Determination 231
- Eccentricity 255
- Education 260
- Executives 289
- Fighting 318
- Fools 326
- Forgiveness 332
- Friendship 344
- Grammar 375
- Happiness 384
- Hell 394
- Home 400
- Ideas 414
- Jokes 441
- Juries 451
- Liberals 477
- Life 492
- Love 507
- Mothers 555
- Nonsense 576
- Poetry 629
- Roads 708
- Secrets 724
- Snow 749
- Style 777
- Thoughts 812
- Translation 826
- The World 882
- Worries 883

Froude, James A. (1818–1894)
- Ability 10
- Animals 55
- Character 132
- Experience 291
- Mistakes 543
- The Poor 639
- Society 752

Fry, Christopher (1907–2005)
- Comedy 156
- Eternity 281
- Tragedy 824

Fujimori, Alberto (1938–)
Liberation 479
Fulbright, J. William (1905–1995)
Dissent 242
Statesmen 763
Thoughts 812
Fulford, Robert (1932–)
The Future 353
Fulghum, Robert (1937–)
Children 140
Laughter 464
Fuller, Margaret (1810–1850)
Knowledge 460
Fuller, R. Buckminster (1895–1983)
Architects 59
Beauty 81
Failure 297
Humanity 407
Technology 801
The Universe 841
War 860
Fuller, Thomas (1608–1661)
Alcohol 42
Bachelors 77
Cats 117
Conversation 176
Courage 186
Courtesy 188
Cowardice 188
Cruelty 198
Debt 211
Despair 226
Determination 231
Education 260
Facts 295
Faults 310
Friendship 344
Fruit 351
Generosity 359
Gifts 363
Giving 364
Health 388
Laziness 469
Love 507
Madness 514
Mind 536
Money 548
The News 572
Plants 623
Power 644
Presents 650
Purpose 665
Revenge 699
Rich and Poor 702
Riches 704
Sadness 712
Skill 745
Slander 745
Society 752
Trees 828
Trust, ...829
Waste 863
Wives 875
Yesterday 892
Zeal 897
Fund, John (1957–)
Rhetoric 701
Fussell, Paul (1924–)
Anxiety 57
Optimism 590
Status 765

G

Gaberino, Geoffrey (1962–)
Ability 10
Gabirol, Solomon ibn (c. 1021–1058)
Wisdom 871
Gable, Clark (1901–1960)
Fishing 319
Gabor, Zsa Zsa (1919–)
Divorce 243
Husbands 412
Marriage 521
Sex 733

Gadamer, Hans-Georg (1900–2002)
Subjectivity 778
Gaiman, Neil (1960–)
Clothes 153
Heaven 393
Hell 394
Gainsbourg, Serge (1928–1991)
Beauty 81
Ugliness 835
Gaius Petronius (c. AD 66)
Laws 466
Galbraith, John Kenneth (1908–2006)
Astrology 70
Banks 78
Capitalism 115
Communism 159
Divorce 243
Economics 257
Ego 264
Error 280
Government 372
Humor 410
Immortality 426
Leadership 471
Memory 531
Modesty 547
Nonsense 576
Organization 592
Policy 632
Politics 637
Wealth 865
Galilei, Galileo (1564–1642)
The Bible 89
Common Sense 158
Discovery 240
Heresy 396
Ignorance 420
Intelligence 437
Principles 653
Reason 679
Senses 730
Stars 761
The Sun 787
Truth 831
Gallagher (1947–)
Television 803
Gallagher, Maggie (1960–)
Mothers 555
Gallegly, Elton (1944–)
Amnesty 49
Gallico, Paul (1897–1976)
Cause and Effect 120
Galloway, George (1954–)
Torture 820
Gallup, George (1901–1984)
God 367
Statistics 764
Galsworthy, John (1867–1933)
Beginnings 85
Endings 269
Galton, Francis (1822–1911)
Cats 117
Gandhi, Indira (1917–1984)
Activity 23
Competition 162
Conflict 167
Statesmen 763
Work, ...881
Gandhi, Mahatma (1869–1948)
Astrology 70
Beginnings 85
Belief 86
Change 129
Conflict 168
Conviction 177
Corruption 185
Cowardice 188
Culture 199
Defeat 216
Despair 226
Forgiveness 332
Freedom 336
The Future 353
Happiness 384
Humanity 407
Humor 410

Gandhi, Mahatma (cont.)
Hunger 411
Imitation 425
Impotence 427
Journalists 444
Laziness 469
Learning 475
Liberty 481
Love 507
Majorities 515
Materialism 524
Mistakes 543
Nonviolence 576
Peace 608
Peace of Mind 609
Personality 614
Politicians 635
The Present 649
Quality 666
Quantity 666
Rationalism 673
Reform 682
Resistance 694
Revenge 699
Sacrifice 711
Self-Respect 729
Silence 739
Slavery 747
Starvation 762
Strength 771
Suicide 785
Teachers 798
Thoughts 812
Tomorrow 819
Torture 820
Totalitarianism 820
Truth 831
Unity 840
Victory 849
Violence 851
Vision 855
Wisdom 871
Worship 884

Garbo, Greta (1905–1990)
Toughness 821
Garcia, Jerry (1942–1995)
Chaos 130
Culture 199
Gardiner, Stephen (1497–1555)
Kingdoms 455
Shelter 736
Gardner, Ed (1901–1963)
Music 563
Gardner, John (1933–1982)
Leadership 471
Gardner, John W. (1912–2002)
Creativity 190
Excellence 287
History 399
Garfield, James A. (1831–1881)
Commerce 157
Crisis 194
Difficulty 236
Education 260
Freedom 336
Justice 452
Luck 512
Power 644
Suicide 785
Warriors 862
Garland, Judy (1922–1969)
Privacy 654
Garofalo, Janeane (1964–)
Kisses 457
Garrett, Leif (1961–)
Songs 754
Garretty, Marion C.
Mothers 555
Garrison, Theodosia (1874–1944)
Ghosts 362
Garrison, William Lloyd (1805–1879)
Apathy 57
Arguments 61
Noise 574
Retreat 698

Garth, Jennie (1972–)
Ability 10
Garvey, Marcus (1887–1940)
Confidence 166
Gaskell, Elizabeth (1810–1865)
Mothers 555
Gates, Bill (1955–)
Computers 164
Promises 657
Research 694
Society 752
Studying 774
Teachers 798
Gauguin, Paul (1848–1903)
Eyes 293
Plagiarism 622
Revenge 699
Gaulle, Charles de (1890–1970)
Achievement 19
The Moon 550
Nationalism 568
Patriotism 605
Politicians 635
Politics 637
Silence 739
Gaultier, Jules de (1858–1942)
Imagination 423
Gauss, Carl Fredrich (1777– 1855)
Mathematics 525
Gautier, Théophile (1811–1872)
Admiration 26
Cats 117
Eyes 293
Reality 677
Gawain, Shakti (1948–)
Body 95
Confidence 166
Intuition 439
Loss 504
Risk 707
Trust 830
The Universe 841
Gay, John (1685–1732)
Mercy 533
Retreat 698
Rogues 709
Gaynor, Gloria (1949–)
Self-Esteem 729
Geary, James (1914–1989)
Information 432
Geertz, Clifford (1926–2006)
Schools 719
Gehry, Frank (1929–)
Architecture 60
Seuss Geisel, Theodore (1904–1991)
Adults 29
Eyes 293
Fantasy 304
Individualism 430
Nonsense 576
Questions 668
Value 845
Gelbart, Larry (1928–)
Humor 410
Laughter 464
Geldof, Bob (1954–)
Teenagers 801
Gellert, Christian Fürchtegott (1715–1769)
Life 492
Geneen, Harold S. (1910–1997)
Business 112
Leadership 471
Managers 517
Mythology 565
Performance 611, 612
Reliability 687
Uncertainty 835
Genet, Jean (1910–1986)
Cunning 200
Liberation 479
Suicide 785
Gentry, Bobbie (1944–)
Lies 487
George III, King (1738–1820)
Traitors 825

George, David Lloyd (1863–1945)
Eloquence 266
Liberty 481
Politicians 635
Sacrifice 711
Statesmen 763
George, Henry (1839–1897)
Desire 225
Mankind 518
Wages 858
George, Susan (1950–)
Corporations 181
Status 765
George, W. L. (1882–1926)
War 860
Gephardt, Dick (1941–)
Campaigns 113
Democrats 223
Géraldy, Paul (1885–1983)
Youth 894
Gest, David (1953–)
Alcohol 42
Getty, J. Paul (1892–1976)
Earth 254
Money 548
Rhetoric 701
Uncertainty 835
Geyer, Georgie Anne (1935–)
Journalists 444
Giamatti, A. Bartlett (1938–1989)
Decency 212
Power 644
Gibbon, Edward (1737–1794)
Ability 10
Crime 192
History 399
Misfortune 542
Style 777
Victory 849
Writing 888
Gibbons, Jim (1944–)
Abortion 13
Gibbons, John (1962–)
Managers 517
Gibran, Kahlil (1883–1931)
Art 64
Beauty 81
Beginnings 85
Blame, ...93
Childhood 137
Death 208
Desire 225
Despair 226
Doubt 248
Dreams 250
Earth 254
Excess 288
Experience 291
Faith 299
Feet 314
Freedom 337
Friendship 344
Generosity 359
Giving 364
Hair 383
Humanity 407
Ideology 416
Indifference 428
Joy 446
Kindness 454
Laughter 464
Liberty 481
Life 492
Mothers 555
Oppression 589
Optimism 590
Pessimism 617
Poetry 629
Pride 651
Rebellion 680
Resolution 695
Rights 706
Sadness 712
Secrets 724
Silence 739

Gibran, Kahil (cont.)
Slavery 747
Sons 755
Sorrow 756
Soul 756
Strength 771
Teachers 798
Tears 800
Togetherness 817
Tolerance 818
Tomorrow 819
Truth 831
Understanding 837
Vision 855
Yesterday 893
Zeal 897
Gibson, William (1948–)
The Future 353
The Internet 438
Giddings, Paula (1947–)
Mothers 555
Gide, André (1869–1951)
Adventure 30
Art 64
Confidence 166
Difficulty 236
Discovery 240
Freedom 337
Hate 387
Hell 394
Humanity 407
Love 507
Mankind 518
Maxims 527
Objectives 579
Sin 742
Truth 831
Gifford, Kathie Lee (1953–)
Showbiz 736
Gilbert, Walter (1912–)
Biology 91
Gildre, George (1939–)
Liberation 479
Gill, Brendan (1914–1997)
Life 492
Gillespie, George (1613–1648)
Reform 682
Gillilan, Strickland (1869–1954)
Mothers 555
Gil Robles y Quiñones, José María (1898–1980)
Democracy 222
Elections 266
Innocence 433
Gilman, Charlotte P. (1860–1935)
Eternity 281
Ginsberg, Allen (1926–1997)
Dissatisfaction 242
Love 507
Solitude 754
Ginsberg, Ruth Bader (1933–)
Abortion 14
Ginott, Haim (1922–1973)
Parenthood 598
Teachers 798
Giraudoux, Jean (1882–1944)
Flowers 322
Lawyers 468
Sincerity 743
Success 780
Gissing, George (1857–1903)
Emotions 267
Mind 536
Gitlin, Todd (1943–)
Corporations 181
Values 845
Gladstone, William (1809–1898)
Delay 219
Evil 284
Justice 452
Liberals 477
Politcal Correctness 633
Gladwell, Malcolm (1963–)
Decisions 214
Emotions 267
Instinct 435

Gladwell, Malcolm (cont.)
Learning 475
Glasgow, Ellen (1873–1945)
Age 37
Gleason, Jackie (1916–1987)
Actors 23
Modesty 547
Glenconner, Pamela (1871–1928)
Parenthood 598
Glover, Crispin (1964–)
Cinema 147
Realism 676
Glover, Danny (1947–)
Literacy 498
Glyn, Elinor (1864–1943)
Divorce 243
Husbands 412
Godard, Jean-Luc (1930–)
Cinema 147
Style 777
Goddard, Robert H. (1882–1945)
Dreams 250
Hope 403
Reality 677
Godden, Rumer (1907–1998)
Cats 117
Godin, Seth (1960–)
Business 112
Godwin, Gail (1937–)
Teachers 798
Godwin, William (1756–1836)
Education 260
Meditation 530
Goering, Hermann (1893–1946)
Guns 381
Pacifism 593
Goethals, George (1858–1928)
Leadership 472
Goethe, Johann Wolfgang von (1749–1832)
Ability 10
Absurdity 17
Architecture 60
Artists 67
Boldness 96
Cause and Effect 120
Character 132
Courtesy 188
Cowardice 188
Criticism 196
Cunning 200
Deception 213
Determination 231
Dreams 250
Duty 253
Encouragement 269
Enemies 270
Enjoyment 273
Faults 310
Feelings 314
Flattery 320
Fools 326
Forgiveness 332
Fortune 334
Generosity 359
Goals 366
Government 372
Ideas 414
Ignorance 420
Imagination 423
Laughter 464
Laws 467
Liberals 477, 478
Life 492
Manners 520
Materialism 524
Maxims 527
Men 532
Motivation 561
Opportunity 586
The Past 602
Persuasion 615, 616
Poetry 629
Promises 657
Purpose 665
Secrets 724

Goethe, Johann Wolfgang von (cont.)
Stupidity 775
Superstition 789
Sympathy 791
Talent 793
Taste 795
Thoughts 812
Trust 830
Understanding 837
Wit 873
Women 876
Words 878
The World 882
Writing 888
Youth 894
Gogol, Nikolai (1809–1852)
Blame 93
Goldberg, Isaac (1887–1938)
Diplomacy 237
Goldberg, Whoopi (1955–)
Mothers, ...555
Politicians 635
Golden, Arthur (1956–)
Adversity 31
Doubt 248
Rivers 708
Victory 849
Golden, Harry (1902–1981)
Luck 512
Goldman, Emma (1869–1940)
Crime 192
Energy 271
Hope 404
Marriage 521
Rogues 709
Safety 713
Violence 851
Voting 857
Goldman, William (1931–)
Death 208
Life 492
Love 507
Goldoni, Carlo (1707–1793)
Sons 755
Goldsmith, James (1933–1997)
Industry 431
Pleasure 625
Goldsmith, James (cont.)
Praise 645
Goldsmith, Joel S. (1892–1964)
Consciousness 173
God 367
Goldsmith, Oliver (1730–1774)
Ability 10
Commerce 157
Conscience 171
Cowardice 188
Defiance 217
Evil 284
Hope 404
Ridicule 705
Scholars 718
Goldthwaite, Bobcat (1962–)
America 48
Countries 185
Goldwater, Barry (1909–1998)
Brains 104
Individuals 430
Moderation 546
Rights 706
Goldwyn, Samuel (1882–1974)
Ability 10
Books 98
Death 208
Health 388
Ideas 414
Television 803
Goncourt, Edmond de (1822–1896)
Art 64
Love 507
Painting 595
Sickness 737
Gondi, Jean-François-Paul de (1614–1679)
Trust 830

Good, John Mason (1764–1827)
Activity 23
Goode, Virgil (1946–)
Amnesty 50
Goodman, Benny (1909–1986)
Losing 502
Goodman, Ellen (1941–)
Clothes 153
Independence 428
Life 492
Normalcy 576
Parenthood 598
Skepticism 744
Values 845
Work 881
Goodman, Paul (1911–1972)
Activity 23
Enjoyment 273
Goodman, Roy M. (1930–)
Happiness 384
Goodman, Walter (1838–1912)
War 860
Gorbachev, Mikhail (1931–)
Capitalism 115
Stars 761
Water 863
Gordimer, Nadine (1923–)
Censorship 124
Rationalism 673
Gordon, Arthur (1909–1974)
Apathy 57
Gordon, Ruth (1896–1985)
Divorce 243
Gores, Joe (1931–)
Dogs 246
Old Age 583
Pets 618
Gorky, Maxim (1868–1936)
Mothers 555
Gorter, Herman (1864–1927)
Crisis 194
Gosling, Ryan (1980–)
Death 208
Suicide 785
Gotti, John (1940–2002)
Bankers 78
Gough, John Ballantine (1817–1886)
Character 132
Eternity 282
Reputation 693
Gould, Elliott (1938–)
Arrogance 62
Gould, Stephen Jay (1941–2002)
Arrogance 62
Consciousness 173
Conviction 177
Evolution 286
Humanity 407
Nonsense 576
Science 720
Stories 767
Gourmont, Remy de (1858–1915)
Burdens 107
Gracian, Baltasar (1601–1658)
Ability 10
Confidence 166
Enemies 270
Giving 364
Luck 512
Power 644
Skill 745
Sleep 748
Talent 793
Time 815
Wrong 891
Grafton, Sue (1940–)
Pleasure 625
Graham, Billy (1918–)
The Bible 89
Christianity 145
Losing 502
Rape 673
Self 727
Strength 771
Tears 800

Graham, Bob (1936–)
The Cold War 154
Graham, Lindsey (1955–)
Elections 266
Graham, Martha (1894–1991)
Body 95
Dance 203
Perfection 611
Graham, Paul (1964–)
Business 112
Clothes 153
Expectations 290
Graham, Ruth Bell (1920–2007)
Mothers 555
Graham, Shelia (1908–1988)
Food 324
Graham, Stephen (1884–1975)
Forests 330
Graham, Virginia (1912–1998)
Tennis 805
Gramm, Phil (1942–)
Prostitution 660
Gramsci, Antonio (1891–1937)
Optimism 590
Pessimism 617
Grant, Ulysses S. (1822–1885)
War 860
Granville, George (1815–1891)
Charity 134
Graves, Robert (1895–1985)
English 272
Poetry 629
Prose 659
Status 765
Gravina, Gian Vincenzo (1664–1718)
Boredom 101
Gray, Farrah (1984–)
Rejection 684
Gray, Frances (1884–1962)
Today 817
Gray, John (1951–)
Children 140
Gray, Spalding (1941–2004)
Suicide 785
Gray, Thomas (1716–1771)
Commerce 157
Fate 308
Smiles 748
Greeley, Andrew (1928–)
Birth Control 93
Catholicism 115
Greeley, Horace (1811–1872)
Apathy 57
Bigotry 90
Democrats 223
Green, Celia (1935–)
Ideology 416-417
Green, Hannah (1932–)
Health 388
Greenblatt, Stephen (1943–)
Shakespeare 735
Greene, Graham (1904–1991)
Heresy 396
Journalists 444
Schools 719
Sentimentality 731
Unhappiness 838
Greene, Peter (1965–)
Suicide 785
Greenleaf, Robert (1904–1990)
Leadership 472
Greenwood, Colin (1969–)
Underground 836
Gregoire, Christine (1947–)
Responsibility 697
Unity 840
Gregory, Dick (1932–)
Alcohol 42
Loss 504
Grellet, Étienne de (1773–1855)
Kindness 454
Grenfell, Sir Wilfred (1865–1940)
Joy 446
Gretzky, Wayne (1961–)
Procrastination 655

Gretzky, Wayne (cont.)
Sports 760
Greville, Fulke (1554–1628)
Imitation 425
Grey, Alex (1959–)
Liberation 479
Grey, Edward (1862–1933)
Alliances 44
Grey, Zane (1872–1939)
Death 208
Suicide 785
Griffith, Melanie (1957–)
Addiction 24
Alcohol 42
Griffith, Thomas (1915–)
Editors 258
Griffiths, Bede (1906–1993)
Tradition 823
Grillparzer, Franz (1791–1872)
Ideas 414
Thoughts 812
Griswold, Alfred Whitney (1906–1963)
Censorship 124
Grizzard, Lewis (1946–1994)
Newspapers 573
Groening, Matt (1954–)
Alcohol 42
Beer 84
Bosses 102
Jesus 441
Pity 622
Grof, Stanislav (1931–)
Buddhism 107
Crisis 194
Death 208
Groom, Winston (1944–)
Chocolate 143
Groot, Huigh de (1583–1645)
Ignorance 420
Gropius, Walter (1883–1969)
Engineering 272
Grosseteste, Robert (1175–1253)
Strangers 768
Guerard, Albert (1914–2000)
Doubt 248
Guest, Edgar (1881–1955)
Roses 709
Guevara, Che (1928–1967)
Silence 739
Guicciardini, Francesco (1483–1540)
Friendship 344
Guillaume, Robert (1927–)
Racism 671
Guiney, Louise (1861–1920)
Quotations 670
Guinon, Albert (1863–1923)
Listening 497
Guitry, Sacha (1885–1957)
Husbands 412
Wit 873
Wives 875
Women 876
Guizot, Francois Pierre Guillaume (1787–1874)
Enthusiasm 276
Guizot, Madam (1773–1827)
Modesty 547
Gunther, John (1901–1970)
Facts 295
Superstition 789
Gunther, Max (1934–1974)
Losing 502
Gurdjieff, G. I. (1872–1949)
Knowledge 460
Self 727
Sin 742
Gurnall, William (1617–1679)
Kisses 457
Scripture 722
Guterson, David (1956–)
Accidents 18
Guthrie, Arlo (1947–)
Greed 380
Light 497
Pacifism 593

Guy, Jasmine (1964–)
Bigotry 90
Sexuality 734
Gwenn, Edmund (1877–1959)
Comedy 156
Gyatso, Tenzin (1935–)
Peace 608

H

Ha'am, Ahad (1856–1927)
Ability 10
Haas, Ernst (1921–1986)
Photography 621
Habermas, Jurgen (1929–)
Terrorism 806
Hacker, Marilyn (1942–)
Poetry 629
Translation 826
Hackford, Taylor (1944–)
Charisma 133
Hackworth, David (1930–2005)
Terrorism 806
Hadfield, J. A. (1883–1967)
Relaxation 686
Haeckel, Ernst (1834–1919)
Biology 91
Hagel, Chuck (1946–)
Alliances 44
Haggard, H. Rider (1856–1925)
Thoughts 812
Hahn, Thich Nhat (1926–)
Flowers 322
Health 388
Joy 446
Peace of Mind 609
Possibilities 642
Smiles 748
Suffering 783
Haig, Douglas (1861–1928)
Crisis 194
Hailey, Elizabeth Forsythe (1938–)
Time 816
Writing 888
Hakuta, Ken (1950–)
Ideas 414
Money 548
Haldane, J. B. S. (1892–1964)
Environment 278
Ideas 414
Responsibility 697
Hale, Edward Everett (1822–1909)
Determination 231
Friendship 344
Survival 790
Hale, Nathan (1755–1776)
Patriotism 605
Regret 683
Hale, Sarah J. (1788–1879)
Mothers 555
Riches 704
Haley, Alex (1921–2002)
Family 302
Racism 671
Half, Robert (1918–)
Ability 10
Haliburton, Thomas C. (1796–1865)
Authority 72
Obedience 578
Punctuality 663
Reform 682
Halifax, Edward Frederick (1881–1959)
Ego 264
Political Parties 634
Hall, Edward T. (1914–)
Self 727
Hall, Barbara (1946–)
Freedom 337
Justice 452
Life 492
Suffering 783
Hall, Conrad (1926–2003)
Shadows 734
Hall, G. Stanley (1844–1924)
Adolescence 28

Hall, Robert (1764–1831)
Friendship 344
Hall, Tom T. (1936–)
Beer 84
Halsey, William Frederick, Jr. (1882–1959)
Challenges 127
Hamann, Johann G. (1730–1788)
Dessert 228
Knowledge 460
Self 727
Hamilton, Alexander (1755–1804)
Anarchy 50
Debt 211
Government 372
Juries 451
Justice 452
Liberty 481
Opinions 584
Questions 668
Hamilton, Edith (1867–1963)
Chaos 130
Education 260
Thoughts 812
Hamilton, Gail (1833–1896)
Ability 10
Hamilton, Laurell K. (1963–)
Editors 258
Hamm, Mia (1972–)
Champions 127
Sports 760
Hammarskjöld, Dag (1905–1961)
Decency 212
Dignity 237
Friendship 344
Loneliness 500
Rights 706
Hammerstein, Oscar, II (1895–1960)
Teachers 798
Trouble 829
Hammett, Dashiell (1894–1961)
Theater 808
Hammon, Jupiter (1711–1806)
Servants 732
Hampton, Christopher (1946–)
Criticism 196
Hampton, Fred (1948–1969)
Revolution 700
Hancock, Herbie (1940–)
Buddhism 107
Creativity 190
Hand, Learned (1872–1961)
Heresy 396
Handke, Peter (1942–)
Stories 767
Handy, Jack (1949–)
Boxing 103
Haney, Lee (1959–)
Obesity 578
Hanks, Tom (1956–)
Food 324
Health 389
Hannah, Daryl (1960–)
Corporations 181
Hansen, Mark Victor (1948–)
The Future 353
Hanson, Pauline (1954–)
Political Correctness 633
Reconciliation 680
Harden, Marcia Gay (1959–)
Beauty 81
Ugliness 835
Harding, Warren G. (1865–1923)
Healing 388
Hardy, G. H. (1877–1947)
Intelligence, ...437
Majorities 515
Hardy, Thomas (1840–1928)
Cruelty 198
Faces 295
Science 720
Silence 739
The Universe 841
Hare, August (1792–1834)
Knowledge 460
Mankind 518
Thoughts 812

Hare, David (1947–)
Smiles 748
Hari, Mata (1876–1917)
Dance 203
Harrelson, Woody (1961–)
Terrorism 806
Harrington, John (1561–1612)
Treason 827
Harris, Corra (1869–1935)
Courage 186
Harris, Paul (1868–1947)
Segregation 726
Harris, Sydney J. (1917–1986)
Adults 29
Arrogance 63
Childhood 137
Children 140
Curiosity 201
Cynicism 202
Democracy 221
Education 260
Indifference 428
Nationalism 568
Parenthood 598
Patriotism 606
Regret 683
Strangers 768
Youth 894
Harris, Townsend (1804–1878)
Commerce 157
Harrison, Jim (1937–)
Vacations 844
Harrison, William Henry (1773–1841)
The Poor 639
Rich and Poor 702
Hart, B. H. Liddell (1895–1970)
Knowledge 460
Hart, B. H. Liddell (cont.)
Satisfaction 717
Hart, Mickey (1943–)
Rhythm 702
Hartford, John (1937–2001)
Rhythm 702
Hartley, Leslie Poles (1895–1972)
The Past 602
Harvey, Paul (1918–)
Enthusiasm 276
Harvey, Will (1967–)
Research 694
Haskell, Colleen (1976–)
Camping 114
Hastings, Alcee (1936–)
Patriots 606
Hatch, Orrin (1934–)
Judges 449
Hatcher, Sims (1983–)
Tomorrow 819
Yesterday 893
Hathaway, Katharine Butler (1890–1942)
Friendship 344
Instinct 435
Hattersley, Roy (1932–)
Acceptance 17
Havel, Vaclav (1936–)
Lies 487
Political Parties 634
Theater 808
Tragedy 824
Truth 831
Havner, Vance (1901–1986)
Abstinence 15
Church 146
Hawke, Bob (1929–)
Economics 257
Hawken, Paul (1946–)
Corporations 181
Hawking, Stephen (1942–)
Computers 164
Disability 238
Human Nature 405
Hawn, Goldie (1945–)
Buddhism 107
Comedy 156
Family 303
Heart 390
Ugliness 835

Hawthorne, Nathaniel (1804–1864)
Autumn 74
Disease 241
Economics 257
Happiness 384
Heart 390
The Moon 551
Real Estate 675
Hay, John (1838–1905)
Luck 512
Hayakawa, Samel Ichiye (1906–1992)
Literature 498
Tyranny 834
Haydon, Benjamin (1786–1846)
Fame 300
Youth 895
Hayek, Salma (1966–)
Beauty 81
Fame 301
Humor 410
Pain 593
Hays, Arthur Garfield (1881–1954)
Freedom, ... 337
Hayes, Helen (1900–1993)
Achievement 20
Childhood 137
Dignity 237
Gardens 357
Legends 476
Life 492
Longevity 501
Love 507
Maturity 526
Success 780
Hayes, Judith (1945–)
Evolution 286
Hayes, Woody (1913–1987)
Persistence 613
Rust 710
Hays, Arthur Garfield (1881–1954)
Liberty 481
The Poor 639
Revolution 700
Hayworth, J. D. (1958–)
Amnesty 50
Democrats 223
Republicans 692
Hazan, Marcella (1924–)
Cooking 178
Hazlitt, William (1778–1830)
Admiration 26
Adversity 31
Aging 38
Conceit 164
Confidence 166
Conversation 176
Cunning 200
Custom 202
Economics 257
Ego 264
Faith 299
Familiarity 302
Faults 311
Favors 311
Genius 361
Grace 375
Greatness 378
Insults 436
Leisure 476
Liberty 481
Persuasion 616
Power 644
Prejudice 648
Prosperity 660
Punctuality 663
Respect 695
Ridicule 705
Satire 716
Scholars 718
Struggle 772
Superstition 789
Taste 795
Thoughts 812
Understanding 837
Value 845
Vocation 856

Hazlitt, William (cont.)
Wit 873
Zeal 898
Healy, Timothy (1855–1931)
Libraries 485
Hearn, Lafcadio (1850–1904)
Adultery 28
Scripture 722
Hearns, Thomas (1958–)
Boxing 103
Heath, Edward (1916–2005)
Unemployment 838
Heat-Moon, William Least (1940–)
Thoughts 812
Hecht, Ben (1893–1964)
Beggars 84
Journalism 442
Newspapers 573
Reading 674
Hedberg, Mitch (1968–2005)
Automobiles 73
Fishing 319
Food 324
Gambling 354
Hegel, Georg W. (1770–1831)
America 48
Heidegger, Martin (1889–1976)
Subjectivity 778
Philosophy 619
Heine, Heinrich (1797–1856)
Boredom 101
Censorship 124
Communism 159
Criticism 197
Fools 326
Kisses 457
Praise 646
Sanity 715
Stupidity 775
Tolerance 818
Heinlein, Robert A. (1907–1988)
Cats 117
Censorship 124
Dogs 246
Excess 288
Experts 292
Fantasy 304
Flowers 322
Goals 366
Insects 434
Irony 440
Life 492
Meals 527
Moderation 546
Optimism 590
Pessimism 617
Poetry 629
The Poor 639
Stories 767
Theology 808
The Universe 841
Writing 888
Heller, Joseph (1923–1999)
Enemies 270
Mediocrity 529
Questions 668
Hellman, Lillian (1905–1984)
Conscience 171
Cynicism, ...202
Fashion 306
Prejudice 648
Hello, Ernest (1828–1885)
Delusion 219
Helms, Ed (1974–)
Corporations 181
Helms, Jessie (1921–)
Bureaucracy 109
Helmsly, Leona (1920–)
Excess 288
Héloïse (1098–1164)
Fate 308
Gifts 363
Helprin, Mark (1947–)
Silence 739
Helps, Sir Arthur (1813–1875)
Admiration 26

Helps, Sir Arthur (cont.)
Books 98
Boredom 101
Bureaucracy 109
Objectives 579
Reading 674
Thoughts 812
Helvétius, Claude-Adrien (1715–1771)
Censorship 124
Discipline 239
Hemingway, Ernest (1899–1961)
Aging 38
Alcohol 42
Aging 38
Alcohol 42
Artists 67
Cheating 136
Cowardice 189
Death 208
Depression 224
Doctors 244
Effort 262
Fiction 316
Fighting 318
Fishing 319
Grace 375
Grammar 375
Listening 497
Losing 502
Patriots 606
Perspective 615
Purpose 665
Sobriety 750
Stars 762
Stories 767
Tragedy 824
Writing 888
Hemingway, Mary (1908–1984)
Worries 883
Hench, John (1908–2004)
Cities 150
Henderson, Arthur (1863–1945)
Anarchy 51
Henderson, Bruce (1915–1992)
Mediocrity 529
Hendrix, Jimi (1942–1970)
Love 507
Peace 608
Wisdom 871
Henley, Beth (1952–)
Racism 671
Henri, Robert (1865–1929)
Emotions 267
The Sea 723
Henriksen, Lance (1940–)
Totalitarianism 820
Henry IV, King (1367–1413)
Reverence 699
Henry, Buck (1930–)
Presidents 650
Henry, Patrick (1736–1799)
Commerce 157
Liberty 481
Slavery 747
Hensley, Ken (1945–)
Addiction 24
Henson, Jim (1936–1990)
Ambition 45
Food 324
Henson, Keith (1942–)
Cults 199
Status 765
Hepburn, Katharine (1907–2003)
Acting 22
Admiration 26
Discipline 239
Enthusiasm 276
Life 492
Heraclitus (c. 535–475 BC)
Alcohol 42
Bigotry 90
Change 129
Character 132
Childhood 137
Cities 150
Fate 308

Heraclitus (cont.)
Injustice 433
Justice 452
Learning 475
Nature 569
Opposition 589
Rivers 708
Seriousness 732
Understanding 837
Wine 869
Herbert, Alan Patrick (1890–1971)
Marriage 521
Herbert, Frank (1920–1986)
Ancestors, ...52
Discipline 239
Discovery 240
Distrust 242
Enlightenment 274
Fear 313
Fiction 316
Freedom 337
Knowledge 460
Liberty 481
Logic 499
Mystery 565
Novels 577
Trust 830
Herbert, George (1593–1633)
Aging 38
Books 98
Confidence 166
Doctors 244
Forgiveness 332
Gardens 357
Greatness 378
Skill 745
Snow 750
Winter 870
Herford, Oliver (1863–1935)
Charm 135
Ego 264
Tact 792
Writing 888
Hermans, Felicia D. (1793–1835)
Mothers 556
Hermocrates (c. 407 BC)
Peace 608
War 860
Herodotus (484–430 BC)
Deeds 215
Eyes 293
Fathers 309
Jealousy, ...440
Knowledge 460
Power 644
Relaxation 686
Risk 707
Herold, Don (1889–1966)
Babies 76
Intelligence 437
Sophistication 755
Herrick, Robert (1591–1674)
Cats 117
Kisses 457
Tears 801
Herrigel, Eugen (1885–1955)
Zen 898
Herriot, James (1916–1995)
Cats 117
Herschel, John (1792–1871)
Self-Respect 729
Hershey, Barbara (1948–)
Aging 38
Hershey, Lenore (1919–1997)
Giving 364
Hershey, Lewis (1893–1977)
Adults 29
Hertzberg, Arthur (1921–2006)
Anti-Semitism 56
Herzl, Theodor (1860–1904)
Anti-Semitism 56
Body 95
Zionism 898
Herzog, Whitey (1931–)
Fishing 319

Hesburgh, Theodore (1917–)
Fathers 309
Leadership 472
Voting 857
Heschel, Abraham J. (1907–1972)
Anger 54
Awe 75
Defiance 217
Dignity 237
Discipline 239
Racism 671
Self-Respect 729
Worship 884
Hesiod (800–720 BC)
Blessings 93
Disaster 238
Evil 284
Misfortune 542
Shame 735
Hesse, Hermann (1877–1962)
Character 132
Eternity 282
Hate 387
Humanity 407
Insanity 434
Money 548
Opposites 588
Pleasure 625
Power 644
Sanity 715
Saviors 717
Heston, Charlton (1924–)
Political Correctness 633
Hewitt, Jennifer Love (1979–)
Dating 206
Heym, Stefan (1913–2001)
Economics 257
Heywood, John (1497–1580)
Horses 405
Hickam, Homer (1943–)
Ignorance 420
Hickenlooper, John (1952–)
Bureaucracy 109
Restaurants 697
Hickman, Greg
Opportunity 586
Hicks, Bill (1961–1994)
Belief 86
Drugs 252
Fear 313
The Garden of Eden 355
Hicks, Granville (1901–1982)
Censorship 124
Higgins, George V. (1939–1999)
Ego 264
Higginson, Thomas Wentworth (1823–1911)
Eyes 293
Mothers 556
Originality 592
Hightower, Jim (1943–)
Campaigns 113
Corporations 181
Ideas 414
Hilbert, David (1862–1943)
Astrology 70
Hill, Daniel H. (1821–1889)
Knights 459
Hill, Napoleon (1833–1970)
Ability 10
Defeat 216
Dreams 250
Enjoyment 273
Enthusiasm 276
Experience 291
Failure 297
Giving 364
Goals 366
Government 373
Greatness 379
Growth 380
Hate 387
Imagination 423
Laziness 469
Mind 536
Opportunity 586
Organization 592

Hill, Napoleon (cont.)
Patience 604
Peace of Mind 609
Perseverance 613
Persistence 613, 614
Perspiration 615
Planning 623
Procrastination 655
Sacrifice 711
Self 727
Success 780
Teamwork 800
Vision 855
Hillary, Edmund (1919–)
Adversity 31
Hillesum, Etty (1914–1943)
Painting 595
Hillman, James (1926–)
Depression 224
Losing 502
Hinckley, John W., Jr.
Guns 381
Hinn, Benny (1952–)
The Bible 89
Hippocrates (460–377 BC)
Astrology 70
Blessings 93
Disease 241
Healing 388
Health 389
Idleness 418
Illness 421
Knowledge 460
Laziness 469
Occupation 582
Prayer 647
Science 721
Hirst, Damien (1909–)
Smoking 749
Suicide 785
Hitchcock, Alfred (1899–1980)
Assassination 69
Books, ...98
Cinema 148
Christianity 145
Generals 358
Murder 562
Plagiarism 622
Psychiatry 661
Revenge 699
Television 803
Hitchens, Christopher (1949–)
Terrorism 806
Hitler, Adolf (1889–1945)
Heaven 393
Hell 394
Leadership 472
Lies 487
The Middle Ages 534
Obstacles 581
Right 706
Rulers 710
Struggle 772
Success 780
War 860
Wrong 891
Hoagland, Edward (1932–)
Solitude 754
Hobbes, John Oliver (1867–1906)
Destiny 229
Hobbes, Thomas (1588–1679)
Absurdity 16
Despair 226
Gluttony 366
Heresy 396
Hope 404
Leisure 476
Philosophy 619
Religion 688
Secrets 724
Understanding 837
Hoch, Edward Ellis (1849–1925)
Gossip 370
Hodge, Alexander (1823–1886)
Faith 299
Superstition 789

Hodge, Charles (1797–1878)
Church 146
Hodges, Leigh Mitchell (1876–1954)
Life 492
Hodges, Luther H. (1898–1974)
Economics 257
Hodgson, Ralph (1871–1962)
Belief 86
Hoffer, Eric (1902–1983)
Achievement 20
Aging 38
Atheism 71
Blessings 93
Cheating 136
Children 140
Creativity 190
Crisis 194
Death 208
Dreams 250
Ego 264
Enemies 270
Etiquette 283
Failure 297
Fatigue 310
Favors 311
Fear 313
Freedom 337
The Future 354
Generalizations 358
Generosity 359
Glory 365
Greatness 378
Heresy 396
Honesty 401
Humanity 407
Imitation 425
Invention 440
Manners 520
Nonconformity 575
Numbers 577
Obstacles 581
Old Age 583
Opportunity 586
Persistence 614
Persuasion 616
The Poor 639
Power 644
Prediction 648
Purpose 665
Religion 688
Riches 704
Sacrifice 711
Saviors 717
Self-Esteem 729
Skill 745
Stories 767
Talent 793
Talk 794
Uniqueness 839
Youth 895
Hoffman, Abbie (1936–1989)
Cannibalism 114
Dignity 237
Duty 253
Repression 691
Revolution 700
Weather 866
Hoffman, Alice (1952–)
Love 508
Mothers 556
Hoffs, Susanna (1959–)
Biological Clock 90
Holbrook, Hal (1925–)
Political Correctness 633
Holland, Brad (1943–)
Tradition 823
Holland, Jack (1947–2004)
Gossip 370
Holland, J. G. (1819–1881)
God 367
Holmes, John Haynes (1879–1964)
Politicians 635
Priests 652
Holmes, Oliver Wendell, Jr. (1841–1935)
America 48
Character 132

Holmes, Oliver Wendell, Jr. (cont.)
Children 140
Competition 162
Devotion 233
Doubt 248
Ego 264
Lawyers 468
Leisure 476
Majorities 515
Mind 536
Opportunity 586
Salvation 714
Holmes, Oliver Wendell, Sr. (1809–1894)
Ability 11
Age 37
Aging 38
Ancestry 52
Democracy 221
Determination 231
Flowers 322
Friendship 344, 345
Ideas 414
Insanity 434
Knowledge 460
Libraries 485
Life 492
Listening 497
Mind 536
Mothers 556
Music 563
Pleasure 625
Quality 666
Quantity 666
Scholars 718
Secrets 724
Studying 774
Summer 787
Thoughts 812
Trees 828
Truth 831
Twilight 833
Vision 855
Youth 895
Holt, Sir John (1642–1710)
Resolution, ...695
Holtz, Lou (1937–)
Ability 11
Life 492
Motivation 561
Holyfield, Evander (1962–)
Boxing 103
Holzer, Jenny (1950–)
Charisma 133
Home, Henry (1696–1782)
Abstinence 15
Homer (800–700 BC)
Age 37
Alcohol 42
Beggars 85
Blessings 93
Deeds 215
Dreams 250
Eloquence 266
Evil, ...284
Fate 308
Fathers 309
Fools 326
Friendship 345
Gifts 363
Glory 365
God 367
Grace 375
Grief 381
Mankind 518
Mind 536
Murder 562
Music 563
Nobility 574
Parenthood 598
Patience 604
Patriotism 606
Persuasion 616
Planning 623
Reverence 699
Rulers 710
Slavery 747

Homer (cont.)
- Sleep 748
- Stories 767
- Strangers 768
- War 860
- Wine 869
- Wisdom 871

Hooker, John Jay (1930–)
- Judges 449

Hooker, John Lee (1917–2001)
- Corporations 181

Hooker, Richard (1554–1600)
- Cause and Effect 120

Hooks, Bell (1952–)
- Books 98

Hoole, John (1727–1803)
- Traitors 825
- Treason 827

Hoover, Herbert (1874–1964)
- Actions 22
- Agnosticism 39
- America 48
- Competition 162
- Engineering 272
- Fishing 319
- The Public 662
- Television 803

Hope, Bob (1903–2003)
- Banks 78
- Bathrooms 80
- Charity 134
- Golf 370
- Laziness 469
- Middle Age 534
- Political Parties 634

Hopper, Edward (1882–1967)
- Artists 67

Horace (65–8 BC)
- Adversity 31
- Avarice 74
- Blessings 94
- Death 208
- Effort 262
- Envy 278
- Excellence 287
- Expectations 290
- Fate 308
- Faults 311
- Fools 326
- Fortune 334
- Gossip 370
- Greatness 378
- Judges 449
- Life 492
- Mediocrity 529
- Money 548
- Opportunity 586
- The Past 602
- Persuasion 616
- Pleasure 625
- Poetry 629
- Poverty 643
- Profit 655
- Prosperity 660
- Rich and Poor 702
- Silence 739
- Talent 793
- Truth 831
- Vice 848
- Wisdom 871
- Wit 873
- Work 881
- Wounds 885
- Yesterday 893
- Youth 895

Horne, Harriet van (1920–1998)
- Cooking 178

Horne, Richard Hengist (1802–1884)
- Agriculture 40

Household, Geoffrey (1900–1988)
- Cats 117

Housman, A. E. (1859–1936)
- Alcohol 42
- Innocence 433

Houston, Jean (1939–)
- Happiness 385

Houston, Jean (cont.)
Laughter 464
The Universe 842
Houston, Sam (1793–1863)
Civil War 150
Community 161
Howard, George William (1892–1964)
Cause and Effect 120
Howard, Jane (1935–1996)
Family 303
Howard, Moe (1897–1975)
Fools 326
Howard, Sidney (1891–1939)
Hunger 411
Women 876
Howard, Vernon (1918–1992)
Cause and Effect 120
Delay 219
Howe, Edgar Watson (1853–1937)
Criticism 197
Fishing 319
Indifference 428
Laughter 464
Men 532
Mothers 556
Neglect 570
Poetry 629
Rights 706
Thieves 810
Women 876
Howe, Joseph (1804–1873)
Libraries 485
Howe, Julia Ward (1819–1910)
Dessert 228
Howell, James (1594–1666)
Policy 632
Respect 695
Howitt, Mary (1799–1888)
Eyes 294
Hoyle, Fred (1915–2001)
The Universe 842
Hubbard, Elbert (1856–1915)
Ability 11
Admiration 26
Appeasement 59
Arguments 61
Character 132
Civilization 151
Cleverness 153
College 155
Criticism 197
Dignity 237
Effort 262
Enemies 270
Enthusiasm 276
Failure 297
Family 303
Friendship 345
Genius 361
Habits 382
Ignorance 420
Journalism 442
Killing 453
Life 492
Love 508
Loyalty 511
Mistakes 544
Newspapers 573
Opinions 584
Persistence 614
Positivity 642
Preachers 647
Progress 656
Punishment 663
Stupidity 775
Success 780
The Supernatural 788
Trade 822
Words 878
Work 881
Hubbard, Kin (1868–1930)
Babies 76
Conversation 176
Efficiency 262
Fish 318
Happiness 385

Hubbard, Kin (cont.)
- Honesty 401
- Husbands 412
- Listening 497
- Money 549
- Mothers 556
- Music 563
- Poverty 643
- Statesmen 763
- Success 780
- Wealth 865
- Weather 866
- Wives 875
- Women 876

Hubbard, L. Ron (1911–1986)
- Artists 68
- Culture 199

Hubbard, Ruth (1924–)
- Orthodoxy 592

Hubble, Edwin Powell (1889–1953)
- Science 721
- Senses 730

Hudson, Oliver (1976–)
- Family 303
- Relatives 685

Hudson, William H. (1841–1922)
- Birds 91
- Senses 730

Hueck, Catherine de (1896–1985)
- Healing 388

Huerta, Dolores (1930–)
- Forgiveness 333

Huffington, Arianna (1950–)
- Liberation 479

Hufstedler, Shirley (1925–)
- Risk 707

Huggins, Miller (1879–1929)
- Managers 517

Hughes, Charles Evans (1862–1948)
- Judges 449
- Property 658

Hughes, John (1950–)
- Belief 86
- Life 492
- Respect 695

Hughes, Langston (1902–1967)
- Dreams 250

Hughes, Thomas (1822–1896)
- Friendship 345
- Gifts 363

Hugo, Victor (1802–1885)
- Adversity 31
- Aging 38, 39
- Boldness 96
- Chaos 130
- Charity 134
- Civil War 150
- Civilization 151
- Darkness 205
- Debt 211
- Dreams 250
- Education 260
- Fame 301
- Flirting 321
- Forests 331
- Friendship 345
- The Future 354
- Glory 365
- Godfathers 376
- Godfathers 376
- Greatness 378
- Happiness 385
- Heart 390
- Hell 394
- Horses 405
- Humanity 407
- Hunger 411
- Ideas 414
- Imagination 423
- Laughter 464
- Laws 467
- Liberation 479
- Life 492, 493
- Love 508
- Melancholy 530
- Misery 541

Hugo, Victor (cont.)
Mothers 556
Names 566
Patience 604
Planning 623
Popularity 640
Progress 656, 657
Prosperity 660
Quality 666
Quantity 666
Respectability 696
Ridicule 705
Roots 709
Sadness 712
Secrets 724
Society 752
Spring 761
Strangers 768
Strength 771
Stupidity 775
Suffering 783
Suicide 785
Tears 801
Thoughts 812, 813
Trade 822
Utopia 843
Vanity 846
Winter 870
Humboldt, Alexander von (1769–1859)
Happiness 385
Unhappiness 839
Humboldt, Wilhelm von (1767–1835)
Devotion 233
Fate 308
Hume, David (1711–1776)
Ambition 46
Arrogance 63
Art 64
Avarice 74
Circumstances 149
Clothes 153
Conflict 168
Government 372
Illusion 422
Liberty 481
Mind 536
Nature 569
Philosophy 619
Poverty 643
Principles 653
Riches 704
Hume, John (1937–)
Banks 78
Humphrey, Hubert H. (1911–1978)
Friendship 345
Heresy 396
Neurosis 571
Statesmen 763
Status Quo 765
Hunt, E. Howard (1918–2007)
Bureaucracy 109
Evil 284
Flowers 323
Hunt, Leigh (1784–1859)
Kisses 457
Suffering 783
Hunter, Kristin (1931–)
Fect 314
Huntington, Samuel P. (1821–1900)
Protestantism 661
Hurok, Sol (1888–1974)
Pleasure 625
Hurston, Zora Neale (1903–1960)
Losing 502
Research 694
Hutchins, Robert M. (1899–1977)
Apathy 57
Education 260
Totalitarianism 820
Hutton, William (1723–1815)
Charity 134
Deeds 215
Huxley, Aldous (1894–1963)
Abstinence 15
Ancestors 52
Boredom 101

Huxley, Aldous
Bureaucracy 109
Cats 117
Change 129
Charm 135
Dehumanization 218
Democracy 221
Dogs 246
Equality 279
Experience 292
Facts 295
Fiction 316
Forgiveness 333
Free Will 339
Habits 382
Hell 395
Losing 502
Malice 516
Music 563
Novels 577
Orthodoxy 592
Popularity 640
Sacrifice 711
Stupidity 775
Teachers 798
Thoughts 813
The Universe 842
Vice 848
Vision 855
Words 878
The World 883
Huxley, Thomas H. (1825–1895)
Ability 11
Agnosticism 39
Authority 73
The Bible 89
Certainty 127
Common Sense 158
Education 260
Error 280
Evolution 286
Hesitation 398
Injustice 433
Knowledge 460
Lies 487
Opinions 584
Rejection 684
Science 721
Truth 831
Hyde, Catherine Ryan (1955–)
Change 129
Ideas 414
Hyman, Mark E. (1958–)
Complaints 163
Hypatia of Alexandria (c. 360–415)
Dogma 244

I

Iacocca, Lee (1924–)
Bosses 102
Business 112
Decisions 214
Economics 257
Family 303
Leadership 472
Lunch 512
Managers 517
Motivation 561
Ibarruri, Dolores (1895–1989)
Cowardice 189
Heroes 397
Ibsen, Henrik (1828–1906)
Community 161
Decency 212
Journalists 444
Leadership 472
Liberty 481
Power 644
Refuge 683
Ibycus (c. 400 BC)
Arguments 61
Ice T (1958–)
Love 508
Passion 601

The I Ching
- Achievement 21
- Chaos 131

Icke, David (1952–)
- Earth 254
- Rebellion 680

Ifill, Gwen (1955–)
- Journalists 444

Ikeda, Daisaku (1928–)
- Struggle 772

Il, Kim Jong (1942–)
- Ideology 417

Iloilo, Josefa (1920–)
- Togetherness 818

Ingalls, John J. (1833–1900)
- Happiness 385

Inge, William Ralph (1860–1954)
- Consciousness 173
- Evolution 286
- Gambling 354
- Opinions 584
- The Past 602
- Plagiarism 622
- Quarrels 667
- Resolution 695
- Reward 701

Ingelow, Jean (1820–1897)
- Children 140

Ingersoll, Robert Green (1833–1899)
- Anger 54
- Astrology 70
- The Bible 89
- Civilization 151
- Conscience 171
- Famine 304
- Forgiveness 333
- Losing 503
- Mediocrity 529
- Mind 536
- Priests 652
- Slavery 747

Inman, Bobby R. (1931–)
- Zealots 898

Ionesco, Eugène (1909–1994)
- Alienation 44
- Bureaucracy 109
- Dreams 250
- Religion 688
- Shakespeare 735

Ireland, Archbishop John (1828–1918)
- Laws 467
- Liberty 481
- Order 591

Ireland, Patricia (1945–)
- Campaigns 113

Irving, John (1942–)
- Writing 888

Irving, Washington (1783–1859)
- Affection 34
- Dignity 237
- Fishing 319
- Heart 390
- Mind 536
- Misfortune 542
- Mothers 556
- Sorrow 756
- Tomorrow 819
- Women 876
- Yesterday 893

Isocrates (436–338 BC)
- Possessions 641
- Wisdom 871

Israel, Steve (1958–)
- Corporations 181
- Corruption 185

Ives, Charles (1874–1953)
- Mediocrity 529

Ivins, Molly (1944–2002)
- Satire 716

Iyengar, B. K. S. (1918–)
- Yoga 893

Iyer, Pico (1957–)
- Comedy 156
- Humor 410

Izzard, Eddie (1962–)
- Catholicism 115

Izzard, Eddie (cont.)
Guns 382

J

Jacobs-Bond, Carrie (1862–1946)
Friendship 345
Jacobsen, Arne (1902–1971)
Architecture 60
Jackson, Alphonso (1945–)
Republicans 692
Jackson, Andrew (1767–1845)
Banks 79
Cowardice 189
Determination 231
Majorities 515
Mothers 556
Jackson, George (1941–1971)
Patience 604
Jackson, Helen Hunt (1830–1885)
Mothers 556
Jackson, Holbrook (1874–1948)
Censorship 124
Jackson, Jesse (1941–)
Leadership 472
Parenthood 598
Presents 650
Students 774
Jackson, Joseph Henry (1894–1955)
Censorship 124
Jackson, Mahalia (1911–1972)
Songs 754
Jackson, Phil (1945–)
Joy 446
Jackson, Robert (1892–1954)
Ambition 46
Jackson, Victoria (1959–)
Entertainment 274
Reality 677
Jagger, Mick (1943–)
Anarchy 51
James I, King (1566–1625)
Smoking 749
James, Alice (1848–1892)
Medicine 528
James, Clive (1939–)
Education 260
Anarchy 51
James, Henry (1843–1916)
Afternoon 35
Books 98
Cats 117
Civilization 151
English 272
Experience 292
Fiction 316
Kindness 454
Literature 498
Mistakes 544
Summer 787
Tact 792
Tradition 823
Understanding 838
Writing 888
James, John Angell (1785–1859)
Devotion 233
James, P. D. (1920–)
Autumn 74
Giving 364
Memory 531
Political Correctness 633
James, Richard D. (1971–)
Rhythm 702
James, Selma (1930–)
Political Correctness 633
James, William (1842–1910)
Acceptance 17
Aging 39
Attitude 71
Choice 144
Conflict 168
Ego 264
Failure 297
Fatigue 310
Feelings 314
Growth 381

James, William (cont.)
Ideas 414
Laughter 464
Materialism 524
Oblivion 579, 580
Persuasion 616
Philosophy 619
Prejudice 648
Principles 653
Psychology 662
Religion 688
Struggle 773
Theories 809
Wisdom 871
Worries 883
Jameson, Anna (1794–1860)
Mind 536
Jameson, Fredric (1934–)
Utopia 843
Jameson, Margaret Storm (1891–1986)
Cooking 178
Happiness 385
Jarman, Derek (1942–1994)
Sexuality 734
Jarman, Joseph (1937–)
Intellectualism 436
Jarrell, Randall (1914–1965)
Culture 199
Intellectuals 437
Jarry, Alfred (1873–1907)
Tradition 823
Jarvis, Anna (1832–1905)
Mothers 556
Jaworski, Ron (1951–)
Positivity 642
Jay, Anthony (1930–)
Policy 632
Jay, John (1745–1829)
Juries 451
Jaynes, Julian (1920–1997)
Civilization 151
Jeans, James (1877–1946)
Space 757
Jeffers, Robinson (1887–1962)
Old Age 583
Youth 895
Jefferson, Charles E. (1860–1937)
Gratitude 376
Jefferson, Thomas (1743–1826)
Abstinence 15
Advertising 32
Aging 39
Alliances 44
Aristocracy 62
Atheism 71
Attitude 71
Banks 79
Blessings 94
Boldness, ...97
Censorship 124
Cities 150
Commerce 157
Corporations 181
Cowardice 189
Danger 204
Debt 211
Defiance 217
Delay 219
Democracy 221
Despair 227
Determination 231
Dreams 250
Education 260
Effort 262
Emotions 268
Error 281
Ethics 283
Exercise 289
Food 324
Friendship 345
Gardens 357
Generals 358
Government 372
Happiness 385
Health 389
Honesty 402

Jefferson, Thomas (cont.)
Independence 428
Inflation 432
Journalism 442
Judges 449
Juries 451
Kings 456
Laws 467
Lawyers 468
Laziness 469
Liberty 481, 482
Luck 512
Majorities 515
Manners 520
Mind 536
Minorities 539
Money 549
Mythology 565
Newspapers 573
Obedience 578
Occupation 582
Oppression 589
Patriots 607
Persuasion 616
Pleasure 625
Power 644
Priests 653
Privilege 654
Progress 657
The Public 662
Reason 679
Rebellion 680
Religion 688
Resistance 694
Rights 706
Speaking 758
Statesmen 763
Strength 771
Talk 794
Taste 795
Thoughts 813
Tourism 821
Trouble 829
Truth 831
Tyranny 834
Vice 848
Virtue 853, 854
War 860
Work 881
Zealots 898
Jeffery, Lord Francis (1773–1850)
Opinions 584
Prejudice 648
Reputation 693
Violence 851
Jekyll, Gertrude (1843–1932)
Gardens 357
Jenkins, Jerry B. (1949–)
Relationships 685
Jenkins, Mark (1943–)
Boldness 97
Jennings, Peter (1938–2005)
Scholars 718
Jensen, Johannes Vilhelm (1873–1950)
Botany 102
Jerome, Saint (c. 342–420)
Charm 135
Deeds 215
Eyes 294
Friendship 345
Heart 390
Horses 405
Mind 537
Mirrors 540
Secrets 724
Virginity 852
Jerome, Jerome K. (1859–1927)
Dogs 246
Idleness 418
Ignorance 420
Kisses 457
Lies 487
Policy 632
Jerrold, Douglas (1803–1857)
Treason 827
Trouble 828

Jewel (1974–)
Forgiveness 333
Jewett, Sarah Orne (1849–1909)
Tact 792
Jiang Zemin (1917–)
Relativity 686
Jillette, Penn (1955–)
The Internet 438
Jinnah, Muhammad Ali (1876–1948)
Ideology 417
Joan of Arc (1412–1431)
Sin 742
Jobs, Steve (1955–)
Death 208
Dogma 245
Expectations 290
Intuition 439
Perseverance 613
Quality 666
Success 780
Joel, Billy (1949–)
Corporations 181
The Garden of Eden 355
Saints 713
Songs 754
Johanson, Sue (1946–)
Teenagers 802
John of Damascus (c. 676–749)
Water 863
John, Gwen (1876–1939)
Timidity 817
John Paul II, Pope (1920–2005)
Alienation 44
Celibacy 122
Socialism 751
Johnson, Andrew (1808–1875)
Aristocracy 62
Tyranny 834
Johnson, Ben (1572–1637)
Honor 402
Johnson, Benjamin (1665–1742)
Eyes 294
Kisses 457
Johnson, Jimmy (1943–)
Objectivity 579
Johnson, Lady Bird (1912–2007)
Children 140
Fear 312
Libraries 485
Pain 593
Johnson, Lyndon B. (1908–1973)
America 48
Economics 257
Football 330
Losing 503
The Past 602
Presidents 651
Quality 666
Quantity 667
Suspicion 790
Tolerance 818
Wrong 891
Johnson, Mordecai Wyatt (1890–1976)
Decency 212
Johnson, Philip (1906–2005)
Architecture 60
Shelter 736
Vacations 844
Johnson, Richard Mentor (1780–1850)
Benevolence 88
Johnson, Samuel (1709–1784)
Abstinence 15
Admiration 26
Adversity 31
Aging 39
Agriculture 40
Ambition 46
Avarice 74
Bachelors 77
Bravery 104
Celebrities 122
Character 132
Cheating 136
College 155
Communism 159
Complaints 163

Johnson, Samuel (cont.)
Confidence 166
Conscience 171
Conversation 176
Curiosity, ...201
Daughters 206
Debt 211
Defiance 217
Dogs 246
Effort 262
Error 281
Excellence 287
Fame 301
Fatigue 310
Flattery 320
Flirting 321
Food 324
Friendship 345
Gambling 355
Generosity 360
Greatness 378
Grief 381
Habits 382
Hope 404
Idleness 418
Imitation 425
Impatience 426
Industry 431
Information 432
Injustice 433
Integrity 436
Justice 452
Knowledge 461
Libraries 485
Lies 487
Life 493
Malevolence 516
Mankind 518
Marriage 521, 522
Meaning 528
Misery 541
Moderation 546
Music 563
Neglect 570
Neutrality 571, 572
Noise 574
Patriotism 606
Perseverance 613
Pleasure 625
Poetry 630
Possibilities 642
Praise 646
Prejudice 648
Pride 652
Promises 657
Prudence 661
Reflection 681
Refuge 683
Ridicule 705
Rivalry 708
Secrets 725
Self-Confidence 728
Silence 739
Sorrow 756
Speaking 758
Studying 775
Superiority 788
Suspicion 790
Teachers 798
Theories 809
Trust 830
Understanding 838
Value 845
Vengeance 847
Vice 848
Vigilance 850
Waste 863
Welfare 867
Wine 869
Wives 875
Words 878
Wounds 885
Writing 889
Wrong 891
Youth 895
Zealots 898

Johnson, Wendell (1906–1965)
Words 878
Johnston, Denis (1901–1984)
Mythology 566
Johnston, Lynn (1947–)
Bravery 104
Children 140
Criticism 197
Dogs 246
Experience 292
Friendship 345
Gifts 363
Ideas 414
Silence 739
Sleep 748
Jones, Franklin P. (1887–1929)
Mistakes 544
The Moon 551
Parenthood 598
Jones, Howard Mumford (1892–1980)
Conformity 169
Machines 513
Persecution 612
Jones, Mother (1830–1930)
Teachers 798
Jones, Thomas (1892–1969)
Enemies 270
Friendship 345
Jones, Timothy (1962–)
Friendship 345
Jones, Sir William Alton (1746–1794)
Talent 793
Jong, Erica (1942–)
Advice 33
Excuses 288
Jealousy 441
Mothers 556
Pain 593
Reading 674
Risk 707
Talent 793
Jonson, Ben (1572–1637)
Adversity 31
Aging 39
Eloquence 266
Force 330
Meaning 528
Jordan, David Starr (1851–1931)
Dogs 246
Skill 745
Virtue 854
Wisdom 871
Jordan, Michael (1963–)
Cats 117
Sports 760
Teamwork 800
Joseph, Akiba ben (c. AD 50–135)
Censorship 124
Joseph, Michael (1872–1940)
Cats 118
Josephus (AD 37–100)
God 368
Religion 688
Joubert, Joseph (1754–1824)
Admiration 26
Fate 308
Grace 375
Imagination 424
Teachers 798
Utility 843
Youth 895
Jowett, Benjamin (1817–1893)
Clergy 152
Joy, Bill (1954–)
Editors 258
Joyce, James (1882–1941)
Artists 68
Discovery 240
Heresy 396
Kingdoms 455
Mistakes 544
Satan 715
Joyner-Kersee, Jackie (1962–)
Regret 683
Juárez, Benito (1806–1972)
Peace 608

Juárez, Benito (cont.)
- Rights 706

Judd, Ashley (1968–)
- Yoga 893

Judd, Walter H. (1898–1994)
- Democracy 221

Jung, Carl (1875–1961)
- Achievement 20
- Addiction 24
- Aging 39
- Alcohol 42
- Apathy 57
- Astrology 70
- Consciousness 173
- Creativity 190
- Difficulty 236
- Dreams 251
- Ego 264
- Emotions 267
- Failure 297
- Fantasy 304
- Fate 308
- Friendship 345
- Imagination, ...424
- Individualism 429
- Love 508
- Mythology 566
- Neurosis 571
- Numbers 577
- Personality 614
- Psychiatry 661
- Sadness 712
- Suffering 783
- Teachers 798
- Understanding 838
- Vision 855

Juvenal (AD 55–127)
- Avarice 74
- Body 95
- Censure 126
- Chance 128
- Children 140
- Fools 326
- Guilt 381
- Mind 537
- Money 549
- Pleasure 626
- Poverty 643
- Prayer 647

K

The Kabbalah
- Fruit 352
- Rhythm 702

Kafka, Franz (1883–1924)
- Alcohol 42
- Beauty 82
- Bureaucracy 109
- Impatience 426
- Intoxication 439
- Life 493
- Patience 604
- Quiet 669
- Revolution 700
- Suspicion 790
- The World 883
- Youth 895

Kahanamoku, Duke (1890–1968)
- Talk 794

Kahane, Meir (1932–1990)
- Decency 212

Kahlo, Frida (1907–1954)
- Art 64
- Death 208
- Feet 314
- Pain 593
- Painting 595

Kahn, Alice (1943–)
- Technology 801

Kahn, Herman (1922–1983)
- Commerce 157
- Decisions 214
- Utilitarianism 843
- Weapons 866

Kahn, Roger (1927–)
Tennis 805
Kaiser, Henry J. (1882–1967)
Life 493
Opportunity 586
Trouble 829
Work 881
Kakuzo, Okakura (1863–1913)
Life 493
Kalam, Abdul (1931–)
Devotion 233
Kaminer, Wendy (1950–)
Liberals 478
Kant, Immanuel (1724–1804)
Authority 73
Awe 75
Discipline 239
Ethics 283
Humanity 407
Laws 467
Mothers 556
Popularity 640
Science 721
Thoughts 813
Wisdom 871
Kanter, Rosabeth Moss (1943–)
Losing 503
Vision 855
Kapoor, Anish (1954–)
Sculpture 723
Kapuscinski, Ryszard (1932–)
The Cold War 154
Crisis 194
Underground 836
Karaszewski, Larry (1961–)
Sex 733
Vision 855
War 859
Karras, Alex (1935–)
Toughness 821
Karzai, Hamid (1957–)
Terrorism 806
Kass, Leon (1939–)
Abortion 14
Sexuality 734
Kaufman, Bel (1911–)
Children 140
Kaufman, George S. (1889–1961)
Satire 716
Kaufman, Herbert (1878- 1947)
Sons 755
Kaufman, Margo (1954–2000)
Divorce 243
Kay, Alan (1940–)
The Future 354
Invention 440
Kazantzakis, Nikos (1883–1957)
Enlightenment 274
Kearney, Denis (1847–1907)
Defiance 217
Keats, John (1795–1821)
Affection 34
Beauty 82
Error 281
Experience 292
Failure 297
Imagination 424
Kisses 457
The Moon 551
Poetry 630
Keats, John (cont.)
Popularity 640
Solitude 754
Truth 832
Keegan, John (1934–)
Pacifism 592
Keenan, Joe (1896–1984)
Newspapers 573
Television 803
Keenan, Maynard James (1964–)
Belief 86
Keillor, Garrison (1942–)
Childhood 137
Children 141

Keillor, Garrison (cont.)
Encouragement 269
Funerals 352
Reality 677
Keitel, Harvey (1942–)
Struggle 773
Keith, Penelope (1940–)
Shyness 737
Keller, Helen (1880–1968)
Ability 11
Achievement 20
Adults 29
Ancestors 52
Apathy 57
Beauty 82
Character 132
College 155
Darkness 205
Determination 231
Discovery 240
Education 260
Faith 299
Fidelity 318
Friendship 346
Happiness 385
Heart 390
Heresy 396
Ideas 415
Joy 446
Life 493
Literature 498
Optimism 590
Patience 604
Peace 608
Peace of Mind 609
Pessimism 617
Pity 622
Security 726
Senses 730
Silence 739
Spirit 759
Strength 771
Suffering 783
Superstition 789
Tolerance 818
Understanding 838
Utopia 843
Vision 855
Words 878
Kellogg, Frank B. (1856–1937)
Alliances, ...44
Kelly, Sue (1936–)
Farming 305
Kemble, Fanny (1809–1863)
Slavery, 7 47
Kempton, Sally (1943–)
Enemies, ...271
Kendall, Felicity (1946–)
Politicians 635
Kendall, Henry W. (1926–1999)
Environment 278
Kennedy, Anthony (1936–)..........
Freedom 337
Kennedy, Caroline (1957–)
Decency 212
Kennedy, Edward M. (1932–)
Conviction 177
Losing 503
Sacrifice 711
Kennedy, Florynce R. (1916–2000)
Abortion 14
Kennedy, John F. (1917–1963)
Belief 86
Censorship 125
Change 129
Communism 159
Conformity 169
Corruption 185
Creativity 190
Crisis 194
Danger 204
Democracy 221
Destiny 229
Devotion 233
Dreams 251
Efficiency 262

Kennedy, John F. (cont.)
Enemies 271
Excellence 287
Freedom 337
History 399
Leadership 472
Learning 475
Liberty 482
Morality 551
Mythology 566
Names 566
Negotiation 571
Ocean 582
Opinions 584
Opportunity 587
Patriotism 606
Peace 608
Policy 632
Politicians 635
Power 644
Quality 666
Quantity 667
Revolution 700
Risk 707
Sacrifice 711
Skepticism 744
Skeptics 744
The Sun 787
Suspicion 790
Thoughts 813
Time 816
Tolerance 818
Truth 832
Violence 851
Vision 856
Wages 858
Warriors 863
Kennedy, Mark (1957–)
Bureaucracy 109
Environment, ...278
Kennedy, Patrick J. (1967–)
Addiction 24
Kennedy, Robert F. (1925–1968)
Achievement 20
Bravery 105
Courage 186
Failure 297
History 399
Injustice 433
Oppression 589
Power 644
Resistance 694
Tragedy 824
Kennedy, Rose F. (1890–1995)
Birds 92
Business 112
Mind 537
Neglect 570
Kent, Allegra (1937–)
Body 95
Kent, Bruce (1929–)
Cannibalism 114
War 860
Kent, Corita (1918–1986)
Energy 271
Liberation 479
Kent, William (1685–1748)
Gardens 357
Kenyon, Lloyd (1805–1869)
Procrastination 655
Kerouac, Jack (1922–1969)
America 48
Kerr, Jean (1922–2003)
Adults 29
Airplanes 40
Babies 76
Beauty 82
Godfathers 376
Lawyers 468
Kerrigan, Nancy (1969–)
Doubt 248
Judgment 450
Kerry, John (1943–)
Abortion 14
America 48

Kerry, John (cont.)
Strategy 770
Kesey, Ken (1935–2001)
Leadership 472
Shakespeare 735
Kettering, Charles F. (1876–1958)
Failure 297
Imagination 424
Invention 440
Tomorrow 819
Yesterday 893
Kevorkian, Jack (1928–)
Suicide 785
Key, Ellen (1849–1926)
Education 260
Mothers 556
Skill 745
Key, Wilson Bryan (1925–)
Alcohol 42
Persuasion 616
Keyes, Alan (1950–)
Bureaucracy 109
Keyes, Ken, Jr. (1921–1995)
Consciousness 173
Keynes, John Maynard (1883–1946)
Bureaucracy 109
Capitalism 115
Difficulty 236
Economics 257
History 399
Ideas 415
Language 462
Taxes 796
Khan, Hazrat Inayat (1882–1927)
Beauty 82
Khan, Imran (1952–)
Losing 503
Khrushchev, Nikita (1894–1971)
Economics 257
Politicians 635
Kiam, Victor (1926–2001)
Opportunity 587
Procrastination 655
Work 881
Kidder, Tracy (1945–)
Teachers 798
Kierkegaard, Søren (1813–1855)
Aging 39
Anxiety 57
Christianity 145
Commerce 157
Depression 224
Enjoyment 273
Existentialism 289
Freedom 337
Idleness 418
Indifference 428
Laziness 469
Life 493
Love 508
Paradox 596
Pleasure 626
Possibilities 642
Purity 664
Strangers 768
Students 774
Talk 794
Teachers 798
Thoughts 813
Trouble 829
Kilmer, Joyce (1886–1918)
Trees 828
Kimball, Spencer W. (1895–1973)
Gardens 357
Mothers 556
Kind, Ron (1963–)
Corporations 181
Economics 257
King, Alan (1927–2004)
Banks 79
Strangers 768
King, Alexander (1899–1965)
Crisis 194
King, B. B. (1925–)
Learning 475

King, Billie Jean (1943–)
Boldness, ...97
Champions 127
Losing 503
Tennis 805
King, Coretta Scott (1927–2006)
Hate 387
King, Martin Luther, Jr. (1929–1968)
Acceptance 17
Accidents 18
Aging 39
Brotherhood 106
Christianity 145
College 155
Conflict 168
Conscience 171
Conservatives 174
Danger 204
Darkness 205
Democracy 221
Dreams 251
Enemies 271
Faith 299
Fear 313
Fools 328
Forgiveness 333
Freedom, ...337
Greatness, ...378
Hate 387
Hell 395
Ignorance 420
Immortality 426
Injustice 433
Justice 452
Laws 467
Leadership 472
Liberals 478
Light 497
Longevity 501
Love 508
Misunderstanding 545
Nonconformity 575
Nonviolence 576
Obscurity 580
Oppression 589, 590
The Past 602
Peace 608
Personality 614
Perspective 615
Progress 657
Rights 706
Salvation 714
Science 721
Segregation 726
Silence 739
Slavery 747
Soldiers 753
Sons 755
Spirituality 759
Stupidity 775
Toughness 821
Tragedy 825
Truth 832
Violence 851
Vision 856
Welfare 867
Wisdom 871
King, Stephen (1947–)
Hell 395
Hope 403
Laughter 464
Prison 653
Writing 889
Kingsley, Ben (1943–)
Cinema 148
Kingsley, Charles (1819–1875)
Enthusiasm 276
Friendship 346
Kisses 457
Winter 870
Kingsley, Rose G. (1845–1908)
Gardens, ...357
Kingsolver, Barbara (1955–)
Civilization 151
Friendship 346
Illusion 422

Kingsolver, Barbara (cont.)
Libraries 485
Mothers 556
Parenthood 598
Kingston, Maxine Hong (1940–)
Work 881
Kipling, Rudyard (1865–1936)
Animals 55
Children 141
Fathers 309
Gardens 357
Mothers 556
Quotations 670
Soldiers 753
Trouble 829
Unity 840
Kirkland, Sally (1944–)
Mothers 556
Kirshner, Mia (1975–)
Sexuality 734
Kirstein, Lincoln (1907–1996)
Anarchy 51
Kissinger, Henry (1923–)
Boredom 101
Celebrities 122
Crisis 194
Friendship 346
Leadership 472
Mind 537
Moderation 546
Policy 632
Politicians 635
Reality 677
Statesmen 763
Success 780
Vision 856
Kitt, Eartha (1927–)
Learning 475
Kiyosaki, Robert (1947–)
Toughness 821
Klee, Paul (1879–1940)
Artists 68
Time 816
Klein, Allen (1931–)
Recovery 680
Zen 898
Klein, Naomi (1909–)
Ideology 417
Kleiser, Grenville (1868–1953)
Character 132
Self-Control 729
Klimt, Gustav (1862–1918)
Relaxation 686
Klug, Aaron (1926–)
Curiosity 201
Knebel, Fletcher (1911–1993)
Politics 637
Smoking 749
Statesmen 763
Statistics 764
Knight, Bobby (1940–)
Journalists 444
Toughness 821
Writing 889
Knight, Charles (1874–1953)
Mediocrity 529
Knopf, Alfred A. (1892–1984)
Economics 257
Knopfler, David (1952–)
Stories 767
Knowles, John (1926–2001)
Teenagers 802
Koestler, Arthur (1905–1983)
Discovery 240
Science 721
Konig, Hans (1586–1642)
Inflation 432
Konigsburg, E.L. (1930–)
Enthusiasm 276
Kool Keith (1964–)
Underground 836
Kooning, Wiiem de (1904–1997)
Desperation 227
Koontz, Dean (1945–)
Intelligence 437

The Koran
- Deeds 216
- Laughter 465
- Martyrs 524
- Paradise 596
- The Poor 640
- Scholars 718

Korda, Michael (1933–)
- Ambition 46
- Hypocrisy 412
- Pleasure 626
- Success 780

Korzybski, Alfred (1879–1950)
- Belief 86
- Doubt 248

Kosinski, Jerzy (1933–1991)
- Banks 79
- Homelessness 401

Kournikova, Anna (1981–)
- Tennis 805

Kozol, Jonathan (1936–)
- Conflict 168

Kraus, Karl (1874–1936)
- Charm 135
- Decisions 214
- Democracy 221
- Doubt 248
- Journalists 444
- Lust 513
- Masturbation 524
- Mental Illness 533
- Religion 688
- Remorse 690
- Scandals 717
- Sexuality 734
- Solitude 754
- Virginity 852

Krauthammer, Charles (1950–)
- The Middle Ages 534

Kravitz, Lenny (1964–)
- Mothers 556

Krishnamurti, Jiddu (1895–1986)
- Mind 537
- The Past 602
- Sanity 715
- Tradition 823

Kroc, Ray (1902–1984)
- Leadership 472

Kronenberger, Louis (1904–1980)
- Privacy 654
- Television 803

Krutch, Joseph Wood (1893–1970)
- Cats 118
- Value 845

Krzyzewski, Mike (1947–)
- Teamwork 800

Kübler-Ross, Elisabeth (1926–2004)
- Choice 144
- Life 493
- Relaxation 686

Kubrick, Stanley (1928–1999)
- Cinema 148
- Risk 707

Kuhn, Thomas (1922–1996)
- Crisis 194

Kulongoski, Ted (1940–)
- Elections 266

Kundera, Milan (1929–)
- Heart 390
- Mind 537
- Nakedness 566
- Novels 577
- Ridicule 705

Kunis, Mila (1983–)
- Teenagers 802

Kunitz, Stanley (1905–2006)
- Desire 225

Kunkel, Fritz (1889–1956)
- Maturity 526

Kunstler, William (1919–1995)
- Cats 118

Kupcinet, Irv (1912–2003)
- God 368

Kuralt, Charles (1934–1997)
- Translation 827

Kurosawa, Akira (1910–1998)
Madness 514
Sanity, ...715
Kurzweil, Ray (1948–)
Order 591
Time 816
Kushner, Rabbi Harold (1935–)
Health 389

L

La Bruyère, Jean de (1645–1696)
Beginnings 85
Generosity 360
Greatness 378
Industry 431
Judges 448
Judgment 450
Loneliness 500
Misfortune 542
The Present 649
Secrets 725
Taste 795
Wit 873
LaBute, Neil (1963–)
Relationships 685
Trust 830
Lacoraire, Jean-Baptiste (1802–1861)
Affection 34
Ladd, Alan (1913–1964)
Strangers 768
La Fontaine, Jean de (1621–1695)
Appearances 58
Faults 311
Flattery 320
Greatness 378
Journalists 444
Sadness 712
Secrets 725
Work 881
Lahiri, Jhumpa (1909–)
Relationships 685
Lahti, Christine (1950–)
Dessert 228
Theater 808
Lahud, Emile (1936–)
Liberation 479
Lahr, John (1941–)
Noise 574
Laing, R. D. (1927–1989)
Disease 241
Insanity 434
Life 493
Sex 733
Lamartine, Alphonse de (1790–1869)
Mothers 557
Lamarr, Hedy (1913–2000)
The Dead, ...207
Subtlety 778
Lamb, Charles (1775–1834)
Children 141
Friendship 346
Lawyers 468
Mothers 557
Nonsense 576
Religion 688
Space 757
Strength 771
Tobacco 817
Weakness 864
Lambert, Madame de (1647–1733)
Pleasure 626
Lamennais (1782–1854)
Sympathy 791
Lamm, Norman (1927–)
Judaism 447
Lamming, George (1927–)
Architecture 60
Lamott, Anne (1954–)
Grace 375
Hope 404
L'Amour, Louis (1908–1988)
Beginnings 86
Democracy 221

Landers, Ann (1918–2002)
Admiration 26
Cheating 136
Conflict 168
Dogs 246
Marriage 522
Opportunity 587
Parenthood 598
The Poor 640
Television 803
Trouble 829
Landon, Letitia Elizabeth (1802–1838)
Devotion 233
Landor, Walter Savage (1775–1864)
Avarice 74
Cooking 178
Thoughts 813
Landrieu, Mary (1955–)
African-Americans 34
Landry, Tom (1924–2000)
Leadership 472
Lang, Andrew (1844–1912)
Books, ...98
Cats 118
Lang, Walter (1896–1972)
Evolution 286
The Garden of Eden 355
Scripture 723
Langella, Frank (1940–)
Taboos 792
Vampires 846
Langland, William (1332–1400)
Necessity 570
Lao-tzu (c. 600 BC) ....
Beauty 82
Beginnings 85
Benevolence 88
Body 95
Desire 225
Disability 238
Disease 241
Endings 269
Feet 314
Greed 380
Guilt 381
Happiness 385
Killing 453
Kindness 454
Kingdoms 455
Knowledge 461
Laws 467
Leadership 472
Love 508
Mourning 561
Mystery 565
Order 591
Patience 604
Patriots 607
Pride 652
Scholars 718
Selfishness 730
Shame 735
Simplicity 741
Status 765
Strength 771
Thieves 810
Ugliness 835
Victory 849
War 860
Water 863, 864
Largent, Steve (1954–)
Cell Phones 122
La Rochefoucauld, François de (1613–1680)
Ability 11
Admiration 27
Advice 33
Aging 39
Ambition 46
Avarice 75
Blessings 94
Bravery 105
Cleverness 153
Conceit 164
Confidence 166
Decency 212
Deeds 215

La Rochefoucauld, François de (cont.)
Diet 235
Envy 278
Failure 297
Fame 301
Faults 311
Flattery 320
Flirting 321
Forgiveness 333
Fortune 335
Friendship 346
Funerals 353
Generosity 360
Glory 365
Grace 375
Gratitude 376
Greatness 378
Health 389
Heart 391
Hypocrisy 412
Illness 421
Jealousy 441
Lies 487
Listening 497
Memory 531
Men 532
Mind 537
Misfortune 542
Motivation 561
Taste 795
Temperament 804
Timidity 517
Treason 827
Valor 840
Vanity 846, 847
Vice 848
Virtue 854
Weakness 864
Wit 873
Larson, Doug (1902–1981)
Age 37
Bosses 102
Computers 164
Conscience 171
English 272
Fools 328
Friendship 346
Snow 750
Spring 761
Utility 843
Lasch, Christopher (1932–1994)
Consumerism 175
Success 781
Lasorda, Tommy (1927–)
Determination 232
La Salle, Saint Jean-Baptiste de (1651–1719)
Manners 520
Laughlin, Robert B. (1950–)
Mothers 557
Lauer, Matt (1957–)
Chocolate 143
Laurents, Arthur (1918–)
Bachelors 77
Lautreamont, Isidore Ducasse (1846–1870)
Despair 227
Doubt 249
Evil 284
Sadness 712
Lavater, Johann Kaspar (1741–1801)
Cheating 136
Crowds 198
God, ...368
Gossip 370
Heroes 397
Men 532
Opportunity 587
Secrets 725
Smiles 749
Trust 830
Law, Vernon Sanders (1930–)
Experience 292
Law, William (1686–1761)
Self 727
Lawrence, D. H. (1885–1930)
Christianity 145
Civilization 151

Lawrence, D. H. (cont.)
- Communism 159
- Democracy 221
- Flowers 323
- Forests 331
- God 368
- Intuition 439, 440
- Men 532
- Mothers 557
- Passion 601
- Pornography 641
- Possessions 642
- Priests 653
- Psychology 662
- Religion 688
- Respectability 696
- Soul 756
- Taste 795
- Togetherness 818
- Trouble 829
- Vision 856

Lawrence, Elizabeth (1904–1985)
- Childhood 137

Lawrence, T. E. (1888–1935)
- Dreams 251

Lawson, Henry (1867–1922)
- Beer 84

Lawson, William (1774–1850)
- Gardens 357

Lay, Kenneth (1942–2006)
- Uncertainty 835

Leach, Penelope (1937–)
- Children 141
- Love 508

Leacock, Stephen (1869–1944)
- Advertising 32
- Dishonesty 241
- Journalism 442
- Newspapers 573
- Suicide 785

Leahy, Frank (1907–1973)
- Ego 264

Leahy, Patrick (1940–)
- Democrats 223
- Opinions 584

Lear, Edward (1812–1888)
- Babies 76

Lear, Norman (1922–)
- Corporations 181

Leary, Timothy (1920–1996)
- Ambition 46
- Men 532

LeBlanc, Matt (1967–)
- Conformity 169

Le Bon, Simon (1958–)
- Love 508
- Style 777

Le Bon, Yasmine (1964–)
- Parenthood 598, 599

Lebowitz, Fran (1950–)
- Achievement 20
- Adults 29
- Alcohol 42
- Children 141
- Consciousness 173
- Conversation 176
- Dogs 246, 247
- Drugs 252
- Food 324, 325
- Humility 409
- Life 493
- Love 508
- Mental Illness 533
- Personality 614
- Pets 618
- Sleep 748
- Stories 767
- Success 781
- Suicide 785
- Writing 889

Lec, Stanislaw (1909–1966)
- Error 281
- Feet 314
- Heaven 393
- Immortality 426

Lec, Stanislaw (cont.)
- Joy 447
- Patience 604
- Silence 739
- Thoughts 813
- Time 816
- Torture 820
- Writing 889

Le Carré, John (1931–)
- The Cold War 155
- Crisis 195

Lecky, W. E. H. (1838–1903)
- Abortion 14

Le Corbusier (1887–1965)
- Architecture 60

Lee, Bruce (1940–1973)
- Achievement 20
- Circumstances 149
- Endurance 269
- Ideas, ...415

Lee, Harold B. (1899–1973)
- Home 400

Lee, Harper (1926–)
- Conscience 171
- Courage 187

Lee, Robert E. (1807–1870)
- Abstinence 15
- War 861

Lee Kuan Yew (1923–)
- Marriage 523

Le Guin, Ursula K. (1929–)
- Adults 29
- Children 141
- Misogyny 543
- Stories 767
- Uncertainty 835

Lehman, John (1942–)
- Ocean 583
- Power 644

Lehrer, Jim, (1934–)
- Journalists 444

Lehrer, Tom (1928–)
- Ability 11
- Communication 158
- Logic 499
- People 610

Leino, Eino (1878–1926)
- Life 493
- Struggle 773

Lem, Stanislaw (1921–2006)
- Dreams 251
- Faith 299
- Reality 677

Lemieux, Mario (1965–)
- Ability 11

Lenclos, Ninon de (1620–1705)
- Boldness 97
- Joy 447
- Love 508
- Starvation 762

L'Engle, Madeleine (1918–)
- Chaos 130
- Maturity 526
- Vulnerability 858

Lenin, Vladimir I. (1870–1924)
- Communism 159
- Fascism 305
- Freedom 337
- Lies 487
- Truth 832

Lennon, John (1940–1980)
- Eyes 294
- God 368
- Life 493
- Love 508
- Misunderstanding 545

Lennon, Sean (1975–)
- Crisis 195

Leno, Jay (1950–)
- Cats 118
- Fish 319
- Friendship 346
- Health 389
- Politicians 635
- Stock Market 766

Leonard, Sugar Ray (1956–)
Boxing 103
Leonardo da Vinci (1452–1519)
Art 64
Authority 73
Censure 126
Clothes 153
Death 208
Determination 232
Experience 292
Genius 362
Judges 449
Kingdoms 455
Mind 537
Nature 569
Obstacels 581
Patience 604
Poetry 630
Praise 646
The Present 649
Punishment 663
Relaxation 686
Rivers 708
Sensuality 731
Simplicity 741
Sophistication 755
Subtlety 778
Theories 809
Understanding 838
Leopold, Aldo (1887–1948)
Conservation 174
Le Pen, Jean-Marie
Anti-Semitism 56
Lerner, Harriet (1944–)
Relationships 685
Lerner, Max (1902–1992)
Censorship 125
Lesage, Alain Rene (1668–1747)
Conceit 164
Lesko, Matthew (1943–)
Lies 487
Salesmen 714
Lessig, Lawrence (1961–)
Anarchy 51
Lessing, Doris (1919–)
Age 37
Aging 39
Cats 118
Faults 311
Happiness 385
Heroes 397
Laughter 464
Learning 475
Political Correctness 633
Sanity 715
Lessing, G. E. (1729–1781)
Heaven 393
Prayer 647
Leszczynski, Stanislaw (1677–1766)
Certainty 127
Doubt 249
Letterman, David (1947–)
Birds 92
Business 112
Statistics 764
Togetherness 818
Letterman, Elmer G. (1897–1982)
Character 132
Letts, Winifred Mary (1882–1936)
Gardens 357
Luntz, Frank (1962–)
Ideology 417
Levant, Oscar (1906–1972)
Alcohol 42
Blame 93
Character 132
Democrats 223
Envy 278
Genius 362
Happiness, ...385
Hollywood 400
Insanity 434
Patients 605
Politicians 635
Republicans 692

Levant, Oscar (cont.)
Time 816
Levenson, Sam (1911–1980)
Birth 92
Children 141
Insanity 434
Parenthood 599
Toys 822
Levin, Bernard (1928–2004)
Tobacco 817
Levi-Strauss, Claude (1908–)
Questions 668
Lewes, George Henry (1817–1878)
Grief 381
Lewin, Kurt (1890–1947)
Achievement 20
Goals 366
Success 781
Lewis, Al (1910–2006)
The Great Depression 379
Lewis, C. S. (1898–1963)
Achievement 20
Adults 29
Affection 34
Art 64
Blessings 94
Christianity 145
Despair 227
Friendship 346
Heaven 393
Hell 395
Jealousy 441
Learning 475
Literature 498
Love 508
Nakedness 566
Nonsense 576
Originality 592
Peace 608
Pride 652
Protestantism 661
Questions 668
Sex 733
War 861
Worship 884
Writing 889
Lewis, John L. (1880–1969)
Corporations 181
Lewis, Ron (1946–)
Conservation 174
Lewis, Sinclair (1885–1951)
Advertising 32
America 48
Emotions 267
Insults 436
Literature 498
Occupation 582
Real Estate 675
Lewis, Wyndham (1882–1957)
The Garden of Eden 356
Ley, Robert (1890–1945)
Burdens 107
Ley, Willy (1906–1969)
Ideas 415
Rivers 708
Libeskind, Daniel (1946–)
Architecture 60
Cities 150
Lichtenberg, Georg C. (1742–1799)
Aging 39
Aristocracy 62
Belief 87
Character 132
Eyes 294
Faces 295
Fallibility 300
Fantasy 304
Fashion 306
Flattery 320
Food 325
Fools 328
Free Will 339
Genius 362
Greatness 378
Ideas 415
Imitation 425

Lichtenberg, Georg C. (cont.)
Journalists 444
Libraries 485
Opinions 584
Peace of Mind 609
Reason 679
Satire 716
Science 721
Sickness 738
Wisdom 871
Liddy, G. Gordon (1930–)
Crime 192
Lieberman, Joe (1942–)
Alliances 44
Community 161
Liebknecht, Karl (1871–1919)
Anarchy 51
Imperialism 427
Liberation 479
Socialism 751
Liebling, A. J. (1904–1963)
Censorship 125
Journalism 442
Newspapers 573
Writing 889
Liebman, Joshua Loth (1907–1948)
Acceptance 17
Light, Judith (1949–)
Bigotry 90
Likert, Rensis (1903–1981)
Loyalty 511
Lille, Alain de (c. 1202)
Gold 369
Lilly, John (1915–2001)
Belief 87
Mind 537
Lin, Maya (1959–)
Resistance 695
Lincoln, Abraham (1809–1865)
Adversity 31
Ancestry 52
Artists 68
Brothers 106
Cats 118
Character 132
Civil War 150
Coffee 154
Corporations 182
Corruption 185
Criticism 197
Democracy 221
Ego 264
Enemies 271
Enjoyment 273
Failure 297
Feelings 314
Fighting 318
Fools 328
Freedom, ...337
Fruit 351
Generals 359
Government 373
Greatness 378
Happiness 385
Ideas 415
Industry 431
Justice 452
Laughter 464
Laws 467
Liberty 482
Lies 487
Life 493
Malice 516
Mercy 534
Nation 567
Oppression 590
Peace 608
Persuasion 616
Policy 632
Popularity 640
Power 645
Presidents 651
Religion 688
Reputation 693
Resolution 695
Responsibility 697

Lincoln, Abraham (cont.)
- Right 706
- Rights 706
- Shepherds 736
- Silence 739
- Slavery 747
- Speaking 758
- Struggle 773
- Success 781
- Tact 792
- Thoughts 813
- Tomorrow 819
- Truth 832
- Unity 840
- Vice, ...848
- Victory 849
- Virtue 854
- Words 878
- Wrong 891

Lindbergh, Anne Morrow (1906–2001)
- Babies 76
- Breakfast 105
- Coffee 154
- Communication 158
- Flowers 323
- Love 508
- Marriage 522
- Quiet 669
- The Sea 723
- Weddings 866
- Wilderness 867
- Winter 870

Lindbergh, Charles August (1902–1974)
- Airplanes 40
- Birds 92
- Loans 499

Linder, John (1942–)
- Patriots 607

Lindh, Anna (1957–2003)
- Terrorism 806

Lindsay, Vachel (1879–1931)
- Cynicism 202

Linklater, Richard (1913–1964)
- Banks 79

Linkletter, Art (1912–)
- Adolescence 28

Lippmann, Walter (1889–1974)
- Ancestors 52
- Leadership 472
- Liberty 482

Lippman, Walter (cont.)
- Opinions 584
- Reality 677
- Seriousness 732
- Statesmen 763
- Thoughts 813

Lisle, Holly (1960–)
- Responsibility 697

Liston, Sonny (1932–1970)
- Boxing 103

Liszt, Franz (1811–1886)
- Artists 68
- Faith 299
- Serenity 731
- Suicide 785

Little Richard (1932–)
- Greed 380

Livingston, Brockholst (1757–1823)
- Judges 449

Lloyd, Robert (1733–1764)
- Affection 34

Lobel, Arnold (1933–1987)
- Books 98

Locke, John (1632–1704)
- Actions 22
- Body 96
- Children 141
- Curiosity 201
- Government 373
- Knowledge 461
- Mind 537
- Society 752
- Thoughts 813

Loesje (1983–)
- Rumors 710

Logan, Joshua (1908–)
Suicide 785
Loggins, Kenny (1948–)
Relationships 685
Lois, George (1937–)
Creativity 190
Originality 592
Lombardi, Vince (1913–1970)
Achievement 20
Champions 127, 128
Confidence 166
Determination 232
Enthusiasm 276
Leadership 472
Losing 503
Society 752
Success 781
Winning 869
London, Jack (1876–1916)
Charity 134
Forests 331
Forgetfulness 331
Inspiration 435
Life 493
Paradox 596
Sharing 736
Long, Barry (1926–2003)
Acceptance 17
Long, Haniel (1888–1956)
Family 303
Loyalty 511
Starvation 762
Long, Russell (1918–)
Taxes 796
Long, Shelley (1949–)
Mothers 557
Longfellow, Henry Wadsworth (1807–1882)
Affection 34
Ambition 46
Books 98
Conceit 164
Destiny 229
Failure 297
Fame 301
Fate 308
Forgiveness 333
Friendship 346
Giving 364
Leadership 472
Mystery 565
The Past 602
Perseverance 613
Simplicity 741
Sorrow 756
Studying 775
Success 781
Tolerance 818
Vision 856
Youth 895
Longworth, Alice Roosevelt (1884–1980)
Ego 264
Philosophy 619
Youth 895
Loomis, Bernard (1923–2006)
Research 694
Lopez, Barry (1945–)
Irony 440
Life 493
Paradox 596
Lorca, Federico Garcia (1898–1936)
The Dead 207
Lorde, Audre (1934–1992)
Revolution 700
Loren, Sophia (1934–)
Beauty 82
Confidence 166
Mistakes 544
Mothers 557
Talent 793
Lorenz, Konrad (1903–1989)
Research 694
Science 721
Lorimer, George Horace (1867–1937)
Money 549

Loti, Pierre (1850–1923)
Cats 118
Kingdoms 455
Lovasik, Lawrence G. (1913–)
Sarcasm 715
Lovecraft, H. P. (1890–1937)
Conformity 169
Dance, ...203
Mercy 534
Mind 537
Lovelock, James (1919–)
Environment 278
Journalists 444
Lowe, Chris (1959–)
Arrogance 63
Lowell, Amy (1874–1925)
Art 64
Personality 614
Lowell, James Russell (1819–1891)
Ancestry 52
Communism 159
Creativity 191
Endurance 269
Fortune, ...335
Mothers 557
Patience 604
Privilege 654
Reputation 693
Twilight 833
Youth 895
Lowell, Lawrence (1856–1943)
Pleasure 626
Lowey, Nita (1937–)
Guns 382
Lowry, Rich (1968–)
Campaigns 113
Lu, Annette (1944–)
Chauvinism 136
Lubac, Henri de (1896–1991)
Habits 382
Lubbock, John (1834–1913)
Solitude 754
Lucado, Max (1955–)
Conflict 168
Lucan (AD 39–65)
Crime 192
Lucas, E. V. (1868–1938)
Cats 118
Cooking 178
Dogs 247
Suspicion 790
Lucas, George (1944–)
Fear 313
Luce, Clare Booth (1903–1987)
Censorship 125
Communism 159
Courage 187
Ego 264
Family 303
Lies 487
Luce, Henry R. (1898–1967)
Journalists 444
Objectivity 579
Lucius Accius (179–86 BC)
Misfortune 542
Lucius Junius Moderatus Columella (c. 100)
Agriculture 40
Luckman, Charles (1909–1999)
America 48
Lucretius (c. 99–55 BC)
Deeds 215
Food 325
Life 493
Rain 672
Religion 689
Struggle 773
Ludwig, Emil (1881–1948)
Friendship 346
Lunden, Joan (1950–)
Anger 54
Forgiveness 333
Positivity 642
Luntz, Frank (1962–)
Corporations 182

Luong, Tran Duc (1937–)
Values 845
Luther, Martin (1483–1546)
Charity 134
Fools 328
Forgiveness 333
God 368
Grace 375
Heart 391
Kingdoms 455
Laughter 464
Marriage 522
Music 563
Preachers 647
Presents 650
Procrastination 655
Prophets 658, 659
Rich and Poor 702
Saints 714
Schools 719
Sin 742
Temperament 804
Truth 832
Violence 851
Luxemburg, Rosa (c. 1870–1919)
Bureaucracy 109
Lynch, Peter (1944–)
Stock Market 766
Lynde, Paul (1926–1982)
Dessert 228
Lynd, Robert (1879–1949)
Birds 92
Lynes, Russell (1910–1991)
Journalists 444
Tennis 805
Lynn, Loretta (1934–)
Babies 76
Lyon, Bill (1865–1943)
Failure 298
Lyons, Jimmy (1931–1986)
Laziness 469
Lyotard, Jean-François (1924–1998)
Self 727

M

Ma, Yo-Yo (1955–)
Strangers 768
MacArthur, General Douglas (1880–1964)
Commanders 155
Earth 254
Leadership 472
Opportunity 587
Security 726
Soldiers 753
Soul 756
Macaulay, Dame Rose (1881–1958)
Books 98
Delusion 219
Doctors 244
Macaulay, Lord Thomas Babington (1800–1859)
Devotion 233
Flattery 320
Generalizations 358
Persuasion 616
Pleasure 626
Power 645
Religion 689
Speaking 758
Trade 522
Virtue 854
Welfare 867
MacDonald, George (1824–1905)
Acceptance 17
Difficulty 236
Friendship 346
Idleness 418
Political Correctness 633
Riches 704
MacDonald, John D. (1916–1986)
Cats 118
MacDonald, Ross (1915–1983)
California 113
Ocean 583
Wrong 891

Machiavelli, Niccolò (1469–1527)
Ambition 46
Community 161
Ego 264
Favors 311
Flattery 321
Free Will 339
Honor 402
Judges 449
Loss 505
Property 658
Revenge 699
Status Quo 766
Vice, ...848
War 861
MacKenzie, Sir Compton (1883–1972)
Cats 118
Mackintosh, James (1765–1832)
Maxims 527
MacLaine, Shirley (1934–)
Fear 313
Laughter 464
Strangers 768
Maclean, Norman (1902–1990)
Floods 322
Time 816
Words 878
MacLeish, Archibald (1892–1982)
Brothers 106
Liberation 479
Libraries 485
Macmillan, Harold (1894–1986)
Decency 212
Politicians 635
Statesmen 763
Tradition 823
Macnee, Patrick (1922–)
Chauvinism 136
Madison, James (1751–1836)
Angels 53
Commerce 157
Majorities 515
Minorities 539
Property 658
Rights 707
Madonna (1958–)
Consciousness 173
Pleasure 626
Virginity 852
Maeterlinck, Maurice (1862–1949)
Abstinence 15
Conformity 169
Mothers 557
Pets 618
Silence 739
Maher, Bill (1956–)
Abstinence 15
Men 532
Suicide 785
Women 876
Worship 884
Maher, Daniel (1881–1916)
Confidence 166
Mahoney, Roger (1936–)
Crisis 195
Mahfouz, Naguib (1911–2006)
Heresy 396
Mailer, Norman (1923–2007)
Change 129
Defiance 217
Heroes 397
Journalism 442
Journalists 444
Men 532
Newspapers 573
Retreat 698
Sentimentality 731
Sex 733
Sophistication 755
Maister, Joseph de (1753–1821)
Pleasure 626
Makiewicz, Herman J. (1897–1953)
Memory 531
Tragedy 825
Malamud, Bernard (1914–1986)
Joy 447

Malamud, Bernard (cont.)
Life 493
Malcolm, Janet (1934–)
Journalists 444
Malcolm X (1925–1965)
Anger 54
Freedom 337
Justice 452
Media 528
Patriotism 606
Peace 608
Power 645
Preachers 648
Reality 677
Mallet, David (1705–1765)
Uncertainty 835
Malloch, Douglas (1877–1938)
Gardens 357
Malloy, Reverend Edward A. (1941–)
Education 260
Malone, Jena (1984–)
Adolescence 28
Homosexuality 401
Malory, Thomas (1405–1471)
Knights 459
Malraux, André (1901–1976)
Communism 159
Duty 253
Leadership 472
Mystery 565
Quotations 670
Maltin, Leonard (1950–)
Cinema 148
Maltz, Maxwell (1899–1975)
Crisis 195
Goals 366
Obstacles 581
Self-Esteem 729
Mamet, David (1947–)
Political Correctness 633
Mandela, Nelson (1918–)
Change 129
Communism 160
Defiance 217
Mandelbrot, Benoit (1924–)
Competition 162
Mandelson, Peter (1953–)
Ambassadors 45
Mandino, Og (1923–1996)
Adversity 31
Conceit 165
Darkness 205
Disease 241
Gold 369
Grace 375
Individualism 430
Life 493
Love 508
Manners 520
Plants 623
Questions 668
Students 774
Success 781
Manet, Edourad (1832–1883)
Insults 436
Manilius (c. 1 BC)
Pleasure 626
Mankiewicz, Herman J. (1897–1953)
Aging 39
Mann, Horace (1796–1859)
Angels 53
Benevolence 88
Books 98
Brains 104
Generosity 360
Habits 382
Humanity 407
Ignorance 420
Reading 674
Rich and Poor 703
Teachers 798
Victory 849
Mann, Thomas (1875–1955)
War 861
Writing 889

Mannes, Marya (1904–1990)
Emotions 267
Generosity 360
Intelligence 437
Reason 679
Seduction 726
Strangers 768
Mansfield, Katherine (1888–1923)
Books 98
Failure 298
Fiction 317
Friendship 346
Individualism 429
Opinions 585
Reading 674
Regret 683
Risk 707
Sharing 736
Manski, Ben (1974–)
Corporations 182
Manson, Charles (1934–)
Remorse 690
Manson, Marilyn (1969–)
Criticism 197
Media 528
Victimization 849
Wishes 873
Manuel, Don Juan (1282–1349)
Praise 646
Manutius, Aldus (1449–1515)
Business 112
Mao Tse-Tung (1893–1976)
Communism 160
Exercise 289
Perseverance 613
Politics 637
Struggle 773
War 861
Weapons 866
Wounds 885
Maramotti, Achille (1927–2005)
Crisis 195
Marc, Franz (1880–1916)
Defiance 217
Marconi, Guglielmo (1874–1937)
Humanity 407
Struggle 773
Marcus Aurelius Antoninus (121–180)
Anger 54
Beauty 82
Change 129
Circumstances 149
Complaints 163
Death 208
Dignity 237
The Future 354
Happiness 385
Heartbreak 392
Love 509
Majorities 515
Oblivion 580
Opinions 585
Pain 593
Passion 601
Performance 612
Perspective 615
Praise 646
Revenge 699
Rich and Poor 703
Soul 757
Strength 771
Thoughts 813
Tomorrow 819
Victory 849
Virtue 854
Yesterday 893
Marcus Fabius Quintilianus (c. AD 35–100)
Ambition 46
Marcus Valerius Martialis (AD 40–103)
Exercise 289
Fatigue 310
Gifts 363
Marden, Orison Swett (1850–1924)
Ability 11
Determination 232

Marden, Orison Swett (cont.)
Enjoyment 273
Failure 298
Forgiveness 333
Fun 352
Imagination 424
Joy 447
Laughter 464
Nature 569
Obstacles 581
Opportunity 587
Thoughts 813
Vision 856
Youth 895
Margolius, Hans (1902–1984)
Perception 610
Quiet 669
Marion, Francis (1732–1795)
Promises 657
Maritain, Jacques (1882–1973)
Gratitude 377
Markham, Edwin (1852–1940)
Eternity 282
Life 493
Rust 710
Marley, Bob (1945–1981)
Music 563
Pain 594
Slavery 747
Wisdom 871
Marlowe, Christopher (1564–1593)
Heaven 393
Hell 395
Murder 562
Sin 742
Marquis, Don (1878–1937)
Delusion 219
Earth 254
Fishing 319
Happiness 385
Honesty 402
Humanity 408
Lies 488
Middle Age 534
Pity 622
Procrastination 655
Punctuality 663
Unhappiness 839
Work 881
Marshall, Alfred (1842–1924)
Economics 257
Marshall, Garry (1934–)
Mistakes 544
Marshall, George C. (1880–1959)
Peace 608
Marshall, John (1755–1835)
Class 152
Marshall, Peter (1902–1949)
Ego 264
Marshall, Thurgood (1908–1993)
Censorship 125
Compassion 162
Decency 212
Marston, John (1576–1634)
Danger 204
Safety 713
Marston, Ralph (1900–1965)
Attitude 72
Marston, William Moulton (1893–1947)
Crisis 195
Marti, Jose (1853–1895)
Suffering 783
Martialis, Marcus Valerius (AD 40–103)
Pleasure 626
Martin, Dean (1917–1995)
Alcohol 42
Martin, Judith (1938–)
America 48
Birth 92
Charm 135
Class 152
Communication 158
Conversation 176
Effort 262
Manners 520

Martin, Mary (1913–1990)
Wishes 872
Martin, Robert (1947–)
Students 774
Martin, Steve (1945–)
Art 64
Chaos 130
Entertainment 274
Kisses 457
Love 509
Mind 537
Martineau, Harriet (1802–1876)
Reading 674
Marx, Chico (1891–1961)
Kisses 457
Marx, Groucho (1890–1977)
Age 37
Books 99
Brides 105
Cats 118
Children 141
Dance 203
Democrats 223
Earthquakes 255
Evening 283
Fruit 351
Justice 452
Money 549
Mothers 557
Music 563
Obscenity 580
Parenthood 599
Reading 674
Relatives 685
Socialism 751
Television 803
Wives 875
Marx, Karl (1818–1883)
Avarice 75
Bureaucracy 109
Class 152
Communism 160
Competition 163
Democracy 221
Fools 328
Machines 513
Masturbation 524
Opportunity 587
Philosophy 619
Reason 679
Rich and Poor 703
Science 721
Struggle 773
Unity 840
Utility 843
Value 845
Wages 858
Masaryk, Jan (1886–1948)
Rulers 710
Masefield, John (1878–1967)
Flowers 323
Laughter 464
Maslow, Abraham (1908–1970)
Ability 11
Conflict 168
Economics 258
Experts 293
Growth 381
Mistakes 544
Objectivity 579
Safety 713
Value 845
Mason, Jackie (1934–)
Health 389
Money 549
Profit 655
Mason, James (1909–1984)
Cats 118
Mason, John Mitchell (1770–1829)
Sincerity 743
Matheson, Richard (1926–)
Hell 394
Mathewson, Christy (1880–1925)
Baseball 79

Matisse, Henri (1869–1954)
Art 64
Artists 68
Fog 323
Rhythm 702
Vision 856
Witchcraft 874
Work 881
Youth 895
Mattea, Kathy (1959–)
Dessert 228
Matthau, Carol (1924–2003)
Age 37
Old Age 583
Mauch, Gene (1925–2005)
Leadership 472
Losing 503
Managers 517
Maugham, W. Somerset (1874–1965)
Age 37
Art 64
Beauty 82
Books 99
Censure 126
Character 132
Children 141
Contempt, ...176
Criticism 197
Death 209
Dignity 237
Ego 264
Excess 288
Fiction 317
Food 325
Forgiveness 333
Friendship 346
The Future 354
Husbands 412
Illusion 422
Indifference 429
Love 509
Mediocrity 529
Mistakes 544
Moderation 546
Money 549
Old Age 583
The Past 602
Pleasure 626
Poetry 630
Police 632
Politicians 635
Praise 646
Prose 659
Reason 679
Refuge 683
Sentimentality 731
Statesmen 763
Time 816
Tolerance 818
Tradition 823
Unity 840
Wives 875
The World 883
Writing 889
Youth 895
Maupassant, Guy de (1850–1893)
Beds 83
Boredom 101
Patriotism 606
Mauriac, François (1885–1970)
Friendship 346
Maurois, André (1885–1967)
Eccentricity 255
Enemies 271
Fiction 317
Humanity 408
Literature 498
Marriage 522
The Middle Ages 535
Modesty 547
Retreat 698
Self-Confidence 728
Style 777
Maxwell, Elsa (1883–1963)
Laughter 464

Maxwell, John (1586–1647)
Life 494
Maxwell, John C. (1947–)
Executives 289
Leadership 473
Lies 488
Motivation 561
Mythology 566
Maxwell, Neil A. (1926–2004)
Blessings 94
May, Lola (1923–2007)
Teachers 798
May, Rollo (1909–1994)
Apathy 57
Conformity 169
Martyrs 523
Maynard, Joyce (1953–)
Home 400
Mazzini, Giuseppe (1805–1872)
Family 303
Heart 391
McAdoo, William G.
Ignorance 420
McAleese, Mary (1951–)
Decency 212
McAlindon, Harold R. (1940–)
Leadership 473
Mind 537
McCambridge, Mercedes (1916–2004)
Alcohol 42
McCarthy, Colman (1938–)
Pacifism 592
McCarthy, Eugene (1916–2005)
Bureaucracy 109
Efficiency 262
Football 330
Liberty 482
Politics 638
McCarthy, John (1815–1893)
Thieves 810
McCarthy, Mary (1912–1989)
Bureaucracy 110
Retreat 698
Status 765
McCord, Kent (1942–)
Teenagers 802
McCormick, Anne O'Hare (1882–1954)
Punishment 663
McCorvey, Norma (1947–)
Abortion 14
McCulloch-Williams, Martha (1848–1934)
Cooking 178
McCullough, David (1933–)
Success 781
Work 881
McDonough, Will (1935–2003)
Journalists 445
McDougal, Karen (1971–)
Dessert 228
McFadden, Cyra (1939–)
Food 325
McFee, William (1881–1966)
Fate 308
McGeady, Sister Mary Rose (1928–)
Joy 447
McGill, Bryant H. (1969–)
Architects 59
Courtesy 188
Forgiveness 333
Love 509
McGraw, Phil (1950–)
Abortion 14
McGuire, Al (1931–2001)
Losing 503
McKay, Claude (1889–1948)
The Moon 551
McKay, David O. (1873–1970 .....
Bigotry 90
Mothers 557
McKellen, Ian (1939–)
The Bible 89
Religion 689
McKenna, Aline Brosh (1967–)
Diet 235
McKenna, Richard (1913–1964)
Banks 79

McKenna, Richard (cont.)
The Dead 207
McKinney, Cynthia (1955–)
African-Americans 35
McLaughlin, John (1942–)
Rhythm 702
McLaughlin, Mignon (1913–1983)
Bosses 102
Children 141
Courage 187
Friendship, ...346
Ignorance 420
Innocence 434
Listening 497
Marriage 522
Opportunity 587
Women 876
McLuhan, Marshall (1911–1980)
Class 152
Debt, ...211
Education 260
Entertainment 274
Media 528
Nationalism 568
Privacy 654
Uselessness 843
McMillan, Terry (1951–)
Siblings 737
McNabb, Vincent (1868–1943)
Beauty 82
McNamara, Robert S. (1916–)
Brains 104
Heart 391
McQuarrie, Christopher (1968–)
Satan 715
McTiernan, John (1951–)
Entertainment 274
McWilliams, Peter (1949–2000)
Blessings 94
Pain 594
Peace 608
Peace of Mind 609
Suicide 785
Thoughts 813
Mead, Edward Shepherd (1914–1994)
Computers 164
Mead, George H. (1863–1931)
Individualism 430
Self 728
Mead, Margaret (1901–1978)
Bathrooms 80
Community 161
Information 432
Sisters 743
Meadows, Tim (1961–)
African-Americans 35
Meaney, Colm (1953–)
Siblings 737
Means, Russell (1939–)
Corporations 182
Medawar, P. B. (1915–)
Ideas 415
Medina, Harold R. (1888–1990)
Censorship 125
Meek, Kendrick (1966–)
Defiance 217
Meir, Golda (1898–1978)
Achievement 20
Heart 391
Killing 453
Liberation 479
The Poor 640
Rich and Poor 703
Mellon, Andrew (1855–1937)
Corporations 182
Mellor, David (1949–)
Lawyers 468
Meltzer, Bernard (1917–1998)
Friendship 346
Melville, Herman (1819–1891)
Cause and Effect 120
Home 400
Humanity 408
Imitation 425
Insanity 434
Leisure 476

Melville, Herman (cont.)
- Ocean 583
- Originality 592
- Words 878

Menander (342–292 BC)
- Bravery 105
- Character 133
- Courage 187
- Culture 199
- Despair 227
- Determination 232
- Hair 383
- Money 549
- Skill 745
- Wisdom 871
- Work 881

Mencius (371–289 BC)
- Heaven 393
- Siblings 737
- Sincerity 743

Mencken, H. L. (1880–1956)
- Adultery 28
- Age 37
- Animals 55
- Babies 76
- Bachelors 78
- Baseball 79
- Belief 87
- Billiards 90
- Boredom 101
- Celebrities 122
- Communism 160
- Conscience 171
- Criticism 197
- Cynicism 202
- Decency 212
- Delusion 220
- Democracy 221, 222
- Distrust 242
- Education 260
- Elections 266
- Fate 308
- Flirting 321
- Flowers 323
- Football 330
- God 368
- Golf 370
- Government 373
- Heaven 393
- Heroes 397
- Honor 402
- Humanity 408
- Husbands 412
- Idealism 413
- Ideas 415
- Imagination 424
- Injustice, ...433
- Journalism 442
- Judges 449
- Juries 451
- Justice 452
- Kisses 457
- Laws 467
- Lies 488
- Love 509
- Money 549
- Morality 551
- Newspapers 573
- Occupation 582
- Oppression 590
- Patriots 607
- Philosophy 619
- Poetry 630
- Politicians 635
- Politics 638
- Prejudice 648
- Privilege 654
- Religion 689
- Republicans 692
- Self-Respect 729
- Suicide 785
- Taxes 796
- Temptaion 804
- Theology 809
- Theories 809
- Trust 830

Mencken, H. L. (cont.)
- Universities 843
- Wages 858
- Wisdom 871
- Women 876
- Worship 884
- Wrong 891

Mendelssohn, Moses (1729–1786)
- Judaism 447

Mendes, Sam (1965–)
- Cinema 148

Menninger, Dr. Karl A. (1893–1990)
- Hope 404
- Listening 497
- Normalcy 577
- Reality 677
- Suicide 785, 786

Mercier, Alfred (1816–1894)
- Pleasure 626

Mercury, Freddie (1946–1991)
- Charisma 133

Meredith, George (1963–)
- Cooking 178
- Eyes 294

Mermillod, Cardinal Gaspard
- Mothers 557

Mermillod, Cardinal Gaspard (cont.)
- Pride 652

Merton, Thomas (1915–1968)
- Art 64
- Choice 144
- Humility 409
- Suffering 783

Metheny, Pat (1954–)
- Rhythm 702

Meynell, Alice (1847–1922)
- Happiness 385

Michaels, Leonard (1933–2003)
- Cats 118

Michelangelo (1475–1564)
- Achievement 20
- Brains 104
- Danger 204
- Desire 225
- Painting 595
- Perfection 611

Midler, Bette (1945–)
- Cats 118
- Conformity 169

Mies van der Rohe, Ludwig (1886–1969)
- Architecture 60

Milarepa (c. 1052–1135)
- Meditation 530

Milgram, Stanley (1933–1984)
- Conformity 170

Milius, John (1944–)
- Morality 551

Mill, John Stuart (1806–1873)
- Bureaucracy 110
- Censorship 125
- Decisions 214
- Eccentricity 255, 256
- Freedom 337
- Imitation 425
- Liberty 482
- Patriotism 606
- Persecution 612
- Power 645
- Protestantism 661
- Safety 713
- Statesmen 764
- Tradition 823
- War 861

Millar, Margaret (1915–1994)
- Conversation 176

Millay, Edna St. Vincent (1892–1950)
- Advice 33
- Childhood 137
- Humanity 408
- Kingdoms, ...455
- Life 494

Mille, Agnes de (1909–1993)
- Destiny 229

Miller, Arthur (1915–2005)
- Alienation 44

Miller, Arthur (cont.)
Failure 298
Fallibility 300
Imitation 425
Politics 638
Profit 655
Spirit 759
Suicide 786
Miller, Alfred W. (1892–1983)
Fishing 319
Miller, Frank (1957–)
Knights 459
Miller, Henry (1891–1980)
Acceptance 18
Anarchy 51
Beauty 82
Body 96
Chaos 130
Devotion 233
Failure 298
Fame 301
Food 325
Force 330
Gender 358
Greatness 379
Growth 381
Heroes 397
Imagination 424
Killing 453
Lies 488
Life 494
Literature 498
Losing 503
Mystery 565
Philosophy 619
Salvation 714
The World 883
Youth 896
Miller, Hugh (1802–1856)
Opportunity 587
Problems 654
Miller, Johnny (1947–)
Serenity 731
Miller, Jonathan (1934–)
Holidays 400
Miller, Keith (191–2004)
Kingdoms 455
Milligan, Spike (1918–2002)
Enemies 271
Money 549
Quiet 669
Millman, Dan (1946–)
Change 129
Moderation 546
Pain 594
Milne, A. A. (1882–1956)
Agnosticism 40
Discovery 240
Human Nature 405
Majorities 515
Minorities 539
Milton, John (1608–1674)
Agriculture 40
Change 129
Childhood 137
Confidence 166
Conscience 171
Free Will 339
Heaven 393
Hell 395
Knowledge 461
Liberty 482
Mind 537
Opinions 585
Mingus, Charles (1922–1979)
Creativity 191
Minnelli, Liza (1946–)
Reality 677
Minow, Newton (1926–)
Responsibility 697
Minsky, Marvin (1927–)
Realism 676
Television 803
Mises, Ludwig von (1881–1973)
Economics 258
Ideology 417

The Mishnah
Leisure 477
Mitchard, Jacquelyn (1955–)
Cats 118
Pets 618
Mitchell, Adrian (1932–)
People 610
Poetry 630
Mitchell, Beverly (1981–)
Teenagers 802
Mitchell, John N. (1913–1988)
Life 494
Mitchell, Margaret (1900–1949)
Hunger 411
Losing 503
Reputation 693
Women 876
Mitford, Nancy (1904–1973)
Aristocracy 62
Miyazawa, Kenji (1896–1933)
Pain 594
Mizner, Wilson (1876–1933)
Birth 92
Mizner, Wilson (cont.)
Death 209
Doubt 249
Education 261
Ego 264
Faith 299
Flattery 321
Friendship 346
Gambling 355
Listening 497
Plagiarism 622
Research 694
Sports 760
Suspicion 790
Writing 889
Wrong 892
Moby (1965–)
Celebrities 122
Mohr, Jay (1970–)
Yankees 892
Molière (1622–1673)
Fruit, ...351
Innocence 434
Insults 436
Integrity 436
Praise 646
Prostitution 660
Slander 745
Sobriety 750
Solitude 754
Speaking 758
Trees 828
Vice 848
Virtue 854
Writing 889
Moltke, Helmuth von (1800–1891)
Risk 707
Monod, Adolph (1802–1856)
Danger 204
Monroe, Marilyn (1926–1962)
Hollywood 400
Monson, Thomas S. (1927–)
Wishes 873
Work 881
Montagu, Ashley (1905–1999)
Certainty 127
Science 721
Montagu, Lady Mary Wortley (1689–1762)
Entertainment 274
Pleasure 626
Reading 674
Sisters 743
Montague, C. E. (1867–1928)
Quotations 670
Montague, William Pepperell (1873–1953)
Skeptics 745
Montaigne, Michel de (1533–1592)
Ambition 46
Appearances 58
Books 99
Conversation 176
Defeat 216
Devotion 234

Montaigne, Michel de (cont.)
- Education 261
- Fame 301
- Fashion 306
- Food 325
- Fools 328
- Friendship 347
- Impatience 426, 427
- Joy 447
- Kingdoms 455
- Kitchens 458
- Lies 488
- Malice 516
- Memory 531
- Men 532
- Noise 574
- Praise 646
- Reason 679
- Valor 844
- Wit 874

Montalvo, Juan Ecuadorean (1832–1889)
- Apathy 57

Montapert, Alfred A. (1906–)
- Fate 308
- Greed 380

Montegut, Jean-Baptiste (1825–1895)
- Music 564

Montesquieu, Charles de (1689–1755)
- Democracy 222
- Equality 280
- Kingdoms 455
- Laws 467
- Tyranny 834
- Writing 889

Montessori, Maria (1870–1952)
- Discipline 239
- Liberty 482
- Teachers 798

Montgomery, Lucy Maud (1874–1942)
- Friendship 347

Moore, Brian (1921–1999)
- Research 694
- Writing 889

Moore, George A. (1852–1933)
- Difficulty 236

Moore, George Edward (1873–1958)
- Home 401
- Husbands 412
- Plagiarism 622

Moore, Grace (1898–1947)
- Ability 11

Moore, Henry (1898–1986)
- Discipline 239

Moore, Marianne (1887–1972)
- Impatience 427
- Sarcasm 715

Moore, Mary Tyler (1936–)
- Bravery 105
- Courage 187
- Pain 594
- Strangers 769

Moore, Michael (1954–)
- Corporations 182

Moore, Roger (1927–)
- Acting 22

Moore, Thomas (1779–1852)
- Healing 388

Moore-Brabazon, Lord John (1884–1964)
- Writing 889

Moraga, Cherrie (1952—)
- Emotions 267
- Hunger 411
- Transformation 826

More, Hannah (1745–1833)
- Devotion 234
- Obstacles 581

More, Sir Thomas (1478–1535)
- Gold 369
- Money 549
- Sorrow 756
- Wounds 885

Moreau, Jeanne (1928–)
- Love 509

Morely, John (1838–1923)
- Censorship 125

Morgan, Julia (1872–1957)
Architecture 60
Morgan, Robin (1941–)
Men 532
Sexism 734
Morgan, Ted (1932–)
Madness 514
Morley, Christopher (1890–1957)
Books, ... 99
Clouds 154
Conflict 168
Happiness 385
Life 494
Mind 537
Nonconformity 575
Old Age 584
Success 781
Telephones 802
The Universe 842
Morley, Robert (1908–1992)
Work 881
Morrison, Jim (1943–1971)
Curiosity 201
Emotions 267
Friendship 347
Hair 383
Music 564
Reality 677
Temperament 804
Morrison, Toni (1931–)
Love 509
Mothers 557
Racism 671
Parenthood 599
Morrissey, Steven (1959–)
Artists 68
Morrow, Dwight (1873–1931)
Ego 264
Motley, Constance Baker (1921–2005)
Segregation 726
Sexism 734
Motley, John L. (1814–1877)
Deeds 215
Mouskouri, Nana (1934–)
Beginnings 85
Moyers, Bill (1934–)
Ideology 417
Journalists 445
Strangers 769
Moynihan, Daniel P. (1927–2003)
Corporations 182
Mozart, Wolfgang Amadeus (1756–1791)
Genius 362
Life 494
Love 509
Praise 646
Mudd, Roger (1928–)
Journalists 445
Muggeridge, Malcolm (1903–1990)
Acceptance 18
Kingdoms 455
Muhammad (c. 570–632)
Perspiration 615
Spirituality 759
Muir, John (1838–1914)
Imagination 424
Mull, Martin (1943–)
Alcohol 42
Muller, Max (1823–1900)
Strangers 769
Muller, Robert (1944–)
Forgiveness 333
Love 509
Mulroney, Brian (1939–)
Bureaucracy 110
Mumford, Ethel (1878–1940)
Family 303
Relatives 685
Mumford, Lewis (1895–1990)
Godfathers 376
Humor 410
Munger, T. T. (1883–1975)
Doubt 249
Personality 614
Munro, Alice (1931–)
Endings 269

Munro, Alice (cont.)
Reconciliation 680
Munro, H. H. (1870–1916)
Age 37
Cats 118
Statesmen 764
Muray, Nickolas (1892–1965)
Photography 621
Murdoch, Iris (1919–1999)
Cunning 200
Dogs 247
Fantasy 304
Indifference 429
Love 509
Morality 552
Murphy, Maureen (1952–)
Politicians 636
Murphy, Timothy (1952–)
Amnesty 50
Murray, Elizabeth (1940–)
Gardens 357
Murray, William, Lord Mansfield (1705–1793)
Popularity 640
Murrow, Edward R. (1908–1965)
Difficulty 236
Prejudice 648
Musa, Said (1944–)
Chauvinism 136
Independence 428
Musashi, Miyamoto (1584–1645)
Acceptance 17
Death 209
Perception 610
Strategy 770
Warriors 863
Mussolini, Benito (1883–1945)
Crowds 198
Epitaphs 279
Fascism 305
Saints 714
Myers, Mike (1963–)
Marriage 522
Political Correctness 633
Myerson, Abraham (1881–1948)
Dissatisfaction 242

N

Nabokov, Vladimir (1899–1977)
Crime 192
Cruelty 198
Oppression 590
Satire 716
Stupidity 775
Nachman, Rabbi (1772–1810)
Riches 704
Nader, Ralph (1934–)
Bureaucracy 110
Corporations 182
Leadership 473
Strangers 769
Nagauji, Hôjô (1432–1519)
Reality 677
Naisbitt, John (1929–)
Lawyers 468
Nanak, Guru (1469–1539)
Delusion 219
Theft 808
Yoga 893
Nansen, Fridjof (1861–1930)
Distrust,....................242
Naoshige, Nabeshima (1538–1618)
Bravery 105
Intelligence 437
Napier, Sir William (1785–1860)
Retreat 698
Napoléon I (1769–1821)
Ability 11
Beds 83
Doctors 244
Enemies 271
Fame 301
Fear 313
Fools 328
Friendship 347

Napoléon I (cont.)
Generals 359
Glory 365
Heroes 397
History 399
Imagination 424
Leadership 473
Martyrs 523
Medicine 528
Mistakes 544
Motivation 561
Noise 574
Obscurity 580
Priests 653
Quiet 669
Religion 689
Remedies 690
Retreat 698
Revolution 701
Rights 707
Secrets 725
Senses 730
Skepticism 744
Soldiers 753
Statesmen 764
Success 781
Victory 850
Virtue 854
Nash, Ogden (1902–1971)
Age 37
Beds 83
Children 141
Dogs 247
Family 303
Gardens 357
Middle Age 534
Parenthood 599
Pets 618
Remorse 690
Strangers 769
Trees 828
Work 881
Nathan, George Jean (1882–1958)
Aristocracy 62
Beer 84
Patriotism 606
Real Estate 675
Navratilova, Martina (1956–)
Disability 238
Losing 503
Victory 850
Nazarbayev, Nursultan (1940–)
Terrorism 806
Neal, Patricia (1926–)
Miracles 540
Positivity 643
Teachers 798
Neaves, Charles (1800–1876)
Ego 264
Neeson, Liam (1952–)
Adultery 29
Nehru, Jawaharlal (1889–1964)
Capitalism 115
Crisis 195
Eyes 294
Facts 295
Free Will 339
Life 494
Objectives 579
Peace 608
Peace of Mind 609
Rich and Poor 703
Risk 707
Socialism 751
War 861
Nelson, Judd (1959–)
Alienation 44
Youth 896
Nelson, Willie (1933–)
Thoughts 813
Netanyahu, Benjamin (1949–)
Defiance 217
Neumann, Johann von (1903–1957)
Mathematics 525

Nevelson, Louise (1900–1988)
Age 37
Creativity 191
Nevill, Dorothy (1826–1913)
Conversation 176
Newcomb, Simon (1835–1909)
Class 152
Newhall, Nancy (1908–1974)
Conservation 174
Humanity 408
Newhart, Bob (1929–)
Happiness 385
Laughter 464
Taboos 792
Newmark, Craig (1952–)
Crime 192
Newman, John Henry (1801–1890)
Ability 11
Facts 295
Torture 820
Pleasure 626
Virtue 854
Newman, Paul (1925–)
Suckers 782
Newton, Sir Isaac (1642–1727)
Discovery 240
Leadership 473
Patience 604
Tact 792
Truth 832
Talent 793
Newton, Juice (1952–)
Yesterday 893
Newton-John, Olivia (1948–)
Possessions 642
Nicarchus (c. 100)
Doctors 244
Nicholson, Ben (1894–1982)
Consumerism 175
Nicholson, Jack (1937–)
Beer 84
Children 141
Nicklaus, Jack (1940–)
Achievement 20
Expectations 290
Remedies 90
Nidetch, Jean (1923–)
Choice 144
Destiny 229
Niebuhr, Reinhold (1892–)
Grace 375
Journalism 442, 443
Journalists 445
Preachers 648
Serenity 732
Nietzsche, Friedrich (1844–1900)
Absurdity 16
Alcohol 42
Arguments 61
Arrogance 63
Art 64
Artists 68
Beggars 85
Blunders 95
Boredom 101
Cause and Effect 120, 121
Chaos 130
Christianity 145
Conformity 170
Consciousness 173
Corruption 185
Dance 203
Danger 204
Determination 232
Distrust 242
Dogs 247
Education 261
Enemies 271
Enjoyment 273
Epitaphs 279
Eyes 294
Facts 296
Fallibility 300
Family 303
Fighting 318

Nietzsche, Friedrich (cont.)
- Forgetfulness 331
- Forgiveness 333
- Frankness 335
- Freedom 337
- Free Will 339
- God 368
- Heaven 393
- Individuals 430
- Insanity 434
- Intoxication 439
- Jesus 441
- Kitchens 458
- Knowledge 461
- Laughter 464
- Lies 488
- Life 494
- Love 509
- Madness 514
- Mankind 518
- Marriage 522
- Memory 531
- Men 532
- Misunderstanding 545
- Morality 552
- Mothers 557
- Music 564
- Nobility 574
- Opinions 585
- The Past 603
- Physics 621
- Poetry 630
- Praise 646
- Pride 652
- Punishment 663
- Questions 668
- Reason 679
- Resolution 695
- Science 721
- Sensuality 731
- Shadows 734
- Shame 735
- Spirit 759
- Stupidity 775
- Suicide 786
- Taste 795
- Thoughts 813
- The Unconcious 836
- Understanding 838
- Unity 840
- Vanity 847
- Wisdom 872
- Wit 874
- Women 876
- The World 883
- Youth 896

Niger, Samuel (1883–1956)
- Libraries 485

Nightingale, Earl (1921–1989)
- Achievement 21
- Actions 22
- Attitude 72
- Creativity 191
- Danger 204
- Excellence 287
- Expectations 290
- Goals 366
- Life 494
- Opportunity 587
- Sympathy 791
- Thoughts 813
- Writing 889

Nightingale, Florence (1820–1910)
- Actions 22

Nikolais, Alwin (1910–1993)
- Cats 118

Nimoy, Leonard (1931–)
- Sharing 736

Nin, Anaïs (1903–1977)
- Anxiety 57
- Courage 187
- Freedom 337
- Friendship 347
- Idealism 413
- Intoxication 439
- Loss 504

Nin, Anaïs (cont.)
Pain 594
Risk 707
The Unconcious 836
Nisker, Wes (1942—)
Revolution 701
Transformation 826
Nistelrooy, Ruud van (1976–)
Losing 503
Nixon, Richard M. (1913–1994)
Bureaucracy 110
Crisis 195
Government 373
Hate 387
Losing 503
Promises 657
Sadness 712
Sports 760
Winning 869
Nizer, Louis (1902–1994)
Fishing 319
Noah, Yannick (1960–)
Tennis 805
Nobel, Alfred Bernhard (1833–1896)
Hope 404
Truth 832
Nolde, Emil (1867–1956)
Artists 68
Noonan, Peggy (1950–)
Cynicism 202
Nordau, Max (1849–1923)
Civilization 151
Norman, Greg (1955–)
Life 494
Norris, Kathleen (1880–1966)
Books 99
Goals 367
Marriage 522
Nouwan, Henri (1932–1996)
Friendship 347
Healing 388
Novalis (1772–1801)
Body 96
The Universe 842
Nowlan, Alden (1933–1983)
Adults 29
Nussbaum, Martha (1947–)
Trust 830
Nye, Bill (1955–)
Humor 410
Irony 440
Laughter 465
Nye, Edgar Wilson (1850–1896)
Music 564

O

Oakley, Ann (1944–)
Mothers 557
Oates, John (1948–)
Relationships 685
Oates, Joyce Carol (1938–)
Boxing 103, 104
Intellectuals 437
Physics 621
Obama, Barack (1961–)
Patriots 607
O'Brien, Conan (1963–)
Alcohol 43
Delusion, ...220
Laughter 465
O'Brien, Ed (1968–)
Corporations 182
O'Casey, Sean (1880–1964)
Eternity 282
The Garden of Eden 356
O'Connor, Carroll (1922–2001)
Entertainment 274
O'Connor, Flannery (1925–1964)
Writing 889
Odom, William (1909–)
Losing, ...503
O'Donoghue, Michael (1940–1994)
Insects 434
O'Faolain, Sean (1900–1991)
Imagination 424

O'Faolain, Sean (cont.)
Reality 677
Ogilvy, David (1911–1999)
Advertising 33
Business 112
Jokes 442
Research 694
O'Hara, Kane (1711–1782)
Judgment 450
Prejudice 648
O'Keefe, Georgia (1887–1986)
Friendship 347
Ideas 415
Okri, Ben (1959-)
Childhood 137
Perfection 611
Politicians 636
Oliphant, Pat (1935–)
Subtlety 778
Olsen, Ken (1926–)
Computers 164
Olson, Barbara (1955–2001)
The Cold War 155
O'Malley, Austin (1858–1932)
Charity 134
Despair 227
Imagination 424
Lies 488
Politicians 636
Reason 679
Statesmen 764
Onassis, Aristotle (1906–1975)
Money 549
Women 876
Onassis, Jacqueline Kennedy (1924–1994)
Parenthood 599
O'Neal, Shaquille (1972–)
Basketball 80
O'Neill, Eugene (1888–1953)
Censorship 125
Curiosity 201
Kingdoms 455
Satisfaction 717
O'Neill, Jennifer (1948–)
Church 146
Ono, Yoko (1933–)
Dance 203
Openheimer, J. Robert (1904–1967)
Error 281
Oppenheim, James (1882–1932)
Happiness 385
Openshaw, Stan (1946–)
Doctors 244
Ophuls, Marcel (1927–)
Misery 541
Orben, Robert (1927–)
Adversity 31
Blame 93
Children 141
Computers 164
Crisis 195
Health 389
Neutrality 572
Politicians 636
Pollution 639
Temptation 804
O'Rourke, P. J. (1947–)
Adults 30
Animals 55
Books 99
Bureaucracy 110
Children 141
Democrats 223
Fish 319
Food 325
Government 373
Individuals 430
Journalists 445
Mourning 561
Parenthood 599
Seriousness 732
Work 881
Orr, Leonard (1938–)
Corporations 182
Ortega y Gasset, Jose (1883–1955)
Activity 23

Ortega y Gasset, Jose (cont.)
Adolescence 28
Adversity 31
Artists 68
Excellence 287
Liberals 478
Poetry 630
Orwell, George (1903–1950)
Acceptance 18
Animals 55
Censorship 125
Class 152
Communism 160
Equality 280
Feelings 314
Food 325
Freedom 338
The Future 354
Generals 359
Happiness 385
Language 462
Liberty 482
Mind 537
Nationalism 568
The Past 603
Political Parties 634
Politicians 636
Politics 638
The Present 649
Prose 659
Saints 714
Sports 760
Technology 801
Vigilance 850
War 861
Writing 889, 890
Osgood, Charles (1933–)
Babies 76
Osler, Sir William (1849–1919)
Ambition 46
Animals 55
Apathy 57
Dogma 245
Ignorance 420
Libraries 485
Life 494
Medicine 528
The Past 603
Patients 605
Teachers 798
Work 881
Osteen, Joel (1963–)
Positivity 643
Ovid (43 BC–AD 17)
Agriculture 40
Alcohol 43
Ancestry 52
Anxiety, ...57
Boldness 97
Cause and Effect 121
Chance 128
Change 129
Cunning 200
Dignity 237
Enemies 271
Evil 284
Fame 301
Forgetfulness 331
Fortune 335
Gifts 363
Habits 382
Judges 449
Love 509
Luck 512
Marriage 522
Medicine 528
Opportunity 587
The Past 603
Pleasure 626
Relaxation 686
Tears 801
Wives 875
Women 876
Owens, Jesse (1913–1980)
Competition 163
Struggle 773

Owens, Major (1936–)
- Schools 719

Owens, Terrell (1973–)
- Basketball 80

Oz, Amos (1939–)
- Rivalry 708

P

Paar, Jack (1918–2004)
- Flattery 321

Packard, David (1912–1996)
- Ego 265

Paddleford, Clementine (1898–1967)
- Beer 84

Paglia, Camille (1947–)
- Cats 119
- Pornography 641

Paige, Leroy "Satchel" (1906–1982)
- Airplanes 40
- Determination 232
- Relaxation 686

Paine, Thomas (1737–1809)
- The Bible 89
- Character 133
- Christianity 145
- Conflict 168
- Crisis 195
- Human Nature 405
- Infidelity 431
- Liberty 482
- Mankind 518
- Moderation 546
- Oppression 590
- Persecution 612
- Planning 623
- Prophets 659
- Reason 679
- Rebellion 680
- Reflection 681
- Religion 689
- Reputation 693
- Smiles 749
- Suspicion 790
- Triumph 828
- Trouble 829
- Value 845
- Virtue 854

Pankhurst, Christabel (1880–1958)
- Ability 11

Palahniuk, Chuck (1962–)
- Accidents 18
- Addiction 24
- Choice 144
- Effort 262
- Freedom 338
- The Future 354
- The Garden of Eden 356
- God 368
- The Great Depression 379
- Hate 387
- Identity 416
- Intellectualism 437
- Life 494
- Martyrs 523
- Masochism 524
- Materialism 525
- Parenthood 599
- Suicide 786
- Survival 790
- Telephones 802

Palmer, Arnold (1929–)
- Confidence 166
- Hunger 411
- Winning 869

Palmer, Jim (1945–)
- Losing 503

Palmer, Samuel (1805–1880)
- Quotations 670

Pandita, Saskya (1182–1251)
- Misfortune 542
- Silence 739

Panin, Ivan (1855–1942)
- Beauty 82

Pankhurst, Christabel (1880–1958)
- Ability 11

Pantoliano, Joe (1951–)
Subjectivity 778
Paracelsus (1493–1541)
Creativity 191
Heaven 393
Thoughts 813
Paramahamsa, Sri Ramakrishna (1836–1886)
Thoughts 814
Traitors 825
Parker, Christopher (1983–)
Procrastination 655
Parker, Dan (1781–1844)
Gambling 355
Parker, Dorothy (1893–1967)
Beauty 82
Books 99
Boredom 101
Childhood 137
Children 141
Curiosity 201
Friendship 347
Gratitude 377
Love 509
Men 532
Money 549
Plagiarism 623
Quotations 670
Ridicule 705
Sorrow 756
Taste 795
Telephones 802
Parker, Theodore (1810–1860)
Learning 475
Reading 674
Sin 742
Parker, Trey (1969–)
Family 303
Parkinson, C. Northcote (1909–1993)
Boredom 101
Parks, Rosa (1913–2005)
Deeds 215
Optimism 590
Racism 671
Parmenter, Ross (1912–1999)
Devotion 234
Parton, Dolly (1946–)
Smiles 749
Pascal, Blaise (1623–1662)
Admiration 27
Conviction 177
Evil 284
Existentialism 289
Falsity 300
Fame 301
The Future 354
Heart 390
Imagination 424
Love 509
Mankind 518
The Past 603
Persuasion 616
The Present 649
Reason 679
Religion 689
Science 721
Self 728
Silence 739
Soldiers 753
Thoughts 814
Unity 840
Virtue 854
Writing 890
Pasternak, Boris (1890–1960)
Art 65
Eloquence 266
Evening 284
Health 389
Majorities 515
Refuge 683
Space 757
Surprise 789
Pasteur, Louis (1822–1895)
Chance 128
Children 141
Goals 367
Luck 512

Pasteur, Louis (cont.)
Observation 581
Science 721
Pataki, George (1945–)
Corporations 182
Pater, Walter (1839–1894)
Curiosity 201
Opinions 585
The Renaissance 691
Paterculus (19 BC–AD 31)
Eloquence 266
Paterno, Joe (1924–)
Losing 503
Publicity 662
Paterson, Katherine (1932–)
Fiction 317
Paterno, Joe (1924–)
Excellence 287
Paton, Alan (1903–1988)
Forgiveness 333
Freedom 338
Reform 682
Responsibility 697
Patrick, John (1905–1995)
Pain 594
Thoughts 814
Wisdom 872
Patterson, John H. (1844–1922)
Corporations 183
Decisions, ...214
Patton, George S. (1885–1945)
Effort 262
Leadership 473
Victory 850
Planning 623
Risk 707
Paul III, Pope (1468–1549)
Redemption 681
Paul VI, Pope (1897–1978)
Brothers 106
Mothers 557
Paul, Alice (1885–1977)
Rights 707
Paul, Jean (1763–1825)
Heroes 397
The Moon 551
Music 564
Pauling, Linus (1901–1994)
Curiosity 201
Facts 296
Paulsen, Pat (1927–1997)
Politics 638
Pavarotti, Luciano (1935–2007)
Devotion 234
Discipline 239
Pavese, Cesare (1908–1950)
Childhood 137
Circumstances 149
Imagination 424
Joy 447
Suicide 786
Pavlov, Ivan (1849–1936)
Science 721
Pavlova, Anna (1885–1931)
Success 781
Payne, John Howard (1791–1852)
Home 401
Paz, Octavio (1914–)
Love 509
Peacock, Thomas Love (1785–1866)
Celibacy 122
Destiny 229
Waste 863
Peale, Norman Vincent (1898–1993)
Attitude 72
Boldness 97
Change 129
Confidence 166
Determination 232
Emotions, ...268
Enthusiasm 276
Expectations 290
Happiness 385
Heart 391
Hope 404
Mediocrity 529

Peale, Norman Vincent (cont.)
Obstacles 581, 582
Possibilities 642
Positivity 643
Success 781
Thoughts 814
Work 881
Pearce, Joseph Chilton (1926–)
God 368
Pearse, Patrick Henry (1879–1916)
Patriots 607
Pearson, Hesketh (1887–1964)
Quotations 670
Pearson, Lester B. (1897–1972)
Politics 638
Peck, M. Scott (1936–2005)
Community 161
Conflict 168
Discipline 239
Enlightenment 274
Love 509
Vulnerability 858
Wisdom 872
Peguy, Charles (1873–1914)
Infidelity 431
Tyranny 834
Pell, Claiborne (1918–)
America 48
Education 261
Penn, William (1644–1718)
Alcohol 43
Arguments 61
Authority 73
Censure 126
Excess 288
Friendship 347
God 368
Horses 405
Language 462
Lies 488
Marriage 522
Mind 537
The Past 603
Popularity 640
Reading 674
Right 706
Scholars 718
Silence 739
Struggle 773
Words 879
Wrong 892
Penney, James Cash (1875–1971)
Teamwork 800
Pepys, Samuel (1633–1703)
Cooking 178
Pérez, Manuel Benítez (1936–)
Bravery 105
Perkins, John (1945–)
Corporations 183
Pericles (490–429 BC)
Trees 828
Perlis, Alan (1922–1990)
Computers 164
Simplicity 741
Perlman, Elliot (1964–)
Personality 614
Perls, Fritz (1893–1970)
Expectations 290
Perot, Henry Ross (1930–)
Leadership 473
Peter of Alcantara, Saint (1499–1562)
Trouble 829
Peter, Dr. Laurence J. (1919–1990)
Ability 11
America 48
Anger 54
Belief 87
Blame 93
Bureaucracy 110
Countries 185
Democracy, ...222
Destiny 229
Economics 258
Education 261
Ego 265
Friendship 347

Peter, Dr. Laurence J. (cont.)
Ignorance 420
Intelligence 437
Lawyers 468
Logic 499
Misers 540
Misfortune 542
Originality 592
Prejudice 648
Psychiatry 661
Regret 683
Status Quo 766
Peters, Bernadette (1948–)
Actors 23
Peters, Charles (1952–)
Bureaucracy 110
Peterson, David (1943–)
Media 528
Petrarch (1304–1374)
Beauty 82
Friendship 347
Suspicion 791
Petty, William (1623–1687)
Banks 79
Phaedrus (15 BC–AD 50)
Fraud 336
Mind 537
Phelps, Austin (1820–1890)
Books 99
Phelps, William Lyon (1865–1943)
Class 152
Leisure 476
Occupation 582
Students 774
Work 881
Philips, Ambrose (1675–1749)
Seasons 724
Phillips, Wendell (1811–1884)
Aristocracy 62
Defeat 216
Liberty 482
Statesmen 764
Vigilance 850
Phocion (402–318 BC)
Gossip 370
Phocylides (c. 550 BC)
Decisions 214
Phoenix, River (1970–1993)
Vegetarianism 847
Piaget, Jean (1896–1980)
Self 728
Picasso, Pablo (1881–1973)
Artists 68
Children 142
Computers 164
Emotions 267
Fame 301
Fashion 306
God 368
Love 509
Painting 595
Reality 677
Sculpture 723
The Sun 787
Taste 795
Tomorrow 519
Vision 856
The World 883
Youth 896
Pickering, Charles W. (1937–)
Bureaucracy 110
Corporations 183
Pickering, Thomas (1931–)
Diplomacy 238
Pickford, Mary (1893–1979)
Failure 298
Mistakes 544
Pierce, Tamora (1954–)
Illusion 422
Piercy, Marge (1936–)
Actions 22
Danger 204
Hair 383
Love 509
Parenthood 599
Power 645

Pike, Albert (1809–1891)
Liberty 482
Self 728
Pike, Kenneth L. (1912–)
Respectability 696
Pilgrim, Peace (1908–1981)
Peace 608
Peace of Mind 609
Pilgrimage 621
Possessions, ...642
Research 694
Simplicity 741
Pinchot, Gifford (1865–1946)
Conservation 174
Preservation 650
Pindar (552–433 BC)
Deeds 215
Immortality 426
Old Age 584
Silence 739
Words 879
Pindar, Peter (1738–1819)
Laughter 465
Pinto, Ricardo (1961–)
Paradise 596
Pirandello, Luigi (1867–1936)
History 399
Ideas 415
Pirsig, Robert M. (1928–)
Disaster 238
Effort 262
Reason 679
Technology 801
Zen 898
Pitino, Rick (1952–)
Excellence 287
Pitt, William (1708–1778)
Eloquence 266
Necessity 570
Pittman, Frank (1935–)
Corporations 183
Pius XI, Pope (1857–1939)
Authority 73
Communism 160
Conscience 171
Pius XII, Pope (1876–1958)
Justice 452
Space 757
Plagens, Peter (1941–)
Disaster 238
Plain, Belva (1919–)
Birds 92
Desire 225
Plato (c. 428–348 BC)
Abstinence 15
Age 37
Anger 54
Animals 55
Arguments 61
Body 96
Cleverness 153
Cunning 200
Curiosity 201
Death 209
Disease 241
Dishonesty 241
Doctors 244
Education 261
Evil 285
Excellence 287
Eyes 294
Fools 328
Friendship 347
Government 373
Greatness 379
Health 389
Honesty 402
Ignorance 420
Immortality 426
Indifference 429
Injustice 433
Knowledge 461
Laws 467
Learning 475
Lies 488
Light 497

Plato (cont.)
Mankind 519
Mathematics 525
Men 532
Mind 537-538
Misfortune 542
Money 549
Names 567
Necessity 570
Opinions 585
Parenthood 599
Poetry 630
Politicians 636
Poverty 643
Punishment 663
Quantity 667
Rhetoric 701
Science 721, 722
Statesmen 764
Strength 771
Studying 775
Talk 794
Taxes 796
Tragedy 825
Truth 832
Tyranny 834
Wealth 865
Platonov, Andrei (1899–1951)
Happiness 385
Materialism 525
Player, Willis (1915–)
Liberals 478
Pliny the Elder (AD 23–79)
Agriculture, ...40
Beginnings 85
Certainty 127
Glory 365
Numbers 577
Uncertainty 835
Pliny the Younger (AD 62–114)
Creativity 191
Laziness 469
Writing 890
Plomer, William (1903–1973)
Research 694
Plutarch (AD 46–120) ....
Achievement 21
Adversity 31
Age 37
Ancestors 52
Cowardice 189
Education 261
Friendship 347
Funerals 353
Glory 365
God 368
Habits 382
Listening 497
Mind 538
Obscurity 580
Perseverance 613
Poverty 643
Prosperity 660
Silence 740
Speaking 758
Time 816
Violence 851
Wealth 865
Podhoretz, John (1961–)
Losing 503
Poe, Edgar Allan (1809–1849)
Cats 119
Cowardice 189
Despair 227
Dreams 251
Fiction 317
Humanity 408
Literature 498
Mobs 545
Mothers 557
Pain 594
Popularity 641
Sensitivity 731
Suffering 783
Words 879

Pohl, Frederik (1919–)
Earthquakes 255
Poincaré, Henri (1854–1912)
Facts 296
Machines 513
Science 722
Pollack, Sydney
Charisma 134
Pollan, Michael (1955–)
Obesity 578
Poverty 643
Polanski, Roman (1933–)
Cinema 148
Pollard, John G. (1871–1937)
Ability 11
Pollock, Channing (1880–1946)
Self-Confidence 728
Pollock, Jackson (1912–1956)
Art 65
Artists 68
Painting 595
Polybius (205–118 BC)
Conscience 171
Victory 850
Pomfret, John (1667–1702)
Journalists 445
Pompidou, Georges (1911–1974)
Nation 567
Politicians 636
Ponsonby, Arthur (1871–1946)
Cats 119
Poore, Benjamin Perley (1820–1887)
Communism 160
Pop, Iggy (1947–)
Nihilism 574
Pope, Alexander (1688–1744)
Agriculture 40
Change 129
Creativity 191
Cunning 200
Curiosity 201
Devotion 234
Fame 301
Fools 328
Forgiveness 333
Generosity 360
Glory 365
Judges 449
Men 532
Praise 646
Riches 704
Satan 715
Satire 716
Science 722
Simplicity 741
Transformation 826
Vengeance 847
Vulgarity 857
Wit 874
Zealots 898
Popper, Karl (1902–1994)
Happiness 386
Misery 541
Porter, Eleanor H. (1868–1920)
Cats 119
Dogs 247
Pets 618
Porter, Jane (1776–1850)
Mobs 545
Porter, Katherine Anne (1894–1980)
Infidelity 431
Porter, Katherine Anne (cont.)
Intuition 440
Perception 611
Porter, Noah (1811–1892)
Belief 87
Porteus, Belby (1731–1808)
Murder 562
Portman, John (1924–)
Architects 59
Architecture 60
Potter, Elisha (1811–1882)
Human Nature 405
Pound, Ezra (1885–1972)
Anti-Semitism 56
Books 99

Pound, Ezra (cont.)
Education 261
Literature 498
Reading 674
Suicide 786
Pound, Rosco (1870–1964)
Laws 467
Poundstone, Paula (1959–)
Adults 30
Banks 79
Wages 858
Powell, Adam Clayton, Jr. (1908–1972)
Brothers 106
Equality 280
Powell, Colin (1937–)
Commanders 155
Ego 265
Excellence 287
Experts 293
Leadership 473
Optimism 591
Success 781
Words 879
Powell, Dawn (1896–1965)
Tragedy 825
Powell, Enoch (1827–1956)
Media 528
Powell, John (1963–)
Acceptance 18
Powell, Lawrence Clark (1906–2001)
Writing 890
Prager, Dennis (1948–)
Bureaucracy 110
Corporations 183
Liberals 478
Pratchett, Terry (1948–)
Cats 119
Darkness 205
Dreams 251
Eyes 294
God 368
Killing 453
Kings 456
Light 497
Meals 527
The Universe 841
Wages 858
Prather, Hugh (1906–1975)
Difficulty 236
Pratt, Victoria (1970–)
Vulnerability 858
Premchand, Munshi (1880–1936)
Bravery 105
Timidity 517
Prentice, George Dennison (1802–1870)
Disease 241
Food 325
Health 389
Smoking 749
Presley, Elvis (1935–1977)
Adversity 31
Music 564
Prosperity 660
Rhythm 702
Songs 754
Truth 832
Preston, Lewis Thompson (1926–1995)
Loans 499
Price, George (1870–1963)
Madness 514
Sanity 715
Pride, Charley (1938–)
Rainbows 672
Priest, Ivy Baker (1905–1975)
Beginnings 85
Priestland, Gerald (1927–1991)
Journalists 445
Priestley, J. B. (1894–1984)
Children 142
Shyness 737
Slang 746
Priestley, Joseph (1733–1804)
Admiration 27
Mind 538
Prior, Matthew (1664–1721)
Devotion 234

Prior, Matthew (cont.)
Hope 404
Talk 795
Pritchett, Victor Sawdon (1900–1997)
Rape 673
Probst, Jeff (1962–)
African-Americans 35
Proudhon, Pierre-Joseph (1809–1865)
Communism 160
Theft 808
Proust, Marcel (1871–1922)
Childhood 137
Discovery 240
Dreams 251
Eyes 294
Friendship 347
Love 509
Paradise 596
Sickness 738
Strength 771
Torture 820
Wisdom 872
Pryor, Richard (1940–2005)
Criticism 197
Lawyers 468
Liberation 479
Marriage 522
Underground 836
Publilius Syrus (c. 100 BC)
Adversity 31
Advice 33
Anger 54
Avarice 75
Caution 121
Corruption 185
Crime 192
Death 209
Decisions, ...214
Desire 225
Disease 241
Education 261
Enemies 271
Equality, ...280
Excellence 287
Eyes 294
Familiarity 302
Favors 311
Fear 313
Fortune 335
Fraud 336
Friendship 347
Giving 364
Goals 367
Happiness 386
Ignorance 420
Learning 475
Medicine 528
Misery 541
Misfortune 542
Money 549
Neglect 571
Opportunity 587
Planning 623
Praise 646
Promises 657
Prosperity 660
Remedies 690
Reputation 693
Silence 740
Speaking 758
Trees 828
Valor 844
Puig, Manuel (1932–1990)
Ideology 417
Realism 676
Pulteney, William (1684–1764)
Judges 449
Pulitzer, Joseph (1847–1911)
Journalists 445
Newspapers 573
Publicity 662
Pulsifer, Catherine (1957–)
Mothers 557
Punshon, William (1824–1881)
Conscience 171

Putin, Vladimir (1952–)
Terrorism 806
Totalitarianism 820
Puzo, Mario (1920–1999)
Anger 54
Enemies 271
Pyrrhus (319–272 BC)
Victory 850
Pythagoras (c. 582–500 BC)
Body 96
Friendship 347
Life 494
Reverence 699
Silence 740
Sobriety 750
Speaking 758
War 861
Words 879

Q

Quammen, David (1948–)
Identity 416
Quarles, Francis (1592–1644)
Fear 313
Honor 403
Idleness 418
Kingdoms 455
Wealth 865
Quayle, Dan (1947–)
The Future 354
Mistakes 544
Pollution 639
Racism 671
Republicans 692
Teachers 799
Quesnel, Pasquier (1634–1719)
Zeal 898
Quigley, Carroll (1910–1977)
Bankers 78
Loans 499
Quidde, Ludwig (1858–1941)
Pacifism 593
Quillen, Robert (1887–1948)
Arguments 61
Quincey, Thomas de (1785–1859)
Procrastination 655
Quindlen, Anna (1953–)
Belief 87
Books 99
Children 142
Diplomacy 238
Exercise 289
Family 303
Feminism 315
Heart 391
Illness 421
Journalists 445
Life 494
Perfection 611
Success 781
Women 877
Quinet, Edgar (1803–1875)
Orthodoxy 592
Quinn, Jane Bryant (1939–)
Lawyers 468
Quintilian (c. AD 35–100)
Crowds 198
Defeat 216
Fools 328
Lies 488
Wisdom 872
Quintus Ennius (239–169 BC)
Funerals 353
Quinn, Don (1900–1967)
Divorce 243
Quisenberry, Dan (1953–1998)
The Future 354

R

Radner, Gilda (1946–1989)
Fashion 306
Uniqueness 839
Raffarin, Jean-Pierre (1948–)
Secularism 725

Rahall, Nick (1949–)
Wilderness 867
Rainey, Robert (1826–1906)
Abstinence 15
Rajneesh, Bhagwan Shree (1931–1990)
Misunderstanding 545
Raleigh, Sir Walter (c. 1552–1618)
Lies 488
Marriage 522
Trade 522
Rameau, Jean-Philippe (1683–1764)
Rhythm 702
Rand, Ayn (1905–1982)
Achievement 21
Brothers 106
Capitalism 115
Choice 144
Civilization 151
Conformity 170
Consciousness 173
Courage 187
Cowardice 189
Devotion 234
Evil 285
Free Will 339
Guilt 381
Happiness 386
Impotence 427
Majorities 515
Meals 527
Opinions 585
Opposites 588
Privacy 654
The Public 662
Rand, Paul (1914–1996)
Expectations 290
Simplicity 741
Randolph, John (1773–1833)
Aristocracy 62
Liberty 483
Randolph, William (1650–1711)
Politicians 636
Rangel, Charles (1930–)
African-Americans 35
Decisions 214
Democracy 222
Rankin, Jeannette (1880–1973)
Crisis 195
Decency 213
War 861
Raskin, Jef (1943–2005)
Computers 164
Raspberry, William (1935–)
Satisfaction 717
Success 781
Rather, Dan (1931–)
Teachers 799
Truth 832
Ratzenberger, John (1947–)
Showbiz 736
Rauschenberg, Robert (1925–)
Artists 68
Ravitch, Diane (1938–)
Bosses 102
Rawls, John (1921–2002)
Campaigns 113
Ray, Man (1890–1976)
Artists 68
Dreams 251
The Unconcious 836
Rayburn, Sam (1882–1961)
Honesty 402
Language 462
Leadership 473
Reagan, Nancy (1921–)
Pornography 641
Reagan, Ron (1958–)
Buddhism 107
Racism 672
Reagan, Ronald (1911–2004)
Abortion 14
America 48
Character 133
Communism 160
Crisis 195

Reagan, Ronald (cont.)
Democrats 223
Destiny 229
Economics 258
Facts 296
Food 325
Political Parties 634
Politics 638
Status Quo 766
Trade 522
Welfare 867
Redford, Robert (1937–)
Ideas 415
Redwood, John (1951–)
Bureaucracy 110
Reed, Lou (1942–)
Nation 567
Reed, Oliver (1938–1999)
Awe 75
Reed, Willis (1942–)
Stars 762
Reesc, Charley (1937–)
Bureaucracy 110
Reeve, Christopher (1952–2004)
Dreams 251
Heroes 397
Obstacles 582
Ocean 583
Reeves, Martha (1941–)
Songs 755
Reich, Robert (1946–)
Bedrooms 83
Conservatives 174
Crisis 195
Reich, Wilhelm (1897–1957)
Abstinence 15
Liberation 479
Theories 809
Reid, Kate (1930–1993)
Acting 22
Emotions 267
Reik, Theodore (1888–1969)
Parenthood 599
Reiner, Carl (1922–)
Snow 750
Reinhardt, Ad (1913–1967)
Artists 68
Reisman, George (1937–)
Economics 258
Reisz, Karel (1926–2002)
Conformity 170
Rell, Jodi (1946–)
Libraries 485
Renan, Ernest (1823–1892)
Communism 160
Renard, Jules (1864–1910)
Atheism 71
Fame 301
Food 325
Humility 409
Laziness 469, 470
Life 494
Literature 498
Quantity 667
Sincerity 743
Talent 794
Writing 890
Renault, Mary (1905–1983)
Evil 285
Rene de Chateaubriand, Francois
Cats 119
Renoir, Auguste (1841–1919)
Artists 68
Renwick, Robin (1937–)
Lunch 512
Media 528
Repkow, Eike von (c. 1220)
Food 325
Repplier, Agnes (1855–1950)
Dogs 247
Happiness 386
Laughter 465
Leisure 476
Pleasure 626
Tourism 821
Truth 832

Repplier, Agnes (cont.)
Vigilance 850
Reston, James (1909–1995)
The News 572
Retton, Mary Lou (1968–)
Ability 11
Children 142
Corporations 183
Retz, Cardinal de
Arguments 61
Reverdy, Pierre (1889–1960)
Creativity 191
Reznikoff, Charles (1894–1976)
Thoughts 814
Reynière, Grimod de la (1758–1838)
Kitchens 458
Reynolds, Sir Joshua (1723–1792)
Industry 431
Ribon, Pamela (1975–)
Death 209
Honesty 402
Winter 870
Ricci, Ruggiero (1918–)
Rhythm 702
Rice, Anne (1941–)
Authority 73
Vampires 846
Youth 896
Rice, Grantland (1880–1954)
Football 330
Sports 760
Rice, Helen Steiner (1900–1981)
Mothers 557
Rich, Adrienne (1929–)
Lies 488
Richardson, Adam (1967–)
Dogma 245
Richardson, Eliot (1920–1999)
Bureaucracy 110
Richards, Ann (1933–2006)
The Great Depression 379
Hair 383
Mistakes 544
Recovery 681
Richards, Keith (1943–)
Authority 73
Feet 314
Richards, M. C. (1916–1999)
Irrelevance 440
Poetry 630
Richardson, Sir Ralph (1902–1983)
Acting 22
Richardson, Samuel (1689–1761)
Affection 34
Punishment 663
Shame 735
Richter, Charles Francis (1900–1985)
Earthquakes 255
Richter, Jean Paul (1763–1825)
Actions 22
Character 133
Charm 135
Children 142
Courage 187
Cowardice 189
Danger 204
Faults 311
Fear 313
Flowers 323
Forgiveness 333
Friendship 347
Moderation 546
Reflection 681
Riches 704
Words 879
Rickenbacker, Edward Vernon (1890–1973)
Character 133
Courage 187
Friendship 347
Rickman, Alan (1946–)
Seduction 726
Rickover, Hyman (1900–1986)
Bureaucracy 110
Ideas 415
The Rig Veda
Malevolence 516

Riley, Pat (1945–)
Excellence 287
The Public 662
Rilke, Rainer Maria (1875–1926)
Beginnings 85
Blame 93
Contemplation 175
Fate 308
Life 494
Opportunity 587
Questions 669
Rimbaud, Arthur (1854–1891)
Hell 395
Recovery 681
Sensitivity 731
Youth 896
Riskin, Robert (1897–1955)
Love 505
Newspapers 572
Rivarol, Antoine (1753–1801)
Devotion 234
Fame 301
Rivers, Joan (1935–)
Babies 76
Birth Control 93
Exercise 289
Parenthood 599
The Present 650
Queens 668
Sex 733
Rizal, Jose (1861–1896)
Tyranny 834
Roach, Jay (1957–)
Addiction 24
Robbins, Anthony (1960–)
Ability 12
Desperation 227
Robbins, Tom (1936–)
Angels 53
Cause and Effect 121
Childhood 137
Government 373
Heaven 393
Humanity 408
Inspiration 435
Religion 689
Robert, Henry M. (1837–1923)
Laws 467
Liberty 483
Roberts, Cokie (1943–)
Children 142
Mothers 557
Parenthood 599
Roberts, J. M. (1928–2003)
Imperialism 427
Roberts, Pat (1936–)
Terrorism 806
Robertson, Pat (1930–)
Feminism 315
Robespierre, Maximilien (1758–1794)
Crime 192
Innocence 434
Zeal 898
Robinson, Chris (1966–)
Corporations 183
Robinson, Jackie (1919–1972)
Losing 503
Robinson, James Harvey (1863–1936)
Campaigns 113
Robinson, Smokey (1940–)
Songs 755
Rockefeller, David (1915–)
Business 112
Corporations 183
Giving 364
Success 781
Rockefeller, John D. (1839–1937)
Ambition 46
Competition 163
Disaster 238
Duty 253
Opportunity 587
Pleasure 626
Rockefeller, John D., Jr. (1874–1960)
Responsibility 697

Rockne, Knute (1888–1931)
Losing 504
Rodgers, Buck (1938–)
Leadership 473
Roddick, Anita (1942–)
Corporations 183
Rodin, Auguste (1840–1917)
Art 65
Artists 69
Contemplation 175
Flowers 323
Sculpture 723
Time 816
Rodriguez, Paul (1955–)
Hunting 411
Roeper, Richard (1960–)
Magazines 514
Roethke, Theodore (1908–1963)
Intelligence 437
Rogers, Carl (1902–1987)
Students 774
Rogers, Fred (1928–2003)
Children 142
Rogers, Wayne (1933–)
Villains 851
Rogers, Will (1879–1935)
Baseball 79
Cinema 148
Cities 150
Civilization 151
Commerce 157
Communism 160
Delusion 220
Democracy 222
Democrats 223
Difficulty 236
Diplomacy 238
Golf 370
Gossip 370, 371
Government 373
Heroes 397
Humor 410
Ignorance 420
Jokes 442
Lawyers 469
Laziness 470
Marriage 522
Patients 605
Political Parties 634
Politicians 636
Politics 638
Popularity 641
Stock Market 766
Taxes 796
Time 816
Traffic 824
War 861
Rolando, Gary (1982–)
Arrogance 63
Ignorance 420
Rollins, Alice Wellington (1847–1897)
Teachers 799
Rollins, Henry (1961–)
Heartbreak 392
Rollins, Kevin (1953–)
Corporations 183
Romero, John (1967–)
Strategy 770
Rooney, Andy (1919–)
Computers 164
Rooney, Mickey (1920–)
Failure 298
Marriage 522
Success 781
Roosevelt, Eleanor (1884–1962)
Accidents 18
Apathy 57
Beauty 82
Character 133
Children 142
Choice 144
Communism 161
Cooperation 179
Criticism 197
Decisions 214
Enthusiasm 276

Roosevelt, Eleanor (cont.)
Experience 292
Fear 313
Friendship 347, 348
The Future 354
Heart 391
Independence 428
Joy 447
Maturity 526
Mothers 558
Opposition 589
Parenthood 599
Philosophy 619
Self 728
Statesmen 764
Suicide 786
War 861
Women 877
Work 882

Roosevelt, Franklin D. (1882–1945)
Achievement 21
Communism 161
Confidence 166
Conservatives 174
Creativity 191
Democracy 222
Determination 232
Doubt 249
Effort 263
Encouragement 269
Failure 298
Fascism 305
Fate 308
Fear 313
Freedom 338
Injustice 433
Lies 488
Majorities 515
Oppression 590
Perseverance 613
Presidents 651
Prosperity 660
Rulers 710
Self-Control 729
Suspicion 791
Taxes 796
Tradition 823
Youth 896

Roosevelt, Theodore (1858–1919)
Ability 12
Achievement 21
Actions 22
Character 133
Courtesy 188
Decency 213
Deeds 215
Defeat 216
Democracy 222
Devotion 234
Discipline 239
Education 261
Effort 263
Enthusiasm 276
Evil 285
Executives 289
Eyes 294
Failure 298
Feet 314
Government 373
Justice 452
Leadership 473
Learning 475
Liberty 483
Order 591
Politicians 636
Rhetoric 701
Stars 762
Thoughts 814
Victory 850

Rorem, Ned (1923–)
Childhood 138

Rose, Aaron (1940–)
Light 497

Rose, Ernestine (1810–1892)
Bachelors 78

Rosenberg, Harold (1906—1978)
Addiction 25
Artists 69
Creativity 191
Criticism 197
Transformation 826
Rosenstock-Huessy, Eugen (1888–1973)
Language 462
Logic 500
Misunderstanding 545
Rosenwald, Julius (1862–1932)
Money 549
Ross, Betsy (1752–1836)
Knights 459
Ross, Rick (1952–)
Adjustment 25
Ross, Stanley Ralph (1937–2000)
Jesus 441
Rossetti, Dante Gabriel (1828–1882)
Atheism 71
Rossetti, Christina G. (1830–1894)
Silence 740
Sisters 743
Snow 750
Songs 755
Spring 761
Winter 870
Rostand, Jean (1894–1977)
Admiration 27
Loneliness 500
Murder 562
Optimism 591
Pessimism 617
Rosten, Leo (1908–1997)
Actors 23
Belief 87
Deception 213
Dogs 247
Martyrs 524
Money 549
Satire 716
Writing 890
Rothenstein, William (1872–1945)
Gardens 357
Rotten, Johnny (1956–)
Noise 575
Rouff, Marcel (1877–1936)
Cooking 178
Rouault, Georges (1871–1958)
Gifts 363
Rousseau, Jean-Jacques (1712–1778)
Cats 119
Childhood 138
Cities 150
Duty 253
Enjoyment 273
Fame 301
Fortune 335
Gratitude 377
Greatness, ...379
Happiness 386
Heroes 397
Kindness 454
Liberty 483
Men 532
Mothers 558
Obedience 578
Pain 594
Pleasure 626
Promises 657
Secrets 725
Silence 740
Soldiers 753
Strength 772
Suicide 786
Superiority 788
Virtue 854
Rowan, Carl T. (1925–2000)
Status Quo 766
Rowland, Cathy (1950–)
Hope 404
Rowland, Helen (1876–1950)
Bachelors 78
Brides 105
Flattery 321

Rowland, Helen (cont.)
Flirting 321
Infidelity 431
Kisses 457
Marriage 522
Men 533
Opportunity 587
Regret 683
Sacrifice 711
Wives 875
Women 877
Rowland, Jeffrey (1974–)
Reading 674
Rowling, J. K. (1965–)
Acceptance 18
Choice 144
Darkness 205
Death 209
Decisions 214
Dreams 251
Fear 313
Forgetfulness 331
Forgiveness 333
Indifference 429
Knowledge 461
Love 510
Music 564
Neglect 571
Pain 594
Recovery 681
Trust 830
Truth 832
Youth 896
Roy, Claude (1915–1997)
Misfortune 542
Roybal-Allard, Lucille (1941–)
Alcohol 43
Rubin, Jerry (1938–1994)
Theater 808
Rubinstein, Arthur (1886–1982)
Accidents 18
Success 781
Love 509
Ruby, Harry (1895–1984)
California 113
Rudner, Rita (1955–)
Dogs 247
Godfathers 376
Husbands 412
Marriage 522
Paranoia 597
Parenthood 599
Pets 618
Tennis 805
Rudolph, Wilma (1940–1994)
Champions 128
Reward 701
Struggle 773
Winning 869
Rukeyser, Muriel (1913–1980)
Beginnings 86
Stories 767
The Universe 841
Rule, Jane (1931–)
Conformity 170
Morality 552
Rumi, Mavlana (1207–1273)
Gardens 357
Rumsfeld, Donald H. (1932–)
Bureaucracy 110
Criticism 197
Knowledge 461
Objectives 579
Planning 623
Runcie, Robert (1921–)
Tourism 821
Rush, Benjamin (1745–1813)
Scandals 717
Rushdie, Salman (1947–)
Books 99
Censorship 125
Fiction 317
Legends 476
Purity 664
Ruskin, John (1819–1900)
Ability 12

Ruskin, John (cont.)
Conceit 165
Endurance 269
Enjoyment 273
Fortune 335
Gambling 355
Greatness 379
Knights 459
Libraries 486
Lies 488
Morality 552
Patience 605
Pride 652
Prison 653
Punishment 663
Reform 682
Schools 719
Taste 795
Technology 801
Vulgarity 857
Weather 866
Work 882
Writing 890
Russell, Bertrand (1872–1970)
Ability 12
Accidents 18
Achievement 21
Addiction 25
Alcohol 42
Belief 87
Caution 121
Certainty 127
Chaos 130
Competition 163
Conflict 168
Conviction 177
Cooperation 179
Crime 192
Cruelty 198
Discipline 239
Dogma 245
Doubt 249
Duty 253
Facts 296
Fear 313
Fools 328
Freedom 338
Golf 370
Gossip 371
Government 374
Happiness 386
Hesitation 398
Ignorance 420
Injustice 433
Instinct 435
Intelligence 437, 438
Killing 453
Knowledge 461
Leisure 477
Liberals 478
Liberty 483
Love 510
Machines 513
Majorities 516
Mankind 519
Materialism 525
Mathematics 526
Morality 552
Mythology 566
Nonsense 576
Obscenity 580
Opinions 585
Order 591
Paradise 596
Parenthood 599
Patriotism 606
Patriots 607
People 610
Philosophy 619
Pity 622
Pleasure 626
Possessions 642
Progress 657
Propaganda 658
Prostitution 660
Psychology 662

Russell, Bertrand (cont.)
The Public 662
Quiet 669
Reading 674
Relaxation 686
Science 722
Secrets 725
Sin 742
Students 774
Suffering 783
Suicide 786
Superstition 789
Teachers 799
Thoughts 814
Trouble 829
Uncertainty 835
Unhappiness 839
The Universe 842
Wisdom 872
Work 882
Wrong 892
Russell, Bill (1934–)
Toughness 821
Russell, Dora (1894–1986)
Repression 691
Russell, George William (1867–1935)
Russell, John (1921–)
Sanity 715
Russell, Rosalind (1908–1976)
Life 494
Starvation 762
Suckers 782
Russo, Richard (1949–)
Cinema 148
Rustin, Bayard (1912–1987)
Bigotry 90
Ruth, George Herman "Babe" Jr. (1895–1948)
Fear 313
Noise 575
Sports 760
Superstition 789
Rutherford, Mark (1831–1913)
Danger 204
Grace 375
Ryan, Lee (1983–)
Ghosts 362
Ryun, Jim (1947–)
Discipline 239
Dreams 251
Motivation 561

S

Saadi (1184–1291)
Friendship 348
Ignorance 420
Silence 740
Saban, Nick (1951–)
The Present 650
Sackville-West, Vita (1892–1962)
Desperation 227
Sade, Marquis de (1740–1814)
Anarchy 51
Lust 513
Safire, William (1929–)
Apathy 57
Sagan, Carl (1934–1996)
Ambition 46
Clergy 152
Delusion 220
Emotions 268
Genius 362
Information 432
Nonsense 576
The Past 603
Prophets 659
Religion 689
Science 722
Skepticism 744
Spirituality 760
Thoughts 814
Truth 832
The Universe 842

Sahl, Mort (1927–)
Liberals 478
Saint-Beuve, Charles Augustin (1804–1869)
Admiration 27
Saint-Exupéry, Antoine de (1900–1944)
Children 142
Cooperation 179
Flirting 321
Freedom 338
Friendship 348
Goals 367
Heart 391
Language 462
Machines 513
Mind 538
Perfection 611
Planning 623
Sacrifice 711
Self-Respect 729
Stars 762
Travel 827
Understanding 838
Saint-Laurent, Yves (1940–)
Fashion 306
Style 777
Saint-Pierre, Michel de (1916–1987)
Age 37
Cats 119
Optimism 591
Pessimism 617
Saki (1870–1916)
Age 37
Salinger, J. D. (1919–)
Artists 69
Happiness 386
Paranoia 597
Salinger, Pierre (1925–2004)
Corporations 183
Salisbury, Lord (1563–1612)
Doctors 244
Salk, Jonas (1914–1995)
Dreams 251
Enthusiasm 276
Salles, Walter (1956–)
Cinema 148
Sallust (86–34 BC)
Ambition 46
Defeat 216
Envy 278
Excellence 287
Friendship, ...348
Injustice 433
Jealousy 441
Liberty 483
Lies 488
Majorities 516
Morality 552
The Poor 640
Samuel, Herbert (1870–1963)
Libraries 486
Samuelson, Paul A. (1915–)
Economics 258
Questions 669
Sanchez, Oscar Arias (1941–)
Freedom 338
Responsibility 697
Sand, George (1804–1876)
Admiration 27
Age 37
Devotion 234
Enthusiasm 276
Kindness 454
Life 494
Novels 577
Pleasure 627
Work 882
Sandburg, Carl (1878–1967)
Admiration 27
America 48
Babies 76
Bedrooms 83
Dance 203
Dreams 251
Fog 323
Grammar 375
Idealism 413

Sandburg, Carl (cont.)
- The Past 603
- Poetry 630
- Religion 689
- Scholars 718
- The Sea 723
- Slang 746
- Solitude 754
- Time 816
- Valor 844
- War 861

Sane, Justin (1973–)
- Corporations 183

Sanford, Edward T. (1865–1930)
- Anarchy 51

Sanger, Margaret (1879–1966)
- Abortion 14
- Mothers 558

Santana, Carlos (1947–)
- Peace 608

Santayana, George (1863–1952)
- Advertising 33
- Age 37
- America 48
- Birth 92
- Blood 94
- Body 96
- Character 133
- Charm 135
- Death 209
- Depression 224
- Destiny 230
- Eccentricity 255
- Effort 263
- Enlightenment 274
- Eyes 294
- Fame 301
- Family 303
- Fashion 306
- Feet 314
- Friendship 348
- Fun 352
- Habits 382
- History 399
- Humanity 408
- Integrity 436
- Intolerance 438
- Judgment 450
- Learning 475
- Madness 514
- Mind 538
- Music 564
- Oaths 578
- The Past 603
- Perception 611
- Philosophy 620
- Poetry 630
- Possessions 642
- Pride 652
- Quality 666
- Quantity 667
- The Renaissance 691
- Sacrifice 711
- Sanity 715
- Science 722
- Skepticism 744
- Spring 761
- Strangers 769
- Theories 809
- Travel 827
- Tyranny 834
- War 861
- Wisdom 872
- Wives 875
- The World 883

Sarandon, Susan (1946–)
- Parenthood 599

Sargent, John Singer (1856–1925)
- Painting 595

Sarnoff, Dorothy (1914–)
- Listening 497

Sarnoff, Robert W. (1918–1997)
- Money 549

Saroyan, William (1908–1981)
- Anger 54
- Doctors 244

Saroyan, William (cont.)
Failure 298
Wisdom 872
Sarraute, Nathalie (1900–1999)
Suspicion 791
Sarton, George (1884–1956)
Friendship 348
Saints 714
Sarton, May (1912–1995)
Certainty 127
Gifts 363
Sartre, Jean-Paul (1905–1980)
Disability 238
Existentialism 290
Generosity 360
Hell 395
Life 494
Loneliness 500
Philosophy 620
The Poor 640
Rich and Poor 703
Sassoon, Siegfried (1886–1967)
Defiance 217
Sai Baba, Sri Sathya (1926–)
Cooperation 179
Love 505
Pilgrimage 621
Publicity 662
Superiority 788
Transformation 826
Welfare 866
Saunders, George (1958–)
Boredom 101
Saurin, Bernard Joseph (1706–1781)
Valor 844
Savant, Marilyn vos (1946–)
Cell Phones 122
Ideas 415
Knowledge 461
Wisdom 872
Savile, George (1633–1695)
Popularity 641
Sawyer, Charles (1868–1954)
Economics 258
Profit 656
Sawyer, Diane (1945–)
Competition 163
Terrorism 806
Sawyer, Robert J. (1960–)
Honor 403
Relaxation 686
Violence 851
Sayers, Dorothy L. (1893–1957)
Books 99
Occupation 582
Passion 601
Work 882
Scalia, Antonin (1936–)
Privacy 654
Schaeffer, Francis (1912–1984)
Christianity 145
Orthodoxy 592
Secularism 725
Schakowsky, Jan (1944–)
Earthquakes 255
Schanberg, Sydney (1934–)
Journalists 445
Schiller, Friedrich von (1759–1805)
Caution 121
Chance 128
Destiny 230
Dreams 251
Fame 301
Fate 308
Majorities 516
Opposition 589
Secrets 725
Stupidity 776
Utility 843
Youth 896
Schiller, Herbert (1919–2000)
Manipulation 517, 518
Neutrality 572
Schlafy, Phyllis (1924–)
Babies 76

Schlafy, Phylils (cont.)
Bureaucracy 110
Judges 449
Political Correctness 633
Schlegel, Friedrich von (1772–1829)
Thoughts 814
Schlessinger, Laura (1947–)
Values 845
Scholz, Tom (1947–)
Corporations 183
Schopenhauer, Arthur (1788–1860)
Ability 12
Absurdity 16
Boredom 101
Childhood 138
Compassion 162
Cowardice 189
Ego 265
Fame 301
Fate 308
Fools 328
Greatness 379
Hate 387
Ignorance 420
Journalists 445
Kindness 454
Loneliness 500
Memory 531
Morality, ...552
Noise 575
Ridicule 705
Sacrifice 711
Suicide 786
Thoughts 814
Truth 832
Schrader, Paul (1946–)
Loneliness 500
Schreiner, Olive (1855–1920)
Mothers 558
Schrempp, Jurgen (1944–)
Business 112
Schroder, Gerhard (1944–)
Unemployment 838
Schroeder, Theodore (1864–1953)
Censorship 125
Schulberg, Budd (1914–)
Life 494
Schuller, Robert H. (1926–)
Determination 232
Dreams 251
Thoughts 814
Toughness 821
Schulman, Tom (1951–)
Ideas 415
Poetry 630
Schulz, Charles M. (1922–2000)
Love 510
Pets 618
Philosophy 620
Sisters 743
Worries 883
Schumer, Charles (1950–)
Judges 449
Schumann, Clara (1819–1896)
Kisses 457
Schumpeter, Josesph A. (1883–1950)
Bureaucracy 111
Schurz, Carl (1829–1906)
Destiny 230
Freedom 338
Idealism 413
Liberty 483
Schwab, Charles (1862–1939)
Enthusiasm 277
Schwartz, Delmore (1913–1966)
Paranoia 597
Schwarzenegger, Arnold (1947–)
Decency, ...213
Democracy 222
Hate 387
Jealousy 441
Service 732
Strength 772
Schwarzkopf, Norman (1934–)
Leadership 473
Strategy 770

Schweitzer, Dr. Albert (1875–1965)
Compassion 162
Destiny 230
Ethics 283
Happiness 386
Health 389
Humanity 408
Kindness 454
Knowledge 461
Nation 567
Optimism 591
Pessimism 617
Sacrifice 712
Spirit 759
Success 781
Thoughts 814
Scott, Adam (1980–)
Food 325
Scott, Howard (1890–1970)
Corporations 183
Crime 192
Scott, Sir Walter (1771–1832)
Duty 253
Fruit 351
Journals 446
Lies 488
Heartbreak 392
Ridicule 705
Risk 708
Snow 750
Society 752
Trees 828
Scott, Willard (1934–)
Tobacco 817
Scott, Zachary (1914–1965)
Regret 683
Scruton, Roger (1944–)
Gardens 357
Sculley, John (1939–)
Teachers 799
Scully, Vin (1927–)
Losing 504
Seacrest, Ryan (1974–)
Showbiz 737
Seale, Bobby (1936–)
Guns 382
Searle, John (1932–)
Subjectivity 778
Secondat, Charles de (1689–1755)
Books 99
Reading 674
Sedaris, David (1956–)
Illusion 422
Writing 890
Sedgwick, Adam (1785–1873)
Materialism 525
Sedley, Sir Charles (1639–1701)
Mothers 558
Seeger, Pete (1919–)
Education 261
Segal, George (1934–)
Farming 305
Seidler, Harry (1923–2006)
Architects 59
Earthquakes 255
Seifert, Jaroslav (1901–1986)
Lies 489
Seinfeld, Jerry (1954–)
Journalism 443
Newspapers 573
Seitz, Frederick (1911–)
Curiosity 201
Selden, John (1584–1654)
Laws 467
Traitors 825
Sendak, Maurice (1928–)
Adults 30
Seneca (5 BC–AD 65)
Abstinence 16
Adversity 31
Alcoholism 43
Ancestors 52
Anger 54
Art 65
Avarice 75

Seneca (cont.)
Body 96
Chance 128
Character 133
Debt 211
Deeds 215
Defiance 217
Delay 219
Difficulty 236
Discipline, ...239
Error 281
Excellence 287
Expectations 290
Failure 298
Fate 308
Fools 328
Forgiveness 333
Freedom 338
Friendship, ...348
Genius 362
Gifts 363
Giving 364
Humanity 408
Ideas 415
Imitation 425
Kingdoms 455
Leadership 473
Learning 475
Leisure 477
Lies 489
Life 494
Madness 514
Manners 520
Mind 538
Mirrors 540
Misfortune 543
Passion 601
Peace of Mind 609
Pleasure 627
Power 645
Praise 646
The Present 650
Prosperity 660
Prudence 661
Punishment 663
Quality 666
Quantity 667
Reading 675
Sensuality 731
Service 733
Shame 735
Silence 740
Sin 742
Slavery 747
Speaking 758
Stories 767
Talent 794
Thankfulness 807
Time 816
Unhappiness 839
Vice 848
Wealth 865
Wisdom 872
Youth 896
Senior, Nassau William (1790–1864)
Quantity 667
Senna, Ayrton (1960–1994)
Idols 418
Women 877
Serling, Rod (1924–1975)
Television 803
Ethics 283
Weapons 866
Sevareid, Eric (1912–1992)
Executives 289
Television 803
Sévigné, Marquise de (1626–1696)
Friendship 348
Sexton, Anne (1928–1974)
Body 96
Sewell, Anna (1820–1878)
Animals 56
Pets 618
Sewell, George (1924–2007)
Conscience 171
Fear 313

Sewell, George (cont.)
Guilt 381
Sextus Propertius (c. 50–2 BC)
Madness 514
Shaffer, Peter (1926–)
Music 564
Talent 794
Tragedy 825
Shah, Idries (1924–1996)
Enlightenment 274
Shahn, Ben (1898–1969)
Artists 69
Shakespeare, William (1564–1616)
Abstinence 16
Achievement 21
Actions 22
Actors 23
Adversity 31
Alcoholism 43
Angels 53
Arguments 61
Beauty 82
Beggars 85
Blood 94
Books 99
Boredom 101
Brains 104
Brothers 106
Cause and Effect 121
Chaos, ...130
Children 142
Conceit 165
Conscience 171, 172
Contemplation 175
Contempt 176
Cooking 178
Corruption 185
Death 209
Debt 211
Deception 213
Deeds 215
Desire 225
Despair 227
Destiny 230
Devotion 234
Doubt 249
Dreams 251
Eloquence 266
England 272
English 272
Expectations 290
Eyes 294
Faith 299
Fame 301
Familiarity 302
Fashion 306
Fathers 309
Favors 311
Fiction 317
Floods, ...322
Food 325
Fools 328
Forgiveness 333
Gardens 357
Gifts 363
Giving 364
Glory 365
Gold 369
Gossip 371
Grief 381
Guilt 381
Habits 382
Heart 390
Heaven 393
Hell 395
Heroes 398
History 399
Holidays 400
Honesty 402
Hope, ...404
Horses 405
Humility 409
Immortality 426
Innocence 434
Jealousy 441
Joy 447

Shakespeare, William (cont.)
Juries 451
Kindness 454
Kings 456
Kisses 457
Language 462
Lawyers 469
Libraries 486
Lies, ...489
Life 495
Love 510
Madness 514
Manners 520
Marriage 522
Mercy 534
Mind 538, 539
Misery 541
Monarchs 547
Mothers 558
Murder 562
Names 567
Neglect 571
Nobility 574
Noise 575
Numbers 578
Pain 594
Parenthood 599
The Past 603
Patience 605
Peace 608
Philosophy 620
Pity 622
Pleasure 627
Prophets 659
Punishment 664
Quarrels 667
Quiet 669
Reflection 681
Remedies 690
Remembrance 690
Remorse 690
Reputation 693
Rich and Poor 703
Scripture 723
Self 728
Sin 742
Society 752
Soldiers 753
Sorrow 756
Speaking 758
Sports 760
Spring 761
Stars 762
Strangers 769
Studying 775
Stupidity 776
Suicide 786
The Sun 788
Suspicion 791
Tact 792
Talk 795
Thoughts 814
Traitors 825
Trust 830
Truth 832
Vice 848
Villains 851
Virtue 854
War 861
Wine 869
Winning 869
Winter 870
Wisdom 872
Wit 874
Wives 875
Women 877
Words 879
Wounds 885
Wrong 892
Youth 896
Shandling, Garry (1949–)
Dating 206
Sex 733
Shankly, Bill (1913–1981)
Football 330
Sports 760

Shantideva (c. 800)
Happiness 386
Worries, ...884
Sharansky, Natan (1948–)
Democracy 222
Skepticism 744
Sharpton, Al (1954–)
Boxing 104
Shatner, William (1931–)
The Supernatural 788
Shaw, George Bernard (1856–1950)
Ability 12
Alcohol 42
America 48
Arguments 61
Aristocracy 62
Art 65
Assassination 70
Baseball 80
Belief 87
The Bible 89
Burdens 107
Censorship 125
Circumstances 149
Class 152
Communism 161
Conversation 177
Conviction 177
Countries 185
Cowardice 189
Creativity 191
Cynicism 202
Dance 203
Danger 204
Death 209
Democracy 222
Desire 225
Despair 227
Destiny 230
Determination 232
Dogs 247
Dreams 251
Duty 253
Economics 258
England 272
English, ...272, 273
Etiquette 283
Family 303
Fighting 318
Flattery 321
Food 325
Fools 329
Forgiveness 333
Gambling 355
Gardens 357
The Golden Rule 369
Happiness 386
Hate, ...387
Heart 390
Hell 395
Heroes 398
History 399
Home 401
Hope 404
Humanity 408
Humility 409
Imagination 424
Indifference 429
Insects 434
Intelligence 438
Joy 447
Kitchens 458
Knowledge 461
Leisure 477
Liberty 483
Life 495
Literature 498
Love 510
Manners 520
Martyrs 524
Men 533
Mistakes 544
Money 549
Morality 552
Murder 562
Music 564

Shaw, George Bernard (cont.)
Observation 581
Pain 594
Parenthood 599
Patriotism 606
Peace 608
Philosophy 620
The Poor 640
Possibilities 642
Poverty 643
Quiet 669
Quotations 671
Reading 675
Reality 677
Reason 679
Respect 695
Respectability 696
Responsibility 697
Rich and Poor 703
Secrets 725
Silence 740
Sin 742
Sincerity 743
Skeptics 745
Slavery 747
Statesmen 764
Stupidity 776
Superstition 789
Teachers 799
Temptation 805
Uselessness 843
Value 845
War 861
Wives 875
Words 879
Writing 890
Youth 896
Shea, Robert (1933–1994)
Insects 434, 435
Shearer, Harry (1943–)
Power 645
Sheehan, George (1918–1993)
Addiction 25
Body 96
Exercise 289
Happiness 386
Mind 539
Pleasure 627
Sheehy, Gail (1937–)
Cooking 178
Leadership 473
Sheen, Charlie (1965–)
Sobriety 750
Uncertainty 835
Sheen, Bishop Fulton J. (1895–1975)
Flattery 321
Mediocrity 529
Sheen, Martin (1940–)
Catholicism 115
Sheffield, John (1648–1721)
Forgiveness 334
Sheldon, William H. (1898–1977)
Happiness 386
Regret 683
Sheldrake, Rupert (1942–)
Skepticism 744
Shelley, Mary (1797–1851)
Mind 539
Purpose 665
Shelley, Percy Bysshe (1792–1822)
Autumn 74
Charm 135
Misery 541
Spring 761
Thoughts 814
Shenstone, William (1714–1763)
Anger 54
Rich and Poor 703
Shepard, Sam (1943–)
Democracy, ...222
Totalitarianism 820
Sheridan, Richard Brinsley (1751–1816)
Courage, ...187
Daughters 206
Doctors 244

Sheridan, Richard Brinsley (cont.)
Facts 296
Humanity 408
Modesty 547
Speaking 758
Sherman, Allan (1924–1973)
Adultery 29
Sherman, William Tecumseh (1820–1891)
Cruelty 198
Hell 395
Journalists 445
War 862
Sherrington, Charles Scott (1857–1952)
Adjustment 25
Shields, Brooke (1965–)
Birth Control 93
Shiller, Robert J. (1946–)
Intelligence 438
Shipley, Jenny (1952–)
Abortion 14
Shockley, William (1910–1989)
Tomorrow 819
Yesterday 893
Shoemaker, Sam (1893–1963)
Prayer 647
Shoemaker, Willie (1931–2003)
Sports 760
Shore, Dinah (1916–1994)
Trouble 829
Short, Martin (1950–)
Eccentricity 256
Short, Solomon (1789–1867)
Danger 204
Shriver, Sargent (1915–)
Racism 672
Sibelius, Jean (1865–1957)
Criticism 197
Sidney, Sir Philip (1554–1586)
Bravery 105
Gossip 371
Knights 459
Loneliness 500
Nobility 574
Parenthood 599
Sigea, Luisa (1522–1560)
Passion 601
Sigourney, Lydia (1791–1865)
Children 142
Mothers 558
Sills, Beverly (1929–2007)
Failure 298
Silone, Ignazio (1900–1978)
Authority 73
Earthquakes 255
Fascism, ...305
Liberty 483
Silverstein, Shel (1930–1999)
Sensitivity 731
Thoughts 814
Simic, Charles (1938-)
Poetry 630
Simmel, Georg (1858–1918)
Cities 150
Strangers 769
Simmons, Charles (1924–)
Bigotry 90
Fools 329
Manners 520
Simms, William Gilmore (1806–1870)
Censure 126
Tact 792
Tears 801
Simon, Herbert (1916–2001)
Informaiton 432
Simon, John (1873–1954)
Democracy 222
Majorities 516
Simon, Neil (1927–)
Life 495
Simon, Paul (1941–)
Alienation 44
Strangers 769
Simonides (556–468 BC)
Dance 203
Necessity 570
Painting 595

Simonides (cont.)
Poetry 630
Simpson, Jessica (1980–)
Camping 114
Sinatra, Frank (1915–1988)
Alcohol 43
Sinclair, Gordon (1900–1984)
Earthquakes 255
Scandals 717
Sinclair, Upton (1878–1968)
Books 99
Fascism 305
Understanding 838
Singer, Isaac Bashevis (1904–1991)
Eternity 282
Singer, Isaac Bashevis (cont.)
Free Will 340
Literature 499
Originality 592
Writing 890
Singer, Peter (1946–)
Utilitarianism 843
Singh, Manmohan (1932–)
Secularism 725
Siodmak, Curtis (1902–2000)
Weapons 866
Sirk, Douglas (1897–1987)
Intellectualism 437
Sitwell, Edith (1887–1964)
Belief 87
Books 99
Eccentricity 256
Flattery 321
Glory 365
Humility 409
Madness 514
Modesty 547
Poetry 630
Reading 675
Silence, ...740
Taste 795
Truth 832
Vulgarity 857
Sivananda, Swami (1887–1963)
Pilgrimage 621
Purity 664
Senses 730
Struggle 773
Thoughts 814
Values 845
Words 879
Skelton, Richard Bernard "Red" (1913–1997)
Laughter 465
Skinner, B. F. (1904–1990)
Education 261
Machines 513
Sladek, John (1937–2000)
The Future 354
Slaughter, Louise (1929–)
Pollution 639
Slick, Grace (1939–)
Literacy, ...498
Sloan, John (1871–1951)
Consistency 175
Quality 666
Slovo, Joe (1926–1995)
Ideology 417
Smedes, Lewis B. (1921–2002)
Forgiveness 334
Smiles, Samuel (1812–1904)
Difficulty 236
Discovery 240
Honesty 402
Injustice 433
Miracles 540
Resolution 695
Time 816
Smirnoff, Yakov (1951–)
Propaganda 658
Television 803
Smith, Adam (1723–1790)
Benevolence 88
The Public 662
Theories 809
Value 845

Smith, Alexander (1830–1867)
Memory 532
The Sea 723
Superiority 788
Smith, Dodie (1896–1990)
Beauty 82
Ugliness 835
Smith, Captain E. J. (1850–1912)
Accidents 19
Fog 324
Smith, George A. (1817–1875)
Seasons 724
Smith, Hannah Whitall (1832–1911)
Advice 33
Mothers 558
Smith, Hedrick (1933–)
Journalists 445
Smith, Kevin (1970–)
Criticism 197
Smith, Lamar S. (1947–)
Judges 449, 450
Smith, Lillian (1897–1966)
Dehumanization 218
Smith, L. Neil (1946–)
Corporations 184
Lies 489
Smith, Liz (1923–)
Weddings 866
Smith, Logan Pearsall (1865–1946)
Age 37
Blood 94
Books 99
Conscience 172
Idealism 413
Leisure 477
Losing 504
Money 549
Reading 675
Reform 682
Style 777
Youth 896
Smith, Margaret Chase (1897–1995)
Character 133
Cowardice 189
Smith, Michael W. (1957–)
Worship 884
Smith, Patti (1946–)
Adjustment 25
Smith, Scott (1965–)
Writing 890
Smith, Stan (1946–)
Confidence 166
Smith, Sydney (1771–1845)
Books 100
Error 281
Ignorance 420
Mistakes 544
Prejudice 648
Reason 679
Rich and Poor 703
Solitude 754
Talent 794
Timidity 817
The World 883
Smith, William Robertson (1846–1894)
Mythology 566
Smothers, Tommy (1937–)
Censorship 125
Snow, C. P. (1905–1980)
Crime 192
Happiness 386
History 399
Obedience 578
Rebellion 680
Snow, John W. (1939–)
Corporations 184
Snow, Tony (1955–)
Voting 857
Sockman, Ralph W. (1889–1970)
Crisis 195
Defeat 216
Knowledge 461
Love 510
Majorities 516
Minorities 539
Self 728

Sockman, Ralph W. (cont.)
Tolerance 818
Victory 850
Socrates (469–399 BC)
Adversity 32
Celibacy 122
Children 142
Depression 224
Enjoyment 273
Envy, ...278
Fame 301
Food 325
Fools 329
Friendship 348
Glory 365
Government 374
Ignorance 421
Inspiration 435
Instinct 435
Jealousy 441
Knowledge 461
Life 495
Marriage 523
Poetry 630
Politicians 636
Praise 646
Prayer 647
Prosperity 660
Reality 677
Reputation 693
Teachers 799
Thoughts 814
Virtue 854
Wealth 865
Wine 869
Soderbergh, Steven (1963–)
Lies 489
Solomon, King (c. 1000–929 BC)
Riches 704
Rivers 708
Solomon, Sylvia (1949–)
Teachers 799
Solon (638-559 BC)
Advice 33
Character 133
Nobility 574
Oaths 578
Solow, Robert (1924–)
Ambition 46
Solzhenitsyn, Alexander (1918–)
Envy 278
Ethics 283
Humanism 406
Life 495
Memory 532
Sondheim, Stephen (1930–)
Songs 755
Sontag, Susan (1933–2004)
Boredom 101
Depression 224
Lies 489
Men 533
Reality 677
Women 877
Sophocles (496–406 BC)
Authority 73
Cheating 136
Contempt 176
Danger 204
Darkness 205
Death 209
Evil 285
Excuses 288
Grief 381
Ignorance 421
Judgment 450
Kindness 454
Knowledge 462
Laws 467
Lies 489
Love 510
Money 549
Mothers 558
Old Age 584
Pain 594

Sophocles (cont.)
- Remorse 690
- Reward 701
- Ruin 710
- Wealth 865
- Wisdom 872

Sorkin, Aaron (1961–)
- War 862

South, Robert (1634–1716)
- Abstinence 16

Southern, Terry (1924–1995)
- Alienation 44

Southey, Robert (1774–1843)
- Authority 73
- Deception 213
- Friendship 348

Sowell, Thomas (1930–)
- Bureaucracy 111
- Communism 161
- Economics 258
- Elections 266
- Etiquette 283
- Honesty 402
- Liberals 478
- Rationalism 673
- Totalitarianism 820
- Welfare 867

Spalding, Bishop John Lancaster (1840–1916)
- Mothers 558

Spears, Aries (1975–)
- Longevity 501

Specter, Arlen (1930–)
- Judges 450
- Voting 857

Spellman, Cardinal Francis (1889–1967)
- God 368
- Prayer 647

Spence, Gerry (1929–)
- Belief 87

Spencer, Herbert (1820–1903)
- Adjustment 25
- Arguments 61
- Billiards 90
- Boldness 97
- Cause and Effect 121
- Education 261
- Fools 329
- Health 389
- Juries 451

Spengler, Oswald (1880–1936)
- Capitalism 115
- Psychology 662

Spenser, Edmund (1552–1599)
- Liberty 483

Spielberg, Steven (1946–)
- Censorship 125

Spinoza, Benedict de (1632–1677)
- Benevolence 88
- Difficulty 236
- Fame 302
- Flattery 321
- Peace 609
- Peace of Mind 609
- Sin 742
- Understanding 838
- War 862

Spock, Benjamin (1903–1998)
- Babies 76
- Discipline 239
- Fathers 310
- Love 510

Spong, John Shelby (1931–)
- Terrorism 806

Springsteen, Bruce (1949–)
- Adults 30

Spurgeon, Charles H. (1834–1892)
- Ego 265
- Fools 329
- Friendship 348
- Human Nature 405
- Knowledge 462
- Laziness 470
- Perseverance 613
- Slander 745
- Wisdom 872

Spurlock, Morgan (1970–)
Obesity 579
The Sri Guru Granth Sahi
Pilgrimage 622
Staël, Madame de (1766–1817)
Remembrance 690
Service 733
Wit 874
Stafford, William (1914–1993)
Dance 203
Stair, Nadine (1906–)
Mistakes 544
Stalin, Joseph (1879–1953)
Death 209
Hair 383
Rich and Poor 703
Statistics 764
Stallone, Sylvester (1946–)
Redemption 681
Rejection 684
Stamp, Josiah (1880–1941)
Banks 79
Stanislaus I (1677–1766)
Difficulty 236
Stanislavsky, Konstantin (1863–1938)
Art 65
Stanton, Elizabeth Cady (1815–1902)
Age 37
Duty 253
Opinions 585
Sacrifice 712
Truth 832
Stark, Koo (1956–)
Buddhism 107
Starr, Anthony (1975–)
Chaos 130
Sports 760
Starr, Ringo (1940–)
Alcohol 43
Statius, Caecilius (220–168 BC)
Trees 828
Stead, Christina (1903–1983)
Money 549
Wealth 865
Steadman, Ralph (1936–)
Doubt 249
Suspicion 791
Steele, Danielle (1947–)
Mothers 558
Steele, Sir Richard (1672–1729)
Admiration 27
Body, ...96
Books 100
Exercise 289
Flattery 321
Fools 329
Mind 539
Reading 675
Stefansson, Vilhjalmur (1879–1962)
Advertising 33
The Middle Ages 535
Stein, Ben (1944–)
Decisions 214
Duty 253
Life 495
Spirit 759
Stein, Gertrude (1874–1946)
America 48
Common Sense 158
Communism 161
Danger 205
Gardens 357
Information 432
Sculpture 723
Writing 890
Steinbeck, John (1902–1968)
Angels 53
Dishonesty 241
Greatness 379
Ideas 415
The Poor 640
Writing 890
Steinem, Gloria (1934–)
Body 96
Corporations 184
Daughters 206

Steinem, Gloria (cont.)
- Evil 285
- Feminism 315
- Fish 319
- Prison 654
- Status Quo 766

Steinem, Gloria (cont.)
- Women 877

Steiner, George (1929–)
- Poetry 630
- Prose 659

Steiner, Rudolf (1861–1925)
- Community 162

St. Johns, Adela Rogers (1894–1988)
- Husbands 412

Stekel, Wilhelm (1868–1940)
- Maturity 526

Stella, Frank (1936–)
- Artists 69
- Sculpture 723

Stendhal (1783–1842)
- Cleverness 153

Stengel, Casey (1890–1975)
- Business 112
- Crisis 195
- Leadership 473

Stepanek, Mattie (1990–2004)
- Teamwork 800

Stephens, James (1882–1950)
- Bravery 105
- Curiosity 201
- Fear 313

Stephenson, Neal (1959–)
- Subtlety 778

Stern, Bill (1907–1971)
- Elections 266

Sterne, G. B. (1890–1973)
- Optimism 591
- Pessimism 617

Sternberg, Robert (1949–)
- Passion 601

Sterne, Lawrence (1713–1768)
- Distrust 242
- Etiquette 283
- Forgiveness 334
- Health 389
- Knowledge 462
- Manners 520
- Oblivion 580
- Respect 695
- Riches 704

Stevens, Cat (1947–)
- Laughter 465

Stevens, John Paul (1920–)
- Decency 213

Stevens, Wallace (1879–1955)
- Pleasure 627
- Poetry 630
- Scholars 718
- Summer 787

Stevenson, Adlai E., II (1900–1965)
- America 49
- Beauty 82
- Beginnings 86
- Belief 87
- Brotherhood 106
- Communism 161
- Corruption, ...185
- Democrats 223
- Editors 258
- Ego 265
- Forgiveness 334
- Freedom 338
- Hesitation 398
- Ignorance 421
- Journalists 445
- Knowledge 462
- Patriotism 606
- Patriots 607
- Policy 632
- Praise 646
- Presidents 651
- Progress 657
- Quiet 669
- Redemption 681
- Republicans 692

Stevenson, Adlai E., II (cont.)
- Statesmen 764
- Strangers 769
- Words 879

Stevenson, Robert Louis (1850–1894)
- Admiration 27
- Cannibalism 114
- Courage 187
- Destiny 230
- Devotion 234
- Failure 298
- Fear 314
- Forests 331
- Freedom 338
- Friendship 348
- Gardens 358
- Identity 416
- Idleness 418
- Lies 489
- Life 495
- Love 510
- Morality 552
- Neglect 571
- Politics 638
- Quality 666
- Silence 740
- Speaking 758
- Spirit 759
- Theories 809
- Travel 827
- Vanity 847
- Wine 869
- Work 882
- Youth 896

Stewart, Jon (1962–)
- Hollywood 400
- Inspiration 435

Stewart, Patrick (1940–)
- Space 757

Stewart, Potter (1915–1985)
- Abotion 14
- Censorship 125

Stewart, Sean (1965–)
- Comedy 156
- Despair 227
- Food 325
- Heartbreak 392
- Pain 594

Stiles, Ezra (1727–1797)
- Aristocracy 62

Stimson, Henry L. (1867–1950)
- Distrust 242
- Trust 830

Stipe, Michael (1960–)
- Arrogance 63
- Sexuality 734

Stoker, Bram (1847–1912)
- Vampires 846

Stolberg, Benjamin (1891–1951)
- Experience 292
- Experts 293

Stoll, Clifford (1950–)
- Chaos 131

Stone, Clement (1902–2002)
- Objectives 579
- Obstacles 582

Stone, I. F. (1907–1989)
- Government 374
- Lies 489

Stone, Matt (1971–)
- Family 303

Stone, Oliver (1946–)
- Cinema 148
- Murder 562
- Realization 678

Stone, Sharon (1958–)
- Men 533

Stone, W. Clement (1902–2002)
- Attitude 72
- Possessions 642
- Salesmen 714
- Smiles 749

Stoppard, Tom (1937–)
- Actors 23

Stoppard, Tom (cont.)
- Age 37
- Childhood 138
- Democracy 222
- Eternity 282
- Ideas 415
- Imagination 424
- Maturity 526
- Quotations 671
- Truth 832

Storey, David (1933–)
- Friendship 348

Stout, Rex (1886–1975)
- Adolescence 28
- Wealth 865

Stout, Ruth (1884–1980)
- Relaxation 686

Stowe, Harriet Beecher (1811–1896)
- Deeds 215
- Parenthood 599
- Punishment 664
- Truth 832
- Words 879

Stowell, Lord William (1745–1836)
- Food 325

Strachey, Lytton (1880–1932)
- Aristocracy 62

Straczynski, J. Michael (1954–)
- Thoughts 814

Strand, Paul (1890–1976)
- Photography, ... 621

Strauss, Richard (1864–1949)
- Losing 504

Stravinsky, Igor (1882–1971)
- Animals 56
- Childhood 138
- Mistakes 544
- Music 564
- Obstacles 582
- Silence 740

Streep, Meryl (1949–)
- Mothers 558

Streisand, Barbra (1942–)
- Mythology 566
- Slander 746
- Trust 830

Strindberg, August (1849–1912)
- Dogs 247
- Pets 618

Strong, Josiah (1847–1916)
- Aristocracy 62

Strunk, William, Jr. (1869–1946)
- Writing 890

Stuart, Jesse (1906–1984)
- Writing 890

Sullivan, Andrew (1963–)
- Homosexuality 401
- Ideology 417

Sullivan, Annie (1866–1936)
- Freedom 338
- Parenthood 599

Sulzberger, Arthur Hays (1891–1968)
- Brains 104
- Journalists 445

Sulzberger, Arthur Ochs (1926–)
- Sentimentality 731

Summers, Larry (1954–)
- Economics 258

Summers, Montague (1880–1948)
- Witchcraft 874

Sunday, William Ashley (1862–1935)
- Talent 794

Sunde, Karen (1942–)
- Heaven 393

Sun Ra (1914–1993)
- Sickness 738

Sun-tzu (c. 544–496 BC)
- Deception 213
- Defeat 216
- Enemies 271
- Fate 308
- Generals 359
- Kingdoms 455
- Opportunity 587
- Resistance 695

Sun-tzu (cont.)
- Self 728
- Strategy 770
- Subtlety 778
- Victory 850
- War 862
- Warriors 863

Suplee, Ethan (1976–)
- Adolescence 28

Suzman, Helen (1917–)
- Debate 210

Suzuki, David (1936–)
- Skepticism 744
- Talent 794

Suzuki, Shinichi (1898–1998)
- Artists 69
- Children 142
- Experience 292
- Experts 293
- Music 564
- Parenthood 600

Suzuki, Shunryu (1904–1971)
- Zen 898

Svanberg, Carl-Henric (1952–)
- Crisis 195

Swann, Lynn (1952–)
- African-Americans 35

Sweet, Matthew (1964–)
- Creativity 191

Swetchine, Anne Sophie (1782–1857)
- Dignity 237
- Friendship 349
- Love 510
- Strength 772
- Vanity 847
- Weakness 864

Swift, Jonathan (1667–1745)
- Alcoholism 43
- Ambition 46
- Censure 126
- Conversation 177
- Corruption 185
- Death 209
- Desire 225
- Dogs 247
- Feet 314
- Hate 387
- Heart 391
- Kingdoms 455
- Kisses 457
- Laughter 465
- Love 510
- Men 533
- Money 549
- Politicians 636
- Riches 704
- Satire 716
- Slavery 747
- Vision 856
- Youth 896

Swindoll, Charles R. (1934–)
- Friendship 349
- The Past 603

Switzer, Barry (1937–)
- Birth 92
- Ego 265

Swope, Herbert Bayard (1882–1958)
- Failure 298
- Success 781

Sydow, Max von (1929–)
- Charisma 134
- Cinema 148

Sylvian, David (1958–)
- Buddhism 107
- Zen 898

Synge, John Millington (1871–1909)
- Poetry 630
- Translation 826

Syrus, Publilius (c. 100 BC)
- Honor 403
- Loss 505

Szasz, Thomas S. (1920–)
- Adults 30
- Children 142
- Forgiveness 334
- Kingdoms 455

Szasz, Thomas S. (cont.)
Medicine 529
Mental Illness 533
Punishment 664
Reward 701
Right 706
Wrong 892
Szent-Gyorgyi, Albert (1893–1986)
Conscience 172
Discovery, ... 240
Judgment 450
Success 782
Thoughts 814
Water 864

T

Taft, William Howard (1857–1930)
Judges 450
Political Parties 634
Welfare 867
Tagore, Rabindranath (1861–1941)
Beauty 82
Children 142
Clouds 154
Faith 299
Friendship 349
Grace 375
Speaking 758
Surprise 789
Tragedy 825
Yoga 893
Talabani, Jalal (1933–)
Amnesty 50
Talese, Gay (1932–)
Restaurants 697
Talleyrand, Charles Maurice de (1754–1838)
Beggars 85
Defiance 219
Statesmen 763
Talmadge, Thomas DeWitt (1832–1902)
Mothers 558
The Talmud
Anger 55
Deeds 215
Guilt 381
Laughter 465
Mind 539
Oblivion 580
The Poor 640
Relatives 685
Repentance 691
Revenge 699
Wealth 865
Tan, Amy (1952–)
Conformity 170
Desperation 227
Fate 309
Imagination 424
Inspiration 435
Language 462
Memory 532
Power 645
Tancredo, Tom (1945–)
Amnesty 50
Tange, Kenzo (1913–2005)
Architects 59
Tradition 823
Tanner, Chuck (1929–)
Funerals 353
Tarantino, Quentin (1963–)
Cinema 148
Murder 562
Writing 890
Tarkovsky, Adrei (1932–1986)
Cinema 148
Tartakower, Savielly Grigorievitch (1887–1956)
Victory 850
Taylor, Ann (1782–1866)
Cats 119
Mothers 558
Taylor, Elizabeth (1932–)
Abstinence 16
Dogs 247

Taylor, Elizabeth (cont.)
- Patience 605
- Vice 849
- Virtue 854

Taylor, Harold (1914–1993)
- Achievement 21
- Roots 709

Taylor, Henry (1800–1866)
- Charm 135
- Generosity 360

Taylor, Jeremy (1613–1667)
- Ignorance 421
- Pleasure 627
- Quiet 670
- Sorrow 756

Taylor, John (1753–1824)
- Wounds 885

Taylor, Sir Henry (1800–1886)
- Money 549

Taylor, Susan (1827–1860)
- Crisis 195
- Eternity 282
- Quiet 670

Taylor, W. N. (1949–)
- Leisure 477

Teale, Edwin Way (1899–1980)
- Autumn 74
- Utility 843

Tecumseh (1768–1813)
- Legends 476

Teeter, Robert (1939–2004)
- Alienation 44
- Bureaucracy 111
- Cynicism 202

Teller, Edward (1908–2003)
- Addiction 25
- Paradox 596
- Physics 621

Temko, Allen (1924–2006)
- Architecture 60

Temple, William (1628–1699)
- Ability 12
- Complaints 163
- Distrust 242
- Ego 265

Templeton, Charles (1915–2001)
- Christianity 145

Tencin, Madame de (1682–1749)
- Friendship 349

Tenney, James (1934–)
- Style 777

Tennyson, Alfred, Lord (1809–1892)
- Actions 22
- Brides 105
- Despair 227
- Happiness 386
- Mothers 558
- Passion 601
- Reverence 699
- Sex 733
- Sin 742
- Strength 772

Terence (185–159 BC)
- Charity 135
- Courage 187
- Fortune 335
- Humanity 408
- Liberty 483
- Moderation 546
- Praise 646
- Questions 669
- Silence 740

Teresa of Avila, Saint (1515–1582)
- Endurance 269
- Satan, ...715
- Tears 801

Teresa, Mother (1910–1997)
- Ability 12
- Abortion 14
- Beginnings 86
- Devotion 234
- God 368
- Hunger 411
- Joy 447
- Judgment 450
- Life 495

Teresa, Mother (cont.)
Love 510
Miracles 540
Paradox 596
Speaking 758
Strength 772
Vocation, ...857
Words 879
Terkel, Louis "Studs" (1912–)
Decency 213
Stories 767
Terry, Randall (1959–)
Babies 76
Heresy 396
Tertullianus, Quintus Septimius (160–230)
Truth 832
Tesich, Steve (1942–1996)
Friendship 349
Tesla, Nikola (1857–1943)
Mathematics 526
Thackery, William Makepeace (1811–1863)
Bravery 105
Cooking 178
Excellence 287
Laughter 465
Mothers 558
Thalmann, Ernst (1886–1944)
Confessions 165
Thatcher, Margaret (1925–)
America 49
Appeasement 59
Arguments 61
Debate 210
Heart 391
Men 533
Patience 605
Rights 707
Society 752
Talk 795
Thaxter, Celia (1835–1894)
Heart 391
Summer 787
Theisman, Joe (1949–)
Football 330
Themistocles (527–460 BC)
Money 550
Persuasion 616
Theophrastus (372–287 BC)
Time 816
Theresa of Jesus, Saint (1515–1582)
Prayer 647
Theroux, Paul (1941–)
Mind 539
Travel 827
Thomas à Kempis (1380–1471)
Idleness 418
Imperfection 427
Laziness 470
Love 510
Peace of Mind 609
Thomas Aquinas, Saint (1225–1274)
Artists 69
Church 146
Community 162
Friendship 349
Conformity 170
Evil 285
Heresy 396
Hunger 411
Judgment 450
Morality 552
Reason 679
Relaxation 687
Saints 714
Salvation 714
Sin 742
Thomas, Clarence (1948–)
Etiquette 283
Manners 520
Thomas, Dylan (1914–1953)
Alcohol 43
Boredom 101
Old Age 584
Thomas, Lewis (1913–1993)
Affection 34

Thomas, Lewis (cont.)
- Humanity 408
- Language 462
- Music 564
- Science 722
- Society 752
- Understanding 838

Thomas, Marlo (1937–)
- Homosexuality 401

Thomas, Norman (1884–1968)
- Life 495

Thompson, Bennie (1948–)
- Corporations 184

Thompson, Dorothy (1893–1961)
- Conflict 168

Thompson, Francis (1859–1907)
- Character 133

Thompson, Fred (1942–)
- Government 374
- Hollywood 400

Thompson, Hunter S. (1937–2005)
- Alcohol 43
- Beer 84
- Crime 192
- Drugs 252
- Hell 395
- Insanity 434
- Thieves 810
- Triumph 828

Thompson, Joseph P. (1937–)
- Glory 365

Thompson, William I. (1938–)
- Celibacy 122

Thomson, J. Arthur (1861–1933)
- Mind 539

Thomson, James (1700–1748)
- Treason 827

Thomson, Peter (1929–)
- Losing 504

Thomson, William, Lord Kelvin (1824–1907)
- Physics 621

Thoreau, Henry David (1817–1862)
- Ability 12
- Alcohol 43
- Artists 69
- Awe 75
- Belief 87
- Birds 92
- Body 96
- Books 100
- Change 130
- Clothes 153
- Conformity 170
- Desperation 227
- Dogs 247
- Dreams 251
- Earth 254
- Emotions 268
- Eternity 282
- Excitement 288
- Failure 298
- Fame 302
- Fashion 306
- Fate 309
- Feet 314
- Fishing 319
- Flowers 323
- Freedom 338
- Friendship 349
- Fruit 351, 352
- Government 374
- Happiness, ...386
- Health 389
- Heresy 396
- Imagination 424
- Laws 467
- Leisure 477
- Life 495
- Love 510
- Majorities 516
- Miracles 540
- Misunderstanding 545
- Morality 552
- Names 567
- The News 572
- Perception 611

Thoreau, Henry David (cont.)
Philosophy 620
Pleasure 627
Poetry 631
Political Parties 634
Poverty 643
Prejudice 649
The Present 650
Priests 653
Prison 654
Purity 664
Reading 675
Reality 677
Regret 683
Relaxation 687
Rich and Poor 703
Rogues 709
Safety 713
Scholars 718
Sensuality 731
Serenity 732
Silence 740
Simplicity 741
Solitude 754
Strangers 769
Stupidity 776
Success 782
Suspicion 791
Sympathy 791
Taxes 796
Teachers 799
Thoughts 814, 815
Time 816
Tragedy 825
Transcendentalism 826
Truth 833
The Universe 842
Virtue 854
Vision 856
Wages 858
Waste 863
Water 864
Wilderness 867
Work 882
The World 883
Writing 891
Youth 897
Thorn, John (1947–)
Sports 760
Thornburgh, Dick (1932–)
Corporations 184
Thorndike, Edward (1874–1949)
Botany 102
Thornley, Kerry (1938–1998)
Chaos 131
Thorpe, Ian (1982–)
Losing 504
Thucydides (c. 460–395 BC)
Adversity 32
Bravery 105
Courage 187
Enthusiasm 277
Fate 309
Freedom 338
Friendship 349
Glory 365
Happiness 386
Profit 656
Suffering 783
Thurber, James (1894–1961)
Anger, ...55
Belief 87
Comedy 156
Consciousness 173
Desperation 227
Dignity 237
Dogs 247
Duty 253
Ego 265
Electricity 266
Glory 365
Heaven 393
Humor 410
Light 497
Nonconformity 575
Numbers 578

Thurber, James (cont.)
People 610
Questions 669
Safety 713
Sophistication 755
Suspicion 791
Wit 874
Thurman, Howard (1900–1981)
Community 162
Tiegs, Cheryl (1947–)
Beauty 82
Tikkanen, Henrik (1924–1984)
Intelligence 438
Madness 514
Tillich, Paul (1886–1965)
Achievement 21
Cruelty 199
Destiny 230
Duty 253
Listening 497
Love 510
Neurosis 571
Tillotson, John (1630–1694)
Ignorance 421
Silence 740
Speaking 758
Zeal 898
Timrod, Henry (1828–1867)
Spring 761
Ting-Fang, Wu (1842–1922)
Education 261
Titus Livius (59 BC–AD 17)
Ability 11
Misfortune 543
Titus Maccius Plautus (254–184 BC)
Evil 285
Friendship 349
Guilt 381
Loss 505
Patience 605
Sports 760
Wisdom 872
Tocqueville, Alexis de (1805–1859)
Crisis 195
Theories 809
Todt, Fritz (1891–1942)
Engineering 272
Toffler, Alvin (1928–)
Bureaucracy 111
Distrust 242
Error 281
Profit 656
Tokugawa, Ieyasu
Life 495
Tolkien, J. R. R. (1892–1973)
Death 209
Faith 299
Food 325
Gold 369
Justice 452
Marriage 523
Safety 713
Time 816
Warriors 863
The World 883
Tolle, Eckhart (1948–)
Life 495
Toller, Ernst (1893–1939)
Realization 678
Tolstoy, Leo (1828–1910)
Abstinence 16
Artists 69
Beauty 83
Belief 87
Boredom 101
Christianity 145
Conceit 165
Delusion 220
Earth 254
Falsity 300
Family 303
Forgiveness, ...334
God 368
Gold 369
Happiness 386

Tolstoy, Leo (cont.)
Illusion 422
Life 495
Losing 504
Love 510
Peace 609
Property 658
Questions 669
Religion 689
Revelation 699
Slavery 747
Style 777
Truth 833
Unity 840
Warriors 863
Witchcraft 874
Tomlin, Lily (1939–)
Cynicism 202
Drugs 252
Feet 315
Language 462
Life 496
Masturbation 524
Politicians 636
Politics 638
Reality 677
Truth 833
Tooker, George (1920–)
Art 65
Painting 595
Toomer, Jean (1894–1967)
Realization 678
Toscanini, Arturo (1865–1957)
Kisses 457
Torturro, John (1957–)
The Past 603
Tournier, Paul (1898–1961)
Marriage 523
Towne, Charles Hanson (1877–1949)
Friendship 349
Townsend, Robert (1957–)
Bureaucracy 111
Conflict 168
Rust 710
Toynbee, Arnold (1889–1975)
America 49
Animals 56
Civilization 151
Goals 367
Leisure 477
Murder 562
Plants 623
Suicide 786
Tracy, Brian (1944–)
Acceptance 18
Parenthood 600
Winning 869
Trebek, Alex (1940–)
Awe 75
Nature 569
Tree, Herbert Beerbohm (1853–1917)
Virginity 852
Trelease, Jim (1941–)
Books 100
Trevanian (1931–2005)
Equality 280
Trevelyan, Charles E. (1807–1886)
Rivalry 708
Trevelyan, G. M. (1876–1962)
Education 261
Madness 514
Reading 675
Responsibility 697
Trevino, Lee (1939–)
Dogs 247
Tribe, Judge Lawrence (1941–)
Bureaucracy 111
Trillin, Calvin (1935–)
Food 325, 326
Meals 527
Parenthood 600
Restaurants 697
Trilling, Lionel (1905–1975)
Fantasy 304
Neurosis 571

Trogdon, William (1939–)
Thoughts 815
Troisgros, Jean (1926–)
Cooking 179
Troisgros, Pierre (1928–)
Cooking 179
Trollope, Anthony (1815–1882)
Real Estate 675
Satire 716
Trotsky, Leon (1879–1940)
Old Age 584
Strategy 770
Struggle 773
Troward, Thomas (1847–1916)
Cause and Effect 121
Trudeau, Pierre (1919–2000)
Babies 76
Baseball 80
Bedrooms 83
Government 374
Kisses 457
Mothers 558
Nation 567
Taboos 792
Truman, Harry S (1884–1972)
Advice 33
Assassination 70
Children 142
Discipline 239
Dogs 247
Enthusiasm 277
Epitaphs 279
Government 374
Hell 395
Kitchens 458
Leadership 473
Mothers 558
Optimism 591
Parenthood 600
Pessimism 617
Politicians 636
Presidents 651
Prison 654
Statesmen 764
Trump, Donald (1946–)
Moderation 546
Money 550
Winning 869
Truth, Sojourner (1797–1883)
Slavery 747
Women 877
Tsiolkovsky, Konstantin E. (1857–1935)
Mind 539
Tsongas, Paul (1941–1997)
Republicans 692
Tuchman, Barbara W. (1912–1989)
Generals 359
Libraries 486
Tucholsky, Kurt (1890–1935)
Hate 387
Tucker, Michael J. (1957–)
Abortion 14
Tunis, John R. (1889–1975)
Losing 504
Tunney, Gene (1897–1978)
Boxing 104
Tupper, Martin Farquhar (1810–1889)
Babies 77
Eloquence 266
Silence 740
Turing, Alan (1912–1954)
Machines 513
Turlington, Christy (1969–)
Addiction 25
Turner, Kathleen (1954–)
Women 877
Turner, Ted (1938–)
Ego 265
Humility 409
Tusser, Thomas (1524–1580)
Food 325
Hunger 411
Tutu, Desmond (1931–)
Dehumanization 218
Family 303
Forgiveness 334

Tutu, Desmond (cont.)
The Future 354
Tversky, Amos (1937–1996)
Experience 293
Experts 293
Twain, Mark (1835–1910)
Ability 12
Adversity 32
Advertising 33
Alcoholism 43
Ambition 46
America 49
Anger 55
Arrogance 63
Authority 73
Babies 77
Bankers 78
The Bible 89
Books 100
Brotherhood 106
Brothers 106
Cats 119
Censorship 126
Charity 134
Clothes 153
College 155
Community 162
Confidence 166
Conformity 170
Conscience 172
Conservatives 174
Consistency 175
Contempt 176
Conviction 177
Courage 187
Cowardice 189
Criticism 197
Custom 202
Dance 203
Danger 205
Death 210
Desire 225
Determination 232
Dogs 247
Duty 253
Education 261
Efficiency 262
Enemies 271
Enjoyment 273
Enthusiasm 277
Exercise 289
Eyes 294
Facts 296
Fear 314
Fiction 317
Flowers 323
Food 325
Fools 329
Forgiveness 334
Fortune 335
Freedom 338
Friendship 349
Funerals 353
Gifts 363
Golf 370
Government 374
Habits 382
Health 389
Heart 391
Heaven 394
Hell 395
Honesty 402
Humanity 408
Humility 409
Humor 411
Ignorance 421
Illusion 422
Imagination 425
Industry 431
Inferiority 431
Journalists 445
Joy 447
Killing 453
Knights 459
Laughter 465
Laws 468

Twain, Mark (cont.)
Learning 475
Liberals 478
Lies 489
Life 496
Loneliness 500
Loyalty 512
Majorities 516
Malice 517
Mankind 519
Marriage 523
Materialism 525
Maxims 527
Memory 532
Miracles 540
Moderation 546
Mothers 558
Mythology 566
Nakedness 566
Native Americans 568
Numbers 578
Oblivion 580
Opinions 585
Optimism 591
Pain 594
Parenthood 600
People 610
Perseverance 613
Pessimism 617
Pets 618
Pleasure 627
Political Parties 634
Politics 638
Popularity 641
Possibilities 642
Praise 646
Prophets 659
Prudence 661
Quantity 667
Reading 675
Real Estate 675
Reform, ...682
Religion 689
Repartee 691
Resistance 695
Rich and Poor 703
Ridicule 705
Right 706
Satan 716
Science 722
Secrets 725
Silence 740
Slavery 747
Sleep 748
Smoking 749
Soldiers 753
Soul 757
Spring 761
Statesmen 764
Stock Market 766
Stories 767
Strangers 769
Success 782
Superiority 788
Superstition 789
Sympathy 791
Talent 794
Temptation 805
Theories 809
Thoughts 815
Time 816
Trade 522
Truth 833
Weather 866
Vice 849
Vulgarity 857
War 862
Wealth 865
Wit 874
Words 879
The World 883
Wrong 892
Youth 897

Tyler, Anne (1941–)
Advice 33
Dogs 248

Tyler, Anne (cont.)
- Luck 512

Tynan, Kenneth (1927–1980)
- Neurosis 571
- Secularism 725
- Theater 808

U

Udall, Stewart L. (1920–)
- Crisis 196
- Power 645

Ueland, Brenda (1891–1985)
- God 368

Ullman, Liv (1938–)
- Babies 77
- Parenthood 600

Ullman, Samuel (1840–1924)
- Enthusiasm 277

Ulmer, Ernestine (1925–)
- Dessert 228

Ulpian (c. 228)
- Justice 452

Ulrich, Laurel Thatcher (1938–)
- Women 877

Ulvaeus, Björn (1945–)
- Values 845

Unamuno, Miguel de (1864–1936)
- Skepticism 744
- Skeptics 745
- Solitude 754

Underhill, Evelyn (1875–1941)
- Deeds 215
- Evil 285

Unitas, Johnny (1933–2002)
- Conceit 165

Updike, John (1932–)
- Activity 23
- Adultery....29
- America 49
- Boredom 101
- Cats 119
- Criticism 197
- Dreams 251
- Fools 329
- Grace 375
- Rain 672
- Taste 796

Urich, Robert (1946–2002)
- Longevity 501

U.S. Declaration of Independence
- Equality 280

Ustinov, Peter (1921–2004)
- Belief 87
- Children 142
- Comedy 156
- Conformity 170
- Corruption 185
- Criticism 197
- Daughters 206
- Doubt 249
- Experience 292
- Experts 293
- Forgiveness 334
- Generals 359
- Humor 411
- Laughter 465
- Love 510
- Nation 567
- Noise 575
- Optimism 591
- War 862

V

Valance, Holly (1983–)
- Insects 435

Valenti, Jack (1921–2007)
- Censorship 126

Valéry, Paul (1871–1945)
- The Future 354
- Indifference 429
- Paradox 596
- Poetry 631
- Politics 638
- Trouble 829

Valois, Marguerite de (1553–1615)
Heart 391
Valvano, Jim (1946–1993)
Enthusiasm 277
Van Ark, Joan (1943–)
Church 146
Vanbrugh, Sir John (1664–1726)
Pleasure 627
Virtue 854
Van Buren, Abigail (1918–)
Age 37
Birth 92
Maturity 526
Old Age 584
Parenthood 600
Wisdom 872
Van Buren, Martin (1782–1862)
Banks 79
Vance, Jack (1916–)
Automobiles 73
Vanderbilt, Gloria (1924–)
Laughter 465
Mothers 558, 559
Vandiver, William Duncan (1854–1932)
Eloquence 267
Van Doren, Carl (1885–1950)
Conformity 170
Van Doren, Mark (1894–1972)
Discovery 240
Teachers 799
Wit 873
Van Dyke, Henry (1852–1933)
Birds 92
Friendship 349
Life 496
Talent 794
Welfare 867
Vaneigem, Raoul (1934–)
Boredom 101
Losing 504
Starvation 762
Subjectivity 778
Van Gogh, Vincent (1853–1890)
Artists 69
Babies 77
Enthusiasm 277
Fate 309
Love 510
Skepticism 744
Spirit 759
Strength 772
Van Horne, William (1843–1915)
Competition 163
van Vechten, Carl (1880–1964)
Cats 119
Van Vliet, Don (1941–)
Automobiles 73
Varése, Edgard (1883–1965)
Genius 362
Vargo, Ed (1930–)
Baseball 80
Vaughan, Bill (1915–1977)
Conformity 170
Nonconformity 575
Prediction 648
Vauvenargues, Marquis de (1715–1747)
Ability 12
Achievement 21
Equality 280
Nature 570
Thoughts 811
Veblen, Thorstein (1857–1929)
Addiction 25
Business 112
Invention 440
Leisure 477
Nationalism 568
Questions 669
Research 694
Travel 827
Vedder, Eddie (1964–)
Caffeine 113
Vega, Lope de (1562–1635)
Profit 656

Vegetius, Flavius Renatus (c. 400)
Peace 609
Valor 844
Vichy-Chamrond, Marie Anne de (1697–1780)
Women 877
Vicious, Sid (1957–1979)
Anarchy 51
Vickrey, William (1914–1996)
Unemployment 838
Victoria, Queen (1819–1901)
Babies 77
Queens 668
Vidal, Gore (1925–)
Advice 33
Atheism 71
Children 142, 143
Corporations 184
Failure 298
Journalism 443
Newspapers 573
Prose 659
Style 777
Theater 808
Voting 857
Villard, Henry (1835–1900)
Journalists 445
Vine, Tim (1966–)
Hunting 412
Vinet, Alexandre Rodolphe (1797–1847)
Imitation 425
Virgil (70–19 BC)
Ability 12
Belief 87
Confidence 166
Courage 187
Experience 292
Experts 293
Fruit 352
Generosity 360
Gifts 363
Hell 395
Rumors 710
Safety 713
Sickness 738
Sleep 748
Strategy 770
Tears 801
Trust 830
Viscott, David (1938–1996)
Love 511
Vivekananda, Swami (1863–1902)
Cause and Effect 121
Mercy 534
Thoughts 815
Worship 884
Vizinczey, Stephen (1933–)
Stupidity 776
Voltaire (1694–1778)
Abstinence 16
Appeasement 59
Assassination 70
Astrology 70
Atheism 71
Belief 87
Boldness 97
Books 100
Boredom 101
Censorship 126
Certainty 127
Christianity 145
Clergy 153
Conformity 170
Conscience 172
Cowardice 189
Crime 192
Dance 203
Danger 205
Disease 241
Doctors 244
Doubt 249
Earthquakes 255
Enemies 271
Equality 280

Voltaire (cont.)
Error 281
Excellence 287
Excess 288
Expectations 290
Fame 302
Faults 311
Fear 314
Frankness 335
Freedom 338
Funerals 353
God 368
Government 374
Guilt 381
History 399
Ignorance 421
Judgment 450
Liberty 483
Life 496
Marriage 523
Medicine 529
Misfortune, ...543
Moderation 546
Morality 552
Murder 562
The News 572
Opinions 585
Philosophy 620
Poetry 631
Prayer 647
Prejudice 649
Pride 652
Priests 653
Punishment 664
Questions 669
Reading 675
Right 706
Satire 716
Silence 740
Speaking 758
Stupidity 776
Style 777
Superstition 789
Tears 801
Thoughts 815
Truth 833
Tyranny 834
Uncertainty 835
Vice 849
Virginity 852
Work 882
Wrong 892
Von Furstenberg, Diane (1945–)
Risk 708
Vonnegut, Kurt, Jr. (1922–2007)
Artists 69
Astrology 70
Church 146
Community 162
Criticism 197
Earth 254
Greed 380
Identity 416
Jokes 442
Laughter 465
Learning 475
Life 496
Loneliness 500
Maturity 526
Nature 570
Novels 577
Political Parties 634
Speaking 758
Tears 801
Television 804
The Universe 842
Utopia 844
War 862
Work 882
Writing 891
Von Sachsen, Friedrich (1463–1525)
Confidence 167
Vries, Gijs de (1956–)
Terrorism 807

W

Wachowski, Andy (1967–)
- Dreams 251
- Humanity 409

Wachowski, Larry (1965–)
- Dreams 251
- Humanity 409

Waddles, Charleszetta (1912–2001)
- Pride 652

Wagner, Jane (1935–)
- Ability 12
- Delusion 220

Wagner, Richard (1813–1883)
- Joy 447

Waite, Terry (1939–)
- Terrorism 807

Waitley, Denis (1933–)
- Determination 232
- Dreams 251
- Enthusiasm 277
- Excitement 288
- Persistence 614
- Perspective 615
- Smiles 749
- Success 782
- Winning 869

Wakoski, Diane (1937–)
- Poetry 631

Walden, Greg (1957–)
- Corporations 184

Wales, Jimmy (1966–)
- Politics 638

Walken, Christopher (1943–)
- Weddings 866

Walker, Alice (1944–)
- Animals 56
- Heart 391
- Mothers 559
- Parenthood 600
- Sisters 743

Walker, Margaret (1915–1998)
- Godfathers 376

Walker, Mort (1923–)
- Laughter 465

Walker, Stanley (1898–1962)
- Etiquette 283

Wall, Larry (1949–)
- Ideology 417

Wallace, Daniel (1959–)
- Love 511

Wallace, George C. (1919–1998)
- Segregation 726

Wallace, Henry A. (1888–1965)
- Bigotry 90

Wallace, Irving (1916–1990)
- Conformity 170
- Individualism 430
- Self 728

Wallace, Mike (1918–)
- Queens 668

Wallace, Randall (1949–)
- Death 210
- Freedom 338
- Life 496

Wallace, William Ross (1819–1881)
- Mothers 559
- Parenthood 600

Wallach, Eli (1915–)
- Criticism 197
- Praise 646

Wallenda, Karl (1905–1978)
- Life 496

Wallop, Malcolm (1933–)
- Alliances 45

Walpole, Horace (1717–1797)
- Comedy 156
- Humor 411
- Ridicule 705
- Tragedy 825

Walpole, Hugh (1884–1941)
- Adjustment 25

Walsh, William (1663–1708)
Despair 227
Hope 404
Walters, Barbara (1929–)
Determination 232
Walters, Richard "Slick Rick" (1965–)
Realism 676
Walton, Anthony (1962–)
America 49
Walton, Izak (1593–1683)
Birds 92
Health 389
Heaven 394
Walton, Sam (1918–1992)
Expectations 290
Wanamaker, John (1838–1922)
Advertising 33
Courtesy 188
Warburton, William (1698–1779)
Reason 679
Ridicule 705
Ward, Mary A. (1851–1920)
Thoughts 815
Ward, William Arthur (1921–1994)
Anger 55
Change 130
Cooperation 179
Curiosity 201
Excuses 288
Forgiveness 334
Friendship 349
Learning 475
Maturity 526
Teachers 799
Ware, Chris (1967–)
Teenagers 802
Warhol, Andy (1928–1987)
Artists 69
Change 130
Dating 206
Fame 302
Fish 319
The Future 354
Kisses 458
Opposites 588
Warner, Charles Dudley (1829–1900)
Conformity 170
Friendship 349
Giving 364
Warren, Earl (18991–1974)
Age 38
Justice 453
Laws 468
Warren, Rick (1909–)
Retirement 698
Servants 732
Service 733
Warren, Robert Penn (1905–1989)
Poetry 631
Sensitivity 731
Washington, Booker T. (1856–1915)
Ability 12
Circumstances 149
Mothers 559
Obstacles 582
Soul 757
Success 782
Washington, Denzel (1954–)
Rain 672
Washington, George (1732–1799)
Adversity 32
Alliances 45
America 49
Burdens 107
Conscience 172
Defiance 219
Destiny 230
Dignity 237
Discipline 239
Freedom 338
Friendship 349
Gambling 355
Government 374
Liberals 478

Washington, George (cont.)
Liberty 483
Mothers 559
Self-Control 729
Washington, Martha (1732–1802)
Happiness 386
Misery 541
Wasserstein, Wendy (1950–2005)
Loneliness 500
Waterman, Pete (1947–)
Losing 504
Waters, John (1946–)
Obsession 581
Waters, Maxine (1938–)
Anger 55
Waters, Roger (1943–)
Losing 504
Watson, Diane (1933–)
African-Americans 35
Music 564
Watson, James D. (1928–)
Biology 91
Evolution 286
Watson, Lillian Eichler (1902–)
Manners 520
Watson, Thomas J. (1874–1956)
Conformity 170
Machines 513
Watson, William (1858–1935)
Abstinence 16
Watterson, Bill (1958–)
Children 143
Conversation 177
Intelligence 438
Mothers 559
Reality 677
Research 694
Ruin 710
The Universe 842
Women 879
Wattleton, Faye (1943–)
Leadership 473
Watts, Alan W. (1915–1973)
Buddhism 107
Illusion 422
Love 511
Mythology 566
Saints 714
Zen 898
Watts, Isaac (1674–1748)
Appearances 58
Certainty 127
Satan 716
Watts, J. C. (1957–)
Losing 504
Watzlawick, Paul (1921–)
Suicide 786
Waugh, Alec (1898–1981)
Praise 647
Success 782
Wine 869
Waugh, Evelyn (1903–1966)
Friendship 350
Waugh, Evelyn (cont.)
Manners 520
Paradise 596
Punctuality 663
Youth 897
Wax, Ruby (1953–)
Mothers 559
Wayans, Damon (1960–)
Struggle 773
Wayne, John (1907–1979)
Acting 22
Courage 187
Ego 265
Tomorrow 819
Weah, George (1966–)
Liberation 479
Weaver, Dennis (1924–2006)
Automobiles 74
Cannibalism 114
Weaver, Earl (1930–)
Cheating 136

Weber, Max (1864–1920)
Questions 669
Webster, Daniel (1782–1852)
Appearances 58
Confessions 165
Conviction 177
Liberty 483
Suicide 786
Webster, John (1580–1632)
Kitchens 458
Lust 513
Weil, Simone (1909–1943)
Duty 254
Evil 285
Fiction 317
Force 330
God 368, 369
Humanism 406
Intelligence 438
Machines 513
The Past 603
Purity 664
Socialism 751
Weinberg, Steven (1933–)
Effort 263
Religion 689
The Universe 842
Weinstein, Joe (1953–)
Pets 618
Weisberger, Laren (1977–)
Diet 235
Weisz, Rachel (1971–)
Eccentricity 256
Weizmann (1874–1952)
Laws 468
Welch, Jack (1935–)
Bureaucracy 111
Leadership 473
Managers 517
Self-Confidence 728
Welles, Orson (1915–1985)
Aging 39
Agnosticism 40
Artists 69
Coffee 154
Countries 185
Food 325
Gluttony 366
Lunch 512
Memory 531
Quotations 671
Shakespeare 735
Style 777
Universities 843
Wellesley, Arthur (1769–1852)
France 335
Journals 446
Wells, Bob (1966–)
Government 374
Wells, Carolyn (1862–1942)
Actions 23
Wells, H. G. (1866–1946)
Adults 30
Crisis 196
Education 261
History 399
Jealousy 441
Mystery 565
Nature 570
Pain 594
The Past 603
Research 694
Writing 891
Welstone, Paul (1944–2002)
Corporations 184
Welty, Eudora (1909–2001)
Cause and Effect 121
Revelation 699
Shelter 736
Wenders, Wim (1945–)
Cinema 148
Criticism 197
Entertainment 274
Wesley, John (1703–1791)
Enthusiasm 277
Giving 364

Wesley, John (cont.)
Witchcraft 874
Wesley, Samuel (1766–1837)
Style 777
West, Jessamyn (1902–1984)
Heart 391
Heartbreak 392
Irony 440
Wounds 885
West, Kanye (1977–)
Addiction 25
Clothes 154
Misery 541
Pleasure 627
West, Mae (1892–1980)
Age 38
Censorship 126
Finance 318
Marriage 523
Mothers 559
Speaking 758
Temptation 805
Trouble 829
Virtue 854
West, Rebecca (1892–1983)
Desire 225
Duty 254
Epitaphs 279
Feminism 316
Friendship 350
Life 496
Nobility 574
Passion 601
Westcott, Brooke Foss (1825–1901)
Crisis 196
Westerfield, Scott (1963–)
Nature 570
Westlake, Donald E. (1933–)
Magazines 514
Westmoreland, William C. (1914–2005)
Censorship 126
Weyrich, Paul (1942–)
Judges 450
Scandals 718
Wharton, Edith (1862–1937)
Age 38
America 49
Art 65
Criticism 197
Friendship 350
Illness 421
Marriage 523
Mirrors 540
Money 550
Old Age 584
Originality 592
Reading 675
Silence 740
Speaking 758
Writing 891
Whately, Richard (1787–1853)
Manners 520
Whichcote, Benjamin (1609–1683)
Ego 265
Whipple, Edwin P. (1819–1886)
Reason 679
White, Byron R. (1917–2002)
Rape 673
White, E. B., (1899–1972)
Democracy 223
Humor 411
Kitchens 458
Nature 570
White, Gilbert (1720–1793)
Botany 102
White, Hugh (1773–1840)
Mistakes 544
White, Minor (1908–1976)
Photography 621
White, Paul D. (1886–1973)
Tobacco 817
White, Richard (1947–)
Life 496
Stories 767
White, Theodore H. (1915–1986)
Kitchens 458

White, Theodore H. (cont.)
Leadership 474
White, William Allen (1868–1944)
Status Quo 766
Tyranny 834
Whitehead, Alfred North (1861–1947)
Ability 12
Age 38
Art 65
Cats 119
Courage 187
Disaster 238
Distrust 242
Dogs 248
Ideas 415
Majorities 516
Opportunity 587
Pacifism 593
Perception 611
Pets 618
Philosophy 620
Poetry 631
Progress 657
Quantity 667
Simplicity 741
Virtue 855
Youth 897
Whitehead, John W. (1946–)
Children 143
Whitehorn, Katharine (1928–)
Listening 498
Money 550
Whitman, Walt (1819–1892)
America 49
Arguments 61
Body 96
Censorship 126
Cities 150
Conflict 168
Defiance 219
Earth 254
Emotions 268
Failure 298
Flowers 323
Fortune 335
Frankness 335
Freedom 339
Friendship 350
Gardens 358
God 369
Humanity 409
Judgment 450
Loneliness 500
Manners 520
Nature 570
The Past 603
Poetry 631
Police 632
Shadows 734
Simplicity 741
Wisdom 872
Youth 897
Whittier, John Greenleaf (1807–1892)
Tradition 823
Whittlesey, Faith (1939–)
Feminism 316
Whitton, Charlotte (1896–1975)
Ability 12
Wicki, Bernhard (1919–2000)
Status 765
Wiesel, Elie (1928–)
Evil 285
Indifference 429
Kingdoms 456
Life 496
Power 645
Racism 672
Shadows 734
Soul 757
Spirit 759
Stories 768
Winning 869
Wieseltier, Leon (1952–)
Certainty 127
Wiesenthal, Simon (1908–2005)
Hate 388

Wiesenthal, Simon (cont.)
Survival 790
Wiggin, Kate Douglas (1856–1923)
Children 143
Mothers 559
Wilberforce, William (1759–1833)
Industry 431
Wilczek, Frank (1951–)
Mathematics 526
Philosophy 620
Physics 621
Wilde, Oscar (1854–1900)
Ability 12
Acting 22
Advice 33
Age 38
Alcohol 43
America 49
Appearances 58
Arguments 61
Art 65
Artists 69
Bachelors 78
Beauty 83
Beginnings 86
Belief 87
Books 100
Breakfast 105
Brotherhood 106
Business 112
Charm 135
Children 143
Civilization 152
Common Sense 158
Confessions 165
Conformity 170
Conscience 172
Consciousness 174
Consistency 175
Conversation 177
Countries 186
Cowardice 189
Crime 192
Culture 199
Curiosity 201
Danger 205
Death 210
Deception 213
Deeds 215
Devotion 234
Divorce 243
Dreams 251
Emotions 268
Enemies 271
England 272
Excess 288
Experience 292
Fantasy 304
Fashion 306
Faults 311
Fiction 317
Fidelity 318
Flirting 322
Flowers 323
Food 325
Forgiveness 334
Friendship 350
Fruit 352
Gambling 355
Genius 362
God 369
Gossip 371
Happiness 386
Hell 395
Ignorance 421
Illusion 422
Imagination 425
Inividualism 429
Inferiority 431
Intoxication 439
Journalism 443
Journalists 445
Kingdoms 456
Language 462
Lies 489
Life 496

Wilde, Oscar (cont.)
Literature 499
Love 511
Mankind 519
Marriage 523
Misfortune 543
Mistakes 544
Misunderstanding 545
Moderation 546
Money 550
The Moon 551
Morality 552
Mothers 559
Mystery 565
Nobility 574
Novels 577
Obedience 578
Occupation 582
Optimism 591
Painting 595
Paradox 596
The Past 603
Perfection 611
Personality 614
Pessimism 617
Pleasure 627
Poetry 631
Political Parties 634
Popularity 641
Prayer 647
Prison 654
Punctuality 663
Punishment 664
Quotations 671
Reason 679
Reform 682
Refuge 683
Reputation 693
Resolution 695
Respectability 696
Rich and Poor 703
Riches 704
Salesmen 714
Scandals 718
Selfishness 730
Senses 730
Seriousness 732
Simplicity 741
Sin 742
Sincerity 743
Soul 757
Starvation 762
Sympathy 791
Tact 792
Talk 795
Taste 796
Temptation 805
Theater 808
Tragedy 825
Trouble 829
Truth 833
Ugliness 835
Utopia 844
Vulgarity 857
Wealth 865
Weather 866
Wisdom 872
Wit 874
Women 877
Worship, ...884
Writing 891
Wrong 892
Youth 897

Wilder, Gene (1933–)
Cancer 114

Wilder, Thornton (1897–1975)
Avarice 75
Humanity 409
Life 496
Nonsense 576

Wiles, Andrew (1953–)
Relaxation 687

Wilhelm, Georg (1770–1831)
Passion 601

Wilhelm, Kaiser, II (1859–1941)
Beer 84

Wilkins, Mary (1852–1930)
Cats 119
Wilkinson, Paul (1937–)
Terrorism 807
Will, George F. (1941–)
Cats 119
Excellence 287
Excess 288
Football 330
Pessimism 617
Sports 760, 761
Toys 822
Willard, Frances E. (1839–1898)
Abstinence 16
William of Wykeham (1324–1404)
Etiquette 283
Manners 520
Williams, Ben (1982–)
Dogs 248
Williams, Charles (1886–1945)
Self 728
Williams, Don, Jr. (1968–)
Beauty 83
Williams, Kenneth (1926–1988)
Comedy 156
Vulgarity 858
Williams, Raymond (1921–1988)
Crisis 196
Williams, Robin (1952–)
Blood, ...94
Comedy 156
Divorce 243
Madness 514
Satire 716
Williams, Serena (1981–)
Sisters 743
Williams, Tad (1957–)
Lies 489
Williams, Tennessee (1911–1983)
Distrust 243
Frankness 335
God 369
Hell 395
Kindness 454
Loneliness 500
Nature 570
Redemption 681
Security 726
Strangers 769
Williams, Walter J. (1953–)
Editors 259
Williams, William Carlos (1883–1963)
Appearances 58
Art 65
Language 463
Poetry 631
Stories 768
Summer 787
Williamson, Hugh (1735–1819)
Rebellion 680
Repression 692
Revolution 701
Williamson, Marianne (1952–)
Cause and Effect 121
Charisma 134
Darkness 205
Fear 314
Political Parties 634
Recovery 681
Transformation 826
Willis, Ellen (1941–2006)
Consumerism 175
Willis, Nathaniel Parker (1806–1867)
Mothers 559
Willkie, Wendell (1892–1944)
Weakness 864
Willson, Meredith (1902–1984)
Pleasure 627
Wilson, August (1945–2005)
African-Americans 35
Wilson, Earl (1934 – 2005)
Adolescence 28
Snow 750
Wilson, Edmund (1895–1972)
Communism 161

Wilson, Edward O. (1929–)
Ideology 417
Transcendentalism 826
Wilson, Eugune S. (1900–1981)
Curiosity 201
Learning 475
Obstacles 582
Wilson, Harold (1916–1995)
Courage 187
Negotiation 571
Wages 859
Wilson, John (1785–1854)
Books 100
Wilson, Malcolm (1914–2000)
Corporations 184
Wilson, Owen (1968–)
Wealth 864
Wilson, Robert Anton (1932–)
Censorship 126
Conservatives 175
Cynicism 202
Idealism 413
Liberals 478
Theology 809
Wilson, Tom (1931–1978)
Honesty 402
Losing 504
Roses 709
Wilson, Woodrow (1856–1924)
Achievement 21
America 49
Brains 104
Caution 121
Character 133
Conservatives 175
Cooperation 179
Crisis 196
Destiny 230
Dreams 251
Duty 254
Fighting 318
Friendship 350
Intelligence 438
Judgment 450
Kingdoms 456
Patriotism 606
Power 645
Reform 682
Repression 692
Revolution 701
Spirit 759
Statesmen 764
Strength 772
Students 774
Studying 775
Suicide 787
Tolerance 818
Tomorrow 819
Winning 869
Worship 884
Youth 897
Winchell, Walter (1897–1972)
Hollywood 400
Winer, Dave (1955–)
Fruit 352
Winfrey, Oprah (1954–)
Biology 91
Blessings 94
Body 96
Censorship 126
Dance 203
Failure 298
Feet 315
Hate 388
Honor 403
Integrity 436
Mothers 559
Philosophy 620
Queens 668
Reverence 699
Service 733
Winkler, Henry (1945–)
Relationships 685
Winsor, Kathleen (1919–2003)
Ability 12

Winterson, Jeanette (1959–)
- Happiness 386
- Risk 708
- Stories 768
- Value 845

Winthrop, John (1588–1649)
- Authority 73
- Liberty 483

Wirt, William (1772–1834)
- Curiosity 201

Wirthlin, Joseph B. (1917–)
- Friendship 350

Witherspoon, John (1723–1794)
- Books 100

Witten, Edward (1951–)
- Relativity 686
- Unity 840

Wittgenstein, Ludwig (1889–1951)
- Life 496
- Mental Illness 533
- Persuasion 616
- Philosophy 620

Wodehouse, P. G. (1881–1975)
- Cats 119
- Misery 542
- Youth 897

Wolf, David T. (1943–)
- Cynicism 202
- Idealism 413

Wolf, Frank R. (1939–)
- Scripture 723

Wolfberg, Dennis (1946–1994)
- Abstinence 16

Wolfe, Gene (1931–)
- Knights 459

Wolfe, Humbert (1885–1940)
- Journalists 445

Wolfe, Thomas (1900–1938)
- Talent 794

Wolfe, Tom (1931–)
- Loneliness 500
- Religion 689
- Vanity 847

Wolfensohn, James (1933–)
- Crisis 196

Wolff, Tobias (1945–)
- Persistence 614

Wollstonecraft, Mary (1759–1797)
- Monarchs 547
- Religion 689
- Slavery 748

Wonder, Stevie (1950–)
- Ability 13
- Mothers 559

Wood, Natalie (1938–1981)
- Bathrooms 80

Woodberry, George E. (1855–1930)
- Faith 299

Wooden, John (1910–)
- Ability 13
- Conceit 165
- Sports 761

Woodhouse, Barbara (1910–1988)
- Dogs 248

Woods, Alan (1944–)
- Blame 93

Woods, Tiger (1975–)
- Basketball 80
- Golf 370

Woodson, Carter G. (1875–1950)
- Conformity 170
- Segregation 726
- Slavery 748

Woodward, Bob (1943–)
- Decisions 214
- Lies 489
- Presidents 651

Woolf, Virginia (1882–1941)
- Food 325
- Gender 358
- Kingdoms 456
- Literature 499
- Self 728

Wordsworth, William (1770–1850)
- Admiration 27
- Homelessness 401

Wordsworth, William (cont.)
Research 694
Teachers 799
Theories 810
Warriors 863
Worrell, Bernie (1944–)
Talk 795
Wotton, Henry (1568–1639)
Ambassadors 45
Wouk, Herman (1915–)
Fiction 317
Taxes 796
Wright, Frank Lloyd (1867–1959)
Age 38
Architecture 60
Art 65
Atheism 71
Belief 87
Culture 199
Devotion 234
Eyes 294
Ideas 415
Imagination 425
Materialism 525
Nature 570
Nobility 574
Salvation 714
Simplicity 741
Television 804
Truth 833
Utility 843
Writing 891
Youth 897
Wright, Orville (1871–1948)
Truth 833
Wright, Steven (1955–)
Babies 77
Cats 119
Curiosity 201
Evolution 286
Fishing 319, 320
Forests 331
Painting 595
Sleep 748
Wright, Wilbur (1867–1912)
Ability 13
Wright, Wilbur (cont.)
Birds 92
Wurtzel, Elizabeth (1967–)
Depression 224
Wylie, Philip (1902–1971)
Bliss 94
Ignorance 421
Oblivion 580
Wyman, Jane (1914–)
Brotherhood 106
Wyse, Lois (1926–2007)
Friendship 350
Godfathers 376

X

Xenocrates (396–314 BC)
Regret 683
Xenophon (430–357 BC)
Aristocracy 62
The Dead 207
Xiaoping, Deng (1904–1997)
Cats 119

Y

Yarbro, Chelsea Quinn (1942–)
Heresy 396
Yeats, William Butler (1865–1939)
Anarchy 51
Communication 158
Dreams 251
Flowers 323
Glory 366
Journalists 446
Language 463
Pity 622
Rogues 709
Shadows 734
Sobriety 750
Strangers 769

Yeats, William Butler (cont.)
- Women 877

Yee, Rodney (1957–)
- Death 210

Yehoshua, A. B. (1936–)
- Zionism 898

Yeltsin, Boris (1931–)
- Communism 161

Yevtushenko, Yevgeny (1933–)
- Translation 826

Yockey, Francis P. (1917–1960)
- Imperialism 427
- Pessimism 617

Yogananda, Paramahansa (1893–1952)
- Smiles 749

Yoo, John (1967–)
- Torture 820

Yoshimasa, Shiba (1350–1410)
- Actions 23

Young, Andrew (1932–)
- Parenthood 600
- Wealth 865

Young, Brigham (1801–1877)
- Daughters 206

Young, Edward (1683–1765)
- Glory 366
- Poetry 631
- Procrastination 655
- Prose 659
- Satire 717

Young, Loretta (1913–2000)
- Love 511

Young, Whitney (1921–1971)
- Nobility 574

Younger, Evelle J. (1918–1989)
- Delay 219

Youngblood, Jack (1950–)
- Losing 504

Younger, Evelle J. (1918–1989)
- Lawyers 469

Youngman, Henny (1906–1998)
- Alcohol 43
- Atheism 71
- Children 143
- Godfathers 376
- Holidays 400
- Reading 675

Yunus, Muhammad (1940–)
- Bankers 78

Yutang, Lin (1895–1976)
- Afternoon 35
- Lawyers 469
- Mothers 559
- Peace of Mind 610

Z

Zaharias, Babe Didrikson (1911–1956)
- Friendship 350

Zangwill, Israel (1864–1926)
- Brothers 106
- Cleverness 153
- Imitation 426

Zapata, Emiliano (1877–1919)
- Feet 315

Zapatero, Jose Luis Rodriguez (1960–)
- Corporations 184
- Terrorism 807

Zappa, Frank (1940–1993)
- America 49
- Art 65
- Books 100
- Communism 161
- Journalism 443
- Laws 468
- Stupidity 776

Zaslow, Michael (1944–1998)
- Vulnerability 858

Zenger, John Peter (1697–1746)
- Liberty 483

Zeno (335–264 BC)
- Goals 367
- Nature 570

Zeuxis (c. 400 BC)
- Criticism 197

Zhang, Ziyi (1979–)
Cinema 149
Zhou En Lai (1898–1976)
Diplomacy 238
Zhuang Zi (369–286 BC)
Reward 701
Ziglar, Zig (1926–)
Ability 13
Determination 232
Effort 263
Gratitude 377
Humanity 409
Integrity 436
Laughter 465
Money 550
Motivation 561
Parenthood 600
Persuasion 616
Positivity 643
Winning 869
Zimbardo, Philip (1933–)
Shyness 737
Zimmermann, Johann Georg von (1728–1795)
Custom 202
Relaxation 687
Retirement 698
Zinn, Howard (1922–)
Nationalism 568
Ziyang, Zhao (1919–2005)
Communism 161
Zola, Émile (1840–1902)
Artists 69
Priests 653
Style 778
Zuniga, Daphne (1962–)
Apathy 57
Zurschmeide, Jeff (1964–)
Mirrors 540

Index by Subject

A

Ability 9-13
Abortion 13-14
Abstinence 14-16
Absurdity 16
Abundance 16-17
Acceptance 17-18
Accidents 18-19
Achievement 19-21
Acting 21-22
Actions 22-23
Activity 23
Actors 23
Addiction 24-25
Adjustment 25
Admiration 25-27
Adolescence 27-28
Adultery 28-29
Adults 29-30
Adversity 30-32
Advertising 32-33
Advice 33-34
Affection 34
African-Americans 34-35
Afternoon 35
Age 36-38
Aging 38-39
Agnosticism 39-40
Agriculture 40
Airplanes 40
Alcohol 40-43
Alcoholism 43
Alienation 43-44
Alliances 44-45
Ambassadors 45
Ambition 45-46
America 47-49
Amnesty 49-50
Anarchy 50-51
Ancestors 51-52
Ancestry 52
Angels 52-53
Anger 53-55
Animals 55-56
Anti-Semitism 56
Anxiety 56-57
Apathy 57-58
Appearances 58
Appeasement 59
Architects 59
Architecture 59-60
Arguments 60-61
Aristocracy 61-62
Arrogance 62-63
Art 63-65
Artists 65-69
Assassination 69-70
Astrology 70
Atheism 70-71
Attitude 71-72
Authority 72-73
Automobiles 73-74
Autumn 74
Avarice 74-75
Awe 75

B

Babies 75-77
Bachelors 77-78
Bankers 78
Banks 78-79
Baseball 79-80
Basketball 80
Bathrooms 80
Beauty 80-83

Bedrooms 83
Beds 83
Beer 84
Beggars 84-85
Beginnings 85-86
Belief 86-87
Benevolence 88
Bible, The 88-89
Bigotry 89-90
Billiards 90
Biological Clock 90
Biology 90-91
Birds 91-92
Birth 92
Birth Control 92-93
Blame 93
Blessings 93-94
Bliss 94
Blood 94
Blunders 94-95
Body 95-96
Boldness 96-97
Books 97-100
Boredom 100-101
Bosses 102
Botany 102
Boxing 102-104
Bravery 104-105
Breakfast 105
Brides 105
Brotherhood 105-106
Brothers 106-107
Buddhism 107
Burdens 107
Bureaucracy 107-111
Business 111-112

C

Caffeine 112-113
California 113
Campaigns 113
Camping 114
Cancer 114
Cannibalism 114
Capitalism 114-115
Catholicism 115
Cats 115-120
Cause and Effect 120-121
Caution 121
Celebrities 122
Celibacy 122
Cell Phones 122
Censorship 122-126
Censure 126
Certainty 126-127
Challenges 127
Champions 127-128
Chance 128
Change 128-130
Chaos 130-131
Character 131-133
Charisma 133-134
Charity 134-135
Charm 135
Chastity 135
Chauvinism 136
Cheating 136
Childhood 136-138
Children 138-143
Chocolate 143-144
Choice 144
Christianity 144-145
Church 145-146
Cinema 146-149
Circumstances 149
Cities 149-150
Civil War 150
Civilization 150-152
Class 152
Clergy 152-153

Cleverness 153
Clothes 153-154
Clouds 154
Coffee 154
Cold War, The 154-155
College 155
Commanders 155
Comedy 155-156
Commerce 156-158
Common Sense 158
Communication 158
Communism 159-161
Community 161-162
Compassion 162
Competition 162-163
Complaints 163
Computers 163-164
Conceit 164-165
Confessions 165
Confidence 165-167
Conflict 167-168
Conformity 168-170
Conscience 170-172
Consciousness 172-174
Conservatives 174-175
Consistency 175
Consumerism 175
Contemplation 175
Contempt 176
Conversation 176-177
Conviction 177
Cooking 177-179
Cooperation 179
Corporations 179-184
Corruption 184-185
Countries 185-186
Courage 186-187
Courtesy 187-188
Cowardice 188-189
Creativity 189-191
Crime 191-192
Crisis 192-196
Criticism 196-197
Crowds 198
Cruelty 198-199
Cults 199
Culture 199
Cunning 200
Curiosity 200-201
Custom 202
Cynicism 202

D

Dance 202-204
Danger 204-205
Darkness 205
Dating 205-206
Daughters 206
Days 206
Dead, The 207
Death 207-210
Debate 210
Debt 210-211
Decency 211-213
Deception 213
Decisions 213-214
Deeds 214-216
Defeat 216
Defiance 216-218
Dehumanization 218
Delay 218-219
Delusion 219-220
Democracy 220-223
Democrats 223
Depression 224
Desire 224-225
Despair 225-227
Desperation 227-228
Dessert 228
Destiny 228-230

Determination 230-233
Devotion....233-234
Diet....235
Difficulty....235-236
Dignity....236-237
Diplomacy....237-238
Disability....238
Disaster....238
Discipline....238-239
Discovery....239-240
Disease....240-241
Dishonesty....241
Dissatisfaction....241-242
Dissent....242
Distrust....242-243
Divorce....243
Doctors....243-244
Dogma....244-245
Dogs....245-248
Doubt....248-249
Dreams....249-252
Drugs....252
Duty....253-254

E

Earth....254
Earthquakes....254-255
Eccentricity....255-256
Economics....256-258
Editors....258-259
Education....259-261
Efficiency....262
Effort....262-263
Ego....263-265
Elections....265-266
Electricity....266
Eloquence....266-267
Emotions....267-268
Employment....268
Encouragement....268-269
Endings....269
Endurance....269
Enemies....270-271
Energy....271
Engineering....272
England....272
English....272-273
Enjoyment....273
Enlightenment....274
Entertainment....274
Enthusiasm....275-277
Environment....277-278
Envy....278-279
Epitaphs....279
Equality....279-280
Error....280-281
Eternity....281-282
Ethics....282-283
Etiquette....283
Evening....283-284
Evil....284-285
Evolution....285-286
Excellence....286-287
Excess....287-288
Excitement....288
Excuses....288
Executives....288-289
Exercise....289
Existentialism....289-290
Expectations....290
Experience....291-292
Experts....292-293
Eyes....293-294

F

Faces....295
Facts....295-296
Failure....296-298
Faith....299-300
Fallibility....300

Falsity 300
Fame 300-302
Familiarity 302
Family 302-303
Famine....................................304
Fantasy 304
Farming....................................304-305
Fascism 305
Fashion 305-306
Fate 306-309
Fathers 309-310
Fatigue 310
Faults....................................310-311
Favors 311
Fear 311-314
Feelings....................................314
Feet 314-315
Feminism....................................315-316
Fiction....................................316-317
Fidelity 317-318
Fighting....................................318
Finance 318
Fish 318-319
Fishing 319-320
Flattery 320-321
Flirting 321-322
Floods 322
Flowers 322-323
Fog 323-324
Food 324-326
Fools 326-329
Football....................................330
Force 330
Forests 330-331
Forgetfulness....................................331
Forgiveness....................................331-334
Fortune 334-335
France 335
Frankness 335
Fraud....................................335-336
Freedom 336-339
Free Will 339-340
Friendship....................................340-351
Fruit 351-352
Fun 352
Funerals....................................352-353
Future, The 353-354

G

Gambling 354-355
Garden of Eden, The 355-356
Gardening....................................356-358
Gender 358
Generalizations....................................358
Generals 358-359
Generosity 359-360
Genius....................................360-362
Ghosts 362
Gifts 362-363
Giving 363-364
Glory....................................364-366
Gluttony....................................366
Goals....................................366-367
God....................................367-369
Gold 369
Golden Rule, The 369-370
Golf....................................370
Gossip....................................370-371
Government 371-374
Grace 374-375
Grammar....................................375
Grandfathers....................................375-376
Grandmothers....................................376
Gratitude 376-377
Greatness 377-379
Great Depression, The....................................379
Greed 379-380
Grief 380
Growth 380-381
Guilt 381

Guns 381-382

H

Habits 382
Hair 383
Happiness 383-387
Hate 387-388
Healing 388
Health 388-389
Heart 390-391
Heartbreak 392
Heaven 392-394
Hell 394-395
Heresy 396
Heroes 396-398
Hesitation 398
History 398-400
Holidays 400
Hollywood 400
Home 400-401
Homelessness 401
Homosexuality 401
Honesty 401-402
Honor 402-403
Hope 403-404
Horses 404-405
Housework 405
Human Nature 405-406
Humanism 406
Humanity 406-409
Humility 409-410
Humor 410-411
Hunger 411
Hunting 411-412
Husbands 412
Hypocrisy 412

I

Idealism 413
Ideas 413-415
Identity 415-416
Ideology 416-417
Idleness 417-418
Idols 418
Ignorance 418-421
Illness 421
Illusion 421-422
Imagination 422-425
Imitation 425-426
Immortality 426
Impatience 426-427
Imperfection 427
Imperialism 427
Impotence 427
Indecision 427-428
Independence 428
Indifference 428-429
Individualism 429
Individuality 429-430
Individuals 430
Industry 430-431
Inferiority 431
Infidelity 431
Inflation 431-432
Information 432
Injustice 432-433
Innocence 433-434
Insanity 434
Insects 434-435
Inspiration 435
Instinct 435
Insults 436
Integrity 436
Intellectualism 436-437
Intellectuals 437
Intelligence 437-438
Internet, The 438
Intoxication 438-439
Intuition 439-440

Invention....................................440
Irony..440
Irrelevance 440

J

Jealousy.....................................440-441
Jesus 441
Jokes 441-442
Journalism.................................442-443
Journalists 443-446
Journals 446
Joy..446-447
Judaism 447
Judges 447-450
Judgment 450
Juries 450-451
Justice 451-453

K

Killing 453
Kindness 454
Kingdoms 454-456
Kings...456
Kisses 456-458
Kitchens 458
Knights 458-459
Knowledge 459-462

L

Language 462-463
Laughter 463-465
Laws 465-468
Lawyers....................................468-469
Laziness 469-470
Leadership 470-474
Learning 474-476
Legends 476
Leisure 476-477
Liberals 477-478
Liberation 478-479
Liberty 479-484
Libraries 484-486
Lies 486-489
Life 489-496
Light 496-497
Listening..................................497-498
Literacy...................................498
Literature 498-499
Loans 499
Logic.......................................499-500
Loneliness...............................500-501
Longevity 501
Losing 501-504
Loss...504-505
Love 505-511
Loyalty 511-512
Luck 512
Lunch 512
Lust...512-513

M

Machines..................................513
Madness 513-514
Magazines...............................514
Majorities 515-516
Malevolence 516
Malice 516-517
Managers 517
Manipulation..........................517-518
Mankind 518-519
Manners 519-521
Marriage 521-523
Martyrs 523-524
Masochism 524
Masturbation 524
Materialism 524-525
Mathematics 525-526

Maturity 526
Maxims 527
Meals....................................527
Meaning 527-528
Media 528
Medicine....................................528-529
Mediocrity 529
Meditation 530
Meetings....................................530
Melancholy 530
Memory 530-532
Men....................................532-533
Mental Illness 533
Mercy 533-534
Middle Age....................................534
Middle Ages, The 534-535
Mind 535-539
Minorities 539
Miracles 539-540
Mirrors 540
Misers 540
Misery....................................540-542
Misfortune 542-543
Misogyny 543
Mistakes 543-545
Misunderstanding....................................545
Mobs....................................545
Moderation....................................545-546
Modesty 546-547
Monarchs 547
Money....................................547-550
Moon, The 550-551
Morality 551-552
Mothers 552-560
Motivation 560-561
Mourning 561
Movies (See Cinema)
Murder 561-562
Music 562-564
Mystery....................................564-565
Mythology 565-566

N

Nakedness 566
Names....................................566-567
Nation....................................567
Nationalism....................................567-568
Native Americans 568
Nature....................................569-570
Necessity 570
Neglect....................................570-571
Negotiation....................................571
Neurosis 571
Neutrality 571-572
News, The 572
Newspapers 572-573
Nihilism 573-574
Nobility 574
Noise 574-575
Nonconformity....................................575
Nonsense 575-576
Nonviolence 576
Normalcy 576-577
Novels....................................577
Numbers....................................577-578

O

Oaths 578
Obedience 578
Obesity....................................578-579
Objectives 579
Objectivity 579
Oblivion 579-580
Obscenity 580
Obscurity 580
Observation 580-581
Obsession 581
Obstacles 581-582
Occupation....................................582

Ocean 582-583
Old Age 583-584
Opinions 584-585
Opportunity 585-588
Opposites 588
Opposition 588-589
Oppression 589-590
Optimism 590-591
Order 591
Organization 591-592
Originality 592
Orthodoxy 592

P

Pacifism 592-593
Pain 593-595
Painting 595
Paradise 595-596
Paradox 596-597
Paranoia 597
Parenthood 597-600
Passion 600-601
Past 601-604
Patience 604-605
Patients 605
Patriotism 605-606
Patriots 606-607
Peace 607-609
Peace of Mind 609-610
People 610
Perception 610-611
Perfection 611
Performance 611-612
Persecution 612
Perseverance 612-613
Persistence 613-614
Personality 614-615
Perspective 615
Perspiration 615
Persuasion 615-616
Pessimism 617
Pets 618
Philosophy 618-620
Photography 620-621
Physics 621
Pilgrimage 621-622
Pity 622
Plagiarism 622-623
Planning 623
Plants 623-624
Pleasure 624-627
Poetry 627-631
Police 631-632
Policy 632
Political Correctness 632-633
Political Party 634
Politicians 634-636
Politics 636-638
Pollution 638-639
Poor, The 639-640
Popularity 640-641
Pornography 641
Possessions 641-642
Possibilities 642
Positivity 642-643
Poverty 643
Power 643-645
Praise 645-647
Prayer 647
Preachers 647-648
Prediction 648
Prejudice 648-649
Present, The 649-650
Presents 650
Preservation 650
Presidents 650-651
Pride 651-652
Priests 652-653
Principles 653
Prison 653-654

Privacy 654
Privilege 654
Problems 654
Procrastination 655
Profit 655-656
Progress 656-657
Promises 657
Propaganda 657-658
Property 658
Prophets 658-659
Prose 659
Prosperity 659-660
Prostitution 660
Protestantism 661
Prudence 661
Psychiatry 661
Public, The 662
Publicity 662
Punctuality 663
Punishment 663-664
Purity 664
Purpose 665

Q

Quality 665-666
Quantity 666-667
Quarrels 667
Queens 667-668
Questions 668-669
Quiet 669-670
Quotations 670-671

R

Racism 671-672
Radio 672
Rain 672
Rainbows 672
Rape 673
Rationalism 673
Reading 673-675
Real Estate 675
Realism 675-676
Reality 676-677
Realization 678
Reason 678-679
Rebellion 680
Reconciliation 680
Recovery 680-681
Redemption 681
Reflection 681
Reform 682
Refuge 682-683
Regret 683
Rejection 684
Rejoice 684
Relationships 684-685
Relatives 685
Relativity 685-686
Relaxation 686-687
Reliability 687
Religion 687-689
Remedies 689-690
Remembrance 690
Remorse 690
Renaissance, The 690-691
Repartee 691
Repentance 691
Repression 691-692
Republicans 692
Reputation 692-693
Research 693-694
Resistance 694-695
Resolution 695
Respect 695
Respectability 696
Responsibility 696-697
Restaurants 697
Retirement 697-698
Retreat 698

Revelation 698-699
Revenge 699
Reverence 699
Revolution 700-701
Reward 701
Rhetoric 701
Rhythm 701-702
Rich and Poor 702-703
Riches 704-705
Ridicule 705
Right 705-706
Rights 706-707
Risk 707-708
Rivalry 708
Rivers 708
Roads 708
Rogues 709
Roots 709
Roses 709
Ruin 709-710
Rulers 710
Rumors 710
Rust 710

S

Sacrifice 711-712
Sadness 712
Safety 713
Saints 713-714
Salesmen 714
Salvation 714
Sanity 714-715
Sarcasm 715
Satan 715-716
Satire 716-717
Satisfaction 717
Saviors 717
Scandals 717-718
Scholars 718
Schools 718-719
Science 719-722
Scripture 722-723
Sculpture 723
Sea, The 723
Seasons 724
Secrets 724-725
Secularism 725
Security 725-726
Seduction 726
Segregation 726
Self 727-728
Self-Confidence 728
Self-Control 728-729
Self-Esteem 729
Self-Respect 729
Selfishness 729-730
Senses 730
Sensitivity 730-731
Sensuality 731
Serenity 731-732
Seriousness 732
Servants 732
Service 732-733
Sex 733
Sexism 734
Sexuality 734
Shadows 734
Shakespeare 735
Shame 735
Sharing 736
Shelter 736
Shepherds 736
Showbiz 736-737
Shyness 737
Siblings 737
Sickness 737-738
Silence 738-740
Simplicity 740-741
Sin 741-742
Sincerity 742-743

Sisters 743
Skepticism 743-744
Skeptics 744-745
Skill 745
Slander 745-746
Slang 746
Slavery 746-748
Sleep 748
Smiles 748-749
Smoking 749
Snow 749-750
Sobriety 750
Socialism 750-751
Society 751-752
Soldiers 752-753
Solitude 753-754
Songs 754-755
Sons 755
Sophistication 755
Sorrow 755-756
Soul 756-757
Space 757
Speaking 757-758
Spirit 758-759
Spirituality 759-760
Sports 760-761
Spring 761
Stars 761-762
Starvation 762
Statesmen 762-764
Statistics 764
Status 764-765
Status Quo 765-766
Stock Market 766
Stories 766-768
Strangers 768-769
Strategy 769-770
Strength 770-772
Struggle 772-773
Students 773-774
Studying 774-775
Stupidity 775-776
Style 776-778
Subjectivity 778
Subtlety 778
Success 778-782
Suckers 782
Suffering 782-783
Suicide 783-787
Summer 787
Sun, The 787-788
Superiority 788
Supernatural, The 788
Superstition 788-789
Surprise 789
Survival 789-790
Suspicion 790-791
Sympathy 791

T

Taboos 792
Tact 792
Talent 793-794
Talk 794-795
Taste 795-796
Taxes 796
Teachers 796-800
Teamwork 800
Tears 800-801
Technology 801
Teenagers 801-802
Telephones 802
Television 802-804
Temperament 804
Temptation 804-805
Tennis 805
Terrorism 805-807
Thankfulness 807
Theater 807-808
Theft 808

Theology....808-809
Theories....809-810
Thieves....810
Thoughts....810-815
Time....815-817
Timidity....817
Tobacco....817
Today....817
Togetherness....817-818
Tolerance....818
Tomorrow....818-819
Torture....819-820
Totalitarianism....820
Toughness....821
Tourism....821
Toys....821-822
Trade....822
Tradition....822-823
Traffic....823-824
Tragedy....824-825
Traitors....825
Transcendentalism....825-826
Transformation....826
Translation....826
Travel....827
Treason....827
Trees....827-828
Triumph....828
Trouble....828-829
Trust....829-830
Truth....830-833
Twilight....833
Tyranny....833-834

U

Ugliness....835
Uncertainty....835
Unconscious, The....836
Underground....836
Understanding....836-838
Unemployment....838
Unhappiness....838-839
Uniqueness....839
Unity....839-840
Universe, The....840-842
Universities....842-843
Uselessness....843
Utilitarianism....843
Utility....843
Utopia....843-844

V

Vacations....844
Valor....844
Value....844-845
Values....845-846
Vampires....846
Vanity....846-847
Vegetarianism....847
Vengeance....847
Vice....847-849
Victimization....849
Victory....849-850
Vigilance....850
Villains....850-851
Violence....851
Virginity....852
Virtue....852-855
Vision....855-856
Vocation....856-857
Voting....857
Vulgarity....857-858
Vulnerability....858

W

Wages....858-859
War....859-862
Warriors....862-863

Waste 863
Water 863-864
Weakness 864
Wealth 864-865
Weapons 865-866
Weather 866
Weddings 866
Welfare 866-867
Wilderness 867
Wine 868
Winning 868-869
Winter 869-870
Wisdom 870-872
Wishes 872-873
Wit 873-874
Witchcraft 874
Wives 874-875
Women 875-877
Words 877-880
Work 880-882
World, The 882-883
Worries 883-884
Worship 884
Wounds 885
Writing 885-891
Wrong 891-892

Y

Yankees 892
Yesterday 892-893
Yoga 893
Youth 893-897

Z

Zeal 897-898
Zealots 898
Zen 898
Zionism 898